Heidegger and Kabbalah

NEW JEWISH PHILOSOPHY AND THOUGHT

Zachary J. Braiterman

HEIDEGGER AND KABBALAH

Hidden Gnosis and the Path of Poiēsis

Elliot R. Wolfson

INDIANA UNIVERSITY PRESS

This book is a publication of

Indiana University Press
Office of Scholarly Publishing
Herman B Wells Library 350
1320 East 10th Street
Bloomington, Indiana 47405 USA

iupress.indiana.edu

 The paper used in this publication meets the minimum requirements of the American National Standard for Information Sciences—Permanence of Paper for Printed Library Materials, ANSI Z39.48-1992.

Manufactured in the United States of America

Library of Congress Cataloging-in-Publication Data
Names: Wolfson, Elliot R., author.
Title: Heidegger and Kabbalah : hidden gnosis and the path of poiesis / Elliot R. Wolfson.
Description: Bloomington : Indiana University Press, 2019. | Series: New Jewish philosophy and thought | Includes bibliographical references and index.
Identifiers: LCCN 2019013600 (print) | ISBN 9780253042569 (hardback : alk. paper) | ISBN 9780253042576 (pbk. : alk. paper)
Subjects: LCSH: Heidegger, Martin, 1889-1976. | Cabala.
Classification: LCC B3279.H49 W6275 2019 (print) | LCC B3279.H49 (ebook)| DDC 193--dc23
LC record available at https://lccn.loc.gov/2019013600
LC ebook record available at https://lccn.loc.gov/2019980138

1 2 3 4 5 24 23 22 21 20 19

TO THE MEMORY OF
David G. Leahy
philosophical dreamer par excellence

L'Univers est une pensée opaque et solitaire qui a déjà bondi dans les yeux clos de l'homme comme l'espace d'un rêve sans rêve.

François Laruelle

If the bleak days scare away all shining radiance, and if all breadth shrivels into the paltriness of narrow conventionality, then the heart must remain the source of what is light and spacious. And the most solitary heart makes the broadest leap into the middle of beyng,
if on all sides the semblance of nonbeings stops its noise.

MARTIN HEIDEGGER,
PONDERINGS V

To those who are superficial and in a hurry, no less than to those who are deliberate and reflective, it must look as though there were no mystery anywhere.

MARTIN HEIDEGGER,
"A DIALOGUE ON LANGUAGE"

Contents

Contents

Heidegger and Kabbalah

Introduction

Belonging Together of the Foreign

The un-rest of questioning is not empty uncertainty; instead, it is the opening-up and guarding of that rest which, as the gathering together into what is most question-worthy (the event), awaits the simple intimacy of the call and endures the extreme wrath of the abandonment by being.

Heidegger, *Contributions to Philosophy (Of the Event)*

To flee into the identical is not dangerous.
To venture into discordance in order to say the Same is the danger.

Heidegger, "Letter on 'Humanism'"

Martin Heidegger is incontestably considered by intellectual foe and friend alike as one of the most influential philosophers of the twentieth century and perhaps one of the greatest thinkers of all time, and this in spite of the controversy surrounding his allegiance to National Socialism and despite, even more damaging, his inability to acknowledge his mistakes publicly and to show remorse or compassion for the victims of the extermination camps.[1] I have explored the topic of Heidegger's flirtation with the right-wing politics of Nazism in a separate monograph.[2] I will not repeat my arguments here, but what is crucial to note is that regardless of how one decides on the relationship between the political and the philosophical, the gift of Heideggerian thought has been enormous, and so, too, the debt of those seized by the reverberations—at times haunting—of his voice, and this includes the impressive aggregate of Jewish students who flocked to the feet of the master or the "philosopher-king," as he was known. And so it is with my own philosophical reflections on Jewish mysticism. For several decades, I have availed myself of certain themes in Heidegger's œuvre to elucidate the phenomenological aspects of kabbalistic esotericism and hermeneutics. In this book, I will expand my earlier insights and think more deeply about the juxtaposition of Heidegger and kabbalah.[3]

Heidegger and Judaism: Review of Previous Scholarship

To contextualize my approach, it would be beneficial to mention some previous analyses that impinge upon this subject. In her provocative study, *La Dette impensée: Heidegger et l'héritage hébraïque,*[4] Marlène Zarader explored the manner in which the Hebraic heritage influenced Heidegger's thought, principally in his appropriation of biblical faith through the medium of Christianity, which, together with Greek thought, comprise the foundations of occidental culture. The very experience of being and language that

Heidegger sought to retrieve from the pre-Socratic thinkers as an alternative to what was forgotten in the history of Western metaphysics can be traced to what has been more overtly expressed—"in letters black on white"—in Jewish sources.[5] And yet, as Zarader also contends, following Ricœur, Heidegger occludes the Hebraic component of his thought "to the point of leaving something like a *blank* space in his text."[6] Zarader thus concludes that Heidegger both "restored to Western thought the determinations central to the Hebraic universe" and "effaced it from thought and, more broadly, from the West itself."[7] Zarader's own effort was to fill the blank space by making explicit the Hebraic dimension of Christianity that was obfuscated or perhaps consciously repressed by Heidegger with his alternate narrative of a *Heilsgeschichte* that revolves linguistically and historically about the poles of ancient Greece and modern Germany.[8] Just as Heidegger spoke of the oblivion of being (*Seinsvergessenheit*) as the obliviousness to the difference between being and beings,[9] so Zarader identifies Judaism as what is left unthought at the heart of his thinking. In line with Heidegger's hermeneutic, the more pronounced the concealment, the more profound the disclosure, the more resonant the silence, the more poignant the bearing witness. Particularly relevant to this study is the author's comparison of Heidegger's conception of nothingness and the domain of being's withdrawal to kabbalistic speculation on *ṣimṣum*, the contraction of infinity to create the vacuum within the plenum, the space wherein, paradoxically, what is ostensibly other than that which has no other can come to be.[10]

When asked in an interview with Dominique Janicaud to respond to Zarader's thesis, Derrida concurred but argued even more forcefully that it was an act of violence on Heidegger's part to disregard Jewish thought so thoroughly and deliberately, a display of disdain that can be explained only as part of an ideological-political agenda,[11] a position that curiously accords with Buber's critique of Heidegger's misrepresentation of the mission of the prophets of ancient Israel, or more expansively the Judeo-Christian tradition, which he contrasts with the prophetic essence of the poet as typified by Hölderlin.[12] Others, such as François Vézin, have drawn an explicit connection between Heidegger's systematic, and apparently conscious, inattentiveness to Jewish philosophers and his apathy toward the millions of Jews brutally and senselessly murdered.[13] It is interesting that, in a similar vein, reading against Heidegger's own explicit assertions, Jean-Luc Nancy surmised that his signature idea of *Ereignis* may have "nothing to do with a destinality engaged solely by the Greeks but everything to do with a different history, one that includes Roman, Judeo-Christian, and 'modern' events in a sense that Heidegger was perhaps never truly capable of apprehending."[14] My own inquiry will lend support to Nancy's conjecture, albeit as it relates more specifically to the affinities between the Heideggerian event of beyng and the kabbalistic emanation of the infinite, a comparison that brings to light the metaontological critique of the onto-theology typically associated with the Jewish esoteric teaching. The validity of juxtaposing Heidegger's *Seinsdenken* and the kabbalistic contemplation of infinity will be strengthened by attending to several other topics worthy of comparative analysis, to wit, the hermeneutical nature of the human experience of history and the contours of tradition, the conception of authentic time as a linear circle that instantiates the replication of difference, the simultaneous disclosure and concealment of the mystery, and the intricate triangulation of language, peoplehood, and land.

Another work that should be mentioned is Johanna Junk's *Metapher und Sprachmagie, Heidegger und die Kabbala: Eine philosophische Untersuchung*. Even though this book is marred by the fact that the author does not seem to possess the philological skills requisite to read kabbalistic material in its primary languages, and thus her analyses are based on the evaluations culled from other scholars, Junk's study yields some important insights and interpretive strategies that substantively enrich the discussion and illumine the fundamental question of the compatibility of Heidegger's path and the esoteric tradition of the kabbalah.[15] Noteworthy as well are Richard Wolin's *Heidegger's Children: Hannah Arendt, Karl Löwith, Hans Jonas, and Herbert Marcuse*,[16] and Samuel Fleischacker's edited collection *Heidegger's Jewish Followers: Essays on Hannah Arendt, Leo Strauss, Hans Jonas, and Emmanuel Levinas*.[17] These works are serious engagements with the complicated relationship that several leading twentieth-century

Jewish thinkers had to Heidegger, but the latter's relationship to kabbalah or Jewish mysticism is not discussed at all in either book. Mention should also be made of Allen Scult's *Being Jewish/Reading Heidegger: An Ontological Encounter*.[18] The author presents an innovative study that underscores the phenomenological resemblance of Judaism as a way of life, grounded in the interpretative relation to a sacred text, and Heidegger's view of philosophical practice as a reading of the founding texts of Western philosophy. In like fashion, Michael Fagenblat has written that "Heidegger maintained, as does traditional Jewish thought, that thinking is saturated with interpretation and therefore conceived philosophy as an endless series of commentaries that forget, restore, and unfold an original truth, as does the Jewish tradition of commentary."[19] This comparison of Jewish commentarial practice with Heideggerian hermeneutics does not make any explicit reference to the kabbalistic material, but the inclusion of the latter would substantiate the thesis considerably. The same can be said for more recent attempts to draw positive analogies between Heidegger's thinking and rabbinic thought by Elad Lapidot and Sergey Dolgopolski.[20]

It is appropriate to recall as well a passing remark of Emil Fackenheim in *Encounters between Judaism and Modern Philosophy: A Preface to Future Jewish Thought*. Fackenheim, an escapee from Nazi Germany, suggested that the power of the later Heidegger "to captivate the Jewish thinker" far exceeded the Heidegger of *Sein und Zeit*. The rationale for this assertion is that Heidegger's insistence on a shift from an original hearing to a derivative seeing demonstrated that he was "engaged in no less startling an enterprise than the Judaization of the entire history of Western philosophy. . . . At least from Plato to Nietzsche there has been a fateful yet inevitable falling away from an original *Denken*-of-Being—fateful because it manifests a *Seinsvergessenheit* and inevitable because it manifests a *Seinsverlassenheit*."[21] Summarizing Heidegger's later thought, Fackenheim remarks that the notion of truth as the unconcealedness of being "is accessible to an original 'thinking,' which is a 'hearing' rather than a 'seeing.'" Drawing on the conventional portrayal of Judaism as privileging the auditory over the visual, Fackenheim concludes that "the later Heidegger Judaizes philosophy, and hence also the view that the Jewish thinker is justified in being attracted to his later thought."[22]

One can challenge the accuracy of this stereotypical characterization of Judaism, but even more important, Fackenheim's observation is based on the faulty conception that the ocular and auditory dimensions of the Heideggerian appropriative event can be separated definitively. The spuriousness of this claim is attested, for instance, in Heidegger's statement about the nature of *Ereignis* as the saying that is the showing (*die Sage ist Zeigen*), or its corollary, the showing of the saying (*das Zeigen der Sage*).[23] Inasmuch as the hearing is at the same time a coming to light, the listening itself must be construed as an act of seeing.[24] Elsewhere Heidegger points out that the transfer from the aural to the visible—as we see in the case of the term for brightness, *Helle*, which derives from *hallen*, to reverberate or to echo, a character of sound and not originally of sight—is indicative of an early power and wisdom of language.[25] Bracketing this criticism, it is remarkable that Fackenheim, a German Jew arrested by the Nazis during Kristallnacht (November 9–10, 1938), and briefly interned in the Sachsenhausen concentration camp, would have no compunction characterizing Heidegger's alleged denunciation of ocularcentrism after the so-called turn (*Kehre*) in the 1930s as the *Judaization of the entire history of Western philosophy*. The astounding nature of this claim is augmented when we recall that in *To Mend the World: Foundations of Post-Holocaust Thought*, Fackenheim, in a manner that is consonant with Buber,[26] is brutally critical of Heidegger's endorsement of the Nazi regime impelled not by personal considerations but by the force of the philosophical path laid out in *Sein und Zeit*.[27]

Heidegger and Kabbalah: Being, Language, Time

In this section, I will review three Heideggerian themes that have been central to my previous efforts to offer a cogent philosophical exposition of the Jewish mystical material: the depiction of truth as the unconcealedness of the concealment of concealment; the construal of language as the house of being within which all beings are disclosed in the nothingness of their being; and the understanding of the origin of time-space arising from an inceptual act that is, concomitantly, a constriction and an expansion, a withholding of the boundless ground that results in the self-extending delineation of boundary.

Turning to the first topic, I have been struck by the way Heidegger's conception of truth as the clearing (*Lichtung*) for the self-concealing (*Sichverbergen*) of beyng, the bringing to light, the lighting-up, of what remains enshrouded, well captures the paradox of secrecy and the meontological understanding of the infinite nonbeing at play in a plethora of kabbalistic sources.[28] The clearing within which beings are unconcealed is the concealment of those very beings; kabbalists would surely assent to the Heideggerian assessment that the nature of nature (φύσις) is such that every being we encounter "keeps to this curious opposition of presence [*Anwesens*] in that it always withholds itself at the same time in a concealedness [*Verborgenheit*]."[29] The concealment that occurs within the clearing is thus a form of dissembling (*Verstellen*) whereby the being that appears "presents itself as other than it is" (*es gibt sich anders, als es ist*).[30] This insight into the concealment that conceals and dissembles itself leads Heidegger to the disquieting conclusion that the unconcealedness (*Unverborgenheit*) is dominated by a denial that takes the form of a *double concealment* (*zwiefache Verbergen*), the concealment of the concealment, such that truth, in its very essence, is un-truth (*die Wahrheit ist in ihrem Wesen Un-wahrheit*), a proposition that is not intended to state that truth is necessarily falsehood (*Falschheit*), but only that, in defiance of the principle of noncontradiction, it is always itself and its opposite; that is, truth is the disclosure regarding which it is essential that it remain concealed.[31]

Much as Heidegger understood that untruth belongs inextricably to the comportment of truth, insofar as the latter is the unconcealment (*alētheia*) of that which is hidden or forgotten (*lēthe*), the mystery that is "the concealing of what is concealed" (*die Verbergung des Verborgenen*), the nonessence (*Unwesen*) that is essential to the essence of truth,[32] the self-withdrawing (*Sichentziehende*)[33] that initiates the nonshowing of beyng in the showing of every nonbeing,[34] so for the kabbalist, divulging the secret is a double negative that yields a positive, the concealment that conceals itself to be revealed. Heidegger accurately, even if unsuspectingly, expressed the guiding principle of kabbalistic esotericism, "A mystery is a mystery only when it does not even come out *that* mystery is at work."[35] Extrapolating the cosmological implications of this hermeneutic of the dissimulation of the dissimulation, Gershom Scholem wrote that the "secret signatures (*rishumim*) that God had placed upon things are as much concealments of His revelation as revelation of His concealment."[36] Prima facie, Scholem's approach is close to my own,[37] but there is a decisive difference: when Scholem writes that the concealment of the divine revelation is a revelation of the divine concealment, he has in mind something akin to Hegel's dialectic,[38] which posits the sublation of antinomies such that there is a synthesis in which one thing becomes its opposite; my hypothesis, by contrast, is more consistent with Heidegger's idea of the belonging together of opposites that remain opposite in their juxtaposition as opposed to the *coincidentia oppositorum* from which one may infer the identity of the identity of nonidentity and the nonidentity of identity. The kabbalistic intonation of the paradox strikes me as far more germane to understanding the Heideggerian notion of the unveiling (*Entbergung*) of beyng than simply viewing the latter as a philosophical appropriation of the theological emphasis on the epiphany of the invisible God common to a presumed Judeo-Christian vocabulary.[39]

Offering a generalization based on the painstaking immersion in particular texts through many years, I am prepared to say that kabbalists extended the hermeneutic of secrecy to their understanding of the nonbeing of being. Thus, like Nicholas of Cusa and Friedrich Wilhelm Joseph Schelling, both of whom may have incorporated elements of kabbalistic theosophy, which, in turn, influenced Heidegger in an ancillary way,[40] kabbalists have staunchly maintained that all that exists is a manifestation of the light of the infinite, but every manifestation of that light perforce must be a concealment, since what is innately hidden can be revealed only insofar as it endures as being hidden. Perhaps most conspicuously, the conceptual footing of the myth of *ṣimṣum*, the primordial act of divine kenosis, an idea whose roots go back to the thirteenth century but which is expressed more explicitly in the sixteenth century, is the paradox that concealment is the cause of disclosure and disclosure the cause of concealment.[41] Translated phenomenologically, every appearance of the infinite is a nonappearance—the nonapparent cannot appear except as inapparent—whence it follows that the infinite is present in the world to the degree that it is absent from the world; indeed, the infinite light is present precisely as that which is absent, not as a presence presently absent nor as an absence absently present, but as the absent presence that continuously withdraws in the spectacle of its present absence.

Kabbalists and Heidegger share the hermeneutical conviction, which is based on the aforementioned cosmological paradox, that there is no naked truth but only truth rendered visible via the cloak of invisibility. This is the import of Heidegger's insistence, mentioned above, on the identification of saying and showing; that is, with respect to the appearing of beyng implied in the *es gibt*, all that we are capable of speaking is seen through the mantle of the name by which the being is denuded.[42] This, I submit, is also the phenomenological basis of Heidegger's contention that beyng is expressed through but is irreducible to the discrete beings of the world, or to be even more precise, the former is disclosed in the latter to the extent that it is occluded by the latter. Thus, like a mantra, Heidegger proclaims in his essay "Der Spruch des Anaximander" (1946), "By revealing itself in the being, being withdraws [*Das Sein entzieht sich, indem es sich in das Seiende entbirgt*]. . . . By bringing the being's unconcealment, it founds, for the first time, the concealment of being."[43] The same dynamic can be attributed to the kabbalistic understanding of the infinite, and thus we can say of both *Seyn* and *Ein Sof* that they illumine—each from its distinctive vantagepoint—all that can be seen but are themselves never seen,[44] the luminescence that facilitates the appearance of all phenomena but itself does not appear phenomenologically.[45] As Heidegger put it in "Der Rückgang in dem Grund der Metaphysik," the introduction he added to the fifth printing of the essay "Was ist Metaphysik?" in 1949, metaphysical thinking always represents beings only as beings and hence being as being (*das Sein als Sein*), which in its essence is the truth as the unconcealing that is the source of the light in which beings appear, remains veiled and unthought.[46] The identification of being as the light that brings all beings into appearance but that does not itself appear calls to mind Heidegger's two translations of the Heraclitean fragment (preserved by Hippolytus) τὰ δὲ πάντα οἰακίζει κεραυνός, "The thunderbolt pilots all things,"[47] as *Das Alles jedoch (des Anwesenden) steuert (ins Anwesen) der Blitz*, "But lighting steers (in presencing) the totality (of what is present),"[48] or as *Das Seiende im Ganzen aber steuert der Blitz*, "But the lightning steers beings as a whole."[49] Heidegger retrieves from Heraclitus the idea of being as the flash of lightning that summons the presencing of all things present while itself remaining concealed from being present, an idea connected as well to Heraclitus's maxim that nature loves to hide, φύσις κρύπτεσθαι φιλεῖ,[50] which conveys the interplay of unhiddenness and hiddenness, that "the essence of being is such that, as a self-revealing, being reveals itself in a way such that a self-concealing—that means, a withdrawal—belongs to this revealing. . . . As a proffering that clears and lights, being is simultaneously withdrawal."[51]

The new thinking about beyng, as opposed to beings, requires one to push beyond the metaphysical binary of presence and absence. Jean Beaufret succinctly expressed the point: "For if presence and absence are qualities which constantly alternate in beings, this can happen only under the immutable horizon of being. Being itself is never a being, but rather the measure according to which all beings can enter into presence or can pull back from presence and disappear in absence. Far more original than the presence-absence of beings is the omnipresence of being, which, losing nothing in its participation in such a vicissitude, encompasses beings without losing itself in that vicissitude."[52] The same can be said about the infinite for the kabbalists, the light of being that manifests all beings but is itself unmanifest. The unconcealment of beings is what secures the concealment of being. Even the eschatological promise that one may elicit from kabbalistic sources, to gaze upon the light without the encumbrance of any garment, amounts to realizing that it is not possible to behold the light but through the garment that is light. The goal on the mystical path may be described as the removal of all barriers to vision—to polish the heart like a translucent mirror, as Sufis are wont to say—but the greatest of barriers is to think that all barriers may be removed.[53] In the end, nothing is revealed to be the truth of which nothing is revealed but the possibility of something to be revealed.[54]

With respect to this matter, the state of contemplation cultivated by the kabbalists may be profitably compared to Heidegger's description of *Besinnung* as musing (*Er-denken*) or heartfelt thinking (*herzhaften Denken*),[55] that is, the contemplative reflection (*besinnliche Nachdenken*) or meditative thinking (*besinnliche Denken*) that occasions the release (*Gelassenheit*) into what is worthy of interrogation with respect to beyng rather than a computational thinking (*rechnende Denken*) that thinks beyng from the perspective of beings and thereby reinforces the metaphysical fallacy of obliterating the ontological difference.[56] Heidegger felicitously called this mode of contemplation "thoughtful configuration" (*denkerische Gestaltung*),[57] an expression that can be applied propitiously to the poetic thinking traversed by kabbalists, which similarly presumes that "the essence of thinking is something other than thinking" (*das Wesen des Denkens sei etwas anderes als Denken*).[58] Embarking on this path of thinking that is other than thinking leads one to the discernment that the Heideggerian *Seyn* and the kabbalistic *Ein Sof* each denote a presence that is always a nonpresence, a presence that can be present only by not being present, the mystery manifest in the nonmanifestation of the mystery, the nothing about which one cannot speak in contrast to there being nothing about which to speak. In Derridean terms, the ultimate secret is the open secret, the secret that there is no secret,[59] and hence the watchword of the secret of secrecy (*secret du secret*) is that "no more secrecy means more secrecy" (*plus de secret, plus de secret*).[60] By continuing in the footprints of Heidegger,[61] Derrida, perhaps unwittingly, came upon a central tenet of kabbalistic esotericism: the truth of the nonbeing of being cannot be unveiled but through the veil of truth, which is to say, the veil of untruth.

The second theme I have explored in previous work centers on the resonances of Heidegger's complex view on the relation between language and beyng with an analogous pattern of thought that may be elicited from the kabbalah.[62] For Heidegger, especially after the *Kehre*, language and beyng stand in the proximity of their remoteness and in the concordance of their discord.[63] As he famously expressed it, "in thinking being comes to language. Language is the house of being. In its home human beings dwell."[64] Rather than positing a direct correspondence between words and things *à la* classical representationalist epistemology undergirding the Aristotelian definition of the human as the *animal rationale*, Heidegger insists that "language is the house of being in which the human being ek-sists by dwelling, in that he belongs to the truth of being, guarding it."[65] In the manner that the house provides the framework within which beings are both exposed and sheltered, language is understood as an opening through which beyng appears to the human in the occlusion of its appearance.[66] In every word spoken, therefore, we must heed the unspoken.

On this score, we find confirmation of the previous point: the showing-saying of language discloses the mystery of beyng it continues to safeguard, concealing the concealment at the heart of the unconcealment, projecting and withholding, not successively but synchronously.[67] Kabbalists would acquiesce to Heidegger's allegation, "That which shows itself and at the same time withdraws is the essential trait of what we call the mystery [*Was auf solche Weise sich zeigt und zugleich sich entzieht, ist der Grundzug dessen, was wir das Geheimnis nennen*]."[68] In similar fashion, Heidegger describes the *unheimlich*—the uncanny, which is the counterpoint to *Geheimnis*, the mystery—as "what looms forth in the essence of human beings and is that which stirs in all stirring and arousal: that which presences and at the same time absences [*das Anwesende und zugleich Abwesende*]."[69] Just as the presence of being at home is experienced most acutely in the absence of not being at home, so the secret necessitates the letting be—that is, the letting appear—of the "hidden essence of being" (*das verborgene Wesen des Seins*),[70] which is concurrently present and absent, present as that which is absent and absent as that which is present. The mystery, therefore, is not a thing, not even a no-thing, but the "open in-between" (*offene Zwischen*) that "is the being-there [*Da-sein*] . . . of the ecstatic region of the disclosure and concealment of being."[71] The open enclosure—the refusal that is the conferral—is the absolute appearance wherein nothing appears, the privation of the privation of privation, the lack of image that surpasses in its ontic deficiency even the image of lack. Metaontologically, presence is not the absence of absence nor is absence the absence of presence; presencing rather is the absencing of the absencing of presencing. Following this line of thinking, we might say that the mystery of language is the self-withdrawing bestowal of the self-bestowing withdrawal of the nothing—the kabbalistic *Ein Sof* and the Heideggerian *Seyn*—which denotes not a nonbeing, the negation of something positive, but the nullity or emptiness that is the origin of all that comes to be in the intricate interweave of beings that make up the fabric of the world.

Heidegger insists that Dasein is uniquely endowed with the language that unveils the veil of beyng. However, the way that language and beyng belong together in this unveiling of the veiling is veiled, not because the matter is presently concealed and eventually will be revealed, but, in a more enduring sense, because not-showing is intrinsic to the showing that is the saying of the unsaying. With this we arrive at an aspect of Heidegger's thinking that resonates deeply with the paradox of esotericism at play in kabbalistic theosophy: every act of revealing is a concealing, for the truth that is inherently a secret cannot be revealed unless it is concealed. Simply put, uncovering is always a cover-up. In Heidegger's own words, "Retaining belongs to concealment [*Das Behalten gehört in die Verborgenheit*]. The mystery [of being] is concealment, which is [at the same time] unconcealing itself as such [*Das Geheimnis ist die sich entbergende Verborgenheit als solche*]."[72] The kabbalists similarly view the performativity of language as revealing and concealing, not sequentially but concurrently; that is, language has the capacity to reveal the nature of being to the extent that the nature of being it reveals is concealed. For the kabbalists, like Heidegger, the unconcealment is not a disrobing of truth but the unveiling of the veil. "All revealing," writes Heidegger in a decidedly kabbalistic tone, "belongs within a harboring and a concealing. But that which frees—the mystery—is concealed and always concealing itself. . . . Freedom is that which conceals in a way that opens to light, in whose clearing shimmers the veil that hides the essential occurrence of all truth and lets the veil appear as what veils."[73] *To let the veil appear as what veils*—this corroborates the point made above concerning the eschatological goal of the mystical way: lifting the veil, ostensibly to see the face laid bare, amounts to discerning that there is no way to see the face but through the veil of the face. Hence, the final veil to lift is the veil that one can see without a veil.[74]

Heidegger's poeticized thinking, as it is enunciated in relation to Greek and to German—a belonging together that connects but also keeps separate thought and poetry—finds a close parallel in the kabbalistic allocation of ontological significance to Hebrew.[75] From the vantage point of the kabbalists, unfailingly and uniformly upheld through the generations, Hebrew is the matrix language and hence it is accorded the status of being most conducive to unmasking the masking of the unmasking, to disclose the secret of the concealing of what is concealed in ascribing a name to the nameless. In addition, the kabbalistic focus on the connection between the holiness of Hebrew, the godliness of the Jewish people, and the sanctity of the land of Israel presents another intriguing analogy to Heidegger's commitment to the nexus between homeland, peoplehood, and language in the case of the Germans. Far from avoiding the difficult political questions that surround this indissoluble link between place, nationality, and speech, in the final chapter, I will show that kabbalistic sources are susceptible to the reproach that has been leveled against Heidegger for what he himself called the folkish thinking (*völkische Denken*),[76] which mandates the ethnolinguistic enrootedness and invocation of historical destiny for a particular people to the exclusion of others. The similarity is all the more remarkable in light of the fact that Heidegger's privileging of Greek and German as the axes about which the history of beyng turns—the first beginning inaugurated by the Greeks and the other beginning entrusted to the Germans—not only marginalizes but demonizes the Jews as the metaphysical enemy excluded from that history.[77] But more than exclusion, the connection forged by Heidegger between the Jewish question (*Judenfrage*) and the question of being (*Seinsfrage*) confers on the Jew—or, more specifically, on *Weltjudentum*—a central part in the philosophical transgression par excellence, the forgetfulness of being: "The question of the role of *world-Judaism* is not a racial question, but a metaphysical one, a question that concerns the kind of human existence which in an *utterly unrestrained* way can undertake as a world-historical 'task' the uprooting of all beings from being."[78] Apparently, Heidegger did not think the Jew was capable of realizing the "innermost structure" of the *metaphysics of Dasein*,[79] which enables the expansion into the *metapolitics "of" the historical people*, that is, the task of belonging to the *Volk* determined not racially or biologically but by an essentially collective and historical destiny that is metapolitical.[80] As Donatella di Cesare has aptly put it, "Heidegger's apocalyptic vision sees the Jew as the figure of an end that obsessively repeats itself, preventing the German people from reaching the 'other beginning,' that is, a new dawn of the West. . . . The *metaphysics of the Jew* gives rise to *the metaphysical Jew*, an abstract figure to which the qualities that supposedly pertain to the 'idea' of the Jew, the fantastic model of the figural Jew, are obscurely transferred. . . . The *metaphysics of the Jew* thus produces a *metaphysical Jew*, the idea of the Jew defined *metaphysically* on the basis of the secular oppositions that relegate the Jew to inauthentic appearance, that reduce him to a soulless abstraction, to a spectral invisibility, and eventually to nothingness."[81]

The third theme in Heidegger that I have invoked as a prism through which to examine kabbalistic texts is the idea of time.[82] In modes of discourse beholden explicitly to Schelling, and by implication to the theosophical gnosis espoused by kabbalists, Heidegger depicts the *Abgrund* as the "primary clearing," or the nameless abyss, the groundlessness that grounds its ground in the holding sway of its grounding, that is, the ungrounding of the nonground, the spot or interval prior to the partition of time and space into the differentiated representations that mark the signposts of humankind's historical destination. Heidegger's understanding of the origin of time-space within the revealing-concealing of the *Abgrund*, which constitutes the essence of truth, is indebted to Schelling's rendering of time as the space of the *Ungrund*, the infinite within which oppositions are preserved in the indifference of their identity. The terminology of Schelling is appropriated from the mystical theosophy of Jacob Böhme,[83] which is ideationally, if not textually, related, in turn, to the *Abgrund* of Eckhart[84]—an intellectual trajectory that Heidegger noted with regard to the paradoxical notion of God becoming the ground of the emergence from himself to himself of that which is not himself[85]—but also may reflect kabbalistic speculation on *Ein Sof*,[86] as is made explicit in the thought of Friedrich Christoph Oetinger.[87] Previous scholarship has documented the possible influence of kabbalistic motifs on Schelling and the probable channels of influence, to wit, Latin translations of zoharic and Lurianic texts published in Christian Knorr von Rosenroth's *Kabbala Denudata*;[88] original treatises of Christian kabbalah by Pico della Mirandola, Johannes Reuchlin, Guillaume Postel, Egidio da Viterbo, Francesco Giorgi, and Paulus Ricius, to name a few of the better-known examples;[89] the writings of European philosophers, particularly in their interpretation of Spinoza spearheaded by Friedrich Heinrich Jacobi and Johann Georg Wachter, as well as the Cambridge Platonist school of Henry More and his disciple Ann Conway,[90] the thought of Gottfried Wilhelm Leibniz, Gotthold Ephraim Lessing, and Johann Georg Hamann; and the works of hermetists, alchemists, and theosophists influenced by Jewish esotericism and the occult, such as Cornelius Agrippa von Nettesheim, Paracelsus, Athanasius Kircher, Böhme, Franciscus Mercurius van Helmont, Oetinger, and Franz von Baader.[91] As Habermas succinctly expressed the matter, "It remains astonishing how productively central motifs of the philosophy of German Idealism shaped so essentially by Protestantism can be developed in terms of the experience of the Jewish tradition. Because the legacy of the Kabballah already flowed into and was absorbed by Idealism, its light seems to refract all the more richly in the spectrum of a spirit in which something of the spirit of Jewish mysticism lives on, in however hidden a way."[92] It is feasible to extend this argument to Heidegger and to assume an incidental influence of Jewish theosophical speculation on his path of inceptual thinking/enowning, an inspiration that remained unspoken and unthought. At the very least, the similarities are striking and call for interpretation.

Belonging Together and the Correlation of Sameness through Difference

This monograph, to the best of my knowledge, presents the first serious attempt to lay out the comparison of the Heideggerian and kabbalistic corpora on the basis of textual-philological criteria. As I already noted, it may very well be that Heidegger became aware indirectly of kabbalistic motifs and symbols through the work of Schelling.[93] With regard to the more general influence of mystical theosophy on Heidegger, which may independently exhibit a symbolic kinship with the kabbalah, the likely vehicles of transmission would have been the Latin and German writings of Eckhart[94] and the theosophical compositions of Böhme.[95] The impact of these thinkers on Heidegger has been duly noted, but no one has paid attention to how the kabbalistic resonances in their works may have inadvertently imprinted Heidegger's thought. An investigation of this sort would certainly contribute to unearthing new facets and dimensions of European intellectual history from the Middle Ages to modernity and into contemporary postmodernism. At various pivotal junctures in the ensuing chapters, I will argue that certain kabbalistic ideas made their way into Heidegger's thought through secondary conduits. The argument in this book primarily, however, assumes a different form. It is not influence that is the focal point of my concern—I am sympathetic to Heidegger's denigration of this kind of analysis[96]—but rather the constellation of themes underlying the respective viewpoints of Heidegger and the kabbalists, a constellation that demonstrates the disarming correlation—as opposed to dialectical coincidence—of sameness through difference, that is, the identity of the nonidentical in the preservation of the nonidentity of the identical.

Without denying the cultural and existential disparities too obvious to warrant specification, it is justifiable nonetheless to bridge the two, to ponder the kabbalah in light of Heideggerian poetic thinking, and the later in light of the former, on three accounts. First, as I noted above, historical connections between Heidegger and kabbalah—through intermediaries like Böhme and Schelling—cannot be ruled out unequivocally. Second, Heidegger's relation to gnostic, mystical, and esoteric currents in Western Christian thought,[97] including principally Meister Eckhart[98] and Angelus Silesius,[99] suggest the possibility that he may have been enamored with ideas from these sources that have strong parallels in the Jewish material. Third, and most important, leaving aside the historiographical question of influence, the comparative analysis is justified methodologically by conceptual affinities. The path of Heidegger's later thought turns in a paradoxical manner—predicated, as it is, on the poetological heeding of the unspoken in what is spoken—that is particularly appropriate for the study of the apophatic dimension of the kabbalah.

The predictable anachronistic charge of anachronism against this approach is readily dismissible as the philological insistence that a text be studied in a diachronically modulated historical context, though valid up to a point, need not be accorded hegemony in the hermeneutical task of constructing meaning. Availing ourselves of the Heideggerian distinction, the analysis in this book may be considered historical as opposed to historiological. To avoid potential misunderstanding, let me be clear that I am not advocating an interpretative method that discards philological competence on the specious grounds that all readings are equally tenable, an erroneous and self-contradictory view that lamentably has gained great currency in the marketplace of ideas. It is fitting to recall the acerbic observation of Nietzsche, "He who wants to mediate between two resolute thinkers shows that he is mediocre: he has no eye for what is unique; seeing things as similar and making things the same is the sign of weak eyes."[100] Lest I be accused of mediocrity and feeble vision, I will state clearly and unambiguously that I have no intention of equating Heidegger and kabbalists on the basis of superficial comparisons that ignore the specificity of the respective historical, social, and cultural environments that informed each body of thinking. On the contrary, I embrace the discipline of philology as the means that is necessary for both the historicist situating of a text in its literary milieu and the deconstructionist deciphering of the textual sense, a venture that doubtlessly would demarcate the substantial differences even as it points to considerable correspondences. Beyond that criterion, however, the meaning one imparts to or elicits from a text should not be corroborated solely on the basis of genealogy or chronology. As Heidegger himself in one place expressed the matter, "It is possible, for example, to ascertain historically down to the last detail what Leibniz said about the Being of beings, and yet not to understand in the least what Leibniz thought when he defined the Being of beings from the perspective of the monad, and defined the monad as the unity of *perceptio* and *appetitus*, as the oneness of perception and appetite."[101]

What Heidegger wished to convey here, and in countless other passages in his voluminous corpus, is that the philosophical understanding may be enhanced by—but it is certainly not confined to—the historical setting, at least if that setting is determined exclusively and predominantly by historiological assumptions. Granted that one's hermeneutical orientation cannot be disentangled from presumptions about experience more generally and especially the elaborate role that memory plays in the psychosocial formation of identity and the eidetic confabulation of time. Criteria that respect these realities foster a broader and more diversified conception of historical enframing that epistemologically problematizes the commonplace belief that we can be certain that the future does not flow into the past through the present or that the past is not as much occasioned by the future as the future is by the past. In contrast to this more conventional standpoint, the temporal presupposition buttressing my hermeneutic embraces the prospect of a reversible timeline—what I have called the timeswerve of linear circularity—such that the present is as much the cause of the past as the past is the cause of the present; the past persists in the present as the trace that is reconfigured anew each moment through the agency of anamnesis. In sync with Benjamin and Heidegger, I view scholarly reconstruction as a type of *futural remembering*,[102] or a *remembering expectation*,[103] an act of recollecting that has the capacity to redeem the past, not by describing how the past really was but by imputing to it meaning that it never had except as the potential to become what it is not. The radical possibility of time as future—a perspective shared by kabbalists and Heidegger—implies that the past itself is only past insofar as it is the reiteration of what is always yet to come. The gesture of mindfulness most apposite to this temporal possibility is the leap (*Sprung*), which "takes us abruptly to where everything is different, so different that it strikes us as strange," as opposed to a "steady progress, where we move unawares from one thing to the next and everything remains alike."[104] The deeper attunement leads to the recognition that appropriation of one's own requires the disappropriation of confronting the stranger. The encounter with the alien is what propels the journey home, the struggle with the unordinary instigates the return to the ordinary.

Accepting this hermeneutic plausibility, it is reasonable to propose that Heidegger can provide a metadiscourse to excavate structures of thought latent in kabbalistic literature. His own words on the nature of "genuine comparing" in *Einleitung in die Philosophie: Denken und Dichten*—a lecture course announced for the 1944–45 winter semester at the University of Freiburg but canceled after the second session as a result of the intrusion of the Nationalist Socialist Party in November 1944—are especially germane: "After all, comparing [*Vergleichen*] is not supposed to result only in the determination of what is the same and different [*die Feststellung von Gleichem und Verschiedenem*]; rather, with real comparison, we aspire to see what is different through the same and through the difference of the same [*durch das Gleiche das Verschiedene und durch das Verschiedene des Gleichen*] to always see into the very essence of that which stands in comparison."[105] In this book, I will seek to achieve the vision of that which stands in comparison so that difference is disclosed through the discernment of the same and the same through the discernment of difference. There is no appeal to a transcendental ideal for the nature of being or to a concept of experience that can be extricated from specific historical contexts, no postulating a metadiscourse or a monolingualism universally applicable to the multiple networks of sociolinguistic meaning. To paraphrase Derrida, even the speaking of one voice requires that there be several voices.[106] As Steven Burik has argued, the circumspect reader may elicit from Heidegger's own work a model of comparative thinking that is not expressive of syncretism or monotonization that would level out all difference, but rather the forging of a bricolage of thought based on convergences marked by deep-seated divergence,[107] or what has been called more recently by Eric Nelson intercultural hermeneutics.[108] In Heidegger's own formulation in the 1929–30 lecture course *Die Grundbegriffe der Metaphysik: Welt—Endlichkeit—Einsamkeit,* the comparative examination is the most approachable and adaptable method "because in the process of making and grasping distinctions we can first really glimpse whatever is coincident [*Übereinstimmende*] and the same [*Selbige*]."[109]

Here it is pertinent to recall that Heidegger was fond of distinguishing between "the identical" (*das Gleiche*) and "the same" (*das Selbe*).[110] Thus, for example, in "Die Onto-Theo-Logische Verfassung der Metaphysik," a lecture delivered on February 24, 1957, in Todtnauberg as part of a seminar on Hegel's *Wissenschaft der Logik,* he put it this way: "But the same is not the merely identical [*Allein das Selbe ist nicht das Gleiche*]. In the merely identical, the difference disappears [*verschwindet die Verschiedenheit*]. In the same the difference appears [*erscheint die Verschiedenheit*], and appears all the more pressingly, the more resolutely thinking is concerned with the same matter in the same way [*von derselben Sache auf dieselbe Weise*]."[111]

In the trialogue between the guide, the scientist, and the scholar on the nature of thinking, written in 1944–45 but published posthumously in 1995 with the title *Feldweg-Gespräche,* Heidegger expressed the difference between selfsameness (*Selbigkeit*) and identicalness (*Gleichheit*) by noting that the quality of belonging togetherness (*Zusammengehörigkeit*) applies to the former and not to the latter. We can say of things that are identical that they "associate well with one another" (*gleich und gleich gestellt sich gern*), but it is the identicalness that precludes the justification of thinking of them as belonging together (*zusammenzugehören*).[112] Things belong together, in other words, only because of the unbridgeable chasm that keeps them separate; sameness is discernible through difference, but not in a dialectical way that sublates the disjuncture of their conjunction.[113]

The centrality of this notion in Heidegger's thought can be gauged from a passing comment in the address he gave in Messkirch on October 30, 1955, commemorating Conradin Kreutzer's 175th birthday: "Meditative thinking demands of us that we engage ourselves with what at first sight does not go together at all [*nicht zusammengeht*]."[114] Unlike computational thinking, which forces us to cling one-sidedly to ideas and to stitch them together homogeneously, the thinking that is meditational compels us to compound that which is heterogeneous. From a comment in *Der Satz vom Grund,* the 1955–56 lecture course on the principle of reason delivered at the University of Freiburg, it can be further deduced that Heidegger considered the matter of sameness as the belonging together of difference an archaic truth of Western thought that perseveres as the unthought yet to be thought, which is to say, the essential thought that is prevented from ever becoming an object that is no longer underway to being thought:

> When we think the same—more precisely, sameness [*Selbigkeit*]—as a belonging together in essence [*Zusammengehörigkeit im Wesen*], then we keep in mind one of the earliest thoughts of Western thinking. Accordingly, "the same" does not mean the empty oneness of the one and the other, nor does it mean the oneness of something with itself. "The same" in the sense of oneness is the indifference [*Gleichgültige*] of an empty, endlessly repeatable identity [*Identität*]: A as A, B as B. Thought in the sense of what in essence belongs together, the same indeed bursts the indifference [*Gleichgültigkeit*] of what belongs together, even more it holds them apart in the most radical dissimilarity [*Ungleichheit*]; it holds them apart and yet does not allow them to fall away from each other and hence disintegrate. This holding-together

> [*Zussamenhalten*] in keeping-apart [*Auseinanderhalten*] is a trait of what we call the same and its sameness. This holding [*Halten*] pertains to a "relation" [*Verhältnis*] that still stands before thinking as what is to be thought.[115]

Utilizing the Schellingian locution, Heidegger thus delineates the same as the relational quality that bursts the indifference of what is conjoined, holding apart what is held together in radical dissimilarity as opposed to the oneness of the indifference of an endlessly repeatable identity. That radical dissimilarity is the underpinning of Heidegger's repeated emphasis on strife, the contentious encounter of combatants bonded in their disunion. The discriminating ear will hear echoes of this Heideggerian theme in Schelling's comment that the "outcome of opposing infinite activities" is a "*static* conflict," which is equivalent to rest. The synthesis has "to be thought of, not as an annihilation of the two activities by each other, but rather as an equilibrium to which they reduce one another, and whose continuance is conditioned by the persistent rivalry between the two."[116] For Schelling, as for Heidegger, the shared task of philosophy and art is to resolve the infinite dichotomy of opposed activities, but the aesthetic production unveils the mechanism of resolution more completely, and especially the primordial intuition of the poetic gift.[117] The oscillation between opposites is resolved by the third activity of juxtaposition, the bringing of the two opposites into a "relative equilibrium," but the latter is predicated on the constant recurrence of the contradiction between the opposites.[118]

The following passage from "Der Satz der Identität," a lecture delivered at the University of Freiburg on June 27, 1957, sheds further light on this critical Heideggerian hermeneutic of sameness as the *bringing-together by keeping apart*:

> If we think of belonging *together* [*Zusammen*gehören] in the customary way, the meaning of belonging is determined by the word together, that is, by its unity. In that case, "to belong" means as much as: to be assigned and placed into the order of a "together," established in the unity of a manifold, combined into the unity of a system, mediated by the unifying center of an authoritative synthesis. . . . However, belonging together can also be thought of as *belonging* together [Zusammen*gehören*]. This means: the "together" is now determined by the belonging.[119]

The belonging is no longer understood solely "in terms of the unity of the together," but rather connotes "experiencing this together in terms of belonging."[120] Heidegger concludes, therefore, that "belonging *together*" represents "belonging in terms of the unity of the together," whereas "*belonging* together" entails "experiencing this together in terms of belonging." Heidegger makes this distinction to explicate the coupling of thinking and being in the celebrated fragment of Parmenides, τὸ γὰρ αὐτὸ νοεῖν ἐστίν τε καὶ εἶναι, which he translates as *Das Selbe nämlich ist Vernehmen (Denken) sowohl als auch Sein*, "For the same perceiving (thinking) as well as being."[121] The choice of the term *das Selbe* to render the Greek *to auto* is quite deliberate on the part of Heidegger. According to his interpretation, "before thinking arrived at the principle of identity," Parmenides expressed the "enigma" (*Rätsel*) of identity in his pronouncement, which is to be decoded as follows: "thinking and Being belong together in the Same and by virtue of this Same" (*Denken und Sein gehören in das Selbe und aus diesem Selben zusammen*).[122]

To understand the mystery of the identity of thinking and being—the originary mystery that embodies the "essence of thinking" sanctioned by the ancient Greek thinkers and eventually abandoned by the "technical interpretation of thinking" advanced by philosophy beginning with the Sophists and Plato[123]—one must probe the nature of the belonging together. Thinking and being belong together in such a way that the togetherness is delimited by the belonging rather than the belonging by the togetherness, and thus the difference of the sameness of that which belongs together is affirmed—they are the same by virtue of being different. In the "Brief über den 'Humanismus,'" Heidegger put it simply, "thinking is the thinking of being. The genitive says something twofold. Thinking is of being inasmuch as thinking, propriated [*ereignet*] by being, belongs to being. At the same time thinking is of being insofar as thinking, belonging to being, listens to being. As the belonging to being that listens, thinking is what it is according to its essential origin."[124] Thinking belongs to being, but it does so as that which listens to being, which is to say, thinking and being belong together as what remain distinct, since the notion of listening—even listening to oneself—presupposes some degree of distance, a breach that can be bridged only by conjoining what remains apart.

Following this insight, the comparison of kabbalah and Heidegger undertaken in this monograph will yield reflections on the same within which the differences shall become more blatant in light of common ground. Given Heidegger's personal involvement with National Socialism, his disparaging use of some standard anti-Semitic tropes, his steadfast silence about the victims of Nazi brutality, and his concerted effort to avoid engaging any Jewish thinker or text, thereby banishing Jews from the history of philosophy,[125] it is all the more remarkable that the path of his thinking can be illumined by and can illumine the theosophical ruminations of the Jewish esoteric tradition.[126] Even more surprising is the fact that in both Heidegger and the kabbalists one can find a coupling of semantic essentialism and ethnocentric chauvinism, that is, the privileging of a particular language as disclosive of the truth of being and the consequent affirmation of a unique cultural destiny of a particular ethnos to be the custodian of that language in the land of its origin,[127] a position that harbors the potential for the disvaluing of others in racial terms.[128]

In a published review of the first three volumes of Heidegger's *Schwarzen Heften*, spanning the years 1931–41, David Krell noted the obvious: the "repeated juxtaposition of Jews and National Socialism in Heidegger's texts" is "repugnant and perverse." Focusing on one passage in particular in which Heidegger writes that his "attack" on Descartes "has been exploited by both Jews and National Socialists with equal vigor," Krell speculates that these words could have been written at the very moment when Kristallnacht occurred.[129] I certainly understand Krell's point and he is to be given credit for pointing out the magnitude of Heidegger's arrogance and insensitivity to pair the victims and the executor in this aberrant and tactless way. However, it is my hope that the juxtaposition of the ostensibly incongruent fields of discourse, the belonging together of what is foreign, Heidegger and kabbalah, will not only enhance our understanding of both, but, in an even more profound sense, will serve as an ethical corrective of their respective ethnocentrisms, thereby illustrating the redemptive capacity of thought to yield new configurations of the unthought colluding on disparate paths of contemplative thinking.

Notes

1. For a summary of Heidegger's affair with National Socialism, see de Beistegui, *New Heidegger*, pp. 155–79, and Kisiel's balanced treatment "Heidegger's Apology: Biography as Philosophy and Ideology" in his *Heidegger's Way of Thought*, pp. 1–35.

2. Wolfson, *Duplicity*.

3. There are many dimensions of the kabbalistic worldview—to wit, the mystical rationales for rituals, meditational and magical practices, contemplative study, inspired exegesis, angelic visitations, revelatory visions, and other paranormal experiences—that have no counterpart in Heidegger. My focus is limited to certain phenomenological and hermeneutical issues. Although I consider these matters to be central to understanding the philosophical anchor of kabbalistic lore and praxis, I make no claim that these are to be accorded more value than the other dimensions that fall outside the purview of my analysis. Let me note, finally, that the method that undergirds this book is related to my larger assumption that the kabbalah is itself an integral part of the Western philosophical tradition. For an early formulation, see my justification for using Irigaray to analyze the gender construction in medieval kabbalistic texts in Wolfson, "Occultation," p. 117n12. The criticism of my comment offered by Idel, *Kabbalah and Eros*, p. 254n28, is based on a narrow geo-cultural understanding of the taxonomy Western philosophy. In response to Idel's question, I would argue that it is perfectly legitimate, if not desirable, to explicate kabbalists from Persia and Yemen—the two countries mentioned by Idel—using Western philosophical concepts. First, this is

justified historically, since even the so-called "Eastern Kabbalists" were influenced, directly or indirectly, by medieval kabbalistic treatises—primarily composed in Provence and Spain—that were influenced by Aristotelian and Neoplatonic texts and ideas that originated in the Occident, even if they do not present the reader with a rigorous epistemology or a thoroughgoing ontology. But second, and more critically, I am committed to the supposition that one may engage kabbalistic sources philosophically and thereby elicit from them insights that will contribute to the ongoing interrogation of speculative questions that have perplexed thinkers through the centuries. This method is to be differentiated from the more historiographical orientation that puts its focus on the relationship of kabbalists to the philosophical literature of their day. As important as this line of research is, my concern is not with a chronological history of ideas, but with the more constructive attempt to delineate the interaction with philosophy that can be excavated from kabbalistic material. See Wolfson, "Retroactive Not Yet," p. 17.

4. Zarader, *Unthought Debt*. The book has commanded several critical reviews, but see especially Bergo, "Marlène Zarader's *The Unthought Debt*."

5. Zarader, *Unthought Debt*, p. 199.

6. Ibid., p. 7.

7. Ibid., p. 185. On the overlap between themes in the Hebrew Bible and Heideggerian thought, see the more recent conjecture of Atkins, *Ethical and Theological Appropriation*, pp. 162–66. In a letter to Shlomo Zemach, the translator of Heidegger's *Origins of the Work of Art* into Hebrew in 1968, Heidegger explicitly acknowledged that he studied Hebrew "at school" and later as part of his "theological studies." The letter is cited in Herskowitz, "Heidegger in Hebrew," p. 11.

8. Caputo, "People of God," pp. 89–92. On p. 89, Caputo argues that Heidegger's narrative of being is "structurally analogous in all of its main points to the biblical model, that is to the narratives of the Jews and their God in the Tanach, but in Heidegger's narrative the Jews are *totally silenced*, one might even say *repressed*" (emphasis in original). Following Zarader's lead, Caputo concludes that, in spite of Heidegger's intentions, the Jews are the unthought debt or what was left unsaid in his thought, and this is related especially to the emphasis in his own rival history of salvation on the need to respond to the inaugural call of being assigned to one people as their unique historical destiny.

9. Heidegger, *Off the Beaten Track*, p. 275; *Holzwege*, p. 364.

10. Zarader, *Unthought Debt*, pp. 130–38. Building on Zarader's conjecture, Goodman, "Give the Word," pp. 155–60, argues that Celan's attraction to Heidegger's speculation on *das Nichts* may have been inspired by his interest in the kabbalistic notion of *Ein Sof*, a curiosity that was stoked primarily by his reading some of Scholem's scholarship. On the possible affinity between the kabbalistic idea of *ṣimṣum* and Heidegger's description of nothingness as the vortex of zeroness, see Steiner, *Grammars of Creation*, pp. 27–28. In the final stages of writing this book, Jeremy Brown brought to my attention the monograph by Meinvielle, *De la Cábala*, which includes several chapters on the influence—or in the author's precise language, the penetration (*penetración*) and invasion (*invasión*)—of kabbalah on the "Christian world" (*mundo Cristiano*), including a brief section on "La línea cabalista de Heidegger," pp. 320–22. The main thrust of Meinvielle's argument is that Heidegger affirms the notion of being that is separate from beings but he rejects identifying it with God, the uncreated being (*ens increatum*) or the supreme being (*summum ens*) of Christian theology. Supplanting the scholastic metaphysics, Heidegger proposes a "gnostic" path that reintroduces the sacred as the impersonal and indeterminate being. Thus, following Löwith, *Heidegger*, p. 156, Meinvielle concludes that Heidegger continued in the footsteps of Hegel, who renewed in a modern philosophical idiom the language of Valentinus. For other attempts to retrieve the gnostic elements of Heidegger's thought, see below, n. 97.

11. Janicaud, *Heidegger in France*, pp. 358–59. Although Heidegger had Jewish students and colleagues, he unfalteringly showed no interest in engaging Jewish thought on its own terms. One possible exception might have been Martin Buber. Heidegger did maintain a personal connection with Buber, but even in this case it is not entirely clear how much of the latter's work, and especially on Jewish themes and figures, he read. Buber, of course, was more explicit about his engagement with Heidegger's thought, his most vital intervention being *Das Problem des Menschen*, based on lectures delivered in Jerusalem in 1938 and first published in Hebrew in 1942 and then in German in 1948, and *Gottesfinsternis: Betrachtungen zur Beziehung zwischen Religion und Philosophie*, published in 1953. On the relationship between the two thinkers, see Fackenheim, *To Mend the World*, pp. 190–92; and in more detail, Mendes-Flohr, "Martin Buber and Martin Heidegger." Mendes-Flohr writes that "Heidegger was apparently an avid reader of Buber's *Tales of the Hasidim* (*Erzählungen*

des Chassidim) and other of his writings as well" (p. 5). In the accompanying n. 17, Mendes-Flohr refers to Pöggeler, *Paths of Heidegger's Life*, p. 67, to substantiate the assumption about "Heidegger's early reading of Buber's Hasidic tales." Unfortunately, Pöggeler refers only to Heidegger's making use of Buber's *Reden und Gleichnisse des Tschuang Tse*. Mendes-Flohr mentions this work as well and recounts the event in Heidelberg in October 1930 when Heidegger read from Buber's edition of the parables of Chuang Tzu. In support of this claim, he cites Petzet, *Encounters and Dialogues*, pp. 18–19. On the reception of and interaction with Taoism in Heidegger and Buber, see the analysis of Nelson, *Chinese and Buddhist Philosophy*, pp. 109–29. On Buber's meeting with Heidegger, see the correspondence between Fackenheim and Scholem in Scholem, *Life in Letters*, pp. 475–76. The original German is published in Scholem, *Briefe III*, pp. 194–95; Fackenheim's letter is reproduced on p. 420, # 179, n. 1. For more evidence of the encounter between Buber and Heidegger, including photographs, see now Weissblei, "German Martin and the Jewish Mordechai." The complex relationship between Heidegger and Buber centered on the question of ontology and human existence is explored by Munro, "On Being Oneself"; Gordon, *Heidegger-Buber Controversy*. On Buber's critique of Heidegger, see Gordon, op. cit., pp. 151–58 and Goldstein, "Buber's Misunderstanding," pp. 156–67; Novak, "Buber's Critique"; Friedman, "Buber, Heschel, and Heidegger"; Urban, "Paradox of Realization," pp. 175–77. On Buber and Heidegger, see also Herskowitz, "Heidegger as a Secularized Kierkegaard," and Hadad, "Fruits of Forgetfulness."

12. Buber, *Eclipse*, p. 73. The passage to which Buber refers is Heidegger, *Elucidations*, pp. 136–37; *Erläuterungen*, pp. 113–14. See ch. 3 at n. 180. On Heidegger's attempt to contrast poetry and prophetism, see Zarader, *Unthought Debt*, pp. 51–56. Finally, it is worth mentioning the passage from Heidegger, *Anmerkungen I–V*, p. 159, cited and analyzed in Wolfson, *Duplicity*, pp. 167–68. In that aphorism, Heidegger remarks that prophecy is an instrument of the will to power and that the great prophets were Jews, "a fact whose secret side has not yet been thought." Anticipating that others would consider his comment prejudicial, he adds a parenthetical gloss, "A footnote for donkeys: this observation has nothing to do with 'anti-Semitism.' Anti-Semitism is as foolish and as objectionable as the bloody and above all the unbloody attack on 'the pagans' by Christianity. That Christianity too condemns anti-Semitism as 'un-Christian' belongs to the highly developed finesse of its technology of power." As I noted in *Duplicity*, p. 265n61, I utilized the translation by Krell, "Troubled Brows," p. 319. For a different rendering and analysis, see di Cesare, *Heidegger and the Jews*, pp. 214–15. Di Cesare attempts to contextualize the passage historically by noting that it was written after Heidegger had been banned from teaching at the university in 1946. She also argues that Heidegger's self-defense that his comment about Jews and prophecy had nothing to do with anti-Semitism should be read against the backdrop of the growing stigmatization of anti-Semitism in the period of de-Nazification (*Entnazifizierung*). This historical contextualization makes sense, and in particular sheds light on why Heidegger would emphasize that Christianity already condemned anti-Semitism as unchristian, but it does not address the crucial nexus Heidegger draws between the prophecy of the Jews and the will to power.

13. See the evidence adduced in Babich, "Heidegger's Jews," pp. 134–35; and Babich, "Heidegger's *Judenfrage*."

14. Derrida, Gadamer, and Lacoue-Labarthe, *Heidegger*, p. x. Also relevant to Heidegger's repression or marginalization of other cultural formations is the essay by Bernasconi, "On Heidegger's Other Sins." See, by contrast, Davis, "Heidegger on the Way"; and see the studies cited in ch. 3 n. 94.

15. Junk, *Metapher und Sprachmagie*.

16. Wolin, *Heidegger's Children*.

17. Fleischacker, ed., *Heidegger's Jewish Followers*. The influence of "Heideggerian themes or, at least, a post-Nietzschean sensibility" on many of the German-Jewish thinkers from the Weimar period is noted by Aschheim in *Beyond the Borders*, p. 93.

18. Scult, *Being Jewish/Reading Heidegger*. See also Scult, "Forgiving 'La Dette Impensée.'" Noteworthy as well is the hermeneutical program for rereading Heidegger, based on the Jewish concept of *teshuvah*, laid out in the essay by Gibbs, "Reading Heidegger."

19. Fagenblat, "'Heidegger' and the Jews," p. 157. See also Fagenblat, "Lévinas, Judaism, Heidegger." According to Fagenblat, not only is Heidegger an indispensable key to comprehending the viability of Levinas's philosophical ethics, but Heideggerian hermeneutics—especially the notion of "formal indication" (*formale Anzeige*), by which Heidegger established a relationship between the Christian experience of enactment (*Vollzug*) and fundamental ontology—can serve as the foundation for a philosophy of Judaism that is not simply predicated on Jewish identity ("Levinas, Judaism, Heidegger," pp. 56–57).

20. Lapidot, "Das Fremde im Denken"; Dolgopolski, "How Else?"

21. Fackenheim, *Encounters*, p. 218. The passage is cited by Fagenblat, "'Heidegger' and the Jews," pp. 157–58.

22. Fackenheim, *Encounters*, p. 219.

23. Heidegger, *On the Way to Language*, p. 127; *Unterwegs zur Sprache*, p. 246. Compare Heidegger, *On the Way to Language*, p. 47 (*Unterwegs zur Sprache*, p. 137), where the expression "saying" (*sagen*) is said to have the meaning of "let appear and let shine [*erscheinen- und scheinenlassen*], but in the manner of hinting." See Wolfson, *Giving*, p. 131. For a different assessment of the status of the visual image in Heidegger's poetic-linguistic ontology, see Gosetti-Ferencei, *Ecstatic Quotidian*, pp. 185–94.

24. Heidegger, *Poetry, Language, Thought*, p. 170; *Vorträge und Aufsätze*, p. 172.

25. Heidegger, *Essence of Truth*, p. 40; *Vom Wesen der Wahrheit*, p. 54.

26. Novak, "Buber's Critique," pp. 134–36.

27. Fackenheim, *To Mend the World*, pp. 168–71. Fackenheim, on pp. 180–81, does note the eventual shift in Heidegger and his critique of Nazism but finds it wanting and inauthentic. Compare Fackenheim's remark in a letter to Scholem (November 26, 1978), in Scholem, *Life in Letters*, p. 475, inquiring about Buber's meeting with Heidegger: "Perhaps I should add that what is at stake for me here is not Heidegger but the philosophical concerns that he so profoundly stirred and that, in my opinion, he failed philosophically (not to mention personally) to carry out: namely, the historical-ness of Being and the question of truth in the Age of Technology." For the original German, see Scholem, *Briefe III*, p. 420, # 179, n. 1

28. Wolfson, *Language*, pp. 13–21. Fagenblat, "'Heidegger' and the Jews," p. 157, correctly notes the "extensive use of Heidegger" in my "research into Kabbalistic language." The author generously refers to some of my previous publications on p. 166n70 and even mentions the present book as a forthcoming project. See also Fagenblatt, "The Thing," p. 18. With no blame intended to the author, this does not tell the whole story, including my noting the influence of kabbalah on Schelling (see reference below, n. 40) as well as drawing attention to the affinities between Heideggerian thought and modern Jewish philosophy, especially Rosenzweig and Levinas, and this includes the possible residuals of kabbalistic concepts, chronicled in great detail in Wolfson, *Giving*, pp. 45–54, 68–69, 80–81, 94–102, 124–32. Fagenblat, "'Heidegger' and the Jews," pp. 152–56, independently discusses the relationship of Heidegger to Rosenzweig, Levinas, Altmann, and Soloveitchik. See also Fagenblatt, "The Thing," pp. 12–20. On Altmann's use of Heidegger in constructing a contemporary Jewish theology, see Wolfson, *Giving*, p. 290n37, where I refer to previous scholarship that I will refrain from repeating in this context. The attraction of Altmann to Heidegger may have also been related to a mutual interest in Gnosticism. Consider the revealing testimony given by Altmann, "Author's Preface," in *Meaning of Jewish Existence*, p. xii: "Hans Jonas's disclosure of the Gnostic world view (1934), which at that time was virtually disregarded in Germany, also found a strong resonance in me, not least in view of the demonic features of the life experience of those days. Herein lies the basis for my long preoccupation with Gnostic motifs in rabbinic literature." On this passage, see Wasserstrom, "Hans Jonas," pp. 59–60. On Altmann's interest in Gnosticism and various studies on it, see Mendes-Flohr, "Theologian before the Abyss," in Altmann, *Meaning of Jewish Existence*, pp. xlv–xlvii. Regarding Heidegger and Soloveitchik, see Wolfson, "Eternal Duration," pp. 208–12n37; Herskowitz, "Rabbi Joseph B. Soloveitchik's Endorsement," pp. 382–86; and Herskowitz, "The Moment and the Future," pp. 97–99. Herskowitz's suggestion that the similarity I detect between Heidegger and Soloveitchik can be explained by the influence of Kierkegaard on both of them is well taken, but I would argue nevertheless that the specific issue of the compresence of the three temporal modes in the moment reflects the kabbalistic idea as transmitted in Ḥabad sources. See, more recently, Shatz, "Contemporary Scholarship," pp. 156, 157n57, 159–60n58, 166–67n85. On balance, I would say, my contributions to the topic of Heidegger and modern Jewish thinkers could be well characterized by Fagenblat's own assertion that the task is not only to trace the "'Hebraic' elements in Heidegger's thought but the becoming-Heideggerian of prominent strands of modern Jewish thought" (Fagenblat, "'Heidegger' and the Jews," p. 158). Finally, mention should be made of Perlman, *Eclipse of Humanity*. I agree with the main thesis of Perlman's study, although I think that in some other areas of phenomenological inquiry, for instance, their respective investigations of temporality, a case can be made for a more striking resemblance between Heschel and Heidegger. I will not respond in length to Perlman's criticism of my use of Heidegger (pp. 29–30n92), but I will say it is disappointing that in a book published in 2016, the author refers only to my monograph published in 1994 and makes no effort to relate to subsequent work in which I have delved more deeply into the affinities

between Heidegger, the kabbalists, and modern Jewish thinkers, including Heschel. On Heschel and Heidegger, see also Held, *Abraham Joshua Heschel*, pp. 46–51, 249–50nn176–77; Herskowitz, "God, Being, Pathos."

29. Heidegger, *Poetry, Language, Thought*, p. 53; *Holzwege*, p. 40. On φύσις as the ever-emerging self-concealment, see Dahlstrom, "Being," pp. 140–46. It is of interest to recall the comment of Boeder, *Seditions*, p. 6: "No light penetrates the darkness of Heidegger's thought so long as reference continues to be made to the double-pivoting of a φύσις that is simultaneously an emergence into appearance and a self-concealment. This reference fades insofar as thinking finds its way out of Nature not only as it is the Nature of what appears but, what is more, out of Nature as the history of self-concealing and thereby severs the history of occidental thought from just this Nature. This was our point of departure from Heideggerian thought." It is beyond the scope of this note for me to evaluate whether this student of Heidegger was able to achieve this departure, but what is most relevant to my discussion is Boeder's recognition of the central place the paradox of the concurrent revealing and concealing occupied in his teacher's thought. On Heidegger's notion of truth as unconcealment or disclosedness, see also Farber, "Heidegger"; Anderson, "Truth"; Stambaugh, *Finitude of Being*, pp. 13–30; Tugendhat, *Wahrheitsbegriff*, pp. 389–93, 396–99, 402–3; Tugendhat, "Heidegger's Idea of Truth"; and the discussion in Zabala, *Hermeneutic Nature*, pp. 25–44; Dahlstrom, *Heidegger's Concept*, pp. 182, 214, 223–31, 238–40, 291–92, 300–1, 314–15, 322–25, 389–92, 397–407, 431–32; Olafson, "Being"; Sallis, "Interrupting Truth"; de Beistegui, *Truth and Genesis*, pp. 122–30, 142–46, 153–54; Wrathall, "Heidegger, Truth, and Reference"; Wrathall, "Heidegger on Plato"; Malpas, *Heidegger's Topology*, pp. 183–201; Gonzalez, *Plato and Heidegger*, pp. 225–55; Blond, *Heidegger and Nietzsche*, pp. 79–98. On the interplay of revealing and concealing in Heidegger, see also Vail, *Heidegger and Ontological Difference*, pp. 25–46.

30. Heidegger, *Poetry, Language, Thought*, p. 54; *Holzwege*, p. 40.

31. Heidegger, *Poetry, Language, Thought*, pp. 54–55; *Holzwege*, p. 41. Heidegger's commitment to the proposition that "the nature of truth is untruth," *das Wesen der Wahrheit ist die Un-Wahrheit* (*Poetry, Language, Thought*, p. 55; *Holzwege*, p. 41) may be related as well to another deep structure of the kabbalistic worldview, viz., the belief that the deceptiveness of the demonic is an inherent aspect of the veracity of the divine. To the extent that evil is the other side and not the privation of good, that darkness is a manifestation and not the occlusion of light, it follows that there can be no truth that is not itself untruth, no rectitude that is not tinged with mendacity. For discussion of the relevance of this motif to Heidegger's ethics and politics, see Wolfson, *Duplicity*, pp. 154–68. In that analysis, I suggested, inter alia, that the kabbalistic idea may have been transmitted to Heidegger through Böhme and Schelling. On Heidegger's use of Böhme's notion of strife and Schelling's idea of rage, see now Bernasconi, "Being is Evil."

32. Heidegger, *Pathmarks*, p. 148; *Wegmarken*, p. 194.

33. Heidegger, *Contributions*, §129, p. 194 (all references are to the translation of Rojcewicz and Vallega-Neu unless otherwise noted); *Beiträge*, p. 246. The passage is discussed in Wolfson, *Giving*, pp. 242–43. See also Maly, "Man and Disclosure," pp. 51–54.

34. Bernasconi, *Question of Language*, pp. 15–27, 87; Wolfson, *Language*, pp. 19, 413n173; Wolfson, *Giving*, pp. 2, 48–52, 130–31, 243. For a critique of the Heideggerian interpretation of *a-lēthēs* and *a-lētheuein* as unconcealment, see Jonas, *Phenomenon of Life*, p. 181.

35. Heidegger, *On the Way to Language*, p. 50 (emphasis in original); *Unterwegs zur Sprache*, p. 140.

36. Scholem, *Messianic Idea*, p. 293. See also Idel, *Old Worlds*, p. 111.

37. Idel, *Old Worlds*, p. 273n11. I am grateful to Idel for acknowledging the affinity between my view on concealment and disclosure in kabbalistic lore and the perspective of Scholem, and for his noting further the Lacanian influence on my thinking. See also Idel, *Kabbalah and Eros*, p. 129. I have certainly been explicit about the impact of Lacan—especially as it relates to his idea of the exposure of the phallus that remains veiled (see Wolfson, "Circumcision, Secrecy"; Wolfson, *Language*, pp. 128–36)—but Heidegger is an equally, if not more, important source, although perhaps one should note the Heideggerian background of Lacan himself on this matter (see ch. 1 n. 131). To complicate the picture, one could argue that Scholem's perspective is close to Eliade's idea of the religious phenomenon as a hierophany wherein the sacred is both manifest and occluded, occluded to the extent that it is manifest and manifest to the extent that it is occluded, a position that has much in common with the Heideggerian hermeneutic and the paradoxical confluence of truth and untruth, concealment and disclosure. See Wolfson, *Abraham Abulafia*, pp. 17n21, 28–29 (see ch. 7 n. 147). For a different approach to Scholem's relationship

to Heidegger, see Magid, "Gershom Scholem's Ambivalence," pp. 246–47: "As we will see, the defining factor for Scholem is his theory of language, which, unlike Buber and Heidegger, is not an adequate tool of communication, but is the fabric of experience and being itself." According to Magid, Scholem's critique of Buber's *Erlebnismystik* (for a more detailed evaluation of this topic, see Mendes-Flohr, "Introductory Essay," pp. 12–14) as allocating ultimate authority to subjective experience was combined with a Cohenian rejection of the Parmenidean identity of being and thought bolstering a pantheistic cosmology, which becomes most pronounced in the rejection of any transcendence in Heidegger's thinking. See the reproach of Heidegger in one of Scholem's poems cited in ch. 6 n. 222. Scholem's possible engagement with Heidegger is noted as well by Wasserstrom, *Religion after Religion*, pp. 136, 229, 310n60. On Scholem's antipathy to Heidegger and his refusal to accept Gadamer's invitation to meet him based on the inability to forgive his past, see Scholem's letter to Fackenheim (December 7, 1978), in Scholem, *Life in Letters*, p. 476; Scholem, *Briefe III*, p. 195. See ch. 8 n. 176. In my work, including in this volume, I offer a different perspective that narrows the gap between Scholem and Heidegger. For both thinkers, language attests to the fabric of being but in such a manner that language unveils the veil of being that remains veiled in the unveiling. The paradox is also expressed by Scholem linguistically in terms of the relationship between the name and the nameless. See, for instance, Scholem, "Name of God," p. 174, and compare ibid., pp. 180, 193–94. I readily acknowledge that with respect to the privileging of paradox in the kabbalistic understanding and expression of truth, I do concur with Scholem. For a criticism of Scholem's description of the kabbalistic view as paradoxical, together with the notion of the mythological, as oversimplifications, see Idel, "On Some Forms," pp. xxxi–xxxii. I would counter that an appreciation of the nature of the mythical or the paradoxical in general, and in particular as the matter may be elicited from kabbalistic texts, hardly merits the label of oversimplification. Idel's claim is based on an inadequate appeal to hermeneutical diversity and the faulty assertion that, by applying these structural categories to the analysis of texts, the scholar is guilty of necessarily adopting an "essentialistic approach" that lacks "open-mindedness."

38. The connection is made explicit in the description of the Lurianic mythology in Scholem, *Kabbalah*, p. 143: "At the same time, side by side with this Gnostic outlook, we find a most astonishing tendency to a mode of contemplative thought that can be called 'dialectic' in the strictest sense of the term as used by Hegel. This tendency is especially prominent in attempts to present formal explanations of such doctrines as that of the *ẓimẓum*, the breaking of the vessels, or the formation of the *parẓufim*." Although Hegel is not mentioned explicitly, the influence of his thinking is evident in the description of the emanation of the *sefirot* from the infinite nothingness in Scholem, *Major Trends*, p. 218: "In other words, the passage from *ain* to *ani* is symbolical of the transformation by which the Nothing passes through the progressive manifestation of its essence in the Sefiroth, into the I—a dialectical process whose thesis and antithesis begin and end in God: surely a remarkable instance of dialectical thought. Here as elsewhere, mysticism, intent on formulating the paradoxes of religious experience, uses the instrument of dialectics to express its meaning. The Kabbalists are by no means the only witnesses to this affinity between mystical and dialectical thinking."

39. Jonas, "Heidegger and Theology," pp. 211–15, reprinted with minor changes in Jonas, *Phenomenon of Life*, pp. 240–44.

40. On the influence of Cusanus on Heidegger, see McDonough, *Martin Heidegger's Being and Time*, p. xxvi n4. The possible impact of Christian kabbalah on Cusanus, related especially to the mystical meaning of the divine names, including the name YHSWH, has been discussed by Schmidt-Biggemann, *Geschichte der christlichen Kabbala*, 1:49–55. On the name YHSWH, see the sources (including a passage from Pico) cited in Wolfson, *Along the Path*, p. 213n104, to which one might add Baader, *Biographie und Briefwechsel*, 461; Schmidt-Biggemann, *Geschichte der christlichen Kabbala*, 1:16–18. For other references to Baader and the kabbalah, see below, n. 91. On the relationship of Schelling and the kabbalah, see Scholem, *Major Trends*, pp. 409n19 and 412n77; Scholem, *Kabbalah*, pp. 134 and 200; Schulze, "Schelling und die Kabbala"; Benz, *Mystical Sources*, pp. 47–58; Idel, *Kabbalah: New Perspectives*, p. 264; Olson, *Hegel and the Spirit*, pp. 42–44; Schulte, "Zimzum in the Works of Schelling" (German version: "Zimzum bei Schelling"); Schulte, "Ẓimẓum in der *Kabbala Denudata*"; Schulte, *Zimzum*, pp. 296–323; Cahnman, "Friedrich Wilhelm Schelling"; Beach, *Potencies of God(s)*, pp. 1–2, 6–13, 25–45, 69–82, 226–30; Bowie, *Schelling*, p. 117; Gibbons, *Spirituality*, pp. 12–13; Koslowski, *Philosophien der Offenbarung*, pp. 565–771; Habermas, "Dialectical Idealism in Transition"; Bielik-Robson, "God of Luria." And compare the discussion of Franz Joseph Molitor, which includes

occasional references to Schelling, in Schmidt-Biggemann, *Geschichte der christlichen Kabbala*, 3:382–425, esp. 401, 408, 413–14, 417. See also Schmidt-Biggemann, "Schellings 'Weltalter,'" pp. 4, 10, 38–40, 62, 77; Wolfson, *Language*, pp. xv–xvi, 99–105, and references to other scholars mentioned on pp. 392–93n2; and see further references cited in ch. 4 n. 279. For the more specific affinity between Schelling and Ḥabad, see Wolfson, *Open Secret*, pp. 101–2; Wolfson, "Achronic Time," pp. 57–73. On Rosenzweig's linking the Lurianic teaching about the "interiorization of God," which precedes the "self-externalization," and the "dark ground" of Schelling's thought, see Wolfson, *Giving*, p. 80, and references cited on p. 346nn332–33. Schelling's embrace of kabbalah, I presume, may also be related to the more positive outlook he adopted regarding the place and the role of Judaism in the history of religion. See Danz, "'Ihre Wahrheit hat die alttestamentliche Religion nur in der Zukunft.'" The influence of kabbalah on German idealism is addressed as well by Meinvielle, *De la Cábala*, pp. 254–65. See also the wide-ranging analysis of Vassányi, *Anima Mundi*, and the remark about Schelling on p. 387; Franks, "Rabbinic Idealism and Kabbalistic Realism," pp. 232–41; Franks, "Peirce's 'Schelling-Fashioned Idealism,'" pp. 745–51; Franks, "Fichte's Kabbalistic Realism." Also relevant here are the studies on the occult nature of Hegel's philosophical incursions by O'Regan, *Heterodox Hegel*, and Magee, *Hegel*. Magee discusses the influence of kabbalism on Hegel on pp. 150–86. See also Simuţ, *F. C. Baur's Synthesis*. On the affinity of Hegel and the kabbalah, see also Franks, "Nothing Comes from Nothing," p. 12, where the proximity between the Lurianic doctrine of *ṣimṣum* and the depiction of divine creativity in Hegel as the negation of self-negativity is noted. For the impact of Böhmean theosophy on Hegel, see Codignola, "Monde sensible." A related but separate issue is Schelling's classification of philosophy as esoteric and inaccessible, a perspective he shared early on with Hegel. See Franks, *All or Nothing*, pp. 82n135, 327–29, 374–76. Finally, many have opined on the intellectual relationship between Schelling and Heidegger. For the purposes of this study, see especially Iber, *Das Andere der Vernunft*, pp. 326–61; Hedley, "Schelling and Heidegger." See below, n. 93.

41. Wolfson, "Divine Suffering," pp. 110–17. See also Wolfson, "Murmuring Secrets," pp. 69–85.

42. Compare the Lacanian text about the nature of the rainbow and the elementary utterance *c'est cela* cited and discussed by Žižek, *Less Than Nothing*, pp. 861–62.

43. Heidegger, *Off the Beaten Track*, p. 254; *Holzwege*, p. 337.

44. The language was used by Funkenstein, *Perceptions of Jewish History*, p. 331, in his comparison of Heidegger's notion of being with Spinoza's idea of substance, which he famously identified as God or nature (*Deus sive natura*).

45. Compare the formulation of Blumenberg, "Light as a Metaphor," p. 31 (cited in ch. 7 at n. 71).

46. Heidegger, *Pathmarks*, pp. 277–78; *Wegmarken*, pp. 365–66. On the motif of the light of being in Heidegger, see Wood, *Path into Metaphysics*, pp. 297–99.

47. Kahn, *Art and Thought of Heraclitus*, pp. 82–83, 271–72.

48. Heidegger, *Early Greek Thinking*, p. 72; *Vorträge und Aufsätze*, p. 227.

49. Heidegger, *Heraklit*, p. 162. I have utilized the translation in Maly and Emad, eds., *Heidegger on Heraclitus*, p. 45. See now Heidegger, *Heraclitus*, p. 123. For an analysis of Heidegger's reading of this Heraclitean fragment, see Korab-Karpowicz, *Presocratics*, pp. 131–33.

50. Kahn, *Art and Thought of Heraclitus*, pp. 32–33, 105.

51. Heidegger, *Principle of Reason*, p. 70; *Satz vom Grund*, p. 104. Heidegger cited and interpreted this Heraclitean dictum frequently in his lectures and writings. Compare Heidegger, *Metaphysical Foundations*, p. 217 (*Metaphysische Anfangsgründe*, p. 281); Heidegger, *Fundamental Concepts*, p. 27 (*Grundbegriffe*, p. 41); Heidegger, *Essence of Truth*, pp. 9–11 (*Vom Wesen der Wahrheit*, pp. 13–15); Heidegger, *Early Greek Thinking*, pp. 113–14 (*Vorträge und Aufsätze*, pp. 277–79); Heidegger, *Introduction to Metaphysics*, pp. 120–21 (*Einführung in die Metaphysik*, p. 122); Heidegger, *Pathmarks*, pp. 229–30 (*Wegmarken*, pp. 300–1); Heidegger, *Heraclitus*, pp. 83–86, 90–91, 131–32 (*Heraklit*, pp. 109–14, 121–22, 175–77). For discussion of Heidegger's interpretation of the Heraclitean saying and the self-concealing of nature, see Scott, "Appearing to Remember Heraclitus," pp. 252–57; Dahlstrom, "Being," pp. 142–43, 150–51; Wolfson, *Giving*, pp. 51–52, 316–17n129. The interpretive history of the aphorism of Heraclitus is traced by Hadot, *Veil of Isis*, pp. 39–87. Heidegger's specific explication thereof is discussed on pp. 303–7.

52. Beaufret, "Heraclitus and Parmenides," pp. 83–84.

53. Wolfson, *Open Secret*, pp. 25–27, 52, 64, 96, 99–100, 113, 114–29, 212, 245, 341n166.

54. I have taken the liberty to repeat the argument in Wolfson, *Giving*, p. 54.

55. Heidegger, *Gelassenheit*, p. 25. I have modified the translation of *herzhaften Denken* as "courageous thinking" in Heidegger, *Discourse on Thinking*, p. 56. Commenting on the expression *herzhaften Denken*, translated as "hearty thinking," in relation to *Gelassenheit*, Schürmann, *Meister Eckhart*, p. 202, noted that the heart, for Heidegger, is not "the seat of the sentiments" but "the place where the totality of beings renders itself essentially present: it is the center or the core of thinking. This 'heart of thought,' then, maintains a nonfortuitous relation with letting-be and the openness to the favors of the mystery." See also Wood, "Heart in Heidegger's Thought."

56. Heidegger, *Discourse on Thinking*, p. 46; *Gelassenheit*, pp. 12–13. See Stambaugh, "Future of Continental Philosophy." On the meditative nature of the Heideggerian *Besinnung*, see also Seidel, "Musing with Kierkegaard," pp. 410–12. On the ontological difference, see Heidegger, *Basic Problems of Phenomenology*, p. 227 (*Grundprobleme der Phänomenologie*, p. 322): "It is not without reason that the problem of the distinction between being in general and beings occurs here in the first place. For the purpose of the discussion of this difference is to make it possible first of all to get to see thematically and put into investigation, in a clear and methodically secure way, the like of being in distinction from beings. The possibility of ontology, of philosophy as a science, stands and falls with the possibility of a sufficiently clear accomplishment of this differentiation between being and beings and accordingly with the possibility of negotiating the passage from the ontical consideration of beings to the ontological thematization of being."

57. Heidegger, *Ponderings VII–XI*, pp. 57–58; *Überlegungen VII–XI*, pp. 75–76.

58. Heidegger, *Country Path Conversations*, p. 68; *Feldweg-Gespräche*, p. 106.

59. Derrida, *Circumfession*, p. 156. See Caputo, "Toward a Postmodern Theology," p. 221; Wolfson, *Giving*, pp. 157 and 194.

60. Derrida, *Gift of Death*, p. 100; *Donner la mort*, p. 137. See Wolfson, *Giving*, pp. 191–92.

61. Caputo, "Toward a Postmodern Theology," p. 223, sharply contrasts the Derridean insight that the truth is that there is no truth, and the secret is that there is no secret, with the Heideggerian *Denken*, "which is steered by a mighty *Geschick*, a destiny and *moira*, our destiny on Derrida's account is 'destinerrance,' destiny gone errant, cut off from destiny and the Truth of Being." In my judgement, the gap between the two thinkers is not so wide insofar as Heidegger, too, disavows an idea of truth that can be surgically disentangled from untruth. I would go so far as to say that the Derridean dissimulation of secrecy is indebted to Heidegger's insight that every truth is enveloped in a veil of untruth. See, however, Bruns, *Inventions*, pp. 95–97; and Bruns, *Hermeneutics*, pp. 222–23.

62. My surmise regarding the affinity of the kabbalistic conception of language and Heidegger can be contrasted with the argument about magical speech and the Frankfurt school proffered by Matern, *Über Sprachgeschichte*. See also Martins, *Adorno und die Kabbala*, pp. 148–56, 163–68. See ch. 3 n. 229. Relevant as well is the comparative analysis of the question of language in Heidegger and Jewish sources in Zarader, *Unthought Debt*, pp. 37–57. See also the study of Fagenblat cited below, n. 75.

63. Bernasconi, *Question of Language*, pp. 21–23.

64. Heidegger, *Pathmarks*, p. 239; *Wegmarken*, p. 312.

65. Heidegger, *Pathmarks*, p. 254; *Wegmarken*, p. 333.

66. For a more detailed discussion of this theme, see Wolfson, *Giving*, pp. 94–102.

67. Courtine, "Phenomenology and/or Tautology," pp. 249–50. For an attempt to relate Heidegger's understanding of secrecy as a form of concealment, which belongs inextricably to truth as unconcealment, to the paradox of the secret affirmed by ancient thinkers, see Bruns, *Inventions*, pp. 17–18.

68. Heidegger, *Discourse on Thinking*, p. 55; *Gelassenheit*, p. 24.

69. Heidegger, *Hölderlin's Hymn "The Ister,"* p. 72; *Hölderlins Hymne "Der Ister,"* p. 89.

70. Heidegger, *Off the Beaten Track*, p. 85; *Holzwege*, p. 112.

71. Heidegger, *Off the Beaten Track*, p. 85; *Holzwege*, p. 113.

72. Heidegger, *Zollikon Seminars*, p. 171; *Zollikoner Seminare: Protokolle*, p. 216. See now Heidegger, *Zollikoner Seminare*, p. 76: "*Behalten* Bergen im Verbergen in die Unverborgenheit Bewahren vor dem Sog in der sich entziehenden *Verborgenheit*. Geheimnis: die sich entziehende Verborgenheit als solche" (emphasis in original). The secret as the withdrawing concealment is occasioned by the safeguarding of the hiding in the unhiddenness.

73. Heidegger, *Basic Writings*, p. 330; *Vorträge und Aufsätze*, p. 26.

74. See above, n. 53.

75. For a position similar to my own, see Fagenblat, "Of Dwelling Prophetically," pp. 252–58.

76. Heidegger, *Ponderings II–VI*, p. 170; *Überlegungen II–VI*, p. 233.

77. Di Cesare, *Heidegger e gli ebrei*, pp. 135–46, 207–13; di Cesare, *Heidegger and the Jews*, pp. 105–15,

164–68, 201–2; di Cesare, "Das Sein und der Jude," pp. 63–66; English translation: "Heidegger's Metaphysical Anti-Semitism," pp. 186–87. See also McCumber, "Heidegger: Beyond Anti-Semitism."

78. Heidegger, *Ponderings XII–XV*, p. 191 (emphasis in original); *Überlegungen XII–XV*, p. 243.

79. Heidegger, *Ponderings II–VI*, p. 91; *Überlegungen II–VI*, p. 124.

80. Lapidot, "People of Knowers," p. 277.

81. Di Cesare, "Being and the Jew," pp. 77–78 (emphasis in original).

82. Wolfson, *Alef*, pp. 30–46.

83. Koenker, "Grund"; Weeks, "Radical Reformation," p. 52. For more detailed studies of Böhme's impact on Schelling, see Benz, *Schellings theologische Geistesahnen*; Brown, *Later Philosophy*; Schulte, "F. W. J. Schellings Ausleihe"; Vieillard-Baron, "Schelling et Jacob Böhme"; Mayer, *Jena Romanticism*, pp. 179–221; and Whistler, "Silvering," pp. 160–67. Heidegger makes use of the term *Abgrund* much more frequently than *Ungrund*, but the latter is found on occasion as well. For instance, see Heidegger, *Contributions*, § 11, p. 27 (*Beiträge*, p. 31): "The grounded ground is at once abyss [*Abgrund*] for the fissure of beyng and distorted ground [*Ungrund*] for the abandonment of beings by being." See also Heidegger, *Contributions*, § 34, p. 61 (*Beiträge*, pp. 76–77): "Beyng as the ground in which all beings first come to their truth (sheltering, instituting, objectivity); the ground in which beings are submerged (abyss) [*Abgrund*]; the ground in which they also claim to be *indifferent* [Gleichgültigkeit] and *self-evident* [Selbstverständlichkeit] (distorted ground) [*Ungrund*]" (emphasis in original). In my opinion, the translation of *Ungrund* as "distorted ground" offered by Rojcewicz and Vallega-Neu should be modified to "nonground." *Abgrund* and *Ungrund* are paired together as well in Heidegger, *Contributions*, § 188, p. 244; *Beiträge*, p. 308. The former is correlated with concealment of being (*Verbergung des Seins*) and nihilation (*Nichtung*), the latter with dissemblance (*Verstellung*) and decomposition (*Verwesung*). See also Heidegger, *Contributions*, § 226, p. 277 (*Beiträge*, p. 351): "Only now can we also see more clearly the origin of *errancy* and the power and possibility of the abandonment by being, the concealment [*die Verbergung*] and the dissembling [*die Ver-stellung*]: the dominance of the distorted ground [*die Herrschaft des Ungrundes*]" (emphasis in original). Once again, I suggest that the translation of *Ungrund* as distorted ground be changed to nonground. See the passage cited in ch. 4 at n. 93.

84. Emmet, "Ground of Being"; Caputo, *Mystical Element*, p. 98.

85. Heidegger, *Schelling's Treatise*, pp. 116–17 (*Schelling: Vom Wesen*, pp. 203–4): "To understand this, we must think God's nature clearly, God, insofar as he is not He himself, that is, God, insofar as he is the ground of himself [*sofern er der Grund seiner selbst ist*], God as the truly originating God [*der eigentlich anfängliche Gott*] who is still completely in his ground, the God as he has not yet emerged from himself to himself [*wie er noch nicht aus sich selbst zu sich selbst herausgetreten ist*]. . . . The whole boldness of Schelling's thinking comes into play here. But it is not the vacuous play of thoughts of a manic hermit, it is only the continuation of an attitude of thinking which begins with Meister Eckhart and is uniquely developed in Jacob Boehme. But when this historical context is cited, one is immediately ready again with jargon, one speaks of 'mysticism' and 'theosophy.' Certainly, one can call it that, but nothing is said by that with regard to the spiritual occurrence and the true creation of thought." Heidegger goes on to deny the application of the title "mystic" to Schelling if that term is understood as denoting "a muddlehead [*Wirrkopf*] who likes to reel in the obscure and finds his pleasure in veils." Schelling probably had Böhme in mind when he spoke of "dogmatists and abstract idealists," who dismiss as "mystics" the "minds that sought the living ground of nature." See Schelling, *Philosophical Investigations*, pp. 27, 147n31; *Philosophische Untersuchungen*, p. 29.

86. On Böhme's *Ungrund* and the kabbalistic *Ein Sof*, see Aubrey, "Influence of Jacob Boehme," p. 36; Schulitz, *Jakob Böhme*, pp. 47–82; Deghaye, "La Philosophie," pp. 249–50; Deghaye, "La Théosophie de Jacob Boehme," p. 157; Deghaye, *De Paracelse à Thomas Mann*, pp. 83–84, 120–21; Hessayon, "Boehme's Life," p. 31; Scholem, *Geheimnisse der Schöpfung*, p. 31; Schmidt-Biggemann, *Philosophia Perennis*, p. 119; Schmidt-Biggemann, "Schellings 'Weltalter,'" p. 25. See the additional references on the affinities between Böhme and Jewish esotericism cited below, n. 95. The Böhmean *Ungrund* was already linked to the kabbalistic *Ein Sof* by Baader. See Baader, *Gesammelte Schriften zur philosophischen Grundwissenschaft*, p. 242; Baader, *Gesammelte Schriften zur Naturphilosophie*, p. 384; Baader, *Vorlesungen und Erläuterungen*, pp. 106, 119, 132, 172, 191, 194; Friesen, "Sophia," p. 132. For comparative studies on Böhme and Heidegger, see Paslick, "Ontological Context," pp. 409–13 (wherein the influence of the kabbalah on Böhme's ontology, including the affinity between the absolute indifference of the *Ungrund* and *Ein Sof* as the plenitude of reality and the emptiness of nothingness, is considered in relation to Heidegger's

positing a unity of poetry and thought); Friedrich, *Ungrund der Freiheit*; Peckler, "Imagination"; Gentzke, "Imaginal Renaissance," pp. 80n223, 92, 143, 184, 200–1, 298n800, 346. See also Caputo, *Mystical Element*, p. 98, and Zarader, *Unthought Debt*, p. 168; and compare the passing remark of Habermas, "Martin Heidegger," pp. 161–62. See below, n. 92.

87. Benz, *Christian Kabbalah*, pp. 67–68; Deghaye, "La Philosophie," pp. 249–51; Deghaye, *De Paracelse à Thomas Mann*, pp. 116–63, esp. 132–34, 146–47. See also Deghaye, "La Théosophie de Friedrich Christoph Oetinger," pp. 149–50; Deghaye, "*Gedulla* et *Gebura*"; Schmidt-Biggemann, "Schellings 'Weltalter,'" p. 41. For a concise introduction to Oetinger's thought, see Piepmeier, "Friedrich Christoph Oetinger." On the influence of Oetinger on Schelling, see also the editor's notes in Schelling, *Nachlass 8*, pp. 31–32, 34, 46, 216–17.

88. See Coudert, "The *Kabbala Denudata*"; Coudert, *Impact of the Kabbalah*, pp. 100–36. See as well the essays that Andreas B. Kilcher edited for vol. 16 of *Morgen-Glantz*, especially Morlok, "Text als Textur"; Burmistrov, "*Pardes Rimmonim*"; Necker, "Geister, Engel und Dämonen"; and Theisohn, "Zur Rezeption."

89. Here I mention a select bibliography of studies on the Renaissance Christian kabbalah: Blau, *Christian Interpretation*; Benz, *Christian Kabbalah*; Secret, *Le Zôhar chez les kabbalistes chrétiens*; Secret, *Kabbalistes Chrétiens*; Wirszubski, "Francesco Giorgio's Commentary"; Wirszubski, *Pico Della Mirandola's Encounter*; Idel, "Magical and Neoplatonic Interpretations"; Idel, "Kabbalistic Backgrounds"; McGinn, "Cabalists and Christians"; Scholem, "Beginnings"; Dan, "Kabbalah"; Reichert, "Christian Kabbalah"; Schmidt-Biggemann, "Einleitung"; Schmidt-Biggemann, "Schellings 'Weltalter'"; Copenhaver, "Number, Shape, and Meaning"; Copenhaver, "Secret of Pico's Oration"; Copenhaver, "Pico risorto"; Ogren, *Renaissance*, pp. 212–63; Ogren, *Beginnings*, pp. 44–59, 117–33; Ogren, "Law of Change"; Bartolucci, "Marsilio Ficino"; Lelli, "Pico, i Da Pisa"; Campanini, "Il commento alle *Conclusiones cabalisticae*"; Copenhaver and Kokin, "Egidio da Viterbo's *Book on Hebrew Letters*"; Kokin, "Entering the Labyrinth"; Rabin, "Whither Kabbalah?"; Buzzetta, "La Cabbale vulgarisée"; Weiss, *Kabbalistic Christian Messiah*. For a comprehensive list of studies on Christian kabbalah, see Wilkinson, *Orientalism*, pp. 5–6n6.

90. Schmidt-Biggemann, "Schellings 'Weltalter,'" pp. 22–34, 37–38; Wirth, *Conspiracy of Life*, pp. 33–64. On the "cabbalistic fanaticism" of Wachter's *Spinozismus im Judenthum* (1699), see the refutation of Spinozism and pantheism in lecture 13 of Mendelssohn, *Morning Hours*, pp. 75–81. More was the author of various works that deal with kabbalistic matters, including *Conjectura Cabbalistica*; *Immortality of the Soul*, pp. 136–37, 159; *Aditus tentatus rationem reddeni nominum*, in *Kabbala Denudata*, vol. 1, pt. 2, pp. 14–27; *Quæstiones & considerationes paucæ brevesque in Tractatum primum Libri Druschim*, in *Kabbala Denudata*, vol. 1, pt. 2, pp. 62–72; *Ad Clarissimum ac Eruditissimum*, in *Kabbala Denudata*, vol. 1, pt. 2, pp. 173–224; *Visionis Ezechieliticæ*, in *Kabbala Denudata*, vol. 1, pt. 2, pp. 225–73; *Catechismus Cabbalisticus*, in *Kabbala Denudata*, vol. 1, pt. 2, pp. 274–92; *Fundamenta philosophiæ*, in *Kabbala Denudata*, vol. 1, pt. 2, pp. 293–312. On the possible resonances of Lurianic kabbalah in Anne Conway, a disciple of Henry More and an influence on Leibniz, see introduction to Conway, *Principles*, eds. Coudert and Corse, pp. xviii–xxii, xxix–xxxiii; Coudert, *Impact of the Kabbalah*, pp. 177–210; Cocker, *Henry More*, pp. 183–99; Hutton, "From Christian Kabbalism"; Hutton, *Anne Conway*, pp. 7–8, 68, 153, 156–76; White, *Legacy*, pp. 50, 53–56, 64. See also the introduction in Conway, *Principles*, ed. Loptson, pp. 17–19, 30–33, 73. Loptson acknowledges the influence of kabbalah on Conway, but he is somewhat more skeptical based on the assumption that some of the references to the sources in *Kabbala Denudata* were added at a later date by More or van Helmont. See the suggestion about Conway's *Divine Dialogues* in Bailey, *Milton and Jakob Boehme*, p. 93: "She makes no direct mention of Boehme, but many of her theories are thoroughly Boehmenistic in tone; the whole work is Neoplatonic with a special leaning to the Kabalah." On More and the kabbalah, see Crocker, *Henry More*, pp. 63–77, 149, 154; Coudert, *Impact of the Kabbalah*, pp. 220–40; White, *Legacy*, p. 126n40; Schmidt-Biggemann, "Christliche Kabbala oder Philosophia Hebraeorum." On the influence of Jewish esoteric doctrine on Leibniz, see Brown, "Leibniz and More's Cabbalistic Circle"; Brown, "Proto-Monadology of the De Summa Rerum," p. 284 and additional references cited there in n. 7; Coudert, *Leibniz and the Kabbalah*; Coudert, "Leibniz and the Kabbalah"; Coudert, "Leibniz, Locke, Newton"; and Coudert, *Impact of the Kabbalah*, pp. 308–29. The relationship between Leibniz and mysticism more generally is explored by Heinekamp, "Leibniz." Also relevant is the informative analysis in Mahlev, "Kabbalah as Philosophia Perennis?" As Mahlev summarizes his argument, p. 235: "Jews were the most significant 'other' in German Protestantism, not only because they were physically present but

also because they served as a mirror image upon which Protestantism constructed its own identity. The fact that the consideration of ancient Judaism and its esoteric knowledge, the Kabbalah, stood at the heart of the *philosophia perennis* debate since the sixteenth century only intensified the tension. For side by side with Protestant controversies concerning the vaunted antiquity and authenticity of kabbalistic wisdom, there were internecine criticisms and concerns over the Christian preoccupation with these materials. Christian Kabbalah—already an established terminus in the seventeenth century—was often depicted as having a dangerous affinity for Judaism, an intrareligious accusation that in turn affected the image of Judaism itself." See the appendix in Morgenstern, ed., *Martin Luther und die Kabbala*, pp. 177–203.

91. See above, n. 40, and below, n. 93. See also Rudolph, "Die Kabbala im Werk des Paracelsus"; Webster, *Paracelsus*, pp. 26–27, 64–65, 156–68, 250–51; Klijnsmit, "F.M. van Helmont: Kabbalist and Phonetician"; Vaughan, *Johann Georg Hamann*, pp. 34–43, 64–68, 76–78, 96–100, 107–25, 127–31; Betanzos, *Franz von Baader's Philosophy*, pp. 14, 55, 64, 79, 176, 178n38. For discussion of Baader's theosophy, see Faivre, *Access to Western Esotericism*, pp. 113–33, 139–46, 201–74; the influence of the kabbalah on the notion of androgyny in Baader is briefly discussed on pp. 218–19, and see p. 272. Koslowski, "Franz Baader," pp. 247–48, compares Baader's allegedly more radical existential ontology of the total reality (*einer existentialen Ontologie der Gesamtwirklichkeit*) to the Heideggerian existential analysis of the human being (*existentiale Seinsanalyse des Menschen*). On Heidegger's engagement with Baader, see reference in ch. 6 n. 27.

92. Habermas, *Philosophical-Political Profiles*, pp. 21–22. And see Franks, "Inner anti-Semitism." The argument of Habermas, and the thesis I have expounded in this monograph, assumes an even more ironic dimension when we recall the comment in Heidegger, *Phenomenological Interpretations of Aristotle*, p. 53 (*Phänomenologische Interpretationen zu Aristoteles*, p. 70), on the possible "degeneration in the embellishment of mythical and theosophical metaphysics and mysticism and in the trance of a preoccupation with piety, which goes by the name of religiosity."

93. On the influence of kabbalistic sources on Schelling, see above, n. 40. See also Tilliette, "Schelling und die Gnosis," pp. 270–71. Schelling's relationship to Baader is explored in detail by Zovko, *Natur und Gott*. For the influence of kabbalah on German romanticism, see also Gardt, *Sprachreflexion in Barock und Frühaufklärung*, pp. 108–28; Kilcher, *Die Sprachtheorie der Kabbala als Ästhetisches Paradigma*, pp. 239–327; Kilcher, "Die Kabbala als Trope"; Schulte, "Kabbala in der deutschen Romantik."

94. Previous works that have contributed to this discussion are Caputo, "Meister Eckhart and the Later Heidegger;" Caputo, *Mystical Element*, pp. 140–217; Schürmann, *Meister Eckhart*, pp. 192–213; Helting, *Heidegger und Meister Eckehart*; Sikka, *Forms of Transcendence*, pp. 109– 86; Rickey, *Revolutionary Saints*, pp. 69–70, 81–87, 97–98; Dalle Pezze, *Martin Heidegger and Meister Eckhart*; Onishi, "Birth of World"; and the following studies in Lewin, Podmore, and Williams, eds., *Mystical Theology*: Pattison, "Role of Mysticism," pp. 139–43; Williams, "Eckhart's Why and Heidegger's What"; and Wojtulewicz, "Meister Eckhart's Speculative Grammar."

95. The following comment about the relationship of the Romantics to Böhme in Hannak, "Boehme and German Romanticism," p. 168, can be applied to Schelling: "In their search for a deeper dimension of being not beyond but rather within reality itself, the Romantics were fascinated by Hermetic, Neoplatonic, and Kabbalistic texts as well as by contemporary Mesmerism. These interests prepared the ground of their reading of Boehme." See the comments on Böhme in Heidegger, "Poverty," pp. 4–5. Speaking of the impact of the notion of the holy Sophia on the "Oriental Church," and particularly in Russia, Heidegger writes, "The efficacy of the spirit as the all-pervading power of enlightenment and wisdom (Sophia) is 'magical.' The ownmost of the magical is as inscrutable and opaque as the ownmost of the pneumatic. Yet, we know that Jacob Böhme, the theosophist and philosopher . . . had recognized the magical in the light of the shoemaker's globe and thought of it as the primal will. Böhme's doctrine of the divine Sophia (theosophy) was known in Russia as early as the seventeenth century. . . . It is thus no exaggeration when I say that what one nowadays conceives shortsightedly and incompletely as merely 'political' or even roughly 'political' and calls Russian Communism comes from a spiritual world about which we know hardly anything." The attempt to trace the spiritual roots of communism to Eastern Orthodoxy, and especially to the theosophy of Böhme, stands in sharp contrast to Heidegger's disavowal of communism, together with capitalism, as technologically driven ideologies, a description he eventually assigned to Nazism as well. For discussion of Böhme and Heidegger, see studies cited above, n. 86. The affinity between the kabbalistic doctrine of *Adam Qadmon*, the Neoplatonic Logos, and Böhme's

speculation on the first man was already implied by Hegel. See the evidence adduced by Muratori, *First German Philosopher*, p. 279. See also Deghaye, "La Philosophie," pp. 273–75. On the speculation about *Adam Qadmon* as the second divinity (*secunda divinitatis*) in relation to *Ein Sof* and Böhme's speculation about the incarnation of Christ as the spoken and pronounced Word (*das sprechende Wort und das ausgesprochene*), see Baader, *Gesammelte Schriften zur Naturphilosophie*, pp. 406–8. Böhme's writings contain some hints that he was aware of the esoteric dimension of Judaism. See the comment in the preface to Böhme, *"Key,"* p. 17: "Also the wise Heathens and Jews have hid the deep Ground of Nature under such Words, as having well understood that the Knowledge of Nature is not for every one, but it belongs to those only, whom God by Nature has chosen for it." In the same work, reference is made to the rabbinic tradition on the Tetragrammaton; see herein ch. 5 n. 70. The kabbalah is invoked with reference to the magical power of the Tetragrammaton and the need to conceal it from the unworthy by Böhme in *Theosophische Fragen oder 177 Fragen von göttlicher Offenbarung*. See Böhme, *Quaestiones Theosophicae*, pp. 286–87 (Böhme, *Sämtliche Schriften* 9:12–13): "And here we have the wonder-working Word in its operation. For the great name of God TETRAGRAMMATON (JeHoVaH) is here the centre of the wonders of God, and it works in both the central fires. This name the evil spirits, in their transmutation according to the centre of the fire's nature, do misuse. And the ground of all cabala and magic [*der Grund der ganzen Cabbala und Magie*] is contained in this principle, these being the active powers whereby the imperceptible co-works in the perceptible [*das Unempfindliche in dem Empfindlichen mitwirket*]. And here the law of Moses forbids misusing this principle on pain of eternal punishment, as may be seen in the ten commandments. For our fellow allies enough has been said, and for the godless a strong bar lies before it [*den Unsern allhie genug gesagt, und den Gottlosen ein Schloß davor*]" (translation slightly modified). See Böhme, *Quaestiones Theosophicae*, pp. 298–99 (*Sämtliche Schriften*, 9:21): "For what the angels will and desire is by their imagination brought into shape and forms [*das wird durch ihre Imaginirung in Bildung und Formen gebracht*], which forms are pure ideas [*eitel Ideen*]. In manner as the Divine powers [*die göttlichen Kräfte*] have shaped themselves into such ideas before the creation of the angels, so is their after-modelling [*Nachmodelung*]. And herein lies the holy cabala of changes [*die heilige Cabbala der Veränderungen*], and the great kingdom of joy [*die grosse Freudenreich*], in which the Divine wisdom and knowledge is fashioned and shaped by the spirits of the central fire and light. And there is such a joy of cognition therein, that for great joy and knowledge they bow and humble themselves eternally before such majesty [*Hoheit*], that the No [*das Nein*] may not get the dominion in them, and they be deprived of such glory." On these passages, see Stoudt, *Jacob Boehme*, p. 89n17; Hessayon, "Boehme's Life," p. 31. The influence of the Christian kabbalistic understanding of the Tetragrammaton and its relationship to Jesus seems to be at play in Böhme, *De Electione Gratiae*, pp. 107–8 (Böhme, *Sämtliche Schriften*, 6:88): "From eternity the name Jesus lay in man, viz. in the likeness of God [*der Gleichnis Gottes*], in an immovable love. . . . Adam before his fall had the divine light from Jehovah, that is, from the one God in which the high name Jesus stood hidden. Not that it was concealed in God, but in the creature, that is to say, in the attraction to the creature." On Böhme and the kabbalah, see also Martensen, *Jacob Boehme*, pp. 28, 74, 123; Schulze, "Jacob Boehme und die Kabbala"; Scholem, *Major Trends*, pp. 237–38; Llewellyn, "Jacob Boehmes Kosmogonie"; Aubrey, "Influence of Jacob Boehme," pp. 16, 30, 36–37, 44–45, 281n40, 291n29, 295–96n28; Benz, *Mystical Sources*, pp. 47–58; Schulitz, *Jakob Böhme und die Kabbalah*; Häussermann, "Theologia Emblematica"; Huber, "Die Kabbala"; Weeks, *Boehme*, pp. 30, 43 (the author presumes without producing any evidence that Böhme could have learned kabbalistic doctrines from Judah Loew ben Bezalel, the Maharal of Prague, during his visit to Görlitz, a hypothesis that I find highly improbable because of the Maharal's reluctance to expose esoteric doctrines openly even to coreligionists), 106, 116, 147, 200, 204–5; Janz, "Jacob Boehme's Theory," pp. 77–79, 194–95; Edel, "Kabbala in der Theosophie Jacob Böhmes"; Edel, *Die Individuelle Substanz bei Böhme und Leibniz*; Edel, "Métaphysique des idées et mystique des lettres"; O'Regan, *Gnostic Apocalypse*, pp. 193–209; Schmidt-Biggemann, "Jakob Böhme und die Kabbala"; Stoudt, *Jacob Boehme*, pp. 22, 88, 89n17, 96, 115; Rusterholz, "Elemente der Kabbala bei Jacob Böhme"; Kaennel, "Protestantisme et cabale," pp. 193–95; O'Donnell, "Böhme and Hegel," pp. 30–31; Böhme, *Aurora*, pp. 43–44. See my own modest contribution to this question in Wolfson, *Language*, pp. 8, 197, 471n435, 485–86n180, and references to other scholars cited on pp. 423n259 and 468n392; and more fully in Wolfson, "Holy Cabala." Weeks, *Boehme*, p. 30, identifies Balthasar Walter, an acquaintance and fellow traveler of Böhme, as a possible conduit through which he may have learned kabbalistic doctrines. Compare Bailey, *Milton and Jakob Boehme*, p. 96. In more detail, see Penman, "A Second Christian Rosencreuz?" On the more specific relationship between Böhme and Christian kabbalah, see Weeks, *Boehme*, p. 205; Schmidt-Biggemann, "Christian Kabbala"; Schmidt-Biggemann, *Philosophia Perennis*, pp. 117–28, 187–92; Penman, "Boehme's Intellectual Networks," pp. 66–71. Let me note, finally, that despite Böhme's attraction to and appropriation of kabbalistic theosophy, one can predictably discover in his published work negative comments about Judaism. For example, see Böhme, *Aurora*, p. 663: "This is why God gave the law to the Jews, so that they should cultivate all gentleness and holiness and love that the entire world might find a mirror in them. But when they instead fell into pride and boasted of their birth rather than of love and turned the law of love into a blade of anger, God thrust the light from them and turned to the heathens instead." In the same treatise, Böhme avails himself of the well-known anti-Semitic trope of the blind Jew (in some passages the blindness is attributed as well to the Turk and the heathen). See Böhme, *Aurora*, pp. 131, 163, 263, 319, 321, 323, 325, 661. In one passage, Böhme insists that Christian, Jew, Turk, and heathen are all equally capable of overcoming the pernicious effect of the devil (*Aurora*, p. 383), but the ostensible egalitarianism does not alleviate the derogatory comments that distinguish the Christian from the other three types of human beings. Compare Böhme, *High and Deep*, pp. 224–25. After stating categorically that God wills to save all people who are lost, Böhme takes the following jab at the Jewish dietary law: "Dost thou know why God did forbid the *Jews* to eat of *some sort of flesh*? Kindle their fat, and consider their property, and thou shalt discern it" (emphasis in original). See Böhme, *High and Deep*, p. 239, where the Pharisees are labeled the "ministers of the dragon," that is, servants of the devil in his lies, who pretended to be the "ministers of God." The historical circumstances of Heidegger and Böhme are very different, and hence one must be wary of simplistic comparisons, but with respect to this point there is a valid analogy: it is possible for a thinker to be influenced, directly or indirectly, by a tradition, while at the same time maligning the people who sociologically uphold that tradition.

96. Heidegger, *Ponderings II–VI*, p. 24 (*Überlegungen II–VI*, p. 32): "Why do eager reviewers and writers so uniformly and definitely *shirk* when it comes to the decisive treatise, 'On the Essence of Ground'? *Enough already here* with the reckoning up of 'influences' and of the dependencies on Husserl, Dilthey, Kierkegaard, and whoever. Here the task was—if anything—to put into effect a confrontation [*Auseinandersetzung*] with antiquity and with the retrieved problem of being. Instead of which, manifest prattle [*Geschwätz*] keeps piling up from week to week" (emphasis in original). Heidegger does not deny the relevance of the matter of influence when examining masters of thought, but he insists that what is important to comprehend is the "peculiarity" (*eigene Sache*) of the influence and not merely to gossip about the repetition of a "general opinion" (*allgemeinen Meinung*) that is "rootless and homeless" (*wurzel- und heimatlose*). The latter amounts to nothing but idle talk (*Gerede*).

97. On the gnostic resonances in Heidegger's thought, perhaps even constituting an esoteric form of Christian gnosis in polemical conflict with mainstream Christian theology, see Taubes, "Gnostic Foundations," p. 157 (cited partially in ch. 4 at n. 60). Also relevant is the thesis of Sacchi, *Apocalypse of Being*. According to Sacchi, the esotericism in Heidegger is connected to his view that being is disclosed not through logical analysis or discursive thinking but through an *experience of affective connaturality* (p. 127) that is a form of poetic mysticism predicated on the abandonment of reason (p. 137). Sacchi's thesis is summarized as follows: "Led by Hölderlin's hands, Heidegger ended up by confusing philosophy with an erratic dithyramb in order to think about things and *Sein* in the midst of the darkness of a language in which the esoteric gnosticism always comes together with the unintelligibility of ravings" (p. 133). On the attempt to locate the source of Heidegger's philosophizing in an esoteric experience, related especially to his avoidance for public discourse, see Trawny, *Adyton*. Parallels between Heidegger's ontology articulated in *Sein und Zeit* and ancient Gnostic sources were noted by Jonas, *Gnosis und spätantiker Geist*, 1:90–91, 107–8, and 2:7, 359–79; Jonas, "Gnosticism and Modern Nihilism," pp. 441–42, 445, 449–50; Jonas, *Gnostic Religion*, pp. 62–65, 320–40 (the epilogue "Gnosticism, Existentialism, and Nihilism" is reprinted in Jonas, *Phenomenon of Life*, pp. 211–34); and see the analysis of Levy, *Hans Jonas*, pp. 25–30. The impact of Heidegger on Jonas's study of Gnosticism is discussed in several essays in Tirosh-Samuelson and Wiese, eds., *Legacy of Hans Jonas*: Hösle, "Hans Jonas's Position," pp. 30–31; Brumlik, "Resentment"; Rudolph, "Hans Jonas," pp. 97, 103–5; Lazier, "Pauline Theology." See also Jakob, *Martin Heidegger und Hans Jonas*; Wolin, *Heidegger's Children*, pp. 101–33; Wiese, "'Revolt Against Empiricism.'" On Heidegger and Gnosticism,

see Baum, *Gnostische Elemente*; Slattery, "Augustine, Heidegger, and Gnosticism." The relationship between Heidegger and Gnosticism is explored from a standpoint of archetypal psychology in Avens, *New Gnosis*. And see herein ch. 4 n. 61.

98. See above, n. 94. On Heidegger's interest more generally in medieval mysticism, including Eckhart, as part of a youthful attempt to formulate a philosophical theology, see McGrath, *Early Heidegger*, pp. 120–50.

99. Especially relevant is the fact that Silesius became acquainted with the works of Böhme, perhaps through his camaraderie with Abraham von Franckenberg, one of Böhme's nobleman friends. See Rusterholz, "Elemente christlicher Kabbala," pp. 194–97. Compare the passage from Baader, which seeks to sum up Böhme's teaching on the mystical nature of God in the vein of Angelus Silesius, cited by Scholem, *Major Trends*, p. 405n109.

100. Nietzsche, *Gay Science*, §228, p. 145.

101. Heidegger, *What Is Called Thinking?*, p. 91; *Was Heißt Denken?*, p. 95.

102. I have elaborated on this theme in Wolfson, "Not Yet Now," pp. 156–80. On the conceptual convergence and divergence between Benjamin and Heidegger, see the evidence adduced in Wolfson, "Not Yet Now," pp. 159–60n122, and the studies in Benjamin and Vardoulakis, eds., *Sparks Will Fly*, esp. Schwebel, "Monad and Time," and Benjamin, "Time and Task." Also relevant is the essay by Wenning, "Adorno, Heidegger, and the Problem of Remembrance."

103. Heidegger, *Contributions*, §242, p. 303; *Beiträge*, pp. 383–84.

104. Heidegger, *What Is Called Thinking?*, p. 12; *Was Heißt Denken?*, p. 15.

105. Heidegger, *Introduction to Philosophy*, p. 43; *Einleitung in die Philosophie*, p. 138.

106. Derrida, *On the Name*, p. 35. See the passages from Derrida cited herein in ch. 8 at nn. 220–22.

107. Burik, *End of Comparative Philosophy*. The approach I have taken is consonant with the observation of Lapidot, "People of Knowers," p. 273, that the configuration of "Heidegger and Jewish Thought" must be pursued "both as a conjunction and as an opposition."

108. Nelson, *Chinese and Buddhist Philosophy*, p. 252: "Heidegger's articulation of philosophy, language, and existence in relation to the nothing and its own questionability . . . is pertinent to the intercultural hermeneutics that would think with and beyond his art of interpretation; we too must face our limits and finitude. . . . One systematizing meta-language from which different encounters with the nothing and emptiness could be categorized and systematized is lacking. There is only the space and the silence in which encounters occur and are missed. As Heidegger indicated in his dialogue with a Japanese visitor, genuine understanding cannot mean the erasure of what is singular and unique; words allow for each to be granted its own appropriate due and measure. We ought to be accordingly cautious and reticent in claiming that we understand the other and that which we do not and perhaps cannot understand." The methodological underpinning of Nelson's claim that the comparison of Heidegger's *Denkweg* to patterns of thinking culled from Asian sources requires noting both congruence and incongruence supports the more deconstructive analysis proffered by Ma, "Mysterious Relations to the East."

109. Heidegger, *Fundamental Concepts*, p. 178 (translation modified); *Grundbegriffe*, p. 264. And compare the articulation in the preliminary considerations for the lecture course given in the winter semester 1931–32 at the University of Freiburg, published in Heidegger, *Essence of Truth*, p. 1 (*Vom Wesen der Wahrheit*, p. 1): "But we discover what is universal to *all* only by comparing *particular* things and observing the sameness of what they have in common" (emphasis in original).

110. See the analysis in Seppi, "'Wenn einer immerfort dasselbe sagt [. . .],'" pp. 67–77.

111. Heidegger, *Identity and Difference*, p. 45; German text: p. 111. Compare Heidegger, *Poetry, Language, Thought*, pp. 218–19; *Vorträge und Aufsätze*, pp. 196–97.

112. Heidegger, *Country Path Conversations*, p. 25; *Feldweg-Gespräche*, p. 39. For discussion of this theme, see "Translator's Foreword," in *Country Path Conversations*, pp. xiv–xv.

113. Heidegger, *Pathmarks*, p. 309; *Wegmarken*, p. 409.

114. Heidegger, *Discourse on Thinking*, p. 53; *Gelassenheit*, p. 22.

115. Heidegger, *Principle of Reason*, pp. 89–90; *Satz vom Grund*, p. 133. The inherent futurity of the Heideggerian sensibility about the unsaid of what has been said and the unthought of what has been thought is expressed poetically by Bigelow, *Conning*, p. xv: "Philosophy is written correctly when it comes out both stillborn and posthumous: it is finished before the author has yet to begin, and it is begun after the author has come to an end."

116. Schelling, *System of Transcendental Idealism*, p. 51 (emphasis in original).

117. Ibid., p. 230.

118. Ibid., p. 72. My understanding of Schelling's idea of indifference and the implied interconnectivity

of opposites predicated on their irreducible autonomy raises questions about the claim of Bielik-Robson, "Between Unity and Chaos," that while Schelling remained beholden to a dialectical resolution of the "original contradiction" of opposites within God, Rosenzweig created a narrative based on a "non-antithetical sequence" such that the Yes and the No are never rigidly opposed. I concur with Bielik-Robson's interpretation of Rosenzweig, but it strikes me that Schelling's critique of Hegel, and his affirmation of indifference—a notion likely indebted to kabbalistic symbolism mediated through Böhme—suggests that he, too, thought that the antithesis or contradiction in the primordial beginning must be based on a doubling that entails a sequential rather than a dialectical movement between opposites. If this were not the case, the one could never become two. Schelling proffers that the Godhead is indivisibly and concurrently the eternal Yes and the eternal No, and hence the symbolic notation for the two forces, which act with free unity within the divine, is A + B. See the texts of Schelling cited and discussed in ch. 5 at nn. 103–5, 112–14. And consider the explanation of indifference in Schelling, *Statement on the True Relationship of the Philosophy of Nature,* p. 95 (*Darlegung des wahren Verhältnisses der Naturphilosophie,* in Schelling, *Sämmtliche Werke,* 7:106–7): "One posits, for example, that if someone were to claim that Herr Fichte and Fr[iedrich] Nicolai are most intimately related to one another and at bottom fully in agreement [*im Grunde völlig einig sehen*], he would seem to have uttered a great paradox. One employs for this relationship the word polarity, and everything is clear. For one sees how despite the most direct opposition, both are one in terms of their foundation [*beide der innersten Grundlage nach dennoch eins sind*] and how they, represented as the two flammable types of gases, Herr Fichte as oxygen, Nicolai as hydrogen, in their mutual penetrations and depotentiation [*in der gegenseitigen Durchdringung und Depotenzirung*] must produce pure indifference [*die reine Indifferenz*], the true water of our age." Already in this work, published in 1806, Schelling deployed a relatively simply example—the antagonism of Fichte and Nicolai, and their symbolic correlation with oxygen and hydrogen—to illustrate that indifference involves the paradox of polarity, that is, two opposing forces that are, at the same time, in full agreement—just as the clashing gases combine to produce water. In my judgment, Schelling's *Indifferenz* served as the basis for Heidegger's *Zusammengehörigkeit,* the belonging together of contraries in the sameness of their difference, a notion that bears affinity to Rosenzweig's insight regarding the conjunctive "and" that bridges the Yes and the No, the two root words that have an immediate relationship to the Nothing. Rosenzweig explicitly contrasts his perspective with the idealist synthesis, but his assertion that the original character of the No is equivalent to that of the Yes was already anticipated by Schelling. See Rosenzweig, *Star of Redemption,* pp. 246–47; *Stern der Erlösung,* pp. 255–56.

119. Heidegger, *Identity and Difference,* p. 29; German text: p. 92.

120. Heidegger, *Identity and Difference,* p. 29; German text: p. 92.

121. Heidegger, *Identity and Difference,* p. 27; German text: p. 90. A more standard translation of the Parmenidean fragment is offered by Freeman, *Ancilla,* p. 42: "For it is the same thing to think and to be." Regarding this Parmenidean dictum, see the more extensive analysis in Heidegger, *Introduction to Metaphysics,* pp. 145–55; *Einführung in die Metaphysik,* pp. 145–55. See ch. 1 n. 17. Also relevant is the second dictum attributed to Parmenides, ταὐτὸν δ' ἐστὶ νοεῖν τε καὶ οὕνεκέν ἐστί νόημα (Fragment 8.34), rendered by Freeman, *Ancilla,* p. 44: "To think is the same as the thought that It Is," which is to say, as the continuation of the aphorism makes clear, without what is, that is, being, there is no thought, and hence thinking and that of which there is thinking are one and the same. See Cordero, *By Being,* pp. 81n339, 86–87. Compare the interpretation of the Parmenidean teaching as an insight into the essence of *phusis* in Heidegger, *Introduction to Metaphysics,* p. 148 (*Einführung in die Metaphysik,* p. 147): "apprehension and that for the sake of which apprehension happens are the same. Apprehension happens for the sake of Being. Being essentially unfolds as appearing, as stepping into unconcealment, only if unconcealment happens, only if a self-opening happens."

122. Heidegger, *Identity and Difference,* p. 27; German text: p. 90.

123. Heidegger, *Pathmarks,* p. 240; *Wegmarken,* p. 316.

124. Heidegger, *Pathmarks,* p. 241; *Wegmarken,* pp. 314–15.

125. See the studies by Babich: "Heidegger's Jews," pp. 134–35, and "Heidegger's *Judenfrage.*" I concur with the assessment of Lapidot, "People of Knowers," p. 269: "At some moments in the current controversy regarding Heidegger's anti-Semitism, the notion of 'Jewish thought' seems even to be the controversial notion itself. As indicated in the introduction to this volume, one paradox or ambivalence in the current debate is that accusing the philosopher of 'anti-

Semitism' very often means accusing him not so much of philosophizing *against* Jews, but of philosophizing Jews at all. This ambivalence is perhaps constitutive for an entire discursive configuration of critique of anti-Semitism, so to speak a discourse of anti-anti-Semitism. The fundamental ambivalence of the anti-anti-Semitic discourse consists in countering anti-Semitism in philosophy by precluding the Jewish from philosophy or thought altogether, a preclusion which at some critical moments risks reproducing anti-Semitic discourse itself" (emphasis in original).

126. This is hardly unique to Heidegger, as we find other thinkers who avowed explicit anti-Semitic views but who were nevertheless influenced by Jewish ideas, including kabbalistic motifs and symbols. See my comments about Böhme in the concluding part of n. 95 above, and consider the account of the anti-Semitic strain in Paracelsus, which attracted the admiration of German nationalists and ideologues in the Nazi period, in Weeks, *Paracelsus*, p. 132. See also the remark of Franks, "Fichte's Kabbalistic Realism," p. 92: "Fichte is notorious for his role in the development of virulent anti-Semitism, including his opposition to Jewish civil rights. This may be thought—quite wrongly—to preclude the deployment of kabbalistic resources in his philosophy and especially in his account of reciprocal recognition." The same logic can be imputed to Heidegger, although in his case there is less recognition of the channels of influence.

127. In previous publications, I have pointed out that, with respect to these issues, there is no appreciable difference between kabbalists across the generations. I have found no kabbalist who would not subscribe to the privileged status of Hebrew as the matrix language of creation and the superior status of the Jewish people and the land of Israel that derives from that assumption. See Wolfson, *Language*, pp. 197–205.

128. In this orientation, Heidegger follows the main lines of nineteenth-century German philology based on the linkage between language and national identity. For a comprehensive study of this topic, see Benes, *In Babel's Shadow*.

129. Krell, "Heidegger's *Black Notebooks*," p. 135. See as well Krell, *Ecstasy*, and Krell, "Troubled Brows."

1

Hermeneutic Circularity

Tradition as Genuine Repetition of Futural Past

> The *eternal*—what the genuinely and always existing being is—has foolishness for its essential characteristic; the eternal—"the world"—is therefore continually outstripped and masked, for itself, by itself, and on account of its essential semblance; it continually overcomes "truth" in the sense of the fixed, but it cannot persist in its *overflowing* without securing at the same time the means of existence for the new appearance, which in turn will overcome it. And *what* does all this mean? That the world excludes itself from truth, where truth is now after all understood as the pure correspondence of representation to the real.
>
> Heidegger, *Interpretation of Nietzsche's Second Untimely Meditation*

The analysis of Heidegger and kabbalah will commence with an examination of the question of tradition as it relates to the intricate interplay of novelty and repetition that is grounded in the principle of hermeneutical circularity—the recurrence of that which always never was—and the related understanding of time as a linear circle. By way of introducing the intricate theme of dynamism and stasis in the respective paths of Heideggerian and kabbalistic thought, let me offer two preliminary procedural stipulations that will establish hermeneutical criteria essential to the method I shall pursue in this monograph. First, my commitment to the proposition that Heidegger is an effective prism through which to examine kabbalistic material and that the kabbalistic material is an effective prism through which to examine Heidegger does not mean that I am suggesting this is the only, or even the best, theoretical template to do this work. There is no overt or clandestine petition that the use of Heidegger by scholars of kabbalah be mandatory. Needless to say, the postmodern preference prejudices us against thinking that one explanatory tool is either necessary or sufficient. Axiomatically, I accept this disavowal of axiom. Nevertheless, long ago, I set my task as a scholar to read the texts of Jewish mysticism through philosophical interpretive lenses, and the one that has seemed most applicable and productive for me has been Heidegger.

Second, over the years I have been criticized either for espousing an essentialism or for offering statements of a categorical nature in my analysis of kabbalistic sources. In an effort to discredit my claims, appeal has been made to multivocality—and, in some cases, to Derridean *différance*, the emphasis on differing and deferring, a privileging of indeterminacy and almost unlimited potential for meaning[1]—but the appeal to multivocality fails to comprehend that my approach is pliable enough to satisfy both the essentialist contention that there are structures and patterns of thought that we can identify as enduring and the constructivist argument that these structures and patterns are always shifting in accord with ever-changing historical conditions. In various publications, I have emphasized that the propensity to partition matters in this way is subject to a logical fallacy that leads invariably to self-implosion: the veracity of the historicist presumption that meaning is always to be determined from context cannot be sufficiently generalized to justify the argument for contextualization. That is, without the ability to step out of context, we could not cultivate the cognitive apparatus necessary to detect the parameters of any context. A perspectivism predicated on an antinomic schism between the predictability of the universal and the unpredictability of the particular cannot be cogently affirmed without negating itself, since every statement avowing the relativity of perspective is subject to the criterion of perspective. Hence, to state unreservedly that we cannot discover truth can be true only if it is false, but it cannot be false unless it is true.[2]

Homogeneity and Heterogeneous Fluctuation

As one who is sympathetic to both deconstruction and postmodernism, not only do I not eschew the call for pluralistic interpretation as an advantageous explanatory tactic, but I would go so far as to say that the heuristic contrivance of univocality is audible only through the chorus of plurivocality—there is no monological speech that is not in truth dialogical. This conviction regarding what Derrida called the interlocution of the plurality of voices[3] does not discount the possibility of identifying unifying conceptual schemes and symbolic structures. A spurious dichotomy has prevailed in recent scholarship on the kabbalah in particular, and on the phenomenon of mysticism more generally, which is based on essentializing the effort to demarcate resemblance from within disparity as a form of essentialism. Despite the bluster in defending an ostensibly polyvalent hermeneutic—in fact, the insistence on polyvalence, I regret to say, can often be a ploy to cloak hegemony—the argument is specious. There is no compelling reason to separate heterogeneity and homogeneity; epistemically, the latter is detectable only against the backdrop of the former. As Jean-Luc Nancy reminds us of this commonsensical point too often obscured by the haze of political correctness, "difference is not the opposite of identity; for difference is what makes identity possible, and by inscribing this possibility at the heart of identity, it exposes it to this: that its meaning cannot be identical to it. We are our identity, and *we* designates—once again, in the simultaneous and undecidable reference to our 'singularities' and our 'community'—an identity that is necessarily shared out, in us and between us. Difference takes place in this sharing, at once a distribution of meaning into all significations and a withdrawal of meaning from all signification—a withdrawal that each signification indicates, at the limit."[4]

Even from a neuroscientific standpoint, the cerebral coding of information precludes positioning the homogeneous and the heterogeneous in binary opposition—we could not recognize deviation empirically without hypothesizing stability ideationally. Expressed somewhat more technically, syncretic processing is assigned to the right hemisphere of the brain and the diacritic processing to the left hemisphere; the activity of signifying—a cornerstone of our cogitative and linguistic aptitude as thinking beings—involves interaction between the two on the basis of what is referred to as a "bimodal reticulation of similarities and differences."[5] Insofar as the brain discerns that things resemble one another only when it perceives that they are inconsonant, we can postulate more abstractly that discrimination facilitates the detection of correspondence. In the words of William J. Clancey, essential to the "architecture of memory and learning" are the ideas of systematicity and compositionality. These ideas "suggest the existence of rule-like pattern comprehension and generation," which "result from categorization of sequences . . . with later reactivation of sequences admitting substitution of subsequences and couplings. The processes of temporal sequencing, substitution, ongoing generalization, and compositional reconstruction provide an explanation of *productivity*, roughly, the ability to understand and produce relatively unbounded expressions from finite means. Most important, the architecture must be such that conceptual structures form without an executive assembly process that interprets a descriptive language of features, parts, types, orderings, semantic associations, and so on. The process of constructing categories, sequences, and compositions of them is the 'language' of thought—although at this level, it can only be a poetic use of the word."[6]

Some have argued that memory is not to be conceived as "one homogeneous function," but rather as "split into different subfunctions and subprocesses." It must be considered, therefore, an "umbrella concept that covers heterogeneity of different functions and processes associated with different neural mechanisms and regions in the brain. Accordingly, what appears to be homogeneous on the conceptual level, turns out to be heterogeneous in neuronal, empirical terms."[7] One could counter, however, that experiential variation cannot be appreciated without the presumption of conceptual uniformity. Similarly, the scholarly task to mark difference can be executed only if some degree of sameness is presumed; indeed, it is the different sameness that engenders the same difference. If it is true that the same is the same in virtue of the other, then it is correspondingly true that the other is other in virtue of the same.

The positing of recurrent patterns does not disallow diversity by ignoring specific details and historical changes that would account for plurality. In line with François Laruelle, I would argue that thinking from the perspective of a principle of unification—what he calls the One—implies generic fluctuation rather than systematic totalization; that is to say, the general is rooted in and must always be tested against the unassimilability of the particular.[8] The deployment of repeated structures in the study of kabbalistic doctrine and practice does not imply that this variegated history should be subsumed monolithically under the stamp of immutable essences. As a religious phenomenon, kabbalism illustrates that the immutability of system occasions diverse interpretation, even to the point that, as we shall see, the feasibility of system may itself be called into question.[9] In the indigenous wisdom of the tradition, something is new if it is old but it is old if it is new. The polysemy at play in these texts, therefore, indicates the vacillating tension between the novelty that repeats and the repetition that is novel. The inflexible bifurcation of innovation and conservation, which has dominated the academic approach to the study of kabbalah, can be avoided if we accept the dialetheic repudiation of the law of noncontradiction based on the assumption that the identification of opposites in the identity of their opposition yields a genuine and irresolvable contradiction; that is, the truth of a statement that presumes the paradoxical form α and $\neg\alpha$, which translates into the disjunctive syllogism *if it is the case that α, then it is not the case that α*, is a direct reproach of the more prevalent logic that for every statement either α or $\neg\alpha$ is true but both cannot be true at the same time and in the same relation.[10]

With this shift in orientation in mind, we can attempt to understand the substratal presupposition of the hermeneutical axiology and the conception of time as a linear circularity based thereon. I have expounded this conundrum in many of my publications by noting that despite the wide diversity that characterizes kabbalistic productivity, it is possible to identify a common thread that ties together the masters of the esoteric wisdom through the centuries: the assumption under which they have labored—and continue to labor—is that the truth already spoken is always yet to be spoken, that the ancient saying may be envisioned as novel to the degree that the novel saying is envisioned as ancient. The chain of tradition is thus constituted by the endlessly distended moments, which should not be envisaged mathematically as spatially discrete points strung together and unified by an internal time consciousness, but rather as the mythopoeic instantiations of an infinitely protracted torrent that implements the eternal reappearance of the same, which is to say, the indefatigable duplication of difference.

The hermeneutical circle that enframes both kabbalistic speculation and Heidegger's thinking is marked by the following temporal paradox: each moment is steadfastly the same because irresolutely different, and hence, originality is construed as the recovery of an archaic truth that is repeatedly discovered as what has not yet been uncovered.[11] Commenting on Heidegger's description and existential grounding of the hermeneutic circle in the anticipatory movement of the ontological structure of the fore-understanding, Hans-Georg Gadamer wrote:

> The circle, then, is not formal in nature. It is neither subjective nor objective, but describes understanding as the interplay of the movement of tradition and the movement of the interpreter. The anticipation of meaning that governs our understanding of a text is not an act of subjectivity, but proceeds from the commonality that binds us to the tradition. But this commonality is constantly being formed in our relation to tradition. Tradition is not simply a permanent precondition; rather, we produce it ourselves inasmuch as we understand, participate in the evolution of tradition, and hence further determine it ourselves.[12]

Parenthetically, I would add that a judicious understanding of Derridean deconstruction leads us to the same conclusion, and with respect to this issue, as we see from the following depiction of his own writing performance, Derrida may be most kabbalistic or, if one prefers, most Heideggerian: "Every time I write something, I have the impression of making a beginning—but in fact that which is the same in texture is ceaselessly exposed to a singularity which is that of the other. . . . Everything appears anew: which means newness and repetition together. . . . In the actual writing, of course, I'm well aware of the fact that at bottom it all unfolds according to the same law that commands these always different things."[13]

The comment leaves little room for opacity or obscurity: everything must appear as new but newness is unintelligible without the presumption of repetition, the aspect of deconstruction that Derrida calls "paleonymy," that is, "the using of an old word—a *paleo,* a very old word—or the preserving of an old word precisely where the signification of this very word has awoken or woken up to *something else.*"[14] Writing proceeds in accord with the dynamic of *the same law commanding things that are always different.* The chronicling of history as a meaningful construct—in contrast to the metaphysical concept of history that is linked to linearity and an entire system of implications about teleology, eschatology, accumulation of meaning, traditionality, and continuity—implies a logic of repetition whereby the trace marks the recurrence of the similar that is entirely dissimilar.[15] This is precisely what is implied by the etymological denotation of kabbalah as the transmission of received tradition, the selfsame wisdom persistently engendering things divergently. What I espouse, therefore, is not an essentialism that silences discord, but rather a hermeneutic that turns on the paradox that the invariable is the condition that stimulates variance. In the interpretive praxis of scholar and practitioner alike, identity and difference are not mutually exclusive; they well forth from the spot where the original is perpetually disparate and the disparate provisionally original.

Origin and the Impossibility of Beginning the Beginning

It will be beneficial to digress briefly and consider David Leahy's notion of *thinking now occurring,* a formidable philosophical challenge that will help sharpen my view of the conception of tradition as genuine repetition that informed the Heideggerian and kabbalistic hermeneutic. I subscribe to Leahy's conjecture that the new path of thinking must be one in which there is a coincidence of thought and existence without the one being reduced to or derived from the other[16]—it is plausible, as Heidegger observed in *Sein und Zeit,*[17] to mark the launch of philosophy by the Parmenidean aphorism that being and thinking are one and the same, a metaphysical precept that implies, as Hegel astutely observed in the first book of the first volume of the *Wissenschaft der Logik,* published in 1812 and in a revised version in 1832, that "thinking [*das Denken*] and the determination of thinking [*die Bestimmungen des Denkens*] are not something alien to the subject matters, but are rather their essence, or that the *things* and the *thinking* of them agree in and for themselves (also our language expresses a kinship between them); that thinking in its immanent determinations, and the true nature of things, are one and the same content."[18]

The change championed by Leahy requires that the absolute novelty of matter, which is itself the identity of thought, is amalgamated notionally into the "the meta-identical transcendence of a meta-identity," and hence "for the first time the *meta* meta-identically exists in essence. Existence for the first time is conceived essentially as itself absolute novelty. This existence is the matter of thought itself."[19] I take issue, however, with the understanding of the temporal interval as it emerges from Leahy's thinking that is now occurring. In my judgment, the discontinuity of a dramatically new commencement can be appropriated only to the extent that we grasp that the present is not only continuous with, but—in its deepest valence—the reverberation of the past that remains open as the future that is to come.[20]

Describing the intent of his *Novitas Mundi*, Leahy writes that the "book sets out for the first time the transcendental limits of the essentially new form of thought which is what the new world's new thinking really is if it be really new."[21] In somewhat more pedantic language, Leahy elaborates:

> The appearance of the transcendental essence of existence itself is, in its being identically what has occurred to it during the course of its worldly being or being in time, that which makes that time *to be* what it is, identifying it through its transcendental essence with existence itself. . . . What we now see is truly seen for the first time. What we now see occurs through no necessity whatsoever. It is the manifest freedom of the fact of creation in history at this time. This critical occurrence of the transcendental essence of existence itself in thought is the essence of its history, manifested in the historical essence it is the *templative authority* of the history in essence of thought. In the essential history of thought, this world's existence is *contemplated* for the first time (a fact made possible by history's *essential indifference* to time); for the first time, what has occurred presents itself in absolute evidence.[22]

Moving beyond the equally abstract options of an apotheosis of the particular into the universal or the incarnation of the universal within the particular, Leahy's thinking that is now occurring is the thinking of the transcendental essence of existence itself, a thinking that is keenly attuned to the contingency of the factual in the present liberated from the constraints of being determined by the past:

> In its faithful attention to the essence of what occurred to being in time, this thinking now existing brings each object into existence on its own terms without making those terms in themselves its object but only the appearance in them of the transcendental essence of existence itself. It is in the historical essence, through which each object in perpetuity is at once made wholly itself within that existence accounting for this world's existence, that everything comes into existence on its own terms. . . . This is the absolute evidence of purely *factual* contingency. This absolute evidence is in the thinking now occurring radically discontinuous in essence with every point of view that encumbers existence with its own perspective, imposing upon it a *logos* of its own, that is, a purely *logical* contingency, essentially unhistorical, by which the past is bound to its thinking, the essence of which is termination in itself, or *world-determination*. . . . But the termination of the transcendental essence of existence itself is the termination of essence in existence; its *appearance*, or *the essence of history*, terminates in existence itself, not in its *de*termination.[23]

I assent to Leahy's call for the need to uphold a new logic that claims the beginning as the middle excluded by the logic of the excluded middle; that is, a beginning that is not the beginning of the end and therefore not a foreshadowing of the end of the beginning, but the beginning of the beginning that is always also the end of the end, albeit in a distinctly nontautological way. Moreover, this logic will exemplify the paradox of being "without meaning but not meaningless," imparting the sense of "*being for the first time*. The logical category would be *being beginning*. Nothing other than being for the first time would be thought. . . . The essence beyond essence—the exception to essence that *is* essence—of a categorically new logic would be the essence of the new."[24]

Two critical questions need to be asked. First, has Leahy articulated the most felicitous understanding of newness, and second, is it possible to speak of a beginning that exists for the first time in history without presuming that there is a concatenation of successive nows, each coexisting in the absolute relativity of its own spatial-temporal dimensionality? Can there be an absolute now that breaks absolutely with the continuum of time? The presumption of such a possibility is what leads Leahy to relate his thinking now occurring in the third millennium—the *looking without a looking glass*[25]—to speculation about the apocalypse. Against the commonplace understanding, Leahy insists that the apocalypse is not about the end of the old world or the beginning of a new world, but rather about the end of the end and the beginning of the beginning. "We are dealing not with beginning now of the world, not with the creation of the world, but with the beginning of the beginning now of the world, not merely with the beginning, but with the beginning of the beginning. We are dealing not with the final now of the world, not with the end of the world, but with the end of the final now of the world, not merely with the end, but with the end of the end."[26] The now of the apocalypse, on this score, is deemed "the first now of the world. Then the beginning of the new heaven and the new earth is the beginning of the universe now beginning.... For the first time the I now speaking is apocalyptic."[27] Implicit in this turn is the collapse of the temporal divide, for the "not-yet is absolutely now."[28] To heed the imperative of the apocalyptic, consequently, is to discern that *tomorrow is now because now is tomorrow*. An absolutely new beginning, however, logically necessitates an absolute ending of the beginning that is now ending. Naturally, Leahy is attentive to this possibility, and thus he argues, "this beginning of fully apocalyptic thinking is anticipated in previous conceptions of mind in the history of thought. But precisely because previous thought *anticipated* this beginning of an essentially new form of mind its actuality before now is precluded."[29]

With all due deference to Leahy, I would argue that the pure immediacy of now entails the reiteration of the new that renders the supposition of an absolute novum untenable. This plainspoken wisdom is deftly expressed by Emmanuel Falque, "The new, in philosophy as in theology, cannot be formulated except insofar as it arises from what was there before."[30] Nuancing and further complicating the argument, I would contend that what was before could never be retrieved except as what has not yet taken place. Hence, rather than speaking of the thinking now occurring as existing for the first time historically, it is more accurate to speak of the present in which that thinking transpires as the reprise of what has always been what is to become. Utilizing a distinction made by Edward Said, we can say that the point of departure is inaccessible because it is not a transitive property determined by an anticipated end or an expected continuity; it is rather a radical and intransitive starting point that has no object other than its own relentless clarification.[31] The beginning is thus "*making* or *producing difference*; but—and here is the great fascination in the subject—difference which is the result of combining the already-familiar with the fertile novelty of human work in language."[32] By his own admission, Said's conception is indebted to the Husserlian phenomenological reduction whereby the search for the absolute beginning leads to its own undermining inasmuch as the beginning shows itself sensuously only as the beginning constructed intentionally in the constitution of the intuitive object that "attains original givenness in and with the *form of a temporal duration*, rendering an encompassing and objective unity possible."[33] Even in its immanent essence as an absolute givenness, the beginning is always noetically at a distance from being the beginning of the beginning of being.[34]

The logic of this argument can be adduced further from Husserl's remark in the lectures on the internal time consciousness of 1905, "But this *question of origin* is directed towards the *primitive* formations of time-consciousness, in which the primitive differences of the temporal become constituted intuitively and properly as the original sources of all the evidences relating to time."[35] Phenomenological apperception is not concerned with the empirical genesis whence the intuitions of objective space and objective time arise, but only in the immanent sense and descriptive content of the experiences (*Erlebnisse*) bracketed from the natural standpoint and the ensuing epistemological inquiry into the presumed existence or nonexistence transcendent to consciousness. As Husserl boldly states, "We do not fit experiences into any reality. We are concerned with reality only insofar as it is reality meant, objectivated, intuited, or conceptually thought. With respect to the problem of time, this means that we are interested in the *experiences* of time.... We seek to bring *the a priori of time* to *clarity* by exploring the *consciousness of time*, by bringing its essential constitution to light, and by exhibiting the apprehension-contents and act-characters that pertain—perhaps specifically—to time and to which the *a priori* temporal laws essentially belong."[36]

The origin, then, is not an objective time that can be calculated instrumentally by the ego in the world of physical things and psychic subjects,[37] but it is rather the interior time of the eidetic experiences accessible phenomenologically and not psychologically.[38] When gauged from this vantagepoint, the origin of time can never be something that originates in time, and thus the essence of the *arche* inessentially is *an-archic*. Husserl himself, it is worth recalling, defined philosophy more generally—although obviously phenomenology is privileged—as "a science of true beginnings, or origins, of *rizōmata pantōn*."[39] But the true beginning is the beginning that cannot begin. The constant quest for origin, which is the watchword of phenomenology as the science of pure phenomena, to go back to the things themselves (*zur Sache selbst*), is perforce a recoiling to the domain where the very question of origin is interrogated as the origin of the question. At the beginning stands the impasse of the beginning. In lieu of a unitary point whence all things originate, we find a fold, duplicity, contravention, the doubling of infringement that marks the way of the beginning in the beginning of the way.

A similar account, albeit betraying the influence of both Husserl and Merleau-Ponty, is offered by John Sallis: "Radical philosophy is a peculiar *return to beginnings*, a turning towards what already determines it. It is a circling which sets out from the beginnings so as to return to them, which it can do only if in its circling it never really leaves them. . . . Radical philosophy, as return to beginnings, is thus simultaneously a turning towards its own beginnings, towards those beginnings with which the return to beginnings is initiated."[40] I would add, by way of amplification and not dissension, that the return to the beginning is a return to where one has never been because the very notion of beginning, as Sallis himself wrote elsewhere, is always a "redoubling—which is to say no beginning at all."[41] The beginning bears the paradox of existing only "after the fact," that is, it "has always already been the beginning," but if this is so, then there is no beginning that has not begun prior to beginning and therefore destabilizing the very possibility of beginning.[42] In Derridean parlance, the onset can never be anything but second, an echo, a trace, the "originary iterability."[43] Only that which is distinct can be duplicated, since what recurs is the same difference that is indifferently the same. As will become increasingly clear from the subsequent analysis in this chapter and the ones that follow, the conception I articulate on the basis of these sources, in contrast to Leahy, can be extricated from both Heidegger and the kabbalah.

Novelty and Repetition of the Altogether Otherwise

Perhaps more efficaciously than any other twentieth-century philosopher, Heidegger has expressed the intonation of time—or, to be more fastidious, what he calls the "primordial temporality" (*ursprünglichen Zeitlichkeit*) experienced in the ecstatic unity of past, present, and future, as opposed to the vulgar understanding (*vulgären Verständnis*) of time as the continual succession of nows (*Jetzt-folge*)—as the concurrence of the heterogeneity of the homogeneous and the homogeneity of the heterogeneous. This confluence is expressed as well in spatial terms as "*the primordial 'outside itself' in and for itself* [das ursprüngliche 'Außer-sich' an und für sich selbst]."[44] That time is extrinsic to itself in the manner of being intrinsic to itself suggests that the temporal flow consists of the recurrence of the same in which the same is the recurrence of difference.[45] Following this notion of time, thinking itself is best characterized as a circular movement (*Kreisbewegung*) by which one is restored to where one has previously not been. In contrast to the path of philosophy, the pedestrian understanding "can only perceive and grasp what lies straight in front of it: it thus wishes to advance in a straight line, moving from the nearest point on to the next one, and so on. This is called progress [*Fortschritt*]."[46]

Heidegger's sarcasm is palpable as he expresses his disdain for the quotidian sense of time that even treats the orbicular motion in a linear fashion as "straightforward progression" (*Geradeausgehen*), culminating in reverting to the starting point and coming to a standstill. The fuller hermeneutical error implied by this conception of the serial progress of time, as it relates more specifically to a historiological as opposed to a historical perspective, is articulated by Heidegger in a meditation on the *mystery of language* from the *Schwarze Hefte*: "we understand a 'result' ['*Erfolg*'] as the effect [*Wirkung*] that *follows* [folgt] upon a cause [*Ursache*]; but is not the result now what *precedes* that which is supposed to count as 'true'? A result is not so much something effectuated [*Bewirkte*] as it is the first properly backward effectuation [*rückwärts Wirkende*], insofar as the result extinguishes all other possibilities, ones which then would have the result of being able to deny the claim to what is true."[47]

The mundane understanding of causality rests on the assumption that the result is cognized as an effect consequent to an antecedent cause, but the result is veritably a backward effectuation that is the "last consequence of the sovereignty of the human being as the historiological animal"; that is, the surrendering of all history to an anthropomorphizing concept of historiology wherein the past is determined completely "from the horizon of planning and using, and the human being is sequestered from all beyng."[48] A historical comprehension (*geschichtlich begriffen*) "shows that the humanity entangled in *results* and in their calculation and production twists history into a constant and increasing backward motion [*Rückwärtsbewegung*] and indeed one behind the obviousness of the progress which everyone can see and which is all that is seen. Both—that regress [*Rückschritt*] and this progress [*Fortschritt*]—belong together."[49] The emphasis on progress is, in truth, regressive, insofar as the preeminent form of the movement of history, and the essential sense of modern humanity based thereon, are pursued through the ascendancy of historiology. Moreover, the "backward effectivity" (*Rückwärtswirken*) of the professed forward evolution erects "the genuine barrier to all meditation on the beginnings [*Anfänge*], because indeed what happened is seen only in the horizon of *results* and precisely *not* out of the origin [*Ur-sprung*] in the sense of the preservation of possibilities pregnant with decisions."[50]

Inasmuch as this sense of regress-progress is the criterion that engulfs the conventional understanding, moving in a circle, which seemingly gets one nowhere but to the place whence one set out, is objectionable—hence the ubiquitous denunciation of circular reasoning, the everyday view that Heidegger summarily dismissed in *Sein und Zeit* as a failure to comprehend the fore-structure (*Vor-struktur*) of understanding (*Verstehen*) grounded in the tripartite nature of interpretation (*Auslegung*) as fore-having (*Vorhabe*), foresight (*Vorsicht*), and fore-conception (*Vorgriff*).[51] When the hermeneutical condition of Dasein is viewed from this perspective, then the matter of the vicious circle (*circulus vitiosus*) commands a response different from the stock dismissal:

> *But to see a* vitiosum *in this circle and to look for ways to avoid it, even to "feel" that it is an inevitable imperfection, is to misunderstand understanding from the ground up.*... What is decisive is not to get out of the circle, but to get into it in the right way. This circle of understanding is not a circle in which any random kind of knowledge operates, but it is rather the expression of the existential *fore-structure* of Dasein itself.... The "circle" in understanding belongs to the structure of meaning, and this phenomenon is rooted in the existential constitution of Dasein, that is, in interpretive understanding.[52]

The forestructure of understanding thus requires one to leap primordially and completely into the circular being of Dasein constituted as care (*Sorge*),[53] the ontological meaning of which relates to the existentiell question about Dasein's potentiality-for-being-a-whole (*Ganzseinkönnen*) and the existential question about the constitution of the being (*Seinsverfassung*) of the end (*Ende*) and the state of wholeness (*Ganzheit*).[54] Responding to the alleged assumption that Dasein is marked by an unfinished quality (*Unabgeschlossenheit*) that is always outstanding (*aussteht*), which makes it impossible both to experience Dasein ontically as an existing whole and to define it ontologically in its wholeness, Heidegger suggests that the latter is made accessible through the anticipatory resoluteness of being-toward-death (*Sein zum Tode*) that is the coming-to-an-end (*Zu-End-kommen*); the consummate ending, which is death, is the only meaningful way that each individual human being in its own sense of mineness (*Jemenigkeit*) or specificity (*Jeweiligkeit*) can be said to be whole.[55] The fragmentariness of human existence is attenuated by the devouring nature of death, but a proper comprehension of the hermeneutical situation of Dasein precludes interpreting that end as merely the recapitulation of the beginning. Heidegger insists that this ending does not mean fulfillment or disappearance, two forms of being-at-an-end (*Zu-Ende-sein*) that apply to an objective presence or something at hand (*Zuhandenes*), but rather the end is delineated as being-toward-the-end (*Sein zum Ende*), which is a feature of Dasein's being ahead of itself (*Sich-vorweg-sein*) as its own not-yet (*Noch-nicht*).[56] To say that being-toward-the-end offers the existential possibility for an existentiell wholeness of Dasein implies that death does not denote a goal that can be achieved but not yet objectively present (*Vorhandenes*); it is the imminence (*Bevorstand*) through which Dasein is "*completely* thrown back upon its ownmost potentiality-of-being."[57] The being-toward-the-end belongs essentially to the thrownness (*Geworfenheit*) of Dasein that reveals itself in attunement (*Stimmung*).[58] Heidegger's ontological analytic of death, therefore, does not presume a successional narrative from the cradle to the grave, but rather an asymptotic circuity by which one's past is always anticipating the future that is always reshaping the past.

Despite the many turns on Heidegger's path, he remained committed to the primacy of the circle as the appropriate geometric symbol to understand the hermeneutical texture of human experience, the comportment of temporality, and the trajectory of thinking. Thus, in one context, he writes that the "essential feature of the circular movement of philosophy does not lie in running around the periphery and returning to the point of departure [*Ausgangsstelle*]. It lies in that view of the center that this circular course [*Kreisgang*] alone can provide. The center, that is, the middle and ground, reveals itself as such only in and for the movement that circles it."[59] Linear thinking is linked to the certainty of progress, whereas the circularity of philosophical thought is bound up with an ambiguity (*Zweideutigkeit*) that is not eliminated or leveled even by means of the synthetic resolution of the conflict between thesis and antithesis according to the Hegelian dialectic.[60] To move at the *center of philosophizing* is to move about not in the place of certitude but in the *ambiguity of philosophizing*, a move that is always a retracing of one's steps to the beginning of the question that calls into question the question of the beginning.[61] As Heidegger expressed it through the voice of the scientist in the imaginary trialogue on the country path, "You philosophers always think backwards. This is surely the basis for the often noted impression that philosophy and its history leave on every straight-thinking mind: that philosophy, in contrast to the progress of scientific research [*Forschung*], stays in the same place and never gets anywhere."[62] The subterfuge here is obvious as the caricature of the circular law of philosophical argumentation, supposedly condemned by Heidegger, is precisely what he affirms as superior to the scientific idea of progress.

This is the import as well of Heidegger's assertion that the "guiding question" (*Leitfrage*) of inceptual thinking (*anfängliche Denken*) concerns "the essentiality of the essence [*die Wesentlichkeit des Wesens*]," which "consists of the greatest possible generality [*größtmöglichen Allgemeinheit*] of the essence." The question of the essence "contains in itself what is decisive [*Entscheidungshafte*], which now from the ground up pervasively determines the question of being [*Seinsfrage*]. . . . The principle of inceptual thinking therefore sounds like something doubled [*gedoppelt*]: all essence is essential occurrence [*alles Wesen ist Wesung*]."[63] The discourse to displace the closed circular movement—and the ancillary assumption that the future truth is already determined by the past—must partake of this doubling and what appears tautological from the perspective of the more prosaic linear logic. For Heidegger, the genuine tautology "names the Same only once, and indeed as itself" (*nur einmal das Selbe nennt sie und zwar als es selbst*).[64] Tautological thinking is thus predicated on the temporal paradox of the same that can be disclosed only once, and in this respect it is the "primordial sense of phenomenology."[65] The task, for Heidegger, as Derrida well understood, is not to circumvent this hermeneutic circulation, as viciously futile or as pointless as it might seem, but to engage in it by going all around it.[66] This is implied in the Heideggerian emphasis on resoluteness (*Entschlossenheit*) and authenticity (*Eigentlichkeit*):

> The experience of the circular closure does not close anything, it suffers neither lack nor negativity. Affirmative experience without voluntarism, without a compulsion to transgression: not to transgress the law of circle and *pas de cercle* but *trust in them*. Of this trust would thought consist. The desire to accede, by this faithful repetition of the circle, to the not-yet-crossed, is not absent. The desire for a new step, albeit a backward one (*Schritt zurück*), *ties and unties* this procedure [*démarche*]. Tie without tie, get across [*franchir*] the circle without getting free [*s'affranchir*] of its law. *Pas sans pas* [step without step/step without not/not without step/not without not].[67]

With regard to the temporal quandary of the law of the circle—the future auguring the reversion to the past where one has never been, the fourfold connotation of the idiomatic expression *pas sans pas*—there is continuity between the so-called earlier and later Heidegger.[68] To cite one relevant passage from *Sein und Zeit*: the three temporal modes are said to commingle around the notion that only the "*being that, as futural* [zukünftiges], *is equiprimordially having-been* [gleichursprünglich gewesend], *can hand down to itself its inherited possibility* [ererbte Möglichkeit], *take over its own thrownness and be in the Moment for 'its time'* [augenblicklich sein für 'seine Zeit']. *Only authentic temporality* [eigentliche Zeitlichkeit] *that is at the same time finite makes something like fate* [Schicksal], *that is, authentic historicity* [eigentliche Geschichtlichkeit], *possible*."[69]

In some measure, Heidegger's early thought bears affinity to Husserl's description of the "eidetic laws of compossibility"—the "rules that govern simultaneous or successive existence and possible existence together"—anchored in the motivation of the transcendental sphere, as opposed to causation, structured as the "universal *unity-form of the flux*," that is, the "*formal regularity pertaining to a universal genesis*, which is such that past, present, and future become unitarily constituted over and over again in a certain noetic-noematic formal structure of flowing modes of givenness."[70] Consciousness constitutes itself for itself in the unity of its history, and in that constitution are contained the constitutions of all the objectivities, whether ideal or real, transcendent or immanent, that exist for that concrete and monadic ego. Heidegger translated Husserl's insight into his own conceptual and terminological registry: the authentic temporality of Dasein—the finitude that makes possible the destiny of our historicity—is distinguished by the anticipatory resoluteness (*vorlaufenden Entschlossenheit*) of appropriating the present moment as the realization of the future recuperating the past. This resoluteness, as it emerges from Heidegger's reflections on Dasein's essential being-guilty (*Schuldigsein*), entails being thrown to the ground of nullity (*Grund der Nichtigkeit*),[71] but this thrownness is possible only if Dasein, as futural, can reclaim the *way that it always already was* (wie es je schon war), that is, its having-been (*Gewesen*). "Only because Dasein in general *is* as I *am*-having-been, can it come futurally toward itself in such a way that it comes-*back*. Authentically futural, Dasein is authentically *having-been*. . . . Dasein can *be* authentically having-been only because it is futural."[72] Once more, we encounter Heidegger's embrace of circularity applied hermeneutically to the structure of temporality: Dasein projects to the future to the extent that Dasein is thrown back to the past, but Dasein is thrown back to the past only to the extent that it projects to the future. From this it follows that the quality of resoluteness "becomes the *repetition* [Wiederholung] of a possibility of existence that has been handed down."[73] That the repetition is deemed a "handing down" (*Überlieferung*) implies that Dasein can mentally recuperate the stations of the journey it has traversed, but this does not mean that there is an exact reenactment of the past.

> The authentic repetition of a possibility of existence that has been . . . is grounded existentially in anticipatory resoluteness; for in resoluteness the choice is first chosen that makes one free for the struggle over what is to follow [*kämpfende Nachfolge*] and fidelity [*Treue*] to what can be repeated. The handing down of a possibility that has been in repeating it, does not, however, disclose the Dasein that has been there in

> order to actualize it again. The repetition of what is possible neither brings back "what is past," nor does it bind the "present" back to what is "outdated." Arising from a resolute self-projection, repetition is not convinced by "something past," in just letting it come back as what was once real. Rather, repetition *responds* to the possibility of existence that has been-there. But responding [*Erwiderung*] to this possibility in a resolution is at the same time, *as a response belonging to the Moment* [als augenblickliche], the *renunciation* [Widerruf] of that which is working itself out in the today as "past." Repetition neither abandons itself to the past, nor does it aim at progress. In the Moment, authentic existence is indifferent [*gleichgültig*] to both of these alternatives. . . . Repetition first makes manifest to Dasein its own history. The occurrence itself and the disclosedness belonging to it, or the appropriation of it, is existentially grounded in the fact that Dasein is ecstatically open as a temporal being.[74]

The resolve to live momentously, to be responsive to the moment, depends on repetition, but an indispensable component of that repetition is renunciation of the past. Authentic existence entails the being-there that is forged neither by a retroactive glance backward nor by a proleptic glance forward but by repeating what is unrivaled with regard to the untruth of the truth that was once true as untrue. To leap to where one is no more is to retreat to where one is yet to be.[75] Thinking on its way (*unterwegs*), therefore, may be construed as a step back (*den Schritt zurück*) out of metaphysics into the essence of metaphysics, as a migration out of the oblivion of difference into the destiny of the withdrawing concealment of perdurance.[76]

In the lecture course *Vom Wesen der Wahrheit: Zu Platons Höhlengleichnis und Theätet*, offered in the winter semester 1931–32 at the University of Freiburg, Heidegger writes, "For in *genuine* historical reflection we take just that distance from the present which allows us room to leap out [*hinauszuspringen*] beyond our own present, i.e. to treat it just as every present as present deserves to be treated, namely as something to be *overcome* [überwunden]. Genuine historical return is the decisive beginning of authentic *futurity* [Zukünftigkeit]. . . . In the end it is *historical* return which brings us into what is actually happening *today*. In the end it is also only a self-evident and therefore doubtful everyday opinion which takes history as something 'past.'"[77] History is emphatically not what happened factually in the past, as the discipline of historiology presumes, but what can be relived in the present as the way to heed the destiny that beckons us into the future. In that regard, the *genuine historical return is the decisive beginning of the authentic futurity*. Striking a concordant note, Heidegger writes in a notebook entry from autumn 1932, "What truly remains in history is the unique [*Einzige*]—*un*repeatable [Un*wiederholbare*]—at once necessary; what can be '*repeated*' in the extrinsic sense [*äußeren Sinne*]—does not *abide*—instead, it vacillates and has no unassailable necessity. It is altogether something else to repeat what is unique [*das Einzige wiederholen*]—i.e., to carry out a proper necessity—and not just calculate [*ausrechnen*]."[78]

Counterintuitively, uniqueness is not antithetical to repetition. Heidegger insists that if we are to speak of an abiding necessity, then the mandate is *to repeat what is unique*. But how does one repeat what is unique such that what is repeated remains unique? As he put it in a second passage from the notebooks written at a later date, for the common understanding of the masses the notion of sameness (*das Selbe*) is set in opposition to what is novel, but "creative individuals" are committed to the "mystery" (*Geheimnis*) of sameness "in its ever-originary essentiality" (*immer ursprünglichen Wesentlichkeit*).[79] In a third passage, Heidegger opines that what is most common is the universal and its universalization arises "from the incapacity to experience the ever-incomparably unique in the same [*das jeweils Unvergleichbare Einzige im Selben*] and to maintain it in its mystery."[80] A similar idea is expressed in the observation in the *Beiträge zur Philosophie (Vom Ereignis)*, composed between 1936 and 1938, that every essential occurrence of the essence of being "is determined out of what is essential in the sense of the original-unique [*Ursprünglich-Einzigen*]."[81] The upheaval in thinking that Heidegger sought to spearhead rests on the distinction between the conservative wish to preserve *what was begun in the wake of the beginning* and the more revolutionary relation to the beginning that demands acting and thinking *from the perspective of the future*. The beginning is always a reemergence of the unprecedented—the origin (*Ursprung*) that is incomparably distinctive (*Einzig*) in each of its potentially countless iterations—and hence requires the "renunciation of the crutches and evasions of the habitual and the usual."[82]

In much the same cadence, Heidegger writes in another section from the *Beiträge* that the wish to navigate the course of the question of being, in the hope of recuperating the lineage of antiquity, can be fulfilled if one comprehends that the matter of repetition means "to *let* the *same*, the uniqueness of being, become a plight *again* and *thereby out of a more original truth*. 'Again' means here precisely 'altogether otherwise' [*'Wieder' besagt hier gerade: ganz anders*]."[83] At first blush, one would not expect the concept of "the same" to be glossed as "the uniqueness of beyng" (*die Einzigkeit des Seyns*), since sameness, by definition, is demonstrably opposed to uniqueness. In Heideggerian terms, however, there is no opposition, for, as I discussed in the introduction, to attend to the same, which he contrasts with the identical, means to heed that which is recurrently different. This hermeneutical assumption furnishes the rationale for the pattern of time that posits the "same" as unique and the "again" as altogether otherwise. In *Einführung in die Metaphysik*, published in 1953 and based on a lecture course offered at the University of Freiburg in the summer semester of 1935, Heidegger writes, "To ask: how does it stand with Being?—this means nothing less than to *repeat and retrieve* [wieder-holen] the inception [*Anfang*] of our historical-spiritual Dasein, in order to transform it into the other inception."[84] The repetition of the novel is the basis for the phenomenological nexus that Heidegger establishes between time (*Zeit*), eternity (*Ewigkeit*), and the moment (*Augenblick*): "The eternal is not the incessant [*das Fort-währende*]; it is instead that which can withdraw [*entziehen*] in a moment so as to recur [*wiederzukehren*] later. What can recur: not as the *identical* [*das* Gleiche] but as the newly transforming [*Verwandelnde*], the one and the unique [*Eine-Einzige*], i.e., beyng, such that it is not immediately recognized, in this manifestation, as the same [*das Selbe*]!"[85] Conspicuously suggestive of both Kierkegaard's idea of eternity as the movement of becoming, which is the fullness of time, and Nietzsche's doctrine of the eternal recurrence of the same, Heidegger insists that eternity is not set in opposition to time; it is rather that which withdraws each moment to recur again the future.[86] What recurs, however, is not the identical but the same, that is, the unique being that is always—originarily—different.

Tradition and the Present of Futurally Having-Been

Inceptual thinking is characterized as the "original repetition" (*ursprünglichere Wiederholung*) of the "first beginning," the appropriating event (*Ereignis*) of being, which is set in confrontation (*Auseinandersetzung*) with the "other beginning." The antagonistic positioning of the two beginnings transfigures the nature of time as the still-to-be-unfolded other beginning as a "re-attaining" (*zurückzugelangen*) of the still-to-be-won-back first beginning, the future past that comes from the questioning of the truth of being that stands at the "origin of philosophy," the dawning of Greek thought that initiated the history of Western metaphysics.[87] Insofar as "every beginning is unsurpassable, it must constantly be repeated and must be placed through confrontation into the uniqueness of its incipience [*die Einzigkeit seiner Anfänglichkeit*] and thus of its ineluctable reaching ahead."[88] Just as the work of art (*Kunst*)—epitomized in poetizing (*Dichtung*)—is inceptual (*anfänglich*) and futural (*künftig*) in tandem, so the event in its eccentricity begins each time as that which was already yet to come.[89] Following the suggestion of Reiner Schürmann, I concur that the "there" of being-in-the world in *Sein und Zeit* was transmuted from an ontological trait to the "possible momentary site," which denotes "the non-generalizable other of all that has passed for universal and necessary. It names the event occurring only once and just this once. . . . The singular event, thought from out of the singular *there*—that is the other of the ontological tradition."[90] Schürmann goes so far as to surmise, "Heidegger is to be read backward, from the last to the first writings. By reading him in this way, one glimpses precisely the motives and paths that led him to raise the question of being for its own sake and out of itself, motives arising from the singular, and paths prompted by the many ways of accentuating the internal conflict arising from singularization."[91]

If one appreciates the extent to which Heidegger's notion of time is shaped by this unwavering sense of singularity, then it is clearly inaccurate to label his thinking as a "regressive path,"[92] since the beginning to which one relapses is always a new and more primeval beginning than the one from which one has departed. The individuals responsible for initiating the second beginning are described as still bringing with them "the past of the concealed history of being, that detour (as it may seem) metaphysics had to take through beings so as *not* to attain being and thus to come to an end which is strong enough for the plight leading toward the other beginning. This beginning at the same time leads back into the originariness [*Ursprünglichkeit*] of the first beginning and transforms the past into something not lost."[93] The way to the future is a detour (*Umweg*) to the past but not in the sense of just going back. The temporal markers of old and new are drastically altered. The old is not the archaic, as understood in historiological terms, but rather that which, as manifest in historical confrontation and meditation, "cannot be surpassed in essentiality by anything younger." Analogously, the new is not the modern that is currently in vogue, but the "freshness of the originariness of the re-beginning, that which ventures out into the concealed future of the first beginning and thus cannot at all be 'new' but must be even *older* than the old."[94] Already in the *Prolegomena zur Geschichte des Zeitbegriffs*, the published version of the lecture course given at the University of Marburg in the summer semester of 1925, Heidegger taught that the portrayal of tradition as genuine repetition (*echte Wiederholung*), in contrast to traditionalism (*Traditionalismus*), does not presume an uncritical revisiting of the past, but rather a return that "goes back *prior* to the questions which were posed in history, and the questions raised by the past are once again originally appropriated. This possibility of assuming history can then also show that the assumption of the question of the sense of being is not merely an external repetition of the question which the Greeks already raised. If this formulation of the question of being is a genuine one, then the repetition must rather bring us to understand that the Greek formulation of the question was conditioned and provisional and, what is more, had to be so."[95] From the specific case of grappling with the philosophical question about being raised by the ancient Greeks, we can induce the following general maxim: to appropriate the past originally is not merely to repeat the past derivatively, but it is to apprehend the unique circumstances that occasioned the past so that it will be reclaimed from a perspective that is always responsive to and changing in accord with the moment at hand. As James Ward observed, "Retrieval is never an exercise in nostalgia and is certainly not, in Heidegger, a moment in the economy of conservatism."[96]

From the Heideggerian perspective, as we find in Rosenzweig as well, albeit with the crucial difference that the latter blatantly utilized the theological categories of creation and redemption,[97] we decidedly cannot say of the end that it shall be precisely as it was in the beginning; the beginning itself is transformed by the projection into the future that is the eternally evolving and constantly regenerated end. The temporal cyclicality—a facet of Heidegger's hermeneutic circle—does not involve relapsing to where one has been, a mere repetition of patterns, but it is rather a reverting to where one has not been and indeed where one can never be. To attend to the past as "the coming of what has been" (*die Ankunft des Gewesen*) is not to commemorate the "passing of the past" (*das Vergehen*) but rather to appropriate "the gathering of what endures" (*die Versammlung des Währenden*).[98] In the celebrated language of the aphorism attributed to Heraclitus, ποταμοῖσι τοῖσιν αὐτοῖσιν ἐμβαίνουσιν ἕτερα καὶ ἕτερα ὕδατα ἐπιρρεῖ, "As they step into the same rivers, other and still other waters flow upon them."[99] The statement is better known by the Platonic paraphrase in the *Cratylus* 402a, "Heraclitus, I believe, says that all things pass and nothing stays [πάντα χωρεῖ καὶ οὐδὲν μένει], and comparing existing things to the flow of a river, he says you could not step twice into the same river [δὶς ἐς τὸν αὐτὸν ποταμὸν οὐκ ἂν ἐμβαίης]."[100] The original dictum, however, is more paradoxical than

Plato's rendering: ontically, the river remains the same precisely on account of its fluctuating waters; if the waters stop flowing, the river would lose its identity as a river. The stepping differently into the same waters, therefore, instructs us about the permanence of impermanence, and this is precisely the mode of eternality that intersects with time, thereby transmuting temporality into diremptive luminosity, the clearing within which the nonrepresentable presentness shines forth as anticipation of the past and recollection of the future. From the "unique and primordial essence of temporality" spring the most extreme contraries (*Gegensätze*), decisive renunciation (*entschiedene Verzichten*) and unconditional awaiting (*unbedingte Erharren*).[101] The motion of time is not a calculable metric but the swaying between the abdication that is an anticipation and the anticipation that is an abdication. The origin is determined by the telos in such a way that both termini are opened—the end in the beginning and the beginning in the end. By anticipating the past and recollecting the future, we are attuned to a mode of time that deviates from the customary chronology determined by a narrative linearity that dominates both the historicist conception of time and the psychologistic conception of identity. If regression is the operative term, then we must proclaim, in the spirit of Heraclitus, that the way back is the way forward. In Heidegger's own language, which lends credence to the aforecited remark of Schürmann, "We still get closer to what *is* if we think everything in reverse—assuming, of course, that we have, in advance, an eye for how differently everything then faces us. A mere reversal, made for its own sake, reveals nothing."[102]

Leaving aside the political ramifications of the prominence Heidegger apportions to the confrontation between the two beginnings, one initiated by the Greeks and the other allocated to the Germans, what is necessary to emphasize is his avowal of the paradox that only what is unique is repeatable, *Nur das Einmalige ist wieder-holbar*, whence it follows that repetition "does not mean the stupid superficiality and impossibility of the mere occurrence of the *same* for a second and third time. Indeed the beginning can never be apprehended as the *same*, since it reaches ahead and thus encroaches differently each time on that which it itself initiates."[103] The temporal line is here inverted, for the beginning, which is typically located in the past, is understood as the futural initiation of the inaugural event. The transposition of time—the destiny of the past is the effect of rather than the cause of the fate of the future[104]—undergirds Heidegger's stance regarding the historicity of Dasein. The "purely historical view" that tradition is what is handed down to us from the past is a "self-deception" in which we are ensnared as long as we are not thinking. Tradition, when considered authentically, is the reality that comes toward us and not the reality that lies behind us. The openness of the past bolsters our ability to hear the language of previous thinkers in the present so that we can enter into a face-to-face conversation (*Zwiesprache*) with them.[105] To think of time in this way is to acquiesce to the "time of thinking," which stands in contrast to the "time of calculation," a chronometric measure of history that is inessential (*wesenlos*). Only the former affords one the opportunity to think within the "sphere of tradition" (*Spielraum der Überlieferung*), which "prevails when it frees us from thinking back [*Nachdenken*] to a thinking forward [*Vordenken*], which is no longer a planning. Only when we turn thoughtfully toward what has already been thought, will we be turned to use for what must still be thought."[106]

In a letter to Eugen Fink from March 30, 1966, Heidegger wrote that to merit being called a student, one must "succeed in experiencing anew the same matter of thinking, experiencing it as ancient and as sheltering something most ancient within it. Such an experience continues to be determined by the tradition and by the spirit of the present age."[107] To think anew that which is ancient, this is the exhortation of one who wishes to embark on the path of phenomenological thinking. The latter is not a "particular direction of philosophy," but a method, a way to pursue knowledge, the possibility for "thinking to attain the 'things themselves' ['*Sachen selbst*'], or to put it more clearly: to attain the matter of thinking [*zu der Sache des Denkens*]."[108] For Heidegger, the Husserlian directive of going back to the things themselves (*zu den Sachen selbst*) can be realized only when one thinks what is sheltered unexpectedly as ancient in this matter of thinking, an experience determined equivalently by the tradition of the past and the spirit of the current moment.

The path has led us to a profound irony. On the one hand, as the publication of some volumes of the *Schwarze Hefte* has demonstratively proven, Heidegger disparagingly reprimands Judaism as a religious culture that is beholden exclusively to a mathematical-technological sense of time, a classification that corresponds to their privileging the historicist orientation (*Historismus*), which denies them proper access to history (*Geschichte*);[109] on the other hand, his own posture with respect to history accords well with the dialogical foundation of the experience of time that shaped the rabbinic conception of the Oral Torah, which in turn provided the ideational and sociological framework for the notion of tradition approved by the kabbalists. The temporal apperception shared by rabbinic sages, kabbalistic masters, and Heidegger fosters intergenerational dialogue by allowing one to blend with—or, in a more contemporary vernacular, to channel—the spiritual demeanor of a luminary from a previous era.[110] The rabbinic and kabbalistic notion of the oral tradition, which complements and expands the written scripture, is well captured in the words of Heidegger cited above, the new refers to the concealed future of the beginning, and hence it is older than the old.[111] The sharp scholarly distinction between innovative and conservative dissolves in light of this hermeneutical principle: what is old is old because it is new, and what is new is new because it is old.

Interestingly, the affinity between Heidegger and Jewish thought on this point was already noted by Alexander Altmann, who proposed in the essay "Was ist jüdische Theologie?" (1933) that "the existential moments, adduced by Heidegger, of 'heritage' (*Erbe*) and 'destiny' (*Schicksal*) could prove to be decisive for an understanding of Jewish existence."[112] Altmann was quick to add that the Heideggerian structures

> are not quite adequate for the singular phenomenon of Jewish existence if they are understood as purely ontological immanent entities. Rather, in the Jewish case these concepts display a very conscious turning toward the transcendent moment of divine revelation. It is characteristic of the Jewish people that they are conscious of their heritage, as well as of their destiny, believing that they are always being addressed anew by God in the course of history. Israel stands anew time and again before the ineradicable givenness of its spiritual heritage which it must somehow master and satisfactorily incorporate.[113]

The "tragic singularity" of the Jewish destiny consists of the need to heed de novo the "actuality" that was revealed in the foundational command of the monotheistic faith, "Hear O Israel, the Lord our God, the Lord is one" (Deuteronomy 6:4).[114] One must hear again and again the divine command, albeit always from a new perspective calibrated to the impending of the future in the theophanous moment at hand. The tensiveness of time implied in the ever-evolving tradition, based on the never-ending revelation, thus consists of the simultaneity of past, present, and future.

A succinct articulation of this idea, which has molded the scholastic piety of rabbinic culture for centuries, is offered by Joseph B. Soloveitchik in his philosophically nuanced account of the typologies of human nature, the first and the second Adam, which are elicited eisegetically from the scriptural narratives about the creation of humanity in the opening two chapters of Genesis: through participation in the faith community (the destiny of Adam II), one can be delivered from the existential angst of being condemned to the ephemerality of the now (the condition of Adam I). Covenantal time is both retrospective and prospective, affording an individual the chance to reexperience the promise of the past and to anticipate the hope of the future in the present in a manner that mimics the eternality of God—signified by the Tetragrammaton—wherein the boundaries separating before, now, and after dissipate.[115] From within the covenantal community, writes Soloveitchik, "not only contemporary individuals but generations are engaged in a colloquy, and each single experience of time is three-dimensional, manifesting itself in memory, actuality, and anticipatory tension."[116] The Jewish conception of tradition (*masorah*) revolves about this "paradoxical time awareness," which "involves the individual in the historic performance of the past and makes him also participate in the dramatic action of an unknown future." The temporality proper to members of this community, therefore, is "not only a formal succession within the framework of calendaric time but the union of the three grammatical tenses in an all-embracing time experience. . . . Covenantal man begins to find redemption from insecurity and to feel at home in the continuum of time. . . . He is no longer an evanescent being. He is rooted in everlasting time, in eternity itself."[117] Eternity is not the timeless opposition to time but the elongation of time realized in the recycling of what is still to come, the expectation of the past through the commemoration of the future. The future thus repeatedly interrupts the present, but interruption does not signal an unmitigated rupture of the past. The timeswerve of circular linearity—also attested in Rosenzweig[118]—dictates that without continuity we could not discern discontinuity. The two elements—which we can also refer to as synchrony and diachrony—coincide in the coalescence of the three temporal modes in the interminable becoming of the moment, which is called the "Lord's world day" (*Welttag des Herrn*).[119] In his description of the eternal God (*der ewige Gott*), which names not a reified state of being but the perpetual process of coming to be, linked to the central events of his religious phenomenology, Rosenzweig affirms a concept of simultaneity (*Gleichzeitigkeit*) that reverses the timeline—or, to be more precise, transmutes the line into a circle that is open at both ends—in a manner that parallels Heidegger's notion of equiprimordiality:

> Do not Creation, Revelation, Redemption mean the same thing that it means for God? Because for God, the times of that day are his own experiences [*eigne Erlebnisse*]; for him, the Creation of the world is becoming the Creator [*das Schöpferwerden*]; Revelation becoming manifest [*das Offenbar-werden*], Redemption becoming the Redeemer [*das Erlöserwerden*]. He becomes in this way till the end. All that happens is a becoming in him [*Alles was geschieht, ist an ihm Werden*]. And yet, since everything that happens, happens simultaneously [*gleichzeitig*], and really Revelation is not later than Creation, and just for this reason even Redemption is not later than the two, therefore that becoming of God is not a self-transformation [*Sichverändern*] for him, nor growth [*Wachsen*], nor increase [*Zunehmen*] but he is from the beginning and is at every moment and is always coming; and it is only because of this simultaneousness [*dieses Zugleichs*] of his everlasting-being all the time and eternally, that the whole must be designated as a becoming [*das Ganze als ein Werden bezeichnen*].[120]

The temporal depiction of the eternality of the divine as the simultaneous and continual becoming of the past, present, and future serves as a model for the temporality experienced by the eternal people in the circular linearity of their sacramental life. For Rosenzweig, the Jewish liturgical calendar transforms time from a linear to a cyclical progression, which is a prefiguration of eternity; participation in Jewish ritual affords the eternal people the task of fulfilling their metahistorical destiny in the circular rotation of time, which is lived experientially as a linear succession that is nevertheless an "inversion of the temporal sequence" (*Verkehrung der Zeitfolge*) that is "God's time" (*Gottes Zeit*), which "establishes the life of the eternal people."[121]

> Its eternal life . . . constantly anticipates the end and makes it therefore into the beginning. In this reversal [*Umkehrung*] it denies time as resolutely as possible and places itself outside of it. To live in time means to live between beginning and end. He who would want to live outside of time—and he who wants to live not that which is temporary, but an eternal life in time, must want this—he who therefore wants this must deny that "between." Such a denial, however, would have to be active, so that there would result not merely a not-living-in time [*Nicht-in-der-Zeit-Leben*], but a positive living-eternally [*Ewig-Leben*]. And the active denial would take place solely in the reversal. To reverse a between means to make its after into the before and its before into the after, the end into the beginning, the beginning into the end. And the eternal people does that. It already lives for itself as if it were the whole world and as if the world were finished; it celebrates in its Sabbaths the sabbatical completion of the world and makes it into the base and starting point of its existence. But that which would be temporally only a starting point, the Law, this it sets as the goal. So it does not experience the between, although it naturally, really naturally, lives in it. It experiences precisely the reversal of the between, and so it disavows the omnipotence of the between and denies time in this way, and the same time is experienced on the eternal way.[122]

For the Jewish people, who live beyond history, the beginning is the end, and the end the beginning. The surpassing of time is experienced in the fullness of the moment that has no before or after. Linear time is eternalized in the circular rhythms of sacred time, a process exemplified especially in the celebration of Sabbath, which instantiates the coalescence of past, present, and future, the temporal correlates of creation, revelation, and redemption. In the life of the Jew, who lives in and from the end, time has been proleptically redeemed and the experience of the between fulfilled. The disavowal of time—or what Levinas referred to as the deformalization of the abstract aspects of time and the consequent concretization of the structures of experience[123]—does not imply an abrogation or even a dialectical surpassing of temporality, but rather its radical deepening, an eradication of time by rooting oneself more firmly in the ground of time. Eternity, accordingly, is not the metaphysical overcoming of or existential escape from time but rather the merging of the three-dimensional structure of lived temporality through eternalization of the present in the continuous becoming of the being that has always been what is yet to come.[124]

Recasting the view shared by Rosenzweig and Soloveitchik in terms of Heidegger's notion of the moment as the recuperation of what is unique, which may well reflect Kierkegaard's view of repetition or Nietzsche's eternal return,[125] we can say that what is unique in each moment is precisely what is repeatable. The dual deportment of tradition as malleable and durable—malleable in its durability and durable in its malleability—rests on the assumption that each moment instantiates the compresence of the recollection of the past, the actuality of the present, and the anticipation of the future. What is actual about the moment is the inversion of this rectilinearity to the extent that it promotes the memory of what will be and the expectancy of what was. Accordingly, the mandate to remember, which legitimately can be called a central pillar of Jewish ritual and self-understanding, comprises not the nostalgic reclamation of a past sealed in its factical obstinacy, but an auspicious proclamation of a future foreseen in its evental unforseeability. The compresence, as Heidegger noted, is not the result of the accumulation (*Anhäufung*) or sequence (*Abfolge*) of the three ecstasies of time but rather of their equiprimordiality (*Gleichursprünglichkeit*); that is, the convergence arises as a result of the temporality that "temporalizes itself out of the authentic future ... in such a way that, futurally having-been [*zukünftig gewesen*], it first arouses the present [*Gegenwart*]. *The primary phenomenon of primordial and authentic temporality is the future.*"[126]

I will evaluate Heidegger's tempocentrism in chapter 6, but what must be borne in mind here is that he was well aware that the future cannot be severed from the other two modalities of time. Most telling is the locution *futurally having-been*, an expression that insinuates the transposal of the causal order such that *the past is the effect of the future rather than the future being the effect of the past*, a reversal of temporal causality that is resonant with similar strategies in psychoanalytic theory, especially the Freudian concept of *nachträglich*, rendered by Lacan as *l'après coup*, that is, "after the fact,"[127] the deferred action that assumes the character of the future perfect tense (*futur antérieur*) in place of the present perfect tense. In Lacan's own words: "What is realized in my history is neither the past definite as what was, since it is no more, nor even the perfect as what has been in what I am, but the future anterior as what I will have been, given what I am in the process of becoming."[128] According to this construal of time, the symptom does not relate primarily to an occurrence in the past but rather to an event that awaits its futural unfolding.[129] Lacan thus tenders a corrective to the time-function of the logic implied by Freud's idea of repeating (*Wiederholen*) and remembering (*Erinnerung*), according to which "the real is that which always comes back to the same place—to the place where the subject in so far as he thinks, where the *res cogitans*, does not meet it."[130] To remember, in its deepest assonance, is to repeat, but to repeat, as I have noted several times, means to come back to the same place where one has always never been. One cannot but be struck by the conceptual proximity of Lacan's privileging of the future to the view of temporality prioritized by Heidegger—especially pertinent is the Heideggerian notion of the "*remembering expectation* [erinnernde Erharren]," that is, awaiting a call of beyng (*einen Zuruf des Seyns*) by recollecting a hidden belonging to beyng (*eine verhüllte Zugehörigkeit zum Seyn*), the remembrance of what is to come as the temporalization (*Zeitigung*) of the "dispensation of the (hesitant) self-withholding [*Fügung des Sichversagens (des zögernden)*]" that "a-byssally grounds the domain of decision [*gründet ab-gründigerweise den Entscheidungsbereich*]"[131]—and I should add, the kabbalistic conception of time as the *retroactive not yet*, an idea that I have argued also betrays affinity with the Derridean trace.[132]

The routine attitude presumes both the irreversibility of time and its spatial homogenization into a series of now-points.[133] Heidegger refers to this notion of the temporal as the "successive flowing away of the 'now' out of the 'not yet now' into the 'no longer now'" as the "representational idea of time . . . which is standard throughout the metaphysics of the West."[134] The intransient nature of time so calculated consists in its periodic passing away. Technically speaking—as Heidegger put it in "Zeit und Sein," a lecture delivered at the University of Freiburg on January 31, 1962—from the metaphysical outlook, which coincides with our ordinary and inauthentic sense of time, past and future are *me on ti*, that is, "something which is not [*etwas nicht Seiendes*], though not an absolute nullity [*schlechthin Nichtiges*], but rather something present [*Anwesendes*] which lacks something [*dem etwas fehlt*]. This lack is named with the 'no longer now' [*'nicht mehr'*] and the 'not yet now' [*'noch nicht'*]. Viewed in this way, time appears as the succession of nows [*Nacheinander der Jetzt*], each of which, barely named, disappears into the 'ago' and is already pursued by the 'soon.'"[135]

Quotidian time is experienced as a string of nows aligned in sequential procession, and hence there is an inescapable asymmetry between the obdurate past and the variable future. By contrast, authentic time is lived from the future retrieval of the past in the present.[136] It is in this sense that tradition is thinking forward and not thinking backward, a thinking that calls to the past as the restoration of that which convenes us from the future. Common to Heidegger and to a dominant orientation within rabbinic Judaism, amplified in kabbalistic literature, is a conception of tradition built on the basis of a sense of history wherein the synchronic and the diachronic axes of time intersect irrevocably at the point where the present—in truth not a point but more like a ripple—temporalizes itself both as the anticipatory reminiscence of the future awaiting the occurrence of the past and as the recollective anticipating of the past awaiting the revival of the future.

The position articulated by Heidegger can well serve as an elucidation of the philosophical underpinnings of the midrashic proclivity to unearth meaning homiletically from the text rather than by appeal to an independent conceptual system, an approach that has informed Jewish thought for millennia and is clearly what inspired the kabbalistic sensibility as well. As Scholem memorably characterized the rabbinic method in his discussion of revelation and tradition, "Truth is given once and for all, and it is laid down with precision. Fundamentally, truth merely needs to be transmitted. . . . The effort of the seeker after truth consists not in having new ideas but rather in subordinating himself to the continuity of the tradition of the divine word and in laying open what he receives from it in the context of his own time. In other words: Not system but *commentary* is the legitimate form through which truth is approached."[137] *Pace* Scholem, I would argue that it is erroneous to separate tradition and revelation in the history of Judaism, and hence, it is not at all obvious that the mediated and conditional status of the former inevitably necessitates the inability to experience the immediacy and unconditionality of the latter. The rabbinic understanding of a continuing revelation, which unfolds through an unbroken chain of interpretation, is not based on a static conception of a timeless Torah set in opposition to time and therefore resistant to the fluctuation of historical contingency. Rather, it is predicated on a conception of temporality that calls into question the aligning of events chronoscopically in a sequence stretched invariably between before and after. The rabbinic hermeneutic advocates a notion of time that is circular in its linearity and linear in its circularity.[138] The study of Torah demands that one be able to imagine each day, indeed each moment of each day, as a potential renewal of the Sinaitic theophany, an idea that is derived from, or hyperliterally linked to, the words "On this day they came to the desert of Sinai" (Exodus 19:1); that is, "on this day" (*ba-yom ha-zeh*), and not merely "on the day" (*ba-yom*), to indicate that it is incumbent on future readers to look upon the holy writ as if it were given afresh each time it is studied. Every interpretative endeavor is a reenactment of the revelatory experience, albeit from a unique vantage point.[139] One can take hold of the ancient truth, therefore, only as the truth that is yet to be disclosed, a truth renewed in the gesticulation of its genuine iteration; the eternity of Torah consists precisely of this temporal resilience.

The midrashic mindset inculcates the interweaving of time and hermeneutics in the discernment of the discontinuity of continuity that characterizes the rabbinic approach to the scriptural verse subject to continual reinterpretation and, even more significantly, to continual rewriting. Consider in this light Heidegger's remark, "The poetry of the poet or the treatise of the thinker stands within its own proper unique word. It compels us to perceive this word again and again as if we were hearing it for the first time. These newborn words transpose us in every case to a new shore."[140] Heidegger's poetic thinking shares with the rabbinic-kabbalistic hermeneutic the assumption that the uniqueness of the word triggers the need to hear it again repetitively as if it were uttered for the first time, a transporting to the new shore where one has already not been. Critical to this strategy of reading is the spatial bridging of past and future in the present constituted transcendentally within the immanence of consciousness. Phenomenologically speaking, what has been and what will be have no temporal density apart from the noematic lived experience of the moment, but the latter has no ideational content except through the noetic synthesis of the intentional acts of retention and protention, which point respectively to the past and the future crisscrossing in the perceptual present that cannot be represented as presence inasmuch as it always exceeds what can be presented, the now, we might say, that is interminably not-now, the temporal interlude that cannot be fathomed conceptually or empirically.

Notes

1. I am here referring to Moshe Idel, who has doggedly sought to discredit my way of thinking by labeling it a form of essentialism, monochromatism, or pansymbolism that obfuscates multivalency and hermeneutic diversity. See, for instance, Idel, *Absorbing Perfections*, pp. 580–81n135; Idel, *Kabbalah and Eros*, pp. 100–1, 128–31; Idel, *Kabbalah in Italy*, pp. 312, 449n106; Idel, *Ben*, pp. 619–20. This is not the context to argue point by point, text by text, but let me state that Idel's criticism suffers from flattening my methodology. One may quibble with any scholarly position but it should not be hastily ignored without consideration of the details upon which it is based. To list assorted symbolic approaches and to petition Derridean *différance*, as Idel does, is neither a serious theoretical challenge to my thinking nor a sophisticated reading of deconstruction. For a partial rejoinder to Idel's criticism, see Wolfson, "Structure," and Wolfson, "Retroactive Not Yet," pp. 30–31. It is well to recall the paraphrase of the statement in Terence's *Phormio* in the *Theological-Political Treatise* of Spinoza, *Collected Works*, p. 249: "As the old adage goes, you can't say anything so correctly that someone can't distort it by misinterpretation." The sagacity of this comment is as relevant today as when it was first uttered.

2. My discussion here is a summary of the more detailed analysis in Wolfson, *Dream*, pp. 23–24, and Wolfson, *Giving*, pp. xiii–xiv.

3. Derrida, *Points*, p. 393.

4. Nancy, *Gravity of Thought*, p. 64. The hermeneutical point enunciated by Nancy regarding the marking of difference through identity is consistent with a basic assumption of scientific methodology: comparison of divergent phenomena is only possible if there is contiguity in the divergence. For instance, consider the following response in Rovelli, *Order of Time*, p. 40, to the question of how we can determine a fixed standard—the privileged time of a real present—to measure the movement of dissimilar objects by two clocks if duration is always relative to the movement of something with a given trajectory: "The correct answer (rarely given) is this: in motion relative to the *only* reference in which the point in space where the two clocks separate is the same point in space where they get back together. There is only a single straight line between two events in spacetime, from A to B: it's the one along which

time is maximum, and the speed *relative to this line* is the one that slows time. If the clocks separate and are not brought together again, there is no point asking which one is fast and which one is slow. If they come together, they can be compared, and the speed of each one becomes a well-defined notion" (emphasis in original). Underlying Rovelli's comment is the notion of simultaneity articulated by Einstein in conjunction with his theory of special relativity; that is, the now of the extended present, which is neither past nor future, is not absolute but relative to the observer's state of motion. See Rovelli, *Order of Time*, pp. 218n27 and 222n62; and in more detail in Rovelli, *Reality*, pp. 69–77. The shortness of the duration of the intermediate zone of the extended present, determined in the distance from a given reference event, is commensurate with the smallness of the scale by and in which quantum gravity is manifest. See Rovelli, *Reality*, pp. 71 and 153.

5. Chevalier, *Scorpions*, p. 4. The comment of Chevalier is previously cited and discussed in Wolfson, *Language*, pp. 89–90.

6. Clancey, *Conceptual Coordination*, p. 68.

7. Northoff, *Minding the Brain*, p. 85.

8. Laruelle, *Philosophies of Difference*, pp. 70–71: "As affected by non-being, Being will remain undetermined in opposition to any 'metaphysical' type of determination. This latter concerns itself with the particularity of beings. The transcendental or unifying (-unified) All will thus be 'ontically' indeterminable, that is, more rigorously, indeterminable in the mode of ontic multiplicity. This indetermination . . . is not decided in relation to beings in general, but only in relation to beings inasmuch as in general they are multiple and particular: to think the intrinsic variety of Being itself is thus not to wish to break its (necessary) relation to beings. . . . Difference in general is a chiasmus and, in its superior or transcendental phase, we know that the chiasmus conserves itself, that it remains an invariant in the passage from ontic diversity to transcendental unity, that the One appears and affirms itself, certainly not in 'itself' but in the form of unifying Difference, of the indivision of Nothingness and Being, in the transcendental and no longer metaphysical sense of these words. . . . Being remains in every way determined, that is, relative to beings and 'beings' themselves in turn (this is the reversibility of ontological Difference)." See also Laruelle, "Generic as Predicate"; and Laruelle, *Principles of Non-Philosophy*, p. 196: "Thought-in-One obligates us to distinguish between the systematic necessity of a body of rules, a still 'transcendent' necessity which works to the benefit of philosophies . . . and a necessity and universality without fold that we say forms a *Uni*-verse [*Uni-vers*] (uni-versal, unilateral, etc.). . . . If philosophy thinks 'system', non-philosophy thinks 'uni-verse' (this evidently concerns transcendental concepts belonging to the theory of thought, not empirico-regional concepts) and the Universe perhaps 'opposed' in particular to the auto-positional 'World' and to the cosmo-political essence of philosophy. . . . Non-philosophy only knows immanent impossibilities (pragmatic and theoretical) but not prohibitions; axioms and hypotheses that are real-in-the-last-instance but not imperatives." Compare the analysis in Smith, "Thinking from the One."

9. For a different approach to the systematic and integrative nature of medieval kabbalistic speculation as a mode of thinking constellated by metaphysical structures, see Idel, "On Some Forms," pp. xxxvii–xlv.

10. My embrace of a logic of dialetheism to articulate thinking the unthinkable at the limits of thought and saying the unsayable at the limits of speech is indebted to the analysis of Priest, *Beyond the Limits of Thought*. See the summary of his method on p. 3: "This book is about a certain kind of limit, not the limits of physical endeavours like running a mile, but the limits of the mind. I will call them limits of thought. . . . One might also describe them as conceptual limits, since they concern the limits of our concepts. . . . For the present, some examples will suffice to indicate what I have in mind: the limit of what can be expressed; the limit of what can be described or conceived; the limit of what can be known; the limit of iteration of some operation or other, the infinite in its mathematical sense. Limits of this kind provide boundaries beyond which certain conceptual processes (describing, knowing, iterating, etc.) cannot go; a sort of conceptual *ne plus ultra*. The thesis of this book is that such limits are dialetheic; that is, that they are the subject, or locus, of true contradictions. The contradiction, in each case, is simply to the effect that the conceptual processes in question *do* cross these boundaries. Thus, the limits of thought are boundaries which cannot be crossed, but yet which are crossed" (emphasis in original). In defiance of the logical principle of noncontradiction, the neologism *dialetheia* signifies that there are true contradictions and thus a statement can be both true and false, the contradictory nature of which is syllogistically diagrammed in the form of "α and it is not the case that α." See Priest, *In Contradiction*, pp. 3–6. For an extended discussion of dialetheism and the problem of truth and falsity, see ibid., pp. 53–72.

The logical and epistemological repercussions of dialetheism are explored critically in the studies in Priest, Beall, and Armour-Garb, eds., *Law of Non-Contradiction*. See as well Jones, "Dialetheism, Paradox, and Nāgārjuna's Way of Thinking." The dialetheic approach, in my view, renders Husserl's attempt to distinguish the psychological possibility of subjectively thinking that a proposition and its negation are both true, on the one hand, from the a priori logical impossibility of proposing this to be the case, on the other hand, to be a distinction without a difference; that is to say, if it is thinkable that α and $\neg\alpha$ are true at the same time and in the same relation, then it compels us to advance a different logic that would challenge whether the law of noncontradiction is an a priori truth. Concerning Husserl's discussion of this law and the contrast between the psychological-subjective and the logical-objective, see Moran, *Edmund Husserl*, pp. 107–8.

11. This theme has been articulated from numerous vantage points in my scholarly œuvre. See Wolfson, *Abraham Abulafia*, p. 20; *Language*, pp. 86–94; *Alef*, pp. 55–61; "Mythopoeic Imagination"; *Open Secret*, pp. 22–24.

12. Gadamer, *Truth and Method*, p. 293. See below, nn. 51–52. Gadamer's rendering of the Heideggerian hermeneutical circle bears similarity to the relation between knowing and being in the notion of the hermeneutical spiral elaborated by Hart, *Unfinished Man and the Imagination*, pp. 60–68. On the nexus of time and hermeneutics from the perspective of analytic philosophy, see Rödl, *Categories of the Temporal*. The author's hypothesis is that time is the form of knowledge in which understanding and sensibility are united, and hence the forms of the finite intellect are forms of temporal thought or what he calls the categories of the temporal. Insofar as all thought is generic, and the subject of a generic thought is a substance form that is a feature of a predicative unity dependent on the anticipatory contingency of the progressive nature of movement, the atemporal logic of inferential relations—and the implicit presumption that truth is timeless—must be grounded in a temporal logic (pp. 172–73, 175–80). Betraying the influence of Wittgenstein's *Philosophical Investigations*, Rödl argues that thought is inherently temporal not in virtue of its content but in virtue of its form of predication. The grammatical forms of time consciousness consist of the bipolar predication of tense and the tripolar predication of aspect (9–10). Alternatively expressed, human thought is tensed in relation to the persistent substance and the changeable state. Summarizing his perspective, Rödl writes, "An intellect that depends on intuition does not think from nowhere, but by means of time. Thereby it is also temporal in the sense that it represents its object as temporal. Both aspects of its temporality are inseparable" (p. 74). Time-consciousness is thus the unity of sensibility and understanding. See ibid, p. 80: "Finite thought represents its object as temporal, because thought that depends on intuition is situational, and situational thought is of the temporal. Hence, the forms in virtue of which thought has sensory content are forms in virtue of which it relates to the temporal, and the pure concepts of the finite intellect are categories of the temporal."

13. Derrida and Ferraris, *Taste for the Secret*, p. 47. See Schuback, "Hermeneutics of Tradition," pp. 70–72: "Transmission of tradition shows omitting or reveals concealing the non-world pulsating in the self-evidence and communicability of the world in tradition. In its system of familiarity and security, the system of self-evidence where everything fits well together and can be perfectly explicated, showing no need for further explanation or inquiry, the world is always passing on and thereby always exposed to a loss. . . . The loss of the world implicated in a life after death and the not yet of a world in a life before birth casts the world of tradition as the world of an in-between, a world without world that appears as a world of rest, a world resting in continuous tradition."

14. Derrida, "Abraham's Melancholy," p. 156 (emphasis in original). On the term *paleonymy*, see also Derrida, *Dissemination*, pp. 6n6, 18nn20–21.

15. Derrida, *Positions*, p. 57.

16. Leahy, *Novitas Mundi*, p. 4. This section is a highly abbreviated version of the much more detailed analysis in Wolfson, "Thinking Now Occurring."

17. Heidegger, *Being and Time*, §36, p. 165 (*Sein und Zeit*, p. 171; all references are to the Niemeyer edition unless otherwise noted): "This Greek interpretation of the existential genesis of science is not a matter of chance. It brings to explicit understanding what was prefigured in the statement of Parmenides: τὸ γὰρ αὐτὸ νοεῖν ἐστίν τε καὶ εἶναι. Being is what shows itself in pure, intuitive perception, and only this seeing discovers being. Primordial and genuine truth lies in pure intuition. This thesis henceforth remains the foundation of Western philosophy. The Hegelian dialectic has its motivation in it, and only on its basis is that dialectic possible." See Heidegger, *Introduction to Metaphysics*, p. 154 (*Einführung in die Metaphysik*, p. 154), where the dictum of Parmenides is designated the "guiding principle [*Leitsatz*] of Western philosophy."

18. Hegel, *Science of Logic*, p. 25; *Wissenschaft der Logik*, vol. 1, bk. 1, p. 29.

19. Leahy, *Foundation*, p. 177 (emphasis in original).

20. For a related critique of Leahy, see Altizer, *Apocalyptic Trinity*, p. 164. After noting that the total realization of the *novitas mundi* only occurs in Leahy's "thinking now occurring for the first time," Altizer counters, "Nevertheless, this radically new thinking is in deep continuity with a purely Catholic thinking, and is even in continuity with the radically Protestant thinking of Kierkegaard, for Leahy's is unquestionably a Christian thinking, and the first Christian thinking since Hegel's which is a universal thinking." This is not to say that Altizer denies the novelty of the new thinking promulgated by Leahy; on the contrary, he extols that newness by insisting that Leahy is "a truly postmodern thinker even as Hegel is a truly modern thinker." I agree, however, with Altizer's insistence that the radically new thinking is in continuity with older Christian sources.

21. Leahy, *Novitas Mundi*, p. xi.

22. Ibid., p. 6 (emphasis in original).

23. Ibid., pp. 7–8 (emphasis in original).

24. Leahy, *Faith and Philosophy*, p. 115 (emphasis in original).

25. Ibid., p. 143.

26. Ibid., p. 146.

27. Ibid., pp. 146–47.

28. Leahy, *Beyond Sovereignty*, p. 232.

29. Leahy, *Faith and Philosophy*, p. 147 (emphasis in original).

30. Falque, *Metamorphosis of Finitude*, p. ix. For a more technical formulation of this point, see Peirce, "Some Consequences of Four Incapacities," in *Collected Papers*, 5.284, p. 170: "It does not, therefore, follow, because a new constituent of thought gets the uppermost that the train of thought which it displaces is broken off altogether. On the contrary, from our second principle, that there is no intuition or cognition not determined by previous cognitions, it follows that the striking in of a new experience is never an instantaneous affair, but is an *event* occupying time, and coming to pass by a continuous process. Its prominence in consciousness, therefore, must probably be the consummation of a growing process; and if so, there is no sufficient cause for the thought which has been the leading one just before, to cease abruptly and instantaneously. . . . There is no exception, therefore, to the law that every thought-sign is translated or interpreted in a subsequent one, unless it be that all thought comes to an abrupt and final end in death" (emphasis in original).

31. Said, *Beginnings*, pp. 72–73.

32. Ibid., p. xvii (emphasis in original).

33. Husserl, *Experience and Judgment*, p. 157 (emphasis in original).

34. Said, *Beginnings*, pp. 48–49.

35. Husserl, *On the Phenomenology of the Consciousness of Internal Time*, p. 9. For an alternative version, see Husserl, *Phenomenology of Internal Time-Consciousness*, p. 28.

36. Husserl, *On the Phenomenology of the Consciousness of Internal Time*, pp. 9–10. Compare Husserl, *Phenomenology of Internal Time-Consciousness*, pp. 28–29.

37. Husserl, *Idea of Phenomenology*, p. 33.

38. Ibid., p. 35.

39. Husserl, *Phenomenology and the Crisis of Philosophy*, p. 146.

40. Sallis, *Phenomenology and the Return to Beginnings*, p. 17 (emphasis in original).

41. Sallis, "Doublings," p. 120. The position I have articulated regarding the circle opened at both termini is to be contrasted with the "closed temporal lines" implied in the scientific assumption (traceable to Kurt Gödel) that the structure of the light cones—the oblique lines that delimit the discrete phenomena that fill the gravitational field of spacetime—displays a continuous trajectory in the present toward the future that returns to the originating event of the past. See Rovelli, *Order of Time*, pp. 52–53. On the illusory nature of the present and, by extension, of time more generally, see Rovelli, *Seven Brief Lessons on Physics*, pp. 59–60; Rovelli, *Reality*, pp. 175–83. Consider the summation offered by Rovelli, *Reality*, pp. 182–83: "We must learn to think of the world not as something that changes in time. . . . Things change only in relation to one another. At a fundamental level, there is no time. Our sense of the common passage of time is only an approximation that is valid for our macroscopic scale. It derives from the fact that we perceive the world in a coarse-grained fashion. Thus, the world described by the theory is far from the one we are familiar with. There is no longer space that 'contains' the world, and no longer time 'during the course of which' events occur. There are elementary processes in which the quanta of space and matter continuously interact with one another. Just as a calm and clear Alpine lake is made up of a rapid dance of a myriad of minuscule water molecules, the illusion of being surrounded by continuous space and time is a product of a farsighted vision of a dense swarming of elementary processes." And see the stark evaluation on p. 252, which underscores the gap separating our ordinary perception and the scientific perspective: "We are

too used to thinking of reality as existing in time. We are beings who live in time: we dwell in time, and are nourished by it. We are an effect of this temporality, produced by average values of microscopic variables. But the limitations of our intuitions should not mislead us. . . . Time is an effect of our overlooking the physical microstates of things. Time is information we don't have. Time is our ignorance."

42. Frey, *Interruptions*, p. 23. See my similar formulation of the paradox of the temporality of the beginning in Wolfson, *Alef*, pp. xiii, 131–32.

43. Derrida, *Specters of Marx*, p. 163. See citation and discussion of some other Derridean sources on the nature of the beginning in Wolfson, *Giving*, pp. 184–85, and the analysis of the circle and the trace in Protevi, *Time and Exteriority*, pp. 76–110.

44. Heidegger, *Being and Time*, §65, p. 314 (emphasis in original); *Sein und Zeit*, p. 329.

45. The view I have expressed here resembles the Deleuzian interpretation of Nietzsche's doctrine of eternal recurrence. See Wolfson, *Giving*, p. 12; Wolfson, "Retroactive Not Yet," pp. 31–33. A similar interpretation of Nietzsche's eternal return and its relationship to the moment as a subversion of the metaphysical motif of presence is offered by Wood, *Deconstruction of Time*, pp. 11–35, esp. 26–30. For a different approach to the relationship between Heidegger and Deleuze on the question of repetition, difference, and self-disclosing singularity, see Scott, *Time of Memory*, pp. 189–90.

46. Heidegger, *Fundamental Concepts*, p. 187; *Grundbegriffe*, p. 276. Compare Heidegger, *Being and Time*, §11, p. 50 (*Sein und Zeit*, p. 51): "But since the positive sciences neither 'can' nor should wait for the ontological work of philosophy, the continuation of research [*der Fortgang der Forschung*] will not be accomplished as 'progress' ['*Fortschritt*']; but, rather, as the *repetition* [Wiederholung] and the ontologically more transparent purification of what has been ontically discovered" (emphasis in original). It is of interest in this context to recall the following observation made in the 1925–26 lectures on truth and time published as Heidegger, *Logic: The Question*, p. 168 (*Logik: Die Frage*, pp. 198–99): "And perhaps you notice how little of philosophy, as it has been practiced up to now, is a matter of philosophical reasoning—only in a few circles and to a limited extent—and how it is dominated much more by common sense. Philosophy can make good its claim to being a science (in fact the basic science) only if we drive common sense out of philosophical reasoning." Heidegger would eventually abandon the classification of philosophy as science, but he preserved and expanded the contrast between the path of thinking and common sense. The upholding of circular reasoning is a primary example of that divergence.

47. Heidegger, *Ponderings VII–XI*, p. 246 (emphasis in original); *Überlegungen VII–XI*, p. 316.

48. Heidegger, *Ponderings VII–XI*, p. 246; *Überlegungen VII–XI*, p. 316.

49. Heidegger, *Ponderings VII–XI*, p. 247 (emphasis in original); *Überlegungen VII–XI*, p. 317. It stands to reason that Heidegger's criticism of the more conventional cause-effect relationship was indebted to Schelling's idea of *Naturbegriffe* as a form of freedom expressed as absolute self-action. See Matthews, *Schelling's Organic Form of Philosophy*, p. 19: "Exploding the linear causality of the mathematical categories, the multivalent causality of nature as a dynamic whole provides Schelling with an understanding of life, as absolute self-action, as the schema of freedom."

50. Heidegger, *Ponderings VII–XI*, p. 247 (emphasis in original); *Überlegungen VII–XI*, p. 317.

51. Heidegger, *Being and Time*, §32, pp. 145–46; *Sein und Zeit*, p. 150. Compare the comments of Heidegger, *On the Way to Language*, p. 51; *Unterwegs zur Sprache*, p. 142. In that later work, Heidegger still affirms the inevitability of the circular motion of thinking—related specifically to the claim that the human being is the message bearer that comes from the very message toward which one is going—but he distances himself from the idea that the circle can give us an originary experience of the hermeneutic relation. On the hermeneutic circularity in Heidegger, see Gadamer, *Truth and Method*, pp. 268–73; de Man, *Blindness and Insight*, pp. 29–31.

52. Heidegger, *Being and Time*, §32, p. 148 (emphasis in original); *Sein und Zeit*, p. 153. See Spanos, "Heidegger, Kierkegaard, and the Hermeneutic Circle"; Spanos, *Heidegger and Criticism*, pp. 53–80; and Bontekoe, *Dimensions of the Hermeneutic Circle*, pp. 62–91.

53. Heidegger, *Being and Time*, §63, pp. 301–2; *Sein und Zeit*, p. 315.

54. Heidegger, *Being and Time*, §46, pp. 227–29; *Sein und Zeit*, pp. 235–37.

55. Heidegger, *Being and Time*, §48, p. 233; *Sein und Zeit*, p. 242. On the connection between death and the sense of mineness, see Winkler, "Time, Singularity and the Impossible."

56. Heidegger, *Being and Time*, §48, p. 236; *Sein und Zeit*, p. 245.

57. Heidegger, *Being and Time*, §50, p. 241 (emphasis in original); *Sein und Zeit*, p. 250.

58. Heidegger, *Being and Time*, §50, p. 241 (emphasis in original); *Sein und Zeit*, p. 251.

59. Heidegger, *Fundamental Concepts*, p. 187; *Grundbegriffe*, p. 276. See the discussion on the relationship between logic and metaphysics in Heidegger, *Heraclitus*, p. 193 (*Heraklit*, pp. 252–53): "This determination of logic as the metaphysics of λόγος does not in fact bring clarity, but passes itself off as information only from out of a place of perplexity [*eine Auskunft der Verlegenheit*]. But this perplexity in which we now find ourselves is unavoidable: for what metaphysics is can in large part only be illuminated through a clarification of the essence of 'logic.' At the same time, the opposite also holds true: what 'logic' is can only be clarified from out of the essence of metaphysics. We move, therefore, in a circle [*Kreis*]. As soon as thinking enters into such a circular path, it is often—though not always—a sign that such thinking can abide in the realm of the essential [*im Umkreis des Wesenhaften*], or can at least draw nearer to its outer precincts." Compare Heidegger, *Hölderlin's Hymn "Remembrance,"* p. 42; *Hölderlins Hymne "Andenken,"* p. 48. Commenting on Hölderlin's use of the image of the blowing of the northeasterly wind in conjunction with the injunction to embark on a voyage, Heidegger writes: "Thus, the line 'But go now and greet,' is indeed departure. Certainly. But departure is not always 'taking leave.' Do we actually know what 'departure' is? Do we even know what the 'blowing' of the wind is, assuming that we do not simply mean the tangible movement of air? Blowing: a coming that goes, and, in going, comes. Departure is not mere release and empty remaining behind. Departure is also not a mere going away and vanishing. . . . Just as the blowing of the wind is a coming and going that reciprocally exceed one another, so the greeting is a remaining behind and yet a going with that reciprocally demand one another." Heidegger's eliciting from the image of the wind blowing the idea that the going is the coming, and the coming is the going, and that bidding farewell is not an end but the greeting of another commencement, coincides with his view that the way of thinking is marked by an open circularity such that departing is always at the same time returning and returning is always at the same time departing.

60. Heidegger, *Fundamental Concepts*, p. 187; *Grundbegriffe*, p. 276.

61. Heidegger, *Fundamental Concepts*, p. 183; *Grundbegriffe*, p. 272. Hass, "Ambiguity of Being," argues that Heidegger's essential thought, the question of being, must always remain ambiguous.

62. Heidegger, *Country Path Conversations*, pp. 13–14; *Feldweg-Gespräche*, p. 21.

63. Heidegger, *Contributions*, §29, p. 53; *Beiträge*, p. 66.

64. Heidegger, *Four Seminars*, p. 79; *Seminare*, p. 397.

65. Heidegger, *Four Seminars*, p. 80; *Seminare*, p. 399.

66. Derrida, *Truth in Painting*, p. 32.

67. Ibid., 33 (emphasis in original).

68. Wood, *Deconstruction of Time*, p. 217.

69. Heidegger, *Being and Time*, §74, p. 366 (emphasis in original); *Sein und Zeit*, p. 385. For a wide-ranging study of this topic, see Ruin, *Enigmatic Origins*.

70. Husserl, *Cartesian Meditations*, p. 75 (emphasis in original).

71. For an analysis of the discussion of guilt and the irretrievable in *Sein und Zeit*, see Coyne, *Heidegger's Confessions*, pp. 144–54.

72. Heidegger, *Being and Time*, §65, p. 311 (emphasis in original); *Sein und Zeit*, pp. 325–26. Compare the passage from *Sein und Zeit* cited in ch. 6 at n. 74.

73. Heidegger, *Being and Time*, §74, p. 367 (emphasis in original); *Sein und Zeit*, p. 385. On Heidegger's notion of repetition as the ontological structure of historicity, see Ruin, *Enigmatic Origins*, pp. 82–83n28, 132–33. See also the analysis of repetition in light of Heidegger's idea of anticipatory resolution (discussed in relation to both Kierkegaard and Deleuze) in Rot, "From Anxiety to Boredom," pp. 152–62. For the possibility that Heidegger's *Wiederholung* reflects the influence of Kierkegaard's idea of repetition, see Spanos, "Heidegger, Kierkegaard, and the Hermeneutic Circle," pp. 122–26, and Spanos, *Heidegger and Criticism*, pp. 60–66. For discussion of the Kierkegaardian idea of repetition, see Melberg, "Repetition"; Crites, "Blissful Security"; Carlisle, *Kierkegaard's Philosophy of Becoming*, pp. 67–89; Ward, *Augenblick*, pp. 1–33, esp. 11–15. On the affinity between Kierkegaard's use of the notion of the eye-blink (*øjeblik*) to shed light on the temporal paradox of the *kairos* as continuous and discontinuous, the moment manifesting both stasis and change, and Heidegger's view of the now as the opening to the future as the retrieval of the unprecedented, see North, *What Is the Present?*, pp. 31–32, 35–39.

74. Heidegger, *Being and Time*, §74, pp. 367–68 (emphasis in original); *Sein und Zeit*, pp. 385–86. See Mehta, *Martin Heidegger*, pp. 282–83.

75. Heidegger returned to this theme in the 1955–56 lecture course at the University of Freiburg on the Leibnizian *principium rationis* that "nothing is without reason" (*Nichts ist ohne Grund*). See Heidegger, *Principle of Reason*, p. 89 (*Satz vom Grund*, p. 132): "Nevertheless the history of Western thinking shows itself as the *Geschick* of being when and only when we glance back upon the whole of Western

thinking *from the point of view of the leap* and when we recollectively preserve it as the *Geschick* of being that has-been. . . . The leap leaves the realm from which one leaps while at the same time recollectively regaining anew what has been left such that what has-been becomes, for the first time, something we cannot lose. That into which the leap anticipatorily leaps is not some region of things present at hand into which one can simply step. Rather, it is the realm of what first approaches as worthy of thought. But this approach is also shaped by the traits of what has-been, and only because of this is it discernible" (emphasis in original). And compare Heidegger, *Principle of Reason*, p. 102 (*Satz vom Grund*, p. 153): "If it rigidifies, a legacy [*Überlieferung*] can degenerate into a burden and a handicap. It can become this because a legacy is genuinely, as its name says, a delivering [*Liefern*] in the sense of *liberare*, of liberating [*Befreiung*]. As a liberating [*Befreien*], a legacy raises concealed riches of what has-been [*Gewesenen*] into the light of day, even if this light is at first only that of a hesitant dawn."

76. Heidegger, *Identity and Difference*, p. 72; German text: p. 141. On the sense of return implicit in the originary reflection of thinking as the task to think what is to-be-thought in the future, see the passage from Heidegger's *Heraklit* cited in ch. 4 n. 14.

77. Heidegger, *Essence of Truth*, p. 7; *Vom Wesen der Wahrheit*, pp. 9–10.

78. Heidegger, *Ponderings II–VI*, p. 144; *Überlegungen II–VI*, p. 196.

79. Heidegger, *Ponderings II–VI*, p. 257; *Überlegungen II–VI*, p. 353.

80. Heidegger, *Ponderings VII–XI*, p. 201 (emphasis in original); *Überlegungen VII–XI*, p. 260.

81. Heidegger, *Contributions*, §29, p. 53; *Beiträge*, p. 66.

82. Heidegger, *Basic Questions*, p. 38; *Grundfragen*, pp. 40–41. The view of the origin against which Heidegger is philosophizing is well summarized by Kant, *Religion within the Boundaries of Mere Reason*, p. 61: "Origin (the first origin) is the descent of an effect from its first cause, i.e. from that cause which is not in turn the effect of another cause of the same kind. It can be considered as either *origin according to reason*, or *origin according to time*. In the first meaning, only the effect's *being* is considered; in the second, its *occurrence*, and hence, as an event, it is referred to its *cause in time*" (emphasis in original). From Heidegger's perspective, both senses are guilty of ontologizing the origin as if it were a being subject to temporal and spatial determinism.

83. Heidegger, *Contributions*, §33, p. 58 (emphasis in original); *Beiträge*, p. 73. For my previous discussions of this aphorism, see Wolfson, *Giving*, pp. 243–44; Wolfson, "Retroactive Not Yet," pp. 33–34. Compare the anecdote about Socrates in Heidegger, *Zollikon Seminars*, p. 24 (*Zollikoner Seminare: Protokolle*, p. 30): "A widely traveled sophist asks Socrates: 'Are you still here and still saying the same thing? You are making light of the matter.' Socrates answers: 'No, you sophists are making light of it because you are always saying what's new and the very latest [news]. You always say something different. To say the same thing is what's difficult. To say the same thing about the same thing is the most difficult [*Das Schwere aber ist, das Selbe zu sagen und das allerschwerste: vom Selben das Selbe zu sagen*].'" For an alternative version, see Heidegger, *Zollikoner Seminare*, p. 143: "Das Schwerste ist nicht nur, das Selbe zu sagen—sondern über das Selbe—das Selbe sagen," "The hardest thing is not just to say the same thing, but to say the same about the same thing." Heidegger is alluding to the comment of Socrates to Callicles in Plato, *Gorgias* 491b, in *Collected Dialogues*, p. 273: "For you claim that I keep saying the same things, and reproach me with it, but I make the opposite statement of you, that you never say the same things about the same subjects." As the translators of the *Zollikon Seminars* note, the anecdote about Socrates is mentioned as well in Heidegger, *What Is a Thing?*, pp. 73–74 (*Frage Nach dem Ding*, p. 74), to elucidate the point that the most difficult learning is to come to know the ground of what we already know. Sophistry consists of pretending that one is always offering something novel, whereas genuine thinking ensues from saying the same thing about the same thing because only that kind of repetition amounts to genuine innovation.

84. Heidegger, *Introduction to Metaphysics*, p. 41 (emphasis in original); *Einführung in die Metaphysik*, p. 42. See Wolfson, "Revealing and Re/veiling," pp. 33–34, and the sources that treat the paradox of the repetition of the origin in Heidegger cited op. cit., p. 34n35. See also Wolfson, *Giving*, pp. 442–43n116.

85. Heidegger, *Contributions*, §238, p. 293 (emphasis in original); *Beiträge*, p. 371.

86. Compare Heidegger, *Zollikoner Seminare*, p. 322: "Das Endliche *ist* unendlich; die Unendlichkeit *ist* das Endliche. Das Endliche—als solches Negation der Negation," "The finite *is* infinite; infinity *is* the finite. The finite—as such negation of negation." See Löwith, "F. Rosenzweig and M. Heidegger," pp. 76–77. For additional bibliographic information, see ch. 2, n. 75. Here I take issue with the contention of Strauss, *Leo Strauss on Nietzsche's* Thus Spoke Zarathustra, p. 187. I concur with Strauss that "Heidegger's

criticism of Nietzsche is very exact and according to Nietzsche's thought. It confirms primarily the doctrine of eternal return, because if that is dropped Nietzsche's whole doctrine is finished." I disagree, however, with Strauss's further claim that Heidegger must totally reject the doctrine of the eternal return since "no reference to eternity is even possible." While it is accurate to say that there is no conventional understanding of the eternal in Heidegger, that is, an eternality that is in opposition to temporality, it is not correct to deny that his conception of time as the replication of difference does affirm a sense of the eternalization of the temporal in a way that may be seen as a continuation of Kierkegaard and Nietzsche. See Ward, *Augenblick*, pp. 97–124, esp. 120–22, and the text of Heidegger cited in ch. 6 at n. 231. On the importance of Kierkegaard in understanding the crucial difference between temporality and time in Heidegger, see Manchester, *Temporality and Trinity*, pp. 10–17, and compare the discussion of temporality and eternity on pp. 55–60. There are phenomenological similarities as well between the Heideggerian (and, in my mind, kabbalistic) conception and the Buddhist teaching concerning the permanent impermanence of time to emerge from the coming to be and passing away of all conditioned entities (*saṃskṛta, saṃskāra*) in an uninterrupted and continuous flow (*santāna*); see von Rospatt, *Buddhist Doctrine of Momentariness*. On the theological attempt to attribute the notion of God's temporality to Heidegger, see the analysis of Ogden, *Reality of God*, pp. 144–63.

87. Heidegger, *Contributions*, §23, pp. 46–47; *Beiträge*, pp. 57–59. See Fell, "Heidegger's Notion of Two Beginnings"; Stambaugh, *Finitude of Being*, pp. 112–14. Heidegger, *Heraclitus*, p. 37 (*Heraklit*, p. 44), elicits from Heraclitus the notion of the "inceptual to-be-thought" (*das anfänglich Zu-denkende*), an idea that well encapsulates the paradoxical relation of beginning and end in the Heideggerian hermeneutic of time: the inception is marked in perpetuity as that which is to be thought, and hence past and future converge in the present, albeit always in the sameness of their difference.

88. Heidegger, *Contributions*, §20, p. 44; *Beiträge*, p. 55.

89. Heidegger, *Ponderings VII–XI*, p. 196; *Überlegungen VII–XI*, p. 254. Compare the paradoxical description of the poetic utterance as *das dem Wort des Seyns nach-sagende Vorsagen* in the essay "Die Einzigkeit des Dichters" (1943) in Heidegger, *Zu Hölderlin*, p. 37. The hermeneutical claim that the word of the poet is a pre-saying that says after the word of beyng rests on the temporal assumption that the future is a repetition of the past in the present as that which is yet to be. In Heidegger's mind, Hölderlin was the poet who uniquely achieved the ability to speak the word that is both predictive and commemorative; the poet's calling is, quite literally, the "after-saying pre-saying of the issued invocation of beyng" (*nachsagenden Vorsagen des ergangenen Rufes des Seyns*). The historical destiny (*Schickung*) that sends forth the poetic saying is thus always emerging from the future, the time that is coming (*aus der Zukunft Kommende: die kommende Zeit*).

90. Schürmann, *Broken Hegemonies*, p. 581. Compare Schürmann, "Brutal Awakening," p. 94: "Yes, since for the phenomenologist of being, *there is* nothing other than singulars. This *there is*, to be sure, is not nothing. It 'is' being itself qua event. But a universal and most intense being, which would be normative for everything else as it locates all things between the top and the bottom of a scale, lacks any phenomenality. Or, rather, it possesses only phantasmic phenomenality, as the one historical illusion" (emphasis in original).

91. Schürmann, *Broken Hegemonies*, pp. 581–82. On the related appeal to read Heidegger's corpus in a unified way despite his reference to the reversal of his path—a turn rather than a break—see the assessment of Schürmann in Critchley and Schürmann, *On Heidegger's Being and Time*, p. 58. See also below, n. 102.

92. Courtine, "Phenomenology and/or Tautology," p. 241.

93. Heidegger, *Contributions*, §259, pp. 342–43 (emphasis in original); *Beiträge*, p. 434.

94. Heidegger, *Contributions*, §259, p. 343 (emphasis in original); *Beiträge*, pp. 434–35.

95. Heidegger, *History of the Concept of Time*, p. 138 (emphasis in original); *Prolegomena zur Geschichte des Zeitbegriffs*, p. 188. On the widespread view of history as repetition in the period of Heidegger's *Sein und Zeit*, see Korab-Karpowicz, *Presocratics*, pp. 37–41.

96. Ward, *Heidegger's Political Thinking*, p. 99.

97. Rosenzweig, *Star of Redemption*, pp. 259–60 (*Stern der Erlösung*, pp. 269–70): "Redemption is therefore the end before which all that has begun turns back to be engulfed in its beginning. It is only in this way that it is com-plete [*Voll-endung*]. All that is still immediately attached to its beginning is not yet in the full sense actual [*ist noch nicht im vollen Sinne tatsächlich*]; for the beginning whence it sprang can always draw it inside again. This is true for the thing that emerged as Yes of the Not-Nothing [*Ja des Nichtnichts*] as well as for the act that emerged as No of the Nothing [*Nein des Nichts*]. True permanence is

always permanence projected into the future and upon the future. That which always was is not that which is lasting: the world was always; nor is it that which is constantly renewed: living experience [*Erlebnis*] is always new; it is only that which is eternally coming: the Kingdom. It is not the thing [*Sache*], it is not the act [*Tat*], it is only the fact [*Tatsache*] that is secure against falling back into the Nothing" (translation slightly modified). Redemption signifies the end that completes the beginning but that beginning whence the end springs forth is renewed continually by that which is both coming eternally and anticipated at every moment. Compare Rosenzweig, *Star of Redemption*, p. 243; *Stern der Erlösung*, pp. 252–53. Permanence, therefore, is not a matter of the past but rather of that which is projected into the future. On the shared notion in Rosenzweig and Heidegger of the present gaining its meaning in terms of the future, see Gordon, *Rosenzweig and Heidegger*, pp. 197–98.

98. Heidegger, *On the Way to Language*, p. 54; *Unterwegs zur Sprache*, p. 146.

99. Kahn, *Art and Thought of Heraclitus*, pp. 52–53; and see analysis on p. 223.

100. Greek original and English translation as cited in Graham, *Texts of Early Greek Philosophy*, pp. 158–59. For discussion of the Platonic paraphrase of the Heraclitean dictum, see Kahn, *Art and Thought of Heraclitus*, pp. 168–69.

101. Heidegger, *Hölderlin's Hymns "Germania" and "The Rhine,"* p. 106; *Hölderlins Hymnen "Germanien" und "Der Rhein,"* p. 117.

102. Heidegger, *Off the Beaten Track*, p. 21 (emphasis in original); *Holzwege*, p. 29. Here again there is an interesting affinity between Heidegger and Rosenzweig, who reported that he accepted the suggestion of reading his *magnum opus* in reverse from the end to the beginning. See Wolfson, *Giving*, pp. 43–44, and references cited on pp. 311–12nn72–74. Finally, it is worth mentioning Heidegger's remark in a letter to Karl Löwith from August 1927 that he was not interested in charting the "development" of his work on the basis of "the sequence of lecture courses and what is only communicated in them" because this "shortwinded consideration forgets the central perspectives and impulses at work both backwards and forwards." I have availed myself of the translation of this letter in Kisiel, "*Kriegsnotsemester* 1919," p. 160. Consider also the parenthetical aside in Heidegger, *Heraclitus*, p. 50 (*Heraklit*, p. 64): "That is why thinkers, and only thinkers, have the experience that they one day come to understand themselves better in light of what they have already thought, in such a way that the entire edifice of their earlier thought suddenly collapses, even though they always think the same. But this 'same' is not the boring emptiness of the identical [*Gleichen*], which is only a semblance of the same [*ein Anschein des Selben*]. There are those, however, who do not know of the restiveness of the same, and who are proud of the fact that they, at seventy, still think the same as what they already thought and knew as high school students." Despite Heidegger's own aversion to temporalizing his work in a chronological manner, scholarship on him—including, ironically, the aforementioned study by Kisiel, which documents the hermeneutic breakthrough in Heidegger's intellectual biography—has been dominated by precisely such an approach. This is most evident in the repeated distinction between the presumed earlier and later stages of Heideggerian thought. For notable exceptions, see Schürmann, *Broken Hegemonies*, pp. 581–82, and Sheehan, *Making Sense*. Summarizing the content of his study (p. 23), Sheehan states his argument is based on three theses: (1) Heidegger's work is phenomenological from beginning to end; (2) what Heidegger means by *das Sein* is the intelligibility of things or their meaningful presence (*Anwesen*) to human intelligence; and (3) the final goal, the thing itself, is what makes this intelligibility possible, *das Ermöglichende*, that is, that which enables the materiality of ex-sistence to assume the appearance of, or to light up as, the thrown-open clearing.

103. Heidegger, *Contributions*, §20, p. 45 (emphasis in original); *Beiträge*, p. 55.

104. Arendt, *Life of the Mind*, 2:43, suggested that Heidegger's insight that the past has its origin in the future is already evident in Hegel. Compare Comay, *Mourning Sickness*, p. 65. Commenting on Hegel's statement that "the deed is not imperishable" (*die Tat ist nicht das Unvergängliche*), Comay writes, "The double negative actually conceals a triple negative: the deed (or fact) is not in-trans-ient. The negation of the negation is not a return to substantial positivity, but rather an exposure to irrecuperable transience. Time remains irreversible. . . . The obduracy of the deed remains, but it no longer confronts me as a stony obstacle. . . . The event is historicized: instead of determining the future, the past is freed to receive a new meaning from the future." See as well Kolb, "Circulation and Constitution at the End of History."

105. Heidegger, *What Is Called Thinking?*, pp. 76–77; *Was Heißt Denken?*, pp. 82–83.

106. Heidegger, *Identity and Difference*, p. 41; German text: p. 106. The threads of the calculative orientation and politics are intertwined in Heidegger's thought. On this entanglement, see Elden, *Speaking against Number*.

107. Heidegger, *Fundamental Concepts*, p. 368; *Grundbegriffe*, p. 534.

108. Heidegger, *Fundamental Concepts*, p. 367; *Grundbegriffe*, p. 534. Compare the related but somewhat different formulation in the address "Dank an die Heimatstadt Meßkirch," delivered September 27, 1959, and printed in Heidegger, *Reden und Andere Zeugnisse*, pp. 558–59: "Denn der Weg im Denken ist nicht nur eine Methode, sondern der Weg gehört im Denken zur Sache selbst, was ich Ihnen kurz so deutlich mache, daß der Übergang meiner kurzen Worte vom Dank zum Denken nicht so schwer ist, wenn man denkt. Denn Danken und Denken sind nicht nur dasselbe Wort, sondern dieselbe Sache."

109. Heidegger, *Überlegungen VII–XI*, pp. 96–97. I have elaborated on this topic in Wolfson, *Duplicity*, pp. 87–108.

110. From a different vantagepoint, and without probing the primary sources, Goodman, "Give the Word," p. 157, suggested in passing that Heidegger's essential thinking and the kabbalah "have the same temporal and receptive contours." This accords with my own view that kabbalists and Heidegger both presume a conception of time that casts the past as open in the present and therefore renders tradition as a thinking forward rather than a thinking backward. Consider Heidegger, *On the Way to Language*, p. 31 (*Unterwegs zur Sprache*, p. 117): "What you learned there has been learned in turn by listening to the thinker's thinking. Each man is in each instance in dialogue with his forebears, and perhaps even more and in a more hidden manner with those who will come after him." The historical nature of what Heidegger calls the "thinking dialogue" with previous thinkers is to be contrasted with the historiographical reports of the past. Relevant here is the study of Dolgopolski, *Open Past*. The author's claim that the dialogical conversations in the Talmud are driven by, and toward, an open past that is radically different from the futuristic orientation of chronological time bears much affinity with my understanding of Heideggerian hermeneutics. Although Heidegger's tempocentrism is oriented toward the future, the future is privileged to the extent that it is the standpoint whence the past can be reconvened as the not yet rather than the no longer. As I have argued elsewhere, Heidegger's embrace of circularity to explain the hermeneutical structure of human understanding and the attendant comportment of temporality is such that distending into the future is an anticipatory leap in the present back to the ground of the past where one is already standing, a return to where one has always never been. See Wolfson, *Duplicity*, pp. 5, 103–4, 116. The genuine legacy of tradition, on this score, is a liberating gesture that delivers us to the past and thereby discloses by bringing to light that which is concealed in darkness. See above, n. 75. The pliability of the past is what distinguishes authentic from inauthentic time. For his part, Dolgopolski, *Open Past*, pp. 21–33, contrasts the ontological-homogenic approach of Heidegger to the heterogenic perspective on the relation of thinking and memory that he elicits from the Jewish tradition exemplified in talmudic literature. See ibid., pp. 92, 312–13nn5–6.

111. See above, n. 94.

112. Altmann, *Meaning of Jewish Existence*, p. 54.

113. Ibid., pp. 54–55.

114. Ibid., p. 55.

115. Soloveitchik, *Lonely Man of Faith*, p. 68.

116. Ibid., pp. 68–69.

117. Ibid. See analysis in Wolfson, "Eternal Duration," pp. 226–28. The affinity between Soloveitchik and Heidegger is discussed at length on pp. 208–12n37. The curious reader will find reference there to other scholars, who have weighed in on the similarities between these two thinkers.

118. See my brief comment in Wolfson, "Eternal Duration," p. 228. For a more detailed comparison, see Cohen, "Halakah, Sacred Events, and Time Consciousness." Cohen mentions my work on pp. 90–91n8. While he accepts that there is a circularity of time in both Rosenzweig and Soloveitchik, related to their shared assumption about the simultaneity of past, present, and future, Cohen maintains that only in Soloveitchik can one make an appeal "to the possibility of simultaneity even within a linear framework in his unique conception of individual repentance." Cohen thus concludes that it is difficult to accept my alleged "conflation of linearity and circularity as simultaneous features of Rosenzweig's conception of sacred time." A careful examination of my work demonstrates that I have not argued that the juxtaposition of linearity and circularity implies their conflation; on the contrary, in the Heideggerian terms that have influenced my own thinking, juxtaposition is decidedly not conflation. What I have suggested is that one can adduce from Rosenzweig's new thinking, as I have elicited from kabbalistic sources, that there is a dual deportment of time, the extending line that rotates like a sphere and the rotating sphere that extends like a line. See Wolfson, "Light Does Not Talk," p. 93, and the revised version in Wolfson, *Giving*, p. 44. To live halakhically, therefore, means to advance in time linearly but in a manner that repeats itself circularly. For a different approach to the

circularity of the temporal in Rosenzweig's thinking as a form of repetition that entails the incursion of eternity in time, see Braiterman, *Shape of Revelation*, pp. 133–65, esp. 162–65. In some respect, his analysis of the image of the spiral in Buber's *Ich und Du* is closer to my reading of Rosenzweig. See Braiterman, p. 151: "Revelation works in a circle that spirals forward into the future.... The spiral is used to juxtapose the extreme sensitivity to decay observed by the severest critics of modern society alongside the hope in radical renewal.... While the motion is profoundly circular, the spiral plot allows the circle to move forward into the future of redemption. Time is unstuck." On the depiction of Judaism as embracing an idea of eternity-in-time, enacted through the cyclical recurrence of the liturgical calendar, see also Gibbs, *Correlations*, pp. 108–11; Gordon, "Franz Rosenzweig," pp. 135–37; Schindler, *Zeit*, pp. 348–52, 359–70, 382, 385–86; Biemann, *Inventing New Beginnings*, pp. 212–17; Pollock, *Franz Rosenzweig and the Systematic Task of Philosophy*, pp. 276–83; Lin, *Intersubjectivity of Time*, pp. 144–47. For a different perspective on Rosenzweig's construal of the sacred time of ritual, see Mosès, *System and Revelation*, pp. 170–200, and my criticism in Wolfson, *Giving*, pp. 57–58.

119. Rosenzweig, *Star of Redemption*, pp. 276–77; *Stern der Erlosung*, p. 287.

120. Rosenzweig, *Star of Redemption*, p. 277; *Stern der Erlosung*, pp. 287–88.

121. Rosenzweig, *Star of Redemption*, p. 443; *Stern der Erlosung*, p. 467. Simultaneity is correlated most pristinely with the eternity of the Jewish people, but Rosenzweig does attribute this comportment to the temporality experienced by Christians, the eternal way, expressed in the act of brotherly love. Compare Rosenzweig, *Star of Redemption*, pp. 366–67 (*Stern der Erlösung*, pp. 383–84): "Simultaneousness [*Gleichzeitigkeit*] is something that does not exist at all in temporality [*Zeitlichkeit*]. In temporality there is only before and after; the moment someone beholds himself can only precede or follow the moment he beholds another; simultaneous beholding of oneself and another in the same moment is impossible. That is the deepest reason why in the pagan world that is of course precisely temporality, it was impossible to love one's neighbor as oneself. But in eternity [*Ewigkeit*] there is simultaneousness. That from the shore all time is simultaneous [*alle Zeit gleichzeitig ist*] goes without saying. But even time that, as eternal way, leads from eternity to eternity admits of simultaneousness. For only insofar as it is center between eternity and eternity is it possible for people to meet in it. He who therefore beholds himself on the way is at the same point, namely the exact central point [*Mittelpunkte*], of time. The brotherliness is that which transposes men into this central point." The matter of simultaneity with respect to the universality and the particularity of the Jewish people is applied to the triad of God, human, and world in Rosenzweig, *Star of Redemption*, pp. 324–25 (*Stern der Erlösung*, pp. 339–40): "For that which is singular [*das Einzelne*] in itself is not eternal for all that, because the whole is outside of it and can only affirm itself in its individuality [*Einzelheit*] by fitting in the whole somehow as part. An individuality therefore that wanted to be eternal as well would have to have the universe entirely in itself. And that would mean that the Jewish people gathers in its own bosom the elements God world man of which of course the universe consists.... God, man, world must have in themselves the difference through which they become God, man, world of the one people, for this one people [*ein Volk*] must be a unique people [*einziges Volk*]. They must conceal the polar oppositions in themselves in order to be able to be singular, definite, something particular, a God, a human, a world, and yet simultaneously [*zugleich*] everything, God, man, the whole world." On the temporalization of God in Rosenzweig's idea of redemption, see Gordon, *Rosenzweig and Heidegger*, p. 205. For a different perspective on the temporality of existence in Rosenzweig's new thinking and the embrace of a radical finitude ground in the nonidentity between thinking and being and the common sense of death, see Björk, *Life Outside Life*, pp. 91–103.

122. Rosenzweig, *Star of Redemption*, p. 443; *Stern der Erlosung*, p. 467.

123. Levinas, *Entre Nous*, pp. 118, 175–77, 232–33; idem, "Foreword," in Mosès, *System and Revelation*, pp. 21–22. Concerning this theme, see Smith, *Toward the Outside*, pp. 106–8; Sugarman, "Emmanuel Levinas"; Morgan, *Discovering Levinas*, pp. 219–27, esp. 220–21; Severson, *Levinas's Philosophy of Time*, pp. 10, 201–6, 238, 247, 264, 267–68, 336–37n2; Micali, "The Deformalization of Time"; Frangeskou, *Levinas, Kant and the Problematic of Temporality*, pp. 8–9, 146–55. On Levinas's analysis of the temporal ecstasies of past, present, and future in Rosenzweig, correlated with the theological categories of creation, revelation, and redemption, see Chanter, *Time, Death, and the Feminine*, pp. 193–97; and compare Gibbs, "Present Imperative," pp. 170–71.

124. To be sure, in some passages, Rosenzweig demarcates the difference between the eternal life of Judaism and the eternal way of Christianity in terms that imply unequivocally that the former is removed from the web of time in contrast to the latter

whose mandate is to be enmeshed therein. A closer examination of these passages, however, suggests that the matter is more complex: insofar as both the star and its rays are necessary elements of the task of redemption, Jews must eternalize temporality through the liturgical calendar and Christians temporalize eternity by preparing for the kingdom in history by converting the pagan externally and internally. See Rosenzweig, *Star of Redemption*, pp. 438–39 (*Stern der Erlosung*, pp. 462–63): "Before God therefore, both, Jew and Christian, are workers on the same task. He cannot dispense with either. Between the two, he set an enmity for all time, and yet he binds them together in the narrowest reciprocity. To us, he gave eternal life by igniting in our heart the fire of the Star of his truth. He placed the Christians on the eternal way by making them hasten after the rays of that Star of his truth into all time until the eternal end. We see therefore in our heart the true likeness of truth [*das treue Gleichnis der Wahrheit*], but for that we turn away from temporal life and the life of time turns away from us [*doch wenden wir uns dafür vom zeitlichen Leben ab und das Leben der Zit sich von uns*]. They on the contrary follow the river of time, but they have the truth only behind them; they are certainly guided by it, for they follow its rays, but they do not see it with their eyes. The truth, the whole truth, belongs therefore neither to them nor to us. For though we indeed carry it in us, yet for this reason too we must first sink our glance into our own inside if we want to see it, and there we do see the Star, but not—the rays. And belonging to the whole truth would be that one would see not only its light, but also what is illuminated by it. They however are destined all the same for all time to see what is illuminated, not the light. And therefore we both have only a share in the whole truth. . . . Immediate sight of the whole truth comes only to him who sees it in God [*Unmittelbare Schau der ganzen Wahrheit wird nur dem, der sie in Gott schaut*]. But this is a seeing beyond life [*Das aber ist ein Schauen jenseits des Lebens*]. A living seeing of the truth, a seeing that is life at the same time, thrives even for us only out of the sinking into our own Jewish heart and even there only in the image and likeness [*im Gleichnis und Abbild*]. And for them, for the sake of the living effect of truth, the live seeing is denied to them altogether. So we both, they like us, and we like them, are creatures just on this account that we do not see the whole truth. Just for this reason we remain within the limits of mortality. Just for this reason—we remain. And we of course want to remain. We of course want to live." From the perspective of history, the whole truth—the seeing of God that is beyond life—belongs neither to the Jew nor to the Christian. Even for the Jew, who turns away from the temporal to fulfill the metahistorical destiny of the eternal people, the seeing of truth must be a seeing that is life, that is, the vision of truth in the form of the image and likeness confabulated in the heart. The manifestation of truth in the mirror of imagination, wherein truth is appearance and appearance is truth, relates to the creatureliness of the Jew, to the finitude and temporal comportment of being in the world, albeit as the people that is beyond the world. See Wolfson, *Giving*, p. 45, and herein ch. 7 n. 199.

125. See above, nn. 73 and 86. For the influence on Rosenzweig of the Kierkegaardian motif of retrieval as rebirth, see Groiser, "Repetition and Renewal." For the influence of Kierkegaard's notion of the moment on Soloveitchik, see Herskowitz, "The Moment and the Future."

126. Heidegger, *Being and Time*, §65, p. 314 (emphasis in original); *Sein und Zeit*, p. 329.

127. Lacan, *Écrits: First Complete Edition*, p. 213; *Écrits*, p. 256. By putting the focus on the restructuring of an event after the fact, Freud "declares that he considers it legitimate, in analyzing the processes, to elide the time intervals during which the event remains latent in the subject. That is to say, he annuls the *times for understanding* [temps pour comprendre] in favor of the *moments of concluding* [moments de conclure] which precipitate the subject's meditation toward deciding the meaning to be attached to the early event" (Lacan, *Écrits: First Complete Edition*, p. 213; *Écrits*, pp. 256–57). See Bistoen, Vanheule, and Craps, "Nachträglichkeit"; Nobus, *Jacques Lacan*, pp. 86–87; Green, "Lacan: *Nachträglichkeit*."

128. Lacan, *Écrits: First Complete Edition*, p. 247; *Écrits*, p. 300.

129. Lacan, *Écrits: First Complete Edition*, p. 711; *Écrits*, p. 839.

130. Lacan, *Four Fundamental Concepts*, p. 49. Lacan discusses at great length the unconscious, repeating, and remembering (pp. 17–64, esp. 48–51) to demonstrate the noncommutativity of repetition and memory in Freudian theory and to substantiate the further implication that the time-function related to these gestures is bound up with the signifying shaping of the real and hence must be viewed as a category that belongs only to the signifier (p. 40).

131. Heidegger, *Contributions*, §242, p. 303 (emphasis in original); *Beiträge*, p. 384. Interestingly, Lacan invokes Heidegger when he discusses the act of remembering (*remémoration*) right before he mentions Freud's *Nachträglichkeit*. See Lacan, *Écrits: First Complete Edition*, p. 212 (*Écrits*, p. 255): "In

Heideggerian language one could say that both types of remembering constitute the subject as *gewesend*—that is, as being the one who has thus been. But in the internal unity of this temporalization, entities [*l'étant*] mark the convergence of the having-beens [*des ayant été*]. In other words, if other encounters are assumed to have occurred since any one of these moments having been, another entity would have issued from it that would cause him to have been altogether differently." See the revealing remark in the seminar on Edgar Allan Poe's "The Purloined Letter" in Lacan, *Écrits: First Complete Edition*, p. 15 (*Écrits*, p. 21): "Thus, when we are open to hearing the way in which Martin Heidegger uncovers for us in the word *alethes* the play of truth, we merely rediscover a secret to which truth has always initiated her lovers, and through which they have learned that it is in hiding that she offers herself to them most *truly*" (emphasis in original). See Janicaud, *Heidegger in France*, p. 131. On Heidegger's notion of truth and revelation, see Lacan, *Écrits: First Complete Edition*, p. 136; *Écrits*, p. 166, and the comment on the true, the real, and Heidegger's term *echt* in Lacan, *Sinthome*, pp. 69 and 229n7. And compare Lacan, *Anxiety*, p. 8: "There stands Heidegger. With my play on the word *jeter*, it was precisely to him and his originative dereliction that I was closest." See ibid., pp. 79 and 90. Heidegger is also mentioned explicitly by Lacan, *Écrits: First Complete Edition*, p. 262 (*Écrits*, p. 318), in his explanation of how death should be considered a limit. And in another passage, *Écrits: First Complete Edition*, p. 323 (*Écrits*, pp. 387–88), Lacan elucidates Freud's *Bejahung* as the primal condition wherein something of the real (*réel*) offers itself up to the revelation of being (*révélation de l'être*) by referring to Heidegger's language of "to be let-be" (*soit laissé-être*). On Heidegger and the meaning of the verb *to be* in its various conjugations, see Lacan, *Psychoses*, pp. 300–1. See as well the revealing comment, *Écrits: First Complete Edition*, p. 438 (*Écrits*, pp. 527–28), where in the context of calling for a reexamination of the human situation in the midst of beings (*la situation de l'homme dans l'étant*), Lacan clarifies his use of a Heideggerianism: "When I speak of Heidegger, or rather when I translate him, I strive to preserve the sovereign signifierness [*significance souveraine*] of the speech he proffers." Mention should be made of Lacan's translation of Heidegger's essay on the Heraclitean fragment on the "Logos" published in *La Psychanalyse*. See Lacan, *Psychoses*, p. 124; Roudinesco, *Jacques Lacan*, pp. 229–30; Lippi, "Héraclite, Lacan"; Janicaud, *Heidegger in France*, p. 453n121; Krell, "Is There a Heidegger?" The relationship between Heidegger and Lacan has been discussed by various scholars. For a representative list, see Casey and Woody, "Hegel, Heidegger, Lacan"; Richardson, "Psychoanalysis and the Being-Question"; Boothby, *Death and Desire*, pp. 203–21; Riera, "Abyssal Grounds"; Roudinesco, *Jacques Lacan*, pp. 219–31; Egginton, *Philosopher's Desire*, pp. 65, 110–12; Žižek, *Less Than Nothing*, pp. 859–903. Compare Derrida, *Heidegger: la question*, p. 97; and see now Derrida, *Heidegger: The Question*, p. 56. Derrida illumines the co-belonging of being and language in Heidegger's thought by citing two passages from Lacan. Regarding the personal interactions of Heidegger and Lacan, see Roudinesco, *Jacques Lacan & Co*, pp. 298–99. On Heidegger and Freudian psychotherapy, see discussion and citation of other relevant sources, especially the work of Medard Boss, in Wolfson, "Not Yet Now," p. 163n138, to which I would add Richardson, "Heidegger and Psychoanalysis"; Brencio, "World, Time and Anxiety"; and Brencio, "Heidegger and Binswanger." For further references, see ch. 7 n. 114.

132. Wolfson, "Retroactive Not Yet," pp. 44–50. On the Freudian *Nachträglichkeit* and the Derridean trace, see Major, *Lacan avec Derrida*, p. vi; Hamrit, "Nachträglichkeit." For an attempt to discern a common approach to time in Heidegger, Derrida, and Lacan—or what is referred to more specifically as the spacing at the heart of temporality—see Egginton, *Philosopher's Desire*, pp. 106–38. An independent, but somewhat related, question is the influence of kabbalah on Lacan. See Haddad, "Judaism," pp. 203–4. The author suggests that the source of Lacan's knowledge of kabbalah was Elie Benamozegh's *Israël et l'humanité*. See also the intriguing passage of Lacan in *Four Fundamental Concepts of Psychoanalysis* on the phallic symbolism of the *fundamentum* in the kabbalah, cited in Wolfson, *Language*, p. 482n119.

133. Heidegger, *Concept of Time* (McNeill trans.), pp. 17–18.

134. Heidegger, *What Is Called Thinking?*, p. 99; *Was Heißt Denken?*, p. 82.

135. Heidegger, *On Time and Being*, p. 11; *Zur Sache des Denkens*, p. 15.

136. Dastur, *Heidegger and the Question of Time*, pp. 37–38. Many others have written about Heidegger's thinking about time, but here I would like to mention the analysis in Harman, *Quadruple Object*, pp. 54–57. I agree with Harman that Heidegger rejects both the idea of time as a sequence of discrete now-points as well as the Bergsonian idea of a continual flux. But I do not accept his argument that Heidegger espouses a form of occasionalism wherein the only thing

that is real is a frozen moment that is "torn in three directions," a present that has nothing to do with the real past or future and hence is a "temporality without time." Heidegger's notion of equiprimordiality enunciates a genuine convergence of the three *ecstases* of time in the moment that projects to the future and thereby affords one the possibility of reclaiming the past in the present. Far from being a temporality without time, the Heideggerian temporality is saturated with an overabundance of time that renders each moment past, present, and future all at once.

137. Scholem, *Messianic Idea*, p. 289 (emphasis in original). See the analysis in Wolfson, *Giving*, pp. 55–56.

138. Wolfson, *Alef*, p. 60.

139. Ibid., pp. 64–65.

140. Heidegger, *Parmenides*, p. 12; *Parmenides* [GA 54], p. 18. The similarity between Heideggerian and rabbinic hermeneutics extends as well to the use of wordplay to elicit new meaning and the underlying assumption that interpretation is a form of translation in the sense of transporting and thereby transforming the past. The point is made effectively by Fay, *Heidegger: The Critique of Logic*, p. 56: "Heidegger, then, is not interested in going back to word roots to determine with the exactness of the philologist the meaning of a word. The work of the philosopher, at least as he conceives of the task of philosophy, starts where the work of philology stops, or more precisely the one is on the level of what Heidegger calls *Historie*, determination of what the past was as past (*Vergangenheit*), while the other is not interested in the past as past, but sees it as somehow living still (*Gewesenheit*) and influencing the present and future. But if the future is to be shaped according to its authentic possibilities the past cannot be simply taken over in an imitative, essentially uncreative, repetition." If we were to substitute the word *exegesis* for philosophy, then Fay's observation would be a perfectly apt description of the hermeneutical foundation of the midrashic effort of rabbinic sages through the centuries to interpret the scriptural word, an enterprise that is aimed not at repetitively uncovering meaning of the text to establish the past mimetically as it was but rather to invest it eisegetically with new meaning, to shape the present and future by laying bare what is still always to be thought in what was previously spoken. I again note the irony of my argument: notwithstanding Heidegger's unyielding neglect of Jewish sources, the path of his own thinking, and indeed the transition from the metaphysical reasoning of philosophy in the past to the meditative thought he ascribes to the new beginning in the future, shares much with the midrashic method of the rabbis.

2

Inceptual Thinking and Nonsystematic Atonality

Philosophy is always a beginning and requires an overcoming of itself. . . . Philosophy and worldview are so incommensurable that no image could possibly depict the distinction between them. Every image would necessarily bring them too close together.

Heidegger, *Contributions to Philosophy (Of the Event)*

And if thinking is the distinguishing mark of the essence of the human, then what is essential to this essence, namely the essence of thinking, can be first properly caught sight of only insofar as we look away from thinking.

Heidegger, *Country Path Conversations*

In this chapter, I will juxtapose Heidegger's postmetaphysical ponderings and the theosophical musings of the kabbalists in an effort to show how these disparate ideational orbits provide examples—each from its idiosyncratic perspective—of a thinking that demands a looking away from thinking. The goal of the path—which we will pursue not by following one single highway but rather by snaking circuitously through a labyrinth of byways that seemingly go nowhere, an excursion with no fixed destination that brings us back to where we have always never been[1]—may very well be to venture beyond the path, but to undergo such an adventure, the code of the road, as it were, requires one to travel the path continuously. Hermeneutically, there is no overcoming except by undergoing.

Kabbalistic Infinitivity and the Meontological Transcendence of Transcendence

The thinking of time diremptively explored in the previous chapter is related to another salient feature of the kabbalistic *mentalité*. The mystical contemplation endorsed by kabbalists—in parallel with Heidegger's meditative thought—does not progress deductively or inferentially from one point to another on the premise that there is an underlying structure holding the parts together in a unified whole. If we are to speak of a semblance of wholeness, it is the permanently inchoate aggregate fashioned embryonically by the striving of individual entities for correlationality. The algorithm of kabbalistic thought—what one anonymous author in the fourteenth century famously referred to as the order of divinity (*ma'arekhet ha-elohut*)[2]—presumes a structure without a reified center within which the particulars harmoniously coalesce. That is to say, the sense of uniformity and consistency ensues not from a single canon of rationality or intellection, as we find in the structuralist conception of an Eleatic unity upholding the surface diversity, but from the untold aspects of infinitude fabricated in our ongoing attempts to imagine the virtually real as really virtual by representing the nonrepresentable and conceptualizing the nonconceptual. By nonrepresentable and nonconceptual I do not intend to posit an invisible entity positioned beyond the periphery of visuality, a something that is innately hidden. These terms, by contrast, allude to the enigma of nothingness prior to the polar division into being and nonbeing—what the kabbalists call *Ein Sof* and Heidegger called *Seyn*—the emptiness at the core of the invisibly visible spectrality glimpsed within but at the same time removed from the panoply of the visibly invisibles that constitute the immanent realities of this world. In my constructivist reading, to speak of the infinite as the invisible does not betoken a transcendent being but rather the principle of falsification of any such being, the signifier of the absence of the signification of the signifier, the delimited negativity of the positivity that makes possible the impossibility of the symbolically real whose reality is symbolic.

As the grounding myth of theosophical kabbalah evolved in the wake of the teachings of Isaac Luria (1534–72), based in great measure on a close but creative reading of zoharic homilies, the amorphous luminescence of infinity assumes the form of the light of the countenance of *Adam Qadmon* (Primal Human), followed by the redistribution of the light in the ten emanations (*sefirot*) refracted through *Atiq Yomin* (Ancient of Days), and then clothed in the five configurations (*parṣufim*)—*Arikh Anpin* (Long Countenance or the Long Suffering), *Abba* (Father), *Imma* (Mother), *Ze'eir Anpin* (Short Countenance or the Impatient), and *Nuqba* (Female), also referred to more fully as *Nuqba di-Ze'eir*—which function as psychological archetypes of the divine family. This pattern is intensified by the assumption that the structure and the play of concealment and disclosure—related prototypically to the essence of the infinite light (*eṣem or ein sof*) and to the world of the line and the contraction (*olam ha-qaw we-ṣimṣum*) that issue therefrom[3]—is replicated in each of the four worlds that make up the multiverse, emanation (*aṣilut*), creation (*beri'ah*), formation (*yeṣirah*), and doing (*asiyyah*).[4] The proliferation and amplification of Lurianic kabbalah, both in texts composed by his disciples and in subsequent expositions, augmented the tendency to multiply distinctions as a way of demarcating the indistinctness of *Ein Sof*, the nonlocalized substratum of all phenomena localized morphodynamically in the mental and somatic landscapes that we impose on this light—the ententional absence that is the condition for all intentional presence—in an effort to enumerate the innumerable, to calculate the incalculable. My identification of the kabbalistic infinity as the absential efficacy of all phenomena is informed by the following view of Terrence W. Deacon:

> What we will discover is that ententional processes have a distinctive and characteristic dynamical circularity, and that their causal power is not located in any ultimate stuff but in this dynamical organization itself. Our ultimate scientific challenge is to precisely characterize this geometry of dynamical forms which leads from thermodynamic processes to living and mental processes, and to explain their dependency relationships with respect to one another. It is a quest to naturalize teleology and its kin, and thereby demonstrate that we are the legitimate heirs of the physical universe. To do this, we must answer one persistent question. How can something not there be the cause of anything? Making sense of this "efficacy of absence" will be the central challenge of this book, and the key to embracing our ententional nature, rather than pretending to ignore or deny its existence.[5]

It may seem that Deacon's scientific naturalism is far from the concerns of the kabbalah, but, in fact, the invisible dimension of the absence of *Ein Sof* functions similarly as the ententional criterion of nonphenomenalizability, that is, the epistemic provision of all phenomenality, the inapparent that resides in and facilitates the appearing of all things apparent but which itself evades appearance. The polygonal nature of this imaginal construct—the incarnation of the finitely infinite in the vestment of the infinitely finite—is meant to preserve the equilibrium between the random formation of the disorderly and the resolute deformation of the orderly. Simply put, since the structure imputes dimensions to the dimensionless, the orderliness of that structure implodes in the potentially unlimited variation that the structure itself stimulates as a consequence of the contemplative attempt to map the complex simplicity of its simple complexity.[6]

From that vantage point, Lurianic doctrine can be considered an antisystem or the system whose convolution drives it beyond the strictures of a system, rendering it effectively *the nonsystematic system*. Alternatively, in the language of cybernetics, kabbalistic theosophy is a multifaceted hypersystem in which the properties are not explained by the unilateral interaction of the component elements and in which compartmentalization of the parts cannot be reductively subsumed under the aggregation of the whole nor the aggregation of the whole under the compartmentalization of the parts.[7] The cognitive-linguistic schematization of the divine pleroma yields a map without territory inasmuch as what is mapped is indexical of what cannot be indexed. Semiotically, the meaningfulness of the sefirotic ciphers is not established by reference to any demonstrable object; on the contrary, these ciphers are metalinguistic insignia of the insignificant, paradigmatic signs of the nothingness to which nothing can be assigned paradigmatically.

We can thus extrapolate the principle—especially prominent in Lurianic and post-Lurianic treatises—that semantic fragmentation is the most propitious mode to envisage the incipient wholeness of infinitivity. Utilizing Levinas's observation regarding the creative contraction of infinity (*la contraction créatrice de l'Infini*), which may reflect the kabbalistic doctrine of *ṣimṣum*,[8] multiplicity and limitation are not only compatible with unitary and limitless perfection, they articulate its very meaning, and in that respect, infinity can be said to be produced only by renouncing the incursion of a totality in a contraction that leaves a place for a separate being (*L'Infini se produit en renonçant à l'envahissement d'une totalité dans une contraction laissant une place à l'être séparé*).[9] However, in contradistinction to Levinas, one could argue that, for the kabbalists, the exteriority of an infinite transcendence is not easily distinguishable from the interiority of a finite immanence, since there is no break in the concatenation of worlds issuing from *Ein Sof*—even the withdrawal of the infinite into itself leaves a trace of light in the punctiform space from which the light has been vacated, a trace that marks the absence of presence as the presence of absence. To speak of a being that is separate from God is a relative assessment at best and thus it is not clear that kabbalists can preserve the absolute transcendence of the infinite, as Scholem sometimes argued,[10] and avoid, at the very least, admitting to, as we find in Scholem's own notion of the dialectic of form (*Dialektik der Gestalt*),[11] the paradox that *God is absent from the world precisely in the manner that God is present in the world.*

To highlight the paradox I have deduced from the kabbalistic sources, let me mention Jacobi's view of Spinoza reported in Mendelssohn's memoranda in reply to Jacobi's account of his meeting with Lessing, which was appended to Mendelssohn's letter to Jacobi dated August 1, 1784: "Spinoza therefore rejected every transition from the infinite to the finite; in general all *causae transitoriae, secundariae* or *remotae* altogether; and instead of an emanating *En-soph* he posited only an immanent one, an indwelling cause of the world, eternally unalterable within itself, one and the same, taken together with all its consequences."[12] Jacobi's criticism seems to be spot on: the consequence of the identification of God and nature implied in the Spinozistic formula *Deus sive Natura* is reducing *Ein Sof* to an immanent principle, the indwelling cause of the world, the collapse of the infinite into the finite, and theism into a pantheism that borders on atheism.[13] By contrast, the kabbalistic discernment that nature is divinity is based, in Heideggerian terms, on a juxtaposition that preserves the identity of their nonidentity in the nonidentity of their identity.[14] To be sure, based on the language of a passage from the *Ra'aya Meheimna* stratum of the zoharic compilation—the major anthology of kabbalistic lore and practice that began to circulate in the thirteenth and fourteenth centuries in fragmentary units, whence, through an extensive process of scribal transmission, whose contours may not be completely available to scholarly acumen, the manuscript witnesses were redacted into the printed editions of Mantua and Cremona, the exemplars for all subsequent versions[15]—a variety of kabbalists and Ḥasidic masters have maintained that the infinite "encompasses all worlds" (*sovev kol almin*) and "fills all worlds" (*memalle kol almin*).[16] One might be tempted to interpret this distinction dualistically such that the description of *Ein Sof* as encompassing all worlds would deflect the pantheistic leaning implied in the competing claim that *Ein Sof* fills all worlds. To interpret in this way, however, is to literalize the metaphor and to lose sight of the fact that neither can be taken in a strictly physical sense.

The flaw in this logic is made explicit by Shneur Zalman of Liadi (1745–1813), the fountainhead of the Ḥabad-Lubavitch dynasty, incontestably one of the most philosophical and speculative of the Ḥasidic factions:

> The matter is in accord with what is said in the *Zohar* that the infinite, blessed be he, encompasses all worlds and fills all worlds. The explanation is that his essence [*aṣmuto*], may he be blessed, is not in the category of emanation at all. Thus it is explained that the light of the infinite [*or ein sof*] refers to the vitality that illumines and extends from him, blessed be he, to sustain the worlds, for it is like the splendor and illumination exclusively like the splendor of the sun vis-à-vis the sun [*ziw ha-shemesh legabbei ha-shemesh*].... Since he, blessed be he, is holy and separate, he is not garbed or grasped in the worlds, and the aspect of garbing does not even apply to the light except after several contractions [*ṣimṣumim*].... The worlds came to be in the aspect of boundary and limit [*gevul we-takhlit*] on account of the various constrictions of the light so that it will not be disclosed in the aspect of infinity [*beḥinat ein sof*] but rather through boundary and measure [*bi-gevul u-middah*], and this is the aspect of filling [all worlds], this is what proceeds in the aspect of disclosure in boundary and measure.... The beginning of the disclosure is in *Ḥokhmah*, and the totality [*kelalut*] of that aspect, when compared to the actual light of the infinite, is not even like a drop in relation to the ocean, for it does not radiate in the aspect of the disclosure and the garbing in the worlds but in the aspect of encompassing all worlds. The meaning of "encompassing" [*sovev*] is not that it encircles from above [*she-maqqif mi-lema'lah*], for "there is no place devoid of him,"[17] but rather that it is not comprehended or grasped.... And it is called "encompassing" in accordance with what is written "as the wheel within the wheel" (Ezekiel 1:16), that is, like a small circle within a bigger circle that encompasses it from all sides, for it is not possible to say that what is encompassing from above is superior to what is encompassing from below within the smaller wheel because the bigger wheel is actually uniform [*shaweh*] from above and below. Thus, it is with the light of the infinite, blessed be he, he renders small and great as equal [*shaweh u-mashweh qaṭon we-gadol*].[18]

As is the case with Ḥabad texts in general, the specific details of the aforecited passage are exquisite in their intricacy, and I could not possibly do justice to them in this context. What is most important to emphasize, however, is the claim that the infinite essence and the light that emanates from it are outside the category of worlds and therefore beyond the ontological demarcation of transcendence and immanence.[19] Even to speak of that light as transcending transcendence is not sufficient if transcendence still implies the ontic sense of the being that exceeds all beings, the being that is called the being that is beyond being.[20] The use of the qualifying expressions "blessed be he" (*barukh hu*) or "may he be blessed" (*yitbarakh*) certainly leave the impression that Shneur Zalman is still envisioning *Ein Sof* ontotheologically. I would acknowledge that up to a point he is doing so, but I would also suggest that within his own thinking—and expanded in the vast literary corpus produced by the subsequent masters of the Ḥasidic sect he established—there is a path beyond the ontotheological: properly speaking, the infinite should not be subject to any metaphoric or linguistic representation. I have deliberately left these expressions in my translation in order not to obscure what I consider to be a genuine tension between the theism of the tradition and the atheistic implications of the mystical teaching that identifies the infinite as the nothingness whose luminosity is the shadow of nonbeing at the core of all being. In relation to this nothingness, any kataphatic depiction, including the very concept of godliness (*elohut*), is too restrictive, amounting to a kind of spiritual idolatry (*eliliyyut ruḥanit*), in the language of Abraham

Isaac Kook (1865–1935).[21] The most personalistic expression to designate the providential care of the divine presence in the world is accordingly turned, based on the meaning of holy (*qadosh*) as that which is separate, into a signifier of the transcendence that is detached from the world and therefore beyond the cosmological distinction between transcendence and immanence. To cite Shneur Zalman again:

> The sages, blessed be their memory, called the Creator, blessed be he, the blessed holy One [*ha-qadosh barukh hu*], for he is holy and separate from all the worlds [*qadosh u-muvdal mi-kol ha-olamot*] . . . and with respect to this matter he is called "encompassing all the worlds," and it is known that the explanation is not that he encompasses and encircles from above . . . but rather that the efflux from him does not come in the aspect of disclosure in the worlds in the aspect of cause and effect . . . for in the concatenation of cause and effect, the effect knows and comprehends some comprehension of its cause, and it is nullified in relation to it by this comprehension, and thus the overflow of the cause in the effect is verily in the aspect of disclosure. This is not the case with respect to the created beings in relation to the light and the potency that overflows in it from the infinite, blessed he, to bring forth something from nothing, for the potency that overflows in it is not comprehended by it at all.[22]

The light of the infinite, which is contrasted with the infinite itself, comports two fundamental characteristics: it encompasses all worlds and it fills all worlds. But, as Shneur Zalman argues, the terms used to delineate transcendence, *sovev* and *maqqif*, encompassing and encircling, cannot to be taken literally because there is no spatial demarcation that applies to this light, and surely not to the infinite essence. Hence, these terms should be interpreted figuratively as a way of communicating the incommunicable, which entails undermining the distinction between the figurative and the literal—only those who do not know the secret distinguish the external and the internal. Moreover, from the perspective of the infinite—a perspective that eradicates all perspective as it is the perspective from which there can be no perspective—transcendence and immanence are indifferently the same, just as in the scriptural example of the wheel within the wheel, the smaller circle is encompassed entirely and evenly within the bigger circle from all sides and thus there is no basis to distinguish above and below.

One might still argue that the ontotheological interpretation I am challenging is reinforced by the application to *Ein Sof* of the rabbinic motto that God is the place of the world but the world is not the place of God,[23] a saying that even made its way, most likely as a later interpolation, into some versions of the long recension of *Sefer Yeṣirah*,[24] a foundational text for kabbalists through the centuries. This asymmetry conveys, at the most basic level, that the divine gives life to and sustains the world—just as the soul gives life to and sustains the body—but it is ontologically separate from and therefore irreducibly transcendent to the world.[25] But, as noted by Ḥayyim Ickovits, the Lithuanian kabbalist better known as Ḥayyim of Volozhin (1749–1821), the deeper meaning of the attribution of the term "place" (*maqom*) to God, a being to whom spatial delimitation clearly does not apply, is that even though the world has the façade of ontic autonomy, in fact it has no existence apart from the life force it receives from the divine.[26] Philosophically translating the secret of the rabbinic slogan—a mystery beyond rational comprehension—we can say that it can be described as affirming both acosmism and occasionalism. In the Volozhiner's own words:

> There is verily nothing besides the blessed One,[27] no reality at all in all the worlds from the highest of the heights to the lowest depths of the depths of the earth, until you could say that there is here no creature or world at all but rather all is filled with the essence of his incomposite oneness. . . . This is also contained in their dictum, may their memory be for a blessing, that he, blessed be he, is the place of the world and the world is not his place, that is, even though all the places are perceived by the senses to exist [*murgashim la-ḥush bi-meṣi'ut*], these places are not independent [*aṣmiyim*], but rather he, blessed be his name, is the place of all places [*ha-maqom shel kol ha-meqomot*], and from his perspective, blessed be he, they are all considered as if they are not in existence at all, even now as it was before creation.[28]

To denominate the divine as the place of the world, therefore, underscores that the world is created anew each moment because it has no self-sufficient reality. This, too, is the esoteric meaning of the statement in *Sefer Yeṣirah*, "Ten intangible *sefirot*, close your mouth from speaking and restrain your heart from contemplating, and if your heart races, return to the place [*shuv la-maqom*] whence you emerged, for thus it is written 'running to and fro' (Ezekiel 1:14)."[29] We comprehend the concept (*muskal*) of God creating the world unceasingly from the sensible image (*dimyon ha-murgash*) of place even though there is no analogy (*erekh*) or similitude (*dimyon*) between the comparison (*mashal*) and what is compared (*nimshal*).[30]

More profoundly, and more germane to our main focus, the notion that God is the place of the world challenges the rigid dichotomization of transcendence and immanence. The full dialetheic sweep of the kabbalistic viewpoint is the simultaneous affirmation of presumably contradictory propositions: infinity encompasses all worlds precisely because infinity fills all worlds, whence it follows that absence from place is the meontological condition that makes presence in place possible. One of the more forthright distillations of this subtle philosophical point was made by the third of the seven Ḥabad-Lubavitch masters, Menaḥem Mendel Schneersohn (1789–1866), known as the Ṣemaḥ Ṣedeq, who described the infinite in a manner that extends the words of his grandfather, Shneur Zalman: "Everything is nullified in relation to it . . . and before it darkness is as light, and above and below are equal, for its substance and its essence [*mahuto we-aṣmuto*] is found below as it is found above, verily without any division or change at all, not in the aspect of 'fills all worlds' or in the aspect of 'encompasses all worlds,' for it is not in the aspect or taxonomy of the worlds at all."[31] Adopting the only language available to him, the Ṣemaḥ Ṣedeq was trying to communicate that *Ein Sof* is outside the ontological economy. Although he continues to personalize the infinite by adding the qualifier "may he be blessed" (*yitbarakh*), and he speaks of its substance (*mahut*) and essence (*aṣmut*), two things are clear. First, *Ein Sof* cannot be personified and hence the qualifying phrase must be taken as a rhetorical device to inculcate reverence, and second, *Ein Sof* has no substance that can be objectified with an identifiable essence. The terms *essence* and *substance*, consequently, purport their very opposite, that is, the essence whose essence consists of having no essence and the substance whose substance consists of having no substance. In light of this clarification, I would suggest that the dyad of transcendence and immanence is also subject to being undermined. Expressed in Deleuzian terms, the import of the kabbalistic teaching is that transcendence is the immanent point of reference in the same manner that immanence is the transcendent point of reference. Instead of viewing immanence and transcendence as polar opposites linked dialectically in an identitarian discourse, we should see them as coterminous forms of mutual differentiality.[32] Attempts to differentiate the interiority of infinity from its exteriority are futile, since there is no outside that is not inside as the outside and no inside that is not outside as the inside. However, if one wishes to retain this language, as we find in the sources themselves, then we must affirm the paradox that *Ein Sof* is immanent in everything as that which is transcendent to everything.

The point is divulged by another kabbalistic maxim, *ein ha-ne'eṣal nifrad min ha-ma'aṣil*, "the emanated is not separate from the emanator."[33] Similar language was used by some kabbalists, for example, David ben Yehudah he-Ḥasid, to express the virtual identity of *Ein Sof* and *Keter*: "There is no difference between the cause and the effect except that this is the cause and that is the effect, and the enlightened will understand and be silent before the Lord."[34] This principle may reflect the language of *Liber de Causis*, a medieval tract based on Proclus's *Elements of Theology*, which was likely known to kabbalists through Hebrew translation,[35] "the effect is in the cause after the mode of the cause, and the cause is in the effect after the mode of the effect."[36] Be that as it may, the appeal to silence on the part of David ben Yehudah he-Ḥasid brings to light the deep secret implied by undercutting the ontological distinction between emanator and emanated and the consequent elimination of any breach in the chain of being.[37] The collapsing of the gap separating cause and effect would logically lead to a pansophic perspective that warrants an all-inclusive knowledge of reality, since ostensibly everything is comprised within the infinite.[38] But even if we were to assume this to be the case, the all-inclusiveness would not necessarily be absorptive in a monistic or even a pantheistic sense, insofar as the root of all being, the nothingness that precedes the partition into being and nonbeing, is not a stable entity with computable specifications but rather a fluctuating process of ceaseless adaptation, a cause determined by the effects determined by their cause.

The kabbalistic assault on the established principle of causation as progressing linearly from cause to effect calls to mind Heidegger's remark in the *Beiträge* that under the influence of the dogmatics of Christianity—and we could widen this to the medieval scholastic theologies of Judaism and Islam—every being is explained as an *ens creatum*, that is, as an effect of the creator, the most certain cause. As a consequence of this way of experiencing the world, the cause-effect relation becomes "the most common, rudimentary, and nearest, which all human calculation and lostness in beings have recourse to in order to explain something, i.e., to place it into the clarity of the common and usual. Here, where beings must be the most usual, beyng is by necessity what is *a fortiori* ordinary and indeed the most ordinary. Yet now in truth beyng 'is' the *least* ordinary [Un*gewöhnlichste*], and thus beyng has here entirely withdrawn and has abandoned beings."[39] From Heidegger's perspective, the essence of *Seyn* was replaced by the supreme being, God, the cause of all beings. Philosophically, the ontotheological view that all beings are made by this one being must yield to the metaontological notion of the withdrawal of beyng from beings, or the abandonment of beings by beyng. But the position of Heidegger is closer to the dialetheism of the kabbalistic perspective insofar as "beyng *conceals itself* in the manifestness of beings [*das Seyn* verbirgt sich *in der Offenbarkeit des Seienden*]. And beyng itself is essentially determined as the self-withdrawing concealment [*das Seyn wird selbst wesentlich als dieses Sichentziehende Verbergen bestimmt*]."[40] *Beyng conceals itself in the manifestness of beings*—hence, beyng is present in the very beings from which it is absent, not as an objective thing that is occluded—the invisible—but as the inapparent that can appear only as not appearing,[41] the mystery that is bestowed in the refusal of bestowal.

Along similar lines, Heidegger distinguishes his idea of the *Gestell* and the instrumentalist understanding of causality: "Thus where everything that presences exhibits itself in the light of a cause-effect coherence, even God, for representational thinking, can lose all that is exalted and holy, the mysteriousness of his distance. In the light of causality, God can sink to the level of a cause, of *causa efficiens*. He then becomes even in theology the God of the philosophers, namely, of those who define the unconcealed and the concealed in terms of the causality of making, without ever considering the essential provenance of this causality."[42] Adapting Heidegger's language, we can say that *Ein Sof* is not the *causa efficiens*, but the cause in the sense of enframing, that is, the revealing of the ordaining of destining, the unconcealment of the concealed that is always concealing itself in what is brought forth into the open.[43]

Interestingly enough, my explication of the kabbalistic credo is corroborated by Agamben's remark regarding the development of the Neoplatonic idea of emanation as a flux (*fayd*) in Avicenna and its later articulation in Albert the Great:

> The first principle acts neither by will nor by choice but simply exists and, from its existence, accomplishes and "flows into" the world. The fact that in the image of flux what is in question is a tendential neutralization of the concept of cause, in the sense of the reciprocal immanence between causing and caused, is implicit in the way in which Albert the Great takes up this idea: "Only that can flow in which flowing and that from which it flows are of the same form, as the river has the same form as the source from which it flows."[44] . . . If one maintains the image of flux, then the most adequate form for thinking mode is that of conceiving it as a vortex in the flux of being. It has no substance other than that of the one being, but, with respect to the latter, it has a figure, a manner, and a movement that belong to it on its own. The modes are eddies in the boundless field of the substance that, by sinking and whirling into itself, disseminates and expresses itself in singularities.[45]

Following this way of thinking about the first principle—a radical reading that somewhat narrows the gap between the Neoplatonic scheme and Heidegger, which does not mean that the latter should be read Neoplatonically—we can say that no metaphysical ipseity is attributable to the infinite nonground posited by the kabbalists; the one being is more fittingly described, like the Heideggerian sense of *Seyn*, as an intricate lattice of codependent interrelationality constellated by the illimitable flux of the inimitable iterations of the eventfulness of beyng that constitutionally escapes the ontological categorization of beings. The activity ascribed to the hidden essence of *Seyn*, accordingly, is outside the confines of the ordinary understanding of causal determinacy: "For Being has no equal whatever. It is not brought about by anything else nor does it itself bring anything about. Being never at any time runs its course within a cause-effect coherence [*einem kausalen Wirkungszusammenhang*]. Nothing that effects, as Being, precedes the mode in which it—Being itself—takes place so as to adapt itself; and no effect, as Being, follows after. Sheerly, out of its own essence of concealedness, Being brings itself to pass [*ereignet sich Sein*] into its epoch."[46] Being is a spontaneous event that is neither the effect of a preceding cause nor the cause of a succeeding effect. The unsettling of the hierarchical relation of transcendent cause and immanent effect leads, moreover, to an epistemic disorientation, a maddening lucidity, which proceeds from the awareness that there is no naked truth to behold, no face behind the mask that is not itself another mask, no essence that is visible unless it is enveloped in the invisibility of the nonessence. Foucault thus described the abyss of unreason extracted from Nicholas of Cusa's account of the experience of God as utterly unutterable, unintelligible, and immeasurable: "The wisdom of God, when man is blinded by it, is not a reason that has long been concealed by a veil, but a depth without measure. There the secret is still fully secret and contradiction contradicts itself, for at the heart of its all surpassing comprehension is this wisdom that seems vertiginous folly."[47] The secret is revealed most transparently when there is nothing to be manifest but the nonmanifestation of the nothing that is manifest. To plumb this impenetrable depth, one must accept a logic whereby contradiction contradicts itself and hence feigns a truth that both is and is not a contradiction. This teaching embodies an elemental tenet of the kabbalah, a foundation, by definition, that is antifoundational in its very foundationalism.

Thinking the Unthought: Radical Immanence and the Given-without-Givenness

Here, too, we note an astonishing affinity of the kabbalistic upending of a logically coherent system with the methodology appropriate to Heidegger's path of thinking. As is well known, Heidegger penned the following motto as the epigraph for the *Gesamtausgabe*, the collection of his writings, *Wege—nicht Werke*, "Ways—not works."[48] "Work" connotes something fixed and susceptible to systematic analysis, whereas "way" is fluid and prone to turns and twists that are capricious and disruptive. We should recall as well the prefatory remark of the *Schwarze Hefte*, "*The entries in the black notebooks* are at their core attempts at simple designation—not statements [*Aussagen*] or even sketches [*Notizen*] for a planned system."[49] Admittedly, the comment is restricted to the notebooks, but I do not think it is unwarranted to extend it to Heidegger's writings after the turn more generally, compositions that are more aphoristic than systematic in nature. In another passage in the notebooks, he comments on the possibility of a Heideggerian philosophy—"to the extent that such exists at all—is always only *represented* by other ones, i.e., embedded as a standpoint and assembled into a nullity."[50] Heidegger disavows the idea of claiming a philosophy of his own, viewing it principally as a construct formed on the basis of and in relation to other philosophical confabulations. The equation of standpoint (*Standpunkt*) and nullity (*Nichtige*) in his characterization of these taxonomic efforts suggests his ardent disapproval of rendering his thinking in systematic terms. Thus, in the opening section of the *Beiträge*, Heidegger writes, "The age of the 'systems' has past. The age that would elaborate the essential form of beings from out of the truth of beyng has not yet come. In the interim, in the transition to the other beginning, philosophy needs to have accomplished something essential: the projection, i.e., the grounding and opening up, of the temporal-spatial playing field of the truth of beyng."[51] In another aphorism, he describes the goal of his teaching as follows: "Not a *proclamation* [Verkündigung] of new doctrines to the bemired bustling about of humans; instead, a *dislodging* [Verrückung] of humans out of the lack of a sense of plight and into the most extreme plight, namely, the plight of lacking a sense of plight [*aus der Notlosigkeit in die Not der Notlosigkeit als die äußerste*]."[52] By Heidegger's self-appraisal, the main purpose of his thinking is to divert others from the dearth of distress into the utmost distress, which consists of becoming distressed by the want of distress, a gnostic awakening that is the initial step in understanding the predicament of being human—*the plight of lacking a sense of plight*. The substance of that awakening is specified in a second passage: "For the task is not to bring to cognition [*Kenntnis*] new representations of beings [*neuen Vorstellungen vom Seienden*] but rather to ground the *being* of the human being [*Mensch*sein] in the truth of beyng and to prepare this grounding in the inventive thinking [*Erdenken*] of being and Da-sein."[53] As he writes in a third passage, with respect to the occurrence of *Seyn* gathering into its essence, "For thinking no longer possesses the advantages of a 'system'; thinking is historical in the peculiar sense that beyng itself as appropriating event bears all history and therefore can never be calculated. In place of systematics and deduction, there now stands historical preparedness for the truth of beyng."[54] Commenting on Heidegger's *Beiträge*, arguably the most important composition after *Sein und Zeit*, Joan Stambaugh perspicaciously noted that "it is less a *train* of thought than a *circling* around what he is trying to say."[55] This evaluation is corroborated by Heidegger's own description of phenomenology as a thinking that precedes "any possible distinction between theory and praxis. To understand this, we need to learn to distinguish between *path* [Weg] and *method* [Methode]. In philosophy, there are only paths; in the sciences, on the contrary, there are only methods, that is, modes of procedure [*Verfahrensweisen*]."[56]

To deny the systematic nature of thinking does not mean, as Gadamer expressed the view of some of Heidegger's critics, that his later thought "no longer stood on solid ground" because it was linked to the "topsy-turvy political folly brought on by his own ambition for power and his intrigue with the Third Reich." Gadamer contests this view vehemently and insists that Heidegger's *Seinsdenken* does not betray, either theologically or prophetically, the "indemonstrable chatter" of a "mythologist and Gnostic" initiated in the secrets of God.[57] Such accusations fail to recognize that the "Heideggerian expressions speak from the antithesis. They have been set with a provocative pungency *against* a certain habituation of thought, which 'posits' something as an entity, negates something, or 'coins' a word. The famous turn, of which Heidegger spoke to show the inadequacy of his transcendental conception of the self in *Being and Time*, is anything but an arbitrary reversal of a habit of thinking about some voluntary decision."[58]

Gadamer goes on to say that the catalyst for this turn in thinking was a "matter of thinking that had come to Heidegger in a way that is true to the inner dynamic of the matter itself" and not some "mystical inspiration."[59] Gadamer's point is well taken: contrary to a widespread misconception, Heidegger does not abandon logic to an "antiscientific irrationalism,"[60] but posits a different criterion as the foundation for logic, a mode of thinking (*Denken*) about the truth of being (*die Wahrheit des Seins*) that is more rigorous (*strenger*) than the conceptual (*das Begriffliche*) even though it is removed from the ontology of metaphysics. And yet, language persists as a problem insofar as the effort to advance thought into the truth of being still requires making that contemplative thinking of the heart—the thinking that repudiates thinking— recognizable and understandable by using the terminology of existing philosophy.[61] Nevertheless, the breakthrough of thought demands a different logic and a distinctive language. As Heidegger writes in the notebooks, "A person whose Dasein is *not* attuned to the essence of beings as a whole and to their chasms and 'grounding' does not need—and does not deserve—any 'logic.' . . . But one who exists in the essence must demand 'logic' for himself. For it is—rightly understood and not as formal technique—the power and intrinsic exercise of the liberation of truth."[62] Demanding logic for oneself is not to be understood solipsistically or even monadologically; what Heidegger intends is that attunement to the truth of being must ensue from the deep-rooted aloneness—as opposed to loneliness—of Dasein's subjectivity.

Noteworthy in this regard is Heidegger's musing in the *Beiträge* on the transitional nature of the "fundamental ontology" of *Sein und Zeit* as the attempt to grasp metaphysics more originally in order to overcome it: "That title came from clear knowledge of the task: no longer beings [*Seiendes*] and beingness [*Seiendheit*], but being [*Sein*]; no longer 'thinking,' but 'time'; the priority no longer given to *thinking*, but to beyng [*Seyn*]. 'Time' as a name for the 'truth' of being; and all this as task, as '*still on the way*' ['unterwegs'], not as 'doctrine' ['*Lehre*'] and dogma [*Dogmatik*]."[63] The truth of being, which is time, cannot be ascertained by a thinking that is doctrinal or dogmatic. To contemplate that truth, one must be *still on the way*, a permanent state of impermanency, and insofar as the path of thinking is always conditional, time, in its deepest inflection, is the content and form of that path. The concluding words of Heidegger's 1919 lecture course "Die Idee der Philosophie und das Weltanschauungsproblem"—a course in which he set out to question the conception of worldview as either the immanent task of philosophy or as its limit[64] and to demonstrate that "the construction of a worldview in no way belongs to philosophy"[65]—on the nature of phenomenology already attest to the hermeneutical intuition that shaped his thinking: "A world view is an objectification and immobilizing of life at a certain point in the life of culture. In contrast, phenomenology is never closed off, it is always provisional in its absolute immersion in life as such. In it no theories are in dispute, but only genuine insights versus the ungenuine."[66] As Heidegger later wrote in the *Schwarze Hefte*, the promulgation (*Verkündigung*) of a worldview (*Weltanschauung*) appears only when the notion of world (*Welt*) "falls out of joint, the passion for world projection flags, and everything must remain a mere substitution."[67] According to another passage from the notebooks, "A worldview is merely an expedient and must break to pieces if it does not turn into a world-grounding [*Welt-gründung*]. . . . '*Worldview*'—a late word—originating from the place where one looks back and classifies—calculates in 'types.' Nothing futural [*Zukünftiges*]—instead, only a standing still [*Anhalten*] and a tying down [*Festlegen*]—the death of all great and fruitful doubt."[68] The unphilosophical character of worldview is cast in temporal terms, for the worldview is a mode of calculation that offers a typology of a past that stands still and thus has nothing of the quality of being futural associated with a healthy skepticism. Heidegger repeats his contempt for the pragmatic nature of worldviews in yet another passage, "'Worldviews' remain outside the sphere of creative thinking (philosophy) and of great art as well. They are ways in which philosophy and art are immediately brought—i.e., directed—to use or rather to misuse by everyone. Therefore, philosophy can never be 'worldview,' nor may philosophy ever think to take over the place of worldview."[69] Reiterating this perspective in "Das Wesen der Sprache" (1957–58), Heidegger sharply contrasted the movement of the way (*Be-wëgung*)—related more specifically to facilitating an experience (*Erfahrung*) with language—and the codification of method: "To the modern mind, whose ideas about everything are punched-out in the die presses of technical-scientific calculation, the object of knowledge is part of the method. And method follows what is in fact the utmost corruption and degeneration of a way."[70] In that context, Heidegger appeals to the *Tao* of Lao-tzu's poetic thinking (*dichtenden Denken*) to convey his understanding of "the mystery of mysteries of thoughtful saying" (*das Geheimnis aller Geheimnisse des denkenden Sagens*) that is "the way that gives all ways, the very source of our power to think what reason, mind, meaning, *logos* properly mean to say—properly, by their proper nature. . . . Perhaps the enigmatic power of today's reign of method also, and indeed pre-eminently, stems from the fact that the methods, notwithstanding their efficiency, are after all merely the runoff of a great hidden stream which moves all things along and makes way for everything. All is way [*Alles ist Weg*]."[71]

Truth, in the end, is not substantiated by means of proofs (*Beweise*) but by being grounded as Dasein's steadfastness (*Inständigkeit*) in the face of the event (*Ereignis*)[72] or the "happening of being" (*Seingeschehnis*).[73] The sway of Heidegger's thinking, portrayed metaphorically in the images of trailmarks

(*Wegmarken*) and woodpaths (*Holzwege*), is diametrically opposed to the ideal of the philosophical system based on repeatable and exchangeable components organized in logical patterns.[74] Reminiscent of, even though not quite identical to, Rosenzweig's insistence that time, and especially the unpredictability of the present, is the most vital component of *Sprachdenken* as opposed to ratiocination,[75] Heidegger privileges the moment, literally, the glance of the eyes (*Augenblick*), whose primary characteristic is the future, and thus thought is characterized as *unterwegs*, always underway, unrelentingly becoming what it has already not been. The modulation of thought, pertinent to the path, can be compared to Penelope's veil—what is spun during the day undoes itself at night, so that the next day it must be spun anew. "Each of Heidegger's writings," Arendt remarked in her tribute to him on his eightieth birthday, "despite occasional references to what was already published, reads as though he were starting from the beginning and only from time to time taking over the language already coined by him—a language, however, in which the concepts are merely 'trail marks,' by which a new course of thought orients itself."[76]

The notion of the way, in contrast to that of the work, evokes an inherent indecisiveness that cannot be settled even by invoking authorial intent, since each time the thought of a thinker is diligently reexamined, it generates new meaning, perhaps even unknown to the author. Insofar as each event of thinking is a recapitulation of the incomparable, there is no justification for privileging even Heidegger's voice in fortifying the text's meaning. As Trawny observed, "Heidegger has no philosophy, no doctrine that could become the model for an academic school. . . . The thinker's writings are open attempts. . . . One can learn from Heidegger that philosophy is a philosophizing, always rather a questioning than an answering."[77] I will return to the matter of philosophy and the question, but what is worthy of emphasis here is that the rethinking of what has been thought "consists in letting every thinker's thought come to us as something in each case unique, never to be repeated, inexhaustible—and being shaken to the depths by what is unthought [*Ungedachte*] in his thought. What is *un*-thought [Un-*Gedachte*] is there in each case only as the un-*thought* [*Un*-gedachte]. The more original the thinking, the richer will be what is unthought in it. The unthought is the greatest gift [*Geschenk*] that thinking can bestow."[78] Derrida correctly noted that just as Heidegger insisted that there is one single and unique thought for every great thinker, so there must also be one unthought that is still to be thought in "a non-negative way" (*de façon non négative*).[79] The unthought is what is left unsaid in every act of saying, an indefinite and irreducible difference, the surfeit of meaning that defies systematization and sublation in either the identity of nonidentity or the nonidentity of identity.

I thus accept the assessment of Gary Shapiro that Heidegger's mode of thinking "aims at subverting the metaphysics of presence by means of a *historical reduction* or bracketing, in which the entire sequence of thought from Plato to Hegel, Nietzsche, and Husserl is put into parentheses. Outside those parentheses lies a different kind of thinking, a play of absence and presence, lighting and concealment, in which truth is not the telos of a system but an inevitably partial dis-closure that always wavers or trembles between presence and absence."[80] Cast in the language of Laruelle, Heidegger's thought of the unthought marks the end of philosophy inasmuch as it presupposes a negative correspondence between philosophy and its inaccessible other, "an alterity, a peripheral residue or an external-internal condition of philosophical activity," the "non-philosophical margin that it tolerates, circumscribes, reappropriates, or which it *uses* in order to expropriate itself: as beyond or other to philosophical mastery."[81] Support for my contention may be drawn from the similar language used by Heribert Boeder to account for the "incipient veiling" and "originary concealment" to which thinking reverts as the ground of the ontological difference that Heidegger upholds between being and beings: "Like Being with respect to beings as such, so too with respect to truth, unconcealedness is that which is nearest to what is unthought. Accordingly, thinking no longer contemplates the true ground of the true and thus of knowledge but is instead concerned with the origin of truth in that which it is not: about the arising of unconcealedness out of concealment, thus out of its other with respect to which it itself is actually the other."[82]

In an implicit critique of Heidegger, Laruelle writes, "It is not the question of the end and the ends of philosophy, but *that of a non-philosophical discovery that we would not yet have made and which would change the face of philosophy.* This discovery, probably, cannot be made without the renunciation of the question of its death, a question which is moreover that of its sufficiency to be adequate to the Real, the real of death."[83] Without simplistically collapsing the considerable differences between Laruelle and Heidegger—indeed non-philosophy is identified as "post-deconstruction" or "non-Heideggerian deconstruction"[84]—I do not think his portrayal of the end of philosophy is accurate. In the ever-elusive quest to overcome metaphysics, there seems to be a preview of one of the central postulates of Laruelle's philosophical non-philosophy.[85] Heidegger does imagine the domain of the new beginning that is brought into effect out of the essential occurrence of the truth of the event of being and the history of that truth, particularly its relation to German idealism,[86] as one in which there is neither ontology nor metaphysics. "No 'ontology,' because the guiding question no longer delimits the measure and the sphere of the inquiry. No 'metaphysics,' because the procedure is not at all to pass from beings as objectively present or objects as known (idealism) and *step over* [hinübergeschritten] to something else. . . . Both are merely transitional names, for the sake of instituting a minimal intelligibility."[87] Notwithstanding this depiction of the other beginning as being unencumbered by either ontology or metaphysics, it is set into motion by the inceptual thinking, which, as I noted previously, Heidegger depicts as a "confrontation with the first beginning in its more original repetition," thereby transposing "its questioning of the truth of beyng *all the way back* into the first beginning as the origin of philosophy."[88] If the future of the other beginning can be thought only by one who wishes to go back to the first beginning, then overcoming does not imply the conventional meaning of *Überwindung,* but rather the sense of *Verwindung* as surpassing through the gesture of meandering.[89] To surpass implicates one in demarcating the limit that has been surpassed; indeed, the act of exceeding safeguards the threshold that has been exceeded. As Catherine Malabou put it, for Heidegger, "every real change is partly comprised of a metamorphic dimension," and this applies to metaphysics as well, which in each epoch is re-formed and thus undergoes a transformation, literally, "a *passage* or *transition* to another form."[90] Heidegger alludes to this principle when he comments that overcoming the metaphysical means bringing metaphysics "back within its own limits" and not "a destruction [*Zerstörung*] nor even a denial [*Verleugnung*] of metaphysics. To intend anything else would be childish presumption and a demeaning of history."[91] To think the truth of beyng is to overcome metaphysics, which is always concerned with representing beyng in the guise of beings, but, as Heidegger acknowledges, "this 'overcoming of metaphysics' does not abolish metaphysics. As long as man remains the *animal rationale,* he is the *animal metaphysicum.*"[92] The effort to go back to the ground of metaphysics might bring about a transformation of metaphysics and, in its wake, a change in the human essence, but the way to the ground, to recall the truth of being, is through the branches of the tree that spring forth from that root. Coming to a similar conclusion, Thomas Sheehan wrote:

> Metaphysics is clearly a matter of *onto*-logy insofar as the operations of questioning and answering (-logy) all bear on *things* (onto-). Heidegger's *meta*-metaphysical inquiry, on the other hand, takes up where metaphysics leaves off. It turns the outcome of the *Leitfrage* into the material object of the *Grundfrage* by taking the very realness of things . . . and puts that under the microscope as the subject matter of a radically new question. What about the realness *itself,* this οὐσία that things "have"? This is the question not about ὂν ᾗ ὄν but about οὐσία ᾗ οὐσία, *Sein als Sein,* and specifically the question about *what accounts for* the fact that there is *Sein* at all (which things are said to "have").[93]

Applying the same logic to Nietzsche's invocation to establish a new hierarchy of the relation between the sensuous and the nonsensuous, Heidegger speaks of the overturning (*Umdrehung*) of Platonism as a twisting free (*Herausdrehung*),[94] which is to say, one remains bound to that from which one is unbound, since one cannot flee without still being tethered to that from which one has absconded. In the *Beiträge*, Heidegger similarly commented on Nietzsche's bringing forward "becoming" (*Werden*) in opposition to "being" (*Sein*) or "beingness" (*Seiendheit*) as the attempt to invert Platonism: "Yet every inversion [*Umkehrung*] is a fortiori a return to and entanglement in the opposite (sensible—supersensible).... Nietzsche is caught up in *metaphysics*: from beings to being.... The first step toward the creative overcoming of the end of metaphysics had to be carried out in such a way that in one respect the directionality [*Richtung*] of thinking is maintained, although in another respect it is thereby at the same time radically raised beyond itself."[95] For Heidegger, therefore, the mindset, or the posture of thinking (*Denkhaltung*), suitable for the end of metaphysics does not summon, as Laruelle intimates, a "post-philosophical innocence" that recovers the "absence of philosophy" or a "pre-speculative state" purportedly superseded by philosophy.[96] It is rather a state of mindfulness by which one contemplates the advent of the new beginning that both regresses to and evolves beyond the first beginning. In criticizing—whether fairly or not—Schelling's falling back into the "rigidified tradition of Western thought without creatively transforming it," and consequently positing the beginning as insurmountable, Heidegger maintains that "a second beginning becomes necessary through the first, but is possible only in the complete transformation [*Verwandlung*] of the first beginning, never by just letting it stand."[97] The first beginning is not wholly conserved in the transformation of the second beginning, but neither is it thoroughly annihilated.

It is instructive to heed carefully Heidegger's exegesis of Nietzsche's statement that the opposite of the overman (*Übermensch*) is the last man (*letzte Mensch*): "That suggests that the end first becomes visible as an end on the basis of the new beginning. To put it the other way around, overman's identity first becomes clear when the last man is perceived as such."[98] We can assume that Nietzsche's idea of the last man, as is the case with the corresponding Heideggerian notion of the last god (*letzte Gott*), is not a chronological demarcation. Concerning this notion of the last, Heidegger writes that it "is what not only needs the longest ante-cedence [*Vor-läuferschaft*] but what itself *is* the most profound beginning [*der tiefste Anfang*] rather than a cessation, the beginning which reaches out the furthest and catches up to itself with the greatest difficulty."[99] The last signifies the beginning that is constantly catching up to itself, that which is always in a state of surpassing (*Überholende*) and hence imperishably withdrawn from calculation,[100] the terminus of a trajectory that opens up to a new undertaking that is both restorative and innovative. In that respect, the expression *das Letzte* denotes commencement and not end. As Heidegger expressed it elsewhere, "With Nietzsche's metaphysics, philosophy is completed.... But with the end of philosophy, thinking is not also at its end, but in transition to another beginning."[101] The bridge that leads from the old to the new is the unthought that is essential to every thinker's thought. In terms of the history of philosophy, beyng is what has remained unthought in metaphysics, and thus the essence of metaphysics is withdrawn from metaphysics itself—in the same manner that the essence of technology is withdrawn from technology—and the overcoming of metaphysics would mean "simply surrendering the metaphysical interpretation of metaphysics."[102]

The unthought in metaphysics is precisely what guides us to the overcoming of metaphysics: "The question 'Being and Time' points to what is unthought in all metaphysics. Metaphysics consists of this unthought matter; what is unthought in metaphysics is therefore not a defect of metaphysics. Still less may we declare metaphysics to be false, or even reject it as a wrong turn, a mistake, on the grounds that it rests upon this unthought matter."[103] The relationship of what is thought to what is unthought is proportionate to the link between the end and the new beginning; that is, the unthought is not the negative correlate of the philosophical concept, a covert exaltation of philosophy's desire to know its other, assimilating what cannot be thought in the purview of what can be thought. On the contrary, Heidegger's invocation of the unthought is not a way of explicitly presuming to know what cannot be known or implicitly precluding the possibility of a nonphilosophical way of knowing. In my reading, Heidegger articulates, albeit in a different terminology, the "inaugurating postulate" of Laruelle's non-philosophy according to which the affiliation between thought and reality is based neither on adequation nor inadequation, a correspondence that can be confirmed only through the deobjectification of knowledge and the rejection of positing the benchmark of philosophical sufficiency that would perforce conceive of the nonphilosophical other reductively as the negative limit of its own discourse.[104]

Contrasting himself with the idea of non-philosophy articulated in post-Kantian philosophers, Laruelle writes, "When 'non-philosophy' ceases to designate a simple philosophical relation to the extra-philosophical in order to designate a relationship to the philosophical itself in its identity and ceases to be an attribute in order to become 'a subject,' it speaks of a thought which, without being subsumed again into philosophy, is no stranger to it; of a new relationship to this thought and of a new practice of philosophy. It is philosophy which then becomes an 'object' of non-philosophy, of a pure and no longer metaphysical or ontico-ontological 'non' transcendental."[105] Non-philosophy liberates philosophy from the epistemological burden of the correlation of thought to the Real and its revision in the philosophies of differ(e/a)nce, evocatively referred to as the "contemporary pathos of alterity," thereby abandoning the terrain of "Being then that of the Other" for a terrain of "the One or of radical immanence that has shown us the Real itself."[106] The fundamental axiom of non-philosophy is thus summarized as *the essence of the Real resides neither in Being nor in the Other, but in the One,* a One that is "vision-in-One, seen-in-One of the World, of Being and of being to which it unconditionally gives phenomenalized being. . . . Nothing of what is not in the One, nothing of Transcendence is negated or destroyed by this phenomenalization."[107] Non-philosophy is not on the margin of philosophy but it is "philosophy that ceases to be the site of non-philosophy or its foundation." As the philosophy of non-philosophy, this transcendental or first science "aims at the One-of-which-it-speaks," "*the being-One (of) the One, the being-Identity (of) Identity.* Philosophy can at most lead only to the being of the One or the being of Identity and bars the One by Being, which represses it."[108]

This is surely not Heidegger's language, but notionally how far are we from his effort to safeguard the destiny of Dasein as the shepherd of being differentiated from beings? Laruelle thus comments on Heidegger's critique of the tradition's failure "to interrogate the dimension of (co-)*belonging* that is the essence of Difference, the essential provenance of the correlation, the truth of Being as such. Thinking should not forsake 'ontological Difference,' but will allow it to come into what it is in its essence-of-Difference, into its 'own.' What metaphysics, according to Heidegger, leaves indeterminate is this essence (of Being), even if it in its own way has to determine Being: simply at the interior of Difference as the correlation of Being and beings and in function of this relation alone."[109] Digging more circumspectly into this correlativity, Laruelle remarks that being is not a generality acquired as a consequence of abstraction from particulars, but it is rather the horizon that we must presume in order to accede to beings. Metaphysics, therefore, "sets itself up in the relation of beings and the *a priori,* a relation that is in turn *a priori,* a prior place of thought. . . . Thus Being refers necessarily to beings, like reality to the real; it intends them in the broadest possible way."[110]

When Heidegger speaks of *Seyn,* in contrast to *Seiende,* he seems to be affirming a similar sense of the Real that manifests itself—albeit by occluding itself insofar as every showing is concurrently a nonshowing—as the radical immanence that is "without the smallest fragment of transcendence within it" and hence it is discriminated "as much from the transcendent One as from the transcendental One."[111] The immanence affirmed by Heidegger, like that of Laruelle, is not the negation of transcendence, that is, the nontranscendental that is still judged from the vantagepoint of the metaphysical binary of transcendence and immanence. Already in *Sein und Zeit,* Heidegger spoke of the "authentic *being*-whole [*Ganzsein*]" of Dasein as the interlude that stretches between birth and death, the two ends that comprise the totality of the trajectory of a human being's life.[112] Writ large, this means that the sense of wholeness is constituted by the fragmentariness of finitude and not by any principle of transcendence, even a transcendence within immanence that would render the latter coherent as the corollary of the dialectical identity of identity and difference.

The radical immanence is transmitted in Heidegger's notion of *es gibt*, which parallels Laruelle's characterization of the "immanence of phenomenal being-given"[113] as the "given-without-givenness."[114] I can well imagine Heidegger acquiescing to the following words even though Laruelle offers them in part as a corrective to him: "The Real must rather be already *given* even outside every operation of givenness, ontological or scientific, which would precisely possibilize it and would take it out of its 'being-given'. We are no longer within philosophical questioning here . . . . but rather in another mode of thought that thinks under the necessary and first condition of the Real as given without presupposition, and which is not itself a presupposed. . . . We can undoubtedly formulate this status of being-given-without-givenness by saying that we *let-it-be-given* to us as first in relation to thought."[115] A cardinal difference in nomenclature is that Heidegger continues to speak of the beingness of that which is given as nothingness, but, as we shall subsequently argue, what he intends by beingness is not so far from Laruelle's notion of the Real as that which is given without presupposition; that is, beingness is no longer conceived in relation to individual beings as an object of representation standing over and against the representing subject, and the implied presentifying (*Gegenwärtigung*) that accords temporal priority to the presencing of that which is present-at-hand.[116]

Temporal Diremption, Atonal Thinking, and the Jointure of the Open System

To circle back to the key point: Heidegger's unthought is neither something that can never be thought nor that which currently is not thought but potentially can be thought; the unthought of which Heidegger thinks is the mystery that pervades all thought as the capacity to be thought unremittingly in the curvature of time. The more original the thinking—the deeper it wells forth from the origin that stays hidden with every disclosure—the more fecund will be the attempts to articulate the unthought in what has been thought. If the criterion by which thought is to be probed is the unthought, it would seem that the structures of thinking cannot be integrated into a system understood as the unity of beings as a whole, for that would prevent releasing past thought about being to its essential destiny as what is unthought,[117] that is, the concealment that conceals itself from concealment, the presence that is never present, not even as the absence of presence, the nonground that has no ground in which to be grounded. The unthought is related to what is thought as the nothingness of being unveiled in the veiling of its unveiling through an infinitely intertwined web of differentiated nothing.

In the next chapter, I will delve more deeply into the comparison of Heidegger's *Seyn* and the kabbalistic *Ein Sof*, but what is necessary to underline at this juncture is that both of these postontological constructs call into question the suitability of systematic thinking applied to the being that is the singular fragmentation of all beings—the transcendental fractality of the fold as the identity of the in-between[118]—but that can never be confined to any particular being.[119] The question of the tenability of applying the notion of system to the theosophical edifices constructed by the kabbalists is illumined by Heidegger's comments on *the immeasurability of inceptual thinking as finite thinking* [Die Unermeßlichkeit des anfänglichen Denkens als des endlichen Denkens]: "This thinking and its order (the unfolded from it) lie outside the question of whether a system belongs to them or not. A 'system' is possible only as the result of the prevailing of mathematical thought (taking 'mathematical' in the broad sense) . . . . A thinking that stands outside of that domain and of its corresponding determination of truth as certainty is therefore essentially systemless, un-systematic. Yet it is not consequently arbitrary and confused. 'Unsystematic' means 'confused' and 'disordered' only if system is the measuring rod."[120] The atonality of thought implied in these words is profitably compared to a musical fugue wherein the various aspects are joined together compositionally into a polyphonic whole in which each "jointure" (*Fuge*) intones the same sequence of notes from a contrapuntal perspective without a tonal center:

> Inceptual thinking in the other beginning [*anderen Anfang*] has a different sort of rigor: the freedom of the joining of its junctures [*die Freiheit der Fügung seiner Fugen*]. Here one thing is joined to the other out of

the sovereignty of the questioning way of belonging [*fragenden Zugehörens*] to the call. . . . The conjuncture is something essentially other than a "system." . . . "Systems" are possible, and toward the end necessary, only in the realm of the history of the answer to the guiding question. Each of the six junctures of the conjuncture [*Fügungen der Fuge*] stands for itself, but only so as to make the essential unity [*wesentliche Einheit*] more impressive. In each of the six junctures, a saying of the same about the same is attempted [*über das Selbe je das Selbe zu sagen versucht*], but in each case out of a different essential domain [*anderen Wesensbereich*] of that which is called the event. If one's gaze is superficial and piecemeal, then "repetitions" will quickly be apparent everywhere. What is most difficult, however, is to carry out purely and conjuncturally [*fugenmäßig rein zu vollziehen*] an abiding [*Verharren*] with the same and thus testify to a genuine steadfastness [*echten Inständlichkeit*] in inceptual thinking.[121]

The passage calls for a thorough analysis, but my emphasis here is more limitedly on the utilization of Heidegger's inceptual thought—the fugal conjuncture of beyng, which is by nature nonconceptual (*unbegriffliches*)[122]—to clarify the notion of system that systematically invalidates the idea of system, the systemless system, or the open system, akin to a poetics wherein the theoretical structures are ever changing and cohere as counterpoints in a cacophonous ensemble.[123] From the perspective of inceptual thinking, repetitions are discerned to be conjunctural, which is to say, the replication of difference in the belonging together of what is irresolutely similar in virtue of being resolutely dissimilar.

Heidegger raises the thorny question about the "ways and modes of presenting [*Darstellung*] and communicating [*Mitteilung*] the conjuncture of inceptual thinking." There is an implicit danger that the elaboration of the conjuncture cannot avoid "being read and taken as a diffuse 'system.'" However, by focusing on individual questions—for example, the origin of the work of art—we "dispense with a uniform opening up and elaborating of the entire domain of conjuncture [*die gleichmäßige Eröffnung und Durchgestaltung des ganzen Fugenbereichs verzichten*]."[124] In a mode of thinking where things coagulate disjunctively rather than schematically, each of the six junctures—the echo (*Anklang*), the playing-forth (*Zuspiel*), the leap (*Sprung*), the grounding (*Gründung*), the ones to come (*Zukünftigen*), and the last god (*letzte Gott*)—expresses the essential unity of what is thought by standing for itself and without being compressed into a unifying whole. The six junctures convey the unity of the sovereignty of the questioning way of belonging by reverberating the same about the same out of distinct and discordant domains, each one tendering a disclosure of the "sheltering truth of the event" (*Bergung der Wahrheit des Ereignisses*), a truth—identified by Heidegger as the strife (*Streit*) of world and earth—that is the "grounded structure (joining) of the 'there,' a structure of transport-captivation [*gegründete Entrückungs-Berückungsgefüge (Fügung) des Da*]."[125]

Notable is Heidegger's use of an image from the realm of music to convey this notion of conjuncture or the repetition of structure from the perspective of a singularity intoning the same as different. The central role accorded this musical topos challenges the generalization offered by Philippe Lacoue-Labarthe that "Heidegger's attention to music is, we know, nearly nil: beyond the discourse on Conradin Kreutzer (or for which Conradin Kreutzer is the pretext), 'Memorial Address' (in *Discourse on Thinking*),[126] which says practically nothing about music, allusions and references to music are extremely rare, and mostly conventional."[127] The one major exception, which the author goes on to analyze in some detail, is Heidegger's discussion of a passage from Nietzsche's *Der Wille zur Macht* about Wagner.[128] Contesting this generalization, we would do well to recall Heidegger's attempt in *Die Grundbegriffe der Metaphysik* to delineate the "fundamental way" (*Grundweise*) of Dasein as attunement (*Stimmung*), which can mean both mood and tuning.[129] Elaborating on the musical connotation, Heidegger writes, "An attunement is a way [*Weise*], not merely a form or a mode, but a way—in the sense of a melody that does not merely hover over the so-called proper being at hand of man, but that sets the tone for such being, i.e., attunes and determines the manner and way of his being."[130] The aforecited text from the *Beiträge* has also escaped Lacoue-Labarthe's consideration, and to this we can add another critical passage from *Der Satz vom Grund*, mentioned already by Peter Hanly,[131] which, in my view, sheds light on the use of the image of the fugue to illumine the structure of thinking: "If we fully think through the polysemic word *Satz* not only as 'statement' [*Aussage*], not only as 'utterance' [*Sagen*], not only as 'leap' [*Sprung*], but at the same time also in the musical sense [*musikalischen Sinne*] of a 'movement,'[132] then we gain for the first time the complete connection to the principle of reason."[133] What Heidegger intends is that this change in tonality (*Tonart*) occasions the "leap from out of the principle of reason as a fundamental principle about beings [*Grundsatz über das Seiende*] into the principle of reason [*Satz vom Grund*] as an utterance of being [*einem Sagen vom Sein*] concealed itself behind the change of tonality of one and the same principle."[134]

Through skillful playfulness with language, Heidegger introduces a major shift in the modality of thinking, availing himself of the aesthetics of music to articulate the notion of movement in thought—the leap into a different kind of hearing—that allows "a unison between being and reason to resound" (*einem Einklang zwischen Sein und Grund anklingen*).[135] The resonance to which Heidegger alludes—the musical thinking apposite to the new beginning, which is to be distinguished from the belief that music speaks through the sounding of tones, a language distinct from the language of words[136]—relates to discerning the belonging together of being and reason, not based on a systematic analysis of the principle *nothing is without reason*, but on an attunement specifically to the words "is" and "reason" in that principle. The juxtaposition of these words illumines the belonging together and hence the sameness of being and reason, albeit in the specific Heideggerian sense according to which things are the same by virtue of their incontrovertible difference.[137] Sameness, therefore, entails a holding-together (*Zussamenhalten*) by keeping-apart (*Auseinanderhalten*).[138] For Heidegger, it is no longer possible or desirable to deduce a single sense from this principle of reason, which serves as the paradigm for the larger claim about the conjunction of what remains disjointed; the principle indoctrinates us to imagine sundry possibilities echoing with one another in the relational whole, that is, the whole made up of the relationality of the particulars.

The characterization of thought as conjuncture in this musical sense of resonance coupled with dissonance well applies to the thinking on display in kabbalistic works, and even in those treatises that are apparently more systematic. The plurivocality of aspects, refracted through the configurations and sefirotic paradigms, are various manifestations of the infinite light deflected from disconsonant vantage-points, each one expressing the same event interactively as entirely different. The hermeneutic aim of the systemless system is not to subjugate particulars under the stamp of generality but rather to demonstrate how generality is sculpted from the variability and volatility of particulars. The drift of thought exemplified by kabbalists corresponds, therefore, to what Heidegger described as the *Grundstimmung*,[139] the "basic disposition," or literally the grounding-attunement, that is, the attunement to the ground as the grounding of the nonground, an attunement that does not loosen the "rigor of the structure [*Gefüge*]" but accepts nevertheless "only the *availability* [Verfügung] of *one* way an individual can traverse while renouncing the possibility of overseeing other, perhaps more essential, ways."[140]

Central to this attunement to the question of the ground is the positing of the question of the ground of the question. Derrida thus perceptively wrote about the "unquestioned privilege of the *Fragen*" on Heidegger's path, the "question of the question," the "essentially questioning form," which marks the "essence and dignity of thought." Heidegger, we are rightly reminded, "*almost* never stopped identifying what is highest and best in thought with the question, with the decision, the call or guarding of the question, this 'piety' of thought."'[141] The comportment of Dasein in relation to being is determined primarily from the viewpoint of the *Seinsfrage*, the questioning of being that "finds its way into the extreme domain of oscillation, into the belonging to the most extreme occurrence, which is the *turning in the event* [*die Kehre im Ereignis*]. . . . This finding of its way happens in the leap, which unfolds as the grounding of Da-sein."[142] To cite Derrida again, "The point of departure in the existential analytic is legitimated first of all and only from the possibility, experience, structure, and regulated modifications of the *Fragen*. Such is the exemplarity of the entity which *we* are, of the *ourselves* in this discursive situation of *Mitsein* in which we can, to ourselves and to others, say *we*."[143]

This sensibility is already in evidence in Heidegger's depiction of science in the *Rektoratsrede* (1933) as the "questioning standing firm [*fragenden Standhalten*] in the midst of the totality of being as it continually conceals itself."[144] Heidegger eventually came to identify the act of questioning as essential to the path of the meditative thinking that he contrasts with the science of calculative thinking. In a passage from the *Schwarze Hefte*, written in the fall of 1932, Heidegger poetically identified *questioning* as "the glowing, consuming, purifying flame" of the fire of the "original essence of truth" whose "metal," or the "genuineness of the ore," is "*beyng*" (Seyn).[145] From a notebook entry of a later date (1938–39), Heidegger defines *Besinnung* as "the courage to track down one's own presuppositions and their rationale and to interrogate the goal positings with regard to their necessity."[146] The attempt to think meditatively, as opposed to computatively, depends on becoming a radical thinker capable of "wandering through the errant paths of the history of philosophy."[147] As he put in another context, philosophical knowledge is "a comprehending disclosure [*Aufschließen*] of something in a specifically determined and directed questioning, which as a questioning never allows what is questioned to become something present at hand [*Vorhandenen*]."[148] To be underway on the path of thinking, one must "become involved in questions that seek what no inventiveness can find."[149] To think is to ask repeatedly what is it to think, an inquiry that defies any definitive response. Only the question, properly speaking, is thought-provoking (*Bedenklichste*), since it is the gift (*Gabe*) that endlessly gives food for thought.[150] Ironically, the Heideggerian theme of *Fragen*, as I noted in a previous study,[151] resonates with the well-documented Jewish penchant to respond to a question by posing an additional question, a stereotype adroitly expressed by Scholem in an essay published in 1919, "The question is an unending cycle; the symbol of this infinitude, in which the possibility of an empirical end is given, is the rhetorical question. This ('Jewish') question can be justly characterized as medial; it knows no answer, which means its answer must in essence be another question; in the innermost basis of Judaism the concept of an answer does not exist."[152] The priority accorded the question is the logical consequence of the commentarial as opposed to systematic nature of Jewish thought. The hermeneutical emphasis demands an open-ended interrogation that prevents the open text from ossifying into a sealed book.

Even more relevant is Scholem's comment in the third of his ten unhistorical aphorisms on the kabbalah. Creatively interpreting a passage in the zoharic anthology where the attributes of *Binah* and *Malkhut*, the third and the tenth of the *sefirot*, are respectively correlated with the interrogative pronouns "who" (*mi*) and "what" (*mah*),[153] Scholem opines about the lack of object of the highest knowledge (*höchsten Erkenntnis*) that the kabbalah yields: "The fundamental nature of this knowledge is revealed in the classical form of the question: knowledge is a question rooted in God to which no answer corresponds [*Erkenntnis als eine in Gott gegründete Frage, die keiner Antwort entspricht*]."[154] If we substitute *Seyn* for God, Heidegger would concur: the question rooted in being—which, as Gadamer incisively noted, "is a verb, a temporal expression, and not at all something that one could articulate as *das* Sein, *the* Sein"[155]—begets not an answer but another question, and so on ad infinitum. In postmodern terms, the emphasis on constant questioning accentuates that, with respect to any structure of thought, the coherence of the parts does not portend absorption of difference in a seamless and disembodied continuum; the infinitude of the circular dynamic of the question precipitating a question is expressive of what I referred to before as the transcendental fractality of the in-between, the ring of the same difference that precludes the stasis of once and for all. The perception of totality that the structure buttresses is a unity embodied in multiplicity, a one that is unremittingly configured by the manifold, in the language of Laruelle, "a One which does not unify but which remains in-One,"[156] that is, a "unity-becoming"[157] through the array of the many rather than through the unification of the one. For Heidegger, it is legitimate to speak of an *originary interconnection of concepts,* but that interconnectivity is "intrinsically historical and is concealed within the history of Dasein. Consequently there is no system of Dasein for the metaphysical interpretation of Dasein. Rather the intrinsic conceptual interconnection is that of the history of Dasein itself, something which, as history, transforms itself. . . . The historicity of Dasein refuses, even more than any system does, any isolation or isolated consideration of individual concepts."[158]

Here it is worth citing a passage from Rosenzweig that transmutes the kabbalistic idea into a philosophical key closely allied with Heidegger's rejection of the Hegelian dialectic and the sublation of the particular:

> The world is neither a shadow, nor a dream, nor a painting; its being is being-there, real being-there—created creation [*ihr Sein ist Dasein, wirkliches Dasein—geschaffene Schöpfung*]. The world is totally concrete [*ganz gegenständlich*], and all action in it, all "making," from the moment that it is in it, is supervening event. . . . The world is made of things; in spite of the unity of its concrete reality, it does not constitute a single object but a multiplicity of objects, precisely things. The thing does not possess stability as long as it is there quite alone. It is conscious of its singularity [*Einzelheit*], of its individuality [*Individualität*], only in the multiplicity of things [*der Vielheit der Dinge*]. The thing can be shown only in connection [*Zusammenhang*] with other things; it is determined by its spatial relationship with other things, within such a connection. Furthermore, as specific thing, it has no essence of its own, it does not exist in itself, it exists only in its relationships. The essence it has is not within it, but in the relationship it keeps according to its genus; it is behind its determination, and not in it that it must seek its essentiality [*Wesentlichkeit*], its universality [*Allgemeinheit*].[159]

Thinking in the footsteps of Rosenzweig, I would proffer that the idea of system to which kabbalists consent does not denote an architectural structure formed by assembling individual stones whose meaning is validated by the sense of the whole conferring essential properties on specific components, but rather the striving on the part of individual entities qua individuals for reciprocity and codependency; the viability of systematicity, therefore, is contingent on affirming a unity perpetually in the making, an aggregate that is always subject to modification,[160] the positing of a truth whose eternality—which, as I have emphasized several times, is to be distinguished from timelessness—is determined by the discontinuity and nondetermination manifest in the continuities and determinations of time. The merit of a system depends on its proposing a unity accruing incessantly, a cohesiveness that exhibits an impulse for order that can be realized only through negotiating—but never abolishing—disorder. In the disarray of chaos, one finds the nucleus where the lines of the system both crystallize and disintegrate by breaking through the parameters of the system. To paraphrase the words of Charles E. Scott, a framework accounts for something alien to the framework insofar as the framework gives occasion for perceptive alertness to the limits of the framing and to an ephemeral escape from the framework that takes place within the framework.[161] This assessment seems remarkably suitable to the mutability and nondirectionality implicit in the kabbalistic idea of system.

In contrast to the Hegelian dialectic that presumes a universal instantiated comprehensively in the particular, a *singular universality,* wherein the finite vanishes in the infinite,[162] the negation of negation, the "concrete, absolute negativity" as opposed to the negation that is the "abstract negativity,"[163] we do better to think of the universal as being constituted relentlessly in light of the random and indiscriminate particulars, the *universal singularity,*[164] wherein the infinite materializes in the finite, the negation of the negation of negation, a universal that is, to borrow the formulation of Nancy, always calibrated from the prospect of "being-with-one-another, circulating in the *with* and as the *with* of this singularly plural coexistence."[165] As Nancy puts it in his exposition of the idea of manifestation and Hegel's negative:

> The "phenomenon" is not appearance: it is the lively transport of self and the leap into manifest existence. Manifesting itself, it is in relation. It singularizes itself. Everything is singular, and the totality is also singular: it is the singularity of manifestation itself. The singularity of manifestation, or of the world: it

> is that singularity manifests itself to nothing other than itself, or to nothing. Manifestation surges up out of nothing, into nothing. . . . Manifestation is therefore of itself or it is of nothing; it is of itself as much as it is of nothing.[166]

The negative of manifestation is not something hidden or nonmanifest but the naked manifestation of the nonmanifestation of the singularity of all being that is nothing.[167] This corresponds to Heidegger's assertion *Alles ist einzig*, "everything is unique," [168] which I assume means that if we are to speak of universality, the sense of allness, or the "univocity of being,"[169] must always be reckoned in conjunction with the absolute inimitability of the individual.[170] Heidegger's *Einzigkeit* corresponds to, and may have been influenced by, what Kierkegaard called *den Enkelte*, the "single," the particular incorporated in the universal as that which is higher than and therefore incapable of being incorporated in the universal,[171] the particular that is *absolutely nonexisting in its existing*, that is, *absolutely nothing but existence*,[172] the "infinite negation of the negation of the finite," which is to say, the *infinite negation of the self-negation of the infinite*.[173]

When viewed in this manner, there is no discrepancy between the general and the particular; the former can be expressed only through the latter, and the latter through the former. This is to be distinguished from Hegel's depiction of the essence as the consciousness of self-consciousness, which implies that the individuality of the individual is but the outer form of the universal in and for itself. From the standpoint of the guiding question of Heidegger's inceptual thinking, the understanding of essence in this view "is determined on the basis of beingness" (*Seiendheit*, which is related to the Greek οὐσία-κοινόν, that is, the common substance), and "the essentiality of the essence consists in the greatest possible generality of the essence." Conversely, this means that "the particular and the manifold, which fall under the concept of the essence and from which this concept is established, are arbitrary; indeed, what is essential is the arbitrariness of beings, which nevertheless is precisely what the belonging to the essence indicates." From the perspective of belonging to the essence of being, the essential nature of the plurality of particular beings is their arbitrariness. However, if "beyng is conceived as event," then "essentiality is determined out of the originality and uniqueness of beyng itself. There the essence is not the general but is the essential occurrence precisely of what is unique in each case and of what constitutes the rank of the being. . . . Every essential occurrence is determined out of what is essential in the sense of the original unique."[174] The essence is precisely what is unique and therefore repeatable only as nonrepeatable. In this sense, we can speak of the kabbalistic *Ein Sof* as the essence of being, that is, the essence that is the absence of essence, an essence that does not, contra Hegel's description of spirit,[175] become actual through the determinate forms of its necessary self-revelation insofar as that revelation is inescapably a concealment of essence. About the essence of *Ein Sof* we can say, therefore, that it is subject to neither apophatic nor kataphatic theology, since it is neither being nor nonbeing, but the event of beingness, an event that is always the same because always different.

The view I have expressed is brought into sharper relief when compared against the depiction of pure experience in Nishida Kitarō:

> From the perspective of concrete thinking, the universality of a concept is not what we usually say it is—that is, an abstraction of similar natures from something concrete. Rather, it is the unifying force of concrete facts. Hegel likewise writes that the universal is the soul of the concrete. Because pure experience is a systematic development, the unifying force that functions at its foundation is the universality of concepts; the development of experience corresponds to the advance of thinking; and the facts of pure experience are the self-actualization of the universal. . . . We ordinarily think we know the universal through thinking and the individual through experience. But apart from the individual there is no universal. That which is truly universal is the concealed power behind the actualization of the individual; the universal is located within the individual as the power that causes the individual to develop. . . . The true universal at the

> base of the unity that is found in the activity of thinking therefore must be the concealed power that takes as its content the individual actuality. The universal and the individual differ only in that one is implicit and the other explicit; the individual is that which is determined by the universal.[176]

Nishida's notion of absolute nothingness as the self-negation of the self-contradictory identity—what has been referred to as the *chiasmatic chorology*, the crevasse of space that encompasses the vertical and the horizontal axes of the indeterminate whole and the determinate parts[177]—bears a strong resemblance to my own view, bolstered by the study of kabbalistic and Heideggerian texts, but I would reverse the end of the aforecited passage. To speak of particularity as the index of universality implies that the commensurability of the universal must be reckoned by the incommensurability of the particular and the incommensurability of the particular by the commensurability of the universal. On occasion, Nishida articulates this precise view:

> The world of reality is essentially the one as well as the many; it is essentially a world of the mutual determination of single beings. That is why I call the world of reality "absolute contradictory self-identity" [or "unity of opposites"]. . . . World cannot be thought [only] as the one of the many, or [only] as the many of the one. It is essentially a world, where the data are something formed, i.e. dialectically given, and which negates itself, [moving] slowly from the formed to the forming. It is impossible to think either the one whole, or the many single beings, as substratum in the depth of this world. . . . That which "is" in reality, is, as determined, through and through "being", and as formed, through and through changing and passing away. It can be said that it is Being as well as Nothingness. Therefore, I have spoken in other places of the world of absolute Nothingness, and I have called it, as a world of endless moving, the world of determination without a determining one.[178]

In my estimation, kabbalistic theosophy and cosmology similarly promote the insight that particularity is not merely the concrete instantiation of universality nor is universality merely the abstract idealization of particularity. Resisting a Hegelian resolution that would sanction the dialectical universalization of the particular in the particularization of the universal, kabbalists uphold—in a manner consonant with Heidegger—the hypothesis that the indeterminacy of the particular is always in the process of being determined by the determinacy of the universal, just as the determinacy of the universal is always in the process of being undetermined by the indeterminacy of the particular.

Availing myself of the language of Merleau-Ponty to expound the kabbalistic material, I would distinguish the bad dialectic of Hegel and the good dialectic or the hyperdialectic—the dialectic that dialectically topples the dialectic deferral of the nondialectic: "The bad dialectic is that which thinks it recomposes being by a thetic thought, by an assemblage of statements, by thesis, antithesis, and synthesis; the good dialectic is that which is conscious of the fact that every *thesis* is an idealization, that Being is not made up of idealizations or of things said, as the old logic believed, but of bound wholes where signification never is except in tendency, where the inertia of the content never permits the defining of one term as positive, another term as negative, and still less a third term as absolute suppression of the negative by itself."[179] Instead of ascribing to *Ein Sof* a structure of being impervious to the instability of the multiple, the oneness of infinity is best visualized through the multiple qua multiple, that is, in Badiou's mathematical calculus, as the *theory of inconsistent multiplicities*, the axial doctrine of being, wherein the multiple is presented as the presented without any other predicate than its multiplicity.[180] The only consistency verified by these multiplicities is the consistency of their inconsistency. "It is therefore certain," writes Badiou, "that the primitive consistency is *prohibited* by the axiom system, which is to say it is ontologically inconsistent, whilst their inconsistency (their pure presentative multiplicity) is *authorized* as ontologically consistent."[181]

The task of the thinker, then, is to frame the predicative description of the singular in terms of the descriptive predication of the universal, albeit in such a way that the equivocal and implicative whimsicality of the former is not obliterated by the univocal and deductive inexorability of the latter. Heidegger, it goes without saying, had a different understanding of the mathematical and its relationship to the poetic and the ontological,[182] but what I have educed from Badiou, the *axiomatic decision* about the "non-being of the one,"[183] reverberates with Heidegger's reflections on being and the event.[184] More important, the wisdom of the kabbalah and the thinking of Heidegger converge on this point of divergence: being, which is the nonessence of the essence as opposed to the essence of the nonessence, denotes the pure multiplicity of an infinitely systemic nondifferentiated differentiation, the singularity oscillating syllogistically between an absolute minimum of everything dissimilar by virtue of being similar and an absolute maximum of everything similar by virtue of being dissimilar.

Notes

1. This is well captured in Heidegger's repeated use of the term *Weg* to characterize the path of thinking, and especially his choice of *Holzwege* to name a collection of his essays, an expression that means woodpath in colloquial German, but which also has the connotation of a way that leads nowhere. See Stambaugh, "Heidegger, Taoism, and the Question of Metaphysics," p. 80: "The function of woodpaths, which the woodcutters leave behind as they cut and gather wood, is not to lead someone from one point to another; rather, the path is almost a necessary byproduct of the woodcutter's activity. For those of us non-woodcutters walking in the forest, we don't know where the woodpaths are leading and if our primary aim were to arrive at some fixed destination in the shortest amount of time, we wouldn't be on a woodpath. Thus the *philosophical* meaning of being on a woodpath is not so much that it doesn't go anywhere but that the meaning of being on it is not to arrive at a known or predetermined destination. One does not necessarily know at the outset where one is going. For Heidegger, woodpaths express the fact that thinking is thoroughly and essentially questioning, a questioning not to be stilled or 'solved' by any answer, a questioning that cannot calculate in advance the direction in which it will be led, let alone the destination at which it will arrive" (emphasis in original). See also Malpas, *Heidegger's Topology*, pp. 174, 363n30.

2. The text was likely written by a Spanish kabbalist in the early part of the fourteenth century; it was published twice in 1558, in Mantua and in Ferrara. For a new edition with corrections made on the basis of manuscripts, see *Ma'arekhet ha-Elohut*.

3. Eliashiv, *Leshem Shevo we-Aḥlamah: Haqdamot u-She'arim*, p. 73.

4. Scholem, *Major Trends*, pp. 269–73. For an attempt to interpret the *parṣufim* through the prism of Jungian archetypes, see Pedaya, *Kabbalah and Psychoanalysis*, pp. 223–25. Also noteworthy is the psychoanalytical analysis of the gender dimensions of the Lurianic symbolism in Gamlieli, *Psychoanalysis and Kabbalah*.

5. Deacon, *Incomplete Nature*, pp. 44–45.

6. My formulation is inspired by the discussion of complexity and chaos as it pertains to the concept of emergence in Deacon, *Incomplete Nature*, pp. 143–81, esp. 169–75.

7. Clancey, "Scientific Antecedents," p. 12: "In identifying parts and wholes, systems thinking does not reject the value of reductionist compartmentalization and componential analysis; rather, systems thinking strives for a 'both-and' perspective . . . that shows how the whole makes the parts what they are and vice versa. For example, in conceptual systems, metonymic relations (tropes or figures of speech) may have a both-and meaning."

8. See Wolfson, *Giving*, p. 101, and reference on pp. 362–63nn83–84 to other studies (including some of my own) wherein the possibility of this influence on Levinas has been discussed.

9. Levinas, *Totality and Infinity*, p. 104; *Totalité et infini*, p. 77.

10. Scholem was not always consistent on this point, reflecting the tension found in the primary sources between a monistic-pantheistic and a dualistic-theistic orientation. For a theistic interpretation of the Lurianic myth of *ṣimṣum*, see Scholem, *Major Trends*, p. 262; Scholem, *On Jews and Judaism*, p. 283. See also the fifth of the "Zehn unhistorische Sätze über Kabbala" in Scholem, *Judaica* 3, pp. 267–68, and analysis in Biale, "Gershom Scholem's Ten Unhistorical Aphorisms," pp. 79–80. For my critique of Scholem, see Wolfson, "Nihilating Nonground," pp. 33–34. See, however, the passage from Scholem cited in ch. 5 n150.

11. Scholem, *On the Mystical Shape*, p. 41; *Von der mystischen Gestalt*, p. 33. On Scholem's use of dialectic, see introduction n. 38.

12. Jacobi, *Main Philosophical Writings*, p. 350. For a recent assessment of Jacobi's encounters with Jewish thought, see Jaeschke, "Vom Atheismus."

13. Compare the remark about Schelling's understanding of Jacobi's interpretation of the system of Spinozism in a letter to Mendelssohn (1785) discussed in Heidegger, *Schelling's Treatise*, pp. 66–67 (*Schelling: Vom Wesen*, p. 115): "Jacobi wants to show here that pantheism is really Spinozism, Spinozism is fatalism, and fatalism is atheism. . . . However, by equating pantheism and Spinozism, Jacobi was indirectly instrumental in newly asking and more sharply defining and answering the question of what pantheism is, and also in bringing the historical interpretation of Spinoza to other paths. To avoid a misunderstanding here, we must emphasize that Spinoza's philosophy cannot be equated with Jewish philosophy. Alone the familiar fact that Spinoza was evicted from the Jewish community is significant. His philosophy is essentially determined by the spirit of the time, Bruno, Descartes, and medieval scholasticism." From Heidegger's perspective, Schelling's criticism of Spinoza is not centered on the theological challenge of pantheism but on its underlying ontology, "which entails the danger of fatalism, of the exclusion of freedom and its misunderstanding" (*Schelling's Treatise*, p. 72; *Schelling: Vom Wesen*, p. 124). The matter is reiterated in Heidegger, *Schelling's Treatise*, p. 90 (*Schelling: Vom Wesen*, p. 155): "Schelling does not fail to point out the hidden, more far-reaching intention of this view. The intention is to warn everyone by way of an inquisition about philosophy in general as something 'ruinous.' For as fatalism, Spinozism is atheism and every upright person must cross himself when confronted with this." Heidegger's reluctance to classify Spinoza's thought as Jewish philosophy sounds like an affront to the Jews, but it is possible that he was actually responding to the Nazi condemnation of Spinoza's works. Concerning this censure, see Sherratt, *Hitler's Philosophers*, pp. 76, 80, 106. Corroboration for my conjecture is found in the testimony of Safranski, *Martin Heidegger*, p. 256, that in a lecture in the mid-1930s Heidegger "defended Spinoza, declaring that if his philosophy was 'Jewish,' then all philosophy from Leibniz to Hegel was Jewish too." See as well Heidegger, *Identity and Difference*, pp. 47–48 (German text, pp. 113–14): "Spinoza appeals always afresh to the whole thinking of German Idealism, and at the same time provokes its contradiction, because he lets thinking begin with the absolute. Kant's path, in contrast, is different, and is even more decisive than Spinoza's system for thinking of absolute idealism and for philosophy generally." See below, n. 119.

14. Wolfson, *Open Secret*, pp. 150, 338–39n146, 358n103.

15. For a thorough review of the *status quaestionis* of this topic, including references to other scholarly views, see Abrams, *Kabbalistic Manuscripts*, pp. 224–438. Of the many scholars discussed by Abrams, special note should be made of the work of Ronit Meroz. See her "Archaeology," and reference to other studies by her cited on p. x, n1. I concur with her assessment (p. xlvi) that "the Zohar is made up of disparate strata, piled one above the other like the layers of an onion," and the methodological assumption that we must try to determine the archaeological stratum of any given text in light of the intensive redactional activity attested in this compilation. I am not so sanguine, however, about the prospect of identifying these earlier, and perhaps in some cases pretextual, layers, and hence I would question her conclusion that "when the synchronicity and conceptual compatibility of apparent zoharic parallels is in question, the relative weight ascribed to data drawn from earlier sources should be increased." A fuller presentation of Meroz's methodology can now be found in her recently published monograph *Spiritual Biography of Rabbi Simeon bar Yochay*. For my modest reflections on this issue, including a brief criticism of Meroz's approach, see Wolfson, "Zoharic Literature," pp. 321–25.

16. *Zohar* 3:225a.

17. *Tiqqunei Zohar*, sec. 70, 122b.

18. Shneur Zalman of Liadi, *Liqquṭei Torah*, vol. 1, Behar, 42a-b. The expression *shaweh u-mashweh qaṭon we-gadol* is derived from the description of God's judicial impartiality in the liturgical poem *ha-oḥez be-yad middat mishpaṭ*, composed by the sixth-century Palestinian poet Yannai. See *Piyyute Yannai*, p. 38.

19. On the distinction between the infinite (*ein sof*) and the light of the infinite (*or ein sof*), see Cordovero, *Shi'ur Qomah*, 15a.

20. Heidegger, *Contributions*, §110, pp. 169–70; *Beiträge*, pp. 216–17.

21. Wolfson, "Secrecy," pp. 143–50. The passage to which I refer from Kook's *Orot* is cited and analyzed on p. 148. Here it is worth recalling as well the comment of Atlan in *Sparks of Randomness*, pp. 346–47: "the ultimate idol is the personal God of theology . . . the only discourse about God that is not idolatrous is necessarily an atheistic discourse. Alternatively, whatever the discourse, the only God who is not an idol is a God who is not a God." The passage was previously cited in Wolfson, *Giving*, p. xvii. See as well Atlan, "Jerusalem," p. 170: "Nothing authentically universal can come about if the grandeur

and the responsibility of atheism are rejected, on the condition that it is a true atheism—atheistic with regard to all the gods comprised within it, the modern and secular gods engendered by ideology. This true atheism has the unrivaled merit of protecting against the enchantment of the holy and the murderous wrath that only it can bring about."

22. Shneur Zalman of Liadi, *Liqquṭei Torah*, vol. 2, Shir ha-Shirim, 40c.

23. Theodor and Albeck, eds., *Bere'shit Rabba*, 68:9, p. 778; Ulmer, ed., *Pesiqta Rabbati*, 21:26, pp. 464–65.

24. Gruenwald, "Preliminary Critical Edition," §38, p. 157; Hayman, *Sefer Yeṣira*, §38, p. 132. See Pines, "Points of Similarity," p. 86n183.

25. Ickovits, *Nefesh ha-Ḥayyim*, 3:1, pp. 207–9. For a different interpretation, see *Zohar* 3:242a–b (*Ra'aya Meheimna*). In that context, the "world" (*olam*) is identified as the *Shekhinah*, for the Aramaic translation of *olam* is *alma*, which is linked to *ulima*, the word for maiden.

26. Ickovits, *Nefesh ha-Ḥayyim*, 3:2, p. 209. For a comparison of Heidegger and this Jewish thinker, albeit from a different conceptual angle, see Lapidot, "People of Knowers." Lapidot's focus concerns the affinity between what he identifies as the historically antimetaphysical epistemo-political mission that Heidegger attributed to the German people and the cosmic-ontological role accorded the people of Israel, the holy nation (*am qadosh*), understood by Ḥayyim of Volozhin as a historical collective identity that is the nonmetaphysical agency of human knowledge (pp. 280–84).

27. Based on Deuteronomy 4:35.

28. Ickovits, *Nefesh ha-Ḥayyim*, 3:2–3, p. 214.

29. Gruenwald, "Preliminary Critical Edition," §5, p. 142; Hayman, *Sefer Yeṣira*, §5, p. 72.

30. Ickovits, *Nefesh ha-Ḥayyim*, 3:2, p. 210.

31. Schneersohn, *Derekh Miṣwotekha*, 124b. Compare Schneersohn, *Or ha-Torah: Ma'amerei Ḥazal we-Inyanim*, p. 120. I have deliberately rendered the references to *Ein Sof* with the neuter pronoun to emphasize the point that it is beyond all personification. The more typical way of translating would have been to leave the masculine third person. This is correct contextually and philologically, but I do think that Ḥabad's thought harbors the possibility of thinking about *Ein Sof* in terms that surpass the hierarchical polarity of the gender dimorphism with which it is infused.

32. My thinking here is in accord with the paradigm of immanence articulated by Barber, *On Diaspora*, pp. 1–11.

33. Moses ben Jacob, *Shoshan Sodot*, p. 2; Ibn Gabbai, *Avodat ha-Qodesh*, 1:2, p. 3, 1:10, p. 24; Cordovero, *Pardes Rimmonim*, 4:1, p. 39; 4:2, p. 40.

34. David ben Yehudah he-Ḥasid, *Book of Mirrors*, p. 80. The expression is repeated ibid., p. 224, and see the discussion by Matt, introduction, p. 22. See also Joseph ben Shalom Ashkenazi, *Perush Sefer Yeṣirah*, 2c, 28b (printed erroneously under the name of Abraham ben David of Posquières). On the identity of *Ein Sof* and *Keter*, see *Tiqqunei Zohar*, sec. 22, 68b: "Just as thought is concealed, so too, it is concealed; it is called *Ein Sof* from within and the supernal *Keter* from without." See also *Zohar* 3:258a (*Ra'aya Meheimna*). For further references, see ch. 3 nn. 160–61. For recent discussions of this issue in early kabbalistic literature, see Wolfson, "Anonymity," pp. 71–72; Bar-Asher, "*Ancient as 'Ein Sof',*" pp. 151–53.

35. Scholem, *Origins*, p. 423n138, mentions this passage from *Liber de Causis* in conjunction with the statement from Azriel of Gerona: "the something is in the nothing in the manner of nothing and the nothing is in the something in the manner of something." Azriel's text is published in Scholem, "New Fragments," p. 207, and translated and analyzed in Scholem, *Origins*, pp. 423–24. See also Wolfson, "Nihilating Nonground," p. 33. On the Hebrew translations of the Latin text of *Liber de Causis*, see Rothschild, "Le *Livre des causes*." An edition of the Hebrew texts is presented in the same volume by Rothschild, "Traductions hébraïques."

36. *Book of Causes*, p. 30. The logic seems to be implied in the following description of the Soul vis-à-vis the Intellect, and that of the Intellect vis-à-vis the One, in Plotinus, *Enneads*, 5.1. 6, p. 33: "But Soul's expression is obscure—for it is a ghost of Intellect—and for this reason it has to look to Intellect; but Intellect in the same way has to look to that god, in order to be Intellect. But it sees him, not as separated from him, but because it comes next after him, and there is nothing between, as also there is not anything between Soul and Intellect. Everything longs for its parent and loves it, especially when parent and offspring are alone; but when the parent is the highest good, the offspring is necessarily with him and separate from him only in otherness." The claim that the Intellect is necessarily with and yet separate from the One only in otherness seems to me equivalent to the kabbalistic adage, perhaps based on Proclus, that there is no difference between the cause and the effect except that *Ein Sof* is the cause and *Keter* is the effect. The philosophical challenge here is to preserve the difference of identity in the face of

the identity of difference, or in Schellingian terms, to posit a sense of indifference that resists the identity of identity and nonidentity.

37. See the explication of the doctrine in Ibn Gabbai, *Avodat ha-Qodesh*, 1:5, p. 12, 1:6, p. 14. Some kabbalists posited an ontological distinction between the two even when affirming the principle that the emanated is not separate from the emanator. See, for instance, Ibn Zimra, *Magen David*, p. 12: "Thus you have learned that the emanator is not separate from the emanated [*she-ein ha-ma'aṣil nifrad min ha-ne'eṣal*]. However, they are two, the emanator and the emanated. The emanated emanates by means of the will of the emanator and is not necessitated from him, and the emanator is prior to the emanated, but not like the priority of the cause to the effect, because the emanator is eternal, and there is no privation [*he'der*] prior to his existence, which is not the case with the emanated, for the privation preceded its being actualized. The emanator and the emanated are called one, since they are bound to one another like a flame bound to the coal, and not because they are one in their substance and in their essence."

38. Rossi, *Logic and the Art of Memory*, p. 38. On the application of the term *pansophism* to Lurianic kabbalah, see Chajes, "Kabbalah and the Diagrammatic Phase," pp. 111–12. The analysis of Chajes builds on the classification of the Lurianic conception of divinity as the encyclopedic perspective offered by Weinstein, *Kabbalah and Jewish Modernity*, pp. 31–43. I cite the English translation but the Hebrew original, which appeared in 2011, is the edition used by Chajes.

39. Heidegger, *Contributions*, §52, p. 88 (emphasis in original); *Beiträge*, p. 110.

40. Heidegger, *Contributions*, §52, p. 88 (emphasis in original); *Beiträge*, p. 111. For an attempt to apply the logic of dialetheism to Heidegger, see Casati, "Being: A Dialetheic Interpretation."

41. The term *inapparent* (*Unscheinbaren*) appears in the analysis of the Parmenidean dictum ἔστι γὰρ εἶναι, which is rendered as "Being namely *is*" (Ist *nämlich Sein*) or as "being *is*" (*das Sein* ist) in Heidegger, *Four Seminars*, pp. 79–80 (*Seminare*, pp. 397–99): "What is to be thought is thus: ἔστι γὰρ εἶναι—'presencing namely presences' ['*anwest nämlich Anwesen*']. . . . We are here in the domain of the inapparent [*Bereich des Unscheinbaren*]: presencing itself presences [*anwest Anwesen selbst*]. . . . Thus understood, phenomenology is a path that leads away to come before . . . and it lets that before which it is led show itself. This phenomenology is a phenomenology of the inapparent [*eine Phänomenologie des Unscheinbaren*]." The inapparent is to be distinguished from the invisible, and thus I take issue with the thesis of Serafin, "Heidegger's Phenomenology," which is based on translating *Phänomenologie des Unscheinbaren* as the "phenomenology of the invisible."

42. Heidegger, *Basic Writings*, p. 331; *Vorträge und Aufsätze*, p. 27. See ch. 3 n. 135.

43. In light of this dimension of Heidegger's *Seinsdenken*, we can appreciate the inadequacy of Levinas's distinction (*Totality and Infinity*, pp. 27–28; *Totalité et infini*, p. xvi) between the Heideggerian conception of disclosing (*dévoiler*) and the Rosenzweigian notion of revelation (*révélation*); the former allegedly presumes a sense of totality in which the relation between the same and the other is always reducible to knowledge of the other by the same, whereas the latter opposes the idea of totality and affirms the manifestation of the other to the same in its irreducible otherness. A less biased interpretation of Heidegger would require a more nuanced understanding that the disclosure of truth is always at the same time a concealment of truth and hence the suggestion that there is a presumed adequation that levels out the difference between being and representation is patently fallacious. Levinas's implicit claim that, for the Heidegger of *Sein und Zeit*, phenomenology—the comprehension effected through bringing to light—constitutes the "ultimate event of being itself" fails to take into account that the disclosing of the event can come to light only through the withdrawing of the event from disclosure.

44. Agamben cites the passage of Albert the Great from Lizzini, *Fluxus*, pp. 10–11.

45. Agamben, *Use of Bodies*, p. 174.

46. Heidegger, *Question Concerning Technology*, p. 44; *Technik*, pp. 42–43.

47. Foucault, *History of Madness*, p. 31.

48. Heidegger, *Frühe Schriften*, p. 437. A facsimile of the motto in Heidegger's hand is reproduced on the second unnumbered page of the volume before the frontispiece. See Wetz, "Wege—Nicht Werke."

49. The comment appears in the unnumbered page preceding the frontispiece in *Ponderings II–VI* (*Überlegungen II–VI*).

50. Heidegger, *Ponderings II–VI*, p. 134 (emphasis in original); *Überlegungen II–VI*, p. 184.

51. Heidegger, *Contributions*, §1, p. 6; *Beiträge*, p. 5. See Vallega-Neu, *Heidegger's Poietic Writings*, p. 24.

52. Heidegger, *Contributions*, §119, p. 185 (emphasis in original); *Beiträge*, p. 235. The conclusion of the passage is rendered a bit more lucidly in the

alternative translation, Heidegger, *Contributions (From Enowning)*, §119, p. 166: "It is not a matter of *proclaiming* new doctrines to a human operation that has run aground, but of *displacing* man out of the lack of distress into the distress of lack of distress, as the utmost distress" (emphasis in original). Here we see clearly that Heidegger wished to express that the utmost distress is the distress of the lack of distress, the alienation from being alienated.

53. Heidegger, *Contributions*, §42, p. 68 (emphasis in original); *Beiträge*, p. 86.

54. Heidegger, *Contributions*, §125, p. 191; *Beiträge*, p. 242. See Heidegger, *Vier Hefte I und II*, p. 37: "Kein System zu bauen; kein setzendes Subjekt anzusetzen; nirgends ein Ansatz, wo 'bloßes' Ereignis." Compare Ward, *Heidegger's Political Thinking*, p. 160: "Among many other things, *Beiträge* is a massive objection to the very idea of scientific philosophy. It is an 'attempt' (*Versuch*) to think from the most originary fundamental positioning in the question of the truth of Being, a 'future thinking'—which is to say, in the manner of Nietzsche, both a *future* thinking and a thinking *of* the future—understood as a process 'through which the as yet hidden realm of the becoming of the essencing [*Wesung*] of Being passes and is first illuminated and reached in its ownmost event-character [*Ereignischarakter*].'" Ward views this objection as part of Heidegger's realization of the failure of his own call for the "reinspiriting of science," which was expressed in the rectoral address, as well as other criticisms of National Socialism as "an exhibition of modernity" found in the later work.

55. Stambaugh, *Finitude of Being*, p. 112.

56. Heidegger, *Four Seminars*, p. 80; *Seminare*, p. 399.

57. Gadamer, *Heidegger's Ways*, pp. 20–21.

58. Ibid., p. 21 (emphasis in original).

59. Ibid. In light of this passage, I am perplexed by the comment of Wolin, *Frankfurt School Revisited*, p. 111, that Gadamer once accused Heidegger "of having lapsed into unintelligible Being-mysticism (*Seinsmystik*)." On p. 277n1, Wolin gives the reference as Gadamer, *Heidegger's Ways*, p. viii. As a matter of fact, not only does Gadamer not make such a claim in that context—or anywhere else as far as I can discern—but he makes the opposite claim, namely, that all his essays on the latter Heidegger were "to offer a view of the task for thinking that confronted Heidegger; they attempt to show that especially the Heidegger who had made this 'turn' [*Kehre*] after *Being and Time* was in truth continuing down the same path when he encountered questions probing the underpinnings of metaphysics and attempted to think an unknown future."

60. Levy, *Hans Jonas*, p. 81. See also p. 27, where Levy contends that Heidegger responded to the miscarriage of his hopes in National Socialism "with a retreat from reason and with a decision to place whatever trust remained in the fragmentary utterances of supposedly prophetic poets." For a critical assessment of this perspective on Heidegger, see Rorty, *Consequences of Pragmatism*, pp. 37–59, esp. 39–41: "Heidegger has done as good a job of putting potential critics on the defensive as any philosopher in history. There is no standard by which one can measure him without begging the question against him. His remarks about the tradition, and his remarks about the limitations the tradition has imposed on the vocabulary and imagination of his contemporaries, are beautifully designed to make one feel foolish when one tries to find a bit of common ground on which to start an argument. . . . Heidegger brilliantly carries to extremes a tactic used by every original philosopher. Heidegger is not the first to have invented a vocabulary whose purpose is to dissolve the problems considered by his predecessors, rather than to propose new solutions to them. . . . Heidegger's later style makes it easy to dismiss him as someone who has simply become tired of arguing, and who, taking refuge in the mystical, abandons the attempt to defend his almost-respectable earlier work. . . . It is as if to be a philosopher one had to have a certain minimal loyalty to the profession—as if one were not permitted to dissolve an old philosophical problem without being ready to put a new one in its place." As Rorty goes on to argue, what distinguishes Heidegger and Dewey is "the depth and extent of their commentary on the details of the tradition." In lieu of a new system of thought, "they each offer us an account of the dialectical course of the tradition. The self-image of a philosopher—his identification of himself as such (rather than as, perhaps, an historian or a mathematician or a poet)—depends almost entirely upon how he sees the history of philosophy."

61. Heidegger, *Pathmarks*, p. 271; *Wegmarken*, p. 357.

62. Heidegger, *Ponderings II–VI*, p. 23 (emphasis in original); *Überlegungen II–VI*, p. 30. The comment from the notebooks can be elucidated from a passage in Heidegger, *Introduction to Metaphysics*, p. 127; *Einführung in die Metaphysik*, pp. 128–29. After noting that logic as the science of *logos* (*epistēmē logikē*)—understood primarily as assertion—was supposed to be the doctrine of thinking, Heidegger warns the reader that "to appeal to logic for purposes of delimiting the essence of thinking is already a questionable enterprise, because logic as such, and not just its individual doctrines and theories, is still

something worthy of questioning. Thus 'logic' must be put in quotation marks. We do so not because we want to abjure 'the logical' (in the sense of correct thinking). In the service of thinking, we seek to attain precisely that which determines the essence of thinking, *alētheia* and *phusis*. Being as unconcealment, and this is precisely what was lost due to 'logic.'" On Heidegger's attempt to liberate thinking from the bonds of a subject-predicate grammar and logic, see Heller-Roazen, *No One's Ways*, pp. 228–38. And see the comprehensive study of Fay, *Heidegger: The Critique of Logic*.

63. Heidegger, *Contributions*, §91, p. 143; *Beiträge*, p. 183.

64. Heidegger, *Towards the Definition*, pp. 6–9; *Zur Bestimmung*, pp. 7–10.

65. Heidegger, *Towards the Definition*, p. 10; *Zur Bestimmung*, p. 12.

66. This passage, which is missing in the printed record of the lecture course, is cited in Kisiel, "*Kriegsnotsemester* 1919," p. 158. As Kisiel remarked (p. 204n7), he made use of Oskar Becker's distillation that was based on Franz Josef Brecht's transcript.

67. Heidegger, *Ponderings II–VI*, p. 275; *Überlegungen II–VI*, p. 378.

68. Heidegger, *Ponderings II–VI*, pp. 159–60 (emphasis in original); *Überlegungen II–VI*, pp. 218–19.

69. Heidegger, *Ponderings II–VI*, p. 208; *Überlegungen II–VI*, pp. 283–84.

70. Heidegger, *On the Way to Language*, p. 91; *Unterwegs zur Sprache*, pp. 185–86.

71. Heidegger, *On the Way to Language*, p. 92; *Unterwegs zur Sprache*, p. 187. For an attempt to think of Heidegger's *Denkweg* in Buddhist terms, see Hecker, "Eine buddhistische Würdigung."

72. Heidegger, *Ponderings II–VI*, p. 199; *Überlegungen II–VI*, p. 271.

73. Heidegger, *Ponderings II–VI*, pp. 6, 22, 23, 25, 44, 45, 47, 49, 72, 73; *Überlegungen II–VI*, pp. 6, 29, 32, 57, 59, 62, 64, 95, 97.

74. Critchley and Schürmann, *On Heidegger's Being and Time*, pp. 62–64.

75. For a fuller analysis of hermeneutics and time in Rosenzweig's new thinking, see Wolfson, *Giving*, pp. 54–64. In that discussion, I commented on affinities between Rosenzweig and Heidegger. See also Löwith, "F. Rosenzweig and M. Heidegger," and the German version with modifications, "M. Heidegger und F. Rosenzweig." A revised version of the English appears in Löwith, *Nature, History, and Existentialism*, pp. 51–78. For references to other scholarly analyses of Rosenzweig and Heidegger, see Wolfson, *Giving*, pp. 303–4n20, to which may be added Brito, *Heidegger et l'hymne*, pp. 477–88 (including a discussion of the motif of sacred time); Higgins, "Speaking and Thinking." Finally, let me note the astute observation of Altmann. Commenting on the fact that in the essay "Was ist Metaphysik?" Heidegger "based the fundamental attitude of metaphysical questioning on the givenness of the Nothing, experienced in dread, as the primary phenomenon" (*Meaning of Jewish Existence*, p. 7), Altmann wrote in the accompanying note (p. 158n27), "The close similarity of this point of departure to the fundamental experience of the reality of death in Franz Rosenzweig, *The Star of Redemption*, is remarkable." For more recent attempts that contrast the perspective on death in Heidegger and Rosenzweig, see Pattison, *Heidegger on Death*, pp. 56–59, 78–79; Bielik-Robson, "Love Strong as Death," pp. 171–76.

76. Arendt, "Martin Heidegger at Eighty," p. 298.

77. Trawny, *Freedom to Fail*, pp. 2–3. See also "Translators' Foreword" in Heidegger, *Parmenides*, p. xiii: "'Ways, not works' (*Wege, nicht Werke*)—that is the motto Heidegger placed at the head of his *Gesamtausgabe*. The difference is surely not that ways are meandering and tentative, works polished and final. . . . Heidegger had in mind something else entirely; perhaps we could say that for him a work is the work of an author but a way is a way of thought."

78. Heidegger, *What Is Called Thinking?*, p. 76 (emphasis in original); *Was Heißt Denken?*, p. 82. Compare the tribute to Heidegger in Arendt, *Thinking*, p. 432: "To me it seems that this life and work have taught us what *thinking* is, and that the writings will remain exemplary of that, and of the courage to venture into the immensity of the untrodden, to open oneself entirely to what is as yet unthought, a courage possessed only by him who turns himself entirely to thinking and its tremendous depth" (emphasis in original).

79. Derrida, *Of Spirit*, p. 11; *De l'esprit*, p. 25.

80. Shapiro, "Subversion of System," p. 3. Compare Mehta, *Martin Heidegger*, pp. 3–4, who noted that the "central thought" that informed all of Heidegger's work was "the unuttered thought of Being, the hidden source within him of all that he has said, but which no particular formulation fully and adequately expresses and which is not exhausted by all his writings taken together. Heidegger's 'philosophy', therefore, though systematic in the extreme, is not a system and, by reason of the very task it has set before itself, cannot be one. It is rather a trail blazed, a path traversed, a way taken by thought . . . toward the one goal enshrining in language, or rather preparing to do so, the unuttered thought of Being." Mehta's characterization of

Heideggerian thought as systematic in the extreme, on the one hand, and yet not conducive to being called a system, on the other hand, corresponds to my notion of the nonsystematic system, the system that subverts the notion of systematicity.

81. Laruelle, *Principles of Non-Philosophy*, p. 2 (emphasis in original).

82. Boeder, *Seditions*, p. 57.

83. Laruelle, *Principles of Non-Philosophy*, p. 20 (emphasis in original).

84. Laruelle, *Philosophy and Non-Philosophy*, pp. 177–210. Particularly pertinent to my argument is Laruelle's comment, pp. 199–200: "This is because the phenomenal content of the real or in general of the 'non-thetic,' which is more primitive than the Other, contains this *a priori* power of having suspended decision and the World. This power belongs to the (non-) One. It ultimately allows us to give a positive sense and a phenomenal content to the term 'non-Heideggerian,' for example, or more generally to the term 'non-philosophical.' It is manifested by the *neither* and the *nor* that suspend decision and position; and by another *nor* that suspends the synthesis or differe(a)nce of the first two negations and therefore decision itself, which can always return and take them up again; and lastly by a final *nor*, the dualitary *nor* that in reality has already preceded the first two, which both remain unitary, as well as the third, which remains that of transcendence as *a priori*, be it non-thetic or not. Here 'non-' is no longer acquired in simple opposition to Heideggerian or Derridean deconstruction, *which would once again be supposed given and given as inevitable*. . . . In this form, the 'non-,' instead of merely procuring for a decision a supplement of alterity masked and given in the symptom, *offers to whichever phenomenon to be interpreted a radical multiplicity of non-thetic attributes or universal points of view*; one would be tempted to say: a radical multiplicity of decisions for the same phenomenon. . . . Thus the concept of a post-deconstruction or of a 'non-Heideggerian' deconstruction . . . is not acquired through a relative and circular *negation* of Heideggerian, Derridean or other practices. . . . The *non-* here receives a more positive content than it could have in any philosophy whatsoever" (emphasis in original).

85. Laruelle, *Principles of Non-Philosophy*, p. 298: "Non-philosophy does not annul philosophy but regards it philosophically, it manifests philosophy as phenomenally sterile state-of-things, leaves it 'in state' as if it were without-philosophy. It accomplishes this outside of metaphysics." Compare the comments on Laruelle and Heidegger in Brassier, *Nihil Unbound*, pp. 121–22.

86. Heidegger, *Contributions*, §23, p. 47; *Beiträge*, p. 58.

87. Heidegger, *Contributions*, §23, p. 48 (emphasis in original); *Beiträge*, p. 59.

88. Heidegger, *Contributions*, §23, p. 47 (emphasis in original); *Beiträge*, p. 58. Consider the insightful comment concerning the phenomenological method undergirding Heidegger's ontology offered by Blumenberg, *Laughter of the Thracian Woman*, pp. 122–23: "Asking about the essence of the thing means getting to the bottom of that very thing, the return to which had been the founding call of phenomenology. It was not to become metaphysics at any price and could only have become that for the price of losing its reputation with the philosophy departments of the time. It did very quickly become metaphysics, whatever else it may be called. And metaphysics . . . always oversteps a boundary; but it does this under the pressure to continue questioning—a pressure which receives its energy from the lifeworld and from those elements of a situation that remain inescapable even after leaving it."

89. Heidegger, *End of Philosophy*, pp. 85 and 91–92; *Vorträge und Aufsätze*, pp. 69 and 77. On the distinction between *Überwindung* and *Verwindung*, see the note of Stambaugh, *End of Philosophy*, p. 84n1; and my own observations in Wolfson, *Giving*, pp. 100, 361n77, 385–86n289. To the sources mentioned in my previous study, one could now add Vattimo, *Of Reality*, pp. 150–51. Understanding overcoming as a form of zigzagging provides a response to the criticism of Rorty, *Consequences of Pragmatism*, pp. 53–54: "Heidegger hoped that a new path would open. But he thought we shall only see it open if we detach ourselves from the problems of men and are still; in that silence we may perhaps hear the word of Being. . . . By offering us 'openness to Being' to replace 'philosophical argument,' Heidegger helps preserve all that was worst in the tradition which he hoped to overcome."

90. Malabou, *Heidegger Change*, p. 21 (emphasis in original). The author acknowledges that Heidegger does not employ the word *Metamorphose*, but he does avail himself of *Verwandlung*, which has "the advantage of rendering change of route and change of form indistinguishable from each other" (p. 22).

91. Heidegger, *On the Way to Language*, p. 20; *Unterwegs zur Sprache*, p. 103. For a description of the transformation of thinking (*Verwandlung des Denkens*) as a passage (*Wanderung*) that requires putting the two sites—one identified as metaphysics and the

other left unnamed—into discussion, see Heidegger, *On the Way to Language*, p. 42; *Unterwegs zur Sprache*, p. 130. This may be a partial rejoinder to the criticism of Heidegger's appeal to the end of metaphysics offered by Jonas, "Heidegger and Theology," p. 223 (*Phenomenon of Life*, p. 252): "Certainly the language of the later Heidegger, in contrast to the rigorously ontological one of *Sein und Zeit*, has become increasingly and obtrusively ontic, and however figurative or poetical such language is meant to be (and poetic it is, even if bad poetry), its ontic meaning is inalienable from it on pain of its becoming empty sound. Let us then not be intimidated by the frown of the 'ontological difference' and acknowledge that, of course, 'being' is hypostatized in Heidegger, as was 'the good' in Plato and the '*causa sui*' in Spinoza, only, to be sure, not in the category of substance."

92. Heidegger, *Pathmarks*, p. 279; *Wegmarken*, p. 367. On Nietzsche's interpretation of the classification of the human as the *animal rationale* as signifying that the human is a willing animal, that is, the essence of human reason consists of the fact that the human is the animal determined through the thinking commensurate to the will to power, compare Heidegger, *Heraclitus*, pp. 169–70 (*Heraklit*, p. 224): "Around the time that Nietzsche was writing his *Zarathustra* and getting closer to his one, unique thought of the will to power (every thinker only thinks one thought); around this time Nietzsche recognized that the human up to this point, the *animal rationale*, was indeed an animal, but the 'animal' whose essence 'has not yet been established.' The task is therefore to understand decisively the essence of the *ratio* that determines the animal human, and according to the direction already set out step-by-step in contemporary thought. The essence of reason—and that means, subjectivity—is not mere thinking and reason, but rather the will: for in the will as self-willing, the positioning of the self toward itself first consummates itself as subjectivity. According to Nietzsche, however, the will is a will to power. The human is that animal who is determined through the thinking will to power, and is only thereby established in its metaphysical essence. . . . The human thus conceived, and therefore willed and also self-willing, goes beyond the prior human, the merely clever animal. As he who goes beyond the prior human, the future human of metaphysics is 'the over-human' ['*der Übermensch*'], the human of the will to power."

93. Sheehan, *Making Sense*, p. 15 (emphasis in original).

94. Heidegger, *Nietzsche*, Vol. 1: *The Will to Power as Art*, pp. 209–10; *Nietzsche: Erster Band*, pp. 212–13. See Sallis, "Twisting Free."

95. Heidegger, *Contributions*, §91, p. 143 (emphasis in original); *Beiträge*, p. 182.

96. Laruelle, *Principles of Non-Philosophy*, pp. 1–2.

97. Heidegger, *Schelling's Treatise*, p. 161; *Schelling: Vom Wesen*, p. 279.

98. Heidegger, *Nietzsche*, Vol. 1: *The Will to Power as Art*, p. 208; *Nietzsche: Erster Band*, p. 211.

99. Heidegger, *Contributions*, §253, p. 321 (emphasis in original); *Beiträge*, p. 405. For an extensive analysis of this motif, especially as it relates to Heidegger's notion of time-space, see Coriando, *Letzte Gott als Anfang*; and see Vallega-Neu, *Heidegger's Poietic Writings*, pp. 56–58. See also the analysis of the "last god's beginning" in Schalow, *Heidegger and the Quest for the Sacred*, pp. 131–62, and compare Vedder, *Heidegger's Philosophy of Religion*, pp. 157–87. And see the reference to my own study in ch. 4 n. 30.

100. Heidegger, *Contributions*, §253, p. 321; *Beiträge*, p. 405.

101. Heidegger, *End of Philosophy*, p. 96; *Vorträge und Aufsätze*, p. 81.

102. Heidegger, *Nietzsche*, Vol. 4: *Nihilism*, p. 227, *Nietzsche: Zweiter Band*, p. 335.

103. Heidegger, *What Is Called Thinking?*, p. 103; *Was Heißt Denken?*, p. 106.

104. Laruelle, *Principles of Non-Philosophy*, p. 2. See also Laruelle, *Non-Philosophy Project*, p. 2.

105. Laruelle, *Principles of Non-Philosophy*, pp. 2–3.

106. Ibid., p. 3. It is well to recall here the comments of Meillassoux, *After Finitude*, pp. 44–45, on the shift in contemporary philosophy from the Kantian unknowability of the thing-in-itself to its unthinkability: "Where the Parmenidean postulate, 'being and thinking are the same', remained the prescription for all philosophy up to and including Kant, it seems that the fundamental postulate of strong correlationism can be formulated thus: '*being and thinking must be thought as capable of being wholly other*'. Again, this is not to say that the correlationist believes herself to be in a position to declare the fundamental incommensurability between thought and being, such as by declaring the actual existence of a God incommensurable with all conceptualization, since this would assume a knowledge of the in-itself which she has completely abjured. But she sees herself as at least able to emphasize a facticity of the thought-being correlation so radical that it deprives her of any right to rule out the possibility of there being no common measure between the in-itself and what thought can conceive. This radicalization of the correlation had given rise to what we might call a '*possible whole alteration*' of thought and being. The unthinkable can only draw us back to

our inability to think otherwise, rather than to the absolute impossibility of things being wholly otherwise. It then becomes clear that this trajectory culminates in the disappearance of the pretension to *think* any absolutes, *but not in the disappearance of absolutes*, since in discovering itself to be marked by an irremediable limitation, correlational reason thereby legitimates *all* those discourses that claim to access an absolute, *the only proviso being that nothing in these discourses resembles a rational justification of their validity*. Far from abolishing the value of the absolute, the process that continues to be referred to today as 'the end of absolutes' grants the latter an unprecedented licence—philosophers seem to ask only one thing of these absolutes: that they be devoid of the slightest pretension to rationality. The end of metaphysics, understood as the 'de-absolutization of thought', is thereby seen to consist in the rational legitimation of any and every variety of religious (or 'poetico-religious') belief in the absolute, so long as the latter invokes no authority beside itself" (emphasis in original).

107. Laruelle, *Theory of Identities*, p. 80. Compare Laruelle, *Dictionary of Non-Philosophy*, p. 39: "Vision-in-One lifts the specific faith-in-the-real of philosophy, i.e. the philosophical hallucination of the Real. But this lifting is still nothing but a partial condition which is completed through another suspension, namely the unilateralizaion of the transcendental One, i.e. philosophy's divided One. . . . Vision-in-One concretely undercuts the importance of such dyads. The object is seen-in-One or dualyzed into a noetic and transcendental side and into a noematic content on the other side, which is the reduction of this object to the state of occasion." Ibid., 44: "Vision-in-One is the Given and gives-without-givenness ." Ibid., p. 165: "*First fundamental concept of non-philosophy, equivalent to the 'One-in-One' or the 'Real.' That which determines in-the-last-instance the theory and pragmatics of world-thought ('philosophy'). Vision-in-One is radically immanent and uni-versal; this is why it gives-without-givenness the givenness of world-thought*" (emphasis in original). For an elaboration of the given-without-givenness, see ibid., pp. 71–72. And compare the discussion of the givenness of non-philosophy in Laruelle, *Principles of Non-Philosophy*, pp. 191–92: "It is precisely this trait of radical actuality or Performed-without-Performation, of being-given identically without excess or reserve, which renders the real-One absolutely invisible for philosophy in its spontaneous state of sufficiency, and which makes this into an object of denegation for it when it is explicitly (or in thought) confronted. . . . In effect, the *phenomenon*, given par excellence with the One-in-One, is what only appears (to) itself without backdrop of non manifestation. It radicalizes the old phenomenological equation appearing = being, and resolves it through identity rather than through the 'same' of appearing and being. No distinction runs through this, sharing it between appearance and disappearance, or even between what appears, the appearing, and its apparition, at the risk of establishing the non-manifestation in manifestation. The One is thus no longer, unlike Being, that which is *prima facie* hidden: it is rather foreclosed *de jure* for all possible thought because it is *prima facie* manifest, on the condition of understanding this '*prima facie*' as primacy in relation to the play of philosophical veiling and unveiling, without possible play with its contrary, and as 'actually' and 'definitively' Manifested-before-all-Manifestation. . . . It gives the Given-without-Givenness which moreover is foreclosed . . . . The Real expects nothing from thought but it liberates it all the more in its specific work of givenness and of position" (emphasis in original). Laruelle's depiction of the Real and the non-phenomenology of givenness, and the rejection of the philosophical emphasis on disclosing the visible of the invisible or the thought of the unthought resembles the critique in Wolfson, *Giving*, pp. 227–60, of the persistent theological tendency to render the given as a gift, a notion of giving that implies volitional agency. In my judgment, as I argue in the aforementioned study, this is the implication of Heidegger's *es gibt* as well and hence, despite Laruelle's obvious criticism of Heidegger, his own views concerning the manifestation of the already-manifested as opposed to the not-still-manifested, may be much closer to the Heideggerian position than he entertained.

108. Laruelle, *Theory of Identities*, p. 82 (emphasis in original).

109. Laruelle, *Philosophies of Difference*, p. 39 (emphasis in original).

110. Ibid., p. 40. For a succinct critique of Heidegger, see Laruelle, *Dictionary of Non-Philosophy*, pp. 40–41: "Heidegger tried to reunite in 'Being' as ontological Difference (with being) the multiple significations and modalities of Being that philosophy had elaborated and dispersed. Thus there is not a more general, more transcendent or more encompassing concept than that of Being and its own unity and provenance (sense, truth, locality, etc.). Heidegger confirms the *telos* of every philosophy, namely, because Being is his main object (Being qua Being) and his element, whether it be a primordial-transcending, an ekstatico-horizontal and temporal opening, a 'clearing' and 'lighting' (Heidegger), or a

void and a pure multiple (Badiou). A law of essence wants the concepts of 'Being' to be inseparable from the duality of a division and of a more or less divided, even disseminated, horizon, i.e. inseparable from a multiple and a void without which it is unthinkable. Hence Heidegger's effort to simultaneously protect it from nothingness, the void and the nihilist 'vapor' in order to be delivered from Being by 'barring' it in a non metaphysical way. But nothing which is concerned with philosophy, with its attempt to think it starting from itself alone and its desire to rid itself of metaphysics can avoid positing Being as a presupposed that has primacy not only over being but also over the One that it affects by its own division, and partially over the Other."

111. Laruelle, *Principles of Non-Philosophy*, p. 5.

112. Heidegger, *Being and Time*, §72, pp. 355–56 (emphasis in original); *Sein und Zeit*, pp. 372–73.

113. Laruelle, *Principles of Non-Philosophy*, p. 5.

114. Ibid., pp. 98–101.

115. Ibid., pp. 92–93, 100 (emphasis in original). See above, n. 107.

116. Heidegger, *Contributions*, §259, p. 336; *Beiträge*, p. 425.

117. Krell, "Hegel Heidegger Heraclitus," pp. 32 and 42.

118. Laruelle, *Theory of Identities*, p. 129.

119. Here it is of interest to recall the critique of the "dominance of the mathematical" in Spinoza's understanding of system in Heidegger, *Schelling's Treatise*, pp. 32–34 (*Schelling: Vom Wesen*, pp. 56–59): "The realm of beings as a whole experienced in a Christian way is *re*-thought and *re*-created according to the lawfulness of thinking determining all Being in the form of a mathematical connection of foundations: *ordo et connexio idearum idem est ac ordo et connexio rerum* (Spinoza, *Ethics*, Part II, Propos. VII).... The sole completed system which is constructed all the way through in its foundational connection is the metaphysics of Spinoza which was published after his death under the title: *Ethica ordine geometrico demonstrata et in quinque partes distincta*.... The title already expresses the dominance of the *mathematical knowledge requirement—ordine geometrico*. The fact that this metaphysics, that is, science of beings as a whole, is called 'Ethics' is indicative that man's actions and behavior are of decisive importance for the kind of procedure in knowledge and the foundations of knowledge. But this system only became possible on the foundation of a peculiar one-sidedness.... The interpretations of Spinoza's system, which are very diverse in their orientation, usually contributed to thinking generally of a 'system' of philosophy as something like this very definite and one-sided system. The fact that Schelling's philosophy was interpreted as Spinozism belongs to that remarkable history of the misinterpretations of all philosophies by contemporaries. If Schelling *fundamentally fought against* a system, it is Spinoza's system" (emphasis in original). See Macherey, *In a Materialist Way*, pp. 125–35, esp. 126–30. On Schelling's critique of system, see the concise and cogent summary offered by Matthews, *Schelling's Organic Form*, pp. xi-xii. As opposed to Hegel's insistence that the systematic nature of philosophy demands that it exhibit a regular structure, Schelling upheld that philosophy must reflect the creative freedom of individual thinkers, and thus any system is, at best, a perspectival and limited account of the universality of human knowledge. In lieu of the mathematical model, Schelling embraced an organic and developmental model such that a system must be viewed as a seed that proliferates in multifarious manifestations. The telos of philosophy, consequently, "lies not in the gradual homogenization of thought into one all embracing logic, but rather in developing a multitude of systems, all of which should offer us ever more diverse and complex ways of understanding our existence."

120. Heidegger, *Contributions*, §28, p. 52; *Beiträge*, p. 65.

121. Heidegger, *Contributions*, §28, p. 52, §39, p. 65; *Beiträge*, pp. 65, 81–82. My analysis has benefited from the discussion in Vallega-Neu, *Heidegger's Contributions to Philosophy*, p. 32.

122. Heidegger, *Contributions*, §13, p. 30; *Beiträge*, p. 36. See the creative and daring examination of Pylkkö, *Aconceptual Mind*. The author explores at great length Heidegger's naturalization and cultural relativization, and even the avowal of Nazism, in light of the presumed aconceptuality of consciousness.

123. Hutcheon, *Poetics of Postmodernism*, p. 14. See also Kisiel, "Schelling's Treatise," pp. 297–300.

124. Heidegger, *Contributions*, §23, p. 48; *Beiträge*, pp. 59–60.

125. Heidegger, *Contributions*, §238, p. 293; *Beiträge*, p. 371.

126. The reference is to the 1955 memorial address offered by Heidegger in honor of Conradin Kreutzer. See Heidegger, *Discourse on Thinking*, pp. 43–57; *Gelassenheit*, pp. 9–26.

127. Lacoue-Labarthe, *Musica Ficta*, p. 91.

128. Heidegger, *Nietzsche*, Vol. 1: *The Will to Power as Art*, pp. 86–91; *Nietzsche: Erster Band*, pp. 85–91. On Heidegger's interpretation of Wagner, see Phillips, *Metaphysics and Music*, pp. 63–81.

129. As noted by Phillips, *Metaphysics and Music*, p. 7, in his discussion of this passage from Heidegger.

130. Heidegger, *Fundamental Concepts*, p. 67; *Grundbegriffe*, p. 101.

131. Hanly, "Dark Celebration," pp. 241–42. I accept Hanly's conclusion that music represents the changing register of thought for Heidegger but one that must be uncovered by discerning that "music will belong to thought precisely in such a way as to preclude its becoming an object of that thought. The silence that governs the presence of music in Heidegger's thinking will, then, belong to the very core of that presence. It is within the reflections on language that the play of a modality governed by the silent presence of music might be brought to light" (p. 242). Hanly makes no mention of the passage in the *Beiträge* that I have analyzed.

132. To be precise, in the original German no phrase corresponds explicitly to the words "of a movement," but this is implied by the statement "*sondern zugleich noch im musikalischen Sinne*," since one of the meanings of *Satz* is "movement" in the musical sense.

133. Heidegger, *Principle of Reason*, p. 89; *Satz vom Grund*, p. 132.

134. Heidegger, *Principle of Reason*, p. 89; *Satz vom Grund*, p. 132.

135. Heidegger, *Principle of Reason*, p. 89; *Satz vom Grund*, p. 132.

136. Heidegger, *Discourse on Thinking*, p. 44; *Gelassenheit*, p. 10.

137. Heidegger, *Principle of Reason*, pp. 89–90; *Satz vom Grund*, p. 133. Heidegger's thinking is elaborated by Boeder, *Seditions*, p. 53: "the ground is not the ground of reason but rather: reason is the reason of the ground. Yet this amounts to reason's dissolution as a form of consciousness and thus of the representation of objects, even if its object be only the longed-for-absolute, which reason knows to be its ground. For striving as the absolute activity of the ground, an activity related to representing, the object (*Gegenstand*) had already had the meaning of resistance (*Widerstand*)." Representational thinking exhausts itself in the experience of the resistant consciousness that opposes the representability of the absolute knowledge of the totality of being.

138. Heidegger, *Principle of Reason*, p. 90; *Satz vom Grund*, p. 133.

139. Heidegger, *Contributions*, §6, p. 18, §249, pp. 313–14; *Beiträge*, pp. 20–23, 395–96.

140. Heidegger, *Contributions*, §39, p. 64 (emphasis in original); *Beiträge*, p. 81. See Wolfson, *Language*, pp. 13–14.

141. Derrida, *Of Spirit*, p. 9 (emphasis in original); *De l'esprit*, pp. 24–25.

142. Heidegger, *Contributions*, §22, p. 46 (emphasis in original); *Beiträge* p. 57.

143. Derrida, *Of Spirit*, p. 17 (emphasis in original); *De l'esprit*, p. 36.

144. Wolin, ed., *Heidegger Controversy*, p. 32; Heidegger, *Selbstbehauptung*, p. 12.

145. Heidegger, *Ponderings II–VI*, p. 130 (emphasis in original); *Überlegungen II–VI*, p. 178.

146. Heidegger, *Ponderings VII–XI*, p. 200; *Überlegungen VII–XI*, p. 258.

147. Heidegger, *Ponderings VII–XI*, p. 176; *Überlegungen VII–XI*, p. 228. On Heidegger's meditative thinking and the need to incorporate aspects of the conceptual and the nonconceptual to reflect the nature of being's temporal becoming, see Rae, *Ontology in Heidegger and Deleuze*, pp. 87–115. As Rae points out, pp. 100–1, Heidegger's turn to poetry plays a crucial role in his effort to embrace a nonconceptual and nonrepresentational mode of thinking. It must be underscored, however, that poetic language is a mode of conveying the nonconceptual conceptually and disclosing the nonrepresentational representationally.

148. Heidegger, *Fundamental Concepts*, p. 292; *Grundbegriffe*, p. 423.

149. Heidegger, *What Is Called Thinking?*, p. 8; *Was Heißt Denken?*, p. 10.

150. Heidegger, *What Is Called Thinking?*, p. 17; *Was Heißt Denken?*, p. 19. On the centrality of questioning as "a fundamental happening of historical Being" (*ein Grundgeschehnis des geschichtlichen Seins*) related to the being of Dasein, see the seven essential points of the orientation (*die wesentlichen Richtpunkte*) for thinking delineated by Heidegger, *Introduction to Metaphysics*, pp. 152–53; *Einführung in die Metaphysik*, p. 152. I will cite the first four: "1. The determination of the human essence is never an answer, but is essentially a question. 2. The asking of this question is historical in the originary sense that this questioning first creates history. 3. This is the case because the question of what humanity is can be asked only in questioning about Being. 4. Only where Being opens itself up in questioning does history happen, and with it that Being of *the human being* [*des* Menschen] by virtue of which the human being ventures the confrontation [*die Auseinandersetzung*] with beings as such" (emphasis in original).

151. Wolfson, "Skepticism," p. 500.

152. Scholem, "On Jonah," p. 356.

153. *Zohar* 1:1b. Interestingly, in *Major Trends*, p. 220, Scholem refers to the kabbalistic identification of *Binah*, the divine intelligence, as *mi*, the "great Who," and surmises that this symbolism might suggest "the idea of an apotheosis of the well-known Jewish penchant for putting questions."

154. Scholem, *Judaica* 3, pp. 265–66. I have used the translation in Biale, "Gershom Scholem's Ten Unhistorical Aphorisms," p. 76.

155. Derrida, Gadamer, and Lacoue-Labarthe, *Heidegger, Philosophy, and Politics*, p. 9 (emphasis in original).

156. Laruelle, *Principles of Non-Philosophy*, p. 5.

157. Ibid., p. 43.

158. Heidegger, *Fundamental Concepts*, p. 298; *Grundbegriffe*, p. 432.

159. Rosenzweig, *Star of Redemption*, pp. 144–45; *Stern der Erlösung*, pp. 147–48. For a more extensive discussion of interconnectivity and the system of philosophy in Rosenzweig, see Wolfson, *Giving*, pp. 39–41. It is plausible that Rosenzweig's perspective is indebted to what Buber expressed in his predialogical philosophy on the relationship of the particular and the totality under the influence of Gustav Landauer. Thus, in a 1901 lecture sponsored by the *Neue Gemeinschaft*, Buber emphasized that the feeling of community (*Gemeinschaftsgefühl*), which stems from the unity of the I and the world, extends the inner commonality (*Gemeinsamkeit*) of the cosmos, experienced in those sacred moments, to the existential particularity (*Eigenheit*) of each thing. In the unending unity of becoming, which is the universe, there is no incongruity between the general and the particular. See Mendes-Flohr, *From Mysticism to Dialogue*, pp. 57–58; Wolfson, "Theolatry," pp. 10–12.

160. Wolfson, *Language*, pp. 88–89; Wolfson, "Structure," pp. 156–59. The novelty of my attempt to discern an affinity between criticism of system, especially as promoted by German idealism, and the resistance to a totalizing thinking that subsumes the multitude of individuals under a universal in both Heidegger and the kabbalah, is highlighted by considering the following remark of Boeder, *Seditions*, p. 243: "The system is thus a totality of totalities, brought to completion in Hegel's *Science of Logic*. This work knows only one idea, the pure concept, which determines itself by way of its methodical distinction within itself. . . . What is thought in this way has to give the impression within the horizon of the pluralistic mentality of being mere quibbling. Its interest would much rather be engaged by the Kabala."

161. Scott, *Time of Memory*, p. 174. The perspective I have articulated can be profitably compared as well to the view regarding the nexus between chaos, system, and the apophatic proffered by Rosen, "Accessing Creativity"; and Rosen, "Lessons From Dada."

162. Hegel, *Science of Logic*, p. 110: "The finite has thus vanished into the infinite and what *is*, is only the *infinite*" (emphasis in original); *Wissenschaft der Logik*, vol. 1, bk. 1, p. 125.

163. Hegel, *Science of Logic*, p. 89; *Wissenschaft der Logik*, vol. 1, bk. 1, p. 103.

164. Badiou and Žižek, *Philosophy in the Present*, pp. 26–48.

165. Nancy, *Being Singular Plural*, p. 3 (emphasis in original). The intent of the state of *being singular plural* is rendered more clearly in Nancy, *Gravity of Thought*, pp. 65–66: "We are the plural that does not multiply a singular—as if we were the collective figure of a sole reality . . . but that, on the contrary, singularizes a common dispersion, this time irreducibly material *and* absolutely spiritual. We are the community of meaning, and this community has no signification; it does not subsume under a Meaning the exteriority of its parts, nor the succession of its moments, since it is the element of meaning only insofar as it is exposed by and to this exteriority and succession. . . . It is as manifest as the face-to-face or the between-us that indefinitely constitutes us. This manifestation is without secret because it is without signification" (emphasis in original). I concur with Nancy but I would argue that it is precisely because the manifestation is without signification that it is a mystery of self-evasion, a secret that can be revealed only to the extent that it is concealed.

166. Nancy, *Hegel*, p. 33. On the phenomenology of singularizing the singularity of the other, see Bozga, *Exasperating Gift of Singularity*, pp. 183–239.

167. Nancy, *Hegel*, p. 38: "What is unsettling is that the negative of manifestation should turn out to be nothing hidden or nonmanifest. The laziness and repose of thought is always to give itself over to some nonmanifest thing, to which one will lend, depending on the occasion, the pomp of the most spectacular figures and ornaments, the imposing glimmer of cults or arts, the prestige of names or powers, and even the enthusiasm or elevation of great thoughts. But the greatness of Thought is in the simplicity of the decision that turns itself toward naked manifestation."

168. The statement is part of the second poetic epigraph in Heidegger, *Über den Anfang*.

169. The expression is appropriated from Tonner, *Heidegger, Metaphysics and the Univocity of Being*.

170. This emphasis on the individual is indicative of Heidegger's turn away from a more monolithic approach in *Sein und Zeit*, especially as it relates to death, which tolerates nothing beyond itself and is therefore functioning like the whole (All-One) in idealism. See Adorno, *Jargon of Authenticity*, p. 140. On uniqueness (*Einmaligkeit*) and singularity (*Einzigkeit*) as they pertain to the event of beyng—the concreteness of the moment—as opposed to the substance of a being, see Ziarek, "On Heidegger's

Einmaligkeit Again"; Vallega-Neu, *Heidegger's Poietic Writings*, pp. 17, 24, 58, 99, 122, 126, 154, 160, 171–72, 179–80, 192. A future investigation that might bear fruit would be to evaluate Heidegger's emphasis on *Einzigkeit* in light of the quantum notion of particularity. For a nontechnical account of this concept, see Rovelli, *Order of Time*, pp. 31–33: "If we think about it carefully, *every configuration is particular*, every configuration is singular, if we look at *all* of its details, since every configuration always has something about it that characterizes it in a unique way. . . .The notion of 'particularity' is born only at the moment we begin to see the universe in a blurred and approximate way. . . . The difference between past and future is deeply linked to this blurring. . . . So if I could take into account all the details of the exact, microscopic state of the world, would the characteristic aspects of the flowing of time disappear? Yes. If I observe the microscopic state of things, then the difference between past and future vanishes. . . . We often say that causes precede effects and yet, in the elementary grammar of things, there is no distinction between 'cause' and 'effect.' There are regularities, represented by what we call physical laws, that link events of different times, but they are symmetric between future and past. In a microscopic description, there can be no sense in which the past is different from the future" (emphasis in original). See ch. 6 n. 140. The quantum insight that particularity is commensurate to the blurring of our perspective (Rovelli, *Order of Time*, p. 34) can be profitably compared to Heidegger's insight that the concealing of untruth is essential to the unveiling of truth.

171. Kierkegaard, *Fear and Trembling*, p. 46n57. I have aligned myself with Kierkegaard's notion of *den Enkelte* without appropriating the religious dimension implied thereby. See Kierkegaard, *Fear and Trembling*, p. 47: "Faith is exactly this paradox, that the single individual is higher than the universal, but in such a way, mind you, that the movement is repeated, so that after having been in the universal he now as the particular keeps to himself as higher than the universal." Kierkegaard's idea of the *Enkelte*, the single individual, is the concept of the limit that delimits the limit of the concept and renders the Absolute unnamable and unknowable. See Kline, *Passion for Nothing*, pp. 37–38. My gratitude to Lucas Wright for drawing my attention to this work. For an abbreviated presentation, see Kline, "Infinite Reduplication."

172. Leahy, *Beyond Sovereignty*, p. 44.

173. Leahy, *Faith and Philosophy*, pp. 62–63. The shared indebtedness to the Kierkegaardian notion of the individual links the reflections on the singularity of being expressed respectively by Heidegger and Leahy, even though the latter is critical of the former. See, for instance, Leahy, *Beyond Sovereignty*, p. 71: "For Badiou what there is is nothing else than differences, what there is is infinite alterity. Infinite alterity *is*, the situation *is*, the world *is*. In the thinking now occurring this infinite alterity that is the essence of the world is otherwise than being—neither being nor not being: infinite alterity/what there is the essence of the world begins absolutely now . . . infinite alterity otherwise than being—essence the exception to essence beginning absolutely now" (emphasis in original). In the continuation of that passage, Leahy attempts to contrast his affirmation of the radical particularity of being implied in the universality of divine omnipotence from Badiou's view that "the world remains as the nonsublatable substrate of infinite differences: differences are subsumed by sameness but not thereby sublated: differences are not contradicted but supplanted by the universal, but therefore supplanted in the form of an infinite procedure, the conception of whose completion is the creative fiction that forces the transformation of the situation." It seems that, in his mind, Leahy proffered an even more radical sense of the infinite alterity for which there is no sameness that would level out the differences of each particular embodied manifestation of the eventfulness of being. See Leahy, *Beyond Sovereignty*, p. 85, where he explains that the claim "same for all" implies a "circulation of sense" that is "infinitely interrupted" and hence "infinitely open to the newness of existence," the "existence of truth as *singularity absolutely particularized*—singularity actually embodied in existing omnipotence." And compare ibid., p. 89: "It follows from the omnipotent unconditioned embodiment of every-thing for the first time that nothing is not contained in nothing. Every-thing except nothing contained in nothing is embodied in omnipotence—every-thing embodied in omnipotence is the actual annulment of the void. There is then nothing but infinite alterity. There is no Same to which the infinity of differences might be compared. There is nothing but the infinitely evental being of existence itself—being-here infinitely that identifies the readiness of consciousness whose readiness for being is the form of faith." I find Leahy's depiction of the omnipotent embodiment of polyontological difference as the annulment of the void to be compatible with Heidegger's reflections on the nothingness of beyng, bracketing the obvious disparity generated by Leahy's commitment to the faith of his Christian heritage. I detect a similarity to Heidegger as well in the rejection of an

idealist resolution to the problem of sameness and difference in Leahy, *Beyond Sovereignty*, p. 104: "The disorganization that *is* organization, the disorder that *is* order, is a not a breaking in two of a One. Nor is unity, unbroken by the infinite alterity of existence itself, a Same. The unity beyond the One—the unity beginning absolutely now—is the absolute otherness of omnipotence itself now embodying that which embodied omnipotence when hitherto omnipotence compared itself to the creature. As such the unity beyond the One, unity *ex abysso*, is the simplicity that is existence itself: the simplicity of omnipotence the embodiment of infinite & unconditional difference(s)" (emphasis in original).

174. Heidegger, *Contributions*, §29, p. 53; *Beiträge*, p. 66. Compare Heidegger, *Heraclitus*, p. 76 (*Heraklit*, pp. 101–2) where *phusis*, identified as "the foundational word of inceptual thinking" (*das Grundwort des anfänglichen Denkens*), is understood as "the pure emerging [*das reine Aufgehen*] in whose prevalence any appearing thing appears and thus 'is,' without specifying any particular being such as mountain, sea, or animal."

175. Hegel, *Philosophy of Mind*, p. 5.

176. Nishida, *Inquiry into the Good*, pp. 17–18. See Nishida, *Intelligibility and the Philosophy of Nothingness*, pp. 71–72: "What is called Self or Ego, is beyond the determinations of space and time; it is the individual in the abyss of the individual in space and time. In thinking such an individual, it is implied that this individual has its place and is determined by a Universal. . . . I have called it the Universal of self-consciousness, because self-consciousness has its place in this Universal, and is determined by it." Compare the articulation of this point in Nishida's 1935 study "The Standpoint of Active Intuition," in *Ontology of Production*, pp. 98–99: "We say that the historical world possesses a circumference, but the transcendent is qua immanent, and the immanent is qua transcendent. What we call active intuition is absolute negation-qua-affirmation, absolute affirmation-qua-negation. That is to speak of the continuity of the absolutely discontinuous, the mutual determination of singularity and singularity; it is to say the many are the one. . . .To say that a thing acts is perforce to say that the totality changes. To say that a singularity determines the singularity itself, to say that the thing acts, is to say that the thing affirms itself on the basis of itself negating itself. . . . The aspect of the self-determination of the dialectical universal, the aspect of the continuity of the discontinuous, must possess the sense of something like a reflecting mirror. To speak of reflection is to say that the absolutely other is the self; it is to say that the figure of the self is the self." See ibid., p. 125: "What exists is determined as a single limit of the dialectical world. It is for this reason that the more what exists is determined, the more singular it is, then the more global it is, that is, the more universal it is. . . . In the dialectical world a singularity must be conceived itself absolutely to determine itself. It is necessarily both that which, being a single limit, is determined and that which is possessed of a single tendency that determines the entire world." See Nishida's formulation in *Place and Dialectic*, p. 108: "The dialectic of absolute negation, however, must be such that individual determination is universal determination and universal determination is individual determination, time is space and space is time. That an individual thing determines itself means that it becomes itself by negating others and in due time becomes universal by negating itself. And that the universal determines itself means that it individuates itself and in due time becomes an individual thing by negating itself." See ibid., p. 120: "Active form is that in which the spatial is temporal and the temporal is spatial. The self-determination of the eternal now, wherein time is space and space is time, is through formative acts." And p. 131: "The self-determination of the eternal now wherein absolutely time is space and space is time would thus have to be thoroughly formative and creative as historical life. . . . We can say that while we are born we are also not born. . . . Only human beings possess a present." On the identification of space and time in Nishida's thought, see ch. 6 n. 39. Nishida's concept of nothingness and the self-determination of the individual has been discussed by a number of scholars: Carter, *Nothingness*, pp. 81–99; Carter, "God and Nothingness"; Carter, *Kyoto School*, pp. 35–40; Nishitani, *Nishida Kitarō*, pp. 49–55, 161–76, 181–82, 205–12, 219–21; Heisig, *Philosophers of Nothingness*, pp. 61–64; Wargo, *Logic of Nothingness*, pp. 75–88.

177. Krummel, *Nishida Kitarō's Chiasmatic Chorology*.

178. Nishida, *Intelligibility and the Philosophy of Nothingness*, pp. 163–64. Compare ibid., p. 231: "In the world of unity of opposites it is identical to say that the individual forms itself, and that the world forms itself. And, the other way round, it is identical to say that the world forms itself, and that the individual forms itself. The many and the one, negating each other, become that which is 'from the formed towards the forming'. . . . To let the individual many live, is the life of the one whole . . . And the life of the whole one is the life of the individual many." See Nishida, *Last Writings*, p. 68: "In what sense, then, is the absolute the true absolute? It is truly absolute by

being opposed to nothing. It is absolute being only if it is opposed to absolutely nothing. Since there can be nothing at all that objectively opposes the absolute, the absolute must relate to itself as a form of self-contradiction. It must express itself by negating itself." See the summary of Nishida's perspective in Krummel, *Nishida Kitarō's Chiasmatic Chorology*, p. 161: "For Nishida, the individual's free act is the world's self-determination, and vice-versa, in dialectical inter-determination. Because the absolute is nothing but the field or place of individuals, history is made by the free acting of individuals qua historical bodies, moving as creative elements of that world's self-creativity. Nishida claims that his dialectic, in contrast to Hegel's, thus permits the individual to be thoroughly individual." Krummel's explication (pp. 21–26) of Nishida's epistemology of the pure experience (*junsui keiken*) of the place (*basho*) of true nothing (*shin no mu*), the field of consciousness that yields the concrete universal that is distinguished from Hegel's view—that is, the undifferentiated wholeness prior to the dichotomization between subject and object, being and nonbeing, ideal and real, the self-forming formlessness of the absolute nothing (*zettai mu*) that assumes the haecceity of the plethora of beings through self-differentiation, the consciousness immersed within the depths of consciousness, the nothing of nothing, the negation of negation (Nishida, *Place and Dialectic*, p. 73)—corresponds to my interpretation of Heidegger's idea of *Seyn/Nichts* and the kabbalistic *Ein Sof* as the nothingness that is beyond the distinction between something and nothing, the voiding of voidness. Concerning the latter expression, see Wargo, *Logic of Nothingness*, p. 84. Krummel, *Nishida Kitarō's Chiasmatic Chorology*, pp. 141–64, offers a more detailed exposition of Nishida and Hegel. For a different perspective, see the extensive analysis in Suares, *Kyoto School's Takeover*, pp. 1–102. On the phenomenological contours of Nishida's Buddhist-inflected idea of pure experience, see Nishida, *Inquiry into the Good*, pp. 3–34; Heisig, *Philosophers of Nothingness*, pp. 42–47; Carter, *Nothingness*, pp. 1–15; Wargo, *Logic of Nothingness*, pp. 34–46; Yusa, *Zen and Philosophy*, pp. 96–102; Botz-Bornstein, "Nishida and Wittgenstein," pp. 56–59. On the topographical dimension of Nishida's concept of *basho* as the place of nothingness, see Nishitani, *Nishida Kitarō*, pp. 162–63, 219–20; Abe, "Nishida's Philosophy of 'Place'"; Carter, *Nothingness*, pp. 16–57; Wargo, *Logic of Nothingness*, pp. 90–178; Yusa, *Zen and Philosophy*, pp. 202–9.

179. Merleau-Ponty, *Visible and the Invisible*, p. 94 (emphasis in original).

180. Badiou, *Being and Event*, p. 28.

181. Ibid., p. 30 (emphasis in original).

182. Ibid., pp. 123–29, esp. 125–26: "For Heidegger, the poetico-natural orientation, which lets-be presentation as non-veiling, is the authentic origin. The mathematico-ideal orientation, which subtracts presence and promotes evidence, is the metaphysical closure, the first step of the forgetting. What I propose is not an overturning but *another* disposition of these two orientations. I willingly admit that absolutely originary thought occurs in poetics and in the letting-be of appearing. . . . Ontology strictly speaking, as native figure of Western philosophy, is not, and cannot be, the arrival of the poem in its attempt to name, in brazen power and coruscation, appearing as the coming-forth of being, or non-latency. . . . What constituted the Greek event is rather the *second* orientation, which thinks being subtractively in the mode of an ideal or axiomatic thought. The particular invention of the Greeks is that being is expressible once a decision of thought subtracts it from any instance of presence. The Greeks did not invent the poem. Rather they *interrupted* the poem with the matheme. . . . The 'Western' configuration of thought combines the accumulative infinity of subtractive ontology and the poetic theme of natural presence" (emphasis in original). See the passage from *Being and Event* cited in ch. 5 at n. 239. On the relationship between scientific/mathematical truths and artistic/poetic truths in Badiou, compare Phelps, "(Theo)poetic Naming." Badiou's critique of Heidegger's poetic ontology is discussed by Phelps, pp. 34–35. On Badiou and Heidegger, see Hallward, *Badiou*, pp. 56–57, 77–78, 199–200, 355n69, 389n17; Hewson, "Heidegger"; Harman, "Badiou's Relation to Heidegger"; and the comments of Kenneth Reinhard in Badiou and Cassin, *Heidegger*, pp. xi–xv.

183. Badiou, *Being and Event*, p. 31.

184. Van der Heiden, *Ontology*, pp. 30–34. The author contrasts Badiou and Heidegger on p. 33.

3

Heidegger's Seyn/Nichts and Kabbalistic Ein Sof

Whatever philosophy is, and however it may exist at any given time, it defines itself solely on its own terms. . . . Its proper essence turns ever toward itself, and the more original a philosophy is, the more purely it soars in turning about itself, and therefore the farther the circumference of its circle presses outward to the brink of nothingness.

Heidegger, *Nietzsche: The Will to Power as Art*

The leitmotif of this chapter revolves around the hypothesis that Heidegger's notion of *Seyn*, which is crucial to his inceptual thinking of a new beginning, can be fruitfully compared to the theosophic speculation on the infinite nothingness attested in kabbalistic texts since the High Middle Ages. Both Heidegger and the kabbalists can be viewed as embracing a path of thought radically open to what is construed as the unthought, or in the language of Nicholas of Cusa, the concept of pure negativity, the negative self-refraction of the not-other that is consummately other.[1] What Heidegger calls *Seyn* is marked semantically by kabbalists as *Ein Sof*,[2] the name that names the name that is beyond all names, the name that is nameless.[3] Here it is worth mentioning the passage from Heidegger's "Brief über den 'Humanismus,'" to the effect that one finds one's way into the nearness of being by learning "to exist in the nameless [*Namenlosen*],"[4] which Derrida already compared to the kabbalistic conception of the "unnameable possibility of the Name."[5] And let us recall as well the comment attributed to the inquirer—a literary cipher that clearly represents Heidegger—in "Aus einem Gespräch von der Sprache," written in 1953–54 on the occasion of a visit by Tezuka Tomio of the Imperial University of Tokyo,[6] as a rejoinder to why the terms *hermeneutics* and *phenomenology* were dropped from the philosophical lexicon: "That was done, not—as is often thought—in order to deny the significance of phenomenology, but in order to abandon my own path of thinking [*Denkweg*] to namelessness [*Namenlosen*]."[7]

The namelessness to which Heidegger alludes is the *Seyn* that is *Nichts*, the beyng that is nothing, which is not to be decoded as the identity of antinomies characteristic of the Hegelian dialectic, but as the belonging together of the same that persists as irreducibly discrete. Heidegger had this in mind when he marked as the ultimate truth (*der letzten Wahrheit*) that "even nothingness itself is not present without being" (*daß selbst das Nichts nicht west ohne das Sein*).[8] This is not to say that nothingness is present as a representable being but rather that nothingness cannot be without being, that nothingness and being are juxtaposed in the sameness of their difference. Nothingness, on this score, is no longer conceived as nonbeing (*Nichtseiende*) in the sense of a negative determination (*negative Bestimmung*); it is rather the nullity (*Nichtige*) or negativity (*Nichthaftigkeit*) of being, the "highest gift" imparted as the "self-withdrawing" of the refusal.[9] As Heidegger writes in his notebooks from October 1931, "We stand before nothingness [*Nichts*]—to be sure, but in such a way that we do not put nothingness and this standing into effect, do not know how to put them into effect—cowardice and blindness before the opening of the being that bears us into beings." Glossing his own remark that we stand before nothingness, Heidegger explains, "Indeed, not before nothingness—instead, before each and every thing, but *as nonbeings* [un-seiendem]."[10]

The import of this statement and the explanatory comment is made clear in a succeeding aphorism: "*Nothingness*—which is higher and deeper than *nonbeings* [Un-Seiende]—too great and worthy for any individual or all together to stand before it. Nonbeings—which are less than nothingness—because expelled from the being that negates all beings [*weil ausgestoßen aus dem Sein, das alles Seiende nichtet*]."[11] Anticipating the ontological difference between being and beings, Heidegger insists that nothingness is higher than all nonbeings—it is the being that negates all beings. Unlike the *Un-Seiende*, which can be imagined as slipping into the "semblance of beyng" (*Anschein des Seyns*),"[12] the *Nichts* is not something negative (*weder negativ*), a *negativum*,[13] but the "nonbeyng" (*Nichtseyn*) that is the essence (*Wesen*) that occurs essentially in the nonessence (*Unwesen*).[14] Interestingly, in another passage from the notebooks, Heidegger writes, "what is most question-worthy is beyng; it is most worthy because it possesses the highest rank of all beings and in all beings. Beyng is the aether in which mankind breathes. Beyng as (event)."[15] In the course of time, Heidegger would modify this view by elevating *Seyn* above being and beings, that is, it is the beyng that is neither being nor nonbeing. He would also let go of the metaphor of the ether—an image coincidentally used by kabbalists to depict *Keter* or the divine nothingness—but he would maintain the depiction of *Seyn* as *Ereignis*, an event or a happening rather than a substance or an entity.

Autoerotic Quivering, Noetic Jouissance, and Divinizing the Infinite

Quite remarkably, Heidegger deploys mythical and polytheistic language to depict the fissure (*Zerklüftung*) "in virtue of which beyng is the realm of decision [*das Entscheidungsreich*] for the battle among the gods. This battle is waged over their advent [*Ankunft*] and absconding [*Flucht*]; it is the battle in which the gods first divinize and bring their god into decision [*Entscheidung*]. Beyng is the trembling of this divinization [*die Erzitterung dieses Götterns*]."[16] In the same spirit, Heidegger wrote in his notebooks, "*Beyng*—self-refusal as the trembling of the divinizing of the last god [*die Verweigerung als die Erzitterung des Götterns des letzten Gottes*]. The trembling is a keeping open [*das Offenhalten*]—indeed even the openness of the spatiotemporal field [*Offene des Zeit-Spiel-Raums*] of the 'there' [*des Da*] for Dasein."[17] Although this rhetoric seems distant from the kabbalists, Heidegger shares with them a disruption of the solipsism of the metaphysical ground of thought thinking itself, the Aristotelian description of God as the unmoved mover,[18] a conception that had a huge impact on the philosophical-theological imagination of Judaism, Christianity, and Islam as it evolved in the Middle Ages. In place of this relatively benign conception, Heidegger proffers a portrait of being that is decidedly belligerent: the primordial fracture inflames the spirit of struggle (*Kampf*) among the gods in which they divinize and bring their god into decision, the self-refusal of being, the *trembling of the divinizing of the last god*. On the surface, the word "divinizing" seems redundant, but the redundancy underscores that the combat itself is essential to the theocratic act of decision that, ironically, results in the flight of the calculable gods (*Götter*) and the dawning of the inestimable essence of divinity (*Gottwesen*),[19] a double concealment in virtue of which the nonbeing of beyng dissembles as the being of nonbeing—the theological corollary of the metaphysical effacing of the ontological difference between beings and beyng,[20] what Heidegger at one point actually labeled the "theological difference" to name the attempt to think the difference of God vis-à-vis beings, beingness, and being (*der Unterschied des Gottes vom Seienden, von der Seiendheit und vom Sein*).[21] As a consequence of the dissimulation of the nullity of beyng as something negative, apparent divinities become indistinguishable from true divinities, the one as the other are present only in the absence of their presence—in the vacuity, or literally the spiritlessness (*Geistlosigkeit*), that is the flight of the gods (*Flucht der Götter*)[22]—and thus are manifest in the nonappearance of their appearance and concealed in the appearance of their nonappearance.[23] The trembling results, moreover, in the openness of the spatiotemporal field—the abyss as time-space—that makes possible the "appropriating event" that "destines the human being to be the property [*Eigentum*] of beyng."[24]

To speak of *Seyn* as *Er-eignis*, and of the belongingness (*Zugehörigkeit*) of the latter as the property that is the distinguishing destiny of the human being, does not imply that the event can ever "be represented immediately and objectively. The appropriation is the oscillation between humans and gods and is precisely this 'between' itself and its essential occurrence which is grounded through and in Da-sein."[25] What Heidegger wished to communicate is clarified by another comment in the *Beiträge*, "The inventive thinking [*Er-denken*] of beyng leaps into beyng as the 'between' [*Zwischen*] in whose self-clearing essential occurrence the gods and humans come to mutual recognition, i.e., decide about their mutual belonging. As this 'between,' beyng 'is' not a supplement to beings, but is what essentially occurs such that in its truth they (beings) can first attain the preservation proper to beings."[26] Heidegger emphatically denies that the notion of god should be equated with the nonmetaphysical event of being: "The god is neither a 'being' ['*seiend*'] nor a 'nonbeing' ['*unseiend*'] and is also not to be identified with *beyng*. Instead, *beyng* essentially occurs in the manner of time-space as that 'between' which can never be grounded in the god and also not in the human being (as some objectively present, living thing) but only in *Da-sein*."[27] The between into which the thinking of beyng leaps is the clearing wherein humans and gods come to the discrimination of their mutual belonging, which, as we have seen, implies the concurrence rather than the coincidence of what remains separate:

> The event consigns [*übereignet*] god to the human being by assigning [*zueignet*] the human being to god. This consigning assignment is the appropriating event [*Diese übereignende Zueignung ist Ereignis*]; in it, the *truth* of beyng is grounded as Da-sein (and the human being is transformed [*verwandelt*], set out into the decision of being-there [*Da-sein*] and being-away [*Weg-sein*]), and history takes its other beginning from beyng. The truth of beyng, however, as the openness of the self-concealing [*Offenheit des Sichverbergens*], is at the same time transposition [*Entrükkung*] into the decision regarding the remoteness and nearness of the gods and so is preparedness for the passing by of the last god. The event is the "between" in regard to both the passing by of the god and the history of mankind.[28]

Humanity and divinity meet in the space of the between that preserves their distinct identities such that they abide in the distance of intimacy.[29] That beyng is identified as the between—concurrently revealed and concealed by Dasein[30] as the playing field of time-space [*Zeit-Spiel-Raum*] within which "the sheltering of the truth of beings interpenetrates with the absconding and advent of the gods"[31]—is another way for Heidegger to articulate the idea that beyng is nothing, the void that engenders and sustains—by withdrawing from—all beings. Noteworthy is the fact that the decision in this case is not made by gods against one another but by humans and gods jointly, and curiously, without being combative. By contrast, the act of theopoiēsis, the divinization of god, is a consequence of the strife between gods and not between humanity and the gods.

An interesting conceptual parallel to the Heideggerian motif of the trembling, which comes into the open as self-refusal, can be found in the teachings promulgated in the late sixteenth and early seventeenth centuries by Israel Saruq[32] about the jouissance (*sha'ashu'a*) associated with the initial withdrawal or constriction (*ṣimṣum*) of the light of infinity.[33] The utilization of the term *sha'ashu'a* to depict God's relation to the Torah prior to the creation of the world is found in older rabbinic sources and is based on the description of Wisdom in Proverbs (8:30) and echoed in Psalms (119:77, 92, 143).[34] The Saruqian materials also reflect the connotation of this term in the writings of previous kabbalists[35]—including especially the zoharic compilation, where it is connected most frequently to the theme of God taking delight with the souls of the righteous in the Garden of Eden,[36] and Moses Cordovero (1522–70), where it connotes, *inter alia*, the infinite's contemplation of its own essence, which is beyond human comprehension,[37] the first stirrings of the divine will to be garbed in the sefirotic gradations.[38] The erotic element amplified in the Lurianic sources is latent in some of the passages in Cordovero's voluminous corpus.[39]

One of the bolder articulations of this myth is found in an anonymous Lurianic text that begins with the startling assertion "Before all the emanation *Ein Sof* was alone bemusing himself" (*qodem kol ha-aṣilut hayah ha-ein sof levado mishta'ashe'a be-aṣmuto*).[40] From the continuation, which describes the emergence of the letter *yod*—a cipher for the seminal point of divine wisdom—from the infinite, we can deduce that this text is a commentary on the notoriously difficult zoharic passage linked to the first verse of Genesis, "In the beginning of the decree of the king, the hardened spark engraved an engraving in the supernal luster" (*be-reish hurmenuta de-malka galif gelufei bi-ṭehiru illa'ah boṣina de-qardinuta*).[41] I render the term *sha'ashu'a* as *bemusement*—understood in an antiquated sense as to gaze meditatively or to ruminate and not in the more conventional connotation to be puzzled or to be bewildered[42]—to capture in a Lacanian fashion the dual connotation of jouissance as erotic rhapsody and noetic bliss.[43] When I translate the idiom of these texts as the infinite bemusing itself, what I have in mind is an ecstatic amusement that is of a contemplative nature. The rapturous nature of the kabbalistic *sha'ashu'a* is simultaneously cerebral and somatic. The theme of the demiurgic playfulness of *Ein Sof* is highlighted by Saruq:

> You must know that prior to everything, the blessed holy One bemused himself [*mishta'ashe'a be-aṣmo*], that is, he was joyous and he took delight. . . . And from the quivering [*ni'anu'a*] of the spark the Torah was created. . . . Know that the quivering that arose from the bemusement consisted of ten quiverings, corresponding to the *yod*, and they are the ten letters whence every tenfold derives.[44] When the blessed holy One was being amused prior to the [existence of the worlds of] emanation, creation, formation, and doing, and before everything, the blessed One filled all the worlds, that is, [he was] the place wherein it was appropriate for all the worlds to be created, he made a garment [*levush*] from the light of his essence, which is the Torah.[45]

Paraphrasing this text, Scholem wrote, "In the beginning *Ein-Sof* took pleasure in its own autarkic self-sufficiency, and this 'pleasure' produced a kind of 'shaking' (*ni'anu'a*) which was the movement of *Ein-Sof* within itself. Next, this movement 'from itself to itself' aroused the root of *Din*, which was still indistinguishably combined with *Raḥamim*. As a result of this 'shaking,' 'primordial points' were engraved in the power of *Din*, thus becoming the first forms to leave their markings in the essence of *Ein-Sof*."[46]

Scholem does not explicitly dwell on the fact that the self-pleasure is a form of erotic arousal.[47] There is no room to doubt, however, that this was the intent of Saruq's elaborate version of the jouissance of *Ein Sof*, and especially the trembling whence the garment of Torah was concocted from the primordial points in the space within the infinitivity that cannot be circumscribed spatially.[48] The sexual innuendo of this mythic structure is more pronounced in a second passage wherein a metaphor from human sensuality is provided to illumine the nature of the infinite's autoerotic throbbing:

> Just as when a person is happy, he pleasures himself [*mishta'ashe'a be-aṣmo*] and plays with himself [*we-soḥeq beino u-vein aṣmo*], and this toying comes from the spleen, which is entirely the remnants of the blood. Thus, the toying comes to a person from the side of the dregs, which is the force of judgment. Similarly, as it were, *Ein Sof*, blessed be he, saw that these worlds that he imagined emanating had the necessity for judgment in order to reward and to punish, and had he not amused himself there would not have been a place for judgment, and there would not have been place even for the engraving that he engraved in his

> essence, for it is judgment in relation to *Ein Sof*. . . . On account of this, he amused himself, for he is like water or fire that quivers when the wind blows upon it, and it shines like lightning to the eyes, and glistens hither and thither. *Ein Sof*, may he be blessed, quivered in himself [*mitna'ane'a be-aṣmo*], and he shone and sparkled from within himself to himself, and that quivering is called bemusement [*sha'ashu'a*], and from that bemusement . . . there comes to be the power of the measure of the engraving [*shi'ur ha-ḥaqiqah*], which is the Torah in potentiality. . . . From the bemusement there is aroused the potency of the force of judgment [*koaḥ de-khoaḥ ha-din*] and from the potency of that force there comes to be the measure of the engraving, as was mentioned, which is the Torah in potentiality. Since *Ein Sof*, blessed be he, is absolutely incomposite [*pashuṭ be-takhlit ha-peshiṭut*], every dimension of movement or image of movement in him is judgment in relation to himself. . . . This engraving is alluded to in the section of *Zohar* on Genesis: "In the beginning of the decree of the king, the hardened spark engraved an engraving in the supernal luster." That is, in the beginning when the bemusement arose in his incomposite will, as we said, which is the beginning of the measure that he conceived in relation to himself so that he would have dominion, and all dominion is from the aspect of judgment. . . . Know that from this bemusement there arose the engraving . . . and this engraving is the light, that is, the Torah that comes to be from the bemusement as has been mentioned. Thus, the measurement is in relation to *Ein Sof* and the engraving is the Torah.[49]

For the purposes of this analysis, emphasis should be placed on the motif of the shaking that produced the "primordial points" engraved by the power of judgment (*din*) suffused in the sea of mercy (*raḥamim*); from these points emerged the primal Torah, the weaving of the garment (*arigat ha-malbush*)[50] out of the 231 gates of letter permutations,[51] what Scholem ably called "the linguistic movement of *Ein-Sof* within itself."[52] One of the clearest presentations of this dimension of Saruq's attempt to explain the inexplicable first actions of the infinite is found in *Shever Yosef*:

> Prior to his creating the worlds, he and his name alone were, "his name" [*shemo*] numerically equals "will" [*raṣon*], and he filled the space of all the worlds. When it arose in his will to emanate the infinite world [*olam ein sof*] and to create the world that would recognize his greatness and to benefit his creatures, he gladdened himself [*sameaḥ be-aṣmo*], and by means of the bliss he bemused himself [*nishta'ashe'a be-aṣmo*]. From the bemusement [*sha'ashu'a*] the power of the force of judgment was aroused whence there came to be the measure of the engraving [*shi'ur ha-ḥaqiqah*], which is the Torah in potentiality. . . . Therefore, it arose in his will to bemuse himself [*lehishta'ashe'a be-aṣmo*] in order to arouse the power of the force of judgment because from the bemusement there is born the measurement, and the measurement is the root of the cause of boundary, and boundary is the cause of movement, that is, the cause of the contraction of the light within the boundary or its expansion, and this is the root of reward and punishment, judgment and mercy.[53]

The logic of the myth transposes the normal sequencing of cause and effect. On the one hand, the self-pleasuring of the omnibenevolent infinite arouses the attribute of judgment, but, on the other hand, that pleasuring is possible only because of the instigation of the force of judgment. In the heterosexual fantasy, phallomorphically conceived, the desire of the male to project is inspired by imagining the female vessel that will receive the seminal overflow. Speaking of the arousal of the force of judgment is not the same as speaking about the creation of the force of judgment; what is aroused existed already in potential, and thus the erotic adventure can be viewed as the outcome, and not the catalyst, of the divine compression.[54] A second passage from *Shever Yosef* makes the point explicitly: "The secret of the engraving, which is the *gelifu* mentioned in the *Zohar*, is that by means of the bemusement . . . he measured in himself the substance [*mahut*] and the capacity [*yekholet*] of every attribute [*middah*] of the ten attributes that were hidden in his essence [*be-aṣmuto*], blessed be his name, and this happened ten times and thus there were ten measurements by means of ten bemusements, for with respect to each attribute he bemused himself, and from every bemusement there arose a measurement. When he reached the tenth measurement, he imagined in himself that through this measurement it would be fitting to establish the world."[55]

Summarizing Saruq's teaching, the seventeenth-century kabbalist Naftali Bachrach writes, "They said concerning the secret of wisdom that it is from the light that emanates from the hidden source, and its source is called the 'source of wisdom,' and it is the secret of the world of the garment [*olam ha-malbush*],[56] which is called the primordial Torah, and concerning it R. Eliezer said, 'Before the world was created he and his name alone were,'[57] and the Tetragrammaton in its permutations comprises all of the world of the garment."[58] Employing one of the oldest Jewish esoteric doctrines centered on the identity of the Torah and the Tetragrammaton,[59] Bachrach's paraphrase stresses that the name, which is the garment, functions in this context as the attribute of judgment—coeternal with *Ein Sof*—that propelled the linguistic delimitation of the limitless light. In another passage, Bachrach adds words of his own to the Saruqian text, which he copied accurately but without attribution, to clarify the nexus between writing, jouissance, and judgment: "From the abundance of happiness [that God] contemplated in relation to the righteous, he amused and delighted himself [*mishta'ashe'a u-mit'anneg*] how he would have a holy nation, and from that movement there was born the potency of the force of judgment, that is, the constricting of the letters [*qimmuṣ ha-otiyyot*], which come to be from the vowel-points [*nequddot*] that were in the trace [*reshimu*] that remained within the circle [after the withdrawal],[60] for each and every letter has a boundary on paper."[61] Carrying the metaphor forward, Bachrach interprets the division of the infinite consequent to the movement of self-contemplation into the aspects of the encompassing (*maqqif*) and the encompassed (*muqqaf*), the former correlated with the engraving and the latter with the surface that is engraved, which is identified as the root of the "dough of all the worlds,"[62] that is, the prime matter whence all beings are fashioned.

What is implied philosophically in Saruq's kabbalah, especially the connection between *ṣimṣum*, *sha'ashu'a*, and the force of *din*, was made explicit in the depiction of the First Cause (*Causa Primera*) offered by his student, Abraham Cohen de Herrera (1570–1635):

> It knows itself and grasps in itself that which each thing and all things are able to participate, imitate, and resemble, because every effect is known and comprehended when that which it participates and receives from its cause is known and comprehended, as well as that which degenerates or falls away from its cause. . . . With this it seems to me we have a good understanding of the primary cause and the ša'šu'a or movement of pleasure [*movimiento de gozo*] and delight [*alegría*] which our divine guide attributes to it. It thus appears that it moves in itself in order somehow to emerge from itself, conceiving in itself. . . . Ḥesed or mercy and the diverse plurality of limited and in some sense imperfect natures that participate in Din or rigor, privation, and potency, which it later produced or gave birth to outside itself. . . . This is the ṣimṣum or shrinking [*encogimiento*] that limits and assigns it to diverse, limited operations and effects. . . . This is the root and origin of the boṣina de-qardinuta or lamp of darkness [*lámpara de oscuridad*] and strength which, as Din or rigor, allots and gives to all things in effect their rays, limits, and measures and is finally the universal place [*lugar*] of all produced ones, which it emptied out of the infinite [*vacío del infinito*], metaphorically speaking.[63]

The implication of the Saruqian doctrine is drawn out as well by the Lithuanian kabbalist Solomon ben Ḥayyim Eliashiv (1841–1926).[64] In his typically methodical manner, he notes that the *sha'ashu'a* of the infinite is the "aspect of the arousal [*hit'orerut*] and the movement [*tenu'ah*] that quivers within himself, and every movement is in the aspect of constriction [*qimmuṣ*] and contraction [*ṣimṣum*] from place to place. That is to say, the movement that is in the bemusement [*sha'ashu'a*] is the aspect of the contraction from himself to himself, and thus there are two aspects, the forces that quiver and the contraction that is made between the forces, and this is the quivering [*ni'anu'a*] and the contraction. These quiverings . . . are in the aspect of the glowing [*hitnoṣeṣut*], for by means of the bemusement the glowing of many lights was revealed and produced, and this is the aspect of the quivering." The glimmerings disclosed through the bemusement of the infinite are the aspect of points. These points and the contraction are identified respectively as mercy and judgment—expressions of the more concealed aspects of the will (*raṣon*) and thought (*maḥashavah*)—the former is the quality of illuminating and the latter the bestowing of boundary. By the profusion of the illumination the points were joined together until they formed the letters of the Torah.[65]

The Lurianic doctrine spotlights an important element in the construction of gender identity underlying the kabbalistic symbolism: the instrument of writing corresponds to the phallus and the written letters to the semen, but the arche-writing, portrayed as sexual self-excitation, is incited by the activation of feminine judgment in the predominantly masculine and merciful world of infinity (*olam ein sof*).[66] When the mythopoiēsis is charted psychoanalytically, it can be said that the will of the infinite to procreate is impelled by the narcissistic yearning of the male to expand the contours of self into the space of the feminine, to extend phallically and to inseminate the receptacle that receives the overflow in order to give boundary to the boundless. The female thus signifies the potential for heterogeneity ensconced in the homogeneity of the infinite. The psychological drive may be viewed as an application of the theosophical myth or, conversely, the theosophical myth may be viewed as an application of the psychological drive. Once more, the path of thinking leads to an inexorable circularity. Be that as it may, the decisive point is that the creative urge to project is rendered symbolically in the image of *Ein Sof* toying with himself, which eventuates in the linguistic gesticulation of shaking, the graphic act of engraving. Elaborating the Saruqian reading of the aforementioned zoharic image, Bachrach remarked that the engraving of the hardened spark involves the "letters that stand in the world of delights [*olam ha-sha'ashu'im*] that surrounds the light of *Ein Sof*."[67] Saruq and those who followed him embellished the zoharic myth of the primordial act of the infinite as a linguistic movement—primarily an act of writing (*gelifu* or *ḥaqiqah*) but one that is at the same time an act of speaking[68]—that involved sexual self-gratification, but this daring depiction of the divine is found already in older sources and is not completely the innovation of later kabbalists. We could go as far as to say that the complicated symbolic structures in this version of Lurianic kabbalah are midrashic embellishments of zoharic passages. That this has been the view of kabbalists themselves, even if academic scholars have not always been sensitive to the issue, is attested, for instance, in the comment of Ḥayyim of Volozhin on the identification of God and the Torah found in several zoharic homilies: "The supernal source of the holy Torah is in the uppermost of the worlds that are called the worlds of the infinite [*olamot ha-ein sof*], the secret of the hidden garment [*sod ha-malbush ha-ne'lam*] mentioned in the mysteries of the wondrous wisdom from the teaching of our master the Ari, blessed be his memory, for it is the beginning of the secret of the letters of the holy Torah."[69]

In comparing the themes of the fissure and the trembling of *Ein Sof* in the Saruqian version of Lurianic kabbalah and the application of similar motifs to the originary leap of *Seyn* in Heidegger's inceptual thinking,[70] we must note the obvious discrepancy: although in both instances there is a mythical underpinning to the conceptual formulation, for Heidegger these issues apparently have no overt or tacit sexual meaning as we find in the kabbalistic texts. Setting aside this difference, some astonishing affinities can be noted. First, just as Heidegger speaks of the leap as a fissure and self-refusal of being that is experienced as a trembling, an enfolding that is an unfolding to create the partition of the ontological disparity, so the kabbalists envision the inception as the withdrawing of the infinite from itself to itself, the rending of the beginning characterized by the pulsating rapture (*sha'ashu'a*) and the ensuing rupture (*beqi'ah*)—a caesura that is expressed, based on a zoharic idiom, as the infinite breaking and not breaking through its own aura (*baqa we-lo baqa awira dileih*)[71]—or the folding of the garment (*qippul ha-malbush*).[72] The commencement is thus marked by the secret of the fold, the doubling of difference, encoded semiotically in the opening letter of the Torah, the *beit* in the word *bere'shit*, the lingual-algebraic encryption for the antecedent that is consequent to the *alef* of the origin.[73]

Second, for the kabbalists, these images attempt to describe a theopoetic process by which the divine becomes manifest iconically as the image that makes absently present the supreme hiddenness and imagelessness of the Godhead beyond God, a theme likely known to Heidegger from both Eckhart[74] and Schelling.[75] It goes without saying that Heidegger does not unconditionally accept the apophatic discourse well attested in the history of Christian mysticism, but he does, in my judgment, elicit from these sources a more radical, and perhaps esoteric, perspective to fabricate his own idea of *Seyn* that breaks with the ontotheological characterization of the divine aseity as *ipsum esse subsistens*, in the formulation of Aquinas, which renders God as a being among beings even though the beingness of the creator is distinguished from all other creatures by the fact that only in the former case are essence and existence not distinct. The suggestion that Heidegger uncovered traces of the nonmetaphysical, or the meta-metaphysical, within the history of metaphysics would be consistent with his claim, discussed in the previous chapter, that overcoming the metaphysical mandates a continual undergoing that brings metaphysics back within its own limits.

Third, the mystery of being connected to the trembling, according to the kabbalah and Heidegger, is disclosed through the garment of language whose task is to manifest the groundless ground of the pure delight and graciousness of the beckoning stillness that is the origin of speech.[76] Commenting on the zoharic reworking of an older aggadic motif that the Torah was revealed in black fire upon white fire,[77] the nineteenth-century Lithuanian kabbalist Yiṣḥaq Eizik Ḥaver Wildmann wrote, "The root of everything is above in the secret of the contraction [*be-sod ha-ṣimṣum*], which are the letters, the splinterings of the light [*nittuqei ha-orot*], the parchment that bears them, and the thread of the infinite, blessed be he, that encompasses them. It is known that the contraction is the root of judgment, and thus it is called fire.... The root of the primordial Torah is in the contraction of the infinite, blessed be he."[78] Needless to say, the reference to the quintessentially theocentric truism that the root of the letters of the Torah originates in the withdrawal of the infinite light is far from Heidegger's concern, and yet his own notion of being assuming the character of the word through the self-concealing disclosure—the bringing forth (*Hervorbringen*) that lets what is not yet present arrive into presencing, an act of autopoiēsis that is the bursting open (*Aufbruch*) and the arising of something from out of itself (*das von-sich-her-Aufgehen*), a deportment that applies equally to nature (φύσις) and to artistic-poetical production[79]—may be his own atheological translation of the Christological dogma of the word becoming flesh, which uncannily does exhibit similarity to the kabbalistic myth.

Comparative Metaontology: From Nothing to Nothing

The nothingness to which the kabbalists and Heidegger allude from their variant perspectives is not a substance subject to the antinomy of being and nonbeing but rather the dynamic event of the immanent transcendence that is the transcendent immanence; that is, the event wherein transcendence and immanence are juxtaposed in the sameness of their difference prior to the division into transcendence and immanence dictated by the dyadic logic of traditional ontotheology. We can impute to both the kabbalistic *Ein Sof* and the Heideggerian *Seyn/Nichts* the remark of Schelling in *Die Weltalter* that "the Godhead, in itself, neither is nor is not [*weder ist noch auch nicht ist*]; or in another expression ... the Godhead is as well as is not [*sowohl ist als auch nicht ist*]. It is not in such a way that Being [*Seyn*] would befit it as something differentiated from its being [*Wesen*], since it is itself its Being and yet Being cannot be denied to it precisely because in it Being is the being itself."[80] Even more kabbalistic in its inflection, including especially the description of God's self-becoming as arising from the yearning of the eternal will to give birth to itself, an idea likely divulged to Schelling through Böhme's portrayal of the theopoetic desire and autogenesis of the *Ungrund*,[81] is the following comment in *Philosophische Untersuchungen über das Wesen menschlichen Freiheit*:

> Since nothing is prior to, or outside of, God, he must have the ground of his existence in himself [*Da nichts vor oder außer ist, so muß er den Grund seiner Existenz in sich selbst haben*].... This ground of his

> existence, which God has in himself, is not God considered absolutely [*ist nicht Gott absolut betrachtet*], that is, in so far as he exists; for it is only the ground of his existence. It [the ground] is *nature*—in God, a being indeed inseparable, yet still distinct, from him [*ein von ihm zwar unabtrennliches, aber doch unterschiedenes Wesen*].[82]

Heidegger incisively ponders the ramification of Schelling's assumption that the being of God is a becoming to himself out of himself (*Das Seyn Gottes ist ein Zusichselbstwerden aus sich selbst*). Prima facie, ordinary thinking—that is, a thinking whose logic is informed by the principle of noncontradiction and the law of the excluded middle—finds two insurmountable difficulties with this assertion. First, a God subject to becoming ostensibly is no God at all, since anything that becomes is finite; second, if God becomes out of his ground, then we are caught in an intractable circle of reasoning: God must be distinguished from the very ground out of which God emerged. From the commonplace standpoint, this circularity is contradictory, and "contradiction is the destruction of all thinkability."[83] However, insofar as Heidegger affirms the circle as the most appropriate symbol to depict both the hermeneutical condition of Dasein and the attendant comportment of temporality, as we discussed in chapter 1, it should come as no surprise that this is the meaning he elicits from Schelling's idea of the becoming of God. One presumes that becoming is a transition from not-yet-being (*Nochnichtseienden*) to being (*Seienden*). But this not-yet-existing of the ground (*das Nochnichtexistente des Grundes*) is what makes existence (*Existenz*) possible, and hence the not-yet (*Nochnicht*) is "that from which precisely what emerges from itself comes. One forgets to notice that in this becoming what becomes is already in the ground as the ground [*schon im Grunde als der Grund ist*]. Becoming is neither a mere relinquishing of the ground nor an annihilation of it, but on the contrary, what exists first lets the ground be its ground [*das Existierende läßt erst den Grund seinen Grund sein*]."[84]

In contrast to the becoming of an object—the example Heidegger invokes is that of a shoe—wherein the procedure of making is outside the finished product and the finished product is removed from the procedure of making, "in the case of the non-thing-like becoming of God [*nichtdinglichen Werden des Gottes*], becoming as the development of essential fullness is included in Being as its essential constituent."[85] In this autopoetic conception of the divine, becoming itself is comprised as the elemental feature of being—that is, the essence itself is to become other than itself—and hence eternality is instantiated in the temporal not-yet, the circling of the ground and existence in the unity of the primordial movement. This unity consists not of identity but of the belonging together that "first makes their separation and the discord possible which builds up into a higher unity."[86] Extracting from Schelling a hint to his own meditation on the nature of *Seyn*, which likewise avoids "making the objective presence or the handiness of things the first and sole criterion of the determination of Being," Heidegger notes that "in the constitution of the Being of beings indicated by ground and existence," two dimensions emerge in the essence of essence: first, "the primordial temporality of becoming," and second, "the necessarily posited dimension of self-increasing, respectively falling beneath, self."[87] From Schelling's teaching, which reverberates with the kabbalistic doctrine, Heidegger concludes that "we must not take the two determinations out of this circle, immobilize them and set what is thus immobilized against each other in a seemingly 'logical' thinking. Here a contradiction undeniably appears. . . . The ground is in itself what supports what emerges and binds it to itself. But as emergence from itself existence is what grounds itself on its ground and founds it explicitly *as its* ground."[88]

In a previous study, I articulated this metaontological way of contemplating the kabbalistic infinity by comparing it to the Mahāyāna Buddhist identification of the indiscriminate emptiness (*śūnyatā*) and the discriminate suchness (*tathātā*) of all that exists. The advantage of this interpretive stratagem is to distance *Ein Sof* from any suspicion of an ousiology or substance-oriented metaphysics. Infinity is the nothingness before the rift between nothing and something, the nothingness that overcomes all differentiation, including the differentiation between differentiation and nondifferentiation, the self-emptying emptiness that must be emptied of the distinction between empty and nonempty.[89] Alternatively expressed, *Ein Sof* is the nonessence that is the essence of all things that have no essence, the essence that is the absolution of essence,[90] the true form of no-form.[91] Relatedly, Heidegger writes in the *Beiträge* that the abysmal ground is neither emptiness nor fullness, presumably because the fullness of beings is the emptiness of being and the fullness of being the emptiness of beings.[92] In another aphorism from that work, Heidegger explains that the less that humans adhere to the beings they find themselves to be, the nearer do they come to being, and then he adds parenthetically "Not a Buddhism! Just the opposite."[93] His protestation notwithstanding, we are justified to juxtapose his thinking about *Seyn* as *Nichts* and Buddhist reflections on *the radiant emptiness of being*.[94] Just as emptiness in the Madhyamka tradition is the linguistic-conceptual marker to denote the lack of intrinsic nature, and not itself a reified lack of such a nature,[95] so for Heidegger, the claim that being is nothing is meant to criticize the core ontological assumption that being is the *primum signatum*, the signified that requires no signification, or in Derridean terms, the transcendental that is logocentrically imperative insofar as in its absence all signifiers lose their signification and are reduced to chaos. This is the import of the 1943 postscript to "Was ist Metaphysik?" (1929): "The nothing, as other than beings, is the veil of being [*Das Nichts als das Andere zum Seienden ist der Schleier des Seins*]."[96] In the 1949 edition, Heidegger glossed the last line: "The nothing: That which annuls, i.e., as difference, is as the veil of being, i.e., of beyng in the sense of the appropriative event of usage [*Das Nichts: das Nichtende, d.h. als Unterschied, ist als Schleier des Seins, d.h. des Seyns im Sinne des Ereignisses des Brauchs*]."[97] That the nothing is the veil of being means that being is revealed through the nothing by which it is reveiled. Being is thus not to be conceived metaphysically as the presencing unmasked as the absence that is absent as presence or as the presence present as absence.

My suggestion is reinforced by the statement about the aforementioned observation placed by Heidegger in the mouth of the Japanese sage in "Aus einem Gespräch von der Sprache," "We marvel to this day how the Europeans could lapse into interpreting as nihilistic the nothingness of which you speak in that lecture. To us, emptiness is the loftiest name for what you mean to say with the word 'Being.'" Through the Inquirer, Heidegger responds that the confusion is related to his use of the term *Sein*, a term that belongs to the "patrimony of the language of metaphysics," but which has the same meaning as nothingness or emptiness, the essential being that we try to think as the other (*das Andere*) to all that is present or absent.[98] This is confirmed anecdotally by the exchange between Heidegger and Bikkhu Maha Mani, a Buddhist monk from Thailand, reported by Heinrich Wiegand Petzet. After Heidegger opined on the topic of release and openness to mystery, he asked Mani what meditation means for "Eastern humanity." The monk responded that meditation entails concentration and gathering oneself without exertion of the will to the point that the "I" dissolves and all that remains is the Nothing. "But this Nothing is not nothing; it is just the opposite—fullness. No one can name this. But it is nothing and everything—fullness." Petzet adds that Heidegger understood the words of Mani and remarked, "This is what I have been saying throughout my whole life."[99]

Long before Heidegger, the kabbalists ascertained that if one speaks of nothingness as nothing, one negates the negation of the negation and thereby renders the negative as positive. The mutual insight of Heidegger and the kabbalists is captured pithily in the language of a verse cited in Asaṅga's *Mahāyānasaṃgraha*, a base text of the Yogācāra school of the Mahāyāna tradition: "The nonbeing of beings appears as being. . . . Thus it is like a magic trick, / Like the empty sky."[100] Piercing through the epistemological sleight of hand, one with eyes truly awakened from the dichotomy of wakefulness and nonwakefulness sees that in its being nonbeing is without the pretense of being, even as one so enlightened knows that the nature of the formless truth, the empty sky beyond words and images, can only be transmitted through forms that accord with the hardwiring of the human brain to cloak invisibility in the veneer of the visible. Consider the comment of Gishin, a high priest of the Japanese Tendai School: "The nature of reality is beyond words. How can it be adequately grasped through conceptualization? Nevertheless the Great Hero [the Buddha] transmitted the truth by relying on forms and images in accordance with [the capabilities of] sentient beings. The noble Buddha was spiritually proficient and assumed subtle language in order to foster the Path."[101] From the standpoint of absolute truth (*paramārtha-satya*), form is empty, and hence there is neither inherent nature nor intrinsic cause and effect, but there is no access to this truth except by way of conventional truth (*saṃvṛti-satya*) predicated on affirming the very precepts that the enlightened consciousness rejects.[102] As K'uei-chi, the founder of Fa-hsiang, the Chinese equivalent of the Indian Yogācāra school of Buddhism, expounds the statement in the *Heart Sutra* that *form itself is emptiness, and emptiness itself is form*:

> The Madhyamikans comment that actually emptiness is neither empty nor not empty. It is for the purpose of turning confusion into understanding that form is said to be empty. It is not that the emptiness of form is definitely empty, for emptiness is also empty. . . . Therefore, this passage of the sutra is aimed at breaking attachment to the existence of form . . . . It is not that Dharma-nature is empty; rather, what the foolish attach to as inherent nature when sensing the marks of form does not exist. The attachment to [the notion of the] nonemptiness [of form] and [the attachment to the notion that] form becomes empty only after it is destroyed are two erroneous views. . . . Although there are no causes and effects to grasp on to, there are attainable functions and effects. Otherwise, there will be no conventional truth; and if there is no conventional truth, there is no ultimate truth either. . . . One should get rid of the two attachments and seek true emptiness. Therefore, resorting to emptiness, one can eliminate both erroneous views. The form of Dharma-nature, in itself, is the true mark (*chen hsiang*), which is not different from emptiness and is nothing but emptiness. . . . It is not that there is emptiness apart from form, and it is not that form and emptiness are definitely the same or different from each other. Therefore, true emptiness and form are neither different nor not different and neither the same nor not the same.[103]

According to the tetralemic logic of the middle way (*madhyamaka*) in the Mahāyāna tradition—S is P; S is ¬P; S is both P and ¬P; S is neither P nor ¬P[104]—to say that form and emptiness are the same and not different implies that they are not the same nor not different. The characteristic of emptiness—language inevitably fails me—is to be discerned from the middle excluded by the logic of the excluded middle, the chiasm where the reality of the unreality is both and therefore neither real nor unreal, where the existence of the nonexistence is both and therefore neither existent nor nonexistent, where the difference of the nondifference is both and therefore neither different nor nondifferent. The conjecture of Brook Ziporyn, based on the Tiantai School of Chinese Buddhism, can be applied suitably to Heidegger and the kabbalists: "To be a being at all is already, for us, to be that X as non-X, or the Asness that is the showing of Xness and non-Xness. Neither the collapsing of Being into beings nor the separation of the two, which makes of Being another being, are possible from this perspective; as we saw already in the early Mahāyāna argument about a relationship between a thing and its marks, we have here a relationship for which both identity and difference are woefully inadequate predicates."[105]

There are limits of thought that cannot be crossed except as the limits that cannot be crossed.[106] The culmination of the mystical path is sometimes expressed—especially prominent in Sufism—as seeing the face of the unseen without a veil, but as I have argued in previous publications, what this means is that one comes to see that one cannot see the face but through a veil, which is to say, the final veil to unfurl is the veil that there is no veil to unfurl.[107] Similarly, the self-effacing interface of *Ein Sof*—the plenitude that is the emptiness of the emptiness of the plenitude, that is, the emptiness that is itself empty, and therefore identical and not identical to the nonemptiness of the emptiness that is the nonlocality of infinite space[108]—lights up as the showing of the being of nonbeing enshrouded in the nonbeing of being. This is attested explicitly by kabbalists, who assert of the infinite that it is "neither something nor nothing" (*lo yesh we-lo ayin*).[109] Expressed metaontologically, nothingness (*ayin*) can be addressed only by the interrogative "what" (*mah*), which signifies the privation of whatness (*he'der ha-mahut*), the threshold of our thinking, since we cannot speak of this nothing as being in existence (*meṣi'ut*).[110] The kabbalistic insight underlies Kook's insistence that the decisive return of the human spirit to the sphere of "pure belief" (*ha-emunah ha-barah*) will take place when the "last subtle shell of corporeality" (*qelippat ha-hagshamah ha-aḥaronah ha-daqqah*) collapses, the shell that consists of the "attribution of existence in general to divinity [*yaḥas ha-meṣi'ut bi-khelalut el ha-elohut*], for in truth all that we define by existence is incalculably removed from divinity." The "shadows of this negation" may resemble the heresy of atheism—denying the existence of God—but in reality, the expunging of any proclivity to represent the divine unity anthropomorphically or anthropopathically is the "highest level of faith."[111] Even if *Ein Sof* is referred to verbally as a being, the apophatic element that renounces our ability to know anything about that being undermines viewing it ontologically. As the Italian kabbalist Immanuel ben Abraham Ḥai Ricchi concisely summarized the point, the First Cause is "called in the mouth of all veritable kabbalists by the name *Ein Sof*, for in truth there is no end [*ein sof*] to his existence, unity, power, and providence.... And if we come to investigate what is the substance of his existence [*mahut meṣi'uto*], our thoughts grow weary and we do not comprehend it at all."[112]

The traditional metaphysical hierarchy is reversed, *existentia* precedes *essentia*; the nature of the latter is determined by the former. On the basis of this assumption, kabbalists cleverly decoded the word *ḥokhmah*, the designation of the second of the ten sefirotic emanations, but in some sense the foundation of them all, as *koaḥ mah*; that is, as the thirteenth-century kabbalist Azriel of Gerona explained, wisdom is the potential of what will be, the incomposite force (*koaḥ pashuṭ*) that imparts the "forms of the interchangeable substances."[113] There is an amalgamation here of two philosophic concepts: wisdom is described as hylic matter, the potential to become, but it is also grasped as the general that comprises its particulars (*kelal ha-tofes et peraṭaw*). Tishby suggested that Azriel's posture is closest to Averroës, for whom the forms are like roots implanted in the soil of the first matter.[114] Without entering into the question of textual influence, I would say that establishing a genealogy of ideas obscures the point that the kabbalists have subverted the very jargon they appropriated from the philosophical lexicon to propagate the idea that with respect to the infinite actuality is the potential; there is nothing more necessary than the pure contingency of necessity and nothing more contingent than the pure necessity of contingency. If *Ḥokhmah*, which is the something (*yesh*) that comes forth from the nothing (*ayin*), is treated as potentiality lacking a determinate substance of its own, then the ontological cord is undercut, and this would assuredly be the case with *Keter* and, all the more so, with *Ein Sof*. The idea is expressed with particular poignancy by the Castilian kabbalist Moses ben Shem Ṭov de León (1240–1305) in his *Sheqel ha-Qodesh*:

> The secret of this matter is the supernal cause, which is the cause concealed from everything, and the first existent [*meṣi'ut ha-ri'shon*] that initially issues from it is the secret of the first point [*ha-nequddah ha-ri'shonah*], and from it there concatenates the secret of existence [*sod ha-meṣi'ut*], for the secret of the single point [*nequddah aḥat*] is the beginning of all beginnings and the commencement of the essences [*ha-hawwayot*], and thus the author of *Sefer Yeṣirah* said, "Before one what can you count?"[115] That is, before the single point what can he who contemplates count and think? For before this one point there is naught but nothing [*ayin*], the secret of the pure ether [*ha-awir ha-zakh*] that is not comprehended... and thus it is called "nothing," that is, there is none that can understand it. The inquirer may ask, "Is there here something [*ha-yesh poh yesh*] that a person could comprehend?" And one responds, "There is not, for the nothing by all accounts is a hidden matter that no one can understand, and concerning this matter you can know that nothing is its secret and its substance.... Hence, you must know that the correct matter is that the secret of his existence, blessed be he, comes forth from this point. Thus it is called *Ḥokhmah*: the matter that is not comprehended and stands in thought.... And they say: What is *Ḥokhmah*? *Ḥakkeh mah*, that is, since the matter is incomprehensible and you cannot apprehend it, wait for what will come and what will be.[116]

Decoding *ḥokhmah* as *ḥakkeh mah* introduces a temporal ingredient into the apophatic mix, as it were, the ineffability and inscrutability of divine wisdom, the beginning whence everything comes forth, imposes the quality of patience apposite to waiting, an inevitable deferment, the deferment of the inevitable, for what will come to be is expressive of the indefinite will of the infinite and therefore concretizes the indistinguishability of necessity and potentiality. Gnosis of the divine wisdom inculcates the sagacity that in the waiting is the realization of what is awaited—indeed, there is no awaited apart from the waiting for the awaited that never comes because it is eternally coming—and thus the effluence of time itself may be deciphered as the disruption of the homogenous continuity wrought by the permanently impermanent alteration of a future that is essential to the inessentiality of the infinite.

The implications of de León's comment are made clear by the source to which he refers as the anonymous "they say," which has been identified[117] as a passage in the *Perush Shem ha-Meforash* by the thirteenth-century Provençal kabbalist Asher ben David:

> The great name [*YHWH*] begins with a *yod*, and by means of those paths [*ha-netivot*] engraved within it,[118] everything was produced within it, and this *sefirah* is called *Ḥokhmah*, that is, [one should] await what [*ḥakkeh mah*] will come and what will be, for everything issues from there according to the will [*raṣon*] that emanates in it from the *alef* that is before it and from it, for it, too, is the will and the thought of the will [*maḥashavah raṣon*] in accord with the efflux [*ha-meshekh*] that issues from the will and thought, since after the will there comes thought. One cannot cogitate about the will and thought except [as] "running to and fro." Therefore, the rabbis, blessed be their memory, said to their students, who delved into these matters with their questions, "Be quiet, thus it arose in thought,"[119] that is, thus it extended from the will and it was placed in thought, which is *Ḥokhmah*.[120]

The first two sefirotic gradations, will and thought, are distinguished inasmuch as the former is identified as nothing and the latter as something and hence the traditional dogma of *creatio ex nihilo* is transposed into a statement about the emanation of *Ḥokhmah* from *Keter*. And yet Asher ben David contests the legitimacy of this distinction, since one cannot contemplate the nature of either of these emanations. Moreover, the conjunction of the two, marked by the expression "thought of the will," suggests that the nature of the *yesh*—the beginning (*re'shit*) that is the origination of the existence (*ro'sh ha-meṣi'ut*) of differentiated beings,[121] the "beginning of all beginnings" (*hatḥalat kol ha-hatḥalot*) and the "initiation of all beings" (*re'shit kol ha-hawwayot*) that constitute the "secret of reality" (*sod ha-meṣi'ut*)[122]—incarnates the abundant emptiness of the *ayin*, the infinite efflux that emanates from the mystery of the *alef*, the nothing that is being. Thus, in a different treatise, the *Sod Eser Sefirot Belimah*, de León glossed the passage from *Sefer Yeṣirah* "Before one what can you count?" (*lifnei eḥad mah attah sofer*) as "prior to the One what is nothing [*qodem eḥad mah hu ayin*] and it is called the point [*nequddah*] or wisdom [*ḥokhmah*]."[123] That is, before the emergence of the point of wisdom—that to which the mathematical quality of oneness can be first attributed—there is no dyad of being and nonbeing and therefore there is nothing of which to speak or not to speak.

In a manner consonant to Heidegger's ponderings on the nature of *Seyn*, the kabbalistic infinity unsettles the philosophical portrayal of God as the *summum ens* and, consequently, provokes the negation of the negation of the negative,[124] a reclaiming of negativity that no longer dialectically contains its own other within the identity of the same; that is, a nullity (*Nichtigkeit*) that is not the negation of some positivity, à la Hegel's idea of true infinity as the negation of negation, opposed to the bad or negative infinity that fails to enable the absorption of the other into the infinite whole and thus does not free itself from the finite.[125] The kabbalistic equation of whatness and nothingness is well encapsulated by Heidegger's assessment that nothingness is "higher than everything 'positive' and 'negative' in the totality of beings."[126] If we presume, as I think we must, that for kabbalists all beings are the manifestation of infinity—the light that, paradoxically, is described in one zoharic passage as not existing in light (*nehora de-lo qayyema bi-nehora*),[127] that is, the light so resplendently hidden that it sheds the garment of light in which it is attired, and in so doing denudes the darkness—and any manifestation of that light is concomitantly an occlusion thereof, insofar as the concealment cannot be revealed unless it is concealed in the guise of being revealed,[128] then it follows that the nothingness of *Ein Sof* can be beneficially described by what Heidegger refers to—in a manner evocative of Böhme's *Unground*, the eternally unmanifest nothingness that is simultaneously present in and yet absent from the multiplicity of beings that are constitutive of nature[129]—as the nihilating (*Nichtige*) of the "original 'not'" (*ursprünglichen 'Nicht'*), the ripeness (*Reife*) of being manifest and hidden through discrete beings in nature.[130] Insofar as "the 'not' [*das Nicht*] belongs to the essence of beyng"—the ripeness expressed as the turning in the event (*Kehre im Ereignis*)—"beyng likewise belongs to the 'not.' In other words, what has genuinely the quality of the 'not' [*das eigentlich Nichtige*] is the negative [*das Nichthafte*] and is in no way whatever mere 'nothingness' ['*Nichts*'] as the latter is grasped through the representational denial of something [*die vorstellende Verneinung des Etwas*], on the basis of which denial one then says, nothingness 'is' not [*das Nichts 'ist' nicht*]. But *nonbeyng* [Nichtseyn] essentially occurs, and beyng [*Seyn*] essentially occurs; *nonbeing essentially occurs in the distorted essence* [das Nichtsein west im Unwesen], *beyng essentially occurs as permeated with negativity* [das Seyn west als nichthaft]."[131] We can assign to the kabbalistic infinity the same property: it is not the nothingness that is not, which is to say, a nothingness defined representationally as the negation of something, but rather the nonbeyng that occurs as the beyng brimming with negativity.

To interpret *Ein Sof* in this way challenges the widespread but unexamined supposition that the kabbalistic infinite should be classified ontotheologically, which in Heideggerian terms is predicated on the assumption that ontology, the question of beings, is necessarily theology, insofar as the ultimate metaphysical substance, that which is beyond beings (ἐπέκεινα τῆς οὐσίας) or the origin of beings (ἀρχή τοῦ ὄντος), possesses the character of the divine (θεῖον) or the god (θεός).[132] Brushing against this grain, I would argue that instead of viewing *Ein Sof* as a substance, or even a hypersubstance, the substance beyond substance, as the One of the Neoplatonic tradition is sometimes described, the nonontological overabundance contained within the bounds of the ontological,[133] it is preferable to grasp it as a semiotic marker of the being that symbolizes the interrelatedness of all beings in the same way that the Buddhist doctrine of dependent co-arising contests the reification of substance as an enduring essence. The undifferentiated oneness of the nothingness of infinity indicates, therefore, that the existence of all beings that issue therefrom, or that are comprised therein, is nonexistent. Medieval kabbalists did not have the language to communicate this idea adequately, and unfortunately, in the course of time even *Ein Sof* was calcified linguistically, as we see, for example, in the expression *ein sof barukh hu*, the infinite, blessed be he, a turn of phrase that translates the nontheistic—or maybe atheistic—notion back into a theistic index.[134] As Cordovero rightly noted, however, it is not justified to attribute the traditional expression *ha-qadosh barukh hu*, the "blessed holy One," to *Ein Sof* because the words *barukh hu* intimate that which is influenced (*mushpa*) by another, that is, an effect and not a cause, and the infinite cannot be considered the effect of any cause.[135] Even to think of *Ein Sof* as a cause requires a break with the customary understanding of causality insofar as the latter requires some degree of reciprocity between cause and effect that is interrupted by the assumption that we have a cause that does not comport the capacity to be an effect. The apophasis with regard to *Ein Sof* is so austere that there is no letter or name that can be ascribed to it; the infinite is the nihility that exceeds and dispels our theopoetic confabulations.

Ereignis and Envisioning Nothing beyond Nothing

In a note to the 1949 edition of "Brief über den 'Humanismus,'" Heidegger referred to *Ereignis* as the "guiding word" (*Leitwort*) of his thinking since 1936.[136] In another note to the same text, Heidegger articulates his view gnomically: "Being as event of appropriation [*Ereignis*], event of appropriation: the saying [*Sage*]; thinking: renunciative saying in response [*Entsagen*] to the saying of the event of appropriation."[137] That this is the term that signals the move beyond the ontological is shown clearly in Heidegger's remark in the summary of the 1962 lecture "Zeit und Sein" that *Ereignis* "is not a new formation of Being in the history of Being," but it indicates that "Being belongs to and is reabsorbed within Appropriation [*das Sein in das Ereignis gehört und dahin zurückgenommen wird*]." This presumes, in turn, that "the history of Being is at an end for thinking *in* Appropriation, that is, for the thinking which enters into Appropriation . . . is no longer what is to be thought explicitly."[138] From the standpoint of *Ereignis*, metaphysics as "the history of the imprints[139] of Being [*die Geschichte des Seinsprägungen*]" is seen as "the history of the self-withdrawal of what is sending in favor of the destinies . . . an actual letting-presence of what is present [*jeweiligen Anwesenlassens des Anwesenden*]." It follows that metaphysics is the "history of the concealment and withdrawal of that which gives Being." To enter into the thinking of *Ereignis*, one must terminate this withdrawal of the withdrawal so that the oblivion of being will be superseded by the "awakening into Appropriation" (*Entwachen in das Ereignis*).[140]

What instigates the shift from the metaphysical is the appreciation of the ontological difference between beyng and beings, the uncovering of which is pivotal to the recovery of the thinking that is proper to the origin to be retrieved in the second beginning, a thinking that can no longer be thought explicitly, that is, the meditative thinking that turns away from thinking. The history of metaphysics is marred by the fact that beyng "is always grasped as the beingness of beings [*Seiendheit des Seienden*] and hence as these beings themselves."[141] In *Der Anfang der Abendländischen Philosophie*, the lecture course Heidegger offered in the summer semester of 1932 at the University of Freiburg, the thesis is stated epigrammatically: "*beings are indeed on the basis of Being, but Being itself is not a being. Being and beings are different*—this *difference* is the most originary one that could ever open up. Therefore the result: Being is not the beings."[142] Oddly, and perhaps somewhat inconsistently, Heidegger's battle with the essentializing tendency of Western metaphysics smacks of its own essentialism,[143] and thus he insists categorically that "all previous thought" is tainted by the failure to disentangle being from beings.[144] The unfolding of metaphysics in Western thinking commences with the forgetfulness of beyng that results in beyng's failure to appear as what cannot appear and thus its truth as what cannot be thought remains unthought.[145]

For Heidegger, the essence of nihilism is related to this history of the eclipse of beyng in the appearance of beings. "Thought in terms of the destiny [*Geschick*] of being, the *nihil* of nihilism means that there is nothing going on with being [*daß es mit dem Sein nichts ist*]. Being does not come to the light of its own essence. In the appearance of beings as such, being itself stays away."[146] Rather than hearing only a "discordant note" (*mißton*) when the word *nihilism* is pronounced, Heidegger imparts to it an agreeable, albeit "discomfiting" (*mißliche*), nuance as the medium to prompt our remembrance (*Andenken*) by which we can ascertain the "being-historical determination of nihilism" (*seinsgeschichtliche Wesen des Nihilismus*). By reclaiming this sense of nihilism, we discern that "the *nihil* (the nothing) is, and is in an essential way, in what it names [*daß in dem, was er nennt, das nihil (nichts) wesentlich ist*]. Nihilism means: with everything in every respect, the nothing is going on [*Es ist mit allem in jeder Hinsicht nichts*]."[147] Heidegger's explanation of nihilism leads him to prioritize the anthropological by insisting that what it means to be human—the being-there of *Da-sein*—is to think of the presencing (*Anwesen*) of there-being as the "presencing out of the truth of presencing,"[148] a presencing that implies the presence omnipresently absent, that is, the mystery of beyng that is in every respect nothing.[149] As Derrida astutely observed, "Heidegger tries to subordinate all the sciences and regional ontologies to fundamental ontology. He tries to insist on access to the *as such* (the essence) as the distinguishing mark of humanity."[150]

In another touch of irony, the kabbalistic tradition provides a major exception to the generalization affirmed uncritically by Heidegger with respect to the obfuscation of beyng and the nihilistic essence of metaphysics. At first glance, my assertion seems unwarranted, since the concept of nihilism is very far from the worldview of kabbalists. But Heidegger's idiosyncratic taxonomy of nihilism as a means to expose the nothingness of beyng has a precedent in kabbalistic theosophy, where the diffusion of the luminal darkness of infinitivity can be described as well as a recoiling into the truth of its "self-concealing shelter" (*das sich verbergende Bergen*) through which "we catch a glimpse of the essence of the mystery in which the truth of being essences."[151] In language that is deeply kabbalistic in its cadence, Heidegger writes, "*Truth* is the clearing-concealing [*lichtende Verbergung*] which occurs as transporting [*Entrückung*] and captivation [*Berückung*]. These, in their unity [*Einheit*] as well as in excess [*Übermaß*], provide the encompassed open realm [*umstellte Offene*] for the play of beings which, in the sheltering of their truth, come to be as thing, tool, machination, work, act, sacrifice. . . . That essence of truth, however, the transporting-captivating clearing and concealing as the origin of the 'there' [*Ursprung des Da*], essentially occurs in its ground which we experience as ap-propriation [*Er-eignung*]."[152]

For the kabbalists, too, the metaontological mystery is beset by the paradox of the clearing-concealing, the clearing that conceals the concealing that clears, the primal absence of absence that results in the coming to presence of the vacuum within the plenum, an act that can be envisioned as transporting and captivating, approaching and absconding, advent and retreat, or in terms more familiar to kabbalistic rhetoric, extension and contraction. The space that emerges in the infinite expanse is both boundless and bounded, an encompassed open, which manifests the surplus of the appearance of beings and conceals the unity of the essence of their being—in Heidegger's language, the leaping ahead into the essential occurrence of beyng, which entails "the thrusting out of its beings so that the truth of beyng might preserve as an impetus the power of beyng to endure historically"[153]—the shelter that gathers in the manner that it projects and projects in the manner that it gathers.

As I noted in the introduction, it is plausible that Heidegger absorbed some kabbalistic motifs through secondary sources, but what is more crucial to my argument at this juncture is that these affinities disrupt his own adverse characterization of Jewish thought as irrefutably metaphysical.[154] Heidegger could have found in the Jewish esoteric lore a precedent to his inceptual thinking, a counternarrative to the story he tells of Western philosophy as the tale of a depreciating forgetfulness of beyng, the philosophical equivalent to the theological account of the fall from grace. Of course, this was demonstrably not the case, as Heidegger was either steadfastly ignorant of or deliberately hid any indebtedness to Jewish thought, let alone the most recondite part of that literary-cultural heritage. The scholarly restitution might, however, be enacted—and here the intellectual agenda cannot be separated from an ethical directive—by positing a hermeneutic of bifocality whereby the reflections on nothing and being enunciated by kabbalists would be scrutinized through the Heideggerian lens even as the reflections on nothing and being enunciated by Heidegger would be scrutinized through the kabbalistic lens. One of the major repercussions of this mode of speculating for the study of kabbalah, as I have already indicated, is a challenge to the depiction of the infinite as a substance with a uniform and stationary essence, even if it is labeled the being beyond being, the being of the one that is nonbeing. Surely, the term *Ein Sof*, as the denomination of ultimate reality, has its roots in the metaphysical terminology of medieval philosophical literature, which was informed, at least in part, by some of the sources of classical Neoplatonism, but the way it functions may have the potential to subvert its own ontotheological presuppositions.[155] Rather than viewing *Ein Sof* as if it were the equivalent to the Neoplatonic *hyperousios*, the beyond-being, which is a being nonetheless, it is more fitting to think of the unthinkable as *proousios*, the expression used by Iamblichus and his school to name the One as the preessential fount of all things,[156] or perhaps even more suitable is *anousios*, literally, that which lacks being, a term applied in some Gnostic treatises to the nonexistent but still not fictitious first principle.[157] *Ein Sof*, similarly, is actual but nonexistent—like the zero that is considered mathematically to be both purely real and purely imaginary insofar as it is the point on the coordinate plane of complex numbers wherein the real and the imaginary axes intersect—the infinite essence that cannot be essentialized, not even as the essence of the nonessence or as the nonessence of the essence, the no-thing of the apophatic tradition, since the illimitable nothingness cannot be constricted by images of negation that affirm the positivity they ostensibly negate.

To substantiate the point textually, I will cite a passage from the *Secret of the Contraction* (*sod ha-ṣimṣum*) attributed to the towering rabbinic leader of the Lithuanian Jewish community, Elijah ben Solomon (1720–97), the Vilna Gaon:

> Know that one cannot think at all about the infinite, blessed be he, for it is forbidden to name it, even as the necessary of existence [*ḥovat ha-meṣi'ut*]. The first *sefirah* is called "nothing" [*ayin*] and the second is named "something" [*yesh*], for we know that it exists, and we comprehend this only with respect to it and not with respect to the first, and all the more so, with respect to the infinite, blessed be he and blessed be his name, as it is forbidden to think at all and even to call it *ein sof*. What we speak with regard to it and the *sefirot*, everything is from his will and his providence so that he will be known from the perspective of his actions. This is the principle [*kelal*] for all the ways of kabbalah. It is known that just as he is without limit so also is his will. Thus the incomposite will is infinite, and it is even forbidden to think of this at all, but it is known that the worlds are finite and everything is enumerated. Therefore, he contracted his will [*ṣimṣem reṣono*] in the creation of the worlds, and this is the contraction [*ṣimṣum*].[158]

The acute apophaticism expressed in this passage is arresting: so excessive is the ineffability of *Ein Sof* that it cannot even be named the *necessary of existence*, the designation for God that entered the Hebrew philosophical lexicon through the translation of Maimonides's borrowing of Avicenna's *wājib al-wujūd*.[159] The author goes so far as to say that it is prohibited not only to deliberate about infinity but even to call it *ein sof*. So beyond linguistic demarcation is the infinite that it cannot be branded as the infinite. Moreover, since *Keter*, the first emanation, is called "nothing," in contrast to *Ḥokhmah*, the second emanation, which is called "something," we can presume that *Ein Sof* is beyond the metaphysical binary of being and nonbeing. Even though there is a modicum of comparability between *Ein Sof* and *Keter* with regard to their mutual incomparability, it seems judicious to ask nevertheless how one can discriminate the nothingness of *Ein Sof* and the nothingness of *Keter*. Can there be gradations of nothingness such that the nothing of the one is greater than the nothing of the other? Through the centuries kabbalists have debated this subtle philosophical point under the pretext of interrogating whether or not *Ein Sof* and *Keter* are identical or different.[160] Some maintained that the two should not be distinguished and thus the name *Ein Sof* is applied to *Keter*,[161] while others insisted on the need to uphold a clear-cut distinction, and still others argued, as I noted in the previous chapter, that the difference between them is solely terminological, that one is called the cause and the other the effect.[162] This belief was originally deemed a very sensitive secret about which one had to hold one's silence, since it narrowed the gap separating emanator and emanated, but later kabbalists interpreted it in a diametrically opposite way as emphasizing the unbridgeable chasm between the cause and the effect.

By the last decades of the thirteenth century, the predominant view—although by no means unanimously accepted—was that the nothingness of *Ein Sof* signifies the absolute transcendence beyond signification, whereas the nothingness of *Keter* signifies the immanentization of transcendence, the preliminary phase of the differentiation within the indifference of infinity, designated as *hashwa'ah* or *aḥdut ha-shaweh*, which correspond, as Scholem noted, to the Latin expressions *indistinctio* and *aequalitas*.[163] The distinction between the nondifferentiated nothing of *Ein Sof* and the differentiated nothing of *Keter* is captured succinctly in the following passage from the zoharic anthology: "*Ein Sof* cannot be known and it does not produce an end or a beginning like the primordial nothing, which brings forth a beginning and an end. . . . There are no wills, no lights, and no radiances in *Ein Sof*. . . . That which knows, but does not know, is none other than the supernal will, the concealed of all concealed, the nothing."[164] Immediately preceding the above citation, *Ein Sof* is described as the incomprehensible and impenetrable "concealment" (*ṣeni'u*) that contains the "will of all wills," a technical reference to the highest facet of *Keter*. The intent of this remark is to draw attention to the inseparability of *Ein Sof* and *Keter*—they are distinguishable and yet coeval—and not to avow that volitional agency can be applied to infinity in and of itself. On the contrary, it is stated explicitly that there is no dimension of will within *Ein Sof*, for to suggest otherwise would imply some need or lack. As David ben Yehudah he-Ḥasid poetically expressed it, the cause of causes (*illat ha-illot*) is "the place to which forgetfulness [*shikheḥah*] and oblivion [*nishshayon*] pertain, as in the expression 'For God has made me forget' [*ki nashshani elohim*] (Genesis 41:51). What is the reason? Because concerning all the gradations and sources their existence should be investigated, searched, and probed from the depth of the supernal Wisdom, and from there one understands one thing from another. However, concerning the cause of causes, there is no aspect in any place to probe, to investigate, or to know of it any knowledge because it is concealed and hidden in the secret of the nothing and the naught. Therefore, with respect to the matter of comprehension of this place, forgetfulness pertains to it."[165]

Grammatically, *ein sof* is a nominal form, but ontically it does not demarcate something that can be named or even nothing that cannot be named but the void disclosed in the annulment of the void, the infinite negation of the negation of the infinite, the concealment of disclosure disclosed through the disclosure of concealment. A critical part of this metaontology—the assumption that the utmost reality is not a definable subject with identifiable properties but rather what Badiou calls *an evental occurrence of being*, that is, an event of presence that is in excess of being present[166]—demands an inversion of the Aristotelian classification of substance (*ousia*). A key to understanding the kabbalistic speculation on infinity, therefore, is the presumption that the projection of being must always be gauged from the standpoint of the nonbeing of the withdrawal of being—the more absent, the more present; the more secreted, the more transparent. What there is can never be there but as not there; what is given cannot be given but as nongiven. This is the phenomenological significance of the doctrine of *ṣimṣum*, the self-depleting bestowal of the insubstantial substantiality of the infinite as it assumes the substantial insubstantiality of the finite through the agency of the sefirotic emanations, the "limited force that is unlimited" (*koaḥ bi-gevul mi-beli gevul*), in the language of Azriel of Gerona.[167] As the fifteenth-century anonymous author of *Sefer ha-Peli'ah* interprets Azriel's words, "Since there is no deficiency in his perfection, we must say that he has a limited force that is unlimited. That which comes forth from him initially are the *sefirot*, which are a perfect force [*koaḥ shalem*] and a deficient force [*koaḥ ḥaser*]; when they receive the efflux that issues from his perfection, they are a perfect force, and when the efflux is thwarted from them, they are a deficient force. Thus they have a potency to act in perfection and in deficiency."[168] According to this interpretation, the two contingencies are mutually exclusive: when the sefirotic gradations receive the overflow, they are complete, but when they do not, they are deficient. It is feasible, however, to explicate Azriel's words differently such that the status of the gradations vis-à-vis the infinite as the *limited force that is unlimited* tenders the possibility of interpreting the two qualities not successively but synchronously: each of the *sefirot* is complete and deficient all at once—the power of infinity is protracted only to the extent that it is retracted.

Metaphor, Dream, and the Parabolic Bridging of Difference

One might still protest that there is no justification for juxtaposing the kabbalists and Heidegger in the manner that I have suggested, since the nothing that nothings affirmed by the latter is impervious to the meontological bedrock of negative theology that allegedly applies to the nothingness affirmed by the former; that is, the assumption that the being of nonbeing is present as absence and the nonbeing of being absent as presence.[169] But the kabbalistic perspective, I submit, can be elucidated by Heidegger's observation that attunement (*Stimmung*) to the mood of anxiety brings to light the repulsion (*Abweisung/Verweisung*) of the nothing, the nihilation (*Nichtung*) that "makes itself known with beings and in beings expressly as a slipping away of the whole."[170] On the face of it, the objection will still be made that this concern seems even more distant from the world of kabbalistic speculation focused, as it is, on the sense of the whole or the one being in which the totality of beings is incorporated. However, the attentive ear will discern that the aforecited words of Heidegger bring to the fore an indispensable but neglected phenomenological factor of the theosophic ruminations about infinity proffered by the kabbalists: the unfathomable and unspeakable *Ein Sof* is not known intellectually by way of deductive inference, or perceptually by way of direct experience, or even intuitively by way of imagistic exemplification, but rather through an encounter with the nothingness that permeates all beings as the being that withdraws from all beings, an encounter that ignites the terror of nonbeing in confronting the unavoidable void of being, the emptiness of the nonemptiness that is the nucleus of all subsistence.

Elaborating this theme from a slightly different perspective, Heidegger writes in *Einführung in die Metaphysik*, commenting on the juxtaposition of nature and hiding in the Heraclitean fragment 123, mentioned briefly in the introduction,[171] φύσις κρύπτεσθαι φιλεῖ, which he translates as *Sein [aufgehendes Erscheinen] neigt in sich zum Sichverbergen*, "Being [emerging appearance] intrinsically inclines toward self-concealment:"

> Being means: to appear in emerging, to step forth out of concealment [*Verborgenheit*]—and for this very reason, concealment and the provenance [*Herkunft*] from concealment essentially belong to Being. Such provenance lies in the essence of Being, of what appears as such.... What maintains itself in becoming is, on the one hand, no longer Nothing [*das Nichts*], but on the other hand it is not yet what it is destined to be. In accordance with this "no longer and not yet," becoming remains shot through with not-Being [*Nichtsein*]. However, it is not a pure Nothing [*reines Nichts*], but no longer this and not yet that, and as such, it is constantly something else. So now it looks like this, now it looks like that. It offers an intrinsically inconstant view. Seen in this way, becoming is a seeming of Being [*Werden ist, so gesehen, ein Schein des Seins*]. In the inceptive disclosure [*anfänglichen Erschließung*] of the Being of beings, then, becoming, as well as seeming, must be opposed to Being. Yet becoming as "arising" ["*Aufgehen*"] nevertheless belongs to *phusis*. If we understand both in a Greek manner, becoming as coming-into-presence [*In-die-Anwesenheit-kommen*] and going-away [*Weg-gehen*] out of presence, Being as emergent and appearing coming to presence [*aufgehend-erscheinendes Anwesen*], not-Being as absence [*Nichtsein als Abwesen*], then the reciprocal relation between emerging [*Aufgehen*] and decaying [*Untergehen*] is appearance [*Erscheinen*], Being itself [*das Sein selbst*]. Just as becoming is the seeming of Being, seeming as appearing is the becoming of Being.[172]

Heidegger characterizes the nature of becoming (*das Werden*) as the *seeming of Being*; he does not mean to suggest that the world of differentiation is a mere acosmic illusion or pure nothing, as would be implied by the metaphysical binary from which he sought to escape. His point is rather that becoming is inundated with *Nichtsein*, the radical alterity of the nonbeing of being that renders every being as always something else, situated unremittingly betwixt that which is no longer and that which is not yet. That the world of becoming is demarcated as the seeming of being implies that reality is a perspectival letting-shine of the semblance of truth that is subject to being untrue.[173] On the one hand, becoming and appearance are opposed to being insofar as being is always withheld in its bestowing and thus can never appear as such; on the other hand, becoming as the wavering between appearing and disappearing, coming into presence and going away from presence, belongs essentially to the nature of being. This leads Heidegger to conclude that appearance (*Erscheinen*) is being itself (*das Sein selbst*), a conclusion that patently contradicts his insistence that being withdraws from the very beings in which it appears.

To some degree, Heidegger's nonbeing bears the trace of Eckhart's apophatic depiction of the Godhead (*divinitas*; *gotheit*) as not a something that is not and therefore a nothing that is pigeonholed within ontotheological boundaries.[174] The Eckhartian God is described variously as not a being, above being, the superessential being (*überwesende wesen*), or the superessential nothingness (*überwesende nitheit*),[175] and hence it follows that every manifestation of the nonmanifest is a concealment and every concealment a manifestation. In this spirit, the kabbalistic infinite may be envisaged as the empty suchness of the moment positioned between no longer and not yet, the interval of permanent impermanence wherein becoming dons and thereby discards the façade of being, the instant that is always the same because interminably different. Like the time of the dream, this moment, which has neither past nor future, is a present without duration, a presence that resists representation except as nonpresent.[176]

The infinity of the kabbalistic imaginaire can be described in the terms that Heidegger employed in his essay "Andenken" (1942), in what reads like a midrashic gloss on the description of the poetic vocation in a passage from Hölderlin's *Werden im Vergehen*, "[in] the state between Being and not-Being, everywhere the possible becomes actual, and this is in the free imitation of art a terrible but divine dream."[177] In a distinct modulation of Schelling's positive philosophy,[178] and especially his identification of the aesthetic sense of the imagination, discernible most pristinely in poetry, as the true organon of philosophy—their close affinity is strengthened by the claim that poetry transports one into an ideal world, whereas philosophy makes the real world vanish before one's eyes[179]—Heidegger writes about poiēsis as a foretelling of what is coming, not in the sense of the Judeo-Christian prophets who utter in advance the word of God, but in the sense of a prognostication that is the poetic calling (*Dichtertum*) that opens space-time for the luminous blaze of the manifestation of the gods, and accords to humanity the historical task of dwelling upon earth to disclose the nonreal (*das Unwirkliche*) that precedes everything real, the fullness of the imponderable gift suspended between the no-longer-actual (*Nichtmehr-Wirkliche*) and the not-yet-actual (*Nochnicht-Wirkliche*), the advent of the holy that appears unexpectedly in the "divinely terrible nonreality" (*furchtbargöttliche Unwirkliche*) of the dream, the space of the "free imagination of poetry" (*freien Bildens der Dichtung*), the state between being (*Seyn*) and nonbeing (*Nichtseyn*), wherein the possible becomes real and the actual ideal.[180] In the lecture course on Hölderlin's "Germanien," delivered in the University of Freiburg in the winter semester of 1934–1935, Heidegger remarked that a "cherished devise" of the poets is "to symbolize what is actually real by means of the most sensuous possible images of what is, in fact, not real."[181] The image of the dream is not invoked in this depiction of the poetic craft but it is undoubtedly relevant inasmuch as the oneiric can be characterized as well by the propensity to symbolize (*versinnbildlichen*) the actually real (*eigentlich Wirkliche*) by means of sensuous images (*sinnliche Bilder*) of what is considered to be unreal (*Unwirkliche*). In the essay "Hölderlin und das Wesen der Dichtung" (1936), Heidegger made the point explicitly: "Poetry awakens the illusion of the unreal and of the dream [*Dichtung erweckt den Schein des Unwirklichen und des Traumes*] as opposed to the tangible and clamorous actuality in which we believe ourselves to be at home. And yet, on the contrary, what the poet says and undertakes to be is what is truly real [*was der Dichter sagt und zu sein übernimmt, das Wirkliche*]."[182] I would tweak Heidegger's language and replace the term "unreal" with "irreal" as it is used by Husserl to name the hyletic immediacy that is given in consciousness without being real or unreal, existent or nonexistent, present or absent. When viewed from within this phenomenological bracket, the irreal is determinative of what is perceived noetically to be real, and as a result, the line separating facticity and fictionality is conspicuously blurred.[183]

Perhaps this is the intent of Heidegger's aside "Poetry makes beings more beingful" (*Dichtung macht das Seiende seiender*).[184] In what way can beings be made more beingful? Heidegger offers a clue in the continuation when he remarks that it is through allegory (*Gleichnis*) that "the illuminating view [*Lichtblick*], the seeing-in-the-light [*Ins-Licht-sehen*], first opens and frees the look for beings."[185] Inasmuch as poetry casts the real parabolically, it is the aesthetic form that cultivates the sense of "freedom as self-binding [*Sich-binden*] to the anticipatory projection of being," which "makes possible a relationship to beings."[186] Here it is apposite to cite in full the following reflections in the *Beiträge* on the relationship of Dasein, imagination, the event, and the clearing:

> To the usual view directed toward "beings," Da-sein, as grounding the openness of self-concealing, appears as nonbeing [*nichtseiend*] and imagined [*eingebildet*]. In fact, *Da-sein, as the projecting-thrown*

> *grounding* [die entwerfende-geworfene Gründung], *is the highest reality in the domain of imagination* [Bereich der Einbildung], assuming we understand the latter not simply as a faculty of the soul and not simply as something transcendental... but as the *event* itself, wherein all *transfiguration* [Verklärung] oscillates. "Imagination" as an occurrence of the *clearing* itself [*Die "Einbildung" als Geschehnis der* Lichtung *selbst*]. Yet "imagination," *imaginatio*, is a name that names from the viewpoint of the immediate apprehending of ὄν and of beings. Calculated in those terms, all beyng and its opening constitute a *formed image* [Gebilde] that is added to what supposedly stands on its own. But all this is inverted [*umgekehrt*]: what is "imagined" [*"eingebildet"*] in the usual sense is always the so-called "really" present at hand [*"wirkliche" Vorhandene*], for that is what is brought to an image [*hereingebildet*], i.e., brought into the clearing, into the "there," so as to appear [*zu Scheinen gebracht in die Lichtung, in das Da*].[187]

In all probability, Heidegger is here translating Schelling's depiction of the imagination as the activity that "wavers in the middle between finitude and infinity," or as the activity "mediating the theoretical and the practical," which produces the symbols for ideas, as opposed to the schema for concepts; the ideas likewise oscillate between finitude and infinity, and thus the imagination is identified as reason in contradistinction to the understanding.[188] Echoing a sentiment expressed by other exponents of German idealism, including Fichte,[189] Schelling goes as far as to say that in the absence of imagination, nothing is actual.[190]

As reformulated by Heidegger, imagination is not primarily a faculty of the soul, and not even the Kantian transcendental imagination, the faculty of apperception that provides the condition for the possibility of knowledge through the synthesis of intuition and thinking, the sensible and the intelligible, a topic he notoriously grappled with in the *Phänomenologische Interpretation von Kants Kritik der reinen Vernunft*, the lecture course delivered at the University of Marburg in the winter semester of 1927–28,[191] and then at greater length in *Kant und das Problem der Metaphysik*, the so-called *Kantbuch*, first published in 1929.[192] The imagination rather is the clearing, the between of Da-sein, "the axis in the turning point of the event [*der Wendungspunkt in der Kehre des Ereignisses*], the self-opening center of the counterplay between call and belonging [*die sich öffnende Mitte des Widerspiels von Zuruf und Zugehörigkeit*],"[193] within which beyng is constituted as a formed image and beings are imagined to be really present at hand.[194] Heidegger's critique and adoption of Kant's theory turns on the close conjunction he establishes between the imaginary and time, on the one hand, and the imaginary and language, on the other hand. Both these topics have suggestive parallels in kabbalistic thought, but I will focus on the latter topic, as I will have the occasion to return to the former in a subsequent chapter.

The inherently linguistic nature of the imagination is bolstered by Heidegger's remark that *Einbildung* is "a name that names from the viewpoint of the immediate apprehending of ὄν and of beings." That is, by virtue of the imagination, Dasein is the "domain of what is proper [*Eigentum*]," the "domain of the principality [*Fürsten-tum*]," the "sovereign center of the appropriating eventuation as the assignment [*die herrschaftliche Mitte der Er-eignung als Zueignung*], of the ones who belong, to the event and at the same time to themselves: becoming a self [*Selbstwerdung*]." The individuating transformation is effectuated through language inasmuch as the image is constituted as the response of Dasein to the call (*Zuruf*) that is both a hearing (*hören*) and a belonging (*gehörig*).[195] The assignment can be narrowed further to the poet because the poetic saying, in particular, provides the site of the trembling or swaying of the event, the transfigured crossing of the leap whereby the beingness of beings—the projecting-opening order of beyng in virtue of which beings are concealed in the deconcealment (*Entbergsamkeit*) of their concealment[196]—is fortified in a manner comparable to oneiric images whose being is solidified in commensurability to their nonbeing. Dreaming, we might say, is a seeing in night—the invisibility that is the epistemic condition of all visibility, the unseeing that enframes every act of seeing—that is beyond the binary of externality and internality insofar as the outside of nocturnality is completely identified with its inside.[197] The undulation of the dream discloses the limit delimited and yet breached by the imagination in divulging the image whence it is disclosed that the stuff of which dreams are made can be phenomenally present only in being absent from being either ontically present or absent.[198]

Rather than viewing the dream as a shadow of the light, it can be regarded as an illumination of the shadow, provided it is further understood that the oneiric phenomenon is, as Heidegger put it, "a kind of absencing on the part of that which illuminates and of that which itself properly appears. . . . [T]his vanishing itself still an appearing, the appearing of a passing away into that which is altogether devoid of radiance, which no longer illuminates. . . . What is dreamlike cannot be crudely [*globig*] and mistakenly notched up to what is merely unreal [*Unwirkliche*], or to the erosion of the real into nullity [*Nichtige*]. The dreamlike and the dream are a vanishing of the light and radiance that itself is already absencing [*Entschwinden des selbst schon abwesenden Lichtes und Glanzes*], of that which presences of its own accord and appears in shining (illuminating) [*dessen, was von sich her anwest und scheinend (leuchtend) erscheint*]. The absencing, as the absencing of such vanishing, is also still a presencing."[199] The shadowlike and fading nature of the dream does not convey that the dream is nothing, but rather that it is the appearing of the nonapparent, that is, the appearing of what abstains from appearing, the presencing of what prevails as absent, not because it is a presence that is not present—the nonbeing measured according to the metrics of being—but because it is present as nonpresent, the nonbeing that belongs to the being of the human being (*Zum Sein des Menschen gehört ein Nichtsein*).[200] What is decisive about the dream is not that it deals with the realm of shadows, thought to be ontically unreal and null, but that, in its fleetingness as shadow, it corroborates that "all presencing is in itself at the same time absencing [*alle Anwesung ist in sich zugleich Abwesung*],"[201] a presencing that perseveres in the absencing of absencing, a disappearing of the appearance that withdraws in the appearing of its disappearance. The dream, therefore, is the real that essentially stretches into the unreal (*Das Wirkliche erstreckt sich wesenhaft in das Unwirkliche*), but insofar as the nonreal (*Nicht-Wirkliche*), each time differently, is "either the no-longer-real or the not-yet-real" (*entweder das Nicht-mehr-Wirkliche oder das Noch-nicht-Wirkliche*), it becomes "the possible for what is actually real [*das Mögliche für das Wirkliche*]. The possible is in this instance never that which is merely null, or pure nonbeing; it is rather more a 'state' between being and nonbeing" [*eher schon ein 'Zustand' zwischen Sein und Nichtsein*]."[202] For this reason, some kabbalists compared gnosis about God to a dream: the sefirotic gradations are the imaginal constructs of an infinite luminescence whose presence at the horizon of the nonphenomenalizable consists of being not present.[203] The comparison to Heidegger is enhanced further by the fact that the process of imputing an image to the imageless, which is at the crux of the kabbalistic *vita contemplativa*, is at the same time an appurtenant beckoning to the nameless declaimed in the investiture of the name.

To illustrate the point, I will cite the following passage from *Ma'amar Yiḥud ha-Yir'ah*, a text that circulated among the students of Moses Ḥayyim Luzzatto (1707–46). There is reason to doubt that Luzzatto is the author, but the contents are unquestionably in accord with the teaching preserved in treatises that he wrote.[204]

> All of the worlds are naught but the disclosure of what was already arrayed in the perfection of the infinite, blessed be he . . . for the reality of all the worlds is naught but as one who dreams a dream and sees the matter in the imagination, and similarly the entire potency of the infinite, blessed be he, which has no temporality [*ein bo zeman*], is seen according to the way of time [*derekh zeman*]. . . . Thus, the infinite, blessed be he, acts in the way of his perfection, and there is placed before him the curtain of withdrawal [*masakh ha-ṣimṣum*] in which are dependent all these colors, and they are all the laws of nature from beginning to end. All of these things vis-à-vis the infinite, blessed be he, are in a verily different manner, which we cannot comprehend. . . . Similarly, the matter of time is nothing at all but how we imagine nature as it appears to us in accord with the withdrawal [*lefi ha-ṣimṣum*]. As we see in the dream itself that days and years pass in one dream, and with respect to the dreamer it seems to him that this is how it actually is [*nir'eh lo she-hu kakh mammash*]. Analogously, when we are awake, we imagine the matters of nature

> in accord with what we see, and we call this imagining time, as if there could be one hour or one moment like the years of a dream, which are in truth a single moment [*rega eḥad*].[205]

The author of this text exploits the archaic trope that the spatiotemporal world is but a dream, an idea that probably originated in Confucianism and Taoism, was then transported into various schools of Hinduism and Buddhism, and ultimately found its way into both Islamic and Jewish sources at the time when kabbalah began to proliferate as a historical phenomenon.[206] The disciple of Luzzatto appropriates this wisdom to explain one of the deepest mysteries of the esoteric tradition. If we assume that everything was contained indiscriminately in the incomposite oneness of *Ein Sof* prior to the *ṣimṣum*, then what appears to us as the progression of time is in fact the manner in which the single instant of eternity—a moment shaped by the paradoxical simultaneity of immeasurable velocity and interminable rest—is manifest on the phenomenal plane. We cannot speak of anything absolutely new occurring as a consequence of the withdrawal, since all was encompassed in the infinite, and hence time would appear to be illusory like a dream; and yet the trace that remains in the space after the withdrawal is the emanated light (*or ne'eṣal*) that provides the "place for all that exists" (*maqom le-khol nimṣa*), and thus it is viewed as a "new light" (*or ḥadash*).[207] The nature of temporality is to be discerned from this image of the trace, which signals not only the novelty of repetition, but also the blurring of boundaries as what is imagined to be real is really imagined.

The comparison of imagining the divine and the dream state is taken up by Luzzatto himself as we see from this passage:

> The form in the *sefirot* is not essential [*aṣmit*] but contingent [*miqrit*] in accord with the prophetic vision [*mar'eh ha-nevu'ah*], according to the secret "through the prophets I was imaged" (Hosea 12:11). For when the supernal will desires to inform a prophet about a secret it shows him the *sefirot* in one image, and afterward when it desires to show him another matter, it shows them in another image, even if it is opposite to the first. And this is verily like a dream, for the subjects change in one moment in accord with the dreamer.[208]

The forms assumed by the *sefirot* are variable and dissonant as we find in the case of dream images. That no absolute veracity can be affixed to the images by which the divine is perceived leads to the disquieting discernment that these images are true insofar as they are false, just as the dream is the *semblance of the simulacrum* par excellence wherein truth is not opposed to error, since the appearance of truthfulness cannot be determined independently of the truthfulness of appearance. Such a position is attested as well in a passage from *Qelaḥ Pitḥei Ḥokhmah*, a treatise that is likely not authored by Luzzatto but which faithfully preserves his teachings: "The *sefirot* can be seen in images that even conflict with one another [*yekholot ha-sefirot lera'ot be-dimyonot afillu hafkiyyim zeh la-zeh*], just as one verily sees in a dream that subjects change before him in one moment [*kemo mammash ha-ro'eh ba-ḥalom she-mitḥallefim ha-nos'im lefanaw be-rega eḥad*]."[209] In contrast to the waking sensation, the dream imagination epitomizes the capacity to picture a matter in varying and conflicting images in tandem, a characteristic of prophetic visions as well. Since the sefirotic emanations are also visualized concurrently in contradictory terms—for example, as circular and linear, as above and below—the oneiropoetic imagination is the epistemic modality best suited to comprehend the paradoxical nature of the imaginal presentation of the infinite beyond all visual and verbal representation.

One can well detect here the aforementioned viewpoint of Schelling that the imagination vacillates between infinity and finitude. This is precisely the role accorded the imagination in kabbalistic lore, the seeing of the heart that makes present that which is absent without collapsing absence into the negation of presence.[210] For both Heidegger and kabbalists, this activity is realized most visibly and ubiquitously in the dream, a sphere of imaginative activity where the real is symbolized by sensuous images of the unreal. The oneiropoetic, therefore, is the means by which truth is dissimulated intentionally in images that are false. From the inherently metaphoric nature of the dream, and the inescapable reflexivity that this implies, we can deduce, to paraphrase Ibn al-ʿArabī's appropriation of the ancient Indian gnosis, that being is apperceived as a dream within a dream, the imagination within an imagination.[211] Furthermore, two other distinct but related postulates ensue therefrom: first, the constitution of metaphor is such that the uncovering of truth is triggered by the recovery of truth in the covering of the uncovering; and second, the metaphor is a verbal leap that purports to bridge the difference that can be bridged only by augmenting the distance between what is bridged. The language of metaphor, as the visuality of the dreamscape, spans the abyss separating literal and figurative, factual and fictional, by bringing together what is kept apart.[212] The truth, accordingly, is the unconcealing of the concealment, which is always also the concealing of the unconcealment. The dream, paradigmatically, embodies the paradigm of the paradigm as the conferring withdrawal of truth as untruth.

Here it is germane to cite the comment of the Vilna Gaon, "All that we say with respect to *Adam Qadmon* and [the worlds of] emanation, creation, formation, and doing, is very much in the lower worlds, for in each world there are [the worlds] of emanation, creation, formation, and doing, and all of these aspects are the backend of the backend [*aḥorim de-aḥoriyyim*] and they are not glowing [*meṣaḥṣaḥim*]. Thus we speak by way of metaphor [*derekh mashal*] and there is no understanding at all."[213] There is no room for equivocation regarding the aporetic skepticism expressed in these words: whatever we say about any of the links in the chain of being, from the primal Adam to the four worlds, is derived from our experience of the lower, dim worlds—the posterior of the posterior—and hence our language of necessity is parabolic in nature; we have no unmediated access to comprehend reality itself. Eliashiv takes issue with those who would interpret the passage of the Gaon as if he meant that the language we use to discuss the divine is in any way arbitrary or inherently metaphorical, the view attributed to Luzzatto that he openly criticizes even as he admits not having studied the latter's compositions in great detail.[214] Relying on a number of other kabbalists, including Cordovero, Eliashiv insists that the *sefirot* are "subtle lights in the absolute spirituality [*orot daqqim be-takhlit ha-ruḥaniyyut*] that are not apprehended at all," and thus it is incorrect to say they are merely an apparition (*mar'eh*) or an image (*dimyon*) seen through the visions of prophets (*mar'ot ha-nevi'im*); they are, rather, "true and complete realities [*meṣi'uyyot gemurim amitiyyim*] that exist continually from the time the emanator, blessed be his name, emanated and brought them forth, and was garbed and unified in them."[215] Eliashiv does admit that there is a precipitous drop in aptitude from the time of Moses to the current epoch, but the symbolic nomenclature still imbibes the authority of an unbroken tradition. The intent of the Gaon's remark, therefore, "is not related to speech [*dibbur*] and language [*lashon*] but exclusively to comprehension [*hassagah*]. All of his words are only to establish in our hearts that we do not apprehend anything, and in order to distance and to remove every thought of an image of a shape [*demut to'ar*] or form [*ṣiyyur*], God forbid. Thus he said that whatever we grasp of these matters is only in the backend of the backend and they do not glimmer, and our comprehension in all of these words and expressions is far from their truth, for we do not understand anything to the point that according to our comprehension all of their words are only in the aspect of a metaphor."[216]

Eliashiv's motivation to contrast the qualifications of past generations and those in the present is evidently a strategy to avoid epistemological relativism and linguistic nominalism. Parenthetically, I note that this view clashes in part with his assertion that the disclosure of esoteric wisdom (*ḥokhmat ha-nistar*) below is greater in the present than in the past as a result of an augmentation of the light of the infinite in the realm of emanation,[217] an idea that is related even more specifically to the historical assertion that from the time of the sixteenth century the dissemination of kabbalistic texts has been intensified in unprecedented ways commensurate with the augmented revelation of that light in the material world stimulated theoretically by the messianic rectification (*tiqqun*) and practically by the technological revolution of the printing press.[218] Bracketing this inconsistency, I want to focus on the implication that, for Eliashiv, there is the possibility that the masters of previous generations were capable of comprehending the divine without the use of figurative language. The task of the critical scholar is to inquire about the soundness of this effort, not simply to codify it as if it were a truth beyond reproach or scrutiny. Granted that the terms used by kabbalists are not arbitrary, but can we really say they afford us direct knowledge of the divine realities? Can speaking about the unspeakable be anything but metaphorical approximation? Is it possible for anyone—even Moses—to flee from the predicament that the imageless can be seen only through the veil of the image? The stipulation of apophatic theology may be to strip the mind of all concepts and images in approaching the unknowable deity, but the radical shattering of all idolatry, including icons of the aniconic, does not preclude the necessity of the formless donning the form of formlessness. This ancient wisdom—and, in my opinion, utilizing William James's celebrated language about the mystical experience of union, hardly altered by differences of clime or creed—can be detected in Pico's statement, *Nulla res spiritualis descendens inferius operatur sine indumento*, "Nothing spiritual, descending below, operates without a garment."[219] Read Neoplatonically, this implies that spiritual entities assume corporal shape when they descend from the intelligible realm into the sensible world. From a postmetaphysical perspective, we can further extrapolate the cognitive axiom that not only do human beings have no experience of the immaterial except through the vestment of the material but that the vestment itself is the manner in which the immaterial materializes, whence it follows that truth is inherently parabolic and, as such, can be apprehended only through another parable.

Eliashiv himself comes to this very conclusion. After stating that the infinite can be described by the attributes consigned to the sefirotic emanations, including especially the anthropomorphic depictions of the *Shi'ur Qomah* speculation, he observes:

> The emanator, blessed be his name, is annulled [*meshullal*] of all these matters in the utmost nullification [*be-takhlit ha-shelilah*], but all of these matters verily [*mammash*] exist in the [world of] emanation. However, these are only attributed to the [world of] emanation by way of analogy [*erekh*], for it is higher than and superior to all of the reality of [the worlds of] creation, formation, and doing. And there is none in all of [the worlds of] creation, formation, and doing, who can comprehend the substance and form of the [world of] emanation as it is. There is no equivalency between the [world of] emanation and the [worlds of] creation, formation, and doing except in name alone. . . . All of these matters that are in the [world of] emanation are only by way of metaphor [*be-derekh mashal*]. The import is in accord with our apprehension of these matters, for certainly there is no analogy or likeness [*erekh we-dimyon*] at all between the true reality that is in them and our comprehension and apprehension of the matter. As we wrote above from the example of the soul that is in the body, even though the soul is actually within us, we do not comprehend its substance at all. According to our comprehension, it is merely an incomposite light, but in truth, there is in it all of the specific faculties of the body. . . . Hence, it is evident that all the aspects of the configurations [*ha-parṣufim*], and all of their matters of which we speak in the [world of] emanation, are in relation to us . . . only by way of metaphor exclusively, for the entirety of the emanation in relation to us is in the aspect of naught and nothing [*efes wa-ayin*]. . . . In all of these matters themselves, there is no metaphor at all, but rather they are truly everything that is said and repeated with respect to them, everything in actuality [*ha-kol mammash*] without any figurative speech [*meliṣah*] or another locution [*lashon*], and without another intention [*kawwanah*].[220]

In the conclusion of this passage, Eliashiv returns to his admonition against interpreting the descriptions of the emanations in a purely figurative manner. He emphasizes that even the use of grossly anthropomorphic images with reference to this realm should not be taken allegorically, if doing so means denying the actuality of that to which these attributes refer. And yet he also unambiguously affirms that we have no positive knowledge of these emanations—they are like nothing in relation to us—and hence whatever we say about them will be a matter of metaphorical construction. The nature of the secret, which is proportionate to the illumination of the light of the infinite in the world of emanation, must be disseminated secretively, that is, in such a manner that the secret is preserved in its exposure. Taking his cue from the portrayal of the zoharic fraternity, Eliashiv notes that Simeon ben Yoḥai and his colleagues shielded the esoteric nature of the mysteries by speaking of them emblematically (*derekh ḥiddah*).[221] This relates, first and foremost, to the depiction of the incorporeal in corporeal terms. Applying the older aggadic motif of the theophanic images (*demuyot*) or the incarnational forms (*dimyonot*) by which God appears—as a warrior at the splitting of the Red Sea, as an elder giving the Torah on Mount Sinai, or as the enthroned Ancient of Days seen by Daniel[222]—Eliashiv promotes a conception of the *imaginal body* to explain how the delimiting of the limitless is situated between the literal and the figurative; that is, the sense of embodiment that is affirmed is not carnal flesh but is nevertheless a concrete phenomenon and not merely a figure of speech. The body, when conceptualized from the perspective of the imaginal, is not subject to the metaphysical distinction between real and imagined; rather, it occupies an intermediate space in which the imaginary is real and the real imaginary, since there is no reality apart from what is imagined to be real, no being that can appear but through the appearance of its nonbeing.[223]

To cite one other passage that exemplifies the complicated way that Eliashiv rejected the metaphorical stance attributed to Luzzatto, and yet affirmed his own version of theosophical language that is neither and therefore both literal and figurative:

> Indeed, when he is garbed in the emanations and constricted by them in all of their matters, it is as it is written "and through the prophets I was imaged" [*u-ve-yad ha-nevi'im adammeh*] (Hosea 12:11).... Thus when the blessed holy One constricts his true simplicity to be revealed to his creatures, this is what is written "and through the prophets I was imaged." However, my intention is not that all the matters that are said in the words of the holy *Zohar* and the Ari, blessed be his memory, are only by way of prophetic visions [*mar'ot ha-nevu'ah*], as we find in the words of some recent kabbalists... for God forbid that my opinion is that the visions of the prophets were apparitions that essentially were only through images [*dimyonot*], and the essence of the visions was not all in the true reality.... On the contrary, all the words of the holy *Zohar* and the Ari, blessed be his memory, are entirely true, and they are in existence as they are written, because by means of this he, blessed be his name, is revealed in the disclosure of the name *YHWH*, blessed be he, whose seal is truth.[224] ... All the words of the holy *Zohar* and the Ari, blessed be his memory, are not a metaphor and symbol [*mashal we-dimyon*], God forbid. Nevertheless, they do not accord with our apprehension and our comprehension, God forbid. Relative to our apprehension in all of these matters, they are in truth only the aspect of metaphor and symbol. But relative to what is attributable to the emanation itself, which is elevated and transcends every created being in all of its minutiae, all things are there veritably as they are actually written.[225]

On the one hand, the divine emanations as they are in themselves—that is, as the incomposite unity of the infinite, the inner light of the Torah (*or penimit ha-torah*), the Tetragrammaton, which is garbed and contracted within them—are not metaphorical but ontically real, albeit not a physical property (*tekhunah gufani*) that can be described by a form (*to'ar*) or an image (*temunah*), and therefore beyond human comprehension;[226] on the other hand, the emanations of the imageless emanator, the hidden roots (*shorashim ne'lamim*) of all that comes to be in the lower three worlds,[227] are personified necessarily through the prism of imagination and hence they rhetorically assume the character of the metaphorical tropes by which the imaginal body—the "stature of the configuration of the anthropos" (*qomat parṣuf adam*)[228]—is constellated.

As it happens, the wisdom of the kabbalists was well appreciated by Adorno, who notoriously pointed out in a letter to Scholem, "the language into which the symbol is translated is itself a symbolic language, which calls to mind Kafka's statement that all his works were symbolic, but only in the sense that they were to be interpreted by new symbols in an endless series of steps."[229] Adorno correctly understood that in presuming the parabolic nature of truth, an orientation that resonates with the symbolic imaginary proffered by medieval kabbalists, Kafka closed the schism separating fact and fiction, and thereby opened the landscape of textuality to the measure of incommensurability, the limitless limit that delimits the interpretative standpoint from which a reader may summon a hermeneutical criterion of objectivity that avoids the extremes of absolute relativism and relative absolutism.[230] Language, poetically conceived as inherently metaphorical, is always an act of translation, a joining of the divergent rather than a harnessing of the same. In the particular cultural ambiance of the kabbalah, language performs this function by expressing the inexpressible, rendering visible the invisible, making apparent the inapparent. The symbol, therefore, brings the unknown into relation with the known, but without reducing the difference that binds the two incongruities into an identity.

Notes

1. See the detailed analysis in Rohstock, *Negative Selbstbezug des Absoluten*, pp. 49–116.

2. On the comparison of the kabbalistic *Ein Sof* and Heidegger's understanding of *Seyn/Nichts*, see Steiner, *Grammars of Creation*, p. 32: "Though, strictly considered, unthinkable, the *En Sof* of the Kabbahlists [*sic*], becomes the root of roots, the font of fonts. The mundane nihilist would forget, would suppress from preconscious witness, the infinite agency *in absentia* of the abyss of God, of that which irradiated the fruitful turbulence of chaos. . . . Precisely as Heidegger posits, after Hegel, there cannot 'be Being' without the eclipse, the inward contraction of non-being. But non-being which, according to the mystics, 'is so that Being can be,' presses on existence as does a vacuum on a membrane."

3. The tradition concerning the nameless God is found in older sources from late antiquity, in part reflecting the Platonic notion that the absolute being has no proper name, an idea that in due course was appropriated by Jewish, Christian, and Muslim theology and religious philosophy. See Stroumsa, "Nameless God"; Wilkinson, *Tetragrammaton*, pp. 9–18.

4. Heidegger, *Pathmarks*, p. 243; *Wegmarken*, p. 319.

5. Derrida, *Writing and Difference*, p. 137. Concerning this passage, see Wolfson, *Giving*, p. 172.

6. Heidegger, *On the Way to Language*, p. 199. See also Park, "Differing Ways"; Ma, *Heidegger on East-West Dialogue*, pp. 19–23.

7. Heidegger, *On the Way to Language*, p. 29; *Unterwegs zur Sprache*, p. 114. In "Das Wesen der Sprache," in *On the Way to Language*, p. 79 (*Unterwegs zur Sprache*, p. 173), Heidegger elicits from the fact that the guest goes unnamed in Stefan George's "Das Neue Reich" the wisdom that the nameless (*Ungenannt*) remains the highest favor that comes to the poet.

8. Heidegger, *Elucidations*, p. 170; *Erläuterungen*, p. 149. On the identity of being and nothing in Heidegger, and the presumed ineffability of both, see Priest, *Beyond the Limits*, pp. 242–43; Casati, "Being: A Dialetheic Interpretation," pp. 87–115. See the Heideggerian passage cited in ch. 4 at n. 314.

9. Heidegger, *Contributions*, §129, pp. 193–94; *Beiträge*, p. 246.

10. Heidegger, *Ponderings II–VI*, p. 6 (emphasis in original); *Überlegungen II–VI*, p. 7.

11. Heidegger, *Ponderings II–VI*, p. 7 (emphasis in original); *Überlegungen II–VI*, pp. 7–8.

12. Heidegger, *Contributions*, §7, p. 21; *Beiträge*, p. 24.

13. Heidegger, *Contributions*, §145, p. 209; *Beiträge*, p. 266.

14. Heidegger, *Contributions*, §146, p. 210; *Beiträge*, p. 267. See Wolfson, "Nihilating Nonground," pp. 40–41.

15. Heidegger, *Ponderings II–VI*, p. 169; *Überlegungen II–VI*, p. 231.

16. Heidegger, *Contributions*, §127, p. 192; *Beiträge*, p. 244.

17. Heidegger, *Ponderings II–VI*, p. 311; *Überlegungen II–VI*, p. 429.

18. Jussaume, "Heidegger and the Nothing," p. vi.

19. Heidegger, *Contributions*, §254, p. 322; *Beiträge*, p. 406.

20. Heidegger, *Ponderings II–VI*, p. 7; *Überlegungen II–VI*, p. 7.

21. Summerell, "Otherness of the Thinking of Being." Heidegger's description of the theological difference, which was communicated to and reported by Max Müller, is cited on p. 114.

22. Heidegger, *Ponderings II–VI*, p. 135; *Überlegungen II–VI*, p. 185. I have modified the translation of *Geistlosigkeit* as "Godlessness" to "spiritlessness." In the previous paragraph of this aphorism, Heidegger does use the term *Gott-losigkeit*.

23. Tropea, *Religion*, pp. 126–27.

24. Heidegger, *Contributions*, §143, p. 207; *Beiträge*, p. 263.

25. Heidegger, *Contributions*, §143, p. 207; *Beiträge*, p. 263.

26. Heidegger, *Contributions*, §259, p. 338; *Beiträge*, p. 428.

27. Heidegger, *Contributions*, §143, p. 207; *Beiträge*, p. 263.

28. Heidegger, *Contributions*, §7, p. 23 (emphasis in original); *Beiträge*, pp. 26–27.

29. Heidegger, *Ponderings VII–XI*, p. 195; *Überlegungen VII–XI*, p. 252.

30. Heidegger, *Contributions*, §11, p. 27; *Beiträge*, p. 31.

31. Heidegger, *Contributions*, §26, p. 50; *Beiträge*, p. 63.

32. In scholarly literature, there is debate whether Saruq was a genuine disciple of Luria, an autonomous and perhaps less authentic interpreter of Lurianic doctrine, part of an independent circle of kabbalists in Safed that evolved alongside Luria's school, or perhaps someone who transformed Cordoverian themes in a Lurianic key. For some representative studies, see Scholem, "Rabbi Israel Sarug"; Meroz, "R. Yisrael Sarug"; Meroz, "Faithful Transmission"; Meroz, "School of Sarug"; Idel, "Between the Kabbalah"; Idel, "Italy in Safed"; Shatil, "Kabbalah of R. Israel Sarug." It is worth noting that Abraham Cohen de Herrera, who studied with Saruq in Ragusa and transmitted oral teachings in his name, considered him to be a disciple of Luria. Moreover, he attributes the doctrines of *sha'ashu'a* and *malbush* to Luria directly and not to Saruq. See the text from *Beit Elohim* in de Herrera, *House of Divinity*, pp. 7–8. See the passage from *Sha'ar ha-Shamayim*, op. cit., p. 488, where the terms contraction (*ṣimṣum*), measurement (*shi'ur*), attribute (*middah*), bemusement (*sha'ashu'a*), movement (*tenu'ah*), and alteration from pleasure (*ḥilluf me-oneg*), are identified and all ascribed to the master (*rav*), that is, Luria. For the original Spanish, see de Herrera, *Puerta del Cielo*, p. 291, and the English translation in de Herrera, *Gate of Heaven*, p. 295. See Necker, *Humanistische Kabbala im Barock*, pp. 156–57, 159n103.

33. For my previous analysis of this motif and reference to other scholars who have discussed it, see Wolfson, *Circle in the Square*, pp. 69–72, 189–92nn174–80. See also Wolfson, *Language*, pp. 271–87; Wolfson, *Alef*, pp. 131–36. The motif of quivering in both Lurianic kabbalah and Heideggerian thought may be profitably compared to the state of trembling (*durchzittern*) in Hegel to mark the tension of the interiorization of alterity when the subject feels like an "other" in relation to itself. See Malabou, *Future of Hegel*, p. 32.

34. Theodor and Albeck, eds., *Bere'shit Rabba*, 1:1, pp. 1–2, 8:1, p. 57; Babylonian Talmud, Shabbat 89a.

35. See, for instance, Wolfson, *Language*, pp. 277–78, where I analyze the motif of *sha'ashu'a* in the *Bahir*.

36. See *Zohar* 1:178b, 245b; 2:173b, 217b, 255a; 3:193a.

37. Cordovero, *Zohar in Perush Or Yaqar*, 1:12: "Before anything emanated came into being *Ein Sof* was alone, and delighted in the comprehension of his essence [*mishta'ashe'a be-hassagat aṣmuto*]." Similar language is used in Cordovero, *Zohar im Perush Or Yaqar*, 6:20, and compare Cordovero, *Shi'ur Qomah*, 53a: "In *Ein Sof* it is not correct [to speak of] action [*asiyyah*], formation [*yeṣirah*], creation [*beri'ah*] or speech [*amirah*]. . . . In his primordiality to all things, *Ein Sof* comprehends himself [with a] perfect comprehension [*massig et aṣmo hassagah sheleimah*]. He and his will are one and there is nothing outside of him. When he was bemused by his essence and the comprehension of his existence [*hishta'ashe'a be-aṣmuto we-hassagat meṣi'uto*], there was nothing distinct from him." See Cordovero, *Shi'ur Qomah*, 58a; Cordovero, *Elimah Rabbati*, p. 8. Given the fact that kabbalists uniformly accepted the Galenic idea that the semen originates in the brain, it stands to reason that self-contemplation and auto-sexual arousal should be deemed two sides of the same coin.

38. Cordovero, *Zohar in Perush Or Yaqar*, 16:37, cited in Sack, *Kabbalah of Rabbi Moshe Cordovero*, pp. 71–72. In some passages, Cordovero emphasizes that the *sha'ashu'a* of *Ein Sof* is related to benefiting the emanations and created beings outside his essence. See, for example, Cordovero, *Zohar im Perush Or Yaqar*, 21:95, where the rabbinic notion of God's taking delight in the Torah is interpreted symbolically as the *sha'ashu'a* of *Ein Sof* related to the unity of *Ḥokhmah*, *Binah*, and *Da'at*. Compare Cordovero, *Shi'ur Qomah*, 13b. On the description of *sha'ashu'a* as the illumination of the light on *Ein Sof* through the unity of *Keter*, *Ḥokhmah*, and *Binah*, see Cordovero, *Shi'ur Qomah*, 15a, 18b-c. The motif of *sha'ashu'a* in Cordovero has been discussed by Ben-Shlomo, *Mystical Theology of Moses Cordovero*, pp. 60–61, 174, 187, 239n202; Scholem, "Name of God," p. 182n62; Sack, "Doctrine of Ṣimṣum," pp. 226–27; Sack, *Kabbalah of Rabbi Moshe Cordovero*, pp. 73–76, 150–76; Shatil, "Kabbalah of R. Israel Sarug," pp. 164–74. For the influence of Cordovero on the Saruqian notion of *sha'ashu'a*, see also Liebes, "Towards a Study," p. 105n24; Meroz, "School of Sarug," p. 154; Beltrán, *Influence of Abraham Cohen de Herrera's Kabbalah*, pp. 33–39.

39. Sack, "Doctrine of Ṣimṣum," p. 226n79, points out that in at least one passage (Cordovero, *Shi'ur Qomah*, 42d–43b) *sha'ashu'a* does have overt sexual connotations. Especially pertinent are the following words (*Shi'ur Qomah*, 43a–b): "It says, 'I will walk [in your midst]' (Leviticus 26:12), for the agent stands by himself; that is, this matter of the journey [*ṭiyyul*]

is something that applies to him alone so that he will participate in the secret of the unity, the disclosure of the light of *Ein Sof* to his creatures. Therefore, it says that he delighted in himself [*mishta'ashe'a be-aṣmo*] and not in something outside him. Rather he went and took delight in himself." See Sack, *Kabbalah of Rabbi Moshe Cordovero*, p. 73n79. Formulations such as this one likely influenced the Lurianic sources. Compare as well Cordovero, *Shi'ur Qomah*, 13b–c. Shatil, "Kabbalah of R. Israel Sarug," p. 169, minimizes the auto-erotic and narcissistic elements of the myth of divine bemusement, emphasizing the speculative element. In my judgment, Shatil is misled by an oversimplified distinction between the Neoplatonic orientation and the mythical approach. She subscribes to the view of Liebes that Cordovero's teaching is "intensely mythical," but she nonetheless downplays the erotic insinuations because of her conviction that he does not ascribe any change to the "abstract infinite unity" of *Ein Sof*.

40. MSS Oxford, Bodleian Library 1783, fol. 48a and 1784, fol. 58a. For a list of other manuscript witnesses of this text, see Meroz, "Redemption," p. 93. According to Meroz, this anonymous text belongs to the first of five stages in the development of Lurianic theosophy. See, in particular, the reading preserved in MS Oxford, Bodleian Library 1741, fol. 128a: "When it arose in the will of the emanator to produce the letters, at first he was alone, delighting in himself." The text is published on the basis of MS New York, Columbia University X893 M6862 in Meroz, "Early Lurianic Compositions," pp. 327–30. The relevant passage appears on p. 327.

41. *Zohar* 1:15a. See Meroz, "Redemption," pp. 111–12. It is noteworthy that Saruq's *Derush ha-Malbush* is presented as an explication of this zoharic passage. See Saruq, *Derush ha Malbush*, p. 7. On the zoharic symbol of the *boṣina de-qardinuta*, see the comments and reference to other sources in Wolfson, *Language*, pp. 137, 321, 487n198, 571–72n200; and the more recent discussion in Necker, "Hans Blumenberg's Metaphorology," pp. 194–98.

42. There is some similarity between my use of the word *bemusement* to designate the contemplative jouissance of the infinite in kabbalistic sources and the pure play of "musement" articulated by Charles S. Peirce as the meditative-experiential basis for belief in God in the essay "A Neglected Argument for the Reality of God." See, in particular, Peirce, *Collected Papers*, 6.458–459, pp. 314–15: "But let religious meditation be allowed to grow up spontaneously out of Pure Play without any breach of continuity, and the Muser will retain the perfect candour proper to Musement. If one who had determined to make trial of Musement as a favorite recreation were to ask me for advice, I should reply as follows: The dawn and the gloaming most invite one to Musement; but I have found no watch of the nychthemeron that has not its own advantages for the pursuit. . . . There is no kind of reasoning that I should wish to discourage in Musement; and I should lament to find anybody confining it to a method of such moderate fertility as logical analysis. Only, the Player should bear in mind that the higher weapons in the arsenal of thought are not playthings, but edge-tools. In any mere Play they can be used by way of exercise alone; while logical analysis can be put to its full efficiency in Musement." And Pierce, *Collected Papers*, 6.465, p. 318: "But however that may be, in the Pure Play of Musement the idea of God's Reality will be sure sooner or later to be found an attractive fancy, which the Muser will develop in various ways. The more he ponders it, the more it will find response in every part of his mind, for its beauty, for its supplying an ideal of life, and for its thoroughly satisfactory explanation of his whole threefold environment." On musement in Peircean thought, see Raposa, *Peirce's Philosophy of Religion*, pp. 117–41; Ochs, *Peirce, Pragmatism and the Logic of Scripture*, pp. 228–29, 241–45, 250–51, 282–83, 288–89; White, *Hidden God*, pp. 165–85.

43. Wolfson, *Language*, pp. 278–79. Mention should also be made here of the account of how the immaterial soul enters the material body in Plotinus, *Enneads*, 4.7.1, p. 389: "How then, since the intelligible is separate, does soul come into body? It is in this way: as much of it as is only intellect has a purely intellectual life in the intelligible and stays there forever without being affected; but that which acquires desire, which follows immediately on that intellect, goes out further in a way by its acquisition of desire, and, desiring to impart order and beauty according to the pattern which it sees in Intellect, is as if pregnant by the intelligibles and labouring to give birth, and so is eager to make, and constructs the world." Even closer to the kabbalistic mythos is the characterization of noetic desire as the impulse for the mind to procreate in the Arabic paraphrase of this Plotinian passage in the *Theology of Aristotle*, translated by Geoffrey Lewis, in *Plotini Opera, II*, p. 219: "*When the mind acquires a desire, it proceeds because of that desire in a certain direction* and does not abide in its original place, *for it desires* greatly to act and *to adorn the things which it has seen in the mind. Like the woman who has conceived and to whom the birth-pangs have come, so that she may bring forth* what is in her womb, so, when the mind is informed with

the form of desire, *it desires to bring out into actuality* the form that is in it, and it longs greatly for that, and the birth-pangs seize it and it brings it (the form) into actuality *because of its desire for the sensible world*" (emphasis in original).

44. It appears that the reference is to the ten *sefirot* that emerge from or correspond to the ten letters of the name *YHWH* when written out in full in one of the following three ways with the respective sums of 45, 63, and 72: *yw"d h"a wa"w h"a; yw"d h"y wa"w h"y; yw"d h"y wy"w h"y*. The fourth permutation of *YHWH*, which has a sum of 52, consists of nine letters: *yw"d h"h w"w h"h*. Another possible explanation is that the four letters of *YHWH* can be written as a sequence of ten letters: *yod, yod heh, yod heh waw, yod heh waw heh*. See Eliashiv, *Leshem Shevo we-Aḥlamah: Haqdamot u-She'arim*, p. 126. On the derivation of the four permutations from the letters of the name *YHWH*, which are set in the garment, see Saruq, *Derush ha-Malbush*, p. 14.

45. Saruq, *Limmudei Aṣilut*, 3a. Compare the version in Delmedigo, *Ta'alumot Ḥokhmah*, 77b, and the introduction to the commentary on *Sifra di-Ṣeni'uta* in Saruq, *Limmudei Aṣilut*, 34c–d.

46. Scholem, *Kabbalah*, p. 132. For a historical sketch of Saruq and some other kabbalists influenced by him, see Scholem, *Major Trends*, pp. 257–58.

47. The same can be said of the summary of Saruq's teaching in Scholem, "Name of God," p. 181: "Here the coming into being of the linguistic movement, which has its original source in the infinite being of God himself, proceeds from the fact that, in God, a joy, a sense of delight or self-rapture, held sway—in Hebrew, *Shi'ashu'a*—which evoked a movement in the *En-sof*. This movement is the original source of all linguistic movement, for, although still elapsing in the *En-sof* itself, it could be explained in those combinations of the 22 letters of the alphabet, which are mentioned in the book of Yetsira. From this a movement comes into being in the *En-sof* 'from itself to itself,' a movement in which that joy of the *En-sof* gives self-expression to itself, but thereby at the same time expresses the mysterious potentialities of all expression. From this innermost movement the original texture—in Hebrew *malbush*—is woven in the substance of the *En-sof* itself."

48. Liebes, "Tsaddiq Yesod Olam," p. 105n167, argues that *sha'ashu'a* in the Saruqian kabbalah is not described in explicit sexual language even though the divine thought has an erotic quality that is actualized in the emanative process. On the sexual connotation of the word *sha'ashu'a* applied to God in Lurianic texts, see Viṭal, *Sha'ar Ma'amerei Rashbi*, p. 171: "This delight is for the sake of the union to bring forth the male waters from above to below. Just as there is delight in the souls of the righteous below for the female waters, so must there be delight to have pleasure in order to produce the male waters in the secret of the wine that gladdens." The word *sha'ashu'a* in this context denotes the sexual foreplay that arouses the male waters above and the female waters below. Compare Viṭal, *Sha'ar Ma'amerei Rashbi*, p. 44, where *Binah* is described as taking delight in the letters in the manner that *Malkhut* takes delight in the souls of the righteous, which are identified as the female waters. Both these sources have been noted by Meroz, "Early Lurianic Compositions," p. 315n22. Meroz perceptively poses the question whether the expression *mishta'ashe'a* suggests the androgynous image of *Ein Sof*. This approach concurs with my own analysis and the conclusions I have reached independently. However, I have placed greater emphasis on the masculine aspect of this act of sexual self-gratification related to what I have called the androgynous male.

49. Saruq, *Limmudei Aṣilut*, 21d–22a.

50. Ibid., 22a. The same expression is used in *Shever Yosef* in Delmedigo, *Ta'alumot Ḥokhmah*, 60a.

51. Gruenwald, "Preliminary Critical Edition," §18, p. 147; Hayman, *Sefer Yeṣira*, §18, pp. 98–100. On Saruq's theory of *malbush* and its possible connection to older Jewish magical techniques, see Idel, *Golem*, pp. 148–54.

52. Scholem, *Kabbalah*, p. 132.

53. Delmedigo, *Ta'alumot Ḥokhmah*, 60a.

54. This point is missed by Shatil, "Kabbalah of R. Israel Sarug," p. 174, who concludes that Saruq maintains "the causal relationship between God and the power of *din*, without making it a fully integral part of Divine essence, as it is in Cordovero's system." Shatil draws this conclusion after quoting the very text from *Shever Yosef* that I have cited, but she neglected to relate to the first part whence it is clear that the ten delimited attributes are comprised within the limitless essence of the infinite. On the concealment of all things in the essence of *Ein Sof*, see the introduction to the commentary on *Sifra di-Ṣeni'uta* in Saruq, *Limmudei Aṣilut*, 34b.

55. Delmedigo, *Ta'alumot Ḥokhmah*, 60a.

56. Bachrach, *Emeq ha-Melekh*, 1:1, p. 113. Compare Wildmann, *Beit Olamim*, 95a–b.

57. *Pirqei Rabbi Eliezer*, ch. 3, 5b.

58. Bachrach, *Emeq ha-Melekh*, 1:4, p. 124. Compare Graf, *Wayaqhel Moshe*, pp. 38–39, cited in ch. 6 at n. 157. On the doctrine of *malbush* in Bachrach, see Shatil, "Doctrine of Secrets," pp. 374–77.

59. Wolfson, *Language*, p. 26, and reference to other scholarly discussions on p. 422n251.

60. Compare Bachrach, *Emeq ha-Melekh*, 1:1, p. 111.

61. Ibid., 1:2, p. 119. See Liebes, "Towards a Study," pp. 117–20. The images of inscription (*gelifu*) and the paper (*neyyar*) upon which the point (*nequddah*) is inscribed, are developed by Graf, *Wayaqhel Moshe*, p. 39.

62. Bachrach, *Emeq ha-Melekh*, 1:2, pp. 119–20. Compare *Shever Yosef* in Delmedigo, *Ta'alumot Ḥokhmah*, 60a, and Delmedigo, *Novelot Ḥokhmah*, 151b–152a.

63. De Herrera, *Gate of Heaven*, pp. 297–98; *Puerto del Cielo*, pp. 293–94. For the Hebrew translation, see the text of *Sha'ar ha-Shamayim* in de Herrera, *House of Divinity*, p. 490. See the analysis in Altmann, "Lurianic Kabbalah," pp. 30–32; Beltrán, *Influence of Abraham Cohen de Herrera's Kabbalah*, pp. 344–46.

64. On Eliashiv's use of the Saruqian version of Lurianic kabbalah, see Baumgarten, "History and Historiosophy," pp. 18–20. I prefer to label Eliashiv an exponent of Lithuanian kabbalah as opposed to a representative of the kabbalistic circle of the Vilna Gaon. On these taxonomies, see the sources cited by Garb, *Modern Kabbalah*, p. 63n55. Garb characterizes Eliashiv as the "leading theoretician" of this school (p. 65). Closer to the mark, in my opinion, is Nadler's description of Eliashiv's *Leshem Shevo we-Aḥlamah* as "a work largely concerned with the elucidation of the GRA's mystical commentaries" in *Faith of the Mithnagdim*, p. 37. Concerning this categorization, see also Meir, "Eclectic Kabbalah"; Shuchat, "Thoughts on Lithuanian Kabbalah." On balance, Eliashiv's kabbalistic knowledge seems to have been derived mostly from his assiduous reading of texts—rarely, if at all, does he mention having received a tradition orally from a particular master, and thus we can apply to him the traditional idiom *mi-pi sefarim we-lo mi-pi soferim*, "from the mouth of texts and not from the mouth of scribes." See, however, Eliashiv, *Leshem Shevo we-Aḥlamah: Haqdamot u-She'arim*, p. 4, where he states explicitly that he received traditions from both his paternal and his maternal ancestors. He claims, moreover, that a branch of his mother's family can be traced to Luria and he mentions as well that he belongs to the lineage of the seventeenth-century Polish kabbalist Samson ben Pesaḥ of Ostropolye.

65. Eliashiv, *Leshem Shevo we-Aḥlamah: Haqdamot u-She'arim*, p. 126. See ibid., p. 135: "The emergence and existence of the letters of the Torah is thus clarified for us: they came to be from the light of the trace that remained in the place of the contraction of the infinite [*be-maqom ha-ṣimṣum de-ein sof*]; its withdrawal from there happened bit by bit, and in the order of it touched and it did not touch [*de-maṭi we-lo maṭi*], it erupted, returned, and erupted [*hitnoṣeṣ we-ḥozer we-hitnoṣeṣ*], for this is the aspect of the bemusement [*ha-sha'ashu'a*]. From this were produced the likeness of the aspect of many points, for they are the splendors of the light of the outburst [*zoharei or de-ha-hitnoṣeṣut*], and by means of their constantly drawing close, in touching and not touching, the points unified with one another and became letters. They began as disparate and they ended in unison. And these are all the letters of the Torah." On the motif of letters of the infinite in Ḥabad thought, see ch. 5 n. 152.

66. This Lurianic motif is based on zoharic passages that explicitly depict the activity of the *boṣina de-qardinuta* in the highest recesses of the infinite as an expression of judgment or even as the catharsis of evil. See *Zohar* 2:254b; 3:292b (*Idra Zuṭa*); Viṭal, *Eṣ Ḥayyim*, 29:7, 24b. On the expression *olam ein sof*, see Saruq, *Limmudei Aṣilut*, 22c. See also Wildmann, *Beit Olamim*, 101b–102a, who writes of the allusion "to the deep secret to understand the bond of the emanation with the world of infinity by means of the matter of the countenance of the head that is not known, and this is the matter of the unity that the kabbalists revealed."

67. Bachrach, *Gan ha-Melekh*, MS Oxford, Bodleian Library 1586, fol. 2a.

68. Scholem, "Name of God," p. 181, surmised that the primal linguistic expression of *Ein Sof*, through which the garment is woven, is an act of writing that comes before the act of speaking. I took a similar position in my analysis of the divine engraving, which I called *erasing the erasure*, in Wolfson, *Circle in the Square*, pp. 49–78. This is justified insofar as the verbs that are used connote the activity of writing, but a more nuanced understanding would be based on the discernment that writing is at the same time speaking, and we can thus presume that the letters written are also vocally proclaimed. For emphasis on the elements of voice and breath in kabbalistic linguistic speculation, see Garb, "Powers of Language."

69. Ickovits, *Nefesh ha-Ḥayyim*, 4:10, pp. 275–76.

70. The Saruqian kabbalah was made accessible to the Christian world through the inclusion of several texts in Christian Knorr von Rosenroth's *Kabbala Denudata*, including sections from Bachrach's *Emeq ha-Melekh* (vol. 2, pt. 1, pp. 152–346); de Herrera's *Puerta del Cielo* (vol. 1, pt. 3, pp. 3–192), and *Casa de la Divinidad* (vol. 2, pt. 2, pp. 188–242). See Schmidt-Biggemann, *Geschichte der christlichen Kabbala*, 3:76–85, 127–30, 132–34; and the essays by Necker and Theisohn cited in the introduction n. 88.

71. *Zohar* 1:15a. See the account of Saruq's kabbalah in Delmedigo, *Ta'alumot Ḥokhmah*, 78b. On the

zoharic style of oxymoron and paradox, see Scholem, *Major Trends*, pp. 166–67.

72. Saruq, *Limmudei Aṣilut*, 36a; Bachrach, *Emeq ha-Melekh*, 4:1, p. 171; Delmedigo, *Novelot Ḥokhmah*, 164a-b. On the folding up of the Torah, see Scholem, "Name of God," p. 182.

73. For an extended discussion of this symbolism, see Wolfson, *Alef*, pp. 123–32.

74. Many scholars have written about this distinction in Eckhart. See, for instance, McGinn, "God beyond God"; Wolfson, "Patriarchy and Motherhood," pp. 1059–75, and reference to other scholars on p. 1060n33.

75. Schelling, *Ages of the World (Fragment)*, p. 25; *Weltalter*, in *Sämmtliche Werke*, 8:236.

76. Heidegger, *On the Way to Language*, pp. 45–46; *Unterwegs zur Sprache*, pp. 134–35.

77. *Zohar* 3:132a (*Idra Rabba*). On the aggadic image of the primordial Torah written as black fire upon white fire, see Scholem, *On the Kabbalah*, pp. 48–49; Idel, "Concept of Torah," pp. 43–45; Idel, *Absorbing Perfections*, pp. 45–69.

78. Wildmann, *Beit Olamim*, 96a.

79. Heidegger, *Question Concerning Technology*, p. 10; *Vorträge und Aufsätze*, p. 12. Heidegger's insight is inspired by the comment of Plato, *Symposium* 205b, ἡ γάρ τοι ἐκ τοῦ μὴ ὄντος εἰς τὸ ὂν ἰόντι ὁτῳοῦν αἰτία πᾶσά ἐστι ποίησις, which he renders as "Every occasion for whatever passes over and goes forward into presencing from that which is not presencing is *poiēsis*, is bringing-forth [*Her-vor-bringen*]."

80. Schelling, *Ages of the World (Fragment)*, p. 26; *Weltalter*, in *Sämmtliche Werke*, 8:237. For Böhme, the *Ungrund*, which is also identified as *Nichts*, is similarly characterized as neither being nor not being. See below n. 129, and the Böhmean passages cited in ch. 4 n. 264. Compare Paslick, "Ontological Context," p. 413. The influence of Böhme on Schelling is duly noted by Paslick, op. cit., pp. 413–14. See Ohashi, "Der Ungrund und das System," p. 248: "der Ungrund kein Gott nichts in Seiendes ist, somit zu keiner Onto-Theologie bzw. Metaphysik mehr gehört." See also Mayer, *Jena Romanticism*, pp. 200 and 203. For other references, see introduction n. 83.

81. See ch. 4 n. 263, and the texts cited there at n. 266 and in ch. 5 n. 71.

82. Schelling, *Philosophical Investigations*, p. 27 (emphasis in original); *Philosophische Untersuchungen*, p. 30.

83. Heidegger, *Schelling's Treatise*, p. 112; *Schelling: Vom Wesen*, pp. 195–96.

84. Heidegger, *Schelling's Treatise*, pp. 112–13; *Schelling: Vom Wesen*, p. 196.

85. Heidegger, *Schelling's Treatise*, p. 113; *Schelling: Vom Wesen*, p. 196.

86. Heidegger, *Schelling's Treatise*, p. 114; *Schelling: Vom Wesen*, pp. 197–98.

87. Heidegger, *Schelling's Treatise*, p. 114; *Schelling: Vom Wesen*, p. 198.

88. Heidegger, *Schelling's Treatise*, p. 114 (emphasis in original); *Schelling: Vom Wesen*, p. 198.

89. Wolfson, *Giving*, p. 198.

90. See ch. 4 n. 218.

91. This is the expression used in the *Wumen Kuan*, a collection of Zen koans assembled by Wumen Huikai (1183–1260). See Yamada, trans., *Gateless Gate*, p. 35. Rather than setting form and formlessness in binary opposition, the true dharma and the mind of nirvana are described as the form of no-form. The true form, therefore, is not the absence of form but the form of formlessness.

92. Heidegger, *Contributions*, §242, p. 303; *Beiträge*, p. 384. The text is cited in Wolfson, *Giving*, p. 245.

93. Heidegger, *Contributions*, §83, p. 134; *Beiträge*, p. 171. See, however, the conversation between Heidegger and Bikkhu Maha Mani in Heidegger, *Reden und Andere Zeugnisse*, pp. 589–93, and discussion of this meeting in Petzet, *Encounters*, pp. 170–81. It is of interest to recall in this context the remark in Heidegger, "Only a God Can Save Us," p. 62: "my conviction is that only in the same place where the modern technical world took its origin can we also prepare a conversion (*Umkehr*) of it. In other words, this cannot happen by taking over Zen-Buddhism or other Eastern experiences of the world. For this conversion of thought we need the help of the European tradition and a new appropriation of it. Thought will be transformed only through thought that has the same origin and determination."

94. The expression is appropriated from the comparison of Heideggerian and Buddhist reflections on emptiness in Stenstad, *Transformations*, pp. 161–71. On the comparison of Heidegger's nothing and the Buddhist emptiness, see also Stambaugh, *Finitude of Being*, pp. 171–83; Nishitani, "Reflections"; May, *Heidegger's Hidden Sources*, pp. 21–34; Zhang, *Heidegger*, pp. 54–61; Ma, *Heidegger on East-West Dialogue*, pp. 178–85; Coriando, "Substance and Emptiness"; and the chapter "Nothingness, Language, Emptiness: Heidegger and Chan Buddhism" in Nelson, *Chinese and Buddhist Philosophy*, pp. 225–52. See also Davis, "Heidegger and Asian Philosophy," pp. 463–68. A more deconstructive approach to Heidegger's interest in Asian culture has been proffered by Ma, "Mysterious Relations to the East." For a survey of the scholarly assessments of

Heidegger's intellectual relation to and engagement with Buddhism, see Hartig, *Lehre des Buddha.*

95. Garfield, *Engaging Buddhism*, p. 66. It is worth recalling here the comments on the identity of being and nothing in Hegel, *Encyclopedia*, p. 140 (*Enzyklopädie*, pp. 187–88): "Again, being may also be represented as absolutely rich and nothing as absolutely poor. But when we regard the entire world and say of it that everything is and nothing further, we leave all determinateness aside and instead of absolute fullness [*absoluten Fülle*] we only retain absolute emptiness [*absolute Leerheit*]. The same comment can be made about its application to the definition of God as mere being. Standing over and against this definition with equal justification is the Buddhist definition that God is nothingness, with its implication that a human being becomes God through self-annihilation [*daß er sich selbst vernichte*]." This remark, labeled as an "addition" (*Zusatz*), is from the annotations of Hegel's students explicating his comments. The supplementary material was added to the posthumous edition of Hegel's works published in 1832. Leaving aside the concluding statement that the Buddhist teaching culminates in the idea that one becomes God through annihilation of the self, there is merit to Hegel's sensitivity to the fact that no ultimate distinction exists between absolute fullness and absolute emptiness, that the suchness of being is the vacuity of nonbeing. See ch. 4 n. 312 and ch. 5 n. 2.

96. Heidegger, *Pathmarks*, p. 238; *Wegmarken*, p. 312.

97. Heidegger, *Pathmarks*, p. 238, note a; *Wegmarken*, p. 312, note a.

98. Heidegger, *On the Way to Language*, p. 19; *Unterwegs zur Sprache*, p. 103. See Ma, *Heidegger on East-West Dialogue*, pp. 188–89.

99. Petzet, *Encounters*, p. 180.

100. Asaṅga, *Summary of the Great Vehicle*, p. 49.

101. Gishin, *Collected Teachings of the Tendai Lotus School*, p. 5.

102. *Paramārtha-satya* is the truth of the universal emptiness, codependence, and impermanence of all things that lies beneath empirical phenomena and beyond verbal expression and conceptual discrimination, whereas *saṃvṛti-satya* relates to the ways that we routinely experience, classify, and describe sentient reality as a patchwork of reified and permanent substances. See Newland, *Two Truths*; Newland, *Appearance and Reality*; Lusthaus, "Two Truths."

103. K'uei-chi, *Comprehensive Commentary on the Heart Sutra*, p. 91.

104. For a more extensive discussion with proper annotation, see Wolfson, *Open Secret*, pp. 109–14. To cite another example, see Daoyuan, *Records of the Transmission of the Lamp*, 1:98: "Delusion and awakening are like darkness and light / Light and dark are not mutually exclusive / Now, handing over the Dharma of darkness and light / It is neither one nor is it two."

105. Ziporyn, *Being and Ambiguity*, p. 316.

106. See the passage from Priest cited in ch. 1 n. 10.

107. See introduction n. 53.

108. Wolfson, *Dream*, p. 27.

109. See Wolfson, *Giving*, p. 173, and references cited on pp. 414–15nn127–29. See also Matt, "*Ayin*," pp. 134 and 153n69. Matt cites several passages from Pseudo-Dionysius that make a similar point as well as the notable description of the Absolute in the *Brhadaranyaka Upanishad* (4:5, 15), *neti, neti*, "not this, not this." An even closer parallel is found in the words of Nicholas Cusa cited in Wolfson, *Giving*, p. 414n137.

110. Arenfeld, *Yira'ukha im Shamesh*, pp. 748–49.

111. Kook, *Orot*, pp. 126–27. The text is previously cited in Wolfson, "Secrecy," p. 149.

112. Ricchi, *Yosher Levav*, p. 21.

113. Azriel of Gerona, *Commentary on Talmudic Aggadoth*, p. 84. See also *Zohar* 3:28a (*Ra'aya Meheimna*), 235b (*Ra'aya Meheimna*); *Tiqqunei Zohar*, introduction, 4a; sec. 19, 40a; sec. 69, 99b, 102b, 111a, 112b.

114. Azriel of Gerona, *Commentary on Talmudic Aggadoth*, p. 84n4.

115. Gruenwald, "Preliminary Critical Edition, §6, p. 142; Hayman, *Sefer Yeṣira*, §6, p. 74.

116. Moses ben Shem Ṭov de León, *Sefer Sheqel ha-Qodesh*, pp. 5 and 22. The second part of the extract was cited and analyzed differently by Matt, "*Ayin*," p. 132.

117. Moses ben Shem Ṭov de León, *Sefer Sheqel ha-Qodesh*, p. 22n183. This identification was already suggested by Tishby in Azriel of Gerona, *Commentary on Talmudic Aggadoth*, p. 84n4, and Scholem, "Two Treatises," p. 375n26. In *Sod Eser Sefirot Belimah*, p. 375, de León quotes the explanation of decoding the word *ḥokhmah* as *ḥakkeh mah* in the name of the "ancients" (*qadmonim*), whereas in *Sheqel ha-Qodesh*, p. 22, it is simply cited as "they said." It is noteworthy that not only was the identity of Asher ben David apparently unknown to de León but he considered the source ancient, presumably in the same manner as he viewed zoharic texts. As difficult as it is for us to appreciate the sincerity of the temporal collapse implied in this sense of the return of the old as new, it is vital for understanding the kabbalistic sensibility of time as the replication of difference. See Wolfson, "Anonymity," pp. 60–63.

118. The reference is to the thirty-two paths of wisdom mentioned at the beginning of *Sefer Yeṣirah*,

the umbrella concept that conjoins the ten *sefirot* and the twenty-two Hebrew letters. See Gruenwald, "Preliminary Critical Edition," §1, p. 140; Hayman, *Sefer Yeṣira*, §1, p. 59.

119. Babylonian Talmud, Menaḥot 29b. See Moses ben Shem Ṭov de León, *Sefer Sheqel ha-Qodesh*, p. 6, and other references to de León's works cited in n. 47.

120. Abrams, *R. Asher ben David*, p. 234.

121. Moses ben Shem Ṭov de León, *Sod Eser Sefirot Belimah*, p. 375.

122. Moses ben Shem Ṭov de León, *Sefer Sheqel ha-Qodesh*, p. 5.

123. Moses ben Shem Ṭov de León, *Sod Eser Sefirot Belimah*, p. 375.

124. A similar point was made by Meinvielle, *De la Cábala*, p. 321.

125. See Steiner, *Real Presences*, p. 133: "But it is only in recent philosophy, in Heidegger's *Nichtigkeit*, in Sartre's *le néant*, a variation on Heidegger, that the concept of absolute zero becomes almost obsessive. Whereas in common grammar, in the logic which that grammar articulates, the negation of negation generates a positive—this is Hegel's crucial dialectical move—it now produces a final nothingness, a midnight of absence. Of this consequent annihilation, deconstruction is the spectral trace." I would counter that the *Nichtigkeit* of Heidegger is not a midnight of absence but rather a midnight wherein neither presence nor absence is clearly palpable, that is, an abyssal moment that precedes the differentiation into presence and absence, being and nonbeing.

126. Heidegger, *Contributions*, §145, p. 210; *Beiträge*, p. 266.

127. *Zohar Ḥadash*, 57a (*Qaw ha-Middah*).

128. Wolfson, *Language*, pp. 25–31.

129. Böhme, *Six Theosophic Points*, p. 10: "And no place or position can be conceived or found where the spirit of the tri-unity is not present, and in every being; but hidden to the being, dwelling in itself, as an essence that at once fills all and yet dwells not in being, but itself has a being in itself; as we are to reflect concerning the ground and unground, how the two are to be understood in reference to each other." And ibid., p. 12: "For in the unground there is no manifestation, but an eternal nothingness; a stillness without being or colours, neither any virtue . . . and is thus hidden in itself, and were eternally not manifest." In Wolfson, *Language*, p. 468n392, I have already remarked that Scholem, *Origins*, p. 436, commented on the resemblance of Azriel of Gerona's characterizations of the infinite and Böhme's *Ungrund*, and on pp. 442–43, Scholem described *Ein Sof* in Böhmean language as the "abyss and *Ungrund* hidden in the absolute nothingness of which we have only a vague intimation." On Scholem's familiarity with Böhme's *Der Weg zu Christo*, see the diary entry of November 11, 1915, in Scholem, *Tagebücher*, 1:179; English translation in *Lamentations*, p. 76. And see Hermann, "Gershom Scholems Weg," p. 47.

130. Heidegger, *Contributions*, §146, p. 211 (emphasis in original); *Beiträge*, p. 268. On the affinity between Heideggerian and kabbalistic speculation on the indissoluble interweaving of being and nothingness, or more precisely, the nihilation, the no-thing, whence being emerges, see di Cesare, *Heidegger e gli ebrei*, pp. 218–19 (di Cesare, *Heidegger and the Jews*, pp. 172–73). I agree with the conjecture of di Cesare, *Heidegger e gli ebrei*, p. 314n480 (*Heidegger and the Jews*, p. 285n483), that this affinity can be explained by the fact that the works of Eckhart and Böhme played a significant role for Heidegger.

131. Heidegger, *Contributions*, §146, p. 210 (emphasis in original); *Beiträge*, p. 267. For a discussion of negation in Heidegger from the standpoint of the paradox that being is an entity (a) and at the same time not an entity ($\neg a$), see Casati, "Being: A Dialetheic Interpretation," pp. 42–46. On Heidegger's confronting the question of the nothing in his meditations on the essence of being as an attack on logic, see Fay, *Heidegger: The Critique of Logic*, pp. 36–48.

132. Heidegger, *Contributions*, §110, p. 165; *Beiträge*, p. 211.

133. See Wolosky, "Two Types of Negative Theology," p. 161: "The beyond being that surfaces in Platonist discourses comes to be seen as a nonontology embedded within the tradition itself, thus escaping or disrupting its own metaphysical claims."

134. The point was duly noted by Matt, "*Ayin*," p. 138. After citing the comment of David ben Abraham ha-Lavan, *Masoret ha-Berit*, p. 31, "If all the powers were to return to *ayin*, then the Primordial One [*ha-qadmon*], the Cause of all [*illah la-kol*], would stand in its unity in the depths of nothingness, in undifferentiated oneness [*be-aḥdut ha-shaweh*], blessed be He and blessed be His name" (the text is cited more fully in ch. 5 at n. 211), Matt remarks, "Typically, the Jewish mystic cannot resist appending a personal formula to the divine, even when his object of contemplation is undifferentiated oneness concealed in the depths of *ayin*."

135. Cordovero, *Pardes Rimmonim*, 5:4, p. 64. To some extent, the dilemma faced by the kabbalists in their depiction of *Ein Sof* as the cause that of necessity cannot be an effect corresponds to Spinoza's concept

of the infinite being as the *causa sui*, the essence that cannot be conceived except as existence and hence the substance that must be identified as the cause that engenders itself. Consider the account offered by Hegel, *Lectures on the History of Philosophy*, 3:258–59 (*Vorlesungen über die Geschichte der Philosophie III*, p. 168): "Spinoza's first definition is of the Cause of itself [*Ursache seiner selbst*]. He says: 'By that which is *causa sui*, its own cause, I understand that whose essence' (or Notion) 'involves existence, or that which cannot be conceived except as existent.' The unity of existence and universal thought is asserted from the very first, and this unity will ever be the question at issue. 'The cause of itself' is . . . the cause which, while it operates and separates an 'other,' at the same time produces only itself, and in the production therefore does away with this distinction. The establishing of itself as an other is loss or degeneration [*Abfall*], and at the same time the negation of this loss [*die Negation dieses Verlustes*]; this is a purely speculative Notion, indeed a fundamental Notion in all speculation. The cause in which the cause is identical with the effect, is the infinite cause [*Das ist die unendliche Ursache, in der die Ursache mit der Wirkung identisch ist*] . . . if Spinoza had further developed what lies in the *causa sui*, substance with him would not have been rigid and unworkable." See Macherey, *Hegel or Spinoza*, pp. 122–27; Morfino, *Plural Temporality*, pp. 34–39. Bracketing the final comment in the aforecited passage of Hegel, he is right to note the contradiction implicit in the Spinozistic idea of the *causa sui*, viz., the very concept of causality implies that the cause cannot be thought except in relation to an effect that is other than itself, but in the case of the *causa sui*, the exteriorization of the cause produces an effect that is identical to itself. In that respect, positing a substance that is its own cause effectively subverts the very notion of causality. The same can be said about the kabbalistic *Ein Sof*, which is identified philosophically as the cause of all causes, an expression that implies the infinite is a cause that has no cause but itself. Moreover, insofar as all is contained in the infinite, it follows that the effect is indistinguishable from the cause, and hence the binary of cause and effect is disrupted by the positing of a causeless ground of all being.

136. Heidegger, *Pathmarks*, p. 241, note b; *Wegmarken*, p. 316, note a.

137. Heidegger, *Pathmarks*, p. 240, note a; *Wegmarken*, p. 315, note a.

138. Heidegger, *On Time and Being*, pp. 40–41 (emphasis in original); *Zur Sache des Denkens*, pp. 49–50.

139. I have altered Stambaugh's translation of *Seinsprägungen* as the "formations of Being" to the "imprints of Being," which seems to better convey the agency of the swaying-ground of the event of *Ereignis*.

140. Heidegger, *On Time and Being*, p. 41; *Zur Sache des Denkens*, p. 50. See the discussion of appropriation and concealment in Stambaugh, *Finitude of Being*, pp. 75–82.

141. Heidegger, *Contributions*, §145, p. 209; *Beiträge*, p. 266.

142. Heidegger, *Beginning*, p. 26 (emphasis in original); *Anfang*, p. 32.

143. On Heidegger's notion of essences as a replacement for metaphysical foundations, see O'Leary, "Theological Resonances," p. 214.

144. Heidegger, *Contributions*, §145, p. 209; *Beiträge*, p. 266.

145. Heidegger, *Off the Beaten Track*, p. 196; *Holzwege*, p. 263.

146. Heidegger, *Off the Beaten Track*, p. 197; *Holzwege*, p. 264.

147. Heidegger, *Off the Beaten Track*, p. 198; *Holzwege*, p. 265.

148. Heidegger, *Off the Beaten Track*, p. 196; *Holzwege*, p. 263.

149. For an analysis of this Heideggerian motif in a distinctly mystical vein, see Reddan, "Heidegger and the Mystery of Being." While I do not accept Reddan's understanding of mysticism as the experience of the transcendent oneness that results in the dissolution of the temporal and the spatial, the attempt to compare Heidegger's notion of the ontological difference and his emphasis on the experience of being to the concepts of the *aperion* in Anaximander and the Platonic *chōra*, based on the assumption that these ideas depict a mystery underlying and therefore prior to the differentiation of sameness and difference, has something in common with my own attempt to align the kabbalistic *Ein Sof* with the Heideggerian idea of the event of beyng, which is the nihilating ground that precedes the distinction into being and nonbeing.

150. Derrida, "On Reading Heidegger," p. 173.

151. Heidegger, *Off the Beaten Track*, p. 197; *Holzwege*, p. 265.

152. Heidegger, *Contributions*, §32, p. 56 (emphasis in original); *Beiträge*, p. 70. For an illuminating study, see Armitage, "Heidegger's *Contributions to Philosophy*." Although the focus of this study is very different from my own, I assent to the statement, "Meontology is ironic in its negating, but beyng itself also proves essentially ironic in its continual refusal as the truth-process of 'clearing-concealment' (*lichtende Verbergung*). Dasein is called to grasp this ironic dimension of beyng qua truth" (p. 576).

153. Heidegger, *Contributions*, §32, p. 57; *Beiträge*, p. 72.

154. Di Cesare, "Das Sein und der Jude," pp. 66–71; di Cesare, "Heidegger's Metaphysical Anti-Semitism," pp. 187–90.

155. My interpretation of kabbalistic sources accords with the reading of medieval Islamic philosophy offered by El-Bizri, "Being and Necessity." See also the discussion of the shift from the principality of essence to the principality of being and the rise of a new ontology or a metaontology in Kamal, *From Essence to Being*, pp. 51–120.

156. Iamblichus, *On the Mysteries*, 8:2, pp. 308–9; 10:5, pp. 350–51. See also Trouillard, "Note sur *proousios*"; Trouillard, "Procession néoplatonicienne," p. 14. As Trouillard argues, the prefix *hyper*, that is, "above" or "beyond" (*au-delà*), is equivalent to within (*en-deçà*), whereas the prefix *pro*, that is, "before," marks an anteriority that preserves a more definite sense of separateness, the preessential source that engenders essence. See also Shaw, *Theurgy and the Soul*, pp. 112–13; Shaw, "*Chôra*," p. 123n95.

157. For example, see the words of Markos the Valentinian cited by Hippolytus, *Refutation*, 6:42.4, p. 455: "When the Father, who is inconceivable, beyond substance [ἀνούσιος], and neither male nor female, first willed his unspeakable nature to be spoken, and the invisible to take shape, he opened his mouth and emanated a Word similar to himself. He, standing alongside him, showed him what he was, having become manifest as the form of the Invisible [αὐτὸς τοῦ ἀοράτοθ μορφὴ φανεὶς]." For a learned note on the philology of the term *anousios*, see Wright, *Religion*, p. 153n242. See also Dillon, "Monotheism," p. 75; Louth, *St John Damascene*, p. 159. The gnostic depiction of the Father that is neither male nor female is notionally on a par with the kabbalistic description of *Ein Sof* in paternal images even though it is presumed to be beyond the gender polarity. See ch. 5 n. 162.

158. Elijah ben Solomon, *Commentary of the Gaon*, p. 138. Concerning the authorship of this text, as well as an annotated edition based on manuscripts, see Shuchat, "Vilna Gaon's Commentary." The passage under discussion appears on p. 288. For the influence of Luzzatto on this passage, see Shuchat, *World Hidden*, pp. 139–40. On the Vilna Gaon's understanding of *ṣimṣum*, see Shuchat, "Vilna Gaon's Commentary," pp. 272–74, and additional sources cited herein in ch. 4 n. 196.

159. Wolfson, "*Via Negativa*," pp. 397–400, and further reference to primary and secondary sources cited on pp. 397–98nn12–13.

160. For a summary of the different viewpoints related to this question, see Cordovero, *Pardes Rimmonim*, 3:1–8, pp. 25–53, and the scholarly assessment in Tishby, *Wisdom of the Zohar*, pp. 242–46.

161. Gikatilla, *Sha'arei Orah*, 1:57, 144, 164, 165, 2:91, 92 (the depth of thought, *omeq ha-maḥashavah*, is identified as "the will that has no limit or boundary," *ha-raṣon be-ein sof u-gevul*), 105 (in that context, the nominal expression *ein sof* is not applied to *Keter*; rather, it is stated concerning the mystery of the secret of *Keter* that "there is no limit to its depth," *ein sof le-omqo*); and see the editor's introduction, 1:30–31. See also Moses ben Shem Ṭov de León, *Sefer Sheqel ha-Qodesh*, p. 19; David ben Yehudah he-Ḥasid, *Book of Mirrors*, pp. 129 and 131; *Zohar* 3:258a (*Ra'aya Meheimna*); *Tiqqunei Zohar*, sec. 22, 68b.

162. See ch. 2 n. 34.

163. Scholem, *Origins*, p. 439. On the term *hashwa'ah*, especially in the writings of Azriel of Gerona, see Wolfson, *Language*, pp. 98–99, and Valabregue-Perry, *Concealed and Revealed*, pp. 232–44.

164. *Zohar* 2:239a.

165. David ben Yehudah he-Ḥasid, *Book of Mirrors*, p. 227. For an alternate translation and discussion of this passage, see Matt's introduction to *Book of Mirrors*, pp. 21–22.

166. Badiou, *Being and Event*, p. 14. The various facets of Badiou's mathematical conception of metaontology are explored in great detail by Baki, *Badiou's Being and Event*. On the excess of presence in Heidegger's thinking about nature, see Balazut, *Heidegger*, pp. 61–81.

167. Azriel of Gerona, *Be'ur Eser Sefirot*, p. 85.

168. *Sefer ha-Peli'ah*, 11b.

169. Here I take issue with the conclusion of Derrida, *On the Name*, p. 96 [*Khôra*, p. 30]: "There is *khōra*; one can even ponder its *physis* and its *dynamis*, or at least ponder these in a preliminary way. But what *there is*, there, is not [*mais ce qu'*il y a *là n'est pas*] . . . this *there is*, which . . . *gives* nothing in giving place or in giving to think [*cet* il y a *qui d'ailleurs ne* donne *rien en donnant lieu ou en donnant à penser*], whereby it will be risky to see in it the equivalent of an *es gibt*, of the *es gibt* which remains without a doubt implicated in every negative theology, unless it is the *es gibt* which always summons negative theology in its Christian history" (emphasis in original). Compare Derrida, *Psyche*, p. 173. It strikes me that one can discern in the caution of identifying *il y a* and *es gibt* a critique of Heidegger and in the final statement that *es gibt* "always summons negative theology in its Christian history" a critique of the view expressed at a later date by Marion. In my judgment, the Heideggerian *es gibt* is closer to Derrida than he acknowledges.

See Wolfson, *Giving*, pp. 237–41; and Flatscher, "Derridas '*coup de don*' und Heideggers '*Es gibt*'." On the comparison of Heidegger's *es gibt* and Levinas's *il y a*, see Wolfson, *Giving*, pp. 99–100, and other sources cited on pp. 360–61n72. I do not accept the distinction made by Holte, *Meaning and Melancholy*, p. 35, that "whereas Heidegger emphasizes the gift-character of the expression '*es gibt*' . . . for Levinas *il y a* has a rather negative significance. *Il y a* refers to the anonymous fact of being or being in general that refuses to take a personal form." Although Heidegger does utilize the language of the gift to characterize his sense of *es gibt*, the latter implies a sense of giving that gives with no will to give and no desire to be given, and hence, in a post-Heideggerian gesture of thinking the unthought in Heidegger, we can speak of the ungifting of the gift. See Wolfson, "Not Yet Now," p. 136.

170. Heidegger, *Pathmarks*, p. 90; *Wegmarken*, p. 111.

171. See references cited in introduction n. 51.

172. Heidegger, *Introduction to Metaphysics*, pp. 121–22; *Einführung in die Metaphysik*, pp. 122–23.

173. See the text of Heidegger's exposition of this theme in Nietzsche cited and analyzed in Wolfson, *Language*, pp. 14–15, and see my comments on p. 409n118.

174. Buber, *Eclipse*, p. 74, already drew a comparison between Eckhart's description of the Godhead as being above being (*Est enim super esse et ens*) and Heidegger's statement that being is more than all that exists and yet is nearer than any existing thing.

175. See the passages of Eckhart cited in Wolfson, "Patriarchy and Motherhood," pp. 1084–85.

176. Wolfson, *Alef*, pp. 71–72. The insight into the compresence of all three temporal modes and the nature of the dream is buttressed by a numerology affirmed in the concluding section in Viṭal, *Mavo She'arim*, p. 447: the letters of the Aramaic term for dream, *ḥelma* (8 + 30 + 40 + 1), have the numerical sum of 79, which is the same sum as the words *hayah* (5 + 10 + 5 = 20), *we-howeh* (6 + 5 + 6 + 5 = 22), and *we-yihyeh* (6 + 10 + 5 + 10 + 5 = 36), with the addition of 1 for the word itself (*im ha-kolel*). The numerology anchors the idea that the time of the dream is like the moment in which there is a convergence of the three temporal ecstasies of what was, what is, and what will be. From that standpoint, dreamtime emulates the eternal temporality that is the esoteric connotation of the Tetragrammaton. The intrinsic connection between the dream and the Tetragrammaton is affirmed by Valle, *Et Leḥenena*, pp. 45–46: "It is already known that Jacob is the secret of diminution [*sod ha-qaṭnut*], and sleep is also the secret of diminution, and the dream is the secret of the augmentation [*sod ha-gadlut*], that is concealed within the diminution, that is, the name *YHWH* is garbed and hidden in the name *Elohim*, which is the secret of diminution. . . . It is in the nature of the dream that the name *YHWH* will be hidden within *Elohim*, not overtly and with a great openness." On the undoing of time and the syntax of the dream interlude, see Wolfson, *Dream*, pp. 219–74, esp. 245–55.

177. The passage is cited in Heidegger, *Elucidations*, p. 136; *Erläuterungen*, p. 113.

178. For a more extensive discussion, see Yates, *Poetic Imagination*.

179. Schelling, *System of Transcendental Idealism*, p. 14.

180. Heidegger, *Elucidations*, pp. 136–37; *Erläuterungen*, pp. 113–14. That Heidegger was not always consistent on this point is attested, for instance, in his criticism of Cassirer's inability to distinguish sharply between dreaming and waking. See Heidegger, *Piety of Thinking*, p. 33.

181. Heidegger, *Hölderlin's Hymns "Germania" and "The Rhine,"* p. 19; *Hölderlins Hymnen "Germanien" und "Der Rhein,"* p. 16. Compare Heidegger, *Hölderlin's Hymn "Remembrance,"* p. 35 (*Hölderlins Hymne "Andenken,"* p. 40): "For now, we should note only that the master key to all 'poetics,' the theory of 'image' in poetry, of 'metaphor,' neither unlocks a single door in the realm of Hölderlin's hymnal poetizing, nor brings us anywhere into the open. Here it suffices to ponder only this one point: even the 'things themselves' [*die 'Dinge selbst'*] are already each time poetized before they become so-called 'symbols.' The only question that remains is in which essential realm and from out of which truth of poetizing." And see the section on "The dream. That which is dreamlike as the unreal or nonexistent" (*Der Traum. Das Traumhafte als das Unwirkliche order Nichtseiende*) in Heidegger, *Hölderlin's Hymn "Remembrance,"* pp. 94–95; *Hölderlins Hymne "Andenken,"* pp. 109–10. According to Heidegger's analysis, on the one hand, what is dreamlike counts as unreal (*Unwirkliche*), or lacking subsistence (*Bestandlose*), and therefore null (*Nichtige*), and yet, on the other hand, the dream betokens a realm of beings and nonbeings (*der Bereich des Seienden und des Nichtseienden*), which challenges the Western-scientific view that equates being with that which brings about a real effect. Attunement to the irreality of dreams breaks the dominance of determining authentic being based on the trichotomous relation of effecting-effective-effected (*Wirkend-Wirksam-Gewirkte*).

182. Heidegger, *Elucidations*, p. 62; *Erläuterungen*, p. 45. For criticism of this text, pejoratively referred

to as a "shortcut" (*Kurzschluß*) and a "truly violent paraphrase" (*recht gewalttätiger Paraphrase*) of a passage from Hölderlin's *Empedocles*, see Adorno, *Noten zu Literatur*, pp. 454–55; English translation in Adorno, *Notes to Literature*, vol. 2, pp. 115–16.

183. Wolfson, *Dream*, pp. 46–57. It is of interest to consider the comment of Peirce in the 1868 essay "Questions Concerning Certain Faculties," in *Writings of Charles S. Peirce*, vol. 2, p. 196: "In trying to give an account of a dream, every accurate person must often have felt that it was a hopeless undertaking to attempt to disentangle waking interpretations and fillings out from the fragmentary images of the dream itself. . . . A dream, as far as its own content goes, is exactly like an actual experience. . . . Besides, even when we wake up, we do not find that the dream differed from reality, except by certain *marks*, darkness and fragmentariness. Not unfrequently a dream is so vivid that the memory of it is mistaken for the memory of an actual occurrence" (emphasis in original). For a more recent assessment along these lines, see Gosetti-Ferencei, *Life of Imagination*, p. 89: "In these cases of pretending and fictionalizing, opposing the perceived and the imagined may mischaracterize the ability of human thinking to relate at once to the fictional and the real. While a hallucinating or dreaming subject may have little recourse to reality outside the hallucination or dream, the child at play, like the fiction writer, is capable of multimodal registration of different sources of thinking, so that neither needs to suppress or deny the real in order to engage or evoke the counterreal." The author's contention that the same object can be intended in two registers at the same time, *as perceived* and *as imagined*, applies as well to the pretense of seeing-as that is characteristic of the oneiric phenomenon.

184. Heidegger, *Essence of Truth*, p. 47; *Vom Wesen der Wahrheit*, p. 64. There also may be a hint here of the Heraclitean view of the dream as the blurring between wakefulness and sleep that is the fire of the lighting-up of human poiēsis. See the exchange on sleep and dream in Heidegger and Fink, *Heraclitus Seminar*, pp. 137–49, and Capuzzi, "Heraclitus," pp. 140–44.

185. Heidegger, *Essence of Truth*, p. 47; *Vom Wesen der Wahrheit*, p. 64.

186. Heidegger, *Essence of Truth*, p. 47; *Vom Wesen der Wahrheit*, p. 64.

187. Heidegger, *Contributions*, §192, p. 247 (emphasis in original); *Beiträge*, p. 312.

188. Schelling, *System of Transcendental Idealism*, p. 176. Here, too, I note the similarity to Fichte, *Science of Knowledge*, pp. 194–95: "Imagination is a faculty that wavers in the middle between determination and nondetermination, between finite and infinite. . . . The task was that of uniting the opposites, self and not-self. By the power of imagination, which reconciles contradictions, they can be perfectly united." See Wolfson, *Giving*, pp. 4 and 274n22.

189. See Fichte, *Science of Knowledge*, p. 202, cited in Wolfson, *Giving*, pp. 2–3.

190. Schelling, *System of Transcendental Idealism*, p. 72.

191. Heidegger, *Phenomenological Interpretation of Kant's Critique*, pp. 179–98; *Phänomenologische Interpretation von Kants Kritik*, pp. 264–92.

192. Heidegger, *Kant and the Problem of Metaphysics*, pp. 87–138; *Kant und das Problem der Metaphysik*, pp. 127–203. Compare Heidegger, *Contributions*, §134, p. 199; *Beiträge*, p. 253; Weatherston, *Heidegger's Interpretation of Kant*, pp. 85–100, 155–77; Elliott, *Phenomenology and Imagination*, pp. 101–36.

193. Heidegger, *Contributions*, §191, p. 246; *Beiträge*, p. 311.

194. Heidegger, *Contributions*, §192, p. 247; *Beiträge*, p. 312. For a detailed analysis of this passage, which has informed my own exegesis, see Yates, *Poetic Imagination*, pp. 144–47.

195. Heidegger, *Contributions*, §191, pp. 246–47; *Beiträge*, p. 311.

196. Heidegger, *Essence of Truth*, p. 53 (*Vom Wesen der Wahrheit*, p. 73): "The unhiddenness [*Unverborgenheit*] of beings happens in and through deconcealment [*Entbergsamkeit*]. It is a projecting-opening order [*entwerfend-eröffnender Auftrag*] that calls for decision [*Entscheidung*]. The essence of unhiddenness is deconcealment."

197. My perspective on the dream can be profitably compared with Nancy, *Fall of Sleep*, pp. 13–15: "The sleeping *self* does not appear: it is not phenomenalized, and if it dreams of itself, that is . . . according to an appearing that leaves no room for a distinction between being and appearing. Sleep does not authorize the analysis of any form of appearance whatsoever, since it shows itself to itself as this appearance that appears only as non-appearing. . . . In this non-appearing, one single thing shows itself. But it does not show itself to others, and in this precise sense it does not appear. . . . The sleeping self is the self of the thing in itself: a self that cannot even distinguish *itself* from what is not 'self,' a self without self, in a way, but that finds or touches in this being-without-self its most genuine autonomous existence" (emphasis in original). And see Nancy, *Fall of Sleep*, pp. 23–25: "The sleeping person closes his eyes so he can open them to night. Inside himself, beneath the eyelids that sink

with sleep and that were already there, throughout the whole day, solely that there might be evoked, lowering their awnings at times, the always possible imminence of a night in broad daylight, the possibility, if not the necessity, of escaping the solicitations of wakefulness, what he sees is nothing other than night itself. For night—through a major difference from day—is no more external than it is internal. . . . Night identifies outside with inside; the eye sees in it the underside of things, the back of the eyelids, the invisible layer of the other side of things, the underpinnings, crypts, skins turned inside out. . . . There is a silent obedience to the difference of the being: to this 'nothing,' to this 'no thing,' to this *ex nihilo* that light first drove back to the heart of darkness in the movement by which it sprang from it. Light shaped nothing as darkness: it configured it as figureless, as the thing removed from all things. . . . Sometimes, dream occurs. 'Perchance,' as Hamlet says. . . . *Perchance* to dream, that is to say, perchance something of night passing into day, by chance, by misfortune or by capricious luck. All of a sudden, awakening finds close to it a scrap left over from sleep. Something was brought back from nothing, and in effect it is a configuration of nothing" (emphasis in original).

198. Wolfson, *Dream*, p. 109.

199. Heidegger, *Hölderlin's Hymn "Remembrance,"* pp. 98–100; *Hölderlins Hymne "Andenken,"* pp. 115–17. Heidegger's analysis is set forth as an exegesis of Pindar's words in the eight *Pythian Ode* as translated by Hölderlin, "Tagwesen. Was aber ist einer? was aber ist einer nicht? Der Schatten Traum, sind Menschen" ("Creatures of day. Yet what is one? yet what is one not? Shadows' dream are human beings"), cited in Heidegger, *Hölderlin's Hymn "Remembrance,"* p. 95; *Hölderlins Hymne "Andenken,"* p. 111. Regarding the image of the shadow in Heidegger's thought, see ch. 5 n. 10 and ch. 7 at nn. 204–6.

200. Heidegger, *Hölderlin's Hymn "Remembrance,"* p. 97; *Hölderlins Hymne "Andenken,"* p. 114.

201. Heidegger, *Hölderlin's Hymn "Remembrance,"* p. 100; *Hölderlins Hymne "Andenken,"* p. 117.

202. Heidegger, *Hölderlin's Hymn "Remembrance,"* p. 100; *Hölderlins Hymne "Andenken,"* pp. 117–18.

203. Wolfson, *Dream*, pp. 198–202.

204. Garb, "Authentic Kabbalistic Writings," pp. 187–88.

205. The text is published in Luzzatto, *Adir ba-Marom*, pt. 2, pp. 150–51. I have previously cited and analyzed this passage in Wolfson, "Retroactive Not Yet," pp. 47–48. See also Garb, *Kabbalist in the Heart of the Storm*, p. 179.

206. Wolfson, *Dream*, pp. 255–74.

207. Luzzatto, *Qelaḥ Pitḥei Ḥokhmah*, p. 66. Concerning the authorship of this text, see below, n. 209. On *ṣimṣum* in Luzzatto's thought, see Wolfson, "Retroactive Not Yet," pp. 44–48, and Garb, *Kabbalist in the Heart of the Storm*, pp. 175–76, 183–84, 197–99.

208. Luzzatto, *Be'urim le-Sefer Oṣerot Ḥayyim*, sec. 18, in *Ginzei Ramḥal*, p. 299.

209. Luzzatto, *Qelaḥ Pitḥei Ḥokhmah*, pp. 26–27, previously cited in Wolfson, *Dream*, p. 199. I accept the conclusion of Garb, "Authentic Kabbalistic Writings," pp. 188–99, that this work was probably not written by Luzzatto, but its content is consistent with the views we find in his genuine writings. On the role of metaphor, imagination, and dream in Luzzatto's approach to the anthropomorphic nature of kabbalistic symbolism, see Wolfson, "*Tiqqun ha-Shekhinah*," p. 292n8, and Garb, *Kabbalist in the Heart of the Storm*, pp. 174–85.

210. Wolfson, "Retroactive Not Yet," pp. 27–30.

211. Ibn al-'Arabī, *Bezels of Wisdom*, pp. 121–25, cited and analyzed in Wolfson, *Dream*, p. 271.

212. Wolfson, *Dream*, pp. 200–2.

213. Elijah ben Solomon, *Commentary of the Gaon*, p. 137. The view that kabbalistic symbolism, including the doctrines of Lurianic theosophy such as *ṣimṣum*, is not to be taken literally but as metaphor (*mashal*), albeit a metaphor for that which is considered to be ontically real, was affirmed by a number of kabbalists. Compare Ergas, *Shomer Emunim*, 1:25, pp. 45–48; Ickovits, *Nefesh ha-Ḥayyim*, 3:7, p. 225; Wildmann, *Pitḥei She'arim*, 1:3a; Kahana, *Toledot Yiṣḥaq*, pt. 2, 1:19–21, 2:14, where the author reports having heard from his teacher, Yiṣḥaq Eizik Ḥaver Wildmann, who heard from Menaḥem Mendel of Shklov, who received from the Vilna Gaon that all the words of Luria are in the aspect of a parable (*beḥinat mashal*). The comment is cited in the introduction by Ḥayyim Friedlander to Wildmann, *Magen we-Ṣinnah*, p. 6. On the historical-textual background of this work, see the comments of Dweck, *Scandal of Kabbalah*, pp. 225–27. On the figurative interpretation of the metaphorical symbols in Lurianic kabbalah by the Vilna Gaon and his school, compare Shuchat, *World Hidden*, pp. 117–23; Shuchat, "Vilna Gaon's Commentary," pp. 267–74. On the metaphorical explanation of *ṣimṣum*, see Brill, "Mystical Path," p. 134, and compare ch. 4 n. 196.

214. Eliashiv, *Leshem Shevo we-Aḥlamah: Sefer ha-De'ah*, pt. 1, pp. 162–63.

215. Ibid., p. 163. See Peleg, "More about Rabbi Shlomo Eliyashov's Controversy," pp. 185–92, and esp. 188n19.

216. Eliashiv, *Leshem Shevo we-Aḥlamah: Ḥeleq ha-Be'urim*, pt. 1, p. 17. On the role of metaphor in Eliashiv,

as it relates in particular to the thought of Luzzatto, see Baumgarten, "History and Historiosophy," pp. 25–41.

217. Eliashiv, *Leshem Shevo we-Aḥlamah: Ḥeleq ha-Be'urim*, pt. 1, p. 75.

218. Ibid., p. 76. Part of the text is cited by Garb, *Modern Kabbalah*, p. 65, and translated into English in that work on p. vii. I agree with Garb's assessment that Eliashiv's insistence on the qualitative as well as the quantitative proliferation of the disclosure of esoteric knowledge was accelerated by the printing revolution. I would note, however, as I have consistently argued, innovation on the part of the kabbalists is linked to their conservatism. Thus, while I accept that it is reasonable to find a historical explanation for the increase in circulation and explication of secrets at this time, I would caution against a rigid historicism that would obscure the paradoxical juxtaposition that, in my judgment, lies at the core of the kabbalistic hermeneutic.

219. Pico della Mirandola, *Conclusiones Cabalistice Numero XLVII. Secundum Secretam Doctrinam Sapientum Hebreorum Cabalistarum, Quorum Memoria sit Semper in Bonum*, 28.35, in *Syncretism in the West*, pp. 358–59.

220. Eliashiv, *Leshem Shevo we-Aḥlamah: Sefer ha-De'ah*, pt. 1, pp. 161–62. I concur with the remark of Brill "Mystical Path," p. 134n10, "R. Eliashiv acknowledges that even though *zimzum* is literal, it is impossible to grasp God's essence, therefore it is only an analogy (*mashal*) for us."

221. Eliashiv, *Leshem Shevo we-Aḥlamah: Ḥeleq ha-Be'urim*, pt. 1, p. 75.

222. For discussion and quotation of some of the key midrashic sources, see Wolfson, *Through a Speculum*, pp. 8–9, 33–41. Compare Eliashiv, *Leshem Shevo we-Aḥlamah: Haqdamot u-She'arim*, p. 28.

223. I have returned to this theme in many of my writings, but for a concise treatment, see Wolfson, "Bifurcating the Androgyne," pp. 88–95.

224. Babylonian Talmud, Shabbat 55a; Yoma 69b; Sanhedrin 64a.

225. Eliashiv, *Leshem Shevo we-Aḥlamah: Ḥeleq ha-Be'urim*, pt. 2, p. 45.

226. Ibid., p. 46.

227. Ibid.

228. Ibid., p. 45.

229. Text cited in Adorno, *Beethoven*, p. 245n305. See Wasserstrom, "Adorno's Kabbalah," pp. 62–66.

230. Wolfson, *Alef*, p. xii. It is worth noting here the comparison of Kafka's work to the rabbinic Haggadah, the narrative portions of the Talmud meant to explicate the Halakhah or the legal disputations, in Benjamin, *Selected Writings*, 2:496 (*Gesammelte Schriften*, 2.2, p. 679): "In other words, everything he describes makes statements about something other than itself. . . . His prose may prove nothing; but it is so constructed that it can be inserted into passages of argument at any time. We may remind ourselves here of the form of the Haggadah, the name Jews have given to the rabbinical stories and anecdotes that serve to explicate and confirm the teachings—the Halachah. Like the haggadic parts of the Talmud, these books, too, are stories; they are a Haggadah that constantly pauses, luxuriating in the most detailed descriptions, in the simultaneous hope and fear that it might encounter the halachic order, the doctrine itself, en route."

4

Ṣimṣum, Lichtung, and Bestowing Refusal

What if that domain of decision as a whole, the absconding or advent of the gods, were precisely the ending itself? What if, over and above that, beyng in its truth had to be grasped for the first time as appropriation, as the eventuating of that which we call *refusal*? That is neither absconding nor advent, and also not absconding as well as advent; instead, it is something originary, the fullness of the bestowal of beyng in the refusal.

Heidegger, *Contributions to Philosophy (Of the Event)*

Picking up where we left off in the last chapter, the aim here is to delve more deeply by investigating a conjecture that might strike some as provocative and others as preposterous: the thinking underway in Heidegger's later philosophy concerning the clearing (*Lichtung*) and the appropriating event (*Ereignis*), wherein beyng and nothing are the same in the identity of their difference, provides a useful template for understanding the path traversed by kabbalists in their attempts to account for the derivation of all beings from the nothingness of the being of *Ein Sof*.[1] One might object to this comparison on the grounds that, for Heidegger, the "guiding problematic" of the question of being (*Seinsfrage*) can only be thought from the finitude (*Endlichkeit*) of Dasein's existence.[2] Heidegger thus speaks of humanity's existential condition of being-in-the-world as a "characteristic of the innermost transcendental finitude of Dasein which is unified with the thrown projection."[3] Although this language applies to the phenomenological ontology of *Sein und Zeit*, the emphasis on transcendence, understood not as a reified *transcendens* but as Dasein's disclosure of its individuation,[4] is a theme that colored Heidegger's interrogation into the meaning of being throughout his life.[5] As the note added to his personal copy of *Sein und Zeit* attests, in spite of the "metaphysical resonance" of the term, *transcendence* denotes the ecstatic timeliness (*Zeitlichkeit*) or temporality (*Temporalität*), which is the horizon whence we discern that "Beyng [*Seyn*] has 'thought beyond' ['*überdacht*'] beyngs [*Seyendes*]. However, transcendence from the truth of beyng [*Seyns*]: the event [*das Ereignis*]."[6] To identify transcendence as the temporal horizon within which the truth of beyng as the event is enframed accentuates its radically finite nature.

How, then, is it justifiable to juxtapose the kabbalistic conception of infinity and the Heideggerian notion of beyng disclosed as *the most finitude in what is finite* through the structural unity of the transcendence of Dasein?[7] It is precisely in the space of this difference that a relatively ignored facet of the kabbalistic doctrine may come to light. Anticipating the postmodern emphasis on the inessential essence of the singular, Heidegger wrote, "Finitude becomes manifest according to its ownmost essence if it is made accessible through unswerving application, accompanied in turn by the originally grasped, basic question of metaphysics which, to be sure, can *never* be claimed as the *only* one possible."[8] Inverting this insight, we can say that, according to the kabbalah, the essential inessentiality of *Ein Sof* is manifest as the potentially infinite concretizations of the finite, the absolute emptiness that no being can ever be except by not being.

Beyng's Fissure and the Self-Concealing Concealment

In language that reads uncannily like a philosophical translation of the kabbalistic myth of the contraction (*ṣimṣum*) of the infinite light, Heidegger speaks in the *Beiträge* of the event as the oscillation or strife between beyng (*Seyn*) and its negative (*Nichthafte*), that is, nonbeing (*Nichtsein*), the withholding of the "hesitant denial" (*zögernde Versagung*) or the "refusal" (*Verweigerung*) and the bestowing of the ripeness (*Reife*) that bears the fruit (*Frucht*) and the gift (*Verschenkung*).[9] To speak of the abyssal ground (*Ab-grund*) as being permeated with negativity does not denote that the ground is negative in opposition to being positive, but rather it conveys in a more originary sense the "not" (*Nicht*) that occurs as the hesitant withholding, the primordial not (*ursprüngliche Nicht*), "the first and highest lighting up of the intimation" (*das erste und höchste Aufleuchten des Winkes*) that pertains to the event of beyng.[10] In similar terms, Heidegger describes the event of the truth as the "resonating [*Anklang*] of beyng as refusal in the abandonment of beings by being [*der Seinsverlassenheit des Seienden*]."[11] The burden of thinking in the other beginning of philosophy requires that one think inventively to bring beyng into its essential occurrence as the event that eventuates in the chasm of the open realm, the vacillation between beyng and beings, which Heidegger insists is not a "void" (*Leere*) but the "abyssal undepletion" (*ab-gründige Unerschöpfung*), the "clearing for self-concealment" (*Lichtung für das Sichverbergen*). The abyss, which is the fullness of the nothingness of beyng that withdraws from all beings, is also identified as the ground in which the truth as the essence of grounding is grounded and as the "time-space (*Zeit-Raum*)—the *site of the moment* of the strife (beyng or nonbeing) [*die* Augenblicks-stätte *des Streites* (*Seyn oder Nichtsein*)]."[12]

I shall return to the matter of the time-space in chapter 6, but suffice it here to note the conceptual affinity between Heidegger's depiction of the nature of beyng as a wavering between being and nonbeing and the kabbalists' *Ein Sof*, the inexhaustible nihility that likewise is both and therefore neither being nor nonbeing, at once desolate and abounding, depleted and overflowing. Furthermore, the kabbalistic infinity can be described in Heideggerian terms as the beyng whose essential nature consists in its self-withdrawing concealment concealed in the unconcealment of beings.[13] We can thus apply to *Ein Sof* Heidegger's characterization of *Lichtung* as the "open center" that "encircles all that is, like the Nothing [*das Nichts*] which we scarcely know. That which is can only be, as a being, if it stands within and stands out within what is lighted in this clearing. Only this clearing grants and guarantees to us humans a passage to those beings that we ourselves are not, and access to the being that we ourselves are."[14] In somewhat different but related language, Heidegger describes the clearing as the "open middle," which "is not surrounded by what-is, but the illuminating middle itself surrounds—like Nothing, which we hardly know—all that is. Every being that is encountered maintains this strangely ambiguous presence, in that it always simultaneously holds itself back in concealment."[15] The openness (*Offenheit*) originates in the clearing, which is referred to by Heidegger, invoking Goethe's expression in his *Maximen und Reflexionen*, as the "primal phenomenon" (*Urphänomen*), a term that does not signify some primordial entity but rather the opening of being that grants the letting-appear (*Scheinenlassen*) of beings in the manifest concealment of their concealed manifestation.[16] The play between light and dark presupposes the openness of the clearing that is "free not only for brightness and darkness, but also for resonance and echo, for sounding and diminishing the sound. The clearing is the open for everything that is present and absent. . . . Accordingly, we may suggest that the day will come when we will not shun the question whether the opening, the free open, may not be that within which alone pure space and ecstatic time and everything present and absent in them have the place which gathers and protects everything."[17]

This description of the Heideggerian clearing as the *free space of the opening* offers a philosophically perspicacious way to explain the Lurianic myth of the formation of the vessel in the vacuum created within the plenum of the infinite by the withdrawal of its light from itself and into itself. As Heidegger opined in a section of the *Beiträge* dedicated to the exposition of the essence of truth related to the *openness of the open realm* (die Offenheit des Offenen) understood as the *clearing for self-concealing*:

> Openness: is that not . . . the *emptiest of the empty*? So it seems, if we try to take it, so to speak, for itself in the manner of a thing. Yet the open realm, which conceals itself at the same time that beings come to stand in it in each case (indeed not only the things most proximately at hand), is in fact something like an *inner recess* [hohle Mitte], e.g., that of a jug. Yet it must be recognized that the inner recess is not just a haphazard emptiness which arises purely on account of the surrounding walls and which happens not to be full of "things." It is just the opposite: the inner recess itself is what determines, shapes, and bears the walling action of the walls and of their surfaces. The walls and surfaces are merely what is radiated out by that original open realm which allows its openness to come into play by summoning up, round about itself and toward itself, such-and-such walls (the particular form of the vessel). That is how the essential occurrence of the open realm radiates back from and in the embracing walls.[18]

The vessel in Lurianic kabbalah is similarly characterized as the openness that encloses or the enclosure that opens, the clearing wherein the concealing is unconcealed and the unconcealing concealed. Moreover, just as Heidegger depicts the open realm as the jug whose inner core gives shape to the external boundaries within which it is circumscribed, so the vessel in kabbalistic lore, which is created by the withdrawal of light, it is not empty but is rather the clearing that delimits the limitless and thereby provides the clearing for the self-concealing revealing of *Ein Sof.*

Strengthening the kabbalistic resonance, I note that in another passage from the *Beiträge*, Heidegger writes about the fissure (*Zerklüftung*) as the "self-contained unfolding [*sich bleibende Entfaltung*] of the intimacy of beyng itself, to the extent that we 'experience' ['*erfahren*'] beyng as refusal [*Verweigerung*] and as the encompassing refusal [*Umweigerung*]."[19] The symbolism is reiterated in a third passage wherein Heidegger describes "the thoughtful projection of beyng [*der denkerische Entwurf des Seyns*]" as a crack (*Durchriß*) that "spreads *all the way through* what then for the first time announces itself as a 'being' ['*Seiendes*'] in the open, that an *errancy*, in clearing, snatches into itself everything to make what is true possible . . . . Thoughtful and explorative questioning [*Erfragen*]: the renunciation [*Verzicht*] that *takes action*, that adheres *to* the refusal and thus brings it into the light."[20] Questioning is an act of renunciation, an arresting act that adheres to and thus brings to light the errancy of the rupture, the bestowal of being that is the refusal of beyng, the event marked by an "intrusion [*Anfall*] and remaining absent [*Ausbleib*], advent [*Ankunft*] and absconding of the gods [*Flucht der Götter*]."[21] Embracing the paradox forthrightly, Heidegger notes that the "*refusal is the first and highest gift of beyng* [daß die erste höchste Schenkung des Seyns], *indeed its primordially essential occurrence itself.*"[22]

Underlying the depiction of the refusal as the supreme gift of beyng is the further assumption, discussed at several junctures in this book, that withholding and bestowal are inseparably linked, in fact, the one is the other, since beyng is bestowed insofar as it is withheld, and it is withheld insofar as it is bestowed. The idea is reiterated in Heidegger's delineation of *Seyn* as "the allocating refusal" (*die zuweisende Verweigerung*),[23] which "eventuates as the withdrawal [*Entzug*] that incorporates into the stillness in which truth, in accord with its essence, comes anew to the decision as to whether it can be grounded as the clearing for self-concealment. This self-concealment is the unconcealment [*das Entbergen*] of the refusal; it is the allowance to belong in the strangeness of another beginning."[24] The allowance to belong in the strangeness of another beginning imparts the idea of the unordinary arising as a consequence of the retreat of the ordinary, the being that comes to be as other vis-à-vis the not-otherness of beyng. The self-concealment as the unconcealment of the refusal, therefore, "is not simply and only the limit of knowledge in any given circumstance, but the beginning of the clearing of what is lighted."[25] The complex of ideas proffered by Heidegger presents a precise theoretical parallel to the kabbalistic presumption that the beginning is initiated by a contraction of the origin that results in the materialization of the infinite light manifest in the concealment of its manifestation and concealed in the manifestation of its concealment.

As the "intrusion of beyng," for Heidegger, "always comes out of the *persistent* remaining absent of beyng"[26]—the arrival of the gods that is in tandem the fleeing of the gods—so for the kabbalists, the infiltration of the straight light (*or yashar*) into the opening of the empty space (*ḥalal*), the point in the center of the expanse of infinitivity that has no center, always issues from the retraction of the returning light (*or ḥozer*). Presence is thus the absence of the presence of absence, a reversal of the metaphysical understanding of absence as the presence of the absence of presence. "The refusal," writes Heidegger, "is the highest nobility of bestowal and is the basic trait of the self-concealment *whose* manifestness constitutes the originary essence of the truth of beyng. Only in this way does beyng become estrangement itself [*die Befremdung selbst*], the stillness of the passing by of the last god."[27] This language can be adopted in explicating the kabbalistic depiction of the ultimate truth of being as the manifestation of the self-concealment arising from the munificent refusal of *Ein Sof*, the withdrawal that is the supreme expression of the magnanimity to bestow. The bestowal itself, as I noted previously, is a refusal, insofar as what is bequeathed must be held in reserve—the concealment of the concealment cannot be revealed unless it is revealed as that which is concealed. Heidegger's insistence that "as refusal, beyng is not mere withholding and seclusion," and hence the "refusal is the intimacy of an allocation,"[28] well expresses the fundamental paradox of the kabbalistic doctrine of *ṣimṣum*, the self-contracting expansion of the self-expanding contraction. Just as Heidegger spoke of the stillness of the passing of the last god, so for kabbalists, the activity of infinity is a motionless motion, a movement that is quintessentially stationary. Even the matter of estrangement is appropriate, since the worlds that unfurl from the folds of infinity do so as a form of alienation of the same in the guise of the other that is other to the same. This, I suggest, is what Heidegger intends by the last god, the semiotic marker of the transition[29] from the end of metaphysics to the other beginning through the twofold movement of being's bestowing withdrawal, the *self-concealment that is the unconcealment of the refusal.*[30]

Calculating the Incalculable: Last God and the Abysmal Between

One might argue that the discussion about Heidegger's last god is tangential and irrelevant for the study of the kabbalah. And yet a closer examination of the topic indicates that this comparison is warranted. The first thing to note is that the last god is continuously coming and therefore always subject to being surpassed; the quality of lastness, accordingly, connotes not what is chronologically the end, but the ultimate in the sense of what is endlessly without end. This is precisely the meaning of *Ein Sof*, literally, without end, which is to say, the end that has no endpoint. Furthermore, just as *Ein Sof* is the onset that is the climax, so the last god is "the inceptual one in the essencing of beyng" (*der anfängliche in der Wesung des Seyns*).[31] From that vantagepoint the notion of the last god may be viewed as an instantiation of Heidegger's open circle, which we discussed in the first chapter, the return to the beginning that never was, the genuine iteration of the "truth of the uniqueness [*Einzigkeit*] and non-repeatability [*Einmaligkeit*] of beyng";[32] *the again that is altogether otherwise.*[33] The last, as Heidegger informs us in the *Beiträge*, "is what not only needs the longest ante-cedence [*Vor-läuferschaft*] but what itself is the most profound beginning rather than a cessation, the beginning which reaches out the furthest and catches up to itself with the greatest difficulty. What is last is therefore withdrawn from all calculation and for that reason must be able to bear the burden of the loudest and most repeated misinterpretation."[34] The most glaring misinterpretation, I might add, is to understand the last god theistically, that is, to attribute to this god the form of transcendence as "something that surpasses objectively present beings, among them also human beings."[35] Similarly, one of the most difficult challenges in grasping the heterodoxical implications of kabbalistic theosophy—a challenge that some kabbalists themselves have not successfully surmounted—is to resist the temptation to render the infinite in monotheistic or polytheistic terms. Needless to say, there is no justification to distinguish dualistically *Ein Sof* from the personal God of Israel, but there is also little doubt that kabbalists ideally maintained that the contemplative ascent culminates in a purging of all metaphorical images from *Ein Sof*, including the belief that the actions of the infinite are purposefully motivated in a manner that is isomorphic with the resolute activity ascribed to the moral agency of human beings. The last rung of the *vita contemplativa* is the abrogation of the personalistic theologism that is homologous with an ego-oriented psychologism even as we acknowledge—in no small measure due to the wisdom transmitted by masters of the kabbalah—that there is no way to the nameless but through the ladder of the name, no way to the formless but through the vehicle of the form, no seeing the face of the imageless but through the image of the mask.

Ein Sof is the origin that is the endless end, the end that has no end and therefore brings one to the end of all ends. We can infer from the following elucidation of Heidegger that the idea of the last god likewise entails an unambiguous rejection of the conception of the end as it relates to both teleology and eschatology: "*The last god*—is not the end—but is instead the other beginning of the immeasurable possibilities of our history. For the sake of that beginning, the previous history must not perish but must indeed be brought to its end; i.e., its transfiguration [*Verklärung*] must be set into the transition [*Übergang*] and into preparedness [*Bereitschaft*]. The last god—the preparation of his appearance is the extreme venture of the truth of beyng; only in virtue of this truth can the retrieval of beings succeed for humanity."[36] Rather than viewing the last god as the end, Heidegger asserts that it signals the other beginning, the "oscillation of the beginning in itself" and thus "the highest form of refusal, since what is inceptual eludes every attempt to grasp onto it and essentially occurs only in protruding beyond all things that, as futural, are already incorporated into it and are delivered over to its determining power."[37] The end that does not end because it cannot begin—it is always the end that is coming—can give rise to the second beginning, however, only by transfiguring the first beginning and bringing it to its end. In the intimation [*Wink*] of the last god, "the intrusion and remaining absent of the advent as well as of the absconding of the gods that essentially occur as having been," beyng attains its maturity (*Reife*), its "readiness to become fruit and bestowal," the "*essential end* required by the beginning but not carried toward it."[38] The end and the last are sharply distinguished: the last, as the most primordial, withdraws unremittingly from the end. The last can appropriate its inceptuality only by transfiguring the first beginning and bringing it to its end. The realization of the beginning in the end, however, does not presume that the end is naught but the circulation back to the beginning. On the contrary, the beginning whither one returns in the end is not the beginning whence one set forth toward the end. From the beginning, then, we can discern the end, albeit from an inverse perspective. That is, the end can be imagined only as the terminus that can never be terminated. In this sense, the preparation of the appearance of the last god is branded the extreme venture of the truth of beyng, a venture incited by the appearance of what cannot appear but as nonapparent.

Expressed in a different terminology, the "nearness of the last god eventuates when the event, as the hesitant self-withholding [*das zögernde Sichversagen*], is elevated into *refusal*." The latter, however, is not "sheer absence" (*die bloße Abwesenheit*), that is, the renunciation of presence; it is rather the absence of the absence of presence and the presence of absence, the nihilating nihilation—the concealing self-concealment—that belongs to the "originary essence of beyng as lit up in the thinking constitutive of the other beginning."[39] The breach of beyng—the resonating of the event as refusal linked to the grounding of the truth of beyng as the time-space of the stillness of the passing by of the last god[40] in the nearness of its extreme remoteness, "a relation that must not be deformed or eliminated by any 'dialectics'"[41]—intimates a form of alienation of the same in the guise of the other that is, in truth, the other arrayed in the guise of the same. The last god, accordingly, is "wholly other than past ones and especially other than the Christian one."[42] Replying to the question whether speaking of the last god is not a degradation of God or even blasphemy, Heidegger writes that the "last god must be so named, because the decision about the gods ultimately leads under and among them and so raises to the highest the essence of the uniqueness of the divine being [*das Wesen der Einzigkeit des Gottwesens*]."[43]

What is implied by the term *Gottwesen*? A clue is offered by Heidegger's contention that the notion of last should not be understood as "sheer stoppage and ending," but rather in the "sense of the most extreme and most compendious decision about what is highest"; that is, as we indicated above, the connotation of the term *last* is ultimate, the paramount aspect that is impossible to comprehend and for which it is impossible to wait, since the finality of this last god cannot be calibrated by a chronological sequence of the coming to be and the passing away of the gods. The last god, as we may infer from the kabbalistic depiction of *Ein Sof*, is the god that can never arrive except as the god that does not arrive, the end that can never stop ending, the future that is perpetually impending.[44] As Heidegger put it in the draft for *Κοινόν: Zur Geschichte des Seyns* (1939–40):

> Yet the god—how so, the god? Ask beyng! And in its silence, in the inceptual essence of the word, the god answers. You may wander through each and every being. Nowhere does the trace of the god show itself [*Nirgends zeigt sich die Spur des Gottes*]. You can rearrange all beings, never will you encounter a free place for housing the god. You may go beyond your beings and will find only the beingness [*die Seiendheit*] once more of that which already counted as beings for you. . . . Yet how are you to become a questioner [*ein Fragender*] who asks beyng rather than investigating a being [*der das Seyn fragt und nicht ein Seiendes erforscht*]? Only through the voice of silence [*die Stimme der Stille*] that tunes your essence to steadfast insistence within Da- sein [*die dein Wesen zur Inständigkeit im Da-sein anstimmt*] and raises what has been attuned to a hearkening to the coming [*das Kommen*]. For the coming alone is capable of fulfilling the essence of godship [*Gottschaft*] in an inceptual manner.[45]

Heidegger instructs the reader to ask beyng rather than to investigate a being in order to discern the nature of god. The response will be heard in the voice of silence, which is the inceptual essence of language. What does one hear in that silence? That god can be grasped only from within the ontological difference: god is not to be found in beings but only in the beyng that is present in the being withdrawn from all that exists. Heidegger thereby undermines the theistic idea of the immanence of the divine in the world: *the trace of god shows itself nowhere*. But it is precisely in the nonshowing that the essence of the godship shows itself. Analogously, the kabbalistic *Ein Sof* is the concealment that is manifest as unmanifest; that is, the being that is present by being absent from being present in the manifold beings of the cosmological chain. Furthermore, in a way intriguingly redolent of the Jewish belief that the possibility of the messiah's coming is predicated on the impossibility of the messiah's arrival—the hope in the return of what is interminably still to come, the quintessential event of the nonevent[46]—Heidegger maintains that the lastness of the last god consists of the fact that the god is relentlessly coming, which provokes a state of continual waiting. The interminable deferral—the measure of time in its most rudimentary and superlative sense—is commensurate to the fact that the coming alone is capable of fulfilling the essence of godship inceptually. "He brings nothing, unless himself; yet even then only as the most coming of that which comes [*als den Kommendsten des Kommenden*]. Ahead of himself, he bears the to-come of the future [*die Zu-kunft*], his time-play-space [*Zeit-Spiel-Raum*] is beyng, a time-play-space that itself waits for the god, in coming, to fulfill it and in coming to come [*im Kommen komme*]. Thus is the god, of his necessity choosing beyng, the most extreme god, who knows no making [*Machen*] or providence [*Vorsehen*]."[47]

The god affirmed by Heidegger is neither the creator nor the one who exercises providential care over history. Thinking about *Gottwesen*, literally, the being or essencing of the divine, is not a "matter of calculation" but "an attempt at meditation [*umzubesinnen*] on the danger of the strange and incalculable [*Befremdlichen und Unberechenbaren*]."[48] But what does Heidegger precisely mean by the strange and incalculable? In response to this inquiry, we can begin by noting that it should not be construed ontotheologically as if Heidegger was reverting to the apophatic source of the kataphatic God of Christian faith, a God beyond God à la Eckhart, the Godhead (*Gottheit*) through which the divinizing of gods is accomplished,[49] the primal experience of *theos* that precedes translation into the theological criteria of specific religiosities.[50] Nor, in my judgment, is there justification to implant in Heidegger "the seeds for a postmodern theology which can restore a sense of the divine mystery, or reaffirm the religious experience of the 'wholly other.' By taking Heidegger's lead, we can determine that there is more than a superficial resemblance between the thought of being and the mystery of God. Indeed, *his thought enables us to address what is distinctive of the divinities as much through the modality of their absence as through their presence.*"[51]

I concur with the final sentence, but I would argue that the modality of absence to which Heidegger alludes is not akin to a mystery of God linked to an inscrutable transcendence, whether understood ontologically as the transcendental or theologically as the transcendent.[52] As Karl Löwith astutely noted with respect to what he calls the existential ontology of *Sein und Zeit*, Heidegger was undoubtedly affected by the rhetoric and symbols of his religious upbringing, but he translated the theological into a *godless theology*.[53] In a similar vein, Hans Jonas argued that the fact that the "secular thinking" in *Sein und Zeit* assimilates elements from Christianity does not justify postulating an "autonomous parallel" between Heidegger and Christian theology. The real challenge, therefore, is not to find validation or corroboration in what Heidegger has borrowed from Christianity, but to examine the philosophical validity of this secularized appropriation.[54] Summarizing his critique, Jonas wrote, "The being whose fate Heidegger ponders is the quintessence of this world, it is *saeculum*. Against this, theology should guard the radical transcendence of its God, whose voice comes not out of being but breaks into the kingdom of being from without."[55] Jonas does not disavow that the gods reappear in Heidegger's thought; he insists nonetheless that *where the gods are, God cannot be*.[56] If this is true about the early Heidegger, how much more so is it applicable to the contemplation of the later Heidegger, which is fueled by the passion to transcend theology, even the idolatry of natural theology,[57] or as George Steiner put it, "Heidegger's poetics of pure immanence are yet one more attempt to liberate our experience of sense and of form from the grip of the theophanic."[58] In the final analysis, for Heidegger, the sanctioning of scientific knowledge by faith is the very opposite of philosophical overcoming (*Überwindung*) and transformation (*Verwandlung*).[59] The latter would require undermining the theological to the point that the unconcealment of the gods is disclosive of the concealment of God. Phenomenologically speaking, the possibility of the appearance of the inapparent coincides with the horizon of the nonphenomenalizable, the givenness of what can be given only as ungiven.

It is pertinent to note as well the surmise of Susan Taubes that there are suppressed currents of Christian theology—and, more specifically, currents of a gnostic and more esoteric nature—that come to expression in Heidegger's antitheology:

> The suggestion is not so strange if we consider that his attack on Christian theology is not at all on naturalistic grounds.... Heidegger's antitheological polemic is thus directed from a more radical theological position. We must recall that Christian theology is syncretistic. We are confronted with a tradition originating in a (gnostic) Jewish heresy which not only absorbed in itself the heterogeneous elements of Hellenistic mystery cults but had to reconcile itself with systems as incompatible with each other as they were alien to itself, first with the Old Testament and then with Aristotelian metaphysics. Heidegger's polemic is directed against the biblical and metaphysical compromise of Christian theology and is thus carrying on a secret, esoteric, heretical, "Christian" tradition.[60]

Although Jonas did not express his view in precisely these terms, he did independently note the residual of gnostic elements incorporated into, and to some degree reinterpreted by, Heidegger's secular atheism.[61] More important, from Jonas's standpoint, an unbridgeable gulf separates this thinking and the faith of theology inasmuch as the biblical conception of God as the self-revealing being obstructs the unveiling of beyng as that which cannot be hypostasized ontically in compliance with the ontological difference. Since the thinking of beyng transcends all particular beings, including the transcendence of the divine being understood as the ultimate reality or supernatural agent that has the capacity to break into the historical world of becoming, the primal thinking is emphatically a "thinking away from God," or at the very least, a "thinking beyond God."[62] These expressions should not be misread as articulations of an apophatic theology that posits a being that transcends predication except for the predicate of being beyond predication, a stance that would embroil one in a form of metaphysical specularization of the impersonal ground of beyng as the personal being that exercises purposeful and providential agency in the world.

Consider this statement in the *Schwarze Hefte*, "Clearer: not 'origin,' but instead *happening of being and happening of truth* [Sein- und Wahrheit-geschehnis]—not 'transcendence' ['*Transzendenz*'] only, but *the world's becoming world* [Ver-welten der Welt], its beginning and existence."[63] What became clearer to Heidegger in this moment? That he is not seeking a transcendental origin (*Ursprung*) but rather the beginning (*Anfang*) and existence (*Existenz*) of the world. There is no longer any appeal to a metaphysical ground, only attending to the happening of being and the happening of truth, the event that is the world becoming world. The relevance of this uncompromising finitude to rethinking theology is made explicit in another entry to the notebooks, "We first find God again when we lose the *world* no longer and truly exist in the power of *world-formation* [Weltbildung]."[64] This statement should not be interpreted pantheistically or panentheistically as if Heidegger were affirming either that the divine is nature or that nature is the divine. To speak meaningfully of God, one must fully embrace the worldliness of the world without any recourse to transcendence, and this alone allows one to exist in and to partake of the power of world-formation.

Here it is worth recalling Heidegger's statement concerning the god of philosophy understood as the generative ground of the self-existent being: "Man can neither pray nor sacrifice to this god. Before the *causa sui*, man can neither fall to his knees in awe nor can he play music and dance before this god. The god-less thinking [*gott-lose Denken*] which must abandon the god of philosophy, god as *causa sui*, is thus perhaps closer to the divine God [*göttlichen Gott*]. Here this means only: god-less thinking is more open to Him than onto-theo-logic would like to admit."[65] The passage reads like an Eckhartian interpretation of Nietzsche's statement on the death of the God of Western metaphysics; that is to say, the atheistic thinking of Nietzsche's madman, predicated on denying the ontotheological conception of the deity, affords one an opportunity to be in more intimate connection with the *divine God*.[66] The import of this oddly redundant locution—*göttlichen Gott*—may be gleaned from what Heidegger writes elsewhere, "All metaphysics and every art that is grounded in metaphysics . . . poetized and thought gods as beings [*Seiendes*], at most as being [*Sein*] itself. However, those who prepare must first come—those who, after all, are capable of thinking be-ing [*Seyn*] and this alone as the distressing need of the godhood of gods. How undisturbed and owned will be then the path of the futural man to the last god [*der Pfad des künftigen Menschen zum letzten Gott*]; how completely devoid of all detours into the escape routes of the transformation of the hitherto will this path be, and how unconfined will it be by the prospects of the calculated?"[67]

The path of futural thinking leads to the last god, but this can be attained only when one is liberated from the anguish of the godhood of the gods (*die Not der Gottschaft der Götter*), a theological necessity that has prevailed in Western metaphysical contemplation and poeticizing about the gods as beings or the eternal God as being.[68] By contrast, in the future—and here futurity names the time that is not subject to the exigencies of time—we will be capable of thinking *Seyn* without concealing everything essential by unconcealing nothing essential.[69] This path is not restricted by previous diverting paths of transformation (*Seitenwege zur flüchtenden Anverwandlung*) or by the prospects of what can be calculated (*Aussichten auf das Gerechnete*). One is nearer to the "en-opening of the most remote" (*Eröffnung des Fernsten*) in the "hardly revealed 'time-space' [*Zeit-Raum*] of the truth of be-ing [*der Wahrheit des Seyns*]," that is, the last god, when the "gods will be more difficult and more rare, but therein more in sway, and yet thereby nearer in their swaying remoteness [*Wesensferne*]. . . . The last god is inflamed [*entbrennt*] to the highest distress [*höchsten Not*] by be-ing as the abysmal 'in-between' [*abgründige Inzwischen*] of beings."[70] If we attend meticulously to these words, we can deduce that Heidegger's last god is not a god in a theological sense—not even in a post-theological sense—but the abyss (*Abgrund*) that is the between, the clearing or the opening, the being that is the empty nothing that bestows and withholds all beings, "the 'unblendedness' [*Schlichte*] and the 'stillness' [*Stille*] out of which all things proceed together [*zussamengehen*] in their most intimate self-belonging [*innigstes Sichgehören*]."[71]

Heidegger's intention is expressed unequivocally in the following comment in the *Beiträge*:

> The most intrinsic finitude of beyng reveals itself here: in the intimation of the last god [*Hier enthüllt sich die innerste Endlichkeit des Seyns: im Wink des letzten Gottes*]. . . . The last god has his own most unique uniqueness [*einzigste Einzigkeit*] and stands outside of the calculative determination [*verrechnenden Bestimmung*] expressed in the labels "mono-theism," "pan-theism," and "a-theism." There has been "mono-theism," and every other sort of "theism," only since the emergence of Judeo-Christian "apologetics," whose thinking presupposes "metaphysics." With the death of this God, all theisms wither away. The multiplicity of gods is not subject to enumeration but, instead, to the inner richness of the grounds and abysses in the site of the moment for the lighting up and concealment of the intimation of the last god [*in der Augenblicksstätte des Aufleuchtens und der Verbergung des Winkes des letzten Gottes*].[72]

Those who would use Heidegger as a foundation to construct a new theological edifice have not grasped the collapse of the polarity of theism and atheism in the intimation of the last god and thus they have not taken to heart the deep-rooted and far-reaching finitude disclosed by this god, an epiphany of nothing to see that imparts knowledge of "the *most concealed* essence of the *'not'* [Nicht], as the 'not yet' [*Noch-nicht*] and the 'not any longer' [*Nicht-mehr*]," the site of the moment that bespeaks the concealing-revealing of the "intimacy and pervasiveness of the negative [*Nichthaften*] in beyng," the "truth of the *not* itself, and consequently also of *nothingness* [Nichts]."[73]

Heidegger on occasion uses language that could easily mislead one into thinking that he was advocating something akin to a postmetaphysical theology. Thus, in one passage in the *Schwarze Hefte* in which Heidegger distinguishes "the many," who identify the beyng (*Seyn*) beyond beings (*über dem Seienden*) as a nonbeing (*Unseienden*), and the "creative ones," who know that beyng is not a nonbeing but the nothing, he concludes, "Consequently, for the many, there must always be *'religions'*—but, for the individuals, there is *God* [*für die Einzelnen aber ist* der Gott]."[74] Allegedly, Heidegger is attributing to the elite belief in God and to the masses conformity to institutional religions. A careful glance at the context, however, reveals the subversive implication of Heidegger's words: *der Gott* is synonymous with *das Seyn*, and the latter is placed "under beings" (*unter das Seiende*), which is to say, beyng is the strange and incalculable surplus, the event that is neither being nor nonbeing. In the same manner, *der Gott* is not subject to any ontic attribution, either positive or negative; like the *Ein Sof* of the kabbalists, the term is a sign that names the residual of the residue that cannot be named even as the unnamable, the residue, as we shall see below, that is the trace of nothing to be traced, the trace effaced in the imprint of its erasure.

The decidedly nontheistic meaning of the term *god* can be culled from another passage in the notebooks in which Heidegger reflects on the notion of culture as it relates to struggle (πόλεμος): "The struggling structure [*kämpferische Gefüge*] of the historical Dasein of a people and its destiny, a Dasein exposed to the gods [*gottausgesetzten*]."[75] What is implied here becomes more transparent in another passage where the nexus between history, peoplehood, god, and world is expanded: "*The concept of world*—a questioning that pushes itself to its limits, where it experiences itself exposed to what is most question-worthy: where the 'there' opens up abyssally [*abgründig*], where the need of preservational disputation necessitates the 'there' (constancy), and history [*Geschichte*], i.e., a people [*ein Volk*], becomes itself; history is the venturing of the gods [*das Gewagtwerden der Götter*] out of a world and for a world [*aus einer Welt für sie*]; this happening [*Geschehnis*] is intrinsically individuation [*Vereinzigung*]."[76] What constitutes the worldhood of the world is that which is most worthy of questioning, the "there" of Dasein that opens up abyssally, that is, opens up to the abyss of the groundless ground, the ground that grounds by pulling away from the ground (*Ab-grund*). In and through that clearing, the concealment-exposure of language, a people becomes itself and professes its place in history, which is further described as a venturing of the gods, both out of and for the world; that is to say, the happening of the historical partitioning, the individuating event that is the essence of beyng,[77] is completely immanent and without any transcendental Archimedean frame of reference. As the venturing of the gods, history discloses "the abyssal character of the gaining through strife [*die Abgründigkeit der Erstreitung*]—sacrifice and consecration."[78] Through an "act of violence of the creating person," the gods "are compelled to their individuation—and a people is—as history. The gods indeed only those of a people: no general god for everyone, i.e., for no one [*Die Götter ja nur die des Volkes: kein allgemeiner Gott für Jedermann, d.h. Keinen*]."[79]

The gods are not transcendental beings outside history; they are historical forces that are individualistically apportioned to and requiring a particular people in the struggle to ground beings in the truth of the beyng from which they are hidden.[80] That is the import of the directive: "Need to create (the event) of *those* gods with whom we can be friends and to whom we need not be slaves."[81] Most significantly, *there is no general god for everyone and therefore there is no general god for anyone*. The matter is elaborated in the *Beiträge*: "A people is a people *only* if it receives its history as allotted to it through finding its god, the god that compels this people beyond itself and thus places the people back amid beings. Only then does a people escape the danger of circling around itself and of idolizing, as its *unconditioned*, what are merely conditions of its subsistence. . . . The essence of a people is grounded in the historicality of those who belong to *themselves through* their belonging to the god."[82] The nature of Dasein is linked to the essence of a people, which is determined by the god allocated to that people. Only by finding that god can a people escape the danger of a solipsistic self-encircling and the consequent idolization of the conditional as unconditioned. Heidegger's elitism comes to the fore when he asserts that a people finds its god through the few seekers, the future ones of the last god (*die Zukünftigen des letzten Gottes*), "who in reticence *seek on behalf* of this people and who . . . must apparently even stand *against* a 'people' that is *not yet* properly a people."[83] It would take us too far afield to unpack this statement and to delve into Heidegger's discussion of the strife that is essential to the future ones in particular and to the people guided by them more generally. What is of most concern for our immediate discussion is the comment posed as a question:

> Will the time of the gods then be *over and done* and a relapse into the mere life of *world*-poor creatures commence, ones for whom the earth has always remained only something to be exploited? Restraint and reticence will be the most intimate celebration of the last god and will attain for themselves the proper mode of confidence in the simplicity of things and the proper stream of the intimacy of the captivating transport of their works. Furthermore, the sheltering of truth will leave concealed what is most concealed and will thus lend it a unique presence.[84]

Through the contestation (*Bestreitung*) that arises from the strife, the future ones become cognizant of the "most diffident and most distant intimation of the last god" by means of which they have access to the incursion of the event of beyng wherein truth assumes presence in its remaining absent. Only one who stands on "the verge of extreme despair" can catch sight of "the full light of the beacon of beyng, the light in which the last god is concealed."[85] This mindfulness creates the unrest (*Unruhe*) that is "the restful enduring of the fissure" (*das ruhige Beständnis der Zerklüftung*).[86] The last god signifies the fissure of beyng—the space of oscillation (*Schwingungsraum*)—that opens and closes in relation to those who practice restraint. Most notably, the epoch of the last god is the time when *the gods will be over and done*, which does not, however, justify the exploitation of the earth, since the primary characteristics of this last god and its seekers are restraint and reticence.

With this in mind, we better understand the following observation in the notebooks: "It is now coming to light that we have already long been living, and will still long live, in the age of the departing gods [*Weltalter der scheidenden Götter*]. The question is whether we will experience in this departure the course of the gods and thus their nearness [*Nähe*], one that moves us while escaping from us [*bewegende-entgehende*]."[87] To be in the age of the departing gods—the period between the termination of the first beginning and the commencement of the second beginning, the "abode of the plight—in which the flight of the gods can be experienced and the waiting for the ones who will come can be carried out"[88]—means to experience the nearness of the gods in the moment as they are passing and becoming ever more remote: "*World*—the opening up of the counterplay [*die Eröffnung des Widerspiels*] between remoteness and nearness, beenness and future: the gods."[89] The term *god*, for Heidegger, is a mythopoetic way of naming both the spatial void, marked by the vacillation between proximity and aloofness, and the temporal expanse, marked by the fluctuation between past and future. Those who would try to elicit from Heidegger an argument for the revitalization of theology are at an even greater distance from the gods to whom one can be attached only by being detached. Heidegger thus categorizes the philosopher as the "questioner exposed to the tumult of the nearness of the gods."[90] To be sure, there is the risk that the philosopher "can still misinterpret everything, and make everything empty. . . . But one can also possess the vocation of bearing the actual tradition of philosophy from peak to peak and of preparing the trembling of the future through one's divinely compelled work [*götterhaft erzwungenes Werk*]."[91] The divinely compelled work is assigned to the philosopher as one who interrogates every presupposition, a questioning fueled by the tumult of the gods occupying a position nearby. What is the clamor caused by this closeness to the gods? The expiring beliefs in whose wake our knowledge of the world is severely destabilized.

The interpretation is corroborated by the following passage that defines the philosophical calling: "*Philosophy*—will not deliver, will not discover things (through research), will not (after the fact) raise any worldview to concepts—instead, philosophy will again know the πόλεμος—*the event*—and will fathom the ground [*Grund*] and the abyss [*Abgrund*] and the nonground [*Ungrund*][92] and thus will become a plight and the necessity—to seize what has been given as task [*Aufgegebene*] and to conquer what has been given as endowment [*Mitgegebene*]—to bring history to a happening [*die Geschichte zum Geschehen bringen*] = to venture the gods once again [*noch einmal die Götter wagen*]."[93] The gods to which Heidegger refers are not to be interpreted theistically but as a component of the relational fabric of beings, the emptiness within which the conflictual event that brings about the historical happening takes place. The task to appropriate the relationality of all being receives its fullest formulation in Heidegger's fourfold (*das Geviert*), which consists of the earth, sky, mortals, and divinities. Consider Andrew J. Mitchell's succinct clarification of this theme: "The fourfold provides an account of the thing that is inherently relational. Thanks to the fourfold, these things unfold themselves ecstatically, opening relations with the world beyond them. Unlike the self-enclosed object of modern metaphysics, the thing is utterly worldly, its essence lying in the relations it maintains throughout the world around it, the world to which it is inextricably bound. The world becomes the medium of the thing's relations. The fourfold is the key to understanding this streaming, mediated, relationality of finite, worldly existence."[94]

The emphasis on the correlationality of the worldly existence provides the critical element for understanding Heidegger's invocation of the gods prior to his articulation of the fourfold as a means to get beyond the theopoetic envisioning of an anthropomorphic and anthropopathic deity. In a stark and evidently Nietzschean assessment, Heidegger writes, "God is gone; things are used up; knowledge is in ruins; action has become blind. In short: *beyng is forgotten*—and a semblance of beings is raging or is fleeing into what was hitherto."[95] The Christian God does not exist and it is only the idols, which are constructed by our calculating ratiocination, that allow us to continue to attribute activity to that God.[96] On this score, Heidegger juxtaposes the "Godlessness of Bolshevism" (*Gott-losigkeit des Bolschewismus*) with the "moribund state of Christianity" (*Abgestorbenheit des Christentums*), since both are "great signs that we have actually and wittingly entered the epoch of the abandonment by being."[97] In another passage, he goes further and labels the "forms of *modern Christianity*" as "the genuine configurations of Godlessness [*die eigentlichen Gestalten der Gott-losigkeit*]."[98] Even Nietzsche's celebrated proclamation that "God is dead" is, according to Heidegger, "spoken in the *Christian* manner, precisely because it is *un*-Christian. And that is why the 'eternal recurrence' is merely a Christian expedient—to give the inconsequential 'life' once again the possibility of importance. And this remains an attempt at salvation in 'beings' versus nihilism of beings."[99]

Heidegger's intent can be illumined from a passage in *Schelling: Vom Wesen der menschlichen Freiheit*, where he noted that the term *theology* first evolves within philosophy and not "in the framework and service of an ecclesiastical system of faith." From that standpoint, every philosophy "is theology in the primordial and essential sense that comprehension (*logos*) of beings as a whole asks about the ground of Being, and this ground is called *theos*, God." In that context, Heidegger reiterates his view that Nietzsche's philosophy, too, is to be considered theological in spite of his declaration of God's death. Rather than viewing modern philosophy as a "secularization of Christian theology," it is more accurate to characterize the latter as the "Christianization of an extra-Christian philosophy." All theology is possible only on the basis of philosophy, even if the latter is identified as the work of the devil. Heidegger concludes, therefore, that the questioning of philosophy "is always and in itself both onto-logical and theological in the very broad sense. Philosophy is *Ontotheology*. The more originally it is both in one, the more truly it is philosophy."[100]

Heidegger's last god is his way of coming to terms with Nietzsche's death of god, which signifies "the abandonment of being in the current appearance of beings;"[101] that is, the last god is the god after there are no more gods,[102] the god depleted of godhood, the god that signals the overcoming of ontotheology and hence the setting of philosophy on the new course of thinking about the open concealedness (*offene Verborgenheit*) of the essential occurrence of beyng, a mode of contemplation set against calculative reasoning and to which he refers by various names, to wit, "originary meditation" (*ursprünglichen Besinnung*),[103] "thoughtful meditation" (*denkerische Besinnung*),[104] and "thoughtful configuration" (*denkerische Gestaltung*).[105] In the liminal epoch between the presence of what is absent and the absence of what is present, Heidegger saw his task as preparing the "future ones" to stand in the "remotest proximity of the last god" by remaining silent about what is essential,[106] but the last god is, as I noted above, the god that is always to come, and therefore can be proximate only by being infinitely remote. In that respect, the last god is the symbolic enactment of the demise of god. Hence, as Heidegger observes in another passage, the "advancing secularism" of the "disempowerment of the beginning," which proceeds from the inceptual entanglement in beyng, requires the "pushing away of beings" and this "will then carry over even to God—as the creator."[107] The god is manifest when what is manifest is no longer a god. One is curiously reminded of Scholem's quip that the atheistic religion brought forth by the secular world endorses the ironic belief that *God will appear as non-God*,[108] a sentiment that may have been informed as well by his understanding of the kabbalistic infinite as the nothingness that transcends theistic representations, the godhead bereft of godliness.

The implications of the last god as an overcoming of the Christian God, and by extension all theistic representations of divinity, are further clarified by this description: "A god who would like to raise himself beyond being, or indeed is thus raised and made into the source (cause) of being (not simply of beings) '*is*' no god and can *be* no god ["ist" *kein Gott und kann kein Gott* sein]. More inceptual than *every* god is beyng [*Anfänglicher denn* jeder *Gott ist das Seyn*]."[109] The last god is so called because it is no god at all, the god released from being godly; it names the beyng that is beyond being, the source or cause of being that is more inceptual and therefore more belated than any god. *Seyn* is no longer thinkable as the otherwise than being either as the transcendental or as the transcendent. The use of the term *Gottwesen* is meant to subvert the positing of an alterity understood in this manner. What Heidegger intends is something far more groundbreaking and paradoxical: the absence of the gods is not to be interpreted either as the absence of presence or as the presence of absence. The absence, in other words, does not mean that the once visible gods are now hidden and therefore invisible; it suggests rather that the unconcealment of the concealment is itself concealed by the unconcealment. There is no reality beneath the veneer of appearance; beyng is nothing but the pure appearance behind which there is nothing but the appearance of being.

The force of the last god as ultimate intimates an atheological surpassing of the ontotheological demarcation by attributing to this being the sense of being that is separate from any being and hence from any nonbeing that would simply be the negation of being. In a passage from the *Beiträge*, after depicting *Seyn* as the trembling of divinization, Heidegger notes that the "trembling expands the temporal-spatial playing field in which the trembling itself comes into the open as refusal.... Beyng must be thought out to this extremity. It thereby illuminates itself as the most finite and richest, the *most abyssal* [Abgründigste] of its own intimacy. For beyng is never a determination of the god as god; rather, beyng is that which the divinization of the god needs so as to remain nevertheless completely distinct from it."[110] Heidegger's rejection of the theological determination of *theīon/deus* could not be clearer: the divinization of the god needs the very beyng—to be distinguished from the beingness of metaphysics—whence it must remain completely distinct! The refusal of beyng is thus designated as the "most intimate compelling of the most originary and ever-inceptual plight, a compelling into the necessity of defense against the plight. The essential defense is not supposed to ward off the plight so as to get rid of it. In resisting it, the defense must instead precisely preserve the plight and extend it into its being carried out in accord with the diffusion of the trembling."[111] In the same manner that the ever-inceptual plight induces the necessity of defense against the plight by preserving the plight, the divinization of the god necessitates the evasion of godliness through the enowning of the trembling of divinization that requires the temporal-spatial playing field for its own decision.[112] The danger of obfuscating the ontological difference—the eliding of nonbeings in the semblance of beyng—results in the self-concealing of the clearing as the remoteness of undecidability that "is at once the farthest... nearness to the god but also the plight of the abandonment by being, which is concealed by the lack of a sense of plight evident in the avoidance of meditation today. In the essential occurrence of the truth of beyng, *in* the event and *as* the event, the last god is hidden."[113]

By *Gottwesen*, Heidegger intends this refusal as linked to the mystery of appropriation (*Geheimnis der Ereignung*) that is inexplicable and immeasurable, the sheltering-clearing that grants the opening to the time-space wherein the being of truth is manifestly concealed as the truth of being. Could we not say analogously that *Ein Sof* is the strange and incalculable essence of divinity—the essence that is the abdication of essence, the essence beyond the metaphysical distinction of transcendence and immanence—that we glimpse precisely when the familiar and calculable god of theistic confabulation takes flight, when the standard configuration of the personal deity in anthropomorphic and anthropopathic images is sabotaged by a mystical atheism that would render all portrayals of God—including the theosophy disseminated by the kabbalists themselves—as conceptual idolatry?[114] We can impute Heidegger's statement that the "most extreme god needs beyng" (*der äußerste Gott bedarf des Seyns*) to *Ein Sof*, insofar as the latter is the being that is nothingness, not because it is emptied of beings but because as the interdependence of all beings it is the delimitation of the limitless, the withholding that makes possible the bestowal of beingness from the being that is the consummate threshold surpassed by the constant crossing of the turning (*Kehre*) that is invariably a counter-turning (*Wider-kehre*), the event that is "the highest reign over the advent and absconding of past gods."[115] Furthermore, just as Heidegger spoke of the intimation of the last god that beckons "the law of the great individuation [*das Gesetz der großen Vereinzelung*] in Da-sein, of the solitude of the sacrifice [*der Einsamkeit des Opfers*], and of the uniqueness of the choice [*der Einzigkeit der Wahl*] regarding the shortest and steepest path,"[116] so we could say with respect to *Ein Sof* that it portends—allusively rather than representationally—the sense of individuation of the self as long as the latter is understood as the solitude of sacrifice by which one embarks on the path wherein "lies the mystery of the unity [*das Geheimnis der Einheit*] of the innermost nearing in the most extreme distance [*innigster Näherung in der äußersten Entfernung*], the traversal of the broadest temporal-spatial playing field of beyng. This extremity of the essential occurrence of beyng requires what is most intrinsic in the plight of the abandonment by being."[117] Translating the Heideggerian insight into the lexicon of kabbalistic theosophy, *Ein Sof* embodies the mystery of the unity of the *innermost nearing in the most extreme distance*; that is, the essential occurrence of beyng that is most contiguous in its infinite aloofness and most aloof in its infinitesimal contiguity, neither transcendent nor immanent and therefore both transcendent and immanent, transcendent in its immanence and immanent in its transcendence, the bestowal that withdraws in its bestowal and bestows in its withdrawal.

Erasure and the Trace of the Untraceable

In another passage from the *Schwarze Hefte*, Heidegger notes that the questioning appropriate to the second beginning is not the metaphysical query par excellence that paved the way of the first beginning, "Why is there at all something rather than nothing?"[118] One might insist that the kabbalistic *ṣimṣum* is suffused with this type of metaphysical thinking. Some disciples of Luria, including Ḥayyim Viṭal (1543–1620), openly presented the cosmological myth as a way to account for the appearance of a purportedly autonomous reality vis-à-vis the infinite; that is, as a way to explain precisely why there is something rather than nothing. A more circumspect reading of the kabbalistic material, however, lends support to Heidegger's stance that the posing of this question blurs the ontological difference between beyng and beings and is thereby implicated in alienating the alien character of the "there" (*das Befremdende der Fremde des Da*). What is most egregious is to advance a theological response to this inquiry: "Not to give a reassuring-theological 'proof' that explains God—not to eliminate the alienation as something extraneous [*nicht Ent-fremden als Fremdheit beseitigen*]—instead, to make even everything *familiar* seem alien [*sondern Befremdung alles* Heimischen]. Where is God? The prior and more proper question: do we have a 'where'? And do we stand within it, such that we can ask about God? The alien character of the 'there' as perseverance of the 'where.'"[119]

The text confirms that the theological—or even the posttheological—arrogation of Heidegger's language about the godhood, the gods, or the last god, is misguided. Discourse about God's existence or the seeking for a proof thereof—a proposition that Heidegger considers to be absurd (*Widersinnige*)[120]—remains bound to the metaphysical worldview that has dominated thinking since the first beginning, a pathway predicated on estranging that which is estranged, that is, alienating the alienation, instead of discerning the familiar in the unfamiliar, the ordinary in the extraordinary, the habitual in the mysterious.[121] As we noted above, it is specifically the stillness of the passing by of the last god that Heidegger identified as the beyng that is foreign and potentially discordant. The use of the theistic term is meant to render the homely as eccentric, the mundane as holy, not in an otherworldly sense, but as deterring the lure of the customary (*Gewohnheit*) so that one might "transform everything difficult into an impelling and thus into a repelling toward the uncustomary [*Ungewöhnliche*]. The latter is the space for the nearness and remoteness of the god."[122]

Inasmuch as the other beginning is "the opening for the time of *the last god*,"[123] the future history of humankind is delegated as "the concealed history of the great stillness in which the sovereignty of the last god opens up beings and configures them [*das Seiende eröffnet und gestaltet*]."[124] The last god is thus functionally on a par with Heidegger's *Lichtung*, the clearing in which beings are disclosed in the concealment of their disclosure: "*Beyng*—the trace [*Spur*] of the divinization of the absconded gods [*der Götterung der entflohenen Götter*], a trace that broadens a clearing. This clearing sets free the self-refusal [*die Verweigerung*] as an assignment of Da-sein, whereby the clearing is grounded [*gegründet*], humans are transformed [*gewandelt*], and beings come to be more fully. That tracing of the divinization [*Spuren der Götterung*], the tracing that in itself is this assignment, may be grasped as the appropriation [*Ereignung*].—To name beyng means to 'think' the *event of appropriation*."[125] In place of the metaphysical conception of being as a durable and self-subsisting substance, and nonbeing as the lack thereof, Heidegger portrays beyng as the trace of the divinization of the gods that have fled. This originary trace presumes that the origin is an event or happening of beyng, a presence that can never be present and therefore is erroneously described as absent.

What Heidegger intended here is developed at greater length in his argument in "Der Spruch des Anaximander" (1946) that not only does the origin remain hidden, "but even the relation between presence [*Anwesen*] and what presences [*Anwesendem*] is still unthought. . . . Unintentionally, presence itself became something present. . . . It is taken to be only the most universal and highest of present beings and hence as one of them. The essence of presence together with the difference between presence and what is present remains forgotten. *The oblivion of being is oblivion to the difference between being and the being* [Die Seinsvergessenheit ist die Vergessenheit des Unterschiedes des Seins zum Seienden]."[126] Heidegger goes on to say, "Oblivion of being belongs to that essence of being which it itself conceals [*Die Vergessenheit des Seins gehört in das durch sie selbst verhüllte Wesen des Seins*]. It belongs so essentially to the destiny [*das Geschick*] of being that the dawn of this destiny begins as the unveiling of what presences in its presence [*die Enthüllung des Anwesenden in seinem Anwesen*]." The beginning is an unveiling of what has been veiled in what Heidegger calls the *event of metaphysics*, that is, the self-veiling essence of being, the forgetting of what has been forgotten, the critical difference between presencing and that which has been present. Heidegger goes so far as to say that "even the early trace [*die frühe Spur*] of the difference is extinguished through presencing, appearing as something present [*das Anwesen wie ein Anwesendes erscheint*] and emerging as the highest of beings that are present [*in einem höchsten Anwesenden*]. . . . The difference between being and the being, however, can be experienced as something forgotten only if it is unveiled along with the presencing of what is present; only if it has left a trace, which remains preserved in the language, to which being comes. . . . Illumination [*Lichtung*] of the difference, therefore, cannot mean that the difference appears as the difference [*der Unterschied als der Unterschied erscheint*]."[127]

Just as in the notebooks Heidegger referred to beyng as the trace of the divinization of the absconded gods, so in this later essay on Anaximander, he speaks of the origin of being as a trace of the presencing occluded in what is present, the oblivion that forgets the oblivion of the ontological difference, an obfuscating of the obfuscation that can be uncovered through the recovery of language as the naming of what remains nameless. Derrida thus commented on the aforecited Heideggerian text:

> What Heidegger wants to mark is this: the difference between Being and beings, the forgotten of metaphysics, has disappeared without leaving a trace. The very trace of difference has been submerged. If we maintain that *différance* (is) (itself) other than absence and presence, if it *traces*, then when it is a matter of the forgetting of the difference (between Being and beings), we would have to speak of a disappearance of the trace of the trace. . . . Since the trace is not a presence but the simulacrum of a presence that dislocates itself, displaces itself, refers itself, it properly has no site—erasure belongs to its structure. . . .

> The paradox of such a structure, in the language of metaphysics, is an inversion of metaphysical concepts, which produces the following effect: the present becomes the sign of the sign, the trace of the trace. . . . It is a trace, and a trace of the erasure of the trace.[128]

Derrida's deconstructionist reading of Heidegger sheds light on the latter's depiction in the *Schwarze Hefte* of *Seyn* as the trace of the divinization of the gods who have fled. The gods of which the clearing is the trace are neither present nor absent, neither being nor nonbeing; the trace is a trace of the erasing of the trace—what Derrida elsewhere calls the arche-trace, the originary trace that is the origin of the origin constituted reciprocally as nonorigin[129]—that disappears in its appearance and appears in its disappearance. From the metaphysical standpoint, the inscription of the trace can only be described as "an erasure of the trace itself. The trace is produced as its own erasure. And it belongs to the trace to erase itself, to elude that which might maintain it in presence. The trace is neither perceptible nor imperceptible."[130] Analogously, the trace of the origin that Heidegger placed at the beginning is not a phenomenal trace of a plenary presence, but a nonphenomenal trace of what can never be present and hence never absent, a trace of the trace of the being that is otherwise than being, the erasure that is the inception of writing, not as a token of difference but as a stroke of *différance*, the originary repetition of the non-self-identical other that cannot be reduced to the same.[131] Additionally, as we noted above, the tracing opens the clearing that endows Dasein with its deportment as the self-refusal that is expressed in naming the namelessness and contemplating the event of appropriation. This self-refusal mimics the dynamic that Heidegger attributes to the truth of beyng as unconcealment:

> But this concealing of its essence and essential origin is the trait in which being's primordial self-illumination occurs . . . so that thinking can precisely *not* pursue it. The being itself does not step into the light of being. . . . By revealing itself in the being, being withdraws [*Das Sein entzieht sich, indem es sich in das Seiende entbirgt*]. . . In this way being, with its truth, keeps to itself. This keeping to itself is the way it discloses itself early on. . . . By bringing the being's unconcealment [*Un-Verborgenheit des Seienden*], it founds, for the first time, the concealment of being [*Verborgenheit des Seins*]. Concealment remains, however, the characteristic of the refusal that keeps to itself.[132]

The elusive nature of the trace of divinization calls attention to the fact that the gods cannot be reified as objective beings ascertainable by thought or classifiable by language; at best, they are disappropriated in the appropriation of the time-space of the world as vestiges of what is most proximate because most remote. Again, we mark the striking resemblance to the engendering paradox of kabbalistic theosophy: the being of *Ein Sof* reveals itself in the beings from which it withdraws. Rather than focusing on the whereabouts of the divine, therefore, it is necessary to ascertain the contours of the world where we stand as the "there," the open place (*offene Stelle*) of nature (φύσις),[133] the space of the between within which we are destined to ask the question of the "where," the unconcealment (ἀλήθεια) that grounds the origin beyond—and obfuscated by—the beginning. Dasein is most question-worthy (*Frag-würdigste*), but this status is determined in relation to the domain of nature, "the *genesis of the gods*, this genesis [*Entstehung*] not meant as production—rather, to come into position [*Stand*] as to emerge and to rise up [*Aufstehen*]; not causal derivation; nor out of misconstrued 'affects' and their impact."[134] The affiliation of nature with the genesis of the gods does not imply causal production but the coming into position as the emerging and arising from the state of concealment.

What is foreshadowed in Heidegger's notebooks is developed further in the essay "Wozu Dichter?" (1946), where he elicits from Hölderlin's elegy "Brod und Wein" that to be a poet in a desolate time is "to attend to the track of the fugitive gods [*die Spur der entflohenen Götter*]. This is why the poet, at the time of the world's night, utters the sacred."[135] The uttering of the sacred is proportionate to the augmentation of nocturnality—epitomized by midnight—to the point that the desolation has become so desolate, it hides the desolation of its own desolation. "The closer it comes to the midnight of the world's night, the more exclusively desolation reigns in such a way that it withdraws its essence. It is not only that the sacred is vanishing as the track of the godhead [*die Spur zur Gottheit*], but that even the tracks to this lost track are almost erased. The more the tracks are effaced, the less an individual mortal who reaches into the abyss can still attend to a hint [*Wink*] or instruction [*Weisung*]."[136] The overpowering of technology, and the privileging of self-assertion (*Sichdurchsetzens*) in a world that is allowed to be only will—in my opinion, we can detect in these words an implicit critique of Nazi Germany—has triggered the withdrawal of the whole (*das Heile*) and the world has become hopeless (*heil-los*). "As a result, not only does the holy [*das Heilige*] remain hidden as the track to the godhead, but even what is whole, the track to the holy, appears to be extinguished. Unless there are still mortals capable of seeing what is unwhole and unhealing threaten *as* unwhole and unhealing [*das Heillose* als *das Heillose*]."[137]

The light of the last god, according to a passage to which I have already referred, is perceived uniquely by one who withstands the utmost despair. However, a proper attunement to Heidegger's words intones that the last god is no god at all, at least not in any conventional connotation. What is lost is not only the trace to the godhead, but the trace of the trace that is lost, the alienation from being alienated, the exile from knowing that one is in exile. Heidegger thus depicts the "basic movement of beyng (a movement which trembles qua modernity)" as a "*de-divinization*" (Entgötterung), which comprises "the unfolding all the way to the end and the entrenchment of decisionlessness about the god."[138] De-divinization is a process of suspended belief in which one remains decisionless about god. But this decisionlessness is what opens the door to the beckoning of the future: "A *god* is only the one and the ones that tear humans away from 'beings' and that compel beyng as the 'between' [*das Zwischen*] for themselves and for humans—those gods that must have first arrived if a people is to find its essence. But the god is never an 'object' ['*Gegenstand*'] of Christian tactics [*christlicher Taktik*] or of political expedients [*politischer Maßnahmen*] or of 'incantations' ['*Beschwörungen*'] drunk on 'lived experiences' ['*Erlebnis*'-*betrunkener*], incantations in which such 'objects' could perhaps become 'perceptible.'"[139] The gods are not transcendent to the world; they are the dimensions of the world that create the space between beings and beyng. It is in this sense that the arrival of the gods facilitates the people's finding its essence, since the latter is not possible unless there is the willingness to question the truth of beyng in the pursuit of the beyng of truth. To interpret that arrival theistically is to obscure Heidegger's resolve that god is not an object we perceive through a lived experience of a theological, political, or magical nature.

What Heidegger wished to communicate is clarified by a comment in the *Beiträge*, cited in the previous chapter but worth repeating here, "The inventive thinking [*Er-denken*] of beyng leaps into beyng as the 'between' in whose self-clearing essential occurrence the gods and humans come to mutual recognition, i.e., decide about their mutual belonging. As this 'between,' beyng 'is' not a supplement to beings, but is what essentially occurs such that in its truth they (beings) can first attain the preservation proper to beings."[140] Heidegger ardently challenges the assumption that god should be understood metaphysically or equated with the nonmetaphysical event of beyng: "The god is neither a 'being' ['*seiend*'] nor a 'nonbeing' ['*unseiend*'] and is also not to be identified with *beyng* [Seyn]. Instead, *beyng* essentially occurs in the manner of time-space as that 'between' which can never be grounded in the god and also not in the human being (as some objectively present, living thing) but only in *Da-sein*."[141] The between into which the thinking of beyng leaps is the clearing wherein humans and gods abide in the distance of their intimacy.[142] The juxtaposition of this mutuality in the space of difference is what makes possible the atheological exceeding of the theological:

> Deliverance [*Erlösung*] from the "*gods*" ["Göttern"] means: from the idols [*Götzen*] to whom belong all "purposes" and "causations" and "causes," all forms and "goals" of machination: "the" science, "the" technology, "the" common usefulness, "the" people—"the" culture. Why this deliverance, and whence the demand for it? From the truth of beyng—so that every being might again find its way back into its simple

ground [*einfachen Grund*] and manifest in all this the abysses of beyng [*die Abgründe des Seyns*], which alone suffice as sites of the decision on whether beyng merely bestows beingness to beings or surmounts itself [*es selbst noch sich überhohe*] toward the trembling of that which is most uncertain [*Ungewissesten*]: the advent or flight of the last god [*der Ankunft oder Flucht des letzten Gottes*].[143]

In contrast to the divinization of theopoiēsis, which is "a circling around 'God'" (*ein Kreisen um "Gott"*) that arises from a technological utility,[144] the decision of dedivinization is the final iconoclastic gesture, the destruction of all the forms of objectification presupposed by the doctrines of causality, teleology, utilitarianism, pragmatism, machination, technology, science, peoplehood, and culture.

Here it is germane to recall Heidegger's explication in "Die Zeit des Weltbildes," a lecture delivered on June 9, 1938, of the loss of gods (*Entgötterung*) as the fifth phenomenon of modernity. This expression is not to be understood as the "crude atheism" of the "mere elimination of the gods." The loss of the gods is a twofold process intimately related to Christianity: "On the one hand, the world picture Christianizes itself [*sich verchristlicht*] inasmuch as the ground of the world is posited as infinite and unconditioned, as the absolute. On the other hand, Christendom reinterprets its Christianity as a world view (the Christian world view) and thus makes itself modern and up to date." Contrary to what one might assume, the loss of the gods does not imply an atheistic abolition of the gods. In a far more complicated and sophisticated way, the loss of the gods is related to the Christianization of the world picture (*Weltbild*), which posits the ground of the world (*Weltgrund*) as the infinite and unconditioned absolute. The shift in orientation results in Christianity becoming a worldview (*Weltanschauung*) that reflects the "condition of indecision [*Entscheidungslosigkeit*] about God and the gods." Heidegger is quick to point out, however, that the loss of the gods does not exclude religiosity (*Religiosität*). Rather, the relation to the gods that ensues from the loss of the gods "is transformed into a religious experience [*Erleben*]. When this happens, the gods have fled [*dann sind die Götter entflohen*]. The resulting void is filled by the historical and psychological investigation of myth."[145]

The nonmetaphysical import of Heidegger's embrace of atheism is amplified in the following insightful reflection in the notebooks:

The "overcoming of metaphysics" will also be readily identified with "*atheism*," especially if metaphysics is understood in terms of cultural Christianity, whereby atheism means the denial of the presence at hand of a God [*Verneinung des Vorhandenseins eines Gottes*]. The overcoming of metaphysics is indeed a-theism—but in a sense unavailable to any theological metaphysics: steadfastness in the dispossession of humans from every preparedness to bring to a first decision the divinity of God [*die Gottschaft des Gottes*] in the encounter with their problematic humanity. The foundational enduring of this "without the decidability of the divinity of God" is incorporated into a moment of the history of beyng and renounces the claim and the public reputation of comparison with any sort of ecclesial or otherwise instituted pursuits of piety and lived experience.... A-theism understood in terms of the history of beyng would measure itself according to a standard that is essentially too low and would pervert its own essence, if it strove to pass itself off merely as a higher piety over and against the ecclesial devoutness of cultural Christianity. For this a-theism is altogether not a piety; in every case, piety must have its ground in the metaphysical interpretation of beings.[146]

Heidegger offers a shrewd analysis of the modern predicament and the role played by Christianity in fostering the religious experience centered on the flight of the gods that results from a worldview that posits God as the absolute that supplants the theistic image. The release from idolatry, which is demanded by the truth of beyng and the need for every being to be restored to the ground that manifests the abysses of beyng, culminates in the removal of the final idol, *the idol of the god personified as the deity that must be worshiped without being idolized*. The monotheistic iconoclasm is transposed philosophically into the assumption that beyng itself will no longer be apprehended ontologically as that which bestows beingness on beings but will transcend itself toward the trembling, the decision that heralds the indecision of whether the last god is arriving or departing. In this matter, there is no intention or will; it is simply the consequence of the *es gibt*, the giving that gives with no will to give and no desire to be given, an idea that is far removed from the postmodern theological efforts to salvage the nature of being as a miraculous gift.[147] As Heidegger put it in another passage from the notebooks, "To *be* in the proximity of the gods—even if this proximity is the remotest remoteness of the undecidability regarding their flight or advent—that cannot be charged to 'good fortune' or to 'misfortune.' The constancy of beyng bears its own measure in itself, provided it at all requires a measure."[148] This measure is immeasurable, which is not to say the computation of a being of colossal proportions, but rather the demarcation of the immeasurability of beyng that is commensurate to the between, the interlude wherein god is present as the excess (*Übermaß*) of the surpassing of all beings, the god that is always yet to come and therefore can never be present.[149] As the presence of nonpresence, as opposed to the nonpresence of presence, the last god is the signpost of the khoric abyss of the "concealment of that self-concealment which radiates as beyng," the space of "great solitude," wherein one can heed the "uncanny silence which indeed still devours the thunder of the passing by of the god."[150]

Configuring Nothing: Disfiguration and the Limits of Imaginality

In a passage from the *Schwarze Hefte*, cited in chapter 3, Heidegger portrays the *self-refusal of beyng* as the "trembling of the divinizing of the last god," which occasions the "openness of the spatiotemporal field," that is, the "there" (*Da*) for the being-there of Dasein.[151] As we have noted, there are conspicuous affinities between Heidegger and the kabbalistic *ṣimṣum* as the nascent withdrawal that opens the opening of the spatial-temporal field that gathers and disperses the beingness of all beings that come to be from and return to the nothingness of being. Another entry from the notebooks reverberates even more poignantly with the Jewish esoteric doctrine: "We never grasp the *inceptual* [Anfängliche]; in order not to become something present at hand [*vorhandenes Gewordenes*] and thereby forfeit itself, the inceptual must constantly withdraw. Therefore, the beginning [*Anfang*] can never present itself; it can only be carried out, namely, in the downgoing of recession [*Untergang des Zurücktretens*], such that the withdrawal truly *remains* a withdrawal."[152] Just as kabbalists relate the incomprehensibility of the beginning to the fact that it bestows by withholding, so Heidegger emphasizes that the inceptual can never be apprehended objectively because the beginning cannot be turned into a thing that is present at hand and hence subject to representation but only carried out or enacted—the word used is *vollziehen*, the predicate form related to *Vollzugssinn*, a term that Heidegger privileged from early on as the expression most suitable to name the appropriating event by which Dasein facilitates the absent presence of the present absence of all that is given—through the undergoing of the retreating, that is, the withdrawal that withdraws from withdrawing and thereby remains a withdrawal.

In another aphorism from the notebooks, Heidegger speculates that "beginnings [*Anfänge*] withdraw from every will to seize hold of them; in withdrawing, they merely leave behind the outset [*Beginn*] as their mask."[153] The outset, we can presume, is a temporal occurrence that, as mask, both conceals and reveals—indeed, reveals in the manner of concealing and conceals in the manner of revealing—the nontemporal beginning, the foundation that can never be incorporated within the ontological provenance of thingness (*Dinglichkeit*). Utilizing Derrida's description of spirit (*Geist*) in Heidegger's thinking, we can say of the inceptual that it "forms part of the series of non-things [*non-choses*]" and thus "in no way allows itself to be thingified [*chosifier*]."[154] I would slightly amend Derrida's words by noting that nonthingness should not be set in opposition to thingness, for to do so is to reinforce the antinomy that Heidegger sought to bypass by casting a bright light on the ontological difference between being and beings. In his words: "The thinking of being seeks no hold in beings. Essential thinking heeds the measured signs of the incalculable and recognizes in the latter the unforeseeable arrival of the unavoidable."[155] To treat being as if it were a being is to obscure the differential relation between being and beings, or as Heidegger puts it, the "complete disempowerment [*Entmachtung*] of being in favor of an undisputed and limitless empowerment [*Vormacht*] of beings."[156] I note, parenthetically, that Heidegger's tireless insistence on distinguishing being and beings is anticipated in Schelling's comment "Since the concept of having being [*Begriff des Seyenden*] includes a differentiation from Being in it [*einen Unterschied von dem Seyn in sich*], a distinction that is denied in regard to the Godhead, and, according to the ancient saying, what is Being itself, has no being (*Ejus quod est Esse, nullum est Esse*)."[157]

Despite his best intentions, Heidegger could not avoid syntactical language when speaking about the basic experience (*Grunderfahrung*) of beyng that cannot be transmitted suitably either through an assertion (*Aussage*) or a proposition (*Satz*).[158] Aware of the dilemma, he writes in a tone familiar to mystic visionaries, "We can never say beyng (event) immediately and therefore not even mediately in the sense of the heightened 'logic' of dialectics. Every saying already speaks *out of* the truth of beyng and can never immediately leap over itself to beyng itself. The laws of bearing silence are higher than those of any logic."[159] One can discern here an intricate conjunction of the apophatic and the kataphatic that is reminiscent of what we find in kabbalistic sources: the truth of being is beyond language but it is not possible for linguistic beings to leap over language to lay bare being as being divested of linguistic attire—and even silence is included under this taxon. In the between of the juxtaposition, the belonging together of the dissimilar, there must be a bridge, and for humankind, language is that bridge. Language imposes itself on Heidegger's efforts to speak of the truth of being beyond language, as we see, for instance, in his depiction of the inceptual as "the grounding of the origin of what is simplest in its uniqueness and unsurpassability."[160]

The formulation is evocative of descriptions of the self-determination and self-actualization of the highest of beings in scholastic metaphysics—cast by Heidegger, as we noted above, in the Spinozistic coinage *causa sui*—but it is imperative not to lose sight of the fact that, for Heidegger, the nothing is no thing and not the antithesis of a thing; the inner ground of all beings is the event of the clearing and not a being that is grounded in either its own being or in the being of another.[161] This is the crux of Heidegger's criticism of German idealism, and particularly as it found expression in Hegel, according to which beings are transfigured into an objectivity (*Gegenständlichkeit*) that extends to the subjectivity of the representing I and to the relation of representing the object and representing the representation.

> Machination as the basic character of beingness [*der Seiendheit*] now lapses into the form of the subject-object dialectic, which, as absolute, plays out to their end and orders together all possibilities of every known realm of beings. Here once again is sought complete security against all uncertainty, i.e., a conclusive grip on the *correctness* of absolute certainty but also, unwittingly, an evasion of the truth of beyng. No bridge leads from here to the other beginning. Yet it is precisely this thinking of German Idealism that we must know, for it brings the machinational power of beingness into its extreme, unconditioned development (it elevates the conditionedness of the *ego cogito* into the unconditioned) and prepares the end.[162]

The absolute certainty about the machinational power of beingness is proportionate to the evasion of the truth of beyng. To retrieve the latter, we must come to the end whence we unearth the "extraordinary character" (*Ungewöhnliche*) of the beginning as that which withdraws constantly and hence is always most ancient and most novel, reaching backward to the farthest past and extending forward to the farthest future.[163] The greatest power accorded the human is to draw near to beyng—that which is most question-worthy—but the beyng to which one can draw near presents itself in the mode of that which is most distant, the self-refusal that is the pure relation of the withdrawal of its being (*Sichentzogenseins*).[164] What is withdrawn in the self-withdrawal is the unique and unsurpassable origin, the *Ursprung*, the source whence the leap (*Sprung*) of the beginning ensues. The beginning is thus depicted as "the veil that conceals the origin—indeed an unavoidable veil. . . . The origin keeps itself concealed in the beginning."[165] The origin is consumed by an incipience (*Anfänglichkeit*) of beyng that withholds itself from what has been commenced in the beginning (*Angefangenen*).[166]

For the kabbalists, too, the beginning may be appositely described as the veil that conceals the origin that both precedes and succeeds it; that is, the divine wisdom (*Ḥokhmah*), symbolized by the letter *beit*, etymologically related to the word *bayit*, is the house within which the agglomeration of beings contained in the *Ein Sof* or the nothingness (*ayin*) of the divine crown (*Keter*), symbolized by the letter *alef*, the wonder (*pele*) that is the master of the world (*alufo shel olam*), take refuge and gain release.[167] Although the expression *alufo shel olam* suggests the traditional theological sense of a volitional creator, scrutiny of its usage in kabbalistic sources indicates that the overtly theistic language actually signifies the very opposite: the *aluf* is the *alef*, which is the *pele*, the mystery outside the polarities imposed by the structure of the world, including the distinction between transcendence and immanence. The *aluf* that is the *pele* of the *alef* names the nameless being of nothing unfurled in the nothing of being, the garment (*levusha*) that garbs the hidden ancient light (*nehora setima attiqa*),[168] the covering (*kissuya*) of that which cannot be uncovered. Hence, the originary event can be described enigmatically as the opening of a cleft in the self-contained unfolding, the inceptual projection that is concurrently a withdrawal, an act expressive of both constrictive judgment and expansive mercy. For Heidegger, as for the kabbalists, we can speak of the "resonating [*Anklang*] of the essential occurrence of beyng [*Wesung des Seyns*] in the abandonment by being."[169] Astoundingly, Heidegger likewise speaks of that resonating as a bestowing that is "*an excess of pure refusal* [das Übermaß der reinen Verweigerung],"[170] the self-withdrawing (*Sichentziehende*) that is the grounding (*Gründung*) that "*clears the self-concealing* [lichtet das Sichverbergen]."[171]

By placing the kabbalah in dialogue with Heidegger, we can better appreciate that the concept of the beginning for the kabbalist is not simply a receding that precedes the extension; the extension itself is a form of receding inasmuch as the line of the infinite (*qaw ha-ein sof*) cannot extend from the light of the infinite (*or ha-ein sof*) into the space emptied of that light unless the character of its infinitivity recoils;[172] we could not even speak of the line coming forth from the circle of infinity (*iggul ha-ein sof*)[173] if the boundlessness were not bounded. Generalizing even more broadly, we can say, following Eliashiv, there is a necessity for contraction in each and every disclosure (*inyan ṣorekh ha-ṣimṣum ha-na'aseh be-khol gilluy we-gilluy*),[174] an idea that conceptually is parallel to the Neoplatonic view that each stage in the procession from the originative monad is simultaneously a retreat, and hence the whole of the emanation can be characterized by diminishing degrees of perfection and likeness to the One, that is, a devolution from similarity to dissimilarity.[175] Scholem was no doubt influenced by an articulation of this sort and thus he emphasized that *ṣimṣum* is not a one-time event but rather constantly repeats itself,[176] the dialectic of expansion (*hitpashshetut*) and withdrawal (*histallequt*) that corresponds to the "two tendencies of perpetual ebb and flow," which "continue to act and react upon each other. Just as the human organism exists through the double process of inhaling and exhaling and the one cannot be conceived without the other, so also the whole of Creation constitutes a gigantic process of divine inhalation and exhalation."[177] I would modify Scholem's view, however, by noting that it is not only that the "perpetual tension" of the cosmic process dialectically entails that every expansion is preceded by withdrawal, but rather, more paradoxically, that the expansion is itself a withdrawal in the same manner that every disclosure (*gilluy*) is a concealment (*he'lem*), since what is disclosed is the concealment and the concealment cannot be disclosed as concealment unless it is concealed.

The underlying axiom of this esoteric wisdom was formulated succinctly by Shalom Dovber Schneersohn (1860–1920), the fifth of the seven masters of the Ḥabad-Lubavitch dynasty: "This is the aspect of the disclosure and the emissions of the light of the infinite, the one who emanates in the worlds of the emanated and created beings, and as it is written 'In your light the light is seen' (Psalms 36:10), for through your essential light of the essence of the light of the infinite, the light is seen in the worlds, and it is known that every disclosure of the light is by means of the garments in which the light is garbed and concealed to the point that there can be the aspect of disclosure."[178] The light can be revealed only if it is concealed, which is to say, the truth is exposed though the veil of truth that is the untruth. That the removal of the veil results in the unfurling of another veil to be unfurled implies that the enunciation of the secret can never coincide with what is enunciated. Inevitably, as Benjamin put it in a fragment on the imagination written in 1920–21, every apparition is a "de-formation [*Entstaltung*] of what has been formed. It is a characteristic of all imagination that it plays a game of dissolution with its forms."[179] Perhaps this is also the intent of Benjamin's somewhat perplexing comment inspired by the apocryphal Ḥasidic dictum, concocted by Scholem,[180] concerning the status of the world to come: "Everything will be the same as here—only a little bit different. Thus it is with the imagination [*die Phantasie*]. It merely draws a veil over the distance. Everything remains as it is, but the veil flutters and everything changes imperceptibly beneath it."[181] As a veil, the imagination conceals the images in its purview by revealing them in forms that are the same but indiscernibly different, different precisely because the same and the same precisely because different. In more technical phenomenological terms, the disfiguration of all figures implies that there is no mode of givenness that is not also a refusal to give.

I would argue, contra Scholem's well-known distinction, that the midrashic connotation of *ṣimṣum* as concentration of the divine presence to a point in place is not diametrically opposed to the kabbalistic connotation of that term as the withdrawal of the divine presence from a point in place.[182] When kabbalists cite or paraphrase the relevant aggadic passage in their interpretation of the doctrine of *ṣimṣum*, and this includes Luria in one of the few texts that he authored,[183] they are doing so because they believed, and with good reason, that their idea flows naturally out of the older sources.[184] The compression of the limitless to a delimited space is perforce a contraction and a retreat. Every creative act of the infinite must be seen through the prism of this twofold process, although I must emphasize again that the two processes occur contemporaneously and not consecutively: the overflowing is itself an act of withholding and the withholding an act of overflowing. According to Luria, the beginning, which conceals and thereby reveals the origin, emerges from the expanding contraction that sets the motion of time as the contracting expansion into place, the clearing within which the cosmic structure lights up as the shadow-play of the plenitudinal void. Temporally speaking, the beginning, the interlude that is the oldest and the youngest—the oldest because the youngest and the youngest because the oldest[185]—displays the quality of the *retroactive not yet*, the achronic fecundity of the future that is the originary abyss continually voiding itself in the generation of the beginning that passes away incessantly, the trace of the untraceable that is both antecedent and consequent to the withdrawal of the light, the past that comes before as what comes after.[186]

The philosophical import of the Lurianic trope is elucidated by Heidegger's Heraclitean understanding of nature (φύσις) as "an emerging and an arising, a self-opening [*das Sichöffnen*], which, while rising, at the same time turns back into what has emerged, and so shrouds within itself [*in dem sich verschließt*] that which on each occasion gives presence to what is present [*was je einem Anwesenden die Anwesung gibt*]. Thought as a fundamental word, φύσις signifies a rising into the open: the lighting of that clearing [*das Lichten jener Lichtung*] into which anything may enter appearing [*erscheinen*], present itself in its outline, show itself in its 'appearance' (εἶδος, ἰδέα) and be present as this or that. Φύσις is that rising-up which goes-back-into-itself; it names the coming to presence of that which dwells in the rising-up and this comes to presence as open."[187] The outpouring of being, which is always in addition a withdrawal into nonbeing—referred to as well as the fullness of "the *truth* as the *clearing* for *self-concealing*" (*der* Wahrheit *als* Lichtung *für das* Sich-verbergen) or as "the essential occurrence of the negative in beyng as event" (*das wesende Nichthafte des Seyns als Ereignis*)[188]—offers a remarkable parallel to the nonontological nothingness[189] promulgated by the kabbalists; that is, the presumption that absolute nothingness, the nothingness that is less than and therefore more than nothing, the infinitesimal source of the negation that is the affirmation of all that exists, can be given only as what is not given.[190] In the formulation of a particularly complex strata of zoharic literature, "the mystery of unity is hidden in the supernal concealment [*raza de-yiḥuda go ṭemira illa'ah setim*] and revealed through the concealed engravings [*we-galya go gelifei ṭemirin*], to ascend in its gradations to be completed above."[191] The secret of divine unity hidden in the supernal concealment can be revealed only by way of the engravings that are concealed. The disclosure is depicted metaphorically as an act of writing, but what is written remains opaque, maintaining a sense of secrecy even in—precisely as a consequence of—the act of exposing. In line with the Derridean description of the trace cited above, we could say that the concealed engravings come about as the result of a form of writing that is itself an erasure. To cite another illustration from a different but equally difficult stratum of the zoharic compilation: "Within the concealment of the concealed [*bi-ṭemiru di-ṭemirin*] was etched a trace [*reshimu*] that was not seen or revealed. That trace was etched and not etched [*rashim we-lo rashim*]. Masters of understanding and of open eyes cannot understand it. It is the foundation of all [*qiyyuma de-kholla*]. That trace is miniscule, it is not seen and not revealed. It abides in the will to establish everything, to receive what it receives from that which has no trace or will, and is not seen."[192] Just as for Heidegger, the giving of *es gibt*, the letting be (*Seinlassen*) of being, is the mystery of the "concealing of what is concealed as a whole [*die Verbergung des Verborgenen im Ganzen*], of beings as such"[193]—and hence what is manifest of necessity is hidden in and by its very manifestation[194]—so for the kabbalist, every bestowal of *Ein Sof*—a trace that is etched and not etched in the concealment of the concealed—is concomitantly a withholding, a veiling of what is unveiled in the unveiling of the veil.

Naming the Nameless and the Being of Nonbeing

Support for my conjecture may be drawn from the following comment of Eliashiv:

> Thus the whole secret of the contraction [*sod ha-ṣimṣum*] was within the light of the infinite itself [*be-tokh or ein sof aṣmo*], in his middle, as is known. And the matter of his middle is, as it were, in the strength of the quality of the aspect of the infinite [*be-toqef eikhuto di-veḥinat ein sof*]. The contraction came about within his very being [*hinneh bo aṣmo na'aseh ṣimṣum*], for it is his opposite, as it were, and the contraction occurred within the infinite itself and it endures within it forever, and this is, as it were, by way of two opposites in one subject [*shenei hafakhim be-nose eḥad*]. . . . And the force of the limit [*koaḥ ha-gevul*] and the limitless [*u-vilti gevul*] stand forever in existence together . . . and this is the aspect of two opposites in one subject.[195]

The mystery of *ṣimṣum* serves prototypically to enunciate the paradox of two opposites within one substratum insofar as it presumes that the limitless is capable of being delimited. This is the import of the contention that the contraction takes place in the middle of the light of *Ein Sof*, a depiction that is palpably absurd, since there can be no middle of that which has no dimensions—the middle of nowhere is everywhere to the degree that the middle of everywhere is nowhere. In terms of the historical debate over whether *ṣimṣum* should be taken literally (*kefshuṭo*) or figuratively (*derekh mashal*), Eliashiv famously defended the former view against the latter, especially as it was formulated by some of the students of the Gaon of Vilna, who followed the position of Moses Ḥayyim Luzzatto.[196] This is surely accurate philologically and textually, but philosophically one must ponder what it means to speak of the *Ein Sof* literally withdrawing its light. In the domain of the infinite, the literal cannot be anything but nonliteral; that is, something is literally true if it is figuratively so and figuratively true if it is literally so,[197] a point that Eliashiv himself affirms, as I noted in the previous chapter.

In another passage, Eliashiv points out that the opinion of the masters of Jewish esoteric lore differs with Maimonides's view that the simple unity of the divine essence necessitates that the attributes must be interpreted negatively. There is agreement that the *via negativa* applies to the infinite essence, but the kabbalists diverge from Maimonides inasmuch as they maintain the paradox, expressed in the language of Azriel of Gerona, that the sefirotic potencies, which collectively are the disclosure of the Tetragrammaton, are the limited force that is unlimited (*koaḥ bi-gevul mi-beli gevul*).[198] This manifestation is possible only when the boundless light compresses itself in each of the ten gradations, an enigma that is related to the midrashic idea of God constricting his presence (*meṣamṣem shekhinato*) between the two poles of the ark of the covenant.[199] Drawing on Azriel's nomenclature, Eliashiv writes that "the boundary that is without boundary [*ha-gevul mi-bilti gevul*] is merely the emanation from concealment to disclosure, and it is evident that the concealment and disclosure are not antinomies, but they are in one subject."[200] According to the principle of noncontradiction, concealment and disclosure are patently antinomical; the sefirotic emanations, however, defy this logic, and thus what appears to be oppositional is neutralized by the idea of two contraries existing together in one subject—the dialetheic assumption that every statement bears the paradox that α and $\neg\alpha$ are coincidentally true. The concealment relates to the nameless light of *Ein Sof* and the disclosure to the light of the manifestations comprised in the Tetragrammaton, but the full scope of the dialetheism leads to the awareness that the concealment of the nameless and the disclosure of the name are phenomenologically transposable:

> The emanation, which is the name *YHWH*, is the infinite itself [*ein sof aṣmo*], for all that the emanation accomplishes for the sublimity and elevation of the name *YHWH*, blessed be he, which is our God [*eloheinu*], is only by means of the light of the infinite [*or ein sof*] that is garbed and unified [*ha-mitlabbesh u-mityaḥed*] there to be one with all of the emanation entirely. . . . Therefore, the name *YHWH* is designated the essential name [*shem ha-eṣem*] because the infinite shows itself [*ein sof aṣmo mitra'eh*] through this name by means of its being garbed and unified [*hitlabbesho we-yiḥudo*] in the emanation.[201]

To be even more precise, Eliashiv argues that the investiture (*hitlabbeshut*) and unity (*yiḥud*) of *Ein Sof* in the *sefirot* takes effect after the rectification (*tiqqun*) of the primordial world of chaos (*olam ha-tohu*) that arises from the name being permutated as *ywd he waw he* (10 + 6 + 4 + 5 + 1 + 6 + 1 + 6 + 5 + 1), which equals 45, the numerology of the word *adam* (1 + 4 + 40). Once the light is appropriately configured in the form of the supernal anthropos, which corresponds to Israel, there is an inseparable unity between the infinite and the emanations. "Thus his names are himself, blessed be he, for the light of the infinite itself is revealed by means of the emanation [*ha-aṣilut*] through the Tetragrammaton, blessed be he, and in the names and epithets that branch out from him, and he and his name are one. However, all of his disclosures in them are only for the sake of the generation and the existence of the worlds of creation [*beri'ah*], formation [*yeṣirah*], and doing [*asiyyah*], for if not for this he would not have been revealed at all, and he would have remained in the aspect of infinity as it was before."[202]

Following the precedent of Viṭal,[203] Eliashiv repeatedly emphasizes that the world of emanation is to be distinguished from the worlds of creation, formation, and doing—the four worlds according to the traditional kabbalistic cosmology—insofar as the first world alone can be considered a manifestation of the light of the essence of the infinite (*or aṣmut ein sof*), which is represented symbolically by the Tetragrammaton. This reflects a distinction traceable to thirteenth-century kabbalists between the world of unity (*olam ha-yiḥud*) and the world of separation (*olam ha-perud*). The force of the mythologic, however, prescribes that, even in the former, the realm of divine emanations, the nameless can be expressed through the name only by remaining inexpressible. This is the mystical rationale for the ritual custom to pronounce the ineffable name by its epithet *Adonai*—by uttering the latter the name is both spoken and unspoken, spoken as the unspoken, a verbal gesticulation that is coerced at all times to say what it does not say. To summon Azriel's language mentioned above, the limited force reveals, and thereby conceals, the incomposite light that is without limit.[204] In one context, after affirming that the vessels of the supernal world are to be considered as light, form, or soul in relation to the worlds beneath it, Eliashiv writes,

> However, in the garments (which are the worlds of creation, formation, and doing), the light of the essence [*or aṣmut*] is not revealed. Therefore, [the worlds of] creation, formation, and doing are not from the aspect of divinity [*mi-beḥinat elohut*] . . . and his light, blessed be his name, is not united with them so that they would be one in the way that the soul is united with the body. . . . Thus, they are called the aspect of garments, for they are not one entity with the body. This is not the case in the [world of] emanation within which the light of the infinite is united, and the emanation becomes one with him. Therefore, the emanation is called body, since it is united with the soul that is within it, and thus it is entirely the complete divinity [*elohut gamur*].[205]

Three levels are discriminated: infinity aligned with the soul; the infinite light dispersed through the world of emanation aligned with the body; and the lower three finite worlds aligned with the garments. One of the more theologically tantalizing implications of this discussion is that the term *elohut* is attributed distinctively to the sphere of the sefirotic emanations inasmuch as they exercise providential governance in the lower worlds.

> All of the emanation entirely is called by the name *YHWH,* blessed be he, and by all the other names as well. . . . But above the emanation is the incomposite infinite light [*or ein sof pashuṭ*] that is without any name at all. Hence, he contracted and expanded [*nitṣamṣem we-hitpasheṭ*] in the light of his essence and he is garbed in the emanation, and consequently, he is called by means of the emanation through the name *YHWH,* blessed be he, and all of the Torah and the worship are directed to him, and all of the prayers completely. We worship him inasmuch as he is garbed in the emanation, for by means of this he is revealed. The intention is not that we worship him through some intermediary, God forbid. Since they are verily one with him, the emanation is not an intermediary at all, but rather he and the emanation are wholly one. However, the emanation is his disclosures, for by means of the emanation he is revealed, and it is possible now to grasp him through the name, which are all the names mentioned in the Torah.[206]

Naturally, Eliashiv wishes to avoid the intimation of dualism and hence he insists that the fact that prayer is directed to the Tetragrammaton does not imply that we worship an intermediary, even though he states that the purpose of the first contraction within the incomposite essence was "to depart from the gradation of infinity [*madregat ein sof*] and to be revealed in the aspect of divinity [*elohut*] in all of the emanations."[207] This is justified by the assumption that the hidden light of the infinite, which is beyond all names, is garbed in the name that comprises all of the divine names. Since the unity of *Ein Sof* is undifferentiated, it is possible to reach the aspect of infinity, which is above the emanation, through the gradations of the emanation.[208] The predictable pivoting to a rhetoric that breaches the divide between the nameless and the name should not obscure the implication that the theopoetic representation of the deity depends on the emanator (*ma'aṣil*) assuming the demiurgical role classified respectively as creator (*bore*), former (*yoṣer*), and maker (*oseh*) in concurrence with the form that the transcendent light takes in each of the lower three worlds. The term *elohut* denotes the light of divinity that emanates and is garbed in these worlds, which is "in truth distant from the gradation of his essential, concealed truth . . . for every word and attribute of divinity through which he, blessed be his name, is called, is, as it were, only the aspect of the fifth gradation from the comprehensive gradations." This is followed immediately by the disclaimer, "And yet, every aspect of his divinity, blessed be his name, is perpetually from the essence of the unity."[209]

It is possible that Eliashiv is deliberately challenging more blatant acosmic or panentheistic interpretations of kabbalistic thought, as we find in some Ḥasidic sources, especially in the texts produced by the Ḥabad-Lubavitch dynasty.[210] My concern, however, is not to adjudicate the questions of historical background or influence but to interrogate philosophically whether Eliashiv himself can maintain this distinction cogently and consistently. Can he truly entertain a break in the chain of being such that the first world is qualitatively different from the other three worlds? In my mind, the answer to this must be negative. This is attested in the remark cited at the end of the last paragraph: the assertion that divinity is most properly attributed to the lowest manifestation—referred to as the last of the gradations, which are the roots of the five aspects of soul in each world (*nefesh, ruaḥ, neshamah, ḥayyah,* and *yeḥidah*)—is subverted by the stipulation that it emanates from the essence of the infinite. Consider as well the following passage:

> The evident intent of the unity of *YHWH Elohim* is that he, blessed be his name, is one with all of existence entirely [*eḥad im kol ha-meṣi'ut kullo*], for the name *Elohim* is his light that expands in the coming to be of all existence, and these are the thirty-two [occurrences of] *Elohim* in the account of creation[211] whence all of existence was fashioned. When they stand in their holiness, as when they emerged from him, blessed be his name, and his light is revealed through them, then he and they are completely unified, and this is the unity of *YHWH Elohim*. The Torah gestured toward it, "On the day that the Lord God [*YHWH Elohim*] made heaven and earth" (Genesis 2:4), for then he, blessed be his name, was one with the whole of existence, for his name and his holiness are discernible and disclosed in all of them. And "the Lord will be one and his name will be one" (Zechariah 14:9), for the worlds of creation, formation, and doing themselves are not divinity at all [*elohut kelal*], but his name is upon them, for he brought them into existence, sustains them, and has providence over them. When they are all sanctified to his name, his name is united with them, for it becomes clear from the entire existence that "our king is true, there is none but him."[212]

The unity of the divine is viewed through the conjunction of *YHWH* and *Elohim*, the former relates to the world of emanation and the latter to the multiple powers that are manifest in the lower three worlds. The pairing of the names suggests that God is one with all existence. That Eliashiv wants to burn the proverbial candle at both ends is apparent from the statement that, on the one hand, the worlds of creation, formation, and doing are not divinity, but on the other hand, the unique name—the essential name that names the essence whose essence it is to have no essence—presides over them. When the lower worlds are sanctified in the name, then the entirety of existence gives witness to the fact that, in the words of the *Aleynu* prayer cited at the end of the passage, "our king is true, there is none but him" (*emet malkenu efes zulato*). This liturgical proclamation, I submit, should not be interpreted as confirmation of the traditional monotheistic belief that there is one deity, rendered in the allegorical language of royalty, but rather in accord with the monistic intent that the infinite is the sole reality, the nothingness in virtue of which everything is transmogrified into nothing. Hence, to affirm that there is nothing besides him, *efes zulato*, ensnares one in the double bind of nothingness, the potential for something other than the being that is nothing must be sought in the capacity of that nothing to become something in the annihilation of its nothingness.

Eliashiv exerted great effort to avoid the panatheistic conclusion that divinity is dissolved in the nihility of the light of the essence—the obverse of the premise that the light of the essence simulates the persona of divinity in the shape of the seemingly independent worlds—but I am not convinced that the patterns of his thinking allow him to dodge this outcome. For instance, in one context, he audaciously speaks of the five disclosures—the light of the infinite (*or ein sof*), the world of the line and the contraction (*olam de-qaw we-ṣimṣum*), the world of the primal anthropos (*olam de-adam qadmon*), the world of emanation (*olam aṣilut*) and the worlds of creation, formation, and doing (*olamot beri'ah yeṣirah asiyyah*)[213]—through which the concealed truth of *Ein Sof* is revealed. The emanation and emission of the light in each of the disclosures comes to be by means of the aspect of the contraction and withdrawal of the light.[214] Or, even more daringly, in a second passage, he comments that through the latent force of the divine powers (*gevurot*) in the infinite does the contraction come to be and the measureless is manifest in the aspect of the line and the measure (*qaw u-middah*). As the forces of judgment coagulate below, the illimitable light is constricted further and the infinity beyond theistic representation assumes the form of the demiurge, who creates and exercises providence over the lower worlds, even to the ultimate terminus, conferring existence on the demonic shells (*qelippot*) and evil. All the disclosures of *Ein*

Sof, accordingly, are "by means of the coming to be of the garments of the line [*hithawwut di-levushin de-ha-qaw*], the contraction, the primal anthropos, the emanation, and afterwards in creation, formation, and doing, which all came to be by means of the aspects of the powers . . . and his disclosure in each one is proportionate to the comportment of the garments."[215] The garment symbolizes the mechanism by which the formless is both hidden and revealed—not consecutively but synchronously. The manifestation of the presence is made possible by the occlusion of the presence; only in the concealment of disclosure is there disclosure of the concealment. Even when Eliashiv speaks of the descent of the worlds into the domain of the shells as a consequence of human transgression, and creation is separated from emanation, and the name *Elohim* is blemished because the light of the unity of the two names vanishes and the light of the infinite is cloaked from donning the garment through which it is rendered visually tangible, he still qualifies the matter by saying that the light shines in concealment.[216] It is not possible for the light to disappear absolutely, as it is the only thing that is real. The following additional comment about the unity of *YHWH* and *Elohim* bolsters my suggestion: "The intention is only with regard to the concealed [*ha-he'lem*] and the hidden [*ha-hester*] that is within them, which is their inwardness [*penimiyyutam*] and the main force of their being [*koaḥ qiyyumam ha-iqqari*]. For as pertains to what is concealed and hidden, God, blessed be his name, is always the place of the world, bearing it in all of its fullness, and it exists and endures only because of him, and he is in the aspect of the soul to the soul and the spirit to the spirt for all its existence and all of its phenomena."[217]

Here we come face to face with the paradox of the paradigm that informs the kabbalistic *Lebenswelt*: the namelessness of the infinite, whose hidden truth is beyond comprehension, can be revealed only by constricting itself in the spiritual light of the four letters of the essential name that comprises the nonessence of the essence of *Ein Sof* manifest as the essence of the nonessence of the sefirotic gradations.[218] The intractable point, which teeters on the edge of inexpressibility, is well expressed in the following comment in the compendium of Lurianic teaching, *Pitḥei She'arim*, composed by Wildmann:

> You must know that all that the kabbalists spoke, and all that the Ari, blessed be his memory, revealed from the secrets of the divine wisdom and about the worlds, we are speaking only about his will, blessed be he, and not about the master of the will, for we do not speak at all about the emanator, blessed be his name. No creature, even the supernal among the supernal, has any comprehension of the master of the will, for he is concealed from every idea and every thought, and there is no apprehension of him at all; we speak only about his will. . . . And this matter is very deep, for in *Pirqei Rabbi Eliezer* it is said "Before the world was created he and his name alone were."[219] These words are very deep for, in truth, the blessed one has no name, "what likeness will you compare unto him" (Isaiah 40:18), for the matter of the name relates to something that is comprehended. . . . Thus it is not appropriate to attribute a name to the emanator, blessed be he, about whom no creature has any comprehension or idea at all. However, the blessed one on account of the abundance of his mercy in wishing to benefit and to create entities that are bounded and limited . . . contracted his will [*ṣimṣem reṣono*]. . . . Consequently, after the contraction [*ha-ṣimṣum*], it is possible to speak of his will and of everything that issues from it. . . . And thus we attribute names to him that are all comprised in the Tetragrammaton . . . and this is what is said that *raṣon* is numerically equal to *shemo*, for his name is his will comprehended by us. Prior to the aspect of this contraction it is not appropriate to attribute a name to him, blessed be he, but his name and he were all one. No one knows his name but the *Ein Sof* himself, blessed be he, and this is what the kabbalists intended when they write that prior to the emanation of the worlds the ten *sefirot* were hidden in the *Ein Sof* like a flame bound to the coal,[220] and this is the way of parable [*derekh mashal*] and a deep matter [*inyan amoq*]. The matter of the ten *sefirot* are his ten names, blessed be he . . . and after the contraction we have the power to speak of them, and it is not appropriate to attribute any name to the aspect that is prior to the contraction, for no one comprehends his name except for him, blessed be he, alone. His name and he are all one. This is the intent as well of R. Eliezer the Great when he said that before the world was created he and his name were one; that is, it is not appropriate to attribute a name at all but rather he, blessed be he, alone and his name were one. Understand these matters because they are deep.[221]

Insofar as the infinite has no name or image—and hence the designation "master of the will" cannot be taken as anything but a figurative trope to name the unnamable—all language and knowledge must relate to the will, which is identified as the name, or more specifically the Tetragrammaton. This idea is buttressed by the statement from *Pirqei Rabbi Eliezer* that prior to creation God and his name alone were and by the numerical equivalence of the respective expressions "will" and "his name," *raṣon* and *shemo*, which both equal 346. Interpreting the aggadic dictum kabbalistically, Wildmann pushes the apophatic to its limit—the name that is coeternal with the nameless names the namelessness of the name and therefore is both a name and not a name. This name is identified further as the ten *sefirot* hidden within *Ein Sof*. In that state—a term whose applicability to what I am trying to describe is questionable—the nameless and the name are distinguished as indistinguishable. After the contraction of the infinite, the name is enunciated in its ineffability as the boundary that issues from the boundless, an activity of symbolic representation linked to the verse "and through the prophets I was imaged" (Hosea 12:11). Since human beings are created in the divine image—that is to say, the image of the imageless—they have the capacity to portray the incorporeal in corporeal imagery. "Thus, everything that is found in the human is spoken of with respect to that which is above by way of parable, as it is written 'from my flesh I will behold God' (Job 19:26)."[222]

Eliashiv offers a similar explanation of the relationship between the name and the nameless:

> For the light of the infinite is clothed in the emanation, and the emanation becomes the aspect of a curtain [*masakh*] to the light of his essence that is above. Thus his light is constricted [*nitṣamṣem*] and diminished [*nitma'eṭ*] by means of this and it becomes fitting from then to be called by the name, and it is called through this by the name *YHWH*, blessed be he, and by all of the names. It follows that the name is merely the light of the emanator itself, and concerning the light of the infinite itself, which is exceedingly beyond [*lema'alah lema'alah*], we can say nothing, since it is outside of the names and above the names. . . . All those names by which he, blessed be his name, is called in relation to us are as a curtain and a window to the light of his essence that is above.[223]

The Tetragrammaton names the unnamed in the form of a curtain or a window through which the light is simultaneously exposed and shrouded. Eliashiv speaks of *Ein Sof* as if it were above, using a spatial metaphor to mark the transcendence of the essence voided of essence. But obviously the image is inadequate and should not be taken literally as a characteristic of infinity, since the latter cannot be bound spatially and still be characterized as infinite. Simply put, the unnamed does not denominate an entity with quantifiable and intelligible boundaries. In the preceding chapter, I mentioned that Derrida noted the affinity between Heidegger and the kabbalists with regard to the relationship of the name and the nameless. Let us recall in this context another remark of Derrida about the name of God in the kabbalah: "The name hidden in its potency possesses a power of manifestation and of occultation, of revelation and encrypting [*crypte*]. What does it hide? Precisely the abyss that is enclosed within it. To open a name is to find in it not something but rather something like an abyss, the abyss as the thing itself."[224] Derrida has articulated well the intent of Eliashiv, and other kabbalists, on the essential name that names the essence that cannot be named. The name names the nameless not as a thing but as no-thing, the abyss. It is mistaken to render these speculations about the name of the namelessness that gesticulates the namelessness of the name ontotheologically. To attribute the predicate "above" to the essence, which is not subject to spatial coordinates and about which we can say nothing, is the analogical means of portraying the incoherence that is the metric of coherence, the systemic limitlessness that delimits the parameters of the system.[225]

Oratorically, the will of the infinite is referred to as the foundation (*yesod*) and the telos (*takhlit*).[226] The purpose of the emanation is thus cast by Eliashiv, following the view expressed by kabbalists already in the thirteenth century, as an apocatastatic restitution of everything to the incomposite and indifferent unity of the infinite.

> The cause of the emanation is the infinite light, which is also from the category of disclosures, and all of them issue from him and are subject to him, for he is the first disclosure that is revealed from his concealed truth in the aspect of the disclosure of the infinite light, and he is the cause of causes and the telos of everything. Only for this did he bring forth everything, to restore everything at the end to him, and in order to effectuate this telos, he initially contracted [*ṣimṣem*] the light of the infinite [*or de-ein sof*] in the aspect of the central point [*nequddah ha-emṣa'it*] that is within him, and he produced therein the place [*maqom*] for the totality of existence, and afterwards he emanated there the line of the infinite [*ha-qaw de-ein sof*] and he brought forth there by means of this the entirety of existence in order to bring them to this goal, for they came forth from the infinite and they will return to the infinite.... Thus the contraction entirely [*kol ha- ṣimṣum*] is verily as it is literally and plainly [*ke-mashma'o ukhe-feshuṭo mammash*].[227]

The logic of the apocatastasis implies a symmetry of the first contraction (*ṣimṣum ha-ri'shon*) and the final rectification (*tiqqun ha-aḥaron*): just as the condensation of the infinite light at the beginning into the central point—the phallic aspect of the kingship of the infinite (*yesod de-ha-malkhut de-ein sof*),[228] the primordial will (*raṣon*), also referred to as the inner point (*nequddah ha-penimit*) of the kingship of the kingship (*malkhut de-malkhut*),[229] the essence (*aṣmut*) that is intermediate between the limited and the limitless[230]—is to be taken literally, so the elevation of all the worlds and the disclosure of the inner light of *malkhut* when it is restored to its source in the aspect of the kingship of the infinite (*malkhut de-ein sof*) at the end must be taken literally.[231]

When one delves beneath these rhetorical casings, however—that is, when one views the matter from the perspective of the garbing of the interior in the interior (*hitlabbeshut ha-penimi be-ha-penimi*) as opposed to the garbing of the exterior in the interior (*hitlabbeshut ha-ḥiṣoni be-ha-penimi*)[232]—one discerns that the foundation is no foundation and the telos is no telos because the nothing at the beginning and the nothing at the end respectively disrupt the notion of a beginning or an end with discernibly fixed boundaries. These terms betoken the emptiness of being rather than the being of emptiness, the ground that is the absence of ground, the goal that is the deprivation of goal. But even more profoundly, as I intimated at the start of the chapter, the groundlessness enframing all that exists suggests that, notwithstanding a commonly held misperception, the act of constriction is not a one-time occurrence; each inundation of the infinite light is possible because that light is diminished as it proliferates. The ideational implications of the kabbalistic teaching are thus on a par with Heidegger's insistence that the enactment of being is always a revocation of nonbeing. For the kabbalists, too, contraction is expansion, and not its opposite, inasmuch as the nameless can manifest itself only through the garment of the name. Phenomenologically, what is given—a givenness lacking etiology or teleology—is always also withheld from being given. From the vantagepoint of the chiasmic middle excluded by the law of the excluded middle, the indeterminate space where opposites converge in their divergence, the giving is the withholding of the withholding that is the giving.

Nihilating Nonground and the Temporal Sway of Becoming

If we follow this line of thinking, then rather than viewing *Ein Sof* as an entity subject to ontotheological conditions, it is more aptly identified as the linguistic signpost for the being that is neither something that is nothing nor nothing that is something, the origin beyond the language of origin, the conceptual marker of the ground that defies conceptualization as ground, the infinity incommensurate to our finite delineations of the infinite. *Ein Sof* thus can be said to correspond to Heidegger's event of thinking that must be constantly thought as unthought, the one true beyng of which all beings are simultaneously the manifestation of the concealment and the concealment of the manifestation. Insofar as the beings reveal the beyng they occlude, what is revealed is naught but the occlusion that is occluded, the mystery exposed as the mystery that hides its exposure as mystery.[233] Correspondingly, the unthought can be thought only through unthinking what is thought. To express the matter in terms derived from Laruelle's nonphilosophy, we could say that *Ein Sof* does not name a transcendental being that is unthinkable because it is beyond thinking but rather the namelessness that is insufficiently thought and therefore must be subject continuously to more questioning, the radically immanent differential that is foreclosed to thought except as what is yet to be thought. That words are inadequate signifies that the one, which is the real, is infinitely effable and not that it is irretrievably ineffable—there is always more to say concerning that about which there is always less to say.[234] Language here expectedly falters for the nihilating nonground—the groundlessness that is the origin of the ground, the abyss that engenders the inessential sameness manifestly concealed in the essential fluctuation of temporal-spatial phenomena—cannot be confined within the margins of an ontological economy.[235]

In previous work, I have suggested that *Ein Sof* should be demarcated as the *postmetaphysical unity of being*,[236] the self-negating negativity that breeds the positivity of the entangled manifold that constitutes the fabric of the world, the effluent emptiness that is the womb of all becoming, the matrixial space where opposites are identical in the opposition of their identity.[237] When infinity is viewed as a transcendent infinite, the multiplicity of finite beings appear to be illusory; one attuned to the emptiness at the nucleus of everything, however, comprehends that the infinity of transcendence as opposed to the transcendence of infinity denotes, in Deleuzian language, an immanence that is "immanent only to itself and consequently captures everything, absorbs All-One, and leaves nothing remaining to which it could be immanent."[238] The positing of *Ein Sof* as the one true being is not to repudiate the existence of the world vis-à-vis a transcendent nothingness but to highlight the fact that the laceration of nothingness[239] by the immanent beingness of beings signals the interfusion and codependency of all that exists, which exhorts us to question the commonsensical assumption about the reified and distinct nature of things. *Ein Sof* is not a single substance, or even the sum of all substances, but the relationality of everything that has existed, presently exists, and will exist in the multiverse. The unspeakable oneness of which the kabbalists insistently speak is constituted by the multivocality of the whole disintegrating in the integration of the parts disintegrating in the integration of the whole. Commuted into the terminological register of quantum physics, we can say the ground of the nonground is the unifying electromagnetic force constantly transformed in compliance with the ever-evolving symbiotic constellations that cohere in the intrarelational field of material nature. The oneness of infinitivity, therefore, does not imply a disembodied and disembedded unity but rather an embedded and embodied concrescence ceaselessly fabricated by the ever-changing prehension of actual entities. The scientific data reinforces the mystical exemplar of a universal singularity predicated on the juxtaposition of the monolithic and the polymorphic, not as antinomies whose conflict can be dialectically sublated, but as coefficient variables divided and thereby conjoined by the erratic constancy of their deviations. Consequently, what is hypothetically common to all that exists conjointly must be enunciated in the idiom that is distinctive to each entity individually.

Thus, employing the technical Lurianic jargon, Eliashiv writes about the "secret of the rectification of the unity" (*sod tiqqun ha-aḥdut*) that is predicated on the "rectification of the order of the interconnectivity" (*tiqqun de-seder ha-kelilut*) of the entirety of existence from the alpha of the six days of creation to the omega of the advent of the messiah. Deflecting a metaphysical-ontotheological explanation, I would postulate that the all-embracing oneness of *Ein Sof* is not a homogeneous totality but rather the heterogeneous congruence of everything in the supernal world of emanation and the lower worlds of creation, formation, and doing, which all derive from the holy sparks that were dispersed with the cataclysmic shattering of the vessels because of their inability to contain the light as it streamed forth from the eyes of the primal anthropos (*adam qadmon*) radiating to the world of points (*olam ha-nequddot*).[240] Insofar as the multiplicity of beings in the differentiated realm originate from the one undifferentiated source, they are interrelated and interdependent (*kol ha-peraṭim kullam she-be-ha-taḥton teluyyim u-mequsharim zeh ba-zeh*) and they will return apocatastatically to the primary interconnectivity (*kelilut ha-ri'shon*) and the secret of the true unity (*sod ha-aḥdut ha-amitti*) that is the light of the infinite.[241] But the interconnective unity of this light is not a stable and uniform entity that can be known conceptually or classified linguistically; it is rather a changeable and multifarious amalgamation, both at the beginning and at the end. Consequently, we are closer to the mark to think of the kabbalistic infinite as the aggregation of the one that is constituted by an open-ended variable, an event of eternal enfolding that is unfolding unceasingly in time, a process that cannot be named or theorized because each and every being is assiduously becoming the nothing it was and continues not to be.[242] Put differently, the infinite cannot be delimited by images of affirmation or negation, since the negative images presuppose the positivity they supposedly negate. Hence, to say of *Ein Sof* that it is nothing is as fallacious as saying of it that it is something. As we read in the text on the secret of contraction attributed to the Vilna Gaon, cited in the previous chapter, the apophatic denial of language is so extreme that it is even improper to consign the term *ein sof* to the infinite.[243] Extrapolating the aporetic implications of this lexical point, Eliashiv writes, "Thus, if not for the emanation, the emanator would not be called by the name 'divinity' [*elohut*] and not by any name at all, but only by the name *Ein Sof* or the name 'emanator' [*ma'aṣil*], for all of these verily are not names at all. The expression *Ein Sof* is only a negative attribute [*to'ar be-derekh shelilah*], for we say that he is without boundary and without limit, and similarly, the expression *ma'aṣil* is only the aspect of an adjective [indicating] that he emanates the emanation, and this is merely in the same manner that we refer to every craftsman by his craft."[244]

Once again we may sharpen our focus by triangulating the kabbalah and Heideggerian thought with the tetralemic logic of the Buddhist *madhyamaka*. Soliciting this comparative perspective, we could say of *Ein Sof*—as Heidegger's *Seyn/Nichts*—that it is both being and nonbeing and therefore neither being nor nonbeing.[245] In the peripheral center, the inclusive middle excluded by the logic of the excluded middle, contradictory properties are attributed and not attributed to the nonsubstance at the same time and in the same relation, whence it follows that the propositions $(\alpha \cdot \neg\alpha)$ and $\neg(\alpha \cdot \neg\alpha)$ converge in the point of their divergence. The syllogistic formula communicates the fundamental meontological paradox of the being of the nonbeing of the nonbeing of being: the kabbalistic *Ein Sof* and the Heideggerian *Seyn/Nichts* are linguistic signposts that point beyond language to the emptiness that is the fullness of the fullness of the emptiness. Surprisingly, this gnosis is encapsulated in an aphorism in *Der cherubinische Wandersmann* of Johann Scheffler (1624–77), better known by his nom de plume, Angelus Silesius, an author that had a notable impact on Heidegger[246]: "The gentle Godhead is nothing and beyond nothing, / Who sees nothing in all things, believe me, sees this" (*Die zarte Gottheit ist das Nichts und Übernichts, / Wer nichts in allem sieht, Mensch glaube, dieser siehts*).[247] To grasp the paradox of the Godhead that is both nothing and beyond nothing, one must be able to perceive the nothing in all things, which is not to ascertain that all things are acosmically nothing but rather to appreciate that the meontological core is the nothing that is everything in virtue of being nothing. Commenting on the passage by Silesius, Schelling elicits the implicit kabbalistic nuance:

> The Godhead is nothing [*nichts*] because nothing can come toward it in a way distinct from its being [*Wesen*] and, again, it is above all nothingness because it itself is everything. It certainly is nothing, but in the way that pure freedom [*lautere Freiheit*] is nothing. It is like the will that wills nothing, that desires no object, for which all things are equal and is therefore moved by none of them. Such a will is nothing and everything. It is nothing insofar as it neither desires to become actual itself nor wants any kind of actuality. It is everything because only from it as eternal freedom comes all force and because it has all things under it, rules everything, and is ruled by nothing.[248]

The affinity of Schelling's words to kabbalistic theosophy is enhanced by his statement that the Godhead in its "highest simplicity" (*höchste Einfalt*) is "above God" (*über Gott*).[249] One might assail this suggestion by noting that the depiction of the Godhead above God calls to mind Eckhart's famous characterization of the nondifferentiated ground in which God is beyond being and distinction, even the distinction of being God—in one sermon, the Dominican monk notoriously prayed to God to make him free of God.[250] I would surely not disagree with that statement, but I would insist nonetheless, as I commented above, that the atheological transcending of the theistic representation of God can be ascribed to *Ein Sof* as well and therefore juxtaposing kabbalah and Schelling, and by extension Heidegger, on this point is not an outlandish proposition. Moreover, just as Schelling speaks of this Super-Godhead (*Übergottheit*)—a turn of phrase that he may have appropriated from Silesius but which he attributes to the "ancients" (*Ältere*)[251]—as the "pure equivalence" (*Gleichgültigkeit*) or "indifference" (*Indifferenz*) "that is nothing and yet everything,"[252] so *Ein Sof* is characterized as the nonground wherein being and nothing do not coincide in the identity of opposites but endure as equal in the opposition of identity, and hence being is nothing in the nothing of being and nothing is being in the being of nothing.

Also noteworthy is Schelling's description of the Godhead as the "eternal freedom" and the "pure will without obsession and craving, the will insofar as it actually does not will,"[253] the will to which one cannot confer either the property of willing or that of not-willing.[254] The "grim fate of all life" is such that every creature desires to return to the originary delimitation (*Einschränkung*) and narrowness (*Enge*) of the "silent nothingness" in which it existed prior to extending outward into the breadth of self,[255] a striving toward the dearth of conation (*des Nichtswollens*).[256] Even more intriguing is Schelling's characterization of the nothingness of pure indifference as being "just like the pure happiness [*reine Frohheit*] that does not know itself, like the equanimous bliss [*gelassene Wonne*] that is entirely self-fulfilled and thinks of nothing, like the calm interiority [*stille Innigkeit*] that does not look after itself and does not become aware of its not Being [*nicht Seyns*]."[257] Amazingly, this description corresponds to the portrayal of the jouissance (*sha'ashu'a*) of *Ein Sof* that we discussed in chapter 3, the noetic-erotic arousal of infinity that has no object outside itself and that delights in the being of its own nonbeing, that is, the being that precedes the dyadic division into being and nonbeing—a theme that resounds even more precisely with the conclusion of the passage of Schelling according to an alternative version, "the calm interiority that rejoices at its nonbeing" (*die stille Innigkeit, die sich freut ihres nicht Seyns*).[258] Schelling's depiction of the pure will of the abyss—the extension of the *undesiring desire* of the zero point of the absolute beginning into the void[259]—corresponds to what is attributed to *Keter* in kabbalistic literature, the first emanation that is coterminous with *Ein Sof*, the absolute will that wills nothing, the will wanting naught but its own willfulness, the pure will—the will of all wills (*ra'awa de-khol ra'awin*)[260]—that does not will anything external. In this matter, it behooves us to note the probable influence on Schelling of Böhme, whose idea of the eternal will of the *Ungrund* and what Ray L. Hart has felicitously called the "abyssal indeterminate desire"[261] that draws itself insofar as there is nothing extrinsic that can be drawn,[262] the craving that stimulates the becoming of the other within the center of the will as the contra-will[263]—that is, the will for the other that is separate from and yet still part of the all-inclusive self—bears a striking resemblance to the kabbalistic conception of the autoerotic stirrings of the will of the infinite to emanate.[264] A concise formulation of the theopoiēsis of desire[265] is given by Böhme in the *Mysterium Pansophicum*:

> The non-ground is an eternal nothing but forms an eternal beginning as a craving [*Sucht*]. For the nothing is a craving for something. And since there is also nothing that may give something, the craving is itself the giving of that which is indeed also a nothing as merely a desiring [*begehrende*] craving. And that is the eternal primal state of *magia* which forms in itself since there is nothing. It forms something from nothing, and that just in itself and, since indeed the same craving is also a nothing as only a mere will, the will has nothing and is also nothing that may give itself something; and it has also no place where it could find or rest itself.[266]

For the kabbalist, the goal of the mystical quest is to be conjoined to the infinite, to reverse the order of creation by transforming something into nothing, the same other returning always as what is already other to the same. The hiddenness of the infinite, therefore, does not signify the transcendence that protects the theistic dogma of divine separateness; the concealment relates rather to the mystery of the disclosure of nothing in the limitless cycle of beings that has neither beginning nor end. From this perspective, nothingness can be regarded as the temporal sway of eternal becoming, the fullness of time that is interminably emptying itself in the coming to be of what passes away persistently, the moment that is the enduring end of the beginning that is the beginning of the end. In the black hole of infinity, time is eternalized in the nonpresent present, the present that can never be present and thus can never be absent. The nothing of *Ein Sof* is the unnamable and unknowable essence of being that permeates and yet escapes all beings, the groundlessness above time and space that is the elemental ground of the temporal-spatial world, the pleromatic vacuum that is neither the nothing of something nor the something of nothing, the nonbeing that continually comes to be in the ephemeral spectacle of being, the void wherein everything possible is actual because what is actual is nothing but the possible,[267] the sheltering-concealing[268] wherein the real is what appears to be real,[269] the clearing in relation to which emptiness is no longer distinguishable from fullness, the matrix within which all beings are revealed in the concealment of their being.

Translated into Heideggerian language, *Ein Sof* can be described as the indescribable nothing that nihilates, the nihilation (*Nichtung*) that resists any attempt to affix nothing within an ontological perimeter, that is, to explain nothing exclusively in terms of beings. In a mystical tenor worthy of any kabbalist, Heidegger writes in "Was ist Metaphysik?" that the nihilation "is neither an annihilation [*Vernichtung*] of beings nor does it spring from a negation [*Verneinung*]. Nihilation will not submit to calculation in terms of annihilation and negation. The nothing itself nihilates [*Das Nichts selbst nichtet*]."[270] Clarifying his position in the 1943 postscript to this text, Heidegger wrote that "we must prepare ourselves solely in readiness to experience in the nothing the pervasive expanse of that which gives every being the warrant to be [*was jedem Seienden die Gewähr gibt, zu sein*]. That is being itself [*Das ist das Sein selbst*]."[271] The kabbalistic infinity likewise may be pondered as the repelling gesture (*abweisende Verweisung*)[272] of nothingness vis-à-vis beings as a whole, the refusal of being that prompts the clearing through and in which the plurality of discrete beings are manifest in the unconcealment (*Unverborgenheit*) of their concealment and therefore can be thought only as unthought (*ungedacht*).[273]

If the nothing is identified as the "negation of the totality of beings," and hence as "nonbeing [*Nicht-Seiende*] pure and simple," then it must be brought "under the determination of the negative [*Nicht-hafen*], viewing it, it seems, as the negated [*Verneinten*]."[274] Developing this insight in the *Beiträge*, Heidegger writes, "From the perspective of beings, beyng [*Seyn*] 'is' *not* a being [*Seiende*]; it 'is' a nonbeing [*Nichtseiende*] and so, according to the usual conception, nothingness [*Nichts*]. This way of thinking is unassailable, especially if beings are taken in the sense of objects [*Gegenständliche*] and objectively present things [*Vorhandene*] and nothingness signifies the utter negation [*Verneinung*] of beings understood in that sense. Thereby negation [*Verneinen*] itself has the character of an objective assertion [*gegenständlichen Aussage*]."[275] In the appendix to "Die Zeit des Weltbildes," Heidegger proposes that the operative metaphor to divulge the paradox of that which gives by withholding is the shadow, understood not in its established sense as the "absence of light," but as "the manifest, though impenetrable, testimony of hidden illumination [*verborgenen Leuchtens*]. Conceiving of the shadow this way, we experience the incalculable [*Unberechenbare*] as that which escapes representation [*Vorstellung*], yet is manifest in beings [*Seienden*] and points to the hidden being [*Sein*]." Hence, the refusal itself—the showing of the unshowing—is the "highest and hardest disclosure of being [*Offenbarung des Seins*]." Like the kabbalists many years before him, Heidegger grasped that the supreme manifestation of light is the "hidden essence of being [*verborgene Wesen des Seins*]," the refusal that "reveals itself first of all as the absolute non-being [*schlechthin Nicht-Seiende*], as the nothing [*Nichts*]."[276] The bestowal of the refusal is thus accorded the status of the nothing that is the *highest and hardest disclosure of being*. But this nothing, as "the nothing of beings [*Nichthafte des Seienden*]," is the "keenest opponent of mere negating [*bloß Nichtigen*]. The nothing is never nothing [*Das Nichts ist niemals nicht*], and neither is it a something [*Etwas*] in the sense of an object [*Gegenstandes*]; it is being itself [*Sein selbst*] whose truth will be given over to man when he has overcome himself as subject [*Subjekt*], when, that is, he no longer represents [*vorstellt*] beings as objects [*Objekt*]."[277] To apprehend—or better to experience—that nothing is being itself, the negating of the polynomial void that cannot be objectified as the nothingness of something or as the something of nothingness, which is to say, the nullity that is neither being nor nonbeing,[278] one must cease representing beings as objects, and this includes representing oneself as a subject.

Ṣimṣum and Being's Self-Concealing Revealing as Nonbeing

Consonant with the kabbalists, Heidegger grasped that the manifestation of the hidden essence of beyng consists of its refusal to be manifest, and hence it can be said of beyng that it reveals itself as the nihilation of being. A likely channel to explain the affinity between Heidegger and the kabbalists on this matter is Schelling, who argued that "the force of contraction [*die Kraft der Zusammenziehung*] is the real and actual beginning of everything. The greatest glory of development is not expected from what easily unfolds. It is expected from what has been excluded and which only decides to unfold with opposition."[279] More specifically, Heidegger advances Schelling's kabbalistically inflected insight that *the ground of revelation is precisely what negates all revelation*[280] by relating the motif of the twofold nature of the unveiling and veiling of being to the character of truth as the unconcealment in which the concealment prevails as the concealing that conceals the unconcealing. Being's "primordial self-illumination" is thus described in "Der Spruch des Anaximander" (1946) as the "unconcealment of the being" that "darkens the light of being," which leads to a rhetorically startling conclusion that coincides with the principal paradox of the kabbalistic understanding of infinity: "*By revealing itself in the being, being withdraws.*"[281] In "Die seinsgeschichtliche Bestimmung des Nihilismus" (1944–46), Heidegger argued that what is necessary is not to overcome the inauthenticity of the essence of nihilism, which is interpreted as the omission of being in the unconcealment of beings, but to encounter being by undertaking a thinking "encouraged by Being itself. . . . Such thinking to encounter [*Entgegendenken*] rests primarily on the recognition *that Being itself withdraws* [Das Sein selbst entzieht sich], *but that as this withdrawal Being is precisely the relationship that claims the essence of man, as the abode of its (Being's) advent* [die Unterkunft seiner (des Seins) Ankunft]. The unconcealment of the being as such is bestowed along with that abode. . . . By thinking to encounter Being itself, thinking no longer omits Being, but admits it: admits it *into* the originary, revealing unconcealment of Being, which is Being itself."[282] The essence of the transformation from human to Dasein is related to the fact that we become through the encounter of thinking the dwelling—the opening of being-there—wherein being reveals itself as the there-being in its withdrawal from being.

At times, Heidegger expresses this motif in more confounding ways that demonstrate an even keener resemblance to the kabbalistic doctrine of *ṣimṣum*, the delimiting of the limitless, a mystery already alluded to in one zoharic passage where the "hidden, supernal concealment" (*ṭemira illa'ah satim*), the "place that has no dimension" (*atar deleit beih shi'ura*), is characterized paradoxically as precipitating the "measure that has no measure" (*shi'ura deleit shi'ura*).[283] In several passages from the *Beiträge*, which can only be regarded as ecstatic in nature, Heidegger describes the eventfulness of beyng variously as the excess (*Über-maß*) that springs from the self-concealment "of all quantification and measurement," the "self-withdrawing [*Sichentziehen*] of *measuring out*,"[284] the "*hesitant self-withholding*" (zögernde Versagung), the "ripeness of 'time'" (*die Reife der "Zeit"*), which is "gravid with the original 'not'" (*ursprünglichen "Nicht"*),[285] the "abyssal ground" (*Ab-grund*) of the "originary essential occurrence of the ground" (*ursprüngliche Wesung des Grundes*), the "staying away of the ground" (*Weg-bleiben des Grundes*), the "essence of truth" (*Wesen der Wahrheit*), the "self-concealing in a protruding that bears" (*das Sichverbergen im tragenden Durchragen*), the "primessential *clearing-concealing*" (*erstwesentliche* lichtende Verbergung), the appropriation that opens itself in the "primordial ground" (*Ur-grund*), the emptiness (*Leere*) of the abyss (*Ab*-grund), the ground that is the repudiation of ground (Ab-*grund*), the nonground (*Un-grund*).[286] Heidegger's threefold characterization of the groundless ground as *Abgrund, Urgrund,* and *Ungrund,* is surely indebted to Schelling,[287] but he has transmuted the latter's thinking into a deeper mystical key, a poetized translation of an older esoteric doctrine—perhaps extracted by Heidegger from the residual of kabbalistic theosophy in Schelling that might have resulted from the influence of a secondary conduit like Böhme or Oetinger[288]—albeit stripped of any theological import.

Moreover, just as Schelling spoke of the primal being as the indecipherable will through which the eternal self-revelation of the Absolute is enacted in the world as a self-affirmation (*Selbstbejahung*)[289] or self-arrayment (*Selbstanziehung*),[290] so Heidegger maintained that the nihilating nothing reveals being in an act of will that is without reason or purpose, the will to nonwilling (*Nicht-Wollen*)[291]—an idea to which he attaches the Eckhartian term *Gelassenheit*[292]—not as the negation of willing (an act of opposing) or the suspension of willing (an act of refusal), which are both variations of willing, the will-not-to-will, in Arendt's language,[293] but as the nonwill (*Nicht-Wille*), "that which is a non-willing [*was ein Nicht-Wollen ist*], that is to say, not a will and thus nothing pertaining to will [*nicht eine Wille und somit überhaupt nichts Willensmäßiges ist*]."[294] The *Gelassenheit* of nonwilling does not entail "to willfully renounce willing" (*willentlich dem Wollen absagen*), but rather "that which does not at all pertain to the will."[295] Whereas not willing is the passive inverse of the assertion of the will, nonwilling is the release that conceals a "higher activity than that found in all the doings of the world and in all the machinations of the realms of humankind," an activity that is not an activity, a willing that does not belong to the will and therefore is "outside the distinction between activity and passivity."[296] The stillness and restraint of renunciation proper to the essence of meditational thinking may "appear as inactivity, as leaving alone . . . but are in fact perhaps the most extensive overflow back into the letting be of being as event [*das Seinlassen des Seins als Ereignis*]."[297] *Gelassenheit* on the part of Dasein thus corresponds to the *Seinlassen* of the open region and free expanse of the clearing.[298] As Heidegger wrote in the *Schwarzen Heften,* "Beyng itself *is* and only beyng is—and as beyng it *is without* a goal. . . . The truth of beyng is to be grounded, because this truth belongs to beyng. . . . Because beyng is only the abyssal ground, it has no goals and averts every setting of a goal."[299]

The self-concealing revealing of beyng's self-revealing concealing is elucidated by the fragment of Heraclitus, cited by Hippolytus, "Time is a child playing a game of draughts; the kingship is in the hands of the child" (αἰὼν παῖς ἐστι παίζων, πεσσεύν . παιδὸς ἡ βασιληίη).[300] The *Seinsgeschick*—the release (*Loslassen*) or the flinging loose (*Loswurf*) of beings that is the venture (*das Wagnis*) of being[301]—is the time that is compared with the child at play, the playing that constitutes the nobleness of the child, the dare to surrender to the risk and chance that is the game.[302] There is no rhyme or reason to the world-play (*Weltspiele*):

> It plays, because it plays [*Es spielet, weil es spielet*]. The because withers away in the play. The play is without "why." It plays since it plays. It simply remains a play: the most elevated and the most profound. But this "simply" is everything, the one [*das Eine*], the only [*Einzige*]. Nothing *is* without *ground/reason* [Grund]. Being and ground/reason: the same [*das Selbe*]. Being as what grounds, has no ground [*Sein als gründendes hat keinen Grund*]; as the abyss [*Ab-Grund*] it plays the play that, as *Geschick,* passes being and ground/reason to us.[303]

With these words, which conclude the last of the thirteen lectures based on the course *Der Satz vom Grund,* Heidegger responds to the question raised in the fifth lecture when he juxtaposed the Leibnizian principle *Nihil sine ratione,* "Nothing is without reason," and the poetic aphorism of Silesius "Ohne warum" from the first book of *Der cherubinische Wandersmann,* "The rose is without why: it blooms because it blooms, / It pays no attention to itself, asks not whether it is seen" (*Die Ros ist ohn warum; sie blühet, weil sie blühet, / Sie acht nicht ihrer selbst, fragt nicht, ob man sie siehet).*[304] On the face of it, the poet's mystical adage utterly contradicts the philosopher's principle of sufficient reason (*principium reddendae rationis*). However, as Heidegger plumbs the depth of thought engrained in the poetic verse, perhaps also influenced by Eckhart's exhortation that the works one does from the inmost ground (*innersten grunde*) should be wrought without why (*sunder warumbe*),[305] he exhumes a more sagacious way to understand the paradox at the nub of the principle of logic, or as Renato Cristin put it, he tears the principle "from its logical tonality (in line with the dictates of calculation)" and then transfers it "to the plane where the analogy between Being and the abyss reigns. Having torn away this shell which hid calculating thought under the camouflage of the obviousness of natural causality, Heidegger can show that behind every basic thesis of metaphysics lies the bugbear of calculation and objectivation."[306]

To say that nothing is without reason means that being and ground are the same—in the specific Heideggerian sense of the same distinguished from the identical—but the abyss of being that grounds has no ground. Like the rose described by Silesius, it has no why and it blooms simply because it blooms. With respect to this play, therefore, absolute necessity is pure contingency. Fortuitousness (*Zu-fälligkeit*) and groundlessness (*Abgründigkeit*) belong to the truth of the essence of being.[307] Heidegger maintains that the inceptual thinking he champions is "intrinsically historical," which means that it is "determined by the plight of the lack of a sense of plight [*Not der Notlosigkeit*]. Such thinking reaches ahead into the necessities connected to the essential shelterings of truth and of the guiding knowledge of it. If it does break out, the plight of the lack of a sense of plight will strike up against the remaining absent of both the advent *and* the absconding of the gods."[308] The plight of the lack of a sense of plight—expressed in the coexistent presence and absence of the gods, not in the sense of a presence presently absent but rather the presence constituted by the absence of presence dissimulating as the presence of absence—corresponds to the poetic wisdom that the rose blooms because it blooms without reason or purpose. The principle that everything has a reason means in fact that there is no reason for anything.

Schelling's concept of the will characterizing the absolute beginning has been linked to the Origenistic tradition upheld as well by Böhme.[309] Without quibbling with this assertion, I would add that the kabbalists, too, routinely speak of the beginning in terms of the infinite will that exceeds willfulness, the will that is not subject to the teleological idea of the will motivated by and directed to a final cause. In Heidegger's view, the task of Dasein to ground the domain of decision making (*Entscheidungsbereich*) about the truth of being requires a "surrendering" (*Entäußerung*) that is the opposite of "self-renunciation" (*Selbstaufgabe*), a relinquishing of self that facilitates the grounding (*Gründung*) by courageously facing the abyss (*Ab-grund*),[310] and similarly kabbalists proffer an ideal of quietistic piety that demands the divestiture of self through encountering and imitating the infinite will by inculcating the activity of no-activity, the willing of nonwilling (*Wollen des Nicht-Wollens*) that is the nonwilling of willing (*Nicht-Wollen des Wollens*).[311] By affirming this will that definitively wills nothing but the indefinite nothingness of the will, kabbalists, too, problematize the advent and the absconding of divinity. This is not to deny that Jewish mystics regularly utilize traditional terms and describe the divine will as if it were a personal volition—this is a crucial factor in the theurgical understanding of the commandments. The limitless will, however, which is the hidden nothing that can be present only by not being present, is a will denuded of will, a will in which what is willed is both unconditionally necessary and necessarily conditional; in the will devoid of will, the emptiness of the divine plentitude, what is most determinate is the indeterminate, what is most actual is the possible, what is most indispensable is the contingent.

Heidegger illumines the Schellingian point, which resonates with the kabbalah, by directing the reader's attention to the proposition in Hegel's *Wissenschaft der Logik*, "Being and nothingness are the same" (*Sein und Nichts ist dasselbe*), a statement prominently cited in the lecture "Was ist Metaphysik?"[312] In one passage, Heidegger explicates Hegel's statement as follows: "Being and nothing do belong together [*gehören zusammen*], not because both—from the point of view of the Hegelian concept of thought—agree in their indeterminateness and immediacy, but rather because being itself is essentially finite and manifests itself only in the transcendence of a Dasein that is held out into the nothing."[313] Comparably, albeit more tersely, in a passage from the *Beiträge*, Heidegger concedes that the Hegelian statement can signify only "a general agreement with regard to bringing together [*Zussamenbringung*] being and nothingness."[314] The principle of noncontradiction does not admit thinking of the "essential occurrence of being" (*Wesung des Seins*) from the standpoint of "the belonging of nothingness to *being*" (*die Zugehörigkeit des Nichts zum* Sein),[315] a juxtaposition that would preclude seeing nothing primarily as either nonbeing in relation to being or as negation in relation to affirmation.

In Heidegger's thinking, as I stated in the introduction, belonging together implies the joining of what lingers as separate. This is the spot where the disparity in the way that Hegel and Heidegger respectively interpret the assertion that being and nothingness are the same comes to light. For Hegel, the sameness entails identity and hence the collapse of difference. Heidegger alludes to this when he writes that from Hegel we can infer that, in the "first stage of what is to be thought in the future as beyng," being is not determinate (*bestimmte*) but rather "*un*-determined" (Un-*bestimmte*) and "unmediated" (Un-*mittelbare*), that is, the "pure negativity [*reine Negativität*] of objectivity and of thinking (beingness and thinking)."[316] From Heidegger's metaontological perspective, Hegel's dialectic is still metaphysically conditioned insofar as the nothing is specified as the negativity of objectivity, which is the only negative that can be thought from within the identity of beingness and thinking. To extricate oneself from this conundrum, one must be mindful of the fact that being is not to be construed as a being and, correspondingly, that nothing is not nonbeing, that is, the negation of being, but it is rather "higher than everything 'positive' and 'negative' in the totality of beings." To say, therefore, that being and nothingness are the same is not an affirmative declaration of their nondifference, the identity of their nonidentity, but a "thoughtful questioning" of their juxtaposition, the bridging that sustains the distance of what is bridged and thus allows one "to experience as the most concealed gift the nihilating in beyng itself [*das Nichtende im Seyn selbst*], which alone genuinely *un-settles* us into beyng and into its truth. Then we will indeed recognize that nothingness can never be reckoned, or balanced, *against* beyng . . . because beyng (i.e., nothingness) is the 'between' [*Inzwischen*] for beings [*das Seiende*] and for divinization [*die Götterung*] and can never become a 'goal.'"[317]

Heidegger's emplacement of *Seyn* as the between and the attempt to distance it from any ontological categorization is clarified from a second passage in the *Beiträge*: "Beyng never *is* more fully than beings but also never less fully than the gods, because the latter 'are' not at all. Beyng 'is' the 'between' amidst beings and the gods, utterly and in every respect incomparable, 'needed' by the gods and withdrawn from beings."[318] Beyng is between beings and the gods, never more fully than beings since it is withdrawn from beings, and never less fully than the gods since the gods are not at all and thus they are in need of beyng to claim some sense of being. The beyng of which Heidegger speaks, therefore, is not a something set over and against nothing but rather over and against the "nonbeyng" (*Nichtseyn*) that may be construed topographically as the unparalleled between in which beings come to be, an advance that is described poetically as the ripening of the "turning in the event" (*Kehre im Ereignis*).[319] In a passage that is incredibly close to the comment of Rosenzweig cited in chapter 2,[320] Heidegger notes, "where beyng is conceived as event, essentiality [*Wesentlichkeit*] is determined out of the originality and uniqueness of beyng itself. There the essence is not the general but is the essential occurrence precisely of what is unique in each case and of what constitutes the rank of the being. . . . The principle of inceptual thinking therefore sounds like something doubled: all essence is essential occurrence [*alles Wesen ist Wesung*]."[321] To say of nothingness that it is not is to continue to be beholden to the metaphysical representation of nothing as the negation of something and of something as the negation of nothing. Heidegger wishes to place nonbeing and being outside the dyadic structure of an ontological classification, but he still maintains that it can be said of both that they essentially occur, or as he expressed it in a passage cited previously, nonbeing is "unessence" (*Unwesen*) and being is "permeated with negativity" (*nichthaft*).[322]

These depictions, which convey a sense of "esoteric turbulence,"[323] correspond well to the kabbalistic notion of *Ein Sof*. Just as Heidegger spoke of alterity as the other of itself, so kabbalists conceive of infinity as the negation of the negation, the absolute negation of the absolute, which generates unqualified difference—the Derridean *différance*—wherein all difference is annihilated in the nondifferentiated indifference, the pure void, neither nothing nor something, in which presence of absence is obscured in the absence of presence. The infinite is the nothingness that is not constricted by images of affirmation or negation, the inchoate essence that has no essence, the being that is otherwise to the otherwise than being.[324] In the language that Derrida deployed to summarize the view of Levinas, we can refer to *Ein Sof* as the "infinitely-other," which "cannot be bound by a concept, cannot be thought on the basis of a horizon; for a horizon is always a horizon of the same, the elementary unity within which eruptions and surprises are always welcomed by understanding and recognized."[325] Inasmuch as *Ein Sof* comprehends the other as part of its otherness, however, and the sefirotic emanations unfold from the very being in which they are enfolded, in the final analysis, we must conclude that difference is comprised in the sameness of the other that is differently the same. The oneness of being, therefore, embraces the truth that being is not one.

Notes

1. On the history of the term *ein sof*, see Scholem, *Origins*, pp. 265–70, 431–43; Scholem, *Major Trends*, pp. 207–9, 214–16; Scholem, *Kabbalah*, pp. 88–96; Tishby, *Wisdom of the Zohar*, pp. 229–55; Valabregue-Perry, *Concealed and Revealed*; Valabregue-Perry, "Concept of Infinity."

2. Heidegger, *Kant and the Problem of Metaphysics*, p. 160; *Kant und das Problem der Metaphysik*, pp. 234–35.

3. Heidegger, *Kant and the Problem of Metaphysics*, p. 161; *Kant und das Problem der Metaphysik*, p. 236.

4. Heidegger, *Being and Time*, §7, p. 36; *Sein und Zeit*, p. 38.

5. Stambaugh, *Finitude of Being*; Magus, *Heidegger's Metahistory*, pp. 85–86.

6. Heidegger, *Being and Time*, §7, p. 36. For the original German, see Heidegger, *Sein und Zeit* [GA 2], 5, note a.

7. Duff, *Heidegger and Politics*, p. 135.

8. Heidegger, *Kant and the Problem of Metaphysics*, p. 161 (emphasis in original); *Kant und das Problem der Metaphysik*, p. 237.

9. Heidegger, *Contributions*, §9, p. 25; *Beiträge*, p. 29. On the hesitant self-withholding and the clearing of beyng within the opening of time-space, see Vallega-Neu, *Heidegger's Poietic Writings*, pp. 37–38.

10. Heidegger, *Contributions*, §242, p. 306; *Beiträge*, p. 388.

11. Heidegger, *Contributions*, §51, p. 86; *Beiträge*, p. 108.

12. Heidegger, *Contributions*, §9, p. 25 (emphasis in original); *Beiträge*, p. 29.

13. Heidegger, *Contributions*, §52, p. 88 (emphasis in original); *Beiträge*, p. 111. The passage is cited in ch. 2 at n. 40.

14. Heidegger, *Poetry, Language, Thought*, p. 53; *Holzwege*, p. 40. Compare Heidegger, *Heraclitus*, p. 167 (*Heraklit*, p. 221): "Depth is the self-opening concealing expanse that continually points to an ever more lightened concealment and gathers itself therein. . . . Only when thinking has thought what is deepest—that is, only when it has begun to think and continues to think the essential and singular to-be-thought—does the re-turn proper to thinking, i.e., the originary reflection, come to itself and come into play originarily." Heidegger combines in this passage two of his most signature ideas: the hermeneutic juxtaposition of concealment and disclosure and the temporal presumption that the return proper to thinking in the present is the mandate to think what is to-be-thought in the future. Both of these characteristics are applicable to the kabbalistic *Ein Sof*. On the essential relation between unconcealment and self-concealment as it pertains to *phusis*, see Heidegger, *Heraclitus*, pp. 129–32; *Heraklit*, pp. 171–77.

15. The comment of Heidegger from the course "Introduction to Metaphysics," offered at the University of Freiburg in the summer semester of 1935, is cited in Parkes, "Thoughts on the Way," p. 137.

16. Heidegger, *On Time and Being*, p. 65; *Zur Sache des Denkens*, p. 81.

17. Heidegger, *On Time and Being*, pp. 65–66; *Zur Sache des Denkens*, p. 81.

18. Heidegger, *Contributions*, §214, p. 268; *Beiträge*, pp. 338–39. I am here expanding my attempt to draw parallels between this Heideggerian passage and Lurianic kabbalah in Wolfson, "Divine Suffering," p. 154n112. Heidegger returned to the image of the jug in several lectures, most notably in "Das Ding" (1950), included in Heidegger, *Poetry, Language, Thought*, pp. 165–86; *Vorträge und Aufsätze*, pp. 167–87. On the basis of the depiction of the jug as a vessel, Heidegger advanced a conception of thingness as the void that holds the gift of the outpouring in the twofold manner of taking and keeping—in Buddhist terms, the suchness of the container consists of its emptiness. For the earlier version of this lecture, see Heidegger, *Bremen and Freiburg Lectures*, pp. 5–22; *Bremer und Freiburger Vorträge*, pp. 5–23. See also Heidegger's explication of the eleventh chapter of the *Daodejing* briefly discussed in ch. 5 n. 10.

19. Heidegger, *Contributions*, §127, p. 192; *Beiträge*, p. 244.

20. Heidegger, *Contributions*, §262, p. 352 (emphasis in original); *Beiträge*, p. 447.

21. Heidegger, *Contributions*, §120, p. 186; *Beiträge*, p. 235.

22. Heidegger, *Contributions*, §123, p. 190 (emphasis in original); *Beiträge*, p. 241.

23. Heidegger, *Contributions*, §123, p. 189; *Beiträge*, p. 240.

24. Heidegger, *Contributions*, §123, p. 190; *Beiträge*, p. 241.

25. Heidegger, *Poetry, Language, Thought*, pp. 53–54; *Holzwege*, p. 40.

26. Heidegger, *Contributions*, §120, p. 186; *Beiträge*, p. 236.

27. Heidegger, *Contributions*, §254, p. 321 (emphasis in original); *Beiträge*, p. 406.

28. Heidegger, *Contributions*, §123, p. 189; *Beiträge*, p. 240.

29. On the transformative nature of the advent of the last god, see Malabou, *Heidegger Change*, p. 10: "The last God appears at the crossing of the arrival and flight of the ancient gods. It does not arise as would a *new* divinity but is born from *the secret transformation* of the previous gods" (emphasis in original). Malabou cites in support of her contention the remark of Heidegger, *Sojourns*, p. 3 (*Aufenthalte*, p. 2): "The gods of Greece and their supreme god, if they ever come, will return only transformed to a world [*nur verwandelt in eine Welt einkehren*] whose overthrow [*umstürzenende Veränderung*] is grounded in the land of the gods of ancient Greece." The fuller context from which this statement is extracted reveals Heidegger's insistence that the task is to open the field to the coming of god, but to do so is predicated on understanding the reversal of the timeline such that the "field lies behind us, not before us. What is of necessity is to look back and reflect on that which an ancient memory has preserved for us and yet, through all the things that we think we know and we possess, remains distorted. However, we could only seek something that, albeit in disguise, is already known." One will readily discern here an echo of the Platonic doctrine of anamnesis according to which the acquisition of knowledge consists of rediscovering what was known beforehand. The other element at play here is Heidegger's insistence that overcoming does not mean overthrowing, but rather undergoing a transformation such that what is overcome in some respect is sustained. See ch. 2 n. 89. On occasion, however, Heidegger does emphasize radical novelty when he writes about the future god, and even speaks of it as "wholly other than past ones." See text cited below at n. 42.

30. See Schalow, *Heidegger and the Quest for the Sacred*, pp. 106–9. For a more detailed exploration of this theme, see Wolfson, "*Gottwesen*." I have taken the liberty of making use of parts of that study in this context.

31. Heidegger, *History of Beyng*, p. 114; *Geschichte des Seyns*, p. 132.

32. Heidegger, *Contributions*, §116, p. 180; *Beiträge*, p. 228.

33. See text cited in ch. 1 at n. 83.

34. Heidegger, *Contributions*, §253, p. 321; *Beiträge*, p. 405.

35. Heidegger, *Contributions*, §7, p. 21; *Beiträge*, p. 24.

36. Heidegger, *Ponderings II–VI*, p. 228 (emphasis in original); *Überlegungen II–VI*, p. 314. The passage is repeated almost verbatim in Heidegger, *Contributions*, §256, p. 326; *Beiträge*, p. 411.

37. Heidegger, *Contributions*, §256, p. 329; *Beiträge*, p. 416.

38. Heidegger, *Contributions*, §256, pp. 324–25 (emphasis in original); *Beiträge*, pp. 409–10. The meaning I elicit from this Heideggerian passage stands in marked contrast to the interpretation offered by Derrida, "Faith and Knowledge," p. 55: whereas Levinas insists that God is the future, Heidegger maintains that the last god announces himself in the very absence of a future. According to my reading, Heidegger's view is closer to the Jewish sense of messianic futurity implied in the Levinasian depiction of God, which is related to his diachronic understanding of time. See Wolfson, *Giving*, pp. 61, 116–17, 120–23, 149–50, and 376n187 (where I suggest an affinity between Levinas's notion of diachrony and

Heidegger's idea of the ecstatic character of time as the temporalizing transcendence); and Wolfson, "Not Yet Now," pp. 139, 186–88. See below, n. 46.

39. Heidegger, *Contributions*, §256, p. 326 (emphasis in original); *Beiträge*, p. 411.

40. Heidegger, *Contributions*, §256, p. 327; *Beiträge*, p. 412.

41. Heidegger, *Contributions*, §256, p. 326; *Beiträge*, p. 412.

42. The passage occurs as the epigraph to the seventh section of the *Beiträge*, "Der Letzte Gott." See Heidegger, *Contributions*, p. 319; *Beiträge*, p. 403; and analysis in Summerell, "Otherness," pp. 126–31.

43. Heidegger, *Contributions*, §254, p. 322; *Beiträge*, p. 406. Rojcewicz and Vallega-Neu render *Gottwesen* as "Godhead," but in order to avoid the peril of lapsing into an ontotheology, I have followed the more literal translation of Emad and Maly in Heidegger, *Contributions to Philosophy (From Enowning)*, §254, p. 286, as "divine being." This is the only section in the *Beiträge* where the expression *Gottwesen* appears.

44. Mitchell, *Fourfold*, pp. 170–71. My interpretation of Heidegger's last god as the god who arrives by not arriving and who appears by not appearing can be compared profitably to Dastur, *Questions of Phenomenology*, pp. 183–84: "This God is the last, not as the last member of a series but rather because it simultaneously constitutes both the most extreme and the highest figure of time, and because in it is gathered the heterogeneous multiplicity of the experiences of the divine, as Hölderlin had sensed. . . . We must therefore not oppose the plurality of the Gods in flight of which Hölderlin spoke to the unicity of the God yet to come, for whom Heidegger wants to prepare the way; rather, and more profoundly, we must understand that the plurality of the Gods has nothing to do with number, but refers instead to the properly temporal dimension of a God who appears only in the instant of his disappearance, and who must therefore be originarily divided in order to 'pass' into time. This thematic of a God who only 'passes' implies that the Christian idea of divine infinitude is abandoned because, for Heidegger, what is unveiled in the sign that the last God addresses to us while passing is 'the most intimate finitude of being.' . . . And such a God, who signals on the basis of death and who exists only through this sign addressed to mortals, is what calls for the 'phenomenology of the inapparent,' with which the later Heidegger is associated."

45. Heidegger, *History of Beyng*, pp. 178–79; *Geschichte des Seyns*, p. 211.

46. For a more extended discussion, see Wolfson, *Duplicity*, pp. 87–108. Many Jewish thinkers have affirmed some form of the paradox of the messianic future as that which comes by not coming, but the two that bear the most resemblance to Heidegger are Levinas and Derrida. See Wolfson, "Not Yet Now," pp. 142–56. The affinity between Heidegger's reflections on the poet's unconditionally awaiting the last god, the god that exceeds all determinable ends, and the Derridean idea of messianicity, that is, messianism without the conventional religious belief in a messiah, is noted by Winkler, "Dwelling and Hospitality," p. 376. For the broader historical and intellectual background of this notion, see Schulte, "Messianism Without Messiah."

47. Heidegger, *History of Beyng*, p. 179; *Geschichte des Seyns*, p. 211. My reading of Heidegger's last god coincides with the interpretation of the Heideggerian sense of overcoming (*Überkommnis*) proffered by Hamacher, "Messianic Not," p. 224, as the "nakedness of a coming beyond every coming of the determinate or even determinable, anticipated or anticipatable, projected or projectable." Hamacher (p. 223) connects the aporetic coming of a beyond-coming with the statement of Nancy in *La pensée dérobée*, "There is the to-come of a naked coming" (*Il y a l'à-venir d'un venir nu*), a statement that logically seems to deny the possibility of the second coming of the messiah whence we can deduce the deconstruction of Christianity. Drawing out the temporal implications of this coming of a beyond-coming, Hamacher writes (pp. 224–25): "If the future is to be thought in its pure movement, if it is to be thought as itself, and thus as mere coming without the arrival (*Ankunft*) of any sort of present, and thus thought without any determination through this present, then it must be thought as come-able—as the mere possibility of coming or as the possibility that is itself nothing other than coming, the coming of the coming without term or determination. If, however, the coming itself is merely coming, then it is in no sense already there; it is not an actual, in some way empirical or sensory coming, nor does it accord with a transcendental schema that would constitute its coming-to-be. It rather voids the sense of its every being present and dissolves the structure that grants the actuality of its being coming; indeed, it can never—so long as it, as coming, is referred to as coming—and at no time (namely, in no coming), *be* a coming. It is not we who wait; the coming itself waits for the coming. It is the already-there of the still-never-having-been-there and of the never-ever-being-there" (emphasis in original).

48. Heidegger, *Contributions*, §254, p. 322; *Beiträge*, pp. 406–7. I have modified the translation

of *Befremdlichen und Unberechenbaren* as "something strange and incalculable," since the word "something" (for which there is no corresponding word in German) gives the spurious impression that Heidegger's idea of *Gottwesen* can be objectified or thingified.

49. Higgins, "Speaking and Thinking," p. 93. But see p. 95, where the author proposes that the last god in Heidegger's thought "is an expression of the divinity, as such, of any manifestation of divinity. . . . The last god is the ultimate, highest aspect (as it were) of divinity. It is the element in which God can be God, analogous to what Eckhart describes as Godhead." See ibid., p. 104. Stambaugh, *Finitude of Being*, p. 91, also assumes that the meaning of "godhead" in Heidegger is identical to the use of the term in Eckhart "to designate the transpersonal ultimacy of the divine." One of the passages to which she refers in support of her contention is from Heidegger, *Poetry, Language, Thought*, p. 150 (*Vorträge und Aufsätze*, p. 151): "The divinities [*Göttlichen*] are the beckoning messengers of the godhead [*Gottheit*]. Out of the holy sway of the godhead, the god appears in his presence or withdraws into his concealment." Stambaugh also refers to a second, almost identical, passage in Heidegger, *Poetry, Language, Thought*, p. 178 (*Vorträge und Aufsätze*, p. 180): "The divinities are the beckoning messengers of the godhead. Out of the hidden sway of the divinities the god emerges as what he is, which removes him from comparison with beings that are present." In both contexts, Heidegger is explaining the nature of divinity, which together with sky, earth, and mortals, constitutes his notion of the fourfold. It is not clear to me what the precise meaning of *Gottheit* is for him beyond its being the source whence the divinities emerge. In my judgment, as I have argued in the body of this chapter, the import of *Gottwesen* is to undermine the positing of an element of divinity understood theistically; the force of the last god as ultimate intimates a surpassing of the ontotheological by affirming beingness separate from any being. An approach close to my own—albeit in language that seems to me still a bit too ontotheological in tone—is found in Thomson, *Heidegger, Art, and Postmodernity*, pp. 36–37: "I find myself increasingly inclined to conclude that 'being as such'—that is, 'be-ing' in its *difference* from the metaphysically conceived understanding of the being of entities—*is* the later Heidegger's unnamed name for this God to come, 'the last or ultimate God' whom he evokes . . . at the climax of his *Contributions to Philosophy (From Enowning)*. Heidegger's post-Christian 'last God' is a phenomenologized (and so secularized) rethinking of Meister Eckhart's 'Godhead' (that is, a finally unnamable source of all our different conceptions of god), one whose name the later Heidegger will tellingly write under erasure in his 'fourfold,' and thereby pluralize (no longer speaking of God but, instead, of gods)" (emphasis in original). Thomson correctly notes that Heidegger dismissed all types of theism, but he nonetheless suggests that his idea of the gods, which is an alternate way of speaking about the last god, may be "tentatively characterized as *polytheistic*." In this regard, it is of interest to consider the passing remark of Proclus, *Commentary on Plato's Parmenides*, p. 37, that the demiurge is "not One in the absolute sense; for he is a god, not God, and the god that is the One is not a god, but God simply." Mention here should be made of the innovative analysis of Yannaras, *On the Absence*. The author accepts Heidegger's criticism of Western metaphysics but turns to apophatic theology, especially garnered from the works attributed to Dionysius the Areopagite, to elicit an alternative explanation such that nothingness is not construed, in the wake of Nietzsche, as the absence of God conceived ontotheologically as the supreme being—a position that leads to nihilism—but as the unknowable God to whom neither being nor nonbeing can be attributed, and not merely, as Derrida famously argued, as the hyperessential being that is the being beyond being. See the summary of the argument in Yannaras, *On the Absence*, p. 22: "We speak then of an *apophaticism* destructive of idols, which under the guise of nihilism is manifest as the 'inner crisis' of western metaphysics. And we are indebted to Heidegger for seeing in this crisis the starting point for its historical understanding. . . . God is either identified with the conceptual notion of an impersonal and abstract 'first cause' of the universe (*causa prima*), or of an absolute 'authority' in ethics (*principium auctoritatis*). In both cases the existence of God is a conceptual necessity, secured by demonstrative argument, but unrelated to historical experience and the existential condition of human beings. Precisely because it offers an absolutized rational affirmation of God, European metaphysics prepares for the possibility of its own rational refutation. The 'death of God' is but the end-result of the historical unfolding of this absolutized and double-edged rationalism, which took place in the nations of Western Europe over the span of approximately a millennium." See also ibid., p. 44: "The western apophatic tradition, from the neo-Platonist Eriugena to Anselm, Abelard and Thomas Aquinas—the attempt to reconcile affirmations and negations, the advocacy

of knowing and of unknowing—bears out this discovery. Natural theology is revealed as the logic of affirmative statements, apophatic theology as the logic of negations." As Yannaras further argues (ibid., p. 29), the trajectory of Western metaphysics leads to the *apophaticism of essence*, the positing of an uncreated and transcendent existence whose essence is unknown, whereas the Christian thought of the Greek East leads to an *apophaticism of the person*, the encountering of God as a person (hypostasis) in the immediacy of a relationship with the other that cannot be exhausted cognitively or conceptually.

50. Higgins, "Speaking and Thinking," p. 112. Compare Meylahn, *Limits and Possibilities*, pp. 74–77.

51. Schalow, *Heidegger and the Quest for the Sacred*, p. 131 (emphasis in original). A similar approach is taken by Kalary, "Heidegger's Thinking," pp. 125–30. See also Vallega-Neu, *Heidegger's Poietic Writings*, pp. 176–77; Tarditi, "Is Ontology the Last Form?", and Keiling, "Dionysius," pp. 91–92. For one of the more thoughtful attempts to posit a Christian response on the basis of Heidegger's analysis of Western nihilism and the *Seinsvergessenheit*, see Hart, *Hidden and the Manifest*, pp. 1–144. The stance I have taken is closer in spirit to the chapter "Jean-Luc Marion and the Contemporary Theological Appropriation of Heidegger" in Hemming, *Heidegger's Atheism*, pp. 249–69.

52. Heidegger, *Nietzsche*, Vol. 4: *Nihilism*, p. 211; *Nietzsche: Zweiter Band*, p. 349. Support for my interpretation may be culled from Heidegger's letter to a young student (June 18, 1950), which was published as the epilogue to "Das Ding." See Heidegger, *Poetry, Language, Thought*, p. 184 (*Vorträge und Aufsätze*, pp. 185–86): "The default of God and the divinities is absence [*Der Fehl Gottes und des Göttlichen ist Abwesenheit*]. But absence is not nothing [*Abwesenheit ist nicht nichts*]; rather it is precisely the presence [*Anwesenheit*], which must first be appropriated, of the hidden fullness of what has been [*der verborgenen Fülle des Gewesenen*] and what, thus gathered, is presencing [*und so versammelt Wesenden*], of the divine in the world of the Greeks, in prophetic Judaism, in the preaching of Jesus. This no longer [*Nicht-mehr*] is in itself a not-yet [*Noch-nicht*] of the veiled arrival [*der verhüllten Ankunft*] of its inexhaustible nature. Since Being is never the merely precisely actual [*da Sein niemals das nur gerade Wirkliche ist*], to guard Being can never be equated with the task of a guard who protects from burglars a treasure stored in a building. Guardianship of Being is not fixated upon something existent" (translation slightly modified). Absence is not nothing, that is, the negation of presence, but rather the presence of the hidden fullness of the being that can never be rendered as something actual or existent, the being that is always suspended between no longer and not yet. It is telling that in this context Heidegger adopts a ecumenical tone and relates his notion of the veiled presencing of being to the pagan divinities of Greece, the epiphanies of the divine in prophetic Judaism, and the spirit of God conjured by the preaching of Jesus. See the recent analysis of this passage in Atkins, *Ethical and Theological Appropriation*, pp. 17–18.

53. Löwith, *My Life in Germany*, p. 31. See also Fehér, "Heidegger's Understanding"; and Hemming, *Heidegger's Atheism*, pp. 41–73.

54. Jonas, "Heidegger and Theology," pp. 211–14; Jonas, *Phenomenon of Life*, pp. 241–43. The appropriation of the method of Christian theology on the part of Heidegger is explored by Dahlstrom, "Heidegger's Method."

55. Jonas, "Heidegger and Theology," p. 219; Jonas, *Phenomenon of Life*, p. 248.

56. Jonas, "Heidegger and Theology," pp. 219–20 (emphasis added); Jonas, *Phenomenon of Life*, p. 248.

57. Connell, "Against Idolatry."

58. Steiner, *Grammars of Creation*, p. 68. See ibid., p. 19n1: "Heidegger's ontology is grounded in a constant 'keeping at bay' of the theological." On Heidegger's critique of theology, see Hemming, *Heidegger's Atheism*, pp. 179–214.

59. Heidegger, *Ponderings II–VI*, pp. 33–34; *Überlegungen II–VI*, p. 44.

60. Taubes, "Gnostic Foundations," p. 157.

61. See introduction n. 97. Mention should be made of the nuanced argument in Schmidt, "Monotheism as a Metapolitical Problem." According to Schmidt, Heidegger subsumes the political theology of an antimonotheism, which includes both Judaism and Christianity, under the concept of metapolitics. The latter, in turn, is expressive of what the author calls "Heidegger's political eschatology of tragedy," which led to his "later theopolitics" based on the "contrast between Greek polytheism and Jewish-Christian monotheism, between the goddess of Aletheia and the Logos Christi." Heidegger's thinking occasions a "Gnostic dissociation of the gods and their eschatological epiphanies at the end of times," which Schmidt interprets "as an effort to turn Jewish-Christian apocalypse against itself, in order to enable the return of the Greek gods" (p. 133). The alleged gnostic underpinning of Heidegger's theopolitics of antimonotheism accords with my own analysis of the implicit gnostic proclivity of Heidegger in Wolfson, *Duplicity*, pp. 109–30, and more extensively

in Wolfson, "*Gottwesen*." On Heidegger's embrace of a "postmonotheist Gnosticism," see also Mjaaland, "Confessions," pp. 270–72.

62. Jonas, "Heidegger and Theology," p. 221; Jonas, *Phenomenon of Life*, p. 250.

63. Heidegger, *Ponderings II–VI*, p. 22 (emphasis in original); *Überlegungen II–VI*, p. 29.

64. Heidegger, *Ponderings II–VI*, p. 24 (emphasis in original); *Überlegungen II–VI*, p. 31.

65. Heidegger, *Identity and Difference*, p. 72; German text: pp. 140–41. See Gschwandtner, *Postmodern Apologetics?*, p. 30.

66. Yannaras, *On the Absence*, p. 51.

67. Heidegger, *Mindfulness*, p. 225; *Besinnung*, pp. 255–56.

68. Heidegger, *Ponderings II–VI*, p. 37; *Überlegungen II–VI*, p. 49. See the chapter "Being after the Death of God: Heidegger from Theo- to Onto-logos," in Smith, *Dialogues between Faith and Reason*, pp. 175–204, esp. 199–200. Smith conjectures that Heidegger's last god is "informed with a kind of Nazi fantasy and infused with an alternate spirit that connects him to contemporary post-Nietzschean theology." I am not certain of the first of these statements and the second also seems problematic insofar as Smith still attempts to elicit from Heidegger "a return of God and a turning to God," even though he does acknowledge that the last god cannot be characterized by any of the ontotheological categories that have been applied traditionally to the God of Christianity. Smith does emphasize—in a manner more congenial with my interpretation of Heidegger—that the last god neither arrives nor departs, indeed, the last god does not come at the end of a linearly conceived period of time but is always passing, disappearing in the wink or trace of its appearance.

69. Heidegger, *Ponderings II–VI*, p. 40; *Überlegungen II–VI*, p. 53.

70. Heidegger, *Mindfulness*, p. 225; *Besinnung*, p. 256. I have slightly modified the translation.

71. Heidegger, *Mindfulness*, p. 225; *Besinnung*, p. 256.

72. Heidegger, *Contributions*, §256, pp. 325–26; *Beiträge*, pp. 410–11.

73. Heidegger, *Contributions*, §256, p. 325 (emphasis in original); *Beiträge*, p. 410.

74. Heidegger, *Ponderings II–VI*, p. 290 (emphasis in original); *Überlegungen II–VI*, p. 398.

75. Heidegger, *Ponderings II–VI*, p. 126; *Überlegungen II–VI*, p. 172. Compare Heidegger, *Ponderings II–VI*, p. 134 (*Überlegungen II–VI*, p. 183): "Will we once again venture the gods and along with them the truth of the people?"

76. Heidegger, *Ponderings II–VI*, pp. 156–57 (emphasis in original); *Überlegungen II–VI*, p. 214.

77. Heidegger, *Ponderings II–VI*, p. 157; *Überlegungen II–VI*, p. 215.

78. Heidegger, *Ponderings II–VI*, p. 157; *Überlegungen II–VI*, p. 214.

79. Heidegger, *Ponderings II–VI*, p. 157; *Überlegungen II–VI*, p. 214.

80. Heidegger, *Ponderings II–VI*, p. 231; *Überlegungen II–VI*, p. 318.

81. Heidegger, *Ponderings II–VI*, p. 177 (emphasis in original); *Überlegungen II–VI*, p. 242.

82. Heidegger, *Contributions*, §251, p. 316 (emphasis in original); *Beiträge*, p. 398.

83. Heidegger, *Contributions*, §251, p. 316 (emphasis in original); *Beiträge*, pp. 398–99.

84. Heidegger, *Contributions*, §252, p. 317 (emphasis in original); *Beiträge*, pp. 399–400.

85. Heidegger, *Ponderings II–VI*, p. 230; *Überlegungen II–VI*, p. 316.

86. Heidegger, *Contributions*, §252, p. 317; *Beiträge*, p. 400.

87. Heidegger, *Ponderings II–VI*, p. 122; *Überlegungen II–VI*, p. 167.

88. Heidegger, *Ponderings II–VI*, p. 163; *Überlegungen II–VI*, p. 223.

89. Heidegger, *Ponderings II–VI*, p. 157 (emphasis in original); *Überlegungen II–VI*, p. 215.

90. Heidegger, *Ponderings II–VI*, p. 125; *Überlegungen II–VI*, p. 172. See Blok, "Question of Faith."

91. Heidegger, *Ponderings II–VI*, pp. 125–26; *Überlegungen II–VI*, p. 172.

92. I have modified the translation of *Ungrund* by Rojcewicz as "deformed ground."

93. Heidegger, *Ponderings II–VI*, p. 159 (emphasis in original); *Überlegungen II–VI*, p. 217. On the utilization of the term *Ungrund* by Heidegger, see the passages cited in the introduction n. 83.

94. Mitchell, *Fourfold*, p. 3. See also Vycinas, *Earth and Gods*, pp. 224–37; Gall, *Beyond Theism*, pp. 74–95. On the holy and the fourfold in Heidegger's later thinking, see Gschwandtner, *Postmodern Apologetics?*, pp. 34–38.

95. Heidegger, *Ponderings I–VI*, p. 169 (emphasis in original); *Überlegungen II–VI*, p. 231.

96. Heidegger, *Ponderings II–VI*, p. 331; *Überlegungen II–VI*, p. 457. Compare the sardonic and somewhat acrimonious comment of Heidegger, *Heraclitus*, pp. 158–59 (*Heraklit*, p. 209): "Has the human already escaped reflection when, for example, as a Christian he thinks of his god? Or is he thereby only concerned with his own salvation? But how

could this be, if only with and through this type of self-concern and this form of self-encounter the power of subjectivity's self-reflection has been released into modern world history and has become hardened in it? Then Christianity, with its belief in, and teaching of, the τέχνη–like notion of Creation (regarded metaphysically), is an essential reason for the rise of modern technology, and also plays an essential role in the formation of the dominance of the self-reflection of subjectivity. As a result, it is precisely Christianity that is unable to overcome this reflection. What else could be the cause of the historical bankruptcy of Christianity and its church in the modern era of world history? Is a third world war needed in order to prove this?" Deciphering the full import of this passage lies beyond my immediate concern, but we can conclude that, for Heidegger, the metaphysical link between Christianity and modern technology relates to the egological implication of the self-reflection of subjectivity and the corresponding theistic depiction of a God who creates by the fiat of the personal will. On Heidegger's critique of Christianity as enhancing the dominance of technology and the obfuscation of being, see discussion and citation of sources in Wolfson, *Duplicity*, pp. 78–80.

97. Heidegger, *Ponderings II–VI*, pp. 255–56; *Überlegungen II–VI*, p. 351.

98. Heidegger, *Ponderings II–VI*, p. 380; *Überlegungen II–VI*, p. 522.

99. Heidegger, *Ponderings II–VI*, p. 58; *Überlegungen II–VI*, p. 76. Compare the aphorism "*On clandestine ways to God* who is 'dead,'" in *Ponderings II–VI*, pp. 55–56; *Überlegungen II–VI*, p. 73. See *Ponderings II–VI*, p. 239 (*Überlegungen II–VI*, p. 329), where Heidegger criticizes the effort of those brimming with "Christian humility," who explain Nietzsche's madness as an "instance of the Christian God punishing and striking down the arrogant." See the discussion of Nietzsche's aphorism and Heidegger's destruction of ontotheology in Gall, *Beyond Theism*, pp. 14–38. See also Zaborowski, "Metaphysics"; Armitage, *Heidegger and the Death of God*; Dastur, *Questions of Phenomenology*, pp. 177–84; and the analysis of God's death as event in Hemming, *Heidegger's Atheism*, pp. 135–77, as well as the chapter "Zarathustra and the Death of God," op. cit., pp. 215–47.

100. Heidegger, *Schelling's Treatise*, pp. 50–51 (emphasis in original); *Schelling: Vom Wesen*, pp. 87–88. I have taken the liberty of amending Stambaugh's translation. For discussion of Heidegger's deconstruction of metaphysics as ontotheology, see Thomson, *Heidegger on Ontotheology*, pp. 7–43.

101. Heidegger, *Ponderings II–VI*, p. 222; *Überlegungen II–VI*, p. 303.

102. Compare Heidegger, *Ponderings II–VI*, p. 218 (*Überlegungen II–VI*, p. 297): "Are not the last death throes of the gods coming over the West? Only one who thinks out into this extreme possibility can fathom the plight concealed behind current history, wherein impotence and violence together seem to constitute the law of motion." Heidegger's speculation on the last god, the god of unmitigated futurity that as such never can arrive, seems to be a direct response to the challenge offered by Nietzsche, *Gay Science*, §108, p. 109: "After Buddha was dead, they still showed his shadow in a cave for centuries—a tremendous, gruesome shadow. God is dead; but given the way people are, there may still for millennia be caves in which they show his shadow.—And we—we must still defeat his shadow as well!" The better-known aphorism about the madman's proclamation of the death of God occurs in Nietzsche, *Gay Science*, §125, pp. 119–20. The position I am criticizing is well captured in Armitage, *Heidegger and the Death of God*, p. 83: "In the *Beiträge's* penultimate chapter, Heidegger discusses his conception of God or the holy as the last God (*der letzte Gott*), which is the ultimate showing of God in and through the current nihilism of modernity. Here God shows himself, out of the event of being/truth, in particular out of the concealed dimension of truth (being), *as* concealed, and as such, as the holy itself. Thus, Heidegger's ontological commitments do then, in a strange way, lead to a kind of theism, albeit one that attempts to overcome 'ontotheology.' Nevertheless, a theism of sorts remains, a phenomenological theism perhaps" (emphasis in original). For an interpretation of Heidegger's last god similar to my own, see Glazer, "From Thinking," pp. 21–23: "The welling up of meaning—both un-possessive and of non-identity that takes place in Enowning [*Ereignis*]—is crucial to understanding this 'last god.' In passing over all the way into and through, this un-possessive owning has no appropriatable content. Whereas the identity of 'God' has seen its demise in its overwhelming appropriation and distortion of content, the un-possessive owning of the 'last god' begins by being emptied of any such appropriatable content. In this sense, the 'last god' passes over both identity and concept, towards the true emptiness that it is meant to be. This emptiness, however, has been stuffed with an overflow of appropriatable content that in no way reveals this truth of this term. Rather this filling only obscures the majesty of this emptiness. Part of the radical recovery in and through the 'last god' is

a relinquishing any owning of this god in terms of form or content. Its meaning is experienced both in and of its passing through. Such a refusal to owning by way of appropriatable content is what Heidegger terms, Enowning [*Ereignis*]. This experience of god is the *last* insofar as it marks the primordially eternal moment *before* the coming of Being from its origin in be-ing. . . . These reflections of the *Denker* upon the *first God* and the *last god* provide a critical response to the proclamation of Nietzsche's parable" (emphasis in original). I concur with Glazer's discerning in this Heideggerian theme a reiteration and transposition of his earlier interpretation of Pauline eschatology and the Christian parousia. See Wolfson, "Not Yet Now," pp. 148–52; Wolfson, *Duplicity*, pp. 87–97. See also van der Heiden, "Experience of Contingency."

103. Heidegger, *Ponderings II–VI*, p. 183; *Überlegungen II–VI*, p. 250.

104. Heidegger, *Ponderings II–VI*, p. 242; *Überlegungen II–VI*, p. 333.

105. Heidegger, *Ponderings VII–XI*, pp. 57–58; *Überlegungen VII–XI*, pp. 75–76.

106. Heidegger, *Ponderings II–VI*, p. 222; *Überlegungen II–VI*, p. 304.

107. Heidegger, *Ponderings II–VI*, p. 68; *Überlegungen II–VI*, p. 90.

108. Scholem, "Zionism," p. 292. Scholem's statement is noted and analyzed by Wasserstrom, *Religion after Religion*, p. 79. Wasserstrom detects in the comment of Scholem a *coincidentia oppositorum* of the skeptic and the gnostic. See also Miron, *Angel of Jewish History*, p. 160. In n38 ad locum, Miron asserts that the concept of nothing implicit in Scholem's comment "is similar to that of Heidegger." On the matter of atheism, see Lucca, "Ateismo e profondità dell'essere." Finally, it is worth noting the skepticism that Scholem displayed in an essay written in honor of Ernst Bloch's ninetieth birthday in July 1975, "Does God Dwell in the Heart of an Atheist?", published in Scholem, *On the Possibility*, pp. 216–23, and see esp. p. 219: "Of course, the statement declared by Bloch's motto is not true: 'Only an atheist can be a good Christian, and only a Christian is able to be a good atheist.' A nice sentence, but one lacking in all meaning. No proof is given in support of this statement; Bloch seems excessively addicted to the game of his 'atheism,' and it is perhaps superfluous to add that he was enamored thereof. . . . May Bloch forgive me, but I do not believe in his atheism." The text of Scholem appeared in German in *Der Spiegel*, July 7, 1975, and was translated into Hebrew in Scholem, *Explications and Implications*, pp. 453–60. May Scholem forgive me, but I do not think he has plumbed the depth of Bloch's remark, which appeared on the cover of the original German edition of *Atheismus in Christentum*, together with four other statements. See Bloch, *Atheism in Christianity*, p. viii, and the comments in the introduction by Peter Thompson, pp. xx–xxii. The first of the statements declares "To think is to step over, to overstep," and the last emphasizes "What is decisive is: to transcend without transcendence." The paradoxical logic leads Bloch to conclude in the second statement, "The best thing about religion is that it makes for heretics." Heresy is the overstepping or transcending of the boundaries of religion, which he understands primarily from the etymology of the term *re-ligio* as binding back to the past, that is, fastening the adherents to the mythical God of the beginning. By this metrics, the eschatological orientation of the Christian belief in the resurrection of the Son of Man—an idea rooted in the futuristic element of redemption revealed in the scriptural name of God as *ehyeh asher ehyeh*, "I will be what I will be" (Exodus 3:14)—is no longer religion. I can appreciate why Scholem rejected this suggestion, but it is crucial to making sense of Bloch's ostensibly jarring assertion that only an atheist can be a good Christian and only a Christian can be a good atheist. The atheism of which he speaks denotes what he calls the "breakthrough in the theocratic concept of Yahweh" (Bloch, *Atheism in Christianity*, pp. 76–81); that is, the overcoming of the reified theological representation of God, a form of idolatry that keeps one bound to the past, and positing instead the openness of the future, the ontology of the not-yet, which is the true intent of the Jewish injunction against images (*Bilderverbot*) and the source of utopian hope. See Bloch, *Atheism in Christianity*, pp. 79, 202–3, and the fuller analysis in Wolfson, "Not Yet Now," pp. 188–93. Bloch's comment seems to be expressing the same sentiment conveyed by Adorno, *Negative Dialectics*, p. 401, that the "one who believes in God cannot believe in God." See Wolfson, "Not Yet Now," p. 181; Wolfson, *Giving*, p. 264n29.

109. Heidegger, *History of Beyng*, p. 114 (emphasis in original); *Geschichte des Seyns*, p. 132.

110. Heidegger, *Contributions*, §123, p. 189; *Beiträge*, pp. 239–40.

111. Heidegger, *Contributions*, §123, p. 189; *Beiträge*, p. 240.

112. For a different interpretation that elicits from Heidegger's comments an idea of the holy as neither a being nor a nonbeing, see Dillard, *Non-Metaphysical Theology*, pp. 23–26.

113. Heidegger, *Contributions*, §7, p. 21 (emphasis in original); *Beiträge*, p. 24.

114. It is of interest to consider my argument in light of the thesis of Schwartz, "Kabbala als Atheismus?"

115. Heidegger, *Contributions*, §255, p. 323; *Beiträge*, pp. 407–8.

116. Heidegger, *Contributions*, §255, p. 323; *Beiträge*, p. 408.

117. Heidegger, *Contributions*, §255, p. 323; *Beiträge*, p. 408.

118. Heidegger, *Ponderings II–VI*, p. 175; *Überlegungen II–VI*, p. 239.

119. Heidegger, *Ponderings II–VI*, p. 175 (emphasis in original); *Überlegungen II–VI*, pp. 239–40.

120. Heidegger, *Ponderings II–VI*, p. 331; *Überlegungen II–VI*, p. 457.

121. Compare Heidegger, *Ponderings II–VI*, p. 193 (*Überlegungen II–VI*, p. 263): "I am slowly learning to experience the true nearness of the great thinkers in what is most foreign about them."

122. Heidegger, *Ponderings II–VI*, p. 259; *Überlegungen II–VI*, p. 356.

123. Heidegger, *Ponderings II–VI*, p. 192 (emphasis in original); *Überlegungen II–VI*, p. 262.

124. Heidegger, *Ponderings II–VI*, p. 201; *Überlegungen II–VI*, p. 274.

125. Heidegger, *Ponderings II–VI*, p. 311 (emphasis in original); *Überlegungen II–VI*, p. 429.

126. Heidegger, *Off the Beaten Track*, pp. 274–75 (emphasis in original); *Holzwege*, p. 364.

127. Heidegger, *Off the Beaten Track*, p. 275 (translation slightly modified); *Holzwege*, pp. 364–65.

128. Derrida, *Margins of Philosophy*, pp. 23–24 (emphasis in original). See my previous analysis of Derrida's commentary on this Heideggerian passage in Wolfson, *Giving*, pp. 195–96, 425–26n271. Compare the discussion of the Derridean trace against the backdrop of Heidegger's thinking in Marrati, *Genesis and Trace*, pp. 87–176. See ch. 5 n. 137.

129. Derrida, *Of Grammatology*, p. 61. See also Derrida, *Spurs/Nietzsche's Styles*, pp. 20–23: "Here the meaning is not someplace else, but with writing it is made and unmade [*fait et défait*]. And if there is such a thing as truth, then this truth too can reside only in the imprint [*cette trace*] of an empty multiplied furrow which is both headless and tailless. It resides there that it should destroy itself.... This writing is of an obscure sort, the sort that obliterates what it imprints and disperses what it says." Regarding the philosopher's constriction to following the trace of truth, see *Spurs/Nietzsche's Styles*, pp. 86–87. On the Derridean trace and arche-writing, see Conley, "Trace of Style"; Gasché, *Tain of the Mirror*, pp. 157, 186–94, 277–78, 289–93; Gasché, *Inventions of Difference*, pp. 25, 40–42, 44–49, 158, 160–70; Caputo, *Prayers and Tears*, pp. 57–61, 319–20; Howells, *Derrida*, pp. 50–52, 74, 134–35; Bennington, *Interrupting Derrida*, pp. 12, 15, 28, 35, 169–71, 178, 196; Harvey, *Derrida*, pp. 153–81; Krell, *Of Memory*, pp. 165–204. On the possible kabbalistic nuance of the Derridean arche-trace and the gesture of writing, see the views of Habermas, Bloom, and Handelman discussed in Wolfson, *Giving*, pp. 155–56, 177–78, 180, 182, 184–86. See ibid., p. 161, where I note the thematic link between time as the originary iterability, the nonidentical identity of the Jew, and the trace as the repetition of the same that is always different.

130. Derrida, *Margins of Philosophy*, p. 65. See ibid., p. 172n16, where Derrida suggests that the closure and transgression of metaphysics related to the trace may have been suggested by Plotinus: "In a sense—or a non-sense—that metaphysics would have excluded from its field, while nevertheless remaining in secret and incessant relation with this sense, form in itself already would be the *trace* (*ikhnos*) of a certain nonpresence, the vestige of the un-formed, which announces-recalls its other, as did Plotinus, perhaps, for all of metaphysics. The trace would not be the mixture, the transition between form and the amorphous, presence and absence . . . but that which, by eluding this opposition, makes it possible in the irreducibility of its excess. Henceforth, the closure of metaphysics, the closure that the audaciousness of the *Enneads* seems to indicate by transgressing it, would not occur *around* a homogeneous and continuous field of metaphysics. Rather, it would fissure the structure and history of metaphysics, *organically* inscribing and systematically *articulating* the traces of the *before* and the *after* both from within and without metaphysics. Thereby producing an infinite, and infinitely surprising, reading" (emphasis in original).

131. On this account, there is affinity between Heidegger's *Spur* and Levinas's notion of the other as the *trace of illeity*. See Levinas, *Collected Philosophical Papers*, pp. 106–7; Levinas, *Otherwise Than Being*, pp. 12, 94; and see the analyses in Wyschogrod, *Emmanuel Levinas*, pp. 158–64, 224, and Wolfson, *Giving*, pp. 98–99, 142, 144–48.

132. Heidegger, *Off the Beaten Track*, pp. 253–54 (emphasis in original); *Holzwege*, pp. 336–37.

133. Heidegger, *Ponderings II–VI*, p. 176; *Überlegungen II–VI*, p. 241. See the analysis in Vycinas, *Earth and Gods*, pp. 174–223.

134. Heidegger, *Ponderings II–VI*, p. 179 (emphasis in original); *Überlegungen II–VI*, p. 245.

135. Heidegger, *Off the Beaten Track*, p. 202; *Holzwege*, p. 272.

136. Heidegger, *Off the Beaten Track*, p. 203; *Holzwege*, pp. 272–73.

137. Heidegger, *Off the Beaten Track*, p. 221 (emphasis in original); *Holzwege*, p. 295. See Mitchell, *Fourfold*, pp. 197–201, esp. 199–200.

138. Heidegger, *Ponderings VII–XI*, p. 20 (emphasis in original); *Überlegungen VII–XI*, p. 25.

139. Heidegger, *Ponderings VII–XI*, p. 20 (emphasis in original); *Überlegungen VII–XI*, p. 25.

140. Heidegger, *Contributions*, §259, p. 338; *Beiträge*, p. 428.

141. Heidegger, *Contributions*, §143, p. 207 (emphasis in original); *Beiträge*, p. 263.

142. Heidegger, *Ponderings VII–XI*, p. 195; *Überlegungen VII–XI*, p. 252.

143. Heidegger, *Ponderings II–VI*, p. 305 (emphasis in original); *Überlegungen II–VI*, p. 420. Compare Heidegger, *Ponderings II–VI*, p. 331 (*Überlegungen II–VI*, p. 456): "The *twilight of the idols* is drawing near. . . . It is not yet the evening twilight; coming first is the morning one. The assembling of the idols is the sign of a long and conclusive flight of the gods" (emphasis in original).

144. Heidegger, *Ponderings II–VI*, p. 309; *Überlegungen II–VI*, p. 426.

145. Heidegger, *Off the Beaten Track*, p. 58; *Holzwege*, p. 76.

146. Heidegger, *Ponderings XII–XV*, p. 19 (emphasis in original); *Überlegungen XII–XV*, pp. 23–24. It is worth considering the observation of Löwith, *Meaning in History*, p. 201: "Radical atheism, too, which is, however, as rare as radical faith, is possible only within a Christian tradition; for the feeling that the world is thoroughly godless and godforsaken presupposes the belief in a transcendent Creator-God who cares for his creatures. To the Christian apologists, the pagans were atheists not because they did not believe in any divinity at all but because they were 'polytheistic atheists.' To the pagans the Christians were atheists because they believed in only one single God transcending the universe and city-state, that is, everything that the ancients had consecrated. The fact that the Christian God has ruled out all the popular gods and protecting spirits of the pagans created the possibility of a radical atheism; for, if the Christian belief in a God who is as distinct from the world as a creator is from his creatures and yet is the source of every being is once discarded, the world becomes emancipated and profane as it never was for the pagans."

147. Wolfson *Giving*, pp. 227–60, esp. 236–46.

148. Heidegger, *Ponderings II–VI*, p. 215 (emphasis in original); *Überlegungen II–VI*, p. 294.

149. Heidegger, *Ponderings II–VI*, p. 253; *Überlegungen II–VI*, p. 347.

150. Heidegger, *Ponderings II–VI*, p. 300; *Überlegungen II–VI*, p. 412.

151. Heidegger, *Ponderings II–VI*, p. 311; *Überlegungen II–VI*, p. 429.

152. Heidegger, *Ponderings II–VI*, p. 243 (emphasis in original); *Überlegungen II–VI*, p. 334. At the end of the entry, Heidegger guides the reader to the "Vortrag über das Kunstwerk" and to the "W.S. 37/8." Trawny decodes the first reference to Heidegger's "Der Ursprung des Kunstwerkes," published in the *Holzwege*, pp. 1–74, and to the essay "Vom Ursprung des Kunstwerks: Erste Ausarbeitung," *Heidegger Studies* 5 (1989): 5–33. The second reference is to the lecture offered as the Winter Seminar 1937–38 and later published as *Grundfragen der Philosophie* and translated as *Basic Questions of Philosophy*.

153. Heidegger, *Ponderings II–VI*, p. 208; *Überlegungen II–VI*, p. 283. On the terminology *Anfang* and *Beginn*, see below, n. 165.

154. Derrida, *Of Spirit*, p. 16; *De l'esprit*, p. 35. See, however, the comment of Jonas cited in ch. 2 n. 91.

155. Heidegger, *Pathmarks*, p. 237; *Wegmarken*, p. 309.

156. Heidegger, *Contributions*, §259, p. 338; *Beiträge*, p. 427.

157. Schelling, *Ages of the World (Fragment)*, p. 26; *Weltalter*, in *Sämmtliche Werke*, 8:237–38. See Iber, *Das Andere der Vernunft*, pp. 346–49.

158. Heidegger, *Contributions*, §38, p. 63; *Beiträge*, p. 80.

159. Heidegger, *Contributions*, §38, p. 63 (emphasis in original); *Beiträge*, p. 79.

160. Heidegger, *Ponderings II–VI*, p. 366; *Überlegungen II–VI*, p. 503.

161. For discussion of Heidegger's critique of the ideal of the *causa sui*, see Vedder, *Heidegger's Philosophy*, pp. 113–32.

162. Heidegger, *Contributions*, §104, p. 159 (emphasis in original); *Beiträge*, p. 203.

163. Heidegger, *Basic Questions*, p. 38; *Grundfragen*, p. 40, cited partially in ch. 1 at n. 82.

164. Heidegger, *Ponderings II–VI*, p. 366; *Überlegungen II–VI*, p. 504.

165. Heidegger, *What Is Called Thinking?*, p. 152; *Was Heißt Denken?*, p. 156. In that context, the words used respectively for origin and beginning are *Anfang* and *Beginn*. See Wolfson, *Alef*, pp. 234–35n15.

166. Heidegger, *Basic Concepts*, p. 92; *Grundbegriffe*, p. 107.

167. On the nexus of *alef*, *pele*, and *alufo shel olam*, see Wolfson, *Open Secret*, p. 333n68. On the symbolization of *Keter* as *alef*, see, for instance, Asher ben David, *Perush Shem ha-Meforash*, in Abrams, *R. Asher ben David*, p. 231. Regarding this symbol

and the relationship of *Ein Sof* and *Keter* in Asher's kabbalah, see Scholem, *Origins*, pp. 432–33. By contrast, some kabbalists emphasized that *Keter* is not represented by a letter of its own but only by the tip (*qoṣ*) of the *yod*, the first letter of the Tetragrammaton and the symbol for *Ḥokhmah*. If the lack of linguistic identification is true of *Keter*, it is all the truer of *Ein Sof*. See Matt, "*Ayin*," p. 130.

168. *Zohar* 3:193b.

169. Heidegger, *Contributions*, §50, p. 85; *Beiträge*, p. 107.

170. Heidegger, *Contributions*, §128, p. 193 (emphasis in original); *Beiträge*, p. 245.

171. Heidegger, *Contributions*, §130, p. 195 (emphasis in original); *Beiträge*, p. 247.

172. Viṭal, *Sha'ar ha-Haqdamot*, p. 35: "By means of this line [*derekh ha-qaw ha-zeh*] the light of the infinite [*or ha-ein sof*] extended and spread forth below into the empty space [*ha-ḥalal*], and then in wisdom he emanated, created, formed, and made all of the worlds." Compare Viṭal, *Eṣ Ḥayyim*, 1:1, 11d; Viṭal, *Mavo She'arim*, p. 11. On the basis of this Lurianic teaching, other kabbalists coined the expression *qaw ha-ein sof*. See, for instance, Sharabi, *Reḥovot ha-Nahar*, 6b; Luzzatto, *Adir ba-Marom*, pt. 1, p. 344; Luzzatto, *Qelaḥ Pitḥei Ḥokhmah*, pp. 80–81, 85, 88; Wildmann, *Pitḥei She'arim*, pt. 1, 7b (there the expression used is *ḥuṭ qaw ha-ein sof*, the thread of the line of the infinite); Yosef Ḥayyim of Baghdad, *Da'at u-Tevunah*, 33a, 39c. See ch. 5 n. 152.

173. Viṭal, *Mavo She'arim*, pp. 10–11.

174. Eliashiv, *Leshem Shevo we-Aḥlamah: Haqdamot u-She'arim*, p. 43. Compare the letter of Eliashiv in Schatz, *Ma'yan Moshe*, p. 238: "Prior to the disclosure of each configuration [*parṣuf*], an aspect of contraction [*ha-ṣimṣum*] preceded it in the light of the configuration related to it, which is the aspect of the infinite vis-à-vis the lower one. . . . Thus, every contraction is verily an aspect of judgment, for it bestows boundary on the light." See Eliashiv, *Leshem Shevo we-Aḥlamah: Sefer ha-De'ah*, pt. 2, p. 42, cited below at n. 215.

175. Proclus, *Elements of Theology*, prop. 64, pp. 60–61: "For if the outgoing proceeds [πρόδος] by a declension [ὕφεσιν] through terms that are akin to the constitutive causes, from the wholly perfect must arise things complete in their kind, and by these latter the origin of things incomplete must be mediated in due sequence: so that there will be one order of substances complete in themselves, and another of incomplete substances." The substances that are complete in themselves fall short of the original monad, in that they are discriminated into a manifold, but they nevertheless are assimilated to that monad by their self-complete existence; whereas the incomplete beings that exist in another fall away from the monad that exists in itself to the point that there is no more assimilation or likeness. In the technical language used by Proclus in *Elements of Theology*, prop. 64, pp. 62–63: "But all procession advances through similars [ὁμοίων] until it reaches the wholly dissimilar [ἀνομοίων]." The matter is elaborated in slightly different language in Proclus, *Commentary on Plato's Parmenides*, pp. 34–35: "Then, shifting to the examination of what is other than the One, they show that these things by participating in the One posit all other things along with themselves, and by not participating in it are deprived of all qualities. Since all these results cannot be applied to the One Being, they conclude with plausibility that the discussion is not only about it but about all things from the primary cause down to the lowest, in which there is privation of all things. (These are thus likened to the primary cause by dissimilarity, for that which is deprived of all qualities by its non-participation in the One is in a sense like that which transcends all things by its non-participation in Being.)" See ibid., p. 34n22, where mention is made of the concept of the similarity of dissimilarity or the similitude of dissimilitude (ἀνόμοιος ὁμοιότης) in Proclus's *Platonic Theology*, I.12. See Proclus, *Théologie Platonicienne*, 1:57. Proclus speaks of the dissimilar similitude of matter to the first, that is, matter is similar to the One by virtue of its being dissimilar. The negation of the dissimilitude with respect to matter relates to the quality of privation or deficiency, whereas with respect to the One it is enunciative of its being exempt from all production because of its supereminence and its imparticipability. Significantly, Proclus notes that each of the negations is affirmative, but one is so paradigmatically (παραδειγματικῶς) and the other iconically (εἰκονικῶς). On the oxymoron ἀνόμοιον ὁμοιότητα, see the supplementary notes in Proclus, *Théologie Platonicienne*, 1:144–45. In the final analysis, we are justified to ask whether anything can be meaningfully marked as wholly dissimilar in a system wherein all things proceed from an original monad and thus are conjoined with or participate in the imparticipable.

176. Scholem, *Major Trends*, p. 261; Scholem, *On Jews and Judaism*, p. 283. Concerning Scholem's approach to the doctrine of *ṣimṣum*, see Wohlfarth, "Haarscharf."

177. Scholem, *Major Trends*, p. 263. See Wolfson, "Divine Suffering," pp. 114–15.

178. Schneersohn, *Sefer ha-Ma'Amarim 5665*, p. 165.

179. Benjamin, *Selected Writings*, 1:280. See analysis in Wolfson, "Not Yet Now," p. 168. Benjamin's idea of deformation (*Entstaltung*) should be compared to his characterization of Kafka's fixation and the sole topic of his work as "the distortion of existence" (*die Entstellung des Daseins*). See Benjamin, *Selected Writings*, 2:496; *Gesammelte Schriften*, 2.2, p. 678. The deformation or disfigurement (*Entstellung*) in Kafka's world is said to have "its roots in the fact that what is great, new, and liberating here manifests itself as atonement, in cases where the past has not seen through itself, confessed, and been finished with. . . . Kafka's writing is simply full of configurations of forgetting [*Konfigurationen des Vergessens*]—of silent pleas to recall things to mind" (Benjamin, *Selected Writings*, 2:498; *Gesammelte Schriften*, 2.2, p. 682). Benjamin's depiction of *Entstellung* in Kafka, including a comparison to the Freudian idea of disfigurement, displacement, and condensation as processes of the dreamwork, is discussed by Weigel, *Walter Benjamin: Images*, pp. 142–43. On the critical assessment of the positive and negative dimensions attributed to the aesthetic role of the image in the different stages of Benjamin's thought, see Ross, *Walter Benjamin's Concept*. The author thus summarizes her argument on p. 5: "Specifically, my hypothesis is that the main shifts and problems of Benjamin's thinking, including the gradual erosion of the system of oppositions that had characterised his early writing, can be grasped by an analysis of his writing on the topic of the image. Furthermore, this approach will be used to show that despite his attack on the 'demonic' expressivity of certain kinds of sensuous forms, Benjamin's major ideas also require and can be shown to avail themselves of an aesthetic mode of presentation in images." The role of thinking-in-images in Benjamin has been discussed by various scholars. For a representative list, see Jacobs, "Walter Benjamin"; Weigel, *Body- and Image-Space*, pp. 49–60; Weigel, *Walter Benjamin: Images*, pp. 183–206; Weigel, "Flash of Knowledge"; Nägele, "Thinking Images." See ch. 7 n. 170.

180. Scholem's authorship of this statement—cited by Benjamin and independently by Bloch—was revealed by him in a letter to Benjamin from July 9, 1934. See Scholem, *Correspondence of Walter Benjamin and Gershom Scholem*, p. 123; *Walter Benjamin/Gershom Scholem*, p. 154. The letter appears as well in Benjamin, *Correspondence*, p. 446. The statement fabricated by Scholem bears some resemblance to the dictum attributed to Israel of Rizhin which he cites in the *Messianic Idea*, pp. 34–35: "Among the most famous sayings of this kind are those of Rabbi Israel of Rizhin, that in the days of the Messiah man will no longer quarrel with his fellow but with himself, or his bold suggestion that the Messianic world will be a world without images, 'in which the image and its object can no longer be related'—which apparently means that a new mode of being will emerge which cannot be pictorially represented." The philosophical import of Scholem's comment is explicated by Blumenberg, *Work on Myth*, p. 226: "Or does everything depend on the possibility of being able to believe that the Messiah has not yet come? The future Messiah is an idea; it can be burdened with all sorts of self-denial and need in the form of anticipation. No dogma is needed to determine who it will be and what nature he will have. The Jews' Messiah is supposed to come as one who is totally unknown—as, in the literal sense, a figure of what has never been present before. Consequently every word about him can be a prohibition of imagery, rejection of myth, suspension of history. Rabbi Israel of Rischin taught that the messianic world would be a world without likenesses, because in it the comparison and what is compared could no longer be related to one another. But that would apparently mean, Gershom Scholem comments, 'that a new mode of being will emerge which cannot be pictorially represented.'" Atkins, *Ethical and Theological Appropriation*, pp. 180–81n24, relates the remark of Blumenberg to Heidegger's insight that "our capacity to think non-metaphysically is dependent upon whether we can think difference as difference, i.e., as singular and irreducible." The comment of Blumenberg is occasioned by his larger effort (*Work on Myth*, pp. 221–22) to link the scriptural prohibition of images, and what he assumes to be the affirmation of an invisible God, to utopian thinking; that latter must be poor in images because any image spoils the ideal. Insightfully, Blumenberg relates this utopian iconoclasm to Barth's dialectical foreign God, Bultmann's kerygma, Heidegger's Being, and Adorno's restoration by negative dialectics of the pure and empty horizon of possibility.

181. Benjamin, *Selected Writings*, 2:664; *Gesammelte Schriften*, 4.1, pp. 419–20. See Ross, *Walter Benjamin's Concept*, pp. 132n37, 146–47n13.

182. Scholem, *Major Trends*, p. 260; Scholem, *Kabbalah*, pp. 129–30. A similar argument contesting Scholem's view was made by Paul Franks, "Contraction and Withdrawal: The Midrashic Roots of Philosophical Conceptions of Tsimtsum," a paper presented at the conference *Tsimtsum and Modernity: Lurianic Heritage in Modern Philosophy and Theology*, sponsored by the Faculty of Divinity, University of Cambridge, May 31–June 1, 2016. I did not have access

to a printed version of the lecture, but I attended the conference and reference the argument from memory. For a philosophically nuanced presentation of Scholem's distinction between the midrashic and kabbalistic perspectives, see Bielik-Robson, "God of Luria," pp. 36–38. Mention here should be made as well of the analysis of the use of the term *ṣimṣum* to denote the consolidation of all the waters to create the dry land in a passage from the *Midrash ha-Ne'lam* stratum of zoharic literature in Wald, *Doctrine of the Divine Name*, pp. 54–57. As Wald correctly noted, the esoteric intent of this imagery is to depict the delimiting of divine mercy by the force of judgment, a delimitation, I would add, that entails both constriction to a point and withdrawal from a point.

183. See text cited in ch. 5 at n. 136.

184. See Eliashiv, *Leshem Shevo we-Aḥlamah: Haqdamot u-She'arim*, p. 128.

185. On the soteriological import of this symbolism—the messiah is the oldest and the youngest inasmuch as he corresponds to the highest aspect of the divine—see Wolfson, "Cut That Binds," pp. 121–22.

186. Wolfson, "Retroactive Not Yet," pp. 48–50.

187. Heidegger, *Elucidations*, p. 79; *Erläuterungen*, p. 56. On Heidegger's interpretation of the Heraclitean notion of *kosmos* as an anticipation of his understanding of *Sein selbst*, that is, being as distinct from beings, see Capobianco, "Heidegger on Heraclitus." See other references cited in the introduction n. 51.

188. Heidegger, *Contributions*, §146, p. 211 (emphasis in original); *Beiträge*, p. 268. Compare the analysis in Romano, *There Is*, pp. 213–36.

189. The expression was coined by Marion, "Nothing."

190. On the question of whether there can be a phenomenology of nothingness and the controversy between Heidegger and Carnap over this matter, see Romano, *There Is*, pp. 177–212.

191. *Zohar Ḥadash*, 56d (*Qaw ha-Middah*).

192. *Zohar* 2:68b (*Tosefta*).

193. Heidegger, *Pathmarks*, p. 148; *Wegmarken*, p. 194. For a more complete citation of this passage and analysis, see Wolfson, *Giving*, p. 129.

194. Heidegger, *Discourse on Thinking*, p. 55; *Gelassenheit*, p. 24. I take issue with the assessment of Bielik-Robson, *Saving Lie*, p. 139: "*Seinsvergessenheit* (forgetfulness of being), which is the movement of *Seyn* (being) itself, and not just a mistake of Western metaphysics, is the forgetfulness of truth, which allows beings to be, that is, to endure, for a while in their error: *Seinlassen* (letting be) is thus a purely negative gesture, a kind of an ontological negligence. Beings come to being when they forget Being as the impossibility of beings." Respectfully, this summary of Heidegger is too one-dimensional because it neglects to mention that the letting be, or the *es gibt*, is hardly just a negative gesture. The very oblivion is what allows for the coming to be of beings just as concealment is the condition that makes unconcealment possible. Heidegger was committed to the belief that by exposing the ontological difference between being and beings, the former would be recovered, but this does not mean for him that the oblivion of being is ever fully amended. In the nature of things, being must be veiled so that there can be beings, in a positive and not merely negative manner. The forgetfulness of truth allows beings to be in their truthfulness.

195. Eliashiv, *Leshem Shevo we-Aḥlamah: Sefer ha-Kelalim*, pt. 1, p. 217.

196. Pachter, "Gaon's Kabbalah," pp. 124–34. See also Shuchat, *World Hidden*, pp. 117–18, and reference to other scholars cited in n32, 122–23n48, 123–24, 137–42. Concerning the Vilna Gaon's interpretation of *ṣimṣum* and the controversy with Ḥasidim, see Nadler, *Faith of the Mithnagdim*, pp. 11–20; Einfeld, *Teaching of the Gra*, pp. 198–218. On *ṣimṣum* in Eliashiv's writings, see the wide-ranging analysis in Bar-Bettelheim, "Concept of *Zimzum*," pp. 97–174, and compare the recent studies of Shuchat, "*Ṣimṣum* Taken Literally" and Vilk, *Sefer ha-Ṣimṣum*, pp. 120–36.

197. For an amplification of this point, see Wolfson, "*Nequddat ha-Reshimu*," pp. 76–81.

198. See ch. 3 n. 167 and discussion of Azriel's language in Eliashiv's letter printed in Schatz, *Ma'yan Moshe*, p. 264.

199. Eliashiv, *Leshem Shevo we-Aḥlamah: Haqdamot u-She'arim*, p. 217.

200. From a letter of Eliashiv printed in Schatz, *Ma'yan Moshe*, p. 238.

201. Eliashiv, *Leshem Shevo we-Aḥlamah: Haqdamot u-She'arim*, p. 88. Compare Eliashiv, *Leshem Shevo we-Aḥlamah: Sefer ha-De'ah*, pt. 1, p. 158. It goes without saying that there were earlier kabbalists who interpreted the designation of the Tetragrammaton as the *shem ha-eṣem* in light of the fact that of all the names this is the one that instructs us about the essence (*aṣmut*) of *Ein Sof*. For instance, see Ibn Zimra, *Magen David*, pp. 53–54.

202. Eliashiv, *Leshem Shevo we-Aḥlamah: Ḥeleq ha-Be'urim*, pt. 1, p. 5. The assumption about the manifestation of the light of the infinite in the Tetragrammaton, and the containment of all the names in that name, is the conceptual basis for explaining the dynamics of the proper intention in

the ritual of prayer. See Eliashiv, *Leshem Shevo we-Aḥlamah: Sefer ha-De'ah*, pt. 1, pp. 160–61.

203. Viṭal, *Eṣ Ḥayyim*, 3:3, 17a. Part of the passage is cited in ch. 5 at n. 148.

204. This theme, which I have emphasized in many writings, is captured in the contemporary kabbalistic work by Arenfeld, *Yira'ukha im Shamesh*, p. 753, in language that strikes me as consistent with the view of Eliashiv: "In the manner that by means of the disclosure of the limited form the concealed and hidden reality is drawn forth, for the limited force from the perspective of its nature conceals and hides the incomposite light of the blessed One, which is not revealed but through measure and boundary. However, in the supernal worlds, which are the worlds of holiness, even though the light comes forth in measure and boundary, it is still apparent and revealed that he, blessed be his name, sustains everything and brings everything into being, and is joined with them in the supreme unity. As is known, even in the world of emanation, the light of *Ein Sof* is united with the *sefirot* in one unity . . . and all the more so with respect to *Adam Qadmon*. However, in the lower worlds, which are the world of separation, so hidden and concealed is his light, blessed be he, that room is given to the aspect of 'whither shall I rule' [*ana emlokh*], which is the something [*yesh*] that is the opposite of holiness, and from it there concatenates below the force of evil, the shells, and the Other Side." The semblance of a reality independent of the divine—the import of the rhetorical *ana emlokh*, that is, the ostensibly prideful claim for autonomy and the denial of divine sovereignty—is viewed as the source of evil and unholiness. On the expression *ana emlokh*, see Yalles, *Qehillat Ya'aqov*, s.v. *benei ḥeit*, 23d. The biblical figure Ḥeit is identified with Hadar, the eighth of the Edomite kings (Genesis 36:39)—on the grounds that the numerical value of *ḥeit* is eight—whose source is the "world of rectification" (*olam ha-tiqqun*), since he was the only king paired with a wife, whereas each of the other seven kings of Edom, the wicked ones who died, were males unbalanced by any female counterpart and thus symbolically represent the effeminate or emasculated males. Insofar as the first seven kings originated in the "world of chaos" (*olam ha-tohu*), to them is attributed the seditious comment "whither shall I rule?" This passage had a significant influence on many Ḥasidic masters. To cite a modest sampling of the many relevant examples: Epstein, *Ma'or wa-Shemesh*, pp. 15, 114, 138, 140, 642; Rabinowitz, *Peri Ṣaddiq*, 1:297; Rabinowitz, *Ṣidqat ha-Ṣaddiq*, sec. 206, p. 113; Rabinowitz, *Maḥashavot Ḥaruṣ*, 9.8, p. 75. An especially interesting use of this theme is found in Rabinowitz, *Resisay Laylah*, sec. 30, p. 49, where the source of the imagination (*shoresh ha-dimyon*)—for all humanity with the exception of Jacob, and to some extent Joseph, because his dreaming was anchored in the image of his father—is said to issue from the break (*shevirah*) that was the repercussion of the thought encapsulated in the words "whither shall I rule?" The waywardness of imagination is linked ethnically to Amaleq, the nemesis of Israel, and the victory of the latter over the former, primarily through the attribute of Joseph, which is to say, through control of excessive sexual desire, is the triumph of the imaginal, the conversion of what is false into what is true, emblematized by the holiday of Purim and the blurring of the boundary between blessed Mordecai and cursed Haman. On the zoharic symbol of the kings of Edom as the primordial forces of evil, see the recent analyses in Har-Shefi, *Myth of the Edomite Kings*, and Hellner-Eshed, *Seekers of the Face*, pp. 167–77. Regrettably, I must say that Har-Shefi's criticism of my gender analysis (*Myth of the Edomite Kings*, p. 175n80) reflects the same misunderstanding attested by many other scholars. To note, as he does, that the feminine—in this case the figure of Meheṭabel, the wife of Hadar—plays an active role does not address the issue I have raised about the derivative or secondary ontological status of the female vis-à-vis the male. It is quite obvious to anyone versed in gender theory that ascribing to the wife the role of complementing and perfecting the last of the Edomite kings only enhances the androcentric perspective. See my discussion in Wolfson, *Language*, pp. 311–12 (a reference tellingly not mentioned by Har-Shefi). For other scholarly discussions of the problem of evil in kabbalistic sources, see Tishby, *Doctrine of Evil*; Tishby, *Wisdom of the Zohar*, pp. 447–74; Scholem, *On the Mystical Shape*, pp. 56–87; Dan, "Samael"; Idel, "Evil Thought"; Idel, *Il male primordiale*; Wolfson, "Left Contained in the Right"; Wolfson, "Light through Darkness" (revised versions of these two essays appear in Wolfson, *Luminal Darkness*, pp. 1–55); Farber-Ginat, "'ShellPrecedes the Fruit'"; Jacobson, "Problem of Evil"; Berman, "Improper Twins"; Berman, "Demonic Writing"; Berman, *Divine and Demonic*; Yisraeli, "Cain."

205. Eliashiv, *Leshem Shevo we-Aḥlamah: Ḥeleq ha-Be'urim*, pt. 1, p. 104.

206. Eliashiv, *Leshem Shevo we-Aḥlamah: Sefer ha-De'ah*, pt. 1, p. 157.

207. Eliashiv, *Leshem Shevo we-Aḥlamah: Haqdamot u-She'arim*, p. 91.

208. Eliashiv, *Leshem Shevo we-Aḥlamah: Sefer ha-De'ah*, pt. 1, p. 159.

209. Eliashiv, *Leshem Shevo we-Aḥlamah: Haqdamot u-She'arim*, p. 29.

210. For a more extensive analysis of acosmism in Ḥabad, or what I have preferred to call apophatic embodiment, see Wolfson, *Open Secret*, pp. 46–47, 66–129, and see references to other scholars cited on p. 338n136. See, more recently, Melamed, "Spinozism, Acosmism, and Hassidism." On Eliashiv's criticism of Naftali Hertz ha-Levi's acosmism, derived from Luzzatto, see Peleg, "More about Rabbi Shlomo Eliyashov's Controversy," pp. 195–97.

211. The reference is to the thirty-two times that the name *Elohim* is mentioned in the first chapter of Genesis.

212. Eliashiv, *Leshem Shevo we-Aḥlamah: Sefer ha-De'ah*, pt. 2, p. 139.

213. Eliashiv, *Leshem Shevo we-Aḥlamah: Haqdamot u-She'arim*, pp. 26–37.

214. Eliashiv, *Leshem Shevo we-Aḥlamah: Haqdamot u-She'arim*, p. 42.

215. Eliashiv, *Leshem Shevo we-Aḥlamah: Sefer ha-Deah*, pt. 2, p. 42.

216. Ibid., p. 138.

217. Ibid., p. 139.

218. See the letter of Eliashiv cited in Schatz, *Ma'yan Moshe*, pp. 183–84. The idea expressed by this kabbalist is by no means unique. My own formulation is indebted to the language of the second-century Yogācāra text *Saṃdhi-nirmocana-sūtra*. See Keenan, trans., *Scripture on the Explication*, pp. 36–37: "The ultimate truth of all things has no-essence, for, from their arising, all things have no-essence. This is what I call the no-essence that is identical with the conditioned arising of things. I also call it the no-essence of ultimate meaning because I preach that among all things, that realm of the purified content of understanding is to be regarded as the no-essence of ultimate meaning.... Moreover, that fully perfected pattern of all things I also term the no-essence of ultimate meaning, for the absence of selfhood in all things whatsoever I call ultimate meaning, or no-essence, because this is the truth of ultimate meaning, because it is manifested by the absence of essence.... Just as empty space is manifested everywhere by the absence of material forms, so is the other aspect the essential no-essence of ultimate meaning, which is manifested everywhere by the absence of selfhood in all things." To say all things have no-essence is not the same as saying that all things have no essence. That is, no-essence is a technical expression to convey the sense of codependent arising, the absence of an inherent selfhood. The lack of an independent self is the ultimate meaning of what is manifest as the "absence of essence" that is the "essential no-essence" of the descriptive marks by which every entity in the natural world is signified. Compare *Scripture on the Explication*, p. 64, where the Buddha explains to Maitreya how the bodhisattvas cultivate quietude and vision: "Good son, because they reflect upon true suchness, they abandon images of doctrine and images of meaning. When they lack anything to be attained in names and name-essences, then they no longer pay any regard to the images that support those [names and name-essences]. In such a fashion they abandon them." As I have argued in chapter 3, the Buddhist insight about the emptiness of being, or the no-self of things, can be applied to the kabbalistic *Ein Sof*, the nonessence that is the essence of all things that have no essence.

219. *Pirqei Rabbi Eliezer*, ch. 3, 5b.

220. Gruenwald, "Preliminary Critical Edition," §6, p. 142; Hayman, *Sefer Yeṣira*, §6, p. 74: "And their measure is ten for they have no limit. Their end is fixed in their beginning and their beginning in their end, as the flame is bound to the coal."

221. Wildmann, *Pitḥei She'arim*, pt. 1, 2a–b.

222. Ibid, 2b.

223. Eliashiv, *Leshem Shevo we-Aḥlamah: Sefer ha-De'ah*, pt. 1, p. 159.

224. Derrida, *Acts of Religion*, p. 214. The comment is from Derrida's essay "The Eyes of Language: The Abyss and the Volcano," an extended analysis of the letter that Scholem wrote to Rosenzweig in 1926 on the peril of the secularization of the Hebrew language. See ch. 7 n. 165. For my previous remarks about Derrida and the Tetragrammaton, including the aforementioned passage, see Wolfson, *Giving*, pp. 170, 174, 176, 184–85. See also Miller, *Name of God*, pp. 53–66, 77–78.

225. My articulation of the kabbalistic teaching on the name and the unnamed has benefited from the analysis in Ziporyn, *Ironies of Oneness and Difference*, p. 145.

226. Eliashiv, *Leshem Shevo we-Aḥlamah: Sefer ha-Kelalim*, pt. 1, p. 2.

227. Eliashiv, *Leshem Shevo we-Aḥlamah: Ḥeleq ha-Be'urim*, pt. 1, p. 18. See the study of Shuchat cited above, n. 196, and see ch. 5 n. 134. On the role assigned to the human as the agent to accomplish the *tiqqun* and the restoration of all things to the infinite, see Eliashiv, *Leshem Shevo we-Aḥlamah: Haqdamot u-She'arim*, pp. 16–17.

228. Eliashiv, *Leshem Shevo we-Aḥlamah: Ḥeleq ha-Be'urim*, pt. 1, p. 20. On *malkhut de-ein sof*, see ch. 6 nn. 154–55. The conceptual link between the locution *malkhut de-ein sof* and the positing of limit within the limitless, the root of judgment in the boundless

mercy of the infinite, expressed in Azriel of Gerona's terminology *koaḥ bi-gevul mi-beli gevul* (above, n. 198) is made by Vilk, *Sefer ha-Ṣimṣum*, pp. 132, 140, and 145.

229. Eliashiv, *Leshem Shevo we-Aḥlamah: Haqdamot u-She'arim*, pp. 129–30. On the identification of *malkhut de-ein sof* as the will that bears existence, see Eliashiv, *Leshem Shevo we-Aḥlamah: Sefer ha-Kelalim*, pt. 1, p. 217.

230. Eliashiv, *Leshem Shevo we-Aḥlamah: Sefer ha-Kelalim*, pt. 1, p. 217.

231. Eliashiv, *Leshem Shevo we-Aḥlamah: Haqdamot u-She'arim*, pp. 110–11. Compare p. 120, where the apocatastasis is described symbolically as the restoration of all things to the womb of *Binah*, the supernal Mother, in the seventh millennium, which is the time of the rule of *Malkhut*.

232. Eliashiv, *Leshem Shevo we-Aḥlamah: Sefer ha-Kelalim*, pt. 1, p. 313.

233. See the passage from Heidegger cited in the introduction at n. 35.

234. Smith, "Thinking from the One," p. 20.

235. Heidegger, *Contributions*, §149, p. 213; *Beiträge*, p. 271. In that context, Heidegger discusses the two determinations of the beingness of beings (*Seiendheit des Seienden*) as τί ἐστιν and ὅτι ἔστιν, the whatness or quiddity (*essentia*) and the mode or the factical existence (*existentia*). From Heidegger's perspective, both of these "are a certain impoverishment of an (in itself already richer) essence of beyng and of its truth (the temporality-spatiality of this truth as abyss)."

236. The expression is appropriated from Backman, *Complicated Presence*. For a summary of the author's thesis, see pp. 4–12, and esp. 7–8: "This study will . . . argue that while the peculiar structure of unity—a dynamic of differentiation that is nevertheless structurally 'simple' and unique—unfolding in Heidegger's work arises out of the tradition itself, it is nonetheless marked by a certain decisive rupture with the unity discovered in the Greek beginning of metaphysics . . . . Whereas the 'protometaphysical' unity disclosed to the narrator-thinker of Parmenides' Poem consists in the absolute simplicity of presence as such, purified of all references to nonpresence, exteriority, and otherness, the postmetaphysical unity traced out by Heidegger's corpus can be characterized as a *complicated presence* . . . . Heidegger's thinking, in its most mature form, sets out from the *singular* presence of an appearing thing and proceeds to unfold *this* presence as a *com*plication, i.e., a folding *together* of multiple dimensions of meaningfulness. . . . A being, a thing, is articulated by the later Heidegger as *im*plying—i.e., as folding into itself—a multidimensional background that as such remains *nonpresent*" (emphasis in original).

237. Wolfson, "Nihilating Nonground"; Wolfson, *Giving*, pp. 78, 171–74, 197–98.

238. Deleuze and Guattari, *What Is Philosophy?*, p. 45.

239. The expression is derived from Bataille, *On Nietzsche*, p. 65: "What gives the impression of transcendence—touching some part of being—is that our perception of it is mediated by nothingness. We only get beyond the particular being that we are through the laceration of nothingness. Nothingness overpowers us, it strikes us down, and we are tempted to offer that which we divine in its darkness the power to dominate us. Consequently, one of the most human moments is to reduce to our scale objects perceived to be beyond collapse. These objects are not flattened, but a moment of sovereign simplicity reveals their intimacy." That Bataille's observations on transcendence, nothingness, and emptiness betray a Buddhist sensibility is supported by the title of the section of the text in which the aforecited passage is found, "The 'Teacup,' 'Zen,' and the Beloved," written February–April 1944.

240. Eliashiv, *Leshem Shevo we-Aḥlamah: Sefer ha-De'ah*, pt. 2, p. 160. Compare ibid., pt. 2, pp. 66–67, 69.

241. Ibid., pt. 1, p. 101. Compare Eliashiv, *Leshem Shevo we-Aḥlamah: Sefer ha-Kelalim*, pt. 1, p. 202.

242. See Viṭal, *Sha'ar ha-Haqdamot*, p. 355: "Know that at the beginning of the emanation the ten *sefirot* were the incomposite essence [*ha-aṣmut ha-pashuṭ*], and each of them were comprised of ten, but they were not discernible in them. The first three were merciful, and thus they had the capacity to receive the light of the infinite, but the other six points were judgement, and thus they could not receive the light of the infinite when it reached them because it is mercy and they are judgment. Since they could not receive it, they were left without the vitality that enlivens them, and they died and were obliterated. These are the secret of those kings who reigned in the land of Edom and were obliterated and died. These kings were below the kingship of the emanation [*malkhut de-aṣilut*], and what remained of them alone was the eighth king, who was called Hadar, because they were male and female, which are *Tif'eret* and *Malkhut*. Thus, they were in need of rectification, and initially they were made into the aspect of vessels for the first point, which is called *Keter*. By means of this the light was ameliorated, for they disseminate and extend by way of veils and vessels, and they could receive the light. Moreover, now all the ten *sefirot* were discernible, which was not the case in the beginning, as was mentioned." Compare Bachrach, *Emeq ha-Melekh*, 6:10, p. 189. The containment of all the *sefirot* in each of the ten as well as the interrelatedness of all the particulars in the

world of rectification (*olam ha-tiqqun*) are said to issue from the spark of the interconnectivity (*niṣoṣ shel ha-kelilut*) of *Keter*.

243. See ch. 3 at n. 158.

244. Eliashiv, *Leshem Shevo we-Aḥlamah: Sefer ha-De'ah*, pt. 1, p. 149.

245. See ch. 3 at n. 103. The interplay of *Seyn* and *Nichts* in Heidegger also betrays kinship with the depiction of the *Tao* as the source of both being (*yu*) and nonbeing (*wu*), or alternatively expressed, being and nonbeing are juxtaposed as the two aspects of the oneness of the *Tao*, the origin of heaven and earth, the mother of the ten thousand things, according to the formulation in the first verse of the *Daodejing*. For Heidegger's relationship to this seminal text, see ch. 5 n. 10.

246. Caputo, *Mystical Element*, pp. 97–103; Andrews, "Religion Without Why."

247. I have utilized the text and translation as they appear in Schelling, *Ages of the World (Fragment)*, p. 24. See Schelling, *Weltalter*, in *Sämmtliche Werke*, 8:234. And compare the slightly different version in *Der Cherubinischer Wandersmann*, 1:111, in Wehr, *Angelus Silesius*, p. 46: "Die zarte Gottheit ist ein Nichts und Übernichts: / Wer nichts in allem sieht, Mensch, glaube, dieser sichts." For discussion of Schelling's interpretation of this aphorism, see Wolfson, *Alef*, p. 39, and Schmidt-Biggemann, "Schellings 'Weltalter' in der Tradition," p. 72.

248. Schelling, *Ages of the World (Fragment)*, p. 24; *Weltalter*, in *Sämmtliche Werke*, 8:235.

249. Schelling, *Ages of the World (Fragmment)*, p. 25; *Weltalter*, in *Sämmtliche Werke*, 8:236. I must take issue with the thesis of Bielik-Robson, "Mysteries of the Promise," that one should distinguish sharply between a Jewish negative theology (exemplified in her study by the German-Jewish thinkers) and the Christian notion of the hidden God (reflected in the Protestant account derived from Kierkegaard, Schelling, and Barth). I am particularly interested in her argument as it pertains to the alleged difference in the respective conceptions of divine concealment in Schelling and the kabbalah. See pp. 261–62: "In Schelling, we find a truly modern syncretic combination of the pagan-masonic image of the veiled Isis-Jehovah, the Pietist vision of Angry God, deriving mostly from Jakob Boehme, as well as a peculiar echo of the Kabbalistic motif of *tsimtsum*, which Schelling interprets in his own way, very far indeed from the manner of Isaac Luria and his twentieth-century German-Jewish followers: Scholem, Benjamin, and Kafka. The theosophy of Schelling, especially when interpreted by Hadot, constitutes a *symmetrical case of influence* where the Lurianic concept of divine contraction becomes accommodated to the Protestant vision of *deus absconditus*. Here, *tsimtsum* is imagined not as a gentle self-withdrawal, a loving act of giving space for creation, but as an 'angry' (*zornig*) self-condensation that gives the hidden God his solid dark ground of existence and constitutes the violent origin of his inscrutability. . . . This hidden God, identified as the principle of being, is a very far cry indeed from the Lurianic God of *tsimtsum* that our twentieth-century 'Kabbalists' will interpret in terms opposed to the tragic, videlicet, in *messianico-antinomian* terms—as a gesture of withdrawing from being, contrary to the gesture of establishing ontological foundations *for* the created world. It will be one of the tasks of this essay to expose the main difference between Christian (especially Protestant) and Jewish modes of perceiving the divine concealedness as organized around a distinction between the *tragic* and the *messianico-antinomian* vision of divine transcendence" (emphasis in original). As the author acknowledges, she depends on the interpretation of Schelling proffered by Hadot, *Veil of Isis*, pp. 300–3. She is also inspired by the discussion of hieroglyphs in Molitor and Scholem offered by Idel, *Old Worlds*, pp. 110–13. There is much with which one can disagree in Bielik-Robson's argument, but for my purposes I want to stress two points. First, in the Lurianic material itself, as I have documented in this study and elsewhere, the act of constriction is not simply an expression of divine love to create the world. Even in the exoteric version of Luria's teaching offered by Viṭal, the lovingkindness by which the world was created is intricately linked to divine judgment, and in the more esoteric reading, represented by Ibn Ṭabul, as Tishby and Scholem long ago noted (see references cited above, n. 204), the act of constriction is the beginning of the catharsis of evil from the Godhead. It would not be inappropriate to understand the kabbalistic doctrine itself as a way of marking a calamity within the economy of the divine related to the quality of anger or stern judgment, although I admit that the precise taxonomy of tragedy is not used by the kabbalists. Second, the interplay between concealment and disclosure, which is crucial to understanding Schelling and later Heidegger (as noted by Hadot, *Veil of Isis*, p. 305), is a faithful rendering of the Lurianic teaching—itself based on much older kabbalistic sources—wherein the infinite is the concealment that can be revealed only by being concealed. The myth of *ṣimṣum* turns on the paradox, stated explicitly by a host of sixteenth-century kabbalists, that the cause of concealment is disclosure and the cause of disclosure is concealment. See reference to my study cited in the introduction n. 41.

250. Eckhart, *Deutschen und lateinischen Werke*, 2:502 (Predigt 52); *Complete Mystical Works*, p. 424 (Sermon 87). See references cited in ch. 3 n. 74, to which may be added Sells, *Mystical Languages*, pp. 187–92.

251. Compare the aphorism "Die Über-Gottheit" in *Der Cherubinischer Wandersmann*, 1:15, in Wehr, *Angelus Silesius*, p. 33: "Was man von Gott gesagt, das gnüget mir noch nicht, / Die Über-Gottheit ist mein Leben und mein Licht." On the possibility that Schelling was influenced by this passage of Silesius and that his use of the term *ancients* refers to those who proffered the *via negativa* according to which "the supergodhead is not God but the indefinable object of philosophy," see the observations of Bolman in his translation of Schelling, *Ages of the World*, pp. 123–24n17. The use of the Pseudo-Dionysian negative theology is apparent in Schelling, *System der Weltalter*, p. 106: "Gott ist sich selbst nicht wesentlich, darum heißt er auch ἀνούσιος. Das für sich ohnmächtige Sein ist ihm wesentlich; dies gehört mit in den ersten Begriff Gottes, daher heißt er auch τὸ ὑπερούσιον, das Freie vom Wesen. Hier ist auch das wahre Anerkenntniß des Nicht-Nichtseins." While this explanation of Schelling's use of the term *ancients* is plausible, it is also possible that he had in mind the kabbalists in a way similar to the designation of the kabbalah as "the oldest Hebraic philosophy" (*die älteste hebräische Philosophie*) in Baader, *Elementarbegriffe über die Zeit*, p. 35.

252. Schelling, *Ages of the World (Fragment)*, p. 25; *Weltalter*, in *Sämmtliche Werke*, 8:236.

253. Schelling, *Ages of the World (Fragment)*, p. 25; *Weltalter*, in *Sämmtliche Werke*, 8:236.

254. Schelling, *Ages of the World (Fragment)*, p. 26; *Weltalter*, in *Sämmtliche Werke*, 8:237. For an attempt to interpret Schelling's speculation on the absolute will of the divine, which freely begets the beginning, in light of Johannine theology, see Schmidt-Biggemann, *Philosophia Perennis*, pp. 452–53.

255. Schelling, *Ages of the World (Fragment)*, p. 89; *Weltalter*, in *Sämmtliche Werke*, 8:320.

256. Schelling, *Ages of the World (Fragment)*, p. 25; *Weltalter*, in *Sämmtliche Werke*, 8:235–36.

257. Schelling, *Ages of the World (Fragment)*, p. 25 (translation modified); *Weltalter*, in *Sämmtliche Werke*, 8:236. For a similar theme in Eckhart's description of the Father delighting in himself, see Wolfson, "Patriarchy and Motherhood," pp. 1077–78.

258. According to the first edition of Schelling's *Die Weltalter in den Urfassungen von 1811 und 1813*, p. 16, cited by Halfwassen, "Freiheit als Transzendenz," p. 186. See also Schmidt-Biggemann, *Philosophia Perennis*, p. 459. On the erotic nature of the Absolute in Schelling, see Iber, *Das Andere der Vernunft*, pp. 261–64.

259. Žižek, *Most Sublime Hysteric*, p. 171. Following Lacan, Žižek identifies the undesiring desire as the "tranquility and beatitude, pure feminine jouissance, an unlimited, non-totalized Whole, the last state of mystical ecstasy, pure expansion in a void that has no consistency, no foundation, and is therefore an abyss [*Un-Grund*] in the proper sense of the word." I am not certain that the jouissance would not be characterized more accurately as phallic, as I have argued with respect to the kabbalistic material. See Wolfson, "Phallic Jewissance," pp. 325–32. Consider Žižek's own reference to "phallic jouissance" in the passage cited below, n. 279.

260. *Zohar* 3:288b (*Idra Zuṭa*).

261. Hart, *God Being Nothing*, p. 80. Hart's summary of Böhme's view (ibid., p. 81) is remarkably close to the meaning I elicit from the Lurianic kabbalistic sources: "*Desire* is Böhme's most comprehensive term for the restless fermentation or effervescence that comprises the internal force field of the wholly internal life of God, as *turba* (from Greek τυρβα: confusion, disorder, chaos) is the term most often used by him to characterize the simultaneity of creativeness and destruction in the indeterminate abyss of Godhead (the *Ungrund*).We spoke of the determination process, the nonserial progression from indeterminate *Ungrund* through *Abgrund* to determinate *Grund*. . . . For Böhme desire as a *concupi-scienta* is a totalizing preknowing of longing itself, insusceptible of compunction, and that because it is compact of both anticipation and remorse, a concupiscence not yet sufficiently determinate to be erotically sexual. What is yearned and longed for is what is lacked, what is wanted, what is not there. What desire in and out and of itself yields is, effectively, *nothing* (emphasis in original). The kabbalists use sexual and erotic images to characterize the desire of *Ein Sof*, but, as I have noted, this act of jouissance is noetic in nature, and the object of the self-contemplation is the lack within the fullness of nothingness, the site of the contraction that yields that which both is and is not *Ein Sof*, in Hart's terms, the determinateness of the indeterminate Godhead. See also ibid., pp. 88–89.

262. Böhme, *Six Theosophic Points*, p. 12.

263. Ibid., p. 11. On the *Ungrund*, theopoetic desire, and the autogenesis of the other in Böhme, see Wolfson, "Holy Cabbala," pp. 35–47. See also the instructive comments in Baader, *Gesammelte Schriften zur Religionsphilosophie*, 3:188, on Böhme's depiction of the primal will (*Urwillen*) of the hidden being (referred to as *Aensoph*) that is breathed out

(*ausgehaucht*) and grasped through the imagination as the revelation of lust (*Offenbarungslust*). The influence of Böhme's theosophy on Schelling is evident in his Stuttgart lectures of 1810 in which he distinguished two principles of God: the first principle is the primordial force (*die erste Urkraft*) whereby the divine exists as a particular, unique, and individual essence (*wodurch er als ein besonderes, einzelnes, individuelles Wesen ist*), the selfhood (*Selbstheit*) or egoism (*Egoismus*) in God, and the second principle is love (*die Liebe*). If only the former principle existed, then there would be no creation but only God's eternal seclusion and absorption in itself (*eine ewige Verschlossenheit und Vertiefung in sich selbst*), the infinite force of a consuming fire that no creature could endure; in virtue of the second principle, however, God can be properly called the essence of all essences (*das Wesen aller Wesen ist*). See Schelling, *Sämmtliche Werke*, 7:438–39. Regarding this passage, see Tillich, *Philosophical Writing*, p. 81; Franks, "Peirce's 'Schelling-Fashioned Idealism,'" p. 748; and compare the text of Schelling's *Weltalter* cited in ch. 5 at n. 105.

264. The affinity to the kabbalistic *sha'ashu'a*, which results in the condensation of light into the darkness of the vessel, is especially palpable in Böhme's words, *Six Theosophic Points*, pp. 13–15: "God, however, desires only light, viz. the lustre from his heart, that he may shine forth in wisdom, and the whole God thus be manifest in himself, and by the forth-going Spirit out of himself, in the virgin of his wisdom; and that there be an eternal perfect joy, delight and satisfaction in him. . . . We now consider Desire, and find that it is a stern attraction, like an eternal elevation or motion. For it draws itself into itself, and makes itself pregnant, so that from the thin freedom where there is nothing a darkness is produced. For the desiring will becomes by the drawing-in thick and full, although there is nothing but darkness. . . . Thus the will draws the more strongly into itself, and its pregnancy becomes the greater, and yet the darkness cannot comprehend the centre of the word or heart of the ternary; for this centre is a degree deeper in itself, and yet is a band. But the first will, in which the gestation of Nature takes place, is deeper still than the centre of the word, for it arises from the eternal Unground or Nothing; and thus the centre of the heart is shut up in the midst, the first will of the Father labouring to the birth of fire." Compare Böhme, *Mysterium Magnum*, p. 28 (*Sämtliche Schriften*, 7:29): "We acknowledge that God in his own essence is no essence [*das Gott in seinem eigenen Wesen kein Wesen ist*] but only the alone power [*die Kraft*] or the understanding to the essence [*der Verstand zum Wesen*], viz. an unsearchable eternal will, wherein all things are couched; and the same is ALL, and yet is only ONE, but yet desireth to manifest itself, and introduce itself into a spiritual essence, which is effected in the power of the light, through the fire in the love-desire." See ibid., p. 32 (*Sämtliche Schriften*, 7:33): "The holy spiritual love-desire, where the holy will of God hath sharpened itself in the harsh impression, and manifested itself through the fire with the power of the omnipotence, that now brings itself forth through the fire in the light; and so in the powers it is introduced into life and motion, in the desire; and herein the holy generation, and the triumphant kingdom of the great love of God, doth consist, and is manifest." And ibid., p. 36 (*Sämtliche Schriften*, 7:37): "The Father is first the will of the abyss [*der Wille des Ungrundes*]: he is outside of all nature or beginnings: the will to something; which will doth conceive itself into a lubet [*Lust*] to its own manifestation [*Selbst-Offenbarung*]. And the lubet is the conceived power of the will, or of the Father, and it is his Son, heart, and seat: the first eternal beginning [*der erste ewige Anfang*] in the will. And he is therefore called a Son, because he receiveth an eternal beginning in the will, with the will's self-conception [*Selbst-Fassung*]." Compare Böhme, *Signature of All Things*, pp. 13–14 (*Sämtliche Schriften*, 6:9–10): "For the eternal nature has produced nothing in its desire [*Begierde*], except a likeness out of itself [*eine Gleichheit aus sich*]; and if there were not an everlasting mixing, there would be an eternal peace in nature, but so nature would not be revealed and made manifest, in the combat [*Streit*] it becomes manifest; so that each thing elevates itself, and would get out of combat into the still rest, and so it runs to and fro, and thereby only awakens and stirs up combat. . . . We understand that without nature there is an eternal stillness and rest, viz. the Nothing [*das Nichts*]; and then we understand that an eternal will [*ein ewiger Wille*] arises in the nothing, to introduce the nothing into something, that the will might find, feel, and behold itself. For in the nothing the will would not be manifest to itself, wherefore we know that the will seeks itself, and finds itself in itself, and its seeking is a desire, and its finding is the essence of the desire, wherein the will finds itself." And see *Signature of All Things*, p. 22 (*Sämtliche Schriften*, 6:18): "We give you to understand this of the divine essence; without nature God is a mystery, understand in the nothing, for without nature is the nothing, which is an eye of eternity, an abyssal eye [*ungründlich Auge*], that stands or sees in the nothing, for it is the abyss [*Ungrund*]; and this same eye is a will, understand a longing [*Sehnen*] after manifestation [*Offenbarung*], to find

the nothing; but now there is nothing before the will, where it might find something, where it might have a place to rest, therefore it enters into itself, and finds itself through nature." On the dialectic of contraction and attraction in the psychology of desire in Böhme and Oetinger, see Deghaye, "Philosophie," pp. 265–66.

265. Hart, *God Being Nothing*, p. 83.

266. Böhme, *Mysterium Pansophicum*, cited in Schelling, *Philosophical Investigations*, p. 85. For the German text and alternate translation, see Böhme, *Aurora*, pp. 796–97. Compare Baader, *Gesammelte Schriften zur Religionsphilosophie*, 2:116.

267. Wolfson, *Language*, pp. 96–97, and, more recently, *Dream*, p. 247. Compare Schelling, *Ages of the World (Fragment)*, p. 26 (*Weltalter*, in *Sämmtliche Werke*, 8:238): "God, in accordance with its highest self [*höchsten Selbst*], is not a necessarily actual essence [*wirkliches Wesen*], but the eternal freedom to be [*die ewige Freiheit zu seyn*]."

268. Heidegger, *Contributions*, §188, p. 216; *Beiträge*, p. 308.

269. On the "inner connection" of being and seeming, see Heidegger, *Introduction to Metaphysics*, pp. 106–7 (*Einführung in die Metaphysik*, p. 108): "We know that Being opens itself up to the Greeks as *phusis*. The emerging-abiding sway [*aufgehend-verweilende Walten*] is in itself at the same time the appearing that seems. . . . Being means appearing [*Sein heißt Erscheinen*]. Appearing does not mean something derivative, which from time to time meets up with Being. Being essentially unfolds *as* appearing [*Sein west* als *Erscheinen*]" (emphasis in original). Compare Heidegger, *Essence of Human Freedom*, p. 49 (*Vom Wesen der menschlichen Freiheit*, p. 71): "the *look* [*Aussehen*] of the thing comes to expression in its producedness, οὐσια, *the being-present of a being as actually present, consists in the* παρουσία of the εἶδος, *i.e. in the presence of its look. Actuality means producedness, there-standingness as the presence of its look*" (emphasis in original). See Guignon, "Being as Appearing," pp. 38–41; Schoenbaum, "Heidegger's Interpretation of *Phusis*," p. 154; and my own discussion in *Language*, pp. 14–16.

270. Heidegger, *Pathmarks*, p. 90; *Wegmarken*, p. 114.

271. Heidegger, *Pathmarks*, p. 233; *Wegmarken*, p. 306.

272. Heidegger, *Pathmarks*, p. 90; *Wegmarken*, p. 114. It is of interest to note the interpretive annotation that Heidegger added in the fifth edition of 1949, cited in *Pathmarks*, p. 90 note b (*Wegmarken*, p. 114 note a): "Repelling: beings by themselves; gesturing toward: the being of beings" (*ab-weisen: das Seiende für sich; ver-weisen: in das Sein des Seienden*).

273. Heidegger, *On the Way to Language*, p. 39; *Unterwegs zur Sprache*, p. 127.

274. Heidegger, *Pathmarks*, p. 85; *Wegmarken*, pp. 107–8.

275. Heidegger, *Contributions*, §129, pp. 193–94; *Beiträge*, p. 246.

276. Heidegger, *Off the Beaten Track*, p. 85; *Holzwege*, p. 112.

277. Heidegger, *Off the Beaten Track*, p. 85; *Holzwege*, pp. 112–13. For an alternate translation, see Heidegger, *Question*, p. 154.

278. Heidegger's position is highlighted if we consider the following account of the determined nothingness of the infinitesimal in the differential calculus of Hermann Cohen in Anckaert, *Critique of Infinity*, p. 35n37: "Nothingness, or the infinite within differential calculus is not a 'void' nothingness, but the 'nil' designates the something of nothingness. Within the differential, the properties of nothingness are linked to something. Nothingness envisaged is always the nothingness of something, a boundary concept or the indication of the limit. Something is, as it were, latent in the womb of the limit or nothingness. The infinitely small contains, unarticulated, the characteristic of the finite quantity." See my comments on Cohen's idea of the nothing of the differential in Wolfson, *Giving*, pp. 77–78, and references to other scholars cited on pp. 344–45nn322–23.

279. Schelling, *Ages of the World (Fragment)*, p. 107; *Weltalter*, in *Sämmtliche Werke*, 8:344. Compare the passage of Schelling cited in ch. 5 at n. 106, and the Lacanian interpretation of Žižek, *Most Sublime Hysteric*, pp. 171–72: "Divine prehistory begins with an initial *contraction* [*Zusammenziehung*], with its own constriction. This is how God gave Himself a solid, dense foundation, consistency as a Oneness, how He made Himself into something that exists, into a *subject*. This contraction is the supreme act of divine egoism, it is the very opposite of love, of pacifying calm. It is a return back onto the self, a destructive fury that annihilates everything that comes into contact with the divine One. . . . All divine life prior to the birth of the Son, before the appearance of the Word, can be summarized by the back-and-forth between the void of limitless expansion and the force that opposes it, which contracts and limits itself, which folds back in on itself. In the course he taught from 1986 to 1987, Jacques-Alain Miller developed the thesis that, for the neo-Platonists, the initial division of the One of jouissance was—to put it in Lacanian mathemes—the division between φ and α. Isn't Schelling's account of the initial division of the

divine *Un-Grund* between contraction and expansion the same as the division between the φ of phallic jouissance and the α of expansion, of limitless dispersion?" (emphasis in original). Schelling's idea of the contraction of God is explored by Brito, *Création selon Schelling*, pp. 162–88, but the author does not note any affinity to the kabbalistic conception of divine withdrawal. See also the discussion of God's withdrawal from the created in Tritten, *Beyond Presence*, pp. 188–99. The Heideggerian undertones of this dimension of Schelling's thought are made explicit on pp. 189–90: "Spirit, as the being, i.e. Spirit in its propriety, is the proper and divine arrangement or mode of being, that which ought to be, *das Seinsollende*. The modalities, as *posterius*, are its visibility. The *prius*, on the other hand, is invisible. This is ontological difference. The doctrine of the potencies/causes reveals that which conceals itself in their tension. The manifestation of the totality corresponds to the concealing of the deed that brought the totality into being. This hints towards Heidegger's forgetting or oblivion of Being (*Seinsvergessenheit*). Being, even when recognizable via the posterior, still remains hidden, still remains in withdrawal, still remains as more than a mere ground for the consequent beings.... Revelation, rather than emanatory becoming, indicates that which remains concealed or withdrawn even in its becoming cognoscible in its effects, i.e. *per posterius*. This is nothing mystical but occurs daily with every free act of the human individual. The question of Being asks not about some meaning, e.g. the first truth, but about the origination of meaning from nothing, about truth's clearing." Despite denying any mystical import to the paradox of concealment and disclosure in Schelling, Tritten, p. 190n54, draws the reader's attention to a similar dynamic in kabbalistic symbolism, whose influence on Schelling he acknowledges. See ibid., p. 185. On the kabbalistic *ṣimṣum* and the thought of Schelling, see the studies mentioned in the introduction n. 40, and compare Anckaert, *Critique of Infinity*, p. 54: "Schelling wants to think the finite in its relation to absolute thought, without positing the finite inside of the absolute. In Schelling, the unbearable proximity of the infinite essence and the infinite freedom in God is solved by the idea of contraction." On the Schellingian idea of contraction, the Lurianic doctrine of *ṣimṣum*, and the speculation of Rosenzweig, see Schindler, *Zeit, Geschichte, Ewigkeit*, pp. 235–46.

280. Schelling, *Ages of the World (Fragment)*, p. 16; *Weltalter*, in *Sämmtliche Werke*, 8:223.

281. Heidegger, *Off the Beaten Track*, p. 253 (emphasis added); *Holzwege*, pp. 336–37.

282. Heidegger, *Nietzsche*, vol. 4: *Nihilism*, pp. 225, 227 (emphasis in original); *Nietzsche: Zweiter Band*, pp. 332, 335.

283. *Zohar Ḥadash*, 56d (*Qaw ha-Middah*).

284. Heidegger, *Contributions*, §131, p. 196 (emphasis in original); *Beiträge*, p. 249.

285. Heidegger, *Contributions*, §146, p. 211 (emphasis in original); *Beiträge*, p. 268.

286. Heidegger, *Contributions*, §242, pp. 299–300 (emphasis in original), *Beiträge*, pp. 379–80.

287. See Seebohm, "Considerations on 'Der Satz vom Grund,'" and my own comments in Wolfson, *Alef*, pp. 34–46.

288. See introduction nn. 40, 83, 86, 87, 91, 93, 95.

289. Schelling, *Philosophical Investigations*, p. 21; *Philosophische Untersuchungen*, p. 23.

290. Schelling, *On the History*, p. 115 (emphasis in original); *Zur Geschichte*, p. 101. I have altered Bowie's translation; see ch. 5 n. 85.

291. Heidegger, *Country Path Conversations*, pp. 48–50, 68; *Feldweg-Gespräche*, pp. 76–79, 106; Davis, *Heidegger and the Will*, pp. 14–17; Rae, *Ontology in Heidegger and Deleuze*, pp. 110–12.

292. On the attempt to distinguish his own sense of the willing of nonwilling and Eckhart's *Gelassenheit*, see Heidegger, *Country Path Conversations*, p. 70; *Feldweg-Gespräche*, p. 109. Many have discussed the Eckhartian term and its influence on Heidegger. See Caputo, *Mystical Element*, pp. 118–27, 173–83; Davis, *Heidegger and the Will*, pp. 18–20, 122–45, 195–97; Rickey, *Revolutionary Saints*, pp. 81–91; Dalle Pezze, *Martin Heidegger and Meister Eckhart*, pp. 127–88; Blok, "Massive Voluntarism." For an attempt to interpret Schelling's reflections on ecstasy as a precursor to the Heideggerian idea of the eradication of the will to will or not to will, see Ohashi, *Ekstase und Gelassenheit*; Cattin, *Sérénité*, pp. 43–75; and the summary in Davis, *Heidegger and the Will*, p. 332n17.

293. Arendt, *Life of the Mind*, 2:172–94. On the relation between Arendt's notion of the will to will and Heidegger's interpretation of the Nietzschean will to power, see Strong, "America as Exemplar," p. 133. See the criticism of Arendt's attempt to link Heidegger's turning away from the will to a "sudden autobiographical event" in Davis, *Heidegger and the Will*, p. 64.

294. Heidegger, *Country Path Conversations*, p. 50; *Feldweg-Gespräche*, p. 79.

295. Heidegger, *Country Path Conversations*, p. 69; *Feldweg-Gespräche*, p. 106.

296. Heidegger, *Country Path Conversations*, p. 70; *Feldweg-Gespräche*, pp. 108–9. The idea of activity that is no-activity, the will that is not-willing, which I have attributed to Heidegger, can be beneficially

compared to the Taoist idea of *wu-wei*, that is, acting through nonaction or doing through nondoing. See Laozi, *Daodejing*, ch. 2, in *Source Book in Chinese Philosophy*, p. 140: "Therefore the sage manages affairs without action and spreads doctrines without words." See ibid., ch. 3, p. 141: "By acting without action, all things will be in order." Ibid., ch. 10, p. 144: "Can you understand all and penetrate all without taking any action? . . . To act, but not to rely on one's own ability, to lead them, but not to master them—This is called profound and secret virtue (*hsüan-te*)." Ibid., ch. 16, p. 147: "Attain complete vacuity, maintain steadfast quietude." Ibid., ch. 37, p. 158: "Tao invariably takes no action, and yet there is nothing left undone. . . . Simplicity, which has no name, is free of desires. Being free of desires, it is tranquil." Ibid., ch. 43, p. 161: "Non-being penetrates that in which there is no space. Through this I know the advantage of taking no action. Few in the world can understand teaching without words and the advantage of taking no action." Ibid., ch. 48, p. 162: "The pursuit of Tao is to decrease day after day. It is to decrease and further decrease until one reaches the point of taking no action. No action is undertaken, and yet nothing is left undone." Ibid., ch. 63, p. 169: "Act without action. Do without ado. Taste without tasting." Ibid., ch. 64, p. 170: "He who takes action fails. He who grasps things loses them. For this reason the sage takes no action and therefore does not fail. He grasps nothing and therefore he does not lose anything." The paradoxical logic that is the foundation of the ethics of *wu-wei* is made explicit in ch. 22, p. 151: "To yield is to be preserved whole. To be bent is to become straight. To be empty is to be full. To be worn out is to be renewed. To have little is to possess. To have plenty is to be perplexed. Therefore the sage embraces the One and becomes the model of the world." See ibid., ch. 36, p. 157: "In order to contract, it is necessary first to expand. In order to weaken, it is necessary first to strengthen. In order to destroy, it is necessary first to promote. In order to grasp, it is necessary first to give. This is called subtle light." On Heidegger and Taoist thought, see ch. 5 n. 10.

297. Heidegger, *Contributions*, §56, p. 93; *Beiträge*, p. 118. Compare Heidegger's description of suffering in *Basic Questions*, p. 151 (*Grundfragen*, p. 175) as "the carrying out of *the* necessity into which the need of the basic disposition compels, the thoughtful questioning of beings as such. . . . The carrying out of the necessity is here a suffering in the sense of this kind of creative tolerance for the unconditioned. This suffering is beyond activity and passivity as commonly understood" (emphasis in original).

298. Davis, *Heidegger and the Will*, pp. 199, 302–3.

299. Heidegger, *Ponderings VII–XI*, p. 113 (emphasis in original); *Überlegungen VII–XI*, p. 147.

300. Freeman, *Ancilla*, p. 28; Greek text in Kahn, *Art and Thought of Heraclitus*, p. 70, and for an alternate translation and analysis, see ibid., pp. 227–29. My discussion is an abbreviation of a longer analysis in Wolfson, *Giving*, pp. 238–39.

301. Heidegger, *Poetry, Language, Thought*, p. 101; *Holzwege*, p. 279.

302. Heidegger, *Poetry, Language, Thought*, p. 102; *Holzwege*, p. 280.

303. Heidegger, *Principle of Reason*, p. 113 (emphasis in original); *Satz vom Grund*, p. 169. On the supremacy of play in Heidegger's thinking, see O'Leary, "Theological Resonances," pp. 241–43.

304. Heidegger, *Principle of Reason*, p. 35; *Satz vom Grund*, p. 53. See the discussion of this principle in Caputo, "Rose is Without Why"; Caputo, *Mystical Element*, pp. 97–139; Blond, *Heidegger and Nietzsche*, pp. 54–78. See also Ruin, "Leibniz and Heidegger"; and the illuminating study by Cristin, *Heidegger and Leibniz*.

305. Eckhart, *Deutschen und lateinischen Werke*, 1:90–92 (Predigt 5b); Eckhart, *Complete Mystical Works*, p. 110 (Sermon 13b): "Out of this inmost ground, all your works should be wrought without Why. I say truly, as long as you do works for the sake of heaven or God or eternal bliss, from without, you are at fault. . . . For whoever seeks God in a special way gets the way and misses God, who lies hidden in it. But whoever seeks God without any special way gets Him as He is in Himself [*als er in im selber ist*], and that man lives with the Son, and he is life itself [*er ist daz leben selbe*]. If a man asked life for a thousand years, '*Why* do you live?' if it could answer it would only say, 'I live because I live' [*ich lebe dar umbe daz ich lebe*]. That is because life lives from its own ground [*eigenen grunde*], and gushes forth from its own. Therefore it lives without *Why*, because it lives for itself. And so, if you were to ask a genuine man who acted from his own ground, 'Why do you act?' if he were to answer properly he would simply say, 'I act because I act' [*ich würke dar umbe daz ich würke*]" (emphasis in original). On this Eckhartian motif, see Soelle, *Silent Cry*, pp. 59–62.

306. Cristin, *Heidegger and Leibniz*, p. 113.

307. Heidegger, *Ponderings II–VI*, p. 46; *Überlegungen II–VI*, p. 60. This entry begins with reference to the principle of sufficient reason (*Satz vom Grunde*).

308. Heidegger, *Contributions*, §120, p. 187 (emphasis in original); *Beiträge*, p. 237. On the characterization of inceptual thinking as a plight consisting of a lack of plight, compare the comment on learning to think the

essence of *logos* in a more originary way in Heidegger, *Heraclitus*, p. 231 (*Heraklit*, p. 308): "Perhaps in taking this path we will succeed in taking one step in our thinking, though even this one step may still be rather clumsy. Compared to the deluge of results and information that the sciences pour out on a daily basis, what our attempt at thinking accomplishes seems pitiful. It appears as though we are not moving about within any clearly defined domain. And not only does it appear this way—it is indeed the case. The thinking being undertaken here is without a domain. Nevertheless, it moves toward one single place. It appears as though this thinking is of no immediate use to us. And not only does it appear this way—it is indeed the case. This thinking is useless and, in that sense, it is unnecessary. Nevertheless, the unnecessary is the most necessary: it is fulfilled through the essential need and necessity of the human essence, and is thereby unavoidable."

309. Schmidt-Biggemann, *Philosophia Perennis*, p. 447.

310. Heidegger, *Contributions*, §8, p. 25; *Beiträge*, pp. 28–29.

311. Heidegger, *Country Path Conversations*, p. 38; *Feldweg-Gespräche*, p. 59.

312. In "Was ist Metaphysik?" Heidegger cites the passage from Hegel's *Wissenschaft der Logik* as "Pure Being and Pure Nothing are therefore the same" ("*Das reine Sein und das reine Nichts ist also dasselbe*"). See Heidegger, *Pathmarks*, p. 94; *Wegmarken*, p. 120.

313. Heidegger, *Pathmarks*, pp. 94–95; *Wegmarken*, p. 120.

314. Heidegger, *Contributions*, §145, p. 209; *Beiträge*, p. 266.

315. Heidegger, *Contributions*, §47, p. 80 (emphasis in original); *Beiträge*, p. 101. And compare Heidegger, *Über den Anfang*, pp. 11–12: "Das Seiende bleibt so entschieden gegen das Seyn durch dieses von diesem unterschieden, daß dem Seienden nicht einmal eigen bleibt das Nichts; denn nur das Seyn hat die Wesung des Nichts. Das Seiende ist das Nichtslose." The essential occurrence of nothingness belongs to beyng, whereas beings are without nothing, literally, nothingless. The distinction between nothingness (*das Nichts*) and nothingless (*das Nichtslose*) is decisive to the ontological difference. The passage is translated and analyzed in Vallega-Neu, *Heidegger's Poietic Writings*, pp. 108–9. On nothingness and the defiance of the law of noncontradiction, see Morton, "Buddhaphobia," pp. 231–41.

316. Heidegger, *Contributions*, §145, pp. 209–10 (emphasis in original); *Beiträge*, p. 266.

317. Heidegger, *Contributions*, §145, p. 210 (emphasis in original); *Beiträge*, pp. 266–67.

318. Heidegger, *Contributions*, §126, p. 192 (emphasis in original); *Beiträge*, p. 244.

319. Heidegger, *Contributions*, §146, p. 210; *Beiträge*, p. 267.

320. See reference in ch. 2 at n. 159.

321. Heidegger, *Contributions*, §29, p. 53; *Beiträge*, p. 66.

322. Heidegger, *Contributions*, §146, p. 210; *Beiträge*, p. 267. See ch. 5 at n. 16.

323. The expression is used by Polt, *Emergency of Being*, pp. 11–18.

324. Wolfson, *Giving*, p. 78. Here it is apposite to mention the observation of Shimon Gershon Rosenberg, *Faith Shattered and Restored*, p. 84, concerning the image of postmodern freedom and divine infinitude: "It is a freedom emanating from infinity itself, which is so lofty as to not even be the source of worlds. It is not even *present as absence*; in fact, God's infinity represents only the negation of limitations and, through that process, the endowment of freedom" (emphasis added). Shagar's comment is, in my opinion, indebted especially to depictions of infinity in Ḥabad literature, but this is a matter that will have to be pursued elsewhere.

325. Derrida, *Writing and Difference*, p. 95.

5

Autogenesis, Nihilating Leap, and Otherness of the Not-Other

Bestowing and grounding have in themselves the unmediated character of what we call a beginning. Yet this unmediated character of a beginning, the peculiarity of a leap out of the unmediable, does not exclude but rather includes the fact that the beginning prepares itself for the longest time and wholly inconspicuously. A genuine beginning, as a leap, is always a head start, in which everything to come is already leaped over, even if as something disguised. The beginning already contains the end latent within itself.

Heidegger, *Poetry, Language, Thought*

In the previous chapter, I attempted to shed new light on Heidegger's notion of *Seyn* and the kabbalistic *Ein Sof* by placing these two seminal constructs of thinking in dialogue. The juxtaposition yielded particularly interesting affinities between the Heideggerian idea of the bestowing refusal of beyng and the Lurianic doctrine of *ṣimṣum*, the primordial contraction that results in the overflow of the infinite radiance and the opening of the open—the empty space of the vessel—wherein the concealment is concealed and thereby revealed as the concealment that is revealed and thereby concealed. This chapter will continue this path of inquiry as I will probe further into the belonging together of these disparate worldviews, focusing especially on the philosophical problem of alterity that comes to the fore from the shared conception of the nihilating leap to the other that transpires within the nihility of the autogenesis of the not-other.

Being Nothing and the Distinction of Indistinction

For Heidegger, to say that being is nothing[1] does not signify, as it does for Hegel,[2] that "nothingness" is grasped as a "nonbeing" understood as a *negativum*, that is, the cancelation of being, the negative transmuted into a positive,[3] the "determinate negation" (*bestimmte Negation*) that "does not resolve itself into a nullity [*Null*], into abstract nothingness [*abstracte Nichts*]."[4] As Hegel argued in the *Phänomenologie des Geistes* (1807), scepticism "only ever sees pure nothingness [*reine Nichts*] in its result and subtracts from the fact that this nothingness is specifically the nothingness of that *from which it results* [*daß diß Nichts, bestimmt das Nichts dessen ist, woraus es resultirt*]. For it is only when it is taken as the result of that from which it emerges, that it is, in fact, the . . . *determinate* nothingness, one which has a *content*. . . . But when . . . the result is conceived as it is in truth, namely, as a *determinate* negation, a new form has thereby immediately arisen, and in the negation the transition is made through which the progress through the complete series of forms comes about of itself."[5] The pure nothingness that the sceptics are wont to posit as a bare abstraction is, in the final analysis, a nothingness that is determined in relation to that from which it derives, and hence it is, properly speaking, a *determinate nothingness* or a *determinate negation*. There is no such thing as an "empty nothing," only a nothing determined dialectically from the standpoint "*of that from which it results*—a result which contains what was true in the preceding knowledge."[6] Anthropologically speaking, the self-certain spirit (*selbst gewisse Geist*) or the beautiful soul (*schöne Seele*), which is knotted in the contradiction between its pure self and the need to externalize and change into an actual existence (*Wirklichkeit*), dwells in the immediacy (*Unmittelbarkeit*) of that antithesis, "an immediacy which alone is the middle term reconciling the antithesis, which has been intensified to its pure abstraction, and is pure being [*reines Seyn*] or empty nothingness [*leere Nichts*]."[7] Let us consider as well what Hegel infers from the proposition that "*Being and nothing are the same* [Sein und Nichts ist dasselbe]" in the *Enzyklopädie der philosophischen Wissenschaften im Grundrisse* (1830):

> And indeed it is one of the hardest thoughts that thinking imposes upon itself, for being and nothing are the opposite in its complete *immediacy*, that is to say, without there already being *posited* in one of them a determination that would contain its relation to the other. And yet, they *do contain* this determination... namely, the determination that is the same in both. The deduction of their *unity* is thus entirely *analytical*, just as in general the whole progression in philosophizing... is nothing other than merely the *positing* of what is already contained in a concept.—But as correct as the unity of being and nothing is, so it is *also* correct that *they are absolutely different*, i.e. that the one is *not* what the other is. However, since at this point the difference has not yet become determinate (for being and nothing are still what is immediate), how it bears on them is something *that cannot be said* [*das* Unsagbare], it is something merely *meant* [*die bloße* Meinung].[8]

Heidegger parts company with Hegel by arguing that his idea of the nothing "is not a negativity because it never takes seriously the not [*Nicht*] and the nihilating [*Nichten*],—it has already sublated the not into the 'yes.'"[9] Trying to forge a suitable language to describe the metaontological insight into how "beyng belongs to the 'not' [*gehört zum Nicht das Seyn*]," Heidegger insists that the nothing is the "essential trembling of beyng itself," the nonbeyng (*Nichtseyn*) that "*is* more than any being [seiender *als jegliches Seiende*],"[10] the "actually nihilating" (*eigentlich Nichtige*)[11] that has the "quality of the 'not' [*Nichthafte*]" but which "is in no way whatever mere 'nothingness' [*bloße 'Nichts'*], as the latter is grasped through the representational denial of something [*die vorstellende Verneinung des Etwas*], on the basis of which denial one then says: nothingness 'is' not [*das Nichts 'ist' nicht*]."[12] We can say, therefore, that being is not (*das Sein ist nicht*) as long as we do not equate it with nothingness (*wir es nicht dem Nichts gleichsetzen*).[13]

Heidegger already opined in "Was ist Metaphysik?" that any question about nothing steadfastly presupposes that nothing is something that "is." If nothing is posited as the negation of being, it is still circumscribed within the metaphysical antinomy of being and nonbeing. Heidegger draws the obvious conclusion from this logical quandary: "Interrogating the nothing—asking what and how it, the nothing, is—turns what is interrogated into its opposite. The question deprives itself of its own object."[14] In an effort to be liberated from this impasse, Heidegger distinguishes nonbeing (*Nichtsein*), which "*essentially occurs in the unessence* [Unwesen],"[15] and beyng (*Seyn*), which "*essentially occurs as permeated with negativity* [nichthaft]." Insofar as beyng is so described, it "*at the same time makes possible and compels otherness* [Andersheit]." Nonbeing is the other to beyng but only as the other of the not-other, that is, *this other that is the other of itself* (*Denn dieses Andere ist das Andere seiner selbst*).[16] Alterity is thus the outcome of the negativity of the nonessence with which the essence of beyng is saturated. In light of this understanding of alterity, we can understand a remark of Heidegger in the *Schwarze Hefte*, "The beginning of the other, however, is obscure—yet already this remains and becomes an essential event: that the other of another beginning and of its plight is experienced [*daß das Andere eines anderen Anfangs und seiner Not erfahren wird*]. To be sure, that requires an intrinsic overcoming [*die innere Überwindung*] of the machinational essence of being [*des machenschaftlichen Wesens des Seyns*]."[17] The other beginning, which will take place when the metaphysical nature of the first beginning is overcome, is clouded in obscurity insofar as it is marked by an alterity so absolute that it can be expressed only by the negative *Not*, the misery or distress of the beginning that does not begin with something that is negated but whose beginningness is the absolute naught that is wrought by the nihilation of the exhaustively fecund otherness.

Heidegger does not subscribe to a dialectical approach to reconcile the antithesis between being and nonbeing, but he is grappling with the same philosophical dilemma that plagued the German idealists: how do we account for otherness in the essence that comprises the nonessence as an integral part of its essence? From the standpoint of the kabbalists, how do we mark the beginning as a transition from the infinite, which purportedly comprehends everything limitlessly, to the finite that is independent and subject to the limitation of space and time? An earlier articulation of the difficulty, and one that may have had a direct influence on some of the thirteenth-century kabbalists, who, in turn, may have shaped the discourse of the Christian kabbalah that indirectly influenced Heidegger, is found in the following delineation of Catholic faith in John Scotus Eriugena's *Periphyseon*:

> God is infinite and more than infinite—for He is the Infinity of infinities—and simple more than simple—for He is the Simplicity of all simple things—and they believe and understand that there is nothing with Him, since He is the periphery of all things that are and that are not and that can be and that cannot be and that appear to be either contrary or opposite *to Him*, not to say like and unlike: for He is the Likeness of like things and the Unlikeness of unlike things, the Oppositeness of opposites, the Contrariness of contraries. For He gathers and puts all things together by a beautiful and ineffable harmony into a single concord: for those things which in the parts of the universe seem to be opposed and contrary to one another are in accord and in tune [when] they are viewed in the most general harmony of the universe itself.[18]

What is the import of the statement that God is "infinite and more than infinite" (*enim deum infinitum esse plusque quam infinitum*)? What is more infinite than infinite? Relatedly, what does it mean to confess that God is "simple more than simple" (*simplicem et plus quam simplicem*)? What is simpler than simple? These paradoxical assertions are meant to underscore that the infinite includes even its own opposite, albeit in a manner that is no longer opposite, since all opposites coincide within it.[19] Infinity, in short, implies nothing exists outside God.[20]

From the assertion that the infinite is both the "likeness of like things" (*similium similitudo*) and the "unlikeness of unlike things" (*dissimilitudo dissimilium*), we can adduce that there can be nothing that is truly opposite to it, no sense of an authentic other. This is the meaning of the characterization of infinity as the "oppositeness of opposites" (*oppositorum oppositio*) and the "contrariness of contraries" (*contrariorum contrarietas*): the opposite of oppositeness is the dissolution of opposition, the contrary of contraries is the disbanding of contrariness. What is divergent and discordant from the perspective of the finite is identical and concordant from the perspective of the infinite. As Nicholas of Cusa famously put it in *De visione dei* (1453), perhaps having been influenced by Eriugena, whose impact is noticeable as well in Azriel of Gerona,[21] "Observe, next, that because of God's supreme simplicity whatever things are predicated of Him cannot differ really, even though we apply different words to God in accordance with different forms. But since God is the Absolute Form of all formable forms [*ratio absoluta omnium formabilium rationum*], He enfolds [*complicat*] in Himself the forms of all things. . . . So although on the basis of one form we ascribe to Him moving and on the basis of another form we ascribe to Him remaining-at-rest, nevertheless because He is Absolute Form in which all otherness is oneness [*omnis alteritas est unitas*] and all diversity is identity [*omnis diversitas identitas*], there cannot be in Him a diversity of forms; for this diversity, as we conceive it, is not identity."[22] Reiterating the point in a second passage from this treatise, Cusanus writes, "In Infinity the oppositeness of opposites is present without oppositeness [*In infinitate est opposito oppositorum sine oppositione*].... And so, there is not anything that is other than You or different from You or opposed to You. For Infinity is not compatible with otherness [*alteritatem*], because there is not anything outside it, since it is Infinity. For Absolute Infinity includes and encompasses all things."[23]

In Nicholas of Cusa's later works, this idea is expressed by the expression "not-other" (*non aliud*). Thus, in *De li non aliud* (1461), the dialogue in which Cusanus set out to clarify this concept most extensively, he cleverly states that not-other cannot be other than not other, which is to say, every aspect of otherness is assimilated and thereby obliterated in that which is not other, and hence the not-other cannot be defined by means of any other.[24] When the multiplicity of the world is perceived through the understanding (*per intellectum*), the mind contemplates the essences (*essentias*) by which the assorted substances are distinguished. However, when those essences are viewed above understanding (*supra intellectum*) and prior to their being discriminated as other (*ante aliud*), that is, prior to the specification of alterity as distinct from unity, then the mind contemplates "no other than the simple Form of essences," which is called "*Not-other* or the Essence of essences, since it is whatever is observed in all the essences."[25] Insofar as there can be no other to what is not-other, then even the distinction between distinction and indistinction is no longer viable: "For in the case of God we must, as far as possible, precede contradictories and embrace them in a simple concept. For example, in God we must not conceive of distinction and indistinction as two contradictories but [must conceive of] them as antecedently present in their own most simple Beginning, where distinction is not anything other than indistinction; and then we will conceive more clearly that the trinity and the oneness are the same thing. For where distinction is indistinction, trinity is oneness; and, conversely, where indistinction is distinction, oneness is trinity."[26]

In *De venatione sapientiae* (1463), Cusanus argues—in an apparently tautological manner—since the "Not-other is not other than Not-other," it is the name that defines itself and all things.[27] The name is attributed to God, who "is not *other* than other, because He defines other. For if Not-other is removed, other does not remain.... Therefore, since Not-other is prior to other, it cannot be made other, and it is actually everything which is at all possible to be." Significantly, in the continuation of the passage, Cusanus emphasizes that the Not-other "does not signify as much as does 'same.' Rather, since same is not other than same, Not-other precedes it and all nameable things. And so, although God is named 'Not-other' because He is not *other* than any other, He is not on this account the same as any other."[28] Cusanus is here trying to offset the charge of pantheism by stressing that the not-otherness of God implies that God is not the same as the same other. Inversely, from the not-other we may deduce that the infinite is identical with the finite precisely because the finite is not identical with the infinite. Hence, Cusanus had already written in *De visione dei*, "Infinity is all things in such way that it is none of them."[29] In another section of that book, he expressed this idea by noting that the absolute face—the "face of faces" (*facies facierum*) and the "truth of all faces" (*veritatem omnium facierum*)—is both "equal to each and every face" and "not equal to any face." All faces, therefore, must be considered images of the face that is uncontractible (*incontrahibilis*) and imparticiable (*imparticipabilis*). It follows, moreover, that every face that looks at the divine face will see "nothing that is *other* than itself or *different* from itself, because it sees its own Truth," but this is so because the truth it sees in the gaze of the face cannot be limited to or participated in by any one gazing face.[30]

Writ large, the cosmos is the locus of theophany, the mirror through which the invisible is specularized—not through physical sight but through mental or intellectual vision—the "contracted shadow" (*in umbra hic contracta*) by which the truth, free of all contraction, is exhibited.[31] As Cusanus ecstatically proclaims, "You have led me to the place where I see Your Absolute Face to be the natural Face of every nature [*videam faciem tuam absolutam esse faciem naturalem omnis naturae*], the Face which is the Absolute Being of all being [*absoluta entitas omnis esse*]."[32] The apophatic entanglement[33] of God and world implied in this statement generates the paradox that the world is God to the extent that God is not the world.[34] In *De docta ignorantia* (1440), Cusanus argued that the universe may be viewed as a *coincidentia oppositorum* of the limited and unlimited, the infinite finitude, an oxymoron captured in the dictum *maximum simul contractum et absolutum*. From the point of view of reason dominated by the logic of the law of noncontradiction, it is absurd to say that the maximum is simultaneously the contracted and the absolute, but through the knowledge of faith, designated alternately as the "learned ignorance" or the spiritual vision of the "absolute seeing power," one apprehends that God as *maximum absolutum* and the universe as *maximum contractum* are indistinguishably the same by virtue of their difference.[35] This implies, moreover, that the finite can expose the infinite only insofar as the infinite is obfuscated by the finite, echoing the kabbalistic approach to the relationship between *Ein Sof* and the world, and notably a relationship assessed as an expression of kenosis, the act of *ṣimṣum*, to which I have already referred. Nature, on this score, is the not-other that cannot be other than and therefore not other in relation to the not-other.

For Cusanus, this is the deepest philosophical meaning of the Christological dogma of filiation, the mystery that facilitates the possibility of deification through the overcoming of the other in which the sameness of the other is no more the same than the otherness of the same is other.

> Therefore, sonship is the removal of all otherness and all difference and is the resolution of all things into one thing—a resolution that is also the imparting of one thing unto all other things. And this imparting is *theosis*. Now, God is one thing in which all things are present as one; He is also the imparting of oneness unto all things, so that all things are that which they are; and in the [aforementioned] intellectual intuition *being something one in which are all things* and *being all things in which there is something one* coincide. Accordingly, we are rightly deified when we are exalted to the point that in a oneness [of being] we are (1) a oneness in which are all things and (2) a oneness [which is] in all things.[36]

In consonance with Cusanus, the kabbalists would accede that within the contours of infinity—about which it can be said that there is nothing apart from it (*ein shum davar zulato*)[37]—we cannot distinguish the difference of identity and the identity of difference. The infinite is thus compared to a circle in which "*other* and *different* are not opposed to identity."[38] Within the absolute simplicity of the maximum essence, the distinction between geometric shapes collapses, for the "infinite line is actually a sphere," in the same manner that absolute possibility coalesces with absolute actuality.[39] This is a particular instantiation of Cusanus's *coincidentia oppositorum*, a coincidence that is, as he writes in *De visione dei*, "contradiction without contradiction" (*contradictio sine contradictione*), for "just as in oneness otherness is present without otherness [*alteritas in unitate est sine alteritate*], because in oneness otherness is oneness, so in Infinity contradiction is present without contradiction [*contradictio in infinitate est sine contradictione*], because in Infinity contradiction is Infinity." God, therefore, is called the "oppositeness of opposites," which implies "oppositeness without oppositeness" (*oppositio oppositorum est oppositio sine oppositione*).[40] In *De li non aliud*, Cusanus goes as far as to say that even Aristotle would have acknowledged this truth and the collapse of opposites implied thereby: "For just as he saw that the contradiction in contradictories is a contradiction of the contradictories, so prior to the contradictories he would have seen Contradiction before the expressed contradiction (even as the theologian Dionysius saw God as the Opposition-of-opposites without opposition [*oppositorum oppositionem sine oppositione*]; for it is not the case that anything is opposed to opposition prior to [there being any] opposites) [*Oppositioni enim ante opposita nihil opponitur*]."[41]

That there is no opposition before opposition is opposed, and the corollary axiom that there is no opposition that can oppose the opposition of opposites without opposition, well capture what many kabbalists have articulated with respect to *Ein Sof*, the unnamable infinity in relation to which there is no contrary.[42] At variance with the Levinasian distinction between totality and infinity, briefly discussed in chapter 2, kabbalists would have readily adopted Cusanus's characterization of infinity as a totality that is "prior to everything which is an other and is all in all [*ante quantitatem atque omne aliud et in omnibus omnia*]."[43] Interestingly, the precise language of Cusanus is detectable in Abraham Cohen de Herrera's remark in *Puerta del cielo* concerning "the theological approach which discusses the First Cause by contradictories, without contradiction, or by contradictions that do not contradict, as if saying that it is the first and the last infinite being and the end of everything, the greatest because it is vast and the least because it is indivisible, or as they say, the maximum and the minimum."[44]

Negating the Negation and the Differentiating Indifference

Centuries later Hegel offered an incisive analysis of the problem raised by Cusanus when he wrote in the *Wissenschaft der Logik* that the infinite (*Unendliche*) is "burdened with the opposition to the finite, and this finite, as an other [*als Anderes*], remains a real existence [*reale Daseyn*] even though in its being-in-itself [*Ansichseyn*], in the infinite, it is at the same time posited as sublated [*aufgehoben*]; this infinite is that which is not finite [*Nicht-endliche*]—a being [*Seyn*] in the determinateness of negation [*Bestimmtheit der Negation*]. Contrasted with the finite, with the series of existent determinacies, of realities, the infinite is indeterminate emptiness [*unbestimmte Leere*], the beyond of the finite [*Jenseits des Endlichen*], whose being-in-itself is not in its existence (which is something determinate)."[45] Considering the matter from the point of view of the connection of the infinite and the finite, "the infinite is only the *limit* of the finite and thus only a determinate, *itself finite infinite* [*selbst endliches Unendliches*]."[46] Expanding the point in another passage from this treatise, Hegel writes,

> This determination of the true infinite cannot be captured in the already criticized *formula* of a *unity* of the finite and the infinite [*einer Einheit des Endlichen und Unendlichen*]; *unity* is abstract, motionless self-sameness [*bewegungslose Sichselbstgleichheit*], and the moments are likewise unmoved beings. But, like both its moments, the infinite is rather essentially only as *becoming* [*Werden*], though a becoming now *further determined* in its moments. Becoming has for its determinations, first, abstract being and nothing [*abstracte Seyn und Nichts*]; as alteration, it has existence [*Daseyende*], something and other [*Etwas und Anderes*]; now as infinite, it has finite and infinite, these two themselves as in becoming. This infinite, as being-turned-back-unto-itself [*In-sich-Zurückgekehrtseyn*], as reference of itself to itself, is *being*—but not indeterminate, abstract being, for it is posited as negating the negation [*negirend die Negation*]; consequently, it is also *existence* or "*thereness*" [*Daseyn*], for it contains negation in general and consequently determinateness. It *is*, and *is there*, present before us [*Es ist, und ist da, present, gegenwärtig*]. . . . True infinity, thus taken in general as *existence* [*Daseyn*] posited as *affirmative* in contrast to abstract negation, is *reality* [*Realität*] in a higher sense than it was earlier as *simply* determined; it has now obtained a concrete content [*Inhalt*]. It is not the finite which is the real [*Reale*], but rather the infinite.[47]

Hegel notes that the image of progression, which implies advancing in a straight line between two limits, cannot be attributed to the infinite, since the latter is bent back on itself in a manner more befitting the image of the circle, "the line that has reached itself, closed and wholly present, without *beginning* and *end*."[48] The mimetic and self-referential movement—the line that has become a circle—is characterized by Hegel as *Schein*, the glimmer of the nonessential (*Unwesentliche*), the "leftover of being" (*Reste des Seyns*), contained in the determinateness of the indeterminate essence (*Wesen*), "an infinite self-contained movement which determines its immediacy [*Unmittelbarkeit*] as negativity [*Negativität*] and its negativity as immediacy, and is thus the shining of itself within itself [*das Scheinen seiner in sich selbst*]. In this, in its self-movement [*Selbstbewegung*], essence is *reflection*. . . . In the becoming of being, it is being which lies at the foundation of determinateness, and determinateness is reference to *an other*. Reflective movement is by contrast the other as *negation in itself*, a negation which has being only as self-referring. Or, since this self-referring is precisely this negating of negation [*Negiren der Negation*], what we have is *negation as negation*, negation that has its being in its being-negated [*Negirtseyn*], as shine."[49]

The other, consequently, "is not *being with negation* or limit, but *negation with negation*. But the *first* over against this other, the immediate or being, is only this self-equality itself of negation [*Gleichheit selbst der Negation*], the negated negation, the absolute negativity."[50] Immediacy is the self-equality of becoming—the unity of being and nothing, the one that is "being as immediate and as reference to nothing," and the other that is "nothing as immediate and as reference to being"[51]—that is the "reflective movement of essence," the "*movement from nothing to nothing and thereby back to itself* [*Bewegung von Nichts zu Nichts, und dadurch zu sich selbst zurück*]." The other that comes to be in this transition (*Übergehen*) "is not the non-being of a being [*das Nichtseyn eines Seyns*] but the nothingness of a nothingness [*das Nichts eines Nichts*], and this, to be the negation of a nothingness [*die Negation eines Nichts*], constitutes being [*Seyn*].—Being is only as the movement of nothingness to nothingness, and so it is essence [*Wesen*]; and this essence does not *have* this movement *in itself*, but the movement is rather the absolute shine [*Schein*] itself, the pure negativity which has nothing outside it which it would negate but which rather negates only its negative, the negative which is only in this negating."[52]

Drawing the Christological implications of the Hegelian dialectic whereby being and nothing are unified in their sublated distinguishedness (*Unterschiedenheit*) as the not-other of each other's other, Merleau-Ponty noted that "to get to the end, the negation is carried to the absolute, becomes negation of itself; at the same time being sinks back to the pure positive, the negation concentrates itself beyond it as absolute subjectivity—and the dialectical movement becomes pure identity of the opposites, ambivalence. It is thus that in Hegel, God, defined as abyss or absolute subjectivity, negates himself in order that the world be, that is, in order that there be a view upon himself that would not be his own and to which he would appear as posterior to being; in other words, God makes himself man—so that the philosophy of Hegel is an ambivalence of the theological and the anthropological."[53] If we were to apply this to the kabbalistic explanation of the emergence of the sefirotic emanations from *Ein Sof*, then the former would constitute the anthropological configuration of the latter, the absolute subjectivity that is the discriminate other in relation to the indiscriminate unity of the abyss that absorbs and thereby nullifies the otherness of every other, the essence that is the determination of what is differentiated from self as a mode of self-determining that relates itself to itself.[54] According to this schematic, the divine gradations would not be designated the nonbeing of being but rather the negation of the nothingness of nothing, the absolute affirmation of pure negativity, that is, the negative that negates and thus affirms the negation of its own negation. The kabbalists, on this reading, would be ensnared in the logic of the dialectic, falling back, in Merleau-Ponty's words, "into the ambivalent image of the Nothingness that sacrifices itself in order that Being be and of the Being that, from the depths of its primacy, tolerates being recognized by the Nothingness."[55]

The thinker whose views on this topic bear an even closer resemblance to the theosophic ruminations of the kabbalists, and the one closer to Heidegger, was Schelling. In *Vom Ich als Princip der Philosophie oder über das Unbedingte in menschlichen Wissen* (1795), Schelling expressed the matter of the beginning in Fichtean terms as the absolute I (*absolute Ich*) going out of itself and opposing a Not-I (*Nicht-Ich*) to itself.[56] Nature is the self-limitation of the infinite and unconditional self-positing I, which divides into the I and Not-I. The unconditioned I may posit the Not-I out of its own freedom, but the question that perseveres is if this Not-I can procure an unalloyed sense of alterity. Within an emanative-monistic scheme, is it possible for the other not to be reduced to an aspect of the same? In *Philosophische Briefe über Dogmatismus und Kriticismus* (1795), Schelling wondered whether it was imaginable to step out of the Absolute and move toward something that is opposed to it.[57] Similarly, in *System des transzendentalen Idealismus* (1800), Schelling argued that the principle to explain everything in transcendental philosophy is that the subjective is the first and only ground of all reality,[58] whence it follows that there is no absolute principle of being behind the theorizing of an ultimate ground of knowledge, the principle of knowledge within knowledge, the limit beyond which one cannot venture. "The claim that there is a highest principle of knowledge is not a *positive* claim, like that on behalf of an absolute principle of being, but a *negative, limiting* one, amounting merely to this: There is an ultimate of some sort, from which all knowledge begins, and beyond which there is no *knowledge*."[59]

For the idealist philosopher the primary knowledge, the fixed point to which everything is attached and from which everything springs forth—the *punctum saliens*—is the "absolute that is both cause and effect of itself—in the absolute identity of the subjective and the objective, which we call nature, and which in its highest potentiality is again nothing else but self-consciousness."[60] Positioning self-consciousness, which is cause and effect in tandem, as the beginning, avoids the logical problem of the infinite regress, but it leaves open the question if we can speak in any meaningful sense of alterity with respect to the materiality vis-à-vis the ideality of nature. Ostensibly, the mind would be entrenched in a form of circular reasoning from which there is no exit. As Schelling lays it out, "*the original content* of knowledge presupposes the *original form*, and conversely, *the original form of knowledge* presupposes its original content, and both are mutually conditioned by each other.—For this purpose we should require to discover in the intellect itself a point at which, by one and the same indivisible act of primordial cognition, both content and form are generated. . . . *The principle of philosophy must thus be one in which content is conditioned by form, and form in turn by content*—not the one presupposing the other, but each in reciprocity."[61]

Diagrammed mathematically, the proposition A = A presupposes the subject A—irrespective of whether A corresponds to something really existing, merely imagined, or even impossible to conceive—the knowledge of which advances beyond the identity of thinking and makes possible the coinciding of the objective and the subjective, the material and the formal, represented by the synthetic judgment A = B.[62] But the latter formula is still subsumed under the identitarian equation of A with itself, as we can infer from the following passage:

> The proposition *self* = *self* fulfills at the same time the second requirement imposed upon the principle of knowledge, that it should simultaneously ground both the form and the content of knowledge. For the supreme formal principle, A = A, is indeed only possible through the *act* expressed in the proposition *self* = *self*—through the act of thinking that becomes an object to itself and is identical with itself. Thus, so far from the *self* = *self* falling under the principle of identity, it is rather the latter that is conditioned by the former.[63]

The reciprocal circularity is cast in temporal terms in Schelling's description of the absolute beginning as the preconscious yearning of the will to be beyond itself that produces the contemplation of self, the duplication that gives rise to difference and identity,[64] a process mirrored in the reflection with which all philosophy begins: "For it is through self-consciousness that all limitation originates, and thus all time as well, this original act cannot itself occur in time; hence, of the rational being as such, one can no more say that it has begun to exist, than that it has existed for all time; the self as self is absolutely eternal, that is, outside time altogether."[65] Through philosophical rumination the self always harbors the possibility of voluntarily interrupting the involuntary time-series and participating in the "wholly extratemporal act whereby all time is first constituted,"[66] the beginning that is the timeless act of self-consciousness that gives all things existence, that appears objectively as *eternal becoming* and subjectively as a *producing without limit*.[67]

Schelling makes a pivotal turn in *Philosophische Untersuchungen über das Wesen menschlichen Freiheit* (1809), where he addressed the problem in language that reveals an astonishing kinship to kabbalistic theosophy in its effort to sketch how the inclusivity of the infinite is such that it must include its own exclusivity, that is, the capacity to be less than infinite. The Schellingian formulation reverberates as well with Böhme's description of the *Ungrund* as the abyss or the nothing, the eternal wisdom without essence, which through the craving (*Sucht*) of the will as the counterwill (*Wiederwille*)—in Schelling's locution, the *divine unwill* (*der* göttliche Unwille)[68]—gives birth to itself from within itself, the contractive self-darkening of the imagination that generates the ground of the primal and unfathomable nonground of which it can be said that it, too, is without essence, and thus, like an image in the mirror, it both exists and does not exist,[69] a conception that may have been indebted to the tenet of Jewish esotericism concerning the coeternality of the nothingness of the infinite and the nothingness of the will, an idea that likely was mediated to the legendary shoemaker from Görlitz through Christian kabbalah.[70] "In the circle out of which everything becomes," writes Schelling, "it is no contradiction that that through which the One is generated may itself be in turn begotten by it. Here there is no first and last because all things mutually presuppose each other, no thing is another thing and yet no thing is not without another thing. God has in himself an inner ground of his existence [*innern Grund seiner Existenz*] that in this respect precedes him in existence; but, precisely in this way, God is again the *prius* of the ground in so far as the ground, even as such, could not exist if God did not exist *actu*." What is distinct and divided from God cannot come to be in God but must become "in a ground different from God." Since nothing is truly outside of God, however, "this contradiction can only be resolved by things having their ground in that which in God himself is not *He Himself* [*was in Gott selbst nicht* Er Selbst ist], that is, in that which is the ground of his existence. If we want to bring this way of being closer to us in human terms, we can say: it is the yearning [*Sehnsucht*] the eternal One feels to give birth to itself [*sich selbst zu gebären*]. The yearning is not the One itself but is after all co-eternal [*gleich ewig*] with it."[71]

The paradox of the all-encompassing One longing to be other than itself can only be explained by imagining an aspect that is coeternal with but not identical to the One—the nondivine that is contained in the divine as the foundation of its existence—an aspect that Schelling also identifies as the will (*Wille*), the "primal Being [*Ursein*] to which alone all predicates of Being apply: groundlessness [*Grundlostigkeit*], eternality [*Ewigkeit*], independence from time [*Unabhängigkeit von der Zeit*], self-affirmation [*Selbstbejahung*]."[72] It is through this "punitive will" (*ahndender Wille*)[73]—a pure and orderly will that comprises the capriciousness of the contra-will[74]—that the "eternal act of self-revelation" (*ewigen Tat der Selbstoffenbarung*) of the infinite is enacted in the finite world of nature.[75] Schelling's depiction of the will in relation to the One bears an extraordinary similarity to the kabbalistic description of *Keter* in relation to *Ein Sof*, which in turn may have influenced the theosophical ruminations of Böhme, as we see, for instance, in this passage:

> Thus the mirror of the eternal eye shines forth in the will, and generates to itself another eternal ground within itself. This is its centre or heart, from which the seeing continually takes its rise from eternity, and through which the will becomes moving and directive, namely of that which the centre brings forth. For all is comprised in the will, and is an essence, which, in the eternal Unground, eternally takes its rise in itself, enters into itself, grasps itself in itself, and makes the centre in itself; but with that which is grasped passes out of itself, manifests itself in the brightness of the eye, and thus shines forth out of the essence in itself and from itself.[76]

Like the kabbalistic *Ein Sof*, the Böhmean *Ungrund* is the "place of all beings and the fulness of all things," but it has no place of its own because it is nothing.[77] Out of this nothing there emerges the devouring fire as the *centrum naturae* that results from the desire of the *Ungrund* to give itself a *Grund*, an idea that is reflected in Schelling's identification of a dark core in divinity, which is part of and yet apart from God, as a way to reconcile the immanence of all in God with the independent existence of evil that is necessary to account for human freedom.[78]

Significantly, in the *Philosophische Untersuchungen*, Schelling compares his conception of evil with the view of Franz von Baader, the person through whom he was introduced to Böhme and who was also well versed in kabbalistic lore: "As disease is admittedly nothing having inherent being [*nichts Wesenhaftes*], really only an apparent picture of life and merely a meteoric appearance of it—an oscillation between

Being and non-Being [*ein Schwanken zwischen Sein und Nichtsein*]—yet announces itself nevertheless as something very real to feeling [*Gefühl*], so it is with evil. In more recent times Franz Baader especially has emphasized this concept of evil, the only correct one, according to which evil resides in a positive perversion [*Verkehrtheit*] or reversal [*Umkehrung*] of the principles, and has explained this through profound analogies, in particular, that of disease."[79] Schelling's portrayal of Baader is corroborated by the latter's explanation of evil as the inhuman that is part and parcel of being human. Given the affinity between Baader's view and the kabbalistic perspective, I will cite the passage in full:

> Thus, there is nonetheless evil—an evil spirit—in man, the recognition of which is independent of all theories and histories: How did this evil spirit come into man or arise in him? And this evil spirit is independent of all direction as to how to expel it again from him, and so forth; but also to the same degree [it] is independent of all theories and systems of those philosophers who would like to deny this evil just because they are not able to explain it. Whereas this evil is by no means neither so dumb nor of so bad [and] common ancestry as they would like to make us believe; and they may only do this to conceal the gap in their system. It is admittedly certain and undeniable that with the divine drive—inasmuch as man silences it in himself little by little—also the divine art (the talent for art) disappears, and that man becomes more unskilled, more inept, also more incomprehensible, more unreasonable or less insightful in respect to the good to the same extent that he becomes tired with it. But then, on the one hand, the insight into that which leads to good still remains with man and that which leads away from it (to evil), and the misuse of this insight to advance good, which falls together with the use of the same insight to advance evil, is exactly this misuse of this insight and of reason; and, on the other hand, however, we observe how reason in such a man admittedly turns into unreason [*zu einer Unvernunft*] but only in that positive sense of a perversity and corruption in which one says that that which is human turns into that which is inhuman [*zum Unmenschlichen*], nature turns into unnature [*zur Unnatur*], form and shape turns into that which is unshaped [*zur Ungestalt*].[80]

Despite the kinship between Baader's perspective on evil and what may be elicited from the kabbalists as well as from Böhme,[81] in another passage in the *Philosophische Untersuchungen*, Schelling distinguishes the dualistic approach that assumes the existence of an evil being alongside the good and the emanative explanation of the kabbalists whereby the evil emanates from the good: "Thus, in order to prove that there are only two manners of explaining evil—the dualistic, according to which there is assumed an evil fundamental being [*Grundwesen*], no matter with which modifications, under or next to the good one, and the Kabbalistic, according to which evil is explained through emanation and distancing—and that every other system therefore must abolish the distinction between good and evil; in order to prove this, nothing less would be required than the full power of a deeply thought-out and thoroughly developed philosophy."[82] Curiously, the position of Baader to which Schelling acquiesces can be found in kabbalistic sources as a challenge to the more monistic orientation.

Distinguishing himself from Fichte in *Zur Geschichte der neueren Philosophie*, a text compiled by the author's son based on lectures delivered in Munich (1833–34), Schelling writes that the beginning is not the finite or human I but the infinite subject (*unendliche Subjekt*) that "can *never* stop being subject, can never be lost in the object, become mere object." The "pure substantiality" (*reinen Substantialität*) of the absolute subject (*das Subjekt überhaupt*) is "free of all being [*frei von allem Sein*], and although *not* nothing [*nicht nichts*], yet *as* nothing [*als nichts*]. Not nothing because it is yet subject, *as* nothing because not object, because it does not exist in objective being [*weil nicht im gegenständlichen Sein seiend*]." The beginning is marked, therefore, by the unconditional and infinite subjectivity (*Subjektivität*) "becoming-finite" and "becoming-object."[83] It follows that in its "pure essentiality" (*reinen Wesentlichkeit*), the subject is deemed "*as* nothing [*als nichts*]—completely devoid of attributes—it is until now only Itself, and thus, as such, a complete freedom from all being and against all being [*eine völlige Freiheit von allem Sein und gegen alles Sein*]; but it inescapably attires itself [*sich selbst anzuziehen*],[84] for it is only a subject *in order that* it become an object to itself [*denn nur dazu ist es Subjekt, daß es sich selbst Objekt werde*], since it has been presupposed that nothing is *outside* it that could become an object for it; but *as* it attires itself [*sich selbst anzieht*], it is no more as *nothing* but *as* something [*ist es nicht mehr als nichts, sondern als Etwas*]—in this self-arrayment [*Selbstanziehung*][85] it makes itself into something; the origin of all becoming something [*Ursprung des Etwas-Seins*], or of objective, concrete being, then, lies in this self-arrayment."[86]

The kabbalistic resonances in Schelling's system are conspicuous to the attentive ear, and the fact that Heidegger dedicated several seminars to his thought, especially the *Philosophische Untersuchungen*, which is the work most influenced by Böhmean theosophy, is ample proof that these esoteric currents may have made an indelible impression on Heidegger's own thinking about the nature of *Seyn* as the trembling of the self-refusing desire to bestow. Just as *Ein Sof* is outside the dyad of the ontological economy, so Schelling refers to the absolute subjectivity, which appears as nothing but is in fact neither nothing nor something, as the essence that cannot "negate itself as *essence*, for it is not just essence in general, but *in an infinite manner*."[87] Insofar as the essence is bereft of all attribution, it is considered to be like nothing but it cannot actually be nothing, since it is everything. Meontologically, the inessential essence is free from all being and, in some sense, against all being. In and of itself the subject is illimitable and therefore cannot be enclosed within the computable boundaries of an object. However, since there is nothing outside the subject, the process by which finite and contingent beings evolve from the infinite and necessary essence—what Schelling calls "construction" (*Konstruktion*)[88]—requires that the subject become an object to itself. Tellingly, Schelling also refers to this activity as *Selbstanziehung*, which I have rendered as "self-arrayment," to capture the fact that the metaphor of investiture delineates how the infinite subject, which can never cease being a subject, becomes objectified as nature. We find a comparable symbol employed by kabbalists, who typically speak of the sefirotic gradations and the worlds that emanate therefrom as the vestments by which the infinite nakedness is adorned, the name by which the nameless is declaimed.[89] In an indisputable kabbalistic inflection, Schelling notes that, through the self-arrayment of the essence, the subject that was nothing is transposed into something. The first being to come forth, the *primum existens*, which is the "first contingency," commences with "dissonance" (*Dissonanz*); that is, unlike the infinite subject, it is no longer identical with itself. Although there is nothing outside the infinite subject, and even prior to the "arrayment of being" (*Zuziehung des Seins*), it is infinite "in its being *in* and *before* itself," Schelling asserts that we can speak of this subject as infinite "only in as much as it still had finitude before itself, but for that reason it is not yet posited there as infinite; to posit itself as infinite it must have cleansed itself [*sich gereinigt*] from this possibility of also being the finite. Thus finitude itself becomes a means for it to posit itself *as* infinite (i.e. as freedom from being [*als Freiheit vom Sein*]), for no other concept is connected here with the word 'infinite'. Only through real opposition [*Gegensatz*] could it be raised into its true essence, could it reach itself *as* infinite."[90]

What Schelling is arguing here is a restatement of his contention in the third version of *Die Weltalter* (c. 1815) regarding the actualization (*Verwirklichung*) of the Godhead (*die Gottheit*):

> But since the Godhead can only actualize itself from out of its free eternity, there must be something between free eternity and the deed of actualization that separates the deed from eternity so that eternity remains free and inviolable. This something can only be time, but not time within eternity itself, but rather time coexisting with eternity. This time outside of eternity is that movement of eternal nature where eternal nature, ascending from the lowest, always attains the highest, and, from the highest, always retreats anew in order to ascend again. Only in this movement does eternal nature discern itself as eternity.[91]

Noteworthy again is the philosophical affiliation with kabbalistic speculation on time and eternity: the Godhead is beyond all time but its eternality should not be reckoned as the amalgamation of all successive moments of time strung together linearly to form a train of timelessness; it is rather the circuitous movement of eternal nature by which the nonbeing of the everlasting being is displayed distinctively in every moment that comes to be and passes away.[92] Hence, time is, as Schelling paraphrases Pindar, "only the simulacrum of eternity [*nur das Scheinbild der Ewigkeit*]. For eternity must not be thought as those moments of time *taken together* [*zusammengenommen*], but rather as co-existing with each single moment [*als jedem einzelnen coexistirend*] so that eternity again sees only its (whole, immeasurable) self in each single one."[93]

To grasp the subtlety of Schelling's point, we would do well to consider his portrayal of the nonground as that which posits an opposition of coincidence in opposition to the coincidence of opposition, an idea that is reminiscent of Böhme's conjecture that the omnipotent and conflictual forces of wrath and love are coextensive in the divine essence.[94] The task, in the formulation of Žižek, is "to locate the source of the split between Good and Evil in God himself *while remaining within the field of monotheism*—the task which German mysticism (Jakob Böhme) and later philosophers who pursued their logic (Schelling, Hegel) tried to accomplish. In other words, the task is to transpose the human 'external reflection' which enacts the split between Good and Evil back *into the One God himself*."[95] As Schelling remarked in the *Philosophische Untersuchungen*,

> there must be a being [*ein Wesen sein*] *before* all ground and before all that exists, thus generally before any duality—how can we call it anything other than the original ground [*Urgrund*] or the *non-ground* [Ungrund]? Since it precedes all opposites, these cannot be distinguishable in it nor can they be present in any way. Therefore, it cannot be described as the identity of opposites; it can only be described as the absolute *indifference* [*Indifferenz*] of both. . . . Indifference is not a product of opposites, nor are they implicitly contained in it, but rather indifference is its own being separate from all opposition, a being against which all opposites ruin themselves [*an dem alle Gegensätze sich brechen*], that is nothing else than their very not-Being [*Nichtsein*] and that, for this reason, also has no predicate, except as the very lacking of a predicate [*Prädikatlosigkeit*], without it being on that account a nothingness [*Nichts*] or non-thing [*Unding*].[96]

Indifference does not arise as a dialectical sublation of opposites; it is opposed to all opposition, even the opposition to opposition, lacking all predication but the lack of predication, but still not nothing or a nonentity. The indifference of the *Ungrund* precludes the possibility of advancing a resolution of antinomical forces in the absolute: "Real and ideal, darkness and light, as we otherwise want to describe the two principles, can never be predicated of the non-ground *as opposites*. But nothing hinders that they be predicated of it as non-opposites [*Nichtgegensätze*], that is, in disjunction and each *for itself* whereby, however, precisely duality (the actual two-ness [*Zweiheit*] of principles) is posited."[97]

Schelling's view on indifference as the difference of identity—that is, the positing of opposites as nonopposites rather than the nonopposition of opposites—is a response to the Hegelian logic of the identity of difference summed up in the *Phänomenologie des Geistes* in the statement that the "absolute Notion of the difference must be represented and understood purely as inner difference [*inner Unterschied*], a repulsion of the selfsame [*Gleichnamigen*], as selfsame, from itself, and likeness of the unlike as unlike [*Gleichseyn des Ungleichen als ungleichen*]. . . . For in the difference which is an inner difference, the opposite [*das entgegengesetzte*] is not merely *one of two*—if it were, it would simply *be*, without being an opposite—but it is the opposite of an opposite [*das entgegengesetzte eines entgegenge*], or the other is itself immediately present in it."[98] For Hegel, opposites are dialectically sublated in the unity that comprises a thing and its opposite such that with respect to any opposite we must say, first and foremost, that it is opposite to itself: "Certainly, I put the 'opposite' here, and the 'other' of which it is the opposite, there; the 'opposite', then, is on one side, is in and for itself without the 'other'. But just because I have the 'opposite' here in and for itself, it is the opposite of itself [*das Gegentheil seiner selbst*], or it has, in fact, the 'other' immediately present in it. . . . Only thus is it difference [*Unterschied*] as *inner* difference, or difference *in its own self* [*an sich selbst*], or difference as an *infinity* [*Unendlichkeit*]."[99]

From Schelling's perspective, this inner difference is no difference at all, since the difference so named is part of a self-identical essence. By contrast, he strives to maintain a bona fide sense of difference by affirming the unity of identity and indifference,[100] that is, a unity that accepts the disjunction of opposites coexisting as nonopposites, a duality that preserves the opposites in contrast to an opposition where the opposites are annulled in the nonidentity of their identity. Schelling describes the relation of the *Ungrund* to the twofold in language that is appropriate to depict the *Ein Sof* in relation to the dual principles that characterize the concealment of the manifestation of its concealment in the sefirotic emanations: "For, precisely because it relates to both as total indifference, it is neutral [*gleichgültig*] toward both. Were it the absolute identity of both, it could be both only *at the same time* [zugleich], that is, both would have to be predicated of it *as opposites* [als Gegensätze] and thereby would themselves be one again. Duality . . . breaks forth therefore immediately from the Neither-Nor [*Weder-Noch*], or indifference, and *without* indifference, that is, *without* a non-ground, there would be no two-ness of principles."[101] In Schelling's post-identity philosophy, shaped as well by Böhme's assumption that light and dark, love and anguish, are differentiated by virtue of the absolute indifference of their identity in the will of the primordial nonground,[102] the *Ungrund* is prior to all opposition and even beyond the overcoming of opposition by preserving the twofoldness of an irreducible duality; it is this quality, above all else, that justifies the characterization of differentiation as a breach of the absolute indifference.

In *Die Weltalter*, Schelling writes that the duality is found "in the primordial beginnings of nature [*Uranfängen der Natur*]" and thus the "ground of the antithesis [*Gegensatzes*] is as old as, nay, is even older than, the world . . . just as in everything living, so already in that which is primordially living, there is a doubling [*Doppelheit*] that has come down, through many stages, to that which has determined itself as what appears to us as light and darkness, masculine and feminine, spiritual and corporeal. Therefore, the oldest teachings [*die ältesten Lehren*] straightforwardly represented the first nature as a being with two conflicting modes of activity."[103] From the beginning, then, there is the doubling of the infinite that renders the first principle, with regard to itself, in a state of contradiction (*Widerspruch*), for if it were not so, it "would be constantly One and would never become Two. It would be an eternal rigidity [*Unbeweglichkeit*] without progress."[104] The "oldest teachings" may very well be a reference to the kabbalah, which Schelling would have imagined to be the archaic tradition of the Jews. Reminiscent of the symbolic representation of the divine in kabbalistic theosophy, God is characterized by the equally primal propulsion to overflow and the compulsion to withdraw, the impetus to bestow on the other and the inclination to retreat from the other: "Therefore, two principles are already in what is necessary of God: the outpouring, outstretching, self-giving being [*sich gebende Wesen*], and an equivalently eternal force of selfhood, of retreat into itself, of Being in itself [*in-sich-Seyns*]. That being and this force are both already God itself, without God's assistance."[105]

Schelling's language about the "beginning" or the "first potency" is even more evocative of the kabbalistic myth of *ṣimṣum* according to which the constriction and withdrawal of the light of the infinite into itself, and the consequent disclosure of the concealment of the concealment, depend on the execution of the quality of strength (*gevurah*):

> That God negates itself [*sich selbst verneint*], restricts its being [*sein Wesen verschließt*], and withdraws into itself [*in sich selbst zurücknimmt*], is the eternal force and might of God. In this manner, the negating force is that which is singularly revealing of God. But the actual being of God is that which is concealed. The whole therefore stands as A that from the outside is B and hence, the whole = (A = B). Therefore, the whole, because God is that which does not have being (is not manifest) in it, inclines, in accord with its essentiality and in relation to what is other, for the most part toward not being that which has being.[106]

Once more, we see that Schelling explicitly rejects the Hegelian dialectic whereby the antithesis of expansiveness and diminution would be overcome in a unity that sublates their difference—a position that is more proximate to the kabbalistic view that the secret of emanation (*sod ha-aṣilut*) depends on the interplay between mercy on the right and judgment on the left,[107] an admixture that is possible because, as Joseph ben Shalom Ashkenazi expressed the hidden matter (*davar ne'lam*), the two opposites emanate from the incomposite force (*koaḥ pashuṭ*) in the equanimous one (*be-aḥdut ha-shaweh*) of the first emanation, the supernal crown (*keter elyon*)[108]—insisting instead that within the Godhead there is a primeval duality such that "what has been set against each other has the same essentiality and originality. The force with which the being closes itself off, denies itself, is actual in its kind as the opposite principle. Each has its own root and neither can be deduced from the other. If this were so, then the antithesis would again immediately come to an end. But it is impossible *per se* that an exact opposite would derive from its exact opposite."[109] If the two primordial forces of contraction and expansion were fully apart, without reciprocal contact, there would be no unity, and we would be forced to posit two deities in the manner of Zoroastrianism. Nevertheless, Schelling maintains that there would be no unity without the presumption of an unyielding binary: "The antithesis rests on this, that each of the two conflicting powers is a being for itself, a real *principle*. The antithesis is only as such if the two conflicting principles conduct themselves as actually independent and separate from each other."[110]

In another passage, Schelling articulates his position in language that is aligned with Böhme's idea of the eternal Yes and the eternal No in the divine will,[111] language that is in accord with one of the most distinctive elements of kabbalistic theosophy:

> We have indicated how the pure Godhead [*die lautere Gottheit*] is indivisibly the eternal Yes [*ewiges Jah*] and the eternal No [*ewiges Nein*] and the free unity of both. From this it automatically followed that the Godhead can be the eternal No = B only insofar as the Godhead is, as such, at the same time the ground of Itself as the eternal Yes. Then from this the reverse also necessarily follows. As B or the eternal No, it is the Godhead only insofar as it is at the same time A, that is, that it posits Itself as the eternal Yes.[112]

To say of the divine essence that it is simultaneously negative and positive is not to conflate the two to the point of eradicating the disparity; it is to postulate the nonduality of oppositional forces in a state of "nondivorce." which is not "free from all difference but rather it is an indifference negating difference" (*Es ist auch hier Indifferenz, Ungeschiedenheit, aber wirkende, nicht eine von aller Differenz freie, sondern eine sie verneinende*).[113] The indifference negating difference does not mean there is no difference of which to speak; it implies rather that the difference persists in the negation of difference qua the difference of negation in the nonduality or the nondivorce of the indifference. Hence, inasmuch as God "is not the cause of the Other through a special volition but through God's mere essence, the Other is certainly not the essence of God, but it belongs to God's essence in a natural and inseparable way. It therefore follows that if the pure Godhead = A, and that the Other = B, then the full concept of the living Godhead which has being is not merely A, but is A + B."[114]

The other is distinguished from God's essence, but it is also said to come to be from that essence and not from a distinct act of will. The concept of the living Godhead, therefore, must be charted formulaically as A + B, the self and the other. This resounds with another rudimentary tenet of kabbalistic theosophy, accentuated by the disciples of Luria: the potential for boundary must be located within the boundless, for if that were not the case, the largesse of the boundlessness would be truncated and the negativity of its infinitude negated. The principle was already enunciated in the thirteen century by Azriel of Gerona: "*Ein Sof* is the perfection without deficit, and if you say that it has a limitless power but does not have a limited power, you diminish its perfection."[115] The perfection of the infinite necessitates the capacity for it to become finite and hence we are led to the paradox that "the delimited way is comprised in the limitless without a limit" (*ha-derekh ha-mugbal kalul be-vilti takhlit beli gevul*).[116] From the standpoint of the principle of the excluded middle—P is either true or not true—the statement is absurd: the limited cannot be contained in the limitless as limited because this would imply that something is both limited and limitless. But it is precisely the paradoxical truth of this excluded middle that we must affirm and thus we say of P that it is both true and not true and therefore neither true nor not true. Contradictory propositions can be both true insofar as they are both false. On this logic, the kabbalists uphold that the bounded is incorporated in the boundless as that which has no boundary.

Like the masters of the kabbalah, Schelling, in great measure due to Böhme, sought to explain the eternal becoming of God by reference to the process by which the nonground of being grounds itself through the activation of the will that is contrary to the will, the dark core in the luminescence of divinity that is and yet is not God.[117] But how can we speak of a will that is legitimately contrary to the will, a counterwill, when the will comprehends the other as part of its not-otherness? The response of Böhme, Schelling, and the kabbalists would be that the otherness of the not-other implies that the infinite is identical with the finite precisely because the finite is not identical with the infinite. The shared paradox opens the way to envisage through the imagination—the temporal mirror of eternity—that difference is the property of the indifferent and multiplicity the provision of the singular.

Engendering the Same Other: From Light of the Vessel to Vessel of the Light

Along these lines, we can reconsider the doctrine of *ṣimṣum* as a means by which kabbalists wrestled with the problem of hypothesizing difference within the indifference of *Ein Sof.* Expressed in gender terms, *ṣimṣum* is related to the *sha'ashu'a* of the masculine propensity to overflow stimulated by the potential of the feminine to receive. The will to bestow—viewed through the lens of the heteroerotic male fantasy—necessitates a vessel to contain the seminal discharge. The female thus functions, as Judith Butler puts it in her analysis of Luce Irigaray, as the "*inscriptional space* of that phallogocentrism, the specular surface which receives the marks of a masculine signifying act only to give back a (false) reflection and guarantee of phallogocentric self-sufficiency, without making any contribution of its own."[118] The possibility of otherness is undermined, since the other is a manifestation of the same, absence a facet of presence, evil an iteration of good, the female a projection of the male. This is not to deny that central to the kabbalistic worldview is the assumption that the male is refined by being conjoined to the female and the female by being conjoined to the male, that the left is contained in the right and the right in the left. To cite one exemplary passage from the zoharic corpus that extols this reciprocity: "This is the praise of the supernal faith, to know that the 'Lord is God' (Deuteronomy 4:35), the male is perfected through the female, and the one is contained in the other, the male is built through the female, and this is the perfect unity, and there is no perfection but in male and female as one."[119] Contrary to the account of the second chapter of Genesis wherein the woman is said to have been constructed from the man—an ontological assumption substantiated philologically by the derivation of *ishshah* from *ish* (Genesis 2:23)—this passage emphasizes that the male is built from the female. The intent of this formulation, however, is not to reverse the supremacy of the male according to the scriptural account, but rather to emphasize that the male, too, is made whole through the female, an idea already alluded to in the mandate that a man should leave his father and mother and cleave to his wife so that they become one flesh (Genesis 2:24). The anthropological assumption reflects the theosophical mystery of the supernal faith: *YHWH,* the masculine potency of mercy, is *Elohim,* the feminine potency of judgment. The identity—and not merely the unity—of the two names signals the repair of the schism in and through which the gender polarity prevailed.

The matter is expressed in miscellaneous ways by the zoharic authorship including this reworking of the rabbinic myth explaining the shift from the parity of the sun and the moon to the latter diminishing itself vis-à-vis the former,[120] a myth that is anchored exegetically in the shift in Genesis 1:16 from the expression "two great lights" (*shenei ha-me'orot ha-gedolim*) to the "great light" (*ha-ma'or ha-gadol*) that ruled by day and the "smaller light" (*ha-ma'or ha-qaṭon*) that ruled by night: "*The two great lights*—initially in one bond [*be-ḥibbura ḥada*], and this mystery is the complete name as one, *YHWH Elohim,* even though it was not revealed but in a concealed manner [*de-lo ihu be-itgalya ella be-oraḥ satim*]."[121] Originally, sun and moon—symbolic ciphers for the masculine *Tif'eret* and the feminine *Malkhut*—were united and as a consequence they were of equal stature, or in the precise language of the text, "at first they dwelled as one in balance" (*yatvei ka-ḥada be-shiqqula*). In that state, both potencies were called by the name *MṢPṢ*, an encoded reference to *YHWH* based on the system of letter permutation known as *Atbash*, i.e., the substitution of *taw* for *alef*, *shin* for *beit*, and so on through the alphabet; this is the import of the statement that the complete name, *YHWH Elohim*, was revealed only in a concealed manner. Subsequently, sun and moon were separated and the latter's light was lessened, which is interpreted zoharically in a more radical fashion as the moon having no light at all except what it receives from the sun (*leit lah nehora bar mi-shimsha*) in the same way that "a woman is enhanced only when she is united with her husband" (*leit itteta be-ribbuya bar be-va'alah ka-ḥada*).[122] I imagine no unbiased reader would deny the androcentrism implied in this statement. But does the original state of balance signify equality of gender?

Let us recall another passage from the same zoharic homily: "When the moon was with the sun in one conjunction [*bi-devequta ḥada*], the moon was resplendent; when it separated from the sun and was appointed over her forces, she diminished herself and diminished her light, and shells upon shells were created to conceal the kernel, and everything was for the sake of arraying the kernel [*tiqquna de-moḥa*] ... and all this was for the sake of arraying the world [*le-tiqquna de-alma*]."[123] In this comment, the hierarchy becomes more transparent, and we discern that even in the state of union or balance, when male and female are marked by the same name, the moon is said to be illumined from the light of the sun but, conversely, the sun is not said to be illumined by the light of the moon. Implicit here is what I have emphasized in my previous work and what needs to be highlighted again: prior to the division into distinct sexuated beings, there is one gender wherein the feminine is dependent ontologically on the masculine in the same way that the limited is comprised in the limitless without any limit. The initiatory act of self-withdrawal results in self-begetting, the splintering of the incandescent light beyond light into light and darkness, the fissuring of the being bereft of being into the polarity of being and nonbeing. The appeal to the duality of indifference notwithstanding, darkness is still conceived as the privation of light and nonexistence as the privation of existence.

The asymmetry is preserved in the state of dimorphic partition: the union of masculine mercy and feminine judgment results in the amelioration of the latter by the former, and not the former by the latter. The point was made succinctly by Moses ben Shem Ṭov de León:

> According to this matter you can know that by all means the secret of the right is the true essence to contain within it the left [*sod ha-yamin hu ha-iqqar ha-amitti likhlol bo ha-semo'l*]. Thus, even though the left is that which arouses the judgment in its power and in its strength, nevertheless [the verse declares] "the right hand of the Lord is triumphant" (Psalms 118:15), that is, the strength is within it. And even though in *Tif'eret* there is the secret of the greatness and the strength, as we have explained, the right is that which comprises the left. Hence, you can know that as long as the right is conjoined to the left, the judgment is placated.[124]

The binary gives way to a monism—even though there is right and left, the latter is ultimately comprised in the former, and thus the verse ascribes the characteristic of the left to the right. The example of *Tif'eret* proves the point: it is a hybrid of greatness and strength, but the conjunction of the two results in the judgment of the feminine left being contained in and mollified by the munificence of the masculine right. The philosophical principle that undergirds the view expressed by de León, which pervades kabbalistic texts, is expressed concisely and clearly by Joseph Ergas (1685–1730) in response to the hypothetical question concerning the attribution of gender to the divine emanations: "Male and female are terms for the donor [*mashpi'a*] and the recipient [*mushpa*], for the donor in relation to its other is called masculine and the one that receives the overflow is feminine. The mystery of the syzygy [*sod ha-ziwwug*] attributed to the *sefirot* is the union [*ḥibbur*] and attachment [*dibbuq*] of the male that overflows with the female that receives, and its matter concerns the sweetening of the severities of the female in the mercies of the male [*hamtaqat gevurot ha-neqevah be-ḥasadim shel ha-zakhar*]."[125] Unquestionably, kabbalistic lore can be byzantine in its oratory and labyrinthine in its architectonic, but with respect to this cardinal point, it is relatively simple: the *hieros gamos* is no more and no less than an elaboration of the rabbinic belief that creation occurs as a consequence of God combining the attribute of mercy and the attribute of judgment so that the fire of austerity is tempered by the water of compassion.[126] There is fluidity to the gender dynamic—the female can become male and the male female—but there is a rigidity that determines that fluidity: the female that bestows is masculinized and the male that receives is feminized. The variability does not measure up to ambiguity. One of the most striking illustrations of the androcentric orientation is the remnant in the zoharic unit *Sifra di-Ṣeniʿuta* of the myth that the creation effectuated by feminine judgment (*Elohim*) without the cooperation of masculine mercy (*YHWH*) was flawed, an idea that has parallels in some ancient Gnostic sources. The more perfect creation is accomplished by the complete name, the combination of *YHWH* and *Elohim*, the coupling of male and female, an idea expressed in the beginning of the text as the scale (*matqela*) upon which the two were balanced in the face-to-face encounter.[127]

Here it is apposite to recall the following comment of Heidegger drawing out the implications in modern Western philosophy, and particularly in German idealism, of the ancient principle that identity is the essential determination of beings:

> In the modern era, identity attains its preeminence in the I; this I is at once grasped as the preeminent identity, i.e., the identity which is *explicitly self*-appertaining and which, by knowing *itself*, is precisely in this knowledge. From here we can begin to see why *knowledge* itself becomes the ground of beingness [*der Grund der Seiendheit*] and thus becomes the most proper being and why for Hegel absolute knowledge is the absolute reality. . . . Owing to the already dominant guideline, *knowledge as self-knowledge* [Wissen als Sichwissendes] is the highest *identity*, the *most proper being*, and as such dwells at the same time in the possibility of conditioning, in its own way as knowledge, all other *objectivities* and indeed not only in a comparatively transcendental sense but—as in Schelling—in such fashion that what is other to the I [*das Andere des Ich*] is itself determined as *visible* spirit [sichtbare *Geist*]. Thereby now once again, and ultimately, identity is raised into the absoluteness of *indifference* [*die Absolutheit der* Indifferenz], which of course does not mean sheer emptiness [*die bloße Leere*].[128]

Insofar as what is other vis-à-vis the I is demarcated as visible spirit, it is not clear that this other betrays a sense of genuine otherness convincingly. On the contrary, identity is marked as the assimilation into "the absoluteness of *indifference*," an inevitable consequence of identifying knowledge as self-knowledge, the pure or unconditioned relation of the *I-think-unity* (Ich-denke-Einheit) whereby "the *self-present present* [selbst gegenwärtige Gegenwart] becomes the paradigm of all beingness."[129]

The logic compels us to confront the question again in a somewhat different terminology: how can that which is purely subjective become objective? We may presume that this is possible only if the potential to become objective is contained in the subject, but then the insinuation would be that there is no objectivity of the object that is not a manifestation of the subjectivity of the subject, no other of the same that is not part of the same of the other, no way to extricate the tautology "being is" from the thetic judgment "I am."[130] Toward the conclusion of the chapter on *Naturphilosophie* in *Zur Geschichte der neueren Philosophie*, Schelling comes around to this very point:

> Now I can indeed think of God as the end and just the result of my thinking, as He was in the old metaphysics, but I cannot think of Him as result of an *objective* process; furthermore, this God which was assumed as result could, if He is God, not have *something outside Himself* [*nicht etwas außer Sich*] (*praeter*

> *se*).... From this—from the last moment, it follows that this God must after all be determined at the end as He also was already at the beginning, therefore that the subject which goes through the whole process is already God at the beginning and during the process, before it also posited in the result *as* God—that in this sense God is admittedly *everything*, that the subject going through nature is also God, only not *as* God [*daß auch das durch die Natur hindurchgehende Subjekt Gott ist, nur nicht als Gott*]—thus God only *outside* His divinity [*also Gott nur außer seiner Gottheit*] or in His externalisation [*Entäußerung*] or in His otherness [*Anderheit*], as an other of *Himself* [*als ein anderer von sich selbst*], as which He only is at the end.[131]

In kabbalistic parlance, if the vessel is itself a manifestation of light, a point to which we shall return subsequently, there does not seem to be room for an actual sense of difference, a Not-I that is not comprised within the absolute I, a nonknowing of the other that is not an aspect of self-knowing.[132] The externalization of the infinite yields an otherness that, at best, can be designated the other of itself, but such an other is veritably no other at all. It is relevant to mention in this connection a second remark in *Zur Geschichte der neueren Philosophie*: "But Spinoza is, of course, an emanationist, admittedly not a physical one but a logical one; he also admittedly does not maintain an external being-separated from its source of that which flows out, as emanation is usually understood (for whether emanation has ever and in any system been comprehensible in this way, e.g., in the Jewish Kabbala [*jüdischen Cabbala*], is still a big question); rather, what follows God remains in God [*sondern das aus Gott Folgende bleibt in Gott*], and, as such, his doctrine can be called an immanent doctrine of emanation."[133] It is beyond my concerns to discuss Schelling's interpretation of Spinoza, but it is noteworthy that he raised doubt about whether the doctrine of emanation in the kabbalah implies that the emanated is separated from the emanator. He is right to frame the paradox of transcendence and immanence as what issues from God remains in God.

Let me exemplify the point by a passage from a short treatise to which I referred in the previous chapter, an explication of the doctrine of *ṣimṣum* believed to have been composed by Luria himself as a commentary on the enigmatic opening of the *Zohar*, "In the beginning of the decree of the king, the hardened spark engraved an engraving in the supernal luster" (*be-reish hurmenuta de-malka galif gelufei bi-ṭehiru illa'ah boṣina de-qardinuta*). As Luria notes, in the egression of the influx from the infinite, there emerges the dyad of light (*or*) and vessel (*keli*)—the former associated with masculine mercy and the latter with feminine judgment[134]—but the vessel is itself constituted by the trace (*reshimu*) of the light that is left behind in the vacuum (*maqom ha-panuy*) from which the light withdrew.

> "Engraved an engraving"—to comprehend whence the vessels came to be in the beginning of the emanation, since the *Ein Sof* is absolute simplicity [*pashuṭ be-takhlit ha-peshiṭut*]. The explanation is that prior to the emanation he and his name alone were[135] and he filled the space of all the worlds. When it arose in his simple will to bring into existence all the worlds and to benefit what is other than himself, he constricted his presence [*ṣimṣem shekhinato*] and his light vanished above and the place [*maqom*] wherein the worlds will be created remained empty [*panuy*]. When the light reverted, it vanished above from the reversion of this light, which is the force of judgment that was there, for by means of it the light vanished above. All the reversion of light is only from the perspective of judgment, for the light extends limitlessly. From that force of judgment that was there... the vessel was made, and from the light that vanished there remained a trace in the empty space in which the light initially extended. By means of the trace that remained the first vessel was made.[136]

The monistic view implied in the assumption that the vessel is made by the trace of light that remained in the space from which the light evacuated—the act of writing that is the erasure that produces the trace as the trace of the trace[137]—is strengthened in a second passage in which the zoharic image of the supernal luster is thus explained by Luria: "The luster [*ṭehiru*] is called the first vessel, the primordial ether [*awir qadmon*]. It is called 'luster' because it is resplendent and it shines exceedingly, and it is not a vessel except in relation to *Ein Sof*, which shines within it."[138] The demarcation "vessel" is not absolute but relative; that is, vis-à-vis the infinite, the luster is a vessel, but, in its own essence, it is light.

Luria's point is amplified by several of his disciples as well as other kabbalists. I will mention three examples. The first illustration is from Saruq's *Derush ha-Malbush*: "Know this one principle that with respect to every spiritual matter, even though the light withdraws, its trace [*reshimu*] remains, and it does not move from its place . . . and when the light of the blessed one is contracted [*nitṣamṣem*] from its trace, it becomes a garment [*malbush*], so that the garment will become a place that is vacant and not vacant [*maqom panuy we-eino panuy*]; that is, when that garment withdraws above that trace always remains below, so that it will be void of the garment itself but not void of the trace. And know that the garment is from the light of his substance, blessed be he."[139] The paradoxical assertion that the garment is the place that is both devoid and not devoid of the "remnant of the infinite" (*reshimu shel ha-ein sof*),[140] also referred to as the "point of the infinite within the trace" (*nequddat ein sof be-tokh ha-reshimu*),[141] accentuates the fact that there is no sense of the other that is not subsumed under the taxonomy of the same. The space created by the contraction "is not called empty except in relation to the garment itself, but with respect to the light of the infinite [*or ein sof*] and the trace of the garment [*reshimu shel ha-malbush*] itself, it is not empty, there is no vacuity [*reiqut*]. And from here begins the root that is in all of the worlds, for even in corporal matters there is no vacuum. The philosophers call this matter the 'world soul' [*nefesh ha-olam*], and the kabbalists call it the 'primordial ether' [*awir qadmon*], for it is the beginning of the governance of the worlds [*teḥillat hanhagat ha-olamot*], which are filled from the ether in a manner that there is no vacuum, and this ether is made from the trace of the garment."[142] The uncompromising denial of any void—space that is empty of anything but the emptiness of space—in all of the worlds strongly intimates that there can be no absolute alterity vis-à-vis the light of infinity.

In a second passage, Saruq reiterates the crucial closure of the gap separating light and vessel in his attenuated account of the breaking of the vessels (*shevirat ha-kelim*):

> This breaking is not, God forbid, a breaking, but rather separation of the letters [*perud ha-otiyyot*], for you already know that these vessels are merely letters of light joined together. When the letters are joined, they have the strength to be in their place, suspended in the ether, but when the letters separate, they do not have strength and they descend below, one here and one there. Hence, the letters of the broken vessels of mercy descend below, and they are the root of judgments that come to be from them afterward, the root of the shells.[143]

The third passage I will cite is from Viṭal, who strikes a similar chord:

> Thus by means of this contraction [*ha-ṣimṣum ha-zeh*] . . . there was in him the aspect of essence [*aṣmut*] and vessels [*kelim*], for the contraction of the light brought about the reality of the vessels . . . but we do not have permission to speak more about this elevated place, and the enlightened will comprehend the beginning of the matter from its end. . . . And yet, it is not actually a vessel [*eino keli mammash*] but in relation to the light that is within it, it is called "vessel." However, it is pure and luminous in the extreme of purity and in the subtlety of luminosity.[144]

That the vessel is itself light seriously neutralizes the argument that kabbalists posited the existence of an alterity that is not absorbed in the infinite totality, since the vessel is the primary symbol to demarcate what is autonomous vis-à-vis the light. I am, of course, aware of the fact that Viṭal's version of the doctrine of *ṣimṣum* addresses the question of how *Ein Sof* can make space for what is allegedly other than itself.[145] This presentation can be tracked to Luria himself, as is attested in the language of the aforecited text, "When it arose in his simple will to bring into existence all the worlds and to benefit what is other than himself [*le-zulato*]." On the face of it, the expression *le-zulato* would lend credence to Scholem's surmise that Luria's teaching promotes a theistic orientation that counterbalances the more pantheistic tendency of earlier kabbalistic sources according to which the line separating God and nature is blurred.[146] This seems to be confirmed as well by another passage from Luria's commentary where he extrapolates from the zoharic language, "In the beginning of the decree of the king," that prior to the creation of the worlds, God and his name alone were, and there was nothing upon which his kingship (*malkhuto*) could hinge;[147] that is, divine governance and providence depend on the existence of a world that is ontically autonomous.

In my opinion, however, it is more accurate to assume that there is an unresolved tension between the theistic and the pantheistic tendencies in the Lurianic material. On the one hand, the light of the infinite is identified as the sole reality of all that exists in the cosmological chain from the highest to the lowest link; nothing could be sustained even for a nanosecond if that light were extinguished. The continuity of being is portrayed symbolically in the image of one anatomic organism: *Ein Sof* is the soul of the soul (*neshamah li-neshamah*) that emanates *Adam Qadmon*, who comprises the four worlds, and the aspect of the essence (*aṣmut*) that is within him consists of the five pneumatic gradations (*nefesh, ruaḥ, neshamah, ḥayyah,* and *yeḥidah*). The world of emanation (*aṣilut*) is identified as the aspect of the body (*guf*) and the worlds of creation (*beri'ah*), formation (*yeṣirah*), and doing (*asiyyah*) as the garments (*malbushim*). The lower three worlds thus constitute one world (*olam eḥad*) that is the apparel of the emanation (*levush ha-aṣilut*), a depiction that doubtless underlines the organic unity of all levels of being. In Viṭal's words: "You have already been informed with respect to all these worlds how this one becomes a body for that one, and this one for that one, such that all the worlds entirely are as one [*kol ha-olamot kullam ke-eḥad*]."[148] On the other hand, in the very same context, Viṭal insists that the world of emanation is distinguished from the other three worlds inasmuch as they are not considered to be from the aspect of divinity (*elohut*).[149] But if we take seriously the logical inference of the claim that the vessel itself is light, then it is not at all clear, irrespective of the effort of the kabbalists to argue otherwise,[150] that we do not end up with a pantheistic monism in which the difference between beings would disappear, and this is so even if, as I myself have argued,[151] it is necessary to avoid thinking of the kabbalistic infinite in ontological terms as the Eleatic unity that comprehends all beings in a totalizing way that negates their singularity.

Notwithstanding the validity of the appeal to posit multiplicity in the very nature of *Ein Sof*,[152] and the implied sense of a fragmented whole—the infinite fractal curve of differentiable points of nondifferentiability—one would be hard pressed to conclude that kabbalists have postulated a valid sense of otherness.[153] I am not certain the kabbalistic infinity avoids being sublated into a totality, however discordant and polyvalent that totality might be, and hence we can assign to it the language that Heidegger used to depict Hegel's concept of the idea, "the absolute self-appearance to itself of the absolute as absolute knowledge [*das absolute Sichselbsterscheinen des Absoluten als absolutes Wissen*]."[154] If, as Hegel argued, the becoming of spirit is identified as the revelatory activity by which it is manifest in its infinite appearance as other in order to be for itself and not merely reflecting back within itself[155]—that is, consciousness exists for itself vis-à-vis the other, indeed, the essential moment is identified as the self-differentiation whereby the other is posited as that for which spirit appears[156]—it would have to follow that since the other exists for consciousness, whose defining characteristic is that its being-in-and-for-itself is the ground of its being in relationship to the other, then the other can exist as other only as it is contained in consciousness, which is to say, in the not-other there is no other.[157] Translated Christologically, the Son is in the Father as the other of God that is within God.[158] In Hegel's own words:

> A further determination is that the substantiality or unity of absolute actuality with itself is only the foundation, only one moment in the definition of God as spirit. The determination, the concrete being, the unity of differentiated determinations, only arises when we proceed further. It presupposes a one and an other, though at the beginning we do not yet have differentiated determinations, a one and an other. At the beginning we have before us only the one, not the other. . . . So if we speak of the beginning, we have this one actuality as a relating of itself to itself and not to an other; we do not yet have an advance, not yet concrete being.[159]

Even if we acknowledge that the infinitivity of *Ein Sof* must be distilled as transfinite or as an increasable actual-infinite—an unbounded succession of ordinal numbers whose unity is formed by an indefinite division beyond mathematical determination—it is still germane to say that *Ein Sof* is the absolute minimum that is the absolute maximum, the infinitesimal whose magnitude comprehends everything incomprehensibly and therefore is incapable of increase or diminution.[160] Moreover, expressed from a gender perspective, as the unadulterated luminosity, *Ein Sof* is the pure benevolence that is aligned exclusively with the masculine.[161] Some of the most renowned kabbalists, accordingly, depicted the infinite in decidedly androcentric imagery as the male without an independent female complement. To be sure, insofar as the catalyst for creation, the boundless impulse of divine love to bestow, must be activated by the stringency of judgment, the capacity to give boundary—a mystery referred to as the "secret of caressing" (*sod ha-ḥibbuq*) induced by the "arousal of the left" (*hit'orerut ha-semo'l*), linked exegetically to the verse "His left hand was under my head, his right arm embraced me" (Song of Songs 2:6), a theme expressed as well by the anatomical image of the female waters (*mayyin nuqvin*) stimulating the male waters (*mayyin dukhrin*)—the very same kabbalists locate the potential of the feminine withholding, which prompts the elongation of the masculine, in the world where femininity is not yet discernible as independent from masculinity.[162] In its most elemental state, the female signifies the potential for difference embedded in the indifference of the infinite and hence it cannot assume the semiotic status of refusing absorption into the whole. Rather, we can apply Hegel's observation that at the beginning we have before us the one and not the other to the theogonic myth of the kabbalists according to which the other is identified similarly as the determinate representation of the indeterminate essence that ensues from the infinite turning back unto itself so that its reflection may appear in and for itself.

The implication of the theosophic symbolism is drawn explicitly by Nathan of Gaza (1643–80), the theologian who provided the kabbalistic framing to bolster the messianic pretense of Sabbatai Ṣevi (1626–76), in his account of the Lurianic myth:

> Know that when there was the contraction in the will of the infinite [*ki ke-she-hayah ha-ṣimṣum hayah be-raṣon ein sof*], there remained a trace [*reshimu*] in that empty space [*ḥalal*] as is known. When the light ascended above, the trace did not exist in the way that it did at the beginning, that is, in its first place, because the movement of the ascent of the light above removed it from its place. The depth of the infinite was great and wondrous to move the trace from its place to another place. . . . Thus, it stood from one side as it was [*mi-ṣad eḥad amad kemo she-hayah*], and that side is called the right . . . for all of the left was comprised in the right [*de-khol sema'la de-itkelil bimina*]. There was produced the movement of the trace that remained from the great light, and thus it was the left. When the light of the straight line [*qaw ha-yosher*] came upon the luster [*ha-ṭehiru*] that stood in its place, the mercies [*ha-ḥasadim*] were constructed to the right side, and when the movement was produced from its place, the strengths [*ha-gevurot*] were constructed to the left. The principle that emerges is that every light of the trace in which no movement was made in the time of the contraction is a root for the right [*shoresh le-yamin*] in the aspect of each and every configuration [*kol parṣuf u-farṣuf*]. . . . This root was produced verily in the time of the contraction, and hence it is called "root" because it is from the very potency of the infinite, but the movements that are produced afterward are not called "root."[163]

Eliciting the gender implications of the symbolism espoused for centuries by kabbalists, Nathan insists that the right side alone should be considered originary since it is the face (*panim*) that derives directly without any motion from the infinite as opposed to the left side that is the back (*aḥor*) that comes to be as a result of the movement of the luster, which is the trace that remains after the space has been purged of the light, a movement that is understood as the endeavor of the residual light to ascend upward to be bound to the light that was withdrawn and weakened as a consequence of the contraction of *Ein Sof*, the light that is described statically as standing in its place (*ha-or she-amad bi-meqomo*).[164]

> Know that in the place that the will of the infinite [*reṣon ein sof*] arose to become the face [*panim*], that is, the actual face of each and every configuration [*panim mammash shel kol parṣuf u-farṣuf*], there was

produced no movement [*tenu'ah*] at all, as it is in the right . . . and in the aspect of the back [*ha-aḥor*], which is to receive these faces, there was movement for the light to go out from its place in concealment [*bi-setiru*], for that light that departs from its place is always hidden in the light that does not move from its place. And this was in the totality of the contraction [*bi-khelalut ha-ṣimṣum*] with regard to the face and the back of each configuration that was in the attribute of *Keter*, which reverted to being entirely facial [*ithaddar kolla panim*].[165]

Given the correlation of the face with the right, which is masculine, and the back with the left, which is feminine, to say of *Keter* that it returns to being entirely facial is another symbolic way of articulating the idea of a single gender—a world of pure masculinity before the dimorphic rupture into male and female.[166] That this dynamic informed Nathan's eschatological vision—the restitution of the beginning at the end—is attested in the following passage from the same treatise: "You must know that there is no perfection of the back of the king except in the root of the back conjoined with the queen, who hides the mystery of her right . . . and it is not possible to separate this back from her except in the future to come when she will be in the secret of the diadem of her husband [*aṭeret ba'lah*] for everything will be restored to the right."[167] The future is marked by the extraction of the posterior from the female because at that time the left will be eliminated as an independent force and everything will be restored to the right, which is to say, there will be only the anterior, a metamorphosis that is symbolized by the scriptural image that describes the woman of valor as the diadem of her husband (Proverbs 12:4). The import of the symbol is made explicit by Nathan in another passage: "And with this you can understand what the sages, blessed be their memory, said that in the future she will be a diadem of her husband . . . she is compared to *Keter* . . . for in the time of the contraction [*be-et ha-ṣimṣum*] it was the right and afterward immediately in the completion of the contraction it became the left, and afterward it returned to the right. However, *Keter* acquired its substance straightaway in the account of the chariot, whereas *Malkhut* did not acquire its substance until the end of the account of creation.[168] . . . For this reason they said that she will be a diadem of her husband, since after her root, which is entirely right, is purified, she has an elevation greater than her husband and she is verily compared to *Keter*."[169] As I have argued in various studies,[170] the image from Proverbs is one of the key metaphors utilized by kabbalists to signify the ascent of the feminine to the masculine and the reconstitution of the male androgyny; in the case of Nathan, this symbol emblematizes the cosmic Sabbath, the seventh millennium, indicative of the messianic status of Sabbatai Ṣevi and the apocatastatic harmony of all differentiated beings.[171]

The axiology underlying this monistic ontology is expressed bluntly by the eighteenth-century kabbalist Baruch of Kosov: "The aspect of lovingkindness [*ḥesed*] is the primordial aspect because *Ein Sof*, which is the absolute primordiality, is the incomposite lovingkindness in the extreme incompositeness, and the aspect of judgment [*din*] is revealed from the profusion of the concatenation of the gradations from cause to effect until the light of the great lovingkindness is diminished and as a consequence the aspect of judgment is revealed. For in the superfluity of the light of the great lovingkindness the aspect of judgment is not discernible or felt at all."[172] The same author accepts the principle of androgyny according to which there is maleness and femaleness in each divine attribute—the former related to the potency to overflow to what is beneath it and the latter to the capacity to receive from what is above it—and he even goes so far as to say that the masculine aspect of bestowal itself displays both aspects insofar as the overflowing is male and the giving of determinate shape to the illumination that overflows so that it can be received is female.[173] Nevertheless, he insists the infinite is pure grace without any admixture of severity and therefore should be classified as utterly masculine.

A similar point may be elicited from Eliashiv:

This is the reason it is forbidden to contemplate *Ein Sof*, may his name be blessed, for the matter of the expression *Ein Sof* is that he is boundless and limitless, and there is nothing at all outside him. . . . Thus, with respect to the aspect of lovingkindness [*ḥesed*], when he is in his essence [*be-aṣmuto*] without any power [*gevurah*] at all, there is no way to distinguish within him something extrinsic to him, for the disclosure of something extrinsic is also only an aspect of one action of his actions, blessed be he, which is the contraction [*ha-ṣimṣum*] . . . but the essence of the lovingkindness has no disclosure related to his actions, and hence there is nothing extrinsic to him . . . and he is concealed in the extreme concealment [*ne'lam be-takhlit ha-he'lem*], verily in the aspect of *Ein Sof*, may his name be blessed forever. Thus it is clarified that the concealment and the disclosure, which are the boundless and the boundary, are themselves the aspect of lovingkindness and power.[174]

To the degree that *ḥesed* is valorized as male and *gevurah* (or *din*) as female, this implies a collapse of difference into a monolithic identity, a mode of thought in which truth is homogenized by the criteria of equality and sameness—something is true in the fullest sense when it is equal to itself.[175] To note, as some of my critics have done, that gender is a correlative phenomenon[176]—we cannot speak of male without female or of female without male—misses the point that in a phallocentric worldview, *correlativity is expressive of a lack of alterity*, since the other is symptomatic of the same, or in the zoharic language utilized by Nathan, the left is contained in the right.[177]

One cannot readily discover in kabbalistic literature—let alone recover—an untainted sense of difference; at best the difference is a difference within indifference, which makes all the difference in the world. Consequently, it is possible to envision masculinity without femininity because the latter is ontologically comprised in the former. The counterpoint, however, is not feasible and thus we cannot visualize femininity without masculinity, a world that is exclusively female—the isolation of the female in this way constitutes the theological transgression of idolatry or in the rabbinic expression for heresy, the cutting of the shoots.[178] Once the single gender splits into the dyad of masculine and feminine, then it is possible to speak of the male contained in the female or the female contained in the male, but prior to the splintering of the male androgyne into the gender dimorphism, there is an asymmetrical containment of the female in the male in a manner that mimics the account of the creation of the human in the second chapter in Genesis according to which woman was comprised in the man.[179] I have argued elsewhere that the kabbalistic logic of a noncorrelative correlativity is buttressed as well by several rabbinic dicta. For example, the maxim that above there is no left, which does not mean that there is a third space that is neither left nor right, but that the godly expanse is entirely right,[180] a characterization that kabbalists attribute to the uppermost dimension of the divine, the sphere of unmitigated compassion.[181] One of the most vivid images to transmit this idea is the portrayal of *Keter*, or the countenance *Arikh Anpin*, as the single eye of mercy without a corresponding eye of judgment, that is, the masculine without an independently existing feminine.[182] As preposterous as it seems, we are obliged to imagine a male that prefigures the bifurcation into male and female, or in the formulation of one zoharic passage describing the status of gender in the highest regions of the divine:

When *Attiqa Qaddisha*, the concealed of the concealed, desires to be adorned [*le'atqena*], everything was adorned in the manner of male and female [*ke'ein dekhar we-nuqba*]. In the place where male and female are integrated, they do not exist but in an alternate way of being male and female [*ba-atar de-itkelilu dekhar we-nuqba lo itqeyyamu ella be-qiyyuma aḥara di-dekhar we-nuqba*]. And when that *Ḥokhmah*, the principle of everything [*kelala de-kholla*], comes forth and is illumined from *Attiqa Qaddisha*, it does not shine but as male and female [*lo itnehir ella bi-dekhar we-nuqba*], for that *Ḥokhmah* emanates and there issues from him *Binah*, and thus male and female are found [*we-ishtekhaḥ dekhar we-nuqba*]. *Ḥokhmah* is the father and *Binah* the mother. *Ḥokhmah and Binah* are balanced on one scale as male and female [*be-ḥad matqela itqalu dekhar we-nuqba*].[183]

Articulated in this passage is one of the axiomatic principles that informed the worldview of theosophic kabbalah: the structure of all being—from the sefirotic emanations to the lowest of the four worlds—assumes the form of the dimorphic constitution of gender, masculine grace and feminine judgment, the potency to overflow and the capacity to receive. In *Attiqa Qaddisha*, however—the paramount configuration of the divine above which is only the aura of the infinite light—masculine and feminine are contained within one another (*itkelilu dekhar we-nuqba*), and since they are not yet demarcated as autonomous, it is as if they do not exist (*lo itqeyyamu*). In that place, maleness and femaleness are not stably distinguished—in the words used by Eliashiv, commenting on this text from the *Idra Zuṭa*, the independent vessels to bring them forth from concealment to disclosure and from potentiality to actuality, that is, the vessel of the masculine for the light of mercy (*or ha-ḥesed*) and the vessel of the feminine for the light of strength (*or ha-gevurah*), had not yet been created[184]—and hence the dimorphism assumes a different complexion. This seems to be implied by the statement "in an alternate way of being male and female" (*be-qiyyuma aḥara di-dekhar we-nuqba*). It is possible that these words should be interpreted as referring to the subsequent stage of emanation when the two genders—represented respectively by *Ḥokhmah and Binah*—are discriminated; that is, male and female exist as distinct genders only in another state of being or on another level of existence (*qiyyuma aḥara*) within the divine pleroma. Either way we interpret this gloss, it does not change the fact that in *Attiqa Qaddisha* there is an overcoming of the gender dimorphism insofar as male and female are contained within one another. But does this containment imply an identity of difference or a difference of identity? Does the instability of gender imply transmutation of substance or merely fluctuation of function? From additional passages in this section of the zoharic compilation, not to mention other strata, the highest aspect of the divine is characterized as uniquely male or as the male that encompasses the dimension of the female that has not been formed independently. I am inclined to read the text in this manner and thus the reference to the alternate way of being male and female implies a state in which there is one gender, the androgynous male that comprises the female. Support for my interpretation may be gleaned from an alternate reading of the passage in question from the *Idra Zuṭa*. After the words *be-qiyyuma aḥara*, some texts preserve the variant *ke'ein dekhar*, "in the manner of the male," in place of *di-dekhar we-nuqba*, "of male and female." This version suggests that at some point in the redactional history it was understood that the statement "in the place where male and female are integrated" (*ba-atar de-itkelilu dekhar we-nuqba*) implies that "they do not exist but in an alternate way in the manner of the male" (*lo itqeyyamu ella be-qiyyuma aḥara ke'ein dekhar*); that is, there is but one gender and the female is contained in the male as the capacity for boundary within the boundless. The gender division into an autonomous masculinity and femininity becomes discernible with the manifestation of the second and third emanations, *Ḥokhmah* and *Binah*, characterized respectfully as the father and the mother.[185]

Generic Multiples and the Fragmentation of the Infinitesimal

Is there a possibility of reading the sources against the grain, of finding a crack in the conceptual edifice that would allow us to avoid the aforementioned collapse, to reclaim an otherness of the same that expresses the inexpressible sameness of the other? Is there a path to conceive of difference as the nonidentical identity of indifference? We turn again to Heidegger as a guide to helping us to see the nonsystematic cohesiveness of the unraveling of the kabbalistic system by probing the profundity of what is be thought from the unthought.

In a manner that is suggestive of both kabbalistic theosophy and Schelling's idealist philosophy, Heidegger envisions the inceptual act—the "self-grounding in the ground which is fathomed and opened up through the beginning"[186]—as a concomitant intensification and attenuation of the lighting up of beyng in the shelter of the self-concealing clearing.[187] I note, in passing, that Heidegger is probably motivated by the comment of Schelling in *Philosophie und Religion*, "there is no continuous transition from the Absolute to the actual; the origin [*Ursprung*] of the phenomenal world is conceivable only as a complete breaking-away [*Abbrechen*] from absoluteness by means of a leap [*Sprung*]. . . . There is no positive effect coming out of the Absolute that creates a conduit or bridge between the infinite and the finite. . . . The Absolute is the only actual; the finite world, by contrast, is not real. Its cause, therefore, cannot lie in an *impartation* [*Mittheilung*] of reality from the Absolute to the finite world or its substrate; it can only lie in a *remove* [*Entfernung*], in a *falling-away* [*Abfall*] from the Absolute."[188]

The shift from infinity to finitude by the falling-away or the removal from the Absolute rather than through a bestowal of reality from the Absolute parallels the contraction/withdrawal of the light of *Ein Sof* according to the teaching propounded by kabbalists overtly since the sixteenth century even though the roots for the idea stretch further back in history.[189] More astonishingly, the comparison is enhanced by the fact that Schelling's view that the world is a mere nonbeing (*Nicht-seyn*) that "can no more come into being as not come into being," and that time is "the principle and necessary form of all that is nonessential" (*Nicht-Wesen*),[190] parallels the acosmism embraced by, or at the very least implied by, some kabbalists and even more explicitly by some Ḥasidic masters.[191] To speak of the cosmos in this way is not to deny Schelling's commitment to the idea that nature is a progressive disclosure of the Absolute, but it does accentuate the paradox that this disclosure perforce must be a concealment, that the darkness contracting into light is the expansion of that light into the constricted forms of the determinate beings that make up the world perceived through the cognitive prism of space and time rendered quantitatively. In my judgment, this is a credible interpretation of kabbalistic cosmology.

Most evocatively, the detachment or elimination from the infinite is designated by Schelling as a leap, which denotes, as we find in some kabbalistic texts, the sense of agency effective outside the strictures of a unidirectional causation. In earlier sources, the leap (*dillug*) denotes the spontaneous elevation that impersonates the movement of the angels, often connected with the ritual leaping required when saying the Trisagion during the *qedushah* prayer,[192] or more generally, a swift motion that is not subject to the temporal and spatial constraints of a linear causality. The miraculous intervention of God is linked specifically to the holiday of Passover, since the Hebrew word *pesah*ʿ denotes skipping over.[193] Building on this symbolism, the image of the leap in later sources—especially pronounced in Hʿabad-Lubavitch masters—signifies the first act of the infinite, the withdrawal of the light, which comes about through a circumvention of any sequence proceeding from cause to effect. As I argued in chapter 3, to think of *Ein Sof* as a cause—indeed, the cause of causes—requires an acausal causality that does not depend on any mutuality because, as of yet, in this nondual oneness (*ahʿdut ehʿad*) there is no division into cause and effect.[194] It is this very discontinuity that propels the continuity of the order of concatenation (*seder ha-hishtalshelut*) disseminated serially through the four worlds.[195] Put differently, the metaphor of the leap conveys that the criterion for predictability can be established unpredictably by a disruption of the noncomputable chaos whence the computational structure materializes imaginally in the concurrent spatialization of time and temporalization of space. The Schellingian-kabbalistic understanding of the leap coincides, therefore, with much of what Heidegger had to say about *Ereignis* in his later philosophy[196] and the assumption that the activity attributed to the hidden essence of *Seyn* is outside the confines of the stock understanding of causal determinacy, that beyng is a spontaneous event that is neither the effect of a preceding cause nor the cause of a succeeding effect.[197] Congruently, as the being that is permeated with the impermeable nothing that is neither being nor nonbeing, neither empty nor nonempty, the infinite oneness that divides infinitesimally, the causal circuit is disrupted with respect to *Ein Sof*, and at best, it can be envisioned as the cause that can have no effect and therefore as not really a cause.

To elucidate the general principle (*kelala de-milta*) of this infinitesimal fragmentation of the agglomerated unity of the infinite, let us consider the formulation by the Bohemian kabbalist Meir ben Judah Leib Poppers (ca. 1624–62):

> The name *YHWH* comprises the five configurations . . . and in each configuration there are ten emanations, the complete stature [*qomah sheleimah*]. In each configuration, there is also the name *YHWH* and it is divided as stated above, the tittle [of the *yod*] is the *Keter* of this configuration and the *waw* is *Ḥokhmah*,

and so on. And thus each configuration divides individually [*bi-feraṭiyyut*] into five configurations. The tittle is the *Arikh* [*Anpin*] of the configuration and the rest of the letters are the remaining configurations, and thus it is with respect to the endless specification of the details [*bi-feraṭei peraṭot ad ein sof*]. And so it is in the worlds of emanation, creation, formation, and doing. In general, there are four worlds, and each one comprises the four, and thus it is in the endless specification of the details. The reason is that each letter of the name perpetually comprises it in its entirety [*kolel kullo*], and hence what is in the part is what is in the whole [*yesh ba-ḥeleq mah she-be-khullo*].[198]

We might say, as Hans-Jost Frey reasonably observed, the fragment has meaning only in relation to the whole that cannot accommodate it, since the fragment by definition is incomplete and thus is precisely what lacks the sense of wholeness.[199] The kabbalistic principle, however, illustrated by the text of Poppers, is that the complete incompleteness of the fragment is determinative of the incomplete completeness of the whole.

To invoke Badiou again, he notes that his thought "both un-binds the Heideggerian connection between being and truth and institutes the subject, not as support or origin, but as *fragment* of the process of a truth."[200] Bracketing the accuracy of his reading of Heidegger, the important point is that Badiou offers an understanding of the fragment vis-à-vis the whole that does not compromise the fragmentariness of the fragment: the *being of the truth* is deduced from the mathematical concept of the unnamable, unconstructible, and indiscernible generic multiple.[201] To be even more precise, we should speak of generic multiples,[202] insofar as the multiple itself is the "absolutely indeterminate" that can never be specified as a unity that defies the principle of subtraction from knowledge of the one.[203] The pure multiple, the multiple of multiples, consists of the one being without-one.[204] The import of the use of the apophatic adjectives to depict the fractional generic is that "a multiple in a given situation solely possesses properties which are more or less 'common' to all the multiples of the situation."[205] The fragmentary nature of the fragment, therefore, is enhanced by the disjointedness of the totality, the "void-multiple, which commands a transmissible thinking," the opening of the infinite text "as the historicity of mathematical deductions."[206]

Closer to the kabbalistic ideal is Frey's own observation that the openness of the fragment "leads to a higher closure. If understanding the fragment from inside is now impossible, it becomes nonetheless possible to understand it through the external circumstances that have prevented its completion. . . . Although the fragment is now no longer treated as whole, it is treated as part of the larger structure of meaning from which it cannot be detached."[207] Needless to say, Frey differs from the kabbalists insofar as he posits a finite whole that is surrounded by the perimeter that cannot be confined within its margins instead of an infinite whole that presumably includes everything and outside of which there is nothing. But the notion of infinity I am proffering in the name of the kabbalists dissolves the divide between these two options. Wholeness implies not an immutable unity of permanent substances but an elaborate web of interrelated processes in which every part can be read as a metonymy for the continually evolving interweave of the cumulative that is resistant to inclusion in a system that would undercut the reciprocal integration of the disintegrated and the disintegration of the integrated.[208]

This is the import of the concluding statement from the aforecited passage of Poppers: what is in the part is what is in the whole. Read from a postmodern perspective, this is not affirming that the particulars are contained immutably in the preordained whole, but rather that the whole itself is constituted incessantly by the ever-changing and seemingly limitless proliferation of the particulars. The kabbalistic principle can be interpreted as an adaptation of two of the thirteen hermeneutical rules attributed to R. Ishmael:[209] (1) *kelal u-feraṭ*, that is, a general statement (*kelal*) followed by a particular specification (*peraṭ*) yields the rule that "there is nothing in the general that is not in the particular" (*ein ba-kelal ella mah she-ba-peraṭ*); and (2) *peraṭ u-khelal*, that is, a particular specification followed by a general statement yields the rule that "the general supplements the particular" (*na'aseh kelal mosif al ha-peraṭ*).[210]

In a totalizing system, we would expect that the validity of the first proposition depends on the validity of its opposite, and hence nothing would be in the general that is not in the particular because nothing would be in the particular that is not in the general. This reciprocity appears to underlie R. Ishmael's seventh rule, the general that needs the particular and the particular that needs the general (*mi-kelal she-hu ṣarikh la-peraṭ u-mi-peraṭ she-hu ṣarikh la-kelal*).

Some kabbalists did espouse this position in describing the divine. A relatively early articulation of this view is found, for instance, in the following words of the fourteenth-century kabbalist David ben Abraham ha-Lavan:

> If all the powers were to return to nothing [*ayin*], then the primordial one [*ha-qadmon*], the cause of all [*illah la-kol*], would stand in its unity in the depths of nothingness, in undifferentiated oneness [*be-aḥdut ha-shaweh*]. . . . With respect to every matter that has no boundary [*gevul*], it is known that it has no beginning [*ro'sh*] or end [*sof*], no telos [*tikhlah*] and no inception [*teḥillah*], and it is the essence [*eṣem*] of everything. Since it is the essence of everything and that which gives boundary to everything, the part is completely in the general [*yesh ba-kelal kol ha-ḥeleq*].[211]

We find the same explanation applied to the rabbinic idea that all of the ten commandments revealed at Sinai were spoken in one word (*dibbur eḥad*) offered by Meir Ibn Gabbai (1480–1540): "This instructs us that there is no difference among them, and the general is the particular and the particular is the general [*we-ha-kelal hu ha-peraṭ we-ha-peraṭ hu ha-kelal*], and there is nothing in the general that is not in the particular and nothing in the particular that is not in the general [*we-ein ba-kelal ella mah she-ba-peraṭ we-ein ba-peraṭ ella mah she-ba-kelal*]."[212] Rehearsing a much older tradition, Ibn Gabbai goes on to identify the Decalogue with the ten utterances (*ma'amarot*) by which the world was created, and these, in turn, with the ten divine emanations (*sefirot*). The hermeneutical claim made about the reversibility of the general and the particular has theosophic implications, and, I should add, this is linked in some sources with the mystery of the androgyne, the general is correlated with the masculine and the particular with the feminine.[213]

Assuredly, any number of kabbalists could be mentioned to demonstrate that the view stated overtly by Ibn Gabbai was hardly eccentric. Often enough, kabbalists posit an equilibrium between the state of affairs before the fracturing of the unity at the beginning and the restoration of that unity at the end: just as everything was assimilated in the light of *Ein Sof* prior to the emanation, so all things will return to be comprised in that light in a perfect unity when the process of rectification (*tiqqun*) of the splintering of the light is brought to fruition. As Viṭal suggests in the first section of his magnum opus, *Eṣ Ḥayyim*, this symmetry is implied by the Tetragrammaton, which, according to an archaic explanation,[214] conveys that all three tenses are coterminous in God, that is, God is, was, and will be all at once, so that there is a compresence of past (*hayah*), present (*howeh*), and future (*yihyeh*): "The great name, which is the name of the four letters *YHWH*, is called this way to instruct about his eternal being and everlasting existence, past, present, and future—prior to the creation, in the time of the perdurance of creation, and after it returns to what was."[215] Reading between the lines, we would presume there is no reality apart from the name in whose unity all particulars are incorporated.[216]

Typical of that approach is the comment of Pinḥas Eliyahu Horowitz of Vilna (1765–1821), which proffers an excellent précis of the Lurianic *Weltanschauung*. Prior to the emanation of the worlds, the Tetragrammaton was hidden in the emanator, which is without a name, like the flame secreted in the coal; once the will arose to emanate and the worlds came into being, the nameless is united with the name like the flame bound to the coal, according to the well-known image used in *Sefer Yeṣirah* to depict the unity of the ten *sefirot*.[217] The name comprises five worlds: the tittle of the *yod* corresponds to *Adam Qadmon*, the *yod* to the world of emanation, the first *he* to the world of creation, the *waw* to the world of formation, and the second *he* to the world of doing. Additionally, the four letters of *YHWH* are correlated with the four elements—fire, spirit, water, and earth—but, on account of its supreme hiddenness, no element is allocated to *Adam Qadmon*. The concealment of *Ein Sof* is even greater and hence it is completely beyond semantic and numeric demarcation. Its thread (*huṭ*), however, is hidden and garbed within *Adam Qadmon* and thus the latter, which sefirotically parallels *Keter* and pneumatically the aspect of *yeḥidah*, is the "containment of all the worlds" (*kelalut kol ha-olamot*). Horowitz concludes by pointing out that the structure repeats itself in each detail that is in every world because "there is nothing in the particular but what is in the general and nothing in the general but what is in the particular."[218]

The worldview presented by Horowitz conforms to the widely accepted symmetrical logic whereby the truth of the postulate that there is nothing in the general that is not in the particular implies the truth of the inverse postulate that there is nothing in the particular that is not in the general. Echoing such a view, Eliashiv wrote, "The principle of things [*kelal ha-devarim*] is that the general and the particular are one [*ha-kelal we-ha-peraṭ eḥad hu*], and as it is in the generality so it is in the particularity [*u-khe-mo she hu bi-khelalut ken hu bi-feraṭut*], and just as it is in the emanation, which is the entire divinity, for there is the disclosures of the emanator, the infinite, may his name be blessed, which is revealed through the name and to bring forth all the worlds of creation, formation, and doing, which are the differentiated worlds, so he brought them into existence as well in accord with the order of all his disclosures revealed in his name, which is in the emanation."[219] What I am proposing, however, is the possibility of eliciting from other kabbalistic texts an asymmetrical logic such that the nature of the general is determined by the particular in a manner that is not reciprocally affirmed with regard to the particular in relation to the general. Perhaps this can be expressed by appeal to another one of the hermeneutical principles transmitted in the name of R. Ishmael: *kelal u-feraṭ u-khelal*, when a general statement is followed by a particular statement, and then by another general statement, one must render a judgment in accord with the particular (*ein attah dan ella ke-ein ha-peraṭ*).[220] The specification is given priority to the generalization, since the latter is molded by the former, and not the former by the latter, as is commonly believed. In this regard, again invoking Frey, "the breaking point of the fragment is the boundary of the possible."[221] That is to say, the limit of possibility—the more-than-possible and hence the impossible[222]—is not determined by the contingent necessity of the whole but rather by the necessary contingency of the part. The primacy accorded the fragmentary in the determination of the aggregate lends support to the conclusion that the complexity of the system renders the very notion of system applicable only as a nonsystem.

Compossibility of the Universal Particular and the Particular Universal

To paraphrase the Yemenite kabbalist Shalom Sharabi (1720–77),[223] since the light of the infinite is attired (*melubbash*) in every detail (*peraṭ*), each detail can be considered the embodiment of divinity in its entirety (*elohut gamur*). The compossible synergy of universality (*derekh kelal*) and particularity (*peraṭut*) is expressed in the presumably inestimable distillations (*berurim*) and rectifications (*tiqqunim*) of the inextensible light.[224] The language is misleading if we presume that it insinuates that *Ein Sof* is a unity that can be surgically abstracted from the infinite multiplicity of the multiple. In my estimation, Sharabi, making explicit what Luria himself implied, is proffering just the opposite: there is no unicity but in the boundless divisibility of the indivisible, no integration but in the indefinite disintegration of the indissoluble. It is worth remembering Scholem's observation that the hidden God "manifests himself to the Kabbalist under ten different aspects, which in turn comprise an endless variety of shades and gradations."[225] A language beyond an ontological syntax was not available to Scholem, but in the main, his emphasis on the endless division of the ten emanations as the prevalent way to express the hiddenness of the infinite brings us to the same conclusion. Noteworthy as well is Scholem's remark that Luria's "special interest in the structure of the spiritual worlds and their emergence through dialectical processes is also expressed in the distinction he makes between the structural 'totality' (*kelalut*) of the forces of emanation and the structural 'individuality' (*peratut*) of each such power that is active in a given overall structure."[226] I would modify this comment by emphasizing that the totality and the individuality cannot be easily separated inasmuch as the former is manifest through the latter, and the latter through the former; the juxtaposition of the two precludes the necessity for a dialectical process by which a presumed difference is sublated. From that standpoint, moreover, the assumption of a symphonic unity of structure collapses under the weight of the particulars that cohere together without a tonal center, as I discussed in the final section of the second chapter.

To return to Sharabi: the dispersal of the light is referred to as the extension (*hitpashsheṭut*), incorporation (*hitkallelut*), and enclothing (*hitlabbeshut*) of the infinite line (*qaw ein sof*) into the circular alignment (*iggulim*) of the fractal whole: "There is no emanation [*sefirah*], soul [*neshamah*], or spark [*niṣoṣ*] that is not comprised of all the worlds from the head of *Adam Qadmon* to the termination of all the worlds, and the autonomous part [*ḥeleq aṣmo*] is not within it except as the unified part [*ḥeleq eḥad*], and the dimension of the measure of the garbing of each configuration [*shi'ur middat halbashat kol parṣuf*] vis-à-vis the configuration above it, and so it is with respect to the measure of the dimension of each world [*middat shi'ur kol olam*] from [the worlds of] emanation, creation, formation, and doing . . . that is, the final detail that all the emanations comprise."[227] It is virtually impossible to communicate discursively the nonsystematic system elaborated by Sharabi—the conceptual framework for the meditational technique at the heart of his kabbalistic school—without inscribing oneself in the intricate maze of the technical language he implements to delineate the indifference of infinity by and through the evidently inexhaustible differentiations. Although pedagogically it is sometimes necessary even for the master to speak in generality (*kelalut*), the truth is always to be found in the specificity (*peraṭut*).[228] And when it comes to the particularities, the distinctions multiply to the point of inscrutability (*ein ḥeqer*).[229] The infinite simplicity marks the prolificacy of the uncompounded one (*aḥdut ha-peshuṭah*) whose absolute determinacy is the indeterminacy of the many. From the particulars one comprehends the singular universal whence one discerns the universal singularity that is the universality of the singular. None of the particulars by itself constitutes the totality of the divine as in the Leibnizian monad, but the aggregation of all the particulars is indexical of the universal instantiated collectively and yet idiosyncratically in each of the particulars. I am reminded of Badiou's comment:

> Thought is nothing other than the desire to finish with the exorbitant excess of the state. Nothing will ever allow one to resign oneself to the innumerable parts. Thought occurs for there to be a cessation—even if it only lasts long enough to indicate that it has not actually been obtained—of the quantitative unmooring of being. It is always a question of a measure being taken of how much the state exceeds the immediate. Thought, strictly speaking, is what un-measure, ontologically proven, cannot satisfy.[230]

Sharabi's language epitomizes the surfeit of thinking that cannot be measured by the canons of rational thought and deductive syllogisms. The unmeasure of *Ein Sof* rests on the premise that the nonbeing of being—as opposed to the being of nonbeing—is manifestly multifarious and thus operationally akin to a differential calculus of the infinitesimal according to which the multiple instructs us about the one rather than the one instructing us about the multiple.[231]

Adopting the mathematical lexicon of Badiou, we could describe *Ein Sof* as the void that is the "subtractive suture to being."[232] Badiou's comment on the *axiom of the void-set*—the set that has no element—could be easily ascribed to the kabbalistic infinitude:

> In its metaontological formulation the axiom says: the unpresentable is presented, as a subtractive term of the presentation of presentation. Or: a multiple is, which is not under the Idea of the multiple. Or: being lets itself be named, within the ontological situation as that from which existence does not exist. . . . We thus arrive at the following remarkable conclusion: *it is because the one is not that the void is unique.*[233]

Ein Sof is the axiom of the foundation that has no axiomatic foundation; as such, it does not signify the supreme being beyond being, a hyperessential essence, but rather the irrevocability of the unpresentation and the unbeing of the multifactorial singular, the event-without-event[234] wherein the supplement of what-is-not-being-qua-being originates.[235]

The Badiouian interpretation of the kabbalistic *Ein Sof* that I have offered closely parallels Heidegger's understanding of *Seyn* as *Nichtseyn*, and this despite Badiou's sharp critique of Heideggerian ontology as well as the fundamental irreconcilability in the role they respectively accord to the poetico-natural and the mathematico-ideal orientations.[236] As Badiou boldly states, "It is possible to reinterrogate the entire history of philosophy, from its Greek origins on, according to the hypothesis of a mathematical regulation of the ontological question. One would then see a continuity and a periodicity unfold quite different to that deployed by Heidegger. In particular, the genealogy of the doctrine of truth will lead to a signposting, through similar interpretations, of how the categories of the event and the indiscernible, unnamed, were at work throughout the metaphysical text."[237] It would be ludicrous to harmonize Heidegger's appeal to truth as the being of the event, which is the event of being, and Badiou's insistence on truth emerging from the conjunction of being and event, but with respect to the issue I have raised, the discordancy can be somewhat ameliorated. Heidegger's poetic idea of the beyng that is nothing, the abyss (*Ab-grund*) that is the nonground (*Un-grund*) of the ground (*Grund*), the essence marked by heterogeneity with respect to that of which it is the essence, and the implied pluralism at the origin rather than a unitary principle,[238] articulate something analogous to Badiou's mathematical concept of the multiple void, the "without-one," the "being as non-being—or un-presentation—fullness . . . being as the non-existing limit of its being."[239] According to Heidegger, as Zarader noted, if we wish to think of being as simple (*l'être comme Simple*), that is, as the same being (*l'être même*), then we can do so only on the basis of understanding being essentially as a fold (*l'être comme Pli*), that is, as difference (*comme différence*).[240] The unitary nature of being, therefore, is predicated on accepting, in Badiou's terms, the "without-being of the One" and the "limitless authority of the multiple," a contemporary ontology fittingly referred to as the *Platonism of the multiple*.[241]

Turning back to the main point of my argument, the Heideggerian leap is comparable to the kabbalistic *ṣimṣum*, insofar as it is the clearing for the self-concealing of the event of beyng, that is, the primal but always yet to be act of nihilation—the nothing that nihilates aboriginally, from the origin hidden within the beginning—the venture of infinity into the province of finitude, the teeming vacuity that precedes the abundant nothingness that becomes something by virtue of being nothing. For both kabbalists and Heidegger, the time-space of the world emerges as a consequence of the distended diminution of the extended leap—beings come to be in the abandonment of the excess of their being. The kabbalistic infinity is well captured by Heidegger's depiction of nothingness as "higher than everything 'positive' and 'negative' in the totality of beings."[242] If we presume, as I think we must, that for kabbalists all being is the manifestation of what contemporary astrophysics might call the gravitational light wave of infinitivity—that is, disturbances in the fabric of the curvature of spacetime generated by accelerated masses that propagate as waves at the speed of light—and any manifestation thereof is synchronously an occlusion, since the infinite cannot be disclosed unless it is concealed in the cloak of the finite, it follows that the nothingness of *Ein Sof* can be beneficially described by the Heideggerian notion of the originary not dissembling in the dissemination of beyng manifest and hidden through the discrete beings of nature.

The kabbalistic tenor of Heidegger's utilization of Schelling is particularly salient in the following passage from the *Beiträge*:

> The leap, that most daring venture in the course of inceptual thinking, jettisons and leaves behind everything conventional [*Geläufige*]. The leap expects nothing immediate from beings; instead, and before all else, it leaps [*erspringt*] into the belonging to beyng [*die Zugehörigkeit zum Seyn*] in the full essential occurrence of beyng as event [*Wesung als Ereignis*]. In this way, the leap appears in the semblance of utter recklessness [*Rücksichtslosesten*], and yet the disposition motivating it is precisely that *diffidence* . . . in which the will to restraint surpasses itself toward steadfastness in withstanding the most remote nearness

of the hesitant withholding [*zögernden Versagung*]. The leap is the venture of a first penetration into the domain of the *history of being* [Seinsgeschichte].[243]

The leap is visualized as the crossing over (*Übergang*) impelled by the inceptual thinking, a movement of thought (*Gedanken-gang*) that springs from the *Ursprung*, the clearing (*Lichtung*), wherein the appropriating event (*Ereignis*) of "the entry of beyng into its truth" (*die Einkehr des Seyns in seine Wahrheit*) can be thought only in "the abandonment of beings by being." In thinking the "nearness to beyng" (*Nähe zum Seyn*) within the "temporal-spatial playing field of Da-sein" (*Zeit-Spiel-Raum des Da-seins*)—a nearness that is far-flung from all that is common—human beings can be said to belong to, or to be enowned by, the abysmal truth of beyng out of which all beings arise.[244] The leap, therefore, is characterized as a risky venture (*Wagnis*)—it comports itself as utter recklessness, an incursion into the history of beyng that requires leaving behind everything conventional; that is, relinquishing the sense of familiarity and security that develops from the commonplace relationship to beings construed primarily as objects of representation constituted noematically in our intentional consciousness, so that we will be equipped for the "going-under" (*Untergang*) that is "the gathering of everything great in the moment of preparedness for the truth of the uniqueness and non-repeatability of beyng. The going-under is the most intimate proximity to the refusal in which the event bestows itself on the human being."[245]

But how does one prepare for a truth that is unique and nonrepeatable? It does not seem possible if we contemplate time solely from the standpoint of a presence that is no more, a presence that is presently at hand, and a presence that is to come—the three tenses of quotidian time that Heidegger relates in *Sein und Zeit* to the "ecstasies of temporality" (*Ekstasen der Zeitlichkeit*), the future (*Zukunft*), the having been (*Gewesenheit*), and the present (*Gegenwart*).[246] It is the possibility of the impossibility of preparing for the unprecedented that underlies the state of temporality that Heidegger links to the bestowal of beyng in the clearing that is "simultaneously the *with-drawal* [Ent-zug] of the event . . . from all representational calculation [*vorstellenden Verrechnung*] and essentially occurs as refusal."[247] As Heidegger formulated the matter elsewhere, presence (*Anwesenheit*) "is never and in no way something [*ein Anwesendes*]; in this regard it is the nothing."[248] Presence is always more and therefore less than being present; even in the absence of being absent, time, like beyng, is neither something that is nothing nor nothing that is something.

The entrance into the history of beyng does not imply a movement that can be calculated in advance, since there is neither progress nor regress of which to speak within the historical domain.[249] In *Der Ursprung des Kunstwerkes*, based on lectures presented in 1935–36 and revised in the 1960 publication, Heidegger remarked that history does not signify a "sequence of events in time," but the "transporting [*Entrückung*] of a people into its appointed task [*Aufgegebenes*] as the entry [*Einrückung*] into its endowment [*Mitgegebenes*]."[250] Appreciably, it is not the avowal but the disavowal that is the "essential occurrence of beyng," the "highest possibility as possibility" that is "thereby the first necessity." The reference to necessity here does not denote something that must transpire but rather what is possible in the purest impulsion of the impossible, the leap of the possibility of possibility that prompts "the expanding of the temporal-spatial playing field in which the trembling itself, as refusal, appropriates to itself the clearing (the 'there'). The intimacy of this trembling requires the most abyssal fissure [*abgründigsten Zerklüftung*], and in the latter the inexhaustibility of beyng might be inventively thought by way of surmises [*ahnend erdenken*]."[251] George Kovacs deftly recapitulated Heidegger's position, "This 'turning' to Being, the understanding of Dasein based on this belonging to Being, represents a leap in thinking Being itself; it breaks with the metaphysical thinking of Being as (a reduction of the richness of Being to) beingness (*Seiendheit*) and inaugurates the saying and thinking of Being itself, of the essence of the truth of Being as event, as appropriation (*Ereignis*), that is, as historical and not dialectical."[252]

The leap is a movement of mindfulness that stands outside the margins of the mathematical and its implied determination of truth as certainty, and hence it betokens a way of thought that is essentially "systemless" (*ohne System*) or "unsystematic" (*un-systematisch*), properties that Heidegger adamantly distinguishes from the "arbitrary" (*willkürlich*) or "confused" (*wirr*).[253] Anticipating his own concerted effort to propose a mode of thinking that departs from the model of the system, the meditative thinking that looks away from calculative thinking, he writes in the introductory remarks of the lecture course on *Abhandlung über das Wesen der menschlichen Freiheit*, given at the University of Freiburg in the summer semester of 1936, that Schelling "had to get stranded in his work because his manner of questioning didn't allow an inner center in the standpoint of philosophy at that time." Heidegger goes on to say that Nietzsche, the only "essential thinker" after Schelling, "broke down in the middle of his real work, *The Will to Power*, for the same reason. But this double, great breakdown of great thinkers is not a failure and nothing negative at all—on the contrary. It is the sign of the advent of something completely different, the heat lightning of a new beginning. Whoever really knew the reason for this breakdown and could conquer it intelligently would have to become the founder of the new beginning of Western philosophy."[254]

The new beginning calls for what Heidegger labeled *inceptual thinking*, which, as we discussed in chapter 2, is configured disjointedly around six conjunctures. Just as, musically, the fugue is a compositional technique based on the reiteration of a theme at different tonal registers, so for Heidegger, structure (*Gefüge*), in contradistinction to system, emerges from the reverberation of the same uniquely in each of the disparate sectors held together in their joinings/fissures. Repetition is thus the perpetuation of the identical in a manner that is always different;[255] that is, to repeat is not the continuation of what has been but the retrieval (*wieder-holen*) of the inception that is "begun again *more originally* [*der Anfang* ursprünglicher *wiederangefangen wird*], and with all the strangeness, darkness, insecurity that a genuine inception brings with it."[256] Alternatively expressed, the event of beyng is calibrated from the standpoint of the originality and uniqueness of beyng itself—the aggregate that is entirely fragmentary inasmuch as "what is as a whole, as what is, itself demands a grounding in openness,"[257] and, as such, the totality is what it is in virtue of what it is to become. Every occurrence is a recurrence of what is yet to be in the fullness of the grounded essence of what has been.[258] The leap, consequently, initiates the beginning constantly surpassed by the prospect of the other beginning that is first insofar as it is second,[259] the beginning in which "the truth of beyng must be ventured as grounding, as inventive thought of Da-sein."[260]

In "Der Ursprung des Kunstwerkes," Heidegger wrote of the leap as the "suddenness of the beginning" (*Unvermittelte des Anfangs*) that is "always a leaping-ahead [*Vorsprung*], a leaping-ahead in which everything to come is already leapt over [*übersprungen*], even if as something veiled. Concealed within itself, the beginning contains already the end."[261] Inasmuch as the leap at the beginning is a leap-ahead, the end can be said to be comprised in the beginning. Heidegger distinguishes the "genuine beginning" from that which is "primitive" on the grounds that the latter has no future "because it lacks the bestowing, grounding leap and the leap-ahead."[262] One might suspect a form of temporal determinacy implied in the statements that "everything to come is already leapt over" and that "the beginning contains already the end." But, in fact, what Heidegger intends is just the opposite: the indefiniteness of the future is secured by the fact that the having-been in the present is grounded as what is to come, the past molded by the future that is molded by the past.[263] As Heidegger put it in a letter to Elisabeth Blochmann from September 12, 1929, the return to the past "is not a passive acceptance of what has been, but its transformation (*Verwandlung*)."[264] Expanding this theme in the 1961 lecture commemorating the seventh centennial of his hometown Meßkirch, Heidegger writes, "But what if we understand the future as that which comes towards us today? In this case the future is not just something that follows upon today, but rather is that which projects into today. Today, then, is not a segment of time existing on its own, self-contained on all sides. Today has its Origin in what-is-as-having-been [*im Gewesen*] and at the same time is opened out onto what comes towards it [*was auf es kommt*]."[265] The distance between the *terminus ad quo* and the *terminus ad quem* is bridged especially by the poiēsis of art, an act that allows truth to arise (*entspringen*) by bringing something into being from the origin (*Ursprung*) by means of the endowing leap (*stiftenden Sprung*).[266]

It is in this sense that Heidegger, partially thinking in the wake of Hegel, can transpose the intent of the statement that the result is the beginning: "The beginning must really be made with the result, since the beginning results from that result."[267] It is imperative to distinguish Heidegger's conception from the uroboric nature of the Hegelian dialectic whereby the end is contained in the beginning as the latter's necessary outcome, and hence in the end the absolute returns to itself as it was in the beginning. Badiou correctly noted that reinforcing this dialectical movement is the "theological circularity which, presupposing the absolute in the seeds of the beginning, leads back to this very beginning once all the stages of its effectuation, its alienation, its-going-outside-itself, and so on, are unfolded. Thus, the dead Son reintegrated into the divisible immanence of the Father *completes* the world-concept of the Christian God, which is the holiness of the Spirit."[268] For Heidegger, by contrast, as I noted in chapter 1, the realization of the beginning in the end does not presume that the end is nothing but the cyclical rotation back to the beginning. On the contrary, in a manner more consonant with the kabbalistic orientation, itself rooted in the Jewish apocalyptic sensibility, the beginning whither one returns in the end is not the beginning whence one set forth toward the end. The timeswerve is not to be conceived as a palindrome, for it entails a return to where one has never been; the temporal sequence, therefore, cannot be read the same backward and forward. It goes without saying that kabbalists unvaryingly have been influenced by the passage in *Sefer Yeṣirah* regarding the *sefirot*, their end is fixed in their beginning and their beginning in their end like a flame bound to the coal.[269] But even this formulation does not necessarily imply a closed and inflexible circle such that we could ascertain the nature of the beginning from the end or that of the end from the beginning. Consider the explication of the critical words "their end in their beginning" preserved in the commentary transmitted in the name of the Provençal kabbalist Isaac the Blind (1160–1235):

> A disseminating wellspring—all that disseminates is from the source, and if the source ceases, everything ceases; and since they disseminate at all times, the beginning has no end. Therefore, it says "their end is in their beginning," for many strands come forth from the coal, which is one; the flame cannot stand on its own but only by means of something else. All the matters and all the attributes, which appear to be separate, have no separation, for all is one like the beginning that unifies everything in a single word.[270]

That the beginning is fixed in the end, and the end in the beginning, signifies the oneness of the multiple beings that come forth from the infinite source of being, but this claim destabilizes the rigidity of beginning and end as temporal indicators. Since the *sefirot* emanate incessantly from *Ein Sof*, the beginning does not begin, which is to say, it is not a beginning, and analogously, we can assume that the ending does not end, which is to say, it is not an ending. The unity of the sefirotic potencies notwithstanding, beginning and end are marked by the distinctiveness of their indistinction.

Ironically, my contention about the similarity between Heidegger's criticism of Hegel's notion of an incontrovertible circle and a divergent view of the open circularity proffered by the kabbalists is consolidated by Heidegger's comment in the rectoral address on the inauguration of Greek science in relation to the mission of the German university in the twentieth century: "The beginning *exists* still. It does not lie *behind* us as something long past, but it stands *before* us. The beginning has—as the greatest moment, which exists in advance—already passed indifferently over and beyond all that is to come and hence over and beyond us as well. The beginning has invaded our future; it stands there as the distant decree that orders us to recapture its greatness."[271] Heidegger urged his listeners to understand that only by obeying the decree to win back the greatness of the beginning will the pursuit of knowledge again become the means to fulfill the spiritual essence of the German people. At this fateful moment, he intuited that the beginning is not the past but the future that has passed *over and beyond all that is to come* and therefore cannot be retrieved simply as the culmination coiled in the commencement.

In the summer course of 1934, several months after assuming the rectorship, Heidegger elaborated on this theme by noting that the essence of being human is determined from that which is essential in the historical moment, but the latter is experienced on the basis of the self-decision (*Selbstentscheidung*) to become who we want to become in the future, and hence the past—what Heidegger names the "beenness" (*Gewesenheit*) or "that which essences from earlier on" (*das von früher her Wesende*)—determines itself from our future. As Heidegger is quick to point out, however, this determination from the future "is not subject to a prediction [*Voraussage*]; it cannot be invented and concocted in a freely suspended manner. It determines itself, rather, from that which essences from earlier on." We come again to the hermeneutical circularity that induces Heidegger's temporal understanding of tradition (*Überlieferung*) and historicity (*Geschichtlichkeit*): "That which essences from earlier on determines itself from the future; the future determines itself from what essences since earlier. . . . That which essences from earlier on has its peculiarity to it in that it has always already grasped over [*hinweggegriffen*] every today and now: It *essences as tradition*. . . . That which essences comes up toward us [*kommt auf uns zu*] in this reaching over [*Übergriff*] from the future [*Zukunft*]." The future comes only to one capable of taking over (*zu übernehmen*) the tradition instead of being lost in the bustle of today. We should not conceive of the past as a present that is no longer nor of the future as a present that is not yet; there is only one "*originally singular and proper time*" (ursprünglich einzige und eigentliche Zeit): the future of the beenness into which we are thrown ahead (*Vorausgeworfensein*).[272]

As the attunement in which thinking abides in the discharge of beyng's withdrawal, the leap "opens the untrodden expanses and concealments of that into which the *grounding* of *Da*-sein must penetrate as belonging to the call of the event."[273] The leap thus heralds the opening of the truth of beyng as the originary swaying of the time-space (*Zeit-Raum*), the abyssal ground (*Ab-grund*),[274] the crevice of the self-concealing disclosure, which demands a thinking that surpasses the Hegelian dialectic and the ideal of truth as the resolution of the antinomy of the ontological difference. Heidegger's inceptual thinking is predicated on a more primal belonging-togetherness (*Zusammengehörigkeit*) of beyng and nothingness that resists the identity of their nonidentity and avows instead the nonidentity of their identity preserved in the juxtaposition of an irreducible divergence. Nothingness is no longer conceived as nonbeing (*Nichtseiende*) in the sense of the negative determination (*negative Bestimmung*) but rather as the nullity (*Nichtiges*) or negativity (*Nichthaftigkeit*) of being, the "highest gift" (*höchste Schenkung*) imparted as the "self-withdrawing" of the refusal.[275]

The matter is expounded oracularly in the following aphorism from *Die Geschichte des Seyns*, a collection of reflections that span the years 1938–40, concerning the nature of the "essential thinking" (*wesentliche Denken*), that is, the "inceptual philosophy" (*anfängliche Philosophie*), which is relevant to the other beginning:

> Der erste Sprung des Denkens denkt: Das Seyn ist das Nichts. Das Nichts nichtet. Die Nichtung verweigert jede Erklärung des Seienden aus Seiendem. Die Verweigerung aber gewährt die Lichtung, in der Seiendes aus- und ein-gehen, als ein solches offenbare und verborgen sein kann.
>
> The first leap of thinking thinks: Beyng is the Nothing. The Nothing nihilates. Nihilation refuses every explanation of beings in terms of beings. Refusal, however, grants the clearing in which beings go in and out, and as such can be manifest and concealed.[276]

The "first leap" does not denote a chronological demarcation but rather the originary beckoning of thought that leads to the paradox of paradoxes, the paradox that being is nothing. Empirically, there can be no verification of such a leap—this is what Heidegger means when he writes that the nihilation refuses every explanation of beings in terms of beings. And yet, this very refusal, the "leap into the abandonment by being as divinization [*die Seinsverlassenheit als Götterung*],"[277] is the nihilating evocation—the unsaying of the said engendered in the saying of the unsaid—through which beings are revealed in their concealment and concealed in their revelation.

The human being is the mediating agency that discerns and negotiates the ontological difference that the nothing opens between beyng and beings. We experience the strangeness (*Befremdlichkeit*) of beings as we come to discern experientially that beings are drastically different from the concealed beyng they manifest. Beings stand out in their disjunction from the beyng that is nothing. Contra Hegel, the Heideggerian nonbeing of beyng is not the counterconcept (*Gegenbegriff*) to beings but rather the nothingness that belongs to their essential unfolding. The nihilation of the nothing is the clearing in which beings are freed to be the beings they are by virtue of not being the being they are not, and thus it entails a double movement, the withdrawal of beings and the withdrawal of nothing, that is, the concealment of concealment, which is the condition for the unconcealment of beyng that allows Dasein to enter into relationship with the beings of the world. As I have emphasized repeatedly, this can be compared fruitfully to one of the most wide-ranging of the theosophical-cosmological doctrines endorsed by the kabbalists, a doctrine rendered poetically by Edmond Jabès: "Thus, an absence within absence could be a perpetual beginning. Could this be God? . . . God, the Absent, but beyond the power of absence, hence bound to be present where all presence is revoked."[278] God is most present in the place from which God is most absent. The world comes into presence by the absenting of this absence, the *ṣimṣum* of *ṣimṣum*, the contraction of contraction, which makes possible the manifest concealment of the concealed manifestation, the material nothingness dissimulating in the façade of the immaterial somethingness.

Notes

1. Heidegger, *Schelling's Treatise*, p. 188: "Being is nothing. It 'is' not a being in the way we know and think we know beings."

2. Hegel, *Science of Logic*, pp. 74–75 (*Wissenschaft der Logik*, vol. 1, bk. 1, p. 86): "This indeterminateness [*Unbestimmtheit*] or abstract negation [*abstracte Negation*] which thus has being [*Seyn*] in it is that to which reflection, whether external or internal, gives voice when it equates such a being with nothing [*Nichts*], when it declares it to be an empty product of thought, a nothingness.—Or, one can say, since being is the indeterminate [*Bestimmungslose*], it is not the (affirmative) determinateness [*Bestimmtheit*] that it is; it is not being but nothing [*die es ist, nicht Seyn, sondern Nichts*]. In the pure reflection of the beginning as it is made in the Logic with *being* as such, the transition is still hidden; because *being* is posited as immediate, the *nothing* only breaks out in it immediately" (emphasis in original). See also Hegel, *Encyclopedia*, pp. 139–40 (*Enzyklopädie*, pp. 186–87): "Now this pure being is a *pure abstraction* and thus the *absolutely negative* which, when likewise taken immediately, is *nothing*. . . . When the opposition is expressed in this immediate way as one of *being* and *nothing*, it seems all too evident that it is null and void for one not to try to dix [upon some determinate sense of] being and to save it from this transition. In this respect, thinking the matter over is bound to fall prey to looking for a fixed determination for being through which it would be differentiated from nothing. . . . However, none of these further and more concrete determinations leave being as *pure being*, as it is here immediately in the beginning. It is *nothing* only in and because of this pure indeterminacy, something *inexpressible*; its difference from nothing is a mere *opinion* [*eine bloße* Meinung]. . . . Being and nothing are at first only *supposed* to be distinguished, i.e. their difference is at first only *in itself*, but not yet *posited*. If we talk about a difference at all, then we have *two* and in each case a determination not to be found in the one applies to the other. But being is absolutely devoid of all determination, and nothing is the very same lack of determination. The difference between these two is only intended—the totally abstract difference that is at the same time no difference" (emphasis in original). For Heidegger's critique of the Hegelian dialectic of negativity, see Gonzalez, "Rest Is *Sigetik*"; Dahlstrom, "Thinking of Nothing"; Jussaume, "Heidegger and the Nothing," pp. 37–73.

3. Hegel, *Encyclopedia*, p. 131 (*Enzyklopädie*, p. 176): "But then philosophy does not rest with the merely negative result of the dialectical as is the case with scepticism. The latter misjudges its result by clinging to it as a mere (i.e. abstract) negation. Because

the dialectic has the negative as a result, the negative is equally positive, precisely as a result, for it contains within itself that from which it results, containing the latter as something it has sublated [*aufgehoben*], and is not without what it has sublated." This passage is from the additional material included in the posthumous edition published in 1832. See ch. 3 n. 95. On skepticism in Hegel's thought, see Forster, *Hegel and Skepticism*; Wolfson, "Skepticism," pp. 497–98.

4. Hegel, *Science of Logic*, p. 33; *Wissenschaft der Logik*, vol. 1, bk. 1, p. 38. For an exhaustive analysis of this theme, see Sparby, *Hegel's Conception of the Determinate Negation*. See also discussion of Hegel's notion of negativity, the lack of being, and the overcoming of death by life in Brencio, "Life and Negativity."

5. Hegel, *Phenomenology of Spirit*, p. 51 (emphasis in original); *Phänomenologie des Geistes*, p. 57.

6. Hegel, *Phenomenology of Spirit*, p. 56 (emphasis in original); *Phänomenologie des Geistes*, p. 61. See the passage from Hegel's *Glauben und Wissen* cited in ch. 8 n. 213.

7. Hegel, *Phenomenology of Spirit*, pp. 406–7; *Phänomenologie des Geistes*, p. 360.

8. Hegel, *Encyclopedia*, pp. 140–41 (emphasis in original); *Enzyklopädie*, p. 188.

9. Heidegger, *Hegel*, p. 37; *Hegel* [GA 68], p. 47.

10. Heidegger, *Contributions*, §145, p. 209; *Beiträge*, p. 266. Many have commented on the nothing at the different stages of Heidegger's thinking. For some representative studies, see Rosen, "Thinking about Nothing"; Motzkin, "Heidegger's Transcendent Nothing"; Marion, "Nothing and Nothing Else"; Polt, "Question of Nothing"; Jussaume, "Heidegger and the Nothing." On the Heideggerian attempt to think of being in relation to nothing, see Stenstad, *Transformations*, pp. 149–55. Consider Fink's criticism that "because Heidegger had not sufficiently insisted on this co-originality of nothingness and being, of absence and presence, that cosmology finally had to subordinate itself to ontology," discussed in Dastur, *Questions of Phenomenology*, pp. 169–70. I concur with Dastur's assessment that this is not an altogether fair or accurate depiction of Heidegger's thought. Fink's assertion, ostensibly contrasting his view with Heidegger, that just as the shadow is not the absence of light but rather belongs to the light, so concealment belongs to being, can be arguably applied to Heidegger himself. Finally, it is worth recalling Heidegger's reading in *Zu Hölderlin*, p. 43, of a passage in the eleventh chapter of Laozi's *Daodejing*: "Das Seiende ergibt die Brauchbarkeit. / Das Nicht-Seiende gewährt das Sein" ("Being yields the utility / Non-being grants being)." From the fuller context of this aphorism, at least according to the Heideggerian interpretation, the nonbeing is the emptiness (*wu*) that bestows being (*yu*), as in the case of the hub of the wheel of a carriage that engenders the possibility of motion, the space that transforms the mass of clay into a utensil, or the openings of the doors and windows that make a room habitable (*Source Book in Chinese Philosophy*, pp. 144–45). The emptiness of nonbeing is thus not the absence or negation of being but the void (*das Nichtige*) of the betweenness (*das Zwischen*), the interim (*Inmitten*) of the meanwhile (*Indessen*). As Heidegger further explains, the in-between (*Inzwischen*) is the gathering that gathers and stretches itself in place and space (*Ort und Raum*) and in the moment and time (*Augenblick und Zeit*). What is most crucial is that Heidegger intuited an affinity between the codependence of emptiness and nonbeing in Laozi and the juxtaposition or belonging together of being and nothing in his own thinking. Compare *Daodejing*, ch. 1, in *Source Book in Chinese Philosophy*, p. 139: "Therefore let there always be non-being so that we may see their subtlety, and let there always be being so we may see their outcome. The two are the same, but after they are produced, they have different names." See ibid., ch. 2, p. 140: "Being and non-being produce each other; difficult and easy complete each other; long and short contrast each other; high and low distinguish each other; sound and voice harmonize with each other; front and back follow each other." The juxtaposition of antinomies here is closer in spirit to Heidegger's idea of belonging together than to Nicholas of Cusa's coincidence of opposites or to the dialectical sublation of binaries validated by Hegel. See *Daodejing*, ch. 40, in *Source Book in Chinese Philosophy*, p. 160: "All things in the world come from being. And being comes from non-being." And compare the description of the Tao in ibid., ch. 14, p. 146: "Infinite and boundless, it cannot be given any name; it reverts to nothingness. This is called shape without shape, form without object." See Zhang, "Coming Time," pp. 73–77. See also Ma, *Heidegger on East-West Dialogue*, pp. 119–43, esp. 133–38; Froese, *Nietzsche, Heidegger, and Daoist Thought*, pp. 129–57. For additional references to Heidegger's engagement with Taoism, see May, *Heidegger's Hidden Sources*, pp. 35–43; Parkes, "Lao-Zhuang and Heidegger"; Burik, *End of Comparative Philosophy*, pp. 148–60; Burik, "Is There Imagination in Daoism?"; Nelson, *Chinese and Buddhist Philosophy*, pp. 109–29; the following studies in *Heidegger and Asian Thought*: Pöggeler, "West-East Dialogue"; Stambaugh, "Heidegger, Taoism, and the Question of Metaphysics"; Hsiao, "Heidegger and

Our Translation"; Parkes, "Thoughts on the Way." A Heideggerian reading of Taoist thought, including the *Daodejing*, is proffered as well by Michael, *In the Shadows of the Dao*, as noted explicitly on p. 81. For an interpretation of Laozi's reflections on the Tao, being, and nonbeing that conforms to Heidegger's view on the belonging together of *Seyn* and *Nichts*, see Yu-Lan, *History of Chinese Philosophy*, 1:178–79: "*Tao* being the all-embracing first principle through which all things are brought into being, *Tao's* actions are of all things. At the same time it is through *Tao* that all things are enabled to be all things.... Thus understood, *Tao*, since it is the first principle of all things, cannot itself be a 'thing'.... Objects can be said to be Being (*yu*), but *Tao* is not an object, and so may only be spoken of as Non-being (*wu*). At the same time, however, *Tao* is what has brought the universe into being, and hence in one way it may also be said to be Being. For this reason *Tao* is spoken of as both Being and Non-being. Non-being refers to its essence; Being to its function.... Being and Non-being have both issued from *Tao*, and thus are two aspects of *Tao*.... I have said that *Tao* is Non-being. Nevertheless, this only means 'Non-being' as opposed to the 'Being' of material objects, and so it is not a mere zero or nothingness."

11. Here I have followed the translation of Emad and Maly in Heidegger, *Contributions (From Enowning)*, §146, p. 188. In this case, I believe they have rendered the German in a manner that better captures the nuance of Heidegger's intent. Rojcewicz and Vallega-Neu in *Contributions*, §146, p. 210, translate *eigentlich Nichtige* as "what has genuinely the quality of the 'not.'"

12. Heidegger, *Contributions*, §§145–46, pp. 209–10; *Beiträge*, pp. 266–67. Compare the comments on Heinrich John Rickert's Neokantian views on negation in Heidegger, *Towards the Definition*, p. 169 (*Zur Bestimmung*, p. 201): "Negation of something. Negation: *formal* function within the region of objectivity. Negation has no determinate regional character, but applies to everything whatsoever. From negation as such there is never determined the *negative* in its what and regional character, but always only from the what of *that which* is negated, and the how of regional oppositions is first determined from this. Oppositions, which express themselves in negation, can therefore be characterized only as *regional*, not through the formal Not" (emphasis in original).

13. Heidegger, *Contributions*, §164, p. 225; *Beiträge*, p. 286.

14. Heidegger, *Pathmarks*, p. 85; *Wegmarken*, p. 107. Compare the elucidation of this crucial point in the 1943 postscript to "Was ist Metaphysik?" in Heidegger, *Pathmarks*, p. 233 (*Wegmarken*, pp. 305–6): "No matter where or to what extent all research investigates beings, it nowhere finds being. It only ever encounters beings, because from the outset it remains intent on explaining beings. Being, however, is not an existing quality found in beings. Unlike beings, being cannot be represented or brought forth in the manner of an object. As that which is altogether other than all beings, being is that which is not. But this nothing essentially prevails as being [*Dies schlechthin Andere zu allem Seienden ist das Nicht-Seiende. Aber dieses Nichts west als das Sein*]."

15. I have modified the translation of *Unwesen* from "distorted essence" to the more literal "unessence."

16. Heidegger, *Contributions*, §146, p. 210 (emphasis in original); *Beiträge*, p. 267.

17. Heidegger, *Ponderings XII–XV*, p. 91 (translation slightly modified); *Überlegungen XII–XV*, p. 116.

18. Eriugena, *Periphyseon*, 1:72, p. 207 (emphasis in original).

19. Moran, "*Spiritualis Incrassatio*," p. 142; Mooney, *Theophany*, p. 70.

20. Eriugena, *Periphyseon*, 1:72, p. 207.

21. On the affinity of Eriugena's statement and the view expressed by Azriel of Gerona, see Scholem, *Origins*, p. 440, and consider the additional evidence educed on pp. 440–41n177. See also Wolfson, *Language*, pp. 96–97, 100, 426–27n310, 428–29n336. As Scholem observed (*Origins*, p. 440), in *De Arte Cabalistica*, Reuchlin notes the similarity between the identity of opposites affirmed in a text of Azriel, where nothing is identified as something and something as nothing, and the teaching of Cusanus, referred to as the German philosopher-archbishop. See Reuchlin, *On the Art of the Kabbalah*, pp. 120–23; Wolfson, *Language*, p. 467n351. On the text of Azriel, see ch. 2 n. 35. For further references to scholarly discussions of Eriugena and the Geronese kabbalists, see Wolfson, *Through a Speculum*, pp. 293–94n88.

22. Nicholas of Cusa, *De visione dei*, ch. 3, in Hopkins, *Nicholas of Cusa's Dialectical Mysticism*, pp. 122–23.

23. Nicholas of Cusa, *De visione dei*, ch. 13, in Hopkins, *Nicholas of Cusa's Dialectical Mysticism*, pp. 182–83.

24. Hopkins, *Nicholas of Cusa on God as Not Other*, pp. 30–31.

25. Ibid., pp. 68–69 (emphasis in original).

26. Hopkins, *On Learned Ignorance*, 1:19, p. 73.

27. Nicholas of Cusa, *De venatione sapientiae*, ch. 14, in *Complete Philosophical and Theological Treatises*, 2:1303.

28. Ibid., 1304 (emphasis in original). On the depiction of God as *non aliud*, see Miller, *Reading Cusanus*, pp. 180–205; Maas, "Divine Omnipotence," pp. 180–81; Hudson, *Becoming God*, pp. 50–56. See also Mojsisch, "Otherness of God."

29. Nicholas of Cusa, *De visione dei*, ch. 13, in Hopkins, *Nicholas of Cusa's Dialectical Mysticism*, pp. 182–83.

30. Ibid., ch. 6, pp. 134–35 (emphasis in original).

31. Ibid.

32. Ibid., ch. 7, pp. 144–45.

33. The expression is used by Keller, *Cloud of the Impossible*, p. 333n75, in her gloss on my comment that, for Cusanus, God both is and is not identical with the world. See reference in the following note.

34. Wolfson, *Language*, pp. 30–31. The paradox of the identity and nonidentity of God vis-à-vis the world has been noted by other scholars. See Hudson, *Becoming God*, pp. 51–53; Keller, *Cloud of the Impossible*, pp. 102–9.

35. Hopkins, *On Learned Ignorance*, 3:1–2, pp. 125–30. See McGinn, "*Maximum Contractum et Absolutum*"; McGinn, "*Unitrinum Seu Triunum*," pp. 96–98. Since Jesus, as the *Verbum incarnatum*, is both divine and human, he exemplifies the *coincidentia oppositorum* of the "absolute maximum" and the "contracted maximum," also referred to as the "contracted maximum individual." See Hopkins, *On Learned Ignorance*, 3:4, pp. 133–35.

36. Nicholas of Cusa, *De filiatione dei*, ch. 3, in *Complete Philosophical and Theological Treatises*, 1:349 (emphasis in original). See also Hudson, *Becoming God*, pp. 158–59.

37. Wildmann, *Pitḥei She'arim*, 3a.

38. Hopkins, *On Learned Ignorance*, 1:21, p. 75 (emphasis in original).

39. Ibid., 1:16, p. 67.

40. Nicholas of Cusa, *De visione dei*, ch. 13, in Hopkins, *Nicholas of Cusa's Dialectical Mysticism*, pp. 180–81.

41. Hopkins, *Nicholas of Cusa on God as Not-Other*, pp. 116–17.

42. Nicholas of Cusa, *De visione dei*, ch. 13, in Hopkins, *Nicholas of Cusa's Dialectical Mysticism*, pp. 182–83.

43. Hopkins, *Nicholas of Cusa on God as Not-Other*, pp. 68–69.

44. De Herrera, *Gate of Heaven*, p. 219. The influence of Cusanus in this passage was noted by Yosha, *Myth and Metaphor*, p. 169. See also Necker, "Circle, Point and Line," pp. 200–201n45.

45. Hegel, *Science of Logic*, pp. 110–11; *Wissenschaft der Logik*, vol. 1, bk. 1, p. 126.

46. Hegel, *Science of Logic*, p. 111 (emphasis in original); *Wissenschaft der Logik*, vol. 1, bk. 1, p. 127. Capturing the paradox of Hegel's thinking, Priest, *Beyond the Limits*, p. 108, observes, "The true infinite is the notion of an object whose finitude is its infinitude, and which is therefore both finite and infinite."

47. Hegel, *Science of Logic*, pp. 118–19 (emphasis in original); *Wissenschaft der Logik*, vol. 1, bk. 1, p. 136.

48. Hegel, *Science of Logic*, p. 119 (emphasis in original); *Wissenschaft der Logik*, vol. 1, bk. 1, p. 136.

49. Hegel, *Science of Logic*, 345–46 (emphasis in original); *Wissenschaft der Logik*, vol. 1, bk. 2, p. 249.

50. Hegel, *Science of Logic*, p. 346 (emphasis in original); *Wissenschaft der Logik*, vol. 1, bk. 2, p. 249.

51. Hegel, *Science of Logic*, p. 80; *Wissenschaft der Logik*, vol. 1, bk. 1, p. 93.

52. Hegel, *Science of Logic*, p. 346 (emphasis in original); *Wissenschaft der Logik*, vol. 1, bk. 2, p. 250.

53. Merleau-Ponty, *Visible and the Invisible*, p. 93. Compare Hegel, *Lectures on the Philosophy of Religion*, 1:126: "This is the key by which the nature of spirit is explicated. God is thus grasped as what he is for himself within himself; God [the Father] makes himself an object for himself (the Son); then, in this object, God remains the undivided essence within this differentiation of himself within himself, and in this differentiation of himself loves himself, i.e., remains identical with himself—this is God as Spirit. Hence if we are to speak of God as spirit, we must grasp God with this very definition, which exists in the church in this childlike mode of representation as the relationship between father and son—a representation that is not yet a matter of the concept. Thus it is just this definition of God by the church as a Trinity that is the concrete determination and nature of God as spirit; and spirit is an empty word if it is not grasped in this determination." See the text cited below in n. 157, and compare Hegel, *Philosophy of Mind*, pp. 264–65: "The absolute spirit in the sublated immediacy and sensoriness of shape and of knowledge is, in content, the spirit that is in and for itself, the spirit of nature and of mind; in form it is initially for the subjective knowledge of *representation*. . . . In the moment of *universality*, of the sphere of pure *thought* or the abstract element of the *essence*, it is therefore the absolute spirit that is first of all the *presupposition*, not, however, self-enclosed and static. As *substantial power* in the reflexion-determination of causality, it is *creator* of heaven and earth; but in this eternal sphere it generates only *its own self* as its *son*; it remains in original identity with what is thus differentiated from itself, but equally this determination—of being what is differentiated from the universal

essence—eternally sublates itself, and, through this mediation of self-sublating mediation, the first substance essentially becomes *concrete individuality* and subjectivity,—is *spirit*. But in the moment of the *particularity* of the judgement, this concrete eternal essence is what is *presupposed*, and its movement is the creation of *appearance*, the disintegration of the eternal moment of mediation, of the unitary son, into independent opposites, on the one hand heaven and earth, elemental and concrete nature, and, on the other hand, spirit as standing in *relationship* with nature, hence *finite* spirit. Spirit, as the extreme of the negativity that is within itself, asserts its independence to the point of evil; it is such an extreme through its relation to a nature confronting it and through its own naturalness which is thereby posited; in this naturalness it is, as thinking, also directed towards the eternal, but it stands in an external relation with it" (emphasis in original).

54. Hegel, *Lectures on the Philosophy of Religion*, 1:426–27: "We have defined essence as the nonfinite, as the negation of the negative—a negation that we call the infinite. So the transition is not made to abstract, arid being but to the being that is negation of the negation. Therein lies the distinction. This being is the distinction that takes itself back into simplicity. Involved within this essence is the determination of what is distinguished; but it is a determining of what is distinguished as it relates itself to itself, a self-determining. Negation is determination. Negation of determination is itself a determining. . . . Distinction does not come into it from outside, for this unrest lies within it as being itself the negation of the negation." See the passage from Hegel cited below at n. 159.

55. Merleau-Ponty, *Visible and the Invisible*, p. 93.

56. Schelling, *Vom Ich als Princip der Philosophie oder über das Unbedingte in menschlichen Wissen*, in *Sämmtliche Werke*, 1:175. See the analysis in Distaso, *Paradox of Existence*, pp. 59–90.

57. Schelling, *Philosophische Briefe über Dogmatismus und Kriticismus*, in *Sämmtliche Werke*, 1:294: "Wie komme ich überhaupt dazu, aus dem Absoluten heraus und auf ein Entgegengesetztes zu gehen?"

58. Schelling, *System of Transcendental Idealism*, p. 7.

59. Ibid., p. 16 (emphasis in original).

60. Ibid., p. 17.

61. Ibid., p. 20 (emphasis in original).

62. Ibid., p. 22.

63. Ibid., p. 30 (emphasis in original). The split between Hegel and Schelling turned on this very issue. Heidegger well summarized the point of contention in *Schelling's Treatise*, p. 12 (*Schelling: Vom Wesen*, p. 19): "This break concerns the concept of the Absolute as the identity and indifference of all opposites which Schelling had made the fundamental principle of philosophy. With regard to this, Hegel says to consider any existence as it is in the *Absolute* consists in nothing else than saying about it that while it is now doubtless spoken of as something specific, yet in the Absolute, in the abstract identity of A = A, there is no such thing at all, for everything is all one there" (emphasis in original).

64. Schmidt-Biggemann, *Philosophia Perennis*, pp. 450–51.

65. Schelling, *System of Transcendental Idealism*, p. 48.

66. Ibid.

67. Ibid., p. 32.

68. Schelling, *System der Weltalter*, p. 124: "Dieser Wille ist ein an sich selbst nichtseinsollender; also dieser Wille ist nach der Analogie der deutschen Wörter, Unkraut, Unfall, Unthat, ein *Unwille*, und da er in Beziehung auf Gott der nichtseinsollende ist, so wäre er in der That in Bezug auf Gott der *göttliche Unwille*" (emphasis in original).

69. See, for example, Böhme, *Six Theosophic Points*, pp. 6–7: "Seeing then the first will is an ungroundedness, to be regarded as an eternal nothing, we recognize it to be like a mirror, wherein one sees his own image; like a life, and yet it is no life, but a figure of life and of the image belonging to life. Thus we recognize the eternal Unground out of Nature to be like a mirror. For it is like an eye which sees, and yet conducts nothing in the seeing wherewith it sees; for seeing is without essence, although it is generated from essence, viz. from the essential life. We are able then to recognize that the eternal Unground out of Nature is a will, like an eye wherein Nature is hidden; like a hidden fire that burns not, which exists and also exists not. . . . It is like a mirror which is a container of the aspect of Nature, and yet comprehends not Nature, as Nature comprehends not the form of the image in the mirror. . . . For if the image depart from the mirror, the mirror is a clear brightness, and its brightness is a nothing; and yet all the form of Nature is hidden therein as a nothing; and yet veritably is, but not in essence." And see ibid., p. 11: "We are now to understand that the first Principle is magical in origin; for it is generated in desire, in the will. Hence its craving and contra-will to bring forth is also magical, namely to bring forth the second Principle." See the passages cited below, nn. 70–71, and compare Baader, *Gesammelte Schriften zur Religionsphilosophie*, 2:112–13; Grunsky, *Jakob Böhme*, pp. 125–36; Deghaye, "Jakob Böhmes Theosophie"; O'Regan, *Gnostic Apocalypse*, p. 38. On the relationship between body, image, and imagination in the Böhmean corpus, see, in more

detail, Gentzke, "Imagining the Image," pp. 114–17, and Wolfson, "Holy Cabala," pp. 28–35.

70. See references cited in introduction nn. 86 and 95. In the *Four Tables of Divine Revelation*, the number one is aligned with the Abyss, which is identified further as the Nothing and the All, and numbers two to four are aligned respectively with the Will of the Abyss, the Delight or Impression of the Will, and Science or Motion. These three numbers constitute the Tetragrammaton and are linked to the Christian trinity: number two is connected to the Father and the letters JE, number three to the Son and the letters HO, and number four to the Spirit and the letters VA. The text is printed in Böhme, *Essential Readings*, pp. 215–17. In Böhme, *"Key,"* p. 22, he writes the following about the name *Jehovah*: "The Ancient Rabins among the *Jews* have partly understood it, for they have said, that this Name is the Highest, and most Holy Name of God; by which they understand the working Deity in Sense: and it is true, for in this working sense lies the true life of all things in Time and Eternity, in the Ground and Abyss; and it is God himself, namely the Divine working Perceptibility, Sensation, Invention, Science, and Love; that is, the true understanding in the working unity, from which the five senses of the true Life spring" (emphasis in original). In the continuation (pp. 22–23), Böhme identifies each of the letters of the name: J is the effluence of the Eternal indivisible unity; E is the threefold I, the Trinity comprised within the unity; H is the Word that comes forth from the breathing of the Trinity; O is the circumference or the Son of God, who speaks from the compressed Delight of the Power and Virtue; V is the joyful effluence of the breathing, the proceeding of the Spirit of God; and A is the Wisdom that issues from the power and virtue, the place wherein the Trinity is manifest. The fact that the rabbis did not discern the trinitarian implications of the name is the reason Böhme began his explication by saying the Jews have only "partly understood it." Summarizing his Christological interpretation of what I assume is the kabbalistic symbol of the Tetragrammaton, Böhme notes, "This Name is nothing else but a speaking forth, or expression of the Threefold working of the Holy Trinity in the unity of God" (p. 23). The role of the name in Böhme's theosophy, including the aforecited passage from the *Clavis*, is discussed by Wilkinson, *Tetragrammaton*, pp. 450–52. On the identification of the Father as the will, the Son as wisdom, and the Spirit as the Word, see Böhme, *Six Theosophic Points*, pp. 8–9. We can assume that the Abyss—the Chaos of the *Mysterium magnum*, the ground whence the polarities of light and darkness, good and evil, life and death, joy and grief, salvation and damnation, emanate (Böhme, *"Key,"* pp. 24–25)—is the nameless that is manifest in the name, which comprises the trinity. See *Four Tables of Divine Revelation*, in Böhme, *Essential Readings*, p. 224: "The word JEHOVAH, is the most holy Name of God, as the Divine sensual life, the only good; whereby the Holy Trinity, with Glory and Omnipotency, is understood; the life of the Abyss, as of the Unity; which chiefly standeth in the only love: And therein also is understood the most holy Name JESUS . . . the ground and fountain of the breathing of Gods Unitie, and a forming of the understanding." And see the first paragraph of the section on the Tetragrammaton in ibid., p. 225: "In this Table is also manifested how the holy Name of the Eternall power, with the knowledge hereof, from Eternity to Eternity; bringing it self into properties, in Nature to eternal light and darkness; and how the word of breathing forth, brings it self into a subject, and how self-will and acceptation of properties arise in the subject, wherein two Essences are always understood; as God's own effluence; and then the properties own acceptation in the free will; in which acceptation another externall kinde of subject is understood; whereby the Unity in its Effluence becomes more external; and thereby the Eternal love bringeth it self into a sensibleness, and like a fiery flame, as in the working of divine Power." It is difficult not to hear the echo of kabbalistic theosophy in this text. In the explanation of the second table in the same treatise, p. 221, Böhme notes the significance of the epithet Adonai, which he relates to the "opening, or free motion of the bottomless Eternal Unity; how the Eternal generation, expansion, and effluence of the Trinity of God is in it self." This description accords with the standard kabbalistic understanding of Adonai as a name for *Malkhut* or the *Shekhinah*, the last of the *sefirot*, which is the divine force immanent in the physical world. On the affinity between the upper three *sefirot* (*Keter*, *Ḥokhmah*, and *Binah*) and Böhme's conception of the immanent Trinity, see Hessayon, "Boehme's Life," p. 31. The connection between Jesus and understanding brings to mind the identification of Christ with the attribute of *Binah* found in the works of the apostate Johann Kemper. See Wolfson, "Messianism," p. 175n94; Wolfson, "Angelic Embodiment," pp. 420–21. Finally, it is worth noting that the role that Böhme assigns to the imagination as the faculty wherein and whereby the Word is incarnate bears a striking similarity to the role attributed to the imagination in kabbalistic texts. See Böhme, *"Key,"* pp. 23–24: "The Wisdom is the Great Mystery of the Divine Nature; for in her,

the Powers, Colours, and Virtues are made manifest; in her is the variation of the power and virtue, namely the understanding: she is the Divine understanding, that is, the Divine vision, wherein the Unity is manifest. She is the true Divine Chaos, wherein all things lie, namely a Divine Imagination, in which the *Ideas* of Angels and Souls have been seen from Eternity, in a Divine Type and Resemblance; yet not then as Creatures, but in resemblance, as when a man beholds his face in a Glass: therefore the Angelical and human *Idea* flowed forth from the wisdom, and was formed into an Image, as *Moses* says, God created Man in his Image, that is, he created the body, and breathed into it the breath of the Divine Effluence, of Divine Knowledge, from all the Three Principles of the Divine Manifestation" (emphasis in original). See the description of the creation of Adam on the sixth day in Böhme, *"Key,"* pp. 43–44. And compare Böhme, *Treatise of the Incarnation*, p. 58: "But that the Word, or the Power of God's Life, has *given in* itself again into the Humanity, *viz.* into the dead and as it were disappeared virginity, and opened again the Virgin-like Life; *at that* we Rejoice, and go with our Imagination into the *Center*, wherein God hath opened himself in the humanity, viz. into his Son's Incarnation. *And so in our Imagination,* which we *introduce* into his Incarnation, we become impregnated of his opened Word, and power of the heavenly and divine Substantiality; not at all with that which is *strange*, yet it seems strange to the earthliness" (emphasis in original).

71. Schelling, *Philosophical Investigations*, p. 28 (emphasis in original); *Philosophische Untersuchungen*, p. 31. See the analysis of Schelling in Sallis, *Return of Nature*, pp. 36–43. The paradoxical assumption affirmed by both Böhme and Schelling, in consonance with the kabbalists, that an aspect of the infinite's limitlessness is its capacity to limit itself, was challenged by Spinoza in his insistence that the possibility of self-restriction cannot be attributed to the *causa sui*. See Melamed, *"Omnis determinatio,"* p. 193. In n. 61, ad locum, Melamed suggests that Spinoza's axiom might have been a response to the Lurianic doctrine of the self-limitation (*ṣimṣum*) of *Ein Sof*. On the formula *omnis determinatio est negatio*, see the extensive analysis in Macherey, *Hegel or Spinoza*, pp. 113–213.

72. Schelling, *Philosophical Investigations*, p. 21; *Philosophische Untersuchungen*, p. 23.

73. I have followed the reading *ein ahndender Wille* in Schelling, *Sämmtliche Werke*, 7:359, which is also the version of the text in *Philosophische Untersuchungen*, p. 32. The translation "a divining will" in Schelling, *Philosophical Investigations*, p. 29, is based on reading the German as *ein ahnender Wille*. For the justification of this rendering (translating the verb *ahnden* or its equivalent *ahnen* as "to divine"), see the extensive comment of Love and Schmidt in Schelling, *Philosophical Investigations*,p. 151n39, which includes the suggestions of previous translators. Sallis, *Return of Nature*, p. 39, translates *ein ahndender Wille* as "an intimating will." Confirmation of the version of the German that I have accepted, and the corresponding translation, may be gleaned from Schelling's own gloss concerning this will in the continuation of the passage from *Philosophische Untersuchungen*, p. 32, *dessen Ahndung der Verstand ist*, "whose punitiveness is the understanding." This reading and translation are more consistent with the kabbalistic and Böhmean assumption that within the boundless mercy of the nonground there is the countering force of vengeful judgment, the constraining aspect of limit within the limitless. The creativity of the infinite comprises both the light of grace and the fire of severity.

74. Žižek, *Ticklish Subject*, pp. 318–19: "Schelling opposed the Will to the 'principle of sufficient reason': pure Willing is always self-identical, it relies on its own act.... Schelling's emphasis on the abyss of pure Willing, of course, targets Hegel's alleged 'panlogicism': what Schelling wants to prove is that the Hegelian universal logical system is in itself *impotent*—it is a system of pure *potentialities* and, as such, in need of the supplementary 'irrational' act of pure Will in order to *actualize* itself" (emphasis in original).

75. Schelling, *Philosophical Investigations*, p. 29; *Philosophische Untersuchungen*, p. 32.

76. Böhme, *Six Theosophic Points*, p. 8. See Brito, *Création selon Schelling*, pp. 340–41; Brito, *Philosophie et Théologie*, pp. 132–34.

77. Böhme, *Six Theosophic Points*, p. 10.

78. See Mayer, *Jena Romanticism*, pp. 200–2. See also Laughland, *Schelling*, pp. 61–91; and Cohen, "L'errance de Dieu," in *Alternances de la Métaphysique*, pp. 49–71. Schelling's interest in the problem of evil is attested already in his 1792 dissertation *De prima malorum humanorum origine philosophematis Gen. III explicandi tentamen criticum et philosophicum*. See Distaso, *Paradox of Existence*, pp. 1–36.

79. Schelling, *Philosophical Investigations*, p. 35; *Philosophische Untersuchungen*, pp. 38–39.

80. Baader, "On the Assertion That There Can Be No Wicked Use of Reason," translated in Schelling, *Philosophical Investigations*, p. 101.

81. The affinity between Böhme's doctrine of the origin of evil in the dark and negative principle of

God's wrath and the kabbalistic symbolism of the divine quality of judgment on the left whence the demonic realm arises was noted by Scholem, *Major Trends*, p. 237.

82. Schelling, *Philosophical Investigations*, p. 73; *Philosophische Untersuchungen*, p. 83.

83. Schelling, *On the History*, p. 114 (emphasis in original); *Zur Geschichte*, p. 99.

84. I have modified Bowie's translation of *sich selbst anzuziehen* as "attracts itself," although in the parenthetical gloss, he adds that the expression conveys "the sense of 'putting on' and thus being inauthentic, and of 'drawing itself to' itself." I agree that the primary meaning here is "putting on" in the sense of being garbed, but I do not think Schelling was trying to communicate a sense of put on as a mode of inauthenticity, deception, or withdrawing. On the contrary, what he is transmitting is the notion that the infinite subject becomes an object to itself through the pretense of arraying. The putting on of the garment, therefore, would have the same function as the reflection of an image in the mirror.

85. In this case as well I have modified Bowie's rendering of *Selbstanziehung* as self-gravitation.

86. Schelling, *On the History*, p. 115 (emphasis in original; translation altered); *Zur Geschichte*, pp. 100–1.

87. Schelling, *On the History*, p. 116 (emphasis in original); *Zur Geschichte*, p. 102.

88. Schelling, *On the History*, p. 116; *Zur Geschichte*, p. 101.

89. Wolfson, "Divine Suffering," pp. 113–14. On Schelling's image of nature as the poem whose enigma can be deciphered, see Hadot, *Veil of Isis*, pp. 204–5, 274.

90. Schelling, *On the History*, p. 116 (emphasis in original; translation slightly modified); *Zur Geschichte*, p. 101.

91. Schelling, *Ages of the World (Fragment)*, pp. 79–80; *Weltalter*, in *Sämmtliche Werke*, 8:306–7.

92. Wolfson, *Alef*, pp. 40–42.

93. Schelling, *Ages of the World (Fragment)*, p. 80 (emphasis in original); *Weltalter*, in *Sämmtliche Werke*, 8:307. For discussion of the reference to Pindar, see the editor's comment in Schelling, *Ages of the World (Fragment)*, p. 145n85. Compare the passage of Schelling cited in ch. 6 at n. 226. On the genealogy of time in Schelling, see Krell, *Tragic Absolute*, pp. 117–30.

94. See Böhme, *Way to Christ*, pp. 126–27 (*Sämtliche Schriften*, 4:98–99): "God is all. He is darkness and light, love and wrath, fire and light. But He calls Himself only God according to the light of His love. There is an eternal *contrarium* between darkness and light. Neither grasps the other, and neither is the other. And yet there is only one being [*einiges Wesen*], but separated by the source and by the will. Yet it is not a divided being, but one *principium* divides it so that each is in the other as a nothing [*ein Nichts*]. But it is there, although not revealed in the characteristic of that which it is." Similar language is used in the opening paragraphs of Böhme, *Three Principles of the Divine Essence*, pp. 9–10. God is all things, which means both good and evil, but the latter is not called God. However, by virtue of being the fountain of wrathfulness in addition to being the source of beneficence, the divine is referred to as angry, wrathful, and zealous. Hence, "there is no difference in God, only when it is enquired from whence Evil and Good proceed, it is to be known, what is the first and original Fountain of Anger, and also of Love, since they both proceed from one and the same Original, out of one Mother, and are one Thing. . . . Therefore the Source or Fountain of the Cause must be sought, *viz.* what is the *Prima Materia*, or first Matter of Evil, and that in the Originality of God as well as in the Creatures; for it is all but one only Thing in the Origin: All is out of God, made out of his Essence, according to the Trinity, as he is one in Essence and threefold in Persons" (p. 10). Compare Koenker, "Grund," pp. 46–47. See, however, Krell, *Tragic Absolute*, pp. 94–95: "The (original) nonground, which is the nonorigin of all grounds, precedes both opposition and identity, all binary sets and straightforwardly oppositional units, every dualism and every monism. It is insufficient to call it a *coincidentia oppositorum*, after the manner of certain well-known systems from Cusa to Böhme and Baader." Krell's point is well taken and demonstrates the inadequacy of Hegel's criticism that Böhme's thought should be characterized as "a barbaric form of presentation and expression" (*eine barbarische Form der Darstellung und des Ausdrucks*), since he lacked the proper concept (*Begriff*) to explain how God is the "profoundest Idea [*die tiefste Idee*] . . . which seeks to bring the most absolute opposites [*die absolutesten Gegensätze*] into unity, and to bind them together." Lacking the speculative acumen and power of expression, Böhme struggled to grasp how the negative is part of the positive, how the devil is in and from the divine, how wrath and love are simultaneously attributed to God. The union of all opposites in God (*die Vereinigung aller Gegensätze in Gott*), according to Hegel, was the fundamental idea of the "absolute divine unity" (*die absolute göttliche Einheit*) in Böhme, but he could not find the appropriate means to convey it. See Hegel, *Vorlesungen über die Geschichte der Philosophie III*, pp. 96–97, 98; *Lectures on the History of Philosophy*, 3:194, 196.

95. Žižek, *Parallax View*, p. 184 (emphasis in original).

96. Schelling, *Philosophical Investigations*, pp. 68–69 (emphasis in original); *Philosophische Untersuchungen*, p. 78. For a more detailed analysis of Hegel and Schelling on this point, see Wolfson, *Language*, pp. 100–4, and Wolfson, *Alef*, pp. 35–40.

97. Schelling, *Philosophical Investigations*, p. 69 (emphasis in original); *Philosophische Untersuchungen*, p. 78. Compare the depiction of the *Ungrund* in Heidegger, *Contributions*, § 34, p. 61; *Beiträge*, pp. 76–77 (cited in the introduction n. 83).

98. Hegel, *Phenomenology of Spirit*, p. 99 (emphasis in original); *Phänomenologie des Geistes*, p. 98.

99. Hegel, *Phenomenology of Spirit*, p. 99 (emphasis in original); *Phänomenologie des Geistes*, pp. 98–99.

100. See Rang, *Identität und Indifferenz*.

101. Schelling, *Philosophical Investigations*, p. 69 (emphasis in original); *Philosophische Untersuchungen*, pp. 78–79.

102. Böhme, *Six Theosophic Points*, p. 18. Paslick, "Ontological Context," pp. 411–12, interprets Böhme's theosophy dialectically in Lurianic terms: "Now no manifestation can occur until this ungrounded will is grounded; and it can be grounded only by positing that which is not itself. But since there exists nothing outside the divine spirit, *it must clear a space within itself*, which is in itself but is not itself. This space is what Boehme calls nature, the dark world of the divine ground, similar to an unreflecting mirror into whose darkness the spirit sacrifices its freedom in its anguished yearning to reveal itself. . . . The desire to manifest demands the creation of real darkness without which the light of manifestation cannot be seen. But the *severe contraction*, by which the dark world is formed in the free spirit, arouses in it the raging desire to escape this prisonhouse of darkness. Of course there is no escape. The paradox is unresolvable. The light which desires to be manifest must desire equally strongly both the creation and the endurance of the darkness which makes manifestation possible. Thus the life process consists in continually overcoming a darkness which can never be completely overcome" (emphasis added). See Deghaye, "Philosophie," pp. 261–63. Compare the comment of Derrida cited below, n. 109.

103. Schelling, *Ages of the World (Fragment)*, p. 6; *Weltalter*, in *Sämmtliche Werke*, 8:211–12.

104. Schelling, *Ages of the World (Fragment)*, p. 12; *Weltalter*, in *Sämmtliche Werke*, 8:219.

105. Schelling, *Ages of the World (Fragment)*, p. 6; *Weltalter*, in *Sämmtliche Werke*, 8:211. Schmidt-Biggemann, *Philosophia Perennis*, pp. 453–54, links the notion of becoming and the movements of expansion and contraction in Schelling to Böhme's doctrine of divine qualities; he makes no mention of the affinity to the kabbalistic symbolism. See the passage from Schelling's 1810 Stuttgart lectures mentioned in ch. 4 n. 263, and compare the reference in this same work (*Sämmtliche Werke*, 7:429) to the act of restriction (*Einschränkung*) or lowering (*Herablassung*) of God that is spontaneous (*freiwilling*), the divine freedom (*die Freiheit Gottes*) that is the explanatory ground of the world (*Erklärungsgrund der Welt*). The creation is further characterized as the "space of revelation" created by God breaking with the absolute identity of his essence (*Nur Gott selbst kann die absolute Identität seines Wesens brechen, und dadurch Raum zu einer Offenbarung machen*).

106. Schelling, *Ages of the World (Fragment)*, p. 15; *Weltalter*, in *Sämmtliche Werke*, 8:223. Compare the passage from Schelling's *Grundriß des Ganzen* cited in Wirth, *Conspiracy of Life*, p. 242n36: "In order to become real from out of an infinite (and insofar ideal) productive activity, it must be inhibited, *retarded*" (emphasis in original). See ch. 4 n. 279.

107. Gikatilla, *Sha'arei Ṣedeq*, 23a.

108. Joseph ben Shalom Ashkenazi, *Perush Sefer Yeṣirah*, 44b. Compare the language of the long recension of the thirteenth-century composition *Sefer ha-Iyyun* in Verman, *Books of Contemplation*, pp. 69–71 (corresponding Hebrew text appears on p. 65): "He is the sustaining power [*koaḥ qiyyum*]; for all that is extant, under the providence of thought [*be-hashgaḥat ha-maḥashavah*], is emanated from the wondrousness of His Unity [*mi-peli'at aḥduto*]. He is unified in the Unity, which does not change, except through His determination. . . . He is united as one, and everything is perfected as one and everything is one intelligence, and every creature is as one, and each law is as one, and each place is as one. And the basis of everything is one will that is the Marvellous Light [*or ha-mufla*], for which He placed one path to be equal amongst us, for the sake of each individual thing. If one thing shall change from the other, everything will go to one place, which is the place of the balanced unity [*ha-aḥdut ha-shaweh*]. Before the Holy One, blessed be He, created any power from amongst these powers, His power was indiscernible—until His nothing appeared as His something [*ad she-nir'eh eino yeshno*]" (translation slightly modified). For a more recent edition of the text, see Porat, ed., *Works of Iyyun*, p. 99.

109. Schelling, *Ages of the World (Fragment)*, p. 6; *Weltalter*, in *Sämmtliche Werke*, 8:211. In contrast to the distinction I am making between Hegel and Schelling, and the further assumption that the latter is more closely aligned with the kabbalistic doctrine of *ṣimṣum*,

consider the following remark of Derrida, *Dissemination*, p. 344: "Interestingly, through the importance it gives to the dot, the air, etc., this Orphic explanation also describes an analogue of the *pleroma*, which is a sort of original space, a pneumatic layer (*tehiru*) in which the *zimzum*, the crisis within God, the 'drama of God' through which God goes out of himself and determines himself, takes place. This contraction into a dot, this withdrawal and then this exit out of self located within the original ether, is of course linked to the mythology of 'Louria,' but it can also arise by way of 'Hegel' 'Boehme,' etc." Concerning this passage, see Wolfson, *Giving*, pp. 168–69. The influence of Scholem's account of the Lurianic myth—especially the language of crisis and drama—is unmistakable in Derrida's words. Compare Scholem, *Major Trends*, p. 260, where Luria's cosmogony is described as "intensely dramatic." And ibid., p. 266: "The cause of this 'breaking of the vessels,' which releases the whole complexity of the cosmological drama and determines man's place in it, appears in Luria's and Vital's doctrine under varying aspects." See ibid., pp. 268, 269, 271, 279, 284. On the use of the term *crisis* to characterize the activity of the infinite, the "break-through of the primordial will," see ibid., p. 217, and for the characterization of Lurianic kabbalah as a response to the crisis of expulsion in Jewish history, see pp. 244, 250. The influence of Scholem on Derrida's understanding of Jewish mysticism is a major contention of Idel, "Jacques Derrida amd Kabbalistic Sources." For a scholarly attempt to read the Orphic myth of creation kabbalistically, see Liebes, *Studies in Jewish Myth*, pp. 65–92.

110. Schelling, *Ages of the World (Fragment)*, p. 10 (emphasis in original); *Weltalter*, in *Sämmtliche Werke*, 8:217.

111. Weeks, *Boehme*, p. 205.

112. Schelling, *Ages of the World (Fragment)*, p. 85; *Weltalter*, in *Sämmtliche Werke*, 8:313.

113. Schelling, *Ages of the World (Fragment)*, p. 87; *Weltalter*, in *Sämmtliche Werke*, 8:317. See the passage of Schelling cited in the introduction n. 118.

114. Schelling, *Ages of the World (Fragment)*, p. 42; *Weltalter*, in *Sämmtliche Werke*, 8:258. On the first cause and the other, see Brito, *Création selon Schelling*, pp. 239–41. It is of interest to note that it is precisely the paradox underlying the kabbalistic assumption about the othering of the divine through the act of contraction that is criticized by Mendelssohn in lecture 14 of his *Morning Hours*, p. 87. On the basis of what he considers a universally known philosophical principle, *No being can actually alienate itself from any degree of its reality*, Mendelssohn concludes, "Just as little can God, by virtue of the fullness of his perfection, think any sort of limited being, together with the actual alienation of his divinity. He thinks for himself a limited degree of his reality with all the weaknesses and incapacities that follow from this limitedness. But He remains himself anything but alienated from his infinite reality." For an alternate rendering, see Mendelssohn, *Last Works*, p. 106. Compare Mendelssohn's remarks in *To the Friends of Lessing: A Supplement to Mr. Jacobi's Correspondence Concerning the Doctrine of Spinoza* (1786), translated in Mendelssohn, *Last Works*, p. 172, and see the excursus on pp. 212–13n43.

115. Azriel of Gerona, *Be'ur Eser Sefirot*, p. 83.

116. Luzzatto, *Qelaḥ Pitḥei Ḥokhmah*, p. 60.

117. See above, n. 71.

118. Butler, *Bodies That Matter*, p. 39 (emphasis in original). The overly sexualized and, in my judgment, pejorative portrayal of the feminine as a vessel is epitomized in the rabbinic dictum (Babylonian Talmud, Sanhedrin 22b), "R. Samuel ben Unya said in the name of Rav: A woman is a shapeless mass [*golem*], and she does not establish a covenant except with one who makes her into a vessel, as it says 'For he who made you will espouse you—his name is Lord of Hosts' (Isaiah 54:5)." This passage is often cited by kabbalists in conjunction with another rabbinic teaching, "A woman does not get pregnant from the first intercourse" (Babylonian Talmud, Yevamot 34b). See, for example, Cordovero, *Pardes Rimmonim*, 5:2, p. 60; Viṭal, *Eṣ Ḥayyim*, 39:7, 72b-c; Viṭal, *Sha'ar ha-Kawwanot*, 4a-b, 23a, 53b, 56d; Bachrach, *Emeq ha-Melekh*, 6:64, p. 296, 6:66, pp. 302–3; Luzzatto, *Adir ba-Marom*, pt. 1, p. 134. The valorizing of the feminine as the vessel that activates the masculine is expressed concisely by Judah Canpanton, *Leqaḥ Ṭov*, MS Oxford-Bodleian 1642, fol. 18a: "The moon is a bride in relation to the sun, and she is in her fullness and radiates. But if not for those faces, which are the faces of the moon that are like the faces of the sun, the sun would not shine upon her." Admittedly, the male potency of the sun to overflow cannot be actualized without the female capacity of the moon to receive, and in this respect a positive role in the creative process is accorded the feminine, but surely the impartial reader will acknowledge that, in the final analysis, to circumscribe the role of the woman as being a vessel to contain the seminal emission of the man is a facet of the phallomorphic prejudice. The point is made in a second passage from Canpanton's *Leqaḥ Ṭov*, MS Oxford-Bodleian 1642, fol. 18b: "The reason for 'This time is bone of my bones' [*zo't ha-pa'am eṣem me-aṣamai*] (Genesis 2:23), that is, like the first time, when they were androgynous [*du parṣufin*], the truth of the essence was unified [*hayah*

amittat ha-eṣem aḥat]. The two were equal [*shawim*] in will and stature, and when they were separated, the creator placed a part of his bones and one limb from his limbs [to create the female counterpart] so that she would listen to him, and he would rule over her and she would be inclined to whatever he wishes. All this happened to Adam on account of Eve just as what occurred to the sun was on account of the grievance of the moon with regard to the sun." Leaving aside the patently androcentric implication of conferring a subservient status to the woman on account of the separation from the state of androgyny, a separation that was caused by her in the same manner that the lessening of the lunar light was caused by the moon complaining about the parallel status of the sun (Babylonian Talmud, Ḥullin 60b), a careful reading of the description of that originary state indicates that the androgyne entailed one essence, that is, one gender, which later bifurcated into two sexuated beings. Compare Judah Canpanton, *Arba'ah Qinyanim*, ed. Blau, p. 22 (I have also made use of MS Cambridge, Trinity College 120, fol. 23b and MS JTSA 2532, fol. 20a): "It may be inferred from what the verse says 'This time is bone of my bones and flesh of my flesh' (Genesis 2:23) that this was not the case the first time.... For since there was in Adam a limb from his limbs prepared for the woman to come to be from him, and she was created from him, it follows that they were created in their perfection, for it was not necessary for the woman to be made from something new but rather from what was already made." This text is yet another corroboration of my argument that the male androgyne is the critical analytic category undergirding the kabbalistic construction of gender; that is, the assertion that male and female were primordially equal does not entail a difference of identity but rather an identity of difference because the woman is still depicted as being comprised in the one essence (or bone) of the man. To say, therefore, that there is no distinction between man and woman, *ein hefresh bein ish le-ishshah* (Canpanton, *Leqaḥ Ṭov*, MS Oxford-Bodleian 1642, fol. 19a) does not imply an egalitarianism that would erase all gender disparity. It signifies rather that the differentiation did not yet occur, a differentiation that is the ontological justification for the ancillary status of the female.

119. *Zohar Ḥadash*, 90c. Compare *Zohar* 1:46a: "R. Judah said, why is it written by each day 'it was evening and it was morning'? To instruct that there is no day without night and no night without day, and they should not be separated." See *Zohar* 3:93b, 134b (*Idra Rabba*). For parallel language, see Moses ben Shem Ṭov de León, *Shushan Edut*, p. 335: "The Written Torah is the general [*kelal*] and the Oral Torah is the particular [*peraṭ*]. However, this is not without that, and that is not without this; the general needs the particular and the particular needs the general. And the secret is there is no day without night or night without day." On the gender implications of the relationship between the general and the particular, see *Zohar* 1:246b; 2:161b. And see the comment in the fragment of the untitled work by Moses ben Shem Ṭov de León preserved in MS Munich, Bayerische Staatsbibliothek Cod. Hebr. 47, fol. 340a: "The secret of the truth [*sod ha-emet*] is the Written Torah and the Oral Torah contained one within the other [*kalul zeh ba-zeh*], and everything is one matter and a proper secret for one who understands [*we-sod nakhon la-mevin*]." (For a somewhat different perspective expressed in this treatise, see the text cited below in n. 124). Concerning this work, see Scholem, "Eine unbekannte mystische Schrift." It is evident that the passages to which I have referred, and many others that could have been cited, do emphasize the correlative nature of the polarities of night and day, the general and the particular, and by extension, the male and the female. It is reasonable to presume, therefore, as many scholars have, that the kabbalah promotes the idea that divine unity is dependent on the pairing of the two poles of the gender dimorphism. However, as I have argued in many studies, this emphasis marks the first stage of the reparation of the split of the male androgyne. The ultimate purpose of the heteroerotic coupling is to pacify judgment by lovingkindness, and hence the second stage entails the containment of the feminine left in the masculine right.

120. Babylonian Talmud, Ḥullin 60b.

121. *Zohar* 1:20a.

122. Ibid.

123. Ibid. My interpretation of the zoharic passage is corroborated in slightly different language by Baḥya ben Asher, *Be'ur al ha-Torah*, 3:204–5 (ad Numbers 28:15). Interpreting the rabbinic aggadah (see above, n. 120) about the diminution of the moon, linked exegetically to the discrepancy in Genesis 1:16 between the initial reference to the sun and the moon as the "great lights" (*ha-me'orot ha-gedolim*) and the subsequent reference to the former as the "great light" (*ha-ma'or ha-gadol*) and the latter as the "small light" (*ha-ma'or ha-qaṭon*), Baḥya writes: "The explanation of this matter is that the word 'great' instructs that the sun and the moon were equal [*shawin*] in illumination, and afterward the moon was diminished ... and it was diminished on account of the complaint that she made saying, 'Is it possible for two kings to make use of one

crown?' For the sake of the glory of God she spoke because it is not possible to make intermediaries such that each one is a light unto itself and the one has no need to receive from the other. It would be almost as if the nations said that God does not have the ability to bestow light on each one . . . . Accordingly, the explanation of the midrash of the rabbis, blessed be their memory, is that at the beginning of creation the sun and the moon were equal in illumination, and this is the language, 'two great lights,' for the sun was upon her face-to-face, and this one shone in the day and the other shone in the night from the perspective of the sun that was upon her. The intent is not that the light of the moon in the beginning of creation was as big as the light of the sun, but rather that both were created in their greatness." Kabbalists offered various opinions regarding this matter, focusing particularly on whether the original equality of sun and moon implied an identity of difference such that the gender dimorphism is neutralized. The various perspectives are well summarized by Cordovero, *Pardes Rimmonim*, 18:1, p. 214.

124. MS Munich, Bayerische Staatsbibliothek Cod. Hebr. 47, fol. 346a. Compare ibid., fol. 340a: "By all means the lovingkindness is the secret of the attribute of the south since it is the supernal right, and the Torah was given in the right . . . as it says 'from his right a fiery law unto them' [*mimino esh dat lamo*] (Deuteronomy 33:2), when the left was contained in the right [*ha-semo'l nikhlal ba-yamin*], and the essence is in the right, which contains the left [*we-ha-iqqar hu ba-yamin she-hu kolel ha-semo'l*]. . . . Thus you can know that since the essence is in the right, in every place it is on top of the left as you find in every matter of the hands when they are directed to be seen [*ha-mekhuwwanim la-re'iyyah*] in the secret of the one who blesses the name, for he, may he be elevated, his secret and the essence of his existence are seen in the secret of the ten *sefirot*, which are the secret of the name of God." See ibid., fol. 340b, where de León substantiates the mystical significance of the liturgical practice with the example of the priestly blessing: the right hand must be elevated over the left to show that the essence is in the right. The supremacy of the right vis-à-vis the left is a foundational axiom in kabbalistic symbolism—I have yet to find one exception in decades of studying this material. Moreover, the ubiquitous correlation of the left with the feminine and the right with the masculine—here, too, I have yet to have discovered one exception—has been the conceptual basis for my pointing out the phallomorphic and androcentric bias of the tradition. Despite the continuous attempts of others to challenge my views, no one has provided any evidence to undermine my assertion regarding the symbolic preeminence accorded by kabbalists to the masculine right over the feminine left and the need to restore the latter to the former and thereby appease judgment by mercy. See the extensive response to my detractors in Wolfson, *Dream*, pp. 439–42n65.

125. Ergas, *Shomer Emunim*, 1:27, p. 48.

126. Theodor and Albeck, eds., *Bere'shit Rabba*, 12:15, pp. 112–13.

127. Meroz, "Archaeology," pp. xlvi–xlix, lxiv–lxvi. I am not convinced by Meroz's attempt to show that the text of *Sifra di-Ṣeni'uta* also preserves the idea that the creation of the masculine potency without the feminine counterpart was defective, but that matter cannot be pursued here. The argument with respect to the faulty creation of the feminine separated from the masculine lends support to my suggestion that the kabbalistic construction of gender parallels what we find in some strands of Gnostic literature from late antiquity: the soteriological emphasis in both traditions involves the restoration of the female to the male. See Wolfson, *Language*, pp. 109–10, 165–67, 389–90, 597n83. On the image of the scale, see below, n. 183.

128. Heidegger, *Contributions*, §102, p. 156 (emphasis in original); *Beiträge*, p. 199.

129. Heidegger, *Contributions*, §102, p. 157 (emphasis in original); *Beiträge*, p. 200.

130. See the discussion of this philosophical complexity in Summerell, "Identity, Subjectivity, and Being Other than the Same."

131. Schelling, *On the History*, pp. 132–33 (emphasis in original); *Zur Geschichte*, pp. 123–24. Compare Schelling, *System der Weltalter*, p. 105: "Die Substanz Gottes, seine Gottheit besteht eben in seinem Thun, *er ist ganz von sich weggehend*, er ist nicht centrum, sondern wesentlich / excentrisch d.h. als Gott ist er nicht das Nothwendige, sondern das nur Seiende, deßen Sein ein *grundloses* ist" (emphasis in original).

132. Nancy, *Hegel*, p. 39.

133. Schelling, *On the History*, p. 78; *Zur Geschichte*, p. 50. For a fuller discussion of Spinoza, deism, monotheism, and pantheism, see Schelling, *System der Weltalter*, pp. 191–96. And consider Schelling, *Weltalter—Fragmente*, 2:186–87, where Spinoza's idea of substance is compared to the *Ein Sof* (*unendlich*), and in the note reference is made to the technical kabbalistic terminology *ze'eir anpin*. See Heidegger, *Schelling's Treatise*, pp. 72–73 (*Schelling: Vom Wesen*, pp. 125–26): "Everything is God, that is, all individual things collected together [*alle einzelnen Dinge in ihrer Zusammenfassung*] are promptly equated with God. God is, so to speak, only their sum total; that

is, God is really nothing [*Gott ist eigentlich nichts*]. Schelling explicitly points out that if this is the meaning of the pantheistic doctrine, Spinoza is not a pantheist and cannot be one. For Spinoza especially separated finite things from the infinite ground [*unendlichen Grund*]. They are what they are only as beings in and according to an other, as consequences of the ground. To the contrary, something primordial can never be posited from a collective sum and a synthesizing of what is merely derived—even if its number were endless." For a more detailed discussion of Schelling's analysis of Spinoza's denial of any transition between the infinite and the finite, on the one hand, and the assumption that the finite has no being except as embraced by the absolute, on the other hand, see Vater, "Schelling's Philosophy of Identity and Spinoza's *Ethica more geometrico*." See also Baader, *Elementarbegriffe über die Zeit*, p. 472. It is of interest to compare Schelling's remarks about Spinozistic emanationism and the kabbalah with Solomon Maimon's summary of the kabbalistic cosmology, influenced partially by his adherence to several of Maimonides's philosophical assumptions, in *Solomon Maimon: An Autobiography*, pp. 103–5: "Before the world was created, the divine being occupied the whole of infinite space alone. But God wished to create a world, in order that He might reveal those attributes of His nature which refer to other beings besides Himself. For this purpose He contracted Himself into the centre of His perfection, and issued into the space thereby left void ten concentric circles of light, out of which arose afterwards manifold figures (*Parzophim*) and gradations down to the present world of sense.... God is prior to the world, not in time, but in His necessary being as the condition of the world. All things besides God must depend on Him as their cause, in regard to their essence as well as their existence. The creation of the world, therefore, could not be thought as a bringing forth *out of nothing*, nor as a formation of something independent of God, but only as a bringing forth *out of Himself*. And as beings are of different grades of perfection, we must assume for their explanation different grades of limitation of the divine being. But since this limitation must be thought as extending from the infinite being down to matter, we represent the beginning of the limitation in a figure as a centre (the lowest point) of the Infinite. In fact, the Cabbalah is nothing but an expanded Spinozism, in which not only is the origin of the world explained by the limitation of the divine being, but also the origin of every kind of being, and its relation to the rest, are derived from a separate attribute of God. God, as the ultimate subject and the ultimate cause of all beings, is called Ensoph (the Infinite, of which, considered in itself, nothing can be predicated). But in relation to the infinite number of beings, positive attributes are ascribed to Him; these are reduced by the Cabbalists to ten, which are called the ten Sephiroth" (emphasis in original). For discussion of this passage in light of Spinoza's claim that finite things are negations of the absolutely indeterminate infinite, see Melamed, "*Omnis determinatio*," pp. 177–78. And compare the comment of Jacobi in *On the Doctrine of Spinoza in Letters to Mr. Moses Mendelssohn*, translated in Schelling, *Philosophical Investigations*, pp. 106–7: "This is likely no other than the very ancient [*uralt*] *a nihilo nihil fit* [nothing comes from nothing] that Spinoza took into consideration according to more abstract concepts than the philosophizing Kabbalists and others before him. In accord with these more abstract concepts, he found that, through each single coming into being in the infinite, and through each single change in the infinite, **something is posited from nothing**.... He rejected thus every **transition** of the infinite to the finite ... and he posited, instead of the emanating, an **immanent** En-Sof; an in-dwelling, **in itself** eternally unchanging, cause for the world that, taken together with all its consequences, would be one and the same" (emphasis in original). For Spinoza's own view of kabbalah, see the disparaging remark in the *Theological-Political Treatise*, in *Collected Works*, p. 217, in the context of criticizing the view that secrets are encoded in the letters or accents of the biblical text: "I've also read, and for that matter, known personally, certain Kabbalistic triflers. I've never been able to be sufficiently amazed by their madness." On Maimon and the kabbalah, see also Buzaglo, *Solomon Maimon*, pp. 133–35; Socher, *Radical Enlightenment*, pp. 5, 29, 32, 57, 62–63, 74–75, 133, 137–39; Franks, "Jewish Philosophy," pp. 64–67, 69–70. The influence of Maimon on Schelling is discussed by Socher, *Radical Enlightenment*, p. 104. See also Franks, "Jewish Philosophy," p. 76n61.

134. Compare the explication of Viṭal in Eliashiv, *Leshem Shevo we-Aḥlamah: Ḥeleq ha- Be'urim*, pt. 1, p. 27. As Eliashiv explains, the place (*maqom*), which is the paradigm of the vessel (*keli*), comes to be from the central point (*nequddah emṣa'it*) of the infinite, the aspect of the root of judgment (*beḥinat shoresh ha-din*). I trust that most readers would agree that it is as difficult to imagine a nucleus of that which is boundless (*beli gevul*) as it is to imagine the root of judgment in the domain characterized as merciful to the extreme (*takhlit ha-raḥamim*). Both formulations

point to the ultimate paradox that must be posited in order to account for differentiated beings emerging from the nondifferentiated being that is the ultimate nothing, that is, the paradox of the capacity for limit is itself a condition of the limitlessness of infinity. On the concealment of these powers, or the forces of judgment, in the light of *Ein Sof*, see Eliashiv, *Leshem Shevo we-Aḥlamah: Sefer ha-De'ah*, pt. 1, p. 221. In that context, presumably to avoid proposing an ontological dualism within the Godhead, Eliashiv emphasizes that the primal forces of judgment, also referred to as refuse, are not intrinsically evil, for there was the potential for them to be ameliorated and transformed into holy judgment; when, however, the 974 wicked generations came forth from them (see ch. 6 n. 25), their evil potential was actualized. Eliashiv's treatment of the problem of evil is too complex to enter into here properly, but I may return to it at another time. Briefly, the consequence of preserving the underlying unity by locating evil in the "dark light" (*or ḥashukh*) of the "vessels of the points" (*kelim de-ha-nequddot*) is that darkness is a modulation of the light and evil a mutation of the good. See Eliashiv, *Leshem Shevo we-Aḥlamah: Sefer ha-De'ah*, pt. 2, p. 36. The logical dilemma underlying this matter is the same as I have argued with regard to the problem of gender: can we preserve a difference of identity in the face of an identity of difference?

135. See ch. 4 n. 219.

136. I have translated from the text cited in Scholem, *Lurianic Kabbalah*, p. 256. This passage raises questions about the conjecture of Scholem, *Major Trends*, p. 262, that Luria's doctrine of *ṣimṣum* was meant to thwart the pantheistic tendencies of the earlier kabbalah, including that of the zoharic anthology, with a more theistic orientation based on a clearer ontic distinction between God and nature. See *Major Trends*, p. 413n87, where Scholem writes that "Luria himself . . . states quite bluntly a purely theistic view which seems to have been somewhat blurred in his later oral teachings." For a theistic interpretation of the Lurianic myth of *ṣimṣum*, see other sources cited in ch. 2 n. 10. However, see the reference to Scholem cited below in n. 150.

137. See the passage from Derrida's *Margins of Philosophy* cited in ch. 4 at n. 128, and compare Derrida, *Writing and Difference*, p. 265: "The problem is even more difficult in that sovereignty simultaneously assigns itself another form of writing: the one that produces the trace as trace. The latter is a trace only if presence is irremediably eluded in it, from its initial promise, and only if it constitutes itself as the possibility of absolute erasure. An unerasable trace is not a trace."

138. Scholem, *Lurianic Kabbalah*, p. 258. Compare the description of *Keter* in Nathan of Gaza, *Sefer ha-Beri'ah*, MS Jewish Theological Seminary of America 1581, fols. 3a–b, as both the light that is proximate to the infinite (*ha-or qarov le-ein sof*) in which the simple thought (*maḥashavah peshuṭah*) arises and the vessel that receives the simplicity of the light of the infinite (*keli leqabbel peshiṭut or ein sof*). Since the vessel itself is constituted by the incomposite light, there is no ontological difference between the light and the vessel, the difference that would serve as the basis for positing a genuine sense of alterity. Consider as well Nathan's explanation of the Lurianic doctrine of the breaking of the vessels (*shevirat ha-kelim*) in ibid., fol. 100a: "All of these matters were desired by the light that has no thought [*or she-ein bo maḥashavah*] whose source is very great, more than the light that is united with the name 'thought.' In order for the thoughts to be actualized, they must be activated by means of the light that is without limit [*or she-ein lo sof*], which is greater than the infinitude of thought [*ein sof shel ha-maḥashavah*]. . . . However, when the straight line [*qaw ha-yashar*], which is the line of thought [*qaw shel ha-maḥashavah*], wanted to fill every vessel of the account of creation with that light, the vessels broke because they did not want to be subsidiary to the light of thought." Notwithstanding the fact that, according to Nathan (ibid., fol. 106b), the cause for the existence of the vessels was the diminution of the light of thought—in the lower worlds of creation, formation, and doing, the vitality of the vessel is strengthened in proportion to the demise of the light, whereas in the world of emanation, which is entirely the essence of divinity (*eṣem elohut*), as the light is removed from or diminished in the vessel, the vitality of the light is amplified and the vessel expires—the vessel is still composed of the light, albeit in a weakened state. On the symbolic status of the vessel in Nathan, see Elqayam, "Mystery of Faith," pp. 328–29n106.

139. Saruq, *Derush ha-Malbush*, p. 9.

140. Ibid., p. 10.

141. Ibid., p. 11.

142. Ibid., p. 25.

143. Delmedigo, *Ta'alumot Ḥokhmah*, 79b.

144. Viṭal, *Eṣ Ḥayyim*, 1:2, 12d.

145. Ibid., 1:2, 11c–d.

146. See above, n. 136.

147. Scholem, *Lurianic Kabbalah*, p. 258.

148. Viṭal, *Eṣ Ḥayyim*, 3:3, 17a.

149. Ibid.

150. See especially Scholem, *Major Trends*, pp. 272–73: "For Luria and his followers, there is no break in this continuous process of evolution. This fact makes the problem of Luria's theism doubly acute, for the pantheistic implications of this doctrine are too manifest to require emphasis. Luria's reply to the question takes the form of a subtle distinction between the world of *Atsiluth* and the three other spheres: the former . . . is conceived as being substantially identical with the divinity and the *En-Sof*, but from then on Luria tries to draw a firm dividing line. Between the world of *Atsiluth* and that of *Beriah*, and similarly between each of the following ones, he postulates a curtain or partition wall which has a double effect. In the first place it causes the divine substance itself to flow upwards; the Light of *En-Sof* is refracted. Secondly, the power which emanates from the substance . . . passes through the filter of the 'curtain.' This power then becomes the substance of the next world, of which again only the power passes into the third, and so through all four spheres." Surely, this is an impressive attempt to deal with the philosophical problem, but I do not think the paradox is resolved. On the contrary, the paradox is intensified, for it is not logically consistent to posit an uninterrupted emanation of the infinite light in all the worlds, on the one hand, and to argue that the lower three worlds should not be considered divinity as is the first world, on the other hand. In the final analysis, one must succumb to an irresolvable tension between the theistic and the pantheistic elements and accept the paradox that *the infinite is transcendent to the world only insofar as it is immanent in the world.*

151. Wolfson, *Giving*, pp. 78, 171–74, 197.

152. With respect to this issue we could note the affinity between the kabbalistic notion and Levinas. See the passage cited in ch. 2 at n. 9. One of the more striking symbols utilized to account for the emergence of division (*hitḥallequt*) and multiplicity (*ribbuy*) in the incomposite oneness (*aḥdut ha-peshuṭah*) of the essentiality of the infinite light (*aṣmiyyut or ein sof*) is the notion of the letters of the infinite (*otiyyot de-ein sof*) promulgated by the Ḥabad-Lubavitch masters. See, for instance, Shneur Zalman of Liadi, *Ma'amerei Admor ha-Zaqen al Nevi'im*, pp. 48–49. In that context, the source of the differentiation within the undifferentiated is identified, more specifically, as the line (*qaw*) and the thread (*ḥuṭ*) that come forth after the contraction of the light (see ch. 4 n. 172) from the letters of infinity. These letters, in other words, constitute the potentiality for plurality wedged in the heart of the indissoluble unity of *Ein Sof*. Concerning the symbol of the letters of the infinite, see the additional sources cited and discussed in Wolfson, *Open Secret*, pp. 59–60, 324n156. The ascription of letters to that which is beyond linguistic demarcation leads the mind to the edge of thought. Clearly, what is meant by this expression of the inexpressible is an apophatic way to delineate the intermediary space between the infinite and the finite, the name of the namelessness and the namelessness of the name. Compare the passage of Eliashiv cited in ch. 3 n. 65. Perhaps in the future I will write an essay comparing the relationship of the letters of the Torah and the light of infinity in Eliashiv and Ḥabad.

153. Wolfson, *Language*, pp. 75–77.

154. Heidegger, *Contributions*, §110, p. 166; *Beiträge*, p. 212.

155. Hegel, *Lectures on the Philosophy of Religion*, 1:120: "Spirit is what manifests itself, what appears but is infinite in its appearance; spirit that does not appear *is not*; it reflects itself back within itself. . . . *That God* (as result) *appears* is what we make into our particular object—God as the *utterly concrete idea* together with its infinite appearance, which is identical with the substance, with the essence [of reality]; this is the content, the specification of this content" (emphasis in original).

156. Ibid., 1:327: "Consciousness is a positing of two that are supposed to be distinct, but this is nothing else than what has been stated, namely this differentiation of the moments themselves. This differentiation takes on the character of a relationship, and in this way the two moments constitute the content of the two sides of the relationship. In consciousness one side is the solid, substantial unity of the idea—God as having being, the God that has being as a self-relating unity. The other side of the distinction is the act of differentiating itself, which is consciousness, the side for which the other, the solid unity, exists; this side consequently takes on the character of being finite. God is thereby determined as an object, as appearance, as having being and appearing for consciousness. . . .The essential moment is self-differentiation; and precisely thereby an other is posited. This differentiation, or the aspect of consciousness, has to be grasped in a reversion to the *absolute affirmation*—an appearing which elevates itself just as eternally to the truth of appearance" (emphasis in original).

157. Ibid., 1:139–40, 142–43, 225, 228. Particularly germane is the description of the concept of God on p. 326: "We have defined the idea as the absolute unity of the spiritual and the natural, and the spiritual as the substantial, so that the 'other' is only something posited by spirit and sustained within

it." In the continuation, Hegel notes that this idea comprises three moments: (1) the substantial, absolute, subjective unity of God and his other, what is referred to as the idea in its self-equivalent affirmation; (2) the differentiation wherein the two moments are distinct, the being for one and for the other; (3) the self-positing of what is differentiated in the absolute affirmation. One will readily discern here Hegel's dialectical logic. Compare the three stages delineated in Hegel, *Philosophy of Mind*, p. 264: the eternal content that remains together with itself in its manifestation; the differentiation of the eternal essence from its manifestation, which becomes through this difference the world of appearance; and the infinite return and reconciliation of the alienated world with the eternal essence, the withdrawal of the essence from appearance into the unity of its fullness. Despite Hegel's effort to sublate difference in the absolute affirmation of the self-positing of what is differentiated, he cannot escape the consequence that if the material other is posited and sustained by spirit, then the otherness of materiality vis-à-vis the spiritual is severely compromised. See Heidegger's summation of Hegel's view cited above, n. 63.

158. Hegel, *Lectures on the Philosophy of Religion*, 1:232: "As religion represents it, there is in God the other of God, God's *Son*, i.e., God as other, the other that remains within love and within divinity; and the Son is the truth of this finite world" (emphasis in original).

159. Ibid., 1:371.

160. My analysis is inspired by the discussion of Cantor's absolute infinity and the transfinite in Priest, *Beyond the Limits*, pp. 113–27, esp. 115–17.

161. Viṭal, *Mavo She'arim*, p. 9. On the metaphorical depiction of *Ein Sof* in masculine terms, consider the remark in the commentary on *Sifra di-Ṣeni'uta* by Cordovero, *Zohar im Perush Or Yaqar*, 23:98. Commenting on the language of the zoharic text, *ad de-reisha de-khissufa de-khol kissufin levushei diqar atqin we-aḥasin*, "Until the head of the desire of all desires arrayed and bestowed garments of glory" (*Zohar* 2:176b), Cordovero writes: "The head of all desires [*reisha de-khol kissufin*], that is, the *Ein Sof*, emanates garments of glory, that is, the dissemination of *Ḥokhmah* through its arrayments in the secret of *Binah* within the interiority of *Keter*, for initially, *Keter* was not arrayed in the arrayments . . . and these arrayments are the branches through which *Ḥokhmah* germinated in its existence, and they are surely garments, since *Keter* is garbed in the dissemination of *Ḥokhmah* and acts through its agency. Thus, they are garments of glory, for *Ḥokhmah* is called glory [*kavod*] and *Keter* is garbed in them, and *Ein Sof* is garbed only in *Keter*; that is, the three principles of governance [*ro'shei ha-hanhagah*]: *Ein Sof* within *Keter*, and *Keter* within *Ḥokhmah* . . . . It says 'arrayed and bestowed,' that is, he arrayed and emanated, for there is no dissemination of *Ḥokhmah* within *Keter* except from the perspective of the secret of the dissemination of the line of measure [*qaw ha-middah*], that is, the essence [*eṣem*] of *Ein Sof* that is within the aspect of *Keter*, for *Ein Sof* is the line of his measure [*qaw middato*]. After he arrayed them, they are not garments in relation to him, but rather he 'bestowed,' he bequeathed them like a person bequeaths to his son. Thus, *Ein Sof*, the cause of all causes, arrayed, emanated, bequeathed, and garbed his son, which is *Keter*, produced by him as the son is produced by the father."

162. Wolfson, *Language*, pp. 76, 95, 181–83, 186–87, 270–71, 311. I will not repeat all the sources I mentioned in that previous study, but I will note one reference where the question about gender dimorphism in the uppermost aspect of the divine (*Attiq* or *Arikh Anpin*) is dealt with in great technical detail: Viṭal, *Eṣ Ḥayyim*, 12:2, 57a–c, and its parallel in Viṭal, *Oṣrot Ḥayyim*, pp. 132–37. The eschatological application of this gender symbolism is made explicit by Bachrach, *Emeq ha-Melekh*, 6:72, p. 324: "The light of this resurrection of the dead is the offspring of *Keter* in the secret of *yeḥidah*, and it has no female [*we-ein lo neqevah*], which is secondary to the male, and this, too, is the secret of the mysteries of the mysteries of Torah, and the final telos of the secrets and mysteries of Torah."

163. Nathan of Gaza, *Sefer ha-Beri'ah*, MS Jewish Theological Seminary of America 1581, fols. 1b–2a. Compare ibid., fols. 102b–103a: "In the time of the contraction everything became left, and in the time of the coming of the light everything was restored to the right. And since there was no left there, the right side in it was strengthened, which is the mystery of thought, so it would not break, and the light of thought extended from within and from without." Concerning this theme in Nathan, and the citation of other textual evidence, see Wolfson, *Language*, p. 511n267. The straight line is referred to by Nathan as both *qaw ha-yashar* and as *qaw ha-yosher*, two linguistic forms attested in the older kabbalistic sources that influenced him. On *ṣimṣum* and the *ṭehiru* in Nathan's Sabbatian theology, see Wirszubski, *Between the Lines*, pp. 153–60.

164. Nathan of Gaza, *Sefer ha-Beri'ah*, MS Jewish Theological Seminary of America 1581, fol. 2b. In the continuation, fols. 2b–3a, Nathan asserts that the

"mystery of the luster" (*sod ha-ṭehiru*) applies to the entirety of the account of creation (*ma'aseh bere'shit*) mentioned by the rabbis, for after the luster separates from its source, it contemplates and gives shape to the ten forms (*ṣiyyurim*) of the *sefirot* to actualize the will of the *Ein Sof*. Even so, he insists that we cannot ascribe to this trace the "essence of divinity" (*eṣem elohut*), for it lacks the "essential life" (*ḥayyim aṣmiyyim*) and thus it bears no similarity to the emanated light (*or ha-ne'eṣal*). For this reason, Nathan (fol. 3a) attributes to the *ṭehiru* the term *golem*, whose numerical value is the same as *ḥokhmah*. On fol. 3b, the *ṭehiru* is identified as the chaos (*tohu*) or as the ether that is not comprehended (*awir she-eino nitpas*), an expression that is applied as well to *Keter*, the divine nothing (*ayin*) that is immutable, or literally, in the state of "standing as it was" (*omed kemo she-hayah*). The term *golem* is also attributed to *Malkhut*; see ibid., fol. 7b. The *ṭehiru* is identified as the source of the shell (*qelippah*) that precedes the fruit (*peri*), which is the light of the straight line (fol. 9b). The "secret of the *ṭehiru*," which is the great dragon (*tannin ha-gadol*), is identified as the *golem* and as *ḥokhmah* (the numerical value of both words is 73) in Nathan of Gaza, *Derush ha-Tanninim*, printed in Scholem, *Be-Iqvot Mashiaḥ*, p. 20. On the depiction of the *ṭehiru* as the "matter that cannot be comprehended" (*davar she-eino nitpas*), see Nathan of Gaza, *Zemir Ariṣim Ya'aneh*, MS Oxford, Bodleian Library 1796, fol. 57b. Nathan's appropriation of the Lurianic doctrine, including the symbol of the *ṭehiru*, is analyzed in detail by Scholem, *Sabbatai Ṣevi*, pp. 299–311. The correlation of left and right respectively with masculine and feminine is discussed by Nathan of Gaza, *Sefer ha-Beri'ah*, MS Jewish Theological Seminary of America 1581, fols. 34b–35a, and compare the discussion of the emergence of the left from the right, ibid., fols. 68b–69a. Following older kabbalistic sources, especially the zoharic literature, the antagonism between left and right is explained as the struggle between the darkness of Esau and the light of the souls of Israel (fols. 69b–70a). See as well the explication on fols. 51b–52a of the transformation of the right of the feminine into the left of the masculine, exemplified in the ritual of the phylacteries of the arm. The principal of the gender dynamic is stated succinctly on fol. 55a: "Thus there is no complete right in the feminine apart from the left of the masculine." On the kabbalistic significance of the phylacteries and the unity proclaimed in the *Shema*, compare ibid., fols. 115a–120b, and analysis in Elqayam, "Mystery of Faith," pp. 140–42.

165. Nathan of Gaza, *Sefer ha-Beri'ah*, MS Jewish Theological Seminary of America 1581, fol. 2b. See also fol. 8a–b. The autoerotic implications of the initial act of withdrawal are alluded to in the following comment of Nathan, ibid., fol. 19a, on the formation of the letters: "The light of wisdom was made in the likeness of lines [*qawim qawim*], elongated serpents [*neḥashim arukkim*], and those serpents entered the womb of *Binah*, and when they emerged afterward from the womb of *Binah*, they took shape except for the *alef*, which took shape from itself without entering into the womb of *Binah*. Rather, the form was produced in that portion of the light from itself, and this alludes to the totality of the contraction . . . for the supernal *yod* corresponds to the upper waters, the lower *yod* corresponds to the lower waters . . . and the line [*qaw*] alludes to the light of the straight line [*le-or qaw ha-yashar*]. . . . The reason that this letter is called *alef* is from the expression *pele*, for it is wondrous and hidden [*mufla'at u-mekhussat*], standing in the place of the supernal mystery [*pele elyon*], which is *Keter*." The *alef* alludes to the *ṣimṣum* insofar as it can be decomposed orthographically into a *yod* on top, a *yod* on bottom, and the *waw* in the middle, which signifies the straight line connecting them. Compare fol. 6a: "Know that the form of the *alef* is bound between *Ḥokhmah* and *Binah* without any form [*ṣiyyur shel alef qashur bein ḥokhmah u-vinah mi-beli shum ṣiyyur*] for the directive about the act of the constriction in its totality [*ma'aseh ha-ṣimṣum bi-khelalut*] instructs about its form in particular with respect to the *yodin*." What is most noteworthy for our purposes is the account of the *alef* coming to being on its own accord without the light of *Ḥokhmah* entering like a serpentine elongation into the uterus of *Binah*. On the description of the letters as elongated serpents, see Nathan's *Derush ha-Menorah*, MS JNUL 8⁰ 1161, fol. 159b, in Scholem, *Be-Iqvot Mashiaḥ*, p. 92. As Scholem, *Sabbatai Ṣevi*, p. 810n321, informed the reader, this text is part of Nathan's treatise *Zemir Ariṣim Ya'aneh*. See MS Oxford, Bodleian Library 1796, fol. 42b.

166. Nathan of Gaza, *Sefer ha-Beri'ah*, fol. 43a: "It is not possible for the lights of the infinite [*me'orot ein sof*] to be revealed, and they are not disclosed unless there is the configuration of a man that is male that has no female [*parṣuf adam zakhar deleit leih nuqba*]. From his power, however, there emanated all of the entities, and this is the matter of the mystery of *Adam Qadmon*, the source of life, for above him are revealed the lights of the infinite, and he contemplates them and draws the essential life from there. This is the purpose and great reason for his emanation, which is concealed from the eyes of all that is living, and there is no light that can comprehend this limit." On the masculine visage that has no feminine, compare ibid., fol. 71b,

and the description of the first of the ten circles of the *ṭehiru*, associated with *Keter*, as having no female, since it was not yet sufficiently purified (*eino kol kakh mevorar*), in Nathan of Gaza, *Derush ha-Tanninim*, in Scholem, *Be-Iqvot Mashiaḥ*, p. 23. Finally, consider the description of *adam yashar* in Nathan of Gaza, *Zemir Ariṣim Ya'aneh*, MS Oxford, Bodleian Library 1796, fol. 88a: "There he is not named as either right or left, for everything is incomposite mercy [*raḥamim peshuṭim*] and limitless worlds are constructed in that human." Insofar as mercy is characterized routinely as masculine, to say that there is neither left nor right because there is only incomposite mercy means the gender binary is overcome when there is maleness without the correlative femaleness.

167. Nathan of Gaza, *Sefer ha-Beri'ah*, MS Jewish Theological Seminary of America 1581, fols. 16b–17a. Compare Nathan of Gaza, *Zemir Ariṣim Ya'aneh*, MS Oxford, Bodleian Library 1796, fol. 91b. The depiction of the future as a state wherein everything is restored to the right, since there is no more back set against the face, is contrasted with the current situation marked by a vacillation between two forms of conjunction of the male and female, either back-to-back or face-to-face. The type of conjunction that prevails depends on human agency, and specifically the liturgical prostration and the need to face the western wall of the Jerusalem temple. See Nathan of Gaza, *Sefer ha-Beri'ah*, MS Jewish Theological Seminary of America 1581, fol. 16b: "And with this we come to explain the matter of prostration, for everyone must turn to the western wall, and the reason is that the eyes and the intellect of the souls [*neshamot*] must always be toward the face of the king, and their souls [*nafsham*] enter into the foundation of Rachel and their spirits [*ruḥam*] into the foundation of *Tif'eret*, to be in the secret of the male waters and the female waters. When the king and the queen stand side by side, they are united, or at times when she is in the rear, her back stands conjoined to his back. Either way the face of the soul is constantly facing the face of the king or queen when the soul ascends." On the secret of prostration, see ibid., fol. 2a–b, and Nathan of Gaza, *Zemir Ariṣim Ya'aneh*, MS Oxford, Bodleian Library 1796, fol. 89b.

168. On Nathan's use of the rabbinic taxonomies *ma'aseh bere'shit* and *ma'aseh merkavah* to name two temporal periods within the infinite, the former prior to the expansion of the straight line and the other after the expansion of the light to fill the vessels, see Wirszubski, *Between the Lines*, pp. 160–61; Elqayam, "Mystery of Faith," pp. 119–24.

169. Nathan of Gaza, *Sefer ha-Beri'ah*, MS Jewish Theological Seminary of America 1581, fol. 12a. Compare fol. 121a: "That the aspect of *Malkhut* will be in the secret of the diadem [*be-sod ha-aṭarah*] in the future to come is only because her root in the time of the constriction was the right, and there is also a line [*qaw*] in the existence of that light, which reaches above to the place to which the light of thought does not ascend." See as well fol. 96a, where the future is described as the ascent of the forces of strength (*gevurot*) in the secret of the diadem. The messianic state is realized proleptically each Sabbath with the elevation of the mystery of the light of thought until it is crowned within *Ein Sof* (fol. 112b).

170. Wolfson, "Coronation," p. 337n96; Wolfson, "*Tiqqun ha-Shekhinah*," pp. 291, 330–32; Wolfson, *Language*, pp. 72 (the inadvertent reference there to Proverbs 12:14 should be corrected to 12:4), 185–86, 375, 387, 459n250, 591n11; Wolfson, *Open Secret*, pp. 176, 178, 203–4, 206–8, 211, 213, 375n41. In my mind, the elevation of the female as the diadem positioned on the head of her husband at the endtime does signify a transposition of gender—also conveyed by the image of the female encircling the male (Jeremiah 31:21)—but not a complete transvaluation insofar as this symbol still implies that the feminine remains inscribed within the phallogocentric axiology, and the female can be redeemed only to the extent that she becomes part of the male. For there to be a true transvaluation and surpassing of patriarchy, the presumption of there being both male and female would have to give way to the discernment that there is neither male nor female, not because the female has been reintegrated into the male but because we are beyond the binary opposition feminine/masculine. The surmounting of the gender binary would thus require a radical dissolution of difference, which, applied socio-culturally, would mean disrupting the particularity of Judaism itself expressed in its ritual practices and doctrinal beliefs. Consider the recent argument that Viṭal's reference to the eschatological image of the righteous sitting with their crowns on their heads, an image that is linked exegetically to the depiction in Proverbs 12:4 of the woman of valor as the diadem of her husband, entails a transposition that is a genuine transvaluation and an overturning of the gender hierarchy offered by Vilk, *Sefer ha-Ṣimṣum*, pp. 9–10: "From this is evident that in the future to come the power and status of the feminine will be greater than the status of the masculine. The intent of this matter is that in the future to come it will be disclosed that the power of reception [*koaḥ ha-qabbalah*] (the feminine) is more important than the power of bestowal [*koaḥ ha-hashpa'ah*] (the masculine); that is, in all the days of the world until

the seventh millennium, the greatest power is the power of bestowal, but in the future to come the matter will be inverted and the power of reception will be strengthened. It will be revealed to all eyes that the greatest level is the potency to receive." Vilk goes on to relate the depth of this matter to the initial acts of divine creativity: the originary withdrawal of light is linked to the power of reception, which is an expression of judgment, and the creation that ensues therefrom is linked to the power of bestowal, an expression of grace. To the extent that the *ṣimṣum* creates the vessel that makes possible the overflow of the life force and the formation of the worlds, the withdrawal can be considered the first expression of the power of receiving, which is identified more technically as the aspect of *malkhut de-ein sof*. The gender transvaluation, according to Vilk, mandates the pietistic task of Jewish men to live a life of humility and deprivation so that they becomes vessels to augment the effluence of the mercy of the infinite, and as a consequence, the true unity will be realized when the opposition of male and female is no longer operative. In Vilk's own words, *Sefer ha-Ṣimṣum*, p. 10: "This is what will be in the future to come, the power of reception will overpower the power of bestowal, for then there will be the perfect unity and it will be disclosed that the power of bestowal and the power of reception are both in complete unity receiving from *Ein Sof*. And then both will be in the aspect of receiving in the manner that the power of bestowal will not come to expression because it, too, will be in the aspect of that which receives. Both will make use of one crown insofar as they receive from the light of *Ein Sof*. This is the depth of what we brought from the Ari, blessed be his memory, that in the future to come the feminine will be the diadem of her husband, for in the future the potency of the feminine, which is the power of reception, will come to expression, whereas the potency of the masculine, the power of bestowal, will not come to expression. On the contrary, both will be in the aspect of that which receives. . . . This matter is rooted in the source of sources, for the perfect unity is the condition of 'there is no other apart from him' (Deuteronomy 4:35), the contraction and the existence will also be comprised entirely in the light of *Ein Sof*, in a manner that the overflow that exists in creation will be completely receiving. The entire existence will be in the aspect of the limit within the limitless [*ha-gevul be-tokh ha-bilti gevul*], which has no name at all, and all 'his existence' will be in the aspect of constriction in the aspect of concealment in the light of *Ein Sof*." To say that the unity to be achieved in the end is one in which all existence will be in the aspect of withdrawal and hidden in the light of infinity implies that the subjugating of the binary of the masculine donor and the feminine recipient betokens the cessation of discriminate beings, the debunking of the erroneous perception that the worlds are ontologically independent of and extrinsic to *Ein Sof*. See Vilk, *Sefer ha-Ṣimṣum*, p. 18, where the spiritual delight (*oneg ruḥani*) of the future is identified explicitly as a state in which all of creation will receive the light of the infinite and be nullified therein. The import of the transposition of the female is that all creation becomes the power of receiving and is thereby incorporated into the boundlessness of the infinite. This comes closest to the view I expressed in Wolfson, "Bifurcating," pp. 112–13: "A bona fide overcoming of the patriarchal hierarchy, however, would require the apophatic erasure of difference to the point that the dyad of giving and receiving is transcended. It is not sufficient for the (feminine) receiver to become the (masculine) giver, as impressive as this may seem; the ideal unity would be one in which there is no more giver or receiver, only the giving that is receiving and the receiving that is giving." The crucial difference between my approach and that of Vilk, however, is that he does not escape from the binarian structure; indeed, his explanation of the supremacy of the feminine over the masculine keeps him tethered to the dichotomy he thinks he has undone. The feminine potency to receive is accorded more value than the masculine potency to bestow, but both male and female are still characterized as female in relation to the infinite, which is the quintessential male insofar as its nature is to bestow light incontrovertibly. In the end, we revert to the status of the feminine in the beginning, the capacity for limit assimilated within the limitless.

171. See the passage of Nathan of Gaza's *Derush ha-Tanninim* in Scholem, *Be-Iqvot Mashiaḥ*, pp. 15–16, cited and explicated in Wolfson, "Engenderment," pp. 235–36. See also Wolfson, "Constructions," pp. 21n30, 71–72n80, and the utilization of my argument with the presentation of additional textual evidence in Rosenstock, "Abraham Miguel Cardoso's Messianism," pp. 93–96. On the harmonious unity of all things and the ascetic ideal of spiritual love in Nathan of Gaza's eschatological teaching (*Sefer ha-Beri'ah*, MS Jewish Theological Seminary of America 1581, fols. 121b–122a), see Wirszubski, *Between the Lines*, pp. 182–83, 210–11. For a different approach to the myth of the androgyne and the erotic in Nathan of Gaza, see Elqayam, "To Know Messiah," pp. 660–66. Rapoport-Albert, in *Women and the Messianic Heresy*, p. 221n221, remarks that

my interpretation of the gender metamorphosis of the female implied in the symbol of coronation and the elevation of the *Shekhinah* does not apply to Frank, who "repeatedly emphasizes the Maiden's femaleness and envisions how the redemption would materialize through her, in fulfilment of the sexual duality existing at every level of being." To the best of my recollection, I have not included the historical phenomenon of Frankism in my previous discussions. Hence, Rapoport-Albert's comment is somewhat gratuitous, but even if correct, it would indicate that Frank's augmenting the spiritual power of the female on the assumption that a more egalitarian approach to gender is a sign of the redemption is a perspective that is at odds with the view proffered by the followers of Sabbatai Ṣevi, who created the conceptual apparatus to spearhead the movement. See Rapoport-Albert's own hesitation on p. 220n215 and, more important, the different assessment in her discussion of Cardoso and Eybeschuetz on p. 223. Her qualification of my perspective on Cardoso in n. 228 makes no sense in light of the fact that her interpretation reinforces my own. Scholem, *Sabbatai Ṣevi*, p. 403, already argued that a sign of the messianic transformation could be seen in the attempts of Sabbatai Ṣevi to change the status of women by including them in ritual deeds from which they were traditionally excluded. On the role of women in the Sabbatian movement, see also Goldish, *Sabbatean Prophets*, pp. 46–47, 100, 106–7, 111; Halperin, *Sabbatai Zevi*, pp. 39, 41, 76, 172; and the copious documentation provided by Rapoport-Albert, *Women and the Messianic Heresy*, pp. 15–156. See also Rapoport-Albert, *Hasidic Studies*, pp. 269–317, and my criticism of her position in Wolfson, "Bifurcating," p. 111n39. As I remarked in that context, I accept that Sabbatai Ṣevi sought to subvert the nomian framework of rabbinic authority by breaking down distinctions between men and women both in terms of ritual practice and in the study of esoteric texts, especially the *Zohar*, but I would still maintain that the egalitarian agenda did not prevent the prevalence of the traditional phallomorphic symbolism on the part of the leading theologians of the Sabbatian movement. See Wolfson, *Language*, pp. 62–63. For the related but independent suggestion that the eventual ascendancy of the antinomian elements—linked especially to sexuality and the erotic sense of touch—was due to the influence of Sabbatai's third wife, see van der Haven, *From Lowly Metaphor to Divine Flesh*, pp. 40–60.

172. Baruch of Kosov, *Yesod ha-Emunah*, p. 271.

173. Ibid., p. 270.

174. Letter of Eliashiv in Schatz, *Ma'yan Moshe*, p. 240.

175. I am here influenced by the argument about Plato in Bergren, "Architecture, Gender, Philosophy," p. 263.

176. Elqayam, "To Know Messiah," p. 665n107, and more recently, Shmueli, "R. Joseph of Hamadan's *Commentary*," p. 251n107. See my various responses in Wolfson, "Constructions," pp. 60–61n153; Wolfson, *Venturing Beyond*, pp. 220–21n118; Wolfson, "Phallic Jewissance," p. 311n69.

177. Compare Nathan of Gaza, *Sefer ha-Beri'ah*, MS Jewish Theological Seminary of America 1581, fol. 9a: "Hence the attribute of *Malkhut* . . . in the time of the contraction was entirely right [*be-et ha-ṣimṣum hayah kolla yamina*]. You must know that even though the root was completely right, there was mixed in it a light that had the property of the back . . . and thus when the supernal attributes wanted to include in it all of their aspects, they placed it in their hinder part to reveal the matter of the back . . . which stood in secrecy, hidden in the light that is the root of the right." See ibid., fol. 11a.

178. See Wolfson, "Iconicity of the Text"; Wolfson, *Language*, pp. 152, 172, 505n200. The ideal, of course, is to maintain the unity of the ten emanations and thus not to separate the tenth from the upper nine or the upper nine from the tenth; both possibilities are deemed to be acts of heresy. Compare *Tiqqunei Zohar*, sec. 69, 117b: "Whoever takes *Malkhut* without the nine *sefirot* cuts the shoots [*meqaṣṣeṣ ba-neṭi'an*] and whoever takes the nine *sefirot* without *Malkhut* is someone who disavows the root [*kofer ba-iqqar*]." As the beginning of the passage states, *Malkhut* is the root or essence of the four letters of the Tetragrammaton (*YHWH*), or the ten letters when that name is written in full (*yod he waw he*), because "it is comprised of the ten *sefirot*, and everything must be contained in it." The text substantiates my claim about asymmetry because the sin of cutting the shoots involves separating the feminine from the upper emanations and the sin of disavowing the root involves not affirming the status of the feminine as being the paradigmatic vessel to contain the upper emanations. These are two ways to express the subordinate and instrumental status of the *Shekhinah*. A different interpretation of this passage is offered by Roi, *Love of the Shekhina*, pp. 120–22.

179. Wolfson, *Language*, pp. 49–55, 63–77; Wolfson, "Bifurcating," pp. 92–102. Confirmation of my perspective can be elicited from the comment of Nathan of Gaza in *Zemir Ariṣim Ya'aneh*, MS Oxford, Bodleian Library 1796, fols. 80b–81a: "From this we learn the matter of the containment of the right in the left and of the left in the right . . . for we have already

learned from our words the matter of the being of *Gevurah*, which is made from the containment of the right in the left; accordingly, even though the left is contained in the right, *Gevurah* does not come to be except subsequently. Thus, the right is contained in the left but the left is not contained in the right." Even in the case of *Binah*, according to Nathan, "the left is not contained in the right except after the right is contained in the left.... After the right is contained in the left in *Binah* there is born the comprehension in *Ḥokhmah* to contain the left in the right" (fol. 81a). In a state of imperfection, the right stands opposite the left and the left opposite the right, but when perfection is achieved, the left is comprised within the right, a unification expressed in the eschatological image of Isaiah 28:5, "In that day, the Lord of Hosts shall become a crown of beauty and a diadem of glory for the remnant of his people" (fol. 93b). For a different and purportedly more egalitarian approach, see Idel, "Androgyny"; Idel, *Kabbalah and Eros*, pp. 53–103, esp. 59–77. My perspective on the male androgyne and kabbalistic phallocentrism is criticized on pp. 99–100, and see also pp. 128–30. I have responded to Idel's presentation of my work elsewhere and will not do so again in this context. But it is worth reiterating my view that the kabbalistic material is closer to older gnostic sources, and maybe also the anthropology promulgated by Paul, according to which redemption consists of rectifying the split of the androgyne by making the female male. It is also of interest to compare what I take to be the dominant kabbalistic perspective and the position of Böhme: the original prelapsarian androgyny, the true likeness of God's image, which will be restored in the eschatological resurrection, is characterized as neither masculine nor feminine. See Simuţ, *F.C. Baur's Synthesis*, pp. 49–51. Does this effacement of gender dimorphism imply an egalitarian overcoming of the phallomorphic hierarchy or does it imply the androcentric suppression of one gender? I hope to discuss the issue in a separate study on the gender implications of Böhme's theosophy.

180. Wolfson, *Venturing Beyond*, pp. 220–21. My interpretation is made explicit in the language of Dunasky, ed., *Midrash Rabbah: Shir ha-Shirim*, 1:45 (on Song of Songs 1:9): "Is there a left above? Is it not the case that it is entirely right [*ha-kol yamin*], as it says 'Your right hand, O Lord, glorious in power, your right hand, O Lord, shatters the foe' (Exodus 15:6)?"

181. *Zohar* 3:129a; Viṭal, *Eṣ Ḥayyim*, 13:13, 68c; Wolfson, *Language*, pp. 179–80.

182. For citation of sources and analysis, see Wolfson, *Venturing Beyond*, pp. 218–24.

183. *Zohar* 3:290a (*Idra Zuṭa*). On the image of the scale as a symbol for the *hieros gamos*, see Wolfson, *Language*, pp. 95, 176, 222, 386, and the reference to the studies of Liebes cited on p. 596n60; Meroz, "Archaeology," pp. lxxii–lxxv. Many passages from a plethora of kabbalistic texts could be cited to support the phallomorphic implications of the image of the scale, but here I will cite as one representative source the following depiction of the rectification of the world at the time of the Sinaitic theophany in Eliashiv, *Leshem Shevo we-Aḥlamah: Sefer ha-De'ah*, pt. 2, p. 381: "Thus he gave them the Torah, for the Torah is from the foundation of the father [*yesod de-abba*] that split and it went outward... and the tablets are the two crowns of knowledge [*iṭrin de-da'at*] that were hidden within it.... Therefore, those who merited the first tablets aroused high above to draw down the concealed light so that it be disclosed below. And this is the mystery of the scale [*ha-raza de-matqela*] that unified everything."

184. Eliashiv, *Leshem Shevo we-Aḥlamah: Sefer ha-De'ah*, pt. 1, p. 16. In the state prior to the emergence of the two distinct vessels, the lights of the male mercy and the female strength "were contained in one vessel" (*kelulim bi-kheli aḥat*) and they had no existence (*qiyyum*) or standing (*ha'amadah*) in their own place. The one vessel could not sustain them because they were "two antinomies contradicting one another" (*shenei hafkiyyim ha-menuggadim zeh la-zeh*).

185. Regarding this passage, see the textual variants and Hebrew translation in Benarroch, "Edition of Early Versions of *Idra Zuta*," p. 193.

186. Heidegger, *Contributions*, §20, p. 44; *Beiträge*, p. 55.

187. See references cited in Wolfson, "Revealing and Re/Veiling," pp. 36–38n43.

188. Schelling, *Philosophy and Religion*, p. 26 (emphasis in original); *Philosophie und Religion*, pp. 34–35. I have taken the liberty of correcting some errors and altering the translation on the basis of the original German. For discussion of this passage, see Franks, "Rabbinic Idealism," pp. 237–38. Franks duly notes the "recognizably Lurianic direction" of Schelling's remark and draws the further implication that "the fall of the human is an image of the fall that is creation itself, which is an exile of divinity from the world, demanding reparation." I agree that in the Lurianic teaching creation can be considered a fall, but I would contend nonetheless that the divine is exiled in the world rather than from the world. See Wolfson, "Divine Suffering," pp. 115–17. It is worth recalling here the contention of Scholem, *Major Trends*, p. 261, that *ṣimṣum* marks the "withdrawal

of God into his own Being in terms of Exile, of banishing Himself from His totality into profound seclusion." The contraction is thus interpreted as the exile of the divine into itself, whereas the breaking of the vessels is the exile of the divine out of itself. The creation of the world is a further step in this process of God being exiled outward. See Scholem, *On the Mystical Shape*, p. 84: "Precisely because God cannot reproduce Himself, His creation must be based upon that estrangement—one might indeed employ the Hegelian term *Entfremdung*—in which evil is embodied within Creation so that it may be itself."

189. See above n. 109, and Schmidt-Biggemann, *Geschichte der christlichen Kabbala*, 3:161–65.

190. Schelling, *Philosophy and Religion*, pp. 32–33; *Philosophie und Religion*, pp. 44–45. Distaso, *Paradox of Existence*, p. 145, summarizes Schelling's perspective lucidly: "Nature and spirit are opposed in their mutual belonging. Nature is characterized by the same inner relation that we find in reason: 'the eternal unity of infinite and finite'. This relation, which is analogous to the paradoxical unconditional-conditional relation . . . is visible only through finiteness and form: finite and infinite, within the Weltseele, are bound by a necessary relation: the true infinite element within infinity itself. Infinity is infinite only as the absolute negation of nothingness or as its own absolute self-affirmation. The true infinite element—from the point of view of reality—is this *absolute bond* . . . between finite and infinite (infinity and finiteness)" (emphasis in original). It seems to me perfectly reasonable to say of the kabbalistic *Ein Sof* that the absolute self-affirmation of its infinity consists of the absolute negation of its nothingness.

191. The most obvious example is the Ḥabad-Lubavitch dynasty. For a comparison of Schelling and Ḥabad thought on this topic, see Wolfson, "Achronic Time," pp. 57–73.

192. On the leap as an ascent from place to place linked to the *qedushah*, see, for example, Viṭal, *Sha'ar ha-Kawwanot*, 39b; Viṭal, *Sha'ar ha-Gilgulim*, p. 135; Viṭal, *Peri Eṣ Ḥayyim*, p. 259.

193. Compare the commentary of Rashi to Exodus 12:11, "The sacrifice is called *pesaḥ* on account of the leap and the skipping [*ha-dillug we-ha-pesiḥah*], for the holy One, blessed be he, skipped over the homes of the Israelites from amongst the homes of the Egyptians, and would jump from Egyptian to Egyptian and the Israelite in the middle was rescued."

194. Baruch of Kosov, *Yesod ha-Emunah*, p. 359. See my comments about the Spinozistic idea of the *causa sui* in ch. 3 n. 135.

195. For a more elaborate discussion, see Wolfson, "Achronic Time," pp. 46–56.

196. See Hellmers, "Reading in *Ereignis*."

197. Heidegger, *Question*, p. 44; *Technik*, pp. 42–43. With respect to the conceptual effacing of the distinction between cause and effect, there is a curious affinity that links Heidegger, the kabbalah, and quantum physics. See the passage cited in ch. 2 n. 170.

198. Poppers, *Mesillot Ḥokhmah*, 3a.

199. Frey, *Interruptions*, p. 25.

200. Badiou, *Being and Event*, p. 15 (emphasis in original).

201. Ibid., p. 355.

202. Ibid., p. 410.

203. Ibid., p. 16.

204. Ibid., pp. 56, 59, 81, 265.

205. Ibid., p. 356.

206. Ibid., p. 126. The description of the univocity of *Ein Sof* vis-à-vis the multiplicity that is both contained therein and emanates therefrom may also be compared profitably to the mathematical argument in Peirce, "Logic of Continuity," pp. 185–86, that every whole number can be considered a multitude that is capable of being completely counted, but the aggregate of all whole numbers cannot be completely counted because such a completion "would suppose that the *last* whole number was included, whereas there is no last whole number. But though the aggregate of all whole numbers cannot be completely counted, that does not prevent our having a distinct idea of the multitude of all whole numbers. We have a conception of the entire collection of whole numbers. It is a *potential* collection indeterminate yet determinable. And we see that the entire collection of whole numbers is more multitudinous than any whole number. In like manner the potential aggregate of all the abnumeral multitudes is more multitudinous that any multitude. This potential aggregate cannot be a multitude of distinct individuals any more than the aggregate of all the whole numbers can be completely counted. But it is a distinct general conception for all that,—a conception of a potentiality" (emphasis in original). The plural singularity that is constitutive of the singular plurality of infinity is precisely the potentiality of the abnumeral multitudes that are concomitantly indeterminate and determinable.

207. Frey, *Interruptions*, p. 26.

208. Ibid., p. 27: "Wholeness is the order in which everything has its place and in which nothing is missing or excessive. Inside the order of the finite whole everything is a part, which means that everything is recognizable in its relationship to the

whole and is therefore read as a metonymy for the whole."

209. For a comprehensive analysis of these principles, see Finkelstein, *Sifra on Leviticus*, 1:120–91. For a critical edition of the text, see Finkelstein, *Sifra on Leviticus*, 2:3–11.

210. Finkelstein, *Sifra on Leviticus*, 2:5–6; Babylonian Talmud, Pesaḥim 6b. See also Palestinian Talmud, Shevu'ot 3:5.

211. David ben Abraham ha-Lavan, *Masoret ha-Berit*, p. 31. The first part of this passage is based on the translation by Matt, "*Ayin*," p. 138 (see ch. 3 n. 134).

212. Ibn Gabbai, *Avodat ha-Qodesh*, 4:33, p. 592. Ibn Gabbai was likely influenced by the text of Azriel of Gerona, *Be'ur Eser Sefirot*, p. 85. Following a conventional Neoplatonic perspective, Azriel states that the one is the foundation of the many, and everything that comes to be in the latter derives from the former. Hence, "the first is the potency of all of them, and the potency of all of them is naught but the primary potency, even though the first is the potency of all of them, for there is nothing in the particular but what is in the general [*she-ein ba-peraṭ ella mah she-ba-kelal*]." Compare Viṭal, *Eṣ Ḥayyim*, 30:6, 30b: "The general and the particular are entirely equal" (*ha-kelal we-ha-peraṭ shawin legamrei*). The specific context that yielded the affirmation of this principle is Viṭal's observation that the five configurations of *Ze'eir Anpin* are comprised within one another to the point that they constitute one configuration. On this principle, see Ḥayyim de la Rosa, *Torat Ḥakham*, 47a, 153a, 153b; Yosef Ḥayyim of Baghdad, *Da'at u-Tevunah*, 52d; and more recently, Arenfeld, *Ma'amar ha-Kelal we-ha-Peraṭ*, pp. 46–47.

213. For a reversal of the gender valence, see *Ma'arekhet ha-Elohut*, ch. 10, p. 219: the *Shekhinah* is referred to as the attribute of the All (*middat ha-kol*), for "she is comprised of everything [*kelulah min ha-kol*] and she is the principle of everything [*kelal ha-kol*], for there is nothing in the particular but what is in the general and nothing in the general but what is in the particular [*ki ein ba-peraṭ ella mah she-ba-kelal we-ein ba-kelal ella mah she-ba-peraṭ*]."

214. Wolfson, *Alef*, p. 74, and references cited on p. 217n118.

215. Viṭal, *Eṣ Ḥayyim*, 1:1, 11a.

216. Compare the interpretation of Viṭal in Arenfeld, *Yira'ukha im Shamesh*, pp. 755–56.

217. See ch. 4 n. 220.

218. Horowitz, *Sefer ha-Berit*, pt. 2, ch. 5, p. 400.

219. Eliashiv, *Leshem Shevo we-Aḥlamah: Haqdamot u-She'arim*, p. 88.

220. Finkelstein, *Sifra on Leviticus*, 2:3. The principle appears in numerous talmudic contexts. For instance, see Babylonian Talmud, Eruvin 27b; Sukkah 50b; Qiddushin 21b; Baba Qama 54a.

221. Frey, *Interruptions*, p. 30.

222. Ibid., p. 31.

223. For an extensive analysis of the mystical practices established by this kabbalist, see Giller, *Shalom Shar'abi*. See also Garb, *Yearnings of the Soul*, pp. 43–46; Meir, *Kabbalistic Circles*, pp. 24–31, 140–59.

224. Sharabi, *Reḥovot ha-Nahar*, 5a. On the history of the use of the term *elohut gamur* in Lurianic and Sabbatian material, see Elqayam, "Mystery of Faith," pp. 149–58.

225. Scholem, *Major Trends*, p. 209.

226. Scholem, *Kabbalah*, p. 131.

227. Sharabi, *Reḥovot ha-Nahar*, 7a.

228. The expression is used with respect to Viṭal's exposition of the female and male waters in *Eṣ Ḥayyim*, 39:1, 65a, by Solomon ha-Kohen, *She'at Raṣon*, 73d: "All these are the words of our master, may his memory be for a blessing; he spoke in generalities but the truth is more with the specificities [*dibber bi-khelalut aval ha-emet hu yoter peraṭut*]." See also the discussion of Sharabi's view on the death of the Edomite kings and the breaking of the vessels in Eliashiv, *Leshem Shevo we-Aḥlamah: Sefer ha-De'ah*, pt. 1, pp. 54–55. In spite of his interest in and diligent study of Sharabi, attested both in his intermittent citation of Sharabi's treatises and in the fact that he wrote marginal glosses on some of them, Eliashiv famously emphasized that there were multiple ways to interpret the Lurianic teaching and hence one should not restrict oneself to the system developed by Sharabi. See Giller, "Between Poland and Jerusalem," p. 239; Giller, *Shalom Shar'abi*, pp. 12–13. On the complex relationship between Eliashiv and Sharabi, see Meir, "Wrestling with the Esoteric," pp. 602–4; Meir, *Kabbalistic Circles*, pp. 65–66.

229. Eliashiv, *Leshem Shevo we-Aḥlamah: Haqdamot u-She'arim*, p. 19. The comment is made specifically with reference to the internal and external aspects of the five gradations of soul, but it can be extended to any subject matter.

230. Badiou, *Being and Event*, p. 282.

231. My thinking here is in accord with Badiou, ibid., p. 32.

232. Ibid., p. 66.

233. Ibid., pp. 67–69 (emphasis in original).

234. Ibid., p. 356.

235. Ibid., p. 15.

236. See ch. 2 n. 182. I express my gratitude for an exchange I had with Kenneth Reinhard on Badiou

and Heidegger. Although my interlocutor did not ultimately agree with my contention, his response helped me sharpen the presentation of my position.

237. Badiou, *Being and Event*, p. 435.

238. O'Leary, "Theological Resonances," pp. 217–36, 243–54.

239. Badiou, *Being and Event*, p. 76. See, however, Hallward, *Badiou*, p. 355n68, who notes the difference between the effort to deconstruct the ontic privileging of the One in Badiou and Heidegger.

240. Zarader, *Heidegger et les paroles*, p. 141.

241. Badiou, *Manifesto for Philosophy*, p. 103.

242. See reference at ch. 4 n. 317.

243. Heidegger, *Contributions*, §115, p. 179 (emphasis in original); *Beiträge*, p. 227.

244. Heidegger, *Contributions*, §116, p. 179; *Beiträge*, pp. 227–28. The expression *Gedanken-gang* is used by Heidegger in his explanation of the official title of the *Beiträge* that is appended to the beginning of the work. See *Contributions*, p. 5; *Beiträge*, p. 3.

245. Heidegger, *Contributions*, §116, p. 180; *Beiträge*, p. 228.

246. Heidegger, *Being and Time*, §65, p. 302; *Sein und Zeit*, pp. 328–29.

247. Heidegger, *Contributions*, §267, p. 370 (emphasis in original); *Beiträge*, p. 470.

248. Heidegger, "Zum Einblick," p. 2, cited in Maly, *Heidegger's Possibility*, p. 26.

249. Heidegger, *Contributions*, §116, p. 180; *Beiträge*, p. 228.

250. Heidegger, *Off the Beaten Track*, p. 49; *Holzwege*, p. 65.

251. Heidegger, *Contributions*, §127, pp. 192–93; *Beiträge*, p. 244.

252. Kovacs, " Leap," p. 40.

253. Heidegger, *Contributions*, §28, p. 52; *Beiträge*, p. 65.

254. Heidegger, *Schelling's Treatise*, p. 3; *Schelling: Vom Wesen*, p. 5.

255. Heidegger, *Contributions*, §28, p. 52, §39, p. 65; *Beiträge*, pp. 65, 81–82.

256. Heidegger, *Introduction to Metaphysics*, p. 41 (emphasis in original); *Einführung in die Metaphysik*, p. 42. On the paradox of the repetition of the origin in Heidegger, see Marrati, *Genesis and Trace*, pp. 109–13. On the "politics of repetition" in Heidegger, see de Beistegui, *Thinking with Heidegger*, pp. 49–60. See also Schrag, "Heidegger on Repetition." On repetition and the experience of poetic language, see Allen, *Ellipsis*, pp. 25–57. For a different approach to poetic creativity, which emphasizes the antithesis between originality and repetition, see Bloom, *Ruin the Sacred Truths*, p. 12.

257. Heidegger, *Off the Beaten Track*, p. 48; *Holzwege*, p. 64.

258. Heidegger, *Contributions*, §29, p. 53; *Beiträge*, p. 66.

259. Heidegger, *Contributions*, §117, p. 180; *Beiträge*, pp. 228–29.

260. Heidegger, *Contributions*, §117, p. 181; *Beiträge*, p. 230.

261. Heidegger, *Off the Beaten Track*, p. 48; *Holzwege*, p. 64.

262. Heidegger, *Off the Beaten Track*, p. 48; *Holzwege*, p. 64.

263. See the passage of Rosenzweig cited in ch. 1 n. 97.

264. Cited in Coyne, *Heidegger's Confessions*, p. 157.

265. Heidegger, "Messkirch's Seventh Centennial," pp. 42–43; Heidegger, *Reden und Andere Zeugnisse*, p. 575.

266. Heidegger, *Off the Beaten Track*, p. 49; *Holzwege*, pp. 65–66.

267. Heidegger, *Identity and Difference*, p. 53; German text, p. 120.

268. Badiou, *Theory of the Subject*, p. 19 (emphasis in original).

269. See above, n. 217.

270. Scholem, *Kabbalah in Provence*, Appendix, p. 6. For a different English rendering, see Sendor, "Emergence of Provençal Kabbalah," 2:69–70.

271. Wolin, ed., *Heidegger Controversy*, p. 32 (emphasis in original); Heidegger, *Selbstbehauptung*, pp. 12–13.

272. Heidegger, *Logic as the Question*, pp. 97–98 (emphasis in original); *Logik als die Frage*, pp. 117–18.

273. Heidegger, *Contributions*, §39, p. 66 (emphasis in original); *Beiträge*, p. 82.

274. Heidegger, *Contributions*, §242, pp. 299–306; *Beiträge*, pp. 379–88.

275. Heidegger, *Contributions*, §129, pp. 193–94; *Beiträge*, p. 246.

276. Heidegger, *History of Beyng*, p. 144; *Geschichte des Seyns*, p. 168. For a different translation and analysis of this passage, see Polt, "Question of Nothing," p. 73.

277. Heidegger, *Contributions*, §126, p. 192; *Beiträge*, p. 244.

278. Jabès, *Book of Questions*, p. 230.

6

Temporalizing and Granting Time-Space

Yet even this that is left behind is no mere "*negativum*"; rather, in ending, it makes appear for the first time the abandonment by being, assuming that the question of the truth of beyng is posed out of the other beginning and thus initiates the encounter with the first beginning.

Heidegger, *Contributions to Philosophy (Of the Event)*

I begin this chapter with a comment of Gustav Landauer from the essay "Durch Absonderung zur Gemeinschaft," published in 1901:

> We are instants of the eternal community of ancestors. It can only help to point out that eternity too follows the rules of time. . . . I am afraid that if we attempt to create timelessness, i.e., stop the process of time and try to see past, present, and future as a kind of "dead simultaneousness" . . . we simply end up with an image of infinite space. Sure, time can be expressed in terms of space, and space in terms of time; time can be swallowed by space and space by time; but to go beyond both notions seems near impossible. To express space through time is maybe one of the most important challenges for the coming generations. All our language is quantitatively spatial and qualitatively facial: the tree, human beings, the mammal—all these categories and many others are built on facial perceptions. It would be good to perceive the world in terms of time instead. Best with the help of hearing. Music can maybe be the simple beginning to this new language.[1]

At the dawn of the twentieth century, Landauer intuited that the great challenge for the coming generations would be to express space through time, to perceive the material world primarily through the temporal prism, to develop a new language based on this change of perception, a language that would be akin to music, an idea that we have encountered in the discussion in chapter 2 of Heidegger's attempt to characterize the structure of inceptual thinking utilizing the image of the fugue. Presumably, following this path would help one avoid expressing time spatially even though it would still fall short of venturing beyond both categories of understanding by which we process the sensory data of our experience of the world mediated through the transcendental-synthetic power of imagination, as Kant forcefully argued. Landauer's words proved to be prescient, as many philosophers and critical theorists in the twentieth century reflected on the crisis of historicity and viewed postmodernism in particular as a way of redressing the predominance of a spatial logic by emphasizing the temporal organization of the pretensions and retentions we fashion into an allegedly coherent narrative about the past and the future determined by and determinative of the present.[2]

What escaped the attention of Landauer—not to mention the barrage of thinkers who have speculated on the priority of time over space—is that an older source for what he projects as the future task of adopting a tempocentric perspective can be found already in the medieval kabbalistic tradition. Here it is apposite to recall that Scholem famously described kabbalah as a "time-bound thought."[3] In support of his contention, he referred to a passage in the treatise *Rav Pe'alim*, composed in the thirteenth century by Isaac Ibn Laṭif (1210–80), "Whatever is found in the heart of the sage without duration and without time is called wisdom, and every image of a true matter that does not exist in itself without time is not wisdom at all. The one who relies upon it is not a sage but a kabbalist."[4] The text of Ibn Laṭif can be utilized as a springboard to reflect on the larger philosophical issue concerning the relationship of time and image.[5] This is not to say that I think this kabbalist, or any other for that matter, presents the reader with a coherent epistemology or a systematic ontology. On the contrary, as I argued in the previous chapter, if we are to impute the notion of system to the kabbalah, it is a system that is nonsystematic; that is, a system that collapses under the weight of the overwhelming specification of details that develop in the attempt to map the fragmented univocity of the infinite. I am nevertheless committed to the supposition that one may engage these sources philosophically and thereby elicit from them insights that will contribute to the ongoing interrogation of speculative questions that have perplexed thinkers through the centuries.

Time-Space, Imagination, and the Fourth Dimension

With this agenda in mind, I will extract from kabbalistic sources a conception of time that involves the expansion of duration into place, a temporal extension that is not constituted either by simultaneity or succession, as Husserl argued,[6] but rather an extension with greater affinity to the monad described by Iamblichus in the *Theologumena arithmeticae*;[7] that is, the nonpositional, zero-dimensional mathematical point that exists prior to the point demarcated by the spatial coordinates of length, width, and breadth or the temporal coordinates of past, present, and future. Time and space are not to be cognized primarily as material substances nor are they conceived respectively as the measure of bodies in motion or as the three-dimensional container in which all bodies are positioned. These commonplace philosophical understandings were undoubtedly known to kabbalists, and even occasionally affirmed by some explicitly,[8] but on the whole they proffered a different conception related to the incarnational investiture of the light of *Ein Sof*, which corresponds to Heidegger's contention that space and time are "the opening [*Ausbruch*] and upsurge [*Anbruch*] of being."[9] Or, as he put in the *Beiträge*, commenting on the relation of time-space and the facticity of Dasein: "Time-space [*Zeit-Raum*] as arising out of, and belonging to, the essence of truth and as the thereby grounded structure (joining) of the 'there,' a structure of transport-captivation [*Entrückungs-Berückungsgefüge*]. (Not yet a 'schema' for the representation of things, not yet mere flowing-by in the order of succession)."[10]

The enumerative representations of space and time materialize out of the more originary time-space that belongs to the truth of the originating essential occurrence of beyng as the event shaped by the more primal qualities of transport (*Entrückung*) and captivation (*Berückung*), correlated respectively with temporalization (*Zeitigung*) and spatialization (*Räumung*): "Time-space is the appropriated sundering [*Erklüftung*] of the turning paths of the event, the sundering of the turning between belonging and call [*Zugehörigkeit und Zuruf*], between abandonment by being and beckoning intimation [*Seinsverlassenheit und Erwinkung*] (the trembling in the oscillation of beyng itself!). Nearness and remoteness [*Nähe und Ferne*], emptiness and bestowal [*Leere und Schenkung*], verve and hesitation [*Schwung und Zögerung*]—in these the hidden essence of time-space resides, and so they cannot be grasped temporally and spatially on the basis of the usual representations of time and space."[11] Brushing against the grain of centuries of philosophical speculation, Heidegger argues that time is not predominantly subjective any more than space is predominantly objective; the essence of time and space must be gleaned from their original unity in time-space, which is the abyssal ground of the "there," that is, the opening/lighting, the clearing ground, the self-opening center that is the between of Dasein,[12] wherein the truth of beyng is revealed in the concealment of its concealment.[13] The abyssal ground—the first occurrence of the grounding of the nonground—is to be grounded in the mode of temporalization and spatialization; these cannot be grasped, however, on the basis of "the usual representations of time and space [*der geläufigen Raum- und Zeit-Vorstellung*]," but "must be determined according to their provenance out of the primessential temporalizing and spatializing [*erstwesentlichen Zeitigen und Räumen*]."[14] The "*originary unity* [ursprüngliche Einheit] of space and time" is thus the "unifying unity [*einigende Einheit*]" of the abyss that allows the spatial and the temporal "to diverge into their separateness [*in ihre Geschiednis auseinandergehen*]."[15] Consistently with his understanding of the idea of juxtaposition, Heidegger emphasizes that the irreducibility of time and space is not compromised by their unity or interpenetration; they are "radically different . . . in their most proper essence, and only in virtue of this extreme difference do they point back to their origin, time-space."[16]

In a tone amazingly evocative of the kabbalistic *ṣimṣum*, Heidegger remarks that the refusal applicable to that time-space is "not nothing," but a "leaving empty" that is "a preeminent kind of opening up. . . . The *lack* of the ground is the lack of the *ground* [*Der* Ab-*grund ist Ab*-grund]. In withholding itself, the ground preeminently brings into the open, namely into the first opening of *that* emptiness which is thereby a determinate one. Inasmuch as the ground, even and precisely as abyss, still grounds and yet does not properly ground [*noch gründet und doch nicht eigentlich gründet*], it abides in hesitancy."[17] The withdrawing-protruding, which kabbalists ascribe to *Ein Sof*, is well captured in Heidegger's claim that the "primordial ground" (*Ur-grund*) opens itself as the self-concealing in the "abyssal ground" (*Ab-grund*), which is then disguised in the "distorted ground" or literally the nonground (*Un-ground*),[18] the ground that simultaneously grounds and does not ground insofar as it is the ground that is the lack of ground. Just as kabbalists portrayed the vacuum, which emerges in the aftermath of the retraction of the light, as an empty fullness, an emptiness whose fullness consists of being empty of its emptiness, so Heidegger writes that the clearing of the concealment is "not the mere emptiness of vacancy [*Unbesetztseins*]; instead, it is the disposed and disposing emptiness of the abyssal ground [*die gestimmt stimmende Leere des Ab-grundes*] which, according to the attuning intimation of the event, is a disposed abyssal ground."[19] Like the kabbalistic infinity, wherein absolute necessity is purely contingent and pure contingency is absolutely necessary, the emptiness of the event of beyng "is actually the fullness of what is still undecided and is to be decided, the abyssal ground that points to the ground, i.e., to the truth of being."[20]

Moreover, Heidegger's identification of time-space as the horizon of being,[21] which is the abyssal ground, translates kabbalistically into the identification of time and space as the elliptical axes of the imaginally configured body of the divine persona. According to this template, the two modalities are conceptually inextricable, linked together in entangled folds of syncopation. Priority, however, is still ascribed to time inasmuch as in its most rudimentary sense—designated by the rabbinic phrase *seder zemannim*[22]—temporality consists of the achronal order that precedes the measurable chronological durée of time, *shi'ur meshekh ha-zeman*,[23] a time before the time in which, according to an aggadic tradition, things were either created or arose in the divine thought prior to the creation,[24] or in the language of another rabbinic legend, the Torah preceded the world by two thousand years,[25] an idea that makes sense only if we presume the ones responsible for propagating it assumed there is a notion of time that does not depend on the physical universe. Extrapolating from these emergent conceptions of a foretime, the kabbalists developed their belief in an originary time that is the measure of the immeasurable ebb and flow of infinity that generates the polarities of light and dark, which translate into the sentient experience of the temporal forged by the bicameral rhythm of day and night, engendered respectively as feminine judgment and masculine mercy.[26]

The idea that I elicit from the kabbalists does not presume, as does Plato's mimetic depiction of time as the moving image of eternity, a gap separating the temporal and the eternal.[27] The conception of the time before time, which informed the kabbalistic thinking, is to be contrasted as well with the notion of timeless eternity, traceable to Parmenides and reinforced in Neoplatonic sources; that is, the delineation of the eternal as that which extends without beginning or end and is therefore devoid of temporal malleability.[28] The kabbalistic understanding, by contrast, rests on the more paradoxical assumption that eternity is archetypically timelike in its capacity for unremitting metamorphosis and that time, inversely, is paradigmatically eternal in its aptitude for irresolute stability.[29] From the standpoint of infinity, the temporality that applies to the *sefirot* is centered in the moment that retrieves the past as that which is perpetually determined to come to be as the indeterminate future. One of the clearest philosophical articulations of the point is found in the following passage from Azriel of Gerona's *Sha'ar ha-Sho'el,* a catechistic commentary on the *sefirot*. After it is established that corporeality (*gashmut*) can be ascribed to the sefirotic gradations vis-à-vis the infinite, insofar as they exhibit the characteristics of boundary (*gevul*), dimension (*shi'ur*), and measure (*middah*), the hypothetical question is posed that tackles one of the thorniest theoretical problems in kabbalistic theosophy: how can we assign a temporal beginning to the emanations if the latter are comprised in the eternality and primordiality of the *Ein Sof*? Alluding to this quandary, the interlocutor in Azriel's dialogue inquires "when were these *sefirot*?" In this seemingly simplistic formulation, the questioner seeks to know how we can demarcate the inception of the emanation of the *sefirot,* the transition from the time of eternity to the eternity of time.[30] If the rejoinder is that the sefirotic potencies came to be in the moment marked as the "now in proximity to the creation of the world" (*attah mi-qarov li-veri'at ha-olam*), then one could probe further: why did the *Ein Sof* intend their emanation in that "now and not from of old" (*attah we-lo me-az*), that is, from eternity? To postulate a beginning in the "now" that is not "of old" would imply a change of mind (*ḥiddush ha-da'at*)[31] on the part of the one that is perfect (*ha-shalem*). In his response, Azriel argues—utilizing language that brings to mind the Neoplatonic quaternity of the One, Intellect, Soul, and Nature—that the first of the *sefirot, Keter,* which is "equal to all of them" (*shaweh le-khullam*), was in the realm of concealment (*ne'lam*), that is, in the potency of the *Ein Sof,* prior to being actualized; the second emanation, *Ḥokhmah,* was in the realm of the intelligible (*muskal*) whence emanated the Torah that preceded the creation of the world; of the remaining *sefirot,* they were either in the realm of the sensible (*murgash*), which corresponds to the third emanation, *Binah,* or in the realm of the natural (*muṭba*), which corresponds to the tenth emanation, *Malkhut*. These *sefirot* were necessary for this world and thus about them we can most suitably say that they emanated in the time of the now that is in proximity to the creation of the world.[32]

The description of the *now that is in proximity to the creation of the world* relates to the instant that signals the time that is not yet time, albeit not timeless, the time before there is time, the midpoint between the nothingness of the eternal origin of time and the somethingness of the temporal beginning of eternity. To the extent that the emanations are contained in the infinite, they should be considered primordial, but this primordiality is to be distinguished from the primordiality of their source in the same manner that the light of a primary candle is to be differentiated from the light of all the ancillary candles that are illumined subsequently from it. We may infer, therefore, that the manifestation of the sefirotic emanations as discrete entities—literally, in the "division of their being" (*be-ḥilluq hawayyatam*)—does not imply that there is any innovation (*ḥiddush*) on the part of the infinite.[33] Even so, we can elicit from Azriel the view, shared by other kabbalists, that the sefirotic gradations are not brought into being in time but are themselves the endurance that determines the contours of the evanescence of temporality. Ultimately, there is no answer to why the emanation occurred now and not before, since the *now,* when properly considered, is itself constituted by the delineation *from before*; that is, the moment is commemorated by an already that has never been, the retroactive not yet, the recurrence of the wholly dissimilar in which there is no time intervening between the first and the last.

To my mind, the kabbalistic orientation is reminiscent of the position elaborated by the Andalusian mystic and poet, Muḥyīddīn Ibn al-ʿArabī (1165–1240): God is the everlasting time (*dahr*), the eternity that is beginningless (*azal*) and endless (*abad*). The enlightened one, who is the "son of the moment" (*ibn waqtihī*), has the capacity to implement this state of temporal eternity, which is a reflection (*maẓhar*) of God's eternal temporality. The temporal (*zamān*), consequently, is most fully realized in the moment (*waqt*) that is the instantiation of divine everlastingness.[34] In contrast with the widespread portrayal of the moment as the *nunc stans*, the steadfast now of the eternal reality wherein the distinction between the three temporal tenses falls away,[35] the Ṣūfi idea promulgated by Ibn al-ʿArabī, which has a strong resemblance to what is expressed by kabbalists, is that the only time that is real is the infinite temporal interval that abides in its nonabiding and flows in the permanence of its impermanence. Rather than viewing the now as the stationary present that has no past or future, the Ṣūfi and kabbalistic conceptions posit an interim of time in which there is a compresence of past, present, and future—what was, what is, and what will be are all occurring at once without the sequentiality or extendedness that is associated with the linear model of time. The moment, therefore, does not entail the abolition of the three tenses but rather their aggregation. Furthermore, on account of this concurrence, which is ascribed by kabbalists, following a much older tradition, to the Tetragrammaton, the moment bears the phenomenological texture of a dream.[36] Prima facie, it might seem that the threefold unity of *YHWH* suggests that the divine being is not subject to the contingencies of time—an argument that is in fact attested in some sources[37]—but other kabbalists insist that the eternality implied by this concomitance signifies the full presence of time and not its absence, a presence that is present always in the excess of being present, ever changing in its changelessness, motionless in its constant motion.[38] Time is thus the disclosive space of the in-between, the metaxy wherein eternal being fluctuates temporally and temporal becoming persists eternally.[39]

The metaxial understanding of time is the notional underpinning of one of the boldest mythologoumena in the Lurianic kabbalah concerning the primordial forces of evil or the unbalanced judgment, the impure thoughts that needed to be purged from the economy of *Ein Sof* prior to the emanation; these forces are referred to in various ways, including, most prevalently, by the scriptural motif of the Edomite kings who reigned before the kings of Israel[40] and the rabbinic image of the worlds created and destroyed before the genesis of this world.[41] The common denominator of these traditions, and the point most relevant to this discussion, is that they presume a temporal element to explain the catharsis within the infinite, a process connected to the motif of the contraction and its repercussion in the breaking of the vessels.[42] Time, on this account, is not simply a property lacking intrinsicality; it is rather the vital energy of the nothingness that is the being that both infuses and retreats from all beings. Already in *Sein und Zeit*, Heidegger defined time as "the transcendental horizon of the question of being;"[43] that is, time is the preobjective and presubjective condition that determines the finitude of Dasein whence the concrete existence of beings can be ascertained.[44] Space, accordingly, is the exteriorization of the interiorization of the horizontal field of presence (*Präsenzfeld*), the domain of fore-giving, the giving before, that must appear in advance of the appearance of any given object, whether as the consequence of immediate presentation (*Gegenwärtigung*) or mediated representation (*Vergegenwärtigung*). In Kantian language, space and time are the "pure forms of intuitions," which are the "conditions for the finitude of intuition, and thereby they are the most acute indicators of the finitude of Dasein, precisely because they must be encountered in advance. Therefore for finite Dasein beings thus uncovered in space and time manifest themselves.... Space and time are *real* and *belong to the factual determination of the factuality of appearances* [*zur* Sachbestimmung der Sachlichkeit der Erscheinungen gehörig]."[45]

Heidegger elicited from Kant the view that the transcendental synthesis of the manifold, which constitutes the nature of apprehension, is structurally a "time-related power of the imagination" (*zeitbezogenen Einbildungskraft*).[46] All our intuitions and concepts, therefore, result from the "imaginative synthesis of the transcendental power of imagination," which "is in itself time-related." But going beyond Kant, Heidegger maintains that "the *power of imagination* is possible only as related to time; or put more clearly, this power *itself* is time understood as original time [*ursprünglichen Zeit*], which we call *temporality* [Zeitlichkeit]."[47] The Heideggerian notion of original time or temporality is sharply contrasted with Kant's understanding of time in the ordinary sense as "the pure succession of nows given in pure intuition: now, and now, and now—that is, a constant sequence of nows. . . . *Time as this pure flowing of a multiplicity of nows is the universal form of representing*, that is, time determines in advance all representing as a sequence of occurrences in the subject—now this representation, now that one, afterward that one, and then that one."[48]

In place of the atomistic depiction of time, Heidegger proffers a more unified conception, which is based on the relatedness of the three components of the Kantian synthesis to the three modes of time: "The synthesis of *apprehension* is related to the *present*, the synthesis of *reproduction* is related to the *past*, and the synthesis of *pre-cognition* is related to the *future. Insofar as all three modes of synthesis are related to time and insofar as these moments of time make up the unity of time itself, the three syntheses maintain their unified ground in the unity of time.*"[49] From his exegesis of Kant, Heidegger concludes that understanding is a "*time-related activity*" and not a "spontaneity independent of time."[50] The phenomenon of time is thus accorded a primary role in the deduction of the categories of transcendental apperception: "*But if the synthesis of understanding*, as synthesis of recognition in the concept, is *related to time and if categories emerge from just* this *synthesis as activity of understanding*, that is, if the three syntheses are interrelated on the basis of time, *then the origin of the categories is time itself*."[51] More important, Heidegger's assertion that the "unified ground"(*einheitlichen Grund*) of the three syntheses secures the transcendentally apperceptive "unity of time" (*Einheit der Zeit*) is the phenomenological basis for his identification of time in its more originary sense with the imagination. According to the Heideggerian interpretation of Kant, temporality, the basic constitution of the subject, is located in the power of imagination, the pure-time synthesis of the three syntheses of reproduction, apprehension, and precognition.[52]

In the later thought of Heidegger, we similarly detect, although from a different vantagepoint, the identification of temporality as the imagination, but understood more specifically as the *Lichtung*, the opening or clearing, wherein the there-being of beings is revealed and concealed by the being-there of Dasein. The idea of the between is also identified as the time-space, a turn of phrase that accentuates the inseparability of the spatial and the temporal combined with privileging the temporal over the spatial in lieu of conceiving time in images that are chiefly derived from the phenomenon of space.[53] In that respect, Heidegger's time-space serves a function analogous to the four-dimensional space-time conceived by physicists—specifically Einstein and Minkowski[54]—as the invariant interval that spawns the variant slices of time and space visually apprehended from different inertial frames of reference.[55] But here we must note an important shift in Heidegger's thinking. Early on, as is attested in the essay "Der Zeitbegriff in der Geschichtswissenschaft," which was based on the lecture "Das Problem der historischen Zeit," delivered before the Philosophy Faculty at the University of Freiburg on July 27, 1915,[56] Heidegger is unequivocally disparaging of natural science for presuming that time is a "simple linear series in which each point . . . is differentiated by its current position as measured from its initial position. Since any given point in time differs from the preceding one only by being the succeeding one, it is possible to measure time and therefore motion." As a consequence of this mathematical conception, the flow of time "freezes, becomes a segment, and only as a segment can it be measured. Time has become a homogeneous ordering of points, a scale, a parameter."[57] The same criticism is leveled against contemporary physics, and particularly the theory of relativity, which "is concerned with the problem of the *measurement* of time and not with time itself. The concept of time is untouched by the theory of relativity; in fact, relativity theory corroborates to the highest degree what we spelled out earlier about the character of the concept of time in natural science, namely, its homogeneous, quantitatively determinable character. Nothing could more clearly express the mathematical character of the concept of time within physics than the fact that time is posited as the fourth dimension alongside three-dimensional space and, together with it, is treated in a non-Euclidean geometry, one with more than three dimensions."[58]

In Heidegger's later thought, he took a more positive view on the identification of time as the fourth dimension. Nature is thus classified as "a four-dimensional spatio-temporal world, wherein time (*t*), added to the three spatial coordinates *x*, *y*, *z*, forms the fourth path along which the relational ordering of locations and sequences of movement can extend."[59] What Heidegger and contemporary physics—considerably amplified and complexified in quantum theory[60]—share is a sense that time is neither nominative nor predicative but adverbial. Time is not the measure of change or that which is measured by change but the interlude in which change happens in its twofold magnitude as measure and measured. To some extent, the seeds for Heidegger's more mature perspective were planted much earlier, as we see, for example, in the distinction he made in *Logik: Die Frage nach der Wahrheit*, the 1925–26 lectures on truth and time, and later expanded in *Sein und Zeit*,[61] between the word *zeitlich*, translated as "temporal," which denotes "that something runs its course, or happens, or takes place *in* time," and *temporal*, translated as "ur-temporal," which means "that something is 'essentially characterized by time.'" The philosophical examination that seeks to investigate the ur-temporality (*Temporalität*) of phenomena is designated a *phenomenological chronology*, but this is contrasted with the chronology assumed by the natural-scientific awareness, that is, the practice or theory of measuring time in history.[62] In contradistinction to the traditional concept of time, Heidegger proffers "that time is not merely and not primarily a schema for determining how changes get ordered. Rather, properly speaking, time is existence [*Dasein*] itself."[63]

Building on Kant's interpretation of time as the "pure pre-viewing of the sequence of nows,"[64] Heidegger asserts that "time itself—the antecedent, constant letting-something-encounter—is itself given, although unthematically. Because it is an unthematic relation to itself, time as the antecedent-constant letting-something-encounter-us lets the 'something' be encountered as the self-same at all times. Only when one holds fast to the genuine now-structure [*Jetztstruktur*] and observes that the primary taking-a-look [*Hinblicknehmen*] at time is unthematic, does one understand what it means to say: time is an original pure and general self-affection [*Selbstaffektion*]."[65] Although time, in its ephemerality, is continuously discontinuous, phenomenologically, we confront the thematically incomprehensible now-sequence (*Jetztfolge*) as the return of the moment that is always different because always the same and always the same because always different:

> Rather, the now-sequence affects in such a way that it lets something be seen—but unthematically, as if the now-sequence itself were constantly retreating and disappearing in its constant referring-to. This affecting is thus something like a constant putting-itself-aside and a liberating letting-something-be-seen.... In other words, this constant, prior letting-something-encounter, this unthematic highlighting of the now... is the pure act of rendering something present [*Gegenwärtigen*]. The now is a now-present [*Gegenwart*].... And the now is a now-present in such a way that it remains unthematic. Likewise, the pre-view of the now is unthematic.... The now is neither a fragment nor a chopped-up now-point that is "merely present" [*weder das Fragment eines beschnittenen und nur vorhandenen Jetztpunktes*], but rather a pointing-toward-something, a letting-something-be-seen [*sondern Weisung auf—als Sehenlassendes*].... By the word "now" I neither name nor speak of anything at all that is just-there [*ein Vorhandenes*]. Rather, with that "now" human existence [*Dasein*] expresses *itself*, not as something just-there but itself in its being unto the world [*Sein zur Welt*], i.e., in the basic form of this being unto the world: the act of making-present [*Gegenwärtigen*].... The present, which is a matter of letting-something-encounter-us,

is not itself present [*anwesend*], it is not something just-there. The present is only a making-present [*Gegenwart ist nur gegenwärtig*], making-present as a comportment.[66]

Notwithstanding Heidegger's criticism of Aristotle's mathematical understanding of time as the measure of bodies in motion, the paradox of the now as the locus of sameness and difference elicited from the Aristotelian analysis of time had a sustained influence on Heidegger's thinking about temporality in all periods of his life. Consider the characterization in *Die Grundprobleme der Phänomenologie* of the "double visage" (*eigentümliches Doppelgesicht*) of the now according to Aristotle:

Time is held together within itself by the now; time's specific continuity is rooted in the now. But conjointly, with respect to the now, time is divided, articulated into the no-longer-now, the earlier, and the not-yet-now, the later. It is only with respect to the now that we can conceive of the then and at-the-time, the later and the earlier. The now that we count in following a motion is *in each instance a different now.* To de nun dia to kineisthai to pheromenon aiei heteron, on account of the transition of the moving thing the now is always another, an advance from one place to the other. In each now the now is a different one, but still each different now is, as now, always now. The ever different nows are, *as different,* nevertheless always exactly *the same,* namely, now. Aristotle summarizes the peculiar nature of the now and thus of time—when he interprets time purely by way of the now . . . that is, in each now it is now; its *essentia,* its what, is always *the same* (tauto)—and nevertheless every now is, by its nature, different in each now . . . nowness, being-now [*Jetztsein*], is always *otherness, being-other* [Anderssein] . . . the now is in a certain way always the same and in a certain way never the same. The now articulates and bounds time with respect to its earlier and later. On the one hand it is indeed always the same, but then it is never the same. . . . This constitutes its always being-now, its otherhood [*Andersheit*]. But what it always already was as that which it is, namely, now—that is the same.[67]

The subversion of the mathematical understanding of a chronological series, and the implied interpretation of time as an objective being or an existing actuality, and the positing of an alternate chronology is elicited by Heidegger from Aristotle's own attentiveness to the quality of *Jetztsein,* the time of the now that personifies otherness in virtue of its being *in a certain way always the same and in a certain way never the same.* It is especially this paradox of the continuity of discontinuity that reverberates with the conception of temporality affirmed by kabbalists, as far back as the thirteenth century, which likewise was not beholden to the Aristotelian ideal of a unilateral evolution from past to future. Essential to the kabbalistic understanding of time is the belief that every now—the present that cannot be presentified noematically except as absence—is continually the same because persistently different and continually different because persistently the same. We can thus apply to the kabbalah Heidegger's commitment to a phenomenological chronology that seeks to ascertain the ur-temporal determinedness of phenomena—the presence-now of the truth of being occluded in its presencing, disappearing in its becoming apparent—without succumbing to the spatial schematization of the temporal.

Heidegger eventually abandoned the rhetoric of phenomenological chronology, but he continued to delve into the determination of being from the standpoint of time rather than the determination of time from the standpoint of being as the experienced objective world, that is, as the measurable and calculable ordering of nature. In his elucidation of Georg Trakl's poem "An einen Frühverstorbenen," Heidegger notes that the premature death of the child Elis—symbolic of the "stranger called to go under"[68]—reveals the wisdom about time fully expressed in the last line, "Golden eye of the beginning, dark patience of the end" (*Goldenes Auge des Anbeginns, dunkle Geduld des Endes*):

Here, the end is not the sequel and fading echo of the beginning. The end—being the end of the decaying kind—precedes the beginning of the unborn kind. But the beginning, the earlier earliness, has already overtaken the end. That earliness preserves the original nature—a nature so far still veiled [*verhüllte*]—of time. This nature will go on being impenetrable to the dominant mode of thinking as long as the

> Aristotelian concept of time, still standard everywhere, retains its currency. According to this concept, time—whether conceived mechanically or dynamically or in terms of atomic decay—is the dimension of the quantitative or qualitative calculation of duration as a sequential progression.[69]

Already in *Sein und Zeit*, as I noted in chapter 1, Heidegger contrasted the primordial temporality and the vulgar understanding of time.[70] The latter coheres with the Aristotelian perspective—the explanation of time that remains on the level of the accidental as opposed to what is fundamental[71]—insofar as time is viewed as the string of interchangeable now-points. As long as this perspective prevails, the true nature of time is veiled. The deeper phenomenology of time (*Temporalität*)—the hermeneutical condition of the possibility of the understanding of being as the ontological constitution of Dasein[72]—discards the serial approach and posits in its place a timeline that can be reversed on the basis of the presumption that the end is antecedent to the beginning that is consequent to the end.[73] The interruption of the sequential order is the import of Heidegger's tautological depiction of the temporalization of temporality (*Zeitigung der Zeitlichkeit*) in the unity of each temporal ecstasis: "Temporalizing does not mean a 'succession' [*'Nacheinander'*] of the ecstasies. The future is *not later* than the having-been, and the having-been is *not earlier* than the present. Temporality temporalizes itself as a future that makes present, in the process of having-been [*Zeitlichkeit zeitigt sich als gewesende-gegenwärtigende Zukunft*]."[74] Taking Nietzsche as the exemplar of the thinker who thinks "beings in their Being [*das Seiende in seinem Sein*]," Heidegger maintained that to think historically, as opposed to historiologically, that is, to think beings in the ecstatic unity of their temporal being, is to discern regarding what is in world history that "what, because it already is, is only coming" (*das, was, weil es schon ist, erst kommt*).[75]

From the kabbalists as well, we can elicit an incalculable calculus related to their experience of time as a linear circularity, a conception of the temporal that is neither a line nor a circle exclusively but rather both a line and a circle concomitantly. Time is construed geometrically as a spiral that returns always to a place it has never been. As I noted in the previous chapter, the principle enunciated in *Sefer Yeṣirah* that the end is fixed in the beginning and the beginning in the end does not mean that the end is simply a reprise of the beginning or that the beginning is merely the preview of the end. The timeswerve implied by this statement is open at both termini and hence the end cannot be ascertained deductively from the beginning nor the beginning from the end; the reversibility of the circular linearity implies not uroboric closure but an ever-changing fluctuation, an indeterminacy that destabilizes the prototype of a palindromic succession proceeding uniformly and bidirectionally from start to finish and from finish to start.

Ecstasies of Time, Equiprimordiality, and the Privileging of the Future

Consonant with Heidegger's analysis in *Sein und Zeit* and other works from that period, the ontological structure of Dasein is grounded in the temporality (*Zeitlichkeit*) that is constituted from the site of being-there in the moment (*Augenblick*), the event of the advent of the nonevent, we might say, the blink of the eye, which occurs beyond presence (*Anwesenheit*), the authentic time that is to be distinguished from the inauthentic time of presencing or making-present (*Gegenwartigkeit*), the calendrical reckoning of the mundane experience. Significantly, Heidegger concludes his magnum opus with the provocative question that sheds much light on the path he eventually traversed, "Does *time* itself reveal itself as the horizon of *being*?"[76] Commenting on this passage, Joan Stambaugh perceptively noted, "To state that temporality is the horizon of Being is not the same as to state that Being is the cause or ground of time. Horizon has to do with directionality and openness, not with causality."[77] Phenomenologically, the horizon is discernible in the momentary present that opens both to the past and to the future, but not simply as the presently occurring now that is a causal bridge wedged between the now that is no longer and the now that is not yet. The moment as the locus of temporalization is characterized rather by the synchronicity of the three modalities of time: "Thus we call the phenomena of future

[*Zukunft*], having-been [*Gewesenheit*], and present [*Gegenwart*] the *ecstasies* of temporality [*die* Ekstasen *der Zeitlichkeit*]. Temporality is not, prior to this, a being that first emerges from *itself*; rather, its essence is temporalizing in the unity of the *ecstasies* [*Zeitigung in der Einheit der* Ekstasen]."[78]

Given the delimitation of Dasein's demeanor as the being that is always "beyond itself" (*über sich hinaus*) or as the being that is "ahead of itself" (*Sich-vorweg*) as its "ownmost potentiality-for-being" (*eigensten Seinkönnen*),[79] priority is allocated to the future. As Heidegger put it in the 1924 lecture "Der Begriff der Zeit":

> In running ahead Dasein *is* its future, in such a way that in this being futural [*Zukünftigsein*] it comes back to its past and present. Dasein, conceived in its most extreme possibility of Being, is *time itself*, not *in* time. . . . Being futural gives time, cultivates the present and allows the past to be repeated in how it is lived. With regard to time, this means that *the fundamental phenomenon of time is the future* (das Grundphänomen der Zeit ist die Zukunft).[80]

The running ahead (*Vorlaufen*) is epitomized in what Heidegger identified as the distinctive property of human existence, the anticipatory resoluteness of being-toward-death (*Sein zum Tode*).[81] The resoluteness consists of Dasein's being authentically futural by claiming its authentically having-been; indeed, insofar as anticipation of the future is a retrieval of the past, the temporal sequence is inverted and the having-been arises from the future (*Die Gewesenheit entspringt in gewisser Weise der Zukunft*).[82]

One would be hard pressed to deny the primacy conferred upon the future in Heidegger's thought. As I noted in chapter 1, however, the notion of equiprimordiality (*Gleichursprünglichkeit*) affirmed by Heidegger presumes the inseparability of the three temporal ecstasies. This is evident in the aforecited passage from "Der Begriff der Zeit": in being futural Dasein comes back to its past and present. In *Sein und Zeit*, Heidegger described the equiprimordiality in the structure of care along similar lines:

> The wholeness of the being [*Seinsganzheit*] of Dasein as care means: ahead-of-itself-already-being-in [*Sich-vorweg-schon-sein-in*] (a world) as being-together-with [*Sein-bei*] (beings encountered within the world). . . . Being-ahead-of-oneself [*Sich-vorweg*] is grounded in the future. Already-being-in . . . makes known having-been. Being-together-with . . . is made possible in making present. . . . The "ahead" does not mean the "before" in the sense of a "not-yet-now, but later." Nor does the "already" mean a "no-longer-now, but earlier." . . . The "before" and the "ahead of" indicate the future that first makes possible in general the fact that Dasein can be in such a way that it is concerned *about* its potentiality-of-being [*Seinkönnen*]. The self-project [*Sichentwerfen*] grounded in the "for the sake of itself" in the future is an essential quality of *existentiality* [Existenzialität]. *Its primary meaning is the future.*[83]

The primordial temporality (*ursprünglichen Zeitlichkeit*) is thus experienced in the ecstatic compresence of past, present, and future, as opposed to the vulgar understanding (*vulgären Verständnis*) of time as the ceaseless succession of nows (*Jetzt-folge*).[84] As Heidegger put it in *Die Grundbegriffe der Metaphysik*, the simultaneity of the present, having-been, and future does not imply that the three perspectives are lined up successively "alongside one another," but rather that they are "originarily simply united in the horizon of time as such. Originarily, there is the *single* and *unitary universal horizon of time*."[85]

Despite the many changes in Heidegger's thinking, there is continuity with regard to the predominance accorded the future as the temporal modality in which all three tenses converge.[86] To demonstrate the point, I will briefly mention the analysis in "Zeit und Sein," a lecture that may be considered both as the completion of the third and unwritten part of *Sein und Zeit*, originally given this title, and as a reversal of the path undertaken in that work, since instead of thinking being within the horizon of time, Heidegger sets out to think being and time together as *Ereignis*, the event of appropriation or enowning, also referred to as the allowing-to-presence (*Anwesenlassen*) of what is "concealed in unconcealment" (*im Entbergen verborgen*), the gift of the unconcealing of being retained in the refusal of the giving—the "there is" (*es gibt*)—of beings.[87] In *Sein und Zeit*, the temporal event is thought from the vantagepoint of the future, whereas in "Zeit und Sein," the event concerns the temporal character of being, or in the more precise and confounding terminology adopted by Heidegger, time is the way that the appropriation appropriates as the presencing of presence without something actually being present, the authentically novel moment that is an event of presence that presences in the twofold absence of the no longer present and the not yet present, the past that comes forward in receding and the future that recedes in coming forward. Thus, we must distinguish the real time of the present as presence (*Anwesenheit*) and the calculable time of the present as the now (*Jetzt*).[88]

We see, once more, that Heidegger privileges the future by noting that the giving of presencing in all three temporal modes is the "constant abiding" (*gereichte Verweilen*) or the reaching (*erreichen*) to and fro that is extended to an individual in time.[89] "Approaching, being not yet present, at the same time gives and brings about what is no longer present, the past, and conversely what has been offers future to itself. The reciprocal relation of both at the same time gives and brings about the present."[90] The expression "at the same time" (*Zugleich*) conveys a sense of "mutual giving" (*Sich-einander-Reichen*) that signals the "unifying unity" (*einigende Einheit*) of the three temporalities. This unity does not imply, however, that they merge into one self-same identity, but rather that they "belong together in the way they offer themselves to one another."[91] The belonging-togetherness (*Zusammengehörigkeit*) preserves difference in the sameness as opposed to identity (*Identität*) or identicalness (*Gleichheit*), wherein all difference disappears,[92] a crucial Heideggerian theme we encountered in the introduction and at several other junctures in this book. The copresencing of past and future in the present is closely aligned with the delineation of time-space as the "openness which opens up in the mutual self-extending [*Einander-sich-reichen*] of futural approach, past and present. This openness exclusively and primarily provides the space in which space as we usually know it can unfold. The self-extending, the opening up, of future, past, and present is itself prespatial [*vor-räumlich*]; only thus can it make room, that is, provide space."[93]

Site of the Moment and the Temporal Bestowing of Place

The construct time-space is identified variously in the *Beiträge* as "the originating essential occurrence of being as event" (*der Erwesung des Seins als Ereignis*),[94] the "essential occurrence of truth" (*Wesung der Wahrheit*),[95] and the "abyssal ground" (*Ab-grund*) that is "the originary essential occurrence of the ground" (*die ursprüngliche Wesung des Grundes*).[96] The positing of this concept as a compound of the spatial and the temporal is obviously meant to modify the tempocentrism of Heidegger's earlier work. The point is addressed explicitly in the following excerpt from the *Beiträge*:

> That to *us*, out of the first beginning and in a retrieving meditation, time appears primarily as the truth of beyng does not mean that the original, full truth of beyng could be grounded only on time. Indeed at first there must on the whole be an attempt to think the essence of time so originarily (in the temporal "ecstases") that time becomes graspable as possible truth for beyng as such. Yet this thinking of time already brings it, through relatedness to the "there" of Da-sein, into essential relation with the spatiality of Da-sein and thereby with space.... Compared to their usual representations, however, time and space are in this case more originary and are entirely time-space, which is not an interconnection but something more originary in the belonging together of time and space. This something points to the essence of truth as the clearing-concealing. The truth of beyng is nothing less than the *essence of truth*, grasped and grounded as the clearing-concealing; it is the occurrence of Da-sein, the occurrence of the axis in the turning as self-opening center.[97]

To think time in its most originary sense is to grasp time as the truth of beyng, but that truth—disclosed through the "there" of Dasein—must also be grounded in space. In contrast to the routine representation (*Vorstellung*) of the temporal and the spatial, Heidegger proposes the idea of time-space as indexical of the essence of the truth of beyng grasped and grounded as the clearing-concealing (*lichtende Verbergung*) in the occurrence of Dasein. In the time-space, the two elements are not coupled together in a pairing (*Verkoppelung*) that obfuscates difference but rather in a belonging together (*Zusammengehörigkeit*) that is a bridging of what remains disparate. Thus, in another passage from the *Beiträge*, Heidegger writes that until the truth is first known in the enactment (*Vollzug*) of the other beginning, time-space is veiled "in the guise of the uncomprehended but familiar naming of 'space' and 'time' together."[98] Not only is it incorrect to construe time-space as merely an aggregation of the phenomena we conventionally label as time and space, but these purported categories of understanding, which produce empirical knowledge in the sense of "labeling" (*Kennzeichnung*) and "pigeonholing" (*Beschilderung*),[99] conceal the true essence of the time span. Moving beyond attempts to determine the pertinent hierarchical order of the temporal and the spatial, Heidegger proffers that from the relation of being and truth we discern that "*time and space* are grounded in their original belonging together [*ursprünglichen Zugehörigkeit*], despite their strangeness [*Fremdheit*]."[100] The conjunction *and* is "in truth the ground of the essence of both space and time, the dislodging into the encompassing open realm which forms presencing and constancy but which could not be experienced or grounded."[101]

Time and space belong together primordially, which implies coextensiveness in their mutual divergence. In Heidegger's words: "Time and space, as belonging [*zugehörig*] to the essence of truth, are originally united in time-space and are the abyssal grounding [*die abgründige Gründung*] of the 'there'; through the 'there,' selfhood and what is true of being first come to be grounded."[102] In the hybridity of time-space—a union that conveys belonging together in difference—the distinctive features of both the spatial and the temporal dissipate. As Schürmann observed, the conjoining of time and space in the singular event of this momentary site destroys them as forms. "Not being the site and time *of* anything, they no longer lend themselves to subsumptions. . . . Space and time thus come to lie beyond the reach of normative co-optation. . . . Instead of their ontological and normative difference, what will have to be thought is a temporal and dispersive discordance."[103] Time-space, consequently, is the prespatial and pretemporal ground, or alternatively, the space that is no space and the time that is no time, whence emerge space (τόπος) as objective and time (χρόνος) as subjective.

A careful examination of Heidegger's reflections on the notion of time-space suggests, however, that he was not able to overcome his tempocentric bias entirely.[104] Thus, for instance, he writes that "time essentially occurs in the essence of truth for beingness [*die Seiendheit*]."[105] To be sure, the statement is qualified immediately by the introduction of the spatial component, but this does not alter the fact that the temporal is identified as the appropriate marker for the essence of the truth of beyng. That the temporal is still privileged is attested as well by the use of the image of the site of the moment (*die Augenblicksstätte*) to depict the origin of time-space as "the uniqueness [*Einzigkeit*] and the intrusion [*Anfall*] of the most luminous transposal [*Entrückung*] into the domain of the intimation out of the gentle captivation by what is self-withholding and hesitant [*Sichversagenden-Zögernden*], nearness and remoteness in the decision, the where and the when of the history of being as self-clearing and self-concealing [*sich lichtend-verbergend*] out of the appropriation of the basic disposition of *restraint*."[106] From this dense and cryptic statement, we can distill that Heidegger envisions the unfolding (*die Entfaltung*) of time-space out of an originary decision tagged as the site of the moment, a decision that comports as the self-withholding of the hesitancy of restraint. The essence of temporalizing (*das Wesen des Zeitigens*) is "the transporting into that which withholds itself" (*der Entrückung in das Sichversagende*).[107] As we remarked in chapter 4, the quality of refusal is juxtaposed with the quality of bestowal and hence the time-space is marked by the "decision regarding the absconding and advent of the gods,"[108] the abyss that manifests the strife between being and nonbeing in the clearing of the withdrawal that exposes and masks the truth as untruth.

The preliminary belonging together of the temporal and the spatial in the abyssal inexhaustibility of the time-space gives way to the emergence of space and time as quantifiable extensions, the where and the when of the history of being. The point is reiterated in slightly different language in the following aphorism:

> Time as transporting and opening up [*entrückende-eröffnende*] is in itself equally a *granting of place* [einräumend]; it creates "space." Space and time are not of the same essence, but each belongs intrinsically to the other. *Space* also must be understood here in the originary sense, as the clearing of a place for something. . . . The unity of temporalizing [*Zeitigung*] *and* the granting of place [*Einräumung*], and indeed in the mode of presencing [*Anwesung*], constitutes the essence of beingness [*Seiendheit*]: the overcrossing [*Überkreuzung*].[109]

The unity of temporalizing and spatializing constitutes the essence of beingness, which is characterized as the overcrossing. The latter term imparts that the time-space is composed of the doubly determined unity of constancy (*Beständigkeit*) and presence (*Anwesenheit*). Temporally, constancy is the "the *enduring* [Ausdauer] of the transporting [*Entrückung*] into the having-been [*Gewesenheit*] and into the to-come [*Zukunft*]," and presence is "the *present* [Gegenwart] in the sense of the gatheredness [*Gesammeltheit*] of the enduring in accord with the withdrawal [*Rückzug*] of the latter out of the transportings." Spatially, constancy is "the filling [*Ausfüllung*] and fulfilling [*Erfüllung*] of space," and presence is the "*granting of a place* [Einräumung] in the sense of giving space for beings which are put back into presence and thus are constant."[110] In the final analysis, the temporal bestows the opening that makes room for and creates the spatial; the appropriation by which the spatial is apportioned—the projection of beingness upon the presencing of the constant presence of the absence that leads to the assumption that space and time are definite beings that can be rendered as present—is clearly temporal in nature. This is what Heidegger intends by his statement that time "should become experienceable as the 'ecstatic' playing field [*Spiel-raum*] of the truth of beyng. Trans-position [*Ent-rückung*] into the cleared region is supposed to ground the clearing itself as the open realm in which beyng gathers itself into its essence."[111]

The crossing over of time into space—a transposition that arrives unexpectedly like a jolt and not as something prognosticated[112]—is depicted by Heidegger as a still movement that is transitory and enduring:

> Time times simultaneously: the has-been, presence, and the present that is waiting for our encounter and is normally called the future. Time in its timing removes us into its threefold simultaneity [*dreifältig Gleich-Zeitiges*], moves us thence while holding out to us the disclosure of what is in the same time [*Sichöffnende des Gleich-Zeitigen*], the concordant oneness [*die Einigkeit*] of the has-been, presence, and the present waiting the encounter. In removing us and bringing toward us, time moves on its way what simultaneity yields and throws open to it: time-space. But time itself, in the wholeness of its nature, does not move; it rests in stillness.[113]

Time—in its threefold synchroneity that yields and opens the conjunctive oneness of the time-space—is both tenaciously moving and haltingly still. We might try to resolve this ostensible contradiction by proposing that what appears from one perspective as motion appears from another perspective as immobility. However, Heidegger questions the validity of this mode of dyadic reasoning, which, as he writes when discussing the inadequacy of the intellect to inquire into the nature of nothing, "disintegrates in the turbulence of a more originary questioning."[114] The thinking that should command our consideration is a thinking that evolves by way of the question, a mindfulness that unsettles the solidity of any ground of meaning, a mindfulness that leads to the discernment that the steadfastness of truth consists of its fluidity. We are justified in applying this remark to the matter of time as well, a topic that Heidegger considered integral to the most elemental interrogation into the nature of being and the human condition. The dichotomy of inertia and mobility collapses in the face of the probing that proceeds from attunement to time's persistent coming to be in its relentless passing away. In its deepest cadence, time is experienced as the arresting kinesis of the moment constantly shifting in its stasis. The obstacle of the initial aporia, therefore, is thwarted by affirming a paradoxical logic that safeguards the question inasmuch as the motion is the stillness and the stillness is the motion. The grounding of Dasein necessitates the appropriation of this originary sense of time, a necessity that "demands stillness and long preparation for the hesitant suddenness of the moments."[115]

It is precisely this logic that underpins Heidegger's description of incipience (*Anfänglichkeit*) as the temporalizing that creates the space for the granting of place. Again, it is worth noting that in spite of his insistence on the initial juxtaposition of time and space as autonomous, he continued to confer priority to the former over the latter. The nature of temporality he esteems as authentic is not the calculation of a sequence of now-points depicted as a line and a perimeter, a conception of time borrowed from the "representation of three-dimensional space." The "true time" consists rather of the "mutual reaching out and opening up [*lichtenden Einander-sich-reichen*] of future, past, and present," which is prior to and independent of the geometric computation.[116] The tempocentric prejudice underscores Heidegger's insistence that dimensionality is constituted by this "reaching out that opens up, in which futural approaching [*Ankunft*] brings about what has been [*Gewesenheit*], what has been brings about futural approaching, and the reciprocal relation of both brings about the opening up of openness [*die Lichtung des Offenen*]."[117] Spatiality is not reckoned from the standpoint of a quantifiable surface but as the reaching out—the opening up—of the three dimensions of time. The giving that gives time—*Das Geben, das Zeit gibt*—empowers us to configure and delimit the area of measurement we call space. The unity of those dimensions, the interplay (*Zuspiel*) of past, present, and future in relation to one another, is identified by Heidegger as the "true extending" that is the fourth dimension of time:

> True time is four-dimensional. But the dimension which we call the fourth in our count is, in the nature of the matter, the first, that is, the giving that determines all. In future, in past, in the present, that giving brings about to each its own presencing, holds them apart thus opened and so holds them toward one another in the nearness by which the three dimensions remain near one another.... This nearing of nearness keeps open the approach coming from the future by withholding the present in the approach.... Time *is* not. There is, It gives time [*Die Zeit ist nicht. Es gibt die Zeit*]. The giving that gives time is determined by denying and withholding nearness. It grants the openness of time-space and preserves what remains denied in what has-been, what is withheld in approach. We call the giving which gives true time an extending which opens and conceals. As extending is itself a giving, the giving of a giving is concealed in true time.[118]

In what can only be called a philosophic poeticizing of Heidegger's thinking, the reader is presented with a profound meditation in which the fourth dimension of time is identified as the intersection of past, present, and future, a unity that holds them together by keeping them apart and keeps them apart by holding them together, the nearing of nearness that determines—in its repudiation of coming near—the giving that gives time. When viewed from this perspective, the ontological nature of time is undercut: time is not (*Die Zeit ist nicht*); in its place is the event of being, the there is, that gives time (*Es gibt die Zeit*). The giving that gives time is the bestowal of the openness of time-space, but the giving is provoked by the denial to give, the extending that simultaneously opens and closes, reveals and conceals. The construal of time as the gathering-dispersal resonates with the kabbalistic description of the bestowal-withholding of the infinite, the giving of the nongiven that creates the space of retraction—the opening of the openness—wherein time expands indefinitely in the oscillation between the incursion of its recoil and the recoil of its incursion.

Time Out of Time and the Eternality of Being's Moment

In the *Beiträge*, we can discern another important turn on Heidegger's path, one that shaped the tracks of his thinking for many decades until his demise. This turn, moreover, brings his thinking into even closer contiguity to what may be deduced from kabbalistic sources. The hyphenated time-space is cast as the open realm (*Offene*) through which the fissure of beyng is made accessible and endurable in Dasein.[119] What Heidegger is alluding to here is that the human being achieves its essential status as historical through summoning the appropriating event that reveals itself concealedly in the sheltering of truth unveiled through the veiling of truth.[120] The privileging of time to this concealing of the unconcealment in the unconcealing of the concealment is evident in Heidegger's further description of the leap into the essential occurrence of the event of beyng as that which "first allows the 'there,' as appertaining and appropriated in the call [*als zugehörig ereignet im Zuruf*], to spring forth as the site of the moment of some 'where' and 'when.' In the directions of its primordial manifestness [*Offenbarkeit*] and concealment [*Verhüllung*], the entire fissure of beyng [*die ganze Zerklüftung des Seyns*] is thereby already co-decided."[121] The leap results in the opening, the "there" of being, springing forth as the *Augenblicksstätte,* a word that combines the spatial and the temporal, the site of the moment, as we noted above, the interval that contains the potential of some determinate place (where) and time (when) in contrast to comporting as "an empty, indeterminate sea of determinability." In that respect, the fissure of beyng in its revealing and reveiling is co-decided. For Heidegger, only a few people "arrive at the leap" and thus "belong to the grounding of Da-sein in the time-space of which beings as beings are preserved and thereby the truth of beyng is sheltered. But beyng is ever in extreme concealment and is transport into the incalculable and unique, at the sharpest and highest crest which both constitutes what is along the abyssal ground of nothingness and itself grounds the abyss. Clearing and concealing constitute the essential occurrence of truth . . . Clearing and concealing, in the manner of transporting and captivation, are the event itself."[122]

Truth is not an object of representational knowledge but a consequence of the thinking that inculcates the dual nature of time-space as the clearing (*Lichtung*) and concealing (*Verbergung*), the transporting-captivating (*entrückend-berückend*) of the event that is always incalculably unique, the uppermost pinnacle—which is the nethermost foothold—of the ever-hidden being that grounds the nothingness of the nonground. Thinking is thus the "most genuine and broadest leap," not because "the essence of beyng could be determined on the basis of *thinking* [Denken] (assertion) but because here, in *knowledge* [Wissen] of the event, the fissure of being [*die Zerklüftung des Seins*] is penetrated the furthest and the possibilities of sheltering the truth in beings can be gauged most extensively. Thinking, as inceptual, grounds the time-space in its structure of transporting and captivating and penetrates the fissure of beyng [*die Zerklüftung des Seyns*] in the uniqueness, freedom, contingency, necessity, possibility, and actuality of the essential occurrence of beyng."[123]

In chapter 4, we discussed the fissure in Heidegger's thought in conjunction with the kabbalistic notion of the contraction/withdrawal of the infinite, at least as understood according to its exoteric meaning, to create an idealized space—the symbolic concretization of the force of potentiality (*koaḥ efsharut*)—for the formation of ostensibly independent worlds.[124] Additionally, we noted that the diminution of light comes about as a result of the stimulation of the aspect of judgment lodged in the boundless mercifulness of infinity, the actualization of the potential for determination within the indeterminable, the enactment of the place of contraction (*maqom ha-ṣimṣum*) in the center of the unlimited expanse of nothingness.[125] The spatial metaphor, however, needs to be complemented by the temporal, for the place that emerges as a consequence of the contraction is an unraveling of the knot of eternity, a process to which we can attribute the words of Heidegger, "*Time becomes space.* But the originary time [*die ursprüngliche Zeit*] becomes the fore-space [*Vor-raum*] of the duration."[126] We may adduce from the kabbalistic speculation on *ṣimṣum* a shared insight into the codependency of time and space as well as the prioritizing of the former inasmuch as the temporal duration of the infinite magnitude creates the forespace of the multifarious worlds in the concatenation of being. Eternality, on this score, is not the privation of time but its deepest inflection as the time before there was time.

Heidegger describes the event of beyng "as the *hesitant self-withholding* and therein the ripeness of 'time,' the mightiness of the fruit, and the greatness of the bestowing, but in the *truth* as *clearing* for *self-concealing*."[127] This sense of ripeness—the vegetal image that intimates the essential feature of time as the future perfect tense, that is, the present perpetually awaiting its futural unfolding[128]—reveals the character of the original not (*ursprünglichen Nicht*), which is expressed as the bestowing that is both not yet and no longer, the withholding of the hesitation, the captivating in the transporting, "the essential occurrence of the negative [*Nichthafte*] in beyng as event."[129] The event of beyng is thus suffused with negativity in the vacillation or strife between being and not-being, the truth of which—as the clearing for self-concealing—is ground in the abyss of time-space,[130] which occurs in the domain of beyng that is neither spatial nor temporal in the sense determined by mathematic-computable representation,[131] but in "the originary open spaciousness" (*die ursprüngliche offene Geräumigkeit*) through which "is thrown the swing of time" (*der Schwung der Zeit*), and in which "the world forms itself."[132] This cogitation seems far from the kabbalists, who adamantly deny that temporal and spatial qualities can be affixed to the infinite. A closer examination, however, complicates this deceptively clear distinction and brings their thought closer to the musings of Heidegger. Explained esoterically, what kabbalists had in mind in their depictions of the initial constraint of the light of *Ein Sof* can be expressed in the spirit of Heidegger as the infinite betraying the dual structure of the time-space through which the fissure of beyng is concealed and revealed, transported and captivated. *Ṣimṣum* is the constriction that creates the moment of the prespatial intermezzo—the space empty of space—in which time as the self-extending withdrawal can unfold. Utilizing Derrida's reformulation of Heidegger, we can say the remnant of the infinite light in the primordial emptiness, whence the luminosity of the infinite withdraws, is "a simulacrum of a presence that dislocates itself, displaces itself . . . the sign of the sign . . . and a trace of the erasure of the trace."[133] Time so conceived is the displacement of place and place the dislocation of time.

Just as Heidegger spoke of the time-space that is neither temporal nor spatial, so the kabbalists obdurately refute the attribution of temporal and spatial qualities to the infinite. For instance, Cordovero states that one cannot inquire why *Ein Sof* did not emanate *Keter* at a prior moment because "there is there no time," and thus we must distinguish between the priority of time (*qadimat zeman*) and the priority of gradation (*qadimat ma'alah*).[134] It is reasonable to appeal to the latter but not to the former in any attempt to demarcate the shift from the nothingness of infinity to the infinity of nothingness. In a somewhat more laborious manner, Viṭal attempts to explain the mystery of the infinite finitude of the beginning emerging from the finite infinitude of the origin:

> Thus it is known that the supernal light, which is endlessly beyond [*lema'lah lema'lah ad ein qeṣ*], is called *Ein Sof*. Its name indicates that concerning it there is no apprehension, no thought, no rumination at all, and it is removed and separated from all thoughts, and it preceded all things emanated, created, formed, and made, and there was in it no time of commencement and beginning, for it existed everlastingly and was established forever, and in it there is no beginning or end at all. . . . However, the emanation of this *Adam Qadmon*, and all the more so the rest of the worlds beneath him, have a beginning and an end, and they have a time for the beginning of their being and their emanation, which is not the case with *Ein Sof*. From the moment and time when the emanation and concatenation of the lights and worlds began, there commenced the coming into being of the created entities one after the other until the matter comes to the existence that is now, and in accord with the order of the emanation and the concatenation like the order of times, one after the other it was accomplished. It was not possible to advance or to delay the creation of this world, for each and every world is created after the creation of the world above it, and all the worlds were created, emanated, and concatenated, and they went one in the place of the other in different and later times, one after the other, until the time of the creation of this world was reached. And then it was created in the time appropriate to it after the creation of the upper worlds above it. This is sufficient because it is not possible to expand and to delve into the explanation of this matter as is necessary concerning how, what, and why.[135]

The explanation of the sequence of time up to the very present can be traced back to the transition from *Ein Sof*, which has no beginning or end, to *Adam Qadmon* and the four worlds, all of which commenced at a given moment in the past that is naught but the future and will terminate at a given moment in the future that is naught but the past. The transference from the origin to the beginning is not a matter of quantitative computation, but the imaginal distension of the illimitable light that is the vitality of being, the contracted elongation of an efflux that has no beginning that is not a novel iteration of what cannot begin without having already begun.

To clarify the import of this claim, let me refer again to what is considered one of the few texts genuinely written by Luria, a commentary on the zoharic passage that seeks to explain the opening verse of Genesis as a symbolic reference to the issuing forth of the *sefirot* from infinity.[136] The key sentence worthy of our attention, "prior to the emanation he and his name alone were and he filled the space of all the worlds,"[137] is based on the celebrated remark from *Pirqei Rabbi Eliezer,* "Before the world was created he and his name alone were."[138] Needless to say, the spatial element, which underlies the description of *Ein Sof* filling all worlds, cannot be understood literally, since before the emanation, there are no worlds of which to speak. I surmise, therefore, that the expression "he filled the space of all the worlds" should be taken as a metaphor to convey its very opposite; that is, the omni-expanisveness of infinitivity subverts the very possibility of topographical allocation. To fill all worlds means there are no worlds to be filled; there is nothing but the utter darkness of the unalloyed luminescence beyond the polarity of light and dark. With respect to the temporal element, by contrast, there is no comparable disavowal; to the contrary, time is ascribed to the infinite. This is implicit in the reference to the coeternity of the ineffable name with the divine prior to creation. The Tetragrammaton, as noted in the previous chapter, signifies the concurrence of the three tenses. One might argue that blurring the boundaries between past, present, and future raises questions about the suitability of applying the category of time to the divine. There is textual evidence that some kabbalists assumed such a position, as we find, for example, in the case of Ergas: "Even though he was [*hayah*], he is [*howeh*], and he will be [*yihyeh*], nonetheless he has no relation to time, because his having been is not the past, his being in the present is not the moment, and his coming to be is not the future. . . . And it is the wonder of the mysteries of his incomposite unity that he is the one that exists without any diffusion of temporal being [*hawwayah zemanit*]."[139]

Notwithstanding this categorical denial, Ergas speaks of the durée (*hemshekh* or *meshekh*) that is prior to creation. Our imagination mistakenly conceives of that duration as if it could be divided into past, present, and future, but the reality is that the duration is a temporal tensiveness in which these three tenses cannot be distinguished and hence there is nothing antecedent (*qodem*) or consequent (*mit'aḥer*), an obvious disruption of the sequential order of cause and effect.[140] Ergas refers to a comment of Naḥmanides (1194–1270) explicating the dictum transmitted in the name of R. Isaac[141] that the name *Ehyeh* is repeated three times in the epiphany to Moses (Exodus 3:14) to indicate that just as God was with the Israelites in the past, so shall he be in the present and in the future: "The explanation of the opinion of R. Isaac is that since the past and future time for the creator is entirely in the present . . . therefore all of the times are called by one name, and this is indicative of the necessary of existence [*ḥiyyuv ha-meṣi'ut*]."[142] Echoing a motif well attested in medieval scholastic philosophy and theology, based on previous thinkers, including Plotinus, Augustine, and Boethius,[143] to name a few of the better known examples, Naḥmanides submits that the Avicennian definition of God, adopted by Maimonides, as the necessarily existent[144] implies that the divine dwells in an eternally abiding instant that knows no temporal distinctions, the *nunc stans* that is the incarnate form of the *nunc aeternitatis,* the standing now of eternity that endures in the interminable flux of time, the timeless nowhere that is temporally omnipresent.[145] From the human perspective, the moment is, as Arendt put it, the "non-time-space in the very heart of time," the present situated between the memory of an infinite past and the anticipation of an infinite future,[146] but from the divine perspective, that moment has no past and no future, and thus it warrants neither recollection nor expectation; it is the quintessential embodiment of time as the union of past, present, and future.[147] The coalescence of the three tenses is indicative of the temporal transcendence of the temporal as masters of Jewish esoteric lore often claimed with respect to the deeper connotation of the Tetragrammaton. To cite one example from Shneur Zalman of Liadi: "The name *YHWH* indicates that he transcends time [*lema'lah min ha-zeman*], for he was, is, and will be in one moment [*hayah howeh we-yihyeh be-rega eḥad*] . . . and he also transcends the aspect of place [*lema'lah mi-beḥinat maqom*], for he constantly brings into being the entire aspect of place from above to below, and to the four sides. Even though he, blessed be he, transcends place and time, he is found also below in place and time; that is, he is united in the aspect of his kingship [*she-mityaḥed be-middat malkhuto*] whence there issue and come to be place and time."[148] The ascription of temporal characteristics to God is categorically denied, but it is precisely the sempiternity implied by the ineffable name that triggers the regeneration of the invariable in the capriciousness of the variable. From that vantage point, the eternality (*niṣḥiyyut*), signified by the compresence of past, present, and future in the Tetragrammaton, is itself an aspect of temporality, the limitless extension of the stream of time. Time is overcome, therefore, in the ubiquity of time as that which lingers in the lapsing of lingering and lapses in the lingering of lapsing. There is no eternity set over and against time, but only the temporal eternity measured against the timelessness of eternal temporality in the manner that the halo of silence envelops the periphery of the verbal or the haze of invisibility permeates the showground of the visible.[149]

YHWH, Ehyeh, and Temporal Emplacement

To appreciate the innovation of Luria's interpretation of the passage from *Pirqei Rabbi Eliezer*, it is worth recalling an explanation offered by Cordovero: either the third person pronoun is decoded as a reference to *Ein Sof* and the name to *Keter*,[150] or the third person pronoun refers to *Keter* and the name to *Ḥokhmah*.[151] Preference is given to the second possibility, but in either case, Cordovero explicitly rejects the interpretation of the midrashic dictum that would imply that *Keter* preceded the emanation and was unified with the emanator as its garment.[152] For Luria and his disciples, the name demarcates the potential for limit within the limitless, the lowest aspect of *Ein Sof* designated as the "kingship within kingship" (*malkhut she-be-malkhut*),[153] and in Saruqian kabbalah[154] and later Sabbatian sources[155] as the "kingship of the infinite" (*malkhut de-ein sof*), the aspect of the feminine contained within a world that is entirely masculine, the inner point (*nequddah penimit*) of the pointless—an ideational point (*nequddah maḥashavit*) rather than a physical point like the nucleus of a circle (*nequddat ha-merkaz*)—wherein the contraction transpires.[156] As Moses ben Menaḥem Graf of Prague (1650–ca.1710) put it in his explanation of how the concealed letters of the Tetragrammaton became manifest:

> Every aspect of the point makes for itself a palace in which to hide, and there came to be from the *yod* three points of the *waw*, and from the first *he* the second *he*. And to this the rabbis, blessed be their memory, alluded in the *midrash*, "R. [Eliezer] said before the blessed holy One created the world, he and his name alone were." That is, the name, mentioned above, was produced from the secret of the measure [*shi'ur*] and the engraving [*gelifu*], which is the attribute of the Torah, and if not for the engraving, which is the Torah, there would have been no possibility for the world to have been created, but by means of the measurement that he measured in himself, as it were, there emerged the engraving, which is the Torah, and afterward in that place the worlds were created . . . and since all the worlds stood within *Malkhut* that is in the essence [*aṣmut*] of the infinite, may he be blessed, which is the secret of the Torah, the Torah says "Through me kings reign" (Proverbs 8:15), and since the Torah emerged from the secret of the arousal [*hit'orerut*], which is the secret of the movement [*tenu'ah*], that is, the bemusement [*sha'ashu'a*], as it were, the Torah said "I will be a source of delight [*sha'ashu'im*] every day" (ibid., 8:30).[157]

By a series of symbolic identifications, the name is equated with the Torah, which is the aspect of kingship embedded within the essence of *Ein Sof*, and the place wherein all the worlds come forth in the manifest concealedness of their concealed manifestation.

Naturally, there were precedents for this approach, as we see in Meir Ibn Gabbai's exposition of the statement from *Pirqei Rabbi Eliezer*, "The secret of the matter as the masters of worship received orally is that prior to the concealed emanation emanating, the unique master, the root of all roots, called by the sages of truth *Ein Sof*, was alone with his name. The import of 'his name' is the supreme gradation [*rom ma'alah*] that is called the primordial ether [*awir ha-qadmon*], for it is primordial like his primordiality, since the name is not separated from the essence."[158] The esoteric intent of the aggadic statement that prior to the creation God and his name alone were is that *Ein Sof* and *Keter* were coterminous, and hence the name is not independent of the essence that is nameless. Similarly, David ben Solomon Ibn Zimra (1479–1573), one of Luria's teachers in Egypt, noted that the Tetragrammaton, which was before the creation of the worlds, was comprised in the divine essence (*kalul be-aṣmuto*).[159] The nameless can encompass the name insofar as infinity contains the determinate as an aspect of its indeterminacy.

The followers of Luria expounded this theme, relating it to what is perhaps the most vexing paradox of kabbalistic theosophy, the positioning of a demarcating point in the sea of infinitude that defies all demarcation. The name—identified variously as the Torah, the garment, and the aspect of the kingship of the infinite—represents the quality of judgment by which the limitlessly expanding light of mercy is delimited.[160] The matter is explained cogently by Eliashiv:

> With regard to the central point that is verily in the middle of his light: the aspect of the point is attributed to the *sefirah* of *Malkhut*, for it is the main source for each *sefirah* and for all of existence, and thus it is called a point, for it is the source, like the seed of the fruit in relation to the fruit. The central point that is in her is on account of the aspect of the foundation [*yesod*] that is in her, the foundation of the kingship [*yesod de-ha-malkhut*], for this is always called the central point; the quiddity of the foundation [*eikhut ha-yesod*] and the inner potency [*koaḥ ha-penimi*] within it are from the knowledge of the central line [*da'at ha-qaw ha-emṣa'i*]. Therefore, the foundation of the kingship is called the central point.... And this is the import here with regard to the aspect of the kingship of the infinite [*malkhut de-ein sof*], and the aspect of the foundation in her is the central point of the kingship of the infinite. Thus all of the contraction was only in the kingship of the infinite and in the aspect of the foundation in her.[161]

The aspect of judgment, which was the catalyst that instigated the contraction of the light, is located in the nucleus earmarked as the feminine, the aspect of *Malkhut*, which is the capacity for boundary (*gevul*) within the boundless and the potential for measure (*middah*) within the immeasurable. It is surely valid to highlight the female dimension of the matrixial point, but the phallic nature of that point is apparent from the emphasis on the aspect of the foundation (*yesod*), which is allied with the knowledge (*da'at*) of the central line (*qaw ha-emṣa'i*), a symbolic reference to the masculine potency of *Tif'eret*. I note, parenthetically, that this text is proof of the thesis I have argued for the better part of the last three decades regarding the phallomorphic bias of the gender construction in the traditional kabbalah, a bias that displays a remarkable uniformity despite the obvious multivalency at play as well—indeed, as I argued in chapter 1, it is the uniformity that engenders the multivalency and the setting of these hermeneutical possibilities in opposition is a vestige of a binarian logic that the texts themselves seriously question. With regard to the matter at hand, from the context it appears, more technically, that the foundation of the kingship refers to the uterus, the place of gestation, but it is also clear that this part of the female anatomy is interpreted through a phallocentric lens.[162] Be that as it may, the Lurianic teaching, exploited by Eliashiv, identifies *malkhut de-ein sof* as the name that was coeternal with the namelessness of the infinite.

Most notably for our analysis, this symbol instills in us the conviction that the origin of time is to be sought in the place of contraction; that is, temporality in its originary modulation is a circle that arises as a consequence—although it may also be viewed as the cause—of the withdrawal of the infinite light that occasions the augmentation of the line so that the formlessness dissembles in the semblance of the form and the namelessness dons the garment of the name. Eliashiv, however, argues that in each and every moment (*rega*), new purifications (*berurim ḥadashim*) emerge to rectify the original fissure and to restore some of the light to its source.[163] The pulsation of time is gauged, therefore, from the event of the present moment that wavers incessantly between the poles of showing and nonshowing, coming to be in passing and passing in coming to be. Writ large, the arc of the temporal duration of the existence of the world (*meshekh zeman de-qiyyum ha-olam*) extends from the contraction of the light of the infinite that engenders the beginning (*hatḥalah*) and inception (*re'shit*) of the line to the final rectification at the end (*sof*) and terminus (*takhlit*) of the line when all the sparks of that light return to the infinite in the secret of the perfect unity (*sod ha-aḥdut ha-sheleimah*).[164]

Time is thus a circle calibrated as the line that extends from and reverts back to *malkhut de-ein sof*, from the fragmented unity of the *ṣimṣum* at the beginning to the unified fragmentation of the *tiqqun* at the end, a process that culminates in the tenth millennium.[165] From the perspective of the "general boundary and measure" (*gevul u-middah kelalit*), there is "one general stature [*qomah kelalit aḥat*] that comprises all of the duration of that time entirely [*kol meshekh otto ha-zeman kullo*] from the moment of the beginning of the time of constriction until the moment of the rectification [*me-et hatḥalat zeman ha-ṣimṣum ad et ha-tiqqun*]."[166] The linear circle can be viewed as well from the perspective of the now (*attah*) molded by the predication of endless details that cannot be probed (*bi-feraṭot uvi-peraṭei peraṭot ad peraṭim ein ḥeqer*):

> That general light [*ha-or ha-kelali*] itself by which *Ein Sof*, blessed be his name, is revealed to illumine the way from the beginning of the time of the contraction and the line until the time of the final rectification, is divided, as it were, into multiple details [*li-feraṭim rabbim*] to the point that in each and every moment [*rega wa-rega*] from the aforementioned general time [*ha-zeman ha-kelali*] there radiates from it a distinctive illumination [*me'ir be-he'arah meyuḥedet mimmennu*]. For as it radiates in one moment, it does not radiate in another moment, but rather each and every moment with an illumination that is distinctive to it, and there is bestowed upon it the measure of the lights [*shi'ur ha-me'orot*] in accord with the measure of the moments of time of the entire duration of the general time [*shi'ur rig'ei ha-zeman de-khol meshekh zeman ha-kelali*] . . . and it receives the illumination of *Ein Sof*, blessed be his name, in each and every moment by way of a different luminescence [*ma'or aḥer*]. With the consummation of the measure of all the lights in it, then there shall be the end and terminus of the whole general stature [*ha-qomah ha-kelali*].[167]

With characteristic lucidity, Eliashiv articulates the kabbalistic discernment of the metrics of time as the extensionality of the disclosure of the infinite light in the various configurations of the divine aligned with their corresponding historical epochs. The open-ended splintering of that concealed light—the details and the details of the details (*ha-peraṭim we-ha-peraṭei peraṭim*)—structurally reflects the potentially unlimited mirroring that stems from the fact that each configuration is composed monadically of all the other configurations, each of which is itself composed of all of them, and so on ad infinitum.[168] In postmodern terms, the virtuality of the universal time of *Ein Sof* is instantiated in the fathomless array and fracturing of the cumulative manifestations of the plurivocality unfolding from the infinitivity enfolded in the one that is more and therefore less than one. Insofar as every moment is infused distinctively with the selfsame radiance of *Ein Sof*, each moment is inimitably different from what comes before and what comes after in the disjointed rotation of time.

Against this background we can turn to the implication of this teaching to understand the kabbalistic version of a fourth dimension arising from the amalgamation of the three tenses in the moment wherein the temporal is eternalized and the eternal temporalized. It goes without saying that I do not wish to argue that Heidegger's views about time are identical to those of the kabbalists nor do I think it is justifiable to treat the complex ruminations of the latter monolithically. Even with respect to the emphasis on futurity, the very topic that will yield the most interesting convergences of these divergent orbits of thinking, there is an unbridgeable chasm that separates Heidegger and the kabbalists. For Heidegger, the ultimate measure of the future is the imperishable perishing that we each must endure in the nonrelational ownmost potentiality of our being-toward-death, the possibility of our absolute impossibility, the constant being there as the prospect of not being there, the not yet no longer that is already no longer not yet.[169] By contrast, the kabbalists understand the future—emblematized by the scriptural name *Ehyeh*—as the surplus of no more that is always not yet, the capability for rejuvenation, which, most profoundly, is the restitution to the undifferentiated nothingness of infinity. In this place of no-place, the distinction between time and timelessness is no longer operative, not because time is subsumed in the timeless, but because timelessness is the measure of the fourth dimension that precedes the triadic division of time.[170]

Momentarily, I shall return to the matter of futurity. Suffice it here to say that, in kabbalistic lore, the future is not determined by the imperishability of our perishability but by the power of regeneration, which is exemplified in the proclivity of repentance—the halakhic foundation for the mystical ideal of *restitutio*—to break the karmic chain of causality so that the fate of an individual is not irrevocably determined by past events.[171] In spite of this and other disparities between the kabbalah and Heideggerian thought, some striking similarities cannot be ignored. The one that is most relevant pertains to the compresence of past, present, and future symbolized by the Tetragrammaton and the viewing of the name as that which fosters the time-space as the open enclosure of all being, the self-revealing concealment of the self-concealing revelation repeatedly renewed in the site of the moment.[172] Lest there be any misunderstanding, let me restate unequivocally that the question of influence—the issue that unfailingly consumes the mind of intellectual and social historians working within the confines of the academy—is not of paramount importance to me. What is far more tantalizing is the fact that there is a constellation of thought based on conceptual correspondences.

The ten emanations, the garments of the infinite light, are contained in the four letters of the ineffable name (*shem ha-meforash*), which is also referred to as the essential name (*shem ha-eṣem*), the name of the essence, forging the paradox of the name that names the nameless, and in so doing, preserves its namelessness. Etymologically, the Tetragrammaton is from the root *hwh* that connotes the sense of isness, and as we have seen, this refers, more specifically, to the simultaneity of what was, is, and will be. Insofar as *YHWH* is a name that cannot be taken nominally, it does not designate the existence of a being per se; it functions rather like a gerund that denotes the eventfulness of being, the beingness that is the center of the encircling nothingness. This is astonishingly close to Heidegger's emphasis on *Ereignis* in relation to *Seyn*; beyng is not a thing that can be objectified but an event that—as *YHWH* vis-à-vis *Ein Sof*—concurrently reveals and conceals the true and hidden essence of the mystery of the being of nonbeing that is the nonbeing of being. Moreover, just as the extension of space is a consequence of what Heidegger called the fourth dimension of time, which is determined by the interplay of the tripartite bestowal that corresponds to the three tenses, so for kabbalists, the space created by the withdrawal of light functions as the fourth dimension in which the temporal modes intermingle.

The convergence associated with the Tetragrammaton is applied to *Ehyeh* as well on account of the triple repetition of this name in Exodus 3:14. An allusion to this is found in *Tiqqunei Zohar*: "*Ehyeh* is atop *YHWH*, and this vapor of the heart guides[173] the voice of *YHWH*; it is the Cause of all Causes, hidden and concealed and not revealed, and it governs and rules over everything. *Ehyeh* illustrates that the Cause of Causes was, is, and will be, and it is the vapor that rises infinitely [*ad ein sof*], and by means of it the Cause of all the Causes governs."[174] In part, the kabbalistic explication is based on the talmudic interpretation of the expression *ehyeh asher ehyeh*, "The blessed holy One said to Moses, Go and tell Israel: I was with you in this servitude and I will be with you in the servitude of the kingdoms."[175] In the zoharic context, the rabbinic gloss is expanded to include past, present, and future, inspired no doubt by the occurrence of the name *Ehyeh* three times in the scriptural context. Theosophically, this name, the first person singular imperfect, signifies that the infinite—designated by the philosophical nomenclature *illat ha-illot* or *illat kol ha-illot*—embodies the undifferentiated unity and synchronicity of the three temporal modes.[176] The view endorsed by the author of the zoharic passage is based on the attribution of the name *Ehyeh* to the first of the sefirotic emanations in some of the earliest thirteenth-century kabbalistic texts,[177] an attribution that signals the determinate indeterminacy of the overflowing nothingness, the pure contingency of absolute necessity, the origin—the *alef*—whence all beings emerge and whither they return.[178] As the Vilna Gaon wrote in his commentary on *Tiqqunei Zohar*, "*Ehyeh* is the language of existence [*meṣi'ut*], and as the commentators explain with regard to *ehyeh asher ehyeh* . . . it instructs about what was, is, and will be; that is to say, it says *Ehyeh* there three times, as they said '*Ehyeh asher ehyeh*, I was with you etc. and I will be with you etc.,' this is the past and the future, and afterward it says 'Go and say *ehyeh*,' which relates to the redemption in the present."[179]

Although three tenses are distinguished in demarcating the efficacy of divine providence, they can all be assimilated into the future inasmuch as they are derived from the three occurrences of *Ehyeh*. The deportment of time to be discerned from this name, or the gradation of *Keter* to which it is ascribed—the apex of the pleromatic void, the emptiness that must be empty of its emptiness to be empty and hence neither empty nor nonempty—is the quality of the primeval futurity. The latter communicates the paradox that the radically novel is the most ancient, that the eternality of time and the temporality of eternity converge in the attribute that symbolizes the primordiality and fecundity of the infinite. Opposites meet—not coincidentally but juxtapositionally—in the nothingness of infinity: the never-beginning future intersects with the never-ending past, and the never-beginning past with the never-ending future. According to the esoteric meaning of the name *Ehyeh*, in each instant, the nothing becomes something that is not what it has become—it shall be what it shall be but what it shall be must always not be what it is.[180] As we discussed in the first chapter, Heidegger not only pinpointed the future as the temporal mode from which our acting and thinking should be oriented, but he also understood the future in its most radical sense as the attunement to the other beginning by way of return to the first beginning in which the event of beyng is always what is to come.[181]

It is not unwarranted, in my opinion, to apply the same criterion to the kabbalistic symbolism associated with *Ehyeh*, the divine nihility that is the potentiality fully actual as the actuality that is fully potential in being nothing. In temporal terms, we can say that *Ehyeh* points to the future recurrently rejuvenated in the breach of the beginning within the origin whence time is engendered from the infinite past constantly renewed in the present. Time, then, is the absolute giving, the giving that is without the intention of a giver to give or to be received as gift, the given of the ungiven,[182] an unreserved graciousness that withholds nothing but the withholding of the grace of reciprocity, the impossible possible, possible because of the impossibility of its ownmost possibility. According to one zoharic passage, we read that *Ehyeh* signifies the "totality of everything" (*kelala de-kholla*), a state in which "everything was hidden and not revealed" (*kolla satim we-lo itgalya*), the "generality with no particularity" (*kelala be-lo perața*);[183] that is, all differentiation comprised in an undifferentiated way. From the concealment of *Keter* emerges the infinitesimal beginning, *Ḥokhmah*—the dimensionless point within which the infinite expansiveness of the pointless is compressed—whence issues forth the seed that impregnates the river, *Binah*, and as a result, it disseminates everything, thereby stimulating the impetus of the infinite will to be summoned to emanate and to produce everything (*zammin le'amshakha u-le'olada kolla*).[184] This process is encrypted in the words *asher ehyeh*, which complete the name.[185] The gesture of beckoning (*zammin*) bespeaks the true nature of time (*zeman*), the indeterminate coming to be of what has already been determined, a paradox that is typically expressed in kabbalistic literature by the term *hitḥaddeshut*, the renewal of the past that is yet to be. The unfathomable mystery is expressed semiotically by the fact that the first letter of the Hebrew alphabet comprises both the general (*kelal*) and the particular (*perat*); that is, the inundation of particulars are symbolized by *elef*, which stands metonymically for the one thousand generations,[186] indiscriminately discriminated in the *alef*.[187] Thus, we read in a midrashic gloss on the name *Ehyeh* in another zoharic text, in which the ten divine names corresponding to the *sefirot* are delineated:

> The first one is *ehyeh*, the supernal concealed one [*setima illa'ah*], like one who says "I am what I am" [*ana ma'n da-ana*],[188] but it is not known who it is [*we-lo ityeda ma'n hu*]. Afterward, *asher ehyeh*, I am summoned to be revealed [*ana de-zammin le'itgalya*] in those crowns. At first it was concealed and then it began to be revealed, until it reached the disclosure of the holy name. Thus it is written by Moses, *ehyeh*—initially, the concealment of everything [*setimu de-kholla*]. I am what I am [*ana hu ma'n da-ana*]. Afterward, *asher ehyeh*—I am summoned to be revealed [*ana zammin le'itgalya*].[189]

The full name transmitted to Moses conveys the confluence of determinacy and indeterminacy. On the one hand, all the emanations were comprised within the supernal crown, "the principle and concealment of the origin" (*kelala u-setima de-qadmita*), the "head of all heads" (*reisha de-khol reishin*), the "concealed name that is not revealed" (*shemeih satim we-lo itgalya*),[190] but, on the other hand, the name attached to that gradation signifies that the predilection of the divine volition is that it will be what it will be, a name that does not denote a circumscribed something but only the void that is the unbounded openness of the future—the time of the undoing of time—in the same way that one says "I am that I am," but no one knows the nature of that being, since its status is determinedly what is still to be determined. As Menaḥem Mendel of Shklov (1750–1827) astutely quipped on the zoharic expression, "*Ehyeh* instructs about the greatness of his concealment, 'I am summoned to be revealed,' but not now."[191] The disclosure of the will of the infinite is always present by being in the future, the now that is perpetually not now.

In slightly more technical terms, Eliashiv makes the same point: "Therefore, *Arikh Anpin* is called by the name *Ehyeh*, for it instructs about the future, I will be summoned to be revealed . . . and this refers to what will be revealed afterward in the four configurations of *Abba*, *Ima*, *Ze'eir*, and *Nuqba*, which are the four letters of the name *YHWH*, blessed be he, but it itself is only in the aspect of *Ehyeh*, for it has no disclosure in the name *YHWH*, blessed be he, except in the tittle of the *yod*."[192] To the extent that time (*zeman*) is dependent on the quality of summoning (*zammin*), we can transpose this into Heideggerian parlance and say that what is to come withholds its presencing, not as a presence that refuses to come to presence at present and is thus presently absent, but as the presence that can only be present as nonpresent and is thus always absently present. The ontological condition of such a being is its becoming. With respect to this hidden name, therefore, absolute necessity is indistinguishable from pure possibility. In the emptiness of the infinite nonemptiness, there is no antithesis between what is foreordained and what is indefinite. Therein lies the essence of temporality in its most originary comportment: time is encapsulated in the name that comprises all the names in the generality of their particularity and the particularity of their generality, the names that, to quote Eliashiv again, are "constantly interchanging in their disclosure in accord with the condition of the world and their merit, according to the moment [*ha-et*] and the time [*ha-zeman*]. One day is not like the other, nor one hour like the other, but all are contained in all, one is concealed and the other disclosed."[193]

Imagining Time and the Futural Givenness of the Nongiven

In the final section of this chapter, I want to explore an additional dimension that may be culled from the Heideggerian and the kabbalistic perspectives on time, the nexus of the temporal and the imaginal. It goes without saying that it is not an easy matter to generalize about a phenomenon as multifaceted as the imagination, but one of its salient characteristics, attested in a variety of disciplinary approaches, including philosophy, psychology, and neurobiology, is the ability to traverse spatial and temporal distances, an ability that is facilitated by the transporting quality of reminiscence, which has long been associated with the imaginative faculty. In Kantian terms, imagination is the faculty of representation, of making present in the intuition what is absent from the senses, catching thereby a glimpse of "what is given to the mind as the nonappearance in the appearances."[194] As Eva Brann expressed it, "To the imagination diverse regions of present space represent different slices of time, insofar as they are invested by different memories. . . . The imagination overcomes the physical necessities of space and time equally."[195] Probing the matter further, we surmise that the ability of the imagination to surmount spatial and temporal boundaries is related to the fact that when we imagine something of the present we not only summon an image of what is indirectly given through sense perception but an image that is lodged between retention and expectation, the no more of the past that is not yet and the not yet of the future that is no more. And thus we return to a point made in the first chapter about the overlap of the hermeneutic and the temporal: the imaginary conflation of the past that is still to be and the future that already was is precisely the key to understanding the paradox of the linear circularity that is at the heart of the midrashic process that has informed the variegated nature of textual reasoning in the history of Jewish thought, accentuated in the kabbalistic teaching. The quest for temporal meaning ensues timelessly in time, not as a sequence subject to mathematical calibration, but as a spontaneous fracture in the spatial spread of the timeline, completely in and of the moment that can be calculated only as incalculable and estimated only as inestimable. The interval of time coalesces in the space of difference in which the moment is effaced in its perseverance and perseveres in its effacement, a time so fully present it defies the possibility of representation, so binding it releases one from all causal links to past or future, a split second wherein and wherewith the superfluity of time divests one of all memory of the past and expectation of the future, the time devoid of time.

As it happens, in the treatise, *Ṣeror ha-Mor,* Ibn Laṭif offers a description of time related to this very conception: "The temporal present of necessity exists but it is impossible to understand it. Rather it is in the image of the intermediary between past and future; the intermediate image, which is between two nothingnesses, is very difficult for the intellect . . . to imagine . . . for there is no intermediary outside the intellect, even for something that exists in actuality, and how much more so for the absolute privation."[196] Ibn Latif is here drawing on an idea that is traceable to Plato: the image is a combination of being and nonbeing; the object we imagine is mentally present but somatically absent, and hence it is, at once, real and unreal.[197] Rendered in the technical language of Husserlian phenomenology, the presentification of the image, whether in the act of recollecting the past or in anticipating the future, is to be contrasted with the appresentationally given object that is symptomatic of the appearance of the present in the impressional consciousness of perception. The intentionality of the imagination is to be distinguished from that of perception insofar as the givenness of the perceived object has the character of actuality, whereas the reproductive givenness of the imagined object is characterized as fictive, and in this sense, it can be given only as nongiven and is, accordingly, more proximate to the retentional consciousness of memory in which the absent is continuously made present by the present being perpetually absent.[198] The insight into the formal kinship between time and imagination is expressed poetically and perspicaciously by Brann: "An image, as a likeness, is composed of Nonbeing and Being *at once,* meaning that it *is not* the original, which in a way it also *is*; an image is the presence of an absence. In time, as the pure structure of Becoming, that 'at once' comes apart as absence turns into presence and presence into absence, as the future that *is not* yet ceaselessly propels the present that *is* now into a past that *is not* anymore; time is thus a present winged by two absences."[199]

Alternatively, we can speak of the image as the coupling of the hidden and the manifest, the visible and the invisible; it both is and is not what it represents.[200] The mutability of time, similarly, exhibits the heterogeneity of the homogeneous in the homogeneity of the heterogeneous. To paraphrase Hegel, the constituent element of becoming as the unity of being and nothing is that it is marked by movement that consists of the reciprocal passing of one opposite into the other.[201] What is available at any moment is the presence of the actual present, the now that appears to us, but this present lacks any presence apart from the presence of the past recollected as future or the presence of the future anticipated as past; that is, a presence that cannot be accorded the reality of being present outside the absence conjured by the affirmation of negation that is central to the imaginative faculty.[202] It follows that the duration of time is not primarily the property of thinghood or the measure of actual bodies in motion, as Aristotle famously argued, but rather the measure of alteration determined by the stretching (*distentio*) of the mind backward and forward, a decisive aspect of Plotinus's reflections on time that had an impact on Augustine's *Confessions* and later thinkers, including especially on Husserl's lectures on the phenomenology of internal time consciousness.[203]

To the extent that becoming marks the being of the nothingness of time, we can conjecture that the facticity of the latter is such that nonbeing and being coalesce, not as the dialectical resolution of antinomies but as the paradoxical juxtaposition of contraries that belong together in virtue of their intractable disjuncture. As Merleau-Ponty put it, "Past and future exist all too well in the world, they exist in the present, and what being itself lacks in order to be temporal is the non-being of the elsewhere, of the bygone, and of tomorrow.... Past and future voluntarily withdraw from being and pass over to the side of subjectivity, to seek there not some real support, but rather a possibility of non-being that harmonizes with their nature."[204] Congruent with the Heideggerian perspective outlined above, Merleau-Ponty maintains that the commonsense conception of time as a string of now-points is meaningful only insofar as it presupposes the synchronization of being and nonbeing in a field of presence that is circumscribed by the absence of the double horizon of past and future. Time and imagination both assume that being is implicated with nonbeing in becoming. Again, to quote Brann: "Imagination and time are related to the brink of identity through memory, which is the presence of what has gone absent through passage.... Therefore, if we want to understand something of imagination, memory, and time, we must mount an inquiry into what it means to say that something is not what it claims to be or is not there or is nonexistent or is affected by Nonbeing."[205]

Kabbalistically, the attribution of temporality to *Ein Sof* and to the sefirotic emanations is predicated on the parallel assumption that time can be thought from the vantagepoint of an apophasis that emerges from pondering the existence of nonexistence, the event of presence that is always present in its nonpresence. Through the intentionality of the nonintentional that is germane to the imagination, every present can become a replication of the past that induces the disruption of the future, the coming to be of what has always never been but the having been of what is always yet to come. Within the imagination, therefore, we find the possibility of affirming the heterogeneity of the homogeneity of the hermeneutic condition, the uncovering of the singularity within that which repeats, the novelty within reiteration, the reoccurrence of the unvarying in which the unvarying is nothing but the reoccurrence of variation. Expressed in a different conceptual idiom, the task of the imagination is to make a presence of an absence by fabricating the image that is a mixture of being and nonbeing.[206] The temporal moment to which that spatial hiatus relates is the present as the recognition of the future remembered in the anticipation of the reproduction of the past.

In a relatively lengthy diary entry from June 17, 1918, Scholem precociously pontificated on the nature of Judaism and time. Although many of the themes discussed in this excursus were later cultivated by Scholem, especially in conjunction with his understanding of kabbalistic symbolism, I have chosen to focus on this text because of its speculative nature unencumbered by the historiographical concerns that eventually came to dominate his phenomenological approach.

> As a religious category, Time becomes the eternal present [*ewige Gegenwart*]. This can be explicated using some related examples. The notion of God correlates to the idea of the messianic realm. God is 'ehje asher 'ehje —"I will be who I will be" [*ich werde sein, der ich sein werde*]. What does this mean? In Hebrew *'ehje* means both the present ("I am") and the future. For God, Time is always in the future. Hebrew has no other means to express the concept of the eternal present than by making the future permanent.[207]

Scholem supports his contention with a citation from Hermann Cohen's *Der Begriff der Religion im System der Philosophie* to the effect that in the future, the meaning of the present will be given and the difference between the two will be reduced, insofar as the present and the future will be bound together in God's being (*Gegenwart und Zukunft werden in diesem Sein Gottes verbunden*).[208] From Cohen's reflections, Scholem educes the following conception of the divine:

> God's true name is thus the Self of Time [*Gottes wahrer Name ist also das Ich der Zeit*]. His name means: "The Divine, which is the eternal present (the foundation [*Grund*], and at the same time the expansion [*Ergänzung*]) of all empirical time, for through all generations God *was* what he will become [*denn was Gott sein wird, das* war *er durch alle Geschlechter*]." The designation of the present [*die Bezeichnung der Gegenwart*] expresses this central point better than the future because the actual unreality [*die reale Unwirklichkeit*] of the present—which only has being as a *source* [*die ja Sein nur als* Ursprung *hat*] . . . from whose nothingness eternal Time distends as the empirical future [*aus deren Nichts die ewige Zeit hervorquillt als empirische Zukunft*]—makes it suitable to express what we intend to say here. This notion of Time corresponds to the messianic realm. . . . The messianic realm is the present of history [*die Gegenwart der Geschichte*]. The prophets could speak about this idea only hypothetically by using the image of the future. . . . The kingdom of God is the *present*, for it is the origin [*Ursprung*] and the end [*Ende*]. It has no metaphysical future. The God who "will be" demands from Time that it "will be." But just as God *is*, so *is* Time. . . . God has no Existence; he has only Being [*Gott hat kein Dasein, nur Sein*]. Being represents itself.[209]

It is instructive that the Neokantian perspective of Cohen yields in Scholem's mind a theological conception of messianic temporality that is consonant with the perspective that he eventually associated with the kabbalah and that, in my judgment, accords as well with Heidegger, and this despite the latter's well-known critique of Neokantianism.[210] The most tangible instantiation of time is the eternal present, which is identified further as the true meaning of the divine name—the reference more specifically is to *ehyeh asher ehyeh*, I shall be as I shall be—since of God it must be said that he always was what he would become, that is, past and future are indistinguishable in the essence of the present that is continually fluctuating and therefore eternally immutable. Just as God has no existence (*Dasein*) but only being (*Sein*)—a formulation that Scholem lifts verbatim from Cohen[211]—so the present is characterized by the oxymoron *actually unreal*, which is to say, it has no concrete or definite existence but it is the nothingness whence eternal time extends into the empirical future. To the extent that the future is privileged in this delineation—from the Cohenian perspective, the foundation of time is the anticipation of the future[212]—time is said to correspond to the messianic, an idea developed in Cohen's Jewish writings, including the *Religion der Vernunft aus den Quellen des Judentums*.[213] But on this point Scholem subverts the expected correlation of the eschatological and futurity by arguing that, even though the prophets rhetorically spoke about the messianic realm in the image of the future, in fact, it relates to the present. The kingdom of God is precisely the present that comprises the origin and the end but without a metaphysical future. Implicit here, even though expressed tentatively, is an allusion to the distinction Scholem would later use to describe the messianic idea in Judaism, the tension between the restorative tendency to return to a past imagined to be ideal and the utopian tendency to create the state of things in the future that has never existed.

> Both tendencies are deeply intertwined and yet at the same time of a contradictory nature; the Messianic idea crystallizes only out of the two of them together. Neither is entirely absent in the historical and ideological manifestations of Messianism. . . . There has never been in Judaism a measured harmony between the restorative and the utopian factor. . . . The reason for this is clear: even the restorative force has a utopian factor, and in utopianism restorative factors are at work. The restorative tendency . . . is nourished to no small degree by a utopian impulse which now appears as projection upon the past instead of projection on the future. . . . The completely new order has elements of the completely old, but even this

> old order does not consist of the actual past; rather, it is a past transformed and transfigured in a dream heightened by the rays of utopianism.[214]

Just as Scholem nascently intimated in the earlier meditation, so in the mature reflection, he explicitly rejects the notion that messianism is predicated on the belief in progress. Redemption is not the product of inner historical developments, but rather the effect of transcendence breaking into history and thereby bending the temporal arc so that the future can reclaim the past that is always what is yet to come.[215] Messianic hope thus hinges on the dialectical intertwining and transposability of the restorative and utopian poles.

The idea of time proffered by Scholem is linked, moreover, to the "metaphysics of Hebrew" according to which the presentation of the present is through the future. Scholem offers three examples to illustrate the point. The first is that the language of a command is future oriented but it applies to the present. Concerning the directive "You should be holy" (Leviticus 19:2), Scholem notes, "you should be, meaning both that you will be and that you are. You *are* holy because I am holy. *Only* this is the meaning of the command to spread holiness into the present moment."[216] The second example is the *waw ha-hippukh* of a narrative; that is, the consecutive or conversive *waw*, the prefix that converts the perfect tense of the predicate into the imperfect tense, as in the case of *we-hayah*, which can mean "and it was" in the past or "and it shall be" in the future. Simply put, if the *waw* of reversal is placed before a verb in the past, the word gets a futuristic meaning, but if it is placed before a verb in the future, the meaning changes into the past. From the relatively simply grammatical rule, Scholem deduces an intricate philosophical assumption about the messianic potential of temporal reversibility: "*Time is transformed through fusion* [In der Verbindung verwandeln sich die Zeiten]: the past is in the future and the future is in the past [*Vergangenheit in Zukunft und Zukunft in Vergangenheit*]. How does this happen? Through the vehicle of the present [*Im Medium der Gegenwart*]. The Time of the *waw ha-hippukh* is the messianic Time."[217] The messianic is not about the appearance of the radically novel diremptively disrupting the flow of time; it is rather the expectation of the unexpected predicated on the repetition of the past in the reversal of the future that both affirms and negates the repetition of the future in the reversal of the past.[218] To dwell within the parameters of that paradox is to bear the hope of the hopelessness of waiting for what already and always is manifest as nonmanifest. The name of God is what "guarantees the metaphysical possibilities of this grammatical construction" because that name signifies that "what can happen again has happened,"[219] but in such a way that, as we saw with respect to Heidegger, the *again* is *altogether otherwise*.[220] Scholem cites another example of the *waw ha-hippukh* to substantiate his claim, the frequently used expression *wa-yelekh*,[221] which denotes that one has left (*er ging*) so that one will go (*wird gehen*). Summarizing the discussion, Scholem writes, "The *Essence* [Wesen] inherent in this construction (as Husserl says) enables the construction. This essence is God's time [*die Zeit Gottes*], which is the present. The past and the future can be transformed through the present because they are equivalent."[222] This leads to Scholem's third example, a command uttered with a *waw ha-hippukh* is "spoken out in the *past*, as an obligatory past." The point is illustrated by *we-ahavta* (Leviticus 19:18, 34; Deuteronomy 6:5, 11:1), "You shall love, which is a command that can only be made because you have already loved [*Du* sollst *lieben, das ist nur möglich, dir zu befehlen, weil du geliebt hast*]." The ostensibly innocuous grammatical principle yields a weighty truth about the intonation of time in Judaism: "The most overpowering thing of all is when the messianic realm makes an appearance in language because messianic beams of light elevate the past. Only a *Jewish* language is capable of such a construction."[223]

We can excuse the ethnocentric pride displayed by Scholem's youthful exuberance, but it is incorrect to limit this notion of the paradoxical nature of the messianic present as the commingling of past and future to Judaism. For our purposes, it is incumbent to recall Heidegger's assertion in the 1936 lectures on *Schelling: Vom Wesen der menschlichen Freiheit* about the becoming of God and the relationship between what conventional thinking mistakenly considers the antinomy between the movement of time and the stillness of eternity:

> We are accustomed not only to "measure" every process and all becoming guided by time, but to follow it this way in general. But the becoming of the God as ground to the God himself as existing [*Das Werden des Gottes als Grund zum Gott selbst als Existierendem*] cannot be represented as "temporal" in the everyday sense. Thus, one is accustomed to attribute eternity to the Being of God. But what does "eternity" mean and how is it to be comprehended in a concept? God's becoming cannot be serialized in individual segments in the succession of ordinary "time." Rather, in this becoming everything "is" "simultaneous" ["*gleichzeitig*"]. But simultaneous does not mean here that past and future give up their nature and turn "into" the pure present. On the contrary, original simul-taneity [*Gleich-Zeitigkeit*] consists in the fact that being past [*Gewesensein*] and being future [*Künftigsein*] assert themselves and mingle with each other together with being present [*Gegenwärtigsein*] as the essential fullness of time itself [*die Wesensfülle der Zeit selbst*]. And this mingling of *true temporality* [eigentlichen Zeitlichkeit], this Moment [*Augenblick*], "is" the essence of eternity [*das Wesen der Ewigkeit*], but not the present which has merely stopped and remains that way, the *nunc stans*. Eternity can only be thought truly, that is, poetically, if we understand it as the most primordial temporality [*ursprünglichste Zeitlichkeit*], but never in the manner of common sense which says to itself: Eternity, that is the opposite of temporality. Thus, in order to understand eternity, all time must be abstracted in thought. What remains in this procedure is not, however, a concept of eternity, but simply a misunderstood and half-baked concept of an illusory time.[224]

Heidegger sets out to explain the paradox that emerges from Schelling's idea of the being of God consisting of "a becoming to himself out of himself,"[225] a paradox that bears an extraordinary conceptual affinity to kabbalistic theosophy, especially as it was articulated in the name of Luria. The Schellingian idea, as I discussed in chapter 3, collapses the prevailing metaphysical binary insofar as the being of God is understood as a process of becoming. But how are we to understand this paradox from a temporal standpoint? Rejecting the metaphysical understanding of eternity as completely pure of any admixture of temporal concepts, Schelling insists that "true eternity does not exclude all time [*all Zeit ausschließt*] but rather contains time (eternal time) subjugated within itself [*selbst sich unterworfen*]. Actual eternity is the overcoming of time [*Ueberwindung der Zeit*], as the richly meaningful Hebrew language expresses 'victory' (which it posits among the first attributes of God) and 'eternity' with a single word (*naezach*)."[226] Conspicuously, Schelling corroborates his understanding of eternal time (*die ewige Zeit*) by noting that the Hebrew word *neṣaḥ* means both victory and eternity. That he had in mind, more specifically, the kabbalistic application of that term is evident from his reference that it denotes one of the first attributes of God (*den ersten Eigenschaften Gottes*).[227]

Heidegger is correct to note, therefore, that, for Schelling, eternity is not in opposition to time; it is rather "the inexhaustible fullness of temporality" (*der unerschöpflichen Fülle der Zeitlichkeit*) realized in the moment characterized by the simultaneity of past, present, and future,[228] a theme that only enhances the kabbalistic connection of which Heidegger was apparently unaware. The contemporaneity of the state of "at once" (*Zumal*) should not be understood as "the contraction of the succession of ordinary time into a 'now' magnified to giant proportions," but rather as the coalescing of the three tenses in the equiprimordiality that is indicative of an original temporality.[229] Commenting on the statement in *Sein und Zeit*, "The now is not pregnant with the not-yet-now, but rather the present arises from the future in the primordial, ecstatic unity of the temporalizing of temporality,"[230] Heidegger remarked in an accompanying note: "We do not need to discuss in detail the fact that the traditional concept of eternity in the significance of the 'standing now' (*nunc stans*) is drawn from the vulgar understanding of time and defined in orientation toward the idea of 'constant' objective presence. If the eternity of *God* could be philosophically 'constructed,' it could be understood only as more primordial and 'infinite' temporality. Whether or not the *via negationis et eminentiae* could offer a possible way remains an open question."[231]

Heidegger is critical of the theological concept of eternity as the *nunc stans* because he assumes it implies a presence that is devoid of movement. A more nuanced approach, however, would indicate that his own idea of eternity as the true temporality—another point of affiliation with Rosenzweig, as we saw in chapter 1—is closer to his medieval predecessors, and especially Eckhart's idea of the eternal now (*nû in êwicheit*) or the essential now (*wesenlîchen nû*), which is the fullness of time (*vüllede der zît*),[232] as well as the reverberation of this mystical sensibility in the poetic aphorism of Silesius "Die Zeit ist Ewigkeit," wherein time is identified as eternity and eternity as time.[233] Analogously, the eternality of the kabbalistic *Ein Sof* is not the absence but the fullness of time expressed in the nondenumerable and durationless moment—the circle that has no beginning or end and therefore must be entirely present[234]—wherein all three temporal modes are contemporaneously entwined in a copresence that disrupts their specificity as discrete and successive intervals on the timeline.

Notes

1. Landauer, *Revolution*, p. 103.

2. See the text of Jameson cited in Wolfson, *Alef*, p. 47. For an in-depth analysis of the relation of time and space, see Protevi, *Time and Exteriority*.

3. Scholem, "Franz Rosenzweig," p. 35. See Wilensky, "Relations," pp. 368–69; Idel, *Old Worlds*, p. 288n24.

4. Ibn Laṭif, *Rav Pe'alim*, sec. 39, 14a; Kasher, "Isaac Ibn Laṭif's Book," p. 27. Wilensky, "Relations," p. 370, suggests that the temporal nature of kabbalistic thought relates to the fact that this wisdom is transmitted orally from master to disciple, a dialogical process that unfurls in time. Ibn Laṭif's theory of temporality has been discussed by several other scholars: Schechterman, "Studies," pp. 107–13; Esudri, "Studies," pp. 208–14; and compare my own reflections in Wolfson, *Dream*, pp. 360–62n37. See the more extensive exploration of this theme by my student González Diéguez, "Isaac ibn Laṭif," pp. 239–325. The chapter begins with the aforementioned passage from *Rav Pe'alim*. In addition, she cites this text on p. 221 in support of her claim that Ibn Laṭif integrates the messianic age "in a temporal scheme of cosmic cycles which he derives from esoteric exegesis of the Bible" (p. 220). This theme is discussed in greater detail on pp. 262–318. I have offered a different explanation of this passage. The temporal implications of Ibn Laṭif's theory of cosmic cycles have also been explored by Wilensky, "Messianism," pp. 221–37; Pedaya, *Naḥmanides*, pp. 22–23, 216–17. Both Wilensky and Pedaya suggest that, with regard to this matter, Ibn Laṭif may have been influenced by Ismāʿīlī theology. For fuller treatment of this topic, see Wilensky, "'First Created Being,'" pp. 272–76 (English translation in *Jewish Intellectual History in the Middle Ages*, pp. 72–74); and see also the wide-ranging study by Krinis, "Cyclical Time." Ibn Laṭif is mentioned only once by Krinis (p. 32), but his analysis opens up many vistas for future exploration of the idea of cosmic cycles appropriated by some kabbalists, a dimension of their conception of temporality that I have not explored. I propose, however, that the hermeneutical dynamic of linear circularity would seem to be operative in this doctrine as well, but the matter requires a separate analysis.

5. Wolfson, "Retroactive Not Yet," pp. 16–30.

6. Husserl, *On the Phenomenology*, pp. 386–87.

7. Plaisance, "Occult Spheres," p. 391.

8. See Ergas, *Shomer Emunim*, 2:17, p. 106.

9. Heidegger, *Ponderings II–VI*, p. 14; *Überlegungen II–VI*, p. 18.

10. Heidegger, *Contributions*, §238, p. 293; *Beiträge*, p. 371.

11. Heidegger, *Contributions*, §239, p. 294; *Beiträge*, p. 372.

12. Heidegger, *Contributions*, §191, p. 247; *Beiträge*, p. 312.

13. Heidegger, *Contributions*, §240, p. 297; *Beiträge*, p. 376.

14. Heidegger, *Contributions*, §242, p. 302; *Beiträge*, p. 383.

15. Heidegger, *Contributions*, §242, p. 299; *Beiträge*, p. 379.

16. Heidegger, *Contributions*, §241, p. 298; *Beiträge*, p. 377.

17. Heidegger, *Contributions*, §242, p. 300 (emphasis in original); *Beiträge*, pp. 379–80.

18. Heidegger, *Contributions*, §242, p. 300; *Beiträge*, p. 380.

19. Heidegger, *Contributions*, §242, p. 301; *Beiträge*, p. 381.

20. Heidegger, *Contributions*, §242, p. 302; *Beiträge*, p. 382.

21. Heidegger, *Ponderings II–VI*, p. 39; *Überlegungen II–VI*, p. 51.

22. Theodor and Albeck, eds., *Bere'shit Rabba*, 3:7, p. 23. See Wolfson, *Alef*, pp. 62, 73, 77–79, 84–88, 94, 109, 111, 217nn108 and 111, 220n151, 222nn178 and 180, 230n283.

23. Eliashiv, *Leshem Shevo we-Aḥlamah: Sefer ha-De'ah*, pt. 2, p. 107.

24. Theodor and Albeck, eds., *Bere'shit Rabba*, 1:4, p. 6.

25. Theodor and Albeck, eds., *Bere'shit Rabba*, 8:2, p. 57. According to another rabbinic dictum, the Torah rested 974 generations in the bosom of God prior to the creation of the world. See Schechter, ed., *Avot de Rabbi Natan*, version A, ch. 31, p. 91, translated in Wolfson, *Language*, p. 550n76. This tradition should be contrasted with the mythologoumenon preserved in several rabbinic sources, including Babylonian Talmud, Ḥagigah 13b–14a, to the effect that God envisaged creating a thousand generations of human beings before the giving of the Torah (based on Psalms 105:8), but because of their wickedness, 974 generations were not created (deduced exegetically from Job 22:16) and the Torah was revealed 26 generations after Adam. Even though it is stated that the generations were not created, the continuation of the talmudic text identifies them with the insolent souls implanted in each generation. Compare Theodor and Albeck, eds., *Bere'shit Rabba*, 28:4, pp. 262–63; Buber, ed., *Midrash Tehillim*, 90:13, 196b; Abrams, *Book Bahir*, sec. 135, p. 219; *Tiqqunei Zohar*, sec. 69, 103a; Moses ben Jacob, *Shoshan Sodot*, pp. 247–48; Eliashiv, *Leshem Shevo we-Aḥlamah: Haqdamot u-She'arim*, p. 183; Eliashiv, *Leshem Shevo we-Aḥlamah: Sefer ha-De'ah*, pt. 1, p. 5; pt. 2, p. 29. Some kabbalists linked the secret meaning of these generations to the primal forces of evil or the worlds created and destroyed, which is further identified in the Lurianic sources as the shattered vessels. See Abulafia, *Sha'ar ha-Razim*, pp. 59–60; Abulafia, *Oṣar ha-Kavod*, 40a; *Ma'arekhet ha-Elohut*, ch. 8, p. 206; Saruq, *Limmudei Aṣilut*, 16a–c; Bachrach, *Emeq ha-Melekh*, 8:30, pp. 207–8; Wildmann, *Afiqei Yam*, pp. 17–18. According to other sources, these generations are identified as the souls that emerged from the world of chaos. See Elijah ben Solomon, *Commentary of the Gaon*, p. 26; Eibeschütz, *Tif'eret Yehonatan*, 145d (ad Deuteronomy 32:4); Wildmann, *Pitḥei She'arim*, pt. 2, 63a; Wildmann, *Beit Olamim*, 97a; Eliashiv, *Leshem Shevo we-Aḥlamah: Sefer ha-De'ah*, pt. 1, pp. 221–22.

26. On time as the conjunction of masculine mercy and feminine judgment, see Wolfson, *Alef*, pp. 79, 91, 98; Wolfson, "Retroactive Not Yet," pp. 42–44. According to some kabbalists, the pulse of time seems to be related to the throbbing of the divine phallus, but according to other kabbalists, time is associated with the feminine *Shekhinah*—particularly the words *et*, *zeman*, and *zo't*—although in some passages, even this association is linked to the heteroerotic coupling of the female and the male, as in the expression *itto de-ṣaddiq*, the moment that belongs to the righteous one. See *Zohar* 3:58a; *Tiqqunei Zohar*, sec. 6, 21a (in that context, *itto de-ṣaddiq* is identified more specifically as the night of Sabbath, commonly held by kabbalists to be the time of the *hieros gamos*), sec. 21, 43a, and sec. 69, 101b; Gikatilla, *Sha'arei Orah*, 1:134–35; Ibn Gabbai, *Avodat ha-Qodesh*, 2:18, p. 135; *Ḥemdat ha-Yamim al Shabbat Qodesh*, p. 266; Horowitz, *Shenei Luḥot ha-Berit*, 1:64; Katz, *Berit Kehunat Olam*, p. 325; Elijah ben Solomon, *Tiqqunei Zohar im Be'ur ha-Gra*, 44a; Wolfson, *Alef*, pp. 88, 100, 104–6, 227n245; Wolfson, "*Imago Templi*," pp. 127–32. Independently, and utilizing a different methodological apparatus, Pedaya, "Divinity as Place and Time," discusses the manner in which the divine is described in terms of the concepts of time and space in kabbalistic sources. Although her primary emphasis is on the spiritualization of the holy place, Pedaya does emphasize the concurrence of the spatial and the temporal such that we have the "ability to feel place as time, or to feel time as place," and this is particularly relevant to the state of redemption (p. 101). For another approach to the issue of time, especially as it relates to the construction of the feminine imaginaire, see Roi, *Love of the Shekhina*, pp. 38–39, 201, 228–29, 320.

27. The perspective of kabbalah on time and eternity is interpreted this way by Baader, *Elementarbegriffe über die Zeit*, pp. 35–36. More specifically, Baader introduces the kabbalistic idea of the four worlds that issue from the Absolute (*Ein Sof*)—emanation (*aṣilut*), or the archetypal world (*mundum archetypum*); creation (*beri'ah*), or the angelic world (*mundum angelicum*); formation (*yeṣirah*), or the sidereal world (*mundum sidereum*); and doing (*asiyyah*), or the elementary world (*mundum elementarem*)—to illustrate the philosophic principle that the eternal can bring forth only another being that is eternal, and hence the temporal creation of the material universe cannot be affirmed as the original or unmediated production of God. Even though the archetypal world comprises all the *sefirot*, depicted Platonically as the "ideals of perfection" (*Ideals die Vollendung*)—Baader goes so far as to assume that Plato's theory of the Ideas is based on the kabbalah—it is identified more specifically with the *Shekhinah*, which is associated in turn with

humanity, the creation that appears last, in accord with the traditional proverb, *Finis coronat opus*, "The end crowns the work." According to Baader, the structure of the four worlds enunciated by kabbalists is instructive of the tenet that he claimed was ignored by the contemporary philosophers who presumed that the temporal could come forth from the eternal. I would argue, however, that the sharp distinction Baader makes between the eternal and the temporal indicates that he did not grasp the subtlety of the kabbalistic teaching on this matter. On Baader's conception of time, see Schumacher, *Begriff der Zeit*. The author mentions the influence of kabbalah on Baader (pp. 81n9, 103–4, 252), but he makes no effort to relate this influence to the main subject of his analysis. For Heidegger's analysis of Baader's negotiation with the topic of time, see Heidegger, *Zollikoner Seminare*, pp. 335–37.

28. Manchester, *Syntax of Time*, pp. 107–8.

29. Ibid., p. 108. The view I have attributed to the kabbalists resembles the argument that has been made with respect to the depiction of eternity as a multitemporality in Spinoza's thought by Morfino, *Plural Temporality*, pp. 148–52, esp. 149: "By making God the immanent rather than the transcendent cause of the world, and by making the will an effect rather than a cause, Spinoza made the temporality of the *res extensa* the only temporality, no longer anchored even to the isomorphism of geometric space, since what we are witness to in Spinoza—far from a mathematisation of being, as one school of criticism would have it—is a historicisation (or politicisation) of physics. Both the temporal continuity of the moments and the discontinuity of a moment with respect to the time-line are based on the transcendence of the divine will: the continuous creation cuts matter into contemporaneous sections, subjugating their plurality to the decision of the divine will (whether it decides in favour of continuity or discontinuity). All this in Spinoza leaves room for a theory of multitemporality, in which the infinite multiplicity of the durations is not liable to totalisation, because eternity cannot be the result of the sum of the durations, hence, an indefinite duration. The concept of *connexio* compels us toward a more radical conception, to conceive of durations as the effects of endless encounters between rhythms. This means that starting from the knowledge of an existing duration, we can access knowledge of the existing durations that exist in relation to it (connected to it), both in the abstract and inadequate form of time—which renders a particular rhythm into an absolute, making it the measure of all the others—as well as in the form of eternity, an adequate conception of the relational nature of time as a complex connection of durations." In my assessment, the eternality of the kabbalistic infinite likewise implies the relational nature of time as the finite interweaving of multiple temporalities. Also noteworthy is the observation of Negri, *Savage Anomaly*, pp. 174–75: "Then, corporeality is raised to the level of eternity: This is not given in the form of determinate existence, but again in the form of the force of attraction exercised on existence toward essence, toward intelligence. . . . Next, the same dimension of the divinity is led back to the dimension of surfaces; God and eternity are placed on the very level of the body." Negri's perspective on Spinoza is summarized on p. 190: "The constitution of reality, in its force and in its dynamic, comprehends time as a dimension implicit to reality. Duration and eternity are based on free necessity." And see ibid., pp. 181–82: "The analytic of time, in the Spinoza of the *Ethics*, is rooted in the paradox presence-eternity, and it is not articulated to the same degree as is the ontological thematic of space. Certainly, it would be possible to begin a reconstruction of an analytic of time in analogy to that of space. That would give us a conception of time as the principal limit of the problem of freedom. . . . But it would be vague, generic. . . . The thematic of real time, then, will be addressed by the critique. But time overturns metaphysics. The metaphysics of time is the destruction of metaphysics. An ontology of time brings the object of analysis down from the horizon of speculation to the horizon of practice." Negri promotes a constitutive praxis as a philosophy of the future linked to what he calls the Spinozian disutopia (pp. 217–23), but this is a matter that is outside the purview of this study.

30. The intent of the passage is made clearer in the version extant in MS London, British Library Or. 1055, fol. 135a: "The eighth question [concerns] one asking when these *sefirot* were, whether proximate to the creation of the world [*im qarov li-veri'at ha-olam*] or whether from of old [that is, from eternity] prior to the world having been created [*im me-az ṭerem nivra ha-olam*]. The response: some of the *sefirot* were in potentiality in the *Ein Sof* prior to their being actualized like the first one, which is *Maḥashavah*, and the second, which is *Ḥokhmah*, is of old [*me-az*]. And some of them are in the sensible [*ba-murgash*] and some of them in the natural [*ba-muṭba*], which are necessary for this world, and there are those that emanated with them in proximity to the creation of the world. And since the potency of one is in the other, in the coming into being of the first two *sefirot*, the

potency of the concealed and the intelligible [*koaḥ ne'lam u-muskal*], that is, the concealed potency is the *Keter Elyon* and the intelligible is what is called the potency of *Ḥokhmah*, their existence is sufficient [*maspiq*] for the subsequent ones."

31. Preserved in some manuscripts, for example, MS Palatina Library, Parma 2784, fol. 19a, is the variant *ḥissaron ha-da'at*, the "deficiency of knowledge." The alternate reading is noted in the edition of Azriel's text, *Perush Eser Sefirot*, p. 5.

32. Azriel of Gerona, *Be'ur Eser Sefirot*, p. 86.

33. Ibid., p. 87.

34. See Böwering, "Ibn al-'Arabī's Concept of Time." See also Wolfson, *Alef*, pp. 71, 102–3, 214n93, 215nn97–98; Coates, *Ibn 'Arabi and Modern Thought*, pp. 81–88. Chittick, *Sufi Path of Knowledge*, p. 395n7, mentions the ḥadith that "God is time" and chronicles its impact on Ibn al-'Arabi's view that the multiplicity of properties experienced in the cosmos—the self-disclosure of the being that remains veiled and unnamed—derive from the diversity of divine names, which are expressions of the beginningless and endless day that is God's time.

35. A classical formulation of the *nunc stans* is found in the description of the Intellect by Plotinus, *Enneads*, 5.1.4, p. 23: "For around Soul things come one after another . . . but Intellect is all things. It has therefore everything at rest in the same place, and it only is, and its 'is' is for ever, and there is no place for the future for then too it is—or for the past—for nothing there has passed away—but all things remain stationary for ever, since they are the same." The depiction of eternity as the ubiquitous present that has no past or future is developed at greater length in Plotinus, *Enneads*, 3.7.3. See also Plotinus, *Enneads*, 4.3.25, p. 113: "We must certainly not attribute memory to God, or real Being or Intellect; for nothing [external] comes to them and there is no time, but eternity in which real being is, and there is neither before nor after, but it is always as it is, in the same state not admitting of any change." The Plotinian passages are based on Plato, *Timaeus* 37e4–38a1, which is itself an elaboration of the account of being in Parmenides. See Freeman, *Ancilla*, p. 43: "Being has no coming-into-being and no destruction. . . . And it never Was, nor Will Be, because it Is now, a Whole all together, One, continuous." For the Greek text and alternate English rendering, see Coxon, *Fragments of Parmenides*, pp. 64–67.

36. See ch. 3 n. 176.

37. Ergas, *Shomer Emunim*, 2:17, pp. 107–8. Ergas unequivocally denies the attribution of time to *Ein Sof* prior to creation, and he even argues that the sefirotic emanations are above time (*zeman*) and the temporal order (*seder zemannim*), but he does attribute to them a duration (*meshekh*) that is like the eternal present that has no past or future.

38. I have here repeated my argument in Wolfson, *Alef*, p. 166. We can elucidate the kabbalistic understanding of the present—the diremptive interval of time that incarnates the eternal nothingness of infinity in a seemingly interminable thread of moments identically different because differently identical—by considering the critique of the Bergsonian model of time as the sheer continuous duration offered by Bachelard, *Intuition of the Instant*, pp. 25–26: "The reason why our opponents posit an endless division of time is that they initially frame their analysis at the level of an entire life summed up by the curve of the élan vital. Since from a macroscopic perspective we live what appears to be an unbroken or continuous duration, a close examination of details would induce us, in their view, to appreciate duration in ever-smaller fractions than our initially chosen units. But the problem would change meaning if we considered the actual construction of time starting from instants, instead of its artificial division starting from duration. We would then see that time multiplies itself following the schema of numerical correspondences, far from dividing itself according to the fragmentation schema of some continuum. . . . For the purposes of analysis, our opponents start from the numerator, which they take to be a homogeneous, continuous quantity, and above all an immediately given quantity. . . . We start from the denominator, on the other hand, as mark of the phenomenon's wealth of instants and our basis for comparison. . . . But again, if we are willing to meditate by going from the phenomenon rich in instants to the phenomenon poor in instants—i.e., from denominator to numerator, and not the reverse—we will realize that we can get along not only without words that evoke the idea of duration (a mere verbal feat), but even without the idea of duration itself, all of which proves that duration could at best play the role of servant in the domain where she used to rule as mistress. . . . Let us suppose the macroscopic phenomenon can be depicted by this first line of dots. . . . We place these dots without regard for the interval separating them, since it is not from the interval, in our view, that duration derives its sense or its schema. For us the continuous interval is nothingness; and nothingness has no more 'length' than it has duration." Bachelard's advocacy for a temporal synchronism based on the continuity of discontinuity is a useful conceptual model to assess the kabbalistic understanding of time

as the eternal unfolding of the temporal eternality of the infinite.

39. See Manchester, *Syntax of Time*, p. 71. Commenting on the Neoplatonic idea of the present, especially in Iamblichus, Manchester writes, "For presence is just as much a feature of the time-metaxy, the 'in-between' in its timelikeness and not in suspension thereof, as it is of the singular Now. As disclosure space, time is the 'metaxy' in which being has its becoming and becoming its being." As the author notes, he is influenced by the idea of metaxy developed by Voegelin, *Anamnesis*. The "experience of being," writes Voegelin, "does not occur in world time from whose perspective the experience of eternity is hard to comprehend; instead it is allowed to take place where it is experienced, in the 'in-between,' the *metaxy* of Plato, which is neither time nor eternity. The tension of being itself, its genesis, exegesis, and interpretation, its ordering effect, its disintegration, and so on, are in fact experienced as a process. But this process occurs in the *metaxy*. . . . To this end let us recall once more that, in the philosophical experience of the tensions between the poles of time and eternity, neither does eternal being become an object in time, nor is temporal being transposed into eternity. We remain in the 'in-between,' in a temporal flow of experience in which eternity is nevertheless present. This flow cannot be dissected into a past, a present, and a future of world-time, for at every point of the flow there persists the tension toward eternal being transcending time. The concept most suitable to express the presence of eternal being in the temporal flow is *flowing presence*" (p. 329, emphasis in original). See my own analysis of Voegelin's reflections on time and the Platonic idea of *metaxy* in Wolfson, *Alef*, p. 57. The view of Voegelin is close to what I have elicited from kabbalistic sources, but there is a crucial difference. In my opinion, we can elicit from the kabbalah an idea of the in-between in which the eternal being is temporalized and the temporal object is eternalized. The tension between the poles of eternity and time is thus resolved in the juxtaposition of opposites that are identical in their opposition. Let me note finally that a similar view may be adduced from Nishida's understanding of the stuff of time being constituted by the confrontation of the past and the future as the unity of opposites in the present. As such, time exhibits a unity in contradiction as it moves endlessly from the formed of the past that has not yet passed to the forming of the future that is manifest as that which is yet to come. See Nishida, *Intelligibility and the Philosophy of Nothingness*, pp. 164–66: "Time is, in the end, neither to be thought from the past, nor from the future. If the present is regarded merely as the moment, as a point on a continuous straight line, then there is no present whatever, and, consequently, no time at all. . . . Time consists essentially in the present coexistence of moments. By saying this I mean that time, as the one of the many as well as the many of the one, consists in the contradictory unity of the present. . . . Touching eternity in a moment of time, the Now, means nothing else than this: that the moment, in becoming a 'true' moment, becomes one of the individual many, which is to say, the moment of the eternal present which is the unity of opposites. Seen from the other side, this means nothing else than that time is constituted as the self-determination of the eternal now. The fact that in the present the past has passed and not yet passed, and the future has not yet come and yet shows itself, means not only, as it is thought in abstract logic, that the past is connected with the future, or becomes one with it; it also means that they become one, by negating each other, and the point, where future and past, negating each other, are one, is the present. Past and future are confronting each other, as the dialectical unity of the present. Just because they are the unity of opposites, past and future are never connected, and there is an eternal movement from the past into the future." See Nishida, *Ontology of Production*, p. 72: "What is thus conceived is the temporal as the linear determination or continuity's determination of the mediation of the continuity of discontinuity. As I said earlier, time must be both linear and circular. So the circular, as the ground of objective time, must be spatial. It may seem absurd, but contradictorily, objective time or true time can be conceived starting from the fact that the instants that can never return are arrayed simultaneously. . . . To speak of time in terms of the self-determination of the mediation of the continuity of discontinuity (temporally speaking) or as the self-determination of the eternal now, each instant, instant by instant, must be thought as an infinite linear progression without regress." Ibid., p. 83: "The self-determination of the world of the eternal now, in which instants are simultaneous, the world of space-qua-time and time-qua-space, must at its core mean reflecting the self within the self." On the self-determination of the singularity of the eternal now as the affirmation of absolute negation, the absolute interruption or rupture between the past that has already passed and the future that has not yet come, see ibid, pp. 99–101, 113–17, 121–28, 136, 145, 158, 164–66, and the passages from Nishida, *Place and Dialectic*, cited in ch. 2 n. 176. Nishida's position is summarized in *Place and Dialectic*, p. 164: "The historical present

refers to the *basho* wherein we can conceive the infinite past and future to be simultaneously existent. We ought to regard what has been determined as actual to be what has been determined by means of the relationship of synchronic existence between past and future, that is, the spatial relationship among the temporal. This is why I speak of the self-determination of the eternal now and say that the present determines itself. . . . We ought to regard the historical present as the self-determination of the eternal now. Therein the temporal is spatial and the spatial is temporal. It is a self-contradictory world as the self-identity of absolute opposites." The full paradox espoused by Nishida is such that the eternal present is permanently stationary and yet constantly in flux, and hence the world is both always changing and changeless. See Nishida, *Place and Dialectic*, p. 109. On Nishida's concept of the temporal flow of consciousness and the eternal present as the flash of timelessness concurrently within and beyond time, see Heisig, *Philosophers of Nothingness*, pp. 51, 58–59, 63; Carter, *Nothingness*, pp. 87–88; Suares, *Kyoto School's Takeover*, pp. 53–54. See also Wargo, *Logic of Nothingness*, pp. 138–40.

40. The source for the image of the Edomite kings is Genesis 36:31–39. See *Zohar* 2:108b, 176b (*Sifra di-Ṣeni'uta*), 3:128b (*Idra Rabba*), 142a (*Idra Rabba*), 292a (*Idra Zuṭa*). See ch. 4 n. 204 and below n. 187.

41. Theodor and Albeck, eds., *Bere'shit Rabba*, 3:7, p. 23, 9:2, p. 68. See *Zohar* 2:34b; Tishby, *Wisdom of the Zohar*, pp. 276, 289, 458; Wolfson, "Light through Darkness," p. 81, and other scholars cited there in nn. 30–31.

42. Scholem, *Major Trends*, pp. 263–64; Scholem, *On the Mystical Shape*, pp. 82–87; Tishby, *Doctrine of Evil*, pp. 21–61.

43. Heidegger, *Being and Time*, §8, p. 37; *Sein und Zeit*, p. 39.

44. Elliott, *Phenomenology and Imagination*, p. 109. On Heidegger's argument in *Sein und Zeit* that Dasein's spatiality is grounded in its temporality, see Protevi, *Time and Exteriority*, pp. 144–45, and for a critique of the Aristotelian subordination of time to space implied in the spatial representation of the temporal, see ibid., pp. 153–82.

45. Heidegger, *Phenomenological Interpretation of Kant's Critique*, p. 107 (emphasis in original); *Phänomenologische Interpretation von Kants Kritik*, pp. 155–56.

46. Heidegger, *Phenomenological Interpretation of Kant's Critique*, p. 231; *Phänomenologische Interpretation von Kants Kritik*, p. 340. See Elliott, *Phenomenology and Imagination*, pp. 114–17.

47. Heidegger, *Phenomenological Interpretation of Kant's Critique*, pp. 231–32 (emphasis in original); *Phänomenologische Interpretation von Kants Kritik*, pp. 341–42.

48. Heidegger, *Phenomenological Interpretation of Kant's Critique*, p. 232 (emphasis in original); *Phänomenologische Interpretation von Kants Kritik*, p. 342. Compare the comment on Kant's conception of time as the unchangeable and permanent substratum of all appearances in Heidegger, *What Is a Thing?*, p. 231 (*Frage nach dem Ding*, p. 233): "In each now time is the same now [*In jedem Jetzt ist die Zeit dasselbe Jetzt*]; time is constantly itself [*sie ist ständig sie selbst*]. Time is that enduring [*Beharrliche*] which always is. Time is pure remaining [*reine Bleiben*], and only insofar as it remains are succession [*Nacheinander*] and alteration [*Wechsel*] possible. Although time has a now-character in each now, each now is unrepeatably this single now, and different from every other now." See the passage cited below at n. 66.

49. Heidegger, *Phenomenological Interpretation of Kant's Critique*, p. 246 (emphasis in original); *Phänomenologische Interpretation von Kants Kritik*, p. 364.

50. Heidegger, *Phenomenological Interpretation of Kant's Critique*, p. 247 (emphasis in original); *Phänomenologische Interpretation von Kants Kritik*, p. 365.

51. Heidegger, *Phenomenological Interpretation of Kant's Critique*, p. 247 (emphasis in original); *Phänomenologische Interpretation von Kants Kritik*, p. 365.

52. Heidegger, *Phenomenological Interpretation of Kant's Critique*, p. 249; *Phänomenologische Interpretation von Kants Kritik*, p. 368.

53. See discussion of this issue in Larrabee, "Time and Spatial Models."

54. The affinity between Einstein's space-time field and Heidegger's four-dimensional *Zeit-Raum* is noted by O'Leary, "Theological Resonances," p. 214.

55. Balashov, "Persistence," pp. 31–35; Camilleri, *Brief History*, pp. 68–72.

56. Heidegger, "Zeitbegriff in der Geschichtswissenschaft," reprinted in Heidegger, *Frühe Schriften*, pp. 415–33. An English version was published as "Concept of Time," in the *Journal of the British Society for Phenomenology* 9 (1978), and reprinted with some revisions in Kisiel and Sheehan, eds., *Becoming Heidegger*, pp. 60–72.

57. Kisiel and Sheehan, eds., *Becoming Heidegger*, p. 66.

58. Ibid., p. 67 (emphasis in original).

59. Heidegger, *Hölderlin's Hymn "The Ister,"* p. 44; *Hölderlins Hymne "Der Ister,"* p. 53.

60. On Heidegger and quantum physics, see Pylkkö, *Aconceptual Mind*, pp. 60–61.

61. Heidegger, *Being and Time*, §5, p. 18 (*Sein und Zeit*, pp. 18–19): "'Time' has long served as the ontological—or rather ontic—criterion for naïvely distinguishing the different regions of beings. . . . 'Temporal' ['*Zeitlich*'] here means as much as being 'in time' ['*in der Zeit' seiend*]. . . . The fact remains that time in the sense of 'being in time' ['*in der Zeit sein*'] serves as a criterion for separating the regions of being. . . . In contrast we must show, on the basis of the question of the meaning of being . . . *that—and in what way—the central range of problems of all ontology is rooted in the phenomenon of time correctly viewed and correctly explained.* If being is to be conceived in terms of time, and if the various modes and derivatives of being in their modifications and derivations are in fact to become intelligible through a consideration of time, then being itself—and not only beings that are 'in time'—is made visible in its 'temporal' character [*in seinem 'zeitlichen' Charakter sichtbar gemacht*]. But then 'temporal' can no longer mean only 'being in time' ['*in der Zeit seiend*']. The 'atemporal' ['*Unzeitliche*'] and the 'supratemporal' ['*Überzeitliche*'] are also 'temporal' with respect to their being. . . . [W]e shall call the original determination of the meaning of being and its characters and modes which devolve from time its *temporal* determination [temporale *Bestimmtheit*]. The fundamental ontological task of the interpretation of being as such thus includes the elaboration of the *temporality of being* [Temporalität des Seins]" (emphasis in original).

62. Heidegger, *Logic: The Question*, p. 169 (emphasis in original); *Logik: Die Frage*, p. 199.

63. Heidegger, *Logic: The Question*, p. 173; *Logik: Die Frage*, p. 205. On the twofold nature of the measuring and the self-measured measure (*messenden und selbst gemessenen Maß*) connected to the future time disclosed through the poetic word, see Heidegger, *Zu Hölderlin*, p. 38.

64. Heidegger, *Logic: The Question*, p. 330; *Logik: Die Frage*, p. 400.

65. Heidegger, *Logic: The Question*, p. 331; *Logik: Die Frage*, p. 400.

66. Heidegger, *Logic: The Question*, pp. 331–32 (emphasis in original); *Logik: Die Frage*, pp. 400–2. Compare Heidegger, *Being and Time*, §6, p. 24; *Sein und Zeit*, p. 25.

67. Heidegger, *Basic Problems*, pp. 247–48 (emphasis in original); *Grundprobleme*, pp. 350–51. The crucial passage on the paradoxical nature of the now as always the same in virtue of its connectivity and always different in virtue of its divisibility appears in Aristotle's *Physics* 222a10–20, in *Complete Works of Aristotle*, 1:375–76: "The 'now' is the link of time . . . (for it connects past and future time), and it is a limit of time (for it is the beginning of the one and the end of the other). But this is not obvious as it is with the point, which is fixed. It divides potentially, and in so far as it is dividing the 'now' is always different, but in so far as it connects it is always the same, as it is with mathematical lines. For the intellect it is not always one and the same point, since it is other and other when one divides the line; but in so far as it is one, it is the same in every respect. So the 'now' also is in one way a potential dividing of time, in another the termination of both parts, and their unity. And the dividing and the uniting are the same thing and in the same reference, but in essence they are not the same." In the final analysis, Aristotle concludes that "time is not composed of indivisible nows any more than any other magnitude is composed of indivisibles" (*Physics* 239b8–9, in *Complete Works*, 1:404). See also the passage about Kant's notion of time cited above, n. 48. For a comparison of the Aristotelian and Kantian perspectives, see Pinosio, *Logic of Kant's Temporal Continuum*, pp. 19–23.

68. Heidegger, *On the Way to Language*, p. 174; *Unterwegs zur Sprache*, p. 50.

69. Heidegger, *On the Way to Language*, p. 176; *Unterwegs zur Sprache*, p. 53.

70. See reference in ch. 1 n. 44.

71. Heidegger, *Logic: The Question*, p. 173; *Logik: Die Frage*, p. 204.

72. Heidegger, *Basic Problems*, pp. 274–76; *Grundprobleme*, pp. 389–91.

73. See the analysis in Derrida, *Animal That Therefore I Am*, pp. 90–92. For a similar theme in Rosenzweig's view of time, see Wolfson, *Giving*, pp. 43–44. And compare Frey, *Interruptions*, p. 24: "The arbitrariness of beginning and end, which are impossible to keep a watch on from the inside of the whole, is the whole's crumbling away at the edges."

74. Heidegger, *Being and Time*, §68, p. 334 (emphasis in original); *Sein und Zeit*, p. 350. Compare Heidegger, *Metaphysical Foundations*, p. 211 (*Metaphysische Anfangsgründe*, p. 273): "Temporality temporalizes itself primarily out of the future. This means that the ecstatic whole of temporality, and hence the unity of horizon, is determined primarily out of the future."

75. Heidegger, *Parmenides*, p. 138; *Parmenides* [GA 54], p. 205.

76. Heidegger, *Being and Time*, §83, p. 415 (emphasis in original); *Sein und Zeit*, p. 437.

77. Heidegger, *On Time and Being*, introduction, p. viii.

78. Heidegger, *Being and Time*, §65, p. 314 (emphasis in original); *Sein und Zeit*, p. 329.

79. Heidegger, *Being and Time*, §41, p. 185; *Sein und Zeit*, pp. 191–92.

80. Heidegger, *Concept of Time* (McNeill trans.), pp. 13–14 (emphasis in original).

81. Heidegger, *Being and Time*, §50, p. 241; *Sein und Zeit*, pp. 250–51.

82. Heidegger, *Being and Time*, §65, p. 311; *Sein und Zeit*, p. 326.

83. Heidegger, *Being and Time*, §65, pp. 312–13 (emphasis in original); *Sein und Zeit*, p. 327. Compare Heidegger, *Basic Problems*, pp. 265–68; *Grundprobleme*, pp. 374–79.

84. Heidegger, *Being and Time*, §65, p. 314; *Sein und Zeit*, p. 329.

85. Heidegger, *Fundamental Concepts*, p. 145 (emphasis in original); *Grundbegriffe*, p. 218.

86. Wood, *Deconstruction of Time*, pp. 224–25.

87. Heidegger, *On Time and Being*, p. 6; *Zur Sache des Denkens*, p. 10. See the analysis in Gonzalez, *Plato and Heidegger*, pp. 293–343.

88. Heidegger, *On Time and Being*, pp. 11–12; *Zur Sache des Denkens*, p. 16. Compare the discussion of being as presence (*Anwesenheit*) or presenting (*Präsenz*), making-present (*Gegenwärtigen*), and the uncoveredness (truth) or presence-now (*Gegenwart*) of something present as modes of time in Heidegger, *Logic: The Question*, pp. 161–63; *Logik: Die Frage*, pp. 191–93.

89. Heidegger, *On Time and Being*, p. 12; *Zur Sache des Denkens*, p. 17.

90. Heidegger, *On Time and Being*, p. 13; *Zur Sache des Denkens*, p. 18.

91. Heidegger, *On Time and Being*, p. 14; *Zur Sache des Denkens*, p. 18.

92. Compare the passage from Heidegger, *Identity and Difference*, cited herein in the introduction, n. 111.

93. Heidegger, *On Time and Being*, p. 14; *Zur Sache des Denkens*, p. 19.

94. Heidegger, *Contributions*, §239, p. 294; *Beiträge*, p. 372.

95. Heidegger, *Contributions*, §239, p. 296; *Beiträge*, p. 375.

96. Heidegger, *Contributions*, §242, p. 299; *Beiträge*, p. 379.

97. Heidegger, *Contributions*, §95, pp. 148–49 (emphasis in original); *Beiträge*, p. 189.

98. Heidegger, *Contributions*, §239, p. 296; *Beiträge*, p. 375.

99. Heidegger, *Contributions*, §51, p. 86; *Beiträge*, p. 108.

100. Heidegger, *Contributions*, §32, p. 56 (emphasis in original); *Beiträge*, p. 69.

101. Heidegger, *Contributions*, §239, p. 296; *Beiträge*, p. 374.

102. Heidegger, *Contributions*, §240, p. 297; *Beiträge*, p. 376.

103. Schürmann, *Broken Hegemonies*, p. 581 (emphasis in original).

104. See Wolfson, *Alef*, pp. 44–46. Backman, *Complicated Presence*, p. 195, notes that *Zeit-Spiel-Raum* is "Heidegger's new formulation of what in fundamental ontology was called the temporality (*Temporalität*) of being. It is the dimensionality that configures the 'instantaneous site' (*Augenblicksstätte*) in which the presence . . . of a being can take place." On Heidegger's privileging temporal becoming in his understanding of being, and this despite his efforts to think the nature of being and Dasein from the perspective of time and space, see Rae, *Ontology in Heidegger and Deleuze*, pp. 34–35.

105. Heidegger, *Contributions*, §98, p. 150; *Beiträge*, p. 192.

106. Heidegger, *Contributions*, §239, p. 296; *Beiträge*, p. 375.

107. Heidegger, *Contributions*, § 242, p. 303; *Beiträge*, p. 384.

108. Heidegger, *Contributions*, §254, p. 321; *Beiträge*, p. 405.

109. Heidegger, *Contributions*, §98, pp. 150–51 (emphasis in original); *Beiträge*, p. 192. See Vallega-Neu, *Heidegger's Poietic Writings*, p. 37: "The clearing of time-space is a temporalizing and spatializing *at once*" (emphasis in original).

110. Heidegger, *Contributions*, §98, p. 151 (emphasis in original); *Beiträge*, p. 192.

111. Heidegger, *Contributions*, §125, pp. 190–91; *Beiträge*, p. 242.

112. Heidegger, *Contributions*, §125, p. 191; *Beiträge*, p. 242.

113. Heidegger, *On the Way to Language*, p. 106; *Unterwegs zur Sprache*, pp. 201–2.

114. Heidegger, *Pathmarks*, p. 92; *Wegmarken*, p. 117.

115. Heidegger, *Contributions*, §245, p. 309; *Beiträge*, p. 391.

116. Heidegger, *On Time and Being*, p. 14; *Zur Sache des Denkens*, p. 19.

117. Heidegger, *On Time and Being*, p. 15; *Zur Sache des Denkens*, p. 19.

118. Heidegger, *On Time and Being*, pp. 15–16 (emphasis in original); *Zur Sache des Denkens*, p. 20. See the analysis in Sikka, *Forms of Transcendence*, pp. 177–79.

119. Heidegger, *Contributions*, §120, p. 186; *Beiträge*, p. 235.

120. Heidegger, *Contributions*, §120, p. 186; *Beiträge*, pp. 235–36.

121. Heidegger, *Contributions*, §120, p. 186; *Beiträge*, p. 236.

122. Heidegger, *Contributions*, §120, p. 186; *Beiträge*, p. 236.

123. Heidegger, *Contributions*, §120, p. 187 (emphasis in original); *Beiträge*, p. 237.

124. Eliashiv, *Leshem Shevo we-Aḥlamah: Sefer ha-De'ah*, pt. 1, p. 222.

125. Ricchi, *Yosher Levav*, p. 10.

126. Heidegger, *Ponderings II–VI*, p. 29 (emphasis in original); *Überlegungen II–VI*, p. 38. The thematic nexus between divine withholding, expressed figuratively as the inhaling of the breath, and the transition from eternality (*le-olam*) to temporality (*le-ittim*), is already implied in a passage in *Sefer ha-Bahir*. See the Heideggerian analysis of this text in Wolfson, *Alef*, pp. 126–33.

127. Heidegger, *Contributions*, §146, p. 211 (emphasis in original); *Beiträge*, p. 268.

128. See discussion in ch. 1 at nn. 127–32.

129. Heidegger, *Contributions*, §146, p. 211; *Beiträge*, p. 268.

130. Heidegger, *Contributions*, §221, p. 273; *Beiträge*, p. 346.

131. Heidegger, *Pathmarks*, p. 254; *Wegmarken*, p. 334.

132. Heidegger, *Ponderings II–VI*, p. 59; *Überlegungen II–VI*, p. 78.

133. Derrida, *Margins of Philosophy*, pp. 23–24.

134. Cordovero, *Zohar im Perush Or Yaqar*, 6:20. On the categorical denial of the attribution of temporality to the divine, see the comments of Horowitz, *Shenei Luḥot ha-Berit*, 1:263.

135. Viṭal, *Eṣ Ḥayyim*, 1:1, 11b. Compare Viṭal, *Sha'ar ha-Haqdamot*, pp. 31–32.

136. The passage is translated in ch. 5 at n. 136.

137. Scholem, *Lurianic Kabbalah*, p. 256.

138. See ch. 3 n. 57.

139. Ergas, *Shomer Emunim*, 2:17, pp. 106–7.

140. Ibid., p. 107. It is noteworthy that the disruption of the linear sequence in the kabbalistic understanding of temporality is in accord with the findings of contemporary physics on the nature of the passage of time. See the concise and straightforward articulation of this point in Rovelli, *Order of Time*, p. 21: "The difference between past and future, between cause and effect, between memory and hope, between regret and intention . . . in the elementary laws that describe the mechanisms of the world, there is no such difference." In somewhat more technical terms, Rovelli notes, pp. 24–25, that there is only one law of physics that is still predicated on a distinction between past and future, one equation that renders absurd the backward projection of a sequence of events, viz., the law of thermal agitation, which dictates that heat can pass from a hot body to a cold one but never from a cold body to a hot one, the basis for the concept of entropy, introduced by Rudolf Clausius, and later formulated as the second principle of thermodynamics. From this we can generalize that "the arrow of time appears *only* where there is heat. The link between time and heat is therefore fundamental: every time a difference is manifested between the past and the future, heat is involved. . . . Only where there is heat is there a distinction between past and future. Thoughts, for instance, unfold from the past to the future, not vice-versa—and, in fact, thinking produces heat in our heads" (emphasis in original). See the passage cited in ch. 2 n. 170, and Rovelli, *Reality*, pp. 249–52. The quantitative metrics notwithstanding, I am not convinced that thinking uniformly displays the quality of unfolding from past to future; it is entirely possible that within the domain of the mind the process equally unfolds from future to past.

141. *Exodus Rabbah* 3:6.

142. Moses ben Naḥman, *Perushei ha-Torah*, 1:292 (ad Exodus 3:13).

143. Plotinus, *Enneads*, 3.7.3; Augustine, *Confessions*, 11:11, pp. 228–29, 11:13, p. 230; Arendt, *Life of the Mind*, 2:12; Arendt, *Love and Saint Augustine*, pp. 15–16. On eternity and time in Plotinus and Augustine, compare Manchester, *Temporality and Trinity*, pp. 69–93. For discussion of this theme in Boethius, see Leftow, *Time and Eternity*, pp. 112–46. Arendt's own contribution was to localize the thinking ego in the *nunc stans*, the space between past and future, drawing into its own presence the twofold absence of no more and not yet. See Arendt, *Life of the Mind*, 2:36, and analysis in Bowen-Moore, *Hannah Arendt's Philosophy*, pp. 96–100; Calcagno, "Role of Forgetting." For a comparison of Benjamin's *Jetztzeit* and Arendt's *nunc stans*, see Kattago, *Memory and Representation*, pp. 117–20.

144. See ch. 3 n. 159. In line with the Aristotelian perspective, Maimonides maintains that time is an accident consequent to motion, which can be applied only to a body, and thus it follows that the being to which no motion can be found does not fall under time. Since the first cause is neither a body nor a force in a body, it is not subject to movement or to time. See Maimonides, *Guide of the Perplexed*, 2:introduction, p. 237; 2:1, p. 246.

145. See above, n. 35, and compare Adamson, "Eternity in Medieval Philosophy." As Adamson shows through close textual analysis, in some of the pertinent sources of the Arabic Plotinus, God is above eternity and time, the former associated with the

intellect, whereas other sources more emphatically attribute eternity to God.

146. Arendt, *Between Past and Future*, p. 13.

147. See description of Hegel's view in Arendt, *Life of the Mind*, 2:43–44.

148. Shneur Zalman of Liadi, *Liqquṭei Amarim: Tanya*, Sha'ar ha-Yiḥud we-ha-Emunah, ch. 7, 82a. Regarding this theme in Ḥabad thought, see Wolfson, *Open Secret*, pp. 62, 279, 325n168, 396nn65–66; Wolfson, "Achronic Time," p. 51. See also the extensive analysis in Tworek, "Time in the Teachings of Rabbi Shneur Zalman of Liadi." Needless to say, the discussion of this matter in Ḥabad literature is complex and thus cannot be adequately addressed in this context. However, I will cite one passage in which the paradoxical perspective is encapsulated in a philosophically poignant way. See Schneersohn, *Be-Sha' ah she-Hiqdimu 5672*, 1:343, "*Adam Qadmon* is the aspect of the intermediary between the light of infinity and the worlds. The matter of the intermediary is in two ways. The first is that it is intermediary between the two gradations within it, the internal aspect [*beḥinah penimit*] of *Adam Qadmon* and the external [*we-ḥiṣonit*] of *Adam Qadmon*, for the internal aspect that is within it is the beginning of the line [*re'shit ha-qaw*] in the pattern of *Attiq*. Even though this is the aspect of the inner light [*or penimi*], nevertheless it is in the aspect of complete separation [*havdalah legamrei*] from the worlds. And the external aspect of *Adam Qadmon* is the aspect of the universal [*kelal*] in relation to the worlds. The second is that it is an intermediary in the matter of being [*be-inyan ha-hithawwut*], for the being of the worlds is in the aspect of the universal and the particular [*kelal u-feraṭ*]. The aspect of *Adam Qadmon* is the aspect of the universal of the worlds [*beḥinat ha-kelal shel ha-olamot*]; that is, it is not only the beginning of being [*re'shit ha-hithawwut*], which is the beginning of existence [*re'shit ha-meṣi'ut*], but it is the aspect of the universal that comprises all that will come to be afterward. Yet, everything is comprised in it but not at all in the aspect of existence, and with respect to this it is the aspect of the intermediary. This can be clarified from the matter of time, for all that comes to be is under time, but in *Adam Qadmon* there is no aspect of time since there is no aspect of existence in it. Even so, it is not entirely above time insofar as it is still an aspect of a single thought [*maḥashavah aḥat*], whence it follows that it is in the aspect of time but not in the aspect of time [*bi-veḥinat zeman we-lo bi-veḥinat zeman*]. Thus, it is an intermediary between the light of infinity, which is entirely above the demarcation of time, and the coming to be of the worlds in the aspect of the temporal orders and time [*seder zemannim u-zeman*]." Ostensibly, a crucial distinction is drawn between the light of infinity and the configuration of the primordial Adam. Whereas the former is entirely transcendent to time, the latter bears the paradox of being concomitantly in time and yet not in time. The dialetheic logic at play here, however, pushes thinking to the point that the statement that *Ein Sof* is entirely above time does not imply a state of timelessness, an eternality devoid of time, as the notion of eternity itself can be applied only to that which falls under the category of time; consequently, eternity is marked by the aspect of *Malkhut* and the compresence of the three temporal ecstasies, which signifies the time above time, the time that has no boundary. Compare Schneersohn, *Be-Sha'ah she-Hiqdimu 5672*, 3:1345: "It is not appropriate to speak about the matter of eternality [*inyan ha-niṣḥiyyut*] with regard to the matter that is entirely above time since it is not at all within the parameters of time [*be-geder ha-zeman*]; it is possible to speak of the matter of eternality only in the matter of time, for the temporal is the aspect of boundary and it is possible to say with respect to it that it is without boundary and thus the time will never cease . . . and this is the aspect of the kingship of the name [*malkhut de-shem*], which is the matter of time, he reigned, he reigns, and he will reign, the past, the present, and the future . . . and when the light of infinity illumines the aspect of kingship, then the time of kingship will be in the aspect of eternality. . . . From the perspective of the illumination of the light of infinity, which is above time, time extends continuously and does not cease. . . . Similarly, by means of the disclosure of the light of infinity in the aspect of the time of kingship, time is in the aspect of eternality that does not ever terminate, and this is the matter of the unity of the blessed holy One and the *Shekhinah*, that is, the unity of *YHWH* and *Elohim*. *YHWH* is above time and *Elohim* is the aspect of time, and the unity of *YHWH* and *Elohim* entails that the aspect that is above time radiates until time is also eternal and does not ever cease. Indeed, the truth of the matter of the unity of *YHWH* and *Elohim* is that *Elohim* will be like *YHWH* in actuality, and thus time itself will be above time [*she-ha-zeman aṣmo yihyeh lema'lah me-ha-zeman*]." See Schneersohn, *Yom Ṭov shel Rosh Hashanah 5666*, p. 301: "Accordingly, we find in the Torah that it is written 'There never arose in Israel another prophet like Moses' [*we-lo qam navi od be-yisra'el ke-mosheh*] (Deuteronomy 34:10). At first blush, it should have said 'there never will arise' [*we-lo yaqum*], in the future tense, so why does it say 'there never arose' [*we-lo qam*], which implies the past tense,

when the intent was that none would similarly arise in the future? Rather, it is because the Torah illumines [the aspect] above time wherein past and future are both as one. And this is the matter of the aspect of Israel, which is the disclosure of the name *YHWH*. It is understood that this is also the unity of *YHWH* and *Elohim* . . . and even though there is here place and time, the place and time, however, do not constrict or conceal at all. This is the unity of *YHWH* and *Elohim* from above to below; that is, the disclosure of the name *YHWH* glows in the name *Elohim* in actuality, and the name *Elohim* does not conceal or hide at all." The correlation of the Tetragrammaton and the aspect beyond time indicates that eternity is characterized by the compresence of the three temporal modes implied by this name. The interpretation of the Tetragrammaton as signifying the temporal eternality of *Ein Sof* is repeated by many other Ḥasidic masters. For instance, see Jacob Joseph of Polonnoye, *Toledot Ya'aqov Yosef*, 2c, 62b, 64b, 84c, 116b, 125c, 194b. See also Twersky, *Yesamaḥ Lev*, printed together with *Me'or Einayim*, pp. 567–68: "As it is written in the holy *Zohar*, 'when it arose in his will to create the world,' in his will precisely, from him and within him [*minneih u-veih*], without any arousal from below, verily in his will. For the beginning of the arising of thought that arose in his incomposite will to create the world was verily from him. And all of this is because the creator, blessed be he, was [*hayah*], is [*howeh*], and will be [*we-yihyeh*] in a single occurrence as one [*be-fa'am aḥat ke-eḥad*], since he is not in time [*she-eino bi-zeman*] as he transcends temporality [*lema'lah mi-zemanniyyut*]. Time is created by the creator and thus in relation to him the past, present, and future are one." Compare Twersky, *Me'or Einayim*, pp. 213–14: "It is known that the Torah consists of the names of the blessed holy One, and God, blessed be he, was, is, and will be, living and persisting eternally, and similarly is the Torah . . . and certainly, in each moment and time [*be-khol et u-zeman*], the Torah is garbed [*mitlabbeshet*] in accord with the needs of the moment and the time." On this quality of time in Ḥasidism (typified by a text by Menaḥem Mendel of Vitebsk) and its possible source in the thought of Judah Halevi, see Wolfson, *Giving*, pp. 321–22n178. For discussion of the topic of eternity and time in the Ḥasidic view of the divine, including citation of some of the passages I have mentioned, see Mayse, "Reflection."

149. I have taken the liberty to offer here a slightly revised version of my observation in Wolfson, *Alef*, p. 107. See ibid., pp. 74- 77, 93, 108–10.

150. Cordovero, *Pardes Rimmonim*, 3:1, p. 25. See ibid., 4:8, pp. 52–53. In *Tiqqunei Zohar*, sec. 19, 40b, the name mentioned in the dictum of *Pirqei Rabbi Eliezer* is decoded as a reference to *Keter*.

151. Cordovero, *Pardes Rimmonim*, 5:4, p. 64.

152. Cordovero, *Pardes Rimmonim*, 3:1, p. 25. The interpretation rejected by Cordovero is affirmed by other kabbalists. See Moses ben Jacob, *Shoshan Sodot*, p. 174; Ibn Gabbai, *Avodat ha-Qodesh*, 1:2, p. 2.

153. Viṭal, *Eṣ Ḥayyim*, 42:1, 89b–c. To be more precise, two gradations are ascribed to the aspect that is designated as *malkhut she-be-malkhut*, the lower one that receives everything from above in the manner of *Malkhut* and the higher one that overflows to that which is below in the manner of *Keter*, the intermediary between the infinite and the emanations. Compare Saruq, *Limmudei Aṣilut*, 24a–b.

154. Delmedigo, *Novelot Ḥokhmah*, 151b.

155. Liebes, *On Sabbateanism*, pp. 308–9n71.

156. Wildmann, *Pitḥei She'arim*, 4a. See, however, Luzzatto, *Qelaḥ Pitḥei Ḥokhmah*, pp. 68–69: "The disclosure that remains after the withdrawal—everything is called as the kingship of the infinite, blessed be he [*kemo malkhut ein sof barukh hu*]. . . . Therefore, this revealed light is called *malkhut*, and it is said that it is like the final part of all that has been withdrawn . . . and thus it is called the trace [*reshimu*] of all that has been withdrawn. . . . And this is the limited way [*derekh ha-mugbal*] that was contained within the infinite, blessed be he." In this respect, the trace is identified as the "place for all that exists," the vacuum (*ḥalal*) that is devoid of the light of the infinite (p. 66).

157. Graf, *Wayaqhel Moshe*, pp. 38–39.

158. Ibn Gabbai, *Avodat ha-Qodesh*, 1:2, p. 2. The same explanation is offered in Ibn Gabbai, *Derekh Emunah*, pp. 23–24, but in that context, it is emphasized that the entire emanation was comprised in potentiality within the name that is *Keter* or the primordial ether. Compare Ibn Gabbai, *Avodat ha-Qodesh*, 1:4, p. 8; 1:14, p. 37 (the name symbolizes all of the emanation that was hidden in the concealment of the infinite).

159. Ibn Zimra, *Magen David*, p. 54.

160. Graf, *Wayaqhel Moshe*, p. 40. Although viewed by some of his contemporaries as championing a radical interpretation of the Lurianic theosophy, a similar approach predicated on the attribution of limit to the limitless—concretized in the image of the contraction of the light by which the namelessness of the secret of the infinite (*raza de-ein sof*) became manifest through the name—was upheld by the Sabbatian thinker Neḥemiah Ḥiya Ḥayon. See the technical analysis in Fischheimer, "'Anyone Who Looks at the Brass Serpent Shall Survive,'" pp. 245–57.

I will not list previous scholarship on this topic as it is amply noted by Fischheimer.

161. Eliashiv, *Leshem Shevo we-Aḥlamah: Ḥeleq ha-Be'urim*, pt. 1, p. 20. Compare Eliashiv, *Leshem Shevo we-Aḥlamah: Haqdamot u-She'arim*, pp. 91–92, 128–29.

162. Wolfson, "Divine Suffering," p. 156n128; Wolfson, *Language*, pp. 77, 458n241. In some sources, it appears that *yesod* of the female refers to the vaginal opening. See Sharabi, *Reḥovot ha-Nahar*, 40b: "The foundation of the feminine is the opening [*ha-yesod shel nuqba hu petaḥ*]."

163. Eliashiv, *Leshem Shevo we-Aḥlamah: Sefer ha-De'ah*, pt. 2, p. 109.

164. Ibid., pt. 2, p. 46.

165. Eliashiv, *Leshem Shevo we-Aḥlamah: Haqdamot u-She'arim*, p. 121. I hope to write a separate study on Eliashiv's conception of time and the historical epochs, but let me state briefly that, in line with the rabbinic tradition, he maintains that the current world order consists of six millennia to be followed by the seventh, the day that is entirely Sabbath or the messianic era, and then the world to come, which comprises the eighth to the tenth millennia. Compare Eliashiv, *Leshem Shevo we-Aḥlamah: Haqdamot u-She'arim*, pp. 179–80, 199. The tenth millennium is the culmination of the apocatastasis, which is described as the return of all things to the kingship of the infinite (*malkhut de-ein sof*) or to the encompassing light of the infinite (*or ein sof ha-maqqif*). See Eliashiv, *Leshem Shevo we-Aḥlamah: Sefer ha-De'ah*, pt. 1, pp. 141–42.

166. Eliashiv, *Leshem Shevo we-Aḥlamah: Sefer ha-De'ah*, pt. 2, p. 46.

167. Ibid. On the hermeneutical basis in Jewish sources for the description of the moment as the site of genuine iteration—instantiating the paradox of being always different because always the same and always the same because always different—see Wolfson, *Alef*, pp. 59–87.

168. Eliashiv, *Leshem Shevo we-Aḥlamah: Haqdamot u-She'arim*, p. 121.

169. Wolfson, "Not Yet Now," pp. 128–42.

170. A previous attempt to compare and contrast the notion of futurity in Heidegger and the biblical conception based on the epiphany of the divine name revealed to Moses in Exodus 3 is offered by Motzkin, "'Ehyeh' and the Future." By comparing Heidegger's conception of the future to the biblical text, Motzkin sets out to highlight the simplicity of the former, although he admits that the complexity of the latter is revealed through the temporal categories and distinctions elaborated in *Sein und Zeit* (p. 174). The doubling of absence and presence that the author discerns in the scriptural narrative with respect to a future that is spoken of but has not yet taken place can be applied in some measure to Heidegger's idea of the future as well (p. 175). I concur with Motzkin's conclusion about the biblical text: "God in this passage in Exodus is also only transcendent within a world, but this transcendence is not marked, as it is for Cohen, by solipsism, or for Heidegger, by finitude. God's transcendence is not out of the world, but in the world, because God is the transcendent principle of becoming and therefore His future is always a future-with rather than an act of individuation. For our Greco-Western tradition, becoming has been viewed as the principle of immanence, and transcendence as signifying a transcendent eternity or being. Here in this text, however, the reverse is true. The principle of becoming is transcendent, and the state of being is immanent within that transcendence. Hence the principle of becoming is in productive tension with time as projection" (p. 182). I am not convinced, however, that Heidegger integrated projection and generation in a way that is at odds with the perspective implied in the theophany to Moses. Leaving that aside, Motzkin's focus is exclusively on the scriptural text, whereas I am concerned with the kabbalistic interpretations thereof, which reverberate more deeply with Heidegger's thinking. For a decidedly different approach regarding Heidegger's inability to consider the futurity of being as it relates to the Tetragrammaton and the name *Ehyeh*, see di Cesare, *Heidegger e gli ebrei*, pp. 268–70 (di Cesare, *Heidegger and the Jews*, pp. 238–39).

171. Wolfson, *Dream*, p. 242.

172. Fagenblat, "The Thing," p. 23, noted the nexus between the Jewish tradition on the compresence of the three temporal tenses in the Tetragrammaton and the Heideggerian notion of the equiprimordiality of the three ecstases of time.

173. Literally, "rides," *rakhiv*. I have rendered the term in accord with its figurative meaning, which is based on the comment of Maimonides, *Guide of the Perplexed*, 1:70, p. 171, that the word *rakhov* "is used figuratively to designate domination over a thing, for a rider dominates over and rules that which he rides." This holds the key to understanding his interpretation of Ezekiel's vision of the chariot (*merkavah*), that is, it provides in poetic form the metaphysical principles that explain divine governance in the natural world.

174. *Tiqqunei Zohar*, sec. 70, 122b.

175. Babylonian Talmud, Berakhot 9b.

176. For the description of *Ehyeh* as signifying the nondifferentiated unity of all things, see *Zohar* 3:65a.

177. Goetschel, "'Ehyeh Asher Ehyeh.'" For other relevant sources, see Ben-Shachar and Weiss,

"Anonymous Geronese Kabbalistic Commentary," p. 166n46.

178. Compare the text, attributed to Azriel of Gerona, in Scholem, "Traditions," p. 231. Interpreting Moses's question to God at the epiphany of the burning bush, "And when they will say to me, what is his name [*mah shemo*], what will I say to them?" (Exodus 3:13), the author writes: "He requested to know the essence [*mahuto*] of the name, for he saw that Pharaoh denied the divinity [*kofer ba-elohut*] and said 'I did not know the Lord' (Exodus 5:2). The meaning of 'I did not know' [*lo yada'ti*] is I knew that there is no comprehension of him except by way of negation [*al derekh lo*], that is, the nothing [*ayin*] and the nullity [*afisah*], which cannot be scrutinized. Thus Moses said, 'I must know in order to respond to Pharaoh and to Israel with a clear answer to their question, for if I do not know the essence of the name, I do not have the power to bring them back.' The blessed holy One answered, 'I shall be as I shall be' [*ehyeh asher ehyeh*]—he intimated to him that everything comes from one root, and a sign for this is that the *alef* is a single letter, and from its vocalization it produces the *he*, and the *he* produces through the power of its vocalization the *yod*, and in the concealment of the vocalization of the *yod* there is the *waw*, and in the concealment of the vocalization of the *waw* there is the letter *he*." The letters *ahw"y*, which are described as emerging from the letter *alef*, were referred to in medieval sources as the vowel letters, but since their numerical sum is twenty-two (1 + 5 + 6 + 10), they also represent the Tetragrammaton, which, according to the kabbalists, comprises all twenty-two letters of the Hebrew alphabet.

179. Elijah ben Solomon, *Tiqqunei Zohar im Be'ur ha-Gra*, 141b.

180. For a more extended discussion, see Wolfson, *Dream*, pp. 244–55.

181. See ch. 1 n. 89.

182. See ch. 3 n. 169.

183. *Zohar* 3:65b. I have followed the alternative reading preserved in both of the first editions of the *Zohar*, Mantua (1558–60) and Cremona (1559–60): *kelala be-lo perata*. In the Margaliot text, as in many other editions, the reading is *kelala de-khol perata*, the "generality of every particularity."

184. Compare Cordovero, *Pardes Rimmonim*, 20:2, p. 231.

185. *Zohar* 3:65b. See my previous discussion of this passage in Wolfson, *Dream*, p. 245.

186. See above, n. 25.

187. Eliashiv, *Leshem Shevo we-Aḥlamah: Sefer ha-De'ah*, pt. 1, p. 5. In some contexts, Eliashiv identifies the primordial Edomite kings as the source of all the existents that will come to be in their specificity in all the different worlds (*kol ha-meṣi'uyyot kullam bi-ferațot uvi-peratei perațot asher be-khol ha-olamot kullam*). The paradox of the novel reiteration of time is embraced explicitly: all that was in the past will be in the future in the course of the temporal duration of the being of the world (*kol mah she-hayah attid lihyot be-khol meshekh zeman de-khol qiyyum ha-olam*). See Eliashiv, *Leshem Shevo we-Aḥlamah: Sefer ha-De'ah*, pt. 1, p. 30. The link between the particulars and the Edomite kings is based on the fact that the act of discrimination is a facet of the attribute of judgment, which is connected to the Edomite kings. See the continuation of Eliashiv, *Leshem Shevo we-Aḥlamah: Sefer ha-De'ah*, pt. 1, p. 30: "Since when it was the will of the [infinite], blessed be his name, to create only the roots of all the existence entirely, he emanated only the sovereignties [*malkhuyyot*]. However, each and every king of the seven kings is comprised of many lights, that is, from ten to ten, and from ten to ten, ad infinitum, and everything is only from the aspect of the sovereignties . . . and their dimension was in accord with the measure of all the particular existents [*shi'ur kol peraței ha-meṣi'uyyot*] in the temporal duration of the existence of the world in its entirety." The mathematical formula underlying Eliashiv's comments can be traced to thirteenth-century kabbalistic sources: the first emanation, *Keter*, which is symbolized by the *alef*, contains all ten emanations, and each of the ten comprises all ten, which equals one hundred, and each of those one hundred comprises all ten, and hence we arrive at one thousand, which in Hebrew is *elef*, a word that contains the same consonants as *alef*. From this we can deduce the identity of *alef* and *elef*, which respectively signify generality (*kelalut*) and particularity (*perațut*).

188. On this expression, see my remarks in Wolfson, *Dream*, p. 449n118.

189. *Zohar* 3:11a.

190. Ibid.

191. Menaḥem Mendel of Shklov, *Kitvei ha-Ga'on*, 1:150. The phallocentric nature of this symbolism is made explicit in the continuation of this passage: "And this is the secret of the creation of the world [*beri'at olam*], and the *alef* of the creation of the world is hidden in the safeguarding of the sign of the covenant, and this is the eternal covenant [*berit olam*], for the sign of the covenant is not revealed except by means of the Torah that will come and be revealed from the Tree of Life, and by means of this the name *Ehyeh* instructs that 'I am summoned to be revealed.'"

192. Eliashiv, *Leshem Shevo we-Aḥlamah: Haqdamot u-She'arim*, p. 71.

193. Ibid., p. 34.

194. Arendt, *Thinking*, pp. 387–89.

195. Brann, *World of the Imagination*, pp. 615–16.

196. Ibn Laṭif, *Ṣeror ha-Mor*, p. 155. I have also consulted MS Paris, Bibliothèque Nationale 982, fol. 80b. For a parallel description of time, see Ibn Laṭif, *Perush Megillat Qohelet*, pp. 19–20. In that context, Ibn Laṭif cites the comment of Maimonides, *Guide of the Perplexed*, 1:73, pp. 196–97, that "the cleverest philosophers were confused by the question of time and that some of them did not understand its notion—so that Galen could say that it is a divine thing, the true reality of which cannot be perceived—this applies all the more to those who pay no attention to the nature of anything."

197. Plato, *Sophist* 240b–c, in *Collected Dialogues*, p. 983. See analysis in Brann, *World of the Imagination*, pp. 389–96.

198. Cairns, *Philosophy of Edmund Husserl*, pp. 72–74. For a more detailed analysis of the problem of the present and the metaphysics of presence in Husserlian phenomenology, see Bernet, "Is the Present Ever Present?" and Bernet, "La présence du passé dans l'analyse husserlienne."

199. Brann, *What, Then, Is Time?*, p. xii (emphasis in original).

200. In a related, though somewhat different, terminological index, Henry Corbin educed from the Ṣūfi understanding of the active imagination (*ḥaḍrat al-khayāl*), especially in the mystical theosophy of Ibn 'Arabī, the depiction of the image as the intermediate plane, which is marked by the coincidence of opposites of the infinite and the finite, the intelligible and the sensible. See Corbin, *Creative Imagination*, pp. 218–19, 249, 272–73, and the discussion in Wolfson, "*Imago Templi*," pp. 123–24.

201. Hegel, *Encyclopedia*, p. 142; *Enzyklopädie*, pp. 190–91. See analysis in Brann, *What, Then, Is Time?*, p. 23.

202. Wolfson, *Language*, p. 5.

203. Wolfson, *Alef*, pp. 8–30. Many of my insights in that discussion correspond to the analysis of Ruin, "Time as Ek-stasis."

204. Merleau-Ponty, *Phenomenology of Perception*, pp. 434–35.

205. Brann, *Ways of Naysaying*, p. xii.

206. Ibid.

207. Scholem, *Lamentations*, p. 245; *Tagebücher*, 2:235.

208. Cohen, *Begriff der Religion*, p. 22.

209. Scholem, *Lamentations*, pp. 245–46 (emphasis in original); *Tagebücher*, 2:235–36. I have amended the translation.

210. On Heidegger's reading of Kant as a critique of Neokantian interpretations prevalent in his day, see Bredeson, "Genesis of Heidegger's Reading of Kant," pp. 157, 189–91, 219n340, 232–33, 263–79. For a decidedly more negative and one-sided assessment of Cohen's messianism, see Scholem, *Messianic Idea*, p. 26: "The restorative factors lost their effect to the degree that the national and historical elements of the Messianic idea were superseded by a purely universalistic interpretation. Hermann Cohen, surely as distinguished a representation of the liberal and rationalistic reinterpretation of the Messianic idea in Judaism as one could find, was driven by his religion of reason into becoming a genuine and unhampered utopian who would have liked to liquidate the restorative factor entirely." Compare Scholem, *On the Possibility*, p. 108. See, by contrast, the more positive evaluation of Cohen's messianic utopianism and his interpretation of the ineffable name in Scholem, "Name of God," pp. 67–68. In the letter to Salman Z. Schocken, dated October 29, 1937, outlining his path to the study of kabbalah, Scholem explicitly mentions that Saadia Gaon, Maimonides, and Cohen all annoyed him because their primary effort was to combat myth and pantheism. See Scholem, *On the Possibility*, p. 4. A similar sentiment is expressed by Scholem, *Major Trends*, p. 38. See as well Scholem's disapproving comments (*Major Trends*, p. 36) on Cohen's conviction that evil is nonexistent, a posture that is linked to the presumed philosophical opposition to myth. On Cohen's impact on Scholem's concern for the crisis of Jewish theology in modernity, see Biale, *Gershom Scholem: Kabbalah and Counter-History*, pp. 108–12. For a different perspective on Scholem's relationship to Cohen's rationalism, see Kaufmann, "Imageless Refuge," pp. 148–50, esp. the summation on p. 150: "Benjamin (through the 1920s) and Scholem (for the rest of his life) remained faithful to the transcendence encoded in Cohen's Kantianism. They avoided as best they could all immanence, every threatened collapse into an immediate knowledge of the metaphysical." The influence of Cohen on Scholem's research on kabbalah is noted by Magid, "Gershom Scholem's Ambivalence," p. 247, and in more detail by Weidner, *Gershom Scholem*, pp. 163–64, 198–99, 319–25.

211. Cohen, *Begriff der Religion*, p. 47. For discussion of this passage, see Wolfson, *Giving*, pp. 17–18.

212. Cohen, *Logik der reinen Erkenntnis*, p. 154: "Diese Vorwegnahme ist die eigentliche, die Grundat der Zeit. Die Antizipation ist das Charakteristikum der Zeit."

213. Cohen, *Religion of Reason*, p. 249: "The ideality of the Messiah, his significance as an idea, is shown in the overcoming of the person of the Messiah

and in the dissolution of the personal image in the pure notion of time, in the concept of the *age*. Time becomes future and only future. Past and present submerge in this time of the future" (emphasis in original). For the impact of Cohen on other thinkers, including Bloch and Levinas, see Wolfson, "Not Yet Now," pp. 191–93.

214. Scholem, *Messianic Idea*, pp. 3–4.

215. Ibid., p. 10. For an echo of this reversion in kabbalistic literature, see ibid., p. 23.

216. Scholem, *Lamentations*, p. 246 (emphasis in original); *Tagebücher*, 2:236. For an analysis of this text, see Weidner, *Gershom Scholem*, pp. 219–21.

217. Scholem, *Lamentations*, p. 246 (emphasis in original); *Tagebücher*, 2:237. I have slightly revised the translation. The identification of the time implied by the *waw ha-hippukh* as messianic is repeated by Scholem, "95 Thesen," in *Tagebücher*, 2:305 (no. 83). The text, an obvious allusion to Luther's Ninety-five Theses (1517), is reprinted in Schäfer and Smith, eds., *Gershom Scholem: Zwischen den Disziplinen*, p. 294. Scholem's theses were written in celebration of Benjamin's twenty-sixth birthday and were dated July 15, 1918. See also Scholem, *Lamentations*, p. 254; *Tagebücher*, 2:253.

218. The implications of Scholem's formulation are made explicit by Hamacher, "95 Theses," p. 39 (no. 79): "Does the pull go from the fore-world to the after-world or the reverse? Or, *at the same time*, the reverse? Is not every reversal a repetition? And every repetition an affirmation *and* an erasure of that which is repeated? Does not every repetition come from another future? 'The time of *waw ha-hippukh* is the messianic time' [Scholem, "95 Theses," no. 83]" (emphasis in original). The text is reprinted in Hamacher, *Minima Philologica*, p. 85.

219. Scholem, *Lamentations*, p. 246.

220. Not only was Scholem blind to any similarity between his articulation of the Jewish conception of time and the perspective of Heidegger, but he was overly dismissive of the latter, although admittedly the criticism relates only to an early study by Heidegger. See the entry from November 14, 1916, in Scholem, *Lamentations*, p. 148 (*Tagebücher*, 1:418): "Heidegger's essay on historical time is really quite ridiculous and unphilosophical. Benjamin really got it right with his assessment of it." The reference is to Heidegger's essay "Zeitbegriff in der Geschichtswissenschaft," cited above, n. 56. The criticism of Benjamin to which Scholem alludes is found in a letter to Scholem from November 11, 1916, in Scholem and Adorno, *Correspondence of Walter Benjamin*, p. 82. See Fenves, *Messianic Reduction*, pp. 118–22; and further discussion and reference to other scholarly analyses in Wolfson, "Not Yet Now," pp. 159–60n122.

221. The verb *wa-yelekh* is correct in the original German (*Tagebücher*, 2:237) but incorrect in the English translation, which has the erroneous *wa-halach* (*Lamentations*, p. 246).

222. Scholem, *Lamentations*, pp. 246–47 (emphasis in original); *Tagebücher*, 2:237. The reference to Husserl is noteworthy and demands further research. For Scholem's praise of this philosopher, see the stanza in the poem "Amtliches Lehrgeducht," composed for Benjamin on December 5, 1927, in Scholem, *Fullness of Time*, pp. 74–75: "Wer heilig ist und hochmodern / Zugleich, halt es mit Husserl gern. / Doch hört man ein Gerücht im Land / Daß Heidegger ihn nicht verstand" ("Whoever is ultramodern and ascetic / Will find Husserl most sympathetic. / Though there is a rumor going through the land / He was someone Heidegger could never understand").

223. Scholem, *Lamentations*, p. 247 (emphasis in original); *Tagebücher*, 2:237.

224. Heidegger, *Schelling's Treatise*, p. 113 (emphasis in original); *Schelling: Vom Wesen*, pp. 196–97. I have corrected the translation in light of the orginal German. Compare Heidegger, *Metaphysik des deutschen Idealismus*, p. 85.

225. Heidegger, *Schelling's Treatise*, p. 112; *Schelling: Vom Wesen*, p. 195.

226. Schelling, *Ages of the World (Fragment)*, p. 43; *Weltalter*, in *Sämmtliche Werke*, 8:260. Compare the version of this passage in Schelling, *Weltalter—Fragmente*, 1:233: "Die Ewigkeit ist keine leere, abgezogne Ewigkeit, sondern die die Zeit selbst umterworfen enthält. Wollen wir uns wirkliche Ewigkeit denken, so kön*n*en wir dieß nicht mit gänzlicher Ausschließung aller Zeitbegriffe. Denken wir uns wirkliche Ewigkeit, so denken wir uns auch ein ewig Gewesenes, ein ewig Seyendes, u. eines, das ewig seyn wird . . . Die wahre Ewigkeit ist nicht die, welche die Zeit in diesem Sin*n* ausschließt; wirkliche Ewigkeit ist die die Zeit überwindet: daher die sin*n*volle hebräische Sprache Sieg (den sie unter den ersten Eigenschaften Gottes begreift) und Ewigkeit mit einem Wort (נצח) ausdrückt."

227. In traditional kabbalistic lore, *neṣaḥ* is the name of the seventh of the ten sefirotic emanations. It is possible, however, that Schelling is influenced by the adaptation of this symbolism by Böhme as referring to seven properties (*Eigenschaften*), or seven spirits (*Geister*) or divine forces (*der Göttlichen krefften*), that constitute the eternal nature of God's body. See the sources cited and analyzed in Wolfson, "Holy Cabala," pp. 31–32. In that context, I neglected to mention that the seven vital spirits (*Vital-geister*) of the Böhmean theosophy and the lower seven *sefirot* affirmed by the kabbalists were already compared

by Baader, *Gesammelte Schriften zur philosophischen Anthropologie*, pp. 252–53n6. See also Baader, *Gesammelte Schriften zur Religionsphilosophie*, 1:191–92.

228. Heidegger, *Schelling's Treatise*, p. 114; *Schelling: Vom Wesen*, p. 197. Compare the discussion of the problem of God's self-becoming and the presumed interval between eternality and temporality in Brito, "Création et temps." See also Brito, *La création*, pp. 548–63. The kernel for Schelling's more mature perspective is already attested in his 1794 study on Plato's *Timaeus*. The mimetic relation between eternity and time, epitomized in the statement that time is the image of eternity, is interpreted by Schelling to mean that eternity becomes time when applied to phenomena; the medium that facilitates the contact between the ideal and invisible world and the real and visible world is the representational faculty of the human intellect. The mediation of the intelligent self-activity (*verständige Selbstthätigkeit*) endows the eternal with temporal form and thereby eternalizes the temporal. See Distaso, *Paradox of Existence*, pp. 43–44. The perspectives of Schelling and Heidegger on eternity and time are contrasted by Žižek, *Indivisible Remainder*, pp. 31–32: "However, in contrast to those who emphasize Schelling's affinity with Heidegger's assertion of temporality as the ultimate, unsurpassable horizon of Being, it should be said that nowhere is Schelling farther from Heidegger, from his analytics of finitude, than in his conception of the relationship between time and eternity. For Schelling, eternity is not a modality of time; rather, it is time itself which is a specific mode (or rather, modification) of eternity: Schelling's supreme effort is to '*deduce' time itself from the deadlock of eternity.* The Absolute 'opens up time', it 'represses' the rotary motion into the past, in order to get rid of the antagonism in its heart which threatens to drag it into the abyss of madness. On the other hand—and, again, in clear contrast to Heidegger—freedom for Schelling is the moment of 'eternity in time', the point of groundless decision by means of which a free creature (man) breaks up, suspends, the temporal chain of reasons and, as it were, directly connects with the *Ungrund* of the Absolute. This Schellingian notion of eternity and time—or, to put it in more contemporary terms, of synchrony and diachrony—is therefore to be opposed to the standard notion of time as the finite/distorted reflection of the eternal Order, as well as the modern notion of eternity as a specific mode of temporality: *eternity itself begets time in order to resolve the deadlock it became entangled in*. For that reason, it is deeply misleading and inadequate to speak about eternity's 'fall into time': the 'beginning of time' is, on the contrary, a triumphant ascent, the act of decision/differentiation by means of which the Absolute resolves the agonizing rotary motion of drives, and breaks out of its vicious cycle into temporal succession" (emphasis in original).

229. Heidegger, *Schelling's Treatise*, p. 113; *Schelling: Vom Wesen*, p. 197. See Kisiel, "Schelling's Treatise," p. 291.

230. Heidegger, *Being and Time*, §81, p. 406; *Sein und Zeit*, p. 427.

231. Heidegger, *Being and Time*, §81, p. 406n13 (emphasis in original); *Sein und Zeit*, p. 427n1. Concerning this passage, see Manchester, *Temporality and Trinity*, pp. 57–58.

232. Wolfson, "Patriarchy and Motherhood," pp. 1070–71, and reference to other scholars cited on p. 1070nn87–88. The analogy between Heidegger and Eckhart on this point is made as well by Sikka, *Forms of Transcendence*, pp. 179–80.

233. *Der cherubinische Wandersmann*, 1:47, in Wehr, *Angelus Silesius*, p. 38: "Die Zeit ist Ewigkeit und Ewigkeit wie Zeit, / So du nur selber nicht machst einen Unterscheid."

234. Wildmann, *Beit Olamim*, 97b: "The concealed brain [*moḥa setima'ah*] is the beginning of faith, and the concealed brain entirely is the secret of the ring, which is the perimeter of the providence of the world [*heqqef hanhagat ha-olam*], as they said, 'a sphere that rotates in the world' [Babylonian Talmud, Shabbat 151b], and there is no beginning or end at all because in the concealed brain everything is in the aspect of the present."

7

Disclosive Language

Poiēsis and Apophatic Occlusion of Occlusion

. . . the essential *being* of language cannot be anything linguistic.

Heidegger, "A Dialogue on Language"

The poet, more easily than others, veils the truth in images and presents it that way to the gaze for preservation.

Heidegger, *Contributions to Philosophy (Of the Event)*

I begin this chapter by invoking the distinction that Heidegger makes in *Sein und Zeit* between hearing (*Hören*) and hearkening (*Horchen*). The former is a psychological state of responding to stimuli, the "sensing of tones and the perception of sounds," whereas the latter is the primordial attunement, a mode of being that entails "hearing that understands."[1] Understanding does not come from talking or from listening; on the contrary, the existential possibility of both is grounded in understanding as a mode of attentiveness that is not simply the physical act of perceiving sound. Inverting what is commonly assumed, Heidegger asserts that one does not gain understanding from listening but rather only one who already understands is able to listen.[2] It is interesting to note that, in his private copy of Heidegger's philosophical *magnum opus*, Celan marked this passage with the word "phenomenology," a marginal gloss that suggests that the poet discerned that the acoustic images specified by Heidegger in that context—the creaking wagon, the motorcycle, the marching column, the north wind, the woodpecker tapping, and the crackling fire—provide an elemental path to get back to the things themselves, as Husserl famously defined the phenomenological task.[3]

Poetic Saying and the Sigetic Origin of Language

But even more important was Celan's marginal note to the succeeding passage in *Sein und Zeit*, where Heidegger articulates his notion that listening to the discourse of the other implies that "we can at the same time hear the way in which it is said, the 'diction,' but this, too, only by previously understanding what is spoken."[4] Because of this attunement, which is predicated on an "antecedent co-understanding" (*vorgängigen Mitverstehen*), we can evaluate whether the manner in which something is said (the diction) is thematically apposite to what has been said. In his annotation of this remark, Celan jotted down "important for poetry."[5] The reader of a poem must be attuned to the twofold nature of the unspoken that the poet both says in the unsaying of what is said and unsays in the saying of what is unsaid.[6] This accords with Heidegger's statement that to keep silent is an "essential possibility of discourse"[7]—he even cautions that taciturnity (*Schweigsamkeit*) requires that one say to oneself daily, "be silent about bearing silence" (*schweigen vom Erschweigen*)[8]—whence we may infer the corollary that speaking excessively does not necessarily facilitate dialogic understanding. It is necessary to "thoroughly fathom the silence, in order to learn *what* may be said and *must* be said."[9] Silence is the indefinite determination (*unbestimmte Bestimmende*) that allows dialogue to succeed.[10] Indeed, the "authentic saying" of genuine dialogue is naught but the "silence about silence."[11] Keeping silent, however, is not identical to being mute nor is it achieved by one accustomed to speak a little:

> Authentic silence is possible only in genuine discourse [*Nur im echten Reden ist eigentliches Schweigen möglich*]. In order to be silent, Dasein must have something to say, that is, must be in command of an authentic and rich disclosedness [*Erschlossenheit*] of itself. . . . As a mode of discourse, reticence [*Verschwiegenheit*] articulates the intelligibility of Dasein so primordially that it gives rise to a genuine potentiality for hearing and to a being-with-one-another that is transparent.[12]

The seed planted by Heidegger in the major composition of his youth flowered in his later thought to become a key component of the role he assigned to language in his poetic thinking as the hearing of what cannot be heard but as unheard, the heeding of silence in the silence of heeding. Thus, Heidegger writes about the "*originary silence* [ursprüngliche Schweigen] as *further* silence in and out of the pre-sentiment of language. But that silence is not inactive—rather, the initially opening listening into (beings)."[13] It is possible that Heidegger was influenced by a remark of Schelling, which itself may be indebted to a kabbalistic theme appropriated by Böhme,[14] that the proclaimed (*ausgesprochene*) or real (*reale*) word is the unity of light and darkness, correlated respectively with vowel (*Selbstlauter*) and consonant (*Mitlauter*);[15] the former is the audible aspect of language and the latter the inaudible.[16] Be that as it may, for Heidegger, the poetic form of language is the privileged means of bespeaking the originary silence and the listening to beings. Poetry, accordingly, is described as "the saying of the unconcealment of beings [*die Sage der Unverborgenheit des Seienden*]. The prevailing language is the happening [*Geschehnis*] of that saying in which its world rises up historically for a people and the earth is preserved as that which remains closed. Projective saying [*entwerfende Sagen*] is that in which the preparation of the sayable [*Sagbaren*] at the same time brings the unsayable [*Unsagbare*] as such to the world."[17]

We detect here a confluence of the apophatic and the kataphatic, a point that is evident as well in the following statement in the *Schwarze Hefte* on the need to conceal and disclose being: "The sheltering concealment [*bergende Verbergung*] in the reticence [*Verschweigung*] of the essence; but the reticence requires precisely disclosive discourse [*entbergenden Rede*] about being. The question of being is necessary, but only as the most proper service to the sovereignty of the essence."[18] The reticence is proportionate to the concealing of the essence, but the former can be preserved only through the discourse that discloses the latter. In virtue of this confluence, language is delineated as "poetry in the essential sense. But since language is that happening in which, each time, beings are first disclosed as beings, poesy, poetry in the narrower sense, is the most primordial form of poetry in the essential sense. Language is not poetry because it is ur-poesy; rather, poesy happens in language because the latter preserves the primordial essence of poetry."[19] And what is that primordial essence? Reversing the view that has dominated Western philosophy since antiquity, Heidegger insists that language is not primarily a form of verbal communication based on words functioning as symbols signifying or representing beings extrinsic to the mind; it is rather the clearing-concealing advent of beyng,[20] the opening within which the giving is withheld, the revealing concealed, and the sayable unsaid. Language thus preserves the primacy of the event such that beings are disclosed in the nonbeing of the being of their nonbeing.

Perhaps influenced by the dismissal of the representational model of the relationship of subject and object in Schelling's *Identitätssystem*,[21] Heidegger sought to find the appropriate language to articulate a mode of discourse wherein the word of being is no longer understood referentially as a sign that corresponds to being, but it is rather an opening that exposes and in so doing shelters "the appropriation in an indicative word," the essential occurrence of beyng,[22] which cannot be reified into an object of representational knowledge. In a section from the *Beiträge* entitled "*Language and the inventive thinking of beyng*" (Das Erdenken des Seyns und die Sprache), Heidegger confronts the dilemma head on: the truth of beyng cannot be expressed in ordinary language since the latter is the language of beings. But can a "new language" (*neue Sprache*) be invented for beyng? Heidegger promptly responds in the negative, but he adds: "Even if it could, and perhaps without artificially formed words, such language would not be one that speaks. All saying must allow the co-emergence of a capacity to hear it. . . . Thus all that matters is this one thing: to say the most nobly emerged language in its simplicity and essential force, to say the language of beings as the language of beyng."[23] The possibility of inventing a new language is not feasible—beyng in its essence is nameless—and hence the best one can accomplish is a transformation (*Verwandlung*) of the language of beings into a mode of speaking about beyng that is beyond our linguistic reach. Heidegger admits that some of his unique locutions, such as the "renunciation of pursuance," the "clearing of concealment," the "appropriating event," or "Da-sein," press upon realms that are still closed. Nevertheless, through the "transformed saying" (*gewandelten Sagen*), there is an "opening of the truth of beyng."[24] The metamorphosis of language is not simply the exchange of one terminology for another; it is an extending of language beyond its limit to the essence of language:

> Language preserves the event because it springs from the word and remains with the word [*Die Sprache wahrt das Ereignis—weil sie dem Wort entspringt und beim Wort bleibt*]. Language is the *promise* [Versprechen] of the event to the evental people [*an den ereigneten Menschen*]. In language and as language, the word of being promises the truth. . . . Speaking and *promising* [*Sprechen und* Versprechen].[25]

Insofar as the word partakes of language as the opening of the openness that exposes the concealment of the self-concealing revealing, language can be spoken of as that which springs from and preserves the event of being. One can discern a residue of the Christological understanding of the word in Heidegger's depiction of language as the promise of the event and as the word of being that promises the truth. To equate speaking with promising strikes me as a philosophical translation of the proleptic hope of the parousia. In Heidegger's gnomic formulation, "The word comes to language, beyng brings itself to the word [*Das Wort kommt zur Sprache, das Seyn bringt sich zum Wort*]."[26] But the language points to its origin in the silence that exceeds the limits of language. Silence is the "inceptual essence of the word" (*anfänglichen Wesen des Wortes*).[27] In the thinking of being, therefore, language is best construed as the attunement (*Stimmung*) to the event, the essencing of being that "essences as the quietness of the departure."[28] As Heidegger put it in his notebooks, "supposing that the human had chosen the disclosability [*die Entbergsamkeit*] of the being of beings and by this choice was placed back into Dasein, must he then not proceed far into the stillness of the happening of being [*die Stille des Seinsgeschehnisses*], a happening which possesses its own time and its own silence [*Schweigen*]? Must he not have long been silent in order to find again the power and might of language and to be borne by them?"[29] Language originates in silence and therefore one must be silent to rediscover the efficacy of language as the sign that gives way to the abjuration of the sign.

In the *Beiträge*, Heidegger introduced the notion of "sigetics" (*die Sigetik*) to name the appropriate logic of a philosophy that "seeks the *truth of the essential occurrence* of beyng, and this truth is the intimating-resonating concealment (the mystery) of the event (the hesitant withholding). . . . Bearing silence arises out of the essentially occurring origin of language itself."[30] As he puts it in a second passage, inceptual thinking is sigetic because of its "bearing silence in the most explicit meditation [*Besinnung*]" as the way to let "beyng protrude into beings out of the silence-bearing utterance of the grasping word [*erschweigenden Sagen des begreifenden Wortes*]."[31] In *Besinnung*, which was written shortly after the completion of the *Beiträge*, futural thinking—the "en-thinking [*Er-denken*] of the preparedness for the history of the crossing [*Übergangs*] (the overcoming [*Über-windung*] of metaphysics)"—is described as "the en-owned saying in imageless word [*das er-eignete Sagen im bildlosen Wort*]."[32] What can be communicated in a saying so described? What does it mean to utter words without images? Heidegger, it seems, anticipated Derrida's idea of *dénégation*, a mode of speaking-not, which is to be distinguished from not-speaking, that is, the gesture of speaking to not speak rather than not speaking to speak.[33] To speak of nothing is not the same as having nothing of which to speak, that is, remaining silent either by saying nothing or by saying that there is nothing to say. Speaking-not is a verbal gesticulation that entails a mode of erasure that erases any and every trace, including especially the trace of its own erasure, constituting thereby the erasure of the trace. We attend to the erasure of erasure by hearing as profoundly as is possible the silence of the imageless word, the language of the crossing beyond language, the language of the overcoming muted in the muteness of poetic vision in which the voice of the soundless resounds in the vocalization of the nameless name, the name of the nameless that is the nothingness of being. By venturing deeper into the infinite listening to this essence, one is led to the deafness and muteness of the inessential, and only then, perhaps, may one be in the position to see what needs to be unseen and to speak what needs to be unspoken.

The apophatic elements of Heidegger's thought and the resonances of his complex view on the relation between language and being can be fruitfully explored in conjunction with a similar pattern of thought that may be elicited from kabbalistic works from the thirteenth century to the present. For Heidegger, as he enunciates with more clarity after the legendary turn, the age-old philosophical truism—traceable to Parmenides—that language and being stand in proximity to one another means that they are brought together as that which is held apart, a theme we have encountered at various junctures in this book. To the extent that Heidegger never abandoned the idea that language is the originary and hence distinctive essence of the being of human beings,[34] and that without language there is no being and without being there is no language, his thought remains anthropocentric. Heidegger confidently and unapologetically affirms the longstanding distinction of the human from plants and animals: the human alone is said "to have language by nature," which is to say, the human "is the living being capable of speech." This implies not only that the human possesses speech, but also that speech "enables man to be the living being he is as man. It is as one who speaks that man is—man." Language, therefore, "belongs to the closest neighborhood of man's being."[35] The metaphor of the neighborhood signals the juxtaposition as opposed to the conflation of language and the human being. The presumption of the belonging together of language and being thus circumvents both the idealist reduction of being to language and the realist reduction of language to being.

Secrecy and Veiling the Veil of Unveiling

Dasein is accorded the special role of guarding the clearing, the primal space of the between, wherein language and being are juxtaposed in the sameness of their difference. The showing-saying of language reveals the name of the namelessness that remains hidden precisely as a result of being exposed as the beyng that cannot be exposed within the deluge of beings that constitute the world. The poet is privileged as the purveyor of the mystery of language that bears witness to the breakaway (*Aufbruch*) through which beyng originarily becomes word and the nameless dons the attire of the name.[36] By saying the unsaid in unsaying the said, the poem mimics the simultaneous appearing and disappearing that is characteristic of the spatiotemporal construction of being,[37] and in that respect, the poet ideally fulfills the task allocated to the human being—the messenger that bears the message of the unconcealment of the twofold (*der Botengänger der Botschaft der Entbergung der Zwiefalt*)—to seek the mystery of the limit (*das Geheimnis der Grenze*) on the path of thinking by probing the boundary of the boundless (*der Grenzgänger des Grenzenlosen*).[38] Poetic language dramatizes into a narratological form the giving of the nongiven, the withholding bestowal of the nihilating ground of the nonground, the unconcealment of being as it conceals itself in the unpresentability of truth that constitutes the condition of the possibility of its presentation as nonpresentable.[39] More than the philosopher and the scientist, the poet knows that language manifests the wholly invisible (*ganz Unsichtbare*) that, above all, determines everything to which the human must correspond out of the ground of his existence (*jedoch allem zuvor alles Bestimmende, dem der Mensch aus dem Grunde seines Daseins entsprechen muß*),[40] the nothing that is more originary than the "not" of negation (*das Nichts ist ursprünglicher als das Nicht und die Verneinung*),[41] the advent of the retreat of the appropriating event, the nullity that precedes the fissure into being and nonbeing.[42] The revealing of nothing perforce must be a concealing, for only by being concealed can nothing be revealed.

Relatedly, the hermeneutic of secrecy espoused through the centuries by kabbalists presumes that the language most suitable to express the secret is the language of secrecy. In the cryptic rumination of Laruelle, "Black is without opposite: even light, which tries to turn it into its opposite, fails in the face of the rigor of its secret. Only the secret sees into the secret, like Black in Black [*Seul le secret voit dans le secret, comme Noir en Noir*]."[43] Just as the singularity of the vision-in-Black (*la vision-en-Noir*) by which we gain access to the world, the transcendental darkness into which one has never entered and from which one will never leave (*transcendantales ténèbres où il n'est jamais entré et qu'il ne quittera jamais*)—the opacity that renders the real invisible in its visibility—is already manifest before any manifestation (*Noir s'est déjà manifesté avant toute opération de manifestation*) and thus no other can be positioned in opposition to it, so the distinction between inner and outer breaks down to the extent that there is nothing to be seen but the secret that is a secret.[44] The tautology brings to light one of the more profound paradoxes of the Jewish esoteric tradition: the secret can be revealed only as the secret that is concealed, for if this were not so, then it would not be a secret that was revealed. The appropriate linguistic means to diffuse the mystery, therefore, is the murmur or the whisper, a form of speaking by speaking not rather than remaining completely silent.[45] Not to be apprised of this paradox is to be ignorant of the protocol of esotericism steadfastly cultivated by kabbalists, hardly altered by variation in time or place, a form of unknowing so thorough that the one who knows is not even aware of not knowing the unknowing, a triple concealment in which the concealment is concealed from being concealed. In this state of alienation—the concealment of the concealment of concealment—not only has the secret been forgotten, but the forgetting itself has been forgotten. Truth is so visibly invisible in this inappropriability of appropriation and impropriety of the proper,[46] the hiddenness so exhaustively hidden, there is no more hiddenness to hide. Redemption—the surmounting of oblivion by remembering the disremembered—consists of restoring the secret to its secrecy, the concealment to its concealment.

Numerous texts could be cited as evidence to corroborate my claim regarding the nature of the secret. I will mention one salient example from Cordovero: "The cause of the disclosure is the cause of the concealment and the cause of the concealment is the cause of the disclosure [*sibbat ha-hitgallut hu sibbat ha-he'lem we-sibbat ha-he'lem hu sibbat ha-hitgallut*]. And the matter is that by the concealing of the strong light and its being garbed in a garment, it is revealed. The light is thus hidden and verily it is disclosed, for if it were not hidden, it would not be disclosed."[47] The duplicity of the secret is such that the secret is not only a potentially threatening idea that for political reasons is revealed to the intellectual elite but must be hidden from the ignorant masses; the inherently secretive nature of the secret dictates that the disclosure of the secret is predicated on its concealment even from the one to whom it has been disclosed. The secret is the mystery that is both hidden and revealed, revealed to the extent that it is hidden and hidden to the extent that it is revealed. The more the secret is exposed, the more it is buried; invertedly, the secret best kept is the secret most widely disseminated.

With regard to this matter there is a conspicuous congruence between kabbalistic esotericism and Heidegger's assumption that the mystery is known not by unveiling but by preserving the mystery as mystery.[48] The affinity is amplified by the fact that just as kabbalists located the origin of the mystery in the autoerotic conatus of the infinite, as I chronicled in the third chapter, so Heidegger utilizes Hölderlin's term *intimacy* (*Innigkeit*) to characterize the "poetic naming" of the "originary unity of the enmity of the powers of what has purely sprung forth. It is the mystery belonging to such beyng."[49] This unity is contrasted with Hegel's concept of the absolute, since the intimacy of beyng is "never simply inexplicable in some respect, in *one* particular level of its beyng; it remains enigma through and through. Intimacy has the nature of a mystery, not because others fail to penetrate it; rather, in itself it prevails in essence as mystery."[50] As the intimacy holds sway, the mystery is preserved. The manifestness of the mystery arises precisely from "a not wanting to explain," a "self-concealing concealment." The mystery is brought to understanding, consequently, as an unveiling that "may be accomplished only in song, in the poetizing."[51] The divulging of the inscrutable transpires uniquely through poetic song because the latter is a manner of speaking that conceals the unveiling in the veiling of the unconcealing. The poetic foundation (*die dichterische Stiftung*) of the intimacy of the fundamental attunement (*Grundstimmung*) in which "the historical Dasein of a people and its decision is meant to find its locale" is appropriated in the power of veiling (*Verhüllen*) that sustains and shields the nexus of images (*Bildzusammenhang*) of the poetizing: "The task of the image is not to clarify, but to veil; not to make familiar, but to make unfamiliar; not to bring closer, but to place into a distance." But a deeper attention to the intimacy of this fundamental attunement intimates that veiling and unveiling—in a manner that emulates the originarily unitary nexus (*der ursprünglich einige Zusammenhang*) of the most extreme contraries (*die äußersten Gegensätze*) identified as the decisive renunciation (*das entschiedene Verzichten*) and the unconditional awaiting (*das unbedingte Erharren*)—are not juxtaposed extrinsically but rather "spring forth out of a unique and primordial essence of temporality."[52]

In "Aus einem Gespräch von der Sprache," Heidegger placed the following comment in the mouth of the Japanese interlocutor: "A mystery is a mystery only when it does not even come out *that* mystery is at work."[53] So concealed is the concealment that the concealment of the concealing is concealed. In the diary that Heidegger wrote chronicling his first trip to Greece in 1962, he commented on the Heraclitean description of Apollo, "He neither reveals, nor hides but rather he shows" (οὔτε λέγει οὔτε κρύπτει ἀλλὰ σημαίνει), in the following way: "To show means to let something be seen, which as such . . . is kept at the same time covered and protected. Such a showing is the proper happening in the field of ἀλήθεια, which founds the sojourn in the antechamber of the holy."[54] To dwell in the abode of the antechamber of the holy, one must be acclimated to the truth of the untruth of the truth as the showing of the nonshowing, the exposure of what is safeguarded in its coming to be exposed. For Heidegger, as I have emphasized at several points in this book, the confluence of opposites does not signify a coincidence but rather a concomitance wherein the same, as opposed to the identical, connotes that which persists in difference. Claiming the middle excluded by the logic of the excluded middle guides Heidegger to the conclusion "The essence of truth is now interrogated out of the essential occurrence of beyng and is grasped as the clearing of what is self-concealing and thus as belonging to the essence of beyng itself. The question of the truth 'of' beyng reveals itself as the question of the beyng 'of' truth."[55] It follows, hermeneutically, that the uncovering is always also a cover-up, and in that sense, untruth is inseparably linked to truth, a juxtaposition that resists the dialectical harmonization of antinomies as the truth is an untruth that is neither and therefore both true and untrue, and hence what is manifest is the concealment in the double form of refusal (*Versagen*) and dissembling (*Verstellen*).[56] "Truth is un-truth [*Die Wahrheit ist Un-Wahrheit*]," writes Heidegger, "insofar as there belongs to it the reservoir of the not-yet uncovered, the un-uncovered, in the sense of concealment. . . . Truth occurs as such in the opposition of clearing and double concealing."[57] Or, as he puts it elsewhere in his explication of sheltering (*Bergung*) as the preservation of the event through the playing out (*Bestreitung*) of strife, "Thus truth essentially occurs as what is in each case true by way of sheltering. Yet this that is true [*Wahre*] is what it is only as the un-true [*Un-wahre*], at once non-being [*unseiend*] and non-grounding [*ungründig*]."[58]

Heidegger repeats this insight on many occasions: truth is not simply the disclosure of what was once hidden; it is the disclosure of what remains hidden. There is a simultaneity of the unconcealment of beings and the concealment of beyng, a simultaneity of truth and untruth that ensures that errancy will always hold sway. Heidegger thus insists that the letting-be of beings "is intrinsically at the same time a concealing. . . . Considered with respect to truth as disclosedness [*Entborgenheit*], concealment is then un-disclosedness [*Un-entborgenheit*] and accordingly the un-truth [*Un-wahrheit*] that is most proper to the essence of truth [*Wahrheitswesen*]."[59] As Heidegger goes on to say, this concealment of beings as a whole, the un-truth proper, "is older than every openedness of this or that being. It is older even than letting-be itself, which in disclosing already holds concealed and comports itself toward concealing." This concealedness is identified as the mystery, which is "not a particular mystery regarding this or that, but rather the one mystery—that, in general, mystery (the concealing of what is concealed) as such holds sway throughout the Da-sein of human beings. In letting beings as a whole be, which discloses and at the same time conceals, it happens that concealing appears as what is first of all concealed."[60] Correspondingly, *Ein Sof* is the most archaic mystery, the withholding of being that fosters the letting be of beings, the eventuation of what is unconcealed in the concealing of the concealment.

For Heidegger, this dynamic is essential to the philosophical enterprise, which involves the "terrifying, though rare, questioning of the truth of beyng. Philosophy is the grounding of truth while simultaneously being deprived of what is true."[61] The essence of being human is *to comport oneself to the unhidden*,[62] but what is unhidden is always still hidden, what is unearthed is the occlusion of the occlusion. His take on the poetic word epitomizes the point: "Beauty is a fateful gift of the essence of truth, and here truth means the disclosure of what keeps itself concealed [*die Entbergung des Sichverbergenden*]."[63] The paradoxical intent of Heidegger's insistence on the *disclosure of what keeps itself concealed* was well understood by Arendt: "Presence and absence, concealing and revealing, nearness and remoteness—their interlinkage and the connections prevailing among them—have next to nothing to do with the truism that there could not be presence unless absence were experienced, nearness without remoteness, discovery without concealment."[64] Commenting on the aletheiological as opposed to the epochal sense of the withdrawal of being in Heidegger, Schürmann noted that concealment as *lēthē* is an integral part of *alētheia*, the "absence that abides *essentially* in the heart of presencing."[65] Heidegger's thought runs deeper than the commonplace conviction that an attribute can be discerned only through its opposite. The belonging together dialectically surpasses the dialectical subjugating of antinomies—the presence is an absence that is neither and therefore both present and absent, what is most immediate is most remote, what is disclosed, in the end, is the concealment of the concealment concealed in the disclosure. Unconcealment is thus not a disrobing of the naked truth but the disposing of the garment in which truth is attired, the investiture that masks the mask exposed as the face that unmasks the face. That there is no truth denuded of the vestment of untruth accords with the assumption of kabbalists that the infinite cannot appear except as the inapparent, that every configuration of the imageless is an imaginal disfiguration of the image. Epistemologically, truth is not visible unless it is enveloped in the veil of invisibility.[66]

The view I have attributed to the kabbalists and to Heidegger can be profitably compared with the discussion on the metaphorics of the naked truth in Hans Blumenberg:

> The reader will surely agree that it is tautologous to speak of the "naked truth." . . . But this metaphor does not mean to bring anything into the *concept* of truth; it projects conjectures and evaluations of a very complex kind over the top of the concept, as it were. The metaphor is intimately linked with the import

and importance of *clothing*, considered as guise or disguise, in relation to which nakedness likewise splits into unmasking, into the uncovering of a deception, on the one hand, and shameless unveiling, the violation of a sacred mystery, on the other.[67]

According to Blumenberg's philosophical metaphorology, the naked truth belongs to the class of absolute metaphors, that is, the "*foundational elements* of philosophical language" that "resist being converted back into authenticity and logicality" and therefore must be analyzed in accord with "their conceptually irredeemable expressive function. . . . That these metaphors are called 'absolute' means only that they prove resistant to terminological claims and cannot be dissolved into conceptuality, not that one metaphor could not be replaced or represented by another, or corrected through a more precise one. Even absolute metaphors therefore have a *history*."[68] To some extent, the notion of the absolute metaphor is useful for interpreting kabbalistic texts and Heidegger,[69] and particularly relevant is the inference that these metaphors "would force us to reconsider the relationship between logos and the imagination. The realm of the imagination could no longer be regarded solely as the substrate for transformations into conceptuality. . . . Through this implicative connection, the relationship of metaphorology to the history of concepts . . . is defined as an ancillary one: metaphorology seeks to burrow down to the substructure of thought, the underground, the nutrient solution of systematic crystallizations."[70]

Seyn and *Ein Sof* can be said to function as absolute metaphors, which signify, like the light of being, as Blumenberg characterizes it, "the 'letting-appear' that does not itself appear, the inaccessible accessibility of things."[71] I would counter nonetheless that the image of a truth that is naked should be problematized insofar as nakedness itself is just another form of apparel, the unmasking that is masking the mask, the unveiling that is veiling the veil.[72] The Heideggerian perspective, which illumines the esoteric stance of the kabbalah, even as the esoteric stance of the kabbalah illumines the Heideggerian perspective, is an inverse of what we presume to be the empirical or commonsensical standpoint: visibility is commensurate to the garment in which the invisible body is arrayed, and hence nudity can neither evince nor conceal the secret of truth divested of its truthfulness. Heidegger relates this intuition to the poetic nature of language, which is intricately linked to another central motif on his path of thinking, the eclipsing that is proper to the essence of truth as the unconcealment of beyng:

> The mystery is not a barrier that lies on the other side of truth, but is itself the highest figure of truth [*die höchste Gestalt der Wahrheit*]; for in order to let the mystery truly be what it is—concealing preservation of authentic beyng [*verbergende Bewahrung des eigentlichen Seyns*]—the mystery must be manifest as such. A mystery that is not known in its power of veiling [*verhüllenden Macht*] is no mystery. The higher our knowing concerning the veiling [*die Verhüllung*] and the more genuine the saying of it as such, the more untouched its concealing power [*verbergende Macht*] remains. Poetic saying of the mystery is *denial* [*die* Verleugnung].[73]

To speak of mystery as the highest figuration of truth means that every act of unconcealing is at the same time an act of concealing: what is exposed is the hiddenness of the exposure. It is at this point that Heidegger's thinking bears an incredible resemblance to what was articulated by the kabbalists, epitomized in the principle that concealment is the cause of disclosure and disclosure the cause of concealment. The one true being, the nameless essence of *Ein Sof*, the essence that is no essence, is manifest through the shroud of the name to the extent that it remains shrouded in its manifestation. Concealment can be revealed as concealment only inasmuch as the concealment is concealed in its unconcealment. Similarly, as we have seen, Heidegger maintains that the mystery is defined as the *concealing preservation of authentic beyng*, that is, the withholding of beyng that is proper to the bestowal of beings. For the mystery to be propagated as mystery, it must be revealed in its veiling power. Translated linguistically, to speak of the mystery presumes the concealing power that precludes the mystery from being spoken except as unspoken. The avowal, therefore, is itself a disavowal, the poetic saying a repudiation of what is said.

It "Is" It Itself: Being's Mystery and Heeding the Unspeakable

Kabbalists would certainly concur with Heidegger that the origin of language is the ability to keep silent. Consider this striking meditation in the *Beiträge* on restraint (*Verhaltenheit*), silence (*Schweigen*), and language (*Sprache*):

> Words fail us; they do so originally and not merely occasionally, whereby some discourse or assertion could indeed be carried out but is left unuttered, i.e., where the saying of something sayable or the re-saying of something already said is simply not carried through. Words do not yet come to speech at all, but it is precisely in failing us that they arrive at the first leap. This failing is the event as intimation and incursion of beyng. This failing us is the inceptual condition for the self-unfolding possibility of an original (poetic) naming of beyng.[74]

Heidegger's notion of ineffability does not entail the saying of the unsayable if the latter is understood as something potentially sayable that is presently not spoken. What he proposed rather is the unsaying of the sayable, which is to say, the belief that every assertion falls short of articulating the words that have yet to assume the character of speech, but this failure is precisely what makes possible the poetic naming of beyng. Insofar as the naming cannot be severed from the nameless that defies naming, the mystery to which language can only allude, the apophatic and the kataphatic are inextricably conjoined in what Heidegger refers to as the possibility of language to express itself as the "telling silence,"[75] or literally, the "saying not-saying" (*sagenden Nichtsagens*).[76] Thus, in a second passage from the *Beiträge*, Heidegger expounded the sigetic theme of "Beyng and its bearing silence" (*Das Seyn und seine Erschweigung*): "Bearing silence is the prudent lawfulness of the silence-bearing activity.... Bearing silence is the 'logic' of philosophy inasmuch as philosophy asks the basic question out of the other beginning."[77] In yet another passage from the *Beiträge*, Heidegger explains that every language of Dasein is in essence silence insofar as it originates in the turning (*Kehre*), or the counter-turning (*Wider-kehre*), of the event that occurs "in between the call (to the one that belongs) and the belonging (of the one that is called).... *The call* to the leap into the appropriation is the great stillness of the most concealed self-knowledge.... The *call* is intrusion *and* remaining absent in the mystery of the appropriation"[78]

Expressed hermeneutically, the saying of thinking (*die Sage des Denkens*) must always remain unspoken (*ungesprochen*), since the spoken (*das Gesprochene*) is never what is said (*das Gesagte*).[79] Hence, in his first lecture course on Hölderlin's poetry, delivered in the University of Freiburg in the winter semester of 1934–35, Heidegger deduces the following from the comparison of "*poetic* telling" (dichterischen *Sagen*) and the "*thoughtful* telling" (denkerischen *Sagen*) of philosophy: "In a real philosophical lecture, for example, the decisive issue is not really what is said directly, but what is kept silent in this saying. For this reason, one can indeed listen to and transcribe philosophical lectures without further ado, and yet in so doing constantly *mishear* [verhören]—and this not in the incidental sense that one incorrectly apprehends individual words or concepts, but in the fundamental sense of an essential mishearing, in which one never notices what is really being spoken of, or to whom it is properly being spoken."[80] Philosophy is contrasted sharply with the sciences: the charge of the latter is "to directly grasp what is said" as opposed to the former where the goal is to "preserve in silence what is essential in one's saying."[81] From the seemingly contradictory claims in the poem "Germania," related to the eagle's injunction to the solitary speaking girl (lines 84–85) to name what is before her eyes so that the unspoken will no longer remain a mystery, on the one hand, and the assertion (lines 93–96) that the veritable thing (*ein Wahres*), which appears and is circumscribed in a threefold manner, must nevertheless remain unspoken, on the other hand, Heidegger elicits the following truism: "The poem is language. Yet who properly speaks in the poem? The author, the 'I,' we, the man, the eagle. They speak of language that is to name (speak) and yet in naming to leave unspoken."[82] The paradox of the apophatic pronouncement is captured concisely and adeptly in the words *in naming to leave unspoken*—the nameless that is unspoken is not what is not spoken but what is unnamed in the poetic act of speaking. The truth of being is thus promulgated through the perplexity of the being of truth, the mystery expressed as the unsaid (*Ungesagte*) and manifest as the unshowable (*Unzeigbare*).[83] The "future first thinker" (*künftige erste Denker*), Heidegger writes in the *Beiträge*, must be capable of affirming the statement "To thinking there remains only the simplest saying [*Sagen*] of the plainest image in purest reticence [*Verschweigung*]."[84] In this spirit, he recommends in an entry from the notebooks—presumably for himself and for others—"Write out of a great reticence" (*Aus einer großen Verschwiegenheit schreiben*).[85]

The alliance of being and language assumes a particular valence for Heidegger that has deep affinity to the apposition of these terms in kabbalistic sources. Just as the kabbalists postulate a commingling of the apophatic and the kataphatic inasmuch as there is no way to reach the nameless but through the name, and hence language reveals the being it conceals, so Heidegger maintains that it is precisely through the act of saying the unsayable that the poet leaves the unsayable unsaid. To illumine the point, let me cite a crucial passage from "Brief über den 'Humanismus'":

> Yet being—what is being? It "is" It itself. The thinking that is to come [*das künftige Denken*] must learn to experience that and to say it [*zu erfahren und zu sagen*]. "Being" ["*Sein*"]—that is not God [*Gott*] and not a cosmic ground [*Weltgrund*]. Being is essentially farther than all beings and is yet nearer to the human being than every being, be it a rock, a beast, a work of art, a machine, be it an angel or God. Being is the nearest. Yet the near remains farthest from the human being. Human beings at first cling always and only to beings. But when thinking represents beings as beings it no doubt relates itself to being. In truth, however, it always thinks only of beings as such; precisely not, and never, being as such. The "question of being" ["*Seinsfrage*"] always remains a question about beings [*die Frage nach dem Seienden*]. It is still not at all what its elusive name indicates: the question in the direction of being [*die Frage nach dem Sein*]. Philosophy, even when it becomes "critical" through Descartes and Kant, always follows the course of metaphysical representation. It thinks from beings back to beings with a glance in passing toward being. For every departure from beings and every return to them stands already in the light of being.[86]

Heidegger here charts the course of thinking for the future centered on learning to experience and to say the proposition that delineates the nondelineable nature of being: *Es "ist" Es selbst*, "It 'is' It itself." Needless to say, this definition sounds like a textbook example of a tautology. As I observed in chapter 1, however, Heidegger approves of tautological thinking insofar as it is expressive of the hermeneutic circularity engendered by the repetition of the same as different and the eruption of the different as the same.[87] What is decreed about being, consequently, is that it is itself. Nothing seems to have been revealed, and we are left to ponder, what is the It that is itself? To answer that positively is to cling to the domain of discriminate beings and thereby succumb to the error of the metaphysical representation of being, which obscures the ontological difference. On this score, it is interesting to note that the quotation marks around the word *is* were not in the first edition of *Wegmarken*.[88] We can surmise that Heidegger added them out of a concern that the reader might be inclined to repeat this error and view the "it" of being from the vantagepoint of beings. Support for this conjecture may be drawn from a second passage in this treatise where Heidegger writes that the expression *it gives* (*es gibt*) "is used preliminarily to avoid the locution 'being is' ['*das Sein ist*']; for 'is' ['*ist*'] is commonly said of some thing that is [*gesagt von solchem, was ist*]. We call such a thing a being [*das Seiende*]. But being [*Sein*] 'is' precisely not 'a being' ['*das Seiende*']. If 'is' is spoken without a closer interpretation of being, then being is all too easily represented as a 'being' [*dann wird das Sein allzuleicht als ein 'Seiendes' vorgestellt*] after the fashion of the familiar sort of beings that act as causes and are actualized as effects."[89] Placing the word *ist* in the phrase *Es "ist" Es selbst* in quotation marks mitigates any obfuscation of Heidegger's main point, which is to pivot from the question about beings to the question of being.

If being is not a being, it is unquestionably nothing and thus not something that could be assessed as either cause or effect. We are compelled nevertheless to ask again, what is the *it* that is affirmed to be itself? Language here is obviously an obstacle, but, as we shall see, a proper understanding of language will provide the resolution to the impediment that is language: the only way to transcend language is through language. To distance himself from a traditional ontotheological perspective, Heidegger tells us categorically that the being of which he speaks is not God or the cosmic ground. The being, which is not a being, is the clearing that is concealed from the concealment of metaphysics. The inherent impossibility of treating this being in proper linguistic or logical terms is offered by Heidegger in his explanation of his singular locution *es gibt*: "For the 'it' that here 'gives' is being itself. The 'gives' names the essence of being that is giving, granting its truth. The self-giving into the open, along with the open region itself, is being itself."[90] The self-giving (*Sichgeben*) is structurally parallel to the Aristotelian definition of the First Mover as thought thinking itself, the uroboric state in which thinker, thinking, and thought are identical. Without effacing the considerable difference between Aristotle's quintessential metaphysical idea and Heidegger's postmetaphysical conception, it seems reasonable to make the comparison and legitimate to translate the tripartite structure of the former into Heideggerian parlance such that the it that gives, the giving, and that which is given, are manifestations of the selfsame nothing of being—as opposed to the being of nothing—revealed in the concealment of the open. The human qua being-there (*Da-sein*) stands uniquely in relation to the clearing, the "open in-between" (*offene Zwischen*), the "ecstatic region [*ekstatischen Bereiches*] of the disclosure and concealment of being,"[91] the "locality of the truth of being amid beings," which "gathers to itself and embraces ek-sistence in its existential, that is, ecstatic, essence."[92] We are susceptible to the ontic condition of falling (*Vefallen*), which is identified as the forgetting of the truth of being that results from ensnarement in the throng of beings unthought in their essence. The alienation is an inevitable consequence of the fact that being assumes the paradoxical character of being nearer to the human than the nearest of beings but, at the same time, at least for ordinary thinking, this nearness is farther than the farthest.[93] "As such," concludes Heidegger, "being remains mysterious [*geheimnisvoll*], the simple nearness of an unobtrusive prevailing [*unaufdringlichen Waltens*]. The nearness occurs essentially as language itself."[94]

Commenting on the Heideggerian idea that the "proximity of being is produced as language," Derrida writes,

> Being is nothing, is not a being; it does not belong to the totality of beings. Its meaning can appear only if beings come to be declared as what they are in their being (i.e., if being is said). But this does not mean that being belongs only to language in the sense in which one might speak of a linguistic being [*d'un être de langage*] in a pejorative sense. A being that was only in and through the word would be nothing but a verbal phenomenon, and so it would not be Being [*l'Être*].[95]

The co-belonging of being and language is an attempt to move beyond the metaphysical paradigm that presumes that language is the essence of the human being represented as the *animal rationale*, the animal that possesses the capacity for reason and discourse, ζῷον λόγον ἔχον. As Heidegger explains this seminal idea in Western philosophy, "the metaphysical-animal explanation of language" (*die metaphysisch-animalische Auslegung der Sprache*) covers up "the essence of language in the history of being. According to this essence, language is the house of being [*Haus des Seins*], which is propriated [*ereignete*] by being and pervaded [*durchfügte*] by being. And so it is proper to think the essence of language from its correspondence [*Entsprechung*] to being and indeed as this correspondence, that is, as the home of the human being's essence [*Behausung des Menschenwesens*]. But the human being is not only a living creature who possesses language along with other capacities. Rather, language is the house of being in which the human being ek-sists by dwelling, in that he belongs to the truth of being, guarding it."[96]

Curiously, Derrida considered Heidegger's metaphorical depictions of language as the house of being and as the home of the human being's essence as resonating rhetorically with the "expressionist-romantico-Nazi style."[97] Even so, he set as his task to ponder whether in this case the metaphor is only metaphor and whether the romantico-Nazi style exhausts the meaningfulness of the metaphor. His answer to both hypothetical questions is assuredly negative, leading him to conclude, "What Heidegger wants to show is that to the extent that there is language only in the clearing of being [*l'éclairement de l'être*] and to the extent that being cannot be a simple product of language, failing which it would not be and thus would not be what it is—to that extent the meaning of being is, let's say without metaphor and abstraction, the condition of possibility of language on which it nonetheless depends. . . . So one must think language on the basis of being and the essence of man on the basis of the possibility of language."[98] The correspondence between being and language, which implicates the human being as well, for the essence of the latter is determined in the space of this correspondence, provides an alternate conception to the metaphysical understanding that emerges from the definition of the human as the rational animal, the animal that has logos. But what is the nature of the correspondence? Surely, Heidegger does not intend by this the conventional correspondence between objects in the external world and words that express ideas in the internal landscape of the mind. The correspondence he affirms relates rather to the image of language as the house of being, the clearing in which being reveals itself in its concealment and within which the human being dwells in proximity to and therefore assumes the guardianship of the truth of that being. Language is no longer apperceived as the property possessed by humans as opposed to other animal species; it is the home where humanity's essence is procured as that which comes to dwell in being as the "dimension of the ecstasis of ek-sistence."[99]

Heidegger's position is illumined further from his remark on the derivation of the word *logos* from *legein*, which "is rooted in *apophainesthai*, to bring forward into appearance [*zum Vorschein bringen*]."[100] On the basis of an eccentric interpretation of a sentence from Plato's *Sophist* 205b, Heidegger explains that this bringing-forth (*Her-vor-bringen*) of "what presences into appearance" (*das Anwesendes in den Vorschein*)—the passing beyond the nonpresent (*Nicht-Anwesenden*) and going forward into presencing (*Anwesen*)—is poiēsis.[101] Poetic activity quintessentially embodies the summoning of thinking and language to bring forth into appearance and concrete imagery the nongiven of what is given. Insofar as the qualifying characteristic of nature is the "arising of something from out of itself," Heidegger equates the two: "*Physis* is indeed *poiēsis* in the highest sense. For what presences by means of *physis* has the irruption [*Aufbruch*] belonging to bringing-forth, e.g., the bursting of a blossom into bloom, in itself (*en heautōi*)."[102] The poetic is the thread that ties together nature and language, two modes of occasioning (*Veranlassung*) that instigate the "presencing of that which at any given time comes to appearance in bringing-forth. Bringing-forth brings out of concealment [*Verborgenheit*] into unconcealment [*Unverborgenheit*]. . . . This coming rests and moves freely within what we call revealing [*das Entbergen*]. The Greeks have the word *alētheia* for revealing. The Romans translated this with *veritas*."[103] Heeding the philological import of the word *alētheia*, Heidegger maintained that truth does not connote the correctness of representation (*Vorstellen*)—understood epistemically as either a perceptual datum or an inferential sign—but the event by which the concealed comes forth into unconcealment. "In every great philosophy, its concealed *way* [Weg]—and its thrust—to the essential *disclosure* [Aufschluß] must be followed. But we must never become fixated on its stated propositions [*ausgesprochenen Sätzen*] . . . because this truth is not a propositional truth [*Satzwahrheit*]—or, better: because the propositions, the essential ones, have a different character as propositions [*Satzcharakter*] than that of a merely correct assertion [*Aussage*]."[104]

The unique stance enunciated by Heidegger is clarified in his comment on the Parmenidean statement ἔστι γὰρ εἶναι, which he translates as "for there is being" ("*Es ist nämlich Sein*"): "The primal mystery for all thinking is concealed in this phrase. Perhaps 'is' can be said only of being in an appropriate way, so that no individual being ever properly 'is.' But because thinking should be directed only toward saying being in its truth, instead of explaining it as a particular being in terms of beings, whether and how being is must remain an open question for the careful attention of thinking."[105] Not only is the primal mystery for all thinking (*das anfängliche Geheimnis für alles Denken*) concealed in this dictum, but it has remained unthought (*ungedacht*). Heidegger exposes the mystery—giving thought to the unthought—by underscoring that the goal of speaking with respect to the truth of being is to say being in its truth and not to explain it as a particular being. Even this objective, however, is complicated by the fact that being cannot be said unless it is left unsaid. The unthought that is to be thought in the Parmenidean dictum concerns the inherently apophatic nature of language as the saying of the unsaying that ensues from the appropriating event of the nonbeing of being.[106]

Heidegger was aware of this difficulty as we may gather from the following words from the *Beiträge*:

> Every saying of beyng [*Sagen des Seyns*] is couched in words and namings which, as expressions of beyng, are liable to be misunderstood when taken in the sense of the everyday view of beings and thought exclusively in that sense. What this requires is not at all primarily a failure of the question (within the realm of the thoughtful interpretation of beyng); rather, the word itself already reveals something . . . and thereby conceals that which is supposed to be brought into the open in thoughtful saying. Nothing can remove this difficulty. Indeed, the attempt to remove it already signifies misunderstanding of all saying of beyng. The difficulty must be accepted and must be grasped in its essential belonging (to the thinking of beyng).[107]

The thinking of beyng must be expressed in a saying that is concomitantly an unsaying, a mode of revealing that conceals the revealed and thereby reveals the concealing. This difficulty cannot be mitigated, since the language used to speak about beyng is drawn invariably from the realm of beings. In this respect, there is a reversal of the metaphysical assumption regarding the humanizing quality of language that is the outcome of thinking of the human as the animal that possesses language. Quite the contrary, the unbridgeable gap between being and beings guarantees the fact that language dehumanizes the human subject as an objectively present living being.[108] Language is still the ground of what it is to be human but it must be construed from this varied perspective that reduces the risk of a rampant egotism and the potentially deleterious effect of an uncompromising anthropomorphization of the world. Tellingly, Heidegger concludes the *Beiträge* with these words: "Language is grounded in silence. Silence is the most concealed holding to the measure [*Maß-halten*]. It *holds* to the measure, in the sense that it first posits measures. Language is thus the positing of measures [*Maß-setzung*] in that which is most internal and most extensive, the positing of measures as the originating essential occurrence of what is fitting [*Fugs*] and of its joining [*Fügung*] (the event)."[109] If the human is the animal that speaks, this is so because the human is the being uniquely endowed with language, the positing of measures that is the originating essential occurrence of the event of beyng, grounded in the holding to measure that is silence.

Kabbalistic Poiēsis: Anxiety, Lament, and the Language of Silence

Identifying the primary task of language as poiēsis, understood as the unconcealment of the concealed, suggests another striking similarity to the kabbalists, who likewise view language—and in particular the matrix language that is Hebrew—principally as the unconcealing of the concealment that is the namelessness uncloaked through the cloak of the name. Simply put, my hypothesis is that the nameless name posited by the kabbalists corresponds to Heidegger's understanding of the nothing (*Nichts*) that is the beyng (*Seyn*) given in but always recoiling from the superfluity of beings (*Seiende*), what he referred to in "Was ist Metaphysik?" as the repelling gesture of the nothing in relation to the entirety of the beings of the world.[110] The fundamental occurrence of Dasein is identified as the unveiling of this beyng through the beings that "conceal from us the nothing we are seeking." Hence, the nothing is not placed before us as a consequence of the "complete negation of the totality of beings," but rather it is precisely the disclosure of the latter that "makes manifest the nothing."[111] For the nothing to be manifest as nothing, it must remain unmanifest in the plethora of beings in which it is manifest.

The beyng of which Heidegger speaks, as the *Ein Sof* of the kabbalists, is not akin to the differential void that may be envisioned either as the something of nothingness or as the nothingness of something.[112] We become attuned to this nothing of beingness by way of anxiety, which is not the fear of the loss of any determinate something but the sense of uncanniness that arises from the dread of there being no determinate something at all. In the face of such trepidation, the indeterminateness comes to the fore and we cannot say anything definitive about that before which we feel uncanny. This feeling of the *unheimlich* is a continuation of what Heidegger analyzed in *Sein und Zeit* in conjunction with the basic attunement (*Grundbefindlichkeit*) to the mood of anxiety that leaves one disoriented as the tranquility and self-assurance of "being-at-home" (*Zuhause-sein*) in the everyday world slip away and one enters the existential state of "uncanniness" (*Unheimlichkeit*), the sense of "not-being-at-home" (*Nicht-zuhause-sein*),[113] an ontological condition in which the familiar becomes strange.[114] Additionally, the *Unheimlichkeit* that one endures in encountering the nothing bears a phenomenological resemblance to the gnostically inflected distress or foreboding, *Bekümmerung*, the term that Heidegger used in an early phase—as a precursor to Augustine's *cura* rendered in *Sein und Zeit* as *Sorge*—to name the "original motivation to philosophize in the face of the very facticity of life."[115] In this state of suspicion, we have no hold on the certainty of the self or of entities in the world—in the *Phänomenologische Interpretationen zu Aristoteles: Einführung in die Phänomenologische Forschung*, the lecture course from the winter semester 1921–22, Heidegger describes this as the "genuine loss" of "letting oneself be diverted from facticity" (*Sichabringenlassen der Faktizität*), which constitutes the existence (*Existenz*) of the "radical existentiell worry" (*radikale existenzielle Bekümmerung*)[116]—and hence the philosophical disposition arises as the clear demarcation of being fades from our purview; the unrest of anxiety reveals the nothing that nothing is not in virtue of not being the nothing that nothing is.[117]

In an extraordinary passage from the *Schwarze Hefte*, which bears the title *Der Mensch und das Sein*, Heidegger avails himself of language that is more strikingly gnostic: the delusion we must break through—fostered by the semblance of being (*Schein des Seins*) that entangles our thinking about being in the question of being (*Seinsfrage*) and thereby impedes a deeper compression (*Verdichtung*) that arises from the "*uniqueness* of the *isolation* of being in nothingness" (Einzigkeit *der* Vereinzelung *des Seins im Nichts*)—is that it is impossible to step outside the relation of humankind to being; on the contrary, it is precisely the vocation of the thinker "to question disclosively [*erfragen*] the whole of this relation." To do so requires that "one would step into nothingness [*das Nichts*]. Yet as long as this is allowed merely as something misthought, contrived, it is only the semblance of that semblance [*der Schein jenes Scheins*]." If, however, "the outermost [*das Äußerste*] is only the innermost [*das Innerste*] of the human being, then the outside [*das Außerhalb*] becomes the inside of the innermost and deepest [*Innerhalb des Innersten und Tiefsten*], becomes that place where the human being has forsaken himself the longest [*sich längst verlassen*] and in the highest mission of his essence has found himself [*in den höchsten Auftrag seines Wesens gefunden hat*]. Have to come back from there as a complete alien [*ein ganz Fremder*] and bring along—set down—the most alien [*das Befremdlichste*]."[118]

When the external is internalized, and the internal externalized, one is centered— to be at home means that one discerns that the inside is the vantagepoint whence one imagines that one is outside and the outside is the vantagepoint whence one imagines that one is inside—in the marginality of alienation, the unsettling experience of being situated in the disconcerting place where one finds oneself by discovering that the self has been abandoned. Heidegger's formulation is evocative of the notion of the redeemed redeemer, the redeemer who is in need of redemption as a consequence of having been trapped in the material world of darkness in the attempt to redeem others. This interpretation of ancient Gnosticism was undoubtedly known to Heidegger from the German *Religionsgeschichtliche Schule* and particularly Richard Reitzenstein,[119] whose perspective was accepted and elaborated by Rudolf Bultmann in his presentation of the unfolding of Hellenistic Christianity by means of gnostic terminology,[120] and continued by his students, including Hans Jonas in his portrayal of the gnostic image of the alien.[121] The degree to which Heidegger was informed by a similar myth of estrangement in the world is made more explicit in this subsequent entry in the notebooks: "The alien *(the human being) and* the great fortuitiveness *(being)*. The throwing into being and the trembling of the thrownness into the essence as *language. Language: the hearth of the world*... *Here* the uniqueness of the revealing-concealing isolation in the simplicity of the aloneness of Dasein. (The unison.)"[122] The kinship of Heidegger's worldview and what German historians of religion in the early twentieth century considered to be the essence of Gnosticism is brought to light when we consider the following summation of Bultmann:

> For the essence of Gnosticism does not lie in its syncretistic mythology but rather in a new understanding... of man and the world; its mythology is only the expression of this understanding. Whereas to ancient man the world had been home... the *utter difference of human existence from all worldly existence* was recognized for the first time in Gnosticism and Christianity, and thus the world became foreign soil to the human self... in fact, in Gnosticism, his prison. Gnostic thought is so radical that to it the impulses of one's own senses, instincts, and desires, by which man is bound to the world, appear alien and hostile—hostile to man's real self, which cannot achieve its own nature in this world at all, and to which this world is a prison in which his real self, related to and derived from the divine world of light, is shackled by the demonic powers of darkness.[123]

In Heidegger's philosophical translation of this myth, the human being *(der Mensch)* is labeled the alien *(der Fremdling)* vis-à-vis the great happenstance *(der große Zufall)* of being *(das Sein)*, the groundlessness *(Abgründigkeit)* of the *essential fortuitiveness of being (die* wesentliche Zu-fälligkeit des Seins) that provokes a fracturing *(Zerklüftung)* experienced affectively as the fearfulness *(Furchtbarkeit)* of the essence of being and the concealment of its blessing *(die Verborgenheit des Segens)*.[124] The existential state of this alienation is further described as the "throwing into being" *(der Wurf in das Sein)* and as "the trembling of the thrownness into the essence as *language*" *(das Erzittern der Geworfenheit in das Wesen als* Sprache).[125] Language is the hearth of the world wherein one finds "the uniqueness of the revealing-concealing isolation [*die Einzigkeit der entbergend-verbergenden Vereinzelung*] in the simplicity of the aloneness [*das Einfache der Allein-heit*] of Dasein."[126] Paradoxically, language is the home that is the place of isolation and aloneness but also the place of unison *(Ein-klang)*, the haven of solitude and the womb of relationality. Moreover, as Heidegger put it in "Was ist Metaphysik?," the experience of the anxiety of being hurled into the abode of language confronting the encompassing nothingness is unnerving, as it "robs us of speech. Because beings as a whole slip away, so that precisely the nothing crowds around, all utterance of the 'is' falls silent in the face of the nothing. That in the uncanniness of anxiety we often try to shatter the vacant stillness with compulsive talk only proves the presence of the nothing."[127] In the postscript to the 1943 edition of this essay, Heidegger reiterates the central point of his argument: "One of the essential sites of speechlessness [*Sprachlosigkeit*] is anxiety in the sense of the horror to which the abyss of the nothing [*Abgrund des Nichts*] attunes human beings."[128]

Significantly, Wittgenstein interpreted Heidegger's notion of anxiety as coming up against the limits of language, expressed most primally in the amazement that one feels that anything at all exists—framed more abstractly as the ultimate metaphysical query about why there is something rather than nothing[129]—a bewilderment so basic that not only is there no satisfactory answer but it cannot even be formulated properly as a question.[130] Elsewhere Wittgenstein delineates this experience of the brute and obstinate facticity of the world as "the mystical" *(das Mystische)*,[131] the inexpressible *(Unaussprechliches)* that "shows itself" *(zeigt sich)*.[132] The onus of the philosophical method stipulates that one say nothing except what can be said *(Nichts zu sagen, als was sich sagen lässt)*,[133] which is to say, to disclose the world as described in the propositional, factual language of the natural sciences but to offer no assurance that the being of the empirical world coincides with the pictures formed by these statements of fact. On this measure, Wittgenstein's own propositions about the nature of language and reality say nothing at all; that is, they are not scientific descriptions of the world, and thus they should be treated as a ladder upon which the reader climbs and then discards. Only when one surmounts (*überwinden*) these propositions does one see the world rightly (*sieht er die Welt richtig*).[134] And this leads Wittgenstein to the seemingly pedestrian but, at the same time, astounding conclusion: "Whereof one cannot speak, thereof one must be silent" (*Wovon man nicht Sprechen kann, darüber muss man schweigen*).[135]

Wittgenstein and Heidegger agree that philosophy has the duty to shed light on the world portrayed in scientific thought but not to provide independent evidence of the facts susceptible to representation. In contrast to Wittgenstein, however, Heidegger does not think it is nonsense to utilize nonscientific language to say the unsayable.[136] The unsayable, in other words, is not what is never uttered but precisely what is always left clandestinely unexpressed in what is overtly expressed. Poetic speech is a pointing to the invisible (*das Zeigen in das Unsichtbare*) through the letting-be heard of the unspoken in the spoken (*das Hörenlassen des Ungesprochenen im Gesprochenen*).[137] Confronting the unsaid of the saying triggers a sense of repulsion, which Heidegger would eventually identify as the "truth of beyng," a disquiet that may be heeded only if one is habituated to the "questioning of nothingness"—the question that cannot be proposed without coaxing one to question the very question of its questionability[138]—whence one discerns that nothingness is "the essential trembling of beyng itself [*die wesentliche Erzitterung des Seyns selbst*] and therefore *is* more than any being."[139]

Still more remarkable than the affinity between the Wittgensteinian and Heideggerian positions is the resemblance of what Heidegger articulated as the mood of anxiety with which one is overcome when mutely facing the nothing of being to what Scholem—perhaps influenced by Benjamin's reflections on the nexus of language and lament[140]—argued in the youthful cogitation "Über Klage und Klagelied," composed in 1917,[141] with respect to the unique status of lamentation:

> All language is infinite. But there is one language whose infinity is deeper and different from all others (besides the language of God). For whereas every language is always a positive expression of a being [*einen positiven Aussdruck eines Wesens*], and its infinity resides in the two bordering lands of the revealed [*Offenbarten*] and the silenced [*Verschwiegenen*], such that it actually stretches out over both realms, this language is different from any other language in that it remains throughout on the border [*Grenze*], exactly on the border between these two realms. This language reveals nothing [*offenbart Nichts*], because the being [*Wesen*] that reveals itself in it has no content (and for that reason one can also say that it reveals everything) and conceals nothing [*verschweigt nichts*], because its entire existence [*Dasein*] is based on a revolution of silence. It is not symbolic, but only points toward the symbol; it is not concrete [*nicht gegenständlich*], but annihilates the object [*vernichtet den Gegenstand*]. This language is lament.[142]

The description of the infinity of language residing between concealment and disclosure—a theme that Scholem would later connect more specifically to the linguistic theory of the kabbalah[143]—is reminiscent of Heidegger's positioning poiēsis on the boundary between speech and speechlessness; that is, poetry is a form of keeping silent by speaking rather than speaking by keeping silent, or in Heidegger's precise formulation to which I referred above, a projective saying through which the preparation of the sayable facilitates the coming to fruition of the unsayable in the world. Analogously, Scholem identifies lament as "nothing other than a language on the border, language of the border itself. Everything it says is infinite, but just and only infinite with regard to the symbol. In lament, nothing is expressed and everything is implied."[144] What is particular about this language is that it does not refer to anything particular but to the condition of being that enframes all beings in an always singularly universal as opposed to a universally singular way: "To be is to be the source of lament [*Sein heißt: Quell von Klage sein*]. Origin and border, as in birth in the sphere of life, converge in the sphere of language within lament."[145]

Furthermore, just as for Heidegger anxiety has no specific object and hence the linguistic response it occasions is, at best, a metaphor of what cannot be rendered metaphorically—the metaphor par excellence that serves as a metaphor that nothing is metaphorical—so for Scholem, lament is a language that both reveals nothing because the being it reveals has no content and conceals nothing because its entire existence is based on a revolution of silence through which there is a restoration (*Zurückführung*) of the symbolic to the revelation that induces mourning's self-overturning (*Sichselbst-überschlagen*) and the consequent reversal (*Umkehrung*) that "allows for the course toward language to emerge as expression."[146] The expression that emerges from this revolution, however, is an expression of the inexpressible, the language of silence, an apophatic proclamation. The poetic elocution, which paradoxically reaches its climax in speaking the unspeakable, is predicated on the agonizing assumption—both liberating and inhibiting—that what is said can never be what is spoken insofar as what is spoken can never be what is said.[147] This is what Scholem intends when he writes that lament is "a completely unsymbolic language, since there is no symbol of a symbol. It is only symbolic in relation to that in mourning, which itself is neither a symbol nor an object, but *was* a symbol and an object; now, however, in annihilation, it signifies the infinite nothing [*das unendliche Nichts*], the zero to an infinite degree [*die Null vom Grade Unendlich*]: the expressionless [*das Ausdruckslose*], the extinguished [*das Erloschene*]."[148] To identify lament as the language of annihilation (*die Sprache der Vernichtung*) means not only that what is declaimed is erased in its very declamation but that the erasure, too, can be erased—and hence be itself— merely through declamation.[149] As Heidegger somewhat enigmatically remarked about the dictum on the basis of which the attunement of the beginning is to be experienced: "*The concealed deep mourning over the veiled decaying of the essence into being as presence* [Die verborgene tiefe Trauer über das verhüllte Ver-wesen des Wesens zum Sein als Anwesenheit]."[150]

It is worth comparing Scholem's tantalizing characterization of lament as an unsymbolic language to the following depiction of language in Heidegger's "Brief über den 'Humanismus'": "In its essence, language is not the utterance [*Äußerung*] of an organism; nor is it the expression [*Ausdruck*] of a living thing. Nor can it ever be thought in an essentially correct way in terms of symbolic character [*Zeichencharakter*], perhaps not even in terms of the character of signification [*Bedeutungscharakter*]. Language is the clearing-concealing advent of being itself [*lichtend-verbergende Ankunft des Seins selbst*]."[151] I do not intend to collapse all the differences between Heidegger and Scholem, but the points of commonality are not without import. For both, language is not primarily a form of chatter or communication, nor is it purely a matter of symbolic signification. It is the opening that reveals and conceals the event of being whose nucleus is nothing. Although the more mature Scholem used the idea of symbol to depict what he considered to be at the heart of the kabbalistic theory of language, it is important to note that his later use of symbol corresponds conceptually to his earlier locution "unsymbolic," that is, the signifier that points to that which is beyond signification. This, in turn, is in the neighborhood of Heidegger's way of speaking about language as the clearing in which beings are disclosed in their hiddenness and hidden in their disclosure.

Here it is well to recall again Wittgenstein's quip in the preface of the *Tractatus*, the second part of which corresponds verbatim to the conclusion of that treatise cited above, that the whole meaning of the book can be summed up as follows: "What can be said at all can be said clearly; and whereof one cannot speak thereof one must be silent." The philosophical burden, then, is to draw the limit (*Grenze*) to thinking (*Denken*), or to be more precise, to the expression of thoughts (*Ausdruck der Gedanken*), to establish the dividing line "to be able to think both sides of this limit," which is to say, to be able to assess what we are capable of thinking and what cannot be thought. The other side to the border of speech, or the limit to thinking, is nonsense (*Unsinn*).[152] Conversely, for both Scholem and Heidegger, the limit is the differentiating point that demarcates the point of nondifferentiation, the borderline between being and nonbeing. From Scholem's standpoint, only lament, the language of the border that marks the liminality of speech, enables one to cross from the silence that has descended into speech to the speech that has ascended unto silence. Hence, in contrast to revelation, whereby "each language is absolutely positive and expresses nothing more than the positivity of the linguistic world," lament entails that "each language suffers death in a truly tragic sense, in that this language expresses nothing, absolutely nothing positive, but only the pure border."[153] Lament is the tragic point of all language, repeatedly attempting to become symbolic but always failing, since as the language of annihilation, every attempt at articulation is, ipso facto, self-annihilation.[154] Alternatively expressed, lament is the silence that cannot be silenced, but, as such, it is the purest and truest form of speech, rendered theologically as the word of God.[155]

> There is no answer to lament, which is to say, there is only one: falling mute [*das Verstummen*]. Here again lament shows itself to be the deep opposition of revelation, which is the linguistic form that absolutely demands an answer and enables one. . . . The teaching that is not expressed, nor alluded to in lament, but that is kept silent, is silence itself. And therefore lament can usurp any language: it is always the not empty, but extinguished expression, in which its death wish and its inability to die join together. The expression of innermost expressionlessness [*der Ausdruck des innerlichst Ausdruckslosen*], the language of silence [*die Sprache des Schweigens*] is lament. This language is infinite, but it has the infinity of annihilation [*die Unendlichkeit der Vernichtung*], which is, as it were, the ultimate power [*Potenz*] of what has been extinguished.[156]

Significantly, as I noted above, Heidegger understood poiēsis as a form of *saying not-saying*.[157] Scholem likewise referred to lament as the *language of silence*, the *expression of the innermost expressionlessness*, the speechless (*das Sprachlose*) that reveals and thereby conceals the nothing at the innermost center (*Mittelpunktes*) of that which has no core (*Kern*).[158] Moreover, in consonance with Heidegger's view that poetic language is "not supposed to express anything, but to leave the unsayable unsaid [*das Unsagbare ungesagt lassen*], and to do so in and through its saying,"[159] Scholem's grappling with the seemingly implacable snare of the apophatic need to speak about not speaking is exemplified in poetic language: "*Every* lament can be expressed as poetry, since its particular liminality [*Grenzhaftigkeit*] between the linguistic realms, its tragic paradox makes it so. . . . Perhaps, indeed, the languages of symbolic objects have no other possibility to become languages of poetry except in the state of lament."[160]

With respect to poetizing in particular and, by extension, language more generally, there is an intertwining of the apophatic and the kataphatic: precisely through the act of saying, the poet leaves the unsayable unsaid, not by being reticent but by saying the unsayable in the unsaying of the sayable. The infinite force that is in each word of lament

> negates itself and sinks back into the infinity of silence, in which the word's emptiness [*Leere*] becomes teaching [*Lehre*] . . . The silent rhythm, the monotony of lament is the only thing that remains: as the only thing that is symbolic in lament—a symbol, namely, of being extinguished [*Erloschenseins*] in the revolution of mourning. . . . But the very inviolability of rhythm in relation to words is what, in the most elementary sense, constitutes all poetry. . . . Lament is thus in poetry what death is in the sphere of life.[161]

Just as death is the only hope for reconciliation in life, lamentation is the restitution of language that occurs through the annihilation of language; that is, the symbolic expression of the inexpressible, which is a form of speaking-not without falling into the silence characteristic of not speaking.[162] The mystical nature of lamentation compels us to discern that the wealth of images utilized by the poet relate to the apparent and not to the objectively real because what the images reveal is the zero point (*Nullpunkt*), expressed mathematically by Scholem as $X \times 0 = 0$.[163] Translating this calculus of the incalculable into an optical metaphor, language can be viewed as the mirror that cannot mirror itself and thus mirrors the image of the nothing that everything is not, the real appearance of what appears to be real.[164]

One can discern the seeds for what Scholem came to identify as the essence of the meaning of language in the Jewish mystical tradition. As he wrote in "Bekenntnis über unsere Sprache," a letter to

Rosenzweig dated December 12, 1926, "The power of the language is hidden within the name; its abyss is sealed therein."[165] Scholem's main concern in the letter is to express the challenge of the secularization of the holiness of the Hebrew language posed by Zionism and the return of the Jewish people to the modern nationalist state, and the threat of being overtaken existentially by an uncanniness (*Unheimlichkeit*) that would ensue from the actualization (*Aktualisierung*) of the language as a vernacular of everyday life and the transition from the sacred to the profane. Hence, the specific language to which Scholem refers in the aforecited remark is Hebrew and the name alludes to the Tetragrammaton. Reworking a rabbinic tradition on the sealing of the cosmic abyss by the letters of the divine name, Scholem speaks of the abyss of language sealed by the name. That abyss, we can assume, is itself inchoate and therefore nameless, an idea that he would notoriously express in a letter to Benjamin, written on September 20, 1934, as the "nothingness of revelation" (*Nichts der Offenbarung*), which he elucidates as "a state in which revelation appears to be without meaning, in which it still asserts itself, in which it has *validity* but no *significance*. A state in which the wealth of meaning is lost and what is in the process of appearing (for revelation is such a process) still does not disappear, even though it is reduced to the zero point of its own content, so to speak."[166]

The connection to Scholem's earlier speculation on lament is obvious: in both instances, he avails himself of the algebraic-geometric concept of the zero point—that is, the inflection point that demarcates the originary nonzero in relation to which all coordinates of the surrounding vector are determined—in order to express the essence of language as the revelation of nothing to be revealed, the appearance of nonappearance, which is to be distinguished from disappearance, for the nonapparent appears, albeit as what does not appear. The nothingness of revelation lays bare language in its most rudimentary form as essentially insignificant—called by some the naked truth but which I prefer to designate the primal investiture, since I do not think we can behold the nakedness of truth except through the veil of truth that unveils the truth of the veil; if divine language comprises the potential for limitless meaning, it cannot be limited to any specific meaning. From the kabbalistic perspective in Scholem's presentation, *Ein Sof* (*das Unendliche*), the concealed Godhead (*die verborgene Gottheit*) without form (*gestaltlos*), dwells indecipherably in the depths of its own being (*in der Tiefe ihres eigenen Wesens unerkennbar ruht*), and thus can be described only negatively, indeed through the negation of all negations (*der Negation aller Negationen*).[167] However, insofar as every expression of the infinite contains the inexpressible, there is an inescapable play of doubleness (*Doppelspiel*), a coincidence of opposites that is labeled by Scholem the *dialectic of form*.[168] To elude interpreting this dialectic in Hegelian terms, I would suggest renaming the phenomenon in Heideggerian jargon as the juxtaposition wherein the autonomous identity of the contraries remains intact: every disclosure is concealment without the concealment being sublated into disclosure, every conferral on creation is a withdrawing from creation without the withdrawal being sublated into conferral.

The concurrent omniabsence of the infinite and its omnipresence thus yields the cosmological paradox that God is present in the world from which God is absent—not that God is absent after being present but rather present and absent at the same time, that is, only present because absent and absent because present. This paradox, in turn, undergirds what Scholem calls the "mystical nihilism" (*mystische Nihilismus*) that has informed kabbalistic metaphysics: inasmuch as "the formless substance" (*die gestaltlose Substanz*) of *Ein Sof* is manifest in every stage of emanation and creation, "there is no thoroughly shaped image [*durchgestaltete Gestalt*] that can completely detach itself from the depths of the formless. . . . The truer the form the more powerful the life of the formless within it."[169] Invoking Benjamin, albeit referred to anonymously as "a great thinker" (*ein großer Denker*),[170] Scholem writes that the kabbalists, by comparing the theory of emanation with mystical linguistic theory of the name of God, were able to grasp that imagelessness is the refuge of all images.[171] Scholem was undeniably correct to detect that Benjamin's claim that the yearning that crosses the threshold of the image to the imageless refuge of all images in the power of the name reverberates with the kabbalistic perspective. But perhaps more pertinent is another observation of Benjamin, mentioned in chapter 4, that the imagination plays a game of dissolution, since there is always a deformation of the image that has been formed.[172] These words cast a light on the central paradox of kabbalistic theosophy underscored by Scholem, and one that, in my opinion, echoes Heidegger's contention regarding the refusal of beyng in relation to the beings it bestows: just as beyng retreats from the beings in which it appears, so the imagelessness of *Ein Sof* is manifestly concealed in the concealedly manifest images of the *sefirot*. Immanuel Ḥai Ricchi succinctly expressed the premise underlying this principle: "the inwardness of the secret [*penimiyyut ha-sod*] is the secret of *Ein Sof*, which sustains the *sefirot*, corresponding to the brain that is within the substance."[173] This insight applies whether the *sefirot* are interpreted as consubstantial with the essence (*aṣmut*) of the divine light or as instruments (*kelim*) through which that light is channeled. That is, whether one adopts the essentialist or the instrumentalist perspective—the two dominant theoretical models to explain the relationship of the sefirotic gradations to *Ein Sof*—one must acknowledge the paradox that the concealment of the infinite can be revealed only insofar as it is concealed, for what is concealed cannot be revealed unless it persists in being concealed. Every act of bestowal, therefore, is concomitantly a withholding. From the perspective of the visionary, the ascent to the pleroma of form is a descent into the abyss of formlessness, and the mystical language that issues therefrom is a speaking that is an unspeaking, the communication of the incommunicable, the imaginal fabrication of a myriad of images in the attempt to reveal and thereby conceal the imagelessness that is devoid of positive content.[174] The imagelessness is preserved in the images by which it is unseen.

Scholem would later identify as the shared characteristic and inner dimension of all mystical traditions the symbolic nature of language, the naming of the absolute concreteness of the word of God that can never assume any particular semantic declension. As he put it in "Der Name Gottes und die Sprachtheorie der Kabbala," based on the lecture given at the Eranos meeting in Ascona in 1970:

> The linguistic theories of mystics frequently diverge when it comes to determining this symbolic nature. But all mystics in quest of the secret of language come to share a common basis, namely the fact that language is used to communicate something which goes way beyond the sphere which allows for expression and formation; the fact, also, that a certain inexpressible something, which only manifests itself in symbols, resonates in every manner of expression; that this something is fundamental to every manner of expression, and . . . flashes through the chinks which exist in the universal structure of expression.[175]

A direct line can be drawn from the reflection on the nature of lament and the speculation on the nature of mystical language.[176] Specifically as it relates to the kabbalah, the original source of all language is the essential name, the name that names the essence but which is not indicative of any specific property or activity. The name, therefore, is the infinitely interpretable wellspring of all signification that itself has no fixed significance.[177] As Scholem expressed it elsewhere, "The word of God must be infinite, or, to put it in a different way, the absolute word is as such meaningless, but it is *pregnant* with meaning. Under human eyes it enters into significant finite embodiments which mark innumerable layers of meaning. . . . Authority no longer resides in a single unmistakable 'meaning' of the divine communication, but in its infinite capacity to take on new forms."[178] Just as the younger Scholem identified lament as the speechlessness at the innermost center of language, so the older Scholem identified the Tetragrammaton, the fulcrum of revelation, as the meaninglessness that enables meaning to be decipherable through exegesis. The primary meaningfulness of language, both human and divine, is not a matter of communication but appeal.[179] This is the crux of Scholem's well-known view that the mystical symbol "'signifies' nothing and communicates nothing, but makes something transparent which is beyond all expression. . . . It is a 'momentary totality' which is perceived intuitively in a mystical *now*—the dimension of time proper to the symbol."[180] What is rendered transparent is not a thing at all; it is the nothingness of revelation, which refers not to the inaccessible transcendence of ontotheological speculation, as some have argued,[181] but to the being exposed in the concealment of its being. The poiēsis of symbolic language renders transparent the transparency of the transparent in the manner of the concavity of the convexity of the mirror mirroring itself. The transparency of this threefold exposure is linked temporally to the now, the modality of time beyond the partition of time, the equiprimordiality of past, present, and future.

The crisis of modernity is the blurring of this transparency that results from the falling silent of tradition, the withdrawal of the name of God from language, and the consequent inability to retrieve the mystery of ineffability. In an oratorical flourish that again calls to mind Heidegger, Scholem insists that poets are the ones who can best address this crisis:

> For poets do not share the doubt that most mystics have in regard to language. And poets have one link with the masters of the Kabbala, even when they reject Kabbalistic theological formulation as being still too emphatic. This link is their belief in language as an absolute, which is as if constantly flung open by dialectics. It is their belief in the mystery of language which has become audible.[182]

Much attention has been paid to the affinities and differences between Benjamin's theory of language and what Scholem elicits about language from the kabbalistic material.[183] There is good historical and textual justification for this comparison. I want to suggest, however, by way of addition and not substitution, that more consideration be given to the views proffered respectively by Scholem and Heidegger. For both, the power of the poet is connected to disclosing the noncommunicable essence of language, the mystery of the nameless that is coiled in the unspoken core of every word spoken. Furthermore, not only were both thinkers keenly aware of the fact that there is no unconcealment that is not also concealment, but they equally understood the current predicament of humanity as one in which the absence—for Heidegger, signifying the obfuscation of beyng by metaphysical machination, and for Scholem, the removal of God from history by ideological secularization—is the most profound presence. Consider Scholem's assessment in his memorial address for Rosenzweig delivered in January 1930:

> The divinity, banished from man by psychology and from the world by sociology, no longer wanting to reside in the heavens, has handed over the throne of justice to dialectical materialism and the seat of mercy to psychoanalysis and has withdrawn to some hidden place and does not disclose Himself. Is He truly undisclosed? Perhaps this last withdrawal is His revelation. Perhaps God's removal to the point of nothingness was a higher need, and He will reveal His kingship only to a world that has been emptied.[184]

Heidegger was less inclined to use such explicit theological terminology, and of course he showed no overt interest in Jewish thought, let alone the complex kabbalistic symbolism lurking behind Scholem's impassioned appraisal of the current existential situation as one in which the name of God has been removed from human language.[185] Notwithstanding these differences, Heidegger would have agreed with Scholem's anarchistic atheology[186] that in a world emptied of all but its own emptiness, occlusion might be the highest form of manifestation. Both thinkers, in addition, seemed keenly aware of the fact that the postphilosophical and metapolitical calling of linguistically revealing the concealment of concealment belongs particularly to the poet, who is endowed with the soteriological task of impelling others to awaken from being oblivious to obliviousness and the consequent need to be redeemed.

In my view, neither Scholem nor Heidegger ever abandoned the allure of the world-negating orientation of Gnosticism, even though in the case of Scholem it was tempered somewhat by the embrace of Zionism and the affirmation of Palestine, later the state of Israel, as the homeland of the Jewish people and Hebrew as the linguistic correlate that grounds the essence of the national identity.[187] One could say that this is equivalent to Heidegger's embrace of Germany and of German as the language most conducive to the disclosure of being, and therefore the most effective language for philosophy and poetry.[188] Just as in Scholem's cultural Zionism, so in Heidegger's attraction to National Socialism, as I will explore in more detail in the next chapter, there is a presumed synergy between language and land—the destiny of one is determinative of and determined by the other. Yet, reading between the lines, one could argue that both Scholem and Heidegger continued to be beleaguered by a disjointedness that was askew with their respective ethno-nationalist ideologies, a melancholic dislocation that led each to feel like a *stranger in a strange land*,[189] even when entrenched in the native soil of either Germany or Palestine-Israel. Moreover, the unassailable sense of the tragic and cataclysmic nature of reality and the saturnine distrust[190] in the prospect of rectification of the world's blemish apart from the restitution of all things to the infinite beyond space and time were critical for Scholem's use of the term *gnostic* as a tool of historical and phenomenological inquiry of kabbalistic sources, especially the depiction of the cosmic drama as a crisis within the inner workings of the Godhead according to the Lurianic teaching and its elaboration in the heretical myth of Sabbatian theology.[191] Scholem's celebrated remark that the messianic idea in Judaism "has compelled a *life lived in deferment*, in which nothing can be done definitively, nothing can be irrevocably accomplished"[192] is indicative of a pessimistic utopianism that rejects the possibility of an enduring sociopolitical redemption even as he maintained that Judaism, in contrast to Christianity, rejected the interiorization of the eschatological ideal without some presentation in the external realm of history.[193] Not only does Scholem declare that Jewish messianism is "in its origins and by its nature—this cannot be sufficiently emphasized—a theory of catastrophe,"[194] but he insists that the "redemption is not the product of immanent developments such as we find it in modern Western reinterpretations of Messianism since the Enlightenment where, secularized as the belief in progress, Messianism still displayed unbroken and immense vigor. It is rather transcendence breaking in upon history, an intrusion in which history itself perishes, transformed in its ruin because it is struck by a beam of light shining into it from an outside source. . . . The apocalyptists have always cherished a pessimistic view of the world. Their optimism, their hope, is not directed to what history will bring forth, but to that which will arise in its ruin, free at last and undisguised."[195]

To my mind, although Scholem's apocalyptic pessimism and the understanding of the messianic as perpetual deferral have deep roots in the Jewish tradition, his particular formulation is in accord with Benjamin's perspective expressed in the "Theologisch-Politisches Fragment":

> Only the Messiah himself completes all history, in the sense that he alone redeems, completes, creates its relation to the messianic. For this reason, nothing that is historical can relate itself, from its own ground, to anything messianic [*Darum kann nichts Historisches von sich aus sich auf Messianisches beziehen wollen*]. Therefore, the Kingdom of God is not the telos of the historical dynamic; it cannot be established as a goal [*Ziel*]. From the standpoint of history, it is not the goal but the terminus [*Ende*]. Therefore, the secular order [*die Ordnung des Profanen*] cannot be built on the idea of the Divine Kingdom, and theocracy has no political but only a religious meaning. . . . For nature is messianic by reason of its eternal and total passing away. To strive for such a passing away—even the passing away of those stages of man that are nature—is the task of world politics, whose method must be called nihilism.[196]

Scholem's interpretation of Jewish messianism, especially as it intersects with Lurianic kabbalah and its aftermath in the Sabbatian and Frankist movements, remains faithful to Benjamin's insight that messianic redemption is not the goal of history but its end, and hence the method most appropriate to *Weltpolitik* is the nihilistic passing away of nature. To be sure, Scholem insists that the constant postponement of messianic redemption—what he calls the "anti-existentialist idea"—accounts for both the greatness and the constitutional weakness of Jewish messianism: whenever the tension between the expectation and the delay has been alleviated by an actual messianic movement, when the abyss that separates the internal-symbolic and the external historical has been crossed, it has been decried or unmasked as pseudo-messianism.[197] The Zionist establishment of the modern state may have been born out of horror and destruction, but it jeopardizes the metahistorical and antipolitical nature of traditional Jewish eschatology, compromising its anarchic and antinomian lifeblood. Scholem thus wondered whether Jewish history "will be able to endure this entry into the concrete realm without perishing in the crisis of the Messianic claim."[198] The apocalyptic spirit stems from the infinite negativity of time, the impossible possibility that makes it always possible that the future that is coming threatens not to be the future one has anticipated. The hopelessness of hope proceeds from the fact that the future we are awaiting can never transpire in time and the homeland we are coveting can never materialize in space.

I note, parenthetically, that the gnostic outlook I ascribe to these two thinkers concurs as well with Rosenzweig's characterization of poetry as "at home neither in time nor in space, but where time and space have their inner origin, in imagistic thinking."[199] The poet, constitutionally, is in a state of *Unheimlichkeit*, a condition that is especially germane to the Jews, since they do not feel at home even in the land promised to them as their inheritance.[200] It should come as no surprise that Rosenzweig signals out the Jewish poet as one who disproportionately bears a sense of disaffection in the world to the point that even language is experienced as a source of exile since it is surrounded by the scriptural word.[201] But beyond just the poet, the whole of the Jewish nation, as the metahistorical reference point in history, is fundamentally at odds with the wheeling and dealing of the sociopolitical world. Curiously, the metahistorical status Rosenzweig assigned to the Jews as the eternal people can be compared profitably to the metapolitical role Heidegger ascribed to the poetic dwelling through which one withdraws from the maneuverings of the mundane. Of course, I do not deny that Rosenzweig advocated a return to life as a conquering of death, but this return is rooted in the belief that redemption is not the consequence of historical development, the effect of a causal chain that links the retention of the past and the protention of the future, but rather the antihistoricist corollary of an expectation that is realized as the expectation of what cannot be realized.[202] Salvation comes by way of eternity diremptively breaking into rather than naturally progressing out of history. In the ritualistic lifecycle of the Jew, typified by the Sabbath, time has been proleptically redeemed. This prolepsis entails the suspension of time, which does not imply a weakening of temporality but its intensification. Eternity is not the exodus from the fluctuations of time into some stationary kingdom of heaven; it is rather the compresence of the three dimensions in the today that is always conscious of being more than today, the tomorrow that is now in virtue of not being now.[203]

The notion of time as a linear circularity operative in Rosenzweig's new thinking militates against the belief that history can redeem itself. Rosenzweig and, I believe, Scholem, would have agreed with Heidegger that enlightenment in the inherently unredeemable world consists of casting light on the shadow so that the shadow is illumined as light. Departing from the Platonic underpinning of the gnostic mythos, there is no escaping the shadowy world by fleeing to the realm of radiant and everlasting truth.[204] The task of the great thinker, Heidegger reminds us, demands jumping over one's shadow, for only through the leap does one surpass the shadow.[205] The surpassing, however, involves abiding within rather than dispelling the shadow. What is dark, Heidegger conjectures, is not dissolved in brightness; it remains concealed and comes to appearance in the light as the nonapparent. True thinking dwells inceptually in the essential space of a dark light.[206] By illumining the dark light and uncovering the shadow as shadow, one is emancipated and thereby reveals that in the showing of the unhidden, beings hide themselves; what is finally disclosed is the concealment that conceals itself in its disclosure.

Notes

1. Heidegger, *Being and Time*, §34, p. 158; *Sein und Zeit*, p. 163. On the centrality of the auditory and the experience of the voice in Heidegger's phenomenology of language, see Groth, *Voice That Thinks*, pp. 73–82.

2. Heidegger, *Being and Time*, §34, p. 159; *Sein und Zeit*, p. 164.

3. Lyon, *Paul Celan*, p. 12.

4. Heidegger, *Being and Time*, §34, p. 158; *Sein und Zeit*, p. 164.

5. Lyon, *Paul Celan*, pp. 12–13.

6. Krell, *Phantoms of the Other*, p. 139. See the discussion of this aspect of Heidegger's thinking about language and silence, informed by the apophatic utterances of medieval Christian mystics, especially Meister Eckhart, in Wolfson, *Language*, pp. 418–19n211. On the influence of Eckhart on Heidegger, see sources cited in the introduction n. 94.

7. Heidegger, *Being and Time*, §34, p. 159; *Sein und Zeit*, p. 165.

8. Heidegger, *Ponderings II–VI*, p. 8; *Überlegungen II–VI*, p. 10. The point is reiterated in Heidegger's "Der Weg zur Sprache," which was part of the lecture series on language arranged in January 1959 by the Bavarian Academy of the Fine Arts and the Academy of the Arts in Berlin. See Heidegger, *On the Way to Language*, pp. 134–35 (*Unterwegs zur Sprache*, p. 255): "Saying will not let itself be captured in any statement. It demands of us that we achieve by silence the appropriating, initiating movement within the being of language [*die ereignende Be-wëgung im Sprachwesen zu erschweigen*]—and do so without talking about silence [*ohne vom Schweigen zu reden*]."

9. Heidegger, *Ponderings II–VI*, p. 13 (emphasis in original); *Überlegungen II–VI*, p. 16.

10. Heidegger, *On the Way to Language*, p. 22; *Unterwegs zur Sprache*, p. 106.

11. Heidegger, *On the Way to Language*, pp. 52–53; *Unterwegs zur Sprache*, p. 144.

12. Heidegger, *Being and Time*, §34, p. 159; *Sein und Zeit*, p. 165. As Heidegger put it in *Hölderlin's Hymn "Remembrance,"* p. 33 (*Hölderlins Hymne "Andenken,"* p. 39), "the first condition for all hearing" is "the quiet passion for the unsaid" (*die stille Leidenschaft für das Ungesagte*).

13. Heidegger, *Ponderings II–VI*, p. 59 (emphasis in original); *Überlegungen II–VI*, p. 78. On talking, listening, and keeping silent, see Bruns, *Heidegger's Estrangements*, pp. 20–26. See also Bruns, *Hermeneutics*, pp. 156–58; Vallega-Neu, "Heidegger's Reticence"; Vallega-Neu, *Heidegger's Poietic Writings*, pp. 9–10, 28, 40, 153, 171–72.

14. See the comments of Wirth in Schelling, *Ages of the World (Fragment)*, pp. 141–42n59, which are repeated in Wirth, *Conspiracy of Life*, pp. 161–62.

15. On the possibility that these terms are derived from Böhme, see Schelling, *Philosophische Untersuchungen*, pp. 128–29n147. See also Schelling, *Philosophical Investigations*, p. 153n50; and the references to Wirth cited in the previous note.

16. Schelling, *Philosophical Investigations*, p. 32; *Philosophische Untersuchungen*, p. 36.

17. Heidegger, *Off the Beaten Track*, p. 46; *Holzwege*, pp. 61–62. Compare Heidegger, *On the Way to Language*, p. 140 (*Unterwegs zur Sprache*, p. 207): "The poetic word of this kind remains an enigma. Its saying has long since returned to silence" [*Ein Rätsel bleibt das dichtende Wort solcher Art, dessen Sagen längst ins Schweigen zurückgegangen*]." See Bruns, *Heidegger's Estrangements*, pp. 163–65. On Heidegger's conception of poetry as a movement from wordlessness into language, see Smith, *Sounding/Silence*. For a representative, and by no means exhaustive, list of other scholarly analyses of Heideggerian poetics, see Wolfson, *Giving*, pp. 333–34n261.

18. Heidegger, *Ponderings II–VI*, p. 56; *Überlegungen II–VI*, p. 74.

19. Heidegger, *Off the Beaten Track*, p. 46; *Holzwege*, p. 62.

20. Heidegger, *Pathmarks*, pp. 248–49; *Wegmarken*, p. 326. See Malpas, *Heidegger's Topology*, pp. 204–5.

21. Whistler, *Schelling's Theory*, pp. 84–85.

22. Heidegger, *Contributions*, §120, p. 187; *Beiträge*, p. 237.

23. Heidegger, *Contributions*, §36, p. 62; *Beiträge*, p. 78.

24. Heidegger, *Contributions*, §36, p. 62; *Beiträge*, p. 78. See Malabou, *Heidegger Change*, pp. 9–10.

25. Heidegger, *Zum Wesen der Sprache*, p. 112.

26. Ibid.

27. Heidegger, *History of Beyng*, p. 178; *Geschichte des Seyns*, p. 211.

28. Heidegger, *Zum Wesen der Sprache*, p. 149, cited in Ziarek, *Language after Heidegger*, p. 64.

29. Heidegger, *Ponderings II–VI*, p. 6; *Überlegungen II–VI*, p. 6. Compare Heidegger, *Vier Hefte I und II*, pp. 35–37: "Die stille *ist* urkundlich in der Sage des Denkens. Sprache ereignet Stille. Die Stille ist der Hort. . . . Das 'im Stillen' gehört nicht nur *auch* zur Sprache—sondern in ihm west das Wesen der Sprache—auch ihr Klang. . . . Die Stille still das Ereignis in die Welt. Die Stille des Wortes ist die weltende Lichtung des Ereignens. Das Wort lichtet den Unterschied; denn es stillt die Stille der Welt. Die Helle ist der Hall der Stille. . . . Das Lichte aus Helle, Helle aus Hall. Hall aus der Stille, Stille aus Welt. . . . Welten ist das Spiel des Spiegels der Stille" (emphasis in original).

30. Heidegger, *Contributions*, §§37–38, p. 63 (emphasis in original); *Beiträge*, pp. 78–79. See Law, "Negative Theology," pp. 145–46; Ænishanslin, "La logique," pp. 364–65; Ziarek, *Language after Heidegger*, pp. 142–74, esp. 149–50.

31. Heidegger, *Contributions*, §23, p. 47; *Beiträge*, p. 58.

32. Heidegger, *Mindfulness*, p. 11; *Besinnung*, p. 15. On the role of the imageless in Heidegger's phenomenology of the nonphenomenalizable, see Vallega-Neu, "Heidegger's Imageless Saying," and Ziarek, "Image-Less Thinking."

33. Wolfson, *Giving*, pp. 171–72, 178, 192, 208–9.

34. Heidegger, *Hölderlin's Hymns "Germania" and "The Rhine,"* p. 62; *Hölderlins Hymnen "Germanien" und "Der Rhein,"* pp. 67–68.

35. Heidegger, *Poetry, Language, Thought*, p. 189; *Unterwegs zur Sprache*, p. 9.

36. Heidegger, *Introduction to Metaphysics*, pp. 182–83; *Einführung in die Metaphysik*, p. 180.

37. Ziarek, *Language after Heidegger*, p. 64.

38. Heidegger, *On the Way to Language*, p. 41; *Unterwegs zur Sprache*, p. 129.

39. Nancy, *Gravity of Thought*, p. 55.

40. Heidegger, *Aus der Erfahrung*, p. 197.

41. Heidegger, *Pathmarks*, p. 86; *Wegmarken*, p. 108.

42. Heidegger, *Contributions*, §129, pp. 193–94; *Beiträge*, p. 246.

43. Laruelle, "On the Black Universe," pp. 106–7. See the analysis of Masciandaro, "Secret," pp. 78–82.

44. Laruelle, "On the Black Universe," pp. 105–6. See the discussion of the mystery in Laruelle, *Mystique non-philosophique*, pp. 60–62, esp. 61: "L'Un-en-Un n'a pas besoin de l'intellect, pas plus d'ailleurs de l'intellect que de l'amour. C'est à cette condition de l'être-forclos de la vision-en-Un, un secret intrinsèque et donc intrinsèquement 'négatif,' sans positivité, insondable à force d'immanence, que le mauvais mystère représentationnel de la mystique peut être éliminé et l'unition devenir l'opération de la connaissance mais non du Réel. La pratique future renonce à pretendre penser l'Un par l'Un, ou avec l'Un, et pense le rapport au mystico-philosophique *selon* l'Un, elle expose le Secret qui fait les Humains par axioms et théorèmes. . . . L'Un comme plan est la métaphysique concentrée sur soi et réalise par consequent comme hallucination transcendantale. Ce n'est pas l'Un-sans-plan, l'Un-sans-unité, *tel* qu'il détermine une authentique connaissance se limitant au champ philosophico-mystique comme à son seul objet. La mystique future détermine cet objet dans un Verbe-fiction non-référentiel sans se fonder sur lui, sans fluer de lui, mais en déterminant son apport. Il n'y a plus de secret ou de mystère 'caché' telle une boîte noire au cœur de l'Un ou de Dieu, en réalité au cœur du Logos. Mais un secret qui reste tel qu'un secret que ne transforme pas sa révélation 'formelle' puisqu'il est déjà révélé. Un révélé-sans révélation, un secret (de) l'Un déjà donné pour le Monde, secret de l'humilité que sa communication n'entame pas" (emphasis in original). Compare the summation of Laruelle's view on the secrecy of the secret in Masciandaro, "Secret," pp. 78–79: "Far from the superficial concept of secrecy as object of knowledge, and farther still from the banal aporia of secret (that there is no secret), the secret of black is exactly that there is **secret**, that **secret** *is*. **Secret** is what remains freely and impenetrably itself, sits securely above intellectual capture, stays outside of opposition as the infinitely open *dual* of light" (emphasis in original).

45. Wolfson, "Murmuring Secrets," pp. 85–99.

46. I have here availed myself of the language of Nancy, *Gravity of Thought*, p. 80.

47. Cordovero, *Pardes Rimmonim*, 5:4, p. 63. For other sixteenth-century sources that preserve variations of this dictum, see reference to my study in the introduction n. 41.

48. Heidegger, *Elucidations*, p. 43; *Erläuterungen*, p. 24. The passage is cited partially in ch. 8 at n. 109.

49. Heidegger, *Hölderlin's Hymns "Germania" and "The Rhine,"* p. 226; *Hölderlins Hymnen "Germanien" und "Der Rhein,"* p. 250.

50. Heidegger, *Hölderlin's Hymns "Germania" and "The Rhine,"* p. 226 (emphasis in original); *Hölderlins Hymnen "Germanien" und "Der Rhein,"* p. 250.

51. Heidegger, *Hölderlin's Hymns "Germania" and "The Rhine,"* pp. 226–27; *Hölderlins Hymnen "Germanien" und "Der Rhein,"* p. 250.

52. Heidegger, *Hölderlin's Hymns "Germania" and "The Rhine,"* pp. 105–6; *Hölderlins Hymnen "Germanien" und "Der Rhein,"* pp. 116–17. On Heidegger's characterization of time in its primordiality as the nexus of withdrawing and transporting, contracting and expanding, see texts cited and analyzed in ch. 6 at nn. 109–11.

53. Heidegger, *On the Way to Language*, p. 50 (emphasis in original); *Unterwegs zur Sprache*, p. 140.

54. Heidegger, *Sojourns*, p. 45; *Aufenthalte*, p. 27a.

55. Heidegger, *Contributions*, §259, p. 338; *Beiträge*, p. 428.

56. Heidegger, *Poetry, Language, Thought*, p. 54; *Holzwege*, p. 41.

57. Heidegger, *Poetry, Language, Thought*, p. 60; *Holzwege*, p. 48.

58. Heidegger, *Contributions*, §246, p. 309; *Beiträge*, p. 392.

59. Heidegger, *Pathmarks*, p. 148; *Wegmarken*, p. 193.

60. Heidegger, *Pathmarks*, p. 148; *Wegmarken*, pp. 193–94.

61. Heidegger, *Contributions*, §14, pp. 30–31; *Beiträge*, p. 36.

62. Heidegger, *Essence of Truth*, p. 20; *Vom Wesen der Wahrheit*, p. 25.

63. Heidegger, *What Is Called Thinking?*, p. 19; *Was Heißt Denken?*, p. 21.

64. Arendt, "Martin Heidegger at Eighty," p. 300.

65. Schürmann, *Heidegger on Being and Acting*, p. 314n46 (emphasis in original).

66. The invisibility of which I speak may be profitably compared to the theoretical and heuristic role accorded dark matter in contemporary

astrophysics, the matter that is not visually detected—seemingly because it does not interact with light in any measurable way—but which is presumed to be causally responsible for the gravitational pull on the matter that is visible. My argument, moreover, is rooted in an epistemological perspectivism according to which we never see all the sides of any phenomenon, and hence everything visible is cloaked in invisibility. This is true of the truth as well, which we can see only partially, and consequently, as Heidegger repeatedly argued, every truth is intertwined with untruth. An entirely different consideration is the phenomenological and neuroscientific issue of our capacity to see absence, not simply as a cognitive deduction on the basis of what we perceive as not being present, but as an actual experience of the absence of objects, to the point perhaps that we visually apprehend presence only through the veneer of absence. For a lucid examination of the paradox of the perception of absence, see Farennikova, "Seeing Absence," and the nuanced rejoinder by Vadiya in "Absence: An Indo-Analytic Inquiry."

67. Blumenberg, *Paradigms for a Metaphorology*, p. 41 (emphasis in original).

68. Blumenberg, *Paradigms for a Metaphorology*, pp. 3–5 (emphasis in original).

69. For an attempt to utilize Blumenberg to illumine the role of metaphors in kabbalistic texts as occupying a position between the poles of midrash and philosophy, see Necker, "Hans Blumenberg's Metaphorology."

70. Blumenberg, *Paradigms for a Metaphorology*, pp. 4–5.

71. Blumenberg, "Light as a Metaphor for Truth," p. 31.

72. The logic of my argument against the possibility of a naked truth is comparable to the argument against the possibility of pinpointing a chronological beginning to time, the hypothetical $t = 0$ postulated by physicists. That is, just as the beginning cannot begin unless it had already begun—hence we must presume that any beginning is a reiteration of a prior beginning—so we cannot get to a truth that is completely denuded inasmuch as the disrobing of truth will always disclose another layer of truth, which is to say untruth, to be disrobed.

73. Heidegger, *Hölderlin's Hymns "Germania" and "The Rhine,"* p. 108 (emphasis in original); *Hölderlins Hymnen "Germanien" und "Der Rhein,"* p. 119. I have taken the opportunity to repeat some of my analysis in Wolfson, *Duplicity*, pp. 116–17.

74. Heidegger, *Contributions*, §13, p. 30; *Beiträge*, p. 36.

75. Heidegger, *Identity and Difference*, p. 73.

76. Ibid., p. 142. The translation appears in Bernasconi, *Question of Language*, p. 77, and see Wolfson, *Giving*, pp. 13 and 283n99.

77. Heidegger, *Contributions*, §§37–38, pp. 62–63 (emphasis in original); *Beiträge*, pp. 78–79. See Brito, *Heidegger et l'hymne du sacré*, pp. 103–13, and other references cited above, n. 30.

78. Heidegger, *Contributions*, §255, p. 323 (emphasis in original); *Beiträge*, pp. 407–8. Compare Heidegger, *Ponderings II–IV*, p. 189 (*Überlegungen II–VI*, p. 258): "Every essential thinker always *thinks* about a decisive leap more originarily than he *speaks* of it; and in *that* thinking he must be grasped and *his* unsaid must be said. . . . Therefore, interpretation is required" (emphasis in original).

79. Heidegger, *Poetry, Language, Thought*, p. 11; *Aus der Erfahrung*, p. 83.

80. Heidegger, *Hölderlin's Hymns "Germania" and "The Rhine,"* p. 40 (emphasis in original); *Hölderlins Hymnen "Germanien" und "Der Rhein,"* p. 41.

81. Heidegger, *Hölderlin's Hymns "Germania" and "The Rhine,"* p. 40; *Hölderlins Hymnen "Germanien" und "Der Rhein,"* p. 41.

82. Heidegger, *Hölderlin's Hymns "Germania" and "The Rhine,"* p. 44; *Hölderlins Hymnen "Germanien" und "Der Rhein,"* p. 45.

83. Heidegger, *On the Way to Language*, pp. 120–22; *Unterwegs zur Sprache*, pp. 240–42.

84. Heidegger, *Contributions*, §32, p. 58; *Beiträge*, p. 72.

85. Heidegger, *Ponderings II–VI*, p. 22; *Überlegungen II–VI*, p. 28.

86. Heidegger, *Pathmarks*, p. 252; *Wegmarken*, p. 331.

87. See ch. 1 at nn. 64–65.

88. Heidegger, *Pathmarks*, p. 375n11.

89. Heidegger, *Pathmarks*, p. 255; *Wegmarken*, p. 334.

90. Heidegger, *Pathmarks*, pp. 254–55; *Wegmarken*, p. 334.

91. Heidegger, *Off the Beaten Track*, p. 85; *Holzwege*, p. 113.

92. Heidegger, *Pathmarks*, p. 253; *Wegmarken*, p. 332.

93. Heidegger, *Pathmarks*, p. 253; *Wegmarken*, p. 332.

94. Heidegger, *Pathmarks*, p. 253; *Wegmarken*, p. 333.

95. Derrida, *Heidegger: The Question*, p. 56; *Heidegger: la question*, p. 97.

96. Heidegger, *Pathmarks*, p. 254; *Wegmarken*, p. 333. See ch. 2 n. 92. And consider the account of the "thoughtful concern for authentic knowing" offered by Heidegger, *Heraclitus*, p. 278 (*Heraklit*, p. 373): "Philosophy is not a 'discipline,' nor an academic 'major' or 'minor': rather, it is a *joint* [Fuge] in which beyng joins [*zu-fügt*] itself to the thinking human, presuming that beyng is the jointure [*Fügung*] that operates as this joint among humans" (emphasis in original).

97. Derrida, *Heidegger: The Question*, p. 57; *Heidegger: la question*, p. 98. In *Duplicity*, p. 140, I noted that Heidegger's apolitical disavowal of the political after stepping away from the office of the rectorate showed a penchant for the esoteric (for other scholars who have weighed in on this issue, see ibid., p. 181n35), but I did not pursue the connection between esotericism, the occult, and National Socialism. Consider the nexus between occultism, capitalism, and totalitarianism in the "Theses against Occultism" by Adorno, in *Minima Moralia*, pp. 239–42: "By its regression to magic under late capitalism, thought is assimilated to late capitalist forms. . . . The hypnotic power exerted by things occult resembles totalitarian terror: in present-day processes the two are merged. The smiling of auguries is amplified in society's sardonic laughter at itself, gloating over the direct material exploitation of souls. The horoscope corresponds to the official directives to the nations, and number-mysticism is preparation for administrative statistics and cartel prices. Integration itself proves in the end to be an ideology for disintegration into power groups which exterminate each other. He who integrates is lost. . . . The power of occultism, as of Fascism, to which it is connected by thought-patterns of the ilk of anti-semitism, is not only pathic. Rather it lies in the fact that in the lesser panaceas, as in superimposed pictures, consciousness famished for truth imagines it is grasping a dimly present knowledge diligently denied to it by official progress in all its forms. . . . Occultists rightly feel drawn towards childishly monstrous scientific fantasies. . . . Occultism is the metaphysic of dunces. The mediocrity of the mediums is no more accidental than the apocryphal triviality of the revelations. . . . The worthless magic is nothing other than the worthless existence it lights up. This is what makes the prosaic so cosy. Facts which differ from what is the case only by not being facts are trumped up as a fourth dimension." Compare Wasserstrom, "Adorno's Kabbalah," pp. 66–69; Josephson-Storm, *Myth of Disenchantment*, pp. 311–12. There has been a wealth of studies on National Socialism and the occult, of which I will here mention two examples: Goodrick-Clarke, *Occult Roots of Nazism*, and Staudenmaier, *Between Occultism and Nazism*. Perhaps I shall return to this important matter in an independent study.

98. Derrida, *Heidegger: The Question*, p. 57; *Heidegger: la question*, p. 99.

99. Heidegger, *Pathmarks*, p. 254; *Wegmarken*, p. 334. On the anthropocentric implications of Heidegger's denying a sense of worldliness and history to plants and animals based on their ostensible lack of language, see the texts cited and analyzed in Wolfson, *Duplicity*, pp. 39–42. Many have weighed in on the construction of animality in Heidegger's thought. For an innovative approach that challenges Heidegger's alleged anthropocentrism, see Iveson, "Animals in Looking-Glass World"; Iveson, "Wo und Ob: Heidegger's Animal Differently."

100. Heidegger, *Basic Writings*, p. 315; *Vorträge und Aufsätze*, p. 11.

101. Heidegger, *Basic Writings*, p. 317; *Vorträge und Aufsätze*, p. 12.

102. Heidegger, *Basic Writings*, p. 317; *Vorträge und Aufsätze*, p. 12.

103. Heidegger, *Basic Writings*, pp. 317–18; *Vorträge und Aufsätze*, p. 13.

104. Heidegger, *Ponderings II–VI*, p. 171 (emphasis in original); *Überlegungen II–VI*, p. 234.

105. Heidegger, *Pathmarks*, p. 255; *Wegmarken*, pp. 334–35.

106. Heidegger, *Contributions*, §276, p. 391; *Beiträge*, p. 497.

107. Heidegger, *Contributions*, §41, p. 66; *Beiträge*, p. 83.

108. Heidegger, *Contributions*, §281, p. 401; *Beiträge*, p. 510.

109. Heidegger, *Contributions*, §281, p. 401 (emphasis in original); *Beiträge*, p. 510.

110. See ch. 4 n. 272.

111. Heidegger, *Pathmarks*, pp. 86–88; *Wegmarken*, pp. 109–11.

112. See the passage cited in ch. 4 at n. 277.

113. Heidegger, *Being and Time*, §40, pp. 182–83; *Sein und Zeit*, pp. 188–89. For an extensive discussion of this theme, see Withy, *Heidegger on Being Uncanny*, pp. 48–101.

114. For comparison of the Freudian *Unheimliche* as a psychological sentiment and Heidegger's *Unheimlichkeit* as an ontological dimension of Dasein, see Masschelein, *Unconcept*, pp. 139–43. The Heideggerian and Freudian approaches to anxiety are analyzed in Rot, "From Anxiety to Boredom."

115. According to the formulation of Kisiel and Sheehan in the annotated glossary in *Becoming Heidegger*, p. 430, s.v. *Bekümmerung*. See ibid., p. 438, s.v. *Sorgen*; Hoffmann, *Heideggers Phänomenologie*, pp. 39–43; Crowe, *Heidegger's Religious Origins*, pp. 38, 57, 79, 172–74; Duff, *Heidegger and Politics*, pp. 33–34, 113, 182–83.

116. Heidegger, *Phenomenological Interpretations of Aristotle*, p. 53; *Phänomenologische Interpretationen zu Aristoteles*, p. 70.

117. Heidegger, *Pathmarks*, p. 88; *Wegmarken*, pp. 111–12. See Bernasconi, *Question of Language*, pp. 54–57; Rot, "From Anxiety to Boredom," pp. 53–54, 57–58.

118. Heidegger, *Ponderings II–VI*, pp. 52–54 (emphasis in original); *Überlegungen II–VI*, pp. 69–71.

119. Reitzenstein, *Hellenistic Mystery-Religions*, p. 354; Schmithals, *Gnosis in Korinth*, pp. 82–134; Rudolph, *Gnosis*, pp. 121–22, 131–32.

120. Bultmann, *Theology of the New Testament*, 1:166–67, 175–77. See the pertinent comments in Macquarrie, *Existential Theology*, pp. 86–87, 173. On Heidegger's dialogue with Bultmann and his participation in the latter's seminar on Paul, see Dastur, "Heidegger et la théologie," p. 234. For criticism of the appropriateness of the gnostic redeemer myth, see Meeks, *Prophet-King*, pp. 14–16.

121. Jonas, *Gnosis und spätantiker Geist*, 1:96–98; Jonas, *Gnostic Religion*, pp. 49–51, 75–80.

122. Heidegger, *Ponderings II–VI*, p. 54 (emphasis in original); *Überlegungen II–VI*, p. 71.

123. Bultmann, *Theology*, 1:165 (emphasis in original).

124. Heidegger, *Ponderings II–VI*, p. 46 (*Überlegungen II–VI*, p. 70): "The *essential fortuitiveness of being* (partitioning) is the fearfulness of its essence and likewise the concealment of the blessing. On the 'ground' of this—namely, *the* fortuitiveness as such in being—the entire superficiality of the *sciences*—causal research—first becomes visible, and therein is manifest how much they foster the semblance of truth and do so merely in a previously dimmed realm. . . . Fortuitiveness and groundlessness and width and breadth of the future of being" (emphasis in original).

125. Jonas, *Gnosis und spätantiker Geist*, 1:106–9, mentioned Heidegger in his discussion of the motif of thrownness (*Geworfensein*) in gnostic sources.

126. Heidegger, *Ponderings II–VI*, p. 54 (emphasis in original); *Überlegungen II–VI*, p. 71. Compare *Ponderings II–VI*, p. 160 (*Überlegungen II–VI*, p. 218): "A history of philosophy is to be presented as the history of the great isolation [*Vereinsamung*]." Contrary to what one might expect, Heidegger maintained that true community (*Gemeinschaft*) can only grow out of the sense of aloneness (*Alleinheit*) of the individual. See Heidegger, *Ponderings II–VI*, p. 45 (*Überlegungen II–VI*, p. 59): "Only if and only as long as this originary *aloneness* of Dasein is experienced can true community grow indigenously; only thus is to be overcome all publicness of those who have come together and are driven together" (emphasis in original). It is of interest to compare Heidegger's view to the perspective on Zionism affirmed by Scholem in "Abschied," an open letter to Siegfried Bernfeld, published in *Jerubbaal, Eine Zeitschrift der jüdischen Jugend* 1 (1918–19): 125–30, and translated in Scholem, *On Jews and Judaism*, pp. 54–60. The relevant passage appears on pp. 55–57: "The great demand of Zionism, which is eternally one, to be a holy people, has a presupposition the misunderstanding of which is in a real sense the chimerical basis for that objective mendacity against which witness is to be given here. Community demands solitude: not the possibility of together desiring the same, but only that of common solitude establishes community. Zion, the source of our nationhood, is the common, indeed in an uncanny sense, the identical solitude of all Jews, and the religious assertion of Zionism is nothing other than this: the midst of solitude happens at the same time to be where all gather together, and there can be no other place for such a gathering together. . . . There is only one place from which Zion can be reached and youth restituted: solitude. And there is only one medium, brought to radiance by labor, that will be the source of renewal: the existence that must be the argument against a youth that has desecrated words." It is of interest to recall Rosenzweig's depiction of Scholem in a letter to Rudolf Hallo, dated May 12, 1921, in Rosenzweig, *Briefe und Tagebücher*, p. 704: "Er ist vielleicht der einzige schon wirklich Heimgekehrte, den es gibt. Aber er ist allein heimgekehrt." Scholem's missive was a critique of what he referred to as the "pseudo-Zionist lie of community" (*On Jews and Judaism*, p. 55) promulgated by the German Zionist youth movement, but his view is related to an idea proffered by a number of thinkers in the early part of the twentieth century, including Landauer and Buber, to the effect that true individuality is expressive of community, that the latter can only proceed from an originary aloneness, that the solitude of the contemplative is precisely what engenders the possibility of genuine sociality. For discussion of this theme and citation of some of the relevant sources, see Wolfson, "Theolatry," pp. 5–9. Recently, Biale, *Gershom Scholem: Master of the Kabbalah*, pp. 60–61, suggested that the tension between desire for community, on the one hand, and the need for solitude, on the other hand, may explain why Scholem "found it so hard to fulfill his Zionist dreams."

127. Heidegger, *Pathmarks*, p. 89; *Wegmarken*, p. 112.

128. Heidegger, *Pathmarks*, p. 238; *Wegmarken*, p. 312. The continuation of this passage is cited in ch. 3 at n. 96.

129. For analysis of this principle, especially as advanced by Leibniz, see Heidegger, *Metaphysical Foundations*, pp. 114–15; *Metaphysische Anfangsgründe*, pp. 141–42.

130. McGuinness, ed., *Ludwig Wittgenstein*, p. 68: "To be sure, I can imagine what Heidegger means by being and anxiety. Man feels the urge to run up

against the limits of language. Think for example of the astonishment that anything at all exists. This astonishment cannot be expressed in the form of a question, and there is also no answer whatsoever. Anything we might say is *a priori* bound to be mere nonsense. Nevertheless we do run up against the limits of language." Wittgenstein adds a note here: "Feeling the world as a limited whole—it is this that is mystical. 'Nothing can happen to me,' that is, whatever may happen, for me it is without significance." The first proposition corresponds to Wittgenstein, *Tractatus*, 6.45, pp. 186–87: "The contemplation [*Anschauung*] of the world sub specie aeterni is its contemplation as a limited whole [*begrenztes—Ganzes*]. The feeling [*Gefühl*] of the world as a limited whole is the mystical feeling." Notably, in the continuation of the passage from his conversation with Waismann, Wittgenstein adds the example of Kierkegaard and the paradox and then identifies the running up against the limits of language as ethics (McGuinness, ed., *Ludwig Wittgenstein*, p. 68). On the similarity between Wittgenstein's anguish over the nature of being and Heidegger's analysis of *Sorge*, see Steiner, *Grammars of Creation*, p. 272.

131. Wittgenstein, *Tractatus*, 6.44, pp. 186–87: "Not *how* the world is, is the mystical, but *that* it is" (*Nicht wie die Welt ist, ist das Mystische, sondern dass sie ist*).

132. Ibid., 6.522, pp. 186–87: "There is indeed the inexpressible. This *shows* itself; it is the mystical" (*Es gibt allerdings Unaussprechliches. Dies zeigt sich, es is das Mystische*). For a comparison of Wittgenstein and James on the demarcation of the mystical as that which can be shown as opposed to the delineation and classification of conceptual-linguistic facts, see Goodman, *Wittgenstein*, pp. 43–50.

133. Wittgenstein, *Tractatus*, 6.53, pp. 188–89.

134. Ibid., 6.54, pp. 188–89. From Wittgenstein's comment that those who understand his own propositions will finally recognize them as senseless (*unsinnig*), I assume that the metaphor of disposing the ladder after one has climbed on it—in Wittgenstein's precise language: *Er muss sozusagen die Leiter wegwerfen, nachdem er auf ihr hinaufgestiegen ist*—is meant in a permanent way. For a different interpretation, see Comay and Ruda, *Dash*, p. 84. Provocatively, the authors suggest that perhaps, even for Wittgenstein, the throwing away of the ladder needs "continual restaging, which would require keeping the ladder on hand if only to be able to keep on demonstrating its superfluity." After tentatively proposing this explanation, the authors offer an alternative that resonates with the approach I have adopted: "or is the whole point of the exercise to demonstrate precisely that *there is no there, there*—an insight that would make any ladder at once superfluous and insufficient?"

135. Wittgenstein, *Tractatus*, 7, pp. 188–89. For an analysis on the connection between grammar and reality in Wittgenstein against the backdrop of semantic ineffability, see McCutcheon, *Religion*, pp. 97–107, esp. 99–101.

136. My analysis has benefited from Carman, "What Science Leaves Unsaid." See also Rorty, "Wittgenstein, Heidegger and the Reification of Language," in *Philosophical Papers*, 2:50–65; and the analysis of Heidegger and the grammar of being in Priest, *Beyond the Limits*, pp. 237–48.

137. Heidegger, *Aus der Erfahrung*, p. 197.

138. Heidegger, *Pathmarks*, p. 85; *Wegmarken*, p. 108.

139. Heidegger, *Contributions*, §145, p. 209 (emphasis in original); *Beiträge*, p. 266.

140. Barouch, "Lamenting Language," pp. 7–16. See also Weidner, *Gershom Scholem*, pp. 191–96; Ferber, "Language of the Border," pp. 165–66, 175–76, 180–85; Ferber, "Lament and Pure Language"; Ferber, "Incline Thine Ear"; Sauter, "Ghost of the Poet"; Schwebel, "Lament and the Shattered Expression"; Schwebel, "Tradition in Ruins." See below, n. 183.

141. The original German was published in Scholem, *Tagebücher*, 2:128–33; an English translation by Lina Barouch and Paula Schwebel appeared as Scholem, "On Lament and Lamentation." A Hebrew translation of the German by Tali Koons was published in *Lamentations: Poetry and Thought in Gershom Scholem's World*, pp. 88–94. Scholem's interest in lament in his early speculation on the nature of language and Jewish thought has been the focus of a number of scholars. In addition to the references cited in the previous note, see Weigel, "Scholems Gedichte"; Weigel, "Role of Lamentation"; Barouch, "Sprache zwischen Klage und Rache"; Barouch, "Erasure and Endurance of Lament"; Barouch, "Dancing on the Rope"; Barouch, *Between German and Hebrew*, pp. 23–76; Bielik-Robson, "Unfallen Silence"; Weidner, "'Movement of Language'"; Ferber, "Gershom Scholem on the Language of Lament."

142. Scholem, "On Lament," p. 313; *Tagebücher*, 2:128.

143. See the passage from Scholem, *Messianic Idea*, p. 293, cited in the introduction at n. 36.

144. Scholem, "On Lament," p. 313; *Tagebücher*, 2:128.

145. Scholem, "Job's Lament," p. 322; *Tagebücher*, 2:546.

146. Scholem, "On Lament," p. 316; *Tagebücher*, 2:130.

147. Barouch, in both "Erasure and Endurance of Lament," pp. 15–16 and "Dancing on the Rope," p. 159, relies on the understanding of apophasis as a linguistic expression that oscillates between the poles of saying and unsaying proffered by Sells, *Mystical Languages*. It appears that Barouch is unaware of my own discussion of the juxtaposition of the kataphatic and the apophatic in kabbalistic texts and other mystical traditions. I concur with Sells in marking apophasis as a verbal act, what I call speaking-not as opposed to not speaking, but I advance a more paradoxical understanding of the paradox by emphasizing that the saying itself is a verbal gesture of unsaying. See Wolfson, *Language*, pp. 215, 217–19, 343; Wolfson, *Venturing Beyond*, pp. 246–48; Wolfson, "Murmuring Secrets," pp. 91–99; Wolfson, "Nihilating Nonground," pp. 38–39. Also pertinent here is the discussion in Wolfson, *Abraham Abulafia*, pp. 10–38, of Scholem's understanding of the nature of the secret and the authentic esoteric tradition that he culls from kabbalistic literature. The paradox of disclosing the secret by concealing it—every disclosure of the concealment is a concealment of the disclosure—corresponds to the demarcation of mystical language as a saying that is an unsaying. See Wolfson, *Abraham Abulafia*, pp. 28–29, where I note the parallel between the inseparability of concealment and unconcealment in Heidegger's understanding of truth and Scholem's assumption that a secret can be revealed only to the extent that it remains hidden. Finally, it is worth recalling that in the 1918 essay "Abschied," Scholem argued that the true power of the Zionist revival of the national language was to be discerned from cultivating the "possibility of being silent in Hebrew." See Scholem, *On Jews and Judaism*, p. 57.

148. Scholem, "On Lament," p. 317 (emphasis in original); *Tagebücher*, 2:131. The similarity between the Heideggerian *Angst* and the Scholemian *Trauer* is mentioned by Bielik-Robson, "Unfallen Silence," p. 144. After noting the affinity, Bielik-Robson draws the following contrast: "But for Scholem being a symbol indicates something more than just a lack of literal objectivity. It is also evidence of a mythic knowledge of the world as a hermetic natural totality, one that is necessarily dark, vague, fluid, and half-concealed, for it lacks an external standpoint of judgment (precisely as in the famous saying of Heraclitus from Fragment 123, *physis kryptesthai philei*, 'nature loves to hide'). While the language of revelation is literality itself—*das Aussprechlichste*, reserving no recess of darkness in its all-revealing light—the mythic knowledge of immanence rests in the silence of the symbol." Heidegger surely uses a different terminology, but what is attributed to Scholem can be elicited from his thinking as well, including the interpretation linked to the Heraclitean dictum, which Heidegger invokes to support his claim that the self-revealing of being is always also a self-concealing. See references to primary and secondary sources cited in the introduction n. 51. And compare Heidegger, *Heraclitus*, p. 282 (*Heraklit*, p. 379): "Light takes up that which is illuminated, and brings it to appearance against darkening and veiling. However, at the same time, the light must relinquish the illuminated."

149. Scholem, "On Lament," p. 314; *Tagebücher*, 2:129.

150. Heidegger, *Ponderings II–VI*, p. 55 (emphasis in original); *Überlegungen II–VI*, p. 72.

151. Heidegger, *Pathmarks*, pp. 248–49; *Wegmarken*, p. 326.

152. Wittgenstein, *Tractatus*, p. 27. See Wolfson, *Language*, pp. 289–91; Knepper, "Ineffability Investigations." For comparative analyses of the topic of silence or the unsayable in the thought of Heidegger and Wittgenstein, see McCormick, "Saying and Showing"; McCormick, *Heidegger and the Language of the World*, pp. 157–71; Bindeman, *Heidegger and Wittgenstein*; and Dhawan, *Impossible Speech*, pp. 122–97. On Heidegger and Wittgenstein, see also Wolfson, *Language*, pp. 15–16, and other studies cited therein on p. 410nn128–29. See as well my remarks, ibid., p. 419n211, and the slightly revised position in Wolfson, "Skepticism," pp. 506–8. See also Philipse, "Heidegger and Wittgenstein."

153. Scholem, "On Lament," p. 314; *Tagebücher*, 2:129.

154. Scholem, "On Lament," p. 314; *Tagebücher*, 2:129.

155. Bielik-Robson, "Unfallen Silence," p. 142, refers to Scholem's understanding of lament as the "counter-revelation" based on its comportment as the *unsilenceable silence*, that is, the silence that is "on par with the most pronounced, *ausprechlichst*, Word Divine. Silence as a tragic counter-revelation, rising up to meet 'revelation proper.'"

156. Scholem, "On Lament," p. 316; *Tagebücher*, 2:130–31.

157. See above, n. 76.

158. Scholem, "On Lament," p. 316; *Tagebücher*, 2:130.

159. Heidegger, *Hölderlin's Hymns "Germania" and "The Rhine,"* p. 108; *Hölderlins Hymnen "Germanien" und "Der Rhein,"* p. 119.

160. Scholem, "On Lament," p. 317 (emphasis in original); *Tagebücher*, 2:130–31. For a different assessment of Scholem's early writings on language and the mystical experience, related specifically to a critique of revelation as an ecstatic experience that must be translated into a poetic dictum, see Biale, *Gershom Scholem: Kabbalah and Counter-History*,

pp. 86–89. Also relevant is the poetic interpretation of some of Scholem's early writings on tradition and his later work on kabbalah and philology offered by Weidner, "Reading Gershom Scholem."

161. Scholem, "On Lament," p. 318; *Tagebücher*, 2:132.

162. Scholem, "On Lament," p. 319; *Tagebücher*, 2:133.

163. Scholem, "Job's Lament," p. 323; *Tagebücher*, 2:547.

164. Scholem, "Job's Lament," 322; *Tagebücher*, 2:546.

165. Scholem, *On the Possibility*, p. 28. A Hebrew version of the letter appeared in Scholem, *Explications and Implications*, pp. 59–60. The text was translated into French by Mosès, "Une lettre inédite" and analyzed by Mosès, "Langage et sécularisation," and Mosès, *Angel of History*, pp. 168–82. See also Brocke, "Franz Rosenzweig und Gerhard Gershom Scholem"; Derrida, *Acts of Religion*, pp. 191–227; Shahar, "Sacred and the Unfamiliar"; Herzog, "'Monolingualism' or the Language of God"; Barouch, *Between German and Hebrew*, pp. 47–48. The essay, which includes a transcription of the original German of the letter, is also available at http://www. steinheim institut.de/ edocs/bpdf/ michael_ brocke-franz_ rosenzweig_ und_ gerhard_ gershom scholem.pdf. According to the signature of the original German, the letter was written on 7 Tevet 5687, which corresponds to December 12, 1926. The date given in the Hebrew, English, and French versions is December 26, 1926, which refers not to the date of composition but the date of the occasion for which the letter was written, namely, the celebration of Rosenzweig's fortieth birthday. To be precise, Rosenzweig's birthdate is December 25, but apparently it was commemorated one day after the Christmas holiday. My gratitude to David Biale for clarifying this issue.

166. Scholem, ed., *Correspondence of Walter Benjamin and Gershom Scholem*, p. 142 (emphasis in original); Scholem, ed., *Walter Benjamin/Gershom Scholem: Briefwechsel*, p. 175. Regarding Scholem's "nothingness of revelation," see Wolfson, *Venturing Beyond*, p. 233, and reference to other scholars cited there in n. 166; and additional sources cited in Wolfson, "Not Yet Now," p. 171n166.

167. Scholem, *On the Mystical Shape*, p. 38; *Von der mystischen Gestalt*, p. 31. Compare the use of the expression *Negation auf Negation* on the part of the kabbalists to refer to the unity of *Ein Sof* in Scholem, *Geheimnisse der Schöpfung*, p. 33. See, however, Scholem, *Major Trends*, p. 11, where the Maimonidean view of God as the "negation of negation" is contrasted with the kabbalistic understanding of the conflict between the known and unknown aspects of God.

168. Scholem, *On the Mystical Shape*, p. 41; *Von der mystischen Gestalt*, p. 33.

169. Scholem, *On the Mystical Shape*, pp. 41–42; *Von der mystischen Gestalt*, 34. See Kaufmann, "Imageless Refuge," pp. 152–53; Wolfson, *Language*, pp. 122–23. Of the many sources that could have been cited to corroborate the paradox of the formless form articulated by Scholem, I mention the following depiction of the divine in *Sefer ha-Iyyun* in Verman, *Books of Contemplation*, p. 69 (Hebrew text, p. 65): "He possesses the power of shape [*demut*] and the power of image [*temunah*] and the power of form [*ṣurah*], which is not perceived [*nikkeret*]. He is unique [*meyuḥad*] and His unity is revealed and covered [*we-yiḥudo megulleh u-mekhusseh*], hidden and secret [*nistar we-ne'lam*]." See the critical edition in Porat, ed., *Works of Iyyun*, p. 99.

170. Scholem, *Von der mystischen Gestalt*, p. 47. The English translation "a great modern thinker" in Scholem, *On the Mystical Shape*, p. 55, is based on the Hebrew translation *hogeh gadol mi-ḥakhmei dorenu*, in Scholem, *Elements of the Kabbalah*, p. 186. The passage that Scholem paraphrases is from an essay of Benjamin published in *Neue schweizer Rundschau* in November 1929. See Benjamin, *Selected Writings*, 2:269 (*Gesammelte Schriften*, 4.1, p. 370): "The unprecedented yearning that had overcome me at the heart of what I had longed for was not the yearning that flies to the image from afar. It was the blissful yearning that has already crossed the threshold of image and possession, and knows only the power of the name—the power from which the loved one lives, is transformed, ages, rejuvenates itself, and imageless [*bildlos*], is the refuge of all images [*Zuflucht aller Bilder*]." See Kaufmann, "Imageless Refuge," p. 153; Wolfson, *Language*, p. 123. For Benjamin, the imageless is closely linked to his concept of the expressionless (*das Ausdruckslose*). See Menninghaus, "Walter Benjamin's Variations."

171. Scholem, *On the Mystical Shape*, p. 55; *Von der mystischen Gestalt*, p. 47.

172. See ch. 4 n. 179.

173. Ricchi, *Mishnat Ḥasidim*, p. 507.

174. Ferber, "Language of the Border," pp. 169–70. Despite the many differences between Scholem and Buber on this point, there is a shared assumption that the imagelessness of the divine is preserved in the images by which it is seen. See Wolfson, "Theolatry," pp. 27–30. Also pertinent is the discussion in Urban, "Paradox of Realization," pp. 185–86, of *Gottesbild* in Buber and his concession that God's unknowability is the presupposition for the translation of images into reality as symbols of the divine.

175. Scholem, "Name of God," p. 61. On the role of the symbol in Scholem's interpretation of the kabbalah, see Rotenstreich, "Symbolism"; Biale, *Gershom Scholem: Kabbalah and Counter-History*, pp. 89–92; Handelman, *Fragments of Redemption*, pp. 104–15; Idel, "Zur Funktion von Symbolen," and English version in Idel, *Old Worlds*, pp. 83–108; Weidner, *Gershom Scholem*, pp. 174–96.

176. Weigel, "Scholems Gedichte," pp. 28–32, and Weigel, "Role of Lamentation," pp. 192–96. According to Weigel, the earlier theory of Scholem centered on lament is an inversion of his later theory focused on the name of God and the linguistic theory of the kabbalah. Weigel acknowledges that the common denominator of the two texts is the addressing and extinction of the word, but she sees a shift from an emphatic theory of poetry, according to which the poem emerges from the transmission of an extinction of words, to a reflection on the potential task of poets alongside the kabbalists to serve as guardians of the knowledge of the name and the mystery of language.

177. Scholem, "Name of God," pp. 193–94.

178. Scholem, *On the Kabbalah*, pp. 12–13 (emphasis in original).

179. Scholem, "Name of God," p. 194.

180. Scholem, *Major Trends*, p. 27 (emphasis in original).

181. Handelman, *Fragments of Redemption*, p. 167.

182. Scholem, "Name of God," p. 194. It is apposite to recall Scholem's comment, in his address upon receiving the Bialik Prize in 1977, on the "tremendous poetic potential within Kabbalah, in its own unique language no less than in its poetry proper." See Scholem, *On the Possibility*, p. 48; Wasserstrom, *Religion*, pp. 108–9; Wolfson, *Language*, p. xi. For a more detailed discussion of the place occupied by poetry in Scholem's thinking, see Wasserstrom, "Fullness of Time." See also Weigel, "Scholems Gedichte;" Weigel, "Role of Lamentation"; Wolfson, *Language*, pp. 421–22n245.

183. See references cited above, n. 140. See also Biale, *Gershom Scholem: Kabbalah and Counter-History*, pp. 103–8; Handelman, *Fragments of Redemption*, pp. 16–33, 90–92; Jacobson, *Metaphysics*, pp. 85–153; Wolfson, *Language*, p. 26, and other references cited therein at pp. 405n74, 406n78; Weidner, *Gershom Scholem*, pp. 79–84; Weigel, "Scholems Gedichte," pp. 32–37; Weigel, "Role of Lamentation," pp. 189–92.

184. Scholem, "Franz Rosenzweig," pp. 27–28.

185. Scholem's analysis is the inspiration behind Agamben, *Fire and the Tale*, pp. 68–70. See the discussion of this passage in ch. 8 at nn. 90–91.

186. I have modified the term "anarchistic theology" used by Biale, *Gershom Scholem: Kabbalah and Counter-History*, pp. 94–100.

187. Scholem, *From Berlin to Jerusalem*, pp. 54–55, 69, 151, 166–67. On Zionism and the problem of the Hebrew language, see Weigel, "Scholems Gedichte," pp. 37–42. The bibliography of scholarly analyses of Scholem's Zionism is immense and I will here mention a modest sampling of the relevant studies: Biale, *Gershom Scholem: Kabbalah and Counter-History*, pp. 8–10, 53–72, 171–96, 207–10; Biale, "Scholem und der moderne Nationalismus"; Biale, *Gershom Scholem: Master of the Kabbalah*, pp. 9–18, 40–41, 60–61, 94; Rotenstreich, "Gershom Scholem's Conception"; Weidner, *Gershom Scholem*, pp. 40–54, 69–73, 91–103, 105–21; Bouretz, *Witnesses for the Future*, pp. 224–351, esp. 231–51, 335–48; Engel, *Gershom Scholem*, pp. 26–61, 94–123, 168–98; Zadoff, *Gershom Scholem*, pp. 3–83. Most relevant to my analysis is the reconsideration of Scholem's affirmation of Zionism and Rosenzweig's critique by Maor, "Scholem and Rosenzweig." For Scholem's own account of his heated discussions with Rosenzweig about the hopes for the future of German Jewry (*Deutschjudentum*) versus the renewal and rebirth of Jewry in the land of Israel, see Scholem, *From Berlin to Jerusalem*, pp. 139–41. See Mosès, "Langage et sécularisation," pp. 87–88; Mosès, *Angel of History*, pp. 171–72. In addition to the passage from Scholem's autobiography, Mosès refers to Rosenzweig's letter to Scholem from January 6, 1922, in which he reproached the latter for positing as a "central dogma" that Judaism in the Diaspora was in a state of apparent death and that only in the land of Israel could it be restored to life (*das Judentum scheintot ist und erst 'drüben' wieder lebendig werden wird*). For the original German, see Rosenzweig, *Briefe und Tagebücher*, p. 741. The material is discussed as well by Derrida, *Acts of Religion*, pp. 192–94, and see Shahar, "Sacred and the Unfamiliar," pp. 302–8. Particularly perceptive is Shahar's noting that Scholem's anxieties about the secularization of Hebrew were shared by Rosenzweig, and indeed the letter written by Scholem in December 1926 to celebrate Rosenzweig's birthday was "a gesture of confession that displays the signature of friendship and rivalry" (p. 303). For both Rosenzweig and Scholem, the essence of Hebrew lies in its holiness and thus it cannot be secularized, normalized, or limited territorially without distortion or destruction (p. 304). Shahar draws the reader's attention to Rosenzweig's "Neuhebräisch? Anläßlich der Übersetzung von Spinozas Ethik," in Rosenzweig, *Zweistromland*, pp. 723–28, a review of Jakob Klatzkin's Hebrew translation of Spinoza's *Ethics*. On p. 727, Rosenzweig criticizes this effort as part of the hope of Zionism to create a genuinely national culture (*"echtnationale" Kultur*) based on a conception of the language that is indigenous (*"bodenwüchsige"*). The sense of newness and future-orientation is misguided

as it obscures the sanctity of Hebrew connected to the past and empowers one to invent a language that is novel and unique. To speak Hebrew correctly, one must speak it as it is and not as one wants it to be: "Man kann eben nicht so Hebräisch sprechen wie man möchte, sondern man muß es schon so sprechen, wie es einmal ist" (p. 727). Rosenzweig agrees that the core of all national existence is language, but he insists that this is a matter of traditional inheritance and not territorial emplacement: "Was hier allgemein gesagt ist, das gilt nun ganz und gar von dem Kern alles nationalen Daseins, won der Sprache. Sie kann nicht werden wie sie will, sondern sie wird werden wie sie muß. Und dieses Muß liegt nicht wie bei jeder natürlich-nationalen Sprache in ihr selber, sondern außerhalb ihrer Gesprochenheit, in der Erbmasse der Vergangenheit und in dem gewahrten Zusammenhang mit denen, deren Judentum notwendig wesentlich das des Erben ist" (p. 728). Rosenzweig's review is translated into English in Glatzer, *Franz Rosenzweig*, pp. 263–71. The passages to which I alluded appear on pp. 268–70. I note, finally, that Scholem reports in *From Berlin to Jerusalem*, p. 140, that Rosenzweig regarded him as a nihilist. This is corroborated in the description of the "evil Scholem" (*der böse Scholem*) in Rosenzweig's letter to Rudolf Hallo, dated March 27, 1922, in *Briefe und Tagebücher*, p. 768: "Am wenigsten mit einem Nihilisten wie Scholem. Der Nihilist behält immer recht. . . . In Scholem steckt das Resentiment des Asketen. . . . Wir haben nicht Nichts, wie Scholem dem zionistischen Dogma zuliebe möchte, aber auch nicht Alles, wie du, verstört von Scholems kalt dir zugeschleudertem 'Nichts', es nun am liebsten bei mir fändest, sondern beide nur Etwas, wirklich und wahrhaftig nur Etwas." The connection Rosenzweig made between nihilism, the resentment of an ascetic, and the Zionist dogma, is a topic that merits a separate discussion.

188. The comparison is explored by Fagenblat, "Of Dwelling Prophetically." On the connection between the rise of Zionism and the waning of Hebrew in the German-Jewish milieu of Scholem's upbringing, see Barouch, *Between German and Hebrew*, pp. 49–60. For discussion of the larger cultural assumption about the potential of the German essence to heal the world, see Staudenmaier, *Between Occultism and Nazism*, pp. 146–78.

189. The expression, which is the scriptural etymology for the name of the firstborn son of Moses and Zipporah, Gershom, *ger hayyiti be-ereṣ nokhriyyah* (Exodus 2:22), is appropriated from Prochnik, *Stranger in a Strange Land*. Scholem's disappointment with Zionism and his sense of personal despair are documented by Engel, *Gershom Scholem*, pp. 109–15, and Zadoff, *Gershom Scholem*, pp. 83–94.

190. See my application of this term to Benjamin in Wolfson, "Not Yet Now," pp. 169–70n160, and the citation there of other studies that address the phenomenon of melancholy in Scholem and Benjamin.

191. Scholem, *Major Trends*, pp. 260–64, 267–68, 269, 279–80, 286; Scholem, *Kabbalah*, p. 143. See also Tishby, "Gnostic Doctrines." See ch. 5 nn. 109 and 188. The Sabbatian and Frankist heresies were also characterized by Scholem as gnostic on account of their nihilism and antinomianism, as well as the positing of a dualism between the hidden God and the demiurgic potency. See Scholem, *Major Trends*, pp. 297–99, 316, 322–23; Scholem, *Messianic Idea*, pp. 104–7; Scholem, *Sabbatai Ṣevi*, pp. 253, 311–12, 797. On the importance of gnosticism in Scholem's historiography of Jewish mysticism, see Idel, "Subversive Catalysts." See also Brenner, "Gnosis and History." Compare Grimstad, *Modern Revival of Gnosticism*, pp. 63–79. For a different approach, see Bielik-Robson, "God of Luria," pp. 40–41.

192. Scholem, *Messianic Idea*, p. 35 (emphasis in original). See the insightful comments on Scholem's view in Blumenberg, *Work on Myth*, pp. 227–28. See below, n. 197.

193. Scholem, *Messianic Idea*, pp. 1–2, 16–17. On the essential lack of relation between human history and the redemption, see ibid., p. 15. And compare the beginning of the poem "Traurige Erlösung," composed in 1926, in Scholem, *Fullness of Time*, pp. 68–69: "Der Glanz aus Zion scheinet vergangen / das Wirkliche hat sich gewehrt. / Wird nun sein Strahl, noch unversehrt / ins Innere der Welt gelangen?" ("The light of Zion is seen no more, / the real now has won the day. / Will its still untarnished ray / attain the world's innermost core?"). The poem ends with an ostensible glimmer of hope: "Nie konnte Gott dir näher sein, / als wo Verzweiflung auch zerbirst: / in Zions selbstversunkenem Licht" ("God never comes more close / than when despair bursts into shards: / in Zion's self-engulfing light"). To my ear, even this image of despair bursting into shards, likely reflecting the language of Lurianic kabbalah, is ambiguous insofar as the hope itself is still framed calamitously in apocalyptic terms. Compare the concluding stanza of the poem "Begegnung mit Zion und der Welt (*Der Untergang*)," dated June 23, 1930, in Scholem, *Fullness of Time*, pp. 88–89: "Was innen war, ist nach Außen / verwandelt, der Traum in Gewalt, / und wieder sind wir draußen / und Zion hat keine Gestalt" ("What was within is now without, / the dream twists into violence, / and once again we stand outside / and Zion is without form or sense"). And see the opening stanzas of the poem "Media in Vita,"

dated 1930–33, in Scholem, *Fullness of Time*, pp. 94–95: "Ich habe den Glauben verloren / der mich hierher gebracht. / Doch seit ich abgeschworen, / ist es um mich Nacht. / Das Dunkel der Niederlage / zieht mich unheimlich an; / seit ich keine Fahne mehr trage, / bin ich ein ehrlicher Mann" ("I have lost the faith / that brought me to this place. / And in the wake of this forsaking, / night is my surrounding space. / I am uncannily attracted / by the darkness of this defeat; / since I no longer carry any banners, / I'm as honest a man you'll ever meet"). My interpretation of Scholem coincides with Maciejko, "Gershom Scholem's Dialectic of Jewish History," pp. 216–19. On the anarchistic and nihilistic dimensions of Scholem's theological politics, see Jacobson, *Metaphysics*, pp. 52–81. For discussion of the German-Jewish background of Scholem's apocalyptic pessimism and the repudiation of the world, see Rabinbach, "Between Enlightenment and Apocalypse," pp. 80–82, and my own reflections on Benjamin's messianic time and historical disjointedness in Wolfson, "Not Yet Now," pp. 156–80. See also the intriguing discussion of the Weimar paradox as it relates to understanding National Socialism as a form of Jewish heresy predicated on the annihilation of Israel and God in Altmann, *German Stranger*, pp. 281–300, esp. 283–87.

194. Scholem, *Messianic Idea*, p. 7.

195. Ibid., p. 10.

196. Benjamin, *Selected Writings*, 3:305–6; *Gesammelte Schriften*, 2.1, pp. 203–4. Compare the detailed analysis of this text in Jacobson, *Metaphysics*, pp. 19–51, and see Bouretz, *Witnesses for the Future*, pp. 165–223, esp. 212–21. See also Gelikman, "Crisis of the Messianic Claim," pp. 173–77.

197. Scholem, *Messianic Idea*, p. 35. I have discussed this aspect of Scholem's understanding of the messianic element in Lurianic kabbalah and Sabbatianism in Wolfson, "Engenderment," pp. 204–6. From Scholem's perspective, the failure of Sabbatian messianism was the split between the political and the mystical, and the eventual privileging of the latter over the former. The inability to keep these two together represents an assault on what Scholem called the "dialectics of Jewish mysticism" according to which the drive inward to the spiritual essence is at the same time a drive outward to the sociopolitical materialization (*Messianic Idea*, p. 17). See Scholem, *History of the Sabbatian Movement*, p. 81. The ahistorical implications of Scholem's construal of what he considered to be the dialectical strength and weakness of the idea of Jewish messianism were at the heart of Jacob Taubes's dispute with Scholem: not the messianic ideal as such but the halakhic orientation of the rabbis was the basis for a suspension of or retreat from the historical. See Taubes, "Price of Messianism," pp. 556–57; Idel, *Messianic Mystics*, pp. 240–41; Macho, "On the Price of Messianism," pp. 34–38. I would somewhat modify my comments about this dispute in Wolfson, "Immanuel Frommann's Commentary," p. 189. The transfiguration of the messianic idea, for Taubes, is not something exterior to Jewish spirituality but can be seen as part of its inner dynamic. Thus, I concur with Taubes's insistence that we must remove the "road-block of interiorization which Scholem has erected to preserve in a dogmatic fashion an 'essential' difference between the '-isms'—Judaism and Christianism," so that "a more coherent reading of the inner logic of the Messianic idea becomes possible. Internalization, or opening the inward realm, belongs essentially to the career of that 'idea,' if such an idea should have a career at all in an unredeemed world" ("Prince of Messianism," p. 553). I would still contend that, in the final analysis, the apocalyptic view promulgated by Taubes as the revelation that discloses the triumph of eternity, the Prince of Life, and the overthrowing of time, the Prince of Death, to be played out on the stage of history with the culmination of the End Time, that is, the end of time in which the temporal order has been sublated, and the related assertions that the freedom of negation—manifest in an act of apostasy (*Ab-fall*)—is the truthfulness of the mystery that is the foundation of history, and that the truthfulness inevitably entails concealment based on the assumption that the labyrinth of this world is constitutionally in a state of error (*Stätte der Irre*), betray a gnostic sensibility that is not so far from either Scholem or Heidegger. See Taubes, *Occidental Eschatology*, pp. 4–6. See ibid., p. 8: "History is the source of revelation for mankind and his pathway through time. In the aeon of sin, existence begins as time, aiming toward death. Time contains the principle which brings death. . . . Time is not the place of life, but contains the pestilential smell of death, and plunges life into the Sheol of the past. Not until the End Time, at the end of time, when transience itself passes away, will eternity triumph over the deadly principle of time." The gnostic underpinnings of Taubes's apocalypticism is a matter that demands a separate analysis, but even a cursory glance at this passage demonstrates beyond doubt that he harbored an unequivocally negative view about time and history: the endtime signifies hyperliterally the end of time and the triumph of eternity. Blumenberg, *Work on Myth*, p. 228, contextualizes Scholem's depicting Jewish messianism as an anti-existentialist

idea in the philosophical school of existentialism, and particularly its emphasis on authenticity: "The messianic idea, as the anticipation of a condition that cannot be grasped by the imagination, is truly antiexistentialist in its retroactive effect on the situation of the person in the present—forcibly depriving it of all claims to unmediated fulfillment. But in regard to the 'essencelessness' [*'Wesenlosigkeit'*] of the future condition, it itself formally complies with the standard of freedom from likenesses, of not being 'carried over' [*übertragen*] and of being incapable of being carried over, to which existentialism gives the title of 'authenticity.'" On the translation of biblical eschatology into the gnostic derision toward creation, see the comments of Blumenberg, *Laughter*, p. 116.

198. Scholem, *Messianic Idea*, p. 36. Scholem's comment that the "utopian return to Zion . . . is bound to history itself and not to meta-history" (ibid., pp. 35–36) strikes me as an implicit criticism of Rosenzweig. It is appropriate to recall the concern that Scholem raised in his letter to Rosenzweig (see above, n. 165) about the danger of the secularization of the Hebrew language that would ensue from the realization of the Zionist yearning to return to history, turning the sacred into the mundane and thereby insufficiently safeguarding against an apocalyptic rebellion of the latent power of the holy language. See Scholem, *On the Possibility*, pp. 27–29: "People talk a great deal here about many things which may make us fail—particularly these days about the Arabs. But another, more serious danger than that of the Arab people threatens us, a danger which follows of necessity from the Zionist enterprise. What will be the result of updating the Hebrew language? Is not the holy language, which we have planted among our children, an abyss that must open up? People here do not know the meaning of what they have done. They think that they have turned Hebrew into a secular language and that they have removed its apocalyptic sting, but it is not so. The secularization of the language is merely empty words, a rhetorical turn of phrase. In reality, it is impossible to empty the words which are filled to bursting with meaning, save at the expense of the language itself. . . . The creators of the Hebrew renaissance believed in the magical powers of language with a blind, almost fanatical faith. Had their eyes been open, they would have been unable to find in their souls the demonic courage to revive a language within an environment in which it could only become a kind of Esperanto. And yet they walked—and continue to walk—on the edge of an abyss, as if in a trance—and the abyss is silent. . . . This Hebrew language is pregnant with catastrophe; it cannot remain in its present state—nor will it remain there. . . . One day the language will turn against its own speakers—and there are moments it does so even now; moments which it is difficult to forget, leaving wounds in which all the presumptuousness of our goal is revealed. Will we then have a youth who will be able to hold fast against the rebellion of a holy tongue? . . . When the power inherent in the language, when the spoken word—that is, the content of the language—will again assume form, our nation will once more be confronted by the holy tradition as a decisive example. And the people will then need to choose between the two: either to submit to it, or to perish in oblivion. God cannot remain silent in a language in which He has been evoked thousands of times to return to our life. The inevitable revolution of a language in which His voice is again heard—that is the only subject not discussed here in the land, because those who renewed the Hebrew language did not believe in the Day of Judgment which they set up for us through their deeds. Would that the lightness of mind which guided us on this apocalyptic path not lead us to destruction." See Biale, *Gershom Scholem: Master of the Kabbalah*, p. 94.

199. Rosenzweig, *Star of Redemption*, p. 263; *Stern der Erlösung*, p. 273. See the passage from Rosenzweig cited and analyzed in ch. 1 n. 124. On the quietistic and gnostic elements of Rosenzweig's thought, see Wolfson, "Facing the Effaced," pp. 63–74; Wolfson, *Giving*, pp. 79–80, and references cited therein at pp. 318n142 and 345–46n330. A different approach to this topic can be found in Pollock, *Franz Rosenzweig's Conversions*. I concur with, and have benefited from, Pollock's uncovering that at the heart of Rosenzweig's early crisis, and near conversion to Christianity, was not the struggle between faith and reason, but rather skepticism about the world and the possibility for personal salvation. Where we differ is that, in my opinion, the sense of world denial does not dissipate in Rosenzweig's theological speculation about world redemption and the possibility of a more politically activist response. See Pollock, "From Nation States." I am still of the opinion that, for Rosenzweig, world redemption—at least when viewed from the vantagepoint of the eternal people—depends on denying the capability of history redeeming itself in time. The eschatology implicit in Rosenzweig's new thinking depends on a gnostic-like denunciation of history as a viable stage for redemption. The reader is told at the conclusion of Rosenzweig's magnum opus (*Star of Redemption*, p. 447; *Stern der Erlösung*, p. 472) that the wings of the gate of the innermost sanctuary of the divine, where no human can remain alive, open

back into life (*Ins Leben*). This return, however, does not bespeak confidence in history as a place that can accommodate a utopian resolution to suffering and injustice. There is no pretense that the disenchanted world can be miraculously enchanted by the ways of either Church or State. One who belongs to the eternal people is granted the opportunity to live an eternal life in time through ritual observance, that is, to anticipate the end constantly and thereby transpose it into the beginning. This reversal "denies time as resolutely as possible and places itself outside of it" (Rosenzweig, *Star of Redemption*, p. 443; *Stern der Erlösung*, p. 467). To live in time means to live between beginning and end, but to live outside time—the necessary comportment of one who lives eternally—this between must be abandoned. Compare Bouretz, *Witnesses for the Future*, pp. 84–164, esp. 137–61.

200. On Rosenzweig's sense of *Unheimlichkeit* as indexical of Jewish particularity, see Batnitzky, *Idolatry and Representation*, pp. 90–94. The similarity and difference between Rosenzweig and Heidegger is noted by the author. For a different approach to the place of poetics in the two thinkers, see Simon, *Art and Responsibility*, pp. 11–12, 14–15, 128–32, 187–88, 214–19. See ch. 8 n. 152. On the lyrical form of the poetic and the visual dimension of the painterly in Rosenzweig's aesthetic, see Braiterman, *Shape of Revelation*, pp. 49–51.

201. Galli, *Franz Rosenzweig and Jehuda Halevi*, p. 177, cited and analyzed in Wolfson, *Giving*, pp. 66–67. See also Wolfson, *Duplicity*, p. 74.

202. The antihistoricist tendency of Rosenzweig's thinking has been the subject of several scholars. See Altmann, "Franz Rosenzweig on History," pp. 132–33: "For this reason God must redeem man not through history but—there is no alternative—through religion. . . . But in *The Star of Redemption* eternity . . . is the triumph of redemption over death, man's glorious release from his temporal existence, the reality of the Kingdom." According to Altmann, Rosenzweig's disappointment with historicism leads him toward religion, which is a "viewpoint outside history itself" (p. 135). See also Yerushalmi, *Zakhor*, pp. 92–93; Katz, "On Historicism and Eternity"; Mendes-Flohr, "Franz Rosenzweig and the Crisis of Historicism"; Funkenstein, *Perceptions of Jewish History*, pp. 257–305, esp. 291–302; Wolfson, "Facing the Effaced," pp. 45–49; Myers, *Resisting History*, pp. 68–105. In my reading, the mastery of time in Rosenzweig's theological ruminations is not effectuated through the overcoming of temporality by eternity (Mendes-Flohr, "Franz Rosenzweig and the Crisis of Historicism," p. 159), but by the concomitant eternalization of time and the temporalization of eternity through the linear circularity of the ritual-liturgical calendar. See Wolfson, "Facing the Effaced," pp. 54–55; Wolfson, *Alef*, pp. 176–77; Wolfson, "Not Yet Now," pp. 150–51. My view is closer to the perspective of Braiterman, *Shape of Revelation*, pp. 140–44. For a different perspective, see Moyn, "Spirit of Jewish History," pp. 88–90; and compare the discussion of the diasporic life of Judaism according to Rosenzweig and the metahistorical status of the eternal people in Björk, *Life Outside Life*, pp. 128–36.

203. I have taken the liberty to restate the argument in Wolfson, *Giving*, pp. 70–71. See also Bielik-Robson, "Nihilism," pp. 47–51.

204. Wolfson, *Duplicity*, pp. 131–53.

205. Heidegger, *What Is a Thing?*, pp. 150–51; *Frage nach dem Ding*, pp. 153–54. Describing the role of the philosopher to transform and to establish a new logic, which would entail constructing metaphysics upon the ground cleared by Kant's *Kritik der reinen Vernunft*, Heidegger surmises that this "did not lie within Kant's capacity, because such a task exceeds even the capacity of a great thinker. It demands nothing less than to jump over one's own shadow [*über den eigenen Schatten zu springen*]. . . . Hegel alone apparently succeeded in jumping over this shadow, but only in such a way that he eliminated the shadow, i.e., the finiteness of man [*die Endlichkeit des Menschen*] and jumped into the sun itself. Hegel skipped over the shadow [*den Schatten übersprungen*], but he did not, because of that, surpass the shadow [*über den Schatten gesprungen*]. Nevertheless, every philosopher *must* want to do this. This 'must' is his vocation. The longer the shadow, the wider the jump [*Je länger der Schatten, um so weiter der Sprung*]" (emphasis in original).

206. Heidegger, *Bremen and Freiburg Lectures*, p. 102; *Bremer und Freiburger Vorträge*, pp. 108–9.

8

Ethnolinguistic Enrootedness and Invocation of Historical Destiny

One must be a god in order to know who is the devil.

Heidegger, *Ponderings V*, §68

As we have noted at several junctures in this book, one of the more arresting affinities between Heidegger and the kabbalists centers on their mutual recognition of the unique role of language as the medium through which the nature of being is concomitantly disclosed and concealed. Both Habermas and Derrida already noted the kinship on this topic between the kabbalists and Heidegger. In his discussion of the subterranean influence of kabbalah on German thought, Habermas glosses the kabbalistic ratification of the divine status of language as follows: "Idealism condemned language as the instrument of knowledge and elevated a divinized art as its substitute. A Jew actually anticipated Heidegger, the *philosophicus teutonicus*, in this peculiarly heightened awareness."[1] For Derrida's part, I refer again to his remark, cited in chapter 3, that compares Heidegger's counsel that to find one's way to the nearness of being, one must learn to exist in the nameless,[2] to the kabbalistic tradition regarding speaking the unnamable name.[3] Derrida rightly perceived that the authentic anonymity embraced by Heidegger—in contradistinction to the inauthentic anonymity of the neutered state of *das Man*, the mode of everyday being-with-one-another, the "they-self" (*Man-selbst*), analyzed in detail in *Sein und Zeit*[4]— promotes the finding of one's way into the nearness of being, which is to say, to let oneself become a dwelling for the truth of being.[5]

Derrida argued that there is a connection between the residual ontotheology of the Jewish esoteric tradition and Heidegger centered on attunement to the thought of being and the articulation of the name that is no name.[6] But the nameless to which Heidegger alludes, and which I contend can be elicited from kabbalistic musings on the infinite, is not an unsignifiable object that transcends signification; it is rather the sign of excess that dissimulates in an endless chain of significations,[7] the nihility that is outside the ontological economy of either positive or negative propositions.[8] For both Heidegger and the kabbalists, the nameless is not the transcendent God worshipped and adulated monotheistically, the being that is beyond being; it is rather the being that cannot be reduced to or identified with any being, even the otherwise than being, the godhead or the divinity that can be approached only atheologically, as it exceeds all theological kataphasis, the one constellated not by the one of singular identity but by the illimitable multiples of the one that is never one, the being that is neither being nor nonbeing but the negation of the negation of negation.

The intent of Derrida's comparison is underscored by another outcome of the suggested juxtaposition of Heidegger and the Jewish esoteric tradition. The spirit of anonymity exemplified by many kabbalists through the centuries, and still in evidence today, can be understood as an expression of the contemplative quest to exist in—that is, to be united with—the unnamable name by eradicating one's own name. This is in accord with Heidegger's affirmation of an anonymity that allows one to subsist in and to be beckoned by the name of the nameless. The quietistic eradication of one's proper name corresponds to the avowal of the disavowal of the namelessness, the signpost that marks that the worldplay of beyng, as we noted in chapter 4, acts without reason or purpose. The ateleological status of the being devoid of referentiality is to be emulated by Dasein's *Gelassenheit*, acting with the will that is depleted of the willfulness to will, the willing of nonwilling that willfully abandons the agency of willing the constraint of causal irrevocability.[9] In the kabbalistic ethos, the transgressive piety, similarly anchored in the willing of nonwilling, is identified as the virtue of humility, the purging of selfhood achieved by the self when it is conjoined to the nothingness of *Keter*, the absolute and infinite will that is beyond both the willing not to will and the willing to relinquish the will to not will.[10]

Metapolitical Triangulation: Land, Language, Peoplehood

In the infamous rectoral address, Heidegger spoke of the essence of the German university related to the "the inexorability of that spiritual mission which impresses onto the fate of the German Volk the stamp of their history."[11] The essential character of the university is self-governance (*Selbstverwaltung*), but the latter involves determining through self-examination (*Selbstbesinnung*) the way to realize the task of becoming what one ought to be.[12] As Heidegger envisioned it, crucial to this task is the act of "self-limitation" (*Selbstbegrenzung*) by which the German people will that essence, and in so willing, assert their own essential being. Self-assertion (*Selbstbehauptung*) is thus understood as a consequence of the nexus between self-governance, self-examination, and self-limitation. In a patently Platonic fashion,[13] the reclaiming of science—the word *Wissenschaft* denotes authentic knowing, in which the question of being occupies a central place, as opposed to more contemporary forms of positivism or empiricism—bespeaks the historical and spiritual mission of the German university, which, in turn, embodies the essence of the German people that can be fully realized only in the state.[14] This knowledge, Heidegger told his audience on that fateful day, could be attained only "when we submit to the power of the *beginning* of our spiritual-historical existence. The beginning [*Anfang*] is the commencement [*Aufbruch*] of Greek philosophy. . . . All science remains bound to that beginning of philosophy and draws from it the strength of its essence, assuming that it still remains at all equal to this beginning."[15]

Several years later, in *Einführung in die Metaphysik*, Heidegger articulated the dilemma of modernity as follows:

> This Europe, in its unholy blindness always on the point of cutting its own throat, lies today in the great pincers between Russia on the one side and America on the other. Russia and America, seen metaphysically, are both the same: the same hopeless frenzy of unchained technology and of the rootless organization of the average man. When the farthest corner of the globe has been conquered technologically and can be exploited economically; when any incident you like, in any place you like, at any time you like, becomes accessible as fast as you like; when you can simultaneously "experience" an assassination attempt against a king in France and a symphony concert in Tokyo; when time is nothing but speed, instantaneity,

> and simultaneity, and time as history has vanished from all Dasein of all peoples; when a boxer counts as the great man of a people; when the tallies of millions at mass meetings are a triumph; then, yes then, there still looms like a specter over all this uproar the question: what for?—where to?—and what then? The spiritual decline of the earth has progressed so far that peoples are in danger of losing their last spiritual strength, the strength that makes it possible even to see the decline [which is meant in relation to the fate of "Being"] and to appraise it as such.[16]

As is well known, the critique of technological machination is a central theme in Heidegger's writings, and in no small measure, this obsession was part of his ill-fated embrace of National Socialism and eventual rejection of it, at least in the concrete form it had taken under Hitler's leadership. There is much to say about this complex matter, but in this context, what I wish to emphasize is that, for Heidegger, the spiritual decline—the pinnacle of which consists of the fact that people no longer perceive the decline, an argument whose structure parallels the gnostic myth of the redeemed redeemer, that is, the redeemer who needs to be redeemed from oblivion to his role as redeemer[17]—is crucially expressed as ethnicities losing their individual sense of history, which is tied principally to the cultural formation mediated through language. Along these lines, the ascendancy of the German *Volk* is related intrinsically to the German language. This is the principle by and through which the Germans "struggle over their most proper *essence*" in the effort to claim their inimitability as the "people of poets and thinkers" ("*Volk der Dichter und Denker*").[18] Although the German language obviously is not restricted to the geographical boundaries of Germany, inasmuch as its roots are embedded in that place, the language and the land are in a synergetic relationship such that the essence of one is disclosive of the essence of the other. For Heidegger, the German essence is both enrooted in the soil of the language and embodied in the language of the soil. It follows that his repeated reflections on the primacy of language, including the notorious claim that language is the house of being,[19] must be interpreted in a particularistic as opposed to a universalistic register. Heidegger thus speaks of the house as "the space opened up for a people as a place in which they can be 'at home,' and thereby fulfill their proper destiny." Insofar as this space "is bestowed by the inviolate earth," it can be said that the "earth houses the peoples in their historical space."[20] For the German *Volk*, that space is the soil of Germany, and the granting of the feeling of homeliness (*das Heimische*), which is the essence of the homeland (*das Wesen der Heimat*),[21] is through the opening of the between that is language.

Heidegger, of course, is not the first thinker who deemed German to be the language most appropriate to the path of thinking.[22] We are reminded, for instance, of Hegel's remark in the preface to the second edition of *Wissenschaft der Logik*, written in 1831, about the relationship between language and thought: "In this respect, the German language has many advantages over other modern languages, for many of its words also have the further peculiarity of carrying, not just different meanings, but opposite ones, and in this one cannot fail to recognize the language's speculative spirit. It can delight thought to come across such words, and to discover in naïve form, already in the lexicon as one word of opposite meanings, that union of opposites which is the result of speculation but to the understanding is nonsensical."[23] Heidegger was heir to this attitude and thus believed that German is loftier than other languages since it is most conducive to the task of thinking. The reader, therefore, is misled if he or she is not cognizant of the fact that Heidegger's many reflections on the nature of *Sprache* are not about language in general but more specifically about German, or to be even more precise, about German and its special relationship to Greek, as Derrida argued in "Interpretations at War: Kant, the Jew, the German,"[24] an alliance that was upheld by other German thinkers, including Hermann Cohen, who argued that both cultural formations displayed the same *Eigentümlichkeit*, the exemplarity based on the paradoxical conjunction of universality and particularity; that is, the national specificity is expressive of the general ideal.[25]

Heidegger's espousal of the Greek-German symbiosis tends toward a racial component as his Germanism, and we can assume his sense of Greekism, is not inclusive of the other precipitously condemned as the barbarian. To insist that Greek and German are the philosophical languages par excellence is further evidence of this ethnocentrism: "For along with the German language, Greek (in regard to the possibilities of thinking) is at once the most powerful and the most spiritual of languages."[26] Despite his growing dissatisfaction with the execution of the Nazi agenda, Heidegger never wavered from the conviction that the retrieval of thinking—the second beginning that comes about as the confrontation with the first beginning and the return to the origin concealed therein—must be realized by the German people through their indigenous language and preferably, I surmise, in their native land. Nor did he abandon the belief that German derives its ultimate worth from being the most applicable means to reclaim Greek, the language of "the intimate people" (*das innige Volk*), according to Hölderlin, "armed with the spirit of the gods."[27] In the Le Thor seminar from 1969, Heidegger offered the following romanticized version of Hellenic thought: "The Greeks are those human beings who lived immediately in the openness of phenomena—through the expressly ek-static capacity of letting the phenomena speak to them (modern man, Cartesian man, *se solum alloquendo*, only talks to himself). No one has ever again reached the heights of the Greek experience of being as phenomenon."[28] To attain those heights was precisely the undertaking Heidegger set for himself.

Engendering Mother Tongue and Fatherland

To assess Heidegger's approach, one must set his thinking in the context of nineteenth-century German philology. Consider the summation given by Tuska Benes:

> Comparative philologists generally interpreted language as evidence of ethnic descent and wove myths of cultural origin around the perceived starting points of national tongues. The first moments in the emergence of a language or nation were considered to be formative; the organic unfolding of a first principle or underlying idea could explain subsequent historical development. This origin paradigm held sway over German linguistic thought through most of the nineteenth century. . . . In this respect, comparative philology epitomized the nineteenth-century German quest for origins. Language scholars worked feverishly to reconstruct the *Ursprache*, or the primordial linguistic forms from which the world's tongues supposedly evolved, especially within the Indo-European language family. Philologists ordered languages and ethnic groups based on the model of branching genealogy from a single point of origin.[29]

Heidegger doubtless accepted this philological quest for origins, but even more important for him is the threefold connection between people, language, and land. If, as Heidegger thought, homelessness (*Heimatlosigkeit*) is a symptom of the oblivion of being (*Seinsvergessenheit*) or the abandonment of beings by being (*Seinsverlassenheit des Seienden*), then homecoming (*Heimkunft*) consists of standing in the nearness to being, the "there" of the being-there that is the clearing of the appropriative event.[30] Perhaps with an eye to criticizing the exploitations of the Nazis, Heidegger states explicitly that the word *homeland* is thought "in an essential sense, not patriotically or nationalistically, but in terms of the history of being."[31] The sincerity of this remark notwithstanding, Heidegger did not escape from a chauvinism that accorded unrivaled status to Germany and its citizens.

Utilizing Heidegger's own distinction in a letter written on December 15, 1945, to Constantin von Dietze,[32] we can propose that he proffered a national as opposed to a nationalistic ideology;[33] that is, he affirmed a worldview that sponsored the cultural-linguistic preeminence of the German people without allocating to them the biological-racial supremacy that would justify vilification of the other.[34] However, as Blanchot rightly noted about Heidegger's distinction, "By saying he preferred the national to nationalism, he was not using one word in place of another; this preference is also at the basis of his thought and expresses his deep attachment to the land, that is, the homeland (*Heimat*), his stance in favor of local and regional roots . . . and his loathing for urban life."[35] I would add that Heidegger made it abundantly clear that the idea of homeland is inextricably linked to the veneration of German as the

Muttersprache. As Heidegger elicits from Hölderlin's poem "Heimkunft," for the Germans to be at home, they must take hold of the peculiar character of "the German" (*das Deutsche*), a possession (*Eigentum*) that encompasses the "still withheld essence of their homeland."[36] The mother tongue, in short, is the conduit that guides one to the fatherland.

In a passage from the *Schwarze Hefte*, Heidegger tacitly disparaged the nationalistic sense of ethnicity (*Volkstum*) promulgated by the Nazis:

> Which of us will then presume, in a "time" that is so confused, to settle for "all eternity" what is German and what is a people and do so at a time which is perhaps itself only the consequence of an essential misunderstanding of what is German, a misunderstanding due to nationalism? And even if one could say something about the German essence, how can one pretend to have grasped the entire essence? Whence this raving blindness which now sets about spoiling the most concealed German possessions?[37]

What is important to emphasize is that even though Heidegger is implicitly ridiculing the Nazi misappropriation of the idea of a German essence—*das Wesen der Deutschen*—because of a confounded sense of nationalism, he denies neither that there is such an essence nor that it is the most concealed of possessions the Germans need to acquire. As he writes in another aphorism from these notebooks, "The Germans will not grasp—let alone fulfill—their Western destiny, unless they are equipped for it by the originality of their language [*die Ursprünglichkeit ihrer Sprache*], which must ever again find its way back to the simple, uncoined word, where the closeness to beyng bears and refreshes the imprintability of discourse [*die Prägsamkeit des Sagens*]."[38]

Parallel to the disquieting claim of kabbalists that Hebrew is the matrix language, that is, the language that is most indicative of the nature of all that exists, Heidegger adamantly affirmed that German is the language most suited to the poeticizing that discloses the concealment of the event of beyng in its unconcealment and thereby provides the conditions for Dasein's historical dwelling on earth.[39] Homecoming is identified with poiēsis, which is further characterized as the ability "to be in the joy which preserves in words the mystery of nearness to the most joyful. . . . The poetic joy is the knowledge that in everything joyful, which already comes to meet us, the joyful greets us while reserving itself."[40] Poetry is depicted by Heidegger in more general terms as "the awakening and delineation of an individual's ownmost essence, through which he reaches back into the ground of his Dasein."[41] Hence, the comportment of a people—and not just the Germans—can be determined by how it stands in relation to the power of poetry.[42] Sounding a similar note in "Hebel—der Hausfreund" (1957), Heidegger opines, "the world is the house that mortals inhabit. . . . Only in the measure that man, as the mortal one, inhabits the house of the world, does he stand in the calling (*Bestimmung*) to build a house for the celestial ones, and a dwelling-place for himself."[43] It follows that the house-friend "is friend to the house which the world is. He is attached to the whole wide dwelling of humankind. Yet his attachment is based on a belongingness to the world and its structure, a belongingness that is primordial but commensurate with each age."[44] It would appear, then, that the assumption that the essence of the house-friend as poet is to be determined from within the framework of the house of the world challenges the conclusion I reached about the ethnic nature of that belonging. In the continuation of his analysis, however, Heidegger retrieves the more culturally and linguistically specific delimitation of dwelling in the world from Hebel's identification of the moon as the genuine house-friend:

> Just as the moon in its shining brings a soft light, so Hebel, the earthly house-friend, brings a light through his sayings, and a light that is soft as well. . . . The light is only the reflection of the light the moon previously received from the sun whose brilliance shines onto the earth too. The reflection of the sun is passed on by the moon to the earth in a softened glow; this glow is the poetic image of that saying which is addressed to the house-friend so that he, thus illuminated, passes on what is addressed to *him* to those who dwell on earth with him. . . . As the first calendar-maker, the moon marks the hourly passage of time. So too does poetic saying lead the way for mortals in their passage from birth to death.[45]

There is much to unpack here, not the least of which is another fascinating parallel to the symbolic nexus in kabbalistic literature of the lunar imagination and the temporality of the poetic image, but I will focus on the fact that Heidegger expounds the view of Hebel by referencing Hölderlin's idea of dwelling poetically on earth as the proper way to understand the autochthonous nature of human inhabitation.[46]

The poet is the house-friend, for just as the glow of the moon's soft light illumines the night and renders transparent all that had been hidden under the cover of darkness, so the poet "gathers the world into a saying whose word remains a softly restrained shining in which the world appears as if being caught sight of for the first time." The essence of the poetic saying is a form of preaching—the German *Predigen*, we are reminded, is from the Latin *praedicare*—which Heidegger interprets as "to let what is to be said appear in its shining [*das zu-Sagende in seinem Glanz erscheinen lassen*]."[47] The saying/showing of the concealed can transpire solely through the poet's native language:

> Man speaks from within that language to which his essence is commended. We call this language "the mother tongue." With regard to the language that has grown historically—that it is the mother tongue—we may say: *It is language, not man, which genuinely speaks. Man speaks only to the extent that he in each case co-responds to language.*[48]

Assuredly, this is confirmation of my assertion that Heidegger never swerved from his commitment to the proposition that language confers the abode in which human beings may dwell,[49] but the language most apposite to that conferral and the awakening of poetry that ensues therefrom is German. The supremacy of German is not to be understood in the ordinary sense of language as an instrument for communication and information—the horrifying upshot of which is the construction of calculating machines (*Rechenmaschinen*), thinking and translating machines (*Denk- und Übersetzungsmaschinen*), and even the language machine (*Sprachmaschine*)[50]—but as that which holds open the opening in and through which Dasein inhabits the house of the world as the one allocated with the poetic shepherding of bringing beings into being.

The linguistic character of poeticizing as the configuring ground (*Grundgefüge*) of historical Dasein should apply to all people without partiality, since language is presumed to constitute the originary essence of the historical being of human beings,[51] and yet it is identified exemplarily as German. In one context, Heidegger pridefully avers that the German song entails the greatest facility to bring one into the nearness of the mystery of beyng because it is the most joyful.[52] Moreover, as we discussed at length in the previous chapter, Heidegger maintained that poetic language—emblematic of language more generally—originates and culminates in the inceptive saying of beyng that is silence. Given his classification of German as the poetic diction par excellence, it follows—as ludicrous as this might seem—that the apophatic unsaying is most effectively gesticulated in German. To the extent that silence is the source of speaking, and speaking entails listening to the unspoken, German is the language in which the stillness of the appropriating-showing saying resounds most effusively.[53] Hölderlin argued that *clarity of presentation* (Klarheit der Darstellung) is natural to the Germans—and included therein, according to Heidegger, is the "ability to grasp," the "designing of projects," the "erection of frameworks and enclosures," the "construction of boundaries and divisions," and "dividing and classifying"—but this native trait does not become authentically their own disposition (*Verfassung*) until they encounter what is foreign (*das Fremde*) and the ability to grasp is tested by the need to grasp the ungraspable (*das Unfaßliche zu fassen*).[54] Heidegger's belief that no language is superior to German in its facility to express the inexpressible and to comprehend the incomprehensible is in accord with the kabbalistic contention that Hebrew, categorically assumed to be the language of creation and revelation, is the most appropriate means for declaiming the ineffable and for conceiving the inconceivable.

Rendered more technically, the name—or, to be more precise, the Tetragrammaton—is the ladder to the nameless, but that name, mystically conceived, is the Torah, which comprises all the twenty-two letters of the Hebrew alphabet.[55] To use the terminology attributed to some of the Provençal and Catalonian kabbalists of the thirteenth century, the climax of the meditative ascent consists of thought cleaving to that which thought cannot comprehend, a state of conjunction (*devequt*) with the divine nothing facilitated by the mind divesting itself of all concepts, images, and words.[56] Some kabbalists (and Ḥasidic masters influenced by them) even identified the goal of the mystical path as conjunction with and incorporation into the expanse of the infinite.[57] In this nondual consciousness, or metaconsciousness, all differentiation is overcome and the suitability of language itself is called into question. As we find in the case of visionaries in other religious communities influenced by the *via negativa*, the state of mystical union and integration is correlated with an apophasis that renders all theistic portrayals of God—including the theosophical speculation propagated by the kabbalists themselves—as conceptual idolatry. The pinnacle of the path is the absorption of the differentiated self into the great sea of nondifferentiation, an assimilation into the formless and boundless light that engenders a mystical atheism.[58]

To be sure, in kabbalistic sources, the apophatic dimension is counterbalanced by an amplification of the kataphatic leaning of the biblical and rabbinic corpora. With respect to this matter, once more I note the accord between kabbalah and the mystical piety nurtured by Christians and Muslims. In all three monotheistic faiths, informed by their respective scriptural legacies, the language germane to the visionary gnosis ensues from the coalition of the kataphatic and the apophatic; that is to say, the very being to whom the disparate forms are ascribed is the being from whom these forms are erased. One of the more sophisticated attempts to communicate this idea is found in the Ḥabad-Lubavitch literature: the transcendence of the light of the infinite beyond visual and verbal anthropomorphization, the figure of the metafigure, the nonhuman (*lo adam* based on 1 Samuel 15:29), corresponding perhaps to the contemporary notion of the posthuman, is set in contrast to the immanence of that light, which assumes the image of the appearance of a human (*demut ke-mar'eh adam*) on the throne of glory (Ezekiel 1:26).[59] Theopoetic discourse arises in the interplay between the present absence of the nonhuman and the absent presence of the human. To say the unsaid, therefore, does not mean to speak about a mysterious transcendent entity whose meaning ineluctably eludes the grasp of our understanding, or even to speak about the reticence of not speaking about such a transcendence, as we find in the romantic understanding of the symbol,[60] but rather to demarcate that chasm of the between, the womb of possibility, by uttering what is always still to be uttered, a nonutterance that renders the inexpressible fully expressible in its inexpressibility. Kabbalistic apophaticism implies not only that every act of unsaying presupposes a previous saying or that every act of saying demands a corrective unsaying, but, more paradoxically, and in line with the position I have attributed to Heidegger, that *every saying is an unsaying*, for what is said can never be what is spoken, insofar as what is spoken can never be what is said. In making claims about the ineffability of the infinite through the gesture of speaking-not, kabbalists, much as Christian and Muslim mystics, availed themselves of images of negation—that is, images that are negative but no less imagistic than the affirmative images they negate—to illustrate the negation of images.[61] Returning to the metaphor previously invoked, one can never dispose of the ladder because the name is not only the means by which one ascends to the nameless; it is the investiture by which the nameless is pronounced and thereby remains unpronounceable.

Speaking of the mystical utterance, there is no end to speaking, since what is spoken is unspeakable. The unspoken is not, however, equally spoken by different languages. For the kabbalists, the most auspicious way to the silence beyond speech is through Hebrew, the sole language considered to be sacred, whereas Heidegger attributed priority to German as the most effective language to express poetically what is inexpressible, a task that he himself considered as naming the holy, the enigma that shines forth in its gathering depth only as it veils itself.[62] For instance, consider Heidegger's comment on the following words of Hölderlin, "Concerning what is highest, I will be silent. / Forbidden fruit, like the laurel, is, however, / Above all the fatherland. Such, however, each / Shall taste last" (Vom Höchsten will ich schweigen. / Verbotene Frucht, wie der Lorbeer, ist aber / Am meisten das Vaterland. Die aber kost' / Ein jeder zuletzt): "The fatherland, our fatherland Germania—most forbidden, withdrawn from the haste of the everyday and the bustle of activity. The highest and therefore most difficult, that which comes last, because fundamentally first—the origin withheld in silence."[63] The confrontation with the "primordial power" of that origin provokes "a questioning that is truly necessitated, one that has the task of once again first bringing about a historically spiritual space. This can occur only if such questioning is necessitated from out of the ownmost need of our historical Dasein. . . . It is the need of needlessness, the need of the complete inability to experience the innermost question-worthiness of Dasein."[64] Heidegger extracts from Hölderlin that only the poetic word—typified in the German language—can awaken humankind to this task of constructing a spiritual space, that is, a space calibrated to the physical wherein the spiritual can materialize.

The full import of Heidegger's reading of Hölderlin can be discerned only if we bear in mind another remark, "*The 'fatherland' is beyng itself*, which from the ground up bears and configures [*trägt und fügt*] the history of a people as an existing [*daseienden*] people: the historicity of its history [*die Geschichtlichkeit seiner Geschichte*]. The fatherland is not some abstract, supratemporal idea in itself. . . . Rather, the beyng of the fatherland—that is, of the historical Dasein of a people—is experienced as the authentic and singular beyng from which the fundamental orientation toward beings as a whole arises and attains its configuration [*Gefüge*]."[65] That the fatherland of Germany is the historical Dasein of the German people implies that it is the beyng whence this people orients itself toward the totality of beings, and in that respect, the fatherland is identified as beyng itself, *Das "Vaterland" ist das Seyn selbst*. The German language, consequently, gives voice in a unique way to the taciturnity of genuine discourse that occasions a "*thoughtful* encounter with the *revelation of beyng*."[66] The homecoming is dependent on kinship with the poet, ostensibly a universal idea, but Heidegger ascribes that homecoming more specifically to "the future of the historical being of the German people. They are the people of poetry *and* of thought."[67] Heidegger unabashedly imputes to the Germans an eminently enviable position by proclaiming *Sie sind das Volk des Dichtens und des Denkens*, a shockingly stark and unapologetic expression of his ethnocentric bias.

As Heidegger audaciously proclaimed in the *Schwarze Hefte*, "Only someone who is German can in an originarily new way poetize being and say being—he alone will conquer anew the essence of θεωρία . . . and finally create *logic*."[68] In an even more ominous tone, Heidegger wrote in the addendum to the lecture course "Parmenides und Heraklit" offered during the winter term 1942–43 at the University of Freiburg:

> The highest form of suffering is dying one's death as a sacrifice for the preservation of the truth of Being. This sacrifice is the purest experience of the voice of Being. What if German humanity is that historical humanity [*geschichtliche Menschentum*] which, like the Greek, is called upon to poetize and think, and what if this German humanity must first perceive the voice of Being! Then must not the sacrifices be as many as the causes immediately eliciting them, since the sacrifice has *in itself* an essence all its own and does not require goals and uses! Thus what if the voice of the beginning should announce itself in our historical destiny?[69]

Unquestionably, the problem to which Heidegger is responding is of universal scope, the oblivion of being and the consequent abandonment of humanity to self-forgetfulness (*Selbstvergessenheit*):

> Primordially, the emergent essence of Being disposes and determines the mode of the sheltering of the unconcealed as the word. The essence of the word disposes and first determines the essence of the humanity corresponding to it and thereby relegates this essence into history, i.e., into the essential beginning and the transformation of the essence of the truth of beings. . . . Only because Being and the truth of Being are essentially beyond all men and humanities [*über alle Menschen und Menschentümer*], can, and

> therefore must, the "Being" or "non-being" of man be at stake where man as historical is determined to the preservation of the truth of Being.[70]

Being and the truth of being are beyond all humanity, and yet, the crucial players in the gnostic drama—the ones called upon to sacrifice for the preservation and transformation of the essence of the truth of being—are the Germans; to them exclusively belongs the historical destiny to ameliorate the forgetfulness of the forgetfulness by heeding the voice of being. Just as kabbalists have dependably identified the Jews as the nation that bears the image of the divine uniquely, and thus exemplify the essence of humanity in their imaginal capacity to imagine the unimaginable and in their linguistic deportment to describe the indescribable, so Heidegger had no compunction about identifying the Germans as the historical humanity: the universal task to unveil the veiling of the veil of unveiling, to disclose the concealment of the unconcealment, can be accomplished most felicitously through the language of this particular ethnos.

In a second study from 1942, a sustained analysis of Hölderlin's "Andenken," Heidegger reiterates his belief that the universal vocation for the futural humanity can be achieved only through the particular destiny of the German people:

> The dwelling near the origin that prepares a foundation is the original dwelling, in which the poetic is first grounded, upon whose ground the sons of the earth are then to dwell, at least if they are *to dwell poetically upon this earth*. The poesis *of the poets* is now what founds everything that remains. What remains is the originary *remembrance* [*das ursprüngliche* Andenken] of the poet. . . . That which remains prepares the historical place in which German humanity [*das Menschentum der Deutschen*] must first learn to become at home, so that, when it is time, it will be able to linger in the moment when destiny lies in the balance. . . . *Remembrance* is a poetic abiding in the essence of what is fitting to poetic activity, which, in the secure destiny of Germany's future history, festively shows the ground of its origin.[71]

This passage buttresses the view that Heidegger did come to reject the purely geopolitical understanding of the ideal of the German homeland and the German people, especially in the distorted and vulgar way disseminated by the Nazis, in favor of a theological-political-poetical sensibility, to paraphrase Lacoue-Labarthe.[72] To be at home means, first and foremost, to dwell poetically on earth. As Jennifer Anna Gosetti-Ferencei explicated this aspect of Heidegger's thinking:

> Poetic dwelling in the later works is characterized by the nonviolence of *Gelassenheit,* a letting-be that escapes representational thinking and refuses the technological objectification of things in favor of a more essential, poetic revealing; this is the "turning around" that also motivates and arises from factical life. Dwelling here reflects Hölderlin's notion of peaceful dwelling . . . . Here is found Heidegger's discovery of the earth, for poetic language offers a different appreciation of nature than that offered by metaphysics. Because poetic language grants the elusive character of presence—that beings are never fully disclosed as actual but belong to the structure of Being's withdrawal—poetic language does not dominate nature as an object to be exhausted in mechanistic laws or in technological manipulation.[73]

How is the poetic dwelling accomplished? Only by those who dwell in the nearness to the origin, a task that is apportioned to the poets, who are entrusted with the responsibility to ground what remains in the originary remembrance. The form of spatialization dependent on poetic abiding is the deeper sense of the historical place wherein German humanity will learn to become at home and secure the destiny of its future. In spite of Heidegger's lofty poetizing, the concreteness of the specific land is not eviscerated; on the contrary, it is reinforced to the degree that the poetic dwelling still depends on the historical place that takes root within the confines of a particular country.

Poetic Homecoming and Proximal Distance

There is good reason, in my judgment, to accept the sincerity of Heidegger's insistence that he distanced himself from several of the main tenets of Nazism; the recently published notebooks, which have been used by some to argue how deeply entrenched Heidegger's thought in this aberrant ideology was, also offer ample evidence of his growing disenchantment with the movement.[74] Irrespective of the veracity of this change of heart, Heidegger never altered or relinquished his acceptance of three foundational and incontrovertible components of the Teutonic spirit of National Socialism, to wit, the superiority of the German people, the German language, and the German soil. Even if we grant, as I think we should, that after resigning from the rectorship, Heidegger retreated from the political arena and cultivated an interest in a poetic thinking that can be considered political only by virtue of being apolitical or metapolitical, his thought was still beholden to a collective myth of the decline of European culture and the need for its renewal to be executed specifically by the Germans or at least by their elites,[75] designated as "the ones to come" (*die Zukünftigen*),[76] or as "the future ones" (*die Künftigen*), "who, in grounding, *hold* beyng open and urgent and developed in the truth of its essence,"[77] the ones for whom what is most proper in philosophy, yet always left unsaid, is kept open.[78] The myth that sustained the necessity for renewal has been identified as the "matrix of generic fascism," since it preserves the exclusionary belief in the distinction of one race and the imparting to that race the task of changing the course of history.[79] Using this measure, we can say without qualification that Heidegger's thinking is prejudicial. This is not to deny, however, that he viewed the particularistic from the standpoint of a greater purpose to serve humankind. The horrors of World War II did effect a change in Heidegger's thinking in this direction, as we see, for example, from the comment in "Brief über den 'Humanismus'": "'German' is not spoken to the world so that the world might be reformed through the German essence; rather, it is spoken to the Germans so that from a destinal belongingness [*geschickhaften Zugehörigkeit*] to other peoples they might become world-historical [*weltgeschichtlich*] along with them."[80] Notwithstanding the effort to contextualize the ethnic-nationalistic in terms of a loftier and more magnanimous rationale, Heidegger continued to locate the universal calling of becoming world-historical in the individuated destiny of the German people and its language.

Here it is pertinent to recall the astute observation of Löwith that Heidegger understood his mission as translating the existential belief of one's ownmost individual Dasein into the more specifically cultural German Dasein,[81] a destiny that is "no less particular by virtue of its generality;"[82] indeed, its generality is expressive of an even more acute particularism insofar as Dasein is delimited most pristinely as German. As Heidegger himself put it in the *Schwarze Hefte*, "The communal-civil [*volklich-staatlich*] happening is to be unfolded in its actuality in order to attack all the harder and sharper and fuller the floundering (rootlessly and without rank) of the new spirit—i.e., in order to guide the awakening actuality of German Dasein to its greatness for the first time, a greatness concealed to this Dasein and waiting for it, a greatness around which the most fearful storm is raging."[83] There is no transition from a Dasein that is always particular to a Dasein that is always universal, since it is the notion of the German Dasein that universalizes the particularity and particularizes the universality.[84] More recently, Vattimo has similarly argued that the destiny allotted to the Germans by Heidegger was seen as the "call of Being, but exactly of a Being that announces itself only as a particular historical sending, within the limits of a situation (the prevailing power of capitalistic America and Stalinist Russia) that is also unreadable—in its perspective—in terms of universal values and essences."[85] Heidegger's support of Nazism did not embroil him in positing any access to metaphysical first principles or absolute truths. The political engagement with National Socialism stemmed precisely from the categorical rejection of categorical absolutes, the debunking of the universal dictates of reason in favor of accepting an uncompromising human finitude.

A consequence of that finitude is the resolute insistence that the meaningfulness of a language be determined from its contextualization in a corresponding topographical setting. Heidegger did not practically, and could not theoretically, welcome the possibility, as Adorno expressed it, of a "language without earth, without subjection to the spell of historical existence, a utopia that lives on unawarely in the childlike use of language."[86] For Heidegger, the notion of language without soil is preposterous as the philological and geomorphological strands cannot be unknotted.[87] I would go so far as to say that Heidegger could not even endorse the decoupling of language and people implied in Arendt's identification of her homeland as the German language separated from the country of Germany,[88] or what Agamben has more recently called, influenced by Scholem's analysis of the linguistic theory of the kabbalah,[89] language without name, which similarly entails the severing of language from the people who speak it as part of their national identity, and by extension, from the land where it is spoken.[90] Canetti and Celan are mentioned by Agamben as individuals who wrote in German without any relation with the German nation, and thus they sought to save the language from its people.[91] Moreover, they serve as models for a future anonymous, anarchic, and antinomian intertwining of politics and poetry. Heidegger did attempt to extend beyond the more constricted nationalism of Nazi ideology, but the political dimension of poetry for which he advocated was still tied to the intricate triangulation of land, language, and peoplehood, and in that respect, the poetic semiologically effaces any genuine sense of cultural plurality or multivocality.[92] As incongruous as it might seem, Heidegger's path converges divergently with the esoteric tradition of the kabbalah.[93] Interestingly, in an interview with Edith Wyschogrod, Levinas described the "Heideggerian idea" as affirming "that the whole of language bears the ultimate secret of the absolute. For him, the absolute is being."[94] Levinas did not overtly make the comparison to the kabbalistic sensibility about language and the nature of being, but the comparison can easily be made. That Heidegger himself was concerned that his approach to language could border on the mystical is corroborated in an interesting aside in *Sein und Zeit*. After discussing the import of rendering the term *alētheia* as unconcealment, he remarked, "In citing such evidence we must guard against uninhibited word-mysticism [*Wort-mystik*]."[95] Heidegger's warning notwithstanding, he does ascribe to language a near mystical power, and specifically, as we have seen, Greek and German occupy a privileged position as the languages that have the ability to disclose the concealed nature of beyng.

In a celebrated passage from the zoharic anthology, which had a significant impact on subsequent kabbalists, we read that the three gradations of God, Torah, and Israel were bound together, and that each one displayed the dual structure of the exoteric and the esoteric.[96] The common denominator of this triad is the ontological status accorded Hebrew, which is not only the language through which all things are created, but the *Ursprache* that reveals the nature of being in a manner that is not duplicated by any other language, even Aramaic, the one other language that is treated by some medieval Jewish thinkers as having an equivalent prominence.[97] Although I am sympathetic with the postmodern proclivity to resist essentializing and generalizing, I am unfamiliar with any kabbalist who would reject either the belief that Hebrew is the holy language and, as such, is to be distinguished from all other languages, or the corollary beliefs that the Jewish people and the land of Israel are endowed with a unique holiness. These matters are well known and I myself have discussed them in previously published studies, and so I will not belabor the point here.[98] I will, however, cite one remarkable articulation of this idea from Eliashiv whence we can deduce that the Jews, in a very fundamental way, are responsible for the theopoetic configuration of the infinite that is beyond figuration:

> The matter concerning all this is that all of the names of the blessed one, which are the disclosures through which the emanator, the *Ein Sof*, blessed be his name, is disclosed in the world of emanation, they are only to illumine and to reveal his divinity below. Thus, they are only appropriate when the lower beings receive his divinity, blessed be he, and acknowledge him. However, if that were not so, God forbid, he would not have been revealed at all, and the emanator, the *Ein Sof*, blessed be his name, would have remained alone in his essence and in his concealed truth as it was prior to the creation. Therefore, all the disclosures, which are the names of the blessed one, do not abide except through his nation Israel, for they constantly receive his divinity and acknowledge him. If not for this, all of the disclosures would be gathered in their source (and existence in its entirety would be immediately annihilated because all of the existence is only the

> activity of the light of his disclosures, and they exist and endure continuously only from the light of his disclosures, blessed be his name). Hence, it follows that only his nation Israel, who acknowledge only him, and direct their intention to him, and continuously mention and extol his name, are the ones that establish all of his disclosures and his names. And it is known that the Torah in its entirety is just his name.[99]

Eliashiv's perspective is hardly idiosyncratic, but even so, the boldness of his formulation cannot be overstated: Israel establishes God's divinity, since the acts of the Jewish people serve as the theurgic catalyst to incite the emanation of the light from the concealed darkness of the infinite. In the absence of that stimulation, the impersonal and godless Godhead would not have donned the persona of the theistic God of history. The imaginal confabulation, in turn, has cosmological ramifications, as the world itself could not exist without the disclosure of that light through the myriad of divine names, which are composed of the Hebrew letters. The existence of both God and world, therefore, depend on the linguistic capability of Israel, the quintessential embodiment of humanity in the sociopolitical sphere.

Despite the politically correct mandate to avoid generalizations and thereby dodge the scourge of being essentialized as an essentialist, it is legitimate to conclude that the traditional kabbalistic literature consistently generalizes about the unique role assigned to Israel and its paradigmatic status of being Adam in the fullest and most perfect sense, the microanthropos arrayed isomorphically in the image of the supernal macroanthropos.[100] Even when the more universalistic element is accentuated by kabbalists—especially when the messianic vision of unity and knowledge of the divine is described as the common telos of the human species—the role delegated to the Jews is still exceptional. The spiritual-ethical goal may well be universal in scope—in the striking language of Eliashiv, the rectification of the absolute oneness (*tiqqun ha-aḥdut ha-gamur*) in the eschaton will be characterized by the unification of all the particulars (*ishim ha-peraṭim*) into one stature (*qomah*) and the entire world will assume the shape of the countenance (*parṣuf*) of one complete human (*adam shalem eḥad*).[101] The responsibility to actualize this rectification, however, is given singularly to the people of Israel and distinctively in the land of Israel. Moreover, the nature of the anthropomorphic form to be brought into being through the poiēsis of the Jewish imagination is the reconfigured archetype of Israel in whose constellation the other—symbolized by Edom—has been assimilated.

One might be inclined to attenuate the geo-ethnocentrism by appealing to the universalism implicit in the particularism—the exclusivity of the chosen people is the means to achieve a greater inclusivity that is the utopian ideal expressed in the prophetic idiom of the ingathering of all nations to worship the one true God of Israel. No less a figure than Hegel tried to liberate Judaism from the longstanding condemnation of its parochial identification of the deity as a national God. He argued that the same is true of other religions, including Christianity; that is, in spite of what is presumed about the universality of Christendom, the consciousness of God for Christians is also, at bottom, the consciousness of a national God. Christianity, therefore, is guilty of a similar parochialism insofar as its God is aligned with the one particular family of Christian believers. But the particularism in Christianity is mitigated by the fact that the national God is also the universal creator and lord of the world. The proclaimed purpose of the religion is to inculcate the cognition of the true God that extends beyond the familial restriction.[102] The same can be said about Judaism: in contradistinction to other "Oriental religions," which "cleave to nationality because with them God is still known in a categorially particular way," the God of the Hebrews "is known in his full universality. Objectively speaking, therefore, God is universal lord, but viewed subjectively the Jewish people alone is his chosen property, because it alone recognizes and worships him. But the extension of this subjective relationship, meaning that the Gentiles also are to be worshippers of Jehovah, is expressed in many writers, particularly in the prophets."[103]

Hegel's vindication of Judaism is substantiated theoretically by appeal to the messianic ambition that arises from the need to strike a balance between the nationalistic spirit and the universalistic aspiration.

As accurate as this may be, one cannot deny the problematic repercussions of grounding the universalist objective as part of a vocational particularity. To state the difference in bold philosophical terms: in lieu of the particularistic universalism impelled by the Hegelian dialectic, reflective of the broader ideal of the German *Aufklärung*, the eschatological posture of Judaism tenaciously embraces a universalist particularism.[104] The friction that has marked the Jewish sensibility through the centuries proceeds logically from this posture: on the one hand, the exclusivity of an ethnocentrism that has deep roots in the biblical metaphor of chosenness; on the other hand, the inclusivity implied in the prophetic-messianic mission of being a light unto the nations. Fluctuating between these poles, Israel's election has assumed the form of an inclusive exclusiveness that is an exclusive inclusiveness.

Any number of thinkers could be invoked in this context to illustrate the point, but let me mention Levinas, who placed the burden of bearing this universal particularism at the heart of Israel's messianic mission. The Jewish predicament is the human predicament, and hence the concern with the specificity of the Jew is always meant didactically to illumine the universal status of humanity; as the consummate stranger, the Jew is the figural token of the alterity that comports the nature of human subjectivity; that is, the Jew stands as witness to the fact that we are the same by virtue of our irreducible difference.[105] In spite of Levinas's rejection of mysticism, with respect to this issue, there is affinity—albeit not identity—between his position and the widespread kabbalistic axiom that the ideal of humanity is embodied socio-culturally in Israel, and consequently, that only with respect to the Jews is the conflict between the individual and the general adequately mediated, that the repair of the world will be enacted primarily through one particular people.

The ethnocentrism is evident even in the extreme case when the obliterating of boundaries, characteristic of the redemption, is anticipated by the conversion to Islam or to Christianity, as in the respective cases of Sabbatianism and Frankism, historical phenomena that I have labeled philosophically as the *othering of the other in the eschatological effacing of ontic boundaries*.[106] On the face of it, conversion challenges the axiological framework that distinguishes Israel as the holy seed from all the other peoples of the earth. Presumably, the ontological dualism is undermined by the border crossing that allows the Jew to become the other in the guise of Edom or Ishmael. But a more circumspect scrutiny of conversion as a prolepsis of the soteriological transmutation—personified in the figure of the messiah as the symbol of alienation from within rather than marginalization from without—reveals that the exclusiveness associated with the Jew is inclusive of its own others. Rather than signifying an exemplarity that is inclusively exceptional, the kabbalistic anthropology—even in its messianic expression—remains exceptionally inclusive.[107] The inclusion of the excluded in the claim to exclusivity thus only renders the inclusivity even more exclusive. One would be hard-pressed to rationalize or justify such a claim to exceptionality masked under the pretense of universality.

What is appropriate to emphasize again is that this dimension of the kabbalistic worldview is conceptually contiguous with Heidegger. First, in the manner that Heidegger affirms that language—in particular Greek and German—reveals the being it conceals, the kabbalists view Hebrew as the language that discloses the light of the infinite by keeping it hidden. From this vantagepoint, the Torah, whose constituent elements are the letters of the Hebrew alphabet, is the garment that exposes the light through its occlusion and occludes the light through its exposure. Second, just as Heidegger believed the capacity of poiēsis was the particular destiny of the German *Volk*, so the masters of Jewish esoteric lore unanimously have ascribed the particular task of being custodians of the language that is the house of being to the Jewish people. Third, we can justifiably infer that kabbalists would assent to Heidegger's demarcation of the homecoming as the return to the nearness of origin, and the consequent assumption that to return home consists "in knowing the mystery of this nearness, or even prior to this, in learning to know it."[108] Nearness to the origin is the mystery of the mystery, an idea that well resonates with the kabbalistic hermeneutic that the secret is illumined by the duplicitous nature of the infinite light that radiates in the obscurity of its darkness and is obscured in the transparency of its luminescence. Moreover, in total fidelity to the kabbalists, Heidegger cautions the reader, "we never know a mystery by unveiling or analyzing it to death, but only in such a way that we preserve the mystery *as* mystery" (*daß wir das Geheimnis als das Geheimnis hüten*).[109] As I have argued often in my work, and several times in this monograph, secrecy for the kabbalists likewise demands a guarding of the secret as secret, since the secret cannot be disclosed except as a secret that is hidden. It is astonishing how well suited are Heidegger's words to enunciate what I consider to be the cardinal dogma of kabbalistic esotericism: no secret is more concealed than the secret that is revealed.

The attitude to Hebrew and the land of Israel in Jewish sources, especially heightened in the kabbalistic material, fulfills a similar function, as German does for Heidegger in grounding the particular in the universal. The bond between linguistic and territorial provincialism lends credence to Altmann's hypothesis in "Was ist jüdische Theologie?," a seminal essay to which I had the occasion to refer in chapter 1: since all thinking is oriented toward the universal, this must also be the case for Jewish theology, which is a manner of thinking; what is distinctive about that theology, however, fails repeatedly to advance into the articulation of what is generally understandable. Altmann draws the conclusion that "If one comprehends this tendency of the Jewish theological attitude, which manifests itself at every step in talmudic and midrashic literature as well as in the facticity of all great theological forms of Judaism, then one cannot uphold whatsoever the talk of an inner rupture of Jewish theology caused by the polarity of universalism and particularism. Rather, one should refer to the formal structure of Jewish theology as essentially particularistic."[110] The particularism is indexical of the universal insofar as the untranslatability and singularity applies to the task of theology more broadly, and not just to Jewish theology: "It is the task of theology to preserve and refine this specific nuance. It is not universalization but differentiation that is the function specific to its nature; through it alone is it able to live and testify to its theological experience."[111] If we substitute *philosophical* for *theological*, Altmann's words could well apply to the perspective of Heidegger that I have outlined above.

With a touch of irony, probably not discernible to Altmann himself, he goes on to say that the particularism he claims for Judaism can be applied universally to every genuine theological thought. In his words, "Theological ideas—and this pertains to all religions—are never concepts that can be schematized and thus universalized in some way without forfeiting the true essence of their being."[112] For every religion, consequently, we must say unconditionally that its specific theology cannot be translated into universalistic terms. The very resistance to universalization is proffered as a universal characteristic of theology. Keeping the focus on Judaism, Altmann hit an important nerve: even the universalist element springs from and returns to the particularistic coloration that defies thematization and translation into a universal abstraction. Thus, in the lecture "Das jüdische Mystik" (1935), Altmann argued, pushing against the grain of the historiographical sketching of the historical manifestations of Jewish mysticism, that it is of interest "to see the constant elements in this process of becoming, or better, the continuity in this becoming. Jewish mysticism has been able to preserve its specifically Jewish singularity to an incomparably greater extent than, e.g., Arab mysticism, the structure of which was substantially altered through its fusion with Indian thought. The basic trait of positive, creative assimilation peculiar to Judaism has proved successful also in this area of its intellectual history."[113]

Candidly, Altmann's distinction between Jewish and Islamic mysticism is not defensible, but his comment about the singularity of the former, which he relates to the capacity for creative assimilation, that is, the ability to integrate alien ideas, provides a plausible and valuable heuristic model. Intriguingly, because of the ostensible tenacity about the Bible, Jewish mystics were able to prevent submersion in the foreign.[114] To cite Altmann verbatim:

> The source of mysticism is, after all, not a philosophical or a scientific concern; its source is, rather, the piety of the believing individual to whom revelation was granted but for whom this gift has now become

> the object of constant contemplation. The mystic thinks his way into revelation with his whole being. What he brings forth out of the well of his contemplation is for him necessarily just as much of a received gift, i.e., *kabbalah*, as is the original text. . . . He remains in proximity to the mystery, he remains *mekubbal*, i.e., recipient. . . . Only mysticism is ultimately and radically serious about positing God as actual. Only mysticism, therefore, is ultimately and radically serious about the word of God. The world of the Bible lies clear and finished and concise before the gaze of the mystic. But all that is finished is dead. Hence the finished state of the Bible, which is the word of the living God, must reveal itself to be mere appearance.[115]

There is much to say about Altmann's portrayal of Jewish mysticism as an existential thinking rooted in and always returning to the biblical configuration of the revealed God,[116] albeit in such a way that the allegedly closed revelation of the divine word turns out to be mere appearance, since what is purportedly finished and dead can be experienced anew in each moment, the midrashic hermeneutic that is affirmed by Heidegger as well;[117] for my purposes, however, I will underline his insight that the radical particularization of the mystical safeguards rather than erodes the boundary separating Jew and non-Jew. Even the idea of *unio mystica*, according to Altmann, "does not presuppose any diffusion of the *I* in the universe, nor any suspension of the will in the Nothing; rather, it reveals its Jewishness in the fusion of contemplation and responsible act, in leading all speculation back to the ground of Torah."[118]

The insistence on the Jewishness of Jewish mysticism, including the motif of mystical union, casts a light brightly on an intractable blind spot of the tradition. This shortcoming is especially conspicuous in kabbalistic and Ḥasidic literature, where we recurrently discover—and here I respectfully disagree with these early ruminations of my teacher—a nonegocentric piety that is ethnocentric in its theopolitics. Only the Jew, as it were, has the wherewithal to be absorbed into the infinite where all distinctions—including the distinction between Jew and non-Jew—are transcended.[119] The shortcoming here is palpable: the emphasis on the interconnectivity and unity of the manifold of beings should problematize the divisiveness that is enhanced by the ascription of uniqueness to one nationalistic-religious entity over and against all others, a uniqueness that is expressed in the ability of the Jew to experience the overcoming of the difference that is denied to others. The logic of this position is not entirely coherent, and yet, Jewish mystics have repeatedly affirmed that only the Jew can close the gap separating Jew and non-Jew by steadfastly widening that gap.

Autochthony and the Homecoming of Belonging Nowhere

In the 1955 memorial address for Kreutzer, which took place in his hometown of Meßkirch, Heidegger ruminated on the nexus between creativity and dwelling in the homeland. Raising the question whether the flourishing of a genuine work depends on its roots in a native soil, Heidegger cites the following comment of Johann Peter Hebel, "We are plants which—whether we like to admit it to ourselves or not—must with our roots rise out of the earth in order to bloom in the ether and to bear fruit."[120] Heidegger then offers the following exposition of the poet's words: "For a truly joyous and salutary human work to flourish, man must be able to mount from the depth of his home ground [*heimatlichen Bodens*] up into the ether. Ether here means the free air of the high heavens, the open realm of the spirit."[121] Using the occasion to delve into the political situation of postwar Germany, Heidegger wonders, "Is there still a life-giving homeland in whose ground man may stand rooted, that is, be autochthonic [*bodenständig*]?" What prompts Heidegger to raise this question is the fact that, as a consequence of the war, many Germans had lost their homeland, and countless others had become strangers by migrating to urban centers, the "wastelands of industrial districts." The dilemma is deeper insofar as many who have stayed on their native soil "are still more homeless than those who have been driven from their homeland. Hourly and daily they are chained to radio and television. Week after week the movies carry them off into uncommon, but often merely common, realms of the imagination, and give the illusion of a world that is no world. Picture magazines are everywhere available."[122] Modern forms of technological communication have alienated human beings from their natural habitat and hence their autochthony (*Bodenständigkeit*) is threatened: "The loss of rootedness is caused not merely by circumstance and fortune, nor does it stem only from the negligence and the superficiality of man's way of life. The loss of autochthony springs from the spirit of the age into which all of us were born."[123]

In the address delivered on July 22, 1961, "Ansprache zum Heimatabend," published as "700 Jahre Meßkirch,"[124] Heidegger reiterated his concern that in the age of augmented technology with its characteristic uniformity of form, humans have lost a sense of home, living predominantly in a state of homelessness, or the uncanny (*das Unheimische*), that is, a state of uprootedness from the earth and alienation from the homeland.[125] Already in the Kreutzer lecture, Heidegger described the spirit of the age as one in which the human being is "encircled ever more tightly by the forces of technology. These forces, which everywhere and every minute claim, enchain, drag along, press and impose upon man under the form of some technical contrivance or other—these forces, since man has not made them, have moved long since beyond his will and outgrown his capacity for decision."[126] The complexity of this matter cannot be discussed here in a satisfactory way; let me focus instead on Heidegger's insistence that, while the forces of technology cannot be reversed, it is still possible for individuals "to pit meditative thinking decisively against merely calculative thinking."[127] As Heidegger clarifies his perspective, however, the goal is not so much to set these two modalities of thinking in opposition but rather to harness them together so that we do not fall into bondage to the ever-increasing influence of technical devices. The comportment (*Haltung*), which both affirms and rejects technology, is designated *the releasement toward things* (die Gelassenheit zu den Dingen).[128] The term *Gelassenheit*, which we encountered previously, in this context denotes specifically *the openness to the mystery* (die Offenheit für das Geheimnis) or the hidden meaning (*verborgenen Sinn*) that pervades technology.

> Releasement toward things and openness to the mystery belong together. . . . They promise us a new ground and foundation upon which we can stand and endure in the world of technology without being imperiled by it. Releasement toward things and openness to the mystery gives us a vision of a new autochthony which someday even might be fit to recapture the old and now rapidly disappearing autochthony in a changed form.[129]

In the moment of history when the greatest threat is the total thoughtlessness (*die totale Gedankenlosigkeit*) that is a consequence of the exclusive dominance of calculative thinking, it is through meditative thinking that one has the capacity to reclaim one's essential nature as a contemplative being (*ein nachdenkendes Wesen*) and to establish a new form of autochthony that may replace the older sense of rootedness in one's homeland.[130] Heidegger has stipulated a path that will lead to a new ground and a retrieving of the message contained in the statement of Hebel, which he repeats at the end of the talk. The attentive ear apprehends that the meaning of the poet's words has been subverted and transposed: the ground of which he speaks is no longer limited to the physical soil of one's birth; it is rather a symbol for the contemplative mode of thinking that combines the releasement toward things and the openness to the mystery that draws near by withdrawing and thereby shows itself in its nonshowing.

As to this understanding of the autochthonous, it is important to recall as well Heidegger's statement, "A poem: something flimsy, without resistance, evanescent, abstruse, and without substance—such a thing belongs nowhere anymore."[131] *To belong nowhere anymore* is surely referring to the alienation and homelessness that mark the contemporary existential condition. But Heidegger's intent exceeds that meaning; the role accorded the uncanny in his understanding of homelessness and homecoming is not constricted by the geopolitical sense of the homeland. Quite to the contrary, the sense of being at home is connected ontologically—or perhaps metaontologically—to that which is foreign. The entwining of *Heimliche* and *Unheimliche* is elaborated by Heidegger in the section on "becoming homely" in the exposition of Hölderlin's "Der Ister" in the lecture course delivered in the summer semester of 1942 at the University of Freiburg. For Germans, to come into one's own is to belong to the fatherland, but whatever is of the fatherland is at home only in relation to what is alien to it in the mother earth. To be at home depends on an encounter between these two axes:

> This *coming to be* at home in one's own in itself entails that human beings are initially, and for a long time, and sometimes forever, not at home. And this is turn entails that human beings fail to recognize, that they deny, and perhaps even have to deny and flee what belongs to the home. Coming to be at home is thus a passage through the foreign. And if the becoming homely of a particular humankind sustains the historicality of its history, then the law of the encounter [*Auseinandersetzung*] between the foreign and one's own is the fundamental truth of history, a truth from out of which the essence of history must unveil itself.[132]

Coming to be at home is thus a passage through the foreign—the precise obverse of the Nazi conception of the indigenous and the demeaning of the non-Aryan, an idea affirmed elsewhere by Heidegger himself in his insistence that the homeland is not only "rootedness in the soil" but also the "way of Being of a people . . . when it interacts with the outside—when it becomes a state,"[133] a conception that led him to denigrate the "Semitic nomads" as individuals to whom the nature of the "German space" would likely never be revealed.[134] A few months after making this statement on February 16, 1934, Heidegger educes from Hölderlin's reading of Sophocles in the lecture course on "Germania," delivered in the winter semester of 1934–35 at the University of Freiburg, that the presence of being at home can be experienced most acutely in the absence of not being at home, occupying the other place that is always the place of the other.

> The uncanny means that which is not "at home," not homely within whatever is homely [*Das Unheimliche meint das, was nicht "daheim," nicht im Heimischen heimisch ist*]. Accordingly, we must therefore think the extraordinary not as the immense, nor merely as that which is not the ordinary, but as that which, without the ordinary, resides within that which is not ordinary. . . . Being unhomely is no mere deviance from the homely, but rather the converse: a seeking and searching out the homely, a seeking that at times does not know itself.[135]

Confrontation with the barbarian—the outside that is not merely the expansion of the homeland into the state but a genuine sense of the extrinsic—affords one the opportunity to attain the state of not being at home within the home, to discover the extraordinary as that which is not ordinary within the ordinary. Moreover, only through this engagement with the foreign—the disposition proper to the poeticizing of the poet—can one recover the historical event that is the question of origin (*Ursprungsfrage*),[136] the "original strife" (*der ursprüngliche Streit*) that arises from "the intimacy of the *'not' in beyng* [*der Innigkeit des* Nicht im Seyn]," that is, the struggle of the oscillation (*Gegenschwung*) between beyng (*Seyn*) and nonbeyng (*Nichtseyn*) in the essence of beyng.[137] The law of destiny that sends forth the poet into the foundation of the history of the fatherland is the love of not being at home for the sake of becoming at home in what is one's own. The truth of which the essence of history unveils itself—an unveiling that is always also a veiling, indeed, an unveiling of the veiling—is the encounter between the foreign and one's own, the unfamiliar and the familiar, the unordinary and the ordinary. The binaries are pointedly destabilized by Heidegger's creative exegesis of Hölderlin.

Further support for this conjecture can be found in the account of the originary remembrance bestowed upon the poet: "It does not only think of what has been and of what is coming; rather, it ponders from where the coming had first been uttered, and thinks back to where what has been must be concealed, so that this foreign element itself can remain what it is even when it is appropriated. Remembrance thinks of the location of the place of origin in thinking of the journey of the voyage through the foreign."[138] As I noted above, Heidegger unearths from Hölderlin the notion of remembrance as a poetic abiding that secures the destiny of the future history of the German people by dwelling in proximity to the origin. And yet, as we see from the aforecited text, the meditative act of remembrance demands that the foreign element—what was concealed in the origin—is preserved in its foreignness even as it is appropriated by the poet, who is representative of Germany at large. At the heart of the appropriation is the disappropriated and unassimilable element of the alien. The return to origin comes about by way of excursion through the foreign. The exhortation is thus for the German poet "to learn the free use of what is his own. That is why the foreign must remain near. That is why, for the future poets, the journey preserves what is unavoidable according to the law whereby they must become-at-home [*Gesetz des Heimischwerdens*]. That is why he who is alone and ponders what is his own at the same time commemorates his companions."[139]

From the intricate relationship of the Greeks and the Germans—a relationship dependent on the essential foreignness of one culture to the other and therefore resistant to either identification or assimilation[140]—Heidegger postulates that instead of integrating or obliterating what is alien, the *modus operandi* is to acknowledge the foreign in its "essential oppositional character" (*wesenhaften Gegensätzlichkeit*), for only by doing so is there "the possibility of a genuine relationship, that is, of a uniting [*der Einigung*] that is not a confused mixing [*wirre Vermischung*] but a conjoining in distinction [*fügende Unterscheidung*]. By contrast, where it remains only a matter of refuting, or even of annihilating the foreign, what necessarily gets lost is the possibility of a passage through the foreign, and thereby the possibility of a return home into one's own [*der Heimkehr ins Eigene*], and thereby that which is one's own itself."[141] Although Heidegger's analysis proceeds from his consideration of the specific relationship of ancient Greece and modern Germany, it seems valid to extend the discussion: the homecoming that he articulates presumes that the mystery of the essence of one's own "unfolds its ownmost essential wealth only from out of a supremely thoughtful acknowledgement of the foreign."[142] The relationship with the other should not foster union or a muddled mixture, but rather genuine opposition, a conjoining through distinction. If the confrontation results in the refutation or the annihilation of the other, then the possibility of the passage through the foreign is compromised and the journey home curtailed.

Translation and Confronting the Foreigner Within

Spotlighting the need to confront the foreign as an essential component of the homecoming stands in blatant contrast to the biological racism propagandized by the Nazis and their denunciation and subjugation of the Jews. This is nowhere articulated more strikingly than in Heidegger's view of translation as a transmogrification of the *Muttersprache* by means of its colliding with the *Fremdsprache*, the transference of the sojourner to the alien shore. As Heidegger put it in his lectures on "Der Ister," "every translation must necessarily accomplish the transition from the spirit of one language into that of another." The transition is tempered by the fact that it is impossible to substitute the word of one language for a word in another language; but precisely because equivalency is not feasible, all translating must be an interpreting, and conversely, all interpreting must be a translating. This leads Heidegger to the astounding conclusion that "translating does not only move between two different languages, but there is a translating within one and the same language."[143] Elaborating this theme in the same lecture, he writes,

> Every translation is interpretation. And all interpreting is translating. To the extent that we have the need to interpret works of poetry and of thought in our own language, it is clear that each historical language is in and of itself in need of translation, and not merely in relation to foreign languages. . . . If becoming homely belongs essentially to historicality, then a historical people can never come to satisfy the essence of its own accord or directly within its own language. A historical people *is* only from the dialogue between its language and foreign languages. . . . "Translating" ["*Übersetzen*"] is not so much a "*trans*-lating" ["Über-*setzen*"] and passing over into a foreign language with the help of one's own. Rather, translation is more an awakening, clarification, and unfolding of one's own language with the help of an encounter with the foreign language.[144]

Heidegger reiterated this critical point in the seminar on Heraclitus, *Der Anfang des abendländischen Denkens*, given the summer semester of 1943:

> Every translation, taken just on its own without its corresponding interpretation, remains subject to all manner of misunderstandings: for every translation is in itself already an interpretation. Silently it carries within itself all the attempts, aspects, and layers of interpretation from out of which it originates. The interpretation itself, on the other hand, is only the carrying out of the translation which, still silent, has not yet been brought into the consummating word. Interpretation and translation are, in the core of their essence, the same. That is why, even in one's own language, translation is constant and necessary, given the fact that the words and texts of the mother tongue are often open to interpretation. All speaking, all call and response, are translation. Therefore, the essence of translating does not consist in two different languages entering into a dialogue. We Germans, for example, must each time translate Kant's *Critique of Pure Reason* in order to understand it. Such translation does not entail degrading the sophisticated language of the work down to the level of everyday speech: rather, it means *trans*porting [über*setzen*] the thinking of this work into a thinking and saying that engages and confronts it. By this process it occasionally appears, strangely, that the interpreter "actually" understands the thinker "better" than the thinker understood himself.[145]

Translation is a mode of interpretation, and interpretation a mode of translation; what the two have in common is that they are hermeneutical processes that arise from the belonging together of the strange, a dislocation that is essential to locating oneself spatially and temporally in the world.[146] This is the implication of Heidegger's assertion that interpretation and translation, in the core of their essence (*Wesenskern*), are the same (*dasselbe*), that is, they are the same in virtue of the difference that distinguishes them as opposed to being identical, which would entail the leveling out of all difference. The sameness consists of the fact that both translating and interpreting are acts of transposal that demand bridging the gap between the primary and secondary languages, a bridging that sustains the very gap that it bridges. Needless to say, there is still a sanctioning of German as the essential language, the "concealed shrine that, in belonging to being, preserves within it the essence of human beings."[147] Specifically, with respect to the Greek language, the exhortation to enter into the singularity of its linguistic spirit is ultimately to help the Germans gain a deeper access to their own language. "We learn the Greek language so that the concealed essence of our own historical commencement can find its way into the clarity of our word.... We may learn the Greek language only when we must learn it out of an essential historical necessity for the sake of our own German language."[148]

The lingering ethnocentricism, however, is modified by the assumption that the encounter with the foreign language through translation is necessary for the sake of appropriating one's own language.[149] At its extreme, the practice of translation as confrontation with the exotic sheds light on the fact that every verbal utterance is an act of translation of the language into itself. As Heidegger expressed it in his lectures on Parmenides:

> It is said that "translating" is the transposing [*Übertragung*] of one language into another, of the foreign language into the mother tongue or vice versa. What we fail to recognize, however, is that we are also already constantly translating our own language, our native tongue, into its genuine word. To speak and to say is in itself a translation, the essence of which can by no means be divided without remainder into those situations where the translating and translated words belong to different languages. In every dialogue and in every soliloquy an original translating holds sway.[150]

The shift from considering every translation an interpretation, and every interpretation a translation, to viewing every utterance as a translation of the language within itself undercuts the rigid line separating self and other. Translation of a foreign word into one's own language requires at the same time the more difficult translation of one's own language into its genuine and ownmost word; the former is the making of that which is foreign familiar, and the latter, the familiar foreign. In either case, the translation and paraphrase "are always subsequent and follow upon the transporting of our whole being into the realm of a transformed truth. Only if we are already appropriated by this transporting are we in the care of the word."[151]

Surprisingly, Heidegger's perspective is illumined by Rosenzweig, who also viewed translation—in his case, limited to the translation of Scripture—as a process of defamiliarization and an embrace of the foreign:

> For the voice of the Bible is not to be enclosed in any space—not in the inner sanctum of a church, not in the linguistic sanctum of a people, not in the circle of heavenly images moving above a nation's sky. Rather this voice seeks again and again to resound from outside—from outside this church, this people, this heaven. . . . If somewhere it has become a familiar, customary possession, it must again and anew, as a foreign and unfamiliar sound, stir up the complacent satedness of its alleged possessor from outside.[152]

To translate is be transported into a realm of transformed truth—a conceptual point bolstered philologically by the fact that the same word, *Übersetzen,* is used to name both activities. The transformation ignites the discernment that not only is the foreign not disposable, but its alterity compels a deeper appreciation of the intimacy of the space of the between where the partition of opponents prevails in the bridging of their discord.

Peter Warnek well expressed the import of the notion of the uncanny in Heidegger's view on translation as the movement into what is most strange in order to encounter what is properly one's own:

> What is *most difficult* is precisely this decisive reversal in which the proper as such finds itself displaced, expropriated *into itself* as strange. This, however, should not be mistaken for the utter abandonment of the proper, should not be confused with the simple privileging of the strange, whereby, through mere inversion, the strange would now be given a priority over the proper. Instead, through this decisive reversal, the proper as such appears itself as the most strange, as if, therefore, it lacked propriety.[153]

It is reasonable to speculate that the estranging movement—the expropriation of the *Muttersprache* by its appropriation of the *Fremdsprache*—is a tacit criticism of the Nazi construal of homeliness. Be that as it may, Heidegger's stance brings to mind Benjamin's thesis in "Die Aufgabe des Übersetzers" (1921), the foreword to his translation of Baudelaire's *Tableaux parisiens,* "As for the posited innermost kinship [*Verhältnis*] of languages, it is marked by a peculiar convergence. This special kinship holds because languages are not strangers to one another, but are, a priori and apart from all historical relationships, interrelated in what they want to express."[154] Translation can be seen, therefore, as a "provisional way of coming to terms with the foreignness [*Fremdheit*] of languages,"[155] but the foreignness of languages is itself a consequence of the kinship of languages. The disjunction between the content and the form of the translation—in contrast to the symmetry between the two that characterizes the original language—both prevents the translation and makes it superfluous.[156]

Benjamin summons a biological image to edify the assumption about the translatability (*Übersetzbarkeit*) of the original: "We may call this connection a natural one, or, more specifically, a vital one. Just as the manifestations of life are intimately connected with the phenomenon of life without being of importance to it, a translation issues from the original—not so much from its life as from its afterlife."[157] As the afterlife (*Überleben*) is not a mimetic repetition of the life that came before, but its continual unfolding (*Entfaltung*), so translation is not the duplication of the original, but the propagation of the polysemy contained therein. Counterintuitively, the translation comes temporally later than the original, but when the process of survival and renewal is scrutinized through the prism of history rather than nature, the timeline is inverted and afterward assumes the character of beforehand.[158] In this respect, every translation is a transformation of the language that is translated:

> To grasp the genuine relationship between an original and a translation requires an investigation analogous in its intention to the argument by which a critique of cognition would have to prove the impossibility of a theory of imitation. In the latter, it is a question of showing that in cognition there could be no objectivity, not even a claim to it, if this were to consist in imitations of the real; in the former, one can demonstrate that no translation would be possible if in its ultimate essence it strove for the likeness to the original. For in its afterlife [*Fortleben*]—which could not be called that if it were not a transformation [*Wandlung*] and a renewal [*Erneuerung*] of something living—the original undergoes a change. Even words with a fixed meaning can undergo a maturing process [*Nachreife*]. . . . To seek the essence of such changes, as well as the equally constant changes in meaning, in the subjectivity of posterity rather than in the very life of language and its works would mean . . . confusing the root cause of a thing with its essence. More precisely, it would mean denying, by an impotence of thought, one of the most powerful and fruitful historical processes. . . .And even if one tried to turn an author's last stroke of the pen into the *coup de grâce* of his work, this still would not save the dead theory of translation. For just as the tenor and the significance of the great works of literature undergo a complete transformation over the centuries, the mother tongue of the translator is transformed as well. While a poet's words endure in his own language, even the greatest translation is destined to become part of the growth of its own language and eventually to perish with its renewal. Translation is so far removed from being the sterile equation of two dead languages that of all literary forms it is the one charged with the special mission of watching over the maturing process of the original language and the birth pangs of its own.[159]

Contained in this passage are the seeds for Benjamin's historical materialism, which presumes the "dialectical reversal" of past and present compared to the experience (*Erfahrung*) of awakening from a dream.[160] We awaken to the present that is the realization of the dream in the calibration of the past as an act of futural remembering. Recollecting the past in the present, however, is not merely replication of what has transpired; it is a mode of consciousness that seeks a "teleological moment" by bestowing new reality on the past, the "moment of waiting" that is akin to the dream that "waits secretly for the awakening."[161]

Benjamin identifies this inversion—waking from the dream that one is waking from the dream—as the *Copernican revolution in historical perception*.[162] In the historian's retelling, as in the remembering of the dream, we find neither the irreversibility nor the repeatability of events but rather the "contemporaneity of the noncontemporaneous," the prognosis of the future rooted in and hence already existent in—even though not yet having occurred—the past that is reshaped in and by the present.[163] It is worth recalling Benjamin's approving citation in "Über das mimetische Vermögen" of Hugo von Hofmannsthal's comment "*Was nie geschrieben wurde, lesen*."[164] How does one read what was never written? Implied in Benjamin's appropriation of this injunction, as we can retrieve from his notes and sketches for "Über den Begriff der Geschichte," is the assumption that the historical method is a philological technique that requires of the historian as reader to transform mimetically the past that never was rather than to recover factually the past that once existed.[165] Reading an unwritten text entails this sense of hermeneutic transformation: history is a text, the historian a reader, and every explication is a rewriting of events. What we remember, therefore, is not the past of a future that is no longer present but the future of a past that has yet to come to light. The same reversal of time underlies Benjamin's admittedly unfinished messianic politics: the redemptive power of the *Jetztzeit* is a consequence of the historian's ability to alter the course of the future by eliciting from the moment the whole of the past abbreviated or condensed in the present. Benjamin thus remarks that the "past carries with it a secret index by which it is referred to redemption." The "secret index" (*heimlichen Index*) relates to the human aptitude for remembering the future that redeems the anticipation of the past.[166] Benjamin also alludes to this potential as the "secret agreement" (*geheime Verabredung*) between past generations and the present, an agreement that turns on the redemptive potential of chronicling and narrating the past, such that nothing is lost to history.[167] One will undoubtedly see the connection between the later insights of Benjamin on history as the unfurling of the past in the reminiscence of the future and his earlier reflections on translation as a transformation of the original through the subsequent ripening in time.

In my judgment, we can elicit from kabbalistic sources a comparable understanding of translation as appropriation by expropriation, the transporting encounter with the alien that enables the return home.[168] I will substantiate this contention by delving into the subject of translation elicited from some zoharic passages focused on the status of Aramaic in relation to Hebrew. Let me commence with the following talmudic dictum that provides the conceptual frame for the ensuing discussion: "It has been taught: R. Judah said, the one who translates a verse literally, he is a liar; if one adds to it, he is a blasphemer and a libeler."[169] The statement is perplexing as one is seemingly left in an insurmountable quandary. What is the correct way to translate if to translate literally is deceit and to translate with explanatory additions is blasphemy and libel? Perhaps the directive transmitted in the name of R. Judah can be decoded in light of Jerome's famous description of his own translating practice in the letter to Pammachius, *non verbum e verbo, sed sensum exprimere de sensu,* "not word for word but to render the sense of the sense."[170] The translator, accordingly, occupies the space between the literal and the nonliteral, a hiatus filled neither by replication of the former nor by embellishment of the latter. But what, then, is the model for translation? The anonymous redactor of the talmudic passage anticipated the question: "Then what is meant by translation? Our translation." The reference is to the standard biblical translation, Targum Onkelos, which apparently satisfies the requirement not to render the *ipsum verbum* in a literal fashion that obscures its meaning but also not to superimpose extraneous layers of sense in order to extricate that meaning.

Whatever else we may glean from the talmudic text, we can assume that the rabbinic sages responsible for it maintained that translation of Scripture is possible because of the reciprocity between the original Hebrew and the target language Aramaic, a reciprocity, however, that preserves the distance it seeks to overcome. Applying Benjamin's terminology, we can say that the Aramaic of the translation is comprised as the afterlife in the Hebrew of the scriptural original. The distance between the two languages is traversed through the collocation of the incongruent and not through the sublation of the dissimilar. That is, in the space of translation—the space between literal and nonliteral—the sameness of their difference becomes apparent, and the foreignness that keeps them apart is consequent to the affiliation that brings them together. Interestingly, Benjamin concludes the aforementioned essay by noting that "just as language and revelation are joined without tension in the original, the translation must write literalness with freedom in the shape of an interlinear version. For to some degree, all great texts contain their potential translation between the lines; this is true above all of sacred writings. The interlinear version of the Scriptures is the prototype or ideal of all translation."[171] To suggest that the original contains the translation implies that they are expressions of an inexpressible meaning that exceeds the linguistic garb of both. In Benjamin's words, "all suprahistorical kinship between languages consists in this: in every one of them as a whole, one and the same thing is meant. Yet this one thing is achievable not by any single language but only by the totality of their intentions supplementing one another: the pure language [*die reine Sprache*]."[172]

It goes without saying that the anonymous kabbalists responsible for the composition and redaction of the zoharic homilies were influenced by divergent viewpoints on the respective nature of Hebrew and Aramaic.[173] To mention two of the most salient examples: Abraham Ibn Ezra famously claimed, building on older rabbinic passages, that Aramaic is the primordial language, even though he also affirmed that there is an underlying unity of Hebrew, Aramaic, and Arabic. Closer to the bone of the kabbalah, as it were, is the view espoused by Judah Halevi. Like Ibn Ezra, Halevi noted the affinity between the three Semitic languages, but he nonetheless venerated Hebrew as the holy language (*leshon ha-qodesh*) compared to the profane (*ḥol*) status of the others.[174] Following Halevi, and in consonance with a trajectory attested in aggadic, magical, and mystical sources, the zoharic authors affirm that Hebrew alone is the matrix language out of which the entities of the world are created. Yet, for Halevi, as for the kabbalists whose opinions are preserved in the zoharic corpus, the topic is more complex: the relationship of the profane to the holy fluctuates between the monistic and dualistic orientations; that is, Hebrew and Aramaic are either semantically transposable or irreconcilably disparate.

The zoharic authors introduce an additional element into the mix: the Hebrew language, which is the divine name and the mystical essence of the Torah, is an expression of the inexpressible. The characterization of the most elemental purpose of language as naming the nameless corresponds to what we gathered from the Heideggerian understanding of the poetic word as the highest grade of silence, which is not to remain speechless, but to let the unsaid appear in speech as unsaid.[175] It is reminiscent as well of another dimension of Benjamin's thinking, that is, the portrayal of the kinship of languages, which makes translation of the multivalency of any one language possible, as the totality of languages that collectively communicate the incommunicable. This idea was explored in more detail in the essay "Über Sprache überhaupt und über die Sprache des Menschen," written in 1916 but unpublished in the author's lifetime. Benjamin begins by arguing that the proposition that *the linguistic being of all things is their language* (Das sprachliche Wesen der Dinge ist ihre Sprache) is not tautological. Prima facie, this is not easy to comprehend, since the statement appears to be a textbook example of a tautology. For Benjamin, however, the statement conveys that the communicable aspect of a mental entity is its language, whence he further deduces that "all language communicates itself *in* itself; it is in the purest sense the 'medium' of the communication."[176] What is communicated *in* and not *through* language is the mental being (*geistige Wesen*) included in the linguistic being (*sprachliche Wesen*). Even though the two are outwardly differentiated, they can be considered identical insofar as the mental being is capable of communication. More specifically, since it is *the linguistic being of man to name things*, Benjamin asserts that the communication of one's mental being in language is through this activity of naming. The fundamental problem of linguistic theory is not only the mediation of the immediacy of mental communication through linguistic communication, but the immediacy that is indicative of the infiniteness (*Unendlichkeit*) of language. "For precisely because nothing is communicated *through* language, what is communicated *in* language cannot be externally limited or measured, and therefore all language contains its own incommensurable, uniquely constituted infinity. Its linguistic being, not its verbal contents, defines its frontier."[177] The limit of speech is delimited by its potential illimitability, the indeterminable boundlessness determined by the linguistic being, which is differentiated from the verbal content of language. Inasmuch as the linguistic being is identical with the mental being, language can be defined as the mental being of things, which expresses itself most purely in the act of naming. "So in name culminate both the intensive totality of language, as the absolutely communicable mental entity, and the extensive totality of language, as the universally communicating (naming) entity. . . . *Man alone has a language that is complete both in its universality and in its intensiveness.*" As the medium of communication, language communicates its mediating relationship as the medium of communication. "*There is no such thing as a content of language; as communication, language communicates a mental entity—something communicable per se.*"[178]

This is the point where Benjamin finds the most intimate connection between the philosophy of religion, the concept of revelation, and linguistic theory: "Within all linguistic formation a conflict is waged between what is expressed and expressible and what is inexpressible and unexpressed."[179] The conflict is related to the theological belief that everything was created by the word of God, which means that all existing things have the potential to be named by human speech and thereby communicated, not that their substance is language. "In the word, creation took place, and God's linguistic being is the word. All human language is only the reflection of the word in name. . . . The infinity of all human language always remains limited and analytic in nature, in comparison to the absolutely unlimited and creative infinity of the divine word."[180] Insofar as the word of language is the "conception of the nameless in the name," translation is at the very heart of Benjamin's linguistic theory: "It is necessary to found the concept of translation at the deepest level of linguistic theory . . . Translation attains its full meaning in the realization that every evolved language . . . can be considered a translation of all the others. . . . Translation is removal from one language into another through a continuum of transformations."[181] Benjamin distinguishes his theory of language as the translation of the nameless into the name from the mystical linguistic theory, which he contends is based on the misunderstanding that "the word is simply the essence of the thing. That is incorrect, because the thing in itself has no word, being created from God's word and known in its name by a human word. . . . For conception and spontaneity together, which are found in this unique union only in the linguistic realm, language has its own word, and this word applies also to that conception of the nameless in the name."[182] Benjamin's desire to distance his view from what he considered to be the erroneous mystical conception notwithstanding, his characterization of the word as the nameless in the name brings his thinking into the vicinity of the kabbalistic and Heideggerian perspectives. The task of the translator is not simply to impart information by converting one language into another; he or she seeks to disclose and thereby conceal the unfathomable and mysterious ineffability of the original, the pure language of which the poet speaks by speaking the unspeakable.

To explicate the conception of translation as an apophatic gesture of unsaying in the zoharic compilation, let me begin with the following words about the hidden and revealed nature of the name and of the Torah:

> That which is more revealed is mentioned to cover that which is hidden and concealed. . . . Accordingly, the supernal name is a hidden and concealed mystery, and it is not mentioned except through a name that is revealed. The one is mentioned, the other is hidden. The one is revealed, the other is secreted. All that which is revealed is mentioned forever. The concealed name is *YHWH*, the revealed name is *Adonai*. Therefore, it is written with the concealed letters and is declaimed with these letters. The one is covered by the other so that the supernal glory will be hidden and concealed forever. For all the ways of the Torah are revealed and concealed. And all the matters of the world, whether this world or the world above, all of them are hidden and revealed.[183]

The revealed and the concealed ways of the Torah are coalescing rather than consecutive states. The zoharic text, in other words, affirms that the Torah is hidden and revealed simultaneously and not sequentially. The ritual practice of vocally substituting *Adonai* for the written *YHWH* provides a useful way to comprehend the coincidence of the hidden and the revealed in the middle excluded by the logic of the excluded middle—the ineffability of the name is secured precisely by its vocalization through the epithet and not by remaining silent. Applied to the Torah, the exoteric and the esoteric exhibit the same convergence—the inner core is displayed through exposing rather than by discarding the external shell, or in the terminology employed in a passage from the zoharic stratum known as *Sabba de-Mishpaṭim*, the secret word revealed by the Torah is seen by the wise, who are full of eyes, through the garment in which it is arrayed and not by divesting the word of its garment.[184] There is no shining of the face in all its nudity, as Levinas put it,[185] because the face can shine only through the mask that is the face.

The zoharic hermeneutic can also be profitably interpreted through Derrida's deconstructionist reading of the biblical narrative of the Tower of Babel.[186] From this story, Derrida infers that the Tetragrammaton "imposes and forbids translation. . . . Translation then becomes necessary and impossible, like the effect of a struggle for the appropriation of the name, necessary and forbidden in the interval between two absolutely proper names."[187] The Tetragrammaton is designated the "translatable-untranslatable name"[188]—translatable inasmuch as it is ineffable and hence unvoiced except through its appellation, and yet, untranslatable insofar as it names the wholly other and absolute singularity that can never be suitably denominated.[189] Derrida presumes that the ineffable name in the Jewish tradition presents the recipient with an absent presence that necessarily must be translated but which is nevertheless impossible to translate. From the specific case of the Tetragrammaton, "the proper name which is never proper,"[190] we can extrapolate about the inexorable necessity and inevitable implausibility of translating every proper name, a double bind that is indicative of language per se as concurrently translatable and untranslatable.[191] The ineffable name thus performs the role of *dénomination*—"at the same time to name and to unname"[192]—implicit in every linguistic utterance, the unsaying that makes each saying both possible and impossible, possible as impossible and impossible as possible.[193]

I propose that the paradox of the impossible possibility of translation lies at the basis of the zoharic understanding of its own multilingualism as the saying of the unsayable, the naming of the nameless. As one might expect, nowhere in zoharic texts do we have a discursive, let alone systematic, treatment of this apophatic gesticulation. The way of reasoning at play in these homilies is scriptural and thus any conceptual framing will emerge from delving into the intricacies of the textual patterns woven by the exegetical prowess of the kabbalists responsible for the shaping of the zoharic material over what appears to be an extended period of several centuries. I will translate what in my mind is the most striking passage about the nature of translation, viewed specifically from the vantage point of the relationship between Hebrew, the language of the divine, and Aramaic, the language of the demonic:

> The *qedushah* that comes at the end is in Aramaic translation [*targum*] ... and thus even an individual can recite it ... but words of the *qedushah* in the holy language may be recited only by ten because the *Shekhinah* is joined together with the holy language, and every *qedushah* accompanied by the *Shekhinah* is only through ten, as it is written "I will be sanctified in the midst of the children of Israel" (Leviticus 22:32). The children of Israel are verily the holy language and not the other nations, who possess another language. And if you inquire, why isn't the *qedushah* of the *qaddish*, which is in Aramaic, recited by the individual? Come and see: This *qedushah* is not like other *qedushot*, which are tripled, but this *qedushah* ascends on all sides above and below, and in all aspects of faith, breaking locks, seals of iron, and the evil shells. This is the praise through which the glory of the blessed holy One is elevated more than any other praise, and this exaltation is more than the rest. What is the reason? Because it is meant to subjugate [*le'itkafya*] the Other Side and to elevate the glory of the blessed holy One above everything. We must recite it in the language of the Other Side and respond with great vigor, "Amen! May his great name be blessed," in order to break the power of the Other Side, and the blessed holy One will be elevated in his glory above everything. And when the power of the Other Side is broken by this *qedushah*, the blessed holy One ascends in his glory, remembering his children and remembering his name. Since the blessed holy One ascends in his glory by means of this *qedushah*, it is only recited by ten. By this language, the Other Side is subdued and its power is broken against its will, and the glory of the blessed holy One ascends, breaking the locks, seals, sturdy chains, and evil shells, and the blessed holy One remembers his name and his children.[194]

In this passage, which illustrates the complex interweaving of the halakhic-ritualistic and mystical-theosophical threads, the zoharic author sets out to explain the liturgical difference between the *qedushah de-sidra* (based on Isaiah 6:3, Ezekiel 3:12, and Psalm 146:10), which comes at the end of the morning prayer as part of *u-va le-ṣiyyon go'el* (Isaiah 59:20), and *qedushah de-yoṣer*, which is recited in the blessing *yoṣer or* before the Shema, recounting Israel's description of the angelic act of sanctification, as well as the *qedushah de-amidah*, recited in the public repetition of the third blessing of the standing prayer, narrating Israel's sanctification of God together with the angels. The *qedushah de-yoṣer* and the *qedushah de-amidah* are exclusively in Hebrew, whereas the *qedushah de-sidra* includes Hebrew and Aramaic. Moreover, the *qedushah de-sidra* can be said by an individual, while the *qedushah de-yoṣer* and the *qedushah de-amidah* require a quorum of ten, since the *Shekhinah* joins those who sanctify the name in Hebrew and such a sanctification requires a minimum of ten worshipers.

The halakhic underpinnings of this passage demand a careful analysis, but what is noteworthy for our purpose is the identification of Aramaic as the language of the Other Side, an idea that builds on the contrast made by Halevi between Hebrew as holy and Aramaic as mundane. Given that the passage is written in Aramaic, it is startling that its author would assert that it is the language of the demonic, a language that belongs essentially to the other nations as opposed to Hebrew, the hallowed language, which is unique to the Jewish people. The discussion of the *qaddish* states more clearly that the power of Aramaic is to break the force of the demonic (*de-yitbar ḥeila de-siṭra aḥara*) and thereby exalt the divine glory over everything, particularly by the vigorous recitation of the words *amen yehei shemeih rabba mevarakh*. Operative here is the principle of fighting fire with fire—one can eradicate the demonic only by commandeering the tactics of the demonic. Because this is the case, even though the *qaddish* is in Aramaic, it is said only in a quorum of ten.

The author of this zoharic passage unqualifiedly posits an ethnolinguistic polarity: the holiness of Israel and Hebrew is pitted against the impurity of the nations and Aramaic. The oneness of God, fittingly, depends on discerning that the Other Side is in conflict with rather than an integral part of the divine. The ultimate task, therefore, is to subdue and to shatter the power of evil, to keep the domains distinct, prohibiting the infiltration of that which is foreign into the consecrated precinct of the holy emanations. Curiously, in a previous part of this homily, the explanation offered for the Aramaic of the *qedushah de-yoṣer* is not to combat the demonic but to be protected from the potential envy that might arise from the fact that with the utterance of this final *qedushah* the Jews exceed the sanctifications recited by the angels. Through concealing the Hebrew in the guise of the Aramaic, the angels are kept in the dark, since, according to a highly influential talmudic tradition,[195] the angels do not understand Aramaic.[196] In a third passage from this zoharic section, the dualism is not only attenuated, it is flatly sabotaged:

> This *qedushah* that the supernal angels sanctify is not recited by an individual. As we have established, the individual is prohibited from uttering any *qedushah* that is in the holy language. The Aramaic translation is always recited individually and not publically; its implementation [*tiqquna*] is surely the individual, but not the multitude. A sign for this mystery: Scripture twice and the Aramaic translation once [*shenayim miqra we-eḥad targum*].[197] "Twice" is an expression that implies multiplicity, for certainly the individual is forbidden to recite the *qedushah* of the holy language. The *qedushah* in Aramaic translation is banned from being recited in public, but always by the individual. We have learned that the Aramaic translation is recited once, not twice and not more. The Aramaic translation necessarily comes to limit [*le-mi'uṭa*]; the holy language necessarily comes to extend [*li-revuyya*], for we elevate in holiness and we do not descend [*ma'alin ba-qodesh we-lo moridin*],[198] but with respect to the Aramaic translation, we descend and do not elevate. We have learned "once" and not more; it is not augmented at all. . . . The other *qedushah* is as an additional holiness and therefore it is subsequent to the prayer, and because it is a holiness that is supplementary to the other *qedushot*, it is after the prayer. Because every person must draw upon himself some of that surplus, the translated *qedushah* was arranged for each individual. If you say, "It includes the *qedushah* in the holy language!" That is so that all of the congregation will be sanctified together by that additional holiness. Since the individual does not have permission to recite it in the holy language, to sanctify himself individually, it was prepared in the language of the Aramaic translation to be recited by the individual, so that each individual could be sanctified by that surplus, to draw upon himself additional holiness.[199]

Reiterating the point of the first passage that we examined, the zoharic author emphasizes that the *qedushah* that recounts the angelic liturgy, the *qedushah de-yoṣer*, is said in Hebrew and thus requires a quorum. The *qedushah* that includes Aramaic, the *qedushah de-sidra*, can be said by the individual worshiper; even when recited publicly, it should be murmured quietly to give the impression that it is not suitable for communal recitation. The point is elucidated further by the talmudic praxis of reading the weekly scriptural text twice and the translation once, whence it is deduced that the Aramaic is restrictive and the Hebrew expansive. This distinction is confirmed by the principle that in matters pertaining to holiness there is elevation and not devaluation, but with respect to translation the inverse is true because we diminish and do not increase, that is, it is recited individually and not jointly. Quite unexpectedly, at this juncture, the zoharic text takes a turn and disrupts the very duality that it previously evoked to explain the use of Aramaic in the *qedushah de-sidra*. The latter is depicted as the "additional sanctification" (*tosefet qedushah*) vis-à-vis the *qedushah de-yoṣer* and the *qedushah de-amidah*. In order for each person to draw down something of this surplus, it was established that it could be said in Aramaic even by the individual. Unlike the previous passage, here there is recognition that the *qedushah de-sidra* includes the holy language as well. The Hebrew is to be recited by the congregation so that everyone will be sanctified together by the superfluity of spirit, but the individual worshiper cannot recite the Hebrew and therefore should avail himself of the Aramaic. Rather than explaining the latter as a means to crush the demonic, it is advanced as the way to obtain the efflux of the extra holiness.

Following this template, we can surmise that Hebrew and Aramaic can be considered antagonistic insofar as they are homologous in shape and substance, and thus what was considered to be the other language, the language of the Other Side, becomes the stranger from without that is within. An analogy that comes to mind is the sculptural portrayal in medieval Europe of the Church and the Synagogue—two female forms that are virtually identical and yet in diametric opposition, the one depicted as upright and triumphant, and the other as downtrodden and subjugated. The philosophical import of this architectural design was to divulge that otherness is detectable only against the backdrop of sameness. In the long and variegated history of Jews and Christians, framed typologically as the struggle between Jacob and Esau, self-definition and definition of the other are inextricably interwoven. As Derrida sagaciously articulated the subject in his depiction of the process of auto-affection (*Selbstaffektion*), a concept that can be traced to Kant,[200] "the same is the same only in being affected by the other, only by becoming the other of the same."[201] The referentiality of self cannot be demarcated in isolation from an intricate web of social interconnectivity. Thus, even if the divine anthropos is identified specifically as the archetype of the Jew, the face of that anthropos is beyond polarities—neither holy nor impure because both holy and impure—and therefore the distinction between Jew and non-Jew must be surpassed in the discernment that the other of the same is not the same as the same of the other. Moving from the abstract to the concrete, we find many instances where a Jewish sage has been swayed by the very doctrine or practice that he discards as blasphemous. Contrariwise, just as appropriating from an external environment is often based on resonance with something internal to the Jewish landscape, so the disposing of something from the outside may actually betray an inherent affinity; the very propinquity to the other demands a sharper demarcation and setting of boundary. The deeper the resemblance, it would seem, the greater the need to discriminate.

The confluence of the two approaches to the relationship of the original language and its translation come together in a passage from the literary unit in the zoharic anthology entitled *Sitrei Torah*:

> "After these things, the word of the Lord came to Abram in a vision" (Genesis 15:1). In every place that it is written in the Torah "in a vision" [*ba-maḥazeh*], it is the name that was revealed to the patriarchs. And which is it? *Shaddai*, as it says, "I appeared to Abraham, Isaac, and Jacob through *El Shaddai*" (Exodus 6:3), and as it is said, "who beholds a vision of *Shaddai*" (Numbers 24:16). This is the prism [*ḥeizu*] through which all the supernal visions are seen like the mirror [*mar'ah*] in which all the images are seen. It is all one—*mar'ah* and *maḥazeh* are identical, the one is the Aramaic translation and the other is the holy language. R. Yose says that many of these abound in the Torah, and thus Onkelos had permission to translate into that language what the blessed holy One revealed in the Torah, and that language is concealed from the supernal angels. "In a vision," it was concealed from the supernal angels, for they did know it when he conversed with Abraham. What is the reason? For Abraham was not circumcised, and having a foreskin, it [the covenant] was hidden in his flesh,[202] and therefore it was concealed from them in the language of the Aramaic translation. Similarly, it is written in the case of Balaam, "who beholds a vision of *Shaddai*." "He beholds" [*yeḥezeh*]—the matter was concealed from the ministering angels, so that they would not have an opening to accuse the blessed holy One of speaking to someone with an impure foreskin. The holy angels have no need for the Aramaic language.... Thus it was revealed to Abraham in a hidden manner so that the holy angels would not pay attention to it, and they would not have an opening to allege that the blessed holy One revealed himself to an uncircumcised man. When was it overtly revealed to him before the supernal angels? When he was given the circumcision of the holy covenant [*berit qeyyama qaddisha*],

> as it is written, "and God spoke to him saying" [*wa-yedabber itto elohim le'mor*] (Genesis 17:3)—*Elohim*, the holy name, and it is not written "in a vision," the name that is disclosed. "Saying" [*le'mor*]—what is the meaning of *saying*? It was spoken and declared in every language, and it was not concealed, and not in an alien language [*be-lishana aḥara*],[203] but in the language that everyone speaks, so that they could converse one with another.[204]

God appears to Abraham through the agency of the *Shekhinah*, to which is affixed the name *Shaddai*. This sefirotic potency is also called *maḥazeh* because it is the prism (*ḥeizu*) through which the supernal forms (*ḥezwan*) are seen in the same manner that images (*diyoqnin*) are made visible in a mirror (*mar'ah*).[205] In fact, *maḥazeh* and *mar'ah* are synonymous and they symbolically allude to the selfsame phenomenon, viz., the divine presence. The only variance is that the former is derived etymologically from an Aramaic root and the latter from Hebrew: *we-kholla ḥad mar'ah maḥazeh ḥad hu da targum we-da leshon ha-qodesh*. The rhetoric of identity could not be clearer: the two are proclaimed to be substantially indistinguishable; the sole difference is their linguistic encasement, a bewildering claim in light of the correlation of Aramaic with the demonic and Hebrew with the divine. The dualism appears to collapse in light of the claim that everything is one. The tone shifts, however, as the author summons the older talmudic tradition that angels do not heed Aramaic—he makes the crucial distinction between knowing and heeding: we must assume the angels know Aramaic but they pay no attention to it. The language that describes the epiphany is precise: God is manifest to Abram in the *maḥazeh*. The Aramaic term is used to communicate that the vision was concealed from the angels. But why should it be concealed? Since God appeared to Abram before he was circumcised, and the sign of the covenant was not yet incised on his flesh—a comparison is made to Balaam, the non-Israelite and hence uncircumcised prophet, who apperceived the divine through the same prism, *maḥazeh shaddai yeḥezeh*—the angels might protest that it was not propitious. But after Abram is circumcised, the term *maḥazeh* is exchanged for *elohim*, an explicit name of the *Shekhinah* that is well known to the angels.

To my ear this text is pivotal as it eviscerates the distinction between Hebrew and Aramaic and the implied conflict between the holy and the unholy. The use of Aramaic is not due to any deficiency in the visionary but rather to the potential antagonism of the angels. Analogously, the lack of circumcision is not viewed as a detriment to Abram's capacity to receive the divine presence and there is no suggestion of an internal change in his spiritual comportment after he is circumcised. Consider, by contrast, the language of a parallel exegesis from what is known as the main body of the *Zohar* on this very verse:

> "The word of the Lord came to Abram in a vision" (Genesis 15:1). What is "in a vision" [*ba-maḥazeh*]? In that prism [*ḥeizu*], the gradation in which all the images are seen [*darga de-khol diyoqnin itḥazyan beih*]. R. Simeon said, Come and see: as long as Abraham was not circumcised, one gradation spoke with him. And which was it? This vision [*maḥazeh*], as it is written, "who beholds a vision of *Shaddai*" [*maḥazeh shaddai yeḥezeh*] (Numbers 24:16). When he was circumcised, all of the gradations rested on this gradation, and then it spoke to him, as it is written, "I appeared to Abraham, Isaac, and Jacob through *El Shaddai*" (Exodus 6:3). Before he was circumcised these gradations did not rest upon him to speak.[206]

According to this passage, there is a transubstantiation of Abraham's body that corresponds to an alteration in his visionary status. Prior to the circumcision, only the *Shekhinah* conversed with him; after the circumcision, all the sefirotic gradations spoke to him as they are refracted through the *Shekhinah*. In the *Sitrei Torah* passage, there is no indication of such a transformation. Before and after the circumcision, the locus of the prophetic vision was exclusively the *Shekhinah*. The change from *maḥazeh* to *mar'ah* or to *Elohim* relates to the appeasement of the angels and not to a modification in Abraham's rank or being.

Especially notable for the larger theme of this chapter is the fact that the author of the *Sitrei Torah* passage positions Abraham on the same level as Balaam. More prevalent in zoharic texts is the reworking of the rabbinic idea of parity between Moses, the supreme prophet of Israel, and Balaam, the outsider who attains the status of the consummate insider, and thus problematizes the rigid distinction between external and internal.[207] In various passages in zoharic literature, the parity is concurrently upheld and toppled; that is, the equivalence between Moses and Balaam is affirmed but also neutralized by the fact that the former is linked to the holy emanations on the right and the latter to the unholy emanations on the left. Kabbalistically, Balaam is the chief magician and the protagonist of the demonic, whose activity corresponds to the theurgic efficacy exhibited by Moses.[208] In the zoharic passage we are considering, Abraham and Balaam are treated as equal. If we further assume, and I think there is justification to do so, that Balaam is a symbolic cipher for Jesus,[209] then the implications of this passage are far-reaching in narrowing the chasm separating Judaism and Christianity. The bridging of that gap can be elicited from the assumption that it is not circumcision that makes Abraham worthy of the vision of God, an older midrashic theme that is reworked in various zoharic homilies.[210] By contrast, in the *Sitrei Torah* passage, the vision bestowed on Abram when he was uncircumcised is the same vision bestowed on Abraham once he was circumcised. The inequity between circumcised and uncircumcised, so central to Jewish particularism and the rift between the two liturgical communities, is no longer vital or decisive.

Even from a linguistic perspective, this text is radically subversive: Aramaic is described as being despicable to the angels but not to God. In fact, as the author rightly notes, the task of translating Scripture into Aramaic is justified by the fact that Aramaic words are found in the body of Scripture and hence the disparity between the two languages cannot be assumed to be absolute. Aramaic is the language of the Other Side, but one of the ways the zoharic text deciphers the meaning of otherness undermines the dyadic nature of difference. Hence, in some contexts, as the one from *Sitrei Torah* that I analyzed, the alterity of *Siṭra Aḥara* is significantly mollified as what is foreign is construed as an instantiation of the familiar. The point is well expressed by Eliashiv in commenting on the statement in the *Ma'amar Adam de-Aṣilut* in Graf's *Wayaqhel Moshe*,[211] that the word *ṭehiru* is the Aramaic translation of the Hebrew word for light, *targumo de-or*:

> This is to teach us that the light of the luster [*or ha-ṭehiru*] is not actually the first light [*ha-or ha-ri'shon mammash*] but rather the dark light [*or ḥashukh*], and it is like the aspect of the Targum vis-à-vis the holy language, which is a much lower level, for all of the Targum is merely the aspect of the backside [*aḥoriyyim*] and judgment [*din*]. . . . And this is what is said, "When it emerged there remained the *ṭehiru*, and it is the Aramaic translation of *or*," which is the dark light. However, all this is only in relation to the supernal light [*ha-or ha-elyon*], which is in the primordial ether [*ha-awir ha-qadmon*] that is above the *ṭehiru*, but in relation to itself, and all the more so in relation to all the worlds that come to be afterwards, the *ṭehiru* is a supremely wondrous light [*or nifla me'od*] and it is also from the supernal radiances [*ha-ṣaḥṣaḥot ha-elyonot*] that are above everything.[212]

Aramaic, the language of the Other Side, is presented here as the backside of Hebrew, the aspect of judgment, but not as autonomous entity, an opposite of equal footing. Driving the point home, Eliashiv depicts translation by the oxymoron *dark light*, that is, a light that is dim but a light nonetheless. The monistic orientation is highlighted at the conclusion with the assertion that the *ṭehiru* may be opaque in comparison to the supernal light of the primordial ether, but it is still in and of itself a supremely wondrous light that comes forth from the supernal radiances, the one source of all being. The structure of the argument is identical to what we saw in chapter 4 with respect to the fact that the vessel, which itself is composed of light, serves as the ultimate signifier of that which is separate from the light. Insofar as the root of difference is implanted in the nondifferentiated, and the nonessence is embedded in the essence, we are led to conclude that heterogeneity is a manifestation of homogeneity. As we have seen at various junctures of this monograph, the infinity of the kabbalists, much as Heidegger's beyng, is not a unity wherein the positing of opposites—diagrammed by Hegel as $+ A - A = 0$—vanishes in the dialectical identity of the pure identity of nonidentity.[213] Rather, the kabbalistic *Ein Sof*, as I interpret it, is more in line with the indifference of the Bohemian-Schellingian *Ungrund*, which corresponds to the belonging together of the Heideggerian *Abgrund*. According to this schema, the holy language and the language of the demonic are the same by virtue of their difference, a sameness that can be discerned only in the face of the obdurate difference of the same.

According to the semantics of the kabbalah—articulated especially in the relationship of Aramaic and Hebrew—translation displays a tension between the monosemiotic and the polysemiotic calculus of signification.[214] On balance, however, knowledge of the profane is crucial to a proper understanding of the sacred. This precise dynamic is offered by Bachrach as an explanation for both the rabbinic decree to recite the Targum weekly and for the composition of the zoharic compendium: "We must give him [the Other Side] a portion of holiness from our faith, and this is the secret of the reading of Scripture twice and the translation once, and this is his portion we bestow on him to be comprised within the holiness. . . . Thus Rashbi and R. Abba, peace and blessing upon them, composed the *Zohar* in the language of the Targum, and not in the holy language, for the light of the radiance [*or nogah*] is constructed entirely from the light of the translation, in which the Torah is completely garbed, in order to give it an overflow so that it will be comprised in holiness. Consequently, there will be no protest regarding the disclosure of the secrets."[215] The Aramaic translation is linked here to *or nogah*, which is the last of the four demonic shells—their names are derived from the zoharic exegesis of Ezekiel 1:4—that is most subtle and closest to the core of holiness.[216] Insofar as the distinction between holiness and impurity begins to be blurred in the location of this shell, which vacillates between the two poles, it is identified as the source of Aramaic, the language that embodies the concept of translation, which, as we saw in the thought of Heidegger, effectuates the unfolding of one's own language with the help of an encounter with what is foreign. The mystical intent of the ritual of reading the translation is to obfuscate the boundary by restoring the unholy to the holy.[217] Most remarkably, Bachrach brought to light one of the profoundest secrets of the scribal activity adopted by the anonymous kabbalists responsible for the composition and redaction of the zoharic corpus: the holiest work in the traditional Jewish canon is written in the language associated with the unholy. As Bachrach explained, underlying this decision is the laudable effort to reintegrate the demonic back into the divine. The deeper implication of this secret, however, is rendered better in terms of Heidegger's unconventional distinction between *das Selbe* and *das Gleiche*: Hebrew and Aramaic are the same but not identical, indeed, they are the same on account of their nonidentity, that is, their similarity is established on the basis of their dissimilarity.

Perhaps we would do well to explain this approach by utilizing Derrida's appeal to the notion of "identity as non-self-identity" to account for the fact that his self-identity as a Jew consisted of not being identical to himself, whence he elicited the paradox of assignation "the less one is Jewish, the more one is Jewish" (*moins on est juif, plus on est juif*).[218] Cast positively, the principle of exemplarity embodied in the figure of the Jew implies that the "more jewish the Jew [*plus le Juif est juif*], the more he would represent the universality of human responsibility for man, and the more he would have to respond to it, to answer for it."[219] The otherness of the Jew perforce must comprise its own other, the universal that transcends the particular in which it is contained. The same relationship, for Derrida, can be detected in the "double postulation" that is the foundation of the "very law of what is called translation," or of the "law itself as translation"—*We only ever speak one language . . . (yes, but)—We never speak only one language* (On ne parle jamais qu'une seule langue . . . (oui mas)—On ne parle jamais une seule langue).[220] From the incompossible and contradictory nature of this antinomy, it follows that one can never claim the language one is destined to speak as one's own—to quote Derrida again, *Yes, I only have one language, yet it is not mine* (Oui, je n'ai qu'une langue, or ce n'est pas la mienne).[221] The monolingual solitude in which one naturally dwells as a consequence of one's sociobiological circumstance is always also the monolingualism of the other, a monolingualism that is, in truth, bilingual or plurilingual. Paradoxically, the impossibility of speaking the language that is one's own necessitates the possibility of speaking a language that is not one's own. As Derrida put it elsewhere, "Two texts, two hands, two visions, two ways of listening. Together simultaneously and separately [*Ensemble à la fois et séparément*]".[222] And with this we return to the issue of the status of Aramaic in relation to Hebrew: to translate the latter into the former is to position oneself in the place where opposites are the same in the opposition of their sameness. Attunement to the zoharic dictum *we-kholla ḥad mar'ah maḥazeh ḥad hu da targum we-da leshon ha-qodesh* inculcates in the reader the truth that collapses the dichotomization of the demonic and the divine in the mirroring of the self as other and the other as self through the glass darkly.

Concluding Reflections: Intimacy and the Belonging Together of the Strange

Utilizing Scholem's interpretation of the kabbalistic linguistic theory according to which the name of God constitutes the origin of all languages,[223] Agamben characterizes the misfortune of modernity as the withdrawal of the name from human language. In an obvious Heideggerian turn, Agamben further suggests that the response to this dilemma is to be garnered from Hölderlin: the language that no longer has a name is the language of poetry.[224] In the absence of God, the people become the object of demand, whence Agamben draws the conclusion that there is a "fundamental nexus between the poet and politics. . . . Hölderlin's poetry marks the point at which the poet, who lives the lack of the people—and of God—as a catastrophe, seeks refuge in philosophy and must turn into a philosopher. . . . But this attempt can be successful only if the philosopher also turns into a poet. Poetry and philosophy can in fact communicate only in the experience of the missing people."[225] The inability of Hegel and Schelling to become poets—which does not mean to write poetry but rather to experience the calamity of language caused by the withdrawal of the name—led to the failure of philosophy to fulfill its political task. Heidegger did attempt to pay this debt, to redress the betrayal of the poetic task, but he was not able to be a poet, and thus, in the end, he had no recourse but to invoke an unnamed god, as in the title of the famous *Der Spiegel* interview of May 1976, *Nur noch ein Gott kann uns retten*, "Only a God can save us."[226] The process set in motion by Hölderlin culminates with the poet and the philosopher speaking in the name of a language that is no longer anchored in the unambiguous sense of peoplehood. Canetti and Celan are mentioned as individuals who wrote in German without any relation to the German nation, and thus they sought to save the language from its people.[227]

Agamben proposes that this is the model for the future dominated by a secular, anarchic, and antinomian messianism:

> But it is only by trying to name the desert that grows in the absence of the name that he will—perhaps—again find the word. If the name was the name of language, he now speaks in a language without name. Only he who has long kept silent in the name can speak in the without-name, the without-law, the without-people. Anonymously, anarchically, aprosodically. Only he has access to the coming politics and poetry.[228]

The language without name—the severing of language from the people, and by extension, from the land—is conceptually on a par with the view of Adorno mentioned above concerning the possibility of language without earth.[229] As I have already surmised, Heidegger could not envision such a possibility: the political dimension of poetry was still tied to the intricate connection between land, language, and peoplehood. The same can be said about the kabbalah and its continual impact on conceptions of Jewish identity, especially as expressed in Zionist right-wing ideology.[230] Celebrations of the diasporic nature of Judaism—epitomized in Steiner's formula that *the text is the homeland*[231]—are commendable, but they are not sufficient to untie the knot of the ethnolinguistic geopolitics that continues to inform the beliefs and actions of segments of the Jewish world.[232] Bifurcating homelessness and homeland leaves one with a sense of displacement that remains dependent dialectically on an emplacement that is determined from the particular framework of Jewishness. The nonbelonging of exile is still a manner of belonging, albeit belonging by not belonging, and therefore I take issue with Butler, as I do not think it is philosophically or culturally tenable to ground the generalizability of the ethical principles of equality and justice—values that will remain Jewish if they are not exclusively Jewish—in the historical phenomenon of dispersion. Relationality may, in fact, depose ontology, but in the history of Judaism, the relation to alterity cannot be disentangled from nationalism and ethnicity as the defining frameworks of collective and individual identity.[233]

Another path may be pursued, however, to destabilize the territorialism and exceptionalism, a poetic—as opposed to a political—breach that opens from the weight of the cultural prejudices themselves and seeks to affirm the homelessness of being at home in contrast to the homeliness of being banished from home. In pursuit of the dispossession of the possessed, we can unearth a genuine sense of alterity—the affirmation of the other as the other to the same rather than as the same to the other—that would depend on the inclusion of exclusiveness in the inclusiveness of the exclusion as opposed to the exclusion of inclusiveness in the exclusiveness of the inclusion. Expounding Hölderlin's line *Alles ist innig*, Heidegger writes, "This means that one is appropriated to the other, but in such a way that thereby it itself remains in what is proper to it, or even first attains to it: gods and men, earth and heaven. Intimacy does not mean the coalescence and obliteration of distinctions. Intimacy names the belonging together of what is foreign, the ruling of the strange, the claim of awe."[234] Bracketing the image of the fourfold order of gods, men, earth, and heaven that is invoked in this passage,[235] what is important to emphasize is Heidegger proposed an ethical-political principle—perhaps it is more accurately classified as postethical and postpolitical—according to which one is appropriated to the other by remaining proper to the inappropriable distillation that is one's own; the intimacy of confronting the other is neither a coalescence (*Verschmelzen*) nor an obliteration (*Verlöschen*) of distinctions, but rather a preserving of them in the belonging together of what is foreign (*das Zusammengehören des Fremden*). The translatability of languages depends on the inherent untranslatability of each language and the resistance of the other to the tedium and potential brutality of sameness.[236] Here it is worthwhile recalling the following observation of Nancy:

> The conditions of meaning are always the same, and if we want to imagine what access to meaning was had by the inhabitants of a world that seems to us to have been immersed in the transparency of meaning (the Christian, Greek, Jewish, Nambikwara, or Zen world, etc.), we must above all understand that this "transparency" is only the interpretation that *we* offer to ourselves of what was also their opacity. Never did a Christian, a Greek, a Jew, a Nambikwara, or a Buddhist, accede to the kingdom of meaning in a procession or ascension of luminous certainties. Nor did a Plato or a Descartes. On the contrary, meaning always made itself known by its obstinate consistence, its resistance to the enslavements of intelligence, its opaque apodicticity. But—and this is history—its figures transform themselves, for example from "Jew" into "Greek" and from "Greek" into "Arab" and from "Arab" into "Christian"—and this transformation itself, this twisting and incessant multiplication of figures, of exposures of meaning, are a part, and not the smallest, of its opacity and resistance.[237]

Taking measure of the role that resistance to the other plays in the transformation of multiple figurations of meaning—traversing one cultural milieu into another—we can say that the semblance of evil is to be sought without subjugating it to the good or reducing its independent opacity by viewing it as the calcified transparency that, in the end, must be restored to the nondifferentiated luminosity of the infinite. Evil and good, darkness and light, are coterminous powers that belong together and oscillate between being and nonbeing in the nothingness of the will bereft of willfulness, an idea of kenosis affirmed by Schelling, perhaps transmitting the kabbalistic tradition as mediated through Böhme.[238] Apropos of this possibility, it is interesting to note that in the *Philosophische Untersuchungen*, Schelling approves of the view of Baader that "evil resides in a positive perversion [*positiven Verkehrtheit*] or reversal [*Umkehrung*] of the principles. . . . All other explanations of evil leave the understanding and moral consciousness equally unsatisfied. They all rest fundamentally on the annihilation [*Vernichtung*] of evil as a positive opposite [*positiven Gegensatzes*] and on the reduction of evil to the so-called *malum metaphysicum* . . . or the negating concept [*verneinenden Begriff*] of the imperfection of creatures."[239] In a second passage from this treatise, Schelling contrasts two explanations of the nature of evil, the dualistic (*die dualistische*), which presumes that evil is a fundamental being (*Grundwesen*) alongside the good, and the kabbalistic (*die kabbalistische*), "according to which evil is explained through emanation and distancing."[240] As it happens, Schelling's presentation of Baader's view is closer to the kabbalistic perspective, which presumes that evil—the *Siṭra Aḥara*—is not an independent metaphysical force or the negating concept of creatures, the light diminished in the process of emanation proceeding from the source, but rather the positive perversion or the positive opposite of the indissoluble principles, the nonessence infused with negativity that belongs to the positivity of the essence, the potential for difference of identity coiled within and yet departing from the identity of difference.

My strategy in this book has been to follow this path, to link two ostensibly disparate corpora in order to illumine the convergence from within the divergence, to demonstrate that otherness of the similar is consequent to the similarity of the other. I have sought to recover from two admittedly independent ideational matrices a logic that preserves the disparity of the uniform by keeping to the uniformity of the disparate. Without denying the demonstrably detrimental attitude that has informed the kabbalistic and Heideggerian constructions of the other—in both cases, although qualitatively and quantitatively different, the theoretical construct has had pernicious practical implications—I contend nonetheless that the negative propensity of a singular universality has the capacity to yield the ethical imperative of a universal singularity: what secures our equality is our diversity. The trespassing of the boundary between self and other need not be accomplished by incorporating or demolishing the other whether in acts of gratuitous compassion or wanton aggression. Applying the dialetheic logic deployed throughout this work, we could say that the indeterminacy of the other is always in the process of being determined by the determinacy of the same and the determinacy of the same by the indeterminacy of the other. Furthermore, assuming a relational rather than a substantialist notion of self, I would argue that in the domain of intersubjectivity one is veritably the singularity of oneself to the extent that one is constantly becoming otherwise than oneself, that the exteriority of the interior is gauged by the interiority of the exterior, that individuality consists of embracing an alterity that is universalizable in such a way that the particularity is preserved: the difference between us is what invariably makes us the same and therefore categorically not subject to the categorical. The menacing solitude of our homelessness—at once overwhelmingly individualistic and compellingly collectivistic—alights the way back home, the longest of paths, not because it leads far away, but because it leads through what is most near.[241] The journey embarked upon in this book, indeed the journey I began many years ago, has been a concerted effort to unveil the truth of this veil, to find the route to the familiar by delving into and dwelling within the domain of the foreign, relentlessly cultivating two ways of seeing and two ways of listening, simultaneously together and separate.

Notes

1. Habermas, *Philosophical-Political Profiles*, p. 24.
2. Heidegger, *Pathmarks*, p. 243; *Wegmarken*, p. 319.
3. Derrida, *Writing and Difference*, p. 137.
4. Heidegger, *Being and Time*, §27, p. 125 (*Sein und Zeit*, p. 129): "The self of everyday Dasein is the *they-self* [Man-selbst], which we distinguish from the *authentic self*, that is, the self which has explicitly grasped itself. As the they-self, Dasein is *dispersed* in the they [*das Man*] and must first find itself. . . . If *Dasein* is familiar with itself as the they-self, this also means that the they prescribes the nearest interpretation of the world and of being-in-the-world. The they itself, for the sake of which Dasein is every day, articulates the referential context of significance" (emphasis in original). See the discussion of falling prey (*Verfallen*) and thrownness (*Geworfenheit*)

in *Being and Time*, §38, pp. 169–73; *Sein und Zeit*, pp. 175–80.

5. Despite the turn in Heidegger's thinking, there is continuity with his earlier thought, as is evident from the following passage in *Sein und Zeit*: "If Dasein explicitly discovers the world and brings it near, if it discloses its authentic being to itself, this discovering [*Entdecken*] of 'world' and disclosing [*Erschließen*] of Dasein always comes about by clearing away [*Wegräumen*] coverings [*Verdeckungen*] and obscurities [*Verdunkelungen*], by breaking up the disguises [*Verstellungen*] with which Dasein cuts itself off from itself" (*Being and Time*, §27, p. 125; *Sein und Zeit*, p. 129). Note that Heidegger speaks of abandoning the inauthentic self and disclosing the authentic self of Dasein by discarding all the obstacles, discovering the world and bringing it near, just as in the "Brief über den 'Humanismus,'" he speaks of advancing to the nearness of being. In the language later espoused by Heidegger, the drawing near is achieved by submitting to the namelessness of being, but in some sense this, too, is anticipated in the same section from *Sein und Zeit*: "If the being of everyday being-with-one-another [*alltäglichen Miteinanderseins*], which seems ontologically to approach mere objective presence [*Vorhandenheit*], is really fundamentally different from that kind of presence, then the being of the authentic self can be understood still less as objective presence. *Authentic being a self* [eigentliche Selbstsein] is not based on an exceptional state of the subject, detached from the they, *but is an existentiell modification of the they as an essential existential*. But, then, the sameness of the authentically existing self is separated ontologically by a gap from the identity of the I maintaining itself in the multiplicity of its experiences [*Erlebnismannigfaltigkeit*]" (*Being and Time*, §27, p. 126 (emphasis in original); *Sein und Zeit*, p. 130). The retrieval of the self, lost in the anonymous they, is a form of self-disclosedness that is not delineated either by an ontological presence or an ontic demarcation of subjectivity in the customary egological sense, that is, a subject that can become an object for itself. The sameness (*Selbigkeit*) of the authentic selfhood—the *existentiell modification of the they as an essential existential*—is distinguished from the identity (*Identität*) of the I that sustains and is sustained by the sum of multiple experiences.

6. Wolfson, *Giving*, p. 172.

7. For a similar argument about namelessness and the excessive signification of immanence, see Barber, *On Diaspora*, pp. 7–9.

8. Wolfson, *Giving*, pp. 172–74.

9. See ch. 4 n. 292.

10. Wolfson, *Venturing Beyond*, pp. 286–316.

11. Wolin, ed., *Heidegger Controversy*, p. 29; Heidegger, *Selbstbehauptung*, p. 9.

12. Wolin, ed., *Heidegger Controversy*, p. 29; Heidegger, *Selbstbehauptung*, p. 9.

13. Sommer, "Métapolitique de l'université."

14. Wolin, ed., *Heidegger Controversy*, p. 30; Heidegger, *Selbstbehauptung*, p. 10. Noteworthy is the comparison Heidegger makes in *Heraclitus*, pp. 147–48 (*Heraklit*, p. 193) between the Greek word ἐπιστήμη and the German *Wissenschaft*.

15. Wolin, ed., *Heidegger Controversy*, p. 31 (emphasis in original); Heidegger, *Selbstbehauptung*, p. 11. I have slightly modified the translation.

16. Heidegger, *Introduction to Metaphysics*, p. 40; *Einführung in die Metaphysik*, pp. 40–41. The bracketed words were added in the 1953 edition.

17. See ch. 7 nn. 119–20.

18. Heidegger, *Ponderings VII–XI*, pp. 8–9 (emphasis in original); *Überlegungen VII–XI*, pp. 10–11. See also Heidegger, *Ponderings VII–XI*, p. 264 (*Überlegungen VII–XI*, p. 339): "*Where have the Germans arrived*? Or have they only always still remained where they have always already were and where ultimately Hölderlin found them and Nietzsche still came across them? . . . But perhaps the essence of the Germans—and perhaps whatever they are 'capable' of comes to light through the 'Americanism' they practice *even more* radically and the 'Romanism' they carry out *even more* 'tirelessly'—*is* that they are called the 'people' of thinkers and poets only because as a 'people' they do *not* want this thinking and poetizing, i.e., are not prepared to see their ground in such danger—but always still and more and more unwittingly—glorify and imitate what is 'foreign.' Indeed who would then say that a '*people*' must and could be that which prepares on behalf of beyng the site of its truth?" (emphasis in original). See Vallega-Neu, *Heidegger's Poietic Writings*, pp. 96–97.

19. See ch. 7 at n. 96.

20. Heidegger, *Elucidations*, p. 35; *Erläuterungen*, pp. 16–17.

21. Heidegger, *Elucidations*, p. 36; *Erläuterungen*, p. 17. On the *Heimat* tradition that informed Heidegger's thinking, including his political engagement with Nazism, see Malpas, *Heidegger's Topology*, pp. 23–27

22. See the comments of Hofstadter in the "Introduction" to Heidegger, *Poetry, Language, Thought*, p. xvi, and the more recent attempt to contextualize Heidegger's understanding of *Volk* in the nationalistic tradition of German Romanticism in Sikka, *Heidegger, Morality and Politics*, pp. 121–55.

23. Hegel, *Science of Logic*, p. 12.

24. Derrida, *Acts of Religion*, pp. 152–53: "The first . . . concerns a German tradition which survives as far as Heidegger: the German holds an absolutely privileged relation to the Greek—descent, *mimesis*, and rivalry with all the consequent paradoxes. . . . No other European people is supposed to share this competitive affinity with Greece. If the Greek tradition is safeguarded in a privileged manner within German culture and more specifically within German philosophy, then the syllogism implies the German spirit. Cohen emphasizes this already at the end of the first paragraph: 'Now, as Christianity is unthinkable without the logos, Hellenism is one of its sources. *But thus, and with equal impact, Hellenism appears as one of the fundamental sources* (Grundquelle) *of Germanity*'" (emphasis in original). Derrida goes on to say that, in spite of the difference in substance and style between Heidegger and Cohen, the synergy they affirm with respect to Greek and German is related to "an interpretation of the sense of being" (p. 153).

25. My comments are indebted to the discussion of Cohen's view, including a comparison to Heidegger, in Erlewine, *Judaism and the West*, pp. 19–20.

26. Heidegger, *Introduction to Metaphysics*, p. 60; *Einführung in die Metaphysik*, p. 61. It is of interest to recall Heidegger's reaction in *Schelling's Treatise*, p. 90 (*Schelling: Vom Wesen*, pp. 155–56) to Schelling's statement that a truly universal philosophy cannot be the property of a single nation, "Thus it was also truly German that Jacobi's appeals 'to the heart, the inner feelings and faith' did not prevail, but that the 'higher light of Idealism,' that is, a more strict thinking, came about and gained control in that Idealism which is therefore called German—a higher kind of thinking which received essential inspiration from Leibniz and a first true foundation in Kant." Even in this context Heidegger rejects the claim to a philosophical universalism and appeals to a nobler form of idealism that is exclusively German in nature. For a critique of Heidegger's position, see Badiou, *Métaphysique du Bonheur réel*, p. 22

27. Heidegger, *Hölderlin's Hymns "Germania" and "The Rhine,"* p. 107; *Hölderlins Hymnen "Germanien" und "Der Rhein,"* p. 118. See Dastur, "Hölderlin and the Orientalisation," pp. 166–69.

28. Heidegger, *Four Seminars*, p. 37; *Seminare*, p. 330. In Heidegger's account of the conception of phenomenology in section 7 of *Sein und Zeit*, the emphasis is not on marking the historical trajectory of the philosophical school, which can be traced to Husserl, but rather on the Greek etymology of the words whence the German term is composed. See Mulhall, *Inheritance and Originality*, pp. 211–12. Many have discussed Heidegger's privileging of the Greeks and their special relation to the Germans. See the recently published analysis of Claxton, *Heidegger's Gods*, pp. 7–41.

29. Benes, *In Babel's Shadow*, p. 10.

30. Heidegger, *Pathmarks*, pp. 257–58; *Wegmarken*, pp. 337–39. Numerous scholars have written on this topic. For two detailed studies, see Mugerauer, *Heidegger and Homecoming*; O'Donoghue, *Poetics of Homecoming*.

31. Heidegger, *Pathmarks*, p. 257; *Wegmarken*, p. 338. For an extended discussion of the myth of the homeland that informed Heidegger's thinking, see Bambach, *Heidegger's Roots*, pp. 12–68. A possible critique of the crude nationalism of the Nazi veneration of the German soil may be discernible in Heidegger, *Hölderlin's Hymn "Remembrance,"* p. 41; *Hölderlins Hymne "Andenken,"* p. 47. Interpreting Hölderlin's remark that he wanted to sing "the angels of the holy fatherland" (*die Engel des heiligen Vaterlands*), Heidegger writes, "thus, it is not the 'gods,' but rather the 'angels' that he wants to sing; it is not the fatherland as a present at hand political constellation [*als vorhandene politische Konsellation*] that he belatedly wants to discuss with verse, but rather the 'holy fatherland,' the fatherland grounded in the holy, that he wants to poetize; indeed not even just this, but rather 'the angels of the holy fatherland.'"

32. Heidegger, *Reden und Andere Zeugnisse*, pp. 409–15.

33. Ibid., p. 414. See the discussion of this passage in Derrida, *Psyche*, p. 32. Derrida mistakenly identified this letter as the one addressed to the rector from November 1945. On Heidegger's distinction between the social-national and the nationalistic, see Hemming, *Heidegger and Marx*, p. 197.

34. Compare Heidegger, *Ponderings II–VI*, p. 123 (*Überlegungen II–VI*, p. 168): "If a truth lies in the power of 'race' (of the native-born one), will and should the Germans then lose their historical essence—abandon it—organize it away—or will they not have to bring it to the supreme tragic denouement? Instead of which, those who are now bred are shortsighted and oblivious!" Also relevant is Heidegger, *Ponderings II–VI*, pp. 126–27 (*Überlegungen II–VI*, p. 173): "The many: ones who now speak 'about' race [*Rasse*] and indigenousness [*Bodenständigkeit*] and who mock themselves in their every word and action and demonstrate that they 'possess' nothing of all this, leaving aside the question of whether they actually *are* well-bred [*rassig*] and indigenous" (emphasis in original). See the aphorism "On the situation" (*Zur Lage*) in Heidegger *Ponderings II–VI*, p. 171 (*Überlegungen II–VI*, p. 233): "Where a people

posits itself as its own goal, egoism has expanded into the gigantic but has gained nothing with regard to the domains and truth—the blindness toward beyng survives in a desolate and crude 'biologism' which promotes a swaggering in words. All this is radically un-German." For criticism of Heidegger's supplanting of biological racism with what has been called metaphysical racism, see Derrida, *Of Spirit*, p. 74 (*De l'esprit*, pp. 118–19); Nancy, *Banality*, pp. 4 and 52; Elden, *Speaking against Numbers*, pp. 90–106, esp. 95–99. See also Bernasconi, "Heidegger's Alleged Challenge"; Sikka, "Heidegger and Race"; Sikka, *Heidegger, Morality and Politics*, pp. 156–84; Wolfson, *Duplicity*, pp. 9–10, 31–32, 33–34, 83. On the political implications of the concept of race specifically in Heidegger's notebooks, see Lettow, "Heideggers Politik."

35. Blanchot, "Thinking the Apocalypse," p. 478.

36. Heidegger, *Elucidations*, p. 33; *Erläuterungen*, p. 14. Compare Polt, "Secret Homeland."

37. Heidegger, *Ponderings VII–XI*, p. 24; *Überlegungen VII–XI*, p. 31.

38. Heidegger, *Ponderings VII–XI*, p. 81; *Überlegungen VII–XI*, p. 104.

39. Heidegger, *Aus der Erfahrung*, pp. 155–80. See Mugerauer, *Heidegger and Homecoming*, p. 444.

40. Heidegger, *Elucidations*, p. 44; *Erläuterungen*, p. 25.

41. Heidegger, *Hölderlin's Hymns "Germania" and "The Rhine,"* p. 7; *Hölderlins Hymnen "Germanien" und "Der Rhein,"* p. 8.

42. Heidegger, *Hölderlin's Hymns "Germania" and "The Rhine,"* p. 23; *Hölderlins Hymnen "Germanien" und "Der Rhein,"* p. 22.

43. Heidegger, "Hebel," p. 93; *Aus der Erfahrung*, p. 139. On Heidegger's interpretation of Hebel, see Allen, "Homecoming."

44. Heidegger, "Hebel," p. 93; *Aus der Erfahrung*, p. 139.

45. Heidegger, "Hebel," p. 94 (emphasis in original); *Aus der Erfahrung*, pp. 140–41.

46. Heidegger, "Hebel," p. 98; *Aus der Erfahrung*, p. 147. On spatiality in Heidegger's thinking and the eventual turn to a poetic understanding of dwelling, with particular reference to Hölderlin, see Malpas, *Heidegger's Topology*, pp. 74–83, 206–9, 267–77, 311–15. For an analysis of the role of the topological in Hölderlin's vision of the world, see Constantine, *Significance of Locality*.

47. Heidegger, "Hebel," p. 96; *Aus der Erfahrung*, p. 143.

48. Heidegger, "Hebel," p. 99 (emphasis in original); *Aus der Erfahrung*, p. 148.

49. Heidegger, *Poetry, Language, Thought*, pp. 191–92; *Unterwegs zur Sprache*, p. 11.

50. Heidegger, "Hebel," p. 100; *Aus der Erfahrung*, p. 149. See the analysis in Heim, "Heidegger and Computers," pp. 405–9.

51. Heidegger, *Hölderlin's Hymns "Germania" and "The Rhine,"* pp. 61–62; *Hölderlins Hymnen "Germanien" und "Der Rhein,"* p. 67.

52. Heidegger, *Elucidations*, p. 44; *Erläuterungen*, p. 26.

53. Heidegger, *On the Way to Language*, p. 131; *Unterwegs zu Sprache*, p. 251.

54. Heidegger, *Elucidations*, pp. 112–13 (emphasis in original); *Erläuterungen*, p. 88.

55. See ch. 3 n. 59.

56. Wolfson, *Language*, pp. 264, 291, 309, 467n360.

57. See the passage of Isaac of Acre discussed in Wolfson, *Language*, pp. 124–25; Epstein, *Ma'or wa-Shemesh*, pp. 183, 718, 730–31. On the desire of all the worlds and all the created beings to be conjoined with *Ein Sof*, see Epstein, *Ma'or wa-Shemesh*, p. 741.

58. On the nexus of mysticism and atheism, see Wolfson, *Giving*, pp. xx, 72–74, 168–70, 341n297, 413n110. In my previous discussion of this matter, I neglected to mention the following passage from Hume, *Dialogues Concerning Natural Religion*, pp. 36–37: "I can readily allow, said *Cleanthes*, that those who maintain the perfect simplicity of the supreme being, to the extent in which you have explained it, are complete *mystics*. . . . They are, in a word, atheists, without knowing it. For though it be allowed, that the deity possesses attributes, of which we have no comprehension; yet ought we never to ascribe to him any attributes, which are absolutely incompatible with that intelligent nature, essential to him. A mind, whose acts and sentiments and ideas are not distinct and successive; one, that is wholly simple, and totally immutable; is a mind, which has no thought, no reason, no will, no sentiment, no love, no hatred; or in a word, is no mind at all. It is an abuse of terms to give it that appellation; and we may as well speak of limited extension without figure, or of number without composition" (emphasis in original). Hume, it seems, was one of the first to discern that if mysticism necessarily implies the utter incomprehensibility of the divine nature (see p. 48), it is conceptually on a par with atheism, since nothing positive can be said about God.

59. Wolfson, *Open Secret*, pp. 240–48.

60. Whistler, *Schelling's Theory*, pp. 27–28, 162–63. The view that Whistler attributes to Schelling, against the usual understanding of the romantic symbol, can be applied to Heidegger and to the kabbalists.

61. See reference to my work cited in ch. 7 n. 147.

62. See the evidence adduced in Perotti, *Heidegger on the Divine*, pp. 94–114, esp. 98–101. The description

of the holy as that which shines forth only as it veils itself is derived from Heidegger's interpretation of the following lines from a poem by Trakl, "Ein Tiergesicht / Erstarrt vor Bläue, ihrer Heiligkeit" ("Animal face / Freezes with blueness, with its holiness"). See Heidegger, *On the Way to Language*, pp. 166–67; *Unterwegs zur Sprache*, pp. 40–42. According to Heidegger's reading, the blue wild game (*das blaue Wild*) to which Trakl refers is "an animal whose animality presumably does not consist in its animal nature [*ein Tier, dessen Tierheit vermutlich nicht im Tierischen*], but in that thoughtfully recalling look [*schauenden Gedenken*] for which the poet calls. This animality is still far away, and barely to be seen. The animality of the animal here intended thus vacillates in the indefinite [*Unbestimmten*]. It has not yet been gathered up into its essential being. This animal—the thinking animal, *animal rationale*, man—is, as Nietzsche said, not yet determined. . . . By the poetic name 'blue wild game' Trakl evokes that human nature [*Menschenwesen*] whose countenance [*Antlitz*], whose countering glance [*Gegenblick*], is sighted by the night's blueness, as it is thinking of the stranger's footfalls and thus is illumined by the holy." See the analysis in Derrida, *Geschlecht III*, pp. 65–69, and compare the passage from Heidegger's *Heraklit* cited in ch. 2 n. 92.

63. Heidegger, *Hölderlin's Hymns "Germania" and "The Rhine,"* p. 4; *Hölderlins Hymnen "Germanien" und "Der Rhein,"* p. 4.

64. Heidegger, *Hölderlin's Hymns "Germania" and "The Rhine,"* p. 119; *Hölderlins Hymnen "Germanien" und "Der Rhein,"* p. 134.

65. Heidegger, *Hölderlin's Hymns "Germania" and "The Rhine,"* p. 109 (emphasis in original); *Hölderlins Hymnen "Germanien" und "Der Rhein,"* pp. 121–22.

66. Heidegger, *Hölderlin's Hymns "Germania" and "The Rhine,"* p. 5 (emphasis in original); *Hölderlins Hymnen "Germanien" und "Der Rhein,"* p. 6.

67. Heidegger, *Elucidations*, p. 48 (emphasis in original); *Erläuterungen*, p. 30.

68. Heidegger, *Ponderings II–VI*, p. 21 (emphasis in original); *Überlegungen II–VI*, p. 27. For an alternate translation, see Trawny, *Heidegger and the Myth*, p. 14. Trawny's comment that this passage is "seemingly from out of the blue" is not justifiable as the textual evidence that he himself supplies attests.

69. Heidegger, *Parmenides*, p. 167 (emphasis in original); *Parmenides* [GA 54], pp. 249–50.

70. Heidegger, *Parmenides*, p. 166; *Parmenides* [GA 54], p. 249.

71. Heidegger, *Elucidations*, p. 171 (emphasis in original); *Erläuterungen*, pp. 149–50. I have slightly modified the translation. On the essential relation between history, the advent of the holy, the event of the beginning as the inceptual greeting, the encounter of gods and humans, and the bridal festival, see Heidegger, *Hölderlin's Hymn "Remembrance,"* p. 62 (*Hölderlins Hymne "Andenken,"* pp. 69–70): "The festival is the event in which gods and humans come to encounter one another [*das Ereignis des Entgegenkommens der Götter und Menschen*]. What is festive in the festival is the ground of this event, which can be neither caused by gods nor made by humans. The festive is the inceptual event that sustains and pervasively attunes all coming to encounter one another in such encountering. The festive is that which inceptually attunes [*anfänglich Stimmende*]. That which attunes in this manner pervasively attunes and determines everything as a silent voice [*eine lautlose Stimme*]. . . . This inceptual greeting is the concealed essence of history. This inceptual greeting is *the* event [das *Ereignis*], *the* commencement [der *Anfang*]. We name this greeting inceptual in the sense of the coming of the holy, because it is first and only in this greeting that the encountering of humans and gods springs forth and has the ground of its source. The festival is the event of the inceptual greeting" (emphasis in original).

72. Lacoue-Labarthe, "Poetry's Courage," pp. 165 and 167. For an alternate translation, see Lacoue-Labarthe, *Heidegger and the Politics of Poetry*, pp. 63 and 66. See, however, p. 104, where the expression "theologico-poetic" is applied to Benjamin in contrast to the expression "theologico-political," which is applied to Heidegger.

73. Gosetti-Ferencei, *Heidegger, Hölderlin, and the Subject of Poetic Language*, p. 49. See also Simon, *Art and Responsibility*, pp. 225–56; Reid, *Being Here Is Glorious*, pp. 62–63, 71.

74. See the passage cited above at n. 37, and further evidence adduced in Wolfson, *Duplicity*, pp. xvi–xvii, 29–30, 33–34, 52, 183–84n42, 199n3.

75. Compare the assessment of Heidegger offered by Bourdieu, *Political Ontology*, p. 52: "Thus his idea of a godless theology informing an initiatory academy, is an attempt to reconcile the esoteric elitism of small circles like the *George-Kreis*, from which he borrows his models of intellectual achievement (such as Hölderlin, rediscovered by Norbert von Hellingrath, or Reinhardt's *Parmenides*), with the ecological mystique of the *Jugendbewegung* or of Steiner's anthroposophy, which preach a return to rural simplicity and sobriety, forest walks, natural food, and hand-woven garments."

76. As I noted in chapter 2, in the *Beiträge*, the category of "the ones to come" is one of six junctures

that Heidegger delineates as essential to the nature of inceptual thinking. See Heidegger, *Contributions*, §1, p. 7, §3, p. 10; *Beiträge*, pp. 6, 9. On the future ones, see also Heidegger, *Contributions*, §§248–52, pp. 313–18; *Beiträge*, pp. 395–401.

77. Heidegger, *Ponderings II–VI*, p. 325 (emphasis in original); *Überlegungen II–VI*, p. 448. Compare Heidegger, *Ponderings II–VI*, p. 222; *Überlegungen II–VI*, p. 304; Heidegger, *Contributions*, §251, p. 316; *Beiträge*, pp. 398–99.

78. Heidegger, *Ponderings II–VI*, p. 287; *Überlegungen II–VI*, p. 393.

79. Feldman, "Between *Geist* and *Zeitgeist*," p. 176.

80. Heidegger, *Pathmarks*, p. 257; *Wegmarken*, p. 338.

81. Löwith, *My Life in Germany*, pp. 34–44.

82. Ibid., p. 38.

83. Heidegger, *Ponderings II–VI*, p. 80; *Überlegungen II–VI*, p. 110. On the elitism implicit in Heidegger's conception of the culturally-historically specific German Dasein, compare *Ponderings II–VI*, p. 88 (*Überlegungen II–VI*, pp. 119–20): "If the dawning German Dasein is great, then it bears millennia before itself—we are constrained by that to think in advance correspondingly—i.e., to anticipate the arising of a completely other being and to prepare its *logic* for it. . . . We have to strive to grasp the whole only on the basis of the few and thereby consider that precisely the few—if indeed in them something great is at work—exist beyond themselves—and yet *are* quite differently from the way they act and speak" (emphasis in original). As we may discern from another entry in the notebooks (*Ponderings II–VI*, p. 81; *Überlegungen II–VI*, p. 110), Heidegger quickly realized that the decision to assume the rectorship—a decision for which he maintained that he was pressured—was acting against his "innermost voice," but one that he took on so that he might "possibly be able to *prevent* one thing or another" (emphasis in original). The task of "building up," however, was impeded by the fact that "the personnel are lacking." We see from this passage as well that, for Heidegger, the rejuvenation of the spirit of the German Dasein was limited to select individuals, who represented the totality in their exceptionality. I would be remiss if I did not note that in an entry that follows these reflections on the rectorship, Heidegger extols Hitler: "The great experience and fortune that the Führer has awakened a new actuality [*eine neue Wirklichkeit*], giving our thinking the correct course and impetus. Otherwise, despite all the thoroughness, it would have remained lost in itself and would only with difficulty have found its way to effectiveness. Literary existence is at an end" (*Ponderings II–VI*, p. 81; *Überlegungen II–VI*, p. 111). Nevertheless, it was the failure of National Socialism to deliver on the promise of a spiritual renewal and a new grounding of the German university that led Heidegger to believe accepting the rectorship was a personal blunder and a professional miscalculation. See Heidegger, *Ponderings II–VI*, p. 119 (*Überlegungen II–VI*, p. 162): "*The end of my rectorate.* April 28, 1934.—My resignation tendered, because a justification no longer possible. *Long live mediocrity and noise!* . . . My rectorate was based on a great mistake [*großen Irrtum*], namely, my wanting to bring *questions* into the temperament and regard of my 'colleagues,' questions from which they were at best *excluded*, to *their* advantage—and undoing" (emphasis in original). See also Heidegger, *Ponderings II–VI*, p. 102 (*Überlegungen II–VI*, p. 139): "*Motto for the rectorate*: you must not evade the constant disillusionments; they clarify the situation and strengthen the genuine volition" (emphasis in original). And compare the sober assessment in Heidegger, *Ponderings II–VI*, pp. 113–14 (*Überlegungen II–VI*, pp. 154–55): "*The essential experience of the rectoral year now coming to an end.* This is the irresistible *end* of the university in every respect, on account of the impotence for a genuine 'self-assertion.' The latter remains as the ultimate demand, growing fainter without any resonance. . . . The mere reacting with National Socialist means of power and with the affiliated functionaries can perhaps from the outside simulate the assertion of a strong position; what use is it, when the entire structure is intrinsically impotent and, moreover, is denied the influx of new and young powers or even only the retention of adaptive teachers? The point in time of my engagement was too early, or better: downright otiose; the opportune 'leadership' should aim not at inner change and self-education but rather at the most visible accumulation of new institutions or else at an emphatic alteration of what was hitherto. In doing so, however, the essential can remain entirely as of old" (emphasis in original). For other references where Heidegger acknowledged his mistake, see Wolfson, *Duplicity*, pp. 9 and 28. For criticism of the bureaucratic role of the rector, and relativizing the affiliation of one who occupies that position as a National Socialist, see Heidegger, *Ponderings II–VI*, p. 96; *Überlegungen II–VI*, p. 131.

84. Löwith, *Martin Heidegger and European Nihilism*, p. 220.

85. Vattimo, *Of Reality*, p. 200.

86. Adorno, *Notes to Literature*, vol. 1, p. 192. See Düttmann, "Without Soil: A Figure in Adorno's Thought."

87. Compare Heidegger's remark in a letter to Victor Schwoerer from October 2, 1929, translated in Heidegger, *Philosophical and Political Writings*,

p. 1: "I take great pleasure, every day, in seeing my work deeply rooted in our native soil." In the same letter, Heidegger infamously referred to the "growing Jewish contamination" of "our *German* spiritual life" (emphasis in original).

88. See Cassin, *Nostalgia*, pp. 41–63. Arendt's view of nostalgia is contrasted with that of Heidegger on pp. 49–52. Cassin accepts that Heidegger's conception of the homeland cannot be reduced to the nationalism of National Socialism (p. 50), but she insists nonetheless that his ontological notion of the homeland is still tied to the specificity of the German language (p. 51). This is correct insofar as, for Heidegger, homelessness is a function of the reduction of language to a means of communication and the consequent obscuring of its true essence as the opening in which beings come to presence through the self-concealing revealing of being. I would stipulate, however, that language, for Heidegger, is never divorced from the land of Germany, and in that sense, I do not agree with Cassin's conclusion that the ontological can be distinguished from the political. On homelessness, wordlessness, and alienation as conditions of the withdrawal of the political in modernity, see Villa, *Arendt and Heidegger*, pp. 10–11, 171–74, 188–201, 226–27.

89. The passage that influenced Agamben is Scholem, "Name of God," pp. 193–94, paraphrased in ch. 7 at n. 177. Part of the text is cited by Agamben, although without proper bibliographical information.

90. Agamben, *Fire and the Tale*, pp. 68–71.

91. Ibid., p. 70.

92. Villa, *Arendt and Heidegger*, p. 253. See as well Vandevelde, *Heidegger and the Romantics*, pp. 85–139, esp. 118–25.

93. See Fagenblat, "Of Dwelling Prophetically," pp. 252–58.

94. Wyschogrod, *Crossover Queries*, p. 291, and see also the comment of Levinas on p. 283, regarding Heidegger's attributing a "special wisdom to language." Compare Levinas, *Oeuvres 1*, p. 328: "Au *Liegen* heideggérien s'oppose la création: l'idée de fondement est inverse—le commencement qui n'est pas un fondement, mais une parole." See the extensive explanation on p. 496n52.

95. Heidegger, *Being and Time*, §44, p. 202; *Sein und Zeit*, p. 220.

96. *Zohar* 3:73a.

97. Regarding the views of Abraham Ibn Ezra and Judah Halevi, see reference cited below, n. 174.

98. For instance, see Wolfson, *Language*, pp. 197–212.

99. Eliashiv, *Leshem Shevo we-Aḥlamah: Sefer ha-De'ah*, pt. 1, p. 160.

100. For a detailed textual analysis of this dimension of the kabbalistic tradition, see Wolfson, *Venturing Beyond*, pp. 17–128. For a different approach, see Koch, *Human Self-Perfection*. I accept Koch's overall attempt to read the so-called *musar* literature as a mystical corpus of spiritual guidebooks, but I am not convinced he has justified the universalistic meaning of the term *human* as it appears in these sources. This humanistic reading is a gallant effort to retrieve the ethical import of this material; in my judgment, however, there is no philological or textual justification to speak of human self-perfection in kabbalistic sources without a caveat on the ethnocentric connotation of that term.

101. Eliashiv, *Leshem Shevo we-Aḥlamah: Sefer ha-De'ah*, pt. 2, p. 160.

102. Hegel, *Lectures on the Philosophy of Religion*, 2:683–86. See the extended note on Hegel's attitude to Judaism, pp. 443–44n551, and compare the monograph of Cohen, *Spectre juif de Hegel*. See, more recently, Bienenstock, "Hegel über das jüdische Volk."

103. Hegel, *Lectures on the Philosophy of Religion*, 2:741–42.

104. The distinction between the "particularist universalism" of German culture and the "universal particularism" of Judaism is made with reference to Hermann Cohen by Cohen, *Natural and Supernatural*, pp. 101–2. On the tension between the universal and the particular in Hermann Cohen, see the additional studies cited in Wolfson, *Giving*, p. 289n28.

105. Wolfson, *Giving*, p. 108, and references to primary and secondary sources on p. 370n142.

106. Wolfson, *Venturing Beyond*, pp. 129–85. Unfortunately, this dimension of my thinking on the problem of alterity and the relationship to the other was ignored by Koch, *Human Self-Perfection*, p. 23, who noted that Magid, "Ethics Disentangled," although "evidently inspired" by me, offered a different approach by arguing that divinity is found in the self and, by extension, in the other. Koch is correct that Magid's study bears the influence of my own work, but the distinction he draws between us is misleading. *Venturing Beyond*, which is my most elaborate statement on this topic, consists of four chapters: the first chapter is the critique of the ethnocentric setting of rigid boundaries based on identifying the human in the most ideal sense with the Jews; the second chapter deals with the crossing of these boundaries enacted through conversion, or what I call "othering the other," which is a prolepsis of the overcoming of distinctions in the messianic era; the third chapter establishes the axiology of the hypernomian, which is a manifestation or application of the crossing of boundaries; and the fourth chapter discusses humility and ascetic renunciation as the pietistic gestures that

quintessentially embody the hypernomian principle. Moreover, the idea that Koch flags as Magid's innovation is precisely the hermeneutical principle that instigated my own analysis of the trope of incarnation in medieval kabbalistic sources, *the setting of boundary and the proximity of the other.* This idea can be found in many of my writings, but it is stated most explicitly in Wolfson, "Textual Flesh," pp. 190–91: "I am well aware that the incarnational tropes to be extracted from Jewish texts are distinct from and in opposition to the Christian formulations; indeed, in my estimation, it is the disparity that justifies the use of the same nomenclature. This is not to deny the adverse portrayal of Christians by Jews and Jews by Christians. The rejection of the 'other' does not, however, mean the other has no impact on the formation of one's own sense of self; on the contrary, condemnation of the other bespeaks contiguity with the other, and this is so even when the other has preached intolerance or perpetrated violence in the sociopolitical arena. By utilizing the term 'incarnation' in explicating kabbalistic texts I do not mean to paint a monolithic picture. Precisely by deploying one term to ponder disparate phenomena I call attention to the rift that both unifies and splits the two. In the long and variegated history of Jews and Christians, framed typologically as the struggle between Jacob and Esau, self-definition and definition of the other are inextricably interwoven."

107. See Wolfson, *Giving*, p. 40.

108. Heidegger, *Elucidations*, pp. 42–43; *Erläuterungen*, pp. 23–24. On homecoming as the recovery of place, see Malpas, *Heidegger's Topology*, pp. 305–11.

109. Heidegger, *Elucidations*, p. 43 (emphasis in original); *Erläuterungen*, p. 24.

110. Altmann, *Meaning of Jewish Existence*, p. 52.

111. Ibid.

112. Ibid.

113. Ibid., p. 71.

114. Ibid., pp. 71–72.

115. Ibid., p. 72.

116. Compare the formulation in Altmann's 1934 essay "The Religious World of the Middle Ages," in *Meaning of Jewish Existence*, pp. 58–59: "For the mystic, the submersion practiced in the act of prayer stands in principle above 'learning' and philosophizing. . . . From its inception Jewish mysticism has not been directed toward philosophical speculation but was determined by religious motives. In this it does not deny its closeness to Gnosticism, which also, according to its goal, is concerned with practical-religious matters and not scientific-theoretical ones."

117. See ch. 1 at n. 140.

118. Altmann, *Meaning of Jewish Existence*, p. 76 (emphasis in original).

119. Wolfson, *Open Secret*, p. 237.

120. Heidegger, *Discourse on Thinking*, p. 47; *Gelassenheit*, p. 14.

121. Heidegger, *Discourse on Thinking*, pp. 47–48; *Gelassenheit*, pp. 14–15.

122. Heidegger, *Discourse on Thinking*, p. 48; *Gelassenheit*, p. 15.

123. Heidegger, *Discourse on Thinking*, p. 49; *Gelassenheit*, p. 16.

124. The lecture is included in Heidegger, *Reden und Andere Zeugnisse*, pp. 574–82, but I will cite the German text provided by Sheehan together with his translation (see the following note). For an earlier rendering of this text, see Heidegger, "Homeland." The lecture is discussed in detail by Mugerauer, *Heidegger and Homecoming*, pp. 479–87.

125. Heidegger, "Messkirch's Seventh Centennial," pp. 48–51.

126. Heidegger, *Discourse on Thinking*, p. 51; *Gelassenheit*, p. 19.

127. Heidegger, *Discourse on Thinking*, p. 53; *Gelassenheit*, p. 21.

128. Heidegger, *Discourse on Thinking*, p. 54; *Gelassenheit*, p. 23.

129. Heidegger, *Discourse on Thinking*, p. 55; *Gelassenheit*, p. 24. On Heidegger's account of *Gelassenheit* as openness to the mystery, see Schürmann, *Meister Eckhart*, pp. 192–210.

130. Heidegger, *Discourse on Thinking*, p. 56; *Gelassenheit*, p. 25.

131. Heidegger, *Hölderlin's Hymns "Germania" and "The Rhine,"* pp. 21–22; *Hölderlins Hymnen "Germanien" und "Der Rhein,"* p. 20.

132. Heidegger, *Hölderlin's Hymn "The Ister,"* p. 49 (emphasis in original); *Hölderlins Hymne "Der Ister,"* pp. 60–61. See the discussion of the theme of homecoming through otherness in Dallmayr, *The Other Heidegger*, pp. 149–80. See also Vallega, *Heidegger and the Issue of Space*; Capobianco, *Engaging Heidegger*, pp. 52–69; O'Donoghue, *Poetics of Homecoming*, pp. 105–65; Gosetti-Ferencei, *Heidegger, Hölderlin, and the Subject of Poetic Language*, pp. 125–28; Claxton, *Heidegger's Gods*, pp. 43–79; Winkler, "Dwelling," pp. 378–80.

133. Heidegger, *Nature, History, State*, p. 55.

134. Ibid., p. 56. See Wolfson, *Duplicity*, pp. 42–43.

135. Heidegger, *Hölderlin's Hymn "The Ister,"* p. 74; *Hölderlins Hymne "Der Ister,"* p. 91. See Warnek, "Translating *Innigkeit*," p. 63. On the description of wonder as the phenomenon wherein the most usual becomes the most unusual, see Heidegger, *Basic Questions*, pp. 144–45; *Grundfragen*, pp. 166–67.

136. Heidegger, *Contributions*, §278, p. 399; *Beiträge*, p. 507.

137. Heidegger, *Contributions*, §144, p. 208; *Beiträge*, p. 264.

138. Heidegger, *Elucidations*, p. 171; *Erläuterungen*, p. 150.

139. Heidegger, *Elucidations*, p. 160; *Erläuterungen*, p. 138. For a more critical assessment of Heidegger's reading of Hölderlin on this point, see Adorno, *Notes to Literature*, vol. 2, p. 117 (*Noten zu Literatur*, p. 456): "Hardly anywhere did Hölderlin prove his posthumous champion more wrong than in his relationship to what is foreign. Hölderlin's relationship to it is a constant irritant for Heidegger. . . . Heidegger's endogamous ideal outweighs even his need for a genealogy of the doctrine of Being. Hölderlin is driven up hill and down dale in the service of a conception of love that circles around inside what one is anyway, fixated narcissistically on one's own people; Heidegger betrays utopia to imprisonment in selfhood." On Adorno's objection to Heidegger's reading of Hölderlin, see Robinson, *Adorno's Poetics of Form*, pp. 28–33.

140. Heidegger, *Hölderlin's Hymn "The Ister,"* p. 54; *Hölderlins Hymne "Der Ister,"* p. 67. The point is repeated in Heidegger, *Hölderlin's Hymn "The Ister,"* p. 124; *Hölderlins Hymne "Der Ister,"* p. 154. See Ward, *Heidegger's Political Thinking*, pp. 221–22.

141. Heidegger, *Hölderlin's Hymn "The Ister,"* p. 54; *Hölderlins Hymne "Der Ister,"* pp. 67–68. See the detailed analysis of the themes of *Heimat*, *Heimkunft*, the holy, and poetic language in Grugan, "Thought and Poetry," pp. 100–56.

142. Heidegger, *Hölderlin's Hymn "The Ister,"* p. 55; *Hölderlins Hymne "Der Ister,"* p. 69.

143. Heidegger, *Hölderlin's Hymn "The Ister,"* p. 62; *Hölderlins Hymne "Der Ister,"* p. 75. For discussion of Heidegger's view of translation, see Groth, *Translating Heidegger*, pp. 115–63. See also the exchange in Schalow, "Conversation with Parvis Emad," pp. 186–87; Ireland, "Heidegger, Hölderlin, and Eccentric Translation"; and Schalow, "Attunement and Translation."

144. Heidegger, *Hölderlin's Hymn "The Ister,"* pp. 65–66 (emphasis in original); *Hölderlins Hymne "Der Ister,"* pp. 79–80. By contrast, see Heidegger, *Ponderings XII–XV*, pp. 188–89 (*Überlegungen XII–XV*, p. 239), where he expresses his disapproval of the "reorganization" and the "prostitution" of the German language and a new colloquial speech related to so-called "German science" (*deutschen Wissenschaft*). Heidegger complains that since the configuration (*Bildung*) of this "new colloquialism" (*Umgangssprache*) involves the participation of non-Germanic peoples (*außerdeutsche Völker*), it can no longer be considered a *German* language (*keine* deutsche *Sprache mehr*) but is rather a vernacular form of an international slang (*internationalen Gaunersprache*).

145. Heidegger, *Heraclitus*, pp. 49–50 (emphasis in original); *Heraklit*, p. 63.

146. Warnek, "Translating *Innigkeit*," pp. 62–63. It strikes me that Heidegger's perspective is discernible in the poignant and brutally honest words about the creative effort to inscribe the unutterable offered by Lacoue-Labarthe, *Phrase*, pp. 89–90: "Whenever I set about writing, writing something like this, whenever I can no longer speak and, whatever the noises outside, leave to the dread of silence the tribute it tirelessly demands as though it were some inalienable right, whenever I remain silent, without for all that wanting to say anything, then, I listen and can hear it, barely audible, not knowing where it comes from, from no voice distinctly articulated, this unknown tongue, no word of which, nor any structure, nor any sound, is identifiable as such, but which has all the appearance of a possible language. . . . The difficult thing, once it's not so much grasped as sensed, on this shifting shoreline at low tide, neither water nor sand, in this faint, imperceptible backwash, is that there is an imperious need to translate it. But everything is missing: words, grammar, agreements, anything that might be transposed. It is well known that a phrase ought to well up. It is almost there, imminent, and all that seems necessary is the patience needed for it to spurt forth and impose itself. But in what language one might call one's own, if the other, the one that came before, absolutely, in which nothing was said, makes each of them, even the solitary tongue from which each of us comes, almost definitively foreign? It is an illusion to place one's trust in one's own voice, which is no more our own than our way of moving or looking."

147. Heidegger, *Hölderlin's Hymn "The Ister,"* p. 66; *Hölderlins Hymne "Der Ister,"* p. 81. With respect to this issue, Heidegger is heir to the romantic notion that the German people are the bearers of European culture through translation. See Vandevelde, "Translation"; Vandevelde, *Heidegger and the Romantics*, pp. 42–43.

148. Heidegger, *Hölderlin's Hymn "The Ister,"* p. 66; *Hölderlins Hymne "Der Ister,"* p. 81.

149. Warnek, "Translating *Innigkeit*," p. 59; Davis, "Heidegger on the Way."

150. Heidegger, *Parmenides*, p. 12; *Parmenides* [GA 54], p. 17. It is worth recalling the fictional exchange in Heidegger, *On the Way to Language*, p. 24 (*Unterwegs zur Sprache*, p. 109), between the Japanese scholar and the inquirer on the experience of translating German texts (including some of

Heidegger's essays) into Japanese: "And while I was translating, I often felt as though I were wandering back and forth between two different language realities, such that at moments a radiance shone on me which let me sense that the wellspring of reality [*Wesensquell*] from which those two fundamentally different languages arise was the same." The response of Heidegger through the voice of the inquirer is telling: "You did not, then, seek for a general concept under which both the Europeans and the Eastasian languages could be subsumed." The Japanese scholar concurs, "Absolutely not." The exchange is significant because it affirms that there may be a common source that sustains the meaningfulness of both languages, a common source whose radiance is accessible through the act of translation, but this does not imply that there is a general concept under which the two disparate languages can be subsumed. This is another example of Heidegger's idea of the juxtaposition or belonging together of the same that remains different.

151. Heidegger, *Parmenides*, p. 12; *Parmenides* [GA 54], p. 18.

152. Rosenzweig, "Scripture and Luther," p. 56. See Batnitzky, "Translation as Transcendence," pp. 92 and 116; Reichert, "It Is Time," pp. 174–76; and the nuanced discussion of the aesthetic of translation, with particular emphasis on the spatial or architectural dimension and the negotiation of the inside-outside dichotomy, in Braiterman, *Shape of Revelation*, pp. 54–59, 105–10, 187–90. Also of note is the detailed comparison of Rosenzweig's view on translation with that of Benjamin in Galli, "Introduction: Translating Is a Mode of Holiness." See also the chapter on "Rosenzweig's Philosophy of Translation," in Galli, *Franz Rosenzweig and Jehuda Halevi*, pp. 322–59. There is clearly a structural similarity between Rosenzweig's approach to translation of the voice of the Hebrew Bible as that which cannot be restricted to any place and his rejection of Zionism. See Batnitzky, *Idolatry and Representation*, p. 141: "Rosenzweig's theory of translation is consonant with his argument that Jews themselves must return to their strange, foreign pathos, both for their own sake and for the sake of the redemption of the world. For Rosenzweig, this meant an embrace of a decidedly diaspora Judaism." A similar point is made concerning Rosenzweig's theo-philological view of Hebrew and his anxieties about Zionism as a mimicry of German nationalism by Shahar, "Sacred and the Unfamiliar," p. 306: "Rosenzweig's argument on the *Unheimlichkeit* of Hebrew, its 'homelessness,' its 'uncanniness,' is bound up with the view that its theological depth and its fullness cannot be reduced to a particular historical or territorial experience, but rather should be attributed to its transcendence, its foreignness, its being like a 'guest.' Hebrew is like an eternal wanderer who lives *un-heimlich* in the world. This is how Hebrew reveals itself as an abyss—the gap, the absence, the wound of *Heimat*." See also Mendes-Flohr, "Hebrew as a Holy Tongue." Compare the contrast of Buber and Rosenzweig in Braiterman, *Shape of Revelation*, p. 154: "The difference between the two was Zionism. Buber sought to set the people in the space of its land, whereas Rosenzweig sought to plant that blood in the temporal rhythm of a ritual calendar." On the messianic import of the act of translation according to Rosenzweig, see the comment cited by Steiner, *After Babel*, p. 257.

153. Warnek, "Translating *Innigkeit*," pp. 61–62 (emphasis in original). It is worthwhile to recall the comments of Schürmann, *Meister Eckhart*, p. 205, on the secular meaning of Heidegger's use of *Gelassenheit* and especially as it relates to the issue of translation: "When Eckhart says *übersetzen*, he has in mind a very precise trajectory, the mind's transition into God. Heidegger, too, speaks of *übersetzen*, but here the passage simply leads thinking to its 'food,' which is the manifestation of being in time—or (later in his career) the manifestation of language in historic utterances. In Eckhart, translation leads the ground of the mind back into the ground of God; in Heidegger, it simply reunites man to being (or to language) as to his 'homeland,' in which forms of life, ever renewed, are possible."

154. Benjamin, *Selected Writings*, 1:255; *Gesammelte Schriften*, 4.1, p. 12.

155. Benjamin, *Selected Writings*, 1:257; *Gesammelte Schriften*, 4.1, p. 14.

156. Benjamin, *Selected Writings*, 1:258; *Gesammelte Schriften*, 4.1, p. 15. Many have opined on Benjamin's theory of translation. See, for example, Barnstone, *Poetics of Translation*, pp. 240–59; Weigel, *Body- and Image-Space*, pp. 128–45; Weigel, "Lost in Translation"; Jacobs, *In the Language*, pp. 75–90.

157. Benjamin, *Selected Writings*, 1:254; *Gesammelte Schriften*, 4.1, p. 10.

158. Benjamin, *Selected Writings*, 1:254–55; *Gesammelte Schriften*, 4.1, p. 11.

159. Benjamin, *Selected Writings*, 1:256; *Gesammelte Schriften*, 4.1, pp. 12–13.

160. Benjamin, *Arcades Project*, p. 838; *Gesammelte Schriften*, 5.2, p. 1006.

161. Benjamin, *Arcades Project*, p. 390; *Gesammelte Schriften*, 5.1, p. 492. On the dream in Benjamin's thought, see Wolfson, *Dream*, pp. 326–27n99, and reference to other scholarly analyses mentioned

there. For other sources, see Wolfson, "Not Yet Now," p. 164n139.

162. Benjamin, *Arcades Project*, pp. 388–89 (emphasis in original); *Gesammelte Schriften*, 5.1, pp. 490–91.

163. Benjamin, *Arcades Project*, p. 464; *Gesammelte Schriften*, 5.1, p. 580.

164. Benjamin, *Selected Writings*, 2:722; *Gesammelte Schriften*, 2.1, p. 213. The passage of Hofmannsthal appears two other times in Benjamin's œuvre. See the epigrams to "Der Flaneur" in Benjamin, *Gesammelte Schriften*, 5.1, p. 524, and the reference cited in the following note.

165. Benjamin, *Gesammelte Schriften*, 1.3, p. 1238: "Die historische Methode ist eine philologische, der das Buch des Lebens zugrunde liegt. 'Was nie geschriebene wurde, lesen' heißt es bei Hofmannsthal. Der Leser, an den hier zu denken ist, ist der wahre Historiker." See Spiegel, "The Task of the Historian," p. 4; Kleinberg, *Haunting History*, p. 51; Wolfson, "Not Yet Now," p. 162. In that context, I cited Hofmannsthal's comment from Richter, *Thought-Images*, p. 50, and not directly from Benjamin.

166. With regard to this temporal reversal, Benjamin's thinking can be compared profitably with the analysis of Bloch's reflections on memory and utopia examined in Geoghegan, "Remembering the Future," and Kaufmann, "Thanks for the Memory." On Benjamin's concept of memory, see also Weigel, *Body- and Image-Space*, pp. 109–27.

167. Benjamin, *Selected Writings*, 4:390; *Gesammelte Schriften*, 1.2, pp. 693–94.

168. On the kabbalistic tenor of Benjamin's approach to translatability and the idea of the pure language, see Steiner, *After Babel*, pp. 66–67. As Steiner insightfully noted, "in terms obviously derived from the Kabbalistic and gnostic tradition, Benjamin founds his metaphysic of translation on the concept of 'universal language.' Translation is both possible and impossible—a dialectical antinomy characteristic of esoteric argument. This antinomy arises from the fact that all known tongues are fragments, whose roots, in a sense which is both algebraic and etymological, can only be found in and validated by 'die reine Sprache.' This 'pure language' . . . is like a hidden spring seeking to force its way through the silted channels of our differing tongues. At the 'messianic end of their history' (again a Kabbalistic or Hasidic formulation), all separate languages will return to their source of common life. In the interim, translation has a task of profound philosophic, ethical, and magical import." On the mystical nature of Benjamin's understanding of the translatability of language, see Steiner, *After Babel*, pp. 262–63. Steiner ends the book, p. 498, by referring to a kabbalistic tradition according to which translation will not only be unnecessary but inconceivable in the future, since words will shake off the servitude of meaning.

169. Babylonian Talmud, Qiddushin 49a.

170. On the historical background and subsequent impact of Jerome's dictum, see Brock, "Aspects of Translation Technique."

171. Benjamin, *Selected Writings*, 1:262–63; *Gesammelte Schriften*, 4.1, p. 21.

172. Benjamin, *Selected Writings*, 1:257; *Gesammelte Schriften*, 4.1, p. 13. See also Steiner, *After Babel*, p. 324.

173. My discussion is based on the more detailed analysis in Wolfson, *Language*, pp. 203 and 517n87. For additional technical studies on the language of the zoharic anthology, see Rapoport-Albert and Kwasman, "Late Aramaic"; Mopsik, "Late Judeo-Aramaic"; Liebes, "Hebrew and Aramaic"; Damsma, "Aramaic of the Zohar."

174. See Wolfson, *Language*, p. 203, and reference to other scholars cited on p. 517n87.

175. Heidegger, *Elucidations*, p. 216; *Erläuterungen*, p. 189.

176. Benjamin, *Selected Writings*, 1:63–64 (emphasis in original); *Gesammelte Schriften*, 2.1, p. 142. On the correspondence between Heidegger and Benjamin on this matter, see Ruin, "Origin in Exile," pp. 151–54. It is of interest to note as well the letter of Adorno to Scholem, dated April 17, 1963, where he asserts that "there are certain astounding, mostly linguistic, similarities between Benjamin and Heidegger" with respect to their interpretations of Hölderlin, and Heidegger's notion of "the poetized" (*das Gedichtete*). See Scholem, *Life in Letters*, p. 392; the original German in Scholem, *Briefe II*, p. 269, # 62, n. 3. Adorno informed Scholem that in a lecture on Hölderlin, which he was preparing to deliver at the annual conference of the Hölderlin-Gesellschaft in Berlin on June 7, 1963, he planned to develop his critique of Heidegger "precisely out of the differences pertaining to things so similar. As will be immediately evident to you, this involves the concept of the mythical. Heidegger holds that the mythical has the last word with Hölderlin; Benjamin shows that for Hölderlin it's the dialectical that counts. Not incidentally, I present certain of Benjamin's categories as having indisputable priority, though I'd like to leave the question open whether Heidegger knew Benjamin's work (which seems unlikely to me). I would be grateful if you could send me a quick comment." The revised version of Adorno's lecture, "Parataxis: Zur späten Lyrik Hölderlins," was first published in *Die*

Neue Rundschau 75 (1964), and reprinted in Adorno, *Noten zu Literatur*, pp. 447–91; English translation in Adorno, *Notes to Literature*, vol. 2, pp. 109–49. In his response (dated April 22, 1963), Scholem clarifies that the date of composition of Benjamin's essay on Hölderlin was either 1914 or 1915, and concludes that he has no reason to assume that Heidegger either received a copy of that essay or even knew of it secondhand. He acknowledges, however, that the similarity of Heidegger's concept of "the poeticized" to Benjamin's analysis did occur to him as well (Scholem, *Life in Letters*, pp. 392–93; Scholem, *Briefe II*, p. 93). I note, parenthetically, that this admission attests that Scholem read, or at the very least was familiar with, some of Heidegger's later work wherein the poetic became the central motif. See introduction n. 37. On Benjamin and Heidegger, compare the discussion and citation of sources in Wolfson, "Not Yet Now," pp. 159–60n122, and the collection of essays in Benjamin and Vardoulakis, eds., *Sparks Will Fly*.

177. Benjamin, *Selected Writings*, 1:63–64 (emphasis in original); *Gesammelte Schriften*, 2.1, pp. 142–43.

178. Benjamin, *Selected Writings*, 1:65–66 (emphasis in original); *Gesammelte Schriften*, 2.1, pp. 145–46.

179. Benjamin, *Selected Writings*, 1:66; *Gesammelte Schriften*, 2.1, p. 146.

180. Benjamin, *Selected Writings*, 1:68; *Gesammelte Schriften*, 2.1, p. 149.

181. Benjamin, *Selected Writings*, 1:69–70; *Gesammelte Schriften*, 2.1, pp. 150–51. See Fenves, "Genesis of Judgment," pp. 88–90.

182. Benjamin, *Selected Writings*, 1:69; *Gesammelte Schriften*, 2.1, p. 150.

183. *Zohar* 2:230b.

184. *Zohar* 2:98b. See analysis in Wolfson, *Luminal Darkness*, pp. 73–74, 264–71.

185. Levinas, *Difficult Freedom*, p. 233. See, however, Wolfson, *Giving*, p. 153, and the passage of Levinas and the interpretation of Wyschogrod cited on p. 402n520, according to which the face must remain a mask.

186. I am here repeating the discussion in Wolfson, *Giving*, p. 185.

187. Derrida, "Des Tours de Babel," p. 170.

188. Ibid., p. 174.

189. On the "double bind" that the name *YHWH* imposes on the recipient as something that necessarily must be translated but which it is impossible to translate, see Derrida, *Ear of the Other*, pp. 102–3; Derrida, "On a Newly Arisen Apocalyptic Tone," p. 117.

190. This formulation is used by Derrida in his response to Marion, "In the Name," p. 45.

191. On the depiction of deconstruction in terms of the conditions of the translatability and untranslatability of language, see Caputo, *Prayers and Tears*, p. 53.

192. Derrida's language in Marion, "In the Name," p. 44.

193. Derrida, *Psyche*, p. 146.

194. *Zohar* 2:129b.

195. Babylonian Talmud, Shabbat 12b. Whatever the original intention of the maxim attributed to R. Yoḥanan, it had important repercussions in the Jewish religious imagination, and this is especially true within the zoharic compilation, wherein Hebrew is privileged, even though much of the text was composed in Aramaic.

196. *Zohar* 2:129b. Compare *Zohar* 1:8b, 74b (*Sitrei Torah*).

197. Babylonian Talmud, Berakhot 8a–b.

198. This maxim appears frequently in rabbinic literature. For example, see Babylonian Talmud, Yoma 12b, Megillah 9b, Menaḥot 39a, Zevaḥim 18a.

199. *Zohar* 2:132b–133a.

200. See references cited in Lohmar, "Husserl's Type," p. 121n43.

201. Derrida, *Speech and Phenomena*, p. 85. On auto-affection, see Zahavi, *Self-Awareness and Alterity*, pp. 110–37; Lawlor, *Derrida and Husserl*, pp. 4, 188–96, 231–32.

202. I have here followed the reading preserved in the Cremona edition of the *Zohar*, Bere'shit, p. 243, *begin de-avraham lo hawah mahul wa-hawah arel we-satim be-visreih*, rather than the version in the Mantua edition, *begin de-avraham lo hawah mahul wa-hawah arel satim bisra*. For another interesting variant, see the Aramaic text prepared for the eleventh volume of the *Pritzker Zohar*, p. 253 (ad *Zohar* 1:88b), http://www.sup.org/ zohar/ ?d= Aramaic% 20Texts&f =index: *begin de-avraham lo hawah gazir wi-qeyyama qaddisha lo ḥatim be-visreih*. And the English rendering in *The Zohar: Pritzker Edition*, vol. 11, p. 655: "It was because Abraham was uncircumcised, and the holy covenant was not sealed in his flesh."

203. On the related expression *lishan aḥara*, see *Zohar* 1:74b (*Sitrei Torah*).

204. *Zohar* 1:88b-89a (*Sitrei Torah*). For discussion of this passage, see Matt, "'New-Ancient Words,'" pp. 188–89.

205. Regarding this symbolism, see Wolfson, *Dream*, pp. 163–64, 166–67, 395–96n96.

206. *Zohar* 1:88b–89a.

207. On the status of Balaam and Moses in the rabbinic, zoharic, and Lurianic corpora, see the extensive analysis in Magid, *From Metaphysics to Midrash*, pp. 143–95. For a more detailed discussion of the use of the figure of Balaam, the archnemesis of Israel, to depict Heidegger's acrimony toward

Judaism, see Wolfson, *Duplicity*, pp. 154–68. Based especially on the parity of the demonic Balaam and the divine Moses that emerges from the kabbalistic material, elaborating on the older rabbinic precedent, I attempted to narrow the gap between the internal and the external by suggesting that the external gives shape to the internal as much as the internal gives shape to the external, that the alienation of the other is part and parcel of the identification of self, not as the dialectical identity of the nonidentity of opposites but rather as the simultaneous nonidentity of opposites juxtaposed in the sameness of their difference, the same difference that is differently the same. To demonize the other as absolutely exterior preserves the false dichotomy of self and other and thereby obstructs one from being able to discern that darkness is an aspect of light and light an aspect of darkness, that the foreign is an inherent part of the familiar, that indecision belongs to the realm of decision. One is here reminded of the incisive words in "John Brown" by Bob Dylan, *The Lyrics*, p. 34: "But the thing that scared me most / Was when my enemy came close / And I saw that his face looked just like mine." These words served as the basis for the essay by Fagenblat, "The Thing," but as the author remarks (p. 8n1), he was indebted to my previous use of Dylan's song in an interview I did with Aubrey Glazer, http://religiondispatches.org/what-does-heideggers-anti-semitism-mean-for-jewish-philosophy/.

208. *Zohar* 2:21b–22a. For a list of other sources, see Wolfson, *Luminal Darkness*, pp. 19–20n18, 215n36; Wolfson, *Venturing Beyond*, pp. 43–44n112, 140–41n46. Compare the text of Gikatilla cited in Wolfson, *Venturing Beyond*, p. 100. I respectfully disagree with Magid's conclusion, *From Metaphysics to Midrash*, p. 160, that the zoharic authors do not primarily view the midrashic equation of Moses and Balaam "in terms of prophecy but rather in terms of leadership (Moses—Israel, Balaam—gentiles)." The point accentuated in various zoharic homilies is the analogy between the theurgy of Moses and the magic of Balaam. The key difference is that Moses, as do other faithful prophets, beholds the divine glory, whereas Balaam gazes through his witchcraft only at the lower crowns. See *Zohar* 3:207b.

209. Urbach, *World of the Sages*, pp. 537–55, and see discussion of Urbach's argument in Magid, *From Metaphysics to Midrash*, pp. 151–53. See also Baskin, *Pharaoh's Counselors*, pp. 91–93; Wolfson, *Venturing Beyond*, pp. 44n112, 56n167, 140n44. On the image of Balaam as Christ in zoharic literature, see now Haskell, *Mystical Resistance*, pp. 66–106.

210. Wolfson, "Circumcision, Vision, and Textual Interpretation."

211. Graf, *Wayaqhel Moshe*, p. 52.

212. Eliashiv, *Leshem Shevo we-Aḥlamah: Haqdamot*, p. 166.

213. Compare the account of Fichte's idea of infinity in Hegel, *Faith and Knowledge*, pp. 112–13: "This yields the true character of thought which is infinity. For the absolute concept is infinity, is in itself the absolute affirmation, but since the concept is turned against the opposite and finite as their identity, thought is absolute negation; and this negation, posited as existent, as real, is the positing of opposites: $+ A - A = 0$. The nothing exists as $+ A - A$, and is in its essence infinity, thought, absolute concept, absolute pure affirmation. . . .
The true infinite is the absolute Idea, identity of the universal and particular, or identity of the infinite and finite themselves (i.e., of the infinite as opposed to a finite). This [opposed] infinite is pure thinking. Posited as this abstraction, it is pure, absolutely formal identity, pure concept, Kant's reason, Fichte's Ego. But when it is set against the finite, it is for this very reason, the absolute nothing of the finite: $+ A - A = 0$. It is the negative side of the absolute Idea."

214. For discussion of these analytic categories, see Ruthrof, *Language and Imaginability*, p. 94.

215. Bachrach, *Emeq ha-Melekh*, p. 1098. The passage is from the *Tiqqunei Shabbat* attributed to Bachrach and appended to this edition of *Emeq ha-Melekh*.

216. For references, see Wolfson, *Venturing Beyond*, pp. 99n331 and 104n359.

217. Compare *Ḥemdat ha-Yamim al Shabbat Qodesh*, p. 83. The anonymous author of this text, which is considered to be of Sabbatian provenance, explains Luria's custom of reading scripture twice and the Aramaic translation once every Friday in light of this symbolism: "There are three shells surrounding the holiness, and the fourth is radiance [*nogah*], sometimes it is in holiness and sometimes it returns to the shell . . . and it is written 'surrounded by radiance' (Ezekiel 1:4), for it surrounds the holiness. Converts receive from this shell that sometimes turns toward holiness and sometimes toward impurity. Onkelos the convert, who was from the aspect of the radiance, wanted to rectify it and produced the translation, for it is of his quality to incorporate it within holiness." The kabbalistic symbolism is the basis for the exposition in Naḥman of Bratslav, *Liqquṭei MoHaRaN*, 19:4, 26a–b. The Aramaic targum is identified as the Tree of Knowledge of Good and Evil because it is the intermediary between the holiness of the Hebrew language and the unholiness of the languages of the seventy nations. Aramaic can be both good and evil—it comprises the aspect of one who enlightens (*maskil*) and the aspect of one who destroys (*meshakkel*)—and thus it has the power to break the shell of impurity.

Not only are the other nations sustained by the holy language through the mechanism of translation, which corresponds to the aspect of *nogah* (19:5, 26c), but the translation elevates the good within the demonic and thereby perfects the holiness of Hebrew (19:6, 26c).

218. Derrida, "Testimony Given," p. 41; "Un témoignage donné," p. 76. Compare Derrida, "Abraham, the Other," p. 16: "I still feel, *at once, at the same time,* as less jewish *and* more jewish than the Jew [*comme moins juif* et *plus juif que le Juif*], as scarcely Jewish and as superlatively Jewish as possible, more than Jew [*plus que Juif*], exemplarily Jew, but also hyperbolically Jew" (emphasis in original). I have restored the French based on the original in Cohen and Zagury-Orly, eds., *Judéités*, p. 24. Compare Derrida, "Avowing—The Impossible," pp. 21–22 (Derrida, *Le dernier des Juifs*, pp. 22–23): "And how does a Jew of whom I know only too well, and from so close, that he will never have been sure of being together with himself in general, a Jew who dares not stop at the hypothesis that this dissociation from self renders him *at once* as less Jewish and as most Jewish [*d'autant moins juif et d'autant mieux juif*]—how could such a split or divided Jew have received this remark?" (emphasis in original).

219. Derrida, "Abraham, the Other," p. 12. The affinity between exemplarity and the Levinasian ethics as first philosophy is noted by Derrida on p. 23. Concerning this theme, see Wolfson, *Giving*, pp. 163–64, and reference to other scholars cited therein on p. 410n63.

220. Derrida, *Monolingualism*, p. 10 (emphasis in original); *Le monolinguisme*, p. 25.

221. Derrida, *Monolingualism*, p. 2 (emphasis in original); *Le monolinguisme*, p. 15.

222. Derrida, *Margins of Philosophy*, p. 65; *Marges de la philosophie*, p. 75.

223. See ch. 7 nn. 175 and 177.

224. Agamben, *Fire and the Tale*, p. 68.

225. Ibid., p. 69.

226. Heidegger, "Only a God Can Save Us." See especially Heidegger's comments on pp. 61–62: "I consider Hölderlin not [just] one poet among others whose work the historians of literature may take as a theme [for study]. For me, Hölderlin is the poet who points into the future, who waits for a god, and who, consequently, should not remain merely an object of research according to the canons of literary history."

227. Agamben, *Fire and the Tale*, p. 70.

228. Ibid., p. 71.

229. See above at n. 86.

230. See Fagenblatt, "The Thing," pp. 20–24. The affinity between Gush Emunim theology and Heidegger's ontology of place is drawn explicitly on pp. 22–23. I note as well the pertinent comment of Žižek, *Courage of Hopelessness*, p. 123. After briefly presenting the scriptural justification for the Jewish claim to the historical right to the land of Israel, an account that is predicated on the destruction of the Canaanites, the previous occupants of that geographical space, Žižek draws the following conclusion about the relevance of tradition to contemporary politics: "The lesson is simply that every legitimization of a claim to land by reference to some mythic past should be rejected. In order to resolve (or contain, at least) the Israeli-Palestinian conflict, we should not dwell in the ancient past—we should, on the contrary, forget the past (which is in any case constantly reinvented to justify present actions). Another, even more crucial, lesson is that the Jewish people themselves will ultimately pay the price for the politics of ethnic fundamentalism that brings them uncannily close to anti-Semitic conservatism. It will push Jews towards becoming just another ethnic group craving for their particular *Blut und Boden*."

231. Steiner, "Our Homeland," p. 24; and the rejoinder of Ezrahi, "Our Homeland"; Ezrahi, *Booking Passage*.

232. For a succinct articulation of the geo-theological position that the land of Israel occupies in the Jewish tradition, see Neher, "Jewish Dimension of Space." On the geo-theology of Judaism, see also Neher, *Jérusalem*, pp. 37–40. Taubes, *Occidental Eschatology*, pp. 24–25, argues that the exilic state of the Jews, their lack of being rooted in the land, or adhering to a state, are not exceptional but rather are part of a larger spiritual heritage of the so-called Aramaic Orient. A similar portrayal of the Jews is offered by other thinkers, on occasion with a decidedly anti-Zionist or post-Zionist slant. For two methodologically distinct attempts to celebrate the diasporic nature of Jewish existence, see Butler, *Parting Ways*, and Boyarin, *Traveling Homeland*. Of relevance as well is the analysis of postcolonialism and the geopolitics of post-Holocaust Jewish thought in Slabodsky, *Decolonial Judaism*. The author's thesis is summarized on p. 27: "Writing after the Holocaust it would hardly be a surprise to contend that Jews fulfilled a barbaric role in the Western imaginary. By exploring this reading I neither imply that the history of Jewish victimhood is the only possible account of Jewish lives nor that all possible Jewish histories culminate in a largely (though not uniquely) European event. I rather suggest that given the

geo-political conditions created by imperial expansion, the Western narrative created networks of barbaric portrayals that included Jews from the fifteenth to the twentieth centuries. This history, which symbolically spans the Jewish expulsion from Spain and the Final Solution during the Holocaust (1492–1942), may not account for the totality of Jewish experiences. . . . But it does describe the relational experiences of a large number of Jews in the Atlantic framework."

233. Butler, *Parting Ways*, p. 5. For a more detailed discussion of Butler's perspective, see Dickinson and Morgan, "Dwelling in Diaspora."

234. Heidegger, *Elucidations*, pp. 224–25; *Erläuterungen*, p. 196. On the contrast between the familiar and the strange in Heidegger's understanding of belonging—related more specifically to the distinction he draws between the human being as "world-forming" (*weltbildend*) and the animal's "deworlding of the world" (*die Entweltlichung der Welt*)—and its impact on Levinas's concept of alterity, see Gordon, "Displaced: Phenomenology and Belonging."

235. See ch. 4 at n. 94.

236. See Budick, "Crises of Alterity."

237. Nancy, *Gravity of Thought*, p. 83 (emphasis in original).

238. See ch. 5 nn. 78 and 94. The affinity between Böhme's account of evil as rooted in the divine nature and the perspective found in kabbalistic sources is noted in the introduction to Böhme, *Genius the Transcendent*, p. 6. See also the reference to Scholem cited in ch. 5 n. 81, and McGinn, *Mysticism in the Reformation*, p. 179.

239. Schelling, *Philosophical Investigations*, pp. 35–36; *Philosophische Untersuchungen*, p. 39.

240. Schelling, *Philosophical Investigations*, p. 73; *Philosophische Untersuchungen*, p. 83.

241. Heidegger, *On the Way to Language*, p. 48; *Unterwegs zur Sprache*, pp. 137–38. Despite the criticism of Heidegger's anthropology offered by Buber, Heidegger would have surely agreed with Buber's assertion that the task for the individual is to overcome solitude without forfeiting its questioning power. See Buber, *Between Man and Man*, p. 236. Moreover, a common element in Heidegger and Buber relates to the assumption that homelessness serves as the catalyst that enables one to understand the fundamental fact of human existence in relation to being, a way of relating to the other that is neither individualistic nor collectivistic. Finally, there are interesting affinities with respect to the notion of the sphere of the between articulated by both thinkers, a topic that demands a separate treatment. See Buber, *Between Man and Man*, pp. 238–41; Munro, "On Being Oneself," pp. 102–10.

Bibliography

Abe, Masao. "Nishida's Philosophy of 'Place.'" *International Philosophical Quarterly* 28 (1988): 355–71.

Abrams, Daniel. *The Book Bahir: An Edition Based on the Earliest Manuscripts*. Los Angeles: Cherub, 1994 (Hebrew).

———. *Kabbalistic Manuscripts and Textual Theory: Methodologies of Textual Scholarship and Editorial Practice in the Study of Jewish Mysticism*. 2nd rev. ed. Foreword by David Greetham. Los Angeles: Cherub, 2013.

———. *R. Asher ben David: His Complete Works and Studies in Kabbalistic Thought*. Los Angeles: Cherub, 1996 (Hebrew).

Abulafia, Ṭodros ben Joseph. *Oṣar ha-Kavod*. Satu Mare: M. L. Hirsch, 1926.

———. *Sha'ar ha-Razim*. Edited with introduction and annotation by Michal Kushnir-Oron. Jerusalem: Bialik Institute, 1989.

Adamson, Peter. "Eternity in Medieval Philosophy." In *Eternity: A History*, edited by Yitzhak Y. Melamed, 75–116. New York: Oxford University Press, 2016.

Adorno, Theodor W. *Beethoven: The Philosophy of Music*. Edited by Rolf Tiedemann. Translated by Edmund Jephcott. Stanford: Stanford University Press, 1998.

———. *The Jargon of Authenticity*. Translated by Knut Tarnowski and Frederic Will. Evanston: Northwestern University Press, 1973.

———. *Minima Moralia: Reflections from Damaged Life*. Translated by E. F. N. Jephcott. London: Verso, 1974.

———. *Negative Dialectics*. Translated by E. B. Ashton. New York: Seabury Press, 1973.

———. *Noten zu Literatur* [*Gesammelte Schriften* 11]. Frankfurt am Main: Suhrkamp, 1974.

———. *Notes to Literature*, vol. 1. Edited by Rolf Tiedemann. Translated by Shierry Weber Nicholsen. New York: Columbia University Press, 1991.

———. *Notes to Literature*, vol. 2. Edited by Rolf Tiedemann. Translated by Shierry Weber Nicholsen. New York: Columbia University Press, 1992.

Ænishanslin, François. "La logique, la pensée, le silence: Un style en transition." In *Heideggers "Beiträge zur Philosophie,"* edited by Emmanuel Mejía and Ingeborg Schüßler, 359–66. International Colloquium May 20–22, 2004, University of Lausanne. Frankfurt am Main: Vittorio Klostermann, 2009.

Agamben, Giorgio. *The Fire and the Tale*. Translated by Lorenzo Chiesa. Stanford: Stanford University Press, 2017.

———. *The Use of Bodies*. Translated by Adam Kotsko. Stanford: Stanford University Press, 2016.

Allen, Jeffner. "Homecoming in Heidegger and Hebel." *Analecta Husserliana* 12 (1982): 267–75.

Allen, William S. *Ellipsis: Of Poetry and the Experience of Language after Heidegger, Hölderlin, and Blanchot*. Albany: State University of New York Press, 2007.

Altizer, Thomas J. J. *The Apocalyptic Trinity*. New York: Palgrave Macmillan, 2012.

Altmann, Alexander. "Franz Rosenzweig on History." In *The Philosophy of Franz Rosenzweig*, edited by Paul Mendes-Flohr, 124–37. Hanover: University Press of New England, 1988.

———. "Lurianic Kabbalah in a Platonic Key: Abraham Cohen Herrera's *Puerta del Cielo*." In *Jewish Thought in the Seventh Century*, edited by Isadore Twersky and Bernard Septimus, 1–37. Cambridge, MA: Harvard University Press, 1987.

———. *The Meaning of Jewish Existence: Theological Essays 1930–1939*. Edited by Alfred L. Ivry. Translated by Edith Ehrlich and Leonard H. Ehrlich. With an introduction by Paul Mendes-Flohr. Hanover: University Press of New England, 1991.

Altmann, William H. F. *The German Stranger: Leo Strauss and National Socialism*. Foreword by Michael Zank. Lanham: Lexington, 2011.

Anckaert, Luc A. *A Critique of Infinity: Rosenzweig and Levinas*. Leuven: Peeters, 2006.

Anderson, John M. "Truth, Process, and Creature in Heidegger's Thought." In *Heidegger and the*

Quest for Truth, edited with an introduction by Manfred S. Frings, 28–61. Chicago: Quadrangle Books, 1968.

Andrews, Michael F. "Religion without Why: Edith Stein and Martin Heidegger on the Overcoming of Metaphysics, with Particular Reference to Angelus Silesius and Denys the Areopagite." *Analecta Husserliana* 89 (2006): 399–427.

Arendt, Hannah. *Between Past and Future: Eight Exercises in Political Thought*. Introduction by Jerome Kohn. New York: Penguin, 1977.

———. *The Life of the Mind*. 2 vols. New York: Harcourt Brace Jovanovich, 1978.

———. *Love and Saint Augustine*. Edited by Joanna Vecchiarelli Scott and Judith Chelius Stark. Chicago: University of Chicago Press, 1996.

———. "Martin Heidegger at Eighty." In *Heidegger and Modern Philosophy: Critical Essays*, edited by Michael Murray, 293–303. New Haven: Yale University Press, 1978.

———. *Thinking without a Banister: Essays in Understanding, 1953–1975*. Edited with an introduction by Jerome Kohn. New York: Schocken, 2018.

Arenfeld, Shmuel. *Ma'amar ha-Kelal we-ha-Peraṭ*. Vol. 3 of *Ke-Ṣe't ha-Shemesh: Be'urim we-Iyyunim al Haqdamat Reḥovot ha-Nahar*. Jerusalem: Makhon Yam ha-Ḥokhmah, 2018.

———. *Yira'ukha im Shamesh*. Jerusalem: Makhon Yam ha-Ḥokhmah, 2012.

Aristotle. *The Complete Works of Aristotle*. Revised Oxford translation. 2 vols. Edited by Jonathan Barnes. Princeton: Princeton University Press, 1995.

Armitage, Duane. *Heidegger and the Death of God: Between Plato and Nietzsche*. New York: Palgrave Macmillan, 2017.

———. "Heidegger's *Contributions to Philosophy*: Pauline Meontology and Lutheran Irony." *Heythrop Journal* 55 (2014): 576–83.

Asaṅga. *The Summary of the Great Vehicle*. Rev. 2nd ed. Translated by John P. Keenan. Berkeley: Numata Center for Buddhist Translation and Research, 2003.

Aschheim, Steven E. *Beyond the Borders: The German-Jewish Legacy Abroad*. Princeton: Princeton University Press, 2007.

A Source Book in Chinese Philosophy. Translated and compiled by Wing-Tsit Chan. Princeton: Princeton University Press, 1963.

Atkins, Zohar. *An Ethical and Theological Appropriation of Heidegger's Critique of Modernity: Unframing Existence*. New York: Palgrave Macmillan, 2018.

Atlan, Henri. "Jerusalem: The Terrestrial, the Celestial." In *Modern French Jewish Thought: Writings on Religion and Politics*, edited by Sarah Hammerschlag, 159–70. Waltham: Brandeis University Press, 2018.

———. *The Sparks of Randomness*. Vol. 2: *The Atheism of Scripture*. Translated by Lenn J. Schramm. Stanford: Stanford University Press, 2013.

Aubrey, Bryan A. "The Influence of Jacob Boehme on the Work of William Blake." PhD diss., Durham University, 1981.

Augustine. *Confessions*. Translated with an introduction and notes by Henry Chadwick. Oxford: Oxford University Press, 1991.

Avens, Robert. *The New Gnosis: Heidegger, Hillman, and Angels*. Dallas: Spring, 1984.

Azriel of Gerona. *Be'ur Eser Sefirot*. In *Ma'yan Moshe*, edited by Moshe Schatz, 81–96. Jerusalem, 2011.

———. *Commentary on Talmudic Aggadoth*. Edited by Isaiah Tishby. Jerusalem: Magnes, 1982 (Hebrew).

———. *Perush Eser Sefirot*. In *Shishah Sefarim Niftaḥim*, edited by Yeruḥam Baqar, 1–10. Jerusalem, 2014.

Baader, Franz Xavier von. *Biographie und Briefwechsel*. Edited by Franz Hoffmann. Leipzig: Hermann Bethmann, 1857.

———. *Elementarbegriffe über die Zeit, Vorlesungen über Philosophie der Societät*. Edited by Christoph Schlüter and Anton Lutterbeck. Leipzig: Herrmann Bethmann, 1851.

———. *Gesammelte Schriften zur Naturphilosophie*. Edited by Franz Hoffmann. Leipzig: Hermann Bethmann, 1852.

———. *Gesammelte Schriften zur philosophischen Anthropologie*. Edited by Franz Hoffmann. Leipzig: Herrmann Bethmann, 1853.

———. *Gesammelte Schriften zur philosophischen Grundwissenschaft oder Metaphysik*. Edited by Franz Hoffmann. Leipzig: Herrmann Bethmann, 1851.

———. *Gesammelte Schriften zur Religionsphilosophie*. 3 vols. Edited by Franz Hoffmann. Leipzig: Herrmann Bethmann, 1854.

———. *Vorlesungen und Erläuterungen zu Jacob Böhme's Lehre*. Edited by Julius Hamberger. Leipzig: Hermann Bethmann, 1855.

Babich, Babette E. "Heidegger's Jews: Inclusion/Exclusion and Heidegger's Anti-Semitism." *Journal of the British Society for Phenomenology* 47 (2016): 133–56.

———. "Heidegger's *Judenfrage*." In *Heidegger and Jewish Thought: Difficult Others*, edited by Elad Lapidot and Micha Brumlik, 135–54. London: Rowman and Littlefield, 2018.

Bachelard, Gaston. *Intuition of the Instant*. Translated by Eileen Rizo-Patron. Evanston: Northwestern University Press, 2013.

Bachrach, Naftali. *Emeq ha-Melekh*. Jerusalem: Yerid ha-Sefarim, 2003.

———. *Gan ha-Melekh*. MS Oxford, Bodleian Library 1586.

Backman, Jussi. *Complicated Presence: Heidegger and the Postmetaphysical Unity of Being*. Albany: State University of New York Press, 2015.

Badiou, Alain. *Being and Event*. Translated by Oliver Feltham. London: Continuum, 2005.

———. *Manifesto for Philosophy*. Translated, edited, and with an introduction by Norman Madarasz. Albany: State University of New York Press, 1999.

———. *Métaphysique du Bonheur réel*. Pairs: Presses Universitaires de France, 2015.

———. *Theory of the Subject*. Translated and with an introduction by Bruno Bosteels. London: Continuum, 2009.

Badiou, Alain, and Barbara Cassin. *Heidegger: His Life and His Philosophy*. Translated by Susan Spitzer. Introduction by Kenneth Reinhard. New York: Columbia University Press, 2016.

Badiou, Alain, and Slavoj Žižek. *Philosophy in the Present*. Edited by Peter Engelman. Translated by Peter Thomas and Alberto Toscano. Cambridge: Polity, 2010.

Baḥya ben Asher. *Be'ur al ha-Torah*. 3 vols. Edited by Ḥayyim D. Chavel. Jerusalem: Mosad ha-Rav Kook, 1981.

Bailey, Margaret Lewis. *Milton and Jakob Boehme: A Study of German Mysticism in Seventeenth-Century England*. New York: Oxford University Press, 1914.

Baki, Burhanuddin. *Badiou's Being and Event and the Mathematics of Set Theory*. London: Bloomsbury, 2015.

Balashov, Yuri. "Persistence." In *The Oxford Handbook of Philosophy of Time*, edited by Craig Callender, 13–40. Oxford: Oxford University Press, 2011.

Balazut, Joël. *Heidegger: une philosophie de la présence*. Paris: L'Harmattan, 2013.

Bambach, Charles. *Heidegger's Roots: Nietzsche, National Socialism, and the Greeks*. Ithaca: Cornell University Press, 2003.

Bar-Asher, Avishai. *"Ancient as 'Ein Sof'*: A Commentary on *'Eser Sefirot* by R. David haKohen, Rashba's Disciple." *Da'at* 82 (2016): 151–58 (Hebrew).

Barber, Daniel Colucciello. *On Diaspora: Christianity, Religion, and Secularity*. Eugene: Cascade, 2011.

Bar-Bettelheim, Lilach. "The Concept of *Zimzum* in the Kabbalah of the Early Twentieth Century." PhD diss., Ben-Gurion University of the Negev, 2012 (Hebrew).

Bardon, Adrian. *A Brief History of the Philosophy of Time*. Oxford: Oxford University Press, 2013.

Barnstone, Willis. *The Poetics of Translation: History, Theory, Practice*. New Haven: Yale University Press, 1993.

Barouch, Lina. *Between German and Hebrew: The Counterlanguages of Gershom Scholem, Werner Kraft and Ludwig Strauss*. Berlin: Walter de Gruyter, 2016.

———. "Dancing on the Rope, Walking on the Boundary: Paradoxical Language and Modernistic Associations in Gershom Scholem's Treatise 'On Lament and Lamentation.'" In *Lamentations: Poetry and Thought in Gershom Scholem's World*, edited by Galili Shahar and Ilit Ferber, 154–74. Jerusalem: Carmel, 2016 (Hebrew).

———. "The Erasure and Endurance of Lament: Gershom Scholem's Early Critique of Zionism and Its Language." *Jewish Studies Quarterly* 21 (2014): 13–26.

———. "Lamenting Language Itself: Gershom Scholem on the Silent Language of Lamentation." *New German Critique* 37 (2010): 1–26.

———. "Sprache zwischen Klage und Rache: Gershom Scholems frühe Schriften zur Sprache (1917–1926)." *Münchner Beiträge zur Jüdischen Geschichte und Kultur* 2 (2007): 48–55.

Bartolucci, Guido. "Marsilio Ficino e le origini della cabala cristiana." In *Giovanni Pico e la cabbalà*, edited by Fabrizio Lelli, 47–67. Firenze: Leo S. Olschki, 2014.

Baruch of Kosov. *Yesod ha-Emunah*. Brooklyn: Yaakov Ilowitz, 2007.

Baskin, Judith. *Pharaoh's Counselors: Job, Jethro, and Balaam in Rabbinic and Patristic Tradition*. Chico: Scholars' Press, 1983.

Bataille, Georges. *On Nietzsche*. Translated and with an introduction by Stuart Kendall. Albany: State University of New York Press, 2015.

Batnitzky, Leora. *Idolatry and Representation: The Philosophy of Franz Rosenzweig Reconsidered*. Princeton: Princeton University Press, 2000.

———. "Translation as Transcendence: A Glimpse into the Workshop of the Buber-Rosenzweig Bible Translation." *New German Critique* 70 (1997): 87–116.

Baum, Wolfgang. *Gnostische Elemente im Denken Martin Heideggers? Eine Studie auf der Grundlage der Religionsphilosophie von Hans Jonas*. Neuried: Ars Una, 1997.

Baumgarten, Eliezer. "History and Historiosophy in the Teachings of Rabbi Shlomo Elyashov." MA thesis, Ben-Gurion University, 2006 (Hebrew).

Beach, Edward Allen. *The Potencies of God(s): Schelling's Philosophy of Mythology*. Albany: State University of New York Press, 1994.

Beaufret, Jean. "Heraclitus and Parmenides." In *Heidegger on Heraclitus: A New Reading*, edited by Kenneth Maly and Parvis Emad, 69–86. Lewiston: Edwin Mellen, 1986.

Beltrán, Miquel. *The Influence of Abraham Cohen de Herrera's Kabbalah on Spinoza's Metaphysics*. Leiden: Brill, 2016.

Benarroch, Jonathan. "An Edition of Early Versions of *Idra Zuta* and An Unknown Hebrew Translation from Ms. Vatican 226, Copied in 1311." *Kabbalah: Journal for the Study of Jewish Mystical Texts* 39 (2017): 157–248 (Hebrew).

Benes, Tuska. *In Babel's Shadow: Language, Philology, and the Nation in Nineteenth-Century Germany*. Detroit: Wayne State University Press, 2008.

Benjamin, Andrew. "Time and Task: Benjamin and Heidegger Showing the Present." In *Sparks Will Fly: Benjamin and Heidegger*, edited by Andrew Benjamin and Dimitris Vardoulakis, 145–74. Albany: State University of New York Press, 2015.

Benjamin, Andrew, and Dimitris Vardoulakis, eds. *Sparks Will Fly: Benjamin and Heidegger*. Albany: State University of New York Press, 2015.

Benjamin, Walter. *The Arcades Project*. Translated by Howard Eiland and Kevin McLaughlin, prepared on the basis of the German volume edited by Rolf Tiedemann. Cambridge, MA: Harvard University Press, 1999.

———. *The Correspondence of Walter Benjamin 1910–1940*. Edited by Gershom Scholem and Theodor W. Adorno. Translated by Manfred R. Jacobson and Evelyn M. Jacobson. Chicago: University of Chicago Press, 1994.

———. *Gesammelte Schriften*, 1.2. Edited by Rolf Tiedemann and Hermann Schweppenhäuser. Frankfurt am Main: Suhrkamp, 1991.

———. *Gesammelte Schriften*, 1.3. Edited by Rolf Tiedemann and Hermann Schweppenhäuser. Frankfurt am Main: Suhrkamp, 1991.

———. *Gesammelte Schriften*, 2.1. Edited by Rolf Tiedemann and Hermann Schweppenhäuser. Frankfurt am Main: Suhrkamp, 1991.

———. *Gesammelte Schriften*, 2.2. Edited by Rolf Tiedemann and Hermann Schweppenhäuser. Frankfurt am Main: Suhrkamp, 1991.

———. *Gesammelte Schriften*, 4.1. Edited by Tillman Rexroth. Frankfurt am Main: Suhrkamp, 1991.

———. *Gesammelte Schriften*, 5.1. Edited by Rolf Tiedemann. Frankfurt am Main: Suhrkamp, 1991.

———. *Gesammelte Schriften*, 5.2. Edited by Rolf Tiedemann. Frankfurt am Main: Suhrkamp, 1991.

———. *Selected Writings*. Vol. 1: *1913–1926*. Edited by Marcus Bullock and Michael W. Jennings. Cambridge, MA: Harvard University Press, 1996.

———. *Selected Writings*. Vol. 2: *1927–1934*. Edited by Michael W. Jennings, Howard Eiland, and Gary Smith. Translated by Rodney Livingstone and Others. Cambridge, MA: Harvard University Press, 1999.

———. *Selected Writings*. Vol. 3: *1935–1938*. Edited by Howard Eiland and Michael W. Jennings. Translated by Edmund Jephcott, Howard Eiland, and Others. Cambridge, MA: Harvard University Press, 2002.

———. *Selected Writings*. Vol. 4: *1938–1940*. Edited by Howard Eiland and Michael W. Jennings. Translated by Edmund Jephcott and Others. Cambridge, MA: Harvard University Press, 2003.

Bennington, Geoffrey. *Interrupting Derrida*. London: Routledge, 2000.

Ben-Shachar, Na'ama, and Tzahi Weiss. "An Anonymous Geronese Kabbalistic Commentary on the Ten Sefirot." *Kabbalah: Journal for the Study of Jewish Mystical Texts* 38 (2017): 159–70 (Hebrew).

Ben-Shlomo, Joseph. *The Mystical Theology of Moses Cordovero*. Jerusalem: Bialik Institute, 1965 (Hebrew).

Benz, Ernst. *Christian Kabbalah: Neglected Child of Theology*. Edited by Robert J. Faas. Translated by Kenneth W. Wesche. St. Paul: Grailstone, 2004.

———. *The Mystical Sources of German Romantic Philosophy*. Translated by Blair R. Reynolds and Eunice M. Paul. Allison Park: Pickwick, 1983.

———. *Schellings theologische Geistesahnen*. Wiesbaden: F. Steiner, 1955.

Bergo, Bettina. "Marlène Zarader's *The Unthought Debt*: The Obfuscation of Heidegger's Jewish Sources." *Philosophy Today* 50 (2006): 117–27.

Bergren, Ann. "Architecture, Gender, Philosophy." In *Innovations of Antiquity: The New Ancient World*, edited by Ralph Hexter and Daniel Selden, 253–305. New York: Routledge, 1992.

Berman, Nathaniel. "Demonic Writing: Textuality, Otherness and Zoharic Proliferation." *Jewish Studies Quarterly* 24 (2017): 356–86.

———. *Divine and Demonic in the Poetic Mythology of the Zohar: The "Other Side" of Kabbalah*. Leiden: Brill, 2018.

———. "'Improper Twins': The Ambivalent 'Other Side' in the Zohar and Kabbalistic Tradition." PhD diss., University College London, 2014.

Bernasconi, Robert. "Being is Evil: Boehme's Strife and Schelling's Rage in Heidegger's "Letter on 'Humanism.'" *Gatherings: The Heidegger Circle Annual* 7 (2017): 164–81.

———. "Heidegger's Alleged Challenge to the Nazi Concepts of Race." In *Appropriating Heidegger,* edited by James E. Faulconer and Mark A. Wrathall, 50–67. Cambridge: Cambridge University Press, 2000.

———. "On Heidegger's Other Sins of Omission: His Exclusion of Asian Thought from the Origins of Occidental Metaphysics and His Denial of the Possibility of Christian Philosophy." *American Catholic Philosophical Quarterly* 69 (1995): 333–50.

———. *The Question of Language in Heidegger's History of Being.* Atlantic Highlands: Humanities, 1985.

Bernet, Rudolf. "Is the Present Ever Present? Phenomenology and the Metaphysics of Presence." *Research in Phenomenology* 12 (1982): 85–112.

———. "La présence du passé dans l'analyse husserlienne de la conscience du temps." *Revue de Métaphysique et de Morale* 88 (1983): 178–98.

Betanzos, Ramón J. *Franz von Baader's Philosophy of Love.* Edited by Martin M. Herman. Vienna: Passagen, 1998.

Biale, David. *Gershom Scholem: Kabbalah and Counter-History.* Cambridge, MA: Harvard University Press, 1979.

———. *Gershom Scholem: Master of the Kabbalah.* New Haven: Yale University Press, 2018.

———. "Gershom Scholem's Ten Unhistorical Aphorisms on Kabbalah: Text and Commentary." *Modern Judaism* 5 (1985): 67–93.

———. "Scholem und der moderne Nationalismus." In *Gershom Scholem: Zwischen den Disziplinen,* edited by Peter Schäfer and Gary Smith, 257–74. Frankfurt am Main: Suhrkamp, 1995.

Bielik-Robson, Agata. "Between Unity and Chaos: 'And' in Rosenzweig's Narrative Philosophy." *Archivio di Filosofia* 86 (2018): 123–32.

———. "The God of Luria, Hegel and Schelling: The Divine Contraction and the Modern Metaphysics of Finitude." In *Mystical Theology and Continental Philosophy: Interchange in the Wake of God,* edited by David Lewin, Simon D. Podmore, and Duane Williams, 32–50. London: Routledge, 2017.

———. "Love Strong as Death: Jews against Heidegger (On the Issue of Finitude)." In *Heidegger's Black Notebooks and the Future of Theology,* edited by Mårten Björk and Jayne Svenungsson, 159–89. New York: Palgrave Macmillan, 2018.

———. "Mysteries of the Promise: Negative Theology in Benjamin and Scholem." In *Negative Theology as Jewish Modernity,* edited by Michael Fagenblat, 258–81. Bloomington: Indiana University Press, 2017.

———. "Nihilism through the Looking Glass: Nietzsche, Rosenzweig, and Scholem on the Condition of Modern Disenchantment." *Revista de Estudos Religião* (September 2007): 39–67.

———. *The Saving Lie: Harold Bloom and Deconstruction.* Evanston: Northwestern University Press, 2011.

———. "The Unfallen Silence: *Kinah* and the Other Origin of Language." In *Lament in Jewish Thought: Philosophical, Theological, and Literary Perspectives,* edited by Ilit Ferber and Paula Schwebel, 133–52. Berlin: Walter de Gruyter, 2014.

Biemann, Asher D. *Inventing New Beginnings: On the Idea of Renaissance in Modern Judaism.* Stanford: Stanford University Press, 2009.

Bienenstock, Myriam. "Hegel über das jüdische Volk: 'eine bewunderungswürdige Festigkeit [. . .] ein Fanatismus der Hartnächkigkeit.'" In *Der Begriff des Judentums in der klassichen deutschen Philosophie,* edited by Amit Kravitz and Jörg Noller, 117–34. Tübingen: Mohr Siebeck, 2018.

Bigelow, Pat. *The Conning, the Cunning of Being: Being a Kierkegaardian Demonstration of the Postmodern Implosion of Metaphysical Sense in Aristotle and the Early Heidegger.* Tallahassee: Florida State University Press, 1990.

Bindeman, Steven L. *Heidegger and Wittgenstein: The Poetics of Silence.* Lanham: University Press of America, 1981.

Bistoen, Gregory, Stijn Vanheule, and Stef Craps. "Nachträglichkeit: A Freudian Perspective on Delayed Traumatic Reactions." *Theory and Psychology* 24 (2014): 668–87.

Björk, Mårten. *Life Outside Life: The Politics of Immortality, 1914–1945.* Göteborg: Institutionen för litteratur, idéhistoria och religion, 2018.

Blanchot, Maurice. "Thinking the Apocalypse: A Letter from Maurice Blanchot to Catherine David." Translated by Paula Wissing. *Critical Inquiry* 15 (1989): 475–80.

Blau, Joseph Leon. *The Christian Interpretation of the Cabala in the Renaissance.* New York: Columbia University Press. 1944.

Bloch, Ernst. *Atheism in Christianity: The Religion of the Exodus and the Kingdom*. Introduction by Peter Thompson, translated by J. T. Swann. London: Verso, 2009.

Blok, Vincent. "Massive Voluntarism or Heidegger's Confrontation with the Will." *Studia Phaenomenologica* 13 (2013): 449–65.

———. "A Question of Faith: Heidegger's Destructed Concept of Faith as the Origin of Questioning in Philosophy." In *Rethinking Faith: Heidegger between Nietzsche and Wittgenstein*, edited by Antonio Cimino and Gert-Jan van der Heiden, 123–42. New York: Bloomsbury, 2017.

Blond, Louis P. *Heidegger and Nietzsche: Overcoming Metaphysics*. London: Continuum, 2010.

Bloom, Harold. *Ruin the Sacred Truths: Poetry and Belief from the Bible to the Present*. Cambridge, MA: Harvard University Press, 1989.

Blumenberg, Hans. *The Laughter of the Thracian Woman: A Protohistory of Theory*. Translated, with annotations and an afterword, by Spencer Hawkins. New York: Bloomsbury, 2015.

———. "Light as a Metaphor for Truth: At the Preliminary Stage of Philosophical Concept Formation." In *Modernity and the Hegemony of Vision*, edited by David Michael Levin, 30–62. Berkeley: University of California Press, 1993.

———. *Paradigms for a Metaphorology*. Translated with an afterword by Robert Savage. Ithaca: Cornell University Press, 2010.

———. *Work on Myth*. Translated by Robert M. Wallace. Cambridge, MA: MIT Press, 1985.

Bodnar, István. "The *Problemata Physica*: An Introduction." In *The Aristotelian* Problemata Physica: *Philosophical and Scientific Investigations*, edited by Robert Mayhew, 1–9. Leiden: Brill, 2015.

Boeder, Heribert. *Seditions: Heidegger and the Limit of Modernity*. Translated, edited, and with an introduction by Marcus Brainard. Albany: State University of New York Press, 1997.

Böhme, Jacob. *Aurora (Morgen Röte im auffgang, 1612) and Ein gründlicher Bericht or A Fundamental Report (Mysterium Pansophicum, 1620)*. Translated by Andrew Weeks and Günther Bonheim in collaboration with Michael Spang. Leiden: Brill, 2013.

———. *De Electione Gratiae and Quaestiones Theosophicae*. Translated by John Rolleston Earle. London: Constable, 1930.

———. *Essential Readings*. Edited and introduced by Robin Waterfield. Wellingborough: Crucible, 1989.

———. *Genius of the Transcendent: Mystical Writings of Jakob Boehme*. Translated by Michael L. Birkel and Jeff Bach. Boston: Shambhala, 2010.

———. *The High and Deep Searching Out of the Threefold Life of Man through or According to the Three Principles*. Translated by John Sparrow. London: John M. Watkins, 1909.

———. *The "Key" of Jacob Boehme with an Illustration of the Deep Principles of Jacob Behmen* by Dionysius Andrew Freher. Translated by William Law. Introductory essay by Adam McLean. Grand Rapids: Phanes, 1991

———. *Mysterium Magnum; or, An Exposition of the First Book of Moses called Genesis*. Translated by John Sparrow. London: John M. Watkins, 1924.

———. *Mysterium Pansophicum Or Thorough Report on the Earthly and Heavenly Mysterium*. In Friedrich Wilhelm Joseph Schelling, *Philosophical Investigations into the Essence of Human Freedom*, translated and with an introduction by Jeff Love and Johannes Schmidt, 85–98. Albany: State University of New York Press, 2006.

———. *Sämtliche Schriften*. 11 vols. Edited by Will-Erich Peuckert and August Faust. Stuttgart: Fr. Frommanns, 1955–96.

———. *The Signature of All Things and Other Writings*. Cambridge: James Clarke, 1969.

———. *Six Theosophic Points*. Introductory essay by Nicolas Berdyaev. Ann Arbor: University of Michigan Press, 1958.

———. *The Three Principles of the Divine Essence of the Eternal Dark, Light, and Temporary World*. In *The Works of Jacob Behmen, the Teutonic Theosopher*, vol. 1. London: M. Richardson, 1764.

———. *The Treatise of the Incarnation in Three Parts*. In *The Works of Jacob Behmen, the Teutonic Theosopher*, vol. 2. London: Joseph Richardson, 1764.

———. *The Way to Christ*. Translated by Peter Erb. Preface by Winfried Zeller. New York: Paulist, 1978.

Bontekoe, Ronald. *Dimensions of the Hermeneutic Circle*. Atlantic Highlands: Humanities, 1996.

Book of Causes, The [*Liber de Causis*]. Translated with an introduction by Dennis J. Brand. Milwaukee: Marquette University Press, 1984.

Boothby, Richard. *Death and Desire: Psychoanalytic Theory in Lacan's Return to Freud*. New York: Routledge, 1991.

Botz-Bornstein, Thorsten. "Nishida and Wittgenstein: From 'Pure Experience' to *Lebensform* or New Perspectives for a Philosophy of Intercultural

Communication." *Asian Philosophy* 13 (2003): 53–70.

Bourdieu, Pierre. *The Political Ontology of Martin Heidegger.* Translated by Peter Collier. Stanford: Stanford University Press, 1991.

Bouretz, Pierre. *Witnesses for the Future: Philosophy and Messianism.* Translated by Michael B. Smith. Baltimore: Johns Hopkins University Press, 2010.

Bowen-Moore, Patricia. *Hannah Arendt's Philosophy of Natality.* Hampshire: Macmillan, 1989.

Böwering, Gerhard. "Ibn al-ʿArabī's Concept of Time." In *Gott is schön und Er liebt die Schönheit: Festschrift für Annemarie Schimmel zum 7. April 1992 dargebracht von Schülern, Freunden und Kollegen*, edited by Alma Giese and J. Christoph Bürgel, 71–91. Bern: Peter Lang, 1994.

Bowie, Andrew. *Schelling and Modern European Philosophy: An Introduction.* London: Routledge, 1993.

Boyarin, Daniel. *A Traveling Homeland: The Babylonian Talmud as Diaspora.* Philadelphia: University of Pennsylvania Press, 2015.

Bozga, Adina. *The Exasperating Gift of Singularity: Husserl, Levinas, Henry.* Bucharest: Zeta Books, 2009.

Braiterman, Zachary. *The Shape of Revelation: Aesthetics and Modern Jewish Thought.* Stanford: Stanford University Press, 2007.

Brann, Eva. *The Ways of Naysaying: No, Not, Nothing, and Nonbeing.* Lanham: Rowman and Littlefield, 2001.

———. *What, Then, Is Time?* Lanham: Rowman and Littlefield, 1999.

———. *The World of the Imagination: Sum and Substance.* Lanham: Rowman and Littlefield, 1991.

Brassier, Ray. *Nihil Unbound: Enlightenment and Extinction.* New York: Palgrave Macmillan, 2010.

Bredeson, Garrett Zantow. "The Genesis of Heidegger's Reading of Kant." PhD diss., Vanderbilt University, 2014.

Brencio, Francesca. "Heidegger and Binswanger: Just a Misunderstanding?" *Humanist Psychologist* 43 (2015): 278–96.

———. "Life and Negativity: The Inner Teleology in Hegel's Philosophy of Nature." *Revista Opinião Filosófica* 5 (2014): 54–68.

———. "World, Time and Anxiety: Heidegger's Existential Analytic and Psychiatry." *Folia Medica* 56 (2014): 297–304.

Brenner, Michael. "Gnosis and History: Polemics of German-Jewish Identity from Graetz to Scholem." *New German Critique* 77 (1999): 45–60.

Brill, Alan. "The Mystical Path of the Vilna Gaon." *Journal of Jewish Thought and Philosophy* 3 (1993): 131–51.

Brito, Emilio. "Création et temps dans la philosophie de Schelling." *Revue Philosophique de Louvain* 84 (1986): 362–84.

———. *La création selon Schelling: Universum.* Leuven: Leuven University Press, 1987.

———. *Heidegger et l'hymne du sacré.* Leuven: Leuven University Press, 1999.

———. *Philosophie et Théologie dans l'œuvre de Schelling.* Paris: Cerf, 2000.

Brock, Sebastian. "Aspects of Translation Technique in Antiquity." *Greek, Roman, and Byzantine Studies* 20 (1979): 69–87.

Brocke, Michael. "Franz Rosenzweig und Gerhard Gershom Scholem." In *Juden in der Weimarer Republik. Skizzen und Porträts*, edited by Walter Grab and Julius H. Schoeps, 127–52. Stuttgart: Burg Verlag, 1986.

Brown, Robert F. *The Later Philosophy of Schelling: The Influence of Böhme on the Works of 1809–15.* Lewisburg: Bucknell University Press, 1977.

Brown, Stuart. "Leibniz and More's Cabbalistic Circle." In *Henry More (1614–1687): Tercentenary Studies*, edited by Sarah Hutton, with a biography and bibliography by Robert Crocker, 77–96. Dordrecht: Kluwer Academic, 1990.

———. "The Proto-Monadology of the De Summa Rerum." In *The Young Leibniz and His Philosophy (1646–76)*, edited by Stuart Brown, 263–87. Dordrecht: Kluwer Academic, 1999.

Brumlik, Micha. "Resentment—A Few Motifs in Hans Jonas's Early Book on Gnosticism." In *The Legacy of Hans Jonas: Judaism and the Phenomenon of Life*, edited by Hava Tirosh-Samuelson and Christian Wiese, 73–90. Leiden: Brill, 2008.

Bruns, Gerald L. *Heidegger's Estrangements: Language, Truth, and Poetry in the Later Writings.* New Haven: Yale University Press, 1989.

———. *Hermeneutics Ancient and Modern.* New Haven: Yale University Press, 1992.

———. *Inventions: Writing, Textuality, and Understanding in Literary History.* New Haven: Yale University Press, 1982.

Buber, Martin. *Between Man and Man.* Tanslated by Ronald Gregor-Smith, with an introduction by Maurice Friedman. London: Routledge, 2002.

———. *Eclipse of God: Studies in the Relation between Religion and Philosophy.* With an introduction by Robert M. Seltzer. Amherst: Humanity Books, 1998.

———. *Gottesfinsternis: Betrachtungen zur Beziehung zwischen Religion und Philosophie*. Zürich: Manesse, 1953.

———. *Das Problem des Menschen*. Heidelberg: Lambert Schneider, 1948.

———, ed. *Reden und Gleichnisse des Tschuang Tse*. Zürich: Manesse, 1951.

Buber, Solomon, ed. *Midrash Tehillim*. Vilnius: Rom, 1891.

Budick, Sanford. "Crises of Alterity: Cultural Untranslatability and the Experience of Secondary Otherness." In *The Translatability of Cultures: Figurations of the Space Between*, edited by Sanford Budick and Wolfgang Iser, 1–22. Stanford: Stanford University Press, 1996.

Bultmann, Rudolf. *Theology of the New Testament*. 2 vols. Translated by Kendrick Grobel. Waco: Baylor University Press, 2007.

Burik, Steven. *The End of Comparative Philosophy and the Task of Comparative Thinking: Heidegger, Derrida, and Daoism*. Albany: State University of New York Press, 2009.

———. "Is There Imagination in Daoism? Kant, Heidegger, and Classical Daoism: Rethinking Imagination and Thinking in Images." In *Imagination: Cross-Cultural Philosophical Analyses*, edited by Hans-Georg Moeller and Andrew K. Whitehead, 79–102. London: Bloomsbury Academic, 2019.

Burmistrov, Konstantin. "*Pardes Rimmonim* und die *Kabbala Denudata*: Zum Stellenwert von Cordoveros Kabbala in Knorrs Projekt." *Morgen-Glantz* 16 (2006): 181–201.

Butler, Judith. *Bodies That Matter: On the Discursive Limits of "Sex."* London: Routledge, 1993.

———. *Parting Ways: Jewishness and the Critique of Zionism*. New York: Columbia University Press, 2012.

Buzaglo, Meir. *Solomon Maimon: Monism, Skepticism, and Mathematics*. Pittsburgh: University of Pittsburgh Press, 2002.

Buzzetta, Flavia. "La Cabbale vulgarisée au XVIe: Niccolo Camerario in cabbaliste oublié." *Accademia: Revue de la Société Marsile Ficin* 16 (2014): 121–34.

Cahnman, Werner J. "Friedrich Wilhelm Schelling and the New Thinking of Judaism." In *Kabbala und Romantik*, edited by Eveline Goodman-Thau, Gert Mattenklott, and Christoph Schulte, 167–205. Tübingen: Max Niemeyer, 1994.

Cairns, Dorion. *The Philosophy of Edmund Husserl*. Edited by Lester Embree. Dordrecht: Springer, 2013.

Calcagno, Antonio. "The Role of Forgetting in Our Experience of Time: Augustine of Hippo and Hannah Arendt." *Parrhesia* 13 (2011): 14–27.

Camilleri, Adrian. *A Brief History of the Philosophy of Time*. Oxford: Oxford University Press, 2013.

Campanini, Saverio. "Il commento alle *Conclusiones cabalisticae* nel Cinquecento." In *Giovanni Pico e la cabbalà*, edited by Fabrizio Lelli, 167–230. Firenze: Leo S. Olschki, 2014.

Canpanton, Judah. *Arba'ah Qinyanim*. Edited by Moshe Y. Blau. Brooklyn: Simcha Graphic, 1997.

———. *Arba'ah Qinyanim*. MS Cambridge, Trinity College 120 and MS JTSA 2532.

———. *Leqaḥ Ṭov*. MS Oxford, Bodleian Library 1642.

Capobianco, Richard. *Engaging Heidegger*. Toronto: University of Toronto Press, 2010.

———. "Heidegger on Heraclitus: *Kosmos*/World as Being Itself." *Epoché* 20 (2016): 465–76.

Caputo, John D. "Meister Eckhart and the Later Heidegger: The Mystical Element in Heidegger's Thought: Part One." *Journal of the History of Philosophy* 12 (1974): 479–94.

———. "Meister Eckhart and the Later Heidegger: The Mystical Element in Heidegger's Thought: Part Two." *Journal of the History of Philosophy* 13 (1975): 61–80.

———. *The Mystical Element in Heidegger's Thought*. Athens: Ohio State University Press, 1978.

———. "People of God, People of Being: The Theological Presuppositions of Heidegger's Path of Thought." In *Appropriating Heidegger*, edited by James E. Faulconer and Mark A. Wrathall, 85–100. Cambridge: Cambridge University Press, 2000.

———. *The Prayers and Tears of Jacques Derrida: Religion without Religion*. Bloomington: Indiana University Press, 1997.

———. "The Rose is without Why: An Interpretation of the Later Heidegger." *Philosophy Today* 15 (1971): 3–15.

———. "Toward a Postmodern Theology of the Cross: Augustine, Heidegger, Derrida." In *Postmodern Philosophy and Christian Thought*, edited by Merold Westphal, 202–25. Bloomington: Indiana University Press, 1999.

Capuzzi, Frank A. "Heraclitus: Fire, Dream, and Oracle." In *Heraclitean Fragments: A Companion Volume to the Heidegger/Fink Seminar on Heraclitus*, edited by John Sallis and Kenneth Maly, 135–48. University, AL: University of Alabama Press, 1980.

Carlisle, Clare. *Kierkegaard's Philosophy of Becoming: Movements and Positions*. Albany: State University of New York Press, 2005.

Carman, Taylor. "What Science Leaves Unsaid." In *Wittgenstein and Heidegger*, edited by David Egan, Stephen Reynolds, and Aaron James Wendland, 133–45. New York: Routledge, 2013.

Carter, Robert E. "God and Nothingness." *Philosophy East & West* 59 (2009): 1–21.

———. *The Kyoto School: An Introduction*. Albany: State University of New York Press, 2013.

———. *The Nothingness Beyond God: An Introduction to the Philosophy of Nishida Kitarō*. New York: Paragon House, 1989.

Casati, Filippo. "Being: A Dialetheic Interpretation of the Late Heidegger." PhD diss., University of St. Andrews, 2017.

Casey, Edward S., and J. Melvin Woody. "Hegel, Heidegger, Lacan: The Dialectic of Desire." In *Interpreting Lacan*, edited by Joseph H. Smith and William Kerrigan, 75–112. New Haven: Yale University Press, 1983.

Cassin, Barbara. *Nostalgia: When Are We Ever at Home?* Translated by Pascale-Anne Brault. New York: Fordham University Press, 2016.

Cattin, Emmanuel. *Sérénité: Eckhart, Schelling, Heidegger*. Paris: Vrin, 2012.

Chajes, Jeffrey H. "Kabbalah and the Diagrammatic Phase of the Scientific Revolution." In *Jewish Culture in Early Modern Europe: Essays in Honor of David B. Ruderman*, edited by Richard I. Cohen, Natalie B. Dohrmann, Adam Shear, and Elchanan Reiner, 109–23. Cincinnati: Hebrew Union College Press, 2014.

Chanter, Tina. *Time, Death, and the Feminine: Levinas with Heidegger*. Stanford: Stanford University Press, 2001.

Chevalier, Jacques M. *Scorpions and the Anatomy of Time*. Montreal: McGill-Queen's University Press, 2002.

Chittick, William C. *The Sufi Path of Knowledge: Ibn al-'Arabi's Metaphysics of Imagination*. Albany: State University of New York Press, 1989.

Clancey, William J. *Conceptual Coordination: How the Mind Orders Experience in Time*. London: Routledge, 1999.

———. "Scientific Antecedents of Situated Cognition." In *The Cambridge Handbook of Situated Cognition*, edited by Philip Robbins and Murat Aydede, 11–34. Cambridge: Cambridge University Press, 2009.

Claxton, Susanne. *Heidegger's Gods: An Ecofeminist Perspective*. London: Rowman and Littlefield, 2017.

Coates, Peter. *Ibn 'Arabi and Modern Thought: The History of Taking Metaphysics Seriously*. Oxford: Anqa Publishing, 2011.

Cocker, Robert. *Henry More, 1614–1687: A Biography of the Cambridge Platonist*. Dordrecht: Kluwer Academic, 2003.

Codignola, Maria Moneti. "Monde sensible—suprasensible—renversé. Influences de Böhme sur la troisième figure de la *Phénoménologie de l'esprit* de Hegel." *Les Études philosophiques* (1999): 181–99.

Cohen, Arthur A. *The Natural and the Supernatural Jew*. New York: Pantheon, 1962.

Cohen, Hermann. *Der Begriff der Religion im System der Philosophie*. Giessen: Alfred Töpelmann, 1915.

———. *Logik der reinen Erkenntnis*. Introduction by Helmut Holzhey. Hildesheim: Georg Olms, 2005.

———. *Religion of Reason Out of the Sources of Judaism*. Translated, with an introduction by Simon Kaplan, introductory essay by Leo Strauss, and introductory essays for the second edition by Steven S. Schwarzschild and Kenneth Seeskin. Atlanta: Scholars' Press, 1995.

Cohen, Jonathan. "The Halakah, Sacred Events, and Time Consciousness in Rosenzweig and Soloveitchik." *Shofar* 35 (2016): 69–94.

Cohen, Joseph. *Alternances de la Métaphysique: Essais sur Emmanuel Levinas*. Paris: Galilée, 2009.

———. *Le spectre juif de Hegel*. Preface by Jean-Luc Nancy. Paris: Galilée, 2005.

Cohen, Joseph and Raphael Zagury-Orly, eds. *Judéités: Questions pour Jacques Derrida*. Paris: Galilée, 2003.

Comay, Rebecca. *Mourning Sickness: Hegel and the French Revolution*. Stanford: Stanford University Press, 2011.

Comay, Rebecca, and Frank Ruda. *The Dash—The Other Side of Absolute Knowing*. Cambridge, MA: MIT Press, 2018.

Constantine, David J. *The Significance of Locality in the Poetry of Friedrich Hölderlin*. London: The Modern Humanities Research Association, 1979.

Conley, Tom. "A Trace of Style." In *Displacement: Derrida and After*, edited by Mark Krupnick, 74–92. Bloomington: Indiana University Press, 1983.

Connell, George. "Against Idolatry: Heidegger and Natural Theology." In *Postmodern Philosophy and Christian Thought*, edited by Merold Westphal, 144–68. Bloomington: Indiana University Press, 1999.

Conway, Ann. *The Principles of the Most Ancient and Modern Philosophy*. 2nd ed. Edited and with an introduction by Peter Loptson. Delmar: Scholars' Facsimiles and Reprints, 1998.

———. *The Principles of the Most Ancient and Modern Philosophy*. Edited by Allison P. Coudert and Taylor Corse. Cambridge: Cambridge University Press, 1996.

Copenhaver, Brian P. "Number, Shape, and Meaning in Pico's Christian Cabala: The Upright Tsade, the Closed Mem, and the Gaping Jaws of Azazel." In *Natural Particulars: Nature and Disciplines in Renaissance Europe*, edited by Anthony Grafton and Nancy Siraisi, 25–76. Cambridge, MA: MIT Press, 1999.

———. "Pico risorto: cabbalà e dignità dell'uomo nell'Italia post-unitaria." In *Giovanni Pico e la cabbalà*, edited by Fabrizio Lelli, 1–18. Firenze: Leo S. Olschki, 2014.

———. "The Secret of Pico's Oration: Cabala and Renaissance Philosophy." In *Renaissance and Early Modern Philosophy*, edited by Peter A. French, Howard K. Wettstein, and Bruce Silver, 56–81. Boston: Blackwell, 2002.

Copenhaver, Brian P., and Daniel Stein Kokin. "Egidio da Viterbo's *Book on Hebrew Letters:* Christian Kabbalah in Papal Rome." *Renaissance Quarterly* 67 (2014): 1–42.

Corbin, Henry. *Creative Imagination in the Sūfism of Ibn 'Arabī*. Translated by Ralph Manheim. Princeton: Princeton University Press, 1969.

Cordero, Néstor-Luis. *By Being, It Is: The Thesis of Parmenides*. Las Vegas: Parmenides, 2004.

Cordovero, Moses. *Elimah Rabbati*. Jerusalem: Nezer Shraga, 2013.

———. *Pardes Rimmonim*. Jerusalem: Yerid ha-Sefarim, 2000.

———. *Shi'ur Qomah*. Jerusalem: Or Ḥadash, 1999.

———. *Zohar im Perush Or Yaqar*. Vol. 1. Jerusalem: Or Yaqar, 1962.

———. *Zohar im Perush Or Yaqar*. Vol. 6. Jerusalem: Or Yaqar, 1974.

———. *Zohar im Perush Or Yaqar*. Vol. 16. Jerusalem: Or Yaqar, 1989.

———. *Zohar im Perush Or Yaqar*. Vol. 21. Jerusalem: Or Yaqar, 1991.

———. *Zohar im Perush Or Yaqar*. Vol. 23. Jerusalem: Or Yaqar, 1995.

Coriando, Paola-Ludovica. *Der letzte Gott als Anfang: Zur ab-gründigen Zeit-Räumlichkeit des Übergangs in Heideggers "Beiträgen zur Philosophie (vom Ereignis)."* Munich: Wilhelm Fink, 1998.

———. "Substance and Emptiness: Preparatory Steps toward a Translational Dialogue between Western and Buddhist Philosophy." In *Heidegger, Translation, and the Task of Thinking: Essays in Honor of Parvis Emad*, edited by Frank Schalow, 135–43. Dordrecht: Springer, 2011.

Coudert, Allison P. *The Impact of the Kabbalah in the Seventeenth Century: The Life and Thought of Francis Mercury van Helmont (1614–1698)*. Leiden: Brill, 1999.

———. "The *Kabbala Denudata*: Converting Jews or Seducing Christians?" In *Jewish Christians and Christian Jews: From Renaissance to the Enlightenment*, edited by Richard H. Popkin and Gordon M. Weiner, 73–96. Dordrecht: Academic, 1994.

———. "Leibniz, Locke, Newton and the Kabbalah." In *The Christian Kabbalah: Jewish Mystical Books and Their Christian Interpreters*, edited by Joseph Dan, 149–79. Cambridge, MA: Harvard College Library, 1997.

———. *Leibniz and the Kabbalah*. Dordrecht: Kluwer Academic, 1995.

———. "Leibniz and the Kabbalah." In *Leibniz, Mysticism, and Religion*, edited by Allison P. Coudert, Richard H. Popkin, and Gordon M. Weiner, 47–83. Dordrecht: Kluwer Academic, 1998.

Courtine, François. "Phenomenology and/or Tautology." In *Reading Heidegger: Commemorations*, edited by John Sallis, 241–57. Bloomington: Indiana University Press, 1993.

Coxon, Allan H. *The Fragments of Parmenides: A Critical Text with Introduction and Translation, the Ancient Testimonia and a Commentary*. Rev. and exp. ed. Edited with new translations by Richard McKiraham. Preface by Malcolm Schofield. Las Vegas: Parmenides, 2009.

Coyne, Ryan. *Heidegger's Confessions: The Remains of Saint Augustine in* Being and Time *and Beyond*. Chicago: University of Chicago Press, 2015.

Cristin, Renato. *Heidegger and Leibniz: Reason and the Path*. Foreword by Hans-Georg Gadamer. Dordrecht: Kluwer Academic, 1998.

Critchley, Simon, and Reiner Schürmann. *On Heidegger's Being and Time*. Edited by Steven Levine. London: Routledge, 2008.

Crites, Stephen. "'The Blissful Security of the Moment': Recollection, Repetition, and Eternal Recurrence." In *International Kierkegaard Commentary: Fear and Trembling and Repetition*, edited by Robert Perkins, 229–45. Macon: Mercer University Press, 1993.

Crocker, Robert. *Henry More, 1614–1687: A Biography of the Cambridge Platonist*. Dordrecht: Kluwer Academic, 2003.

Crowe, Benjamin D. *Heidegger's Religious Origins: Destruction and Authenticity*. Bloomington: Indiana University Press, 2006.

Dahlstrom, Daniel O. "Being at the Beginning: Heidegger's Interpretation of Heraclitus." In *Interpreting Heidegger: Critical Essays*, edited by Daniel O. Dahlstrom, 135–55. Cambridge: Cambridge University Press, 2011.

———. *Heidegger's Concept of Truth*. Cambridge: Cambridge University Press, 1994.

———. "Heidegger's Method: Philosophical Concepts as Formal Indications." *Review of Metaphysics* 47 (1994): 775–95.

———. "Thinking of Nothing: Heidegger's Criticism of Hegel's Conception of Negativity." In *A Companion to Hegel*, edited by Stephen Houlgate and Michael Baur, 519–36. Malden: Wiley-Blackwell, 2011.

Dalle Pezze, Barbara. *Martin Heidegger and Meister Eckhart: A Path Towards Gelassenheit*. Foreword by Timothy O'Leary. Lewiston: Edwin Mellen, 2008.

Dallmayr, Fred. *The Other Heidegger*. Ithaca: Cornell University Press, 1993.

Damsma, Alinda. "The Aramaic of the Zohar: The *Status Quaestionis*." In *Jewish Languages in Historical Perspective*, edited by Lily Kahn, 9–38. Leiden: Brill, 2018.

Dan, Joseph. "The Kabbalah of Johannes Reuchlin and Its Historical Significance." In *The Christian Kabbalah: Jewish Mystical Books and Their Christian Interpreters*, edited by Joseph Dan, 55–95. Cambridge, MA: Harvard College Library, 1997.

———. "Samael, Lilith, and the Concept of Evil in Early Kabbalah." *Association for Jewish Studies Review* 5 (1980): 17–40.

Danz, Christian. "'Ihre Wahrheit hat die alttestamentliche Religion nur in der Zukunft': Schellings religionsgeschichtliche Deutung des Judentums." In *Der Begriff des Judentums in der klassichen deutschen Philosophie*, edited by Amit Kravitz and Jörg Noller, 101–15. Tübingen: Mohr Siebeck, 2018.

Daoyuan. *Records of the Transmission of the Lamp (Jingde Chuandeng Lu)*. 2 vols. Translated by Randolph S. Whitfield. Munich: Books on Demand, 2015.

Dastur, Françoise. *Heidegger and the Question of Time*. Translated by François Raffoul and David Pettigrew. Atlantic Highlands: Humanities, 1998.

———. "Heidegger et la théologie." *Revue philosophique de Louvain* 92 (1994): 226–45.

———. "Hölderlin and the Orientalisation of Greece." *Pli* 10 (2000): 156–73.

———. *Questions of Phenomenology: Language, Alterity, Temporality, Finitude*. Translated by Robert Vallier. New York: Fordham University Press, 2017.

David ben Abraham ha-Lavan. *Masoret ha-Berit*. Edited by Gershom Scholem. *Qoveṣ al Yad* 1 (1936): 27–42.

David ben Yehudah he-Ḥasid. *The Book of Mirrors: Sefer Mar'ot ha-Ẓove'ot*. Edited by Daniel C. Matt. Chico: Scholars' Press, 1982.

Davis, Bret W. "Heidegger and Asian Philosophy." In *The Bloomsbury Companion to Heidegger*, edited by François Raffoul and Eric S. Nelson, 459–71. London: Bloomsbury, 2013.

———. *Heidegger and the Will: On the Way to Gelassenheit*. Evanston: Northwestern University Press, 2007.

———. "Heidegger on the Way from Onto-Historical Ethnocentrism to East-West Dialogue." *Gatherings* 6 (2016): 130–56.

Deacon, Terrence W. *Incomplete Nature: How Mind Emerged from Matter*. New York: Norton, 2012.

De Beistegui, Miguel. *The New Heidegger*. London: Continuum, 2005.

———. *Thinking with Heidegger: Displacements*. Bloomington: Indiana University Press, 2003.

———. *Truth and Genesis: Philosophy as Differential Ontology*. Bloomington: Indiana University Press, 2004.

Deghaye, Pierre. *De Paracelse à Thomas Mann: Les avatars de l'hermétisme allemand*. Paris: Dervy, 2000.

———. "*Gedulla* et *Gebura*: Le dictionnaire biblique et emblématique de Friedrich Christoph Oetinger (1776)." In *Ésotérisme, gnoses and imaginaire symbolique: mélanges offerts à Antoine Faivre*, edited by Richard Caron, Joscelyn Godwin, Wouter J. Hanegraff, and Jean-Louis Vieillard-Baron, 233–47. Leuven: Peeters, 2001.

———. "Jakob Böhmes Theosophie: die Theophanie in der ewigen Natur." In *Gnosis und Mystik in der Geschichte der Philosophie*, edited by Peter Koslowski, 151–67. Zürich: Artemis, 1988.

———. "La Philosophie sacrée d'Oetinger." In *Kabbalistes Chrétiens*, 233–78. Paris: Albin Michel, 1979.

———. "La Théosophie de Friedrich Christoph Oetinger." *Les Études philosophiques* (1983): 147–61.

———. "La Théosophie de Jacob Boehme. Les Trois Mystères du livre *De La Signature des Choses*." *Les Études philosophiques* (1999): 147–65.

De Herrera, Abraham Cohen. *Gate of Heaven*. Translated with introduction and notes by Kenneth Krabbenhoft. Leiden: Brill, 2002.

———. *House of Divinity (Casa de la Divinidad), Gate of Heaven (Puerta del Cielo)*. Translated by Nissim Yosha. Jerusalem: Ben-Zvi Institute, 2002 (Hebrew).

———. *Puerta del Cielo*. Edited by Miquel Beltrán. Madrid: Editorial Trotta, 2015.

Deleuze, Gilles, and Félix Guattari. *What Is Philosophy?* Translated by Hugh Tomlinson and Graham Burchell. New York: Columbia University Press, 1994.

Delmedigo, Joseph Solomon. *Novelot Ḥokhmah*. Basel, 1631.

———. *Ta'alumot Ḥokhmah*. Basel, 1629.

De Man, Paul. *Blindness and Insight: Essays in the Rhetoric of Contemporary Criticism*. 2nd ed., rev. Introduction by Wlad Godzich. Minneapolis: University of Minnesota Press, 1983.

Derrida, Jacques. "Abraham, the Other." In *Judeities: Questions for Jacques Derrida*, edited by Bettina Bergo, Joseph Cohen, and Raphael Zagury-Orly, 1–35. Translated by Bettina Bergo and Michael B. Smith. New York: Fordham University Press, 2007.

———. "Abraham's Melancholy: An Interview with Michal Ben-Naftali." Translated by Ellie Anderson and Philippe Lynes. *Oxford Literary Review* 39 (2017): 153–88.

———. *Acts of Religion*. Edited and with an introduction by Gil Anidjar. New York: Routledge, 2002.

———. *The Animal That Therefore I Am*. Edited by Marie-Louise Mallet. New York: Fordham University Press, 2008.

———. "Avowing—The Impossible: 'Returns,' Repentance, and Reconciliation." In *Living Together: Jacque Derrida's Communities of Violence and Peace*, edited by Elisabeth Weber, 18–41. New York: Fordham University Press, 2013.

———. "Circumfession." In *Jacques Derrida*, edited by Geoffrey Bennington and Jacques Derrida. Translated by Geoffrey Bennington. Chicago: University of Chicago Press, 1993.

———. *De l'esprit: Heidegger et la question*. Paris: Galilée, 1987.

———. *Le dernier des Juifs*. Paris: Galilée, 2014.

———. "Des Tours de Babel." In *Difference in Translation*, edited by Joseph F. Graham, 165–207. Ithaca: Cornell University Press, 1985.

———. *Dissemination*. Translated with an introduction and additional notes by Barbara Johnson. Chicago: University of Chicago Press, 1981.

———. *Donner la mort*. Paris: Galilée, 1999.

———. *The Ear of the Other: Otiobiography, Transference, Translation*. Edited by Christie McDonald. Translated by Peggy Kamuf. Lincoln: University of Nebraska Press, 1998.

———. "Faith and Knowledge: The Two Sources of 'Religion' at the Limits of Reason Alone." In *Religion*, edited by Jacques Derrida and Gianni Vattimo, 1–78. Stanford: Stanford University, 1998.

———. *Geschlecht III: Sexe, race, nation, humanité*. Paris: Éditions du Seuil, 2018.

———. *The Gift of Death*. Translated by David Wills. Chicago: University of Chicago Press, 1995.

———. *Heidegger: la question de l'Être et l'Histoire: Cours de l'ENS-Ulm, 1964–1965*. Edited by Thomas Dutoit with the assistance of Marguerite Derrida. Paris: Galilée, 2013.

———. *Heidegger: The Question of Being and History*. Edited by Thomas Dutoit with the assistance of Marguerite Derrida. Translated by Geoffrey Bennington. Chicago: University of Chicago Press, 2016.

———. *Khôra*. Paris: Galilée, 1993.

———. *Marges de la philosophie*. Paris: Éditions de Minuit, 1972.

———. *Margins of Philosophy*. Translated by Alan Bass. Chicago: University of Chicago Press, 1982.

———. *Monolingualism of the Other; or, The Prosthesis of Origin*. Translated by Patrick Mensah. Stanford: Stanford University Press, 1998.

———. *Le monolinguisme de l'autre; ou la prothèse d'origine*. Paris: Galilée, 1996.

———. *Of Grammatology*. Translated by Gayatri Spivak, corrected ed. Baltimore: Johns Hopkins University Press, 1997.

———. *Of Spirit: Heidegger and the Question*. Translated by Geoffrey Bennington and Rachel Bowlby. Chicago: University of Chicago Press, 1989.

———. "On a Newly Arisen Apocalyptic Tone in Philosophy." In *Raising the Tone of Philosophy: Late Essays by Immanuel Kant, Transformative Critique by Jacques Derrida*, edited by Peter Fenves, 117–71. Baltimore: Johns Hopkins University Press, 1993.

———. "On Reading Heidegger: An Outline of Remarks to the Essex Colloquium." *Research in Phenomenology* 17 (1987): 171–85.

———. *On the Name*. Edited by Thomas Dutoit. Translated by David Wood, John P. Leavey Jr., and Ian McLeod. Stanford: Stanford University Press, 1995.

———. *Points . . . Interviews, 1974–1994*. Edited by Elisabeth Weber. Translated by Peggy Kamuf and Others. Stanford: Stanford University Press, 1995.

———. *Positions*. Translated and annotated by Alan Bass. Chicago: University of Chicago Press, 1981.

———. *Psyche: Inventions of the Other*. Vol. 2. Edited by Peggy Kamuf and Elizabeth Rottenberg. Stanford: Stanford University Press, 2008.

———. *Specters of Marx: The State of Debt, the Work of Mourning, and the New International*. Translated by Peggy Kamuf. Introduction by Bernd Magnus and Stephen Cullenberg. New York: Routledge, 1994.

———. *Speech and Phenomena and Other Essays on Husserl's Theory of Signs*. Translated with an introduction by David B. Allison. Preface by Newton Garver. Evanston: Northwestern University Press, 1973.

———. *Spurs/Nietzsche's Styles*. Translated by Barbara Harlow. Chicago: University of Chicago Press, 1978.

———. "A Testimony Given. . . ." In *Questioning Judaism: Interviews by Elisabeth Weber*. Translated by Rachel Bowlby, 39–58. Stanford: Stanford University Press, 2004. French version: "Un témoignage donné" in *Questions au judaïsme. Entretiens avec Elisabeth Weber*, 73–104. Paris: Desclée de Brouwer, 1996.

———. *The Truth in Painting*. Translated by Geoff Bennington and Ian McLeod. Chicago: University of Chicago Press, 1987.

———. *Writing and Difference*. Translated with an introduction and additional notes by Alan Bass. Chicago: University of Chicago Press, 1978.

Derrida, Jacques, and Maurizio Ferraris. *A Taste for the Secret*. Edited by Giacomo Donis and David Webb. Translated by Giacomo Donis. Cambridge: Polity, 2001.

Derrida, Jacques, Hans-Georg Gadamer, and Phillipe Lacoue-Labarthe. *Heidegger, Philosophy, and Politics: The Heidelberg Conference*. Edited by Mireille Calle-Gruber. Translated by Jeff Fort. Preface by Jean-Luc Nancy. New York: Fordham University Press, 2016.

Dhawan, Nikita. *Impossible Speech: On the Politics of Silence and Violence*. Sankt Augustin: Academia, 2007.

Di Cesare, Donatella. "Being and the Jew: Between Heidegger and Levinas." In *Heidegger and Jewish Thought: Difficult Others*, edited by Elad Lapidot and Micha Brumlik, 75–86. London: Rowman and Littlefield, 2018.

———. *Heidegger and the Jews: The Black Notebooks*. Translated by Murtha Baca. Cambridge: Polity Press, 2018.

———. *Heidegger e gli ebrei. I "Quaderni neri"*. Turin: Bollati Boringhieri, 2014.

———. "Heidegger's Metaphysical Anti-Semitism." In *Reading Heidegger's Black Notebooks 1931–1941*, edited by Ingo Farin and Jeff Malpas, 181–94. Cambridge, MA: MIT Press, 2016.

———. "Das Sein und der Jude: Heideggers metaphysischer Antisemitismus." In *Heidegger, die Juden, noch einmal*, edited by Peter Trawny and Andrew J. Mitchell, 55–74. Frankfurt am Main: Vittorio Klostermann, 2015.

Dickinson, Colby, and Silas Morgan. "Dwelling in Diaspora: Judith Butler's Post-secular Paradigm." *European Legacy: Toward New Paradigms* 20 (2015): 136–50.

Diéguez, Guadalupe González. "Isaac ibn Laṭif (1210–1280) between Philosophy and Kabbalah: Timeless and Timebound Wisdom." PhD diss., New York University, 2014.

Dillard, Peter S. *Non-Metaphysical Theology after Heidegger*. New York: Palgrave Macmillan, 2016.

Dillon, John. "Monotheism in the Gnostic Tradition." In *Pagan Monotheism in Late Antiquity*, edited by Polymnia Athanassiadi and Michael Frede, 69–79. Oxford: Oxford University Press, 1999.

Distaso, Leonardo V. *The Paradox of Existence: Philosophy and Aesthetics in the Young Schelling*. Dordrecht: Kluwer Academic, 2004.

Dolgopolski, Sergey. "How Else Can One Think Earth? The Talmuds and Pre-Socratics." In *Heidegger and Jewish Thought: Difficult Others*, edited by Elad Lapidot and Micha Brumlik, 221–44. London: Rowman and Littlefield, 2018.

———. *The Open Past: Subjectivity and Remembering in the Talmud*. New York: Fordham University Press, 2013.

Duff, Alexander S. *Heidegger and Politics: The Ontology of Radical Discontent*. Cambridge: Cambridge University Press, 2015.

Dunasky, Shimon, ed. *Midrash Rabbah: Shir ha-Shirim*. Jerusalem: Dvir, 1980.

Düttmann, Alexander García. "Without Soil: A Figure in Adorno's Thought." In *Language without Soil: Adorno and Late Philosophical Modernity*, edited by Gerhard Richter, 10–16. New York: Fordham University Press, 2010.

Dweck, Yaacob. *The Scandal of Kabbalah: Leon Modena, Jewish Mysticism, Early Modern Venice*. Princeton: Princeton University Press, 2011.

Dylan, Bob. *The Lyrics*. New York: Simon and Schuster, 2014.

Eckhart, Meister. *The Complete Mystical Works of Meister Eckhart*. Translated and edited by Maurice O'C. Walshe. Revised with a foreword by Bernard McGinn. New York: Herder and Herder, 2009.

———. *Die deutschen und lateinischen Werke*. Vol. 1. Edited by Josef Quint. Stuttgart: W. Kohlhammer, 1958.

———. *Die deutschen und lateinischen Werke*. Vol. 2. Edited by Josef Quint. Stuttgart: W. Kohlhammer, 1971.

Edel, Susanne. *Die individuelle Substanz bei Böhme und Leibniz: Die Kabbala als tertium comparationis für eine rezeptionsgeschichtliche Untersuchung*. Stuttgart: Franz Steiner, 1995.

———. "Kabbala in der Theosophie Jacob Böhmes und in der Metaphysik Leibnizens." In *Religion und Religiosität im Zeitalter des Barock*, edited by Dieter Breuer, 2:845–56. Wiesbaden: Harrassowitz, 1995.

———. "Métaphysique des idées et mystique des lettres: Leibniz, Böhme et la Kabbale prophétique." *Revue de l'Histoire des Religions* 213 (1996): 443–66.

Egginton, William. *The Philosopher's Desire: Psychoanalysis, Interpretation, and Truth*. Stanford: Stanford University Press, 2007.

Eibeschütz, Jonathan. *Tif'eret Yehonatan*. Yozifov, 1873.

Einfeld, Tzvi. *The Teaching of the Gra and the Doctrine of Ḥasidism: These and Those Are the Words of the Living God*. Jerusalem: Mosad ha-Rav Kook, 2010 (Hebrew).

El-Bizri, Nader. "Being and Necessity: A Phenomenological Investigation of Avicenna's Metaphysics and Cosmology." In *Islamic Philosophy and Occidental Phenomenology on the Perennial Issue of Microcosm and Macrocosm*, 243–61. Dordrecht: Springer, 2006.

Elden, Stuart. *Speaking against Number: Heidegger, Language and the Politics of Calculation*. Edinburgh: Edinburgh University Press, 2006.

Eliashiv, Solomon ben Ḥayyim. *Leshem Shevo we-Aḥlamah: Ḥaqdamot u-She'arim*. Jerusalem: Aaron Barzanai, 2006.

———. *Leshem Shevo we-Aḥlamah: Ḥeleq ha-Be'urim*. Jerusalem: Aaron Barzanai, 2011.

———. *Leshem Shevo we-Aḥlamah: Sefer ha-De'ah*. Jerusalem: Aaron Barzanai, 2005.

———. *Leshem Shevo we-Aḥlamah: Sefer ha-Kelalim*. Jerusalem: Aaron Barzanai, 2010.

Elijah ben Solomon. *The Commentary of the Gaon Rabbi Elijah of Vilna to Sifra di-Zeni'uta*. Edited by Bezalel Naor. Jerusalem, 1998 (Hebrew).

———. *Tiqqunei Zohar im Be'ur ha-Gra*. Vilnius: Shemaryahu Zuckerman, 1867.

Elliott, Brian. *Phenomenology and Imagination in Husserl and Heidegger*. London: Routledge, 2005.

Elqayam, Abraham. "The Mystery of Faith in the Writings of Nathan of Gaza." PhD diss., Hebrew University, 1993 (Hebrew).

———. "To Know Messiah—The Dialectics of Sexual Discourse in the Messianic Thought of Nathan of Gaza." *Tarbiz* 65 (1996): 637–70 (Hebrew).

Emmet, Dorothy. "The Ground of Being." *Journal of Theological Studies* 15 (1964): 280–92.

Engel, Amir. *Gershom Scholem: An Intellectual Biography*. Chicago: University of Chicago Press, 2017.

Epstein, Qalonymus Qalman. *Ma'or wa-Shemesh*. Jerusalem: Mir, 2005.

Ergas, Joseph. *Shomer Emunim*. Jerusalem: Ahavat Shalom, 2010.

Eriugena, John Scotus. *Periphyseon (De Divisione Naturae)*. 3 vols. Edited by I. P. Sheldon-Williams with the collaboration of Ludwig Bieler. Dublin: Dublin Institute for Advanced Studies, 1972–81.

Erlewine, Robert. *Judaism and the West: From Hermann Cohen to Joseph Soloveitchik*. Bloomington: Indiana University Press, 2016.

Esudri, Yossi. "Studies on the Philosophy of R. Isaac Ibn Latif: Profile, Knowledge and Prophecy, and a Critical Edition of *Zurat 'Olam*." PhD diss., Hebrew University, 2008 (Hebrew).

Ezrahi, Sidra DeKoven. *Booking Passage: Exile and Homecoming in the Modern Jewish Imagination*. Berkeley: University of California Press, 2000.

———. "Our Homeland, the Text . . . Our Text the Homeland: Exile and Homecoming in Modern Jewish Imagination." *Michigan Quarterly Review* 31 (1992): 463–97.

Fackenheim, Emil L. *Encounters between Judaism and Modern Philosophy: A Preface to Future Jewish Thought*. New York: Schocken, 1980.

———. *To Mend the World: Foundations of Post-Holocaust Jewish Thought*. New York: Schocken, 1989.

Fagenblat, Michael. "'Heidegger' and the Jews." In *Reading Heidegger's Black Notebooks 1931–1941*, edited by Ingo Farin and Jeff Malpas, 145–68. Cambridge, MA: MIT Press, 2016.

———. "Lévinas, Judaism, Heidegger." In *Judaism in Contemporary Thought: Traces and Influence*, edited by Agata Bielik-Robson and Adam Lipszyc, 51–63. London: Routledge, 2014.

———. "Of Dwelling Prophetically: On Heidegger and Jewish Political Theology." In *Heidegger and Jewish Thought: Difficult Others*, edited by Elad Lapidot and Micha Brumlik, 245–67. London: Rowman and Littlefield, 2018.

———. "The Thing That Scares Me Most: Heidegger's Anti-Semitism and the Return to Zion." *Journal for Cultural and Religious Theory* 14 (2014): 8–24.

Faivre, Antoine. *Access to Western Esotericism*. Albany: State University of New York Press, 1994.

Falque, Emmanuel. *The Metamorphosis of Finitude: An Essay on Birth and Resurrection*. Translated by George Hughes. New York: Fordham University Press, 2012.

Farber, Marvin. "Heidegger on the Essence of Truth." *Philosophy and Phenomenological Research* 18 (1958): 523–32.

Farber-Ginat, Asi. "'The Shell Precedes the Fruit'—On the Question of the Origin of Metaphysical Evil in Early Kabbalistic Thought." In *Myth and Judaism*, edited by Haviva Pedaya, 118–42. Jerusalem: Bialik Institute, 1996 (Hebrew).

Farennikova, Anna. "Seeing Absence." *Philosophical Studies* 166 (2012): 429–54.

Fay, Thomas A. *Heidegger: The Critique of Logic*. The Hague: Martinus Nijhoff, 1977.

Fehér, István M. "Heidegger's Understanding of the Atheism of Philosophy: Philosophy, Theology, and Religion in His Early Lecture Courses up to *Being and Time*." *American Catholic Philosophical Quarterly* 69 (1995): 189–228.

Feldman, Matthew. "Between *Geist* and *Zeitgeist*: Martin Heidegger as Ideologue of 'Metapolitical Fascism.'" *Politics, Religion, and Ideology* 6 (2005): 175–98.

Fell, Joseph P. "Heidegger's Notion of Two Beginnings." *Review of Metaphysics* 25 (1971): 213–37.

Fenves, Peter. "The Genesis of Judgment: Spatiality, Analogy, and Metaphor in Benjamin's 'On Language as Such and On Human Language.'" In *Walter Benjamin: Theoretical Questions*, edited by David S. Ferris, 75–93. Stanford: Stanford University Press, 1996.

———. *The Messianic Reduction: Walter Benjamin and the Shape of Time*. Stanford: Stanford University Press, 2011.

Ferber, Ilit. "Gershom Scholem on the Language of Lament." In *Lamentations: Poetry and Thought in Gershom Scholem's World*, edited by Galili Shahar and Ilit Ferber, 127–53. Jerusalem: Carmel, 2016 (Hebrew).

———. "'Incline Thine Ear unto Me, and Hear My Speech': Scholem, Benjamin, and Cohen on Lament." In *Lament in Jewish Thought: Philosophical, Theological, and Literary Perspectives*, edited by Ilit Ferber and Paula Schwebel, 111–30. Berlin: Walter de Gruyter, 2014.

———. "Lament and Pure Language: Scholem, Benjamin and Kant." *Jewish Studies Quarterly* 21 (2014): 42–54.

———. "A Language of the Border: On Scholem's Theory of Lament." *Journal of Jewish Thought and Philosophy* 21 (2013): 161–86.

Fichte, Johann Gottlieb. *Science of Knowledge with the First and Second Introductions*. Edited and translated by Peter Heath and John Lachs. Cambridge: Cambridge University Press, 1982.

Finkelstein, Louis. *Sifra on Leviticus according to Vatican Manuscript Assemani 66 with Variants from the Other Manuscripts, Genizah Fragments, Early Editions and Quotations by Medieval Authorities, and with References to Parallel Passages and Commentaries*, vols. 1–2. New York: Jewish Theological Seminary of America, 1983–89.

Fischheimer, Matanya. "'Anyone Who Looks at the Brass Serpent Shall Survive'—A New Inquiry into the Thought of Neḥemiah Ḥayon." *Kabbalah: Journal for the Study of Jewish Mystical Texts* 24 (2011): 241–61 (Hebrew).

Flatscher, Matthias. "Derridas *'coup de don'* und Heideggers *'Es gibt'*. Bemerkungen zur Un-Möglichkeit der Gabe." In *Kreuzungen Jacques Derridas Geistergespräche zwischen Philosophie und Theologie*, edited by Peter Zeillinger and Matthias Flatscher, 35–53. Vienna: Turia + Kant, 2004.

Fleischacker, Samuel, ed. *Heidegger's Jewish Followers: Essays on Hannah Arendt, Leo Strauss, Hans Jonas, and Emmanuel Levinas*. Pittsburgh: Duquesne University Press, 2008.

Forster, Michael N. *Hegel and Skepticism*. Cambridge, MA: Harvard University Press, 1989.

Foucault, Michel. *History of Madness*. Edited by Jean Khalfa. Translated by Jonathan Murphy and Jean Khalfa. London: Routledge, 2006.

Frangeskou, Adonis. *Levinas, Kant and the Problematic of Temporality*. New York: Palgrave Macmillan, 2017.

Franks, Paul W. *All or Nothing: Systematicity, Transcendental Arguments, and Skepticism in German Idealism*. Cambridge, MA: Harvard University Press, 2005.

———. "Fichte's Kabbalistic Realism: Summons as *Ẓimẓum*." In *Fichte's Foundations of Natural Right: A Critical Guide*, edited by Gabriel Gottlieb, 82–116. Cambridge: Cambridge University Press, 2016.

———. "Inner anti-Semitism or Kabbalistic Legacy? German Idealism's Relationship to Judaism." *International Yearbook of German Idealism* 7 (2010): 254–79.

———. "Jewish Philosophy after Kant: The Legacy of Salomon Maimon." In *The Cambridge Companion to Modern Jewish Philosophy*, edited by Michael L. Morgan and Peter E. Gordon, 53–79. Cambridge: Cambridge University Press, 2007.

———. "'Nothing Comes from Nothing': Judaism, the Orient, and Kabbalah in Hegel's Reception of Spinoza." In *Oxford Handbooks Online: The Oxford Handbook of Spinoza*, edited by Michael Della Rocca (2015): 1–22. http://www.oxfordhandbooks.com/view/10.1093/oxfordhb/9780195335828.001.0001/oxfordhb-9780195335828-e-24.

———. "Peirce's 'Schelling-Fashioned Idealism' and 'The Monstrous Mysticism of the East.'" *British Journal for the History of Philosophy* 23 (2015): 732–55.

———. "Rabbinic Idealism and Kabbalistic Realism: Jewish Dimensions of Idealism and Idealist Dimensions of Judaism." In *The Impact of Idealism: The Legacy of Post-Kantian German Thought*. Vol. 4: *Religion*, edited by Nicholas Boyle, Liz Disley, and Nicholas Adams, 219–45. Cambridge: Cambridge University Press, 2013.

Freeman, Kathleen. *Ancilla to the Pre-Socratic Philosophers*. Cambridge, MA: Harvard University Press, 1978.

Frey, Hans-Jost. *Interruptions*. Translated and with an introduction by Georgia Albert. Albany: State University of New York Press, 1996.

Friedman, Maurice. "Buber, Heschel, and Heidegger: Two Jewish Existentialists Confront a Great German Existentialist." *Journal of Humanistic Psychology* 51 (2011): 129–34.

Friedrich, Hans-Joachim. *Der Ungrund der Freiheit in Denken von Böhme, Schelling und Heidegger*. Stuttgart: Frommann-Holzboog, 2009.

Friesen, J. Glenn. "Sophia, Androgyny and the Feminine in Franz von Baader's Christian Theosophy." *Religions* 8 (2016): 130–45.

Froese, Katrin. *Nietzsche, Heidegger, and Daoist Thought*. Albany: State University of New York Press, 2006.

Funkenstein, Amos. *Perceptions of Jewish History*. Berkeley: University of California Press, 1993.

Gadamer, Hans-Georg. *Heidegger's Ways*. Translated by John W. Stanley. Albany: State University of New York Press, 1994.

———. *Truth and Method*. 2nd rev. ed. Translation revised by Joel Weinsheimer and Donald G. Marshall. New York: Continuum, 1989.

Gall, Robert S. *Beyond Theism and Atheism: Heidegger's Significance for Religious Thinking*. Dordrecht: Martinus Nijhoff, 1987.

Galli, Barbara E. *Franz Rosenzweig and Jehuda Halevi: Translating, Translations, and Translators*. Foreword by Paul Mendes-Flohr. Montreal: McGill-Queen's University Press, 1995.

———. "Introduction: Translating Is a Mode of Holiness." In *Cultural Writings of Franz Rosenzweig*, edited and translated by Barbara E. Galli, 3–57. Syracuse: Syracuse University Press, 2000.

Gamlieli, Dvorah Bat-David. *Psychoanalysis and Kabbalah: The Masculine and Feminine in Lurianic Kabbalah*. Los Angeles: Cherub, 2006 (Hebrew).

Garb, Jonathan. "The Authentic Kabbalistic Writings of R. Moses Hayyim Luzzatto." *Kabbalah: Journal for the Study of Jewish Mystical Texts* 25 (2011): 165–222 (Hebrew).

———. *Kabbalist in the Heart of the Storm: R. Moshe Hayyim Luzzatto*. Tel Aviv: Tel Aviv University Press, 2014 (Hebrew).

———. *Modern Kabbalah as an Autonomous Domain of Research*. Los Angeles: Cherub, 2016 (Hebrew).

———. "Powers of Language in Kabbalah: Comparative Reflections." In *The Poetics of Grammar and the Metaphysics of Sound and Sign*, edited by Sergio La Porta and David Shulman, 233–69. Leiden: Brill, 2007.

———. *Yearnings of the Soul: Psychological Thought in Modern Kabbalah*. Chicago: University of Chicago Press, 2015.

Gardt, Andreas. *Sprachreflexion in Barock und Frühaufklärung: Entwürfe von Böhme bis Leibniz*. Berlin: Walter de Gruyter, 1994.

Garfield, Jay L. *Engaging Buddhism: Why It Matters to Philosophy*. Oxford: Oxford University Press, 2015.

Gasché, Rodolphe. *Inventions of Difference: On Jacques Derrida*. Cambridge, MA: Harvard University Press, 1994.

———. *The Tain of the Mirror: Derrida and the Philosophy of Reflection*. Cambridge, MA: Harvard University Press, 1986.

Gelikman, Oleg. "The Crisis of the Messianic Claim: Scholem, Benjamin, Baudelaire." In *Messianic Thought Outside Theology*, edited by Anna Glazova and Paul North, 171–94. New York: Fordham University Press, 2014.

Gentzke, Joshua Levi Ian. "Imaginal Renaissance: Desire, Corporeality, & Rebirth in the Work of Jacob Böhme." PhD diss., Stanford University, 2016.

———. "Imagining the Image of God: Corporeal Envisioning in the Theosophy of Jacob Böhme." In *Lux in Tenebris: The Visual and the Symbolic in Western Esotericism*, edited by Peter J. Forshaw, 103–29. Leiden: Brill, 2017.

Geoghegan, Vincent. "Remembering the Future." In *Not Yet: Reconsidering Ernst Bloch*, edited by Jamie Owen Daniel and Tom Moylan, 15–32. London: Verso, 1997.

Gibbons, B. J. *Spirituality and the Occult: From the Renaissance to the Modern Age*. Abingdon: Routledge, 2001.

Gibbs, Robert. *Correlations in Rosenzweig and Levinas*. Princeton: Princeton University Press, 1992.

———. "Present Imperative: Ethics and Temporality." *Soundings: An Interdisciplinary Journal* 76 (1993): 163–72.

———. "Reading Heidegger: Destruction, Thinking, Return." In *Tainted Greatness: Antisemitism and Cultural Heroes*, edited by Nancy A. Harrowitz, 157–72. Philadelphia: Temple University Press, 1994.

Gikatilla, Joseph. *Sha'arei Orah*. 2 vols. Edited by Joseph Ben-Shlomo. Jerusalem: Bialik Institute, 1981.

———. *Sha'arei Ṣedeq*. Cracow: Fischer and Deutscher, 1881.

Giller, Pinchas. "Between Poland and Jerusalem: Kabbalistic Prayer in Early Modernity." *Modern Judaism* 24 (2004): 226–50.

———. *Shalom Shar'abi and the Kabbalists of Beit El*. Oxford: Oxford University Press, 2008.

Gishin. *The Collected Teachings of the Tendai Lotus School*. Translated by Paul L. Swanson. Berkeley: Numata Center for Buddhist Translation and Research, 1995.

Glatzer, Nahum N. *Franz Rosenzweig: His Life and Thought*. Philadelphia: Jewish Publication Society of America, 1953.

Glazer, Aubrey L. "From Thinking the Last God of Thought to the Poetic God without End: Between Heidegger's *das denkende Dichten* (thinking poetry) & Celan's *das Gedicht dem Anderen* (poetics of alterity)." *Religiologiques* 30 (2004): 13–44.

Goetschel, Roland. "'Ehyeh Asher Ehyeh' in the Works of the Gerona Kabbalists." *Jerusalem Studies in Jewish Thought* 6, nos. 3–4 (1987): 287–98 (Hebrew).

Goldish, Matt. *The Sabbatean Prophets*. Cambridge, MA: Harvard University Press, 2004.

Goldstein, Jeffrey. "Buber's Misunderstanding of Heidegger." *Philosophy Today* 22 (1978): 156–67.

Gonzalez, Francisco J. "And the Rest Is *Sigetik*: Silencing Logic and Dialectic in Heidegger's *Beiträge zur Philosophie*." *Research in Phenomenology* 38 (2008): 358–91.

———. *Plato and Heidegger: A Question of Dialogue*. University Park: Pennsylvania State University Press, 2009.

Goodman, Mark. "Give the Word: Levinas and Heidegger on Language." PhD diss., Boston College, 2000.

Goodman, Russell B. *Wittgenstein and William James*. Cambridge: Cambridge University Press, 2002.

Goodrick-Clarke, Nicholas. *The Occult Roots of Nazism: Secret Aryan Cults and Their Influence on Nazi Ideology*. London: Tauris Parke, 2004.

Gordon, Haim. *The Heidegger-Buber Controversy: The Status of the I-Thou*. Westport: Greenwood, 2001.

Gordon, Peter E. "Displaced: Phenomenology and Belonging in Levinas and Heidegger." In *Between Levinas and Heidegger*, edited by John E. Drabinski and Eric S. Nelson, 209–25. Albany: State University of New York Press, 2014.

———. "Franz Rosenzweig and the Philosophy of Jewish Existence." In *The Cambridge Companion to Modern Jewish Philosophy*, edited by Michael L. Morgan and Peter E. Gordon, 122–46. Cambridge: Cambridge University Press, 2007.

———. *Rosenzweig and Heidegger: Between Judaism and German Philosophy*. Berkeley: University of California Press, 2003.

Gosetti-Ferencei, Jennifer Anna. *The Ecstatic Quotidian: Phenomenological Sightings in Modern Art and Literature*. University Park: Pennsylvania State University Press, 2007.

———. *Heidegger, Hölderlin, and the Subject of Poetic Language: Towards a New Poetics of Dasein*. New York: Fordham University Press, 2004.

———. *The Life of Imagination: Revealing and Making the World*. New York: Columbia University Press, 2018.

Graf, Moshe ben Menaḥem. *Wayaqhel Moshe*. Jerusalem: Yerid ha-Sefarim, 2005.

Graham, Daniel W., trans. and ed. *The Texts of Early Greek Philosophy: The Complete Fragments and Selected Testimonies of the Major Presocratics* (Part I). Cambridge: Cambridge University Press, 2010.

Green, Sharon. "Lacan: *Nachträglichkeit*, Shame and Ethical Time." In *Temporality and Shame: Perspectives from Psychoanalysis and Philosophy*, edited by Ladson Hinton and Hessel Willemsen, 74–100. London: Routledge, 2018.

Grimstad, Kristen J. *The Modern Revival of Gnosticism and Thomas Mann's Doktor Faustus*. Rochester: Camden House, 2002.

Groiser, David. "Repetition and Renewal: Kierkegaard, Rosenzweig, and the German-Jewish Renaissance." In *Die Gegenwärtigkeit deutsch-jüdischen Denkens: Festschrift für Paul Mendes-Flohr*, edited by Julia Matveev and Ashraf Noor, 265–301. Munich: Wilhelm Funk, 2011.

Groth, Miles. *Translating Heidegger*. Amherst: Humanity Books, 2004.

———. *The Voice That Thinks: Heidegger Studies with Bibliography of English Translations, 1949–2015*. 2nd ed., rev. New York: ENI, 2016.

Gruenwald, Ithamar. "A Preliminary Critical Edition of *Sefer Yezira*." *Israel Oriental Studies* 1 (1971): 132–77.

Grugan, Arthur Anthony. "Thought and Poetry: Language as Man's Homecoming. A Study of Martin Heidegger's Question of Being and Its Ties to Friedrich Hölderlin's Experience of the Holy." PhD diss., Duquesne University, 1972.

Grunsky, Hans. *Jakob Böhme*. Stuttgart: Frommanns, 1956.

Gschwandtner, Christina M. *Postmodern Apologetics?Arguments for God in Contemporary Philosophy*. New York: Fordham University Press, 2013.

Guignon, Charles. "Being as Appearing: Retrieving the Greek Experience of *Phusis*." In *A Companion to Heidegger's Introduction of Metaphysics*, edited by Richard Polt and Gregory Fried, 34–56. New Haven: Yale University Press, 2001.

Habermas, Jürgen. "Dialectical Idealism in Transition to Materialism: Schelling's Idea of a Contraction of God and Its Consequences for the Philosophy of History." In *The New Schelling*, edited by Judith Norman and Alistair Welchman, 43–89. London: Continuum, 2004.

———. "Martin Heidegger: On the Publication of Lectures from the Year 1935." *Graduate Faculty Philosophy Journal* 6 (1977): 155–80.

———. *Philosophical-Political Profiles*. Translated by Frederick G. Lawrence. Cambridge, MA: MIT Press, 1983.

Hadad, Yemima. "Fruits of Forgetfulness: Politics and Nationalism in the Philosophies of Martin Buber and Martin Heidegger." In *Heidegger and Jewish Thought: Difficult Others*, edited by Elad Lapidot and Micha Brumlik, 201–20. London: Rowman and Littlefield, 2018.

Haddad, Gérard. "Judaism in the Life and Work of Jacques Lacan: A Preliminary Study." *Yale French Studies* 85 (1994): 201–16.

Hadot, Pierre. *The Veil of Isis: An Essay on the History of the Idea of Nature*. Translated by Michael Chase. Cambridge, MA: Harvard University Press, 2006.

Halfwassen, Jens. "Freiheit als Transzendenz bei Schelling und Plotin." In *Platonismus im Idealismus: Die platonische Tradition in der klasischen deutschen Philosophie*, edited by Burkhard Mojsisch and Orrin F. Summerell, 175–94. Munich: K. G. Saur, 2003.

Hallward, Peter. *Badiou: A Subject to Truth*. Foreword by Slavoj Žižek. Minneapolis: University of Minnesota Press, 2003.

Halperin, David J. *Sabbatai Zevi: Testimonies to a Fallen Messiah*. Oxford: Littman Library of Jewish Civilization, 2007.

Hamacher, Werner. "Messianic Not." In *Messianic Thought Outside Theology*, edited by Anna Glazova and Paul North, 221–34. New York: Fordham University Press, 2014.

———. *Minima Philologica*. Translated by Catharine Diehl and Jason Groves. New York: Fordham University Press, 2015.

———. "95 Theses on Philology." *Diacritics* 39 (2009): 25–44.

Hamrit, Jacqueline. "Nachträglichkeit." *PsyArt: An Online Journal for the Psychological Study of the Arts* (2008).

Handelman, Susan A. *Fragments of Redemption: Jewish Thought and Literary Theory in Benjamin, Scholem, and Levinas*. Bloomington: Indiana University Press, 1991.

Hanly, Peter. "Dark Celebration: Heidegger's Silent Music." In *Heidegger and Language*, edited by Jeffrey Powell, 240–64. Bloomington: Indiana University Press, 2013.

Hannak, Kristine. "Boehme and German Romanticism." In *An Introduction to Jacob Boehme: Four Centuries of Thought and Reception*, edited by Ariel Hessayon and Sarah Apetrei, 162–79. New York: Routledge, 2014.

Harman, Graham. "Badiou's Relation to Heidegger in *Theory of the Subject*." In *Badiou and Philosophy*, edited by Sean Bowden and Simon Duffy, 225–43. Edinburgh: Edinburgh University Press, 2012.

———. *The Quadruple Object*. Winchester: Zero, 2011.

Har-Shefi, Avishar. *The Myth of the Edomite Kings in Zoharic Literature: Creation and Revelation in the Idrot Texts of the Zohar*. Los Angeles: Cherub, 2014 (Hebrew).

Hart, David Bentley. *The Hidden and the Manifest: Essays in Theology and Metaphysics*. Grand Rapids: William B. Eerdmans, 2017.

Hart, Ray L. *God Being Nothing: Toward a Theogony*. Chicago: University of Chicago Press, 2016.

———. *Unfinished Man and the Imagination: Toward an Ontology and a Rhetoric of Revelation*. New York: Herder and Herder, 1968.

Hartig, Willfred. *Die Lehre des Buddha und Heidegger: Beiträge zum Ost-West Dialog des Denkens im 20. Jahrhundert*. Konstanz: Universität Konstanz, 1997.

Harvey, Irene E. *Derrida and the Economy of Différance*. Bloomington: Indiana University Press, 1986.

Haskell, Ellen D. *Mystical Resistance: Uncovering the Zohar's Conversations with Christianity*. New York: Oxford University Press, 2016.

Hass, Andrew. "The Ambiguity of Being." In *Heidegger in the Twenty-First Century*, edited by Tziovanis Georgakis and Paul J. Ennis, 9–22. Dordrecht: Springer, 2015.

Häussermann, Friedrich. "Theologia Emblematica: Kabbalistische und alchemistische Symbolik bei F. Chr. Oetinger und deren Analogien bei Jakob Böhme." *Blätter für Württembergische Kirchengeschichte* (1968–69): 207–346.

Hayman, A. Peter. *Sefer Yeṣira: Edition, Translation, and Text-Critical Commentary*. Tübingen: Mohr Siebeck, 2004.

Ḥayyim de la Rosa. *Torat Ḥakham*. Thessaloníki: Daniel Faraggi, 1848.

Hecker, Helmuth. "Eine buddhistische Würdigung Heideggers." In Willfred Hartig, *Die Lehre des Buddha und Heidegger: Beiträge zum Ost-West Dialog des Denkens im 20. Jahrhundert*, 204–90. Konstanz: Universität Konstanz, 1997.

Hedley, Douglas. "Schelling and Heidegger: The Mystical Legacy and Romantic Affinities." In *Heidegger, German Idealism, and Neo-Kantianism*, edited by Tom Rockmore, 141–55. Amherst: Humanity Books, 2000.

Hegel, Georg Wilhelm Friedrich. *Encyclopedia of the Philosophical Sciences in Basic Outline, Part I: Science of Logic*. Translated and edited by Klaus Brinkman and Daniel O. Dahlstrom. Cambridge: Cambridge University Press, 2010.

———. *Enzyklopädie der philosophischen Wissenschaften im Grundrisse 1830. Erster Teil. Die Wissenschaft der Logik. Mit den mündlichen Zusätzen* [Werke 8]. Frankfurt am Main: Suhrkamp, 1986.

———. *Faith and Knowledge*. Translated by Walter Cerf and Henry S. Harris. Albany: State University of New York Press, 1977.

———. *Lectures on the History of Philosophy*. 3 vols. Translated by Elizabeth S. Haldane and Frances H. Simson. New York: Humanities, 1974.

———. *Lectures on the Philosophy of Religion*. 3 vols. Edited by Peter C. Hodgson. Translated by R. F. Brown, P. C. Hodgson, and J. M. Stewart. Berkeley: University of California Press, 1984–87.

———. *Phänomenologie des Geistes* [Hauptwerke 2]. Hamburg: Felix Meiner, 2015.

———. *Phenomenology of Spirit*. Translated by A. V. Miller. Analysis and foreword by J. N. Findlay. Oxford: Oxford University Press, 1977.

———. *Philosophy of Mind*. Translated by W. Wallace and A. V. Miller. Revised with introduction and commentary by Michael Inwood. Oxford: Oxford University Press, 2007.

———. *The Science of Logic*. Translated and edited by George di Giovanni. Cambridge: Cambridge University Press, 2010.

———. *Vorlesungen über die Geschichte der Philosophie III*. Frankfurt am Main: Suhrkamp, 1986.

———. *Wissenschaft der Logik*. Vol. 1: *Die objective Logik*. Bk. 1, *Die Lehre vom Sein (1832)*. [Hauptwerke 3]. Hamburg: Felix Meiner, 2015.

———. *Wissenschaft der Logik*. Vol. 1: *Die objective Logik*. Bk. 2, *Die Lehre vom Wesen (1813)* [Hauptwerke 3]. Hamburg: Felix Meiner, 2015.

Heidegger, Martin. *Der Anfang der Abendländischen Philosophie: Auslegung des Anaximander und Parmenides* [GA 35]. Frankfurt am Main: Vittorio Klostermann, 2012.

———. *Anmerkungen I–V (Schwarze Hefte 1942–1948)* [GA 97]. Frankfurt am Main: Vittorio Klostermann, 2015.

———. *Aufenthalte*. Frankfurt am Main: Vittorio Klostermann, 1989.

———. *Aus der Erfahrung des Denkens 1910–1976* [GA 13]. Frankfurt am Main: Vittorio Klostermann, 2002.

———. *Basic Concepts*. Translated by Gary E. Aylesworth. Bloomington: Indiana University Press, 1993.

———. *The Basic Problems of Phenomenology*. Translated with introduction and lexicon by Albert Hofstadter. Bloomington: Indiana University Press, 1982.

———. *Basic Questions of Philosophy: Selected "Problems" of "Logic."* Translated by Richard Rojcewicz and André Schuwer. Bloomington: Indiana University Press, 1994.

———. *Basic Writings*. Rev. and exp. ed. Edited by David Farrell Krell. Foreword by Taylor Carman. London: Harper Perennial, 2008.

———. *The Beginning of Western Philosophy: Interpretation of Anaximander and Parmenides*. Translated by Richard Rojcewicz. Bloomington: Indiana University Press, 2015.

———. *Being and Time*. Translated by Joan Stambaugh. Revised and with a foreword by Dennis J. Schmidt. Albany: State University of New York Press, 2010.

———. *Beiträge zur Philosophie (vom Ereignis)* [GA 65]. Frankfurt am Main: Vittorio Klostermann, 1989.
———. *Besinnung* [GA 66]. Frankfurt am Main: Vittorio Klostermann, 1997.
———. *Bremen and Freiburg Lectures: Insight into That Which Is and Basic Principles of Thinking*. Translated by Andrew J. Mitchell. Bloomington: Indiana University Press, 2012.
———. *Bremer und Freiburger Vorträge* [GA 79]. Frankfurt am Main: Vittorio Klostermann, 1994.
———. *The Concept of Time*. Translated by Ingo Farin with Alex Skinner. London: Continuum, 2011.
———. *The Concept of Time*. Translated by William McNeill. Oxford: Blackwell, 1992.
———. "The Concept of Time in the Science of History." Translated by Harry S. Taylor and Hans W. Uffelmann. *Journal of the British Society for Phenomenology* 9 (1978): 3–10.
———. *Contributions to Philosophy (From Enowning)*. Translated by Parvis Emad and Kenneth Maly. Bloomington: Indiana University Press, 1999.
———. *Contributions to Philosophy (Of the Event)*. Translated by Richard Rojcewicz and Daniela Vallega-Neu. Bloomington: Indiana University Press, 2012.
———. *Country Path Conversations*. Translated by Bret W. Davis. Bloomington: Indiana University Press, 2010.
———. *Discourse on Thinking*. Translated by John M. Anderson and E. Hans Freund, with an introduction by John M. Anderson. New York: Harper and Row, 1966.
———. *Early Greek Thinking*. Translated by David Farrell Krell and Frank A. Capuzzi. New York: Harper and Row, 1975.
———. *Einführung in die Metaphysik* [GA 40]. Frankfurt am Main: Vittorio Klostermann, 1983.
———. *Einleitung in die Philosophie: Denken und Dichten* [GA 50]. Frankfurt am Main: Vittorio Klostermann, 1990.
———. *Elucidations of Hölderlin's Poetry*. Translated by Keith Hoeller. Amherst: Humanity Books, 2000.
———. *The End of Philosophy*. Translated and with an introduction by Joan Stambaugh. Chicago: University of Chicago Press, 2003.
———. *Erläuterungen zu Hölderlins Dichtung* [GA 4]. Frankfurt am Main: Vittorio Klostermann, 1996.
———. *The Essence of Human Freedom: An Introduction to Philosophy*. Translated by Ted Sadler. London: Continuum, 2002.
———. *The Essence of Truth: On Plato's Cave Allegory and Theaetetus*. Translated by Ted Sadler. New York: Continuum, 2002.
———. *Feldweg-Gespräche* [GA 77]. Frankfurt am Main: Vittorio Klostermann, 1995.
———. *Four Seminars: Le Thor 1966, 1968, 1969, Zähringen 1973*. Translated by Andrew Mitchell and François Raffoul. Bloomington: Indiana University Press, 2003.
———. *Die Frage nach dem Ding: Zu Kants Lehre von den Transzendentalen Grundsätzen* [GA 41]. Frankfurt am Main: Vittorio Klostermann, 1984.
———. *Frühe Schriften* [GA 1]. Frankfurt am Main: Vittorio Klostermann, 1978.
———. *The Fundamental Concepts of Metaphysics: World, Finitude, Solitude*. Translated by William McNeill and Nicholas Walker. Bloomington: Indiana University Press, 1995.
———. *Gelassenheit*. Stuttgart: Neske, 1959.
———. *Die Geschichte des Seyns* [GA 69]. Frankfurt am Main: Vittorio Klostermann, 1998.
———. *Grundbegriffe* [GA 51]. Frankfurt am Main: Vittorio Klostermann, 1981.
———. *Die Grundbegriffe der Metaphysik: Welt—Endlichkeit—Einsamkeit* [GA 29/30]. Frankfurt am Main: Vittorio Klostermann, 1983.
———. *Grundfragen der Philosophie: Ausgewählte "Probleme" der "Logik"* [GA 45]. Frankfurt am Main: Vittorio Klostermann, 1992.
———. *Die Grundprobleme der Phänomenologie* [GA 24]. Frankfurt am Main: Vittorio Klostermann, 1997.
———. "Hebel—Friend of the House." Translated by Bruce V. Foltz and Michael Heim. *Contemporary German Philosophy* 3 (1983): 89–101.
———. *Hegel* [GA 68]. Frankfurt am Main: Vittorio Klostermann, 2009.
———. *Hegel*. Translated by Joseph Arel and Niels Feuerhahn. Bloomington: Indiana University Press, 2015.
———. "Heidegger and Schmitt: The Bottom Line." *Telos* 72 (1987): 132.
———. *Heraclitus: The Inception of Occidental Thinking and Logic: Heraclitus's Doctrine of the Logos*. Translated by Julia Goesser Assaiante and S. Montgomery Ewegen. London: Bloomsbury Academic, 2018.
———. *Heraklit. 1. Der Anfang des Abendländischen Denkens. 2. Logik. Heraklits Lehre vom Logos* [GA 55]. Frankfurt am Main: Vittorio Klostermann, 1979.
———. *The History of Beyng*. Translated by William McNeill and Jeffrey Powell. Bloomington: Indiana University Press, 2015.
———. *History of the Concept of Time: Prolegomena*. Translated by Theodore Kisiel. Bloomington: Indiana University Press, 1985.

———. *Hölderlin's Hymn "Remembrance."* Translated by William McNeill and Julia Ireland. Bloomington: Indiana University Press, 2018.

———. *Hölderlin's Hymn "The Ister."* Translated by William McNeill and Julia Davis. Bloomington: Indiana University Press, 1996.

———. *Hölderlin's Hymns "Germania" and "The Rhine."* Translated by William McNeill and Julia Ireland. Bloomington: Indiana University Press, 2014.

———. *Hölderlins Hymne "Andenken"* [GA 52]. Frankfurt am Main: Vittorio Klostermann, 1992.

———. *Hölderlins Hymne "Der Ister"* [GA 53]. Frankfurt am Main: Vittorio Klostermann, 1993.

———. *Hölderlins Hymnen "Germanien" und "Der Rhein"* [GA 39]. Frankfurt am Main: Vittorio Klostermann, 1999.

———. *Holzwege* [GA 5]. Frankfurt am Main: Vittorio Klostermann, 1977.

———. "Homeland." Translated by Thomas F. O'Meara. *Listening* 6 (1971): 231–38.

———. *Identity and Difference.* Translated and with an introduction by Joan Stambaugh. New York: Harper and Row, 1969.

———. *Introduction to Metaphysics.* Translated by Gregory Fried and Richard Polt. New Haven: Yale University Press, 2000.

———. *Introduction to Philosophy—Thinking and Poetizing.* Translated by Phillip Jacques Braunstein. Bloomington: Indiana University Press, 2011.

———. *Kant and the Problem of Metaphysics.* Fourth ed. Translated by Richard Taft. Bloomington: Indiana University Press, 1990.

———. *Kant und das Problem der Metaphysik* [GA 3]. Frankfurt am Main: Vittorio Klostermann, 1998.

———. *Logic: The Question of Truth.* Translated by Thomas Sheehan. Bloomington: Indiana University Press, 2010.

———. *Logic as the Question Concerning the Essence of Language.* Translated by Wanda Torres Gregory and Yvonne Unna. Albany: State University of New York Press, 2009.

———. *Logik: Die Frage nach der Wahrheit* [GA 21]. Frankfurt am Main: Vittorio Klostermann, 1976.

———. *Logik als die Frage nach dem Wesen der Sprache* [GA 38]. Frankfurt am Main: Vittorio Klostermann, 1998.

———. "Logos." Translated by Jacques Lacan. *Psychanalyse* 1 (1956): 59–79.

———. "Messkirch's Seventh Centennial." Translated by Thomas J. Sheehan. *Listening* 8 (1973): 40–57.

———. *The Metaphysical Foundations of Logic.* Translated by Michael Heim. Bloomington: Indiana University Press, 1984.

———. *Die Metaphysik des deutschen Idealismus* [GA 49]. Frankfurt am Main: Vittorio Klostermann, 1991.

———. *Metaphysische Anfangsgründe der Logik im Ausgang von Leibniz* [GA 26]. Frankfurt am Main: Vittorio Klostermann, 1978.

———. *Mindfulness.* Translated by Parvis Emad and Thomas Kalary. London: Continuum, 2006.

———. *Nature, History, State 1933–1934.* Translated and edited by Gregory Fried and Richard Polt. London: Bloomsbury, 2013.

———. *Nietzsche.* Vol. 1: *The Will to Power as Art.* Translated by David Farrell Krell. New York: Harper and Row, 1979.

———. *Nietzsche.* Vol. 4: *Nihilism.* Translated by Frank A. Capuzzi. Edited by David Farrell Krell. New York: Harper and Row, 1982.

———. *Nietzsche: Erster Band* [GA 6.1]. Frankfurt am Main: Vittorio Klostermann, 1996.

———. *Nietzsche: Zweiter Band* [GA 6.2]. Frankfurt am Main: Vittorio Klostermann, 1997.

———. *Off the Beaten Track.* Edited and translated by Julian Young and Kenneth Haynes. Cambridge: Cambridge University Press, 2002.

———. "Only a God Can Save Us." Translated by William Richardson. In *Heidegger: The Man and the Thinker.* Edited by Thomas Sheehan, 45–67. Chicago: Precedent, 1981.

———. *On the Essence of Language: The Metaphysics of Language and the Essencing of the Word, Concerning Herder's Treatise On the Origin of Language.* Translated by Wanda Torres Gregory and Yvonne Unna. Albany: State University of New York Press, 2004.

———. *On the Way to Language.* Translated by Peter D. Hertz. New York: Harper and Row, 1971.

———. *On Time and Being.* Translated by Joan Stambaugh. New York: Harper and Row, 1972.

———. *Parmenides* [GA 54]. Frankfurt am Main: Vittorio Klostermann, 1992.

———. *Parmenides.* Translated by André Schuwer and Richard Rojcewicz. Bloomington: Indiana University Press, 1992.

———. *Pathmarks.* Edited by William McNeill. Cambridge: Cambridge University Press, 1998.

———. *Phänomenologie des religiösen Lebens* [GA 60].Frankfurt am Main: Vittorio Klostermann, 1995.

———. *Phänomenologische Interpretation von Kants Kritik der reinen Vernunft* [GA 25]. Frankfurt am Main: Vittorio Klostermann, 1995.

———. *Phänomenologische Interpretationen zu Aristoteles: Einführung in die Phänomenologische Forschung* [GA 61]. Frankfurt am Main: Vittorio Klostermann, 1994.

———. *Phenomenological Interpretation of Kant's Critique of Pure Reason*. Translated by Parvis Emad and Kenneth Maly. Bloomington: Indiana University Press, 1997.

———. *Phenomenological Interpretations of Aristotle: Initiation into Phenomenological Research*. Translated by Richard Rojcewicz. Bloomington: Indiana University Press, 2001.

———. *The Phenomenology of Religious Life*. Translated by Matthias Fritsch and Jennifer Anna Gosetti-Ferencei. Bloomington: Indiana University Press, 2004.

———. *Philosophical and Political Writings*. Edited by Manfred Stassen. New York: Continuum, 2003.

———. *The Piety of Thinking: Essays by Martin Heidegger*. Translated by James G. Hart and John C. Maraldo. Bloomington: Indiana University Press, 1977.

———. *Poetry, Language, Thought*. Translated by Albert Hofstadter. New York: Harper and Row, 1971.

———. *Ponderings II–VI: Black Notebooks 1931–1938*. Translated by Richard Rojcewicz. Bloomington: Indiana University Press, 2016.

———. *Ponderings VII–XI: Black Notebooks 1938–1939*. Translated by Richard Rojcewicz. Bloomington: Indiana University Press, 2017.

———. *Ponderings XII–XV: Black Notebooks 1939–1941*. Translated by Richard Rojcewicz. Bloomington: Indiana University Press, 2017.

———. "Poverty." Translated by Thomas Kalary and Frank Schalow. In *Heidegger, Translation, and the Task of Thinking: Essays in Honor of Parvis Emad*, edited by Frank Schalow, 3–10. Dordrecht: Springer, 2011.

———. *The Principle of Reason*. Translated by Reginald Lilly. Bloomington: Indiana University Press, 1991.

———. *Prolegomena zur Geschichte des Zeitbegriffs* [GA 20]. Frankfurt am Main: Vittorio Klostermann, 1979.

———. *The Question Concerning Technology and Other Essays*. Translated by William Lovitt. New York: Harper and Row, 1977.

———. *Reden und Andere Zeugnisse eines Lebensweges 1910–1976* [GA 16]. Frankfurt am Main: Vittorio Klostermann, 2000.

———. *Der Satz vom Grund* [GA 10]. Frankfurt am Main: Vittorio Klostermann, 1997.

———. *Schelling: Vom Wesen der menschlichen Freiheit (1809)* [GA 42]. Frankfurt am Main: Vittorio Klostermann, 1988.

———. *Schelling's Treatise on the Essence of Human Freedom*. Translated by Joan Stambaugh. Athens: Ohio University Press, 1985.

———. *Sein und Wahrheit* [GA 36/37]. Frankfurt am Main: Vittorio Klostermann, 2001.

———. *Sein und Zeit*. Tübingen: Max Niemeyer, 1993.

———. *Sein und Zeit* [GA 2]. Frankfurt am Main: Vittorio Klostermann, 1977.

———. *Die Selbstbehauptung der Deutschen Universität: Rede, gehalten bei der feierlichen Übernahme des Rektorats der Universität Freiburg i. Br. am 27.5.1933; Das Rektorat 1933/34: Tatsachen und Gedanken*. Frankfurt am Main: Vittorio Klostermann, 1983.

———. "The Self-Assertion of the German University: Address, Delivered on the Solemn Assumption of the Rectorate of the University Freiburg; The Rectorate 1933/34: Facts and Thoughts." Translated with an introduction by Karsten Harries. *Review of Metaphysics* 38 (1985): 467–502.

———. *Seminare* [GA 15]. Frankfurt am Main: Vittorio Klostermann, 2005.

———. *Sojourns: The Journey to Greece*. Translated by John Panteleimon Manoussakis. Foreword by John Sallis. Albany: State University of New York Press, 2005.

———. *Die Technik und die Kehre*. Pfullingen: Neske, 1962.

———. *Towards the Definition of Philosophy*. Translated by Ted Sadler. London: Athlone, 2000.

———. *Über den Anfang* [GA 70]. Frankfurt am Main: Vittorio Klostermann, 2005.

———. *Überlegungen II–VI (Schwarze Hefte 1931–1938)* [GA 94]. Frankfurt am Main: Vittorio Klostermann, 2014.

———. *Überlegungen VII–XI (Schwarze Hefte 1938/39)* [GA 95]. Frankfurt am Main: Vittorio Klostermann, 2014.

———. *Überlegungen XII–XV (Schwarze Hefte 1939–1941)* [GA 96]. Frankfurt am Main: Vittorio Klostermann, 2014.

———. *Unterwegs zur Sprache* [GA 12]. Frankfurt am Main: Vittorio Klostermann, 1985.

———. *Vier Hefte I und II (Schwarze Hefte 1947–1950)* [GA 99]. Frankfurt am Main: Vittorio Klostermann, 2019.

———. "Vom Ursprung des Kunstwerks: Erste Ausarbeitung." *Heidegger Studies* 5 (1989): 5–33.

———. *Vom Wesen der menschlichen Freiheit: Einleitung in die Philosophie* [GA 31]. Frankfurt am Main: Vittorio Klostermann, 1994.

———. *Vom Wesen der Sprache: Die Metaphysik der Sprache und Die Wesung des Wortes, Zu Herders Abhandlung "Über den Ursprung der Sprache"* [GA 85]. Frankfurt am Main: Vittorio Klostermann, 1999.

———. *Vom Wesen der Wahrheit: Zu Platons Höhlengleichnis und Theätet* [GA 34]. Frankfurt am Main: Vittorio Klostermann, 1988.

———. *Vorträge und Aufsätze* [GA 7]. Frankfurt am Main: Vittorio Klostermann, 2000.

———. *Was Heißt Denken?* [GA 8]. Frankfurt am Main: Vittorio Klostermann, 2002.

———. *Wegmarken* [GA 9]. Frankfurt am Main: Vittorio Klostermann, 1996.

———. *What Is a Thing?* Translated by W. B. Barton Jr. and Vera Deutsch. Chicago: Henry Regnery, 1967.

———. *What Is Called Thinking?* Translated by Fred W. Wieck and J. Glenn Gray. Introduction by J. Glenn Gray. New York: Harper and Row, 1968.

———. "Der Zeitbegriff in der Geschichtswissenschaft." *Zeitschrift für Philosophie und philosophische Kritik* 161 (1916): 173–88.

———. *Zollikon Seminars: Protocols—Conversations—Letters*. Edited by Medard Boss. Translated from the German and with notes and afterwords by Franz Mayr and Richard Askay. Evanston: Northwestern University Press, 2001.

———. *Zollikoner Seminare* [GA 89]. Frankfurt: Vittorio Klostermann, 2018.

———. *Zollikoner Seminare: Protokolle—Zwiegespräche—Briefe*. Edited by Medard Boss. Frankfurt am Main: Vittorio Klostermann, 2006.

———. *Zu Hölderlin: Griechenlandreisen* [GA 75]. Frankfurt am Main: Vittorio Klostermann, 2000.

———. "Zum Einblick in die Notwendigkeit der Kehre." In *Vom Rätsel des Begriffs: Festschrift für Friedrich-Wilhelm von Hermann zum 65. Geburtstag*, edited by Paola-Ludovika Coriando, 1–3. Berlin: Duncker und Humblot, 1999.

———. *Zum Ereignis-Denken* [GA 73.1]. Frankfurt am Main: Vittorio Klostermann, 2013.

———. *Zum Ereignis-Denken* [GA 73.2]. Frankfurt am Main: Vittorio Klostermann, 2013.

———. *Zum Wesen der Sprache und Zur Frage nach der Kunst* [GA 74]. Frankfurt am Main: Vittorio Klostermann, 2010.

———. *Zur Bestimmung der Philosophie* [GA 56/57]. Frankfurt am Main: Vittorio Klostermann, 1987.

———. *Zur Sache des Denkens* [GA 14]. Frankfurt am Main: Vittorio Klostermann, 2007.

Heidegger, Martin, and Eugen Fink. *Heraclitus Seminar 1966/67*. Translated by Charles H. Seibert. Tuscaloosa: University of Alabama Press, 1979.

Heim, Michael. "Heidegger and Computers." In *The Question of Hermeneutics: Essays in Honor of Joseph J. Kockelmans*, edited by Timothy J. Stapleton, 397–423. Dordrecht: Kluwer Academic, 1994.

Heinekamp, Albert. "Leibniz und die Mystik." In *Gnosis und Mystik in der Geschichte der Philosophie*, edited by Peter Koslowski, 183–206. Zürich: Artemis, 1988.

Heisig, James W. *Philosophers of Nothingness: An Essay on the Kyoto School*. Honolulu: University of Hawaii Press, 2001.

Held, Shai. *Abraham Joshua Heschel: The Call of Transcendence*. Bloomington: Indiana University Press, 2013.

Heller-Roazen, Daniel. *No One's Ways: An Essay on Infinite Naming*. New York: Zone Books, 2017.

Hellmers, Ryan S. "Reading in *Ereignis*: Schelling's System of Freedom and the *Beiträge*." *Epoché* 13 (2008): 133–62.

Hellner-Eshed, Melila. *Seekers of the Face: The Secrets of the Idra Rabba (The Great Assembly) of the Zohar*. Rishon LeZion: Yedioth Ahronoth, 2017 (Hebrew).

Helting, Holger. *Heidegger und Meister Eckehart: Vorbereitende Überlegungen zu ihrem Gottesdenken*. Berlin: Duncker and Humblot, 1997.

Ḥemdat ha-Yamim al Shabbat Qodesh. Jerusalem: Yerid Sefarim, 2003.

Hemming, Laurence Paul. *Heidegger and Marx: A Productive Dialogue over the Language of Humanism*. Evanston: Northwestern University Press, 2013.

———. *Heidegger's Atheism: The Refusal of a Theological Voice*. Notre Dame: University of Notre Dame Press, 2002.

Hermann, Klaus. "Gershom Scholems Weg zur Kabbala." In *Gershom Scholem in Deutschland: Zwischen Seelenverwandtschaft und Sprachlosigkeit*, edited by Gerold Necker, Elke Morlok, and Matthias Morgenstern, 37–71. Tübingen: Mohr Siebeck, 2014.

Herskowitz, Daniel. "God, Being, Pathos: Abraham Joshua Heschel's Theological Rejoinder to Heidegger." *Journal of Jewish Thought and Philosophy* 26 (2018): 94–117.

———. "Heidegger as a Secularized Kierkegaard: Martin Buber and Hugo Bergmann Read *Sein und Zeit*." In *Heidegger and Jewish Thought: Difficult Others*, edited by Elad Lapidot and

Micha Brumlik, 155–74. London: Rowman and Littlefield, 2018.

———. "Heidegger in Hebrew: Translation, Politics, Reconciliation." *New German Critique* 45 (2018): 97–128.

———. "The Moment and the Future: Kierkegaard's Øieblikket and Soloveitchik's View of Repentance." *Association for Jewish Studies Review* 40 (2016): 87–99.

———. "Rabbi Joseph B. Soloveitchik's Endorsement and Critique of Volkish Thought." *Journal of Modern Jewish Studies* 14 (2015): 373–90.

Herzog, Annabel. "'Monolingualism' or the Language of God: Scholem and Derrida on Hebrew and Politics." *Modern Judaism* 29 (2009): 226–38.

Hessayon, Ariel. "Boehme's Life and Times." In *An Introduction to Jacob Boehme: Four Centuries of Thought and Reception*, edited by Ariel Hessayon and Sarah Apetrei, 13–37. New York: Routledge, 2014.

Hewson, Mark. "Heidegger." In *Alain Badiou: Key Concepts*, edited by Adam J. Bartlett and Justin Clemens, 146–54. Durham: Acumen, 2010.

Higgins, Paul Murphy. "Speaking and Thinking about God in Rosenzweig and Heidegger." PhD diss., Catholic University of America, 2013.

Hippolytus. *Refutation of All Heresies*. Translated with an introduction and notes by M. David Litwa. Atlanta: Society of Biblical Literature, 2016.

Hoffmann, Gisbert. *Heideggers Phänomenologie: Bewusstsein—Reflexion—Selbst (Ich) und Zeit in Frühwerk*. Würzburg: Königshausen and Neumann, 2005.

Holte, Stine. *Meaning and Melancholy in the Thought of Emmanuel Levinas*. Göttingen: Vandenhoeck and Ruprecht, 2015.

Hopkins, Jasper. *Nicholas of Cusa on God as Not-Other: A Translation and an Appraisal of De Li Non Aliud*. Minneapolis: University of Minnesota Press, 1979.

———. *Nicholas of Cusa's Dialectical Mysticism: Text, Translation, and Interpretive Study of De Visione Dei*. Minneapolis: Arthur J. Banning, 1985.

———. *On Learned Ignorance: A Translation and an Appraisal of De Docta Ignorantia*. Minneapolis: Arthur J. Banning, 1990.

Horowitz, Isaiah. *Shenei Luḥot ha-Berit ha-Shalem*. 5 vols. Jerusalem: Oz we-Hadar, 1993.

Horowitz, Pinḥas Eliyahu. *Sefer ha-Berit ha-Shalem*. Jerusalem: S. Krauss, 1990.

Hösle, Vittorio. "Hans Jonas's Position in the History of German Philosophy." In *The Legacy of Hans Jonas: Judaism and the Phenomenon of Life*, edited by Hava Tirosh-Samuelson and Christian Wiese, 19–37. Leiden: Brill, 2008.

Howells, Christina. *Derrida: Deconstruction from Phenomenology to Ethics*. Cambridge: Polity, 1999.

Hsiao, Paul Shih-yi. "Heidegger and Our Translation of the Tao Te Ching." In *Heidegger and Asian Thought*, edited by Graham Parkes, 93–103. Honolulu: University of Hawaii Press, 1987.

Huber, Wolfgang. "Die Kabbala als Quelle zur Anthropologie Jakob Böhmes." *Kairos* 13 (1971): 131–50.

Hudson, Nancy J. *Becoming God: The Doctrine of Theosis in Nicholas of Cusa*. Washington, DC: Catholic University Press, 2007.

Hume, David. *Dialogues Concerning Natural Religion and Other Writings*. Edited by Dorothy Coleman. Cambridge: Cambridge University Press, 2007.

Husserl, Edmund. *Cartesian Meditations: An Introduction to Phenomenology*. Translated by Dorion Cairns. The Hague: Martinus Nijhoff, 1977.

———. *Experience and Judgment: Investigations in a Genealogy of Logic*. Revised and edited by Ludwig Landgrebe. Translated by James S. Churchill and Karl Ameriks. Introduction by James S. Churchill, afterword by Lothar Eley. London: Routledge and Kegan Paul, 1973.

———. *The Idea of Phenomenology*. Translated by Lee Hardy. Dordrecht: Kluwer Academic, 1999.

———. *On the Phenomenology of the Consciousness of Internal Time (1893–1917)*. Translated by John Barnett Brough. Dordrecht: Kluwer Academic, 1990.

———. *Phenomenology and the Crisis of Philosophy*. Translated with an introduction by Quentin Lauer. New York: Harper and Row, 1965.

———. *The Phenomenology of Internal Time-Consciousness*. Edited by Martin Heidegger. Translated by James S. Churchill. Introduction by Calvin O. Schrag. Bloomington: Indiana University Press, 1964.

Hutcheon, Linda. *A Poetics of Postmodernism: History, Theory, Fiction*. London: Routledge, 1988.

Hutton, Sarah. *Anne Conway: A Woman Philosopher*. Cambridge: Cambridge University Press, 2004.

———. "From Christian Kabbalism to Kabbalistic Quakerism: The Kabbalistic Dialogues of Ann Conway, Henry More, and George Keith." In *Christliche Kabbala*, edited by Wilhelm Schmidt-Biggemann, 199–209. Ostfildem: Jan Thorbecke, 2003.

Iamblichus. *On the Mysteries*. Translated with an introduction and notes by Emma C. Clarke, John M. Dillon and Jackson R. Hershbell. Atlanta: Society of Biblical Literature, 2003.

Iber, Christian. *Das Andere der Vernunft als ihr Prinzip: Grundzüge der philosophischen Entwicklung Schellings mit einem Ausblick auf die nachidealistischen Philosophiekonzeptionen Heideggers und Adornos*. Berlin: Walter de Gruyter, 1994.

Ibn al-ʿArabī, Muḥyīddīn. *The Bezels of Wisdom*. Translated by Ralph W. J. Austin. Preface by Titus Burckhardt. New York: Paulist, 1980.

Ibn Gabbai, Meir. *Avodat ha-Qodesh*. Jerusalem: Yerid ha-Sefarim, 2004.

———. *Derekh Emunah*. Jerusalem: Shevilei Orḥot ha-Ḥayyim, 2006.

Ibn Laṭif, Isaac. *Perush Megillat Qohelet*. Jerusalem: Maqor, 1969.

———. *Rav Peʿalim*. Edited by Samuel Schoenblum. Lemberg: Anna Wajdowicz, 1885.

———. *Ṣeror ha-Mor*. Edited by Adolph Jellinek. *Kerem Ḥemed* 9 (1856): 154–59.

Ibn Zimra, David ben Solomon. *Magen David*. Jerusalem: Yerid ha-Sefarim, 2007.

Ickovits, Ḥayyim. *Nefesh ha-Ḥayyim*. Edited and annotated by Joshua Lipschitz. Jerusalem, 2016.

Idel, Moshe. *Absorbing Perfections: Kabbalah and Interpretation*. Foreword by Harold Bloom. New Haven: Yale University Press, 2002.

———. "Androgyny and Equality in the Theosophico-Theurgical Kabbalah," *Diogenes* 52 (2005): 27–38.

———. *Ben: Sonship and Jewish Mysticism*. London: Continuum, 2007.

———. "Between the Kabbalah of Jerusalem and the Kabbalah of Israel Sarug." *Shalem* 6 (1992): 165–73 (Hebrew).

———. "The Concept of Torah in Hekhalot Literature and Its Metamorphosis in Kabbalah." *Jerusalem Studies in Jewish Thought* 1 (1981): 23–84 (Hebrew).

———. "The Evil Thought of the Deity." *Tarbiz* 49 (1980): 356–64 (Hebrew).

———. *Golem: Jewish Magical and Mystical Traditions on the Artificial Anthropoid*. Albany: State University of New York Press, 1990.

———. "Italy in Safed, Safed in Italy: Toward an Interactive History of Sixteenth-Century Kabbalah." In *Cultural Intermediaries: Jewish Intellectuals in Early Modern Italy*, edited by David B. Ruderman and Giuseppe Veltri, 239–69. Philadelphia: University of Pennsylvania Press, 2004.

———. "Jacques Derrida and Kabbalistic Sources." In *Judeities: Questions for Jacques Derrida*, edited by Bettina Bergo, Joseph Cohen, and Raphael Zagury-Orly, 111–30. Translated by Bettina Bergo and Michael B. Smith. New York: Fordham University Press, 2007.

———. *Kabbalah: New Perspectives*. New Haven: Yale University Press, 1988.

———. *Kabbalah and Eros*. New Haven: Yale University Press, 2005.

———. *Kabbalah in Italy 1280–1510: A Survey*. New Haven: Yale University Press, 2011.

———. "The Kabbalistic Backgrounds of the 'Son of God' in Giovanni Pico Della Mirandola's Thought." In *Giovanni Pico e la cabbalà*, edited by Fabrizio Lelli, 19–45. Firenze: Leo S. Olschki, 2014.

———. "The Magical and Neoplatonic Interpretations of the Kabbalah in the Renaissance." In *Jewish Thought in the Sixteenth Century*, edited by Bernard Dov Cooperman, 186–242. Cambridge, MA: Harvard University Press, 1983.

———. *Il male primordiale nella Qabbalah: Totalità, perfezionamento, perfettibilità*. Translated by Fabrizio Lelli. Milan: Adelphi, 2016.

———. *Messianic Mystics*. New Haven: Yale University Press, 1998.

———. *Old Worlds, New Mirrors: On Jewish Mysticism and Twentieth-Century Thought*. Philadelphia: University of Pennsylvania Press, 2010.

———. "On Some Forms of Order in Kabbalah." *Daʿat* 50/52 (2003): xxxi–lviii.

———. "Subversive Catalysts: Gnosticism and Messianism in Gershom Scholem's View of Jewish Mysticism." In *The Jewish Past Revisited: Reflections on Modern Jewish Historians*, edited by David N. Myers and David B. Ruderman, 39–76. New Haven: Yale University Press, 1998.

———. "Zur Funktion von Symbolen bei G. G. Scholem." In *Gershom Scholem: Literatur und Rhetorik*, edited by Stéphane Mosès and Sigrid Weigel, 51–92. Cologne: Böhlau, 2000.

Ijsseling, Samuel. "Heidegger and Politics." In *Ethics and Danger: Essays on Heidegger and Continental Thought*, edited by Arleen B. Dallery and Charles E. Scott with P. Holley Roberts, 3–10. Albany: State University of New York Press, 1992.

Ireland, Julia A. "Heidegger, Hölderlin, and Eccentric Translation." In *Heidegger, Translation, and the Task of Thinking: Essays in Honor of Parvis Emad*, edited by Frank Schalow, 253–67. Dordrecht: Springer, 2011.

Iveson, Richard. "Animals in Looking-Glass World: Fables of Überhumanism and Posthumanism

in Heidegger and Nietzsche." *Humanimalia* 1:2 (2010): 46–85.
———. "Wo und Ob: Heidegger's Animal Differently." *Café Dissensus*, December 31, 2017. https://cafedissensus.com/2017/12/31/wo-und-ob-heideggers-animal-differently.
Jabès, Edmond. *The Book of Questions*. Vol. 2: *Yael, Elya, Aely, El; or, The Last Book*. Translated by Rosmarie Waldrop. Hanover: Wesleyan University Press, 1991.
Jacob Joseph of Polonnoye. *Toledot Ya'aqov Yosef.* Korzec, 1780.
Jacobi, Friedrich Heinrich. *The Main Philosophical Writings and the Novel Allwill*. Translated with an introductory study, notes, and bibliography by George di Giovanni. Montreal: McGill-Queen's University Press, 1994.
Jacobs, Carol. *In the Language of Walter Benjamin*. Baltimore: Johns Hopkins University Press, 1999.
———. "Walter Benjamin: Topographically Speaking." In *Walter Benjamin: Theoretical Questions*, edited by David S. Ferris, 94–117. Stanford: Stanford University Press, 1996.
Jacobson, Eric. *Metaphysics of the Profane: The Political Theology of Walter Benjamin and Gershom Scholem*. New York: Columbia University Press, 2003.
Jacobson, Yoram. "The Problem of Evil and Its Sanctification in Kabbalistic Thought." In *The Problem of Evil and Its Symbols in Jewish and Christian Tradition*, edited by Henning Graf Reventlow and Yair Hoffman, 97–121. London: T and T Clark, 2004.
Jaeschke, Walter. "Vom Atheismus der Vernunft zum Theismus der Vernunft. Jacobis Begegnungen mit jüdischen Denkern und jüdischem Denken." In *Der Begriff des Judentums in der klassichen deutschen Philosophie*, edited by Amit Kravitz and Jörg Noller, 43–57. Tübingen: Mohr Siebeck, 2018.
Jakob, Eric. *Martin Heidegger und Hans Jonas: Die Metaphysik der Subjektivität und die Krise der technologischen Zivilisation*. Tübingen: Francke, 1996.
Janicaud, Dominique. *Heidegger in France*. Translated by François Raffoul and David Pettigrew. Bloomington: Indiana University Press, 2015.
Janz, Bruce. "Jacob Boehme's Theory of Knowledge in *Mysterium Magnum*." PhD diss., University of Waterloo, 1991.
Jonas, Hans. *Gnosis und spätantiker Geist*. 2 vols. Göttingen: Vandenhoeck and Ruprecht, 1988–93.
———. "Gnosticism and Modern Nihilism." *Social Research* 19 (1952): 430–52.
———. *The Gnostic Religion: The Message of the Alien God and the Beginnings of Christianity*. Boston: Beacon, 1963.
———. "Heidegger and Theology." *Review of Metaphysics* 18 (1964): 207–33.
———. *The Phenomenon of Life: Toward a Philosophical Biology*. Foreword by Lawrence Vogel. Evanston: Northwestern University Press, 2001.
Jones, Richard H. "Dialetheism, Paradox, and Nāgārjuna's Way of Thinking." *Comparative Philosophy* 9 (2018): 41–68.
Joseph ben Shalom Ashkenazi. *Perush Sefer Yeṣirah*. Jerusalem: Yeshivat Kol Yehudah, 1990. Printed erroneously under the name of Abraham ben David of Posquières.
Josephson-Storm, Jason A. *The Myth of Disenchantment: Magic, Modernity, and the Birth of the Human Sciences*. Chicago: University of Chicago Press, 2017.
Junk, Johanna. *Metapher und Sprachmagie, Heidegger und die Kabbala: Eine philosophische Untersuchung*. Bodenheim: Syndikat Buchgesellschaft, 1998.
Jussaume, Timothy. "Heidegger and the Nothing: Transcendence after Metaphysics." PhD diss., Villanova University, 2014.
Kabbala Denudata, seu, Doctrina hebræorum transcendentalis et metaphysica atqve theologica: opus antiquissimæ philosophiæ barbaricæ variis speciminibus refertissimum, edited by Christian Knorr von Rosenroth, 2 vols. Sulzbach: Abraham Lichtenthaler, 1677–84.
Kaennel, Lucie. "Protestantisme et cabale: chronique d'un mésamour." In *Réceptions de la cabale*, edited by Pierre Gisel and Lucie Kaennel, 185–210. Paris: L'éclat, 2007.
Kahana, Isaac. *Toledot Yiṣḥaq*, pt. 2, vols. 1–2. New York: Machon HaGra, 2003–9.
Kahn, Charles H. *The Art and Thought of Heraclitus: An Edition of the Fragments with Translation and Commentary*. Cambridge: Cambridge University Press, 1979.
Kalary, Thomas. "Heidegger's Thinking of Difference and the God-Question." In *Heidegger, Translation, and the Task of Thinking: Essays in Honor of Parvis Emad*, edited by Frank Schalow, 111–33. Dordrecht: Springer, 2011.
Kamal, Muhammad. *From Essence to Being: The Philosophy of Mulla Sadra and Martin Heidegger*. London: ICAS, 2010.
Kant, Immanuel. *Religion within the Boundaries of Mere Reason and Other Writings*. Translated and

edited by Allen Wood and George Di Giovanni. Introduction by Robert Merrihew Adams. Cambridge: Cambridge University Press, 1998.

Kasher, Hannah. "Isaac Ibn Laṭif's Book 'Rav Pe'alim'." MA thesis, Bar-Ilan University, 1974 (Hebrew).

Kattago, Siobhan. *Memory and Representation in Contemporary Europe: The Persistence of the Past.* London: Routledge, 2012.

Katz, Steven T. "On Historicism and Eternity: Reflections on the 100th Birthday of Franz Rosenzweig." In *Der Philosoph Franz Rosenzweig (1886–1929): Internationaler Kongreß—Kassel 1986.* 2 vols., edited by Wolfdietrich Schmied-Kowarzik, 745–69. Freiburg: Karl Alber, 1988.

Katz, Yiṣḥaq Isaac. *Berit Kehunat Olam.* Jerusalem: Weiss, 1950.

Kaufmann, David. "Imageless Refuge for All Images: Scholem in the Wake of Philosophy." *Modern Judaism* 20 (2000): 147–58.

———. "Thanks for the Memory: Bloch, Benjamin, and the Philosophy of History." In *Not Yet: Reconsidering Ernst Bloch,* edited by Jamie Owen Daniel and Tom Moylan, 33–52. London: Verso, 1997.

Keenan, John P., trans. *The Scripture on the Explication of the Underlying Meaning.* Berkeley: Numata Center for Buddhist Translation and Research, 2000.

Keiling, Tobias. "Dionysius, Apollo and Other *Göttliche*: Denial and Excess of Meaning in Nietzsche, Heidegger and Wittgenstein." In *Rethinking Faith: Heidegger between Nietzsche and Wittgenstein,* edited by Antonio Cimino and Gert-Jan van der Heiden, 83–102. New York: Bloomsbury, 2017.

Keller, Catherine. *Cloud of the Impossible: Negative Theology and Planetary Entanglement.* New York: Columbia University Press, 2015.

Kierkegaard, Søren. *Fear and Trembling.* Edited by C. Stephen Evans and Sylvia Walsh. Translated by Sylvia Walsh. Cambridge: Cambridge University Press, 2006.

Kilcher, Andreas. "Die Kabbala als Trope im ästhetischen Diskurs der Frühromantik." In *Kabbala und die Literatur der Romantik: Zwischen Magie und Trope,* edited by Eveline Goodman-Thau, Gert Mattenklott, and Christoph Schulte, 135–66. Tübingen: Max Niemeyer, 1999.

———. *Die Sprachtheorie der Kabbala als Ästhetisches Paradigma: Die Konstruktion einer Ästhetischen Kabbala Seit der Frühen Neuzeit.* Stuttgart: J. B. Metzler, 1998.

Kisiel, Theodore. *Heidegger's Way of Thought: Critical and Interpretive Signposts.* Edited by Alfred Denker and Marion Heinz. New York: Continuum, 2002.

———. "*Kriegsnotsemester* 1919: Heidegger's Hermeneutic Breakthrough." In *The Question of Hermeneutics: Essays in Honor of Joseph K. Kockelmans,* edited by Timothy J. Stapleton, 155–208. Dordrecht: Kluwer Academic, 1994.

———. "Schelling's Treatise on Freedom and Heidegger's *Sein und Zeit.*" In *Schelling: Zwischen Fichte und Hegel,* edited by Christoph Asmuth, Alfred Denker, Michael Vater, 287–302. Amsterdam: B. R. Grüner, 2000.

Kisiel, Theodore, and Thomas Sheehan, eds. *Becoming Heidegger: On the Trail of His Early Occasional Writings, 1910–1927.* Evanston: Northwestern University Press, 2007.

Kleinberg, Ethan. *Haunting History: Deconstructive Approach to the Past.* Stanford: Stanford University Press, 2017.

Klijnsmit, Anthony J. "F. M. van Helmont: Kabbalist and Phonetician." *Studia Rosenthaliana* 30 (1996): 267–81.

Kline, Peter. "Infinite Reduplication: Kierkegaard's Negative Concept of God." In *Contemporary Debates in Negative Theology and Philosophy,* edited by Nahum Brown and J. Aaron Simmons, 163–84. New York: Palgrave Macmillan, 2017.

———. *Passion for Nothing: Kierkegaard's Apophatic Theology.* Minneapolis: Fortress, 2017.

Knepper, Timothy D. "Ineffability Investigations: What the Later Wittgenstein Has to Offer to the Study of Ineffability." *International Journal for Philosophy of Religion* 65 (2009): 65–76.

Koch, Patrick B. *Human Self-Perfection: A Re-Assessment of Kabbalistic Musar-Literature of Sixteenth-Century Safed.* Los Angeles: Cherub, 2015.

Koenker, Ernest B. "Grund and Ungrund in Jacob Boehme." *Philosophy Today* 15 (1971): 45–51.

Kokin, Daniel Stein. "Entering the Labyrinth: On the Hebraic and Kabbalistic Universe of Egidio da Viterbo." In *Hebraic Aspects of the Renaissance: Sources and Encounters,* edited by Ilana Zinguer, Abraham Melamed, and Zur Shalev, 27–42. Leiden: Brill, 2011.

Kolb, David. "Circulation and Constitution at the End of History." In *Endings: Questions of Memory in Hegel and Heidegger,* edited by Rebecca Comay and John McCumber, 57–76. Evanston: Northwestern University Press, 1999.

Kook, Abraham Isaac. *Orot.* Jerusalem: Mosad ha-Rav Kook, 1993.

Korab-Karpowicz, W. Julian. *The Presocratics in the Thought of Martin Heidegger.* New York: Peter Lang, 2016.

Koslowski, Peter. "Franz Baader: Spekulative Dogmatik als christliche Gnosis." In *Gnosis und Mystik in der Geschichte der Philosophie,* edited by Peter Koslowski, 243–59. Zürich: Artemis, 1988.

———. *Philosophien der Offenbarung: Antiker Gnostizismus, Franz von Baader, Schelling.* Paderborn: Ferdinand Schöningh, 2001.

Kovacs, George. "The Leap (*der Sprung*) for Being in Heidegger's *Beiträge zur Philosophie (Vom Ereignis).*" *Man and World* 25 (1992): 39–59.

Krell, David Farrell. *Ecstasy, Catastrophe: Heidegger from Being and Time to the Black Notebooks.* Albany: State University of New York Press, 2015.

———. "Hegel Heidegger Heraclitus." In *Heraclitean Fragments: A Companion Volume to the Heidegger/Fink Seminar on Heraclitus,* edited by John Sallis and Kenneth Maly, 22–42. University, AL: University of Alabama Press, 1980.

———. "Heidegger's *Black Notebooks, 1931–1941.*" *Research in Phenomenology* 45 (2015): 127–60.

———. "Is There a Heidegger—or, for That Matter, a Lacan—beyond All Gathering? διαφερόμενον in Heidegger's 'Logos: Heraclitus B 50' as a Possible Response to Derrida's Disquiet." In *Heidegger and Language,* edited by Jeffrey Powell, 201–23. Bloomington: Indiana University Press, 2013.

———. *Of Memory, Reminiscence, and Writing.* Bloomington: Indiana University Press, 1990.

———. *Phantoms of the Other: Four Generations of Derrida's Geschlecht.* Albany: State University of New York Press, 2015.

———. *The Tragic Absolute: German Idealism and the Languishing of God.* Bloomington: Indiana University Press, 2005.

———. "Troubled Brows: Heidegger's *Black Notebooks, 1942–1948.*" *Research in Phenomenology* 46 (2016): 309–35.

Krinis, Ehud. "Cyclical Time in the Ismāʿīlī Circle of Ikhwān al-ṣafāʾ (Tenth Century) and in Early Jewish Kabbalists Circles (Thirteenth and Fourteenth Centuries)." *Studia Islamica* 111 (2016): 20–108.

Krummel, John W. M. *Nishida Kitarō's Chiasmatic Chorology: Place of Dialectic, Dialectic of Place.* Bloomington: Indiana University Press, 2015.

K'uei-chi. *A Comprehensive Commentary on the Heart Sutra (Prajñāpāramita-Hṛdaya-Sūtra).* Translated by Heng-ching Shih in collaboration with Dan Lusthaus. Berkeley: Numata Center for Buddhist Translation and Research, 2001.

Lacan, Jacques. *Anxiety.* Book 10 in *The Seminar of Jacques Lacan.* Edited by Jacques-Alain Miller. Translated by Adrian R. Price. Cambridge: Polity, 2014.

———. *Écrits.* Paris: Éditions du Seuil, 1966.

———. *Écrits: The First Complete Edition in English.* Translated by Bruce Fink, in collaboration with Héloïse Fink and Russell Grigg. New York: Norton, 2006.

———. *The Four Fundamental Concepts of Psychoanalysis.* Book 11 in *The Seminar of Jacques Lacan.* Edited by Jacques-Alain Miller. Translated by Alan Sheridan. New York: Norton, 1981.

———. *The Psychoses 1955–1956.* Book 3 in *The Seminar of Jacques Lacan.* Edited by Jacques-Alan Miller. by Russell Grigg. New York: Norton, 1993.

———. *The Sinthome.* Book 23 in *The Seminar of Jacques Lacan.* Edited by Jacques-Alain Miller. Cambridge: Polity, 2016.

Lacoue-Labarthe, Philippe. *Heidegger and the Politics of Poetry.* Translated by Jeff Fort. Urbana: University of Illinois Press, 2007.

———. *Musica Ficta (Figures of Wagner).* Translated by Felicia McCarren. Stanford: Stanford University Press, 1994.

———. *Phrase.* Translated by Leslie Hill. Albany: State University of New York Press, 2018.

———. "Poetry's Courage." In *Walter Benjamin and Romanticism,* edited by Beatrice Hanssen and Andrew Benjamin, 163–79. London: Continuum, 2002.

Landauer, Gustav. *Revolution and Other Writings: A Political Reader.* Edited and translated by Gabriel Kuhn. Preface by Richard J. F. Day. Oakland: PM Press, 2010.

Lapidot, Elad. "Das Fremde im Denken." In *Heidegger und der Antisemitismus: Positionen im Widerstreit, mit Briefen von Martin und Fritz Heidegger,* edited by Walter Homolka and Arnulf Heidegger, 269–76. Freiburg: Herder, 2016.

———. "People of Knowers: On the Political Epistemology of Heidegger and R. Chaim of Volozhin." In *Heidegger and Jewish Thought: Difficult Others,* edited by Elad Lapidot and Micha Brumlik, 269–89. London: Rowman and Littlefield, 2018.

Lapidot, Elad, and Micha Brumlik, eds. *Heidegger and Jewish Thought: Difficult Others.* London: Rowman and Littlefield, 2018.

Larrabee, Mary Jeanne. "Time and Spatial Models: Temporality in Husserl." *Philosophy and Phenomenological Research* 49 (1989): 373–92.

Laruelle, François. *Dictionary of Non-Philosophy*. Translated by Taylor Adkins. Minneapolis: Univocal, 2013.

———. "The Generic as Predicate and Constant: Non-Philosophy and Materialism." In *The Speculative Turn: Continental Materialism and Realism*, edited by Levi Bryant, Nick Srnicek, and Graham Harman, 237–60. Melbourne: Re.press, 2011.

———. *Mystique non-philosophique à l'usage des contemporains*. Paris: L'Harmattan, 2007.

———. *The Non-Philosophy Project: Essays by François Laruelle*. Edited by Gabriel Alkon and Boris Gunjevic. New York: Telos, 2012.

———. "On the Black Universe: In the Human Foundations of Color." In Eugene Thacker, Daniel Colucciello Barber, Nicola Masciandaro, Alexander R. Galloway, and Aaron Metté, *Dark Nights of the Universe*, 102–9. Miami: [Name], 2013.

———. *Philosophies of Difference: A Critical Introduction to Non-Philosophy*. Translated by Rocco Gangle. New York: Continuum, 2010.

———. *Philosophy and Non-Philosophy*. Translated by Taylor Adkins. Minneapolis: Univocal, 2013.

———. *Principles of Non-Philosophy*. Translated by Nicola Rubczak and Anthony Paul Smith. London: Bloomsbury, 2013.

———. *Theory of Identities*. Translated by Alyosha Edlebi. New York: Columbia University Press 2016.

Laughland, John. *Schelling versus Hegel: From German Idealism to Christian Metaphysics*. Burlington: Ashgate, 2007.

Law, David R. "Negative Theology in Heidegger's *Beiträge zur Philosophie*." *International Journal for Philosophy of Religion* 48 (2000): 139–56.

Lawlor, Leonard. *Derrida and Husserl: The Basic Problem of Phenomenology*. Bloomington: Indiana University Press, 2002.

Lazier, Benjamin. "Pauline Theology in the Weimar Republic: Hans Jonas, Karl Barth, and Martin Heidegger." In *The Legacy of Hans Jonas: Judaism and the Phenomenon of Life*, edited by Hava Tirosh-Samuelson and Christian Wiese, 107–29. Leiden: Brill, 2008.

Leahy, David G. *Beyond Sovereignty: A New Global Ethics and Morality*. Aurora: Davies, 2010.

———. *Faith and Philosophy: The Historical Impact*. Burlington: Ashgate, 2003.

———. *Foundation: Matter the Body Itself*. Albany: State University of New York Press, 1996.

———. *Novitas Mundi: Perception of the History of Being*. Albany: State University of New York Press, 1994.

Leftow, Brian. *Time and Eternity*. Ithaca: Cornell University Press, 1991.

Lelli, Fabrizio. "Pico, i Da Pisa e 'Eliyyà Ḥayyim da Genazzano." In *Giovanni Pico e la cabbalà*, edited by Fabrizio Lelli, 93–120. Firenze: Leo S. Olschki, 2014.

Lettow, Susanne. "Heideggers Politik des Rassenbegriffs. Die *Schwarzen Hefte* im Kontext." In *Martin Heideggers "Schwarze Hefte": Eine philosophisch-politische Debatte*, edited by Marion Heinz and Sidonie Kellerer, with the collaboration of Tobias Bender, 234–50. Berlin: Suhrkamp, 2016.

Levinas, Emmanuel. *Collected Philosophical Papers*. Translated by Alphonso Lingis. Dordrecht: Martinus Nijhoff, 1987.

———. *Difficult Freedom: Essays on Judaism*. Translated by Seán Hand. Baltimore: Johns Hopkins University Press, 1990.

———. *Entre Nous: On Thinking-of-the-Other*. Translated by Michael B. Smith and Barbara Harshav. New York: Columbia University Press, 1998.

———. *Oeuvres 1: Carnets de captivité suivi de Écrits sur la captivité et Notes philosophiques diverses*. Edited and annotated by Rodolphe Calin, preface and explanatory notes by Rodolphe Calin and Catherine Chalier, general preface by Jean-Luc Marion. Paris: Grasset and Fasquelle, 2009.

———. *Otherwise Than Being or Beyond Essence*. Translated by Alphonso Lingis. Dordrecht: Kluwer Academic, 1991.

———. *Totalité et infini: Essai sur l'extériorité*. The Hague: Martinus Nijhoff, 1980.

———. *Totality and Infinity: An Essay on Exteriority*. Translated by Alphonso Lingis. Dordrecht: Kluwer Academic, 1969.

Levy, David J. *Hans Jonas: The Integrity of Thinking*. Columbia: University of Missouri Press, 2002.

Liebes, Yehuda. "Hebrew and Aramaic as Languages of the Zohar." *Aramaic Studies* 4 (2006): 35–52.

———. *On Sabbateanism and Its Kabbalah: Collected Essays*. Jerusalem: Bialik Institute, 1995 (Hebrew).

———. *Studies in Jewish Myth and Jewish Messianism*. Translated by Batya Stein. Albany: State University of New York Press, 1993.

———. "Towards a Study of the Author of *Emek ha-Melekh*: His Personality, Writings and Kabbalah." *Jerusalem Studies in Jewish Thought* 11 (1993): 101–37 (Hebrew).

———. "'Tsaddiq Yesod Olam'—A Sabbatian Myth." *Da'at* 1 (1978): 73–120 (Hebrew).

Lin, Yael. *The Intersubjectivity of Time: Levinas and Infinite Responsibility*. Pittsburgh: Duquesne University Press, 2013.

Lippi, Silvia. "Héraclite, Lacan: du logos au significant." *Recherches en Psychanalyse* 9 (2010): 55–62.

Lizzini, Olga. *Fluxus (fayd): Indagine sui fondamenti della Metafisica e della Fisica di Avicenna*. Bari: Pagina, 2011.

Llewellyn, Robert T. "Jacob Boehmes Kosmogonie in ihrer Beziehung zur Kabbala." *Antaios* 5 (1963): 237–50.

Lohmar, Dieter. "Husserl's Type and Kant's Schemata." In *The New Husserl: A Critical Reader*, edited by Donn Welton, 93–124. Bloomington: Indiana University Press, 2003.

Louth, Andrew. *St John Damascene: Tradition and Originality in Byzantine Theology*. Oxford: Oxford University Press, 2002.

Löwith, Karl. "F. Rosenzweig and M. Heidegger on Temporality and Eternity." *Philosophy and Phenomenological Research* 3 (1942): 53–77.

———. *Heidegger, pensador de un tiempo indigente*. Madrid: Rialp, 1956.

———. "M. Heidegger und F. Rosenzweig: Ein Nachtrag zu 'Sein und Zeit.'" *Zeitschrift für philosophische Forschung* 12 (1958): 161–87.

———. *Martin Heidegger and European Nihilism*. Edited by Richard Wolin. New York: Columbia University Press, 1995.

———. *Meaning in History: The Theological Implications of the Philosophy of History*. Chicago: University of Chicago Press, 1949.

———. *My Life in Germany before and after 1933: A Report*. Translated by Elizabeth King. London: Athlone, 1994.

———. *Nature, History, and Existentialism*. Edited by Arnold Levison. Evanston: Northwestern University Press, 1966.

Lucca, Enrico. "Ateismo e profondità dell'essere. Un breve scambio epistolare tra Furio Jesi e Gershom Scholem." *Scienza e Politica* 26 (2013): 111–16.

Lusthaus, Dan. "The Two Truths (*Saṃvṛti-satya* and *Paramārtha-satya*) in Early Yogācāra." *Journal of Buddhist Studies* 7 (2010): 101–52.

Luzzatto, Moses Ḥayyim. *Adir ba-Marom*, pt. 1. Edited by Joseph Spinner. Jerusalem, 1990.

———. *Adir ba-Marom*, pt. 2. Edited by Joseph Spinner. Jerusalem, 1988.

———. *Ginzei Ramḥal*. Edited by Ḥayyim Friedlander. Benei Beraq, 1984.

———. *Qelaḥ Pitḥei Ḥokhmah*. Edited by Ḥayyim Friedlander. Benei Beraq, 1992.

Lyon, James K. *Paul Celan and Martin Heidegger: An Unresolved Conversation, 1951–1970*. Baltimore: Johns Hopkins University Press, 2006.

Ma, Lin. *Heidegger on East-West Dialogue: Anticipating the Event*. New York: Routledge, 2008.

———. "The Mysterious Relations to the East." *Journal of the British Society for Phenomenology* 39 (2008): 275–92.

Ma'arekhet ha-Elohut. Jerusalem: J. Becker, 2003.

Maas, Frans. "Divine Omnipotence in the View of Nicholas of Cusa." In *Conflict and Reconciliation: Perspectives on Nicholas of Cusa*, edited by Inigo Bocken, 177–87. Leiden: Brill, 2004.

Macherey, Pierre. *Hegel or Spinoza*. Translated by Susan M. Ruddick. Minneapolis: University of Minnesota Press, 2011.

———. *In a Materialist Way: Selected Essays*. Edited by Warren Montag. Translated by Ted Stolze. London: Verso, 1998.

Macho, Thomas. "On the Price of Messianism: The Intellectual Rift between Gershom Scholem and Jacob Taubes." In *Messianic Thought Outside Theology*, edited by Anna Glazova and Paul North, 28–42. New York: Fordham University Press, 2014.

Maciejko, Pawel. "Gershom Scholem's Dialectic of Jewish History: The Case of Sabbatianism." *Journal of Modern Jewish Studies* 3 (2004): 207–20.

Macquarrie, John. *An Existential Theology: A Comparison of Heidegger and Bultmann*. Foreword by Rudolf Bultmann. London: SCM, 1955.

Magee, Glenn Alexander. *Hegel and the Hermetic Tradition*. Ithaca: Cornell University Press, 2001.

Magid, Shaul. "Ethics Disentangled from the Law: Incarnation, the Universal, and Hasidic Ethics." *Kabbalah: Journal for the Study of Jewish Mystical Texts* 15 (2006): 31–75.

———. *From Metaphysics to Midrash: Myth, History, and the Interpretation of Scripture in Lurianic Kabbala*. Bloomington: Indiana University Press, 2008.

———. "Gershom Scholem's Ambivalence toward Mystical Experience and His Critique of Martin Buber in Light of Hans Jonas and Martin Heidegger." *Journal of Jewish Thought and Philosophy* 4 (1995): 245–69.

Magus, Bernd. *Heidegger's Metahistory of Philosophy: Amor Fati, Being and Truth*. The Hague: Martinus Nijhoff, 1970.

Mahlev, Haim. "Kabbalah as Philosophia Perennis? The Image of Judaism in the German Early

Enlightenment: Three Studies." *Jewish Quarterly Review* 104 (2014): 234–57.

Maimon, Solomon. *Solomon Maimon: An Autobiography*. Translated by J. Clark Murray, introduction by Michael Shapiro. Urbana: University of Illinois Press, 2001.

Maimonides, Moses. *The Guide of the Perplexed*. Translated with an introduction and notes by Shlomo Pines, with an introductory essay by Leo Strauss. Chicago: University of Chicago Press, 1963.

Major, René. *Lacan avec Derrida: Analyse désistencielle*. Paris: Flammarion, 2001.

Malabou, Catherine. *The Future of Hegel: Plasticity, Temporality, and Dialectic*. Translated by Lisabeth During. London: Routledge, 2005.

———. *The Heidegger Change: On the Fantastic in Philosophy*. Translated and edited by Peter Skafish. Albany: State University of New York Press, 2011.

Malpas, Jeff. *Heidegger's Topology: Being, Place, World*. Cambridge, MA: MIT Press, 2006.

Maly, Kenneth. *Heidegger's Possibility: Language, Emergence-Saying Be-ing*. Toronto: University of Toronto Press, 2008.

———. "Man and Disclosure." In *Heraclitean Fragments: A Companion Volume to the Heidegger/Fink Seminar on Heraclitus*, edited by John Sallis and Kenneth Maly, 43–60. University, AL: University of Alabama Press, 1980.

Maly, Kenneth, and Parvis Emad, eds. *Heidegger on Heraclitus: A New Reading*. Lewiston: Edwin Mellen, 1986.

Manchester, Peter. *Temporality and Trinity*. New York: Fordham University Press, 2015.

———. *The Syntax of Time: The Phenomenology of Time in Greek Physics and Speculative Logic from Iamblichus to Anaximander*. Leiden: Brill, 2005.

Maor, Zohar. "Scholem and Rosenzweig: Redemption and (Anti-)Zionism." *Modern Judaism* 37 (2017): 1–23.

Marcuse, Herbert. *Heideggerian Marxism*. Edited by Richard Wolin and John Abromeit. Lincoln: University of Nebraska Press, 2005.

Marion, Jean-Luc. "In the Name: How to Avoid Speaking of 'Negative Theology.'" In *God, the Gift, and Postmodernism*, edited by John D. Caputo and Michael J. Scanlon, 20–53. Bloomington: Indiana University Press, 1999.

———. "Nothing and Nothing Else." In *The Ancients and the Moderns*, edited by Reginald Lilly, 183–95. Bloomington: Indiana University Press, 1996.

Marrati, Paola. *Genesis and Trace: Derrida Reading Husserl and Heidegger*. Stanford: Stanford University Press, 2005.

Martensen, Hans Lassen. *Jacob Boehme: His Life and Teaching or Studies in Theosophy*. Translated by T. Rhys Evans. London: Hodder and Stoughton, 1885.

Martins, Ansgar. *Adorno und die Kabbala*. Potsdam: Universitätsverlag Potsdam, 2016.

Masciandaro, Nicola. "Secret: No Light Has Ever Seen the Black Universe." In Eugene Thacker, Daniel Colucciello Barber, Nicola Masciandaro, Alexander R. Galloway, and Aaron Metté, *Dark Nights of the Universe*, 45–87. Miami: [Name], 2013.

Masschelein, Anneleen. *The Unconcept: The Freudian Uncanny in Late-Twentieth-Century Theory*. Albany: State University of New York Press, 2011.

Matern, Reinhard. *Über Sprachgeschichte und die Kabbala bei Horkheimer und Adorno*. Duisburg: Matern, 2000.

Matt, Daniel C. "*Ayin*: The Concept of Nothingness in Jewish Mysticism." In *The Problem of Pure Consciousness: Mysticism and Philosophy*, edited by Robert K. C. Forman, 121–59. Oxford: Oxford University Press, 1990.

———. "'New-Ancient Words': The Aura of Secrecy in the Zohar." In *Gershom Scholem's Major Trends in Jewish Mysticism: 50 Years After*, edited by Peter Schäfer and Joseph Dan, 181–207. Tübingen: Mohr Siebeck, 1993.

Matthews, Bruce. *Schelling's Organic Form of Philosophy: Life as the Schema of Freedom*. Albany: State University of New York Press, 2011.

May, Reinhard. *Heidegger's Hidden Sources: East Asian Influences on His Work*. Translated by Graham Parkes. London: Routledge, 1996.

Mayer, Paola. *Jena Romanticism and Its Appropriation of Jakob Böhme: Theosophy—Hagiography—Literature*. Montreal: McGill-Queen's University Press, 1999.

Mayse, Ariel. "Reflection: Eternity in Hasidism: Time and Presence." In *Eternity: A History*, edited by Yitzhak Y. Melamed, 231–38. New York: Oxford University Press, 2016.

McCormick, Peter J. *Heidegger and the Language of the World: An Argumentative Reading of the Later Heidegger's Meditations on Language*. Ottawa: University of Ottawa Press, 1976.

———. "Saying and Showing in Heidegger and Wittgenstein." *Journal of the British Society of Phenomenology* 3 (1972): 27–35.

McCumber, John. "Heidegger: Beyond Anti-Semitism and *Seinsgeschichte*." In *After Heidegger?*, edited by Gregory Fried and Richard Polt, 101–10. London: Rowman and Littlefield, 2018.

McCutcheon, Felicity. *Religion within the Limits of Language Alone: Wittgenstein on Philosophy and Religion*. Aldershot: Ashgate, 2001.

McDonough, Richard M. *Martin Heidegger's Being and Time*. New York: Peter Lang, 2006.

McGinn, Bernard. "Cabalists and Christians: Reflections on Cabala in Medieval and Renaissance Thought." In *Jewish Christians and Christian Jews: From Renaissance to the Enlightenment*, edited by Richard H. Popkin and Gordon M. Weiner, 11–34. Dordrecht: Academic, 1994.

———. "The God beyond God: Theology and Mysticism in the Thought of Meister Eckhart." *Journal of Religion* 61 (1981): 1–19.

———. "*Maximum Contractum et Absolutum*: The Motive for the Incarnation in Nicholas of Cusanus and His Predecessors." In *Nicholas of Cusa and His Age: Intellect and Spirituality: Essays Dedicated to the Memory of F. Edward Cranz, Thomas P. McTighe and Charles Trinkaus*, edited by Thomas M. Izbicki and Christopher M. Bellitto, 151–75. Leiden: Brill, 2002.

———. *Mysticism in the Reformation (1500–1650)*. Vol. 6, part 1, of *The Presence of God: A History of Western Christian Mysticism*. New York: Herder and Herder, 2016.

———. "*Unitrinum Seu Triunum*: Nicholas of Cusa's Trinitarian Mysticism." In *Mystics: Presence and Aporia*, edited by Michael Kessler and Christian Sheppard, 90–117. Chicago: University of Chicago Press, 2003.

McGrath, Sean J. *The Early Heidegger and Medieval Philosophy: Phenomenology for the Godforsaken*. Washington, DC: Catholic University Press, 2006.

McGuinness, Brian, ed. *Ludwig Wittgenstein and the Vienna Circle: Conversations Recorded by Friedrich Waismann*. Translated by Joachim Schulte and Brian McGuinness. New York: Barnes and Noble, 1979.

Meeks, Wayne A. *The Prophet-King: Moses Traditions and the Johannine Christology*. Leiden: Brill, 1967.

Mehta, Jarava Lai. *Martin Heidegger: The Way and the Vision*. Honolulu: University of Hawaii Press, 1976.

Meillassoux, Quentin. *After Finitude: An Essay on the Necessity of Contingency*. Translated by Ray Brassier. London: Continuum, 2008.

Meinvielle, Julio. *De la Cábala al Progresismo*. Vatican City: Verbo Incarnato, 2013.

Meir, Jonathan. "The Eclectic Kabbalah of R. Shimon Horowitz (A Critical Note on the Term 'The Lithuanian Kabbalah')." *Kabbalah: Journal for the Study of Jewish Mystical Texts* 31 (2014): 311–20 (Hebrew).

———. *Kabbalistic Circles in Jerusalem (1896–1948)*. Translated by Avi Aronsky. Leiden: Brill, 2016.

———. "Wrestling with the Esoteric: Hillel Zeitlin, Yehudah Ashlag, and Kabbalah in the Land of Israel." In *Judaism, Topics, Fragments, Faces Identities: Jubilee Volume in Honor of Rivka*, edited by Ḥaviva Pedaya and Ephraim Meir, 585–647. Beer Sheva: Ben-Gurion University Press, 2007 (Hebrew).

Melamed, Yitzhak Y. "'*Omnis determinatio est negatio*': Determination, Negation, and Self-Negation in Spinoza, Kant, and Hegel." In *Spinoza and German Idealism*, edited by Eckart Förster and Yitzhak Y. Melamed, 175–96. Cambridge: Cambridge University Press, 2012.

———. "Spinozism, Acosmism, and Hassidism: A Closed Circle." In *Der Begriff des Judentums in der klassichen deutschen Philosophie*, edited by Amit Kravitz and Jörg Noller, 75–85. Tübingen: Mohr Siebeck, 2018.

Melberg, Arne. "Repetition (in the Kierkegaardian Sense of the Term)." *Diacritics* 20 (1990): 71–87.

Menaḥem Mendel of Shklov. *Kitvei ha-Ga'on Rabbi Menaḥem Mendel of Shklov*. 2 vols. Jerusalem, 2001.

Mendelssohn, Moses. *Last Works*. Translated with an introduction and commentary by Bruce Rosenstock. Urbana: University of Illinois Press, 2012.

———. *Morning Hours: Lectures on God's Existence*. Translated by Daniel O. Dahlstrom and Corey Dyck. Dordrecht: Springer, 2011.

Mendes-Flohr, Paul. "Franz Rosenzweig and the Crisis of Historicism." In *The Philosophy of Franz Rosenzweig*, edited by Paul Mendes-Flohr, 138–61. Hanover: University Press of New England, 1988.

———. *From Mysticism to Dialogue: Martin Buber's Transformation of German Social Thought*. Detroit: Wayne State University Press, 1989.

———. "Hebrew as a Holy Tongue: Franz Rosenzweig and the Renewal of Hebrew." In *Hebrew in Ashkenaz: A Language in Exile*, edited by Lewis Gilbert, 222–41. Oxford: Oxford University Press, 1993.

———. "Introductory Essay: The Spiritual Quest of the Philologist." In *Gershom Scholem: The Man and His Work*, edited by Paul Mendes-Flohr,

1–28. Albany: State University of New York Press, 1994.

———. "Martin Buber and Martin Heidegger in Dialogue." *Journal of Religion* 94 (2014): 2–25.

Menninghaus, Winfried. "Walter Benjamin's Variations of Imagelessness." *Critical Horizons* 14 (2013): 407–28.

Merleau-Ponty, Maurice. *Phenomenology of Perception*. Translated by Donald A. Landes. London: Routledge, 2012.

———. *The Visible and the Invisible: Followed by Working Notes*. Edited by Claude Lefort. Translated by Alphonso Lingis. Evanston: Northwestern University Press, 1968.

Meroz, Ronit. "The Archaeology of the Zohar—*Sifra Ditseni'uta* as a Sample Text." *Da'at* 82 (2016): ix–lxxxv.

———. "Early Lurianic Compositions." In *Massu'ot: Studies in Kabbalistic Literature and Jewish Philosophy in Memory of Prof. Ephraim Gottlieb*, edited by Michal Oron and Amos Goldreich, 311–36. Jerusalem: Bialik Institute, 1994 (Hebrew).

———. "Faithful Transmission versus Innovation: Luria and His Disciples." In *Gershom Scholem's Major Trends in Jewish Mysticism: 50 Years After*, edited by Peter Schäfer and Joseph Dan, 257–75. Tübingen: Mohr Siebeck, 1993.

———. "Redemption in the Lurianic Teaching." PhD diss., Hebrew University, Jerusalem, 1988 (Hebrew).

———. "R. Yisrael Sarug—Luria's Disciple: A Research Controversy Reconsidered." *Da'at* 28 (1992): 41–50 (Hebrew).

———. "The School of Sarug—A New History." *Shalem* 7 (2002): 151–93 (Hebrew).

———. *The Spiritual Biography of Rabbi Simeon bar Yochay: An Analysis of the Zohar's Textual Components*. Jerusalem: Bialik Institute, 2018 (Hebrew).

Meylahn, Johann-Albrecht. *The Limits and Possibilities of Postmetaphysical God-Talk: A Conversation between Heidegger, Levinas and Derrida*. Leuven: Peeters, 2013.

Micali, Stefano. "The Deformalization of Time." In *Debating Levinas' Legacy*, edited by Andris Breitling, Chris Bremmers, and Arthur Cools, 69–80. Leiden: Brill, 2015.

Michael, Thomas. *In the Shadows of the Dao: Laozi, the Sage, and the Daodejing*. Albany: State University of New York Press, 2015.

Miller, Clyde Lee. *Reading Cusanus: Metaphor and Dialectic in a Conjectural Universe*. Washington, DC: Catholic University Press, 2003.

Miller, Michael T. *The Name of God in Jewish Thought: A Philosophical Analysis of Mystical Traditions from Apocalypse to Kabbalah*. London: Routledge, 2016.

Miron, Ronny. *The Angel of Jewish History: The Image of the Jewish Past in the Twentieth Century*. Boston: Academic Studies, 2014.

Mitchell, Andrew J. "Contamination, Essence, and Decomposition: Heidegger and Derrida." In *French Interpretations of Heidegger: An Exceptional Reception*, edited by David Pettigrew and François Raffoul, 131–50. Albany: State University of New York Press, 2008.

———. *The Fourfold: Reading the Late Heidegger*. Evanston: Northwestern University Press, 2015.

———. "Heidegger's Breakdown: Health and Healing under the Care of Dr. V. E. von Gebsattel." *Research in Phenomenology* 46 (2016): 70–97.

Mjaaland, Marius Timmann. "Confessions and Considerations: Heidegger's Early Black Notebooks and His Lecture on Augustine's Theory of Time." In *Heidegger's Black Notebooks and the Future of Theology*, edited by Mårten Björk and Jayne Svenungsson, 257–75. New York: Palgrave Macmillan, 2018.

Mojsisch, Burkhard. "The Otherness of God as Coincidence, Negation and Not-Otherness in Nicholas of Cusa: An Explication and Critique." In *The Otherness of God*, edited by Orrin F. Summerell, 60–77. Charlottesville: University Press of Virginia, 1998.

Mooney, Hilary Anne-Marie. *Theophany: The Appearing of God According to the Writings of Johannes Scotus Eriugena*. Tübingen: Mohr Siebeck, 2009.

Mopsik, Charles. "Late Judeo-Aramaic: The Language of Theosophic Kabbalah." *Aramaic Studies* 4 (2006): 21–33.

Moran, Dermot. *Edmund Husserl: Founder of Phenomenology*. Cambridge: Polity Press, 2005.

———. "*Spiritualis Incrassatio*: Eriugena's Intellectualist Immaterialism: Is It an Idealism?" In *Eriugena, Berkeley, and the Idealist Tradition*, edited by Stephen Gersh and Dermot Moran, 123–50. Notre Dame: University of Notre Dame Press, 2006.

More, Henry. *Ad Clarissimum ac Eruditissimum virum N. N. De rebus in Amica sua Reponsione contentis Ulterior Disquisitio*. In *Kabbala Denudata, seu, Doctrina hebræorum transcendentalis et metaphysica atqve theologica: opus antiquissimæ philosophiæ barbaricæ variis speciminibus refertissimum*, edited by Christian Knorr von

Rosenroth, vol. 1 pt. 2, 173–224. Sulzbach: Abraham Lichtenthaler, 1677.

———. *Aditus tentatus rationem reddeni nominum & ordinis decem Sephirotharum in duabus Tabulis Cabbalisticis ex Scriptura, Platonismo, ratione que libera*. In *Kabbala Denudata, seu, Doctrina hebræorum transcendentalis et metaphysica atqve theologica: opus antiquissimæ philosophiæ barbaricæ variis speciminibus refertissimum*, edited by Christian Knorr von Rosenroth, vol. 1 pt. 2, 14–27. Sulzbach: Abraham Lichtenthaler, 1677.

———. *Catechismus Cabbalisticus, sive Mercavæus, quo, in Divinis Mysteriis Mercavæ Ezechieliticæ Explicandis & memoria retinendis, decem sephirotharum usus egregie illustrator*. In *Kabbala Denudata, seu, Doctrina hebræorum transcendentalis et metaphysica atqve theologica: opus antiquissimæ philosophiæ barbaricæ variis speciminibus refertissimum*, edited by Christian Knorr von Rosenroth, vol. 1 pt. 2, 274–92. Sulzbach: Abraham Lichtenthaler, 1677.

———. *Conjectura Cabbalistica: Or, A Conjectural Essay of Interpreting the Mind of Moses in the Three First Chapters of Genesis According to a Threefold Cabbala: viz. Literal, Philosophical, Mystical, or, Divinely Moral*. London: Joseph Downing, 1713.

———. *Fundamenta Philosophiæ, sive Cabbalæ Aëto-Pædo-Melissææ*. In *Kabbala Denudata, seu, Doctrina hebræorum transcendentalis et metaphysica atqve theologica: opus antiquissimæ philosophiæ barbaricæ variis speciminibus refertissimum*, edited by Christian Knorr von Rosenroth, vol. 1, pt. 2, 293–312. Sulzbach: Abraham Lichtenthaler, 1677.

———. *The Immortality of the Soul, So Far Forth as It Is Demonstrable From the Knowledge of Nature, and the Light of Reason*. London: Joseph Downing, 1713.

———. *Quæstiones & considerationes paucæ brevesque in Tractatum primum Libri Druschim, sive Introductionem metaphysicam ad Cabbalam genuinam, autore R. Isaaco Loriensi*. In *Kabbala Denudata, seu, Doctrina hebræorum transcendentalis et metaphysica atqve theologica: opus antiquissimæ philosophiæ barbaricæ variis speciminibus refertissimum*, edited by Christian Knorr von Rosenroth, vol. 1, pt. 2, 62–72. Sulzbach: Abraham Lichtenthaler, 1677.

———. *Visionis Ezechieliticæ, sive Mecavæ expositio*. In *Kabbala Denudata, seu, Doctrina hebræorum transcendentalis et metaphysica atqve theologica: opus antiquissimæ philosophiæ barbaricæ variis speciminibus refertissimum*, edited by Christian Knorr von Rosenroth, vol. 1, pt. 2, 225–73. Sulzbach: Abraham Lichtenthaler, 1677.

Morfino, Vittorio. *Plural Temporality: Transindividuality and the Aleatory between Spinoza and Althusser*. Leiden: Brill, 2014.

Morgan, Michael L. *Discovering Levinas*. Cambridge: Cambridge University Press, 2007.

Morgenstern, Matthias, ed. *Martin Luther und die Kabbala: Vom Schem Hamephorasch und vom Geschlecht Christi*. Berlin: Berlin University Press, 2017.

Morlok, Elke. "Text als Textur bei Rabbi Joseph Gikatilla und in der *Kabbala Denudata*. Die Rekonstruktion der Struktur der Gottesnamen aus *Sha'are Ora* in der Lexiographie der *Kabbala Denudata*." *Morgen-Glantz* 16 (2006): 161–79.

Morton, Timothy. "Buddhaphobia: Nothingness and the Fear of Things." In Marcus Boon, Eric Cazdyn, Timothy Morton, *Nothing: Three Inquiries in Buddhism*, 185–266. Chicago: University of Chicago Press, 2015.

Mosès, Stéphane. *The Angel of History: Rosenzweig, Benjamin, Scholem*. Translated by Barbara Harshav. Stanford: Stanford University Press, 2009.

———. "Langage et sécularisation chez Gershom Scholem." *Archives de sciences sociales des religions* 60 (1985): 85–96.

———. "Une lettre inédite de Gershom Scholem a Franz Rosenzweig. A propos de notre langue. Une confession." *Archives de sciences sociales des religions* 60 (1985): 83–84.

———. *System and Revelation: The Philosophy of Franz Rosenzweig*. Foreword by Emmanuel Lévinas, translated by Catherine Tihanyi. Detroit: Wayne State University Press, 1992.

———. "Walter Benjamin and Franz Rosenzweig." *Philosophical Forum* 15 (1983–84): 188–205.

Moses ben Jacob. *Shoshan Sodot*. Jerusalem: Birkat Yiṣḥaq, 2012.

Moses ben Naḥman. *Perushei ha-Torah le-R. Mosheh ben Naḥman*, 2 vols. Edited by Ḥayyim D. Chavel. Jerusalem: Mosad ha-Rav Kook, 1959.

Moses ben Shem Ṭov de León. Fragment of an untitled work. MS Munich, Bayerische Staatsbibliothek Cod. Hebr. 47.

———. *Sefer Sheqel ha-Qodesh*. Edited by Charles Mopsik. Introduction by Moshe Idel. Los Angeles: Cherub, 1996.

———. *Shushan Edut*. Edited by Gershom Scholem, "Two Treatises by Moses de León." *Qoveṣ al Yad* 8 (1976): 330–70 (Hebrew).

———. *Sod Eser Sefirot Belimah*. Edited by Gershom Scholem, "Two Treatises by Moses de León." *Qoveṣ al Yad* 8 (1976): 371–84 (Hebrew).

Motzkin, Gabriel. "'Ehyeh' and the Future: 'God' and Heidegger's Concept of 'Becoming' Compared."

In *Ocular Desire: Sehnsucht des Auges*, edited by Aharon R. E. Agus and Jan Assmann, 173–82. Berlin: Akademie, 1994.

———. "Heidegger's Transcendent Nothing." In *Languages of the Unsayable: The Play of Negativity in Literature and Literary Theory*, edited by Sanford Budick and Wolfgang Iser, 95–116. New York: Columbia University Press, 1996.

Moyn, Samuel. "The Spirit of Jewish History." In *The Modern Era*, vol. 2 of *The Cambridge History of Jewish Philosophy*, edited by Martin Kavka, Zachary Braiterman, and David Novak, 75–96. Cambridge: Cambridge University Press, 2012.

Mugerauer, Robert. *Heidegger and Homecoming: The Leitmotif in the Later Writings*. Toronto: University of Toronto Press, 2008.

Mulhall, Stephen. *Inheritance and Originality: Wittgenstein, Heidegger, Kierkegaard*. Oxford: Oxford University Press, 2001.

Munro, J. P. L. "On Being Oneself: A Comparison of Heidegger and Buber on Personal Identity." PhD diss., University of Edinburgh, 1979.

Muratori, Cecilia. *The First German Philosopher: The Mysticism of Jakob Böhme as Interpreted by Hegel*. Translated by Richard Dixon and Raphaëlle Burns. Dordrecht: Springer, 2016.

Myers, David N. *Resisting History: Historicism and Its Discontents in German-Jewish Thought*. Princeton: Princeton University Press, 2003.

Nadler, Allan. *The Faith of the Mithnagdim: Rabbinic Responses to Hasidic Rapture*. Baltimore: Johns Hopkins University Press, 1997.

Nagel, Mechthild. "Thrownness, Playing-in the-World, and the Question of Authenticity." In *Feminist Interpretations of Martin Heidegger*, edited by Nancy J. Holland and Patricia Huntington, 289–306. University Park: Pennsylvania State University Press, 2001.

Nägele, Rainer. "Thinking Images." In *Benjamin's Ghosts: Interventions in Contemporary Literary and Cultural Theory*, edited by Gerhard Richter, 23–40. Stanford: Stanford University Press, 2002.

Naḥman of Bratslav. *Liqquṭei MoHaRaN*. Benei Beraq: Yeshivat Bratslav, 1972.

Nancy, Jean-Luc. *The Banality of Heidegger*. Translated by Jeff Fort. New York: Fordham University Press, 2017.

———. *Being Singular Plural*. Translated by Robert D. Richardson. Stanford: Stanford University Press, 2000.

———. *The Fall of Sleep*. Translated by Charlotte Mandell. New York: Fordham University Press, 2009.

———. *The Gravity of Thought*. Translated by François Raffoul and Gregory Recco. Amherst: Humanity Books, 1997.

———. *Hegel: The Restlessness of the Negative*. Translated by Jason Smith and Steven Miller. Minneapolis: University of Minnesota Press, 2002.

Nancy, Jean-Luc, and Aurélien Barrau. *What's These Worlds Coming To?* Translated by Travis Holloway and Flor Méchain. Foreword by David Pettigrew. New York: Fordham University Press, 2015.

Nathan of Gaza. *Sefer ha-Beri'ah*. MS Jewish Theological Seminary of America 1581.

———. *Zemir Ariṣim Ya'aneh*. MS Oxford, Bodleian Library 1796.

Necker, Gerold. "Circle, Point and Line: A Lurianic Myth in the *Puerta del Cielo*." In *Creation and Re-Creation in Jewish Thought: Festschrift in Honor of Joseph Dan on the Occasion of his Seventieth Birthday*, edited by Rachel Elior and Peter Schäfer, 193–207. Tübingen: Mohr Siebeck, 2005.

———. "Geister, Engel und Dämonen: Abraham Cohen de Herreras Seelenlehre in der *Kabbala Denudata*." *Morgen-Glantz* 16 (2006): 203–20.

———. "Hans Blumenberg's Metaphorology and the Historical Perspective of Mystical Terminology." *Jewish Studies Quarterly* 22 (2015): 184–203.

———. *Humanistische Kabbala im Barock: Leben und Werk des Abraham Cohen de Herrera*. Berlin: Walter de Gruyter, 2011.

Negri, Antonio. *The Savage Anomaly: The Power of Spinoza's Metaphysics and Politics*. Translated by Michael Hardt. Minneapolis: University of Minnesota Press, 1991.

Neher, André. *Jérusalem, vécu juif et message*. Monaco: Rocher, 1984.

———. "The Jewish Dimension of Space: Zionism." In *Modern French Jewish Thought: Writings on Religion and Politics*, edited by Sarah Hammerschlag, 151–58. Waltham: Brandeis University Press, 2018.

Nelson, Eric S. *Chinese and Buddhist Philosophy in Early Twentieth-Century German Thought*. London: Bloomsbury, 2017.

Newland, Guy. *Appearance and Reality: The Two Truths in the Four Buddhist Tenet Systems*. Ithaca: Snow Lion, 1999.

———. *The Two Truths in the Mādhyamika Philosophy of the Ge-luk-ba Order of Tibetan Buddhism*. Ithaca: Snow Lion, 1992.

Nicholas of Cusa. *Complete Philosophical and Theological Treatises of Nicholas of Cusa*. 2 vols. Translated by Jasper Hopkins. Minneapolis: Arthur J. Banning, 2001.

Nietzsche, Friedrich. *The Gay Science, with a Prelude in German Rhymes and an Appendix of Songs*. Edited by Bernard Williams. Translated by Josephine Nauckhoff. Poems translated by Adrian del Caro. Cambridge: Cambridge University Press, 2001.

———. *The Will to Power*. Translated by Walter Kaufmann and R. J. Hollingdale. Edited by Walter Kaufmann. New York: Random House, 1967.

Nishida Kitarō. *An Inquiry into the Good*. Translated by Masao Abe and Christopher Ives. Introduction by Masao Abe. New Haven: Yale University Press, 1990.

———. *Intelligibility and the Philosophy of Nothingness: Three Philosophical Essays*. Translated with an introduction by Robert Schinzinger. Honolulu: East-West Center Press, 1958.

———. *Last Writings: Nothingness and the Religious Worldview*. Translated with an introduction by David A. Dilworth. Honolulu: University of Hawaii Press, 1987.

———. *Ontology of Production: Three Essays*. Translated with an introduction by William Haver. Durham: Duke University Press, 2012.

———. *Place and Dialectic: Two Essays by Nishida Kitarō*. Translated by John W. M. Krummel and Shigenori Nagatomo. Oxford: Oxford University Press, 2012.

Nishitani Keiji. *Nishida Kitarō*. Berkeley: University of California Press, 1991.

———. "Reflections on Two Addresses by Martin Heidegger." In *Heidegger and Asian Thought*, edited by Graham Parkes, 145–54. Honolulu: University of Hawaii Press, 1987.

Nobus, Dany. *Jacques Lacan and the Freudian Practice of Psychoanalysis*. London: Routledge, 2000.

North, Michael. *What Is the Present?* Princeton: Princeton University Press, 2018.

North, Paul. *The Yield: Kafka's Atheological Reformation*. Stanford: Stanford University Press, 2015.

Northoff, Georg. *Minding the Brain: A Guide to Philosophy and Neuroscience*. New York: Palgrave Macmillan, 2014.

Novak, David. "Buber's Critique of Heidegger." *Modern Judaism* 5 (1985): 125–40.

Oberst, Joachim L. *Heidegger on Language and Death: The Intrinsic Connection in Human Existence*. London: Continuum, 2009.

Ochs, Peter. *Peirce, Pragmatism and the Logic of Scripture*. Cambridge: Cambridge University Press, 1998.

O'Donnell, Neil. "Böhme and Hegel: A Study of Their Intellectual Development and Shared Readings of Two Christian Theologoumena." MLitt. thesis, National University of Ireland, Maynooth, 2008.

O'Donoghue, Brendan. *A Poetics of Homecoming: Heidegger, Homelessness and the Homecoming Venture*. Newcastle: Cambridge Scholars, 2011.

Ogden, Schubert M. *The Reality of God and Other Essays*. San Francisco: Harper and Row, 1977.

Ogren, Brian. *The Beginnings of the World in Renaissance Jewish Thought: Ma'aseh Bereshit in Italian Jewish Philosophy and Kabbalah, 1492–1535*. Leiden: Brill, 2016.

———. "The Law of Change and the Nature of the Chameleon: Yosef ben Šalom 'Aškenazi and Giovanni Pico della Mirandola." In *Giovanni Pico e la cabbalà*, edited by Fabrizio Lelli, 121–33. Firenze: Leo S. Olschki, 2014.

———. *Renaissance and Rebirth: Reincarnation in Early Modern Italian Kabbalah*. Leiden: Brill, 2009.

Ohashi, Ryosuke. *Ekstase und Gelassenheit: Zu Schelling und Heidegger*. Munich: Wilhelm Fink, 1975.

———. "Der Ungrund und das System." In *F.W.J. Schelling: Über das Wesen der menschlichen Freiheit*, edited by Otfried Höffe and Annemarie Pieper, 235–52. Berlin: Akademie, 1995.

Olafson, Frederick A. "Being, Truth, and Presence in Heidegger's Thought." *Inquiry* 41 (1998): 45–64.

O'Leary, Joseph S. "Theological Resonances of *Der Satz vom Grund*." In *Martin Heidegger: Critical Assessments*, vol. 1: *Philosophy*, edited by Christopher Macann, 213–56. Routledge: London, 1992.

Olson, Alan M. *Hegel and the Spirit: Philosophy as Pneumatology*. Princeton: Princeton University Press, 1992.

Onishi, Bradley B. "The Birth of World: The Spark of Eckhart in Heidegger and Bataille." PhD diss., University of California, Santa Barbara, 2014.

O'Regan, Cyril. *Gnostic Apocalypse: Jacob Boehme's Haunted Narrative*. Albany: State University of New York Press, 2002.

———. *The Heterodox Hegel*. Foreword by Louis Dupré. Albany: State University of New York Press, 1994.

Ott, Hugo. *Martin Heidegger: A Political Life*. Translated by Allan Blunden. New York: Basic Books, 1993.

Pachter, Mordechai. "The Gaon's Kabbalah from the Perspective of Two Traditions." In *The Vilna Gaon and His Disciples*, edited by Moshe Hallamish, Yosef Rivlin, and Raphael Shuchat, 119–36. Ramat Gan: Bar-Ilan University Press, 2003 (Hebrew).

Park, Bradley Douglas. "Differing Ways, *Dao* and *Weg*: Comparative, Metaphysical, and Methodological Considerations in Heidegger's 'Aus einem Gespräch von der Sprache.'" *Continental Philosophy Review* 37 (2004): 309–39.

Parkes, Graham. "Lao-Zhuang and Heidegger on Nature and Technology." *Journal of Chinese Philosophy* 39 (2012): 112–33.

———. "Thoughts on the Way: *Being and Time* via Lao-Chuang." In *Heidegger and Asian Thought*, edited by Graham Parkes, 105–44. Honolulu: University of Hawaii Press, 1987.

Paslick, Robert H. "The Ontological Context of Gadamer's 'Fusion': Boehme, Heidegger, and Non-Duality." *Man and World* 18 (1985): 405–22.

Pattison, George. *Heidegger on Death: A Critical Theological Essay*. Burlington: Ashgate, 2013.

———. "The Role of Mysticism in the Formation of Heidegger's Phenomenology." In *Mystical Theology and Continental Philosophy: Interchange in the Wake of God*, edited by David Lewin, Simon D. Podmore, and Duane Williams, 131–46. London: Routledge, 2017.

Peckler, Mark A. "Imagination, Religious Practice, and World Transformations: Sophia, Heidegger, and Jacob Böhme's *The Way to Christ*." PhD diss., University of Denver and Iliff School of Theology, 2009.

Pedaya, Ḥaviva. "The Divinity as Place and Time and the Holy Place in Jewish Mysticism." In *Sacred Space: Shrine, City, Land—Proceedings of the International Conference in Memory of Joshua Prawer*, edited by Benjamin Z. Kedar and R. J. Zwi Werblowsky, 84–111. Jerusalem: Israel Academy of Sciences and Humanities, 1998.

———. *Kabbalah and Psychoanalysis: An Inner Journey in the Path of Jewish Mysticism*. Tel-Aviv: Yedioth Ahronoth, 2015 (Hebrew).

———. *Naḥmanides: Cyclical Times and Holy Text*. Tel-Aviv: Am Oved, 2003 (Hebrew).

Peirce, Charles S. "The Logic of Continuity." In *Philosophy of Mathematics: Selected Writings*, edited by Matthew E. Moore, 179–88. Bloomington: Indiana University Press, 2010.

———. "A Neglected Argument for the Reality of God." In *Collected Papers of Charles Sanders Peirce*, vol. 6, edited by Charles Hartshorne and Paul Weiss, 311–39. Cambridge, MA: Harvard University Press, 1935.

———. "Questions Concerning Certain Faculties." In *Writings of Charles S. Peirce: A Chronological Edition*, vol. 2, edited by the Peirce Edition Project, 193–211. Bloomington: Indiana University Press, 1984.

———. "Some Consequences of Four Incapacities." In *Collected Papers of Charles Sanders Peirce*, vol. 5, edited by Charles Hartshorne and Paul Weiss, 156–89. Cambridge, MA: Harvard University Press, 1934.

Peleg, Erez. "More about Rabbi Shlomo Eliyashov's Controversy against 'The Kabbalists in our Day.'" *Da'at* 79–80 (2015): 183–203 (Hebrew).

Penman, Leigh T. I. "Boehme's Intellectual Networks and the Heterodox Milieu of His Theosophy, 1600–1624." In *An Introduction to Jacob Boehme: Four Centuries of Thought and Reception*, edited by Ariel Hessayon and Sarah Apetrei, 57–76. New York: Routledge, 2014.

———. "A Second Christian Rosencreuz? Jakob Böhme's Disciple Balthasar Walther (1558–c. 1630) and the Kabbalah, with a Bibliography of Walther's Printed Works." *Scripta instituti donneriani Aboensis* 20 (2014): 154–72.

Perlman, Lawrence. *The Eclipse of Humanity: Heschel's Critique of Heidegger*. Berlin: Walter de Gruyter, 2016.

Perotti, James L. *Heidegger on the Divine: The Thinker, the Poet and God*. Athens: Ohio University Press, 1974.

Petzet, Heinrich W. *Encounters and Dialogues with Martin Heidegger 1929–1976*. Translated by Parvis Emad and Kenneth Maly. Chicago: University of Chicago Press, 1993.

Phelps, Hollis. "(Theo)poetic Naming and the Advent of Truths: The Function of Poetics in the Philosophy of Alain Badiou." In *Theopoetic Folds: Philosophizing Multifariousness*, edited by Roland Faber and Jeremy Fackenthal, 30–46. New York: Fordham University Press, 2013.

Philipse, Herman. "Heidegger and Wittgenstein on External World Skepticism." In *Wittgenstein and Heidegger*, edited by David Egan, Stephen Reynolds, and Aaron James Wendland, 116–32. New York: Routledge, 2013.

———. *Heidegger's Philosophy of Being: A Critical Interpretation*. Princeton: Princeton University Press, 1998.

Phillips, Wesley. *Metaphysics and Music in Adorno and Heidegger*. New York: Palgrave Macmillan, 2015.

Pico della Mirandola. *Syncretism in the West: Pico's 900 Theses (1486): The Evolution of Traditional Religious and Philosophical Systems*. Edited and translated by Stephen Alan Farmer. Tempe: Medieval and Renaissance Texts and Studies, 1998.

Piepmeier, Rainer. "Friedrich Christoph Oetinger." In *Gnosis und Mystik in der Geschichte der*

Philosophie, edited by Peter Koslowski, 207–25. Zürich: Artemis, 1988.

Pines, Shlomo. "Points of Similarity between the Exposition of the Doctrine of the Sefirot in the Sefer Yeẓira and a Text of the Pseudo-Clementine Homilies: The Implications of This Resemblance." *Proceedings of the Israel Academy of Sciences and Humanities* 7 (1989): 63–142.

Pinosio, Riccardo. *The Logic of Kant's Temporal Continuum*. Amsterdam: Institute for Logic, Language, and Computation Dissertation Series, 2017.

Pirqei Rabbi Eliezer. Edited by David Luria. Warsaw, 1852.

Piyyute Yannai: Liturgical Poems of Yannai. Edited by Menahem Zulay. Berlin: Schocken, 1938 (Hebrew).

Plaisance, Christopher A. "Occult Spheres, Planes, and Dimensions: Geometric Terminology and Analogy in Modern Esoteric Discourse." *Journal of Religious History* 40 (2016): 385–404.

Plato. *The Collected Dialogues of Plato Including the Letters*. Edited by Edith Hamilton and Huntington Cairns, with introduction and prefatory notes. Princeton: Princeton University Press, 1961.

Plotini Opera, II: Enneades IV–V. Edited by Paul Henry and Hans-Rudolf Schwyzer. Paris: Desclée de Brouwer, 1959.

Plotinus. *Enneads*. 7 vols. Translated by Arthur H. Armstrong. Cambridge, MA: Harvard University Press, 1966–88.

Pöggeler, Otto. *The Paths of Heidegger's Life and Thought*. Translated by John Bailiff. Atlantic Highlands: Humanities, 1997.

———. "West-East Dialogue: Heidegger and Lao-tzu." In *Heidegger and Asian Thought*, edited by Graham Parkes, 47–78. Honolulu: University of Hawaii Press, 1987.

Pollock, Benjamin. *Franz Rosenzweig and the Systematic Task of Philosophy*. Cambridge: Cambridge University Press, 2009.

———. *Franz Rosenzweig's Conversions: World Denial and World Redemption*. Bloomington: Indiana University Press, 2014.

———. "From Nation States to World Empire: Franz Rosenzweig's Redemptive Imperialism." *Jewish Studies Quarterly* 11 (2004): 332–53.

Polt, Richard. *The Emergency of Being: On Heidegger's Contribution to Philosophy*. Ithaca: Cornell University Press, 2006.

———. "The Question of Nothing." In *A Companion to Heidegger's Introduction of Metaphysics*, edited by Richard Polt and Gregory Fried, 57–82. New Haven: Yale University Press, 2001.

———. "The Secret Homeland of Speech: Heidegger on Language, 1933–1934." In *Heidegger and Language*, edited by Jeffrey Powell, 63–85. Bloomington: Indiana University Press, 2013.

Poppers, Meir ben Judah Leib. *Mesillot Ḥokhmah*. Cracow: Yosef Fisher and Shaul Deutscher, 1881.

Porat, Oded, ed. *The Works of Iyyun: Critical Editions*. Los Angeles: Cherub, 2013 (Hebrew).

Priest, Graham. *Beyond the Limits of Thought*. Oxford: Oxford University Press, 2002.

———. *In Contradiction: A Study of the Transconsistent*. 2nd ed. Oxford: Oxford University Press, 2006.

Priest, Graham, J. C. Beall, and Bradley Armour-Garb, eds. *The Law of Non-Contradiction: New Philosophical Essays*. Oxford: Oxford University Press, 2004.

Prochnik, George. *Stranger in a Strange Land: Searching for Gershom Scholem and Jerusalem*. New York: Other, 2016.

Proclus. *Commentary on Plato's Parmenides*. Translated by Glenn R. Morrow and John M. Dillon, with introduction and notes by John M. Dillon. Princeton: Princeton University Press, 1987.

———. *The Elements of Theology*. 2nd ed. rev. Translated by Eric R. Dodds. Oxford: Oxford University Press, 1963.

———. *Théologie Platonicienne*. 6 vols. Edited and translated by H. D. Saffrey and L. G. Westerink. Paris: Belles Lettres, 2003.

Protevi, John. *Time and Exteriority: Aristotle, Heidegger, Derrida*. Lewisburg: Bucknell University Press, 1994.

Pylkkö, Pauli. *The Aconceptual Mind: Heideggerian Themes in Holistic Naturalism*. Amsterdam: John Benjamins, 1998.

Rabin, Sheila J. "Whither Kabbalah? Giovanni Pico Della Mirandola, Kabbalah, and the *Disputations Against Judicial Astrology*." In *Hebraic Aspects of the Renaissance Sources and Encounters*, edited by Ilana Zinguer, Abraham Melamed, and Zur Shalev, 43–52. Leiden: Brill, 2011.

Rabinbach, Anson. "Between Enlightenment and Apocalypse: Benjamin, Bloch and Modern German Jewish Messianism." *New German Critique* 34 (1985): 78–124.

Rabinowitz, Ṣadoq ha-Kohen. *Maḥashavot Ḥaruṣ*. Jerusalem: Har Berakhah, 2006.

———. *Peri Ṣaddiq*, vol. 1. Jerusalem: Mesamḥei Lev, 1999.

———. *Resisay Laylah.* Jerusalem: Har Berakhah, 2003.

———. *Ṣidqat ha-Ṣaddiq.* Jerusalem: Har Berakhah, 2005.

Rae, Gavin. *Ontology in Heidegger and Deleuze: A Comparative Analysis.* New York: Palgrave Macmillan, 2014.

Rang, Bernhard. *Identität und Indifferenz: Eine Untersuchung zu Schellings Identitätsphilosophie.* Frankfurt am Main: Vittorio Klostermann, 2000.

Rapoport-Albert, Ada. *Hasidic Studies: Essays in History and Gender,* with an introduction by Moshe Rosman. Oxford: Litman Library of Jewish Civilization, 2018.

———. *Women and the Messianic Heresy of Sabbatai Zevi 1666–1816.* Oxford: Littman Library of Jewish Civilization, 2011.

Rapoport-Albert Ada and Theodore Kwasman. "Late Aramaic: The Literary and Linguistic Context of the Zohar." *Aramaic Studies* 4 (2006): 5–19.

Raposa, Michael L. *Peirce's Philosophy of Religion.* Bloomington: Indiana University Press, 1989.

Reddan, Marion. "Heidegger and the Mystery of Being." PhD diss., University of Wollongong, 2009.

Reichert, Klaus. "Christian Kabbalah in the Seventeenth Century." In *The Christian Kabbalah: Jewish Mystical Books and Their Christian Interpreters,* edited by Joseph Dan, 127–47. Cambridge, MA: Harvard College Library, 1997.

———. "'It Is Time': The Buber-Rosenzweig Bible Translation in Context." In *The Translatability of Cultures: Figurations of the Space Between,* edited by Sanford Budick and Wolfgang Iser, 169–85. Stanford: Stanford University Press, 1996.

Reid, James D. *Being Here Is Glorious: On Rilke, Poetry, and Philosophy.* Evanston: Northwestern University Press, 2015.

Reitzenstein, Richard. *Hellenistic Mystery-Religions: Their Basic Idea and Significance.* Translated by John E. Steely. Pittsburgh: Pickwick, 1978.

Reuchlin, Johann. *On the Art of the Kabbalah.* Translated by Martin and Sarah Goodman. Introduction by G. Lloyd Jones. New York: Abaris, 1983.

Ricchi, Immanuel ben Abraham Ḥai. *Mishnat Ḥasidim.* Jerusalem: Makhon Mishnat Ḥasidim, 2015.

———. *Yosher Levav.* Jerusalem: Alei Ayin, 2010.

Richardson, William J. "Heidegger and Psychoanalysis?" *Natureza Humana* 5 (2003): 9–38.

———. "Psychoanalysis and the Being-Question." In *Interpreting Lacan,* edited by Joseph H. Smith and William Kerrigan, 139–59. New Haven: Yale University Press, 1983.

Richter, Gerhard. *Thought-Images: Frankfurt School Writers' Reflections from Damaged Life.* Stanford: Stanford University Press, 2007.

Rickey, Christopher. *Revolutionary Saints: Heidegger, National Socialism, and Antinomian Politics.* University Park: Pennsylvania State University Press, 2002.

Riera, Gabriel. "Abyssal Grounds: Lacan and Heidegger on Truth." *Qui Parle* 9 (1996): 61–76.

Robinson, Josh. *Adorno's Poetics of Form.* Albany: State University of New York Press, 2018.

Rödl, Sebastian. *Categories of the Temporal: An Inquiry into the Forms of the Finite Intellect.* Translated by Sibylle Salewski. Cambridge, MA: Harvard University Press, 2012.

Rohstock, Max. *Der Negative Selbstbezug des Absoluten: Untersuchungen zu Nicolaus Cusanus' Konzept des Nicht-Anderen.* Berlin: Walter de Gruyter, 2014.

Roi, Biti. *Love of the Shekhina: Mysticism and Poetics in Tiqqunei ha-Zohar.* Ramat Gan: Bar-Ilan University Press, 2017 (Hebrew).

Romano, Claude. *There Is: The Event and the Finitude of Appearing.* Translated by Michael B. Smith. New York: Fordham University Press, 2016.

Rorty, Richard. *Consequences of Pragmatism (Essays: 1972–1980).* Minneapolis: University of Minnesota Press, 1982.

———. *Philosophical Papers.* Vol. 2: *Essays on Heidegger and Others.* New York: Cambridge University Press, 1991.

Rosen, Diane. "Accessing Creativity: Jungian Night Sea Journeys, Wandering Minds, and Chaos." *Nonlinear Dynamics, Psychology, and Life Sciences* 20 (2016): 117–39.

———. "Lessons from Dada and Chaos: Unknowing as a Creative Heuristic." *Chaos and Complexity Letters* 11 (2017): 193–201.

Rosen, Stanley. "Thinking about Nothing." In *Heidegger and Modern Philosophy: Critical Essays,* edited by Michael Murray, 116–37. New Haven: Yale University Press, 1978.

Rosenberg, Shimon Gershon. *Faith Shattered and Restored: Judaism in the Postmodern Age.* Translated by Elie Leshem, edited by Zohar Maor. Jerusalem: Maggid Books, 2017.

Rosenstock, Bruce. "Abraham Miguel Cardoso's Messianism." *Association for Jewish Studies Review* 23 (1998): 63–104.

Rosenzweig, Franz. *Briefe und Tagebücher.* Vol. 1 of *Der Mensch und sein Werk: Gesammelte Schriften.* Edited by Rachel Rosenzweig and Edith Rosenzweig-Scheinmann, with the collaboration of Bernhard Casper, vol. 2: 1918–1929. The Hague: Martinus Nijhoff, 1979.

———. "Scripture and Luther." In Martin Buber and Franz Rosenzweig, *Scripture and Translation.* Translated by Lawrence Rosenwald with Everett Fox, 47–69. Bloomington: Indiana University Press, 1994.

———. *The Star of Redemption.* Translated by Barbara E. Galli. Madison: University of Wisconsin Press, 2000.

———. *Der Stern der Erlösung.* Vol. 2 of *Der Mensch und sein Werk: Gesammelte Schriften.* The Hague: Martinus Nijhoff, 1976.

———. *Zweistromland: Kleinere Schriften zu Glauben und Denken.* Vol. 3 of *Der Mensch und sein Werk: Gesammelte Schriften.* Edited by Reinhold and Annemarie Mayer. The Hague: Martinus Nijhoff, 1984.

Rospatt, Alexander von. *The Buddhist Doctrine of Momentariness: A Survey of the Origins and Early Phase of This Doctrine Up to Vasubandhu.* Stuttgart: Franz Steiner, 1995.

Ross, Alison. *Walter Benjamin's Concept of the Image.* London: Routledge, 2015.

Rossi, Pablo. *Logic and the Art of Memory: The Quest for a Universal Language.* Translated by Stephen Clucas. Chicago: University of Chicago Press, 2000.

Rot, Avraham. "From Anxiety to Boredom: Heidegger, Freud, and the Emotional History of Secularization." PhD diss., Johns Hopkins University, 2016.

Rotenstreich, Nathan. "Gershom Scholem's Conception of Jewish Nationalism." In *Gershom Scholem: The Man and His Work,* edited by Paul Mendes-Flohr, 104–19. Albany: State University of New York, Press, 1994.

———. "Symbolism and Transcendence: On Some Philosophical Aspects of Gershom Scholem's Opus." *Review of Metaphysics* 31 (1978): 604–14.

Rothschild, Jean-Pierre. "Le Livre des causes du latin à l'hébreu: textes, problèmes, réception." In *Texts in Contexts.* Vol. 2 of *Latin-into-Hebrew: Texts and Studies,* edited by Alexander Fidora, Harvey J. Hames, and Yossef Schwartz, 47–84. Leiden: Brill, 2013.

———. "Les traductions hébraïques du *Livre des causes* latin, édition synoptique." In *Texts in Contexts.* Vol. 2 of *Latin-into-Hebrew: Texts and Studies,* edited by Alexander Fidora, Harvey J. Hames, and Yossef Schwartz, 289–368. Leiden: Brill, 2013.

Roudinesco, Elisabeth. *Jacques Lacan.* Translated by Barbara Bray. New York: Columbia University Press, 1997.

———. *Jacques Lacan & Co.: A History of Psychoanalysis in France, 1925–1985.* Translated by Jeffrey Mehlman. Chicago: University of Chicago Press, 1990.

Rovelli, Carlo. *The Order of Time.* Translated by Erica Segre and Simon Carnell. New York: Riverhead, 2018.

———. *Reality Is Not What It Seems: The Journey to Quantum Gravity.* Translated by Simon Carnell and Erica Segre. New York: Riverhead, 2017.

———. *Seven Brief Lessons on Physics.* Translated by Simon Carnell and Erica Segre. New York: Riverhead, 2016.

Rudolph, Hartmut. "Die Kabbala im Werk des Paracelsus." In *Christliche Kabbala,* edited by Wilhelm Schmidt-Biggemann, 109–20. Ostfildem: Jan Thorbecke, 2003.

Rudolph, Kurt. *Gnosis: The Nature and History of Gnosticism.* Translated and edited by Robert McLachlan Wilson. San Francisco: Harper and Row, 1983.

———. "Hans Jonas and Research on Gnosticism from a Contemporary Perspective." In *The Legacy of Hans Jonas: Judaism and the Phenomenon of Life,* edited by Hava Tirosh-Samuelson and Christian Wiese, 91–106. Leiden: Brill, 2008.

Ruin, Hans. *Enigmatic Origins: Tracing the Theme of Historicity through Heidegger's Works.* Stockholm: Almqvist and Wiksell, 1994.

———. "Leibniz and Heidegger on Sufficient Reason." *Studia Leibnitiana* 30 (1998): 49–67.

———. "Origin in Exile: Heidegger and Benjamin on Language, Truth, and Translation." *Research in Phenomenology* 29 (1999): 141–60.

———. "Time as Ek-stasis and Trace of the Other." In *Rethinking Time: Essays on History, Memory, and Representation,* edited by Hans Ruin and Andrus Ers, 51–61. Huddinge: Södertörns Högskola, 2011.

Rusterholz, Sibylle. "Elemente christlicher Kabbala bei Abraham von Franckenberg." In *Christliche Kabbala,* edited by Wilhelm Schmidt-Biggemann, 183–97. Ostfildem: Jan Thorbecke, 2003.

———. "Elemente der Kabbala bei Jacob Böhme." In *Mystik und Schriftkommentierung* [*Böhme-Studien 1. Beiträge zu Philosophie und Philologie*], edited

by Günther Bonheim and Petra Kattner, 15–45. Berlin: Weißensee, 2007.
Ruthrof, Horst. *Language and Imaginability.* Newcastle: Cambridge Scholars, 2014.
Sacchi, Mario Enrique. *The Apocalypse of Being: The Esoteric Gnosis of Martin Heidegger.* Translated by Gabriel Xavier Martinez. Foreword by Ralph McInerny. South Bend: St. Augustine's, 2002.
Sack, Bracha. "The Doctrine of Ṣimṣum of R. Moses Cordovero." *Tarbiz* 58 (1989): 207–37 (Hebrew).
———. *The Kabbalah of Rabbi Moshe Cordovero.* Beer Sheva: Ben-Gurion University Press, 1995 (Hebrew).
Safranski, Rüdiger. *Martin Heidegger: Between Good and Evil.* Translated by Ewald Osers. Cambridge, MA: Harvard University Press, 1998.
Said, Edward W. *Beginnings: Intention and Method.* New York: Basic Books, 1975.
Sallis, John. "Doublings." In *Derrida: A Critical Reader,* edited by David Wood, 120–36. Oxford: Blackwell, 1992.
———. "Interrupting Truth." In *Heidegger toward the Turn: Essays on the Work of the 1930s,* edited by James Risser, 19–30. Albany: State University of New York Press, 1999.
———. *Phenomenology and the Return to Beginnings.* Pittsburgh: Duquesne University Press, 2003.
———. *The Return of Nature: On the Beyond of Sense.* Bloomington: Indiana University Press, 2016.
———. "Twisting Free: Being to an Extent Sensible." *Research in Phenomenology* 17 (1987): 1–22.
Saruq, Israel. *Derush ha-Malbush we-ha-Ṣimṣum.* Edited by Matthias Safrin. Jerusalem: Matthias Safrin, 2001.
———. *Limmudei Aṣilut.* Munkács: Blayer and Kohn, 1897.
Sauter, Caroline. "The Ghost of the Poet: Lament in Walter Benjamin's Early Poetry, Theory, and Translation." In *Lament in Jewish Thought: Philosophical, Theological, and Literary Perspectives,* edited by Ilit Ferber and Paula Schwebel, 205–20. Berlin: Walter de Gruyter, 2014.
Schäfer, Peter, and Gary Smith, eds. *Gershom Scholem: Zwischen den Disziplinen.* Frankfurt am Main: Suhrkamp, 1995.
Schalow, Frank. "Attunement and Translation." In *Heidegger, Translation, and the Task of Thinking: Essays in Honor of Parvis Emad,* edited by Frank Schalow, 291–311. Dordrecht: Springer, 2011.
———. "A Conversation with Parvis Emad on the Question of Translation in Heidegger." In *Heidegger, Translation, and the Task of Thinking: Essays in Honor of Parvis Emad,* edited by Frank Schalow, 175–89. Dordrecht: Springer, 2011.
———. *Heidegger and the Quest for the Sacred: From Thought to the Sanctuary of Faith.* Dordrecht: Kluwer Academic, 2001.
Schatz, Moshe. *Ma'yan Moshe.* Jerusalem, 2011.
Schechter, Solomon, ed. *Avot de-Rabbi Natan.* Vienna: Ch. D. Lippe, 1887.
Schechterman, Deborah. "Studies in the Short Version of Sha'ar ha-Shamayim of Isaac Ibn Laṭif." MA thesis, University of Haifa, 1980 (Hebrew).
Schelling, Friedrich Wilhelm Joseph. *The Ages of the World.* Translated with introduction and notes by Frederik de Wolfe Bolman Jr. New York: Columbia University Press, 1942.
———. *The Ages of the World (Fragment) from the Handwritten Remains, Third Version (c. 1815).* Translated with an introduction by Jason M. Wirth. Albany: State University of New York Press, 2000.
———. *Nachlass 8: Stuttgarter Privatvorlesungen (1810).* Edited by Vicki Müller-Lüneschloss. Stuttgart: Frommann-Holzboog, 2017.
———. *On the History of Modern Philosophy.* Translated by Andrew Bowie. Cambridge: Cambridge University Press, 1994.
———. *Philosophical Investigations into the Essence of Human Freedom.* Translated and with an introduction by Jeff Love and Johannes Schmidt. Albany: State University of New York Press, 2006.
———. *Philosophie und Religion.* Tübingen: I. G. Cotta'schen Buchhandlung, 1804.
———. *Philosophische Untersuchungen über das Wesen der menschlichen Freiheit und die damit zusammenhängenden Gegenstände.* Edited by Thomas Buchheim. Hamburg: Felix Meiner, 1997.
———. *Philosophy and Religion (1804).* Translated, annotated, and with an introduction by Klaus Ottmann. Putnam: Spring, 2010.
———. *Sämmtliche Werke 1792–1797.* Edited by Karl Friedrich August Schelling, vol. 1. Stuttgart: Cotta, 1856.
———. *Sämmtliche Werke 1804.* Edited by Karl Friedrich August Schelling, vol. 6. Stuttgart: Cotta, 1860.
———. *Sämmtliche Werke 1805–1810.* Edited by Karl Friedrich August Schelling, vol. 7. Stuttgart: Cotta, 1860.
———. *Sämmtliche Werke 1811–1815.* Edited by Karl Friedrich August Schelling, vol. 8. Stuttgart: Cotta, 1861.

———. *Statement on the True Relationship of the Philosophy of Nature to the Revised Fichtean Doctrine: An Elucidation of the Former.* Translated with an introduction and notes by Dale E. Snow. Albany: State University of New York Press, 2018.

———. *System der Weltalter: Münchener Vorlesung 1827/28 in einer Nachschrift von Ernst von Lasaulx.* Edited by Siegbert Peetz. Frankfurt am Main: Vittorio Klostermann, 1998.

———. *System of Transcendental Idealism (1800).* Translated by Peter Heath. Introduction by Michael Vater. Charlottesville: University Press of Virginia, 1978.

———. *Weltalter—Fragmente.* 2 vols. Edited by Klaus Grotsch. Introduction by Wilhelm Schmidt-Biggemann. Stuttgart: Frommann-Holzboog, 2002.

———. *Die Weltalter in den Urfassungen von 1811 und 1813 (Nachlaßband).* Edited by Manfred Schröter. Munich: Biederstein and Leibniz, 1946.

———. *Zur Geschichte der neueren Philosophie: Münchener Vorlesungen.* Edited by Arthur Drews. Leipzig: Dürr'schen Buchhandlung, 1902.

Schindler, Renate. *Zeit, Geschichte, Ewigkeit in Franz Rosenzweigs* Stern der Erlösung. Berlin: Parerga, 2007.

Schmidt, Christoph. "Monotheism as a Metapolitical Problem: Heidegger's War against Jewish Christian Monotheism." In *Heidegger's Black Notebooks and the Future of Theology*, edited by Mårten Björk and Jayne Svenungsson, 131–57. New York: Palgrave Macmillan, 2018.

Schmidt-Biggemann, Wilhelm. "The Christian Kabbala: Joseph Gikatilla (1247–1305), Johannes Reuchlin (1455–1522), Paulus Ricius (d. 1541), and Jacob Böhme (1575–1624)." In *The Language of Adam/Die Sprache Adams*, edited by Allison Coudert, 81–121. Wiesbaden: Harrassowitz, 1999.

———. "Christliche Kabbala oder Philosophia Hebraeorum: Die Debate zwischen Knorr von Rosenroth und Henry More um die rechte Deutung der Kabbala." *Morgen-Glantz* 16 (2006): 285–322.

———. "Einleitung: Johannes Reuchlin und die Anfänge der christlichen Kabbala." In *Christliche Kabbala,* edited by Wilhelm Schmidt-Biggemann, 9–48. Ostfildem: Jan Thorbecke, 2003.

———. *Geschichte der christlichen Kabbala.* Vol. 1: *15. und 16. Jahrhundert.* Stuttgart: Frommann-Holzboog, 2012.

———. *Geschichte der christlichen Kabbala.* Vol. 3: *1660–1850.* Stuttgart: Frommann-Holzboog, 2013.

———. "Jakob Böhme und die Kabbala." In *Christliche Kabbala,* edited by Wilhelm Schmidt-Biggemann, 157–81. Ostfildem: Jan Thorbecke, 2003.

———. *Philosophia Perennis: Historical Outlines of Western Spirituality in Ancient, Medieval and Early Modern Thought.* Dordrecht: Springer, 2004.

———. "Schellings 'Weltalter' in der Tradition abendländischer Spiritualität: Einleitung zur Edition des Weltalter-Fragmente." In Friedrich Wilhelm Joseph Schelling, *Weltalter-Fragmente.* 2 vols., edited by Klaus Grotsch, 1:1–78. Stuttgart: Frommann-Holzboog, 2002.

Schmithals, Walter. *Die Gnosis in Korinth: Eine Untersuchung zu den Korintherbriefen.* Göttingen: Vandenhoeck and Ruprecht, 1956.

Schmitz-Berning, Cornelia. *Vokabular des Nationalsozialismus.* Berlin: Walter de Gruyter, 2007.

Schneersohn, Menaḥem Mendel. *Derekh Miṣwotekha.* Brooklyn: Kehot, 1993.

———. *Or ha-Torah: Ma'amerei Ḥazal we-Inyanim.* Brooklyn: Kehot, 2013.

Schneersohn, Shalom Dovber. *Be-Sha'ah she-Hiqdimu 5672.* 3 vols. Brooklyn: Kehot, 2011.

———. *Sefer ha-Ma'amarim 5665.* Brooklyn: Kehot, 1987.

———. *Yom Ṭov shel Rosh Hashanah 5666.* Brooklyn: Kehot, 2010.

Schoenbaum, Susan. "Heidegger's Interpretation of *Phusis* in *Introduction to Metaphysics.*" In *A Companion to Heidegger's Introduction of Metaphysics,* edited by Richard Polt and Gregory Fried, 143–60. New Haven: Yale University Press, 2001.

Scholem, Gershom. "The Beginnings of the Christian Kabbalah." In *The Christian Kabbalah: Jewish Mystical Books and Their Christian Interpreters,* edited by Joseph Dan, 17–51. Cambridge, MA: Harvard College Library, 1997.

———. *Be-Iqvot Mashiaḥ.* Jerusalem: Sifrei Tarshish, 1944.

———. *Briefe II, 1948–1970.* Edited by Thomas Sparr. Munich: C. H. Beck, 1995.

———. *Briefe III, 1971–1982.* Edited by Itta Shedletzky. Munich: C. H. Beck, 1999.

———, ed. *The Correspondence of Walter Benjamin and Gershom Scholem 1932–1940.* Translated by Gary Smith and Andre Lefevere. Introduction by Anson Rabinbach. New York: Schocken, 1989.

———. "Eine unbekannte mystische Schrift des Mose de Leon." *Monatsschrift für Geschichte und Wissenschaft des Judentums* 71 (1927): 109–23.

———. *Elements of the Kabbalah and Its Symbolism*. Translated by Joseph Ben-Shlomo. Jerusalem: Bialik Institute, 1976 (Hebrew).

———. *Explications and Implications: Writings on Jewish Heritage and Renaissance*. Vol. 2. Edited by Avraham Shapira. Tel Aviv: Am Oved, 1989 (Hebrew).

———. "Franz Rosenzweig and His Book *The Star of Redemption*." In *The Philosophy of Franz Rosenzweig*, edited by Paul Mendes-Flohr, 20–41. Hanover: University Press of New England, 1988.

———. *From Berlin to Jerusalem: Memories of My Youth*. Translated by Harry Zohn. New York: Schocken, 1980.

———. *The Fullness of Time: Poems*. Translated by Richard Sieburth, introduced and annotated by Steven M. Wasserstrom. Jerusalem: Ibis, 2003.

———. *Die Geheimnisse der Schöpfung: Ein Kapitel aus dem kabbalistischen Buche Sohar*. Frankfurt am Main: Jüdischer Verlag, 1992.

———. *History of the Sabbatian Movement*. Edited by Jonathan Meir and Shinichi Yamamoto. Jerusalem: Schocken, 2018 (Hebrew).

———. "Job's Lament." In *Lament in Jewish Thought: Philosophical, Theological, and Literary Perspectives*, edited by Ilit Ferber and Paula Schwebel, 321–23. Berlin: Walter de Gruyter, 2014. Hebrew translation by Tali Koons in *Lamentations: Poetry and Thought in Gershom Scholem's World*, edited by Galili Shahar and Ilit Ferber, 102–3. Jerusalem: Carmel, 2016 (Hebrew).

———. *Judaica 3: Studien zur jüdischen Mystik*. Frankfurt am Main: Suhrkamp, 1973.

———. *Kabbalah*. Jerusalem: Keter, 1974.

———. *The Kabbalah in Provence*. Edited by Rivkah Schatz. Jerusalem: Akadamon, 1970 (Hebrew).

———. *Lamentations of Youth: The Diaries of Gershom Scholem, 1913–1919*. Edited and translated by Anthony David Skinner. Cambridge, MA: Harvard University Press, 2007.

———. *A Life in Letters, 1914–1982*. Edited and translated by Anthony David Skinner. Cambridge, MA: Harvard University Press, 2002.

———. *Lurianic Kabbalah: Collected Studies*. Edited by Daniel Abrams. Los Angeles: Cherub, 2008 (Hebrew).

———. *Major Trends in Jewish Mysticism*. New York: Schocken, 1956.

———. *The Messianic Idea and Other Essays on Jewish Spirituality*. New York: Schocken, 1971.

———. "The Name of God and the Linguistic Theory of the Kabbala (Part I)." *Diogenes* 79 (1972): 59–80.

———. "The Name of God and the Linguistic Theory of the Kabbala (Part II)." *Diogenes* 80 (1972): 164–94.

———. "New Fragments from the Writings of R. Azriel of Gerona." In *Memorial Volume for Asher Gulak and Samuel Klein*, 201–22. Jerusalem: Hebrew University, 1942 (Hebrew).

———. "95 Thesen über Judentum und Zionismus." In *Gershom Scholem: Zwischen den Disziplinen*, edited by Peter Schäfer and Gary Smith, 287–95. Frankfurt am Main: Suhrkamp, 1995.

———. *On Jews and Judaism in Crisis: Selected Essays*. Edited by Werner J. Dannhauser. New York: Schocken, 1976.

———. "On Jonah and the Concept of Justice." *Critical Inquiry* 25 (1999): 353–61.

———. "On Lament and Lamentation." In *Lament in Jewish Thought: Philosophical, Theological, and Literary Perspectives*, edited by Ilit Ferber and Paula Schwebel, 313–19. Berlin: Walter de Gruyter, 2014. Hebrew translation by Tali Koons in *Lamentations: Poetry and Thought in Gershom Scholem's World*, edited by Galili Shahar and Ilit Ferber, 88–94. Jerusalem: Carmel, 2016 (Hebrew).

———. *On the Kabbalah and Its Symbolism*. Translated by Ralph Manheim. New York: Schocken, 1965.

———. *On the Mystical Shape of the Godhead: Basic Concepts in the Kabbalah*. Translated by Joachim Neugroschel. Edited by Jonathan Chipman. Foreword by Joseph Dan. New York: Schocken, 1991.

———. *On the Possibility of Jewish Mysticism in Our Time and Other Essays*. Edited by Avraham Shapira. Translated by Jonathan Chipman. Philadelphia: Jewish Publication Society of America, 1997.

———. *Origins of the Kabbalah*. Edited by R. J. Zwi Werblowsky. Translated by Allan Arkush. Princeton: Princeton University Press, 1987.

———. "Rabbi Israel Sarug: A Student of Luria?" *Zion* 5 (1940): 214–43 (Hebrew).

———. *Sabbatai Ṣevi: The Mystical Messiah 1626–1676*. Translated R. J. Zwi Werblowsky. Princeton: Princeton University Press, 1973.

———. *Tagebücher nebst Aufsätzen und Entwürfen bis 1923*. Vol. 1: *1913–1917*. Edited by Karlfried Gründer and Friedrich Niewöhner, with the cooperation of Herbert Kopp-Oberstebrink. Frankfurt am Main: Jüdischer Verlag, 1995.

———. *Tagebücher nebst Aufsätzen und Entwürfen bis 1923*. Vol. 2: *1917–1923*. Edited by Karlfried

Gründer, Herbert Kopp-Oberstebrink, and Friedrich Niewöhner, with the assistance of Karl E. Grözinger. Frankfurt am Main: Jüdischer Verlag, 2000.

———. "The Traditions of R. Jacob and R. Isaac ben Jacob ha-Kohen." *Madda'ei ha-Yahadut* 2 (1927): 165–293 (Hebrew).

———. "Two Treatises of R. Moses de León." *Qoveṣ al Yad* 8 (1976): 327–84 (Hebrew).

———. *Von der mystischen Gestalt der Gottheit: Studien zu Grundbegriffen der Kabbala*. Frankfurt am Main: Suhrkamp, 1995.

———, ed., *Walter Benjamin/Gershom Scholem: Briefwechsel*. Frankfurt am Main: Suhrkamp, 1980.

———. "Zionism—Dialectic of Continuity and Rebellion." In *Unease in Zion*, edited by Ehud Ben Ezer, 263–96. Foreword by Robert Alter. New York: Quadrangle, 1974.

Scholem, Gershom, and Theodor W. Adorno, eds. *The Correspondence of Walter Benjamin 1910–1940*. Translated by Manfred R. Jacobson and Evelyn M. Jacobson. Chicago: University of Chicago Press, 1994.

Schrag, Calvin O. "Heidegger on Repetition and Historical Understanding." *Philosophy East and West* 20 (1970): 287–95.

Schuback, Marcia Sá Cavalcante. "Hermeneutics of Tradition." In *Rethinking Time: Essays on History, Memory, and Representation*, edited by Hans Ruin and Andrus Ers, 63–74. Huddinge: Södertörns Högskola, 2011.

Schulitz, John. *Jakob Böhme und die Kabbalah: Eine vergleichende Werkanalyse*. Frankfurt am Main: Peter Lang, 1993.

Schulte, Christoph. "F. W. J. Schellings Ausleihe von Hand- und Druckschriften." *Zeitschrift für Religion und Geistesgeschichte* 45 (1993): 267–77.

———. "Kabbala in der deutschen Romantik. Zur Einleitung." In *Kabbala und Romantik*, edited by Eveline Goodman-Thau, Gert Mattenklott, and Christoph Schulte, 1–19. Tübingen: Max Niemeyer, 1994.

———. "Messianism without Messiah: Messianism, Religion, and Secularization in Modern Jewish Thought." In *Secularism in Question: Jews and Judaism in Modern Times*, edited by Ari Joskowicz and Ethan B. Katz, 79–97. Philadelphia: University of Pennsylvania Press, 2015.

———. *Zimzum: Gott und Weltursprung*. Berlin: Suhrkamp, 2014.

———. "Zimzum bei Schelling." In *Kabbala und Romantik*, edited by Eveline Goodman-Thau, Gert Mattenklott, and Christoph Schulte, 97–118. Tübingen: Max Niemeyer, 1994.

———. "Ẓimẓum in der *Kabbala Denudata*." *Morgen-Glantz* 7 (1997): 127–40.

———. "Zimzum in the Works of Schelling." *Iyyun* 41 (1992): 21–40.

Schulze, Wilhelm August. "Jacob Boehme und die Kabbala." *Judaica* 11 (1955): 12–29.

———. "Schelling und die Kabbala." *Judaica* 13 (1957): 65–99, 143–70, 210–32.

Schumacher, Ferdinand. *Der Begriff der Zeit bei Franz von Baader*. Freiburg: Karl Alber, 1983.

Schürmann, Reiner. *Broken Hegemonies*. Translated by Reginald Lilly. Bloomington: Indiana University Press, 2003.

———. "A Brutal Awakening to the Tragic Condition of Being: On Heidegger's *Beiträge zur Philosophie*." In *Martin Heidegger: Politics, Art, and Technology*, edited by Karsten Harries and Christoph Jamme, 89–105. New York: Holmes and Meier, 1994.

———. *Heidegger on Being and Acting: From Principles to Anarchy*. Translated by Christine-Marie Gros. Bloomington: Indiana University Press, 1990.

———. *Meister Eckhart: Mystic and Philosopher*. Bloomington: Indiana University Press, 1978.

Schwartz, Yossef. "Kabbala als Atheismus? Die *Kabbala Denudata* und die religiösen Krise des 17. Jahrhunderts." *Morgen-Glantz* 16 (2006): 259–84.

Schwebel, Paula. "Lament and the Shattered Expression of Mourning: Gershom Scholem and Walter Benjamin." *Jewish Studies Quarterly* 21 (2014): 27–41.

———. "Monad and Time: Reading Leibniz with Heidegger and Benjamin." In *Sparks Will Fly: Benjamin and Heidegger*, edited by Andrew Benjamin and Dimitris Vardoulakis, 123–44. Albany: State University of New York Press, 2015.

———. "The Tradition in Ruins: Walter Benjamin and Gershom Scholem on Language and Lament." In *Lament in Jewish Thought: Philosophical, Theological, and Literary Perspectives*, edited by Ilit Ferber and Paula Schwebel, 277–301. Berlin: Walter de Gruyter, 2014.

Scott, Charles E. "Appearing to Remember Heraclitus." In *The Presocratics after Heidegger*, edited by David C. Jacobs, 249–61. Albany: State University of New York Press, 1999.

———. *The Time of Memory*. Albany: State University of New York Press, 1999.

Scult, Allen. *Being Jewish/Reading Heidegger: An Ontological Encounter*. New York: Fordham University Press, 2004.

———. "Forgiving 'La Dette Impensée': Being Jewish and Reading Heidegger." In *French Interpretations of Heidegger: An Exceptional*

Reception, edited by David Pettigrew and François Raffoul, 231–44. Albany: State University of New York Press, 2008.

Secret, François. *Les kabbalistes chrétiens de la Renaissance*. Paris: Dunod, 1964.

———. *Le Zôhar chez les kabbalistes chrétiens de la Renaissance*. Paris: Durlacher, 1958.

Seebohm, Thomas M. "Considerations on 'Der Satz vom Grund.'" In *The Question of Hermeneutics: Essays in Honor of Joseph J. Kockelmans*, edited by Timothy J. Stapleton, 237–51. Dordrecht: Kluwer Academic, 1994.

Sefer ha-Peli'ah. Przemyśl: Zupnik, Knoller, and Hammerschmidt, 1883.

Sefer ha-Zohar. 3 vols. Edited by Reuven Margaliot. Jerusalem: Mosad ha-Rav Kook, 1978.

Seidel, George J. "Musing with Kierkegaard: Heidegger's *Besinnung*." *Continental Philosophy Review* 34 (2001): 403–18.

Sells, Michael A. *Mystical Languages of Unsaying*. Chicago: University of Chicago Press, 1994.

Sendor, Mark B. "The Emergence of Provençal Kabbalah: Rabbi Isaac the Blind's *Commentary on Sefer Yeẓirah*: Translation and Annotation." PhD diss., Harvard University, 1994.

Seppi, Angelika. "'Wenn einer immerfort dasselbe sagt [. . .]': Heidegger, die Tautologie und ein gewisser Idiot." In *Martin Heidegger: Die Falte der Sprache*, edited by Michael Friedman and Angelika Seppi, 53–88. Vienna: Turia + Kant, 2017.

Serafin, Andrzej. "Heidegger's Phenomenology of the Invisible." *Argument: Biannual Philosophical Journal* 6 (2016): 313–22.

Severson, Eric. *Levinas's Philosophy of Time: Gift, Responsibility, Diachrony, Hope*. Pittsburgh: Duquesne University Press, 2013.

Shahar, Galili. "The Sacred and the Unfamiliar: Gershom Scholem and the Anxieties of the New Hebrew." *The Germanic Review: Literature, Culture, Theory* 83 (2008): 299–320.

Shapiro, Gary. "Subversion of System/Systems of Subversion." In *Writing the Politics of Difference*, edited by Hugh J. Silverman, 1–11. Albany: State University of New York Press, 1991.

Sharabi, Shalom. *Reḥovot ha-Nahar*, introduction to *Nahar Shalom*. Printed as the third part in Ḥayyim Viṭal, *Eṣ Ḥayyim*. Jerusalem: Sitrei Ḥayyim, 2013.

Shatil, Sharron. "The Doctrine of Secrets of *Emeq Ha-Melech*." *Jewish Studies Quarterly* 17 (2010): 358–95.

———. "The Kabbalah of R. Israel Sarug: A Lurianic-Cordoverian Encounter." *Review of Rabbinic Judaism* 14 (2011): 158–87.

Shatz, David. "Contemporary Scholarship on Rabbi Soloveitchik's Thought: Where We Are, Where We Can Go." In *Scholarly Man of Faith: Studies in the Thought and Writings of Rabbi Joseph B. Soloveitchik*, edited by Ephraim Kanarfogel and Dov Schwartz, 135–96. New York: Ktav, 2018.

Shaw, Gregory. "The *Chôra* of the *Timaeus* and Iamblichean Theurgy." *Horizons* 3 (2012): 103–29.

———. *Theurgy and the Soul: The Neoplatonism of Iamblichus*. University Park: Pennsylvania State University Press, 1995.

Sheehan, Thomas. *Making Sense of Heidegger: A Paradigm Shift*. London: Rowman and Littlefield, 2015.

Sherratt, Yvonne. *Hitler's Philosophers*. New Haven: Yale University Press, 2013.

Shmueli, Leore Sachs. "R. Joseph of Hamadan's *Commentary to the Ten Sefirot*." *Kabbalah: Journal for the Study of Jewish Mystical Texts* 32 (2014): 227–321 (Hebrew).

Shneur Zalman of Liadi. *Liqquṭei Amarim: Tanya*. Brooklyn: Kehot, 1979.

———. *Liqquṭei Torah*, vol. 1. Brooklyn: Kehot, 1996.

———. *Liqquṭei Torah*, vol. 2. Brooklyn: Kehot, 1998.

———. *Ma'amerei Admor ha-Zaqen al Nevi'im*. Brooklyn: Kehot, 1984.

Shuchat, Raphael. "*Ṣimṣum* Taken Literally—An Investigation into the Thinking of Emanuel Ḥai Ricci and R. Solomon Eliasov." *Kabbalah: Journal for the Study of Jewish Mystical Texts* 37 (2017): 271–301 (Hebrew).

———. "Thoughts on Lithuanian Kabbalah: A Study in the Lurianic Concept of *Igulim* and *Yosher*." *Da'at* 79–80 (2015): 11–32 (Hebrew).

———. "The Vilna Gaon's Commentary to *Mishnat Ḥasidim*: The *Mashal* and the *Nimshal* in Lurianic Works." *Kabbalah: Journal for the Study of Jewish Mystical Texts* 3 (1998): 265–302 (Hebrew).

———. *A World Hidden in the Dimensions of Time: The Theory of Redemption in the Writings of the Vilna Gaon Its Sources and Influence on Later Generations*. Ramat Gan: Bar-Ilan University Press, 2008 (Hebrew).

Sikka, Sonya. *Heidegger, Morality and Politics: Questioning the Shepherd of Being*. Cambridge: Cambridge University Press, 2018.

———. "Heidegger and Race." In *Race and Racism in Continental Philosophy*, edited by Robert Bernasconi with Sybol Cook, 74–97. Bloomington: Indiana University Press, 2003.

———. *Forms of Transcendence: Heidegger and Medieval Mystical Theology*. Albany: State University of New York Press, 1997.

Sifre on Deuteronomy. Edited by Louis Finkelstein. New York: Jewish Theological Seminary of America, 1969.

Simon, Jules. *Art and Responsibility: A Phenomenology of the Diverging Paths of Rosenzweig and Heidegger.* New York: Continuum, 2011.

Simuţ, Corneliu C. *F. C. Baur's Synthesis of Böhme and Hegel: Redefining Christian Theology as a Gnostic Philosophy of Religion.* Leiden: Brill, 2015.

Slabodsky, Santiago. *Decolonial Judaism: Triumphal Failures of Barbaric Thinking.* New York: Palgrave Macmillan, 2014.

Slattery, Michael. "Augustine, Heidegger, and Gnosticism." In *Martin Heidegger's Interpretations of Saint Augustine: Sein und Zeit und Ewigkeit,* edited by Frederick Van Fleteren, 185–210. Lewiston: Edwin Mellen, 2005.

Smith, Anthony Paul. "Thinking from the One: Science and the Ancient Philosophical Figure of the One." In *Laruelle and Non-Philosophy,* edited by John Mullarkey and Anthony Paul Smith, 19–41. Edinburgh: Edinburgh University Press, 2012.

Smith, David Nowell. *Sounding/Silence: Martin Heidegger at the Limits of Poetics.* New York: Fordham University Press, 2013.

Smith, John H. *Dialogues between Faith and Reason: The Death and Return of God in Modern German Thought.* Ithaca: Cornell University Press 2011.

Smith, Michael B. *Toward the Outside: Concepts and Themes in Emmanuel Levinas.* Pittsburgh: Duquesne University Press, 2005.

Socher, Abraham P. *The Radical Enlightenment of Solomon Maimon: Judaism, Heresy, and Philosophy.* Stanford: Stanford University Press, 2006.

Soelle, Dorothee. *The Silent Cry: Mysticism and Resistance.* Translated by Barbara and Martin Rumscheidt. Minneapolis: Fortress, 2001.

Solomon ha-Kohen. *She'at Raṣon.* Thessaloníki: Beṣalel ha-Levi Ashkenazi, 1820.

Soloveitchik, Joseph B. *The Lonely Man of Faith.* New York: Doubleday, 2006.

Sommer, Christian. "Métapolitique de l'université. Le programme platonicien de Heidegger." *Les Études philosophiques* (2010): 255–75.

Spanos, William V. "Heidegger, Kierkegaard, and the Hermeneutic Circle: Towards a Postmodern Theory of Interpretation and Dis-closure." In *Martin Heidegger and the Question of Literature: Towards a Postmodern Literary Hermeneutics,* edited by William V. Spanos, 115–48. Bloomington: Indiana University Press, 1979.

———. *Heidegger and Criticism: Retrieving the Cultural Politics of Destruction.* Foreword by Donald E. Pease. Minneapolis: University of Minnesota Press, 1993.

Sparby, Terje. *Hegel's Conception of the Determinate Negation.* Leiden: Brill, 2015.

Spiegel, Gabrielle M. "The Task of the Historian." *American Historical Review* 114 (2009): 1–15.

Spinoza, Baruch. *The Collected Works of Spinoza.* Edited and translated by Edwin Curley. Princeton: Princeton University Press, 2016.

Stambaugh, Joan. *The Finitude of Being.* Albany: State University of New York Press, 1992.

———. "The Future of Continental Philosophy." In *Writing and the Politics of Difference,* edited by Hugh J. Silverman, 275–82. Albany: State University of New York Press, 1991.

———. "Heidegger, Taoism, and the Question of Metaphysics." In *Heidegger and Asian Thought,* edited by Graham Parkes, 79–91. Honolulu: University of Hawaii Press, 1987.

Staudenmaier, Peter. *Between Occultism and Nazism: Anthroposophy and the Politics of Race in the Fascist Era.* Leiden: Brill, 2014.

Steiner, George. *After Babel: Aspects of Language and Translation.* 3rd ed. Oxford: Oxford University Press, 1998.

———. *Grammars of Creation: Originating in the Gifford Lectures for 1990.* New Haven: Yale University Press, 2001.

———. "Our Homeland, the Text." *Salmagundi* 66 (1985): 4–25.

———. *Real Presences.* Chicago: University of Chicago Press, 1989.

Stenstad, Gail. *Transformations: Thinking after Heidegger.* Madison: University of Wisconsin Press, 2006.

Stoudt, John Yost. *Jacob Boehme: His Life and Thought.* Foreword by Paul Tillich. New York: Seabury, 1957.

Strauss, Leo. *Leo Strauss on Nietzsche's* Thus Spoke Zarathustra. Edited by Richard L. Velkley. Chicago: University of Chicago Press, 2017.

Strong, Tracy B. "America as Exemplar: The *Denktagebuch* of 1951." In *Artifacts of Thinking: Reading Hannah Arendt's* Denktagebuch, edited by Roger Berkowitz and Ian Storey, 124–42. New York: Fordham University Press, 2017.

Stroumsa, Gedaliahu G. "A Nameless God: Judaeo-Christian and Gnostic 'Theologies of the Name.'" In *The Image of the Judaeo-Christians in Ancient Jewish and Christian Literature,* edited by Peter J. Tomson and Doris Lambers-Petry, 230–43. Tübingen: Mohr Siebeck, 2003.

Suares, Peter. *The Kyoto School's Takeover of Hegel: Nishida, Nishitani, and Tanabe Remake the*

Philosophy of Spirit. Lanham: Rowman and Littlefield, 2011.

Sugarman, Richard I. "Emmanuel Levinas and the Deformalization of Time." *Analecta Husserliana* 90 (2006): 253–69.

Summerell, Orrin F. "Identity, Subjectivity, and Being Other than the Same: Thinking beyond Hegel and Heidegger." *The New Yearbook for Phenomenology and Phenomenological Research* 2 (2002): 179–203.

———. "The Otherness of the Thinking of Being: Heidegger's Conception of the Theological Difference." In *The Otherness of God*, edited by Orrin F. Summerell, 111–34. Charlottesville: University Press of Virginia, 1998.

Tarditi, Claudio. "Is Ontology the Last Form of Idolatry? A Dialogue between Heidegger and Marion." In *Rethinking Faith: Heidegger between Nietzsche and Wittgenstein*, edited by Antonio Cimino and Gert-Jan van der Heiden, 23–37. New York: Bloomsbury, 2017.

Taubes, Jacob. *Occidental Eschatology*. Translated by David Ratmoko. Stanford: Stanford University Press, 2009.

———. "The Price of Messianism." In *Essential Papers on Messianic Movements and Personalities in Jewish History*, edited by Marc Saperstein, 551–57. New York: New York University Press, 1992.

Taubes, Susan A. "The Gnostic Foundations of Heidegger's Nihilism." *Journal of Religion* 34 (1954): 155–72.

Theisohn, Philipp. "Zur Rezeption von Naphtali Herz Bacharachs *Sefer Emeq ha-Melech* in der *Kabbala Denudata*." *Morgen-Glantz* 16 (2006): 221–41.

Theodor, Julius, and Chanoch Albeck, eds. *Bere'shit Rabba*. Jerusalem: Wahrmann, 1965.

Thomä, Dieter. "Heidegger und der Nationalsozialismus. In der Dunkelkammer der Seinsgeschichte." In *Heidegger-Handbuch: Leben—Werk—Wirkung*. Rev. and exp. ed., edited by Dieter Thomä, in collaboration with Florian Grosser, Katrin Meyer, and Hans Bernhard Schmid, 108–33. Stuttgart: J. B. Metzler, 2013.

Thomson, Iain D. *Heidegger, Art, and Postmodernity*. Cambridge: Cambridge University Press, 2011.

———. *Heidegger on Ontotheology: Technology and the Politics of Education*. Cambridge: Cambridge University Press, 2005.

Tillich, Paul. *Philosophical Writings/Philosophische Schriften*. Edited by Gunther Wenz. Berlin: Walter de Gruyter, 1989.

Tilliette, Xavier. "Schelling und die Gnosis." In *Gnosis und Mystik in der Geschichte der Philosophie*, edited by Peter Koslowski, 260–75. Zürich: Artemis, 1988.

Tiqqunei Zohar. Edited by Reuven Margaliot. Jerusalem: Mosad ha-Rav Kook, 1978.

Tirosh-Samuelson, Hava, and Christian Wiese, eds. *The Legacy of Hans Jonas: Judaism and the Phenomenon of Life*. Leiden: Brill, 2008.

Tishby, Isaiah. *The Doctrine of Evil and the "Kelippah" in Lurianic Kabbalism*. Jerusalem: Magnes, 1984 (Hebrew).

———. "Gnostic Doctrines in Sixteenth-Century Jewish Mysticism." *Journal of Jewish Studies* 6 (1955): 146–52.

———. *The Wisdom of the Zohar: An Anthology of Texts*. Translated by David Goldstein. Oxford: Oxford University Press, 1989.

Tonner, Philip. *Heidegger, Metaphysics and the Univocity of Being*. London: Continuum, 2010.

Trawny, Peter. *Adyton: Heideggers esoterische Philosophie*. Berlin: Matthes & Seitz, 2014.

———. *Freedom to Fail: Heidegger's Anarchy*. Translated by Ian Alexander Moore and Christopher Turner. Cambridge: Polity, 2015.

———. *Heidegger and the Myth of a Jewish World Conspiracy*. Translated by Andrew J. Mitchell. Chicago: University of Chicago Press, 2015.

Tritten, Tyler. *Beyond Presence: The Late F. W. J. Schelling's Criticism of Metaphysics*. Berlin: Walter de Gruyter, 2012.

Tropea, Gregory. *Religion, Ideology, and Heidegger's Concept of Falling*. Atlanta: Scholars' Press, 1987.

Trouillard, Jean. "Note sur *proousios* et *pronoia* chez Proclus." *Revue des études grecques* 73 (1960): 80–87.

———. "Procession néoplatonicienne et création Judeo-Chrétien." In *Néoplatonisme, mélanges offerts à Jean Trouillard*, 1–30. Fontenay-aux-Roses: Les Cahiers de Fontenay, 1981.

Tugendhat, Ernst. *Der Wahrheitsbegriff bei Husserl und Heidegger*. Berlin: Walter de Gruyter, 1967.

———. "Heidegger's Idea of Truth." In *The Heidegger Controversy: A Critical Reader*, edited by Richard Wolin, 245–63. Cambridge, MA: MIT Press, 1993.

Twersky, Menaḥem Naḥum. *Me'or Einayim*. New Square: Me'or ha-Torah, 1997.

Tworek, Wojciech. "Time in the Teachings of Rabbi Shneur Zalman of Liadi." PhD diss., University College London, 2014.

Ulmer, Rivka, ed. *Pesiqta Rabbati: A Synoptic Edition based upon All Extant Manuscripts and the Editio Princeps*. Atlanta: Scholars' Press, 1997.

Urbach, Ephraim E. *The World of the Sages: Collected Studies*. Jerusalem: Magnes, 1988 (Hebrew).

Urban, Martina. "The Paradox of Realization: Buber on the Transcendental Boundary of Spatial Images." In *Martin Buber: His Intellectual and Scholarly Legacy*, edited by Sam Berrin Shonkoff, 171–93. Leiden: Brill, 2018.

Vadiya, Anand Jayprakash. "Absence: An Indo-Analytic Inquiry." *Sophia* 55 (2016): 491–513.

Vail, Loy M. *Heidegger and Ontological Difference.* University Park: Pennsylvania State University Press, 1972.

Valabregue-Perry, Sandra. *Concealed and Revealed: 'Ein Sof' in Theosophic Kabbalah.* Los Angeles: Cherub, 2010 (Hebrew).

———. "The Concept of Infinity (*Eyn-sof*) and the Rise of Theosophical Kabbalah." *Jewish Quarterly Review* 102 (2012): 405–30.

Valle, Moses David. *Et Leḥenena*, vol. 1. Jerusalem: Joseph Spinner, 2017.

Vallega, Alejandro A. *Heidegger and the Issue of Space: Thinking on Exilic Grounds.* University Park: Pennsylvania State University Press, 2003.

Vallega-Neu, Daniela. *Heidegger's Contributions to Philosophy: An Introduction.* Bloomington: Indiana University Press, 2003.

_____. "Heidegger's Imageless Saying of the Event." *Continental Philosophy Review* 47 (2014): 315–33.

———. *Heidegger's Poietic Writings: From* Contributions to Philosophy *to* The Event. Bloomington: Indiana University Press, 2018.

———. "Heidegger's Reticence: From *Contributions* to *Das Ereignis* and toward *Gelassenheit*." *Research in Phenomenology* 45 (2015): 1–32.

Van der Haven, Alexander. *From Lowly Metaphor to Divine Flesh: Sarah the Ashkenazi, Sabbatai Tsevi's Messianic Queen and the Sabbatian Movement.* Amsterdam: Menasseh ben Israel Instituut, 2012.

Van der Heiden, Gert-Jan. "The Experience of Contingency and the Attitude of Life: Nietzsche and Heidegger on Paul." In *Rethinking Faith: Heidegger between Nietzsche and Wittgenstein*, edited by Antonio Cimino and Gert-Jan van der Heiden, 161–77. New York: Bloomsbury, 2017.

———. *Ontology after Ontotheology: Plurality, Event, and Contingency in Contemporary Philosophy.* Pittsburgh: Duquesne University Press, 2014.

Vandevelde, Pol. *Heidegger and the Romantics: The Literary Invention of Meaning.* New York: Routledge, 2012.

———. "Translation as a Mode of Poetry: Heidegger's Reformulation of the Romantic Project." In *Phenomenology and Literature: Historical Perspectives and Systematic Accounts*, edited by Pol Vandevelde, 93–113. Würzburg: Königshausen and Neumann, 2010.

Vassányi, Miklós. *Anima Mundi: The Rise of the World Soul Theory in Modern German Philosophy.* Dordrecht: Springer, 2011.

Vater, Michael. "Schelling's Philosophy of Identity and Spinoza's *Ethica more geometrico*." In *Spinoza and German Idealism*, edited by Eckart Förster and Yitzhak Y. Melamed, 156–74. Cambridge: Cambridge University Press, 2012.

Vattimo, Gianni. *Of Reality: The Purposes of Philosophy.* Translated by Robert T. Valgenti. New York: Columbia University Press, 2016.

Vaughan, Larry. *Johann Georg Hamann: Metaphysics of Language and Vision of History.* New York: Peter Lang, 1989.

Vedder, Ben. *Heidegger's Philosophy of Religion: From God to the Gods.* Pittsburgh: Duquesne University Press, 2007.

Verman, Mark. *The Books of Contemplation: Medieval Jewish Mystical Sources.* Albany: State University of New York Press, 1992.

Vieillard-Baron, Jean-Louis. "Schelling et Jacob Böhme: Les Recherches de 1809 et la lecture de la *Lettre pastorale*." *Les Études philosophiques* (1999): 223–42.

Vilk, Yisrael. *Sefer ha-Ṣimṣum we-ha-Meṣi'ut: Berur Ḥadash be-Inyenei ha-Ṣimṣum u-Meṣi'ut ha-Sefirot.* Beit Shemesh, 2018.

Villa, Dana. *Arendt and Heidegger: The Fate of the Political.* Princeton: Princeton University Press, 1996.

Viṭal, Ḥayyim. *Eṣ Ḥayyim.* Jerusalem: Sitrei Ḥayyim, 2013.

———. *Mavo She'arim.* Jerusalem: Sha'arei Yiṣḥaq, 2016.

———. *Oṣrot Ḥayyim.* Jerusalem: Sha'arei Yiṣḥaq, 2018.

———. *Peri Eṣ Ḥayyim.* Jerusalem: Or ha-Bahir, 1980.

———. *Sha'ar ha-Gilgulim.* Jerusalem: Yeshivat Qol Yehudah, 1995.

———. *Sha'ar ha-Haqdamot.* Jerusalem: Sha'arei Yiṣḥaq, 2018.

———. *Sha'ar ha-Kawwanot.* Jerusalem: Meqor Ḥayyim, 1963.

———. *Sha'ar Ma'amerei Rashbi.* Jerusalem: Sitrei Ḥayyim, 2014.

Voegelin, Eric. *Anamnesis: On the Theory of History and Politics.* Translated by M. J. Hanak, based on the abbreviated version translated by Gerhart Niemeyer. Edited with an introduction by David Walsh. Columbia: University of Missouri Press, 2002.

Vycinas, Vincent. *Earth and Gods: An Introduction to the Philosophy of Martin Heidegger.* The Hague: Martinus Nijhoff, 1961.

Wald, Stephen G. *The Doctrine of the Divine Name: An Introduction to Classical Kabbalistic Theology.* Atlanta: Scholars' Press, 1988.

Ward, James F. *Heidegger's Political Thinking.* Amherst: University of Massachusetts Press, 1995.

Ward, Koral. *Augenblick: The Concept of the "Decisive Moment" in 19th- and 20th-Century Western Philosophy.* Burlington: Ashgate, 2008.

Wargo, Robert J. J. *The Logic of Nothingness: A Study of Nishida Kitarō.* Honolulu: University of Hawaii Press, 2005.

Warnek, Peter. "Translating *Innigkeit*: The Belonging Together of the Strange." In *Heidegger and the Greeks: Interpretive Essays,* edited by Drew A. Hyland and John Panteleimon Manoussakis, 57–82. Bloomington: Indiana University Press, 2006.

Wasserstrom, Steven M. "Adorno's Kabbalah: Some Preliminary Observations." In *Polemical Encounters: Esoteric Discourse and Its Others,* edited by Olav Hammer and Kocku von Stuckrad, 55–79. Leiden: Brill, 2007.

———. "The Fullness of Time: Some Thoughts on the Poetry of Gershom Scholem." In Gershom Scholem, *The Fullness of Time: Poems.* Translated by Richard Sieburth. Introduced and annotated by Steven M. Wasserstrom, 13–41. Jerusalem: Ibis, 2003.

———. "Hans Jonas in Marburg, 1928." In *The Legacy of Hans Jonas: Judaism and the Phenomenon of Life,* edited by Hava Tirosh-Samuelson and Christian Wiese, 39–72. Leiden: Brill, 2008.

———. *Religion after Religion: Gershom Scholem, Mircea Eliade, and Henry Corbin at Eranos.* Princeton: Princeton University Press, 1999.

Weatherston, Martin. *Heidegger's Interpretation of Kant: Categories, Imagination and Temporality.* Hampshire: Palgrave Macmillan, 2002.

Webster, Charles. *Paracelsus: Medicine, Magic and Mission at the End of Time.* New Haven: Yale University Press, 2008.

Weeks, Andrew. *Boehme: An Intellectual Biography of the Seventeenth-Century Philosopher and Mystic.* Albany: State University of New York Press, 1991.

———. *Paracelsus: Speculative Theory and the Crisis of the Early Reformation.* Albany: State University of New York Press, 1997.

———. "Radical Reformation and the Anticipation of Modernism in Jacob Boehme." In *An Introduction to Jacob Boehme: Four Centuries of Thought and Reception,* edited by Ariel Hessayon and Sarah Apetrei, 38–56. New York: Routledge, 2014.

Wehr, Gerhard. *Angelus Silesius: Textauswahl und Kommentar.* Wiesbaden: Marixverlag, 2011.

Weidner, Daniel. *Gershom Scholem: Politisches, esoterisches und historiographisches Schreiben.* Munich: Wilhelm Fink, 2003.

———. "'Movement of Language' and Transience: Lament, Mourning, and the Tradition of Elegy in Early Scholem." In *Lament in Jewish Thought: Philosophical, Theological, and Literary Perspectives,* edited by Ilit Ferber and Paula Schwebel, 237–54. Berlin: Walter de Gruyter, 2014.

———. "Reading Gershom Scholem." *Jewish Quarterly Review* 96 (2006): 203–31.

Weigel, Sigrid. *Body- and Image-Space: Re-reading Walter Benjamin.* Translated by Georgina Paul with Rachel McNicholl and Jeremy Gaines. London: Routledge, 1996.

———. "The Flash of Knowledge and the Temporality of Images: Walter Benjamin's Image-Based Epistemology and Its Preconditions in Visual Arts and Media History." *Critical Inquiry* 41 (2015): 344–66.

———. "Lost in Translation: Vom Verlust des Bilddenkens in Übersetzungen Benjaminscher Schriften." *Benjamin Studies* 1 (2002): 47–63.

———. "The Role of Lamentation for Scholem's Theory of Poetry and Language." In *Lament in Jewish Thought: Philosophical, Theological, and Literary Perspectives,* edited by Ilit Ferber and Paula Schwebel, 185–203. Berlin: Walter de Gruyter, 2014.

———. "Scholems Gedichte und seine Dichtungstheorie: Klage Adressierung, Gabe und das Problem einer biblischen Sprache in unserer Zeit." In *Gershom Scholem: Literatur und Rhetorik,* edited by Stéphane Mosès and Sigrid Weigel, 16–47. Köln: Böhlau, 2000.

———. *Walter Benjamin: Images, the Creaturely, and the Holy.* Translated by Chadwick Truscott Smith. Stanford: Stanford University Press, 2013.

Weinstein, Roni. *Kabbalah and Jewish Modernity.* Oxford: Littman Library of Jewish Civilization, 2016.

Weiss, Judith. *A Kabbalistic Christian Messiah in the Renaissance: Guillaume Postel and the Book of Zohar.* Tel Aviv: Hakibbutz Hameuchad, 2016 (Hebrew).

Weissblei, Gil. "The German Martin and the Jewish Mordechai: A Meeting between Buber and

Heidegger, 1957." http://web.nli.org.il/sites/NLI/English/collections/personalsites/Israel-Germany/Division-of-Germany/Pages/Buber-Heidegger.aspx.

Wenning, Mario. "Adorno, Heidegger, and the Problem of Remembrance." In *Adorno and Heidegger: Philosophical Questions*, edited by Iain Macdonald and Krzysztof Ziarek, 155–66. Stanford: Stanford University Press, 2008.

Wetz, Franz Josef. "Wege—Nicht Werke: Zur Gesamtausgabe Martin Heidegger." *Zeitschrift für philosophische Forschung* 41 (1987): 444–55.

Whistler, Daniel. *Schelling's Theory of Symbolic Language: Forming the System of Identity*. Oxford: Oxford University Press, 2013.

———. "Silvering, Or the Role of Mysticism in German Idealism." *Glossator: Practice and Theory of the Commentary* 7 (2013): 151–85.

White, Carol Wayne. *The Legacy of Anne Conway (1631–1679): Reverberations of a Mystical Naturalism*. Albany: State University of New York Press, 2008.

White, Ryan. *The Hidden God: Pragmatism and Posthuman in American Thought*. New York: Columbia University Press, 2015.

Wiese, Christian. "'Revolt against Empiricism': Hans Jonas's Response to Martin Heidegger." In *Heidegger's Jewish Followers: Essays on Hannah Arendt, Leo Strauss, Hans Jonas, and Emmanuel Levinas*, edited by Samuel Fleischacker, 151–77. Pittsburgh: Duquesne University Press, 2008.

Wildmann, Yiṣḥaq Eizik Ḥaver. *Afiqei Yam*. Jerusalem: Makhon Sha'arei Ziv, 1994.

———. *Beit Olamim*. Warsaw: Meir Yeḥiel Halter, 1889.

———. *Magen we-Ṣinnah*. Benei Beraq: Neṣaḥ, 1985.

———. *Pitḥei She'arim*. Warsaw: Meir Yeḥiel Halter, 1888.

Wilensky, Sara O. Heller. "The 'First Created Being' in Early Kabbalah and Its Philosophical Sources." In *Studies in Jewish Thought*, edited by Sara O. Heller Wilensky and Moshe Idel, 261–76. Jerusalem: Magnes, 1989 (Hebrew). English translation in *Jewish Intellectual History in the Middle Ages*. Vol. 3 of *Binah: Studies in Jewish History, Thought, and Culture*, edited by Joseph Dan, 65–77. Westport: Praeger, 1994.

———. "Messianism, Eschatology, and Utopia in the Philosophic-Mystical Current of Kabbalah in the Thirteenth Century." In *Messianism and Eschatology: A Collection of Essays*, edited by Zvi Baras, 221–37. Jerusalem: Zalman Shazar, 1983 (Hebrew).

———. "The Relations between Mysticism and Philosophy in the Teachings of Rabbi Isaac Ibn Latif." *Jerusalem Studies in Jewish Thought* 6, 3–4 (1987): 367–82 (Hebrew).

Wilkinson, Robert J. *Orientalism, Aramaic and Kabbalah in the Catholic Reformation: The First Printing of the Syriac New Testament*. Leiden: Brill, 2007.

———. *Tetragrammaton: Western Christians and the Hebrew Name of God from the Beginnings to the Seventeenth Century*. Leiden: Brill, 2015.

Williams, Duane. "Eckhart's Why and Heidegger's What: Beyond Subjectivistic Thought to Groundless Ground." In *Mystical Theology and Continental Philosophy: Interchange in the Wake of God*, edited by David Lewin, Simon D. Podmore, and Duane Williams, 147–63. London: Routledge, 2017.

Winkler, Rafael. "Dwelling and Hospitality: Heidegger and Hölderlin." *Research in Phenomenology* 47 (2017): 366–87.

———. "Time, Singularity and the Impossible: Heidegger and Derrida on Dying." *Research in Phenomenology* 46 (2016): 405–25.

Wirszubski, Chaim. *Between the Lines: Kabbalah, Christian Kabbalah and Sabbatianism*. Edited by Moshe Idel. Jerusalem: Magnes, 1990 (Hebrew).

———. "Francesco Giorgio's Commentary on Giovanni Pico's Kabbalistic Theses." *Journal of the Warburg and Courtauld Institutes* 37 (1974): 145–56.

———. *Pico Della Mirandola's Encounter With Jewish Mysticism*. Cambridge, MA: Harvard University Press, 1989.

Wirth, Jason M. *The Conspiracy of Life: Meditations on Schelling and His Time*. Albany: State University of New York Press, 2003.

———. *Schelling's Practice of the Wild: Time, Art, Imagination*. Albany: State University of New York Press, 2015.

Withy, Katherine. *Heidegger on Being Uncanny*. Cambridge, MA: Harvard University Press, 2015.

Wittgenstein, Ludwig. *Tractatus Logico-Philosophicus*. Translated by Charles K. Ogden, with introduction by Bertrand Russell. London: Routledge, 1995.

Wohlfarth, Irving. "Haarscharf an der Grenze zwischen Religion und Nihilismus. Zum Motiv des Zimzum bei Gershom Scholem." In *Gershom Scholem: Zwischen den Disziplinen*, edited by Peter Schäfer and Gary Smith, 176–256. Frankfurt am Main: Suhrkamp, 1995.

Wojtulewicz, Christopher M. "Meister Eckhart's Speculative Grammar: A Foreshadowing of Heidegger's *Der Satz vom Grund*?" In *Mystical Theology and Continental Philosophy: Interchange in the Wake of God*, edited by David Lewin, Simon D. Podmore, and Duane Williams, 164–78. London: Routledge, 2017.

Wolfson, Elliot R. *Abraham Abulafia—Kabbalist and Prophet: Hermeneutics, Theosophy and Theurgy*. Los Angeles: Cherub, 2001.

———. "Achronic Time, Messianic Expectation, and the Secret of the Leap in Ḥabad." In *Habad Hasidism: History, Thought, and Image*, edited by Jonatan Meir and Gadi Sagiv, 45–86 (English section). Jerusalem: Zalman Shazar, 2016.

———. *Alef, Mem, Tau: Kabbalistic Musings on Time, Truth, and Death*. Berkeley: University of California Press, 2006.

———. *Along the Path: Studies in Kabbalistic Myth, Symbolism, and Hermeneutics*. Albany: State University of New York Press, 1995.

———. "Angelic Embodiment and the Feminine Representation of Jesus: Reconstructing Carnality in the Christian Kabbalah of Johann Kemper." In *The Jewish Body: Corporeality, Society, and Identity in the Renaissance and Early Modern Period*, edited by Maria Diemling and Giuseppe Veltri, 395–426. Leiden: Brill, 2009.

———. "Anonymity and the Kabbalistic Ethos: A Fourteenth-Century Supercommentary on the Commentary on the Sefirot." *Kabbalah: Journal for the Study of Jewish Mystical Texts* 35 (2016): 55–112.

———. "Bifurcating the Androgyne and Engendering Sin: A Zoharic Reading of Gen 1–3." In *Hidden Truths from Eden: Esoteric Readings of Genesis 1–3*, edited by Caroline Vander Stichele and Susanne Scholz, 87–119. Atlanta: SBL, 2014.

———. *Circle in the Square: Studies in the Use of Gender in Kabbalistic Symbolism*. Albany: State University of New York Press, 1995.

———. "Circumcision, Secrecy, and the Veiling of the Veil: Phallomorphic Exposure and Kabbalistic Esotericism." In *The Covenant of Circumcision: New Perspectives on an Ancient Jewish Rite*, edited by Elizabeth Wyner Mark, 58–70. Hanover: University Press of New England, 2003.

———. "Circumcision, Vision of God, and Textual Interpretation: From Midrashic Trope to Mystical Symbol." *History of Religions* 27 (1987): 189–215.

———. "Constructions of the *Shekhinah* in the Sabbatian Theology of Abraham Cardoso, with a Critical Edition of *Derush ha-Shekhinah*." *Kabbalah: Journal for the Study of Jewish Mystical Texts* 3 (1998): 11–143.

———. "Coronation of the Sabbath Bride: Kabbalistic Myth and the Ritual of Androgynisation." *Journal of Jewish Thought and Philosophy* 6 (1997): 301–43.

———. "The Cut That Binds: Time, Memory, and the Ascetic Impulse." In *God's Voice from the Void: Old and New Studies in Bratslav Hasidism*, edited by Shaul Magid, 103–54. Albany: State University of New York Press, 2002.

———. "Divine Suffering and the Hermeneutics of Reading: Philosophical Reflections on Lurianic Mythology." In *Suffering Religion*, edited by Robert Gibbs and Elliot R. Wolfson, 101–62. New York: Routledge, 2002.

———. *A Dream Interpreted within a Dream: Oneiropoiesis and the Prism of Imagination*. New York: Zone, 2011.

———. *The Duplicity of Philosophy's Shadow: Heidegger, Nazism, and the Jewish Other*. New York: Columbia University Press, 2018.

———. "The Engenderment of Messianic Politics: Symbolic Significance of Sabbatai Ṣevi's Coronation." In *Toward the Millennium: Messianic Expectations From the Bible to Waco*, edited by Peter Schäfer and Mark Cohen, 203–58. Leiden: Brill, 1998.

———. "Eternal Duration and Temporal Compresence: The Influence of Ḥabad on Joseph B. Soloveitchik." In *The Value of the Particular: Lessons from Judaism and the Modern Jewish Experience: Essays in Honor of Steven T. Katz on the Occasion of his Seventieth Birthday*, edited by Ingrid Anderson and Michael Zank, 195–238. Leiden: Brill, 2015.

———. "Facing the Effaced: Mystical Eschatology and the Idealistic Orientation in the Thought of Franz Rosenzweig." *Zeitschrift für Neuere Theologiegeschichte* 4 (1997): 39–81.

———. *Giving beyond the Gift: Apophasis and Overcoming Theomania*. New York: Fordham University Press, 2014.

———. "*Gottwesen* and the De-Divinization of the Last God: Heidegger's Meditation on the Strange and Incalculable." In *Heidegger's Black Notebooks and the Future of Theology*, edited by Mårten Björk and Jayne Svenungsson, 211–55. New York: Palgrave Macmillan, 2018.

———. "The Holy Cabala of Changes: Jacob Böhme and Jewish Esotericism." *Aries—Journal for the Study of Western Esotericism* 18 (2018): 21–53.

———. "Iconicity of the Text: Reification of the Torah and the Idolatrous Impulse of Zoharic Kabbalah." *Jewish Studies Quarterly* 11 (2004): 215–42.

———. "*Imago Templi* and the Meeting of the Two Seas: Liturgical Time-Space and the Feminine Imaginary in Zoharic Kabbalah." *RES: Anthropology and Aesthetics* 51 (2007): 121–35.

———. "Immanuel Frommann's Commentary on Luke and the Christianizing of Kabbalah." In *Holy Dissent: Jews and Christian Mystics in Eastern Europe*, edited by Glenn Dynner, 171–222. Detroit: Wayne State University Press, 2011.

———. *Language, Eros, Being: Kabbalistic Hermeneutics and Poetic Imagination*. New York: Fordham University Press, 2005.

———. "Left Contained in the Right: A Study in Zoharic Hermeneutics." *Association for Jewish Studies Review* 11 (1986): 27–52.

———. "Light Does Not Talk but Shines: Apophasis and Vision in Rosenzweig's Theopoetic Temporality." In *New Studies in Jewish Philosophy*, 87–148, edited by Aaron Hughes and Elliot R. Wolfson. Bloomington: Indiana University Press, 2010.

———. "Light through Darkness: The Ideal of Human Perfection in the Zohar." *Harvard Theological Review* 81 (1988): 73–95.

———. *Luminal Darkness: Imaginal Gleanings from Zoharic Literature*. Oxford: Oneworld, 2007.

———. "Messianism in the Christian Kabbalah of Johann Kemper." In *Millenarianism and Messianism in Early Modern European Culture*. Vol. 1: *Jewish Messianism in the Early Modern World*, edited by Matt D. Goldish and Richard H. Popkin, 139–87. Dordrecht: Kluwer Academic, 2001.

———. "Murmuring Secrets: Eroticism and Esotericism in Medieval Kabbalah." In *Hidden Intercourse: Eros and Sexuality in the History of Western Esotericism*, edited by Wouter J. Hanegraaff and Jeffrey J. Kripal, 65–109. Leiden: Brill, 2008.

———. "Mythopoeic Imagination and the Hermeneutic Bridging of Temporal Spacing: On Michael Fishbane's *Biblical Myth and Rabbinic Mythmaking*." *Jewish Quarterly Review* 96 (2006): 233–38.

———. "*Nequddat ha-Reshimu*—The Trace of Transcendence and the Transcendence of the Trace: The Paradox of *Ṣimṣum* in the RaShaB's *Hemshekh Ayin Beit*." *Kabbalah: Journal for the Study of Jewish Mystical Texts* 30 (2013): 75–120.

———. "Nihilating Nonground and the Temporal Sway of Becoming: Kabbalistically Envisioning Nothing beyond Nothing." *Angelaki* 17 (2012): 31–45.

———. "Not Yet Now: Speaking of the End and the End of Speaking." In *Elliot R. Wolfson: Poetic Thinking*, edited by Hava Tirosh-Samuelson and Aaron W. Hughes, 127–93. Leiden: Brill, 2015.

———. "Occultation of the Feminine and the Body of Secrecy in Medieval Kabbalah." In *Rending the Veil: Concealment and Revelation of Secrets in the History of Religions*, edited by Elliot R. Wolfson, 113–54. New York: Seven Bridges Press, 1999.

———. *Open Secret: Postmessianic Messianism and the Mystical Revision of Menaḥem Mendel Schneerson*. New York: Columbia University Press, 2009.

———. "Patriarchy and the Motherhood of God in Zoharic Kabbalah and Meister Eckhart." In *Envisioning Judaism: Studies in Honor of Peter Schäfer on the Occasion of his Seventieth Birthday*, edited by Raʿanan Boustan, Klaus Hermann, Reimund Leicht, Annette Yoshiko Reed, and Giuseppe Veltri, with the collaboration of Alex Ramos, 1049–88. Tübingen: Mohr Siebeck, 2013.

———. "Phallic Jewissance and the Pleasure of No Pleasure." In *Talmudic Transgressions: Engaging the Work of Daniel Boyarin*, edited by Charlotte Elisheva Fonrobert, Ishay Rosen-Zvi, Aharon Shemesh, Moulie Vidas, in collaboration with James Adam Redfield, 293–335. Leiden: Brill, 2017.

———. "Retroactive Not Yet: Linear Circularity and Kabbalistic Temporality." In *Time and Eternity in Jewish Mysticism: That Which Is Before and That Which Is After*, edited by Brian Ogren, 15–50. Leiden: Brill, 2015.

———. "Revealing and Re/veiling Menaḥem Mendel Schneerson's Messianic Secret." *Kabbalah: Journal for the Study of Jewish Mystical Texts* 26 (2012): 25–96.

———. "Secrecy, Apophasis, and Atheistic Faith in the Teachings of Rav Kook." In *Negative Theology as Jewish Modernity*, edited by Michael Fagenblat, 131–60. Bloomington: Indiana University Press, 2017.

———. "Skepticism and the Philosopher's Keeping Faith." In *Jewish Philosophy for the Twenty-First Century: Personal Reflections*, edited by Hava Tirosh-Samuelson and Aaron W. Hughes, 481–515. Leiden: Brill, 2014.

———. "Structure, Innovation, and Diremptive Temporality: The Use of Models to Study Continuity and Discontinuity in Kabbalistic Tradition." *Journal for the Study of Religions and Ideologies* 6 (2007): 143–67.

———. "Textual Flesh, Incarnation, and the Imaginal Body: Abraham Abulafia's Polemic with Christianity." In *Studies in Medieval Jewish Intellectual and Social History: Festschrift in Honor of Robert Chazan*, edited by David Engel, Lawrence H. Schiffman, and Elliot R. Wolfson, 189–226. Leiden: Brill, 2012.

———. "Theolatry and the Making-Present of the Nonrepresentable: Undoing (A)Theism in Eckhart and Buber." In *Martin Buber: His Intellectual and Scholarly Legacy*, edited by Sam Berrin Shonkoff, 3–32. Leiden: Brill, 2018.

———. "Thinking Now Occurring: Temporal Diremption and the Novelty of Genuine Repetition." In *D. G. Leahy and the Thinking Now Occurring*, edited by Lissa McCullough and Elliot R. Wolfson. Albany: State University of New York Press, 2020.

———. *Through a Speculum That Shines: Vision and Imagination in Medieval Jewish Mysticism*. Princeton: Princeton University Press, 1994.

———. "*Tiqqun ha-Shekhinah*: Redemption and the Overcoming of Gender Dimorphism in the Messianic Kabbalah of Moses Ḥayyim Luzzatto." *History of Religions* 36 (1997): 289–332.

———. *Venturing Beyond: Law and Morality in Kabbalistic Mysticism*. Oxford: Oxford University Press, 2006.

———. "*Via Negativa* in Maimonides and Its Impact on Thirteenth-Century Kabbalah." *Maimonidean Studies* 5 (2008): 393–442.

———. "Zoharic Literature and Midrashic Temporality." In *Midrash Unbound: Transformations and Innovations*, edited by Michael Fishbane and Joanna Weinberg, 321–43. Oxford: Littman Library of Jewish Civilization, 2013.

Wolin, Richard. *The Frankfurt School Revisited and Other Essays on Politics and Society*. New York: Routledge, 2006.

———, ed. *The Heidegger Controversy: A Critical Reader*. Cambridge, MA: MIT Press, 1993.

———. *Heidegger's Children: Hannah Arendt, Karl Löwith, Hans Jonas, and Herbert Marcuse*. Princeton: Princeton University Press, 2001.

Wolosky, Shira. "Two Types of Negative Theology; or, What Does Negative Theology Negate?" In *Negative Theology as Jewish Modernity*, edited by Michael Fagenblat, 161–79. Bloomington: Indiana University Press, 2017.

Wood, David. *The Deconstruction of Time*. Evanston: Northwestern University Press, 2001.

Wood, Robert E. "The Heart in Heidegger's Thought." *Continental Philosophical Review* 48 (2015): 445–62.

———. *A Path into Metaphysics: Phenomenological, Hermeneutical, and Dialogical Studies*. Albany: State University of New York Press, 1990.

Wrathall, Mark A. *Heidegger and Unconcealment: Truth, Language, and History*. Cambridge: Cambridge University Press, 2011.

———. "Heidegger on Plato, Truth, and Unconcealment: The 1931–32 Lecture on *The Essence of Truth*." *Inquiry* 47 (2004): 443–63.

———. "Heidegger, Truth, and Reference." *Inquiry* 45 (2002): 217–28.

Wright, George. *Religion, Politics and Thomas Hobbes*. Dordrecht: Springer, 2006.

Wyschogrod, Edith. *Crossover Queries: Dwelling with Negatives, Embodying Philosophy's Others*. New York: Fordham University Press, 2006.

———. *Emmanuel Levinas: The Problem of Ethical Metaphysics*, 2nd ed. New York: Fordham University Press, 2000.

Yalles, Ya'aqov Ṣevi. *Qehillat Ya'aqov*. Lemberg, 1870.

Yamada, Kōun, trans. *The Gateless Gate: The Classic Book of Zen Koans*. Boston: Wisdom, 2004.

Yannaras, Christos. *On the Absence and Unknowability of God: Heidegger and the Areopagite*. Edited and with an introduction by Andrew Louth. Translated by Haralambos Ventis. London: T and T Clark, 2005.

Yates, Christopher. *The Poetic Imagination in Heidegger and Schelling*. London: Bloomsbury, 2013.

Yerushalmi, Yosef. *Zakhor: Jewish History and Jewish Memory*. Seattle: University of Washington Press, 1982.

Yisraeli, Oded. "Cain as the Scion of Satan: The Evolution of a Gnostic Myth in the *Zohar*." *Harvard Theological Review* 109 (2016): 56–74.

Yosef Ḥayyim of Baghdad. *Da'at u-Tevunah*. Jerusalem: Meqor Ḥayyim, 1965.

Yosha, Nissim. *Myth and Metaphor: Abraham Cohen Herrera's Philosophic Interpretation of Lurianic Kabbalah*. Jerusalem: Ben-Zvi Institute, 1984 (Hebrew).

Yu-Lan, Fung. *A History of Chinese Philosophy*. 2 vols. Translated by Derk Bodde. Princeton: Princeton University Press, 1952.

Yusa, Michiko. *Zen and Philosophy: An Intellectual Biography of Nishida Kitarō*. Honolulu: University of Hawaii Press, 2002.

Zabala, Santiago. *The Hermeneutic Nature of Analytic Philosophy: A Study of Ernst Tugendhat*. Foreword by Gianni Vattimo. New York: Columbia University Press, 2008.

Zaborowski, Holger. "Metaphysics, Christianity, and the 'Death of God' in Heidegger's *Black*

Notebooks (1931–1941)." In *Reading Heidegger's Black Notebooks 1931–1941*, edited by Ingo Farin and Jeff Malpas, 195–204. Cambridge, MA: MIT Press, 2016.

Zadoff, Noam. *Gershom Scholem: From Berlin to Jerusalem and Back*. Translated by Jeffrey Green. Lebanon, NH: University Press of New England, 2018.

Zahavi, Dan. *Self-Awareness and Alterity: A Phenomenological Investigation*. Evanston: Northwestern University Press, 1999.

Zarader, Marlène. *Heidegger et les paroles de l'origine*. Preface by Emmanuel Levinas, 2nd rev. ed. Paris: Vrin, 1990.

———. *The Unthought Debt: Heidegger and the Hebraic Heritage*. Translated by Bettina Bergo. Stanford: Stanford University Press, 2006.

Zhang, Wei. *Heidegger, Rorty, and the Eastern Thinkers*. Albany: State University of New York Press, 2006.

Zhang, Xianglong. "The Coming Time 'Between' Being and Daoist Emptiness: An Analysis of Heidegger's Article Inquiring into the Uniqueness of the Poet via the *Lao Zi*." *Philosophy East and West* 59 (2009): 71–87.

Ziarek, Krzysztof. "Image-Less Thinking: The Time-Space for the Imagination in Heidegger." *International Yearbook for Hermeneutics/Internationales Jahrbuch für Hermeneutik* 14 (2015): 145–62.

———. *Language after Heidegger*. Bloomington: Indiana University Press, 2013.

———. "On Heidegger's *Einmaligkeit* Again: The Single Turn of the Event." *Gatherings* 6 (2016): 91–113.

Ziporyn, Brook. *Being and Ambiguity: Philosophical Experiments with Tiantai Buddhism*. Chicago: Open Court, 2004.

———. *Ironies of Oneness and Difference: Coherence in Early Chinese Thought; Prolegomena to the Study of Li*. Albany: State University of New York Press, 2012.

Žižek, Slavoj. *The Courage of Hopelessness: Chronicles of a Year Acting Dangerously*. London: Allen Lane, 2017.

———. *The Indivisible Remainder: On Schelling and Related Matters*. London: Verso, 1996.

———. *Less Than Nothing: Hegel and the Shadow of Dialectical Materialism*. London: Verso, 2012.

———. *The Most Sublime Hysteric: Hegel with Lacan*. Translated by Thomas Scott-Railton. Cambridge: Polity, 2014.

———. *The Parallax View*. Cambridge, MA: MIT Press, 2006.

———. *The Ticklish Subject: The Absent Centre of Political Ontology*. London: Verso, 2000.

Zohar Ḥadash. Edited by Reuven Margaliot. Jerusalem: Mosad ha-Rav Kook, 1978.

The Zohar: Pritzker Edition, vol. 11. Translation and commentary by Joel Hecker. Stanford: Stanford University Press, 2016.

Zovko, Marie-Elise. *Natur und Gott: Das wirkungsgeschichtliche Verhältnis Schellings und Baaders*. Würzburg: Königshausen and Neumann, 1996.

Index